BRITISH WRITERS

BRITISH WRITERS

JAY PARINI

Editor

RETROSPECTIVE SUPPLEMENT II

Charles Scribner's Sons

an imprint of the Gale Group

New York • Detroit • San Francisco • London • Boston • Woodbridge, CT

Charles Scribner's Sons
an imprint of The Gale Group
27500 Drake Rd.
Farmington Hills, MI 483331-3535

Library of Congress Cataloging-in-Publication Data

British Writers Retrospective Supplement II/Jay Parini, editor
    p. cm.
    Includes bibliographical references and index.
    ISBN 0-684-31228-X (alk. paper)
    1.English literature—Bio-bibliography. 2. English literature—History and criticism. 3. Authors, English—Biography. I Parini, Jay.

PR85.B688 Retro Suppl. 2
820.9—dc21
[B]   2002001442

The paper used in this publication meets the requirements of ANSI/NIS Z39.48-1992 (Permanance of Paper).

Acknowledgments

Acknowledgment is gratefully made to those publishers and individuals who permitted the use of the following materials in copyright:

ROBERT BROWNING Altick, Richard D. From "Andrea Del Sarto: The Kingdom of God is Within," in *Browning: Men and Women and Other Poems*. Edited by J. R. Watson. Macmillan, 1974.—Parr, Catherine. From "Preface," in *Robert Browning: The Poems, Volume II*. Edited by John Pettigrew. Yale University Press, 1981. All rights reserved. Reproduced by permission of Penguin Books Ltd.

GEORGE ELIOT Eliot, George. From "Daniel Deronda," in *Journey Without Maps*. Penguin Books, 1980.

T. S. ELIOT Eliot, T. S. From "Ash Wednesday," "Four Quartets," "The Hollow Men," "Rhapsody on a Windy Night," in *Collected Poems, 1909–1962*. Harcourt Brace & Company, 1963. Copyright © 1963 by T. S. Eliot. All rights reserved. Reproduced by permission of Harcourt Brace & Company. In the UK by permission of Faber and Faber Ltd.—Eliot, T. S. From "Geronition," "The Love Song of J. Alfred Prufrock," "Preludes," "The Waste Land," in *Collected Poems, 1909–1962*. Harcourt Brace & Company, 1963. Copyright © 1963 by T. S. Eliot. All rights reserved. Reproduced by permission of Faber and Faber Ltd.

GRAHAM GREENE Greene, Graham. From *Brighton Rock*. William Heinemann, 1938. Copyright 1938 by Graham Greene. Reproduced by permission of David Higham Associates Ltd., on behalf of the author.—Greene, Graham. From *The Comedians*. The Bodley Head, 1966. Copyright 1965, 1966 by Graham Greene. Reproduced by permission of Random House UK Limited.—Greene, Graham. From *The Confidential Agent*. William Heinemann, 1939.—Greene, Graham. From *The End of the Affair*. William Heinemann, 1951.—Greene, Graham. From *The Heart of the Matter*. William Heinemann, 1948. Copyright 1948 by Graham Greene. Reproduced by permission of David Higham Associates Ltd., on behalf of the author.—Greene, Graham. From *The Honorary Consul*. The Bodley Head, 1973. Copyright 1973 by Graham Greene. Reproduced by permission of Random House UK Limited.—Greene, Graham. From *Journey Without Maps*. William Heinemann, 1936. Copyright 1936 by Graham Greene. Reproduced by permission of David Higham Associates Ltd., on behalf of the author.—Greene, Graham. From *The Power and the Glory*. William Heinemann, 1940. Copyright 1940 by Graham Greene. Reproduced by permission of David Higham Associates Ltd., on behalf of the author.—Greene, Graham. From *The Quiet American*. William Heinemann, 1955—Greene, Graham. From "The Virtue of Disloyalty," in *Reflections*. Reinhardt Books, 1990. © Graham Greene, 1990. All rights reserved. Reproduced by permission of Random House UK Limited.

GEORGE HERBERT Aubrey, John. From *George Herbert: The Critical Heritage*. Edited by C. A. Patrides. Routledge & Kegan Paul, 1983. Routledge & Kegan Paul, 1983.—Ferrar, Nicholas. From *George Herbert: The Critical Heritage*. Edited by C. A. Patrides. Routledge & Kegan Paul, 1983. Routledge & Kegan Paul, 1983— Larkin, Philip. From "Church Going," in *The Less Deceived*. The Marvell Press, 1955. The Specator, 1932. Reproduced by permission of Faber & Faber Ltd.—Herbert, George. From "Aaron," "Afflication (I)," "Afflication (IV)," "The Church-floore," "The Collar," "The Deniall," "Early Sonnet," "Easter-wings," "Employment (I)," "Employment (II)," "The Flower," "The Forerunners," "The Holy Scriptures II," "Jordan (II)," "Love (III)," "Man," "Mans medley," "Mattens," "The Pearl, Matth. 13.45," "Praise (II)," "Prayer (I)," "Providence," "The Quidditie," "The Windows," in *The Works of George Herbert*. Edited by F. E. Hutchinson. Oxford at the Clarendon Press, 1941. Reproduced by permission of Oxford University Press.

GERARD MANLEY HOPKINS House, Humphry. From "Preface," in *The Journals and Papers of Gerard Manley Hopkins*. Edited by Humphry House. Oxford University Press, 1966. © The Society of Jesus 1959. Reproduced by permission.

TED HUGHES Hughes, Ted. From "Fate Playing," "Fulbright Scholars," "The Rabbit Catcher," "Red," "St. Botolph's," in *Birthday Letters*. Faber and Faber, 1998. © Ted Hughes, 1998. All rights reserved. Reproduced by permission of Faber & Faber Ltd.— Hughes, Ted. From "A Horrible Religious Error," "Crow Tyrannosaurus," "Crow's Last Stand," "Examination at the Womb-door," in *Crow: From the Life*

Editorial and Production Staff

Project Editor
PAMELA PARKINSON

Copyeditors
TONY COULTER
LINDA SANDERS

Proofreader
CAROL HOLMES

Indexer
LAURIE ANDRIOT

Permission Researchers
UMA KUKATHAS
JULIE VAN PELT

Production Manager
EVI SEOUD

Buyer
STACY MELSON

Associate Publisher
TIMOTHY DEWERFF

Publisher
FRANK MENCHACA

Contents

Contents...xi

Introduction..xiii

Chronology...xv

List of Contributors lxix

Subjects in Retrospective Supplement II

JANE AUSTEN / *Claire Harman* 1

ROBERT BROWNING / *Julie Hearn*...17

GEOFFREY CHAUCER / *N. S. Thompson* 33

SAMUEL TAYLOR COLERIDGE / *David Wheatley* 51

JOSEPH CONRAD / *Thomas Gavin* 69

JOHN DONNE / *Andrew Zawacki* 85

GEORGE ELIOT / *Patricia Welsch* 101

T. S. ELIOT / *Jay Parini*...119

E. M. FORSTER / *Neil Powell*..135

GRAHAM GREENE / *Cates Baldridge* 151

GEORGE HERBERT / *Peter Scupham* 169

GERARD MANLEY HOPKINS / *Jay Parini* 185

TED HUGHES / *Gerry Cambridge* 199

D. H. LAWRENCE / *John Redmond*..221

SIR THOMAS MALORY / *Scott Ashley* 237

ANDREW MARVELL / *Sandie Byrne*...253

JOHN MILTON / *Robert Faggen* 269

OLD ENGLISH LITERATURE / *Paul Bibire* 291

GEORGE BERNARD SHAW / *John Bertolini*...309

SIR PHILIP SIDNEY / *Diana E. Henderson* 327

TOM STOPPARD / *John Wilders*...343

OSCAR WILDE / *Thomas Wright*..359

MASTER INDEX TO Volumes I–VII, Supplements I–VII, Retrospective Supplements I–II......................375

Introduction

In his preface to *Sesame and Lilies*, John Ruskin wrote: "Life being short and the quiet hours of it few, we ought to waste none of them in reading valueless books." Most readers will, I think, agree with Ruskin; there is no point in wasting time on books that will not make a lasting impact. In this supplement to *British Writers*, we present twenty-two essays on classic authors (or literary periods, in the case of an essay on Old English Literature), confident that these writers produced books that will waste nobody's time.

This supplement of *British Writers* adds to a series originally modeled on *American Writers* (1974-), another series published by Scribners (an imprint of Gale). In the original set of *British Writers*, published between 1979 and 1984, seven volumes were produced, each of them an anthology that featured articles on the lives and works of well-known poets, novelists, playwrights, essayists and autobiographers from the Anglo-Saxon era to the present. This set was followed by several supplemental volumes that covered authors who, for various reasons, had been neglected in the original series.

Throughout the series, we have attempted to provide transparent, knowledgeable essays aimed at the general, literate reader. Most of the critics writing for this supplement, as in the previous volumes, are professionals: teachers, scholars, and writers. As anyone glancing through this anthology will see, the critics have held to the highest standards of scholarship and writing. Their work often rises to a high level of craft and critical vision as they survey the life and work of a writer who has made a genuine impact on the course of British, Irish, or Anglophone literature. The biographical context for works is provided so that readers can appreciate the historical ground beneath the texts under discussion. The essays each conclude with a select bibliography intended to direct the reading of those should want to pursue the subject in greater detail.

In this collection, we examine the work of many of Britain's most central authors, reaching back to Old English Literature and some of its most revered texts, such as *Beowulf*. From the fourteenth century, we include an essay on Geoffrey Chaucer, whom many regard as the father of English literature, famous for his *Canterbury Tales* and other works. The fifteenth century writer, Sir Thomas Mallory, is another early author discussed here, with a close look at *Le Morte D'Arthur* and the question of Arthurian Romance. A wide range of poets are discussed, including Sir Philip Sidney, Andrew Marvell, John Donne, George Herbert, John Milton, Samuel Taylor Coleridge, Gerard Manley Hopkins, Robert Browning, T.S. Eliot, and Ted Hughes—a galaxy of stars. In each case, we pay close attention to major poems and lyric sequences, providing a good deal of context for each poet. In some cases, the poets (Sidney, Milton, Coleridge, Hopkins, and Eliot) were also excellent writers of prose, even major critics in their own right. The whole career is examined in each instance, and the relationship between the poet's verse and prose considered.

The English novel is represented here with essays on Jane Austen, George Eliot, Joseph Conrad, D. H. Lawrence, E. M. Forster, and Graham Greene—all of these firmly in what F. R. Leavis called "the great tradition." Attention is paid especially to the major novels produced by these authors, such as *Pride and Prejudice, Middlemarch, Heart of Darkness, Sons and Lovers, Passage to India*, and *The Heart of the Matter*. Readers will, I think, find uncanny connections among these writers.

English drama is represented here by three of its most influential modern writers: Oscar Wilde, George Bernard Shaw, and Tom Stoppard. The latter, of course, is still a dramatist in full flight, but the essay on his work brings his career up to date, with a close look at his recent masterwork,

Arcadia. These vivid, exuberant careers are studied with great sensitivity and care. In all, this volume provides a cornucopia of readable, lively criticism, designed to stimulate students and general readers, to guide them in their reading and thinking, and to suggest directions for further study. No one of these authors will waste the reader's time, and we hope the essays on their work will be deemed valuable as well.

JAY PARINI

Chronology

731 An Anglo-Saxon monk, Bede, writes *Ecclesiastical History of the English People*

732 The Battle of Tours halts the Moorish conquest of Europe

735 Egbert serves as the first archbishop in England's second archbishopric, located in York

793 The first recorded appearance of the Vikings comes from the island of Lindisfarne, Scotland.

800 Charlemagne is crowned Emperor of the western Roman Empire

896 England's Alfred the Great ends the threat of the Danes

899 Death of Alfred the Great

959–975 Reign of Edgar (great-grandson of Alfred the Great and first king of a united England)

975–978 Reign of Edward (the Martyr)

978–1016 Reign of Aethelred (the Unready)

999 Eastern and western Europeans fear the end of the world

1016 Reign of Edmund

1016–1035 Reign of Canute, by conquest

1037–1040 Reign of Harold I

1040 Duncan I, King of Scotland, is murdered, and Macbeth assumes his thrown until 1057, when Macbeth is murdered by Duncan's son

1040–1042 Reign of Harthacanute

1065 Westminster Abbey is consecrated.

1042–1066 Reign of Edward (the Confessor)

1066 Reign of Harold II

1066 At the Battle of Stamford Bridge, Harold II's army defeats Harald III, king of Norway, and his men, who have invaded England

1066 The Normans, led by William the Bastard (to become William the Conqueror), defeat Harold II at the Battle of Hastings and conquer England

1066–1087 Reign of Norman William I (William the Conqueror)

1085–1086 The Doomsday Book, a census of England, is ordered by King William the Conqueror

1087–1100 Reign of William II (Rufus)

1095 At the Council of Clermont, Pope Urban II called Christians to war; the first crusade lasts until 1099, and other crusades follow until the fall of the last Christian stronghold in 1291

1100–1135 Reign of Henry I

12th century Oxford University is founded

1120 Anglo-Saxon scientist Welcher of Malvern pioneers the measurement of the earth in degrees, minutes, and seconds of latitude and longitude

French philosopher Peter Abelard's *Sic et non*

1121 Concordat of Worms

1128 Scotland's David I founds the Abbey of Holyrood

1135–1154 Reign of Stephen

1136 Abelard's *Historia Calamitatum*

1139 Matilda, daughter of Henry I and cousin of King Stephen, challenges for the throne of England, but withdraws her claim in 1148

1140 Matilda is elected "Lady of the English"

1141 King Stephen is captured during the siege of Lincoln Castle, and Matilda rules for 6 months

1154–1189 Reign of Henry II

1159 John of Salisbury writes his *Policraticus,* a work of political philosophy

CHRONOLOGY

1164	At the Council of Clarendon, King Henry II issues the Constitutions of Clarendon, extending jurisdictions of civil over church courts
1170	Thomas Becket, long-time foe of King Henry II, is murdered by King Henry's men in Canterbury Cathedral
1189–1199	**Reign of Richard the Lionheart (Coeur de Lion)**
1199–1116	**Reign of John**
1215	The Magna Carta, a charter limiting the power of the monarchy, is reluctantly signed by King John
1216–1272	**Reign of Henry III**
1217	Cambridge University is founded
1247	Death of Robin Hood, identified as Robert, Earl of Huntington
1266–1273	St. Thomas Aquinas' *Summa theologiae*
1272–1307	**Reign of Edward I**
1276	The prince of North Wales, Llewelyn II, refuses to pay homage to England's Edward I, who invades North Wales and forces Llewelyn to surrender
1282	Llewelyn II leads a second attack against Edward and fails; Wales falls to English rule
1297	William Wallace (Bravehart) leads attacks against British troops in an attempt for Scottish sovereignty
1305	William Wallace is captured, tried, and hanged
1307–1327	**Reign of Edward II**
ca. 1325	John Wycliffe born
	John Gower born
1327–1377	**Reign of Edward III**
ca. 1332	William Langland born
1337	Beginning of the Hundred Years' War
ca. 1340	**Geoffrey Chaucer born**
1346	The Battle of Crécy
1348	The Black Death (further outbreaks in 1361 and 1369)
ca. 1350	Boccaccio's *Decameron*
	Langland's *Piers Plowman*

1351	The Statute of Laborers pegs laborers' wages at rates in effect preceding the plague
1356	The Battle of Poitiers
1360	The Treaty of Brétigny: end of the first phase of the Hundred Years' War
1362	Pleadings in the law courts conducted in English
	Parliaments opened by speeches in English
1369	Chaucer's *The Book of the Duchess*, an elegy to Blanche of Lancaster, wife of John of Gaunt
1369–1377	Victorious French campaigns under du Guesclin
ca. 1370	John Lydgate born
1371	Sir John Mandeville's *Travels*
1372	Chaucer travels to Italy
1372–1382	Wycliffe active in Oxford
1373–1393	William of Wykeham founds Winchester College and New College, Oxford
ca. 1375–1400	*Sir Gawain and the Green Knight*
1376	Death of Edward the Black Prince
1377–1399	**Reign of Richard II**
ca. 1379	Gower's *Vox clamantis*
ca. 1380	Chaucer's *Troilus and Criseyde*
1381	The Peasants' Revolt
1386	Chaucer's *Canterbury Tales* begun
	Chaucer sits in Parliament
	Gower's *Confessio amantis*
1399–1413	**Reign of Henry IV**
ca. 1400	Death of William Langland
1400	Death of Geoffrey Chaucer
1408	Death of John Gower
ca. 1410	**Sir Thomas Malory Born**
1412–1420	Lydgate's *Troy Book*
1413–1422	**Reign of Henry V**
1415	The Battle of Agincourt
1420–1422	Lydgate's *Siege of Thebes*
1422–1461	**Reign of Henry VI**
1431	François Villon born
	Joan of Arc burned at Rouen

CHRONOLOGY

1434	Jan van Eyck's *Giovanni Arnolfini and His Wife*
1436	Guillaume Dufay's Nuper rosarum flores
1440–1441	Henry VI founds Eton College and King's College, Cambridge
1444	Truce of Tours
1450	Jack Cade's rebellion
ca. 1451	Death of John Lydgate
1452	Leonardo da Vinci born
1453	End of the Hundred Years' War
	The fall of Constantinople
1455–1485	The Wars of the Roses
1455	Gutenberg uses movable-type printing press to print bible
ca. 1455	Donatello's *Magdalen*
ca. 1460	John Skelton born
1461–1470	**Reign of Edward IV**
1463	Villon disappears
1466	Death of Donatello
1469	Machiavelli born
1470–1471	**Reign of Henry VI**
1471	Death of Sir Thomas Malory
1471–1483	**Reign of Edward IV**
1475	Michelangelo born
1476–1483	Caxton's press set up: *The Canterbury Tales*, *Morte d'Arthur*, and *The Golden Legend* printed
1478	Sir Thomas More born
1483–1485	**Reign of Richard III**
1483	François Rabelais and Raphael born
1485	The Battle of Bosworth Field: end of the Wars of the Roses
ca. 1485	Thomas Cromwell born
	Botticelli's *The Birth of Venus*
1485–1509	**Reign of Henry VII**
1486	Marriage of Henry VII and Elizabeth of York unites the rival houses of Lancaster and York
	Bartholomew Diaz rounds the Cape of Good Hope
ca. 1490	Giovanni Bellini's *Allegory*
1492	Columbus's first voyage to the New World
1493	Pope Alexander VI divides undiscovered territories between Spain and Portugal
1497–1498	John Cabot's voyages to Newfoundland and Labrador
1497–1499	Vasco da Gama's voyage to India
1498	Leonardo paints *The Last Supper*
1499	Amerigo Vespucci's first voyage to America
	Erasmus's first visit to England
1503	Thomas Wyatt born
	Leonardo begins *Mona Lisa* (completed 1506)
1505	John Colet appointed dean of St. Paul's: founds St. Paul's School
1509–1547	**Reign of Henry VIII**
1509	The king marries Catherine of Aragon
	Raphael and assistants begin painting the Stanze (completed 1514)
	John Calvin born
1511	Erasmus's *Praise of Folly* published
1512	Michelangelo's Sistine ceiling unveiled.
1513	Invasion by the Scots defeated at Flodden Field
1515	Wolsey appointed lord chancellor
1516	Sir Thomas More's *Utopia*
	Ludovico Ariosto's *Orlando furioso* (first edition)
1517	Martin Luther's theses against indulgences published at Wittenberg
	Henry Howard (earl of Surrey) born
1518	Titian's *Assumption of the Virgin*
	Vives's *Fabula de homine*
	Erasmus's *Colloquia*
1519	Charles V of Spain becomes Holy Roman Emperor
	Death of Leonardo
1519–1521	Spanish conquest of Mexico
1519–1522	Magellan circumnavigates the globe
1520	Death of Raphael
1522	Skelton's *Collyn Clout*

CHRONOLOGY

1523–1524	Holbein the Younger's *Dance of Death* (1st edition)
1525	Cardinal College, the forerunner of Christ Church, founded at Oxford
	Pietro Aretino's *La Cortegiana*
1526	Tyndale's English translation of the New Testament imported from Holland
1527	Death of Machiavelli
1528	Baldassare Castiglione's *Il libro del cortegiano*
1529	Fall of Cardinal Wolsey
	Death of John Skelton
1529–1536	The "Reformation" Parliament
1531	Henry VIII proclaimed head of Church of England
	Sir Thomas Elyot's *The Governour* published
1532	Thomas Cranmer appointed archbishop of Canterbury
	Machiavelli's *The Prince*
	Rabelais's *Pantagruel*
1533	The king secretly marries Anne Boleyn
	Cranmer pronounces the king's marriage with Catherine "against divine law"
1534	The Act of Supremacy constitutes the king as head of the Church of England
	Rabelais's *Gargantua*
1535	Sir Thomas More executed
	Thomas Cromwell appointed vicar general of the Church of England
1536	The Pilgrimage of Grace: risings against the king's religious, social, and economic reforms
	Calvin's *Institutio Christiana*
	Anne Boleyn executed
	Michelangelo begins *Last Judgement* (unveiled 1541)
	The king marries Jane Seymour
1537	The dissolution of the monasteries: confiscation of ecclesiastical properties and assets; increase in royal revenues
	Jane Seymour dies

1538	First complete English Bible published and placed in all churches
1540	The king marries Anne of Cleves
	Marriage dissolved
	The king marries Catherine Howard
	Fall and execution of Thomas Cromwell
1542	Catherine Howard executed
	Death of Sir Thomas Wyatt
1543	The king marries Catherine Parr
	Copernicus's *De revolutionibus orbium coelestium*
	Andreas Vesalius's *De humani corporis fabrica*
1546	Trinity College, Cambridge, refounded
1547	The earl of Surrey executed
	Benevuto Cellini's *Perseus* (completed 1554)
	Cervantes born
1547–1553	**Reign of Edward VI**
1548–1552	Hall's *Chronicle*
1550	Giorgio Vasari's *Vite de' più eccelenti architetti, pittori, et scultori italiani*
1552	The second Book of Common Prayer
ca. 1552	Edmund Spenser born
1553	Lady Jane Grey proclaimed queen
	Death of Rabelais
1553–1558	**Reign of Mary I (Mary Tudor)**
ca. 1554	Births of Walter Ralegh, Richard Hooker, and John Lyly
1554	Lady Jane Grey executed
	Mary I marries Philip II of Spain
	Bandello's *Novelle*
	Philip Sidney born
1555	Louise Labbé's *Sonnets*
ca. 1556	George Peele born
1557	Tottel's *Miscellany*, including the poems of Wyatt and Surrey, published
ca. 1558	Thomas Kyd born
1558	Calais, the last English possession in France, is lost
	Mary I dies
1558–1603	**Reign of Elizabeth I**

CHRONOLOGY

1559	John Knox arrives in Scotland
	Rebellion against the French regent
ca. 1559	George Chapman born
1561	Mary Queen of Scots (Mary Stuart) arrives in Edinburgh
	Thomas Hoby's translation of Castiglione's *The Courtier Gorboduc*, the first English play in blank verse
	Francis Bacon born
1562	Civil war in France
	English expedition sent to support the Huguenots
	Benevuto Cellini's *Autobiography*
1562–1568	Sir John Hawkins's voyages to Africa
1563	John Foxe's *Book of Martyrs*
1564	Births of Christopher Marlowe, William Shakespeare, and Galileo Galilei
	Death of Michelangelo and John Calvin
1565	Mary Queen of Scots marries Lord Darnley
	Santa Teresa's *Libro de la vida*
1566	William Painter's *Palace of Pleasure*, a miscellany of prose stories, the source of many dramatists' plots
1567	Darnley murdered at Kirk o' Field
	Mary Queen of Scots marries the earl of Bothwell
1569	Rebellion of the English northern earls suppressed
	Gerardus Mercator publishes map of the world
1570	Roger Ascham's *The Schoolmaster*
1571	Defeat of the Turkish fleet at Lepanto
ca. 1572	Ben Jonson born
1572	St. Bartholomew's Day massacre
	John Donne born
1574	The earl of Leicester's theater company formed
1575	Tasso's *Gerusalemme liberata* written (published 1581)
ca. 1575	Cyril Tourneur born
1576	The Theater, the first permanent theater building in London, opened
	The first Blackfriars Theater opened with performances by the Children of St. Paul's
	John Marston born
1576–1578	Martin Frobisher's voyages to Labrador and the northwest
1577–1580	Sir Francis Drake sails around the world
1577	Holinshed's *Chronicles of England, Scotlande, and Irelande*
1578	Ronsard's *Sonnets pour Hélène*
1579	John Lyly's *Euphues: The Anatomy of Wit*
	Thomas North's translation of *Plutarch's Lives*
	John Fletcher born
1579–1580	Sir Philip Sidney's *The Defence of Poetry*
1580	Montaigne's *Essais*, I and II
ca. 1580	Thomas Middleton born
1581	The Levant Company founded
	Seneca's *Ten Tragedies* translated
1582	Richard Hakluyt's *Divers Voyages Touching the Discoverie of America*
1583	San Juan de la Cruz's *Noche Oscura*
1584	Sir Walter Ralegh lands on Roanoke Island
	Giordano Bruno's *De la Causa, Principio, et Uno*
	George Peele's *The Arraignment of Paris*
ca. 1584	Francis Beaumont born
1584–1585	Sir John Davis's first voyage to Greenland
1585	First English settlement in America, the "Lost Colony" comprising 108 men under Ralph Lane, founded at Roanoke Island, off the coast of North Carolina
1586	Kyd's *Spanish Tragedy*
	John Ford born
	Marlowe's *Tamburlaine*
	William Camden's *Britannia*
	The Babington conspiracy against Queen Elizabeth
	Death of Sir Philip Sidney

CHRONOLOGY

1587   Mary Queen of Scots executed

Birth of Virginia Dare, first English child born in America, at Roanoke Island

Claudio Monteverdi completes first book of madrigals

1588   Defeat of the Spanish Armada

Marlowe's *Dr. Faustus*

Montaigne *Essais*, III

1589   William Byrd's *Cantiones sacrae, Songs of Sundrie Natures*

1590   Spenser's *The Faerie Queen*, Cantos 1–3

1591   Robert Herrick born

1591–1592   Shakespeare's *Henry VI* (authored)

1592   Outbreak of plague in London: theaters closed

1593   Death of Christopher Marlowe

George Herbert born

Izaak Walton born

Richard Hooker's *Of the Laws of Ecclesiastical Polity* (first four books)

1594   The Lord Chamberlain's Men, the company to which Shakespeare belonged, founded

The Swan Theater opened

Death of Thomas Kyd

1595   Ralegh's expedition to Guiana

Sidney's *Apology for Poetry*

ca. 1595   Thomas Carew born

1596   The Earl of Essex's expedition captures Cadiz

René Descartes born

The second Blackfriars Theater opened

ca. 1597   Death of George Peele

1597   Bacon's first collection of *Essays*

Shakespeare's *Romeo and Juliet*

Jacopo Peri's *Dafne* (the first opera)

1598   The Edict of Nantes

Jonson's *Every Man in His Humor*

1598–1600   Richard Hakluyt's *Principal Navigations, Voyages, Traffics, and Discoveries of the English Nation*

1599   The Globe Theater opened and *Julius Caesar* performed for first known time

Oliver Cromwell born

Death of Edmund Spenser

1600   Death of Richard Hooker

Shakespeare's *A Midsummer Night's Dream*

1601   Rebellion and execution of the Earl of Essex

Donne's *The Progresse of the Soule*

1602   The East India Company founded

The Bodleian Library reopened at Oxford

1603–1625   Reign of James I

1603   John Florio's translation of Montaigne's *Essays*

Cervantes's *Don Quixote* (Part 1)

Shakespeare's *Hamlet*

The Gunpowder Plot

1604   Kepler's *Astronomia pars Optica*

John Marston's *The Malcontent*

Tourneur's *The Revenger's Tragedy*

ca. 1604   Shakespeare's *Othello* (written)

1605   Thomas Browne born

Bacon's *Advancement of Learning*

ca. 1605   Shakespeare's *Macbeth*

1606   Jonson's *Volpone*

Death of John Lyly

Edmund Waller born

1607   The first permanent English colony established at Jamestown, Virginia

John Fletcher's and Francis Beaumont's *Knight of the Burning Pestle*

Monteverdi's *Orfeo*

1608   **John Milton born**

Shakespeare's *King Lear*

1609   Kepler's *Astronomia nova*

John Suckling born

1610   Galileo's *Sidereus nuncius*

1611   The Authorized Version of the Bible

Shakespeare's *The Tempest* (authored)

1612 Death of Prince Henry, King James's eldest son

Webster's *The White Devil*

Bacon's second collection of *Essays*

1613 The Globe Theatre destroyed by fire

ca. 1613 Richard Crashaw born

Webster's *The Duchess of Malfi*

1614 Ralegh's *History of the World*

1616 George Chapman's translation of Homer's *Odyssey*

Deaths of William Shakespeare, Francis Beaumont, and Miguel Cervantes

ca. 1618 Richard Lovelace born

1618 The Thirty Years' War begins

Sir Walter Ralegh executed

Abraham Cowley born

1619 The General Assembly, the first legislative assembly on American soil, meets in Virginia

Slavery introduced at Jamestown

1620 The Pilgrims land in Massachusetts

John Evelyn born

1621 Francis Bacon impeached and fined

Robert Burton's *Anatomy of Melancholy*

Andrew Marvell born

ca. 1621 Henry Vaughan born

1622 Middleton's *The Changeling*

1623 The First Folio of Shakespeare's plays

Visit of Prince Charles and the duke of Buckingham to Spain; failure of attempts to negotiate a Spanish marriage

1624 War against Spain

1625–1649 Reign of Charles I

1625 Death of John Fletcher

Bacon's last collection of *Essays*

Heinrich Schütz's *Cantiones Sacrae*

1626 Bacon's *New Atlantis*, appended to *Sylva sylvarum*

Dutch found New Amsterdam

Death of Cyril Tourneur

Death of Francis Bacon

1627 Ford's *'Tis Pity She's a Whore*

Cardinal Richelieu establishes the Company of New France with monopoly over trade and land in Canada

Buckingham's expedition to the Isle of Ré to relieve La Rochelle

Death of Thomas Middleton

1627–1628 Revolt and siege of La Rochelle, the principal Huguenot city of France

1628 Buckingham assassinated

Surrender of La Rochelle

William Harvey's treatise on the circulation of the blood (*De motu cordis et sanguinis*)

John Bunyan born

1629 Ford's *The Broken Heart*

King Charles dismisses his third Parliament, imprisons nine members, and proceeds to rule for eleven years without Parliament

The Massachusetts Bay Company formed

1629–1630 Peace treaties with France and Spain

1630 Thomas Slater publishes *The True Travels, Adventures, and Observations of Captain John Smith*

1631 John Dryden born

Death of John Donne

1632 Rembrandt's *Anatomy Lesson of Dr. Tulp*

1633 William Laud appointed archbishop of Canterbury

Death of George Herbert; *The Temple* published posthumously

Samuel Pepys born

1634 Death of George Chapman

Death of John Marston

1635 The Académie Française founded

George Etherege born

ca. 1635 Sir Thomas Browne's *Religio Medici* (authored)

1636 Pierre Corneille's *Le Cid*

Harvard College founded

1637 Milton's "Lycidas"

Descartes's *Discours de la méthode*

CHRONOLOGY

King Charles's levy of ship money challenged in the courts by John Hampden

The introduction of the new English Book of Common Prayer strongly opposed in Scotland

Death of Ben Jonson

ca. 1637 Thomas Traherne born

1638 The Scots draw up a National Covenant to defend their religion
Galileo's *Discorsi e dimostrazioni matematiche intorno a due nove scienze*
Sir John Suckling's *The Goblins*

ca. 1638 Death of John Webster

1639 Parliament reassembled to raise taxes

ca. 1639 Death of John Ford
Charles Sedley born

1639–1640 The two Bishops' Wars with Scotland

1640 The Long Parliament assembled
The king's advisers, Archbishop Laud and the earl of Strafford, impeached
Aphra Behn born
Death of Thomas Carew

1641 Strafford executed
Acts passed abolishing extraparliamentary taxation, the king's extraordinary courts, and his power to order a dissolution without parliamentary consent
The Grand Remonstrance censuring royal policy passed by eleven votes
William Wycherley born

1642 Parliament submits the nineteen Propositions, which King Charles rejects as annihilating the royal power
The Civil War begins
The theaters close
Royalist victory at Edgehill; King Charles established at Oxford
Deaths of Sir John Suckling and Galileo

1643 Parliament concludes the Solemn League and Covenant with the Scots
Louis XIV crowned king of France
Charles Sackville, earl of Dorset, born

1644 Parliamentary victory at Marston Moor
The New Model army raised
Milton's *Areopagitica*

1645 Parliamentary victory under Fairfax and Cromwell at Naseby
Fairfax captures Bristol
Archbishop Laud executed
Edmund Waller's *Poems*

1646 Fairfax besieges King Charles at Oxford
King Charles takes refuge in Scotland; end of the First Civil War
King Charles attempts negotiations with the Scots
Parliament's proposals sent to the king and rejected
Richard Crashaw's *Steps to the Temple*

1647 Conflict between Parliament and the army
A general council of the army established that discusses representational government within the army
The Agreement of the People drawn up by the Levelers; its proposals include manhood suffrage
King Charles concludes an agreement with the Scots
George Fox begins to preach
John Wilmot, earl of Rochester, born

1648 Cromwell dismisses the general council of the army
The Second Civil War begins
Fairfax defeats the Kentish royalists at Maidstone
Cromwell defeats the Scots at Preston
The Thirty Years' War ended by the treaty of Westphalia
Parliament purged by the army
Thomas Herrick's *Hesperides*

1649–1660 Commonwealth

1649 King Charles I tried and executed
The monarchy and the House of Lords abolished
The Commonwealth proclaimed

xxii

Cromwell invades Ireland and defeats the royalist Catholic forces
Death of Richard Crashaw

Richard Lovelace's *Lucasta*

1650 Cromwell defeats the Scots at Dunbar

Henry Vaughan's *Silex Scintillans* (first part)
Death of Descartes

1651 Charles II crowned king of the Scots, at Scone
Charles II invades England, is defeated at Worcester, escapes to France
Thomas Hobbes's *Leviathan*

William Harvey's *Essays on the Generation of Animals*

1652 War with Holland

1653 The Rump Parliament dissolved by the army
A new Parliament and council of state nominated; Cromwell becomes Lord Protector
Walton's *The Compleat Angler*

1654 Peace concluded with Holland

War against Spain

1655 Parliament attempts to reduce the army and is dissolved
Rule of the major-generals

1656 Sir William Davenant produces *The Siege of Rhodes*, one of the first English operas
Abraham Cowley's *Davideis*

1657 Second Parliament of the Protectorate

Cromwell is offered and declines the throne
Death of Richard Lovelace

1658 Death of Oliver Cromwell

Richard Cromwell succeeds as Protector

1659 Conflict between Parliament and the army

1660 General Monck negotiates with Charles II
Charles II offers the conciliatory Declaration of Breda and accepts Parliament's invitation to return
Will's Coffee House established

Sir William Davenant and Thomas Killigrew licensed to set up two companies of players, the Duke of York's and the King's Servants, including actors and actresses
Daniel Defoe born

Pepys's *Diary* begun

1660–1685 Reign of Charles II

1661 Parliament passes the Act of Uniformity, enjoining the use of the Book of Common Prayer; many Puritan and dissenting clergy leave their livings

1662 Peace Treaty with Spain

King Charles II marries Catherine of Braganza
The Royal Society incorporated (founded in 1660)

1664 War against Holland

New Amsterdam captured and becomes New York
Molière's *Tartuffe*

Heinrich Schütz's *Christmas Oratorio*

John Vanbrugh born

1665 The Great Plague

Newton discovers the binomial theorem and invents the integral and differential calculus, at Cambridge

1666 The Great Fire of London

Bunyan's *Grace Abounding*

Molière's *Le Misanthrope*

London *Gazette* founded

1667 The Dutch fleet sails up the Medway and burns English ships
The war with Holland ended by the Treaty of Breda
Milton's *Paradise Lost*

Thomas Sprat's *History of the Royal Society*

Jonathan Swift born

Death of Abraham Cowley

1668 Sir Christopher Wren begins St. Paul's Cathedral (completed 1710)
Triple Alliance formed with Holland and Sweden against France
Dryden's *Essay of Dramatick Poesy*

CHRONOLOGY

1670   Alliance formed with France through the secret Treaty of Dover

Pascal's *Pensées*

The Hudson's Bay Company founded

William Congreve born

1671   Milton's *Samson Agonistes* and *Paradise Regained*

1672   War against Holland

Wycherley's *The Country Wife*

Joseph Addison born

Richard Steele born

King Charles issues the Declaration of Indulgence, suspending penal laws against Nonconformists and Catholics

1673   Parliament passes the Test Act, making acceptance of the doctrines of the Church of England a condition for holding public office

1674   War with Holland ended by the Treaty of Westminster

Death of John Milton

Death of Robert Herrick

Death of Thomas Traherne

1676   George Etherege's *The Man of Mode*

1677   Aphra Behn's *The Rover* (1st part)

Baruch Spinoza's *Ethics*

Jean Racine's *Phèdre*

King Charles's niece, Mary, marries her cousin William of Orange

1678   Fabrication of the so-called popish plot by Titus Oates

Bunyan's *Pilgrim's Progress*

Dryden's *All for Love*

Marie de La Vergne de La Fayette's *La Princesse de Clèves*

Death of Andrew Marvell

George Farquhar born

1679   Parliament passes the Habeas Corpus Act

Rochester's *A Satire Against Mankind*

1680   Death of John Wilmot, earl of Rochester

1681   Dryden's *Absalom and Achitophel* (Part 1)

Andrew Marvell's *Miscellaneous Poems*

1682   Dryden's *Absalom and Achitophel* (Part 2)

Thomas Otway's *Venice Preserv'd*

Philadelphia founded

Death of Sir Thomas Browne

1683   The Ashmolean Museum, the world's first public museum, opens at Oxford

Death of Izaak Walton

1685–1688   Reign of James II

1685   Rebellion and execution of James Scott, duke of Monmouth

John Gay born

1686   The first book of Newton's *Principia—De motu corporum*, containing his theory of gravitation—presented to the Royal Society

Aphra Behn's *The Lover's Watch*

1687   James II issues the Declaration of Indulgence

Dryden's *The Hind and the Panther*

Death of Edmund Waller

1688   James II reissues the Declaration of Indulgence, renewing freedom of worship and suspending the provisions of the Test Act

Acquittal of the seven bishops imprisoned for protesting against the Declaration

William of Orange lands at Torbay, Devon

James II takes refuge in France

Death of John Bunyan

Alexander Pope born

1689–1702   Reign of William III

1689   Parliament formulates the Declaration of Rights

William and Mary accept the Declaration and the crown

The Grand Alliance concluded between the Holy Roman Empire, England, Holland, and Spain

War declared against France

King William's War, 1689–1697 (the first of the French and Indian wars)

CHRONOLOGY

Peter the Great begins reform of Russia

Death of Aphra Behn

Samuel Richardson born

1690 James II lands in Ireland with French support, but is defeated at the battle of the Boyne

John Locke's *An Essay Concerning Human Understanding*

1692 Salem witchcraft trials

Death of Sir George Etherege

1694 George Fox's *Journal*

Voltaire (François Marie Arouet) born

Death of Mary II

1695 Congreve's *Love for Love*

Death of Henry Vaughan

1697 War with France ended by the Treaty of Ryswick

Vanbrugh's *The Relapse*

1698 Jeremy Collier's *A Short View of the Immorality and Profaneness of the English Stage*

1699 Fénelon's *Les Aventures de Télémaque*

1700 Congreve's *The Way of the World*

Defoe's *The True-Born Englishman*

Death of John Dryden

James Thomson born

1701 War of the Spanish Succession, 1701–1714 (Queen Anne's War in America, 1702–1713)

Death of Sir Charles Sedley

1702–1714 Reign of Queen Anne

1702 Clarendon's *History of the Rebellion* (1702–1704)

Defoe's *The Shortest Way with the Dissenters*

1703 Defoe is arrested, fined, and pilloried for writing *The Shortest Way*

Death of Samuel Pepys

1704 John Churchill, duke of Marlborough, and Prince Eugene of Savoy defeat the French at Blenheim

Capture of Gibraltar

Swift's *A Tale of a Tub* and *The Battle of the Books*

The Review founded (1704–1713)

1706 Farquhar's *The Recruiting Officer*

Benjamin Franklin born

Deaths of John Evelyn

Death of Charles Sackville, earl of Dorset

1707 Farquhar's *The Beaux' Stratagem*

Act of Union joining England and Scotland

Death of George Farquhar

Henry Fielding born

1709 The *Tatler* founded (1709–1711)

Nicholas Rowe's edition of Shakespeare

Samuel Johnson born

Marlborough defeats the French at Malplaquet

Charles XII of Sweden defeated at Poltava

1710 South Sea Company founded

First copyright act

George Berkeley's *Treatise Concerning the Principles of Human Knowledge*

1711 Swift's *The Conduct of the Allies*

The *Spectator* founded (1711–1712; 1714)

Marlborough dismissed

David Hume born

1712 Pope's *The Rape of the Lock* (Cantos 1–2)

Antonio Vivaldi's Concertos, Op. 3

Jean-Jacques Rousseau born

1713 War with France ended by the Treaty of Utrecht

The *Guardian* founded

Swift becomes dean of St. Patrick's, Dublin

Addison's *Cato*

Ann Finch's *Miscellany Poems, on Several Occasions*

Laurence Sterne born

1714–1727 Reign of George I

CHRONOLOGY

1714   Pope's expended version of *The Rape of the Lock* (Cantos 1–5)

1715   The Jacobite rebellion in Scotland

Pope's translation of Homer's *Iliad* (1715–1720)

Death of Louis XIV

Louis XV crowned King of France

1716   Death of William Wycherley

Thomas Gray born

1717   Pope's *Eloisa to Abelard*

David Garrick born

Horace Walpole born

1718   Quadruple Alliance (Britain, France, the Netherlands, the German Empire) in war against Spain

1719   Defoe's *Robinson Crusoe*

Death of Joseph Addison

1720   Inoculation against smallpox introduced in Boston

War against Spain

The South Sea Bubble

Defoe's *Captain Singleton* and *Memoirs of a Cavalier*

1721   Tobias Smollett born

William Collins born

1722   Defoe's *Moll Flanders*, *Journal of the Plague Year*, and *Colonel Jack*

Sir Richard Steele's *The Conscious Lovers*

1724   Defoe's *Roxana*

Swift's *The Drapier's Letters*

1725   Pope's translation of Homer's *Odyssey* (1725–1726)

1726   Swift's *Gulliver's Travels*

Voltaire in England (1726–1729)

Death of Sir John Vanbrugh

1727–1760   Reign of George II

Handel's *Coronation Anthem*

1728   Gay's *The Beggar's Opera*

Pope's *The Dunciad* (Books 1–2)

Oliver Goldsmith born

1729   Bach's *St. Matthew Passion*

Swift's *A Modest Proposal*

Edmund Burke born

Deaths of William Congreve

Death Sir Richard Steele

1731   Navigation improved by introduction of the quadrant

Pope's *Moral Essays* (1731–1735)

Franklin begins publishing *Poor Richard's Almanac*

Death of Daniel Defoe

William Cowper born

1732   Death of John Gay

William Hogarth's *A Harlot's Progress*

1733   Pope's *Essay on Man* (1733–1734)

Lewis Theobald's edition of Shakespeare

1734   Voltaire's *Lettres philosophiques*

1737   Edward Gibbon born

1738   Johnson's *London*

1739   Hume's *Treatise on Human Nature*

1740   War of the Austrian Succession, 1740–1748 (King George's War in America, 1744–1748)

George Anson begins his circumnavigation of the world (1740–1744)

Frederick the Great becomes king of Prussia (1740–1786)

Richardson's *Pamela* (1740–1741)

James Boswell born

1742   Bach's *Goldberg Variations*

Fielding's *Joseph Andrews*

Edward Young's *Night Thoughts* (1742–1745)

Pope's *The New Dunciad* (Book 4)

1744   Johnson's *Life of Mr. Richard Savage*

Death of Alexander Pope

1745   Second Jacobite rebellion, led by Charles Edward, the Young Pretender

Death of Jonathan Swift

1746   The Young Pretender defeated at Culloden

Collins's *Odes on Several Descriptive and Allegorical Subjects*

Jonathan Edwards's *A Treatise Concerning the Religious Affections*

CHRONOLOGY

1747 Richardson's *Clarissa Harlowe* (1747–1748)

Franklin's experiments with electricity announced

Voltaire's *Essai sur les moeurs*

1748 War of the Austrian Succession ended by the Peace of Aix-la-Chapelle

Smollett's *Adventures of Roderick Random*

Hume's *Enquiry Concerning Human Understanding*

Montesquieu's *L'Esprit des lois*

1749 Bach's *The Art of the Fugue*

Johann Wolfgang von Goethe born

Fielding's *Tom Jones*

Johnson's *The Vanity of Human Wishes*

Bolingbroke's *Idea of a Patriot King*

1750 The *Rambler* founded (1750–1752)

1751 Gray's *Elegy Written in a Country Churchyard*

Fielding's *Amelia*

Smollett's *Adventures of Peregrine Pickle*

Denis Diderot and Jean le Rond d'Alembert begin to publish the *Encyclopédie* (1751–1765)

Richard Brinsley Sheridan born

1752 Frances Burney and Thomas Chatterton born

Charlotte Lenox's *The Female Quixote*

1753 Richardson's *History of Sir Charles Grandison* (1753–1754)

Smollett's *The Adventures of Ferdinand Count Fathom*

1754 Hume's *History of England* (1754–1762)

Death of Henry Fielding

George Crabbe born

1755 Lisbon destroyed by earthquake

Fielding's *Journal of a Voyage to Lisbon* published posthumously

Johnson's *Dictionary of the English Language*

1756 The Seven Years' War against France, 1756–1763 (the French and Indian War in America, 1755–1760)

William Pitt the elder becomes prime minister

Johnson's proposal for an edition of Shakespeare

1757 Robert Clive wins the battle of Plassey, in India

Gray's "The Progress of Poesy" and "The Bard"

Burke's *Philosophical Enquiry into the Origin of Our Ideas of the Sublime and Beautiful*

Hume's *Natural History of Religion*

William Blake born

1758 The *Idler* founded (1758–1760)

1759 Capture of Quebec by General James Wolfe

Johnson's *History of Rasselas, Prince of Abyssinia*

Voltaire's *Candide*

The British Museum opens

Sterne's *The Life and Opinions of Tristram Shandy* (1759–1767)

Death of William Collins

Mary Wollstonecraft born

Robert Burns born

1760–1820 Reign of George III

1760 James Macpherson's *Fragments of Ancient Poetry Collected in the Highlands of Scotland*

William Beckford born

1761 Rousseau's *Julie, ou la nouvelle Héloïse*

Death of Samuel Richardson

1762 Rousseau's *Du Contrat social* and *Émile*

Catherine the Great becomes czarina of Russia (1762–1796)

1763 The Seven Years' War ended by the Peace of Paris

Smart's *A Song to David*

1764 James Hargreaves invents the spinning jenny

1765 Parliament passes the Stamp Act to tax the American colonies

CHRONOLOGY

Johnson's edition of Shakespeare

Walpole's *The Castle of Otranto*

Thomas Percy's *Reliques of Ancient English Poetry*

Blackstone's *Commentaries on the Laws of England* (1765–1769)

1766   The Stamp Act repealed

Swift's *Journal to Stella* first published in a collection of his letters

Goldsmith's *The Vicar of Wakefield*

Smollett's *Travels Through France and Italy*

Lessing's *Laokoon*

Rousseau in England (1766–1767)

Germaine de Staël born

1768   Mozart's *Bastien und Bastienne*

Sterne's *A Sentimental Journey Through France and Italy*

The Royal Academy founded by George III

First edition of the *Encyclopaedia Britannica*

Maria Edgeworth born

Death of Laurence Sterne

1769   David Garrick organizes the Shakespeare Jubilee at Stratford-upon-Avon

Sir Joshua Reynolds's *Discourses* (1769–1790)

Richard Arkwright invents the spinning water frame

Elizabeth Griffith's *The Delicate Distress*

Napoleon Bonaparte born

1770   Boston Massacre

William Billings's *The New England Psalm Singer*

Burke's *Thoughts on the Cause of the Present Discontents*

Goldsmith's *The Deserted Village*

Death of Thomas Chatterton

William Wordsworth born

1771   Arkwright's first spinning mill founded

Benjamin Franklin begins *The Autobiography*

Death of Thomas Gray

Death of Tobias Smollett

Walter Scott born

1772   **Samuel Taylor Coleridge born**

1773   Boston Tea Party

Anna Laetitia Aikin's *Poems*

Goldsmith's *She Stoops to Conquer*

Goethe's *Götz von Berlichingen*

1774   The first Continental Congress meets in Philadelphia

Goethe's *Sorrows of Young Werther*

Joseph Priestly discovers oxygen

Death of Oliver Goldsmith

Robert Southey born

1775   Burke's speech on American taxation

American War of Independence begins with the battles of Lexington and Concord

Johnson's *Journey to the Western Islands of Scotland*

Richard Brinsley Sheridan's *The Rivals* and *The Duenna*

Beaumarchais's *Le Barbier de Séville*

James Watt and Matthew Boulton begin building steam engines in England

Birth of Jane Austen

Birth of Charles Lamb

Birth of Walter Savage Landor

Birth of Matthew Lewis

1776   American Declaration of Independence

Gibbon's *Decline and Fall of the Roman Empire* (to 1788)

Adam Smith's *Inquiry into the Nature & Causes of the Wealth of Nations*

Thomas Paine's *Common Sense*

Death of David Hume

1777   Maurice Morgann's *Essay on the Dramatic Character of Sir John Falstaff*

Sheridan's *The School for Scandal* first performed (published 1780)

General Burgoyne surrenders at Saratoga

CHRONOLOGY

1778 The American colonies allied with France

Britain and France at war

Captain James Cook discovers Hawaii

Deaths of William Pitt, first earl of Chatham, of Jean Jacques Rousseau, and of Voltaire

William Hazlitt born

1779 Johnson's *Prefaces to the Works of the English Poets* (1779–1781); reissued in 1781 as *The Lives of the Most Eminent English Poets*

Sheridan's *The Critic*

Samuel Crompton invents the spinning mule

Death of David Garrick

1780 The Gordon Riots in London

1781 Charles Cornwallis surrenders at Yorktown

Jean Antoine Houdon's *Voltaire*

Immanuel Kant's *Critique of Pure Reason*

Rousseau's *Confessions* published posthumously (to 1788)

Friedrich von Schiller's *Die Räuber*

1782 Frances Burney's *Cecilia*

William Cowper's "The Journey of John Gilpin" published in the *Public Advertiser*

Choderlos de Laclos's *Les Liaisons dangereuses*

Ignatius Sancho's *Letters of the Late Iganatius Sancho, an African*

1783 American War of Independence ended by the Definitive Treaty of Peace, signed at Paris

William Blake's *Poetical Sketches*

George Crabbe's *The Village*

William Pitt the younger becomes prime minister

Marie-Henri Beyle (Stendhal) born

1784 Beaumarchais's *Le Mariage de Figaro* first performed (published 1785)

Death of Samuel Johnson

1785 Warren Hastings returns to England from India

James Boswell's *The Journey of a Tour of the Hebrides, with Samuel Johnson, LL.D.*

Cowper's *The Task*

Edmund Cartwright invents the power loom

Thomas De Quincey born

Thomas Love Peacock born

1786 William Beckford's *Vathek* published in English (originally written in French in 1782)

Robert Burns's *Poems Chiefly in the Scottish Dialect*

Mozart's *The Marriage of Figaro*

Death of Frederick the Great

1787 The Committee for the Abolition of the Slave Trade founded in England

The Constitutional Convention meets at Philadelphia; the Constitution is signed

William Bligh and crew begin voyage to Tahiti in the H.M.S. *Bounty*

Jefferson's *Notes on the State of Virginia*

Thomas Taylor's translation of *Concerning the Beautiful* (Plotinus)

1788 The trial of Hastings begins on charges of corruption of the government in India

The Estates-General of France summoned

U.S. Constitution is ratified

George Washington elected president of the United States

Giovanni Casanova's *Histoire de ma fuite* (first manuscript of his memoirs)

The *Daily Universal Register* becomes the *Times* (London)

George Gordon, Lord Byron born

1789 The Estates-General meets at Versailles

The National Assembly (Assemblée Nationale) convened

The fall of the Bastille marks the beginning of the French Revolution

The National Assembly draws up the Declaration of Rights of Man and of the Citizen

CHRONOLOGY

First U.S. Congress meets in New York

Blake's *Songs of Innocence*

Jeremy Bentham's *Introduction to the Principles of Morals and Legislation* introduces the theory of utilitarianism

Erasmus Darwin's *The Botanic Garden*

Gilbert White's *Natural History of Selborne*

1790   Congress sets permanent capital city site on the Potomac River

First U.S. Census

Burke's *Reflections on the Revolution in France*

Blake's *The Marriage of Heaven and Hell*

Edmund Malone's edition of Shakespeare

Wollstonecraft's *A Vindication of the Rights of Man*

Death of Benjamin Franklin

1791   French royal family's flight from Paris and capture at Varennes; imprisonment in the Tuileries

Anti-Jacobin riots at Birmingham

Bill of Rights is ratified

Paine's *The Rights of Man* (1791–1792)

Boswell's *The Life of Johnson*

Burns's *Tam o'Shanter*

The *Observer* founded

Mozart's *Requiem*

1792   The Prussians invade France and are repulsed at Valmy

September massacres

The National Convention declares royalty abolished in France

Washington reelected president of the United States

New York Stock Exchange opens

Samuel Rogers's *Pleasure of Memory*

Mary Wollstonecraft's *Vindication of the Rights of Woman*

Percy Bysshe Shelley born

1793   Trial and execution of Louis XVI and Marie-Antoinette

France declares war against England

Reign of Terror begins

The Committee of Public Safety (Comité de Salut Public) established

Eli Whitney devises the cotton gin

William Godwin's *An Enquiry Concerning Political Justice*

Blake's *Visions of the Daughters of Albion and America*

Olaudah Equiano's *The Interesting Narrative of the Life of Olaudah Equiano*

Wordsworth's *An Evening Walk* and *Descriptive Sketches*

1794   Execution of Georges Danton and Maximilien de Robespierre

Paine's *The Age of Reason* (1794–1796)

Blake's *Songs of Experience*

Ann Radcliffe's *The Mysteries of Udolpho*

Erasumus Darwin's *Zoonomia*

Death of Edward Gibbon

1795   The government of the Directory established (1795–1799)

Hastings acquitted

Landor's *Poems*

Goethe's *Wilhelm Meister*

Death of James Boswell

John Keats and Thomas Carlyle born

1796   Napoleon takes command in Italy

Edward Jenner performs first smallpox vaccination

Coleridge's *Poems on Various Subjects*

Matthew Lewis's *The Monk*

Watson's *Apology for the Bible*

Death of Robert Burns

1797   The peace of Campo Formio: extinction of the Venetian Republic

XYZ Affair

John Adams elected second president of the United States

Mutinies in the Royal Navy at Spithead and the Nore

CHRONOLOGY

Thomas Bewick's *History of British Birds*

Blake's *Vala, Or the Four Zoas* (first version)

Ann Radcliffe's *The Italian*

Mary Shelley born

Death of Edmund Burke

Death of Mary Wollstonecraft

Death of Horace Walpole

1798   Napoleon invades Egypt

Horatio Nelson wins the battle of the Nile

Wordsworth's and Coleridge's *Lyrical Ballads*

Landor's *Gebir*

Charles Lloyd's *Edmund Oliver*

Malthus's *Essay on the Principle of Population*

1799   Napoleon becomes first consul

Pitt introduces first income tax in Great Britain

Beethoven's *Pathetique*

Mary Hays's *The Victim of Prejudice*

Sheridan's *Pizarro*

Honoré de Balzac born

Thomas Hood born

Alexander Pushkin born

1800   Thomas Jefferson elected third president of the United States

Alessandro Volta produces electricity from a cell

Library of Congress established

Maria Edgeworth's *Castle Rackrent*

Francisco Goya's *Family of Charles IV*

Thomas Babington Macaulay born

Death of William Cowper

1801   First census taken in England

ca. 1801   Oliver Evans invents high-pressure steam engine

1802   The Treaty of Amiens marks the end of the French Revolutionary War

The *Edinburgh Review* founded

Paley's *Natural Theology*

Scott's *Minstrelsy of the Scottish Border* begun

1803   England's war with France renewed

The Louisiana Purchase

Robert Fulton propels a boat by steam power on the Seine

Joseph Mallord William Turner's *Calais Pier*

1804   Napoleon crowned emperor of the French

Jefferson reelected president of the United States

Blake's *Milton* (1804–1808) and *Jerusalem*

The Code Napoleon promulgated in France

Beethoven's *Eroica* Symphony

Schiller's *Wilhelm Tell*

Benjamin Disraeli born

1805   Napoleon plans the invasion of England

Battle of Trafalgar

Battle of Austerlitz

Beethoven's *Fidelio* first produced

Scott's *Lay of the Last Minstrel*

1806   Beethoven's Violin Concerto, Op. 61

Lady Morgan's *The Wild Irish Girl*

Scott's *Marmion*

Deaths of William Pitt and Charles James Fox

Elizabeth Barrett born

1807   France invades Portugal

Aaron Burr tried for treason and acquitted

Byron's *Hours of Idleness*

Charles and Mary Lamb's *Tales from Shakespeare*

Thomas Moore's *Irish Melodies*

Wordsworth's *Ode on the Intimations of Immortality*

1808   National uprising in Spain against the French invasion

The Peninsular War begins

James Madison elected president of the United States

CHRONOLOGY

Covent Garden theater burned down

Goethe's *Faust* (Part 1)

Beethoven's Fifth Symphony completed

Lamb's *Specimens of English Dramatic Poets*

1809   Drury Lane theater burned down and rebuilt

The *Quarterly Review* founded

Byron's *English Bards and Scotch Reviewers*

Byron sails for the Mediterranean

Goya's *Los Desastres de la guerra* (1809–1814)

Births of Alfred Tennyson and Edward Fitzgerald

1810   Crabbe's *The Borough*

Scott's *The Lady of the Lake*

Southey's *Curse of Kehama*

Germaine de Staël's *De l'Allemagne*

Elizabeth Gaskell born

1811–1820   Regency of George IV

1811   Luddite Riots begin

Coleridge's *Lectures on Shakespeare* (1811–1814)

Austen's *Sense and Sensibility*

Schubert's first *Lieder*

Shelley's *The Necessity of Atheism*

John Constable's *Dedham Vale*

William Makepeace Thackeray born

1812   Napoleon invades Russia; captures and retreats from Moscow

United States declares war against England

Henry Bell's steamship *Comet* is launched on the Clyde river

Madison reelected president of the United States

Byron's *Childe Harold* (Cantos 1–2)

The Brothers Grimm's *Fairy Tales* (1812–1815)

Hegel's *The Science of Logic*

Birth of Charles Dickens

Birth of Robert Browning

1813   Wellington wins the battle of Vitoria and enters France

Austen's *Pride and Prejudice*

Byron's *The Giaour* and *The Bride of Abydos*

Shelley's *Queen Mab*

Southey's *Life of Nelson*

1814   Napoleon abdicates and is exiled to Elba; Bourbon restoration with Louis XVIII

Treaty of Ghent ends the war between Britain and the United States

Jane Austen's *Mansfield Park*

Byron's *The Corsair* and *Lara*

Scott's *Waverley*

Wordsworth's *The Excursion*

1815   Napoleon returns to France (the Hundred Days); is defeated at Waterloo and exiled to St. Helena

U.S.S. *Fulton*, the first steam warship, built

Scott's *Guy Mannering*

Schlegel's *Lectures on Dramatic Art and Literature* translated

Wordsworth's *The White Doe of Rylstone*

Anthony Trollope born

1816   Byron leaves England permanently

The Elgin Marbles exhibited in the British Museum

James Monroe elected president of the United States

Austen's *Emma*

Byron's *Childe Harold* (Canto 3)

Coleridge's *Christabel, Kubla Khan: A Vision, The Pains of Sleep*

Benjamin Constant's *Adolphe*

Goethe's *Italienische Reise*

Peacock's *Headlong Hall*

Scott's *The Antiquary*

Shelley's *Alastor*

Rossini's *Il Barbiere di Siviglia*

Death of Richard Brinsley Sheridan

Charlotte Brontë born

CHRONOLOGY

1817   *Blackwood's Edinburgh* magazine founded

Austen's *Northanger Abbey* and *Persuasion*

Byron's *Manfred*

Coleridge's *Biographia Literaria*

Hazlitt's *The Characters of Shakespeare's Plays* and *The Round Table*

Keats's *Poems*

Peacock's *Melincourt*

David Ricardo's *Principles of Political Economy and Taxation*

Deaths of Jane Austen and Germaine de Staël Branwell Brontë and Henry David Thoreau born

1818   Byron's *Childe Harold* (Canto 4), and *Beppo*

John Evelyn's *Diary*

Hazlitt's *Lectures on the English Poets*

Keats's *Endymion*

Peacock's *Nightmare Abbey*

Scott's *Rob Roy* and *The Heart of Mid-Lothian*

Mary Shelley's *Frankenstein*

Percy Shelley's *The Revolt of Islam*

Emily Brontë born

Karl Marx born

Ivan Sergeyevich Turgenev born

1819   The *Savannah* becomes the first steamship to cross the Atlantic (in 26 days)

Peterloo massacre in Manchester

Byron's *Don Juan* (to 1824) and *Mazeppa*

Crabbe's *Tales of the Hall*

Géricault's *Raft of the Medusa*

Hazlitt's *Lectures on the English Comic Writers*

William Hone's *The Political House that Jack Built*

Arthur Schopenhauer's *Die Welt als Wille und Vorstellung (The World as Will and Idea)*

Scott's *The Bride of Lammermoor* and *A Legend of Montrose*

Shelley's *The Cenci*, "The Masque of Anarchy," and "Ode to the West Wind" Wordsworth's *Peter Bell*

Queen Victoria born

Mary Ann Evans (George Eliot) born

1819–1820   Washington Irving's *The Sketch Book of Geoffrey Crayon, Gent*

1820–1830   Reign of George IV

1820   Trial of Queen Caroline

Cato Street Conspiracy suppressed; Arthur Thistlewood hanged

Monroe reelected president of the United States

Missouri Compromise

The *London* magazine founded

Keats's *Lamia, Isabella, The Eve of St. Agnes, and Other Poems*

Hazlitt's *Lectures Chiefly on the Dramatic Literature of the Age of Elizabeth*

Charles Maturin's *Melmoth the Wanderer*

Scott's *Ivanhoe* and *The Monastery*

Shelley's *Prometheus Unbound*

Anne Brontë born

1821   Greek War of Independence begins

Liberia founded as a colony for freed slaves

Byron's *Cain, Marino Faliero, The Two Foscari*, and *Sardanapalus*

John Constable's *Hay Wain*

De Quincey's *Confessions of an English Opium-Eater*

Hazlitt's *Table Talk* (1821–1822)

Scott's *Kenilworth*

Shelley's *Adonais* and *Epipsychidion*

Death of John Keats

Death of Napoleon Bonaparte

Charles Baudelaire born

Fyodor Dostoyevsky born

Gustave Flaubert born

1822   The Massacres of Chios (Greeks rebel against Turkish rule)

CHRONOLOGY

Byron's *The Vision of Judgment*

Peacock's *Maid Marian*

Scott's *Peveril of the Peak*

Shelley's *Hellas*

Death of Percy Bysshe Shelley

Matthew Arnold born

1823 Monroe Doctrine proclaimed

Byron's *The Age of Bronze* and *The Island*

Hazlitt's *Liber Amoris*

Lamb's *Essays of Elia*

Scott's *Quentin Durward*

1824 The National Gallery opened in London

John Quincy Adams elected president of the United States

The *Westminster Review* founded

Beethoven's Ninth Symphony first performed

James Hogg's *The Private Memoirs and Confessions of a Justified Sinner*

Landor's *Imaginary Conversations* (1824–1829)

Scott's *Redgauntlet*

Death of George Gordon, Lord Byron

1825 Inauguration of steam-powered passenger and freight service on the Stockton and Darlington railway

Bolivia and Brazil become independent

Hazlitt's *The Spirit of the Age*

Alessandro Manzoni's *I Promessi Sposi* (1825–1826)

Felix Mendelssohn's String Octet

1826 André-Marie Ampère's *Mémoire sur la théorie mathématique des phénomènes électrodynamiques*

James Fenimore Cooper's *The Last of the Mohicans*

Disraeli's *Vivian Grey* (1826–1827)

Scott's *Woodstock*

1827 The battle of Navarino ensures the independence of Greece

Josef Ressel obtains patent for the screw propeller for steamships

Beethoven's Quartet, Op. 131

Heinrich Heine's *Buch der Lieder*

Thomas Hood's *Other Poems*

Death of William Blake

1828 Andrew Jackson elected president of the United States

Birth of Henrik Ibsen

Birth of George Meredith

Birth of Dante Gabriel Rossetti

Birth of Leo Tolstoy

1829 The Catholic Emancipation Act

Robert Peel establishes the metropolitan police force

Greek independence recognized by Turkey

Balzac begins *La Comédie humaine* (1829–1848)

Hector Berlioz's *Symphonie Fantastique*

Eugène Delacroix's *Sardanapalus*

Peacock's *The Misfortunes of Elphin*

J. M. W. Turner's *Ulysses Deriding Polyphemus*

1830–1837 Reign of William IV

1830 Charles X of France abdicates and is succeeded by Louis-Philippe

The Liverpool-Manchester railway opened

Tennyson's *Poems, Chiefly Lyrical*

Death of William Hazlitt

Christina Rossetti born

1831 Michael Faraday discovers electromagnetic induction

Charles Darwin's voyage on H.M.S. *Beagle* begins (1831–1836)

The Barbizon school of artists' first exhibition

Nat Turner slave revolt crushed in Virginia

Peacock's *Crotchet Castle*

Stendhal's *Le Rouge et le noir*

Edward Trelawny's *The Adventures of a Younger Son*

1832 The first Reform Bill

Samuel Morse invents the telegraph

CHRONOLOGY

Jackson reelected president of the United States

Disraeli's *Contarini Fleming*

Goethe's *Faust* (Part 2)

Tennyson's *Poems, Chiefly Lyrical*, including "The Lotus-Eaters" and "The Lady of Shalott"

Death of Johann Wolfgang von Goethe

Death of Sir Walter Scott

Death of George Crabbe

Lewis Carroll born

1833   Robert Browning's *Pauline*

John Keble launches the Oxford Movement

American Anti-Slavery Society founded

Lamb's *Last Essays of Elia*

Carlyle's *Sartor Resartus* (1833–1834)

Pushkin's *Eugene Onegin*

Mendelssohn's *Italian Symphony* first performed

1834   Abolition of slavery in the British Empire

Louis Braille's alphabet for the blind

Balzac's *Le Père Goriot*

Gogol's *Dead Souls* (Part 1, 1834–1842)

Death of Samuel Taylor Coleridge

Death of Charles Lamb

William Morris born

1835   Hans Christian Andersen's *Fairy Tales* (1st ser.)

Robert Browning's *Paracelsus*

Samuel Butler born

Alexis de Tocqueville's *De la Democratie en Amerique* (1835–1840)

1836   Martin Van Buren elected president of the United States

Dickens's *Sketches by Boz* (1836–1837)

Landor's *Pericles and Aspasia*

1837–1901   **Reign of Queen Victoria**

1837   Carlyle's *The French Revolution*

Dickens's *Oliver Twist* (1837–1838) and *Pickwick Papers*

Disraeli's *Venetia* and *Henrietta Temple*

Death of Alexander Pushkin

1838   Chartist movement in England

National Gallery in London opened

Elizabeth Barrett Browning's *The Seraphim and Other Poems*

Louis Daguerre takes first photographs

Dickens's *Nicholas Nickleby* (1838–1839)

Robert Schumann's *Kinderszenen, Kriesleriana*

1839   Louis Daguerre perfects process for producing an image on a silver-coated copper plate

Faraday's *Experimental Researches in Electricity* (1839–1855)

First Chartist riots

Opium War between Great Britain and China

Carlyle's *Chartism*

1840   Canadian Act of Union

Queen Victoria marries Prince Albert

Charles Barry begins construction of the Houses of Parliament (1840–1852)

William Henry Harrison elected president of the United States

Robert Browning's *Sordello*

Mikhail Lermontov's *A Hero of Our Time*

Thomas Hardy born

Death of Frances Burney

1841   New Zealand proclaimed a British colony

James Clark Ross discovers the Antarctic continent

Punch founded

John Tyler succeeds to the presidency after the death of Harrison

Carlyle's *Heroes and Hero-Worship*

Dickens's *The Old Curiosity Shop*

1842   Chartist riots

Income tax revived in Great Britain

CHRONOLOGY

The Mines Act, forbidding work underground by women or by children under the age of ten

Charles Edward Mudie's Lending Library founded in London

Dickens visits America

Robert Browning's *Dramatic Lyrics*

Macaulay's *Lays of Ancient Rome*

Tennyson's *Poems*, including "Morte d'Arthur," "St. Simeon Stylites," and "Ulysses"

Wordsworth's *Poems*

Death of Stendhal

1843　Marc Isambard Brunel's Thames tunnel opened

The Economist founded

Carlyle's *Past and Present*

Dickens's *A Christmas Carol*

Sören Kierkegaard's *Fear and Trembling*

John Stuart Mill's *Logic*

Macaulay's *Critical and Historical Essays*

John Ruskin's *Modern Painters* (1843–1860)

Death of Robert Southey

1844　Rochdale Society of Equitable Pioneers, one of the first consumers' cooperatives, founded by twenty-eight Lancashire weavers

James K. Polk elected president of the United States

Elizabeth Barrett Browning's *Poems*, including "The Cry of the Children"

Dickens's *Martin Chuzzlewit*

Disraeli's *Coningsby*

Turner's *Rain, Steam and Speed*

Gerard Manley Hopkins born

Death of William Beckford

1845　The great potato famine in Ireland begins (1845–1849)

Disraeli's *Sybil*

Richard Wagner's *Tannhäuser*

Death of Thomas Hood

1846　Repeal of the Corn Laws

The *Daily News* founded (edited by Dickens the first three weeks)

Standard-gauge railway introduced in Britain

The Brontës' pseudonymous *Poems by Currer, Ellis and Acton Bell*

Frederick Douglass's *Narrative of the Life of Frederick Douglass an American Slave*

Lear's *Book of Nonsense*

1847　The Ten Hours Factory Act

James Simpson uses chloroform as an anesthetic

Anne Brontë's *Agnes Grey*

Charlotte Brontë's *Jane Eyre*

Emily Brontë's *Wuthering Heights*

Bram Stoker born

Tennyson's *The Princess*

Giuseppe Verdi's *Macbeth*

1848　The year of revolutions in France, Germany, Italy, Hungary, Poland

Marx and Engels issue *The Communist Manifesto*

The Chartist Petition

The Pre-Raphaelite Brotherhood founded

Zachary Taylor elected president of the United States

Anne Brontë's *The Tenant of Wildfell Hall*

Dickens's *Dombey and Son*

Elizabeth Gaskell's *Mary Barton*

Macaulay's *History of England* (1848–1861)

Mill's *Principles of Political Economy*

Thackeray's *Vanity Fair*

Death of Emily Brontë

1849　Bedford College for women founded

Arnold's *The Strayed Reveller*

Charlotte Brontë's *Shirley*

Ruskin's *The Seven Lamps of Architecture*

Death of Anne Brontë

Death of Maria Edgeworth

CHRONOLOGY

1850 The Public Libraries Act

First submarine telegraph cable laid between Dover and Calais

Millard Fillmore succeeds to the presidency after the death of Taylor

Elizabeth Barrett Browning's *Sonnets from the Portuguese*

Carlyle's *Latter-Day Pamphlets*

Dickens's *Household Words* (1850–1859) and *David Copperfield*

Emerson's *Representative Men*

Hawthorne's *The Scarlet Letter*

Charles Kingsley's *Alton Locke*

The Pre-Raphaelites publish the *Germ*

Robert Louis Stevenson born

Tennyson's *In Memoriam*

Thackeray's *The History of Pendennis*

Richard Wagner's *Lohengrin*

Death of Wordsworth; *The Prelude* is published posthumously

Death of Honoré de Balzac

1851 The Great Exhibition opens at the Crystal Palace in Hyde Park

Louis Napoleon seizes power in France

Gold strike in Victoria incites Australian gold rush

Elizabeth Gaskell's *Cranford* (1851–1853)

Melville's *Moby Dick*

Meredith's *Poems*

Ruskin's *The Stones of Venice* (1851–1853)

1852 The Second Empire proclaimed with Napoleon III as emperor

David Livingstone begins to explore the Zambezi (1852–1856)

Franklin Pierce elected president of the United States

Arnold's *Empedocles on Etna*

Harriet Beecher Stowe's *Uncle Tom's Cabin*

Thackeray's *The History of Henry Esmond, Esq.*

1853 Crimean War (1853–1856)

Arnold's *Poems*, including "The Scholar Gypsy" and "Sohrab and Rustum"

Charlotte Brontë's *Villette*

Elizabeth Gaskell's *Crawford and Ruth*

1854 Frederick D. Maurice's Working Men's College founded in London with more than 130 pupils

Battle of Balaklava

Dickens's *Hard Times*

John Mitchel's *Jail Journal*

Theodor Mommsen's *History of Rome* (1854–1856)

Tennyson's "The Charge of the Light Brigade"

Thoreau's *Walden*

Florence Nightingale in the Crimea (1854–1856)

Births of **Oscar Wilde** and James George Frazer

1855 David Livingstone discovers the Victoria Falls

Robert Browning's *Men and Women*

Elizabeth Gaskell's *North and South*

Franz Liszt's *Faust* Symphony

Olive Schreiner born

Tennyson's *Maud*

Thackeray's *The Newcomes*

Trollope's *The Warden*

Whitman's *Leaves of Grass* (first version)

Death of Charlotte Brontë

1856 The Treaty of Paris ends the Crimean War

Henry Bessemer's steel process invented

James Buchanan elected president of the United States

Flaubert's *Madame Bovary*

Henry Rider Haggard born

George Bernard Shaw born

1857 The Indian Mutiny begins; crushed in 1858

Joseph Conrad is born

The Matrimonial Causes Act

CHRONOLOGY

Charlotte Brontë's *The Professor*

Elizabeth Barrett Browning's *Aurora Leigh*

Baudelaire's *Les Fleurs du Mal*

Dickens's *Little Dorritt*

Elizabeth Gaskell's *The Life of Charlotte Brontë*

Thomas Hughes's *Tom Brown's School Days*

Trollope's *Barchester Towers*

1858 Carlyle's *History of Frederick the Great* (1858–1865)

George Eliot's *Scenes of Clerical Life*

Morris's *The Defense of Guinevere*

Trollope's *Dr. Thorne*

1859 Charles Darwin's *The Origin of Species*

Dickens's *A Tale of Two Cities*

Arthur Conan Doyle born

George Eliot's *Adam Bede*

Fitzgerald's *The Rubaiyat of Omar Khayyám*

Meredith's *The Ordeal of Richard Feverel*

Mill's *On Liberty*

Samuel Smiles's *Self-Help*

Tennyson's *Idylls of the King*

Death of Thomas De Quincey

Death of Thomas Babington Macaulay

1860 Abraham Lincoln elected president of the United States

The *Cornhill* magazine founded with Thackeray as editor

James M. Barrie born

William Wilkie Collins's *The Woman in White*

George Eliot's *The Mill on the Floss*

1861 American Civil War begins

Louis Pasteur presents the germ theory of disease

Arnold's *Lectures on Translating Homer*

Dickens's *Great Expectations*

George Eliot's *Silas Marner*

Meredith's *Evan Harrington*

Francis Turner Palgrave's *The Golden Treasury*

Trollope's *Framley Parsonage*

Peacock's *Gryll Grange*

Death of Prince Albert

1862 George Eliot's *Romola*

Meredith's *Modern Love*

Christina Rossetti's *Goblin Market*

Ruskin's *Unto This Last*

Trollope's *Orley Farm*

Turgenev's *Fathers and Sons*

1863 Thomas Huxley's *Man's Place in Nature*

Death of William Makepeace Thackeray

1864 The Geneva Red Cross Convention signed by twelve nations

Lincoln reelected president of the United States

Johannes Brahms's Piano Quintet in F minor

Robert Browning's *Dramatis Personae*

John Henry Newman's *Apologia pro vita sua*

Tennyson's *Enoch Arden*

Trollope's *The Small House at Allington*

1865 Assassination of Lincoln; Andrew Johnson succeeds to the presidency

Arnold's *Essays in Criticism* (1st ser.)

Carroll's *Alice's Adventures in Wonderland*

Dickens's *Our Mutual Friend*

Sir Samuel Ferguson's *Lays of the Western Gael*

Meredith's *Rhoda Fleming*

A. C. Swinburne's *Atalanta in Calydon*

William Butler Yeats born

Death of Elizabeth Gaskell

1866 First successful transatlantic telegraph cable laid

George Eliot's *Felix Holt, the Radical*

CHRONOLOGY

Elizabeth Gaskell's *Wives and Daughters* (posthumously)

Beatrix Potter born

Swinburne's *Poems and Ballads*

Death of Thomas Love Peacock

1867 The second Reform Bill

Arnold's *New Poems*

Bagehot's *The English Constitution*

Carlyle's *Shooting Niagara*

Dostoyevsky's *Crime and Punishment*

Marx's *Das Kapital* (vol. 1)

Johann Strauss's *On The Beautiful Blue Danube*

Trollope's *The Last Chronicle of Barset*

Giuseppe Verdi's *Don Carlos*

Death of Charles Baudelaire

1868 Gladstone becomes prime minister (1868–1874)

Johnson impeached by House of Representatives; acquitted by Senate

Ulysses S. Grant elected president of the United States

Christopher L. Sholes patents the typewriter

Robert Browning's *The Ring and the Book* (1868–1869)

Collins's *The Moonstone*

John Bigelow publishes complete version of Franklin's *The Autobiography*

1869 The Suez Canal opened

Girton College, Cambridge, founded

Arnold's *Culture and Anarchy*

Mill's *The Subjection of Women*

Tolstoy's *War and Peace*

Trollope's *Phineas Finn*

1870 The Elementary Education Act establishes schools under the aegis of local boards

Dickens's *Edwin Drood*

Disraeli's *Lothair*

Morris's *The Earthly Paradise*

Dante Gabriel Rossetti's *Poems*

1871 Trade unions legalized

Newnham College, Cambridge, founded for women students

Carroll's *Through the Looking Glass*

Darwin's *The Descent of Man*

Meredith's *The Adventures of Harry Richmond*

Swinburne's *Songs Before Sunrise*

John Millington Synge born

1872 Max Beerbohm born

Samuel Butler's *Erewhon*

George Eliot's *Middlemarch*

Grant reelected president of the United States

Hardy's *Under the Greenwood Tree*

Charles Lever's *Lord Kilgobbin*

Nietzsche's *The Birth of Tragedy*

1873 Arnold's *Literature and Dogma*

Mill's *Autobiography*

Pater's *Studies in the History of the Renaissance*

Rimbaud's *Une Saison en enfer*

Trollope's *The Eustace Diamonds*

1874 Disraeli becomes prime minister

Cézanne's *A Modern Olympia* (completed)

Hardy's *Far from the Madding Crowd*

James Thomson's *The City of Dreadful Night*

1875 Britain buys Suez Canal shares

Tchaikovsky's Piano Concerto No. 1

Thomas Eakins's *Gross Clinic*

Trollope's *The Way We Live Now*

ca. 1875 Alexander Graham Bell, with the assistence of Thomas Watson, devises an apparatus for transmitting sound by electricity

1876 F. H. Bradley's *Ethical Studies*

George Eliot's *Daniel Deronda*

Henry James's *Roderick Hudson*

Meredith's *Beauchamp's Career*

Morris's *Sigurd the Volsung*

CHRONOLOGY

Trollope's *The Prime Minister*

1877 Rutherford B. Hayes elected president of the United States after Electoral Commission awards him disputed votes

Johannes Brahms's First and Second Symphonies

Henry James's *The American*

Tolstoy's *Anna Karenina*

1878 Electric street lighting introduced in London

Hardy's *The Return of the Native*

Swinburne's *Poems and Ballads* (2d ser.)

Edward Thomas born

1879 Somerville College and Lady Margaret Hall opened at Oxford for women

The London telephone exchange built

Gladstone's Midlothian campaign (1879–1880)

Robert Browning's *Dramatic Idyls*

Ibsen's *A Doll House*

Meredith's *The Egoist*

E. M. Forster born

1880 Gladstone's second term as prime minister (1880–1885)

James A. Garfield elected president of the United States

George Eastman invents dry, rolled film and the hand-held camera

Thomas Edison invents the light bulb

Robert Browning's *Dramatic Idyls Second Series*

Disraeli's *Endymion*

Dostoyevsky's *The Brothers Karamazov*

Hardy's *The Trumpet-Major*

Lytton Strachey born

Death of Gustave Flaubert

Death of Mary Ann Evans (George Eliot)

1881 Garfield assassinated; Chester A. Arthur succeeds to the presidency

Henry James's *The Portrait of a Lady* and *Washington Square*

Joachuim Maria Machado de Assis's *Memórias póstumas de Brás Cubas*

Renoir's *Luncheon of the Boating Party*

Dante Gabriel Rossetti's *Ballads and Sonnets*

P. G. Wodehouse born

Death of Fyodor Dostoyevsky

Death of Benjamin Disraeli

1882 Triple Alliance formed between German empire, Austrian empire, and Italy

Leslie Stephen begins to edit the *Dictionary of National Biography*

Married Women's Property Act passed in Britain

Britain occupies Egypt and the Sudan

Births of James Joyce and Virginia Woolf

Deaths of Anthony Trollope and Christina Rossetti

1883 Uprising of the Mahdi: Britain evacuates the Sudan

Royal College of Music opens

T. H. Green's *Ethics*

Ralph Iron's (Olive Schreiner) *The Story of an African Farm*

Nietzsche's *Thus Spake Zarathustra* (to 1885)

Stevenson's *Treasure Island*

Deaths of Karl Marx and Ivan Sergeyevich Turgenev

1884 The Mahdi captures Omdurman: General Gordon appointed to command the garrison of Khartoum

Grover Cleveland elected president of the United States

The *Oxford English Dictionary* begins publishing

The Fabian Society founded

Hiram Maxim's recoil-operated machine gun invented

Louis Pasteur inoculates against rabies

Mark Twain's *Huckleberry Finn*

1885 The Mahdi captures Khartoum: General Gordon killed

Haggard's *King Solomon's Mines*

Marx's *Das Kapital* (vol. 2)

CHRONOLOGY

Meredith's *Diana of the Crossways*

Pater's *Marius the Epicurean*

D. H. Lawrence born

1886 The Canadian Pacific Railway completed

Gold discovered in the Transvaal

Ronald Firbank born

Henry James's *The Bostonians* and *The Princess Casamassima*

Georges Seurat's *Sunday on the Island of La Grande Jatte*

Stevenson's *The Strange Case of Dr. Jekyll and Mr. Hyde*

1887 Queen Victoria's Golden Jubilee

Rupert Brooke born

Anton Bruckner's *Te Deum*

Haggard's *Allan Quatermain* and *She*

Hardy's *The Woodlanders*

Giuseppe Verdi's *Othello*

1888 Benjamin Harrison elected president of the United States

Henry James's *The Aspern Papers*

Kipling's *Plain Tales from the Hills*

Rimsky-Korsakov's *Scheherazade*

Births of T. E. Lawrence and **T. S. Eliot**

Death of Gerard Manley Hopkins

1889 Yeats's *The Wanderings of Oisin*

Eiffel Tower completed

Vincent Van Gogh's *The Starry Night*

Deaths of Robert Browning and Matthew Arnold

1890 Morris founds the Kelmscott Press

Agatha Christie born

Dickinson's *Poems by Emily Dickinson* (posthumously)

Frazer's *The Golden Bough* (1st ed.)

Henry James's *The Tragic Muse*

Morris's *News From Nowhere*

Richard Strauss's *Death and Transfiguration*

Jean Rhys born

1891 George Gissing's *New Grub Street*

Hardy's *Tess of the d'Urbervilles*

Wilde's *The Picture of Dorian Gray*

1892 Grover Cleveland elected president of the United States

Conan Doyle's *The Adventures of Sherlock Holmes*

Shaw's *Widower's Houses*

Wilde's *Lady Windermere's Fan*

Birth of J. R. R. Tolkien

Birth of Rebecca West

Death of Alfred, Lord Tennyson

1893 George Moore's *Modern Painting*

Wilde's *A Woman of No Importance* and *Salomé*

Louis Sullivan's *Transportation Building* at World's Columbian Exhibition in Chicago

1894 Kipling's *The Jungle Book*

George Moore's *Esther Waters*

Marx's *Das Kapital* (vol. 3)

Audrey Beardsley's *The Yellow Book* begins to appear quarterly

Gauguin's *The Day of the God*

Shaw's *Arms and the Man*

Death of Robert Louis Stevenson

1895 Trial and imprisonment of Oscar Wilde

William Ramsay announces discovery of helium

The National Trust founded

Radio is born when Guglielmo Marconi transmits electric signals through the air from one end of his house to the other

Conrad's *Almayer's Folly*

Hardy's *Jude the Obscure*

Wells's *The Time Machine*

Wilde's *The Importance of Being Earnest*

Yeats's *Poems*

ca. 1895 Loie Fuller's *La Danse du Feu*

1896 William McKinley elected president of the United States

Failure of the Jameson Raid on the Transvaal

CHRONOLOGY

Housman's *A Shropshire Lad*

Two of Thomas Traherne's manuscripts discovered in a London bookstall

Death of William Morris

1897 Queen Victoria's Diamond Jubilee

Conrad's *The Nigger of the Narcissus*

Havelock Ellis's *Studies in the Psychology of Sex* begins publication

Henry James's *The Spoils of Poynton* and *What Maisie Knew*

Kipling's *Captains Courageous*

Stèphane Mallarmè's *Un Coup de Dés*

Shaw's *Candida*

Stoker's *Dracula*

Wells's *The Invisible Man*

1898 Kitchener defeats the Mahdist forces at Omdurman: the Sudan reoccupied

Hardy's *Wessex Poems*

Henry James's *The Turn of the Screw*

C. S. Lewis born

Shaw's *Caesar and Cleopatra* and *You Never Can Tell*

Wells's *The War of the Worlds*

Wilde's *The Ballad of Reading Gaol*

Death of Lewis Carroll

1899 The Boer War begins

Chopin's *The Awakening*

Elgar's *Enigma Variations*

Winslow Homer's *The Gulf Stream*

Kipling's *Stalky and Co.*

Arnold Schoenberg's *Transfigured Night*

Birth of Elizabeth Bowen

Birth of Noël Coward

1900 McKinley reelected president of the United States

British Labour party founded

Boxer Rebellion in China

Reginald A. Fessenden transmits speech by wireless

First Zeppelin trial flight

Max Planck presents his first paper on the quantum theory

Conrad's *Lord Jim*

Elgar's *The Dream of Gerontius*

Sigmund Freud's *The Interpretation of Dreams*

Yeats's *The Shadowy Waters*

V. S. Pritchett born

Death of Oscar Wilde

1901–1910   Reign of King Edward VII

1901 William McKinley assassinated; Theodore Roosevelt succeeds to the presidency

First transatlantic wireless telegraph signal transmitted

Max Planck develops quantum theory

Chekhov's *Three Sisters*

Freud's *The Psychopathology of Everyday Life*

Rudyard Kipling's *Kim*

Thomas Mann's *Buddenbrooks*

Potter's *The Tale of Peter Rabbit*

Shaw's *Captain Brassbound's Conversion*

August Strindberg's *The Dance of Death*

1902 Barrie's *The Admirable Crichton*

Arnold Bennett's *Anna of the Five Towns*

Cézanne's *Le Lac D'Annecy*

Conrad's *Heart of Darkness*

Claude Debussy's opera *Pelléas et Mélisande* first performed

Henry James's *The Wings of the Dove*

William James's *The Varieties of Religious Experience*

Kipling's *Just So Stories*

Maugham's *Mrs. Cradock*

Stevie Smith born

Death of Samuel Butler

Times Literary Supplement begins publishing

CHRONOLOGY

1903   At its London congress the Russian Social Democratic Party divides into Mensheviks, led by Plekhanov, and Bolsheviks, led by Lenin

The treaty of Panama places the Canal Zone in U.S. hands for a nominal rent

Motor cars regulated in Britain to a 20-mile-per-hour limit

The Wright brothers make a successful flight in the United States

Burlington magazine founded

Samuel Butler's *The Way of All Flesh* published posthumously

Cyril Connolly born

Claude Debussy begins *La Mer* (completed 1905)

W. E. B. Du Bois's *The Soul of Black Folks*

George Gissing's *The Private Papers of Henry Ryecroft*

Hardy's *The Dynasts*

Henry James's *The Ambassadors*

Alan Paton born

Shaw's *Man and Superman*

Synge's *Riders to the Sea* produced in Dublin

Yeats's *In the Seven Woods* and *On Baile's Strand*

1904   Roosevelt elected president of the United States

Russo-Japanese war (1904–1905)

Construction of the Panama Canal begins

The ultraviolet lamp invented

The engineering firm of Rolls Royce founded

Barrie's *Peter Pan* first performed

Cecil Day Lewis born

Chekhov's *The Cherry Orchard*

Conrad's *Nostromo*

Antoni Gaudí's Casa Batlló begun

Henry James's *The Golden Bowl*

Kipling's *Traffics and Discoveries*

Georges Rouault's *Head of a Tragic Clown*

G. M. Trevelyan's *England Under the Stuarts*

Puccini's *Madame Butterfly*

First Shaw-Granville Barker season at the Royal Court Theatre

The Abbey Theatre founded in Dublin

Graham Greene born

1905   Russian sailors on the battleship Potemkin mutiny

After riots and a general strike the czar concedes demands by the Duma for legislative powers, a wider franchise, and civil liberties

Albert Einstein publishes his first theory of relativity

The Austin Motor Company founded

Bennett's *Tales of the Five Towns*

Claude Debussy's *La Mer*

E. M. Forster's *Where Angels Fear to Tread*

Henry Green born

Matisse's *The Open Window*

Richard Strauss's *Salome*

H. G. Wells's *Kipps*

Wilde's *De Profundis*

1906   Liberals win a landslide victory in the British general election

The Trades Disputes Act legitimizes peaceful picketing in Britain

Captain Dreyfus rehabilitated in France

J. J. Thomson begins research on gamma rays

Reginald Fessenden transmits first radio broadcast

The U.S. Pure Food and Drug Act passed

Samuel Beckett born

Churchill's *Lord Randolph Churchill*

William Empson born

Galsworthy's *The Man of Property*

Charles Ives's *The Unanswered Question*

Kipling's *Puck of Pook's Hill*

Shaw's *The Doctor's Dilemma*

CHRONOLOGY

Yeats's *Poems 1899–1905*

1907 Exhibition of cubist paintings in Paris

Henry Adams's *The Education of Henry Adams*

W. H. Auden born

Henri Bergson's *Creative Evolution*

Conrad's *The Secret Agent*

Daphne du Maurier born

Firbank's *A Disciple from the Country*

Forster's *The Longest Journey*

Christopher Fry born

André Gide's *La Porte étroite*

Shaw's *John Bull's Other Island* and *Major Barbara*

Synge's *The Playboy of the Western World*

Trevelyan's *Garibaldi's Defence of the Roman Republic*

1908 Herbert Asquith becomes prime minister

David Lloyd George becomes chancellor of the exchequer

William Howard Taft elected president of the United States

The Young Turks seize power in Istanbul

Henry Ford's Model T car produced

Bennett's *The Old Wives' Tale*

Pierre Bonnard's *Nude Against the Light*

Georges Braque's *House at L'Estaque*

Chesterton's *The Man Who Was Thursday*

Jacob Epstein's *Figures* erected in London

Forster's *A Room with a View*

Anatole France's *L'Ile des Pingouins*

Henri Matisse's *Bonheur de Vivre*

Henri Rousseau's *The Jungle*

Elgar's First Symphony

Ford Madox Ford founds the *English Review*

Alexander Scriabin completes *Le poème de l'extase*

1909 The Young Turks depose Sultan Abdul Hamid

The Anglo-Persian Oil Company formed

Louis Bleriot crosses the English Channel from France by monoplane

Admiral Robert Peary reaches the North Pole

Freud lectures at Clark University (Worcester, Mass.) on psychoanalysis

Serge Diaghilev's Ballets Russes opens in Paris

Galsworthy's *Strife*

Hardy's *Time's Laughingstocks*

Malcolm Lowry born

Claude Monet's *Water Lilies*

Stephen Spender born

Trevelyan's *Garibaldi and the Thousand*

Wells's *Tono-Bungay* first published (book form, 1909)

Frank Lloyd Wright's Robie House, Chicago

Eudora Welty born

1910–1936 Reign of King George V

1910 The Liberals win the British general election

Marie Curie's *Treatise on Radiography*

Arthur Evans excavates Knossos

Edouard Manet and the first post-impressionist exhibition in London

Filippo Marinetti publishes "Manifesto of the Futurist Painters"

Norman Angell's *The Great Illusion*

Bennett's *Clayhanger*

Forster's *Howards End*

Galsworthy's *Justice* and *The Silver Box*

Kipling's *Rewards and Fairies*

Rimsky-Korsakov's *Le Coq d'or*

Bertrand Russell's and Alfred North Whitehead's *Principia Mathematica*

Stravinsky's *The Firebird*

Vaughan Williams's *A Sea Symphony*

Wells's *The History of Mr. Polly*

CHRONOLOGY

Wells's *The New Machiavelli* first published (in book form, 1911)

Wodehouse's *Psmith in the City*

1911 Lloyd George introduces National Health Insurance Bill

Suffragette riots in Whitehall

Roald Amundsen reaches the South Pole

Bennett's *The Card*

Chagall's *Self Portrait with Seven Fingers*

Conrad's *Under Western Eyes*

William Golding born

Alfred Jarry's *Exploits and Opinions of Doctor Faustroll*

D. H. Lawrence's *The White Peacock*

Katherine Mansfield's *In a German Pension*

Edward Marsh edits *Georgian Poetry*

George Moore's *Hail and Farewell* (1911–1914)

Flann O'Brien born

Picasso's *Ma Jolie* (Woman with Zither or Guitar)

Strauss's *Der Rosenkavalier*

Stravinsky's *Petrouchka*

Trevelyan's *Garibaldi and the Making of Italy*

Wells's *The New Machiavelli*

Mahler's *Das Lied von der Erde*

1912 Woodrow Wilson elected president of the United States

SS *Titanic* sinks on its maiden voyage

Five million Americans go to the movies daily; London has four hundred movie theaters

Second post-impressionist exhibition in London

Bennett's and Edward Knoblock's *Milestones*

Constantin Brancusi's *Maiastra*

Marcel Duchamp's *Nude Descending a Staircase*

Wassily Kandinsky's *Black Lines*

D. H. Lawrence's *The Trespasser*

Death of Bram Stoker

1913 Second Balkan War begins

Henry Ford pioneers factory assembly technique through conveyor belts

Guillaume Apollinaire's *Alcools*

Epstein's *Tomb of Oscar Wilde*

New York Armory Show introduces modern art to the world

Alain Fournier's *Le Grand Meaulnes*

Freud's *Totem and Tabu*

D. H. Lawrence's *Sons and Lovers*

Mann's *Death in Venice*

Proust's *Du Côté de chez Swann* (first volume of *À la recherche du temps perdu*, 1913–1922)

Barbara Pym born

Ravel's *Daphnis and Chloé*

Igor Stravinsky's *The Rite of Spring*

1914 The Panama Canal opens (formal dedication on 12 July 1920)

Irish Home Rule Bill passed in the House of Commons

Archduke Franz Ferdinand assassinated at Sarajevo

World War I begins

Battles of the Marne, Masurian Lakes, and Falkland Islands

Joyce's *Dubliners*

Shaw's *Pygmalion* and *Androcles and the Lion*

Gertrude Stein's *Tender Buttons*

Yeats's *Responsibilities*

Wyndham Lewis publishes *Blast* magazine and *The Vorticist Manifesto*

1915 The Dardanelles campaign begins

Britain and Germany begin naval and submarine blockades

The *Lusitania* is sunk

Hugo Junkers manufactures the first fighter aircraft

Poison gas used for the first time

First Zeppelin raid in London

Brooke's *1914: Five Sonnets*

Norman Douglas's *Old Calabria*

CHRONOLOGY

D. W. Griffith's *The Birth of a Nation*

Gustav Holst's *The Planets*

D. H. Lawrence's *The Rainbow*

Wyndham Lewis's *The Crowd*

Maugham's *Of Human Bondage*

Picasso's *Harlequin*

Sibelius's Fifth Symphony

Death of Rupert Brooke

1916 Evacuation of Gallipoli and the Dardanelles

Battles of the Somme, Jutland, and Verdun

Britain introduces conscription

The Easter Rebellion in Dublin

Asquith resigns and David Lloyd George

becomes prime minister

The Sykes-Picot agreement on the partition of Turkey

First military tanks used

Wilson reelected president president of the United States

Henri Barbusse's *Le Feu*

Griffith's *Intolerance*

Joyce's *Portrait of the Artist as a Young Man*

Jung's *Psychology of the Unconscious*

Moore's *The Brook Kerith*

Edith Sitwell edits *Wheels* (1916–1921)

Wells's *Mr. Britling Sees It Through*

1917 United States enters World War I

Czar Nicholas II abdicates

The Balfour Declaration on a Jewish national home in Palestine

The Bolshevik Revolution

Georges Clemenceau elected prime minister of France

Lenin appointed chief commissar; Trotsky appointed minister of foreign affairs

Conrad's *The Shadow-Line*

Douglas' *South Wind*

Eliot's *Prufrock and Other Observations*

Modigliani's *Nude with Necklace*

Sassoon's *The Old Huntsman*

Prokofiev's *Classical Symphony*

Yeats's *The Wild Swans at Coole*

Death of Edward Thomas; *Poems* published posthumously

1918 Wilson puts forward Fourteen Points for World Peace

Central Powers and Russia sign the Treaty of Brest-Litovsk

Execution of Czar Nicholas II and his family

Kaiser Wilhelm II abdicates

The Armistice signed

Women granted the vote at age thirty in Britain

Rupert Brooke's *Collected Poems* (posthumously)

Gerard Manley Hopkins's *Poems* (posthumously)

Joyce's *Exiles*

Lewis's *Tarr*

Sassoon's *Counter-Attack*

Oswald Spengler's *The Decline of the West*

Strachey's *Eminent Victorians*

Béla Bartók's *Bluebeard's Castle*

Charlie Chaplin's *Shoulder Arms*

1919 The Versailles Peace Treaty signed

J. W. Alcock and A. W. Brown make first transatlantic flight

Ross Smith flies from London to Australia

National Socialist party founded in Germany

Benito Mussolini founds the Fascist party in Italy

Sinn Fein Congress adopts declaration of independence in Dublin

Eamon De Valera elected president of Sinn Fein party

Communist Third International founded

Lady Astor elected first woman Member of Parliament

Prohibition in the United States

John Maynard Keynes's *The Economic Consequences of the Peace*

Eliot's *Poems*

Maugham's *The Moon and Sixpence*

Eric Satie's *Socrate*

Shaw's *Heartbreak House*

The Bauhaus school of design, building, and crafts founded by Walter Gropius

Amedeo Modigliani's *Self-Portrait*

Doris Lessing born

1920 The League of Nations established

Warren G. Harding elected president of the United States

Senate votes against joining the League

and rejects the Treaty of Versailles

The Nineteenth Amendment gives women the right to vote in the United States

White Russian forces of Denikin and Kolchak defeated by the Bolsheviks

Karel Čapek's *R.U.R.*

Galsworthy's *In Chancery* and *The Skin Game*

Sinclair Lewis's *Main Street*

Katherine Mansfield's *Bliss*

Matisse's *Odalisques* (1920–1925)

Ezra Pound's *Hugh Selwyn Mauberly*

Paul Valéry's *Le Cimetière Marin*

Yeats's *Michael Robartes and the Dancer*

Death of Olive Schreiner

1921 Britain signs peace with Ireland

First medium-wave radio broadcast in the United States

The British Broadcasting Corporation founded

Braque's *Still Life with Guitar*

Chaplin's *The Kid*

Aldous Huxley's *Crome Yellow*

Paul Klee's *The Fish*

D. H. Lawrence's *Women in Love*

John McTaggart's *The Nature of Existence* (vol. 1)

Moore's *Héloïse and Abélard*

Eugene O'Neill's *The Emperor Jones*

Luigi Pirandello's *Six Characters in Search of an Author*

Shaw's *Back to Methuselah*

Strachey's *Queen Victoria*

1922 Lloyd George's Coalition government succeeded by Bonar Law's Conservative government

Benito Mussolini marches on Rome and forms a government

William Cosgrave elected president of the Irish Free State

The BBC begins broadcasting in London

Lord Carnarvon and Howard Carter discover Tutankhamen's tomb

The PEN club founded in London

The *Criterion* founded with T. S. Eliot as editor

Kingsley Amis born

Eliot's *The Waste Land*

A. E. Housman's *Last Poems*

Joyce's *Ulysses*

D. H. Lawrence's *Aaron's Rod* and *England, My England*

Sinclair Lewis's *Babbitt*

O'Neill's *Anna Christie*

Pirandello's *Henry IV*

Edith Sitwell's *Façade*

Kurt Schwitters begins *Ursonate* (completed 1932)

Gertrude Stein's *Geography and Plays*

Virginia Woolf's *Jacob's Room*

Yeats's *The Trembling of the Veil*

1923 The Union of Soviet Socialist Republics established

French and Belgian troops occupy the Ruhr in consequence of Germany's failure to pay reparations

Mustafa Kemal (Ataturk) proclaims Turkey a republic and is elected president

Warren G. Harding dies; Calvin Coolidge becomes president

Stanley Baldwin succeeds Bonar Law as prime minister

Adolf Hitler's attempted coup in Munich fails

Time magazine begins publishing

E. N. da C. Andrade's *The Structure of the Atom*

Brendan Behan born

Bennett's *Riceyman Steps*

Churchill's *The World Crisis* (1923–1927)

Henry Cowell's *Aeolian Harp*

J. E. Flecker's *Hassan* produced

Nadine Gordimer born

Paul Klee's *Magic Theatre*

D. H. Lawrence's *Kangaroo*

Rainer Maria Rilke's *Duino Elegies* and *Sonnets to Orpheus*

Arnold Schoenberg's *Suite*, Op. 25

Jean Sibelius's *Sixth Symphony*

Picasso's *Seated Woman*

William Walton's *Façade*

1924 Ramsay MacDonald forms first Labour government, loses general election, and is succeeded by Stanley Baldwin

Calvin Coolidge elected president of the United States

Early sound film, *Hawthorne*, shown in New York

Noël Coward's *The Vortex*

Forster's *A Passage to India*

Fernand Léger's *Élément Mécanique*

Mann's *The Magic Mountain*

Pablo Neruda's *Twenty Love Poems and a Song of Despair*

Shaw's *St. Joan*

Death of Joseph Conrad

1925 Reza Khan becomes shah of Iran

First surrealist exhibition held in Paris

Louis Armstrong organizes his Hot Five

Jean Arp's *Lunar Frog*

Alban Berg's *Wozzeck*

Chaplin's *The Gold Rush*

John Dos Passos's *Manhattan Transfer*

Theodore Dreiser's *An American Tragedy*

Sergei Eisenstein's *Battleship Potemkin*

F. Scott Fitzgerald's *The Great Gatsby*

André Gide's *Les Faux Monnayeurs*

Hardy's *Human Shows and Far Phantasies*

Huxley's *Those Barren Leaves*

Kafka's *The Trial*

O'Casey's *Juno and the Paycock*

Virginia Woolf's *Mrs. Dalloway* and *The Common Reader*

Constantin Brancusi's *Bird in Space*

Shostakovich's *First Symphony*

Sibelius's *Tapiola*

Gertrude Stein's *The Making of Americans*

Death of Sir Henry Rider Haggard

1926 George Antheil's *Ballet mécanique*

Isaac Babel's *Red Calvary*

Walter Gropius's Bauhaus completed

Ford's *A Man Could Stand Up*

Gide's *Si le grain ne meurt*

Hemingway's *The Sun also Rises*

Kafka's *The Castle*

D. H. Lawrence's *The Plumed Serpent*

T. E. Lawrence's *Seven Pillars of Wisdom* privately circulated

Maugham's *The Casuarina Tree*

O'Casey's *The Plough and the Stars*

Puccini's *Turandot*

Death of Ronald Firbank

1927 General Chiang Kai-shek becomes prime minister in China

CHRONOLOGY

Trotsky expelled by the Communist party as a deviationist; Stalin becomes leader of the party and dictator of the Soviet Union

Charles Lindbergh flies from New York to Paris

Philo T. Farnsworth transmits first television image

J. W. Dunne's *An Experiment with Time*

Freud's *Autobiography* translated into English

Buckminster Fuller's Dymaxion House

Albert Giacometti's *Observing Head*

Ernest Hemingway's *Men Without Women*

Fritz Lang's *Metropolis*

Wyndham Lewis's *Time and Western Man*

F. W. Murnau's *Sunrise*

Proust's *Le Temps retrouvé* posthumously published

Stravinsky's *Oedipus Rex*

Virginia Woolf's *To the Lighthouse*

1928　The Kellogg-Briand Pact, outlawing war and providing for peaceful settlement of disputes, signed in Paris by sixty-two nations, including the Soviet Union

Herbert Hoover elected president of the United States

Women's suffrage granted at age twenty-one in Britain

Alexander Fleming discovers penicillin

Bertolt Brecht and Kurt Weill's *The Three-Penny Opera*

Eisenstein's *October*

Huxley's *Point Counter Point*

Christopher Isherwood's *All the Conspirators*

D. H. Lawrence's *Lady Chatterley's Lover*

Wyndham Lewis's *The Childermass*

Matisse's *Seated Odalisque*

Munch's *Girl on a Sofa*

Shaw's *Intelligent Woman's Guide to Socialism*

Mikhail Sholokov begins publishing *And Quiet Flows the Don* (completed 1940)

Anton Webern's Symphony

Rebecca West's *The Strange Necessity*

Virginia Woolf's *Orlando*

Yeats's *The Tower*

Death of Thomas Hardy

1929　The Labour party wins British general election

Trotsky expelled from the Soviet Union

Museum of Modern Art opens in New York

Collapse of U.S. stock exchange begins world economic crisis

Robert Bridges's *The Testament of Beauty*

Max Ernst's *La Femme 100 Têtes*

William Faulkner's *The Sound and the Fury*

Robert Graves's *Goodbye to All That*

Hemingway's *A Farewell to Arms*

Ernst Junger's *The Storm of Steel*

Hugo von Hoffmansthal's *Poems*

Henry Moore's *Reclining Figure*

Georgia O'Keeffe's *Black Cross, New Mexico*

J. B. Priestley's *The Good Companions*

Erich Maria Remarque's *All Quiet on the Western Front*

Shaw's *The Applecart*

R. C. Sheriff's *Journey's End*

Edith Sitwell's *Gold Coast Customs*

Thomas Wolfe's *Look Homeward, Angel*

Virginia Woolf's *A Room of One's Own*

Yeats's *The Winding Stair*

Second surrealist manifesto; Salvador Dali joins the surrealists

CHRONOLOGY

Epstein's *Night and Day*

Mondrian's *Composition with Yellow Blue*

1930　Allied occupation of the Rhineland ends

Mohandas Gandhi opens civil disobedience campaign in India

The *Daily Worker*, journal of the British Communist party, begins publishing

J. W. Reppe makes artificial fabrics from an acetylene base

John Arden born

Auden's *Poems*

Coward's *Private Lives*

Ruth Crawford Seeger's *Study in Mixed Accents*:orde

Eliot's *Ash Wednesday*

Ted Hughes Born

Freud's *Civilization and its Discontents*

Wyndham Lewis's *The Apes of God*

Maugham's *Cakes and Ale*

Harold Pinter born

Ezra Pound's *XXX Cantos*

Evelyn Waugh's *Vile Bodies*

Deaths of D. H. Lawrence and Sir Arthur Conan Doyle

1931　The failure of the Credit Anstalt in Austria starts a financial collapse in Central Europe

Britain abandons the gold standard; the pound falls by twenty-five percent

Mutiny in the Royal Navy at Invergordon over pay cuts

Ramsay MacDonald resigns, splits the Cabinet, and is expelled by the Labour party; in the general election the National Government wins by a majority of five hundred seats

The Statute of Westminster defines dominion status

Ninette de Valois founds the Vic-Wells Ballet (eventually the Royal Ballet)

Coward's *Cavalcade*

Dali's The *Persistence of Memory*

John le Carré born

Hugh MacDiarmid's *First Hymm to Lenin*

O'Neill's *Mourning Becomes Electra*

Anthony Powell's *Afternoon Men*

Antoine de Saint-Exupéry's *Vol de nuit*

Walton's *Belshazzar's Feast*

Edgard Varèse's *Ionisation*

Virginia Woolf's *The Waves*

1932　Franklin D. Roosevelt elected president of the United States

Paul von Hindenburg elected president of Germany; Franz von Papen elected chancellor

Sir Oswald Mosley founds British Union of Fascists

The BBC takes over development of television from J. L. Baird's company

Basic English of 850 words designed as a prospective international language

The Folger Library opens in Washington, D.C.

The Shakespeare Memorial Theatre opens in Stratford-upon-Avon

Faulkner's *Light in August*

Huxley's *Brave New World*

F. R. Leavis' *New Bearings in English Poetry*

Boris Pasternak's *Second Birth*

Ravel's *Concerto for Left Hand*

Rouault's *Christ Mocked by Soldiers*

Waugh's *Black Mischief*

Yeats's *Words for Music Perhaps*

Death of Lytton Strachey

1933　Roosevelt inaugurates the New Deal

Hitler becomes chancellor of Germany

The Reichstag set on fire

Hitler suspends civil liberties and freedom of the press; German trade unions suppressed

George Balanchine and Lincoln Kirstein found the School of American Ballet

Paul Hindemith's *Mathis der Maler*

CHRONOLOGY

Lowry's *Ultramarine*

André Malraux's *La Condition humaine*

Olivier Messiaen's *L'Ascension*

Orwell's *Down and Out in Paris and London*

Gertrude Stein's *The Autobiography of Alice B. Toklas*

Arnold Toynbee's *A Study of History*

1934 The League Disarmament Conference ends in failure

The Soviet Union admitted to the League

Hitler becomes Führer

Civil war in Austria; Engelbert Dollfuss assassinated in attempted Nazi coup

Frédéric Joliot and Irene Joliot-Curie discover artificial (induced) radioactivity

Einstein's *My Philosophy*

Fitzgerald's *Tender Is the Night*

Graves's *I, Claudius* and *Claudius the God*

Toynbee's *A Study of History* begins publication (1934–1954)

Waugh's *A Handful of Dust*

Agatha Christie's *Murder on the Orient Express*

1935 Grigori Zinoviev and other Soviet leaders convicted of treason

Stanley Baldwin becomes prime minister in National Government; National Government wins general election in Britain

Italy invades Abyssinia

Germany repudiates disarmament clauses of Treaty of Versailles

Germany reintroduces compulsory military service and outlaws the Jews

Robert Watson-Watt builds first practical radar equipment

Karl Jaspers's *Suffering and Existence*

Ivy Compton-Burnett's *A House and Its Head*

Alban Berg's *Violin Concerto*

Eliot's *Murder in the Cathedral*

Barbara Hepworth's *Three Forms*

George Gershwin's *Porgy and Bess*

Greene's *England Made Me*

Isherwood's *Mr. Norris Changes Trains*

Malraux's *Le Temps du mépris*

Yeats's *Dramatis Personae*

Klee's *Child Consecrated to Suffering*

Benedict Nicholson's *White Relief*

Death of T. E. Lawrence

1936 Edward VII accedes to the throne in January; abdicates in December

1936–1952 Reign of George VI

German troops occupy the Rhineland

Ninety-nine percent of German electorate vote for Nazi candidates

The Popular Front wins general election in France; Léon Blum becomes prime minister

Roosevelt reelected president of the United States

The Popular Front wins general election in Spain

Spanish Civil War begins

Italian troops occupy Addis Ababa; Abyssinia annexed by Italy

BBC begins television service from Alexandra Palace

Auden's *Look, Stranger!*

Auden and Isherwood's *The Ascent of F-6*

A. J. Ayer's *Language, Truth and Logic*

Djuna Barnes's *Nightwood*

Walter Benjamin's "The Work of Art in the Age of Mechanical Reproduction"

Chaplin's *Modern Times*

Faulkner's *Absalom, Absalom!*

Greene's *A Gun for Sale*

Huxley's *Eyeless in Gaza*

Keynes's *General Theory of Employment*

F. R. Leavis's *Revaluation*

CHRONOLOGY

Federico García Lorca's *The House of Bernarda Alba*

Mondrian's *Composition in Red and Blue*

Dylan Thomas's *Twenty-five Poems*

Wells's *The Shape of Things to Come* filmed

Rebecca West's *The Thinking Reed*

Frank Lloyd Wright's *Falling Water*

1937   Trial of Karl Radek and other Soviet leaders

Neville Chamberlain succeeds Stanley Baldwin as prime minister

China and Japan at war

Frank Whittle designs jet engine

Picasso's *Guernica*

Shostakovich's Fifth Symphony

Magritte's *La Reproduction interdite*

Hemingway's *To Have and Have Not*

Malraux's *L'Espoir*

Orwell's *The Road to Wigan Pier*

Priestley's *Time and the Conways*

Tolkien's *The Hobbit*

Virginia Woolf's *The Years*

Tom Stoppard born

Death of James M. Barrie

1938   Trial of Nikolai Bukharin and other Soviet political leaders

Austria occupied by German troops and declared part of the Reich

Hitler states his determination to annex Sudetenland from Czechoslovakia

Britain, France, Germany, and Italy sign the Munich agreement

German troops occupy Sudetenland

Antonin Artaud's *The Theatre and Its Double*

Chester F. Carlson makes his first dry-copy, which led to modern xerographic printing

Edward Hulton founds *Picture Post*

Cyril Connolly's *Enemies of Promise*

du Maurier's *Rebecca*

Faulkner's *The Unvanquished*

Greene's *Brighton Rock*

Hindemith's *Mathis der Maler*

Leni Riefenstahl's *Olympia*

Jean Renoir's *La Grande Illusion*

Jean-Paul Sartre's *La Nausée*

Yeats's *New Poems*

Anthony Asquith's *Pygmalion* and Walt Disney's *Snow White*

1939   German troops occupy Bohemia and Moravia; Czechoslovakia incorporated into Third Reich

Madrid surrenders to General Franco; the Spanish Civil War ends

Italy invades Albania

Spain joins Germany, Italy, and Japan in anti-Comintern Pact

Britain and France pledge support to Poland, Romania, and Greece

The Soviet Union proposes defensive alliance with Britain; British military mission visits Moscow

The Soviet Union and Germany sign nonaggression treaty, secretly providing for partition of Poland between them

Germany invades Poland; Britain, France, and Germany at war

The Soviet Union invades Finland

New York World's Fair opens

Brecht's *Galileo*

Eliot's *The Family Reunion*

Isherwood's *Good-bye to Berlin*

Joyce's *Finnegans Wake* (1922–1939)

MacNeice's *Autumn Journal*

Flann O'Brien's *At Swim-Two Birds*

Powell's *What's Become of Waring?*

Seamus Heaney born

Death of William Butler Yeats

1940   Churchill becomes prime minister

Italy declares war on France, Britain, and Greece

General de Gaulle founds Free French Movement

The Battle of Britain and the bombing of London

CHRONOLOGY

Roosevelt reelected president of the United States for third term

Betjeman's *Old Lights for New Chancels*

Brecht's *The Good Woman of Setzuan*

Angela Carter born

Chaplin's *The Great Dictator*

Disney's *Fantasia*

Greene's *The Power and the Glory*

Hemingway's *For Whom the Bell Tolls*

C. P. Snow's *Strangers and Brothers* (retitled *George Passant* in 1970, when entire sequence of ten novels, published 1940–1970, was entitled *Strangers and Brothers*)

George R. Stibitz demonstrates first complex computer

Richard Wright's *Native Son*

1941 German forces occupy Yugoslavia, Greece, and Crete, and invade the Soviet Union

Lend-Lease agreement between the United States and Britain

President Roosevelt and Winston Churchill sign the Atlantic Charter

Japanese forces attack Pearl Harbor; United States declares war on Japan, Germany, Italy; Britain on Japan

Auden's *New Year Letter*

James Burnham's *The Managerial Revolution*

F. Scott Fitzgerald's *The Last Tycoon*

Huxley's *Grey Eminence*

Shostakovich's *Seventh Symphony*

Tippett's *A Child of Our Time*

Orson Welles's *Citizen Kane*

Virginia Woolf's *Between the Acts*

Deaths of James Joyce and Virginia Woolf

1942 Japanese forces capture Singapore, Hong Kong, Bataan, Manila

German forces capture Tobruk

U.S. fleet defeats the Japanese in the Coral Sea, captures Guadalcanal

Battle of El Alamein

Allied forces land in French North Africa

Atom first split at University of Chicago

William Beveridge's *Social Insurance and Allied Services*

Albert Camus's *L'Étranger*

Joyce Cary's *To Be a Pilgrim*

Camilo José Cela's *La Familia de Pascual Duarte*

Dmitri Shostakovich's *Leningrad Symphony*

Edith Sitwell's *Street Songs*

Waugh's *Put Out More Flags*

1943 German forces surrender at Stalingrad

German and Italian forces surrender in North Africa

Italy surrenders to Allies and declares war on Germany

Cairo conference between Roosevelt, Churchill, Chiang Kai-shek

Teheran conference between Roosevelt, Churchill, Stalin

Eliot's *Four Quartets*

Henry Moore's *Madonna and Child*

Sartre's *Les Mouches*

Vaughan Williams's *Fifth Symphony*

Death of Beatrix Potter

1944 Allied forces land in Normandy and southern France

Allied forces enter Rome

Attempted assassination of Hitler fails

Liberation of Paris

U.S. forces land in Philippines

German offensive in the Ardennes halted

Roosevelt reelected president of the United States for fourth term

Education Act passed in Britain

Pay-as-You-Earn income tax introduced

Beveridge's *Full Employment in a Free Society*

Jorge Luis Borges's *Ficciónes*

Cary's *The Horse's Mouth*

CHRONOLOGY

E. E. Cummings's *1 X 1*

F. A. Hayek's *The Road to Serfdom*

Huxley's *Time Must Have a Stop*

Maugham's *The Razor's Edge*

Sartre's *Huis Clos*

Edith Sitwell's *Green Song and Other Poems*

Graham Sutherland's *Christ on the Cross*

Trevelyan's *English Social History*

1945   British and Indian forces open offensive in Burma

Yalta conference between Roosevelt, Churchill, Stalin

Mussolini executed by Italian partisans

Roosevelt dies; Harry S. Truman becomes president

Hitler commits suicide; German forces surrender

The Potsdam Peace Conference

The United Nations Charter ratified in San Francisco

The Labour Party wins British General Election

Atomic bombs dropped on Hiroshima and Nagasaki

Surrender of Japanese forces ends World War II

Trial of Nazi war criminals opens at Nuremberg

All-India Congress demands British withdrawal from India

De Gaulle elected president of French Provisional Government; resigns the next year

Betjeman's *New Bats in Old Belfries*

Britten's *Peter Grimes*

Orwell's *Animal Farm*

Charlie Parker records "Koko" and "Now's The Time"

Russell's *History of Western Philosophy*

Sartre's *The Age of Reason*

Edith Sitwell's *The Song of the Cold*

Waugh's *Brideshead Revisited*

1946   Bills to nationalize railways, coal mines, and the Bank of England passed in Britain

Nuremberg Trials concluded

United Nations General Assembly meets in New York as its permanent headquarters

The Arab Council inaugurated in Britain

Frederick Ashton's *Symphonic Variations*

ineBritten's *The Rape of Lucretia*

Martha Graham's *Cave of the Heart*

Barbara Hepworth's *Pelagos*

David Lean's *Great Expectations*

Robert Matta's *Being With*

O'Neill's *The Iceman Cometh*

Roberto Rosselini's *Paisà*

Dylan Thomas's *Deaths and Entrances*

1947   President Truman announces program of aid to Greece and Turkey and outlines the "Truman Doctrine"

Independence of India proclaimed; partition between India and Pakistan, and communal strife between Hindus and Moslems follows

General Marshall calls for a European recovery program

First supersonic air flight

Britain's first atomic pile at Harwell comes into operation

Edinburgh festival established

Discovery of the Dead Sea Scrolls in Palestine

Princess Elizabeth marries Philip Mountbatten, duke of Edinburgh

Auden's *Age of Anxiety*

Camus's *La Peste*

Chaplin's *Monsieur Verdoux*

Lowry's *Under the Volcano*

Jackson Pollock's *Full Fathom Five*

Priestley's *An Inspector Calls*

Raymond Queneau's *Excercises in Style*

Edith Sitwell's *The Shadow of Cain*

CHRONOLOGY

Waugh's *Scott-King's Modern Europe*

1948   Gandhi assassinated

Czech Communist Party seizes power

Pan-European movement (1948–1958) begins with the formation of the permanent Organization for European Economic Cooperation (OEEC)

Berlin airlift begins as the Soviet Union halts road and rail traffic to the city

British mandate in Palestine ends; Israeli provisional government formed

Yugoslavia expelled from Soviet bloc

Columbia Records introduces the long-playing record

Truman elected of the United States for second term

John Cage's *Sonatas and Interludes*

Greene's *The Heart of the Matter*

Huxley's *Ape and Essence*

Leavis's *The Great Tradition*

James Hillier patents the electron microscope

Andrew J. Moyer's discoveries lead to industrial penicillin production

Olivier Messiaen's *3 Talas*

Pound's *Cantos*

Priestley's *The Linden Tree*

Pierre Schaeffer produces first musique concrète recordings

Waugh's *The Loved One*

1949   North Atlantic Treaty Organization established with headquarters in Brussels

Berlin blockade lifted

German Federal Republic recognized; capital established at Bonn

Konrad Adenauer becomes German chancellor

Mao Tse-tung becomes chairman of the People's Republic of China following Communist victory over the Nationalists

Simone de Beauvoir's *The Second Sex*

Cary's *A Fearful Joy*

Arthur Miller's *Death of a Salesman*

Orwell's *Nineteen Eighty-four*

1950   Korean War breaks out

Nobel Prize for literature awarded to Bertrand Russell

Heinrich Böll's *Traveler, if You Come to Spa...*

R. H. S. Crossman's *The God That Failed*

T. S. Eliot's *The Cocktail Party*

Fry's *Venus Observed*

Doris Lessing's *The Grass Is Singing*

C. S. Lewis' *The Chronicles of Narnia* (1950–1956)

Wyndham Lewis's *Rude Assignment*

George Orwell's *Shooting an Elephant*

Carol Reed's *The Third Man*

Isaac Bashevis Singer's *The Family Moskat*

Dylan Thomas's *Twenty-six Poems*

ca. 1950   Agatha Christie's *Mousetrap*

1951   Guy Burgess and Donald Maclean defect from Britain to the Soviet Union

The Conservative party under Winston Churchill wins British general election

The Festival of Britain celebrates both the centenary of the Crystal Palace Exhibition and British postwar recovery

Electric power is produced by atomic energy at Arcon, Idaho

W. H. Auden's *Nones*

Beckett's *Molloy* and *Malone Dies*

Benjamin Britten's *Billy Budd*

Camilo José Cela's *La Colmena*

Greene's *The End of the Affair*

Langston Hughes's *Montage of a Dream Deferred*

Akira Kurosawa's *Rashomon*

Wyndham Lewis's *Rotting Hill*

Anthony Powell's *A Question of Upbringing* (first volume of *A Dance to the Music of Time*, 1951–1975)

J. D. Salinger's *The Catcher in the Rye*

CHRONOLOGY

David Smith's *Hudson River Landscape*

C. P. Snow's *The Masters*

Igor Stravinsky's *The Rake's Progress*

1952   **Reign of Elizabeth II**

At Eniwetok Atoll the United States detonates the first hydrogen bomb

The European Coal and Steel Community comes into being

Radiocarbon dating introduced to archaeology

Michael Ventris deciphers Linear B script

Dwight D. Eisenhower elected president of the United States

Beckett's *Waiting for Godot*

Charles Chaplin's *Limelight*

Ralph Ellison's *Invisible Man*

Ernest Hemingway's *The Old Man and the Sea*

Eugène Ionesco's *The Chairs*

Arthur Koestler's *Arrow in the Blue*

F. R. Leavis's *The Common Pursuit*

Lessing's *Martha Quest* (first volume of *The Children of Violence*, 1952–1965)

C. S. Lewis's *Mere Christianity*

Thomas's *Collected Poems*

Amos Tutuola's *The Palm-Wine Drunkard*

Evelyn Waugh's *Men at Arms* (first volume of *Sword of Honour*, 1952–1961)

Angus Wilson's *Hemlock and After*

1953   Constitution for a European political community drafted

Julius and Ethel Rosenberg executed for passing U.S. secrets to the Soviet Union

Cease-fire declared in Korea

Edmund Hillary and his Sherpa guide, Tenzing Norkay, scale Mt. Everest

Nobel Prize for literature awarded to Winston Churchill

General Mohammed Naguib proclaims Egypt a republic

James Baldwin's *Go Tell It on the Mountain*

Beckett's *Watt*

Joyce Cary's *Except the Lord*

Robert Graves's *Poems 1953*

1954   First atomic submarine, *Nautilus,* is launched by the United States

Dien Bien Phu captured by the Vietminh

Geneva Conference ends French dominion over Indochina

U.S. Supreme Court declares racial segregation in schools unconstitutional

Nasser becomes president of Egypt

Nobel Prize for literature awarded to Ernest Hemingway

Kingsley Amis's *Lucky Jim*

Brendan Behan's *The Quare Fellow*

John Betjeman's *A Few Late Chrysanthemums*

William Golding's *Lord of the Flies*

Frank B. Colton develops first oral contraception: Enovid

Christopher Isherwood's *The World in the Evening*

Koestler's *The Invisible Writing*

Iris Murdoch's *Under the Net*

C. P. Snow's *The New Men*

Karlheinz Stockhausen's *Kontra-Punkte*

Thomas's *Under Milk Wood* published posthumously

Tolkien's *Lord of the Rings* (to 1955)

1955   Warsaw Pact signed

West Germany enters NATO as Allied occupation ends

The Conservative party under Anthony Eden wins British general election

Cary's *Not Honour More*

Willem de Kooning's *Woman as Landscape*

Greene's *The Quiet American*

Jasper John's *Green Target*

Philip Larkin's *The Less Deceived*

F. R. Leavis's *D. H. Lawrence, Novelist*

Le Corbusier's Notre-Dame-du-Haut Chapel completed

Vladimir Nabokov's *Lolita*

Patrick White's *The Tree of Man*

1956 Nasser's nationalization of the Suez Canal leads to Israeli, British, and French armed intervention

Uprising in Hungary suppressed by Soviet troops

Khrushchev denounces Stalin at Twentieth Communist Party Congress

Eisenhower reelected president of the United States

Anthony Burgess's *Time for a Tiger*

Allen Ginsberg's *Howl and Other Poems*

Golding's *Pincher Martin*

Naguib Mahfouz's *Palace Walk* (Book I of the Cairo Trilogy)

Murdoch's *Flight from the Enchanter*

John Osborne's *Look Back in Anger*

Snow's *Homecomings*

Edmund Wilson's *Anglo-Saxon Attitudes*

1957 The Soviet Union launches the first artificial earth satellite, *Sputnik I*

Eden succeeded by Harold Macmillan

Suez Canal reopened

Eisenhower Doctrine formulated

Parliament receives the Wolfenden Report on Homosexuality and Prostitution

Nobel Prize for literature awarded to Albert Camus

Beckett's *Endgame* and *All That Fall*

Lawrence Durrell's *Justine* (first volume of *The Alexandria Quartet*, 1957–1960)

Ted Hughes's *The Hawk in the Rain*

Naguib Mahfouz's *Palace of Desire* (Book II of the Cairo Trilogy) and *Sugar Street* (Book III of the Cairo Trilogy)

Murdoch's *The Sandcastle*

V. S. Naipaul's *The Mystic Masseur*

Eugene O'Neill's *Long Day's Journey into Night*

Osborne's *The Entertainer*

Harold Pinter's *The Room*

Muriel Spark's *The Comforters*

White's *Voss*

1958 European Economic Community established

Khrushchev succeeds Bulganin as Soviet premier

Charles de Gaulle becomes head of France's newly constituted Fifth Republic

The United Arab Republic formed by Egypt and Syria

The United States sends troops into Lebanon

First U.S. satellite, *Explorer 1*, launched

Nobel Prize for literature awarded to Boris Pasternak

Beckett's *Krapp's Last Tape*

Merce Cunningham's *Summerspace*

John Kenneth Galbraith's *The Affluent Society*

Greene's *Our Man in Havana*

Murdoch's *The Bell*

Eduardo Paolozzi's *Japanese War God*

Pasternak's *Dr. Zhivago*

Snow's *The Conscience of the Rich*

1959 Fidel Castro assumes power in Cuba

St. Lawrence Seaway opens

The European Free Trade Association founded

Alaska and Hawaii become the forty-ninth and fiftieth states

The Conservative party under Harold Macmillan wins British general election

Brendan Behan's *The Hostage*

William S. Burroughs's *Naked Lunch*

Alexander Calder's *Big Red*

Eliot Carter's *String Quartet* No. 2

Odysseus Elytis's *To Áxion estí*

CHRONOLOGY

Golding's *Free Fall*

Günter Grass's *The Tin Drum*

Graves's *Collected Poems*

Koestler's *The Sleepwalkers*

Pinter's *The Birthday Party*

Robert Raushenberg's *Monogram*

Snow's *The Two Cultures and the Scientific Revolution*

Spark's *Memento Mori*

Charles Townes invents the maser and the laser

1960   South Africa bans the African National Congress and Pan-African Congress

The Congo achieves independence

John F. Kennedy elected president of the United States

The U.S. bathyscaphe *Trieste* descends to 35,800 feet

Publication of the unexpurgated *Lady Chatterley's Lover* permitted by court

Auden's *Hommage to Clio*

John Barth's *The Sot-Weed Factor*

Luciano Berio's *In Circles*

Betjeman's *Summoned by Bells*

Elias Canetti's *Crowds and Power*

Louise Nevelson's *Royal Tide V*

Pinter's *The Caretaker*

Claude Simon's *La Route des Flandres*

Snow's *The Affair*

David Storey's *This Sporting Life*

1961   South Africa leaves the British Commonwealth

Sierra Leone and Tanganyika achieve independence

The Berlin Wall erected

The New English Bible published

Beckett's *How It Is*

Greene's *A Burnt-Out Case*

Koestler's *The Lotus and the Robot*

Murdoch's *A Severed Head*

Naipaul's *A House for Mr Biswas*

Osborne's *Luther*

Spark's *The Prime of Miss Jean Brodie*

White's *Riders in the Chariot*

1962   John Glenn becomes first U.S. astronaut to orbit earth

The United States launches the spacecraft *Mariner* to explore Venus

Algeria achieves independence

Cuban missile crisis ends in withdrawal of Soviet missiles from Cuba

Adolf Eichmann executed in Israel for Nazi war crimes

Second Vatican Council convened by Pope John XXIII

Nobel Prize for literature awarded to John Steinbeck

Edward Albee's *Who's Afraid of Virginia Woolf?*

Francis Bacon's *One of three studies for a Crucifixion*

Beckett's *Happy Days*

Benjamin Britten's *War Requiem*

Anthony Burgess' *A Clockwork Orange* and *The Wanting Seed*

Aldous Huxley's *Island*

Isherwood's *Down There on a Visit*

Lessing's *The Golden Notebook*

Marshall McLuhan's *The Gutenberg Galaxy*

Nabokov's *Pale Fire*

Mary Quant introduces the miniskirt

Aleksandr Solzhenitsyn's *One Day in the Life of Ivan Denisovich*

John Tavener's *3 Holy Sonnets*

Derek Walcott's *In a Green Night*

Andy Warhol's *210 Coca-Cola Bottles*

William Carlos Williams's *Patterson* (begun 1946)

ca. 1962   Joseph Cornell's *Eclipse series*

1963   Britain, the United States, and the Soviet Union sign a test-ban treaty

Britain refused entry to the European Economic Community

The Soviet Union puts into orbit the first woman astronaut, Valentina Tereshkova

CHRONOLOGY

Paul VI becomes pope

President Kennedy assassinated; Lyndon B. Johnson assumes office

Nobel Prize for literature awarded to George Seferis

Britten's *War Requiem*

John le Carré's *The Spy Who Came in from the Cold*

John Fowles's *The Collector*

David Hockney's *Picture emphasizing stillness*

Allen Jones's *Hermaphrodite*

Philip King's *Genghis Khan*

Murdoch's *The Unicorn*

Thomas Pynchon's *V.*

Wole Soyinka's *A Dance of the Forests* (published)

Spark's *The Girls of Slender Means*

Storey's *Radcliffe*

John Updike's *The Centaur*

1964   Tonkin Gulf incident leads to retaliatory strikes by U.S. aircraft against North Vietnam

Greece and Turkey contend for control of Cyprus

Britain grants licenses to drill for oil in the North Sea

The Shakespeare Quatercentenary celebrated

Lyndon Johnson elected president of the United States

The Labour party under Harold Wilson wins British general election

Nobel Prize for literature awarded to Jean-Paul Sartre

Saul Bellow's *Herzog*

Stan Brakhage's *Dog Star Man* (completed)

Burgess's *Nothing Like the Sun*

John Furnival's *Tour de Babel Changées en Ponts*

Golding's *The Spire*

Isherwood's *A Single Man*

Stanley Kubrick's *Dr. Strangelove*

Larkin's *The Whitsun Weddings*

Naipaul's *An Area of Darkness*

Peter Shaffer's *The Royal Hunt of the Sun*

Snow's *Corridors of Power*

Death of Brendan Behan

1965   The first U.S. combat forces land in Vietnam

The U.S. spacecraft Mariner transmits photographs of Mars

British Petroleum Company finds oil in the North Sea

War breaks out between India and Pakistan

Rhodesia declares its independence

Ontario power failure blacks out the Canadian and U.S. east coasts

Nobel Prize for literature awarded to Mikhail Sholokhov

Robert Lowell's *For the Union Dead*

Norman Mailer's *An American Dream*

Osborne's *Inadmissible Evidence*

Pinter's *The Homecoming*

Spark's *The Mandelbaum Gate*

Stockhausen's *Mikrophonie II*

Death of T. S. Eliot

1966   The Labour party under Harold Wilson wins British general election

The Archbishop of Canterbury visits Pope Paul VI

Florence, Italy, severely damaged by floods

Paris exhibition celebrates Picasso's eighty-fifth birthday

Julio Cortàzar's *Hopscotch*

Fowles's *The Magus*

Greene's *The Comedians*

Allan Kaprow's *Assemblage, Environments & Happenings*

Osborne's *A Patriot for Me*

Rhy's *Wide Sargasso Sea*

Paul Scott's *The Jewel in the Crown* (first volume of *The Raj Quartet*, 1966–1975)

White's *The Solid Mandala*

CHRONOLOGY

1967 Thurgood Marshall becomes first black U.S. Supreme Court justice

Six-Day War pits Israel against Egypt and Syria

Biafra's secession from Nigeria leads to civil war

Francis Chichester completes solo circumnavigation of the globe

Dr. Christiaan Barnard performs first heart transplant operation, in South Africa

China explodes its first hydrogen bomb

Anthony Caro's *Prairie*

Bob Dylan's *Times they are A-Changin'*

García Márquez's *One Hundred Years of Solitude*

Golding's *The Pyramid*

Heaney's *Death of a Naturalist*

Hughes's *Wodwo*

Isherwood's *A Meeting by the River*

Naipaul's *The Mimic Men*

Kenzaburo Oé's *The Silent Cry*

Tom Stoppard's *Rosencrantz and Guildenstern Are Dead*

Orson Welles's *Chimes at Midnight*

Angus Wilson's *No Laughing Matter*

1968 Violent student protests erupt in France and West Germany

Warsaw Pact troops occupy Czechoslovakia

Violence in Northern Ireland causes Britain to send in troops

Tet offensive by Communist forces launched against South Vietnam's cities

Theater censorship ended in Britain

Robert Kennedy and Martin Luther King, Jr., assassinated

Richard M. Nixon elected president of the United States

Booker Prize for fiction established

Luciano Berio's *Sinfonia*

Durrell's *Tunc*

Graves's *Poems 1965–1968*

Peter Handke's *Kaspar*

B.S. Johnson's *You're Human Like the Rest of Them*

Miës van der Rohe's Neu Nationalgalerie completed

Osborne's *The Hotel in Amsterdam*

Snow's *The Sleep of Reason*

Solzhenitsyn's *The First Circle* and *Cancer Ward*

Spark's *The Public Image*

1969 Humans set foot on the moon for the first time when astronauts descend to its surface in a landing vehicle from the U.S. spacecraft *Apollo 11*

The Soviet unmanned spacecraft *Venus V* lands on Venus

Capital punishment abolished in Britain

Colonel Muammar Qaddafi seizes power in Libya

Solzhenitsyn expelled from the Soviet Union

Nobel Prize for literature awarded to Samuel Beckett

Angela Carter's *The Magic Toyshop*

Fowles's *The French Lieutenant's Woman*

Eva Hesse's *Expanded Expansion*

P. H. Newby's *Something to Answer For*

Georges Perec's *La Disparition*

Storey's *The Contractor*

1970 Civil war in Nigeria ends with Biafra's surrender

U.S. planes bomb Cambodia

The Conservative party under Edward Heath wins British general election

Nobel Prize for literature awarded to Aleksandr Solzhenitsyn

Durrell's *Nunquam*

Gordimer's *A Guest of Honor*

Hughes's *Crow*

F. R. Leavis's and Q. D. Leavis's *Dickens the Novelist*

Toni Morrison's *The Bluest Eye*

Joyce Carol Oates's *The Wheel of Love*

CHRONOLOGY

Bernice Rubens's *The Elected Member*

Snow's *Last Things*

Spark's *The Driver's Seat*

1971 Communist China given Nationalist China's UN seat
Decimal currency introduced to Britain
Indira Gandhi becomes India's prime minister
Nobel Prize for literature awarded to Heinrich Böll
Bond's *The Pope's Wedding*
Gavin Bryars's *Jesus' Blood Never Failed Me Yet*
Raymond Federman's *Double or Nothing*
Ian Hamilton Finlay's *Poems to Hear and See*
Eugenio Montale's *Satura*
Naipaul's *In a Free State*
Pinter's *Old Times*
Spark's *Not to Disturb*

1972 The civil strife of "Bloody Sunday" causes Northern Ireland to come under the direct rule of Westminster
Nixon becomes the first U.S. president to visit Moscow and Beijing
The Watergate break-in precipitates scandal in the United States
Eleven Israeli athletes killed by terrorists at Munich Olympics
Nixon reelected president of the United States
John Berger's *G*
Bond's *Lear*
Alex Comfort's *The Joy of Sex*
Peter Handke's *A Sorrow Beyond Dreams*
Pinter's *Monologue*
Snow's *The Malcontents*
Wole Soyinka's *The Man Died*
Stoppard's *Jumpers*
Eudora Welty's *The Optimist's Daughter*

1973 Britain, Ireland, and Denmark enter European Economic Community

Egypt and Syria attack Israel in the Yom Kippur War
Energy crisis in Britain reduces production to a three-day week
Nobel Prize for literature awarded to Patrick White
Stan Cohen and Herb Boyer prove that DNA cloning is feasible
Bond's *The Sea*
Joseph Brodsky's *Selected Poems*
J. G. Farrell's *The Siege of Krishnapur*
Edward Gorey's *Amphigorey*
Greene's *The Honorary Consul*
Lessing's *The Summer Before the Dark*
Murdoch's *The Black Prince*
Thomas Pynchon's *Gravity's Rainbow*
Shaffer's *Equus*
White's *The Eye of the Storm*
Death of J.R.R. Tolkien

1974 Miners strike in Britain
Greece's military junta overthrown
Emperor Haile Selassie of Ethiopia deposed
President Makarios of Cyprus replaced by military coup
Nixon resigns as U.S. president and is succeeded by Gerald R. Ford
Betjeman's *A Nip in the Air*
Bond's *Bingo*
Louise Bourgeois's *Destruction of the Father*
Durrell's *Monsieur* (first volume of *The Avignon Quintet*, 1974–1985)
Gordimer's *The Conservationist*
Larkin's *The High Windows*
Stanley Middleton's *Holiday*
Pinter's *No Man's Land*
Solzhenitsyn's *The Gulag Archipelago*
Spark's *The Abbess of Crewe*

1975 The U.S. *Apollo* and Soviet *Soyuz* spacecrafts rendezvous in space
The Helsinki Accords on human rights signed
U.S. forces leave Vietnam

CHRONOLOGY

King Juan Carlos succeeds Franco as Spain's head of state

Nobel Prize for literature awarded to Eugenio Montale

Death of Sir P. G. Wodehouse

John Ashbery's *Self-portrait in a Convex Mirror*

Christo begins *The Pont Neuf Wrapped* (completed 1985)

E. L. Doctorow's *Ragtime*

Ruth Prawer Jhabvala's *Heat and Dust*

E. O. Wilson's *Sociobiology*

1976 New U.S. copyright law goes into effect

Israeli commandos free hostages from hijacked plane at Entebbe, Uganda

British and French SST Concordes make first regularly scheduled commercial flights

The United States celebrates its bicentennial

Jimmy Carter elected president of the United States

Byron and Shelley manuscripts discovered in Barclay's Bank, Pall Mall

Bob Cobbing's *Bill Jubobe*

Richard Dawkins's *The Selfish Gene*

Heaney's *North*

Hughes's *Seasons' Songs*

Koestler's *The Thirteenth Tribe*

David Storey's *Saville*

Spark's *The Take-over*

White's *A Fringe of Leaves*

Death of Agatha Christie

1977 Silver jubilee of Queen Elizabeth II celebrated

Egyptian president Anwar el-Sadat visits Israel

"Gang of Four" expelled from Chinese Communist party

First woman ordained in the U.S. Episcopal church

After twenty-nine years in power, Israel's Labour party is defeated by the Likud party

Fowles's *Daniel Martin*

Hughes's *Gaudete*

Paul Scott's *Staying On*

1978 Treaty between Israel and Egypt negotiated at Camp David

Pope John Paul I dies a month after his coronation and is succeeded by Karol Cardinal Wojtyla, who takes the name John Paul II

Former Italian premier Aldo Moro murdered by left-wing terrorists

Nobel Prize for literature awarded to Isaac Bashevis Singer

Greene's *The Human Factor*

Hughes's *Cave Birds*

Murdoch's *The Sea, The Sea*

Kenzaburo Oé's *Teach Us to Outgrow Our Madness* (published in Japanese in 1969)

1979 The United States and China establish diplomatic relations

Ayatollah Khomeini takes power in Iran and his supporters hold U.S. embassy staff hostage in Teheran

Rhodesia becomes Zimbabwe

Earl Mountbatten assassinated

The Soviet Union invades Afghanistan

The Conservative party under Margaret Thatcher wins British general election

Nobel Prize for literature awarded to Odysseus Elytis

Penelope Fitzgerald's *Offshore*

Golding's *Darkness Visible*

Heaney's *Field Work*

Hughes's *Moortown*

Lessing's *Shikasta* (first volume of *Canopus in Argos, Archives*)

Naipaul's *A Bend in the River*

Pinter's *Betrayal*

Spark's *Territorial Rights*

White's *The Twyborn Affair*

Death of Jean Rhys

1980 Iran-Iraq war begins

Strikes in Gdansk give rise to the Solidarity movement

CHRONOLOGY

Mt. St. Helen's erupts in Washington State

British steelworkers strike for the first time since 1926

More than fifty nations boycott Moscow Olympics

Ronald Reagan elected president of the United States

Burgess's *Earthly Powers*

Golding's *Rites of Passage*

Heaney's *Preoccupations*

Tom Phillips's *A Humument*

Pinter's *Family Voices*

Shaffer's *Amadeus*

Storey's *A Prodigal Child*

Angus Wilson's *Setting the World on Fire*

1981 Greece admitted to the European Economic Community

Iran hostage crisis ends with release of U.S. embassy staff

Twelve Labour MPs and nine peers found British Social Democratic party

Socialist party under François Mitterand wins French general election

Rupert Murdoch buys *The Times* of London

Turkish gunman wounds Pope John Paul II in assassination attempt

U.S. gunman wounds President Reagan in assassination attempt

President Sadat of Egypt assassinated

Nobel Prize for literature awarded to Elias Canetti

Rushdie's *Midnight's Children*

Spark's *Loitering with Intent*

Wislawa Szymborska's *Sounds, Feelings, Thoughts*

1982 Britain drives Argentina's invasion force out of the Falkland Islands

U.S. space shuttle makes first successful trip

Yuri Andropov becomes general secretary of the Central Committee of the Soviet Communist party

Israel invades Lebanon

First artificial heart implanted at Salt Lake City hospital

John Arden's *Silence Among the Weapons*

Bellow's *The Dean's December*

Gao Xingjian's *Signal Alarm*

Greene's *Monsignor Quixote*

Thomas Keneally's *Schindler's Ark*

1983 South Korean airliner with 269 aboard shot down after straying into Soviet airspace

U.S. forces invade Grenada following left-wing coup

Widespread protests erupt over placement of nuclear missiles in Europe

The £1 coin comes into circulation in Britain

Australia wins the America's Cup

Nobel Prize for literature awarded to William Golding

J. M. Coetzee's *Life and Times of Michael K.*

Gao Xingjian's *Bus Stop*

Hughes's *River*

Murdoch's *The Philosopher's Pupil*

Alice Walker wins Pulitzer Prize for fiction with *The Color Purple*

Death of Rebecca West

1984 Konstantin Chernenko becomes general secretary of the Central Committee of the Soviet Communist party

Prime Minister Indira Gandhi of India assassinated by Sikh bodyguards

Reagan reelected president of the United States

Toxic gas leak at Bhopal, India, plant kills 2,000

British miners go on strike

Irish Republican Army attempts to kill Prime Minister Thatcher with bomb detonated at a Brighton hotel

World Court holds against U.S. mining of Nicaraguan harbors

Anita Brookner's *Hotel du Lac*

Golding's *The Paper Men*

Heaney's *Station Island*

Milan Kundera's *The Unbearable Lightness of Being*

Lessing's *The Diary of Jane Somers*

Pinter's *One for the Road*

Spark's *The Only Problem*

1985   United States deploys cruise missiles in Europe

Mikhail Gorbachev becomes general secretary of the Soviet Communist party following death of Konstantin Chernenko

Riots break out in Handsworth district (Birmingham) and Brixton

Republic of Ireland gains consultative role in Northern Ireland

State of emergency is declared in South Africa

Nobel Prize for literature awarded to Claude Simon

Margaret Atwood's *The Handmaid's Tale*

Keri Hulme's *The Bone People*

A. N. Wilson's *Gentlemen in England*

Lessing's *The Good Terrorist*

Richard Long's *A Hundred Sticks Placed on a Beaver Lodge*

Murdoch's *The Good Apprentice*

Fowles's *A Maggot*

1986   U.S. space shuttle *Challenger* explodes

United States attacks Libya

Atomic power plant at Chernobyl destroyed in accident

Corazon Aquino becomes president of the Philippines

Giotto spacecraft encounters Comet Halley

Nobel Prize for literature awarded to Wole Soyinka

Final volume of *Oxford English Dictionary* supplement published

Amis's *The Old Devils*

Clark Coolidge's *Solution Passage*

Ishiguro's *An Artist of the Floating World*

A. N. Wilson's *Love Unknown*

Powell's *The Fisher King*

1987   Gorbachev begins reform of Communist party of the Soviet Union

Stock market collapses

Iran-contra affair reveals that Reagan administration used money from arms sales to Iran to fund Nicaraguan rebels

Palestinian uprising begins in Israeli-occupied territories

Nobel Prize for literature awarded to Joseph Brodsky

Burgess's *Little Wilson and Big God*

Drabble's *The Radiant Way*

Jas H. Duke's *Poems of War and Peace*

Golding's *Close Quarters*

Andy Goldsworthy's *Clearly Broken Pebbles Sratched White*

Heaney's *The Haw Lantern*

Toni Morrison's *Beloved*

Penelope Lively's *Moon Tiger*

1988   Soviet Union begins withdrawing troops from Afghanistan

Iranian airliner shot down by U.S. Navy over Persian Gulf

War between Iran and Iraq ends

George Bush elected president of the United States

Pan American flight 103 destroyed over Lockerbie, Scotland

Nobel Prize for literature awarded to Naguib Mafouz

Amis's *Difficulties with Girls*

Peter Carey's *Oscar and Lucinda*

Greene's *The Captain and the Enemy*

Rushdie's *Satanic Verses*

1989   Ayatollah Khomeini pronounces death sentence on Salman Rushdie; Great Britain and Iran sever diplomatic relations

F. W. de Klerk becomes president of South Africa

Chinese government crushes student demonstration in Tiananmen Square

Communist regimes are weakened or abolished in Poland, Czechoslovakia, Hungary, East Germany, and Romania

CHRONOLOGY

Lithuania nullifies its inclusion in Soviet Union

Nobel Prize for literature awarded to José Cela

Second edition of *Oxford English Dictionary* published

Amis's *London Fields*

Drabble's *A Natural Curiosity*

Ishiguro's *The Remains of the Day*

Murdoch's *The Message to the Planet*

David Nash's *Red Shrine*

Death of Samuel Beckett

1990 Communist monopoly ends in Bulgaria

Riots break out against community charge in England

Nelson Mandela released from prison in South Africa

Civil war breaks out in Yugoslavia; Croatia and Slovenia declare independence

Bush and Gorbachev sign START agreement to reduce nuclear-weapons arsenals

President Jean-Baptiste Aristide overthrown by military in Haiti

Dissolution of the Soviet Union

A. S. Byatt's *Possession*

Derek Walcott's *Omeros*

1991 Allied forces bomb Baghdad following Iraqi invasion of Kuwait

Boris Yeltsin assumes presidency of Russia

Nobel Prize for literature awarded to Nadine Gordimer

Pat Barker's *The Regeneration Trilogy*

Ben Okri's *The Famished Road*

Pinter's *Party Time*

Death of Graham Greene

1992 U.N. Conference on Environment and Development (the "Earth Summit") meets in Rio de Janeiro

Prince and Princess of Wales separate

War in Bosnia-Herzegovina intensifies

Bill Clinton elected president of the United States in three-way race with Bush and independent candidate H. Ross Perot

Nobel Prize for literature awarded to Derek Walcott

Heaney's *Seeing Things*

Michael Ondaatje's *The English Patient*

Barry Unsworth's *Sacred Hunger*

Death of Angela Carter

1993 Czechoslovakia divides into the Czech Republic and Slovakia; playwright Vaclav Havel elected president of the Czech Republic

Britain ratifies Treaty on European Union (the "Maastricht Treaty")

U.S. troops provide humanitarian aid amid famine in Somalia

United States, Canada, and Mexico sign North American Free Trade Agreement

Nobel Prize for literature awarded to Toni Morrison

Roddy Doyle's *Paddy Clarke Ha Ha Ha*

Pinter's *Moonlight*

1994 Nelson Mandela elected president in South Africa's first post-apartheid election

Jean-Baptiste Aristide restored to presidency of Haiti

Clinton health care reforms rejected by Congress

Civil war in Rwanda

Republicans win control of both houses of Congress for first time in forty years

Prime Minister Albert Reynolds of Ireland meets with Gerry Adams, president of Sinn Fein

First women ordained priests in Church of England

Nobel Prize for literature awarded to Kenzaburo Õe

Amis's *You Can't Do Both*

James Kelman's *How Late It Was, How Late*

CHRONOLOGY

Naipaul's *A Way in the World*

1995   Britain and Irish Republican Army engage in diplomatic talks

Barings Bank forced into bankruptcy as a result of a maverick bond trader's losses

United States restores full diplomatic relations with Vietnam

NATO initiates air strikes in Bosnia

Death of Stephen Spender

Israeli Prime Minister Yitzhak Rabin assassinated

Microsoft founder, Bill Gates, is world's richest individual with 12.9 billion dollars

Timothy McVeigh bombs federal building in Oklahoma City

Nobel Prize for literature awarded to Seamus Heaney

Pat Barker's *The Ghost Road*

Death of Sir Kingsley Amis

1996   IRA breaks cease-fire; Sein Fein representatives barred from Northern Ireland peace talks

Prince and Princess of Wales divorce

Cease-fire agreement in Chechnia; Russian forces begin to withdraw

Boris Yeltsin reelected president of Russia

Bill Clinton reelected president of the United States

Nobel Prize for literature awarded to Wislawa Szymborska

British government destroys approximately 100,000 cows suspected of infection with Creutzfeldt-Jakob, or "mad cow" disease

Pinter's *Ashes to Ashes*

Graham Swift's *Last Orders*

1997   China resumes rule of Hong Kong

Diana, Princess of Wales, dies in an automobile accident

Unveiling of first fully-cloned adult animal, a sheep named Dolly

Peter Carey's *Jack Maggs*

Arundhati Roy's *The God of Small Things* wins Booker McConnell Prize for fiction

1998   United States renews bombing of Bagdad, Iraq

Independent legislature and Parliaments return to Scotland and Wales

Ted Hughes, Symbolist poet and husband of Sylvia Plath, dies

Tony Cragg's *Envelope*

Ian McEwan's *Amsterdam* wins Booker McConnell Prize for fiction

Nobel Prize for literature awarded to Jose Saramago

1999   King Hussein of Jordan dies

United Nations responds militarily to Serbian President Slobodan Milosevic's escalation of crisis in Kosovo

J. M. Coetzee's *Disgrace* wins Booker McConnell Prize for fiction

Nobel Prize for literature awarded to Gunter Grass

Jared Diamond's *Guns, Germs, and Steel*

Pinter's *Celebration*

Anita Desai's *Fasting, Feasting*

2000   Penelope Fitzgerald dies

J. K. Rowling's *Harry Potter and the Goblet of Fire* sells more than 300,000 copies in its first day

Oil blockades by fuel haulers protesting high oil taxes bring much of Britain to a standstill

Slobodan Milosevic loses Serbian general election to Vojislav Kostunica

Death of Scotland's First Minister, Donald Dewar

Nobel Prize for literature awarded to Gao Xingjian

George W. Bush, son of former president George Bush, becomes president of the United States after Supreme Court halts recount of closest election in history

Death of former Canadian Prime Minister Pierre Elliot Trudeau

Human Genome Project researchers complete map of the genetic code of a human chromosome

Vladimir Putin succeeds Boris Yeltsin as president of Russia

British Prime Minister Tony Blair's son Leo is born, making him the first child born to a sitting prime minister in 152 years

Margaret Atwood's *The Blind Assassin* wins Booker McConnell Prize for fiction

Kazuo Ishiguro's *When We Were Orphans*

Trezza Azzopardi's *The Hiding Place*

2001   In Britain, the House of Lords passes legislation that legalizes the creation of cloned human embryos

British Prime Minister Tony Blair wins second term

In the United States, terrorists attack World Trade Center and Pentagon with hijacked airplanes, resulting in the collapse of the World Trade Center towers and the deaths of thousands

In response to the terrorist attacks, the United States begins "war on terrorism" with airstrikes in Afghanistan.

Ian McEwan's *An Atonement*

Rushdie's *Fury*

Peter Carey's *True History of the Kelly Gang*

Death of Eudora Welty

2002   Former Yugoslav leader Slobodan Milosevic put on trial at the Hague for alleged war crimes in Croatia, Bosnia, and Kosovo

Princess Margaret, the younger sister of Queen Elizabeth II, dies

List of Contributors

SCOTT ASHLEY. Sir James Knott Research Fellow in History at the University of Newcastle. He has just completed a book on images of barbarians in the early Middle Ages and is beginning one on primitivism in Britain and Ireland from 1750 to 1950. **Sir Thomas Malory**

CATES BALDRIDGE. Professor and writer. He received his B.A. from the Johns Hopkins University and his Ph.D. from the University of Virginia. He is currently professor of English at Middlebury College in Vermont and is the author of *The Dialogics of Dissent in the English Novel* (1984) and *Graham Greene's Fictions: The Virtues of Extremity* (2000). **Graham Greene**

JOHN A. BERTOLINI. Ellis Professor of the Liberal Arts at Middlebury College, Vermont where he teaches film and literature. He has written *The Playwrighting Self of Bernard Shaw*, edited *Shaw and Other Playwrights*, and published articles on Renaissance drama, modern British drama, and Alfred Hitchcock. He is currently working on a study of Terence Rattigan's plays. **George Bernard Shaw**

PAUL BIBIRE. Writer and lecturer. Formerly a lecturer in the School of English, University of St. Andrews, and of the Department of Anglo-Saxon, Norse, and Celtic, University of Cambridge. Since retirement he has been an honorary lecturer at the University of St. Andrews in Scotland in the Department of Medieval History in the School of History. Research includes Old English and Old Norse language and literature; West and North Germanic philology; the historical development of the phonological and morphological systems of Old English and Old Norse from their Indo-European and Germanic origins; Old English dialects; the development of Germanic legend and its representation in early English and Scandinavian poetry; Norse paganism and pagan mythology (sources for its knowledge and modes of its understanding); Icelandic sagas and other prose (in particular formal analysis); Norse court (*skaldic*) poetry. **Old English Literature**

SANDIE BYRNE. Fellow in English at Balliol College, Oxford. Her publications include works on eighteenth and nineteenth-century fiction and twentieth-century poetry. **Andrew Marvell**

GERRY CAMBRIDGE. Poet. Books of verse include *The Shell House* (Scottish Cultural Press, Aberdeen, 1995) with an introduction by George Mackay Brown, and *'Nothing But Heather!': Scottish Nature in Poems, Photographs and Prose* (Luath Press, Edinburgh 1999), which was illustrated with his own natural history photography. His next book of poems, *Madame Fi Fi's Farewell* (Luath Press, Edinburgh) will be published in mid-2002. Cambridge was the 1997–1999 Brownsbank Fellow, based at Hugh MacDiarmid's former home, Brownsbank Cottage, near Biggar in Scotland. He founded and edits the Scottish-American poetry magazine, *The Dark Horse.* **Ted Hughes**

ROBERT FAGGEN. Associate Professor of Literature at Claremont McKenna College. He is the author of *Robert Frost and the Challenge of Darwin* (University of Michigan Press); editor of *The Cambridge Companion to Robert Frost*; *Selected Poems of E. A. Robinson* (Penguin); *Early Poems of Robert Frost*; *Striving Towards Being: The Letters of Thomas Merton and Czeslaw Milosz* (Farrar, Straus & Giroux). A National Endowment for the Humanities Fellow, he is currently editing *The Notebooks of Robert Frost* for Harvard University Press. **John Milton**

THOMAS GAVIN. Writer and professor. Thomas Gavin's first novel, *Kinghill*, was named one of the Notable Books of 1977 by the American Library Association and listed as an "Editor's Choice" by *Time Magazine*. An excerpt from his novel in progress, *Bridge of Lost Boys*, has appeared in *Icarus: New Writing from Around the World*. An emeritus professor of English at The University of Rochester, Gavin has also held teaching positions at Middlebury College in Vermont and Delta College in Michigan. He has taught writing workshops at several conferences and received fellowships from the National Endowment for the Arts, the Andrew W. Mellon Foundation, and the Bread Loaf Writers' Conference. **Joseph Conrad**

CLAIRE HARMAN. Writer. Coordinating Editor of the literary magazine *PN Review* in the 1980s. She published her first biography, of Sylvia Townsend Warner, in 1989. Her biography of the eighteenth century novelist Fanny Burney appeared in 2000 and she is currently engaged in writing a life of Robert Louis Stevenson, whose *Essays and Poems* and *Selected Stories* she has edited for Everyman Editions. She has also edited Sylvia Townsend Warner's *Collected Poems* and *Diaries* and reviews regularly in the British literary press. She lives in Oxford, England. **Jane Austen**

JULIE HEARN. Writer. Former journalist who, in 1999, received an M.St in women's studies from Oxford University. It is a continuing source of amusement to her that she went from writing a weekly mother and baby column for the national Daily Star to researching witch-hunting and maternal power in early modern England. Her first novel is to be published by Oxford University Press in January 2003. **Robert Browning**

DIANA HENDERSON. Associate Professor of Literature at Massachusetts Institute of Technology. Author of *Passion Made Public: Elizabethan Lyric, Gender, and Performance*(University of Illinois Press, 1995) and numerous articles, including essays on early modern drama, poetry, domestic culture, Shakespeare on film, James Joyce, and Virginia Woolf. She is working on a book titled *Uneasy Collaborations: Transforming Shakespeare across Time and Media*. **Sir Philip Sidney**

JAY PARINI. Axinn Professor of English at Middlebury College in Vermont. A poet, novelist, and biographer, his most recent book is a novel, *The Apprentice Lover*. He serves as editor in chief of Scribners' *British Writers* and *American Writers* series. **Gerard Manley Hopkins and T. S. Eliot**

NEIL POWELL. Poet, biographer, editor, and lecturer. His books include five collections of poetry—*At the Edge* (1977), *A Season of Calm Weather* (1982), *True Colours* (1991), *The Stones on Thorpeness Beach* (1994), and *Selected Poems* (1998)—as well as *Carpenters of Light* (1979), *Roy Fuller: Writer and Society* (1995), and *The Language of Jazz* (1997). He lives in Suffolk, England and is working on a biography of George Crabbe. **E. M. Forster**

JOHN REDMOND. Visiting Assistant Professor at Macalester College in St. Paul, Minnesota. He took his doctorate at St. Hugh's College, Oxford, and has taught at Queen Mary and Westfield College, London. An assistant editor of the poetry magazine *Thumbscrew*, he has also written for the *London Review of Books* and the *Times Literary Supplement*. His first collection of poems, *Thumb's Width*, was published by Carcanet in 2001 and nominated for the Guardian First Book Award. **D. H. Lawrence**

PETER SCUPHAM. Poet. Has published ten collections, mostly with Oxford University Press. *Night Watch*, his most recent collection, was published by Anvil Press in 1999. His *Collected Poems* was published by Oxford/Carcanet in October 2002. He is a fellow of the Royal Society of Literature and has received a Cholmondeley award for poetry. **George Herbert**

N. S. THOMPSON. Lecturer in English at Christ Church, Oxford. He is the author of *Chaucer, Boccaccio and the Debate of Love* (1997) and articles on medieval and modern literature for a variety of journals, as well as many reviews for the *Times Literary Supplement*. He has translated several works from the Italian and a selection of his poetry was included in *Oxford Poets 2001: An Anthology*. **Geoffrey Chaucer**

TRICIA WELSCH. Associate Professor and chair of the Department of Film Studies at Bowdoin College in Maine. She received her Ph.D. in English from the University of Virginia. Her work has appeared in numerous film journals, including *Film Quarterly*, *Griffithiana*, *Film Criticism*, *The Journal of Film and Video*, and *Cinema Journal*. She is currently writing a book on Fox Films before the company's merger with Twentieth Century in 1935. She is a passionate devotee of the silent cinema. **George Eliot**

DAVID WHEATLEY. Lecturer in English at the University of Hull. He has published two collections of poetry, *Thirst*(1997) and *Misery Hill* (2000, both Gallery Press) and is coeditor of the poetry journal*Metre*. His articles and reviews have appeared in many journals, including *London Review of Books*, *The Times Literary Supplement*, *Journal of Studies Beckett* and *Poetry Review*. **Samuel Taylor Coleridge**

JOHN WILDERS. Emeritus Fellow of Worcester College, Oxford and Emeritus Professor of the Humanities at Middlebury College, Vermont. He has also taught at the University of Bristol, Princeton University, and the University of California, Santa Barbara and was visiting Research Fellow at the Australian National University in Canberra. He has published books on Shakespeare and was literary consultant for the BBC Television productions of the complete plays of Shakespeare. **Tom Stoppard**

THOMAS WRIGHT. Writer. Editor of the recently published *Table Talk. Oscar Wilde*, the first ever anthology of Wilde's spoken stories. He has written a number of articles on Wilde and related topics in publications such as the *Times Literary Supplement*. He published an interview with Peter Ackroyd in *The Sunday Telegraph Magazine* and wrote the entry on Peter Ackroyd for *British Writers, Supplement VI*. He recently edited and introduced *The Collection*, an anthology of Peter Ackroyd's journalism and miscellaneous writing. He regularly reviews books for *The Daily Telegraph*. **Oscar Wilde**

ANDREW ZAWACKI. Writer. Coeditor of the international journal *Verse* and a reviewer for *Boston Review*, he is the author of a book of poetry, *By Reason of Breakings* (University of Georgia Press, 2002), and a chapbook, *Masquerade* (Vagabond Press, 2001). A former fellow of the Slovenian Writers' Association, he edited the anthology *Afterwards: Slovenian Writing 1945–1995* (White Pine Press, 1999). He studies in the Committee on Social Thought at the University of Chicago. **John Donne**

BRITISH WRITERS

JANE AUSTEN

(1775–1817)

Claire Harman

WHEN JANE AUSTEN's brother Henry wrote the first "Biographical Notice" about the author for the posthumous publication of *Northanger Abbey* and *Persuasion* in 1818, he clearly thought his would be the last words on the subject. "Short and easy will be the task of the mere biographer," he wrote. "A life of usefulness, literature, and religion was not by any means a life of event." Almost two hundred years and thousands of books on Austen later, her fame and readership worldwide continue to grow. Her six completed novels—of which four were published in her lifetime—are among the best-known, best-loved, most-studied works in the English language, and there seems more to say about Austen and the cultural, social, and literary milieu in which she worked than ever before.

Because relatively little has survived (or ever existed) of Austen's personal papers, the "uneventfulness" of her life has itself become an area of study and speculation. Jane Austen guarded her privacy, publishing her works anonymously and resisting the scant opportunities available to exploit their immediate popularity. If she kept a journal or diary, no trace of one has survived, and very few of her letters remain. It is generally believed that her sister, Cassandra, pruned the archive ruthlessly after Jane's death in a deliberate attempt to control what posterity could know (though this assumption is currently being challenged by scholars). Certainly the Austen family was self-contained and self-supporting and closed ranks on the subject of Jane's authorship even before her early death in 1817 at the age of forty two; afterwards, Henry Austen's "Biographical Notice" was thought more than enough to satisfy public curiosity about her. The few remaining letters were bequeathed as keepsakes to favored relations, and Jane's siblings aged and died secure in the belief that their sister's fame was fading with them.

Austen's novels went through a period of relative obscurity in the mid-nineteenth century—heyday of the Victorian triple-decker novel—but by the 1870s public interest had revived to the extent that the Austen family felt the need for a biography and elected one of their own number, Jane's nephew James Austen-Leigh, to compile a *Memoir of Jane Austen*. The *Memoir* remains the main source of biographical information, incorporating family reminiscences and extracts from letters and anecdotes about Austen's life as a writer which, combined with Austen-Leigh's saccharine portrait of his aunt—"there was scarcely a charm in her most delightful characters that was not a true reflection of her own sweet temper and loving heart" (*Memoir*, p. 2)—established at a stroke the highly popular and durable cult of Jane Austen's extreme gentility. "Janeite" books—most of them fanciful—appeared in quantity throughout the 1890s and the first decades of the twentieth century (a period of intense anxiety about the rise of feminism), all corroborating the idea of Austen's sweetness, ladylike passivity, and refinement.

A properly researched, scholarly biography of the author (by Elizabeth Jenkins) did not appear until 1938. That book, and Mary Lascelles's classic study, *Jane Austen and Her Art* (1939) were part of a new Austen industry arising from R. W. Chapman's editorial work on the novels and letters in the 1930s and 1940s. Scholarly interest has grown steadily ever since, and Austen, whose prominent place in the literary canon has never seriously been disputed, is now the subject of hundreds of critical texts.

Nevertheless, the late Victorian cult of "Divine Jane" persists in the popular imagination despite many radically revisionist views of Austen and the significance and meaning of her writing. She has achieved the status of a national treasure, an iconic author in whose work the collective unconscious of an idealized England seems to be given perfect expression. A genuinely popular author as well as a great one, she exists, more obviously than any other English writer, in several mutually exclusive spheres at once. What appears to one reader as a biting satire on eighteenth-century provincial life is read by another purely for its nostalgia value; the feminist message of, say, *Pride and Prejudice,* translates as a paean to sexual pragmatism and the virtues of the status quo; the frustrations of the thwarted professional writer evident in Austen's letters strike some as marks of a delightfully unworldly amateurism. In his influential essay "Regulated Hatred," the critic D. W. Harding claimed that this paradox was "an essential part of [Austen's] complex intention as a writer: her books are, as she meant them to be, read and enjoyed by precisely the sort of people whom she disliked; she is a literary classic of the society which attitudes like hers, held widely enough, would undermine." (p. 347)

LIFE AND PUBLICATION HISTORY

JANE Austen was born on 16 December 1775 into a moderately well-off family on the edges of the gentry. Her scholarly father, George, was rector of the village of Steventon in Hampshire; her mother was a member of the aristocratic Leigh family (her uncle was Theophilus Leigh, master of Balliol College, Oxford). Jane was the sixth of their eight children. She had six brothers and one sister from whom she was virtually inseparable, Cassandra, her elder by two years.

The Austen home was in essence a small school, since Reverend Austen took in boarding pupils, making the rectory at Steventon a noisy and lively environment in which to grow up. Jane had the run of her father's library as well as the benefit of his teaching and was indulged from an early age in her love of reading. She was sent away to three different schools during her youth—in Oxford, Southampton, and Reading— emerging rather better educated than was thought

absolutely necessary for girls at the time, but in no sense a bluestocking. There was no intellectual snobbery in the Austen household ("*our* family . . . are great Novel-readers & not ashamed of being so" she wrote [*Letters*, p. 26]) and Jane shared her father's relish for the Gothic delights of Mrs. Radcliffe and Matthew "Monk" Lewis, books she satirized mercilessly in her own later novel *Northanger Abbey.*

The Austen family seems a paradigm of rock-solid eighteenth-century standards—tolerant, educated, Church of England Tories—but recent biographies have stressed the fluidity within this model and the pragmatism underlying its stability. Elements that did not fit in were expelled, such as Jane's elder brother George, who seems to have suffered some mental or physical disability and was "given away" in infancy (living on to the age of seventy-eight in an asylum). People were taken into the household, such as the orphaned Martha Lloyd, who became part of the Austen family (her sister Mary had married Jane's eldest brother, James, in 1797, and Martha made a late match with Francis Austen in 1828). Opportunities of betterment were taken where they arose, such as the Austens' allowing their rich, childless cousins to adopt their third son, Edward. He took their name, Knight, and was propelled into a higher social stratum, ending up far richer and more powerful than any of his siblings, owner of a large estate in Kent and property in Hampshire.

In the early 1790s, when Jane Austen was in her mid-teens, her brother James instigated a series of private theatricals in the barn at Steventon, in which Jane participated enthusiastically. Star of these productions was the Reverend Austen's niece Eliza Hancock, who had been brought up in India (she is thought to have been the illegitimate daughter of the governor-general, Warren Hastings) and had married a French count, Jean de Feuillide, guillotined in 1794. Jane admired her glamorous cousin intensely, and Eliza, who later married Henry Austen, can be seen as a model for many of the attractive extroverts in Austen's novels. It is notable, however, that Austen did not exploit the intense drama of Eliza's life story in fiction, just as she did not use any material derived from her brother Frank's war experiences (he was part of the naval convoy that went to rescue Sir John Moore at Corunna) or the distressing episode in 1799 when her aunt, Jane Leigh Perrot, was jailed for shoplifting. Given the wealth of dramatic incident in the lives of those around her, Austen's preference for writing, as she said to her niece Anna in 1814, of "3 or 4 Families in a Country Village" (*Letters,* p. 275) was from deliberate choice rather than paucity of experience.

In about the same period as the family theatricals, James Austen was editor of an Oxford college magazine called the *Loiterer,* to which his younger sister may have contributed anonymously. She was a writer at an early age; three notebooks of juvenilia survive, including the satirical story "Jack and Alice," in which a country landowner fends off his female admirers by the strategic placement of mantraps around his estate. Her "History of England," completed before her sixteenth birthday, is similarly satirical and is inscribed "by a partial, prejudiced & ignorant Historian." Like all Austen's juvenilia, it reads as if it was composed primarily for the amusement of her family and is remarkable for its precocity.

Before the age of twenty Austen had written a short epistolary novel called "Lady Susan" (notable for its ruthlessly manipulative central character) and had begun another novel, provisionally titled "Elinor and Marianne," which eventually became her first published work, *Sense and Sensibility.* In 1796 she was at work on "First Impressions," an early version of *Pride and Prejudice,* and by 1798 had begun "Susan," later *Northanger Abbey.* Her father was so impressed with "First Impressions" that he sent it to the publisher Thomas Cadell almost as soon as the manuscript was finished in 1797. Cadell refused it sight unseen, but far from being discouraged, Austen worked assiduously throughout the years 1795–1800 in a way that indicates she was definitely aiming at eventual publication of her growing hoard of manuscripts.

What little is known of Jane's romantic attachments in her youth suggests a sympathetic alignment with her sister. When Jane was seventeen Cassandra threatened to break up the uninterrupted intimacy of their girlhood by getting engaged to a young cleric. Her fiancé, Tom Fowle, died of fever in 1797 while on duty as an army chaplain in the West Indies, and Cassandra entered into a sort of symbolic widowhood, seemingly giving up the thought of marriage (which, since she had been left money by her fiancé, was just about a viable option for her).

At the time of Cassandra's engagement Jane was known as something of a flirt, a "husband-hunting butterfly," as one family friend described her. She was lively and sociable, loved dances, and was subject to fits of high spirits. At the age of twenty she had a brief romance with a handsome young family friend, Tom Lefroy, who was thought too young to marry, went off to make his fortune in the law, was spectacularly successful at it, but never came back to recommence the affair with Jane. Three years afterward Jane was still mentioning him in her letters with a certain wistfulness, but by that time Cassandra's fiancé was dead. The sisters, by then in their mid and late twenties respectively, seemed to give up actively looking for husbands and settled down at home together as spinsters. All their brothers (except the disabled George) married, and all except Henry had children.

In 1801 the Reverend and Mrs. Austen decided to move from rural Hampshire to the elegant and rapidly expanding spa town of Bath in Somerset, taking their two dependent daughters with them. This was by all accounts an unwanted and unhappy move for Austen, leading to a period of dearth and stasis in her writing life. They lived in Bath for five years (1801–1806), during which period the Reverend Austen died, leaving his widow and daughters partly dependent on the support of the Austen sons, especially Edward and James, the latter having inherited his father's living at Steventon. In 1806 the women moved to lodgings in Southampton, where they stayed almost three years. During this period Austen revised "Susan" and sold it for £10 to the publisher Crosby, who did not, however, go on to publish it. Possibly stalled by the uncertain fate of this work, Austen did not begin anything else, apart from "The Watsons," a fragmentary first draft of a novel, until 1811.

Austen's unhappiness during these years may have been exacerbated by another failed romance, which according to family legend took place in the summer of 1801 when the Austens were on holiday on the Devonshire coast. In this uncorroborated story, Jane met and fell mutually in love with a young clergyman of highly congenial temperament. At the end of several weeks they had come to "an understanding" and the young man was expected to propose within the year, but when they next heard from his family it was with news of his death.

We only have Cassandra Austen's word for it that this shadowy, anonymous lover died, or existed at all; no letters at all survive from just before the period in question to three years after it. The long silence has seemed suggestive to some commentators, as has the poignancy with which Austen depicts the loss of a potentially ideal partner in *Persuasion.* Other possible parallels between her works and life are detectable in an incident that happened the following year, 1802. During a visit by the Austen sisters to the country home of their friends the Bigg-Withers, the son, Harris, proposed to Jane and she accepted him. Regretting this decision overnight, Jane withdrew her acceptance next morning and left abruptly with Cassandra. Harris was only twenty-one, and clearly Austen's attachment to him was not strong: most biographers have suggested, plausibly, that she was homesick in Bath and tempted by a scheme that would reinstate her in Hampshire. A similar temptation faces Anne Elliot, the heroine of *Persuasion,* when her cousin Walter, heir to her own family home, presents himself as a suitor: "the idea of . . . calling it her home again, her home for ever, was a charm which she could not immediately resist" (*Persuasion,* p. 160).

The years in Bath and Southampton came to a welcome end in 1809 when Austen's brother Edward was able to provide his mother and sisters with a cottage on his estates (inherited from the Knights) in Chawton, a Hampshire village not far from Austen's original Steventon home. The eight years she lived there were astonishingly productive. She revised *Sense and Sensibility,* solicited its publication, and saw it in print—her long-awaited first book—by 1811. The same year she began *Mansfield Park* and revised "First Impressions" into *Pride and Prejudice* (the books were published in 1814 and 1813 respectively). *Emma* was written in 1814–1815 and published late in 1816; overlapping this was *Persuasion,* begun in 1815 and finished in 1816. The manuscript of "Susan," the novel languishing in Crosby's offices, was bought back in 1816 and revised extensively, appearing eventually as *Northanger Abbey.*

This remarkable output of work afforded Austen a brief period of material and critical success in her lifetime. Her reknown was such that the prince regent invited her to dedicate her next book (*Emma*) to him, an offer the author was, of course, unable to refuse. More valuable was Sir Walter Scott's review of the same book in the *Quarterly Review* (October 1815), an appreciation of the anonymous author's powers as an innovator; privately Scott was even more admiring, writing in his journal in 1826: "That young lady had a talent for describing the involvements and feelings and characters of ordinary life, which is to me the most wonderful I ever met with" (*Journals,* 14 March 1826).

Austen's flow of ideas and energy slowed in 1816 with the first indications that she was not well. early in 1817 she began another novel, "Sanditon," but was only able to work on it for two months. By late spring her health was failing rapidly; she made her will and moved with Cassandra to lodgings in Winchester to be nearer her doctors. She died on 18 July 1817, at age forty-two, of uncertain cause. An article by Sir Zachary Cope in the *British Medical Journal* (18 July 1964) suggested plausibly that Austen suffered from Addison's disease, a liver dysfunction; other commentators believe that she probably died from some form of cancer.

NORTHANGER ABBEY

Northanger Abbey was published after Austen's death but belongs at the start of her public career, being the first of her manuscripts to be accepted by a publisher. It seems in many ways Austen's least sophisticated work, sharing with the juvenilia a relentlessly mocking tone and fixed, by its extensive satire on the "Horrid School" of fiction of the 1790s, in a previous age. Despite the revisions that transformed "Susan" into *Northanger Abbey*, Austen seems to have been aware of how out-of-date her book had become by 1810 and apologized in a foreword: "The public are entreated to bear in mind that thirteen years have passed since it was finished."

Young Catherine Morland is depicted from the beginning as ironically hopeless heroine material, "a thin awkward figure, a sallow skin without colour, dark lank hair, and strong features." But the question is not simply one about the definition of a heroine, but of what constitutes femininity itself—or what constructs it. Catherine's tomboy childhood was spent rolling down hills in sensual abandon and "boys' play;" "she was moreover noisy and wild, hated confinement and cleanliness" (p. 14). This is put an end to—partly—by the onset of puberty, but the transition is difficult and not wholly successful. Catherine struggles to acquire the traditional female drawing-room accomplishments of playing the piano, sketching, and writing poetry, but she is never going to be good enough at them to blazon her worth to a prospective lover. Her ambition to become a heroine is in many respects a reaction to having become a mediocre woman.

Catherine's guide through the maze of gender definition is a most unusual hero, Henry Tilney. "Not quite handsome," and not the heir to his domineering father's estate, tastes, manners, or gruff masculinity, Henry is a surprisingly ambivalent character, an acute and sometimes waspish commentator with a wide knowledge of fiction (conventionally a female interest) and fashion. His conversation at the ball about his purchase of some Indian muslin for his sister may be entirely facetious and is certainly quite camp; while his male friends are depicted as having nothing to discuss apart from dogs, horses, and carriages, Henry is exchanging shopping tips with foolish Mrs. Allen. "You must be a great comfort to your sister, sir," Mrs. Allen remarks approvingly. The remark is two-edged; women may want such a

companionably feminine man as a brother, but will he do as a husband?

Henry is not just feminine but a feminist, as is evident in his exchange with Catherine at the same ball. Henry teases her with some supposedly flattering remarks about the superiority of women's letter writing: "Every body allows that the talent of writing agreeable letters is peculiarly female. Nature may have done something, but I am sure it must be essentially assisted by the practice of keeping a journal." Catherine, unable to judge the tone of this, recognizes it as an exaggeration all the same, and counters it politely, to which Henry—after more banter—responds with his true (opposite) view of the subject:

I should no more lay it down as a general rule that women write better letters than men, than that they sing better duets, or draw better landscapes. In every power, of which taste is the foundation, excellence is pretty fairly divided between the sexes.

(p. 28)

This rational, egalitarian view, expressed (unlike the rest of Henry's speech) in plain language, forms the ground bass to the novel and is the point to which the hero and heroine tend through all the artificial convolutions of Catherine's self-dramatizing romancing. Having at first invented Henry as the hero of her story, she discovers that he is the hero in real life.

Northanger Abbey itself, modernized and comfortable, does not answer to Catherine's Gothic ideal, though she is prepared to swallow her disappointment, constructing instead a world of possible narratives for the place—of dark secrets, dungeons, skeletons, sexual terrorism, and murder. But Catherine is by no means the only romancer in Northanger Abbey—General Tilney, Henry's father, invites her to visit in the mistaken belief that she is an heiress and will therefore be a useful match for his younger son. Nor is Catherine a fool. Her fantasies, like her appetite for fiction, are symptoms of a craving for experience, and many of her instincts about people (formed by her reading) are shown to be correct in the end. General Tilney may not be the Bluebeard figure she has daydreamed, but he is exposed as something almost as bad—a greedy, calculating, hard-hearted monster—when, discovering his mistake over Catherine's status, he ejects her peremptorily from the abbey.

Northanger Abbey is an exception among Austen's works for its sustained satire on the popular literature of the day, the Gothic romances of Ann Radcliffe, Regina Maria Roche, Elizabeth Parsons, and Matthew Lewis that had set trends in sensibility as much as in style. This was a pretty soft target, and Austen knew it; more important and impressive is her authorial intervention (in chapter 5) in defense of the novel as a form. It is addressed not to the reader but to other novelists, particularly those who deliberately exclude novel reading from their characters' range of everyday experience (much in the way that soap-opera characters today are seldom depicted watching television): "Alas! If the heroine of one novel be not patronized by the heroine of another, from whom can she expect protection and regard?" (p. 37) Austen says wittily. The novel itself, from which the heroines of novels seem to shrink, is something to celebrate and be proud of, "work in which the greatest powers of the mind are displayed, in which the most thorough knowledge of human nature, the happiest delineation of its varieties, the liveliest effusions of wit and humour are conveyed to the world in the best chosen language" (p. 38). In an age when there was very little literary criticism, and almost none of the novel, the passage stands out as a sort of rallying cry or manifesto.

SENSE AND SENSIBILITY

IN Elinor and Marianne Dashwood, the heroines of Austen's second completed novel, one finds a celebration of sisterly intimacy that presumably owes a great deal to Austen's love of her own sister and closest female friends. It is not doting but tolerant, not dependent on the superficial signals that govern courtship but on long observation of character and informed analysis. It presents a model, in other words, for an ideal marriage of true minds and tastes, the very state toward which all Austen's plots impend but are never shown reaching.

Each of the sisters is broadly characterized by one of the qualities of the title (Elinor, sense, Marianne, sensibility) but not to the exclusion of the other. Although the title sounds oppositional, the whole thrust of the book is toward identifying people, places, and states of mind that complement each other.

The sisters' dual love stories, running in parallel and ending, predictably enough, with their marriages, multiply the book's social and sexual messages by rather more than a factor of two. The pairings and partings that take place, the number of second attachments (either by betrothal or marriage) that are exposed or withheld like partner-changes in a dance, broaden the moral scope of this notably didactic book. All Austen's novels contain examples of marriages already in place by which to judge the likely outcome for each new heroine and potential hero, and in *Sense and Sensibility* the marriages on show are depressingly compromised. Sir John and Lady Middleton only survive as a couple by keeping to mutually exclusive spheres: "Sir John was a sportsman, Lady Middleton a mother. He hunted and shot, and she humoured her children; and these were their only resources" (p. 32). John Dashwood, half-brother to Elinor, Marianne, and Margaret and usurper of their comfortable home at Norland, seems a much closer match with his wife, Fanny, but their like-mindedness is really nothing more than self-protective and ruthless self-interest. It promotes their own comfort and prosperity efficiently but is destructive of wider family and social ties.

The John Dashwoods represent a crude, asocial form of the instinct for survival embodied in Elinor's "sense." But where their goal is to dominate, Elinor's is to spare others unnecessary pain or trouble, to regulate her personal feelings for the good of the many. She has a strongly practical nature, upon which her family has come to rely, and early in the book it is made clear that to keep the group functioning she must pretend to feel less than they do. When Henry Dashwood dies suddenly (precipitating the family's dispossession), Elinor's mother and sister give themselves up "wholly" to sorrow, "seeking increase of wretchedness in every reflection that could afford it, and resolved against ever admitting consolation in future" (p. 7). They are willfully magnifying and multiplying wretchedness in the belief that expressions of sensibility are the marks of an exalted nature. What they really show is lack of judgment and a dangerous egocentricity. Marianne's exaggerated response to a short separation from her lover, Willoughby, prepares the reader for the critical decline she enters later in the book when he has left her for good. Excessive sensibility is shown as destructive of the self and useless to others. Elinor understands this when she decides not to share with her mother or sisters the devastating news that her suitor, Edward Ferrars, is secretly engaged to Lucy Steele: "their tenderness and sorrow must add to her distress, while her self-command would neither receive encouragement from their example nor from their praise. She was stronger alone. . . ." (p. 141).

Austen modifies with great subtlety what might have become a restrictive polarization between the sisters' respective virtues by allowing each of them a temporary access to the other's state of mind. In Marianne's case this is effected by her long illness, which subdues her physically and imposes a state of reflectiveness she seldom experiences otherwise. Her mistakes and culpability become immediately clear to her: "Long before I was enough recovered to talk, I was perfectly able to reflect. . . . My illness, I well knew, had been entirely brought on by myself. . . . Had I died, it would have been self-destruction" (p. 345). Elinor goes through something similar, is put in her sister's shoes, in the extraordinary interview she has late in the story with Willoughby, who has come back to give some account of his dreadful behavior toward Marianne (who is too ill to admit him herself). Willoughby's penitential visit suggests he is a more decent character than Elinor had thought possible; his physical presence and considerable charm also work on her like a spell:

> She felt that his influence over her mind was heightened by circumstances which ought not in reason to have weight; by that person of uncommon attraction, that open, affectionate and lively manner which it was no merit to possess; and by that still ardent love for Marianne, which it was not even in-

nocent to indulge. But she felt that it was so, long, long before she could feel his influence less.

> (p. 333)

The contrast between the sisters is therefore not so much in their different temperaments but in the extent to which, at the beginning of the book at least, they are able to govern their feelings. Marianne has much more to learn in this respect, and does so traumatically, almost dying in her anorexic decline following Willoughby's jilting and being rewarded at the conclusion of the story with marriage to the worthier but less exciting (and older) Colonel Brandon. For a romantic novel this is not quite as affirmative or celebratory an ending as one might expect. In the last sentence the focus is still on the sister-sister bond as the more enduring and rewarding:

> among the merits and the happiness of Elinor and Marianne, let it not be ranked as the least considerable, that though sisters, and living almost within sight of each other, they could live without disagreement between themselves, or producing coolness between their husbands.

> (p. 380)

PRIDE AND PREJUDICE

AUSTEN was thirty-seven years old when her second novel was published in 1813, but she had been living with the story for sixteen or seventeen years, since the time, that is, when she had been exactly the same age as the book's heroine, Elizabeth Bennet. It is the work of a mature woman without illusions but retains a freshness and optimism from those youthful origins.

The manuscript of the early version of the story has not survived, but "First Impressions" is believed to have been an epistolary novel. By the time the book was sold to a publisher in 1812 as *Pride and Prejudice* it had been "lop't and crop't" and rewritten as a third-person narrative. There are still more than forty letters in the novel, but recasting the book made it possible for Austen to concentrate on one point of view, that of literature's first really unconventional romantic heroine.

Pride and Prejudice is a feminist novel, albeit of a type we might not instantly recognize today, and Elizabeth Bennet a thoroughly amiable heroine whose "prejudice" is easily forgiven. Unlike Emma Woodhouse, she is mature and judicious from the start, and where she has choices to make (though in a narrower sphere of influence than Emma's) she surprises everyone with the strength of her convictions, refusing to marry the odious cleric Collins, and then, most surprisingly, refusing Darcy too. The rashness of this action would have struck contemporary readers forcibly, since ultra-eligible Darcy is, after all, that rare creature "a single man in possession of a good fortune," who the novel's famous first sentence has told us "must be in want of a wife."

In Austen's world, a world of harsh realities for women of the Bennet class, whether that single man is good or not is of secondary importance. Elizabeth is just able to make an independent choice, although by doing so she antagonizes her parents more than if she had actually disgraced them, as her sister Lydia does by eloping with Wickham. Other women are not so lucky. Elizabeth's friend Charlotte Lucas represents the woman condemned to make the best of it. She accepts Collins only three days after he has been rejected by Elizabeth, whose reaction is one of shock: "she could not have supposed it possible . . . that [Charlotte] would have sacrificed every better feeling to worldly advantage." The reader has been prepared by an earlier conversation between the two friends in which Charlotte states:

> Happiness in marriage is entirely a matter of chance. If the dispositions of the parties are ever so well known to each other, or ever so similar beforehand, it does not advance their felicity in the least. They always continue to grow sufficiently unlike afterwards to have their share of vexation; and it is better to know as little as possible of the defects of the person with whom you are to pass your life.
>
> (p. 23)

Elizabeth laughs this off nervously as "not sound," but it is clear that Charlotte, as a plain woman of twenty-seven dependent on her brothers, doesn't have the same choices as her friend. Being romantic is not one of her options.

The extent of Charlotte's compromise is made clear when Elizabeth visits her after her marriage. Charlotte is already practicing the shutdown of her powers of perception and thereby her powers of judgment: "When Mr. Collins said anything of which his wife might reasonably be ashamed, which certainly was not unseldom, [Elizabeth] involuntarily turned her eye on Charlotte. Once or twice she could discern a faint blush; but in general Charlotte wisely did not hear" (p. 156). Mr. and Mrs. Bennet are another example of a couple who try—unsuccessfully—to ignore each other's defects, but Elizabeth acts in entirely the opposite way during her gradual adjustment of opinion about Darcy (a process in which the words "admit" and "allow" are recurrent). She opens her eyes and her mind to get a fuller, broader, picture, symbolized elegantly in the episode when she visits Darcy's magnificent country house, Pemberley, during the period of their estrangement. Elizabeth is forced to go there out of politeness while visiting her aunt and uncle in Derbyshire and submits because she believes Darcy is not at home. Seeing his surroundings for the first time she is impressed by their splendor but also by his genuine taste, and hearing the housekeeper speak in high praise of her master, whom she has known since birth, Elizabeth begins to see him from a new and flattering angle. Standing for some time before a large portrait of Darcy, Elizabeth is able to contemplate him at leisure:

> There was certainly at this moment, in Elizabeth's mind, a more gentle sensation towards the original, than she had ever felt in the height of their acquaintance. . . . Every idea that had been brought forward by the housekeeper was favourable to his character, and as she stood before the canvas, on which he was represented, and fixed his eyes upon herself, she thought of his regard with a deeper sentiment of gratitude than it had ever raised before; she remembered its warmth, and softened its impropriety of expression.
>
> (pp. 250–251)

This subtle passage, in which Elizabeth is able to synthesize her own and other people's views of Darcy for the first time, reaching a sort of Platonic revelation, indicates the power and novelty of Austen's characterization. Elizabeth is both seeing and preparing to be seen (she "fixed his eyes upon herself"), picturing certain possibilities for the first time, particularly the idea of Darcy as a husband.

Darcy is the nearest Jane Austen ever got to depicting a "demon-lover" type in her novels, similar to the sexually attractive but duplicitous cads and seducers of eighteenth-century romances. This is not Darcy's real character, of course, but a projection onto him of Elizabeth's "prejudice," which in this instance also encompasses her romantic ideas and stereotypes derived from her reading. Darcy's "pride" and apparent unfeelingness are actually symptoms of his modesty and reticence, and by the end of the novel he is revealed as a closet philanthropist of the worthiest sort, as well as being wealthy, fastidious, and intellectual.

The unimpassioned resolution of the courtship plot, rapidly described in reported speech, is wholly in keeping with Austen's unsentimental views of love, even true love. An accommodation has been reached, but it is the process that interests Austen more than the outcome, a process in which women often lose as much as they gain. As Sandra Gilbert and Susan Gubar observe in their study of nineteenth-century literary imagination, *The Madwoman in the Attic*, "the comedy of Austen's novels explores the tensions between the freedom of her art and the dependency of her characters: while they stutter and sputter and lapse into silence and even haste to perfect felicity, she attains a woman's language that is magnificently duplicitous" (p. 169).

MANSFIELD PARK

In a letter to her sister announcing the arrival of her first copy of *Pride and Prejudice*, Austen gave an indication of the new work she had in mind: "it shall be a complete change of subject—ordination." Although ordination did not end up as the predominant theme of *Mansfield Park*, there is a somberness and soberness about the book—and two overtly Christian central characters—that do mark a significant change.

Courtship and marriage provide the narrative structure, as usual, but the element of romance, so enlivening to the earlier books, has all but

disappeared. The book is complex and disturbing, and such comic aspects as it contains are much darker than in any other Austen novel. Mrs. Norris is a powerfully convincing portrait of gratuitous evil, and the threat of the existing order collapsing is not just possible but imminent. At the resolution of the romantic plot, the world of Mansfield Park is still precariously balanced. Rather than harmony having been created, chaos has only just been fended off.

The heroine of the story has proved the least popular in all Austen's fiction. Fanny Price is sickly, virtuous, long-suffering, self-abnegating, and passive. Compared with Mary Crawford, friend to Fanny's cousins the Bertrams, Fanny is almost hopelessly unattractive. Mary is—or seems to be—a character in the Elizabeth Bennet mold, vigorous, witty, alert. She is associated with movement, laughing, dancing, riding at a gallop. "Resting fatigues me," she says to Fanny. "I must move."

Fanny's immobility, on the other hand, seems to augur ill from the start. Far from going at life at a gallop, Fanny is so physically weak that she has to be lifted onto her horse and can only ride at walking pace. When at the beginning of the book she is sent from her impoverished and unkempt home in Portsmouth to be adopted into the family of her rich uncle Sir Thomas Bertram at Mansfield Park, Fanny's debility links her immediately with her inert sofa-bound aunt, Lady Bertram. It seems perverse of Austen to have awarded such an unexciting character the position of heroine, and the reader is understandably suspicious of what the author's overall design might be.

But *Mansfield Park* is not a novel of self-discovery as Austen's other novels are. The resolution of the book's problems depends not on Fanny Price transforming or adjusting her character but in keeping it exactly intact. She endures, she persists, and her qualities are eventually recognized and valued. Her stillness, her conservatism, are the benchmarks by which other behavior is judged and for the most part found wanting.

Fanny's reception at Mansfield Park is chill, both figuratively and literally, for she is given an unheated room far away at the top of the house and made to feel all the misery of the poor relation, taken in out of duty. Mrs. Norris, whose malevolence is not perceived by Sir Thomas and Lady Bertram, conducts a campaign of persecution against Fanny, who naturally enough pines for home in this inhospitable atmosphere. An important turning point is reached, however, when Fanny has the chance to return briefly to Portsmouth. The remembered "bustle" of home is in fact chaos, as Austen says: "Nobody was in their right place, nothing was done as it ought to be"; her family has not missed her, her mother is distracted and negligent, her father shallow, drunken, and feckless. Fanny's dismay as she realizes all this for the first time is evident:

> she could think of nothing but Mansfield, its beloved inmates, its happy ways....The elegance, propriety, regularity, harmony—and perhaps, above all, the peace and tranquillity of Mansfield, were brought to her remembrance every hour of the day, by the prevalence of everything opposite to them *here.*
>
> (p. 391)

Fanny's sensitivity to the word and concept of "home" marks her out as a guardian of certain principles. Lady Bertram is blind to them. "It can make very little difference to you, whether you are in one house or the other" (p. 25), she says to Fanny, but Fanny recognizes Mansfield as a material embodiment of that social, political, and emotional solidity toward which all her deepest feelings gravitate.

Fanny's concern with continuity throws into relief the dangerous variability of the other characters, of which the visit to Mr. Rushworth's estate at Sotherton is a brilliant dramatization. Rushworth intends to improve his property in the ultra-fashionable landscaping style of the time, and Henry Crawford, the arch-tamperer, is to advise him. But when the party sets off into the grounds (laid out as formal garden surrounded by artificial wilderness, which in turn borders on parkland) they begin to wander in more ways than one. Mary Crawford, stung by her recent knowledge that Edmund Bertram wishes to join the clergy, takes him along a sequestered and symbolically zigzagging path while she tries to talk him out of it. Maria Bertram is engaged to Mr. Rushworth but takes too ardent an interest in Henry Crawford. His presence and all the talk of "improvements" work on her dangerously, and seeing the locked iron gates opening onto the parkland, she determines to get through them, fixing on a distant hill from which, she is sure, they will be able to see better. While Rushworth is off fetching the key, Maria grows impatient and, with Henry's encouragement, finds there is a way to squeeze through the gates. "I think it might be done," he says, "if you really wished to be more at large, and could allow yourself to think it not prohibited." Fanny, who overhears this, understands that more than a physical boundary is being transgressed here. Her forebodings are borne out later in the plot when Henry runs off with Maria after her marriage, a scandalous turn of events, but one that is almost inevitable in a world where "nobody was in their right place and nothing was done as it ought to be."

The episode of the theatricals in *Mansfield Park* draws the themes together beautifully and is rightly considered a high point of Austen's artistry. From the start there are problems, including the fact that Sir Thomas, head of the household, is known to disapprove and that it is only his absence makes the enterprise possible. The participants quarrel about the choice of play (*Lovers' Vows,* a sentimental melodrama adapted by Elizabeth Inchbald from a play by Kotzebue), and then about roles, and then about involving outsiders in order to perform at all. Only Edmund and Fanny dispprove and refuse to join in, Fanny saying emphatically, "I could not act anything if you were to give me the world. No indeed, I cannot act" (p. 145). Henry Crawford is considered an accomplished actor, and his sister, Mary, is also in her element on the stage. The pull of being able to assume another role, to abandon one's self, is too much even for virtuous Edmund, the would-be clergyman. Under Mary's persuasion he joins in the play, taking the role of a stage clergyman indulging in a love affair, an absurd travesty of his real calling and the real role he should be assuming. Only Fanny keeps out of this chaos of appearances. As audience she is the only member of the group who sees while others act, the only person left in a position to judge.

EMMA

JUDGMENT and interpretation of evidence are the themes dealt with brilliantly in Austen's fourth published novel, *Emma* (1816). The heroine, twenty-year-old Emma Woodhouse, is characterized in the ominously bright opening sentence as "handsome, clever, and rich, with a comfortable home and a happy disposition." She "seemed to unite some of the best blessings of existence; and had lived nearly twenty-one years in the world with very little to distress or vex her." But Emma's advantages of birth and intellect, her indulged childhood at the hands of her father and a governess "who had such an affection for her as could never find fault" (p. 6), seem to have rendered her incapable of judging correctly, to an extent that would quickly alienate the reader if, for instance, it was Emma's slower-witted, unpromising friend Harriet Smith who made all the disastrous mistakes of the novel. But Emma's restless imagination, her preeminently verbal intelligence, mark her as a worthy candidate for a stringent moral trial.

What establishes the novel's great comic potential is that Emma not only colludes in but to a great extent manipulates her own testing. There is a very close identification—at times overlap—between the narrative voice in *Emma* and the heroine's own thoughts, to which we are given unusual access. The structure of the book is therefore formed around her point of view, with richly comic effect; it allows the reader to appreciate the irony underlying Emma's self-satisfaction, emphasizing that she is the subject of her own—as well as the book's—affectionately sardonic commentary. This is how Emma's faults are made tolerable, and the author never needs to conceal the facts that Emma is spoiled and selfish, snobbish and proud, that she has authority and abuses it. There is a deliberately facetious tone to many of her speeches, such as the one she makes to her father and Mr. Knightley, crediting herself with having masterminded the Westons' marriage:

> Mr Weston certainly would never marry again. Some people even talked of a promise to his wife on her death-bed, and others of the son and the uncle not letting him. All manner of solemn nonsense was talked on the subject, but I believed none of it. Ever since the day (about four years ago) that Miss Taylor and I met with him in Broadway-lane. . . . I made up my mind on the subject. I planned the match from that hour.
>
> (p. 12)

It is typical of Emma that she overlooks the parts Miss Taylor and Mr. Weston played in the match, or affects to. Her imagination is capricious and dangerously unemployed, and she treats everything—even the interpretation of past events—as opportunities for play. Emma displays a childlike egocentricity in her confidence that all her whims will be indulged, but she also chafes at being indulged. She is a child no longer (a fact emphasized by the removal of Miss Taylor from the household and the establishment of a parental role toward her own increasingly childlike father) and is in fact desperately bored in an adult world that seems not to pose enough challenges or companions equal to her lively mind. We are shown her restlessness in various occupations. Mr. Knightley tells of reading lists Emma is in the habit of compiling while never actually reading the books, and a little later, when Emma undertakes to draw Harriet's portrait, her portfolio turns out to be full of pictures not one of which had ever been finished: "Her many beginnings were displayed. Miniatures, half-lengths, whole lengths, pencil, crayon, and water colours had all been tried in turn. She had always wanted to do everything" (p. 44).

The world of Highbury is one where, as the curate Mr. Elton comments, "every body has their level" (p. 132). Change is a constant threat to its peaceful workings: the novel begins with the change wrought by "poor Miss Taylor's" marriage to the prosperous and amiable Mr. Weston, by which Emma's former governess is transformed into someone just below Emma in the social hierarchy. Emma has no ambitions beyond Highbury, claustrophobically limited as it is, but it is clear from the start (to the reader if not the heroine) that merely in order to remain where she is, Emma will have to be open to change.

The very first scene between Emma and her hypochondriacal old father shows her surviving an evening at home only by means of the most careful strategy, and it serves as a warning of evenings to come, pandering to Mr. Woodhouse's "habits of gentle selfishness." The direction of change is clear too from Emma's first scene with their gentleman neighbor Mr. Knightley; their familiar, *married* manners are ample evidence of compatability. Knightley's attachment to Emma, though still at this stage kept in a pseudo-paternal sphere, is already in place, as is Harriet Smith's attachment (and suitability) to Robert Martin. Frank Churchill and Jane Fairfax, who have yet to appear in the story, are already secretly engaged in Weymouth. It is only Emma's insistence that she knows best that disrupts what is presented as inevitable from the outset; she precipitates the crises which then have to be resolved.

The crucial episode in Emma's journey towards self-knowledge is the expedition to Box Hill of a group connected through Emma; she ought to make the party cohere but in fact divides it. Sensing "a want of union" (p. 367) she does nothing constructive but falls back selfishly on trying to extract amusement from others. Her flirtatious repartee with Frank Churchill and the fatuous game of witticisms he instigates (which leads to Emma's cruel snubbing of Miss Bates) are the products of an idle and dissatisfied mind. Although any truthful reader would admit that it is a relief to have garrulous Miss Bates cut short for once, the pleasure of Emma's joke is extremely fleeting, overtaken at once by the shock of anyone having made it. Even when Emma begins to feel sorry for her part in "the very questionable enjoyments of this day" (p. 374), she tries to divert blame from herself by arguing with Knightley, whose response is to remind her of Miss Bates's situation—a nicely suggestive word—and her own.

Knightley's chivalric-sounding name is no accident, nor is the name of Emma's home, Hartfield, that she must prove mistress of before she can share Knightley's Donwell, with its overtones of success. Knightley puts Emma in her place in more senses than one, encouraging her to earn by merit the position in society she inherited by accident of birth. The inequalities of life in Highbury are to some extent elided in the process, as the Marxist critic Arnold Kettle remarked (in *The Rise of the Novel,* ed. Watt, 1963, p. 123): "the value of *Emma* is limited, not just relatively, but objectively and always." Austen's most charming heroine remains, to use a phrase that appears toward the end of the book, "faultless in spite of her faults" (p. 356).

PERSUASION

"You may *perhaps* like the Heroine, as she is almost too good for me," Jane Austen wrote to her niece Fanny of Anne Elliot, the heroine of *Persuasion.* Austen's reservations have been shared by many readers. Submissive, dutiful, passive—Anne seems not to come from the same pen as Elizabeth Bennet or Emma Woodhouse, having none of their charm and sex appeal and attendant optimism.

All Austen's novels revolve around single women moving or maneuvering toward marriage, but Anne Elliot is the only really spinsterish one, self-appointedly and disappointedly unmarried. For her the usual Austen plot has gone into reverse: the ideal husband is not waiting to be discovered, but seven years gone. Anne's situation seems poignantly unresolvable; in the past she was "persuaded" (by her friend and mother-substitute, Lady Russell) not to follow her inclination but to give up her highly desirable lover, Captain Wentworth, on the grounds that the connection between a baronet's daughter and an unmoneyed naval officer would be "indiscreet, improper, hardly capable of success and not deserving it" (p. 27). This done, there is nothing left for Anne but the practice of stoicism, for it would make nonsense out of her sacrifice to accept anyone else.

In the intervening years Anne has come to realize that the decision to abandon Wentworth was wrong, weak-minded, and very damaging (though she generously doesn't hold a grudge against its initiator, Lady Russell). When Wentworth's sister, Sophia Croft, and her husband become the tenants of the Elliot family home, Kellynch, a meeting between the two ex-lovers is hard to avoid. Anne's endurance of this brief encounter at her sister Mary Musgrove's house is brilliantly conveyed in disjointed, distracted, and breathless phrases:

> Her eye half met Captain Wentworth's; a bow, a curtsey passed; she heard his voice—he talked to Mary, said all that was right; said something to the Miss Musgroves, enough to mark an easy footing: the room seemed full—full of persons and voices—but a few minutes ended it. Charles shewed himself at the window, all was ready, their visitor had bowed and was gone.
>
> (p. 59)

Anne's response to this meeting reflects an inner battle between conduct and feeling that is characteristic of her. The rush of elation she experiences at having been once again in the same room as the lost lover only reminds her how inappropriate it is to have such feelings, and how painfully agitating. Their strength becomes a frighteningly destructive force if not reciprocated, and she resolves to "try to be feeling less" (p. 60). This in turn has to be adjusted when Mary reports what Wentworth has remarked in parting, that Anne has altered so much he would not have known her. Recognizing in this comment a species of disappointment, even disgust, at her loss of looks and spirits (both the result of the earlier breakup), Anne is propelled into a chilly zone of remorseless self-criticism: "Her power with him was gone for ever" (p. 61). Her task in the future is not "to be feeling less" but not to be feeling at all.

Wentworth's vigor, prosperity, and increased maturity—which she is forced to witness during his visits to the Musgroves—only emphasize the dimensions of Anne's loss. Freed from years of simmering regret, Wentworth "had a heart for either of the Miss Musgroves, if they could catch it; a heart, in short, for any pleasing young woman who came in his way, excepting Anne Elliot" (p. 61). He values in Louisa Musgrove the very qualities of assertiveness and self-will that Anne disastrously lacked in the past, though

when Louisa's assertiveness leads to the crisis on the Cobb at Lyme Regis (where she suffers a fall and seems to have died), Anne is the only character with enough presence of mind to be signally useful.

Given the hopeless outlook at the beginning of the book, Anne Elliot's eventual reunion with Wentworth is the most drastically romantic of all Austen's fictional pairings-off. The latter stages of the book are notable for the heroine's ardent speeches on constancy and vivid descriptions of pent-up erotic feelings: "It was agitation, pain, pleasure, a something between delight and misery." "Agitation" is the predominant emotion, not pleasure; for this and the novel's many fleeting autobiographical references, Anne Elliot has often been thought to reflect Jane Austen's own experience of love more closely than that of the more sparkling and cheerful heroines she created. Unflattering though the portrait might be at times, Anne Elliot, in the words of one of Austen's friends—"was herself."

THE LETTERS

WHAT has survived of Jane Austen's correspondence (some 160 letters only, mostly to her sister, Cassandra) suggests that she did not think of the form in terms of its literary potential. She seems to have done nothing to encourage or maintain correspondence with people outside her immediate family circle, and wrote mainly to convey domestic news and gossip. When R. W. Chapman's first edition of the letters was published in 1932, a number of critics found their unliterariness positively irritating: H. W. Garrod described them as "a desert of trivialities punctuated by occasional clever malice" while Harold Nicolson thought them "trivial and dull," the work of a mind "like a very small, sharp pair of scissors."

Many subsequent commentators have leapt to Austen's defense over the letters' apparent dullness, pointing out that Cassandra Austen had sole charge of her sister's papers after Jane's death and is thought to have destroyed a great deal. The evidence is fairly strong that Cassandra did censor the correspondence: one niece, Caroline

Austen, said that many of the letters Cassandra gave out among the family as keepsakes in the years after 1817 had portions cut out, and it is noticeable that the really long gaps in the surviving correspondence tend to cover eventful periods in Jane's life, such as the summer of 1801 (after which there is a three year lacuna).

Aside from the fact that we do not know what proportion of Austen's correspondence has been left to us, the question of their tone and manner (the "desert of trivialities punctuated by occasional clever malice"), thought to be characteristic of the letters, is perhaps characteristic only of the relationship between Jane and her sister, recipient of most of them. Cassandra was the dominant sibling, as evidenced in Mrs. Austen's often-quoted remark about her daughters: "If Cassandra were going to have her head cut off, Jane would insist on sharing her fate" (*Memoir*, p. 16). In her short study of Austen, the novelist Carol Shields suggests that Jane may have designed the letters "to please an aspect of her sister's misanthropy" (*Jane Austen*, p. 7) and that they may be more expressive of tensions and inequalities in that relationship than has been previously recognized.

The sisters' close relationship has been the subject in recent years of scholarly analysis, in particular Terry Castle's now-famous article for the *London Review of Books* entitled "Sister-Sister" (3 August 1995). The cover line "Was Jane Austen Gay?" helped to fuel a sensationalist reading of Castle's article, to which the author responded in a subsequent issue (24 August 1995) in the following terms:

> To point to a homoerotic dimension in the Austen/Cassandra relationship is in one sense simply to state a truth about the lives of many English women in the early nineteenth century: that their closest affectional ties were with female relations and friends rather than with men.

The furor that attended Castle's original article reached as far as the tabloid press, so affronting was the suggestion that Austen may have had sexual feelings of any sort. As David Nokes observed in the *Times Literary Supplement* soon after, "chief among Austen's traditionally English virtues is an instinctive reticence about sex. . . .

it is evident that cherished notions of the integrity of Austen's art are intimately associated with a symbolic fetishization of the physical intactness of her body" (15 September 1995).

On the whole, the "clever malice" in Austen's letters to Cassandra is cruder than any equivalent effects in her novels: "Miss Langley is like any other short girl with a broad nose & wide mouth, fashionable dress, & exposed bosom" (*Letters*, p. 86). "Miss Debary, Susan & Sally . . . made their appearance, & I was as civil to them as their bad breath would allow" (p. 61). Austen has difficulty establishing a comic tone in her letters to her sister; her irony simply stalls in places, exposing a desolate undertone, as in this description of a party in 1799: "There was the same kind of supper as last Year, & the same want of chairs. . . . I do not think I was very much in request. People were rather apt not to ask me till they could not help it" (p. 35).

Austen's interest in the minutiae of daily life—especially anything to do with money—finds copious expression. Reporting on a shopping trip in London in 1813, she wrote home:

> I was very lucky in my gloves, got them at the first shop I went to, though I went into it rather because it was near than because it looked at all like a glove shop, & gave only four Shillings for them; upon hearing which, everybody at Chawton will be hoping & predicting that they cannot be good for anything, & their worth certainly remains to be proved, but I think they look very well.
>
> (pp. 209–210)

The insistent materialism of Austen's letters provides many essential correctives to the view of her promulgated by the family after her death. Austen's shrewdness as a businesswoman is clear, as is her pleasure in a degree of self-sufficiency. As a single woman Austen owned her own copyrights and manuscripts (if she had been married, her husband would have had legal possession of them) and paid for one set of printing costs out of the last book's profits. Henry Austen claimed that "neither the hope of fame nor profit mixed with her early motives" ("Biographical Notice"), but the letters show Austen reveling in her own money-making potential, as in this response to news that her authorship was beginning to be fairly widely known: "People shall pay for their knowledge if I can make them" (*Letters,* p. 231).

CONCLUSION

THE contemporary of Samuel Taylor Coleridge, J. M. W. Turner, and the Marquis de Sade, Jane Austen lived through one of the most turbulent periods in the history of Europe, a true age of revolution both in society and in art. In the time of Romantic self-revelation, an age of autobiography, she chose to abnegate the self; in a time of almost constant wars against Napoleon, she chose to write of "3 or 4 Families in a Country Village." The colorful, even scandalous, events in and around her own family do not find any equivalent in her fictions; this deliberate regulation of material is now treated by scholars as extraordinary, even pivotal.

Jane Austen's life, like her books, was woman-centered, and no aspect of female psychology escaped her. She was not simply ahead of her time in anticipating much of what we would now call the psychology of sex, but she is in many respects ahead of our time too. Her attitudes toward marriage and self-dependence are similar to those stated by Mary Wollstonecraft in *Vindication of the Rights of Woman,* but very differently expressed in her fiction and in her life choices. Indeed it is interesting to see how far Jane Austen was able to achieve a degree of autonomy, both financial and artistic, while Wollstonecraft's more public and adventurous life made the maintenance of her principles impossible. The pragmatism that shaped Austen's life allowed her an intellectual freedom that no woman of her class and circumstances had exploited before. She became the shaper of the modern novel (a form addressing a predominantly female audience) not despite the revolutionary times she lived in, but because of them.

SELECTED BIBLIOGRAPHY

I. FIRST EDITIONS OF INIVIDUAL WORKS. *Sense and Sensibility* (London, 1811); *Pride and Prejudice* (London, 1813); *Mansfield Park* (London, 1814); *Emma* (London, 1816); *Northanger Abbey* and *Persuasion* (London, 1818); *Love and Friendship* (London, 1922); *Sanditon* (London, 1925).

II. MODERN EDITIONS. *The Novels of Jane Austen,* ed. by R.W. Chapman, 5 vols., 3d ed. (London, 1933; repr. with revisions 1965–1966); *Minor Works,* ed. by R. W. Chapman (London, 1954; repr. with revisions 1969); *Persuasion,* ed. by D. W. Harding (Harmondsworth, U.K., and Baltimore, 1965); *Emma,* ed. by Ronald Blythe (Harmondsworth, U.K., and Baltimore, 1966); *Mansfield Park,* ed. by Tony Tanner (Harmondsworth, U.K., and Baltimore, 1966); *Sense and Sensibility,* ed. by Tony Tanner (Harmondsworth, U.K., 1969); *Pride and Prejudice,* ed. by Tony Tanner (Harmondsworth, U.K., 1972); *Northanger Abbey,* ed. by Anne Henry Ehrenpreis (Harmondsworth, U.K., 1972); *Catharine and Other Writings,* ed. by Margaret Anne Doody and Douglas Murray (Oxford, 1993); *Jane Austen's Letters,* ed. by Deirdre Le Faye (Oxford, 1995); *Collected Poems and Verse of the Austen Family/Jane Austen,* ed. by David Selwyn (Manchester, 1996).

III. CRITICAL AND BIOGRAPHICAL STUDIES. Sir Walter Scott, review of *Emma,* in *Quarterly Review* 14 (October 1815); Henry Austen, "Biographical Notice of the Author," in *Northanger Abbey* and *Persuasion* (London, 1818); James Austen-Leigh, *Memoir of Jane Austen* (London, 1870); Virginia Woolf, *The Common Reader* (London and New York, 1925); Elizabeth Jenkins, *Jane Austen: A Biography* (London, 1938); D. W. Harding, "Regulated Hatred: An Aspect of the Work of Jane Austen," in *Scrutiny* 8 (1939–1940); Mary Lascelles, *Jane Austen and Her Art* (Oxford, 1939); R. W. Chapman, *Jane Austen: Facts and Problems* (Oxford, 1948); Marvin Mudrick, *Jane Austen: Irony as Defense and Discovery* (Princeton and London, 1952); Caroline Austen, *My Aunt Jane Austen* (London, 1952).

Ian P. Watt, ed., *Jane Austen: A Collection of Critical Essays* (Englewood Cliffs, N.J., 1963); B. C. Southam, ed., *Jane Austen: The Critical Heritage,* 2 vols. (London and New York, 1968–1987); Margharita Laski, *Jane Austen and Her World* (London and New York, 1969); F. B.Pinion, *A Jane Austen Companion* (London and New York, 1973); Barry Roth and Joel Weinsheimer, *An Annotated Bibliography of Jane Austen Studies, 1952–1972* (Charlottesville, Va., 1973); Marilyn Butler, *Jane Austen and the War of Ideas* (Oxford, 1975); Sandra Gilbert and Susan Gubar, *The Madwoman in the Attic: The Woman Writer and the Nineteenth-Century Literary Imagination* (New Haven, 1979).

Margaret Kirkham, *Jane Austen: Feminism and Fiction* (Brighton, U.K., and Totowa, N. J., 1983); John Halperin, *The Life of Jane Austen* (Baltimore, 1984); Barry Roth, *An Annotated Bibliography of Jane Austen Studies, 1973–1983* (Charlottesville, Va., 1985); Caroline Austen, *Reminiscences of Caroline Austen* (Winchester, U.K., 1986); Jane Spencer, *The Rise of the Woman Novelist: From Aphra Behn to Jane Austen* (Oxford and New York, 1986); Park Honan, *Jane Austen: Her Life* (London, 1987; New York, 1988); William Austen-Leigh and Richard Arthur Austen-Leigh, *Jane Austen, A Family Record,* rev. and enl. by Deirdre Le Faye (London and Boston, 1989)

Oliver MacDonagh, *Jane Austen: Real and Imagined Worlds* (London and New Haven, Conn., 1991); John Wiltshire, *Jane Austen and the Body: "The Picture of Health"*

(Cambridge, 1992); David Nokes, *Jane Austen: A Life* (London, 1995; New York, 1997); Claire Tomalin, *Jane Austen, A Life* (London, 1995; New York, 1997); Barry Roth, *An Annotated Bibliography of Jane Austen Studies, 1984– 1994* (Athens, Ohio, 1996); Carol Shields, *Jane Austen* (London and New York, 2001).

ROBERT BROWNING

(1812–1889)

Julie Hearn

"YOU ARE WORSE than the worst Alpine Glacier I ever crossed. Bright & deep enough truly, but so full of clefts that half the journey has to be done with ladder and hatchet."

So wrote John Ruskin, to Robert Browning, on 2 December 1855, following the publication of *Men and Women*. Browning, ever sensitive to criticism, was quick to defend his art. Would Ruskin, he wondered, expect a "Druid stone-circle" to be traced for him with as few breaks to the eye as the "crescents of a suburb?" Discontinuity and manipulation of perspective had become, by then, integral to Browning's poetic style. He was exploring new territory through his use of the dramatic monologue and making no apology for either the density of his vision or his intractable treatment of form.

George Eliot, writing for *The Westminster Review* in January 1856, noted perceptively that "in Browning's best poems he makes us feel that what we took for obscurity in him was superficiality in ourselves...he sets our thoughts at work rather than our emotions." Still, Ruskin's Alpine metaphor, with its intimation of a slow struggle across unpredictable terrain, encapsulates an impression of Browning which was to linger long after the poet's eventual fame put him on a par with Tennyson. Even now, approaching the collected works of Robert Browning can seem a daunting task, requiring every analytical tool at the reader's disposal simply to pry some meaning from *Sordello*. *The Ring and the Book* alone runs to nearly 22,000 lines of blank verse, and charges of obscurity which still cling to Browning's literary reputation can make the prospect of trawling through the man's life work seem like an exercise in tedium.

Start traversing the "Glacier," however, and the journey can prove exhilarating.

Oscar Wilde considered Browning unrivalled in his sense of dramatic situation, and comparable to Shakespeare as a creator of character. In 1890, the year after the poet's death, he wrote:

If Shakespeare could sing with myriad lips, Browning could stammer through a thousand mouths. Even now, as I am speaking. . .there glides through the room the pageant of his persons. There creeps Fra Lippo Lippi with his cheeks still burning from some girl's hot kiss. There, stands dread Saul with the lordly male-sapphires gleaming in his turban. Mildred Tresham is there, and the Spanish monk, yellow with hatred. . .The spawn of Setebos gibbers in the corner, and Sebald, hearing Pippa pass by, looks on Ottima's haggard face and loathes her, and his own sin and himself. Pale as the white satin of his doublet, the melancholy king watches with dreamy treacherous eyes too loyal Strafford pass to his doom, and Andrea shudders as he hears the cousin's whistle in the garden, and bids his perfect wife go down.

(From "The True Function and Value of Criticism," *Nineteenth Century* [July 1890] xxviii, pp.123–47, quoted in *Browning: The Critical Heritage*, p. 525.)

Wilde's appreciation of Browning's vitality was at odds with the Browning Society's portrayal of the poet in the decade or so after his death as a purveyor of great religious truths. As a number of contemporary critics have noted, this emphasis on Browning as a didactic artist did little to enhance his reputation, particularly at a time when Victorian writers were being relegated to the socio-cultural scrap heap like so many over-stuffed sofas and dusty aspidistras. For a while, to quote critic Adam Roberts, it seemed as if Browning were being made to "stand in the corner of the classroom with a placard round his neck saying 'God's in his heaven—All's right with the world!'" (*Robert Browning Revisited*, p.

155). As a post-Romantic pre-Modernist, he simply was not fashionable. Although Pound was an admirer, and Yeats admitted a certain indebtedness, it was not until after World War II that Browning's reputation began to re-ascend. During the 1950s, interest in his formal and stylistic innovations took a narrowly scholastic form. Twenty years later, deconstructionist critics seized upon the dramatic monologues, with their problematics of selfhood, and resistance to closure, and gave Browning studies a new lease of life.

EARLY LIFE

THE Brownings can be traced back to the time of Henry VII, when they were landowners in Dorset. The poet's grandfather, also named Robert Browning, moved to London at the age of twenty to take up a clerkship at the Bank of England. He quickly became principal clerk at the Bank Stock Office, a position which earned him £500 a year and the right to sign his name "Robert Browning, Esquire." In 1778, he married Margaret Tittle, whose family owned a sugar plantation on the West Indian island of Saint Kitts. Margaret died eleven years later, leaving behind a small fortune and a young son—the second Robert Browning, and father of the poet. The elder Browning married again, and went on to have nine more children.

When he was nineteen, the poet's father was sent to Saint Kitts to administer the family's plantation. Repelled by slavery, he very soon returned to England, much to the anger of Browning senior, who refused to support him in his plans to become an artist, or to afford him a university education. Forced to make his own way, the young Robert found a position at the Bank of England, where he worked until 1852. In 1811 he married Sarah Anna Wiedemann, the daughter of a Dundee shipowner and, at 39, ten years his senior. The couple took a cottage in Camberwell—then an unspoiled suburb of London, surrounded by fields and meadows—and settled into a life of quiet contentment and modest prosperity. Their first child, the poet Robert

Browning, was born on 7 May 1812, followed twenty months later by his sister Sarianna.

The four Brownings were a close-knit family. As Nonconformists, Robert and Sarah saw religion as a force for political reform and cultural enlightment, and fed their son's inquiring mind accordingly. The young Robert was sent, briefly, to the local dame school, only to be removed, according to family legend, for being too clever. At seven, he went to a weekly boarding school in Peckham where he remained until he was fourteen. It was at home, however, that his imagination and intellect truly flourished. His father, a bibliophile with a penchant for literary rarities, introduced him to Homer when he was five; quoted from Dryden's *Essays on Satire* during their walks, and gave him the run of his remarkable library of more than 6,000 books. Towards the end of his life, in the poem "Development," Browning acknowledges his debt to: "— that instructor sage / My Father, who knew better than to turn straight / Learning's full flare on weak-eyed ignorance, / Or, worse yet, leave weak eyes to go sand-blind, / Content with darkness and vacuity" (*Robert Browning, The Poems*, Vol. II, p. 918).

The father's taste for the macabre (he kept a dead rat for a while, in his desk at the Bank of England, to dissect during quiet moments) extended to his literary collection. "Childe Roland to the Dark Tower Came"—of all Browning's poems, the most deeply rooted in archetypal terrors—owes much to the poet's fascination, as a child, with such tomes as Gerard de Lairesse's *The Art of Painting in All Its Branches* (1707) with its chapter on all things "deformed and broken," and Nathaniel Wanley's *Wonders of the Little World* (1678) which contains accounts of torture, execution, and monstrous births. A lingering preoccupation with the grotesque courses through Browning's work. He was accused, in his day, of excessive morbidity, yet such poems as "Childe Roland," "Porphyria's Lover" and "My Last Duchess," with their fusion of savagery and lyrical beauty, are now seen as going beyond the simply grisly to stand as complex studies of the darker side of human nature.

ROBERT BROWNING

In October 1828, after two years of home tutoring, Browning enrolled at the newly formed nonsectarian University of London, to study Greek, Latin, and German. He left after six months, disappointed by the lectures and the monotony of student life. Back home with his family, he continued to educate himself, becoming, over the next four years, so widely read in art, science, theology, history, politics, and philosophy that he has been ranked with Milton as the most learned of English poets. His parents suggested a career in medicine, but the young Browning was not enthusiastic. Apart from a brief flicker of interest in joining the diplomatic service, he was content to stay at home, supported by his father, while he tried his hand at writing.

It was a challenging time in which to begin writing poems. When we think of Browning as a "great Victorian" we run the risk of forgetting that he grew up in the age of Shelley and Keats and was an inheritor, along with Tennyson, of powerful Romantic influences. The second generation of Romantic poets all died in the 1820s (Keats in 1820, Shelley in 1822, Byron in 1824). Coleridge and Wordsworth lived longer but wrote little after the 1820s that is considered great. Science, and the novel, were rivaling poetry as purveyors of important ideas. Browning, although he didn't know it then, was part of a seismic shift away from Romantic to Victorian poetry. The challenge was, to be original.

EARLY WORKS

BROWNING began his literary career in 1833 when his aunt, Mrs. Christiana Silverthorne, supplied the £30 he needed to get *Pauline: A Fragment of a Confession* into print. A narrative account of a young poet's development, *Pauline* reflects Browning's own struggle, at this time, to reconcile his intense admiration of Shelley with Christian doctrine. Shelley—whose work was still repressed on the the grounds of atheism and political radicalism when Browning discovered him in the mid 1820s—is the "Sun-treader" in *Pauline*. He is the radiant being whom the young narrator follows, as heedlessly as one of

Browning's rats follows the Pied Piper of Hamelin, until he realizes, in a scene reminiscent of Canto IV of Dante's *Inferno*, that:

My powers were greater: as some temple seemed
My soul, where nought is changed, and incense rolls
Around the altar – only God is gone,
And some dark spirit sitteth in his seat!

(Vol. I, p. 18)

Torn between his need for God and his conviction that, as a poet himself, he must either embrace or re-define Shelleyan abandon, the narrator leaves the godless temple of his idol to tread his own literary path. Precisely where this path will take him is hard to tell, for, having reaffirmed his need for God, lest old age find him "a wreck linked to a soul / Yet fluttering, or mind-broken and aware / Of my decay" (p. 19), he betrays an equal need for the eternal feminine principle embodied in Pauline—the poem's enigmatic muse and addressee. Nor can he totally repudiate the glorious Sun-treader, to whom he turns in the final stanza, imploring: "Thou must be ever with me, most in gloom / If such must come, but chiefly when I die, / For I seem, dying, as one going in the dark / To fight a giant. . ." (p. 33)

Tapping multiple sources of inspiration is, of course, no bad thing for a poet—Browning was to excel at it, eventually—but the naive and contradictory outpourings of *Pauline*'s young narrator suggest a creative mind which is too immature, and too much in thrall to powerful Romantic influences, to write something distinctive and original.

Browning was only 20 when he wrote *Pauline*. He published it anonymously, much to his later relief. It failed to sell a single copy, and a volume sent to John Stuart Mill, for review, came back liberally annotated with such harsh remarks as: ". . .the writer seems to me possessed with a more intense and morbid self-consciousness than I ever knew in any sane human being." Mill also wrote "Beautiful," "deeply true," and "good descriptive writing" in the margins, but it is his emphasis on the poem's hypersensitivity, along with a distaste for the sexual politics implied in the narrator's objectification of Pauline which have stuck.

Paracelsus, published in 1835, is longer than *Pauline*, but more tightly structured. Its protagonist, the sixteenth-century physician, seeks absolute knowledge at the expense of human affection, while his foil, the Shelleyan poet, Aprile, repudiates knowledge in pursuit of love. The poem works in dialectical, discontinuous movement, reflecting its concern with the stability of truth. Browning felt confident enough to put his name to *Paracelsus*, and was heartened by a number of favorable reviews. Then, in 1840, he published his epic, *Sordello*, and the critics responded with blistering disdain. Written in rhyming couplets (unusually, for Browning) and in verse narrative rather than dramatic form, *Sordello* reflects, yet again, Browning's fascination with a poet's struggle towards self-definition. The setting is historical—Sordello is a thirteenth-century troubadour, mentioned fleetingly in Dante's *Purgatorio*—but Browning had yet to create characters and situations of complexity and compulsive readability. *Sordello*, for all its stylistic ingenuity, ultimately failed. Few readers could be bothered to finish, let alone analyze, it. Thomas Carlyle wrote to say that his wife *had* read the poem with great interest, but wished to know whether Sordello was a man or a city or a book. Douglas Jerrold, so literary legend has it, turned to a copy of *Sordello* while recovering from an illness; put it down almost immediately and said: "My God!. . .My health is restored, but my mind's gone. I can't understand two consecutive lines of an English poem." (quoted in Chesterton, *Robert Browning*, p. 35).

Stung, but not defeated by the dismal reception of his epic, Browning worked hard to redeem his reputation. At the suggestion of his publisher, Edward Moxon, he decided to publish his poems and plays in a series of inexpensive pamphlets, under the general title *Bells and Pomegranates*. The first of these, *Pippa Passes*, combines narrative, lyric, and dramatic modes, and is widely considered the first substantial poem in which Browning fuses the power of poetry with the psychological insight that marks his greatest works.

Set in the town of Asolo, in northeastern Italy, *Pippa* is divided between the assumptions made by a young factory girl as she "passes" four sites associated with people she knows and envies, and the quite different reality going on behind the scenes. Ironically, the song Pippa sings as she passes, affects those who hear it and radically alters the course of their lives. Appearances throughout the poem are deceptive. Hearing is selective and language contorted. Desire, too, is ambivalent, with role-playing and self-projection the predominant expressions of love. Impoverished spiritually, emotionally or materially, the characters in *Pippa* take refuge in various forms of self-delusion. The "poor girls" sitting on the steps of the Duomo Santa Maria take turns making wishes, but even this simple form of escapism strikes a sour note when the first girl is accused of harping on a romanticized personal experience.

FIRST GIRL.   My turn.
  Spring's come, and summer's coming. I would wear
A long loose gown, down to the feet and hands,
With plaits here, close about the throat, all day;
And all night lie, the cool long nights, in bed;
And have new milk to drink, apples to eat,
Deuzans and junetings, leather coats. . .ah, I should say,
This is away in the fields – miles!

THIRD GIRL.   Say at once
  You'd be home: she'd always be at home!
Now comes the story of the farm among
The cherry orchards, and how April snowed
White blossoms on her as she ran. Why, fool,
They've rubbed the chalk mark out, how tall you were,
Twisted your starling's neck, broken his cage,
Made a dung-hill of your garden!
                  (Vol. I, pp. 333–334)

Sustaining oneself by assuming a role. . .Expressing a subjective thought, without inciting ridicule. . .Pleasing an audience, without diminishing the purity of a creative purpose. . .Browning would have been struggling with precisely these issues at this point in his career. The critical reception of *Sordello* and, to a lesser extent, *Pauline*, had certainly "made a dung-hill" of his carefully tended aspirations. *Pippa Passes* marked a shift away from limited introspection towards a technique he made so much his own that it is frequently cited as wholly his invention.

THE DRAMATIC MONOLOGUE

BROWNING never wrote an ode and disliked the sonnet form. The meditative "Home Thoughts from Abroad," although one of his best-known and most frequently-quoted poems ("Oh to be in England / Now that April's there. . .") is not typical. Browning was a dramatist. For ten years he wrote for the stage, penning historical dramas which received, at best, lukewarm acclaim. *Strafford* (1837), *King Victor and King Charles* (1842), *The Return of the Druses* (1843), *A Blot in the 'Scutcheon* (1843), *Colombe's Birthday* (1844) and *A Soul's Tragedy* and *Luria* (1846) may not have set the theatrical world alight, but they did serve as excellent preparation for Browning's subsequent blending of the lyric and the dramatic in his poems.

Browning himself did not use the term "dramatic monologue," referring, instead to the "dramatic lyric" (a presentation of an emotional or psychological state) and the "dramatic romance" (a story). Certainly, he was neither the first to explore this particular genre (the Old English poem *The Wanderer,* Horace's *Epistles* and Ovid's *Heroides* are among many precursors which could be said to fit the mold) nor the only Victorian to do so (Tennyson, in particular, is often cited as having "invented" the dramatic monologue at more or less the same time). He was, however, in a league of his own when it came to exploiting the genre's full potential.

Batting around contesting definitions of the dramatic monologue has occupied many a critic since Robert Langbaum, in his influential study *The Poetry of Experience: The Dramatic Monologue in Modern Literary Tradition* (1957), stressed the necessary tension between sympathy and moral judgement in the auditor's or reader's understanding of the monologist. In their desire to define at least some unifying principles and fix on a "pure" form of the genre, critics have tended to waver between definitions which are either too restrictive or so expansive that almost every poet from Chaucer to Eliot fits in somewhere on the

scale. However, to talk of "pure" dramatic monologue, reduced to a set of generic rules, and then to judge Browning in relation to such an archetype, does little justice to the poet's startling manipulation of the form. It also elides the fact that all of his work had its roots deep in Victorian culture. George MacBeth, in his introduction to the Penguin Classic *Victorian Verse* (1986), points out that Browning, along with Tennyson, Kipling, Hardy, Morris, Rossetti, Locker-Lampson, Thornbury, Dobson and a host of other Victorian writers, found the dramatic monologue invaluable because, put bluntly, it allowed them to lie while appearing to tell the truth:

> It enabled the Victorian poet to indulge the most cruel and heterodox—though not admittedly blasphemous or sexually frank — opinions while at the same time making it quite clear that he didn't hold them himself. In other words, it completed the revolution in sensibility of the Romantic movement while at the same time preventing the subversion of English society.
>
> (p. 25)

A multifaceted consideration of Browning's dramatic monologues, taking account of their historical roots and cultural influences, and, also, of Browning's experimental—and, at the time, fairly avant-garde—use of the genre, produces the following list of broadly definitive features:

1. Browning's monologues are at once performative and causative. The speaker seeks some kind of effect or transformation and fashions his narrative in order to achieve it.

2. A dramatic situation is inferred rather than clearly stated. As reader (silent listener) we tend to come across the speaker in the act of talking to another person, or to an imagined audience. Quite often, the effect is of having walked into the middle of an emotionally charged scenario within which we must look for clues as to what has gone before.

3. Speakers tend to be historically or culturally remote. This effectively distances them from the author, thereby legitimizing utterances which, however eloquent, are ironically betraying of some hidden motive or intent. As reader/listener we must "de-code" the text as we would any act of speech. The monologue, therefore, de-centers both speaker and reader, and questions the construction of mean-

ing and subjectivity in language.

4. The 'distancing' effect noted above enables Browning to explore potentially controversial issues of gender relations, religious dissent and extreme states of mind in an objective way. The textual sophistication of the form allows for "adventure within order, for excitement within bounds and for imaginative exploration within moral conformity."

(*Victorian Verse*, p. 25).

"So many utterances of so many imaginary persons, not mine" reads the disclaimer Browning attached to his 1842 *Dramatic Lyrics* (*Bells and Pomegranates* No. III). earlier, unflattering, criticism of his Romantic confessional style had clearly hit home. This time round, no-one would be able to accuse him of excessive self-absorption. Two monologues in this collection—"Porphyria's Lover" and "Johannes Agricola in Meditation"—provide an objective and extremely sophisticated analysis of the kind of abnormal psychology that inspires violent psychosexual tendencies on the one hand and religious mania on the other. Both poems are written in exactly the same form—twelve five-line stanzas in iambic pentameters, rhyming *ababb*—and the fact that they were originally paired under the title "Madhouse Cells" suggests that Browning fully intended them to stand as companion studies of lunacy. Religious insanity, in Browning's day, was more commonly associated with delusions of possession than with Johannes Agricola's ecstatic spirituality. Yet, to call this second poem, as some have done, a satire on the Calvinist doctrine of predestination is to miss the wider, more serious, point. Johannes Agricola, believing he has a prior bargain with God, considers himself exempt from the need to offer praise or do good works. For he is "smiled on, full fed," unlike

Priest, doctor, hermit, monk grown white
  With prayer, the broken-hearted nun,
The martyr, the wan acolyte,
  The incense-swinging child—undone
Before God fashioned star or sun!

(Vol. I, p. 379)

The narrator of "Porphyria's Lover" appears equally self-deluded as he describes strangling Porphyria with her hair ("she felt no pain / I am quite sure she felt no pain") for no other reason, it seems, than to immortalize a fleetingly beautiful moment. In both monologues, an unnerving sense of derangement arises from the speakers' obliteration of the listener as they create, out of their delusions, an illusory temporality within which they obsessively "read" themselves.

"My Last Duchess," another of Browning's early monologues, is frequently cited as his most incisive and disturbing exploration of warped psychology:

That's my last Duchess painted on the wall,
Looking as if she were alive. I call
That piece a wonder, now: Fra Pandolf's hands
Worked busily a day, and there she stands.
Will't please you to sit and look at her?

(Vol. I, p. 349)

Browning stretched metrical forms to the limit to make verse imitate, as far as possible, the idioms, the lilt and the diction of human speech. He does it so well that, in many instances, "the speakers give the impression that, had they not been in a poem by Browning, they would still have spoken in the same way." (Woolford and Karlin ed., *Robert Browning*, p. 57).). In "My Last Duchess," a combination of enjambment and colloquial hesitation override the poem's formal properties of rhyme and meter, giving rhetorical weight to the duke's speech as he reveals both the portrait, and something of his amorality, to the envoy from his next intended bride. As readers/silent listeners we very soon decode the implication that the duke had his "last duchess" killed because she displeased him. Yet the man's arrogance and poise sweep up the reader, as well as the hapless envoy, making us more attracted by his outrageousness than repulsed by his crime. The duke effectively disparages both the image and the memory of his "last duchess" ("painted on the wall" is more suggestive of graffiti than something framed and precious, and there is an aspect both lascivious and slapdash to the image of the painter's hands working "busily a day") and when he invites us to "sit and look at her" he obtains our collusion. The very act of continuing to read (listen) as the duke persists in vilifying the dead girl and conflating his own superiority marks our collusion. The last two and a half lines, hammer it home:

> Notice Neptune, though
> Taming a sea-horse, thought a rarity,
> Which Claus of Innsbruck cast in bronze for me!
>
> (p. 350)

The duke cannot resist showing off yet another object in his collection. And we, beguiled into following him this far, cannot help peering over the envoy's shoulder to admire it.

LOVE

On Friday 10 January, 1845, Browning sat down to compose an introductory letter to a fellow poet. "I love your verse with all my heart, dear Miss Barrett," he wrote, followed, just a few paragraphs later, by the somewhat presumptuous "and I love you too." Thus began one of the longest and fullest correspondences in literary history. Browning had yet to meet Elizabeth Barrett when he penned his first of the 573 extant letters they were to exchange. Nor would he meet her for another four months, even though they both lived in London (Browning with his parents and sister in suburban New Cross, Barrett with her family at the address they made famous—50 Wimpole Street) and were soon writing earnestly to one another, on a regular basis.

On a professional level, Barrett was the better-known poet of the two. She had just published a collection (*Poems*, 2 vols., 1844) and was receiving the kind of critical acclaim Browning would have to wait another twenty years to enjoy. Her home-life, however, was dismal. As a child, she had suffered from tuberculosis, leaving her with a weakened constitution. By the time Browning began writing to her she was an invalid and a virtual recluse, lying most of the day on a couch in a darkened room. The eldest of eleven children, she was still mourning the deaths, five years earlier, of her brothers Samuel and Edward — the former from yellow fever, contracted in Jamaica, the latter in a boating accident. Her mother had died in 1828 and her father, Edward Moulton Barrett, was resolutely opposed to any

of his surviving children marrying. Elizabeth Barrett was 38 years old, and wary of Robert Browning's advances. "Winters shut me up as they do a dormouse's eyes: in the spring, *we shall see. . .*" she wrote, to keep him at a distance. (E.B. to R.B., 11 January 1845).

Much has been made of Browning's subsequent Perseus-like rescuing of Barrett from her tyrannical father; their clandestine marriage, which took place on 12 September 1846, and their elopement to Italy, where they lived until Barrett's death, in June 1861. Rudolf Besier's play *The Barretts of Wimpole Street* (1930) so sentimentalized the Browning/Barrett union that the couple's literary reputations—Barrett's in particular—suffered from a surfeit of schmaltz. Virginia Woolf's *Flush: A Biography* (1933) recounts Browning's courtship from the point of view of Barrett's cocker spaniel. Clearly typical of the wry contempt Modernists felt towards their Victorian predecessors, this was hardly conducive to a serious consideration of the Browning/Barrett correspondence, or of anything else they wrote.

The myth of the perfect union has inevitably been countered by the myth that Browning grew disenchanted with his marriage once the reality of living abroad with an ailing wife eroded his initial idealization of Barrett as "my dearest siren, and muse, and Mistress" (R.B. to E.B., Sunday, 24 May 1846). Neither myth nor counter-myth is necessarily accurate, and although both have been used in analyses of Browning's love poetry, the reader should beware of assuming that the male-female relationships of his characters reflect Browning's own experience and opinions.

Happy marriages, like happy lovers, are the exception in Browning's poems, but this could simply be because: "happiness is for the most part not a complex phenomenon, and Browning liked complexity" (Woolford and Karlin, *Robert Browning*, p. 151). Even "By The Fire-Side," an apparently rare example of full and perfect communion between mature lovers, contains enough jagged and discontinuous imagery to suggest an aggression born of sexual frustration and fear of aging. Sensory details of the autumnal landscape hint at brutality and decay. Small ferns "fit their teeth to the polished block" of boulders; a mat of moss is "Elf-needled" and the ruined chapel, halfway up an Alpine gorge, is indistinguishable from the "Blackish-grey and mostly wet" stones of the one-arched bridge, "Where the water is stopped in a stagnant pond/ Danced over by the midge" (Vol. I, p. 554). Such an accumulation of detail destabilizes the speaker's conventionally Romantic talk of souls which "mix as mists do" and encourages the reader to look beyond his depiction of domestic bliss. He and his "perfect" wife, we are led to believe, have a telepathic understanding:

When if I think but deep enough,
    You are wont to answer, prompt as rhyme;
And you, too, find without rebuff
    Response your soul seeks many a time
Piercing its fine flesh-stuff.

(p. 556)

We wonder, however, if this devotion is reciprocated. For the strongest visual image the speaker provides of his wife shows a woman sitting "mute" beside the fire. Two lines, used twice in the poem in relation to different moments, lay particular stress on her "spirit-small hand" propping her "great brow." Laying aside associations with Elizabeth Barrett (who had a particularly broad, pale forehead), it is an attitude more suggestive of a migraine than marital fulfillment.

The central conflict in Browning's love poetry revolves invariably around the intangible influences which encourage or destroy intimacy between two people. Quite often, the passionate intensity of romantic love is at odds with and problematized by the conventional moral codes of society (see, for example, "In a Gondola," "Too Late," "The Flight of the Duchess," "Respectability" and "In a Balcony"). The provocative "The Statue and the Bust" attracted hostile criticism from Victorian readers for apparently encouraging adultery. In this poem, the Grand duke Ferdinand's passion for a married lady is reciprocated, but never consummated, as the two spend days then months, then years, gazing longingly at one another across a square. Dramatic disguise is so thin that Browning appears, for once, to have cast it off altogether as he judges the couple, not for their adulterous yearnings but for being too faint-hearted to gratify them: "the

sin I impute to each frustrate ghost / Is—the unlit lamp and the ungirt loin." (Vol. I, p. 603). Action—even in pursuit of an immoral end—is far better, in Browning's understanding, than passivity and cowardice. For how else, if not through direct engagement with moral conflict, can the soul develop, and the individual ultimately redeem himself either on earth or in a life hereafter?

No lamps are left unlit, or loins ungirted in "The Flight of the Duchess" as the woman of the title jumps at the chance to escape from her inadequate husband ("the pertest little ape / That ever affronted human shape" [Vol. I, p. 427]). "Art thou the tree that props the plant / Or the climbing plant that seeks the tree?" an old Gipsy woman asks (p. 440), neatly encapsulating the power-struggle in sexual relationships which Browning explored so beautifully.

In "A Woman's Last Word" the speaker attempts to mend a quarrel by shoring up her lover's ego. The poem's tense stanzaic form belies the seeming tenderness of the moment, while the speaker's hectoring tone undermines her attempt at conciliation:

Be a god and hold me
    With a charm!
Be a man and fold me
    With thine arm!

Teach me, only teach, Love!
    As I ought
I will speak thy speech, Love,
    Think thy thought—

(Vol. I, pp. 539–540)

In the fifth stanza the "we" of the third line, which we take to mean the speaker and her lover, is shown, in the fourth line, to stand for something else entirely.

Where the apple reddens
    Never pry—
Lest we lose our Edens,
    Eve and I.

This speaker, even as she strives towards compatibility, is distancing herself from men in general and her lover in particular. We can compare this poem to "A Lover's Quarrel" in which a man reflecting on the loss of his lover recalls the high-spirited way in which they transgressed the boundaries of male-female identity as part of their love making:

See, how she looks now, dressed
In a sledging cap and vest!
    'Tis a huge fur cloak—
    Like a reindeer's yoke
Falls the lappet along the breast:
    Sleeves for her arms to rest,
Or to hang, as my Love likes best.

Teach me to flirt a fan
As the Spanish ladies can,
    Or I tint your lip
    With a burnt stick's tip
And you turn into such a man!
    Just the two spots that span
Half the bill of the young male swan.

(Vol. I, p. 531)

During the winter months, living "blocked up with snow" these two created and re-created one another to keep passion alive. Clearly, it was not enough—at least not for the woman. Now spring is coming, but it is not the bitter torment one might expect for the supposedly lovelorn speaker. His first words are: "Oh, what a dawn of day! / How the March sun feels like May / All is blue again / After last night's rain," making the subsequent "And the South dries the hawthorn-spray. / Only, my Love's away! / I'd as lief that the blue were grey" (p. 529) appear contrived. We may suspect this man of forcing himself into a melancholic Keatsian pose purely for effect. His lover will not return—but that, the poem suggests, is an inevitable consequence of imagining somebody to a point at which she might as well not exist.

A tendency to lump *Fifine at the Fair* (1872) among the morass of Browning's later, less critically acclaimed work has obscured the poem's subtle analysis of the sexual myth that depicts women as either madonnas or whores. Its speaker, Don Juan, is nowhere near as complacent as the Don Juans of Molière or Byron, as he swings, in 2,355 rolling alexandrine couplets, between loyalty to his "daisy meek" wife and passion for Fifine, a gypsy girl. The poem's clogged syntax and convoluted arguments neatly reflect the anxiety and fear of impotence that lie behind the legendary seducer's relations with women. Ironically, it was probably the poem's very obscurity that prevented Victorian readers from being scandalized by it.

RELIGION

"And then Christianity is a worthy *myth* & poetically acceptable"

(E.B. to R.B. 20 March 1845)

CHRISTMAS-*Eve and Easter-Day* (1850) finds Browning dealing specifically with organized religion and, unusually for him, seeming to reflect something of his own beliefs. It is possible that he turned to religion, as a subject, following the death of his mother in England—a loss he had to bear shortly after the birth of his only child, Robert "Pen" Wiedemann Barrett Browning on 9 March 1849. To what extent the poems are colored by his personal opinions is debatable and, arguably, irrelevant.

"Christmas Eve," a monologue addressed to an unnamed auditor, evaluates the relative merits of three styles of worship—a sermon in a dissenting chapel; a Catholic mass in Rome and a rationalist lecture given by a "hawk-nosed" German professor with a cough "like a drouthy piston." So cleverly does Browning undermine all three, that when the speaker cleaves, eventually, to the dissenting position it seems merely the best of a bad choice. Browning's Christianity was of a liberal humanist sort, based on New Testament principles of love and forgiveness. Although raised as a Dissenter, he was not a great church-goer in later life. He thus may well have concurred with his "Christmas Eve" monologist's ultimate positioning of himself, beyond all dogma, with "Thee" who "head and heart alike discernest / Looking below light speech we utter, / When frothy spume and frequent sputter / Prove that the soul's depths boil in earnest!" (Vol. I, p. 496).

"Easter Day" searches for tenable grounds upon which to base Christian faith. It is a somewhat stodgy poem, despite some interesting use of metaphor, and has never been popular, except in studies reflecting on its apparent disavowal of the Keatsian world of nature, or its perceived relation to Browning's own philosophical creed. The critical reception of Tennyson's *In Memoriam* totally eclipsed *Christmas Eve and Easter Day*, which was not even widely reviewed.

On the other hand, the religious poems in *Men and Women* (1855) have come to be considered among Browning's finest work. Here we find Bishop Blougram, defending his personal, and highly questionable, slant on Catholicism to an agnostic journalist; Karshish, the Arab Physician, at a loss to cope with the mystery of Lazarus's resurrection; Cleon, a Greek contemporary of the Apostle Paul, revealing his own spiritual impoverishment while dismissing rumours of a Christian deity; and the boy, David, running "o'er the sand burnt to powder," with lilies twined around the strings of his harp, to prophesy the Incarnation to King Saul.

These are extraordinary characters, so cunningly portrayed that they practically leap from the page. Because they speak, despite their historicality, on something approaching our own level, we are struck by the immense range of responses possible to the notion of Christianity. It is not dogma embodied in these poems but conjecture of the most intelligent and thought-provoking order.

Reviews of *Men and Woman* were, on the whole, disappointing. Ironically, it was the more theoretically dry works in *Dramatis Personae* (1864), that brought Browning the success and critical acclaim he had waited so long for. Perhaps, as Browning's biographers William Irvine and Park Honan, suggest, "reviewers were partly making amends to a perverse Anglo-Italian who had proved to be a brave widower and an almost lucid Englishman" (*The Book, The Ring and The Poet*, p. 398). Maybe the intellectual climate was simply ripe, by the mid 1860s, for the poet's difficult, yet powerful treatment of universal themes. "Powerful" is certainly an apt word for the religious poems in *Dramatis Personae*. Like the collection's love poems ("James Lee's Wife," "The Worst of It," "Dis Alter Visum," "Too Late," and "Youth and Art") they struggle with the dualism of ideal and actual— and with the need, and the difficulty, of keeping faith in an ever-changing world.

"A Death in the Desert," which dramatizes the last days of St. John, appeals directly to the post-Enlightenment attempt to re-establish some sense of spirituality. Acknowledging the problematics of textual transmission ("It is a parchment, of my rolls the fifth, / Hath three skins glued together, is all Greek / And goeth from *Epsilon* down to *Mu*" [Vol. I, p. 787]) it posits, nonetheless, man's need to acknowledge Christ's love and God's Truth intuitively, if not intellectually:

Will ye renounce this pact of creatureship?
The pattern on the Mount subsists no more,
Seemed awhile, then returned to nothingness;
But copies, Moses strove to make thereby,
Serve still and are replaced as time requires:
By these, make newest vessels, reach the type!

(p. 803)

"Caliban upon Setebos" shows, in truly grotesque style, the bleakness of human existence when the only great powers one can conceive of are either cruel or indifferent. There is bleakness, too, in "Abt Vogler" as the soliloquizer comes back down to earth, "Sliding by semitones, till I sink to the minor —" (Vol. I, p. 780), after extemporizing the music that lifts him towards the sublime. A combination of rising and falling lines, with the number of syllables per line varying from twelve to seventeen, re-creates the brilliance of musical improvisation, reaching a climax in the seventh stanza before falling away as Vogler returns to a more normal perspective.

"Mr Sludge, 'The Medium'" combines an attack on the kind of table-tapping spiritualism that was popular in Browning's day with a more complex exploration of the way other 'mediums,' including poetry, claim representation of the infinite within the finite:

so Sludge lies!

Why, he's at worst your poet, who sings how Greeks
That never were, in Troy which never was,
Did this or the other impossible great thing!
He's Lowell—it's a world (you smile applause),
Of his own invention—wondrous Longfellow,

Surprising Hawthorne! Sludge does more than they,
And acts the books they write: the more his praise!

(Vol. I, p 858)

Sludge was based on the American medium Daniel Dunglas Home, whom Browning met at a seance in 1855 and detested—much to the chagrin of Elizabeth Barrett, who was herself drawn to clairvoyance. As a character, he makes little appeal to the imagination. Victorian readers admired the poem, but the tendency among later critics has been to compare it unfavorably with the more vivid portrayals in *Men and Women*.

Taken as a whole, the religious poems in *Dramatis Personae* can be seen as a comment on the Victorian crisis of faith most famously embodied in Darwin's *The Origin of Species* (1859). For, as Patricia M. Ball remarks, in her essay "Browning's Godot":

Wherever God enters the poems, he comes as a property of the speaker's self-made universe: he is not the poet's ultimate, for Browning's faith rests upon the one certainty—human uncertainty, the ignorance or doubt of any such ultimate... the more heartily committed voices should be recognized as emerging from little shelters built to keep out the vast and unresponding night.

(in *Browning's Men and Women and other Poems: A Casebook*, pp. 176–7)

ART

THE Ruskinian argument that the highest art results from the perception of moral truth is, typically, held up for some very close scrutiny by Browning. "Pictor Ignotus," in *Dramatic Romances & Lyrics* (1845), explores the alienation felt by a minor Florentine painter who longs to paint in the new, realistic, style but never does, in case an undiscerning public misunderstands his vision. Instead:

My heart sinks as monotonous I paint
These endless cloisters and eternal aisles
  With the same series, Virgin, Babe and Saint,
With the same cold calm beautiful regard —

(Vol. I, p. 398)

A translation of the poem's title—"Painter Unknown"—reminds us that, by the nineteenth century, many an Italian painter's name had been forgotten. This empirical perspective encourages a sympathetic response to the speaker's lament that, had he only dared try, he might have rivaled Raphael ("I could have painted pictures like that youth's / Ye praise so. How my soul springs up!" [p. 397]). It also leads us, perhaps, to a wider consideration of how any individual can become entangled, to the point of paralysis, in the conventions and ideologies of a particular historical moment.

By the time he came to write "Fra Lippo Lippi" and "Andrea del Sarto" for *Men and Women*, Browning had lived for several years in Italy, made a first-hand study of the Bolognese, Venetian, and High Renaissance schools of art, and been inspired by Vasari's *Lives of the Painters*, which he read in the original Italian. Lippi, one of the earliest masters of the Florentine Renaissance, had a wild sexual reputation. Browning exploited this to the full, grafting "his" Lippi's nonconformist yet irrepressible love of all things sensual to a justification of aesthetic freedom. Lippi paints instinctively, and realistically, and has been chastised for it:

The monks closed in a circle and praised loud
Till checked, taught what to see and not to see,
Being simple bodies—"That's the very man!
Look at the boy who stoops to pat the dog!
That woman's like the Prior's niece who comes
To care about his asthma: it's the life!"
But there my triumph's straw-fire flared and funked;
Their betters took their turn to see and say:
The Prior and the learned pulled a face
And stopped all that in no time

(Vol. I, p. 544)

Still, Lippi goes his own way, convinced that all art is praise and that to be responsive to life, in all its richness, makes for a democratic artistic vision that must surely meet with his own Creator's approval. For: "This world's no blot for us, / Nor blank; it means intensely and means good: / To find its meaning is my meat and drink" (p. 548).

"Andrea del Sarto" is parenthetically entitled "The Faultless Painter," and therein lies its chief irony. The technical brilliance of Andrea's paintings is paradoxically matched to his depression and spiritual vacuity as he broods over his wife's infidelity ("My serpentining beauty. . .My face, my moon, my everybody's moon" [Vol. I, p. 644]). His monologue is laden with past conditionals, the grammatical mode of regret. The predominant color throughout is as bleak as his mood ("A common greyness silvers everything" [p. 644]) yet, as in Tennyson's "Tithonus," flashes of fire and gold (Lucrezia's hair, the jingle of a monarch's chain) intrude symbolically, so that: "The whole poem, so quiet in superficial impression, is in fact made dramatic by the sustained tension between Andrea's wish to live out what life remains for him in a sort of drugged repose and the uncontrollable devil-pricks of his self-knowledge" (Richard D. Altick, "Andrea Del Sarto: The Kingdom of Hell Is Within," in *Browning's Men and Women and other Poems: A Casebook*, p. 228).

The Pre-Raphaelite brotherhood, in particular Dante Gabriel Rossetti, adored Browning's poetry for its pictorial vividness—what Isobel Armstrong calls its "still-wet perceptual freshness" (Armstrong, ed. *Robert Browning,* p. 268). "Eurydice to Orpheus" (in *Dramatis Personae,*) was inspired by Frederic Leighton's painting of the same name. Little known, and, at only eight lines, as fleeting as the glance it inscribes, it remains a powerful comment on perspective, the ambiguous nature of myth and the precariousness of sexual identity. Recognizing what twentieth-century feminists have defined as the objectifying nature of the gaze, it gives what is essentially a gendered concept a startling spin. One look, from Orpheus, condemned Eurydice to eternity in the underworld, and determined her place in mythology. So is it her lover Eurydice is addressing here, or the silent reader (listener) whose response might re-define her?

But give them me, the mouth, the eyes, the brow!
Let them once more absorb me! One look now
    Will lap me round forever, not to pass
Out of its light, though darkness lie beyond:
Hold me but safe again within the bond
    Of one immortal look! All woe that was,
Forgotten, and all terror that may be,
Defied—no past is mine, no future: look at me!

                                        (Vol. I, p 816)

THE RING AND THE BOOK

ON a June day, in 1860, Browning picked up a shabby old book at a second-hand market in Florence. It was to become the inspiration for his longest, most ambitious venture—one that sealed his reputation, among Victorian critics and readers alike, as a truly great poet.

Contained, in the *Old Yellow Book* were documents relating to the trial of one Count Guido Franceschini, in 1698, for the murder of his wife and two members of her family. Re-settled in London, following the death of Elizabeth Barrett, Browning turned this "Roman murder-case" into a dramatic poem of epic proportions—twelve books published in four installments between November 1868 and February 1869.

That there is much more to this poem than a sensational yarn is made immediately clear in Book I when Browning gives his readers ("British public, ye, who like me not," [p. 34]) an edited version of the case, complete with moral judgments. What *The Ring and the Book* proceeds to give us is a series of monologues in which nine speakers, including the count, his dying wife, a couple of gossips, the pope, and representatives of the law, offer perspectives which constantly intersect, contradict, qualify, and supplement each other.

Before we enter this labyrinth, Browning invites us to scrutinize a series of objects with more than usual intensity. Among odds and ends on the Florentine market stall are "Bronze angel-heads once knobs attached to chests, / (Handled when ancient dames chose forth brocade). . .A wreck of tapestry, proudly-purposed web / When reds and blues were indeed red and blue, / Now offered as a mat to save bare feet / (Since carpets constitute a cruel cost)" (p. 24). The implication, so imaginatively stated, is that all judgments are partial—including the ones we are about to make as we encounter speakers with a personal, vested, or simply morbid, interest in the Franceschini trial.

Relativist and deconstructionist literary critics have read into *The Ring and the Book* a giving way of the unified Romantic sense of "self" to the Derridean position, which contests the idea of truth as recoverable and objective. Yet

Browning's conception of truth—any truth—was always more relational than relative. He also loved riddles. "Childe Roland" for example, has been variously interpreted as a fearsome pilgrimage into the realms of the psyche; a reflection of Browning's fear of failure as a poet; an extemporization on Gnostic meaning, and a critique of masculine values and the coercive ideology of heroism. Browning, however, only ever said that the idea for "Childe Roland" came to him in a dream, after which he felt compelled to write it down.

Browning certainly knew better than to pin a definitive meaning on *The Ring and the Book* —a work that recognizes, above all, the subtle shades between such binary oppositions as male and female, good and evil, false and true. The sarcastic and somewhat patronizing tone Browning adopts towards readers in Books I and XII reminds us that our judgments of Guido, Pompilia, and the other speakers are bound to be swayed, to some extent, by our own sociocultural conditioning and inevitable blind spots in our perspective. As Clyde de L. Ryals has said: "A right interpretation of the Franceschini case, like that of the Bible, is. . .in Browning's view always provisional: an approximation of the truth for the time being" (*The Life of Robert Browning*, p. 170).

LATER LIFE AND WORK

Will our generation, or a later one, discover that Browning did not fall asleep in 1869?
(Park Honan, in *Victorian Poets: A Guide to Research*, p. 117)

GIVEN the critical neglect of Browning's later work, it can come as a surprise to discover that he wrote more in the single decade of the 1870s, than in the 1830s, 1840s, and 1850s put together. The years 1870–1875 were exceptionally prolific, with the publication of six new titles —*Balaustion's Adventure* (1871), *Prince Hohenstiel-Schwangau* (1871), *Fifine at the Fair* (1872), *Red Cotton Night-Cap Country* (1873), *Aristophanes' Apology* (1875) and *The Inn Album* (1875).

The general opinion, until fairly recently, was that the great man went into his dotage producing nothing but acres of verbiage full of erudite allusion and hopelessly esoteric arguments. However, contemporary critics, including Adam Roberts, Roma King, and Clyde de L. Ryals, see, in the poet's increasingly complex use of perspective, syntax, and language, a radical attempt to transcend the boundaries of art, and a deepening apprehension of the partiality of truths. Ryals writes of the mature Browning's "doctrine of evanescence"—perhaps the only aspect of the poet's thought that can be characterized as doctrinaire:

The universe of Browning's later poetry is very nearly one of absurdity, where man is depicted dealing with fictions in order to reach the "Truth," which in itself may be only the supreme fiction. Almost everything takes on an "as if" quality. A man works as if he were accomplishing something; he lives as if life were meaningful—and because he does, it is.
(*Browning's Later Poetry*, p. 243)

Before considering the more significant longer works, it is worth noting that Browning's late collections of short poems (notably *Pacchiarotto and How He Worked in Distemper* [1876] and *Dramatic Idyls: First Series* [1879]) contain some little gems, in which the poet's racy, colloquial style is as fresh as ever. Here he is in "House," expounding on the subject of his privacy as he invites readers to contemplate the insides of a building, "shaven sheer" by an earthquake:

The owner? Oh, he had been crushed to death, no doubt!
'Odd tables and chairs for a man of wealth!
What a parcel of musty old books about!
He smoked—no wonder he lost his health!

'I doubt if he bathed before he dressed.
A brasier? — the pagan, he burned perfumes!
You see it is proved, what the neighbours guessed:
His wife and himself had separate rooms.'
(*Robert Browning: The Poems*, Vol. II, pp. 438–439)

And here, in "Ned Bratts," satirizing the punishments meted out "one daft Midsummer's Day" at a Bedfordshire court:

> Full-measure, the gentles enjoyed their
> fun,
> As a twenty-five were tried, rank puritans caught at
> prayer
> In a cow-house and laid by the heels—have at 'em,
> devil may
> care!—
> And ten were prescribed the whip, and ten a brand on
> the cheek,
> And five a slit of the nose — just leaving enough to
> tweak.
>
> (Vol. II, p. 606)

Browning's fascination with the intellectualism and Dionysiac irrationalism of Greek literature and culture found its ultimate expression during the 1870's. *Balaustion's Adventure* , although rightly described by Adam Roberts as "a relative lightweight in the Browning canon" (*Robert Browning Revisited*, p. 112) contains a beautiful re-telling of Euripides' *Alkestis*. The tale, re-told by a Rhodian girl seeking refuge with the Syracusans, is challenged by a "critic and whippersnapper" who questions her fidelity to the original text. This raises one of Browning's pet issues, namely his insistence that imaginative re-creation is more vital to poetry, than a slavish attention to particulars.

> Look at Baccheion's beauty opposite,
> The temple with the pillars at the porch!
> See you not something besides masonry?
> What if my words wind in and out the stone
> As yonder ivy, the God's parasite?
> Though they leap all the way the pillar leads,
> Festoon about the marble, foot to frieze,
> And serpentiningly enrich the roof,
> Toy with some few bees and a bird or two—
> What then? The column holds the cornice up.
>
> (Vol. I, p. 877)

Aristophanes' Apology: Including a Transcript from Euripides, Being the Last Adventure of Balaustion (1875) is as complex as its name suggests. It is widely considered the most truly difficult of Browning's poems, yet readers who have taken the time to work through surface difficulties consider it a masterpiece. Catharine Parr, in her preface to volume II of the Yale edition of Browning's poems, claims that the ideal Browning annotator needs to know by heart the Bible, and the plays of Euripides and Aristophanes, as well as Victorian scholarship on them; to be thoroughly versed in art, music, and at least seven languages, and to possess an outstanding knowledge of the more obscure recesses of Italian history. It also helps, she says, to have lived "an eon or two" with unimpaired faculties and to possess the kind of diligence that brings sweat to the brow. *Aristophanes' Apology*, in its day, bewildered critics and readers alike. Well-annotated, it can be a joy, although, as Parr points out, with tongue firmly in cheek, it will not appeal to readers who are not prepared to be fascinated by such things as "the proper method of cooking Copaic eels, the lost plays of Euripides, the curious position adopted by Euripides in writing his plays and the mysterious place in which he is buried, the rival claims of comic and tragic art, the astonishingly fertile mind of the father of comic drama and the grandeur of the old Sophocles" (preface, Vol. II, pp. xxii–xxiii).

Aristophanes' Apology, the third longest of Browning's works (after *The Ring and the Book* and *Sordello*), was to be the last of his long dramatic monologues. His next work, *The Inn Album*, embeds a series of short monologues within a narrative and has generally been seen as a manifestation of the continental realism most famously explored in the novels of Honoré de Balzac and Émile Zola. Crammed with tawdry sensationalism and topical allusions, *The Inn Album* uses melodrama to highlight the vulgarization of art and literature. Victorian critics tended to be uncomfortable whenever Browning probed too closely beneath appearances, to reveal the "spider [in] the communion cup" and "a toad in the christening—font" ("Gold Hair" Vol I, p. 762), *The Inn Album* received half-hearted reviews. So too did *Red Cotton Night-Cap Country*, an earlier first-person narrative, in blank verse, which portrays violence and suicide as an indirect result of stifling marriage conventions. Sensationalism, it was generally agreed, was not a fitting vehicle for a poet of Browning's stature.

Nearly all the poems Browning published between 1876 and 1883 are concerned, either explicitly or implicitly, with justice, judgment, and fame. He also produced a translation of *The*

Agamemnon of Aeschylus (1877) and wrote a philosophical elegy, *La Saisiaz* (1878)—the latter inspired by the unexpected death of Mrs. Anne Egerton Smith, a close friend and traveling companion. The two series of *Dramatic Idyls* published in 1879 and 1880 were well-received although the use of the term 'Idyl' in the title annoyed the Laureate, Tennyson, who considered it, despite the spelling, too close to his own *English Idylls* or *Idylls of the King*.

In 1881 a group of admirers, headed by the Shakespearean and Chaucerian scholar Frederick James Furnivall, founded the Browning Society "for the study and discussion of the works of the poet. . .and the publication of essays on them." Within three years there were twenty-two Browning Societies around the world. America, in particular, experienced something approaching "Browningmania," with society ladies dressed in brown serving brown bread, on brown china, in brown-curtained rooms. *Pauline*, *Paracelsus*, and *Sordello* were printed on railway timetables in Chicago, where bookstores could not keep up with a demand for copies of the poet's work. Mark Twain held Browning classes and gave readings throughout the country, boasting "I can read Browning so Browning himself can understand it" (quoted in *The Life of Robert Browning*, p. 218).

Far from resting on his laurels, Browning continued to write, and to set himself new boundaries. *Jocoseria* (1883), a miscellany of lyric, dramatic, and narrative poems, and *Ferishtah's Fancies* (1884), which traces the spiritual development of an eponymous Persian sage via a series of analogies and parables, were both well-received. *Parleyings with Certain People of Importance in Their Day* (1887) has been called the closest Browning ever came to writing his autobiography. Typically, it is a poem of encyclopedic scope, modeled on *Faust* and the *Divine Comedy*, in which the narrator invokes representative figures to 'parley' with and thereby sketch a poetic vision of his life. In the autumn of 1889 Browning visited Italy with his sister. They stayed with Pen Browning and his wife, Fannie, at their home in Venice. In late November the poet confessed to a cold, which was diagnosed as bronchitis and a weakened heart. On December 12 *Asolando: Fancies and Facts* was published. A collection of short poems in a variety of genres, it includes the infamous 'Epilogue' which greatly influenced Browning's subsequent reputation as an unflinching optimist: "One who never turned his back but marched breast forward, / Never doubted clouds would break" (Vol II, p. 931).

Reviews appeared promptly, and were telegraphed to Venice. Browning rallied just long enough to hear that this last fruit of an extraordinary lifetime's work had been enthusiastically received and that the first edition, printed only that day, was almost sold out. He died later that night and his body was taken home to London, to be buried at Poet's Corner in Westminster Abbey.

More than a century later, the centrality of Browning in the history of English poetry has come to be taken for granted. He is an institution, admired more than read, and approached, more often than not, on tiptoe. He would have hated that. "Zooks!" he might have said, in the manner of Fra Lippo Lippi, to a twenty-first century student rendered pale and anxious by a complete edition of his works. "Your hand sir, and goodbye: no lights, no lights! / The street's hushed and I know my own way back, / Don't fear me!" (Vol I, p. 550).

SELECTED BIBLIOGRAPHY

All poetry quotations are from the New Haven and London Yale University Press collections of Robert Browning's work.

I. Editions Published In Browning's Lifetime *Pauline: A Fragment of a Confession* (London, 1833); *Paracelsus* (London, 1835); *Strafford: An Historical Tragedy* (London, 1837); *Sordello* (London, 1840); *Bells and Pomegranates, No. I—Pippa Passes* (London, 1841); *Bells and Pomegranates, No. II—King Victor and King Charles* (London, 1842); *Bells and Pomegranates, No. III – Dramatic Lyrics* (London, 1842); *Bells and Pomegranates, No. IV — The Return of the Druses* (London, 1843); *Bells and Pomegranates, No V—A Blot in the 'Scutcheon* (London, 1843); *Bells and Pomegranates, No VI—Colombe's Birthday* (London, 1844); *Bells and Pomegranates, No. VII — Dramatic Romances & Lyrics* (London, 1845); *Bells and Pomegranates, No. VIII And Last — Luria and A Soul's Tragedy* (London, 1846); *Poems* 2 vols. (London 1849). This collection contained heavily revised versions of *Paracelsus*, and *Pippa Passes*, but omitted *Strafford* and *Sordello*; *Christmas-Eve and Easter-Day: A Poem* (London, 1850); *Men and Women* (London, 1855);

The Poetical Works of Robert Browning 3 vols. (London, 1863). This collection included a revised *Sordello*. Browning also redistributed the poems of *Dramatic Lyrics, Dramatic Romances and Lyrics* and *Men and Women* under the titles 'Dramatic Lyrics', 'Dramatic Romances' and 'Men and Women'. This format was retained, with minor changes, in the collections of 1868 and 1888–1889; *Dramatis Personae* (London, 1864); *The Poetical Works of Robert Browning, M.A., Honorary Fellow of Balliol College, Oxford* 6 vols. (London, 1868); *The Ring and the Book* 4 vols. (London 1868–9); *Balaustion's Adventure: Including a Transcript from Euripides* (London, 1871); *Prince Hohenstiel-Schwangau, Saviour of Society* (London, 1871); *Fifine at the Fair* (London, 1872); *Red Cotton Night-Cap Country* (London, 1873); *Aristophanes' Apology: Including a Transcript from Euripides, Being the Last Adventure of Balaustion* (London, 1875); *The Inn Album* (London, 1875); *Pacchiarotto and How He Worked in Distemper: With Other Poems* (London, 1876); *The Agamemnon of Aeschylus Transcribed by Robert Browning* (London, 1877); *La Saisiaz; The Two Poets of Croisic* (London, 1878); *Dramatic Idyls* (London, 1879); *Dramatic Idyls, Second Series* (London, 1880); *Jocoseria* (London, 1883); *Ferishtah's Fancies* (London, 1884); *Parleyings with Certain People of Importance in Their Day* (London, 1887); *The Poetical Works of Robert Browning* 16 vols. (London, 1888–1869); *Asolando: Fancies and Facts* (London, 1889).

II. MODERN COLLECTIONS. James F. Loucks, ed., *Robert Browning's Poetry: Authoritative Texts. Criticism* (New York and London, 1979); Richard D. Altick, ed., *Robert Browning: The Ring and the Book* (London, 1971 and New Haven, 1981); John Pettigrew, ed., *Robert Browning: The Poems,* Vols. I and II (New Haven and London, 1981).

III. SECONDARY SOURCES. William Clyde DeVane, *A Browning Handbook*, 2nd edn. (New York, 1955); Park Honan, "Robert Browning" in Frederic E. Faverty, ed., *The Victorian Poets: A Guide to Research*, 2nd edn. (Cambridge, Mass., 1968); G. K. Chesterton, *Robert Browning* (New York, 1967); Mary Rose Sullivan, *Browning's Voices in The Ring and the Book* (Canada, 1969); Philip Drew, *The Poetry of Robert Browning: A Critical Introduction* (London, 1970); Boyd Litzinger and Donald Smalley, eds., *Browning: The Critical Heritage* (London, 1970); Ian Jack, *Browning's Major Poetry* (Oxford, 1973); Isobel Armstrong, "Browning and Victorian Poetry of Sexual Love" in Isobel Armstrong, ed., *Robert Browning* (London, 1974); Patricia M. Ball, "Browning's Godot" (1965) and Richard D. Altick, "Andrea Del Sarto: The Kingdom of Hell Is Within" (1968) in J. R. Watson, ed., *Browning's Men and Women and Other Poems: A Casebook* (London, 1974; repr. 1994); Clyde de L. Ryals, *Browning's Later Poetry, 1871–1889* (Ithaca, N.Y., 1975); Harold Bloom and Adrienne Munich, eds., *Robert Browning: A Collection of Critical Essays* (Englewood Cliffs, N.J., 1979); Herbert Tucker, *Browning's Beginnings: The Art of Disclosure* (Minneapolis, 1980); Donald Thomas, *Robert Browning, A Life Within Life* (London, 1982); Loy D. Martin, *Browning's Dramatic Monologues and the Post-Romantic Subject* (Baltimore and London, 1985); May Ellis Gibson, *History and the Prism of Art: Browning's Poetic Experiments* (Columbus, 1987); Daniel Karlin, ed., *Robert Browning and Elizabeth Barrett: The Courtship Correspondence, 1845–1846* (Oxford, 1989); Gertrude Reese Hudson, *Robert Browning's Literary Life: From First Work to Masterpiece* (Austin, 1992); Daniel Karlin, *Browning's Hatreds* (Oxford, 1993); Clyde de L. Ryals, *The Life of Robert Browning* (Oxford, 1993); Patricia O'Neill, *Robert Browning and Twentieth Century Criticism* (Columbia, 1995); Adam Roberts, *Robert Browning Revisited* (New York and London, 1996); John Woolford and Daniel Karlin, *Robert Browning* (New York, 1996); Esther Loehndorf, *The Master's Voices: Robert Browning, the Dramatic Monologue and Modern Poetry* (Tubingen, 1997); Donald S. Hair, *Robert Browning's Language* (Toronto and London, 1999).

IV. FURHTER READOMG. Robert Langbaum, *The Poetry of Experience: The Dramatic Monologue in Modern Literary Tradition* (New York, 1957, repr. 1963); George MacBeth, intro. to *The Penguin Book of Victorian Verse* (Harmondsworth, U.K., 1969, repr. 1986); Isobel Armstrong, *Victorian Poetry: Poetry, Poetics and Politics* (London and New York, 1993, repr. 1996); Joseph Bristow, ed., *The Cambridge Companion to Victorian Poetry* (Cambridge, 2000); Bernard Richards, ed., *English Poetry of the Victorian Period, 1830–1890*, 2nd edn. (London, 2001).

GEOFFREY CHAUCER

(c. 1340–1400)

N. S. Thompson

IF JOHN DRYDEN in 1700 was able to propose Geoffrey Chaucer as the "Father of English Poetry," earlier generations had not only been copious with praise, but also had been quite specific about the nature of the medieval poet's merits. For William Caxton (1478), Chaucer was "the worshipful fader & first fondeur & enbellisher of ornate eloquence in our englissh," and earlier that century he had been noted as a "noble Rethor" by John Lydgate (c. 1370–1450), for his moral "vertue" by Henry Scogan (c. 1407), and as "the floure of rethoryk / In englisshe tong & excellent poete" by John Walton (c. 1410), while his contemporary Thomas Usk (d. 1388) called him "the noble philosophical poete" and the French poet Eustache Deschamps (c. 1340–?1404) called him a "great Ovid" and a "great translator." Not only was Chaucer the recipient of accolades from his fellow poets John Gower (c. 1330?–1408) and Thomas Hoccleve (c. 1370–c.1450) along with Lydgate, the latter two claimed him as a direct influence, while later Scottish poets in the fifteenth century—Robert Henryson (c.1420–before 1505–1506), William Dunbar (c. 1460–1513), and Gavin Douglas (c. 1475–1522)—were equally happy to claim poetic paternity from him and became known as the "Scottish Chaucerians." Plaudits continued in print during the Renaissance: Edmund Spenser remarked that Chaucer's language was the "well of English undefiled" and Shakespeare's *Troilus and Cressida* owed much to his reading of Chaucer's *Troilus and Criseyde*. The Augustan poets were not stinting in praise, with John Dryden publishing his versions of the tales of the Nun's priest and the Wife of Bath in his *Fables Ancient and Modern* (1700), and later Alexander Pope his imitations of "The Merchant's Tale" and the Wife of Bath's "Prologue" in popular miscellanies of his day. If Chaucer was not seen by the Romantics as a purveyor of eloquence (in a memorandum book of 1807 Lord Byron thought him "obscene and contemptible"), then the many positive references to him serve as a reminder of how we see Chaucer today, not so much as the father of English poetry but rather as the founder of English realism. The story of how he could become this out of the heavily stylized (for some, Gothic) literature of his day paradoxically reveals Chaucer's profound engagement with the literature of his time as he develops into the mature writer who created *The Canterbury Tales*.

LIFE

ALTHOUGH the exact year of his birth is not known, it is safe to say that Chaucer was born in London, around the year 1340, the son of a prosperous wine merchant, John Chaucer (1312–1366) and his wife, Agnes de Copton (d. 1381). The family lived in the Vintry, a medieval ward north of Thames Street, where John Chaucer owned a tenement, which would have housed his wine cellars, as well other properties inherited after the Black Death. In 1347 John was appointed deputy in Southampton to the king's chief butler, overseeing the import of wine for the king. Although he resigned from the post two years later, this appointment may be the reason the Chaucer family escaped the Black Death, which hit London in 1348; it also points to a close connection with the crown, which was later to offer Geoffrey employment for the whole of his adult life, first as a courtier, then as a civil servant.

Little is known of Chaucer's formal education, but the evidence of his work points to his having benefited from the privileges that a prominent family in the capital city were able to enjoy. There was no shortage of grammar schools, where he would have been instructed in Latin; French and Italian could have been taught him by foreign residents in and around the Vintry or the Cordwainers' wards, where many continental merchants had taken up permanent residence. Many were involved in exporting English wool and importing wine, spices, and luxury goods. Chaucer's literary works show ample evidence of his deep knowledge of French, Italian, and Latin, but the primary motive for acquiring them would initially have been for a career in diplomacy or business. At this time there were continuous hostilities with France (known as the Hundred Years' War), when the British crown laid claim to territories in France, while Italian bankers were the most powerfully organized in Europe, giving many loans to Edward III (reigned 1327–1377).

Chaucer is unusual as a medieval writer in that a large amount of his life is documented in public records by virtue of his career in public service; little is known of his literary contacts or milieu, although much can be gathered of his reading. The first written record of Chaucer is in 1357 in the service of Elizabeth, countess of Ulster, the wife of Lionel, earl of Ulster, later duke of Clarence, the second surviving son of Edward III. Most probably as a page in this royal household, Chaucer would have continued his wider education in anything from sports to martial arts, from the refinements of letters to the refinements of courtly behavior, while also performing the duties allotted him. When Lionel reached his majority, the countess's household merged with that of her husband, with whom Chaucer was captured on a campaign in France in 1360. Later still we find him first a valet (*valettus*), then an esquire in the service of King Edward himself, a position he retained for the rest of his life, despite his services elsewhere. These generic titles offer little detail as to what Chaucer's daily duties were, but—lasting forty-three years—they mention annual payments of salary, livery, and gifts, as well as monies received for various trips abroad on the king's business. At some time before 1366 Chaucer married his wife, Philippa, thought to be a daughter of Sir Payne de Roet, and therefore sister to the Katherine who married Sir Hugh Swynford and was later mistress and eventually wife to John of Gaunt, the King's eldest son. The records show two sons from Chaucer's marriage, Thomas (c. 1367–1434) and Lewis (born c. 1380), with possibly two daughters as well. What the details of this marriage were, given that Philippa was also in royal service as a lady-in-waiting, as well as the possible connection with a notorious sister, has given rise to much conjecture, but there is little to suggest that Geoffrey and Philippa actually led separate lives, as has sometimes been suggested.

Whatever his personal circumstances, Chaucer clearly prospered at court, either as an administrator or literary man or perhaps even both, becoming an "esquire of the king's chamber" in 1371. This did not mean that he was any closer to the king but was simply higher in rank among the six hundred other esquires in an organization that was in effect the civil service and the government combined. While he retained this title, together with its annuities, Chaucer saw an important change in duties in 1374 when he was appointed as controller in the port of London for the export of "hides, skins and wools." This might be thought a demotion from the rarified circles of the court, except that England's long-fiber wool was the country's most important export, Edward III placing the famous woolsack for the lord chancellor's seat in Parliament as a reminder of the fact. The sums of money involved in customs duties were large and of vital importance to the crown, hence a trustworthy man was needed. The post was later to incorporate not only the wool export but also the petty custom, which included the import of luxury goods, including spices. Chaucer performed this role for the next twelve years until 1385, the records showing that he spent longer or shorter periods on duties in other ports and also abroad. A house owned by the City of London over the city gate at Aldgate was leased to him rent-free during this time.

Thus the evidence points to Chaucer as a highly valued official in public service. The fact that he served under three different monarchs during his life suggests that he was not the favorite of any particular one, but rather that he could be relied upon as a loyal servant of the crown no matter who was on the throne. Furthermore, his trips abroad suggest a valued negotiator and diplomat, no doubt aided by his ability with languages.

During these trips Chaucer was permitted to appoint a deputy or deputies, but in 1385 the deputy became permanent when, in view of a threatened invasion from France, Chaucer was made a member of the commission for peace in Kent. In addition to being a justice of the peace, he was also elected a member of the House of Commons for Kent the following year. Whether Chaucer actually moved to Kent or not is unclear, but he would certainly have been in London for sessions of Parliament and in 1386 gave testimony in the famous Scrope-Grosvenor case, when two well-known families disputed the right to bear a certain coat of arms. In the same year he gave up his lease on the Aldgate house and and a new controller was appointed at the customs. In the next year, Philippa Chaucer's disappearance from the records is generally taken as evidence of her death. Nothing is known of this period, except that he appears to have survived the purge of the Appellants party, enemies of the king who succeeded in having four of Chaucer's close associates executed: two members of the peace commission and a collector of customs, as well as the poet Thomas Usk. Despite these events, or perhaps because of them, Chaucer is considered to have begun work on the *Canterbury Tales* about this time; he would continue to work on them until his death.

With Richard back in control of his Parliament by the summer of 1389, Chaucer was appointed to what amounted to the top civil service job of his day, namely clerk of the king's works, where he was responsible for the fabric of all royal residences, from palaces to hunting lodges, including the Tower of London and Westminster Palace, the seat of government. Although it only lasted two years, it was a demanding job with a large budget, and Chaucer's salary reflected that. The records also show that he was robbed and possibly wounded when out and about on the business of his clerkship, but he was not required to repay the money. Indeed, when he left the position in the summer of 1391, it was Chaucer who

was owed more than he had earned during his time of office. His next job was perhaps less demanding but no less responsible, as deputy forester of a royal estate in Somerset, which seems a regular appointment for a man of his age and status. He continued to receive extra gifts and grants from the crown as well as his usual emoluments.

It is not known if Chaucer moved to the forest at North Pemberton in Somerset, but if he did he was well away from the ensuing political unrest that ended in the deposition of Richard II and the coronation of Henry IV. In 1397 the king moved against his enemies, the Appellants, purging them, then the next year exiling John of Gaunt's son, Henry, one of their prominent members. When Gaunt himself died in 1399 Richard confiscated his estates, causing Henry to return and successfully claim the throne. At the end of this tumultuous year Chaucer took a lease on a house on the grounds of Westminster Abbey, where he is presumed to have died in 1400. As the presence of several other tombs suggests, a mark of favor to royal servants appears to have been burial in the abbey, along with the monarchs they served; but as a tenant and parishioner of the abbey, Chaucer also had a right to burial in the grounds. Whatever the reason, his final resting place was in the abbey's St. Benedict's Chapel, his tomb later transferred and embellished in 1555 to become the first occupant of the abbey's Poet's Corner, with the date of his death given as 25 October 1400.

THE DREAM POEMS

CHAUCER'S first major poems, apart from lyrics and translations he may have written in his youth, form part of that distinctive medieval genre known as the "dream vision." They comprise, with approximate dates of composition, *The Book of the Duchess* (after 1368), *The House of Fame* (1380s), *The Parliament of Fowls* (1380s), and the "Prologue" to *The Legend of Good Women* (after 1385). These poems do not form a cohesive or even coherent group, especially as the genre itself allowed for considerable variety, but all exhibit an oblique narrative, the record of a dream experienced by a narrator, whose voice recalls the dream's events.

Dream visions go back to the Bible. From the dreams of Joseph and Pharaoh in Genesis, through Daniel and Ezekiel to the Book of Revelation, all bring some divine message of truth, be it personal or collective, simple or allegorical. Similarly in classical literature, messages from the gods are revealed in dreams, especially in Ovid's *Metamorphoses*, Book 11, where the God of Sleep sends one of his sons, Morpheus, to visit Alcyone as she sleeps to bring her the truth of her lost husband, Ceyx, a narrative Chaucer himself utilized. A lively tradition of dream visions continued in the Middle Ages, ranging from works of cosmology to visions of courtly love. Two of the most widely read books throughout the period were Cicero's *Somnium Scipionis* ("The Dream of Scipio") from *De re publica*, and its commentary by the fourth-century writer Macrobius, which gave a widely used categorization of different kinds of dreams. The other text was by the fifth-century author Boethius, whose *Consolation of Philosophy* was a dream vision of the author meeting Dame Philosophy and a record of her answers to his questions. It was notable for resolving the paradox of man's free will as against God's omniscience, and therefore his foreknowledge of events, both fundamental tenets of Christianity. The most popular of all was *Le Roman de la Rose* ("The Romance of the Rose"), created by two different writers during the thirteenth century. The first part was written by Guillaume de Lorris, who created a courtly vision of a walled paradise garden in which dwells the Rose, and he narrates the travails of the Lover to attain her. In a dream landscape, the Lover meets many allegorical personifications (for example, Disdain, False Seeming) who either rebuff or help him toward his goal. Unfortunately the work was incomplete on the death of Guillaume, c. 1237, but manuscripts circulated, and in the third quarter of the century one of the professors at the University of Paris, Jean de Meun, took up the story and provided a 21,000-line continuation to the work's original 4,000, retaining the original structure but taking the work onto wider horizons.

Hence the Lover meets many more kinds of allegorical personifications (Fortune, Friendship, Nature, Reason) and the work becomes a lively discussion on the issues that exercised the medieval mind from women to nature to love, the poem ending with a thinly veiled description of the Lover finally attaining his Rose. Although not strictly defined as a dream vision, Dante's *Divine Comedy* has all the hallmarks of one, as the author finds himself "full of sleep" in the middle of a dark wood in the middle years of his life (*Inferno* 1: 1–12). Naturally, its compendious structure and discussion of the rights and wrongs of history in the Christian dispensation make it a spiritual journey without parallel as Dante travels through Hell, Purgatory, and Paradise, meeting its various denizens, both learning from them and disagreeing with them. More immediately, a series of fourteenth-century French authors had refined the love vision in such works as Guillaume de Machaut's *Dits* and *Jugements* and Jean Froissart's *Fontienne Amoureuse*, which influenced Chaucer directly.

Thus a dream vision could by turns be courtly, philosophical, religious, or satirical. It could reflect an allegorical landscape or indeed the eternal otherworlds of the Christian universe. But the central structure was of a dreamer (often the narrator) who would find some vital truth(s) in the dream to bring back and reveal to humanity. Chaucer's dream poems show him to be a master of narrative and characterization, introducing us to his comic and curious alter ego, the bookish poet of courtly love who, paradoxically, has never experienced love himself, yet who is eager for the knowledge that the dream appears to offer him. But in the end, the dreams are strangely enigmatic, and in two cases—*The House of Fame* and "Prologue" to *The Legend of Good Women*—apparently unfinished.

In *The Book of the Duchess,* 1,334 lines of octosyllabic couplets, the narrator even has difficulty getting to sleep in the first place, so affected is he by lovesickness and melancholy. He picks up a "romance" and reads the tale of Ceyx and Alcyone from Ovid's *Metamorphoses* 11, changing the narrative slightly by the addition of comic elements. In answer to Alcyone's plea for help, Juno sends her messenger to Morpheus, here the god of sleep, who has to blow his horn right in the god's ear to wake him. Morpheus finds the body of Alcyone's dead husband, Ceyx, and takes it to her, letting Ceyx reveal his death. The outcome of the loving royal couple's metamorphosis into kingfishers seems to escape the dreamer, who marvels that any god can bring sleep and calls on Morpheus, Juno or "som wight elles" ("anyone else") for help, even offering a gift of featherbed or pillow as a reward. Suddenly he is asleep and dreams himself to be in bed, on a May morning, hearing a hunt go by.

From the beauties of the morning associated with spring renewal and the adventures of love, the narrator describes the beauties of his chamber, the windows glazed with fine glass, both windows and walls painted with scenes from medieval romances on the theme of Troy and *Le Roman de la Rose*; as a hunt goes by, he flies onto his horse to follow; but when the hunt, led by the Emperor Octavian, comes to an end without catching its prey of a hart, the narrator comes across a lamenting knight dressed in black. The lament is a formal piece, "a lay, a maner songe" ("a poem, a kind of song"), but not sung, only recited, expressing the loss of a lady:

I have of sorwe so gret won
That joye gete I never non,
Now that I see my lady bright,
Which I have loved with al my myght,
Is fro me ded and ys agoon.

(lines 475–479)

["I have such a great dwelling in sorrow that I never have joy, now that I see that my bright lady, whom I have loved with all my power, has died and gone from me."]

For the rest of the poem that follows, the narrator both defers to the black knight as his superior both socially and in love but, as if he had not understood the words of the lay, then interrogates him about the nature of his sorrow. In answer the knight remonstrates against the cruel ways of Fortune, still personified in the Middle Ages as the late Roman goddess Fortuna, who has played a game of chess with him and taken his queen. The narrator gives the knight good reasons (taken from the *Consolation of Philosophy*) why he should be patient with Fortune, but they are unheeded; the knight continues to expand on his falling in love with an idealized description of the lady and her moral virtues, how he became a poet praising her, was unsuccessful in his suit, then gained her, only to lose in the end. Many of the knight's lines are taken from Machaut's *Le Jugement du Roy de Behaingne* ("The Judgment of the King of Bohemia") and his *Remede de Fortune* ("Love's Remedy"), among other French works. From these courtly expressions of love, full of classical allusions and delicate rhetorical forms, the reader is led to what is in effect the poem's climactic interchange between the two men, the narrator still not having understood that the knight is mourning for the lady (named "White") he has lost:

"God wot, allas! Ryght that was she!"
"Allas, sir, how? What may that be?",
"She ys ded!" "Nay!" "Yis, be my trouthe!"
"Is that youre los? Be God, hyt is routhe!"

(lines 1,306–1,310)

[God knows, alas! That was her truly!—Alas, sir, how? What is it?—She is dead!—No!—Yes, that's the truth!—Is that your loss? By God, that is pitiable.]

This brisk interchange undercuts all the intricate tracery of allusion, courtliness, and sophistication that has gone before, all now whisked away in one pointed interchange, a moment of truth-telling that has little to do with poetry but everything to do with a plain message that produces an honest and heartfelt reaction from the narrator. The poem concludes on several lines of allusion to the knight's circumstances that link him to John of Gaunt, the duke of Lancaster who lived at Richmond (line 1,319: "ryche hil") and had a "long castel" (line 1,318, playing on an erroneous etymology of "Lancaster"). John of Gaunt's wife, Blanche, had died in 1368 and, although Gaunt remarried, was remembered by him in various ways after her death. The poem has often been thought to be a memorial or elegy for this Blanche (as the black knight's "Lady White"), but the stylization and obliquity are too great for any direct identification. It is very possible that this poem, including its levity, is a general philosophical treatment on loss and Fortune that was presented to Gaunt as part of a later commemoration for Blanche. But the poem also has a sting in its tail about the nature of courtly poetry that has become so stylized that its truth or reception cannot be guaranteed. If we can see *The Book of the Duchess* as a philosophical debate on the nature of mutability and how to cope with it, it is also—by means of the pun on hart/heart—a process of "herte hunting," of seeking out the roots of poetry and what it can offer. This can indeed be a record, elegy, or commemoration, but it cannot guarantee true consolation and understanding. The fascination of the poem lies in these indeterminacies that reflect the paradoxes of art.

Chaucer's next dream vision is another narrative of 2,158 lines, again in octosyllabic rhyming couplets, divided into three books. *The House of Fame* continues the oblique look at the nature of poetry in a dream centered on the narrator himself. After a reflection on the nature of dreams and an invocation to the "god of slep," the narrator describes the wonderful dream he had on 10 December, when he found himself in a temple of glass where, among gods and goddesses, the story of Aeneas is depicted, which he describes in an admirable précis, giving the story more the emphasis of Ovid in his *Heroides* 7, which criticizes Aeneas for betraying Dido, rather than Virgil's commendation in the *Aeneid* of his "pius" ("respectful") hero who must not tarry in his mission to found the Roman empire. Indeed, by way of amplification Chaucer includes a list of other supposed heroes who betray their lovers. Having passed through the temple, the narrator finds himself in a desert, and looking up sees an eagle coming at him out of the sun. After another invocation, this time to Venus, Book 2 continues in a comic vein as, much to the narrator's consternation, the eagle swoops down and carries him off into the skies. The narrator wonders what this can mean: Does Jove intend to turn him into a star? With an allusion to Dante's words at the beginning of his journey into Hell (*Inferno* 2, 32), he says in self-deprecation that he is not Enoch, Elijah, nor Romulus or Ganymede, all of whom had spectacular journeys into the heavens, and that he is not worthy of the honor. The eagle addresses him as "Geoffrey" and tells him he has been sent by Jupiter, who sees that he has had no reward for all his service in poetry to "Cupido" and "faire Venus," wherefore Jupiter has sent the eagle to take him where he might gather "tydynges / Of Love's folk" (lines 644–645: "news of Love's people"). Accordingly the eagle is to take him to a place called the House of Fame where he may indeed learn news of "Loves folk." But this is no courtly Garden of Love; instead, in a brilliant listing of all the travails of love, the eagle prepares his charge for the worst (lines 672–700).

After an invocation to Apollo at the beginning of Book 3, the dreamer is left by a rock of ice on which he sees the names of "famous folkes," but a symbolic representation of Fame's mutability shows the names melting away on one side, while not the other. On top of this rock stands Fame's dwelling, a wonderful Gothic edifice covered with images and statues in niches of famous minstrels, pastoral poets, trumpeters, and even wizards. Once in the castle hall, he sees statues of famous writers on metal pillars lined up there, leading to the curious figure of Fame herself, with her head in the stars, as many eyes as feathers on a bird, and as many ears and tongues as hairs on a beast (lines 1,360–1,392). He then witnesses the fact that she is the sister of the capricious figure of Fortune as nine groups of petitioners, deserving and undeserving, are given favorable or unfavorable reputations—or even none at all—without any consideration as to their true merit. This does not seem to upset the narrator, who says to an unnamed person that he knows very well how he stands and only hopes that posterity will think of him in the same way. This person then shows the narrator the real source of Fame below the castle in a valley, an enormous wicker house called a "labyrinth"; full of whispering people, this structure lets truth and lies out and in, but which is truth and which lies is unclear:

Thus saugh I fals and truth compouned
Togeder fle for oo tydynge.

(lines 2,108–2,109)

[Thus I saw a lie and a truth mingled together fly out as one item.]

If the narrator—or reader—expects the usual authority figure to bring order out of this chaos, both are frustrated. A "man of gret auctorite" emerges from the crowd, but the text tantalizingly ends at this point. The manuscript evidence shows that the work was taken to end there, although modern editions usually conclude with suspension dots. Obviously the poem is a satiric look at the mutability of fame, on which there can be no concluding authority, but it also looks engagingly at the nature of the literary enterprise itself in that the reader is also in the place of the narrator standing before the many ambiguous messages coming from the House of Rumour and must know where to stand when faced with the cacophany of tidings (lines 1,960–1,976). What is most apparent is that a dream journey supposed to reveal tidings of Love's folk ends not in the Garden of Love but in the ambiguous tidings of real life:

ful of rounynges and of jangles
Of werres, of pes, of mariages,
Of rest, of labour, of viages,
Of abood, of deeth, of lyf,
Of love, of hate, acord, of stryf . . .

(lines 1,960–1,964)

[. . . full of whisperings and gossip of wars, of peace, of marriages, of rest, of work, of journeys, of staying home, of death, of life, of love, of hate, harmony, of strife . . .]

The *Parliament of Fowls* is the third major dream poem, written in rime royal (*ababbcc*), possibly based on the Italian *ottava rima* stanza (*ababbacc*) using a long decasyllabic line, again possibly imitating the Italian hendecasyllable. The poem apparently celebrates St. Valentine's Day, when the narrator relates a meeting of birds as they choose for "the commune profyt" their mates for the season. The poem is yet another look askance at the matter of courtly love poetry, this time setting the deliberations of a group of aristocratic eagles against the commonsense arguments of the "commoner" birds. Before this, however, the narrator presents himself in the same way that the eagle in *The House of Fame* presented "Geoffrey": a bookish student of love who has never experienced love himself. In his quest for knowledge he reads Cicero's *Somnium Scipionis* and gives a précis of the work, as Scipio the Younger is taken in a dream by his ancestor Scipio the Elder (known as "Africanus" for his North African victories) to be shown the Earth and, beyond it, the Milky Way, where human souls abide after death. Scipio is also instructed in the virtuous life that will bring his soul to this pure place. After reading the book, the narrator himself dreams he is guided by the elder Scipio ("Affrycan"), who takes him to a walled park with a gate over which words reminiscent of those over the gates of Dante's Hell (*Inferno* 3:1–3) promise both a "blysful place" (line 127) in golden letters, while black letters also warn that "Disdayn" and "Daunger" will lead to "mortal strokes of the spere" (line 135). Understandably baffled by this ambiguous gate, the narrator finds himself unceremoniously pushed by Scipio into the park, which at first seems to be the paradisaical Garden of Love, except that an ambiguous array of allegorical personifications—from vices to virtues—congregates in the vicinity of the temple of Venus, where Priapus stands with "hys sceptre" in his hand and the goddess herself lies almost naked on a bed of gold (lines 253–273). In this dark hothouse, he discerns the stories of a mixed group of lovers painted on the walls, all of whom were overcome by love, naturally or unnaturally. Although no moralizing takes place, the lesson about not letting love become an obsession is clear. Next, out in the light, the narrator sees a hill of flowers on which stands the goddess Nature, as devised by the twelfth-century writer Alain of Lille in *De Planctu Naturae* ("The Complaint of Nature"), an important dream poem on the necessity of living by the laws of Nature; a message against the sexual abuses of the cenobitical life and also against the sexual asceticism enjoined on the laity by the clergy. Nature presides over the gathering of birds, who are described individually and also as belonging to separate classes following a hierarchy devised by Aristotle: birds of prey (aristocrats), worm eaters (middle classes), and seed eaters (lower classes), with another class given as "water fowl." On her hand, Nature has a female eagle for whom a mate has to be found and three male eagles offer their love in courtly fashion, each one as stylized as the next. The lower birds find this kind of gentility literally a hoot and mock the proceedings, only to be called to order by Nature, who says that a "tercelet" (young male eagle) has been chosen to adjudicate the male eagles' claims. He says that the female should herself choose which is the worthiest of the three, which sparks off a comic debate about the nature of courtly service: the "gentil foules" ("noble birds") think that the two not chosen should remain faithful, and the commonsense voices of the other birds ridicule this. Eventually, in the face of a choice that is perhaps no choice at all (all three males presenting exactly the same refined statements of courtly love), the female asks Nature for the grace of a year in which to make her decision, whereupon the other birds are free to choose their mates.

Although not an explicit attack on the culture of courtly love, *The Parliament of Fowls* certainly does not present the courtship offered by the eagles in an idyllic light; rather this courtship is surrounded by the scorn of common sense and results in the stasis of Nature's "commune profyte" as the procreation of the species among the aristocratic birds is put on hold. Again the vibrant interplay between realistic viewpoints and the ideals of courtly courtship is seen in stark contrast and shows yet another critical perspective on the ideals of courtly culture that come under scrutiny in these dream poems.

A final essay in the dream vision genre, "Prologue" to *The Legend of Good Women*, is a later work (written after *Troilus and Criseyde*) that purports to show the goodness of women by narrating the stories of classical heroines who were faithful in love, in contrast to the author's portrayal of Criseyde's faithlessness. It exists in two versions: the "F" manuscript is dated around 1386 and the later "G" manuscript is dated about 1394. Again, it presents Chaucer in a comic vein, arraigned before the God of Love for having portrayed women unfavorably in *Troilus* and in a translation of the *Roman de la Rose*. Queen Alceste (the Greek queen Alcestis) comes to plead on the narrator's behalf, and he is handed over to

her judgment. As a penance she decides he must write the narratives that follow: Cleopatra, Thisbe, Dido, Hipsipyle and Medea, Lucrece, Ariadne, Phildomela, Phyllis, Hypermnestra. The "F" prologue is noted for its praise of the daisy, which is associated with Alceste and has its roots in the symbolism of Froissart's "Marguerite" ("daisy") poems, rather than the actual flower. Discussion over the poem has been much divided, given its ambiguous blend of comedy and seriousness.

TROILUS AND CRISEYDE

WRITTEN between 1381 and 1386, *Troilus and Criseyde* is in many ways Chaucer's masterpiece. To begin with, it is a complete work, a single long narrative of 8,239 decasyllabic lines in rime royal, divided more or less equally into five books. Books 2 through 4 have a formal prologue (*prohemium*) where the narrator comments on the narrative and his own part in relating it, often asking for help or inspiration from a classical deity or muse. It is, moreover, Chaucer's most sustained work in that not only does it closely follow a source in Giovanni Boccaccio's *Il Filostrato* (written c. 1339), but it amplifies and expands the original's 5,704 lines by more than a third to create a work that, while it often translates many lines stanza for stanza, yet transforms the original into a work of greater depth and reference. Historical source texts known to Boccaccio, and which Chaucer names (and may have consulted), are the mid-twelfth-century *Roman de Troie* by Benoît de Sainte-Maure (where the narrative in episodic form first occurs), which in turn was influenced by two Latin prose histories by Dares Phrygius and Dictys Cretensis. Boccaccio may also have been influenced by a Latin prose redaction of these completed in 1287 by Guido delle Colonne. On the literary side Chaucer is also indebted to Dante for many allusions and images (especially of lovers tragically transformed) and to Boethius for his philosophical perspective on nature, fortune, and love.

Essentially the core narrative is a love story set in ancient Troy as it is beseiged by the Greeks after the elopement of Helen, wife of King Menelaus, with the Trojan prince Paris. Inside the city, love creates more turmoil as Troilus, another son of Priam, king of Troy, falls in love with a beautiful young widow named Criseyde, the daughter of Calchas, the seer who has prophesied the fall of the city and decamped to the Greeks, leaving his daughter at the mercy of the Trojan citizens. Fortunately Hector—the eldest prince—decides she merits protection. Given these difficult circumstances, the two lovers act out the anachronistic conventions of courtly love in an entirely realistic way. The inexperienced Troilus, in love for the first time, is overcome with lovesickness and manages to disburden himself to his older friend Pandarus, Criseyde's uncle, who says he will act as the conventional go-between for the two lovers. He is able to arrange a tryst and the affair is painfully launched, continuing for roughly three years. Calchas, however, wishes to have his daughter spared and has the Greeks make overtures to exchange her for a Trojan prisoner, Antenor (the traitor who will steal Troy's sacred Palladium with Aeneas). Caught up, it appears, in the world of politics and diplomacy, the two lovers can do nothing but bewail their fate and suggest wild solutions of escape. Ultimately, however, they acquiesce to the turn of events. Troilus again plunges into a sorrow from which Pandarus tries in vain to raise him and eventually finds his death at the hands of Achilles on the field of battle, having seen the brooch he had given Criseyde on the cloak of Diomede, knowing then that she has been unfaithful to him. Despite much heart searching and protestations at finding no way to return to Troy as she had promised, Criseyde finds a new lover in the Greek hero Diomede, her affirmations of love for him sounding rather hollow after those given ardently to Troilus.

Boccaccio uses this basic narrative to moralize in comic vein on the code of courtly love. In a prose prologue he establishes himself as the lover Filostrato ("one vanquished by love") whose beloved Filomena has left Naples for another city. The narrative of Troiolo is thus directed to Filomena and meant to show the terrible sufferings of a man for a woman with the aim of caus-

ing her to return. But if Filostrato the narrator is to be identified with Troiolo, what is to be made of the dismissive "*il mal concetto amore di Troiolo*" (part 8, stanza 28: "Troiolo's ill-conceived love"), and what of the identification of Filomena with Criseida, who is described as "villana" (ignoble) for her betrayal in the very same stanza? Furthermore, in a worldly-wise tone at the very end of the work, the narrator concludes that as young women such as Criseida are fickle, young men should try an older woman for love (part 8, stanza 32). Thus Boccaccio establishes a complex and perhaps not entirely well connected series of frames around the narrative, with the result that the core narrative of a courtly love betrayed is seen in ironic perspective. Filostrato is a self-involved narrator who cannot see the full implications of sending his narrative to Filomena, while Criseida—who is ultimately censored in terms of courtly love—is presented as a lively, attractive figure throughout the narrative. Finally, the conclusion seems to undermine the narrative's courtliness, which has already seemed suspect with the rapid course of the love affair.

It is these ironies or inconsistencies that would have proved most attractive to a poet who was entirely used to looking tangentially at the ideals of courtly or "refined" love, as the contemporary usage was (Old French: *fin' amors*). But where Boccaccio's three protagonists seem to act, despite the war, in the youthful camaraderie of a never-land, with Pandaro, Criseida's cousin and Troiolo's great friend, Chaucer creates a much more detailed (one is tempted to say "Gothic") world where the classic impediments to *fin' amors* that necessitate letters, a go-between, sighs, and heightened emotions, become the dire realities of a Troy besieged; where Criseyde's presence is only tolerated through Hector's good wishes; where we feel that Troilus would be much more usefully employed in the defense of his city, and where Pandarus becomes a much older man, Criseyde's uncle, who should perhaps be protecting his niece from any ventures likely to put her further at risk. Chaucer also complicates his characters by giving them significant moments of introspection, even if they do not act upon those reflections.

Troilus is not only an inexperienced lover, but a young man who has actively scorned love. One day in a springtime ceremony in the temple of Palladion, he is smitten by love's arrows and made to fall in love in accordance with the natural order. Whether this is because of the purposeful agency of the god of love or nature or Troilus's own volition is left purposely unclear. Unused to love, Troilus assumes the stereotypical behavior of the courtly lover. Overcome by his vision of Criseyde, he takes to his bed in a welter of painful longing, and only the careful probing of the older Pandarus allows Troilus to reveal the name of his secret love. Unexpectedly, Pandarus is delighted to be of help. In the course of his machinations, it emerges he has never been successful in love himself, although purported to be an expert in the craft (2:695: "Th'olde daunce")—a trait that has often drawn comparison with the narrator of *The Book of the Duchess* or the figure of "Geoffrey" in *The House of Fame*—so that the reader is led to believe that his enjoyment in bringing the two lovers together is a vicarious pleasure, bringing to fruition what he has never been able to accomplish himself. Although Chaucer's narrator calls his work a "tragedye" (5:1,786), based on the medieval definition of the fall of a noble character from high to low, the interplay of characters as Pandarus seeks to bring the two lovers together contains moments of high comedy, from Troilus's hyperbolic straining to Criseyde's coquetry to Pandarus's eager manipulation of the two, all achieved in a rich blend of soliloquies, dialogues, letters, proverbial sayings, appeals to the high art of *fin' amors*, the low "daunce" of love, the movements of the heavens, fate, the gods, even the weather. And, of course, at the center of all this cultural machinery lie three very fallible and understandable human beings. Thus Chaucer's interest is in looking not at the ideals of love but in seeing actuality played out against these and other expectations, and how three individual characters wrestle with the immensities of life and love.

In addition to these players, human and cosmological, Chaucer also amplifies the figure of the narrator over and above that in *Il Filostrato* to become, as many critics have said, almost a character in his own right, commenting on events in the narrative, favorably and unfavorably, while at the same time deferring to an inscribed audience of courtly lovers who are presented as its auditors from the beginning of the work. Overall he is seen to have difficulty with the narrative career of Criseyde as she betrays Troilus, the narrative indeed presenting more of her psychological difficulties and giving more vacillations than in Boccaccio's original. This narrator is crucial to an understanding of the poem because it presents inside the work a figure as critic, whose presence acts as a stimulus to a critical perspective in the reader. Indeed, the characters of Troilus and Criseyde are established in the narrative precisely for the reader's critical judgment. Obviously the excesses of Troilus as lover, often seen today as a "feminized" hero, are going to cause comment, in the same way that Criseyde is paradoxically both her "owene womman" (2:750) with a perfect right to act as she wishes, but also "Tendreherted, slydynge of corage" (5:825: "Tender hearted and fickle/changeable").

Given these views, one of the most useful ways of seeing the work is as an exemplary tale, a cautionary tale that teaches about the effects of love, beneficial and detrimental. Like words on the gate leading into the walled garden of *The Parliament of Fowls,* love has both possibilites; it depends on the path one takes. Boccaccio's poem was in essence meant to be exemplary and instructive, yet it is subverted by humorous ironies (as one might expect of the author of the *Decameron*) that create a critical stance around the excesses of *fin' amors*. In Chaucer's work the ironies are serious, and the lessons deeper, but it also shows that whatever path one takes, events and circumstances may get in the way. Troilus is an exemplary courtly lover who, as hero, is made gentle by love, his sufferings so great they can only be assuaged by the attentions or "grace" of the beloved, depicted as an angelic creature. Not only this, but Troilus looks for ultimate meanings in his love for Criseyde. If he sees her as a divine creature that is not only because of the hyperbole of *fin' amors*, but because he really does feel a sense of eternal love in her regard. In sum, he is a young idealist caught up with his first major love, and an absolutist who sees no wavering from the path where he feels fate and fortune have led him. In contrast Criseyde is a much more pragmatic character. She loves no less passionately than Troilus (although some past critics have tried to argue against this), but having been married and, presumably, in love before, she takes a more considered look at the prospect before her, once Pandarus has told her of Troilus's love and suffering. Her deliberations give a very modern view of a young woman who is going to make up her own mind, not be swayed in any way, and who shows an attractive power of ratiocination in thinking things through. The same can not be said for Pandarus, who is all business, but who seems to have no idea about the seriousness of the lovers. For him it is all a game—the "olde daunce." Or is there a serious vicariousness underneath his japing? At the same time, Pandarus is acting as more than a go-between; he is an active persuader who will say anything to obtain his wishes, or those of Troilus, as on the night of the consummation when he swears that Troilus will not be there when Criseyde comes to dinner. Once the lovers find themselves in bed, after Troilus has to be actually placed there, Troilus says that finally she is "caught," but Criseyde turns to him and says quite clearly she is there under her own volition:

This Troilus in armes gan her streyne,
And seyde, "O swete, as evere mot I gon,
Now be ye kaught; now is ther but we tweyne!
Now yeldeth you, for other bote is non!"
To that Criseyde answerde thus anon,
"Ne hadde I er now, my swete herte deere,
Ben yolde, ywis, I were now nought heere!"

(3:1,205–1,211)

[Troilus clasped her tightly in his arms and said, "O sweet, for the life of me, you are now caught; now there is only the two of us. Now you must yield, there is no other remedy." To which Criseyde answered directly, "If I had not yielded before this point, my dear sweet heart, I should not be here now!"]

On the other hand, when she sees Troilus go by, it is as if she has no volition at all and is under the spell of a love potion (3:651). So the two lovers are embedded in much more than love; they are caught up in the world of cause and effect. Criseyde believes she acts of her own free will, especially in love, but she is perhaps really under the spell of love, while Troilus believes that he has no free will and is at the mercy of fortune (5:260–280). Nevertheless the exchange has to take place and cuts into both their lives.

And what does the narrator make of it all? At various points he seems no better than Pandarus, enjoying the fact of the lovers' consummation, while at the same time reminding the real life Christian audience of the cost of such a thought:

O blisful nyght, of hem so longe isought, How blithe unto hem bothe two thow weere! Why nad I swich oon with my soule ybought, Ye, or the leeste joie that was theere?

(3:1,317–1,320)

[O blissful night, sought so long by them, how joyous to both of them you were! Why have I never bought such a night with (read: "at the cost of") my soul—yes, even the smallest joy that was there?]

But he is ever deferential to what the inscribed audience of courtly lovers thinks and a few lines later, as part of Chaucer's careful stimulation of the real audience, graciously defers to their judgment:

For myne words, heere and every part,
I speke hem alle under correccioun
Of yow that felyng han in loves art,
And putte it al in youre discrecioun
To encresse or maken dymynucioun
Of my langage. . . .

(3:1,331–1,336)

[I speak my words here and in every part under the judgment of you who have understanding in the art of love, and put it to your discretion to augment or make less of what I say. . . .]

But on the other hand, he is a careful manipulator of Criseyde and seeks to mitigate any negative judgement of her. Once she is in the Greek camp, receiving the attentions of Diomede, he mentions other books of Troy saying how she tended Diomede's wounds and then how "Men seyn—I not—that she yaf hym hire herte"

(5:1,050: "Men say—but I am not sure—that she gave him her heart"), then goes on to say that there was never a woman who grieved more than when she betrayed Troilus (5:1,051–1,052), leading up to his special pleading for pity or compassion when considering her:

Ne me ne liste this sely woman for to chyde
Forther than the storye wol devyse.
Hire name, allas, is publysshed so wide
That for hire gilt it oughte ynough suffise.
And if I myghte excuse hire any wise,
For she so sory was for hire untrouthe,
I wis, I wolde excuse hire yet for routhe.

(5:1,093–1,099)

[I would not like to reproach this unfortunate woman more than the story will relate. Alas, her name is spread so wide that her guilt should be sufficiently known. But if I could excuse her in any way, because she was so sorry for her falsehood, I know I would excuse her out of pity.]

This again sets up a critical perspective in the reader, who wonders at the narrator's sympathy (whether right or wrong or simply misguided). Criseyde does offend against the code of love, and also against a code of honor, having said that she would be true to Troilus no matter what. Here she is none other than the daughter of Calchas, the traitor par excellence. But of course there are mitigating circumstances for the reader to discern. Essentially Criseyde is a woman at the mercy of the world of men, from her father, Calchas, to her prince, Hector; from her uncle, Pandarus, to her lover, Troilus. Given a bad name by one, she is beholden to the others to maintain her good name. Is it any wonder, then, that she does fall for Diomede when patently she would be in need of some friend and protector in what is essentially an enemy camp? Naturally there is no need to sleep with the enemy, but the narrative enjoins us to think what the real personal and political reasons might have been, and we see those set against the more idealistic expectations of Troilus and *fin' amors*. Thus, using the narrator and his comments, Chaucer beautifully complicates Boccaccio's narrative to produce differing planes of perspective around Criseyde. He is equally surprising in introducing an ending for Troilus beyond his death in battle, taking three stanzas

from the ending of another poem by Boccaccio, *Il Teseida* (the "Theseiad," or " book of Theseus," a source for the *Knight's Tale*), where the spirit of Arcita rises up to the hollow of the eighth sphere (the influence of the planet Mercury) and looks back on his travails in love from a truly eternal perspective. Accordingly Troilus finds himself in this knight's spot in the "holughnesse of the eighthe spere" (5:1,809: "hollowness of the eighth sphere") looking down on the "litel spot of erthe" and, seeing love in true perspective, has not a care for his "eternal" feelings for Criseyde and simply laughs at the ridiculous torsion of human love.

Using this perspective, Chaucer brings a final Christian frame of reference to his pagan narrative, this time adopting a stanza from *Il Filostrato* and giving it a much greater import. Where Boccaccio has his narrator warn young men ("*giovinetti*") of the fate and false love of Troiolo, Chaucer's narrator expands the sentiment to a general application to all young lovers, admonishing them to eschew earthly loves and only put their trust in the eternal love of God:

O yonge, fresshe folkes, he or she.
In which that love up groweth with youre age,
Repeyreth hom from worldly vanyte,
And of youre herte up casteth the visage
To thilke God that after his ymage
Yow made, and thynketh al nys but a faire,
This world that passeth soone as floures faire.

(5:1,835–1,841)

[O fresh young people, male and female, in which that love grows with your age, turn to your home (that is, "in heaven") away from the vanity of this world, and lift the face of your heart up to that God who made you after his image and consider that this world is nothing but a fair that passes away as soon as beautiful flowers.]

This may sound like a standard medieval moral, but how could it be taken literally when the narrator continues to say that God should be the only object of human love (5:1,842–1,848)? If humanity decided to love God alone, what would happen to the human race, which is God's creation? It perhaps sounds a far-fetched question today, but in the climate of the fourteenth-century Church, with its premium on virgin purity, the question was more culturally vital, if perhaps still academic and equally impractical. This rhetorical question is crucial: "What nedeth feynede loves for the seke?" (5:1,848: "What is the need of seeking false loves?"). Ultimately, as with the birds in *The Parliament of Fowls,* the answer is to procreate the earth. But equally, human love must be kept in perspective with the ultimate need to love God. Thus in showing the excesses, failings, and virtues of love in a pagan world, Chaucer creates a laboratory situation for looking at love in all its many manifestations from courtly to cosmological, where his characters play out the issue of free will and predestination. Chaucer's great creation here is in portraying the individual against these giant forces: while not denying the ultimate authority of his Christian God, he presents the reader with the experience of love caught up among the terrible unknowns of human existence and thus, in the guise of an ancient tale, presents one of the first real humanist works of love.

THE CANTERBURY TALES

CHAUCER's most celebrated work is the collection of medieval narratives known as *The Canterbury Tales,* written between 1385 and 1400. It is beyond the scope of this introduction to give close readings of each individual narrative; instead it will consider the identity of the work as a whole, which was unique for its time in its linking structure known as the "frame." Although it appears to be a compendium of popular tales compiled for the contemporary market, the number of extant manuscripts (fifty-five complete, another twenty-eight fragmentary) suggest it was well known, but the work is far removed from any modern idea of a popular anthology. Firstly, the narratives are not heterogeneous, nor are they all narratives: "The Tale of Melibee" is a moral treatise, "The Parson's Tale" a conflation of two short works on penitence and the seven deadly sins, and several tales are left unfinished either on purpose or because *The Canterbury Tales* itself is unfinished ("The Cook's Tale," "The Squire's Tale," "The Tale of Sir Thopas," "The Monk's Tale"). Although anthologies were "popular" in

Chaucer's day, the word needs to be carefully qualified. Given that literacy was still restricted to the educated laity and clergy, any popular text would be something that corresponded to this limited market. Anthologies were either spiritual or moral works for a person's edification (especially versions of the Bible, Bible stories, or stories of saints, such as *The Golden Legend*), and excerpts from classical or medieval authors for the use of students or the learned layman. Obviously medieval romances (courtly and less than courtly) circulated, as did other popular tales (known as "fabliaux"), but they were not collected and dignified with the name of "literature" (a term that does not appear until the eighteenth century). A medieval best-seller was something like the *Le Roman de la Rose* (for all its humor, a serious work), Macrobius's *Commentary* on the *Sominum Scipionis,* or the *Consolation of Philosophy* by Boethius. Many book owners created their own anthologies by binding their favorite works together (such as the Auchinleck Manuscript), in which case many very different kinds of texts were created as a book by the owner. Thus *The Canterbury Tales* is unique and not strictly speaking of its time in that it is an investigation of literature and its range of possibilities, written before people even began to think what literature could mean. In this respect it is an avant-garde text in that it puts together many diverse kinds of writing in order to allow the reader to see how these different "texts" compare and contrast with one another and how the different kinds of writing each work in a different way. On top of this, the collection also includes the voices of narrators and the pilgrim audience, who comment on the texts and their differences.

The work has a single title and has been considered as a whole for many centuries, being one of the first works printed by Caxton (1478) and enjoying an unbroken readership in manuscript and print since Chaucer's death in 1400. But a crucial question remains about the nature of its unity. In terms of precedents, the closest parallel is Boccaccio's *Decameron,* written shortly after the great plague of 1348, which relates that a group of ten young nobles (seven women, three men) leave their native town of Florence to escape the pestilence and settle down in a succession of villas in the surrounding countryside to amuse themselves by telling stories to each other. Thus, telling one tale a day over a period of ten days, ten narrators relate a total of one hundred short tales, or *novelle,* to one another, each day coming under the leadership of a "king" or "queen" who can impose a theme for the day or not. Overall there are many kinds of narratives, but in the main they reflect the contemporary world of fourteenth-century Italy. The company of young people discuss the *novelle* as reflections of the world and, moreover, as a reflection of what fiction can and cannot do.

The Canterbury Tales takes this idea and puts it on a more symbolic level. The group of young people in the *Decameron* are escaping the plague and at the same time refreshing themselves by deploying fiction to understand humanity at a point where it seems close to annihilation. Chaucer equally sets up a frame story in which his narrators are a group of pilgrims on the road from London to visit the popular shrine of Saint Thomas à Becket in Canterbury Cathedral. Although pilgrimages had long become holiday affairs, the valency of spiritual quest remains in the fourfold level of meaning common to the medieval understanding. The pilgrimage to Canterbury can be seen firstly as a literal journey; secondly, in a metaphorical sense as the journey of life; thirdly, as the individual's quest for God, and, fourthly, as the individual soul's journey back to its origin in eternity with God (the literal, metaphorical, moral, and anagogical levels). What is more, Chaucer is able to show how humanity fails on these various pilgrimages, not only in the fiction of the tales but in the frame as well, depicting the foibles of the pilgrims and the fact that they prefer to while away the time on anything but spiritual renewal. This satirical view can be savage or gentle according to the dynamics of the group and the particular tale, often recalling the narrator's tolerance in *Troilus and Criseyde,* although the final placing of the "Parson's Tale" suggests the ultimate authority of God.

The pilgrimage frame opens with an inspired evocation of spring, the season of renewal, when pilgrims set out on their journeys as a means of recalling the God who created them and their obedience to him. But as soon as the company is described in the Tabard Inn, Southwark (a new suburb south of the Thames), it becomes clear that not all are going to benefit from the spiritual exercise. This "General Prologue," with which the work begins, is thus a collection of character sketches of most of the twenty-nine pilgrims about to set out with the Tabard's innkeeper, Harry Bailey (the Host), who so likes the company he decides to go with them as guide. The pilgrims are a Knight, Squire, Yeoman, Prioress, Nun, three Priests, Monk, Friar, Merchant, Clerk, Sergeant of the Law, Franklin, Haberdasher, Carpenter, Weaver, Dyer, Tapestry Weaver, Cook, Shipman, Physician, Wife of Bath, Parson, Ploughman, Reeve, Miller, Summoner, Pardoner, and Manciple. Some of the pilgrim narrators are described later in the collection (the Nun's Priest and a latecomer, the Canon's Yeoman), but—apart from the Nun—those not described (two of the priests, the Haberdasher, Carpenter, Weaver, Dyer, Tapestry Weaver) do not narrate a tale. Thus from thirty-one pilgrims, plus Chaucer as a pilgrim narrator who tells two tales, a total of twenty-four narratives emerges, in contrast to the stated aim that each pilgrim tell two tales on the way there and two on the way back. Obviously a much larger work was envisaged. Although the work is unfinished, a good number of narratives are interconnected on the basis of the prologues and endlinks to create ten fragments in all, usually given in the order of the Ellesmere Manuscript (c. 1410): 1: Knight, Miller, Reeve, Cook; 2: Man of Law; 3: Wife of Bath, Friar, Summoner; 4: Clerk, Merchant; 5: Squire, Franklin; 6: Physician, Pardoner; 7: Shipman, Prioress, Sir Thopas, Melibee, Monk, Nun's Priest; 8: Second Nun, Canon's Yeoman: 9: Manciple; 10: Parson. As a whole, this company is a reflection of the changing society of the later Middle Ages, in which the old model of feudal society (peasants, clergy, aristocracy) is now complicated by the rising middle classes engaged in mercantile trades in the burgeoning towns and cities. The Knight and Squire represent the old order and were anachronistic by the end of the fourteenth century; the Knight's description is a conflation of earlier traits and campaigns that represent an impossibly long career, adding up to a symbolic rather than realistic presence. Of the peasantry there is only the Ploughman, although the Franklin, Yeoman, Reeve, and Miller come from the prosperous agricultural base. The clergy has a large presence, with lay characters also representing the church in the Pardoner, who sells indulgences for money on behalf of religious houses, and a Summoner, employed by the ecclesiastical court to bring offenders to justice.

Although the sketches of these characters appear to be in the eyewitness report of Chaucer the pilgrim, they often contain more information than he could have gleaned in conversation, but also conceal other information that he might have known. Furthermore, he famously defers to what might be called the character's own appraisal of themselves, loosely agreeing that they are the best representative of their kind, an ambiguous statement given the discrepancy revealed between the individual and the office or position they fill. Several are involved in the abuse of their position or trade, cheating in order to fill their pockets (Miller, Reeve, Shipman, Physician, Summoner, Pardoner), and others appear to live out a fantasy life as part of their self-indulgence and abuse. The Monk enjoys a life of hunting, finery, and exotic diet more associated with the aristocracy, while the Prioress appears to think of herself as a heroine out of romance, calling herself "Madame Eglentyne" ("General Prologue," line 121) and caring more for her pet dogs and ornaments than she does about the care of souls. In all, the unsavory portraits outweigh the good and add up to a version of the medieval genre known as "estates satire," where the hierarchical order of the estates (social classes), which ideally should work each for the other, is seen to disintegrate into self interest and abuse of office. The manifestly virtuous characters are the Parson, his brother the Ploughman, and the Knight; the Second Nun is merely pious.

From this frame, a clear picture emerges of the values of an "old" world eroded by those of the "new," primarily the acquisition of money: the collective enterprise of agrarian feudal society has been overtaken by the cash nexus of the new urban classes, whose push for status has also corrupted the clergy, demonstrated by the fine manners and ways of the Monk, Prioress, and Friar. This is clearly reflected in the narratives themselves, from the ridicule of older wealthy men marrying younger women in the tales of the Miller and the Merchant, to the materialistic values expressed by the Wife of Bath in her prologue; from the portrait of a merchant in the tale of the Shipman to portraits of a grasping Friar and Summoner in tales told each against the other. The focal point of this critical view is the Pardoner, who freely outlines his selfish desires. But then, with the conundrum of "For though myself be a ful vicious man, / A moral tale yet I yow telle kan" (6:459–460: "For though I am a very evil man, yet I can tell you a moral tale") the Pardoner delivers what is virtually a sermon on the text of 1 Timothy 6:10: "*Radix malorum est cupiditas*" (Greed is the root of evil) in the exemplum (illustrative tale) on the "thre rioters" who find a stash of gold and end up killing each other for it. Deception for gain is pilloried in many tales, often based on the popular fabliaux, which often dealt in tit-for-tat situations. They could result either in people receiving a well-deserved comeuppance or, indeed, managing to pull off a bravura scam, such as the Canon of the *Canon's Yeoman's Tale,* who pretends to have discovered the alchemists' secret of creating gold and sells the "formula" to a greedy priest.

Naturally, following from the portraits of the pilgrims, a picture of a corrupt church emerges from the tales of the Miller, Friar, Summoner, and Pardoner. This was nothing new in the fourteenth century, when the church was a standard topic of debate, especially following the Babylonian Captivity, when the papacy was moved to Avignon (1309–1374), and even more so when a rival pope was replaced in Rome, creating the Great Schism (1377–1417). Dante's *Divine Comedy* cataloged many of the church's sins, and there were numerous grassroots movements calling for reform. Many people's reaction to an immensely powerful, landowning, and wealthy church was to call for a return to its apostolic status, whereby it merely preached the word of God, sentiments expressed in the movement of the Lollards active in the later part of Chaucer's life. Given Chaucer's unvarnished view of the urban clergy, but his praise for the work of the poor parish priest, many readers have felt that Chaucer supported the Lollards, or at least was sympathetic to their ideals.

Another institution that comes under scrutiny both in the tales and in discussion among the pilgrims is marriage. early-twentieth-century studies that suggested the interconnectedness of *The Canterbury Tales* identified a "marriage debate" among the tales of Merchant, Clerk, Franklin, and Wife of Bath, whose prologue gives a candid account of her view of marriage as a business, exemplified by her five times at the altar, and her aspiration for a sixth (3:45) The Merchant's story of the cuckolding of the aged January by his young wife, May, clearly shows the imbalances of a marriage based on wealth and lust, while the Clerk's tale of "patient Griselda" is actually an allegory about the patient soul, but of course acts as a stimulus to debate about the role of women. The Franklin's tale of a courtly suitor who relinquishes the claim he has on a foolish wife is an exemplum of the benefits of "gentillese" (moral virtue), while the Wife's tale of an old hag's transformation into a comely maiden, after the young knight to whom she is married relinquishes the sovereignty he has over her, has led critics to see the narratives as a debate about sovereignty in marriage.

It is the more realistic portraits of marriages in the tales of the Miller, Reeve, and Shipman (and also the Maniciple's mythic tale of Phoebus Apollo, his wife, and the crow) that show how and why marriages go wrong because of imbalances and unrealistic demands. Indeed, it might be said that running through the tales is a more general theme of power and the misuse and abuse to which it is put in the arenas of the church, marriage, and general relations of human beings with one another. As more positive guides to behavior, the tales of the Man of Law, Melibee, the Second Nun, and the Parson serve as sober reminders of the straight and narrow. But what is obvious from the narratives as a whole is the lack of authorial intervention with regard to a moral viewpoint.

If the tales are a mixed bag, one has to remember that the frame tale has them as examples offered in a tale-telling competition organized by the Host as a way of passing the time, his guiding rule being that they are "Tales of best sentence and moost solaas" (798: "stories of the best meaning and most pleasure"). But we also learn that tales are told in "earnest" and in "game"; indeed the high-minded expectation of the competition is quickly brought crashing down when the Reeve takes umbrage at the drunken Miller's depiction of a carpenter, because long ago he was once a carpenter himself and decides to "quyte" (pay back) the man, not the tale, by a story of a foolish miller. Similarly the Friar and the Summoner each relate stories against each other, and other arguments break out between the Clerk and the Wife of Bath, the Host and the Pardoner, and the Reeve and the Shipman. Thus the competition becomes skewed in highly personal ways, with the tales reflecting personal motives rather than a "pure" search for a winning story. At the very center of this search is Chaucer the pilgrim, whose tail-rhyme romance of the feminine Sir Thopas is bawled off the stage by the Host as all "game," to be replaced by "Melibee," which is all earnest. Similarly the Knight calls a halt to the Monk's tale, which is actually a catalog of the "tragedies," the falls of famous men (and one woman), a tale that is too much to bear after the seventeenth example.

Thus this first compendium of medieval narratives in English exhibits a variety of literary genres and their reception by a group of self-interested people, each giving their readings and misreadings of one other, as well as their tales. The largest group of connected tales, Fragment 7, has been called the "literature group," comprising six different genres: fabliau (Shipman), saint's legend (Prioress), tail-rhyme romance (Chaucer's *Sir Thopas*), moral treatise (Chaucer's *Melibee*), tragedies (Monk), and beast fable (Nun's Priest). Although each tale is different, all end up reflected in various ways in the *"Nun's Priest's*

Tale" of Chantecleer and the Fox, which has such an overload of potential meanings, from those enunciated by the cockerel, the fox, and the narrator (7:3,426–3,446) to those seen by critics, such as an allegory of the Fall and redemption. Narratives that also reflect on the problems of narration are seen in the prolixity of the Wife's prologue, the Manciple's warning about telling tales at all, and the slippery usage of words in many of the others. In all, *The Canterbury Tales* is an investigation of the art of narrative as well as an investigation in the art of living. If the moral signposts are not as firmly in place as medieval authorities normally declare, that is in order to make a pilgrim of the reader, who must negotiate narrators and narratives alike as if treading a labyrinth until coming to the straight and narrow of "The Parson's Tale" and its emphasis on penance, the only true way to God.

OTHER WORKS

THE Riverside Chaucer contains a number of short poems confidently attributable to Chaucer, which range from a conventional religious lyric poem through poems on "Fortune," "Truth," and "Gentilesse" to the risqué "Complaint to His Purse," the last poem Chaucer is known to have composed, shortly before his death. It also contains four poems of debatable authorship. Although Chaucer is known to have translated *Le Roman de la Rose*, both on his own admission and by contemporary witness, the translation known as *The Romaunt of the Rose* included in the *Riverside* is also of debated authorship. His translation of Boethius's *Consolation of Philosophy* (*Boece*), however, is authentic, as is *A Treatise on the Astrolabe*, a manual on the scientific instrument written for his son Lewis. Although not included in the *Riverside*, the astronomical work known as *The Equatorie of Planets* is now not only accepted as Chaucer's, but the manuscript is thought to be in his own hand. Among other apocrypha, the most notable are fifteen French love poems signed "Ch" found in a manuscript now held at the University of Pennsylvania published by James I. Wimsatt, *Chaucer and the Poems of "Ch"* (Cambridge and Totowa, N.J., 1982).

All quotations are from *The Riverside Chaucer* (1998).

SELECTED BIBLIOGRAPHY

I. COLLECTED WORKS. *The Complete Poetry and Prose of Geoffrey Chaucer,* ed. by John H. Fisher (New York, 1977); *The Variorum Edition of the Works of Geoffrey Chaucer,* Paul G. Ruggiers, general ed. (Norman, Okla., 1979–); *The Riverside Chaucer,* 3d ed., ed. by Larry D. Benson (Oxford and Boston, 1988).

II. INDIVIDUAL EDITIONS. *The Parlement of Foulys,* ed. by D. S. Brewer (London, 1960); *The Canterbury Tales by Geoffrey Chaucer, Edited from the Hengwrt Manuscript,* ed. by B. A. Windeatt (London and New York,1984); *Chaucer's Dream Poetry,* ed. by Helen Phillips and Nick Havely (London and New York, 1997).

III. TRANSLATIONS. Nevill Coghill, trans., *The Canterbury Tales* (Harmondsworth, U.K., 1951, 1977); A. Kent Hieatt and Constance B. Hieatt, eds. and trans., *The Canterbury Tales* [dual text] (New York, 1964); Nevill Coghill, trans., *Troilus and Criseyde,* Harmondsworth, U.K., 1971); Brian Stone, ed. and trans., *Love Visions* [*The Book of the Duchess, The House of Fame, The Parliament of Birds, The Legend of Good Women*] (Harmondsworth, U.K., and New York, 1983); B. A. Windeatt, trans., *Troilus and Criseyde* (Oxford, 1998); David Wright, trans., *The Canterbury Tales* [verse] (Oxford, 1998).

IV. CONCORDANCES. Arthur G. Kennedy and John S. P. Tatlock, *A Concordance to the Complete Works of Geoffrey Chaucer and to* The Romaunt of the Rose (Gloucester, Mass., 1963); Larry D. Benson, *A Glossarial Concordance to* The Riverside Chaucer (New York and London, 1993).

V. LANGAUAGE. Ralph W. V. Elliot, *Chaucer's English* (London, 1974); Helge Kökeritz, *A Guide to Chaucer's Pronunciation* (Toronto and Buffalo, 1978); Norman Davis et al., *A Chaucer Glossary* (Oxford and New York, 1979); David Burnley, *A Guide to Chaucer's Language* (Norman, Okla., 1983); J. J. Smith, ed., *The English of Chaucer and His Contemporaries* (Aberdeen, 1988); Christopher Cannon, *The Making of Chaucer's English* (Cambridge and New York, 1998).

VI. SOURCES AND BACKGRUNDS. Charles Muscatine, *Chaucer and the French Tradition* (Berkeley, Calif., 1957); William Frank Bryan and G. Dempster, *Sources and Analogues of Chaucer's* Canterbury Tales (New York, 1958); Martin M. Crow and Clair C. Olson, *Chaucer Life Records* (Oxford and Austin, Tex., 1966); Larry D. Benson and Theodore M. Andersson, *The Literary Context of Chaucer's Fabliaux* (Indianapolis, 1971); Robert P. Miller, *Chaucer: Sources and Backgrounds* (Oxford and New York, 1977); R. K. Gordon, *The Story of Troilus* (Toronto, 1978); N. R. Havely, *Chaucer's Boccaccio* (Cambridge, 1980); B. A. Windeatt, *Chaucer's Dream Poetry: Sources and Analogues* (Cambridge, 1982); Piero Boitani, ed., *Chaucer and the Italian Trecento* (Cambridge and New York, 1983); David Lyle Jeffrey, ed., *Chaucer and Scriptural Tradition* (Ottawa,

1984); J. D. North, *Chaucer's Universe* (Oxford and New York, 1988); Karla Taylor, *Chaucer Reads* The Divine Comedy (Stanford, Calif., 1989); James I. Wimsatt, *Chaucer and His French Contemporaries* (London and Buffalo, 1991); Barbara A. Hanawalt, ed., *Chaucer's England* (Minneapolis, 1992); Derek Pearsall, *The Life of Geoffrey Chaucer* (Oxford, 1992); N. S. Thompson, *Chaucer, Boccaccio, and the Debate of Love* (Oxford and New York, 1996); Leonard Michael Koff and Brenda Dean Schildgen, eds., *The Decameron and the Canterbury Tale: New Essays on an Old Question* (London and Madison, Wis., 2000).

VII. GENERAL GUIDES. Richard J. Schoeck and Jerome Taylor, *Chaucer Criticism*, 2 vols. (Notre Dame, Ind., 1960); Muriel Bowden, *A Reader's Guide to Geoffrey Chaucer* (New York, 1964); Beryl Rowland, *A Companion to Chaucer Studies* (Oxford and New York, 1968); J. A. Burrow, ed., *Geoffrey Chaucer: A Critical Anthology* (Harmondsworth, U.K., and Baltimore, 1969); P. M. Kean, *Chaucer and the Making of English Poetry,* 2 vols. (London and Boston, 1972); Derek Brewer, *Writers and Their Background: Geoffrey Chaucer* (London, 1974; Woodbridge, Suffolk, U.K., and Rochester, N.Y., 1990); John Gardner, *The Poetry of Chaucer* (Carbondale, Ill., 1977); Derek Brewer, ed., *Chaucer: The Critical Heritage*, 2 vols. (London, 1978); S. S. Hussey, *Chaucer: An Introduction* (London, 1981); G. Kane, *Chaucer* (Oxford and New York, 1984); David Aers, *Chaucer* (Atlantic Highlands, N.J., 1986); Piero Boitani and Jill Mann, eds., *The Cambridge Chaucer Companion* (Cambridge, 1986); Jill Mann, *Geoffrey Chaucer* (London and Atlantic Highlands, N.J., 1991); Valerie Allen and Ares Axiotis, eds., *Chaucer* (London and New York, 1997).

VIII. CRITICAL STUDIES: THE DREAM POEMS. J. A. W. Bennett, The Parlement of Foules: *An Interpretation* (Oxford, 1957); Wolfgang Clemen, *Chaucer's early Poetry* (London, 1963); B. G. Koonce, *Chaucer and the Tradition of Fame* (Princeton, N.J., 1966); J. A. W. Bennett, *Chaucer's "Book of Fame"* (Oxford, 1968); James I. Wimsatt, *Chaucer and the French Love Poets* (Chapel Hill, N.C., 1968); Sheila Delaney, *Chaucer's House of Fame: The Poetics of Skeptical Fideism* (Chicago, 1972); James Winny, *Chaucer's Dream Poems* (London and New York, 1973); A. C. Spearing, *Medieval Dream-Poetry* (Cambridge and New York, 1976); Piero Boitani, *Chaucer and the Imaginary World of Fame* (Cambridge and Totowa, N.J., 1984); A. J. Minnis, *Oxford Guides to Chaucer:The Shorter Poems* (Oxford and New York, 1995).

IX. TROILUS AND CRISEYDE. S. B. Meech, *Design in Chaucer's* Troilus (Syracuse, N.Y., 1959); A. C. Spearing, *Chaucer:* Troilus and Criseyde, (London, 1976); Mary Salu, ed., *Essays on* Troilus and Criseyde (Cambridge and Totowa, N.J., 1980); D. J. Wallace, *Chaucer and the early Writings of Boccaccio* (Cambridge, 1985); Piero Boitani, ed., *The European Tragedy of* Troilus (Oxford and New York, 1989); C. David Benson, ed., *Critical Essays on Chaucer's* Troilus and Criseyde *and His Major early Poems* (Toronto and Buffalo, 1991); B. A. Windeatt, *Troilus and Criseyde* (Oxford, 1992).

X. THE CANTERBURY TALES. Janette Richardson, *Blameth Nat Me* (The Hague, 1970); Jill Mann, *Chaucer and Medieval Estates Satire* (Cambridge, 1973); Peter Elbow, *Oppositions in Chaucer* (Middletown, Conn., 1975); Alfred David, *The Strumpet Muse: Art and Morals in Chaucer's Poetry* (Bloomington, Ind., 1976); Donald R. Howard, *The Idea of* The Canterbury Tales (London and Berkeley, Calif., 1976); R. M. Lumiansky, *Of Sondry Folk: The Dramatic Principle in* The Canterbury Tales (Austin, Tex., 1980); Justin Boyce Allen and Theresa Anne Moritz, *A Distinction of Stories* (Columbus, Ohio, 1981); Judith Ferster, *Chaucer on Interpretation* (Cambridge and New York, 1985); Derek Pearsall, *The Canterbury Tales* (London and New York, 1985); Paul Strohm, *Social Chaucer* (London and Cambridge, Mass., 1989); Helen Cooper, *The Canterbury Tales* (Oxford, 1990); Peggy Knapp, *Chaucer and the Social Contest* (New York, 1990); Lee Patterson, *Chaucer and the Subject of History* (Madison, Wis., 1991); Elaine Tuttle Hansen, *Chaucer and the Fictions of Gender* (Oxford and Berkeley, Calif., 1992); Susan Crane, *Gender and Romance in Chaucer's* Canterbury Tales (Princeton, N.J., 1994); Helen Phillips, *An Introduction to* The Canterbury Tales: *Reading, Fiction, Context* (New York, 1999, and Basingstoke, 2000).

XI. PERIODICALS. *Chaucer Review,* 1966– ; *Studies in the Age of Chaucer,* 1979– .

XII. BIBLIOGRAPHIES. Dudley David Griffith, *Bibliography of Chaucer, 1908–1953* (Seattle, 1955); William R. Crawford, *Bibliography of Chaucer, 1954–63* (Seattle and London, 1967); Lorraine Y. Baird-Lange, *A Bibliography of Chaucer, 1964–1973* (Boston and London, 1977); *The Chaucer Bibliographies* (London and Buffalo, N.Y., 1983–); John Leyerle and Anne Quick, *Chaucer: A Bibliographical Introduction* (Toronto and Buffalo, 1986); Mark Allen and John H. Fisher, *The Essential Chaucer: An Annotated Bibliography of Major Modern Studies* (Boston, 1987); Lorraine Y. Baird-Lange and Hildegard Schnuttgen, *A Bibliography of Chaucer, 1974–1985* (Cambridge and Hamden, Conn., 1988).

SAMUEL TAYLOR COLERIDGE

(1772–1834)

David Wheatley

HE IS THE only person I ever knew who answered to the idea of genius. He is the only person from whom I ever learnt anything. . . . He talked on for ever; and you wished him to talk on for ever. His thoughts did not seem to come with labour and effort; but as if borne on the gusts of genius, and as if the wings of imagination lifted him from off his feet. . . . In his descriptions, you . . . saw the progress of human happiness and liberty in bright and never-ending succession, like the steps of Jacob's ladder, with airy shapes ascending and descending, and with the voice of God at the top of the ladder.

(William Hazlitt,
Lectures on the English Poets)

EARLY LIFE AND WORK

SAMUEL Taylor Coleridge is best known as the author of two great visionary poems, "Kubla Khan" and *The Rime of the Ancient Mariner.* As William Wordsworth's collaborator on *Lyrical Ballads,* he is one of the founding fathers of English Romanticism, but also one of its most elusive spirits: Coleridge was not just a poet, but a critic, playwright, political journalist, pamphleteer, lecturer, translator, prodigious letter-writer, keeper of notebooks, and conversationalist. Unlike Wordsworth, he left no epic comparable to *The Prelude,* and much of his oeuvre remained in uncollected, unpublished, or fragmentary form during his lifetime. This erratic dimension of his personality is suggestively conveyed in Charles Lamb's description of him as "an Arch Angel a little damaged." After the promising beginnings of *Lyrical Ballads,* Coleridge's reputation was quickly eclipsed by Wordsworth's and suffered numerous reverses and attacks, but by the time of his death his position as a cultural sage was unique and unchallengeable. The publication of editions of his letters and notebooks did much to secure his position in the twentieth century, and even today, as the monumental Bollingen Series edition of his *Collected Works* approaches completion, the scale and range of his work continues to surprise. The corpus of poems on which Coleridge's reputation as a major poet rests, however, is unusually small. In his essay "The Snake in the Oak" Ted Hughes restricts Coleridge's period of true creativity to less than a year, from the autumn of 1797 to early summer 1798, and to the three major poems "Kubla Khan," *The Rime of the Ancient Mariner,* and *Christabel.* To this list of frequently anthologized pieces can be added "This Lime-Tree Bower My Prison," "The Eolian Harp," "Frost at Midnight," "Dejection: An Ode," "The Pains of Sleep," and "Fears in Solitude," but despite the efforts of sympathetic modern editors much of Coleridge's later poetry is routinely neglected when not simply ignored.

Coleridge was born at Ottery St. Mary, Devonshire, on 21 October 1772, the youngest of ten children. His father was the local vicar and master of a grammar school. Coleridge was a temperamental and difficult child; after an incident in which he threatened his brother Frank with a kitchen knife, he ran away, spending the night on the banks of the Otter before being retrieved by a neighbor the following morning. Running away and depending on the kindly intervention of friends was a pattern he was to repeat time and time again in his adult life. After the death of his father in 1781 he was sent as a charity scholar to Christ's Hospital in London, where he befriended Charles Lamb and Leigh Hunt. The separation from Devonshire was keenly felt; he had been "from the spot where first I sprang to light / Too soon transplanted," as he wrote in a poem for his brother, "To the Rev. George Coleridge." From Christ's Hospital he went on to Jesus College, Cambridge, where he ran up debts, wrote a Greek prize poem on the slave trade, and read widely in philosophy and politics. Like his fellow undergraduates, Coleridge was greatly excited by events in France. He took the radical side in the great debate on the French Revolution initiated by Edmund Burke and Thomas Paine, and in 1793 abandoned Cambridge to enlist with the dragoons. After a farcical military career of four months, his brother George won a discharge for him on grounds of insanity.

Coleridge's radical phase was brief but eventful, and the cause of no small embarrassment to him in later life. Fired with idealism, in 1794 he hatched a scheme with Robert Southey for the founding of an egalitarian "Pantisocratic" community on the banks of the Susquehanna River in the United States. Southey was engaged at the time to Edith Fricker, and persuaded a reluctant Coleridge to propose to her sister Sara. The marriage was not a success, and would become the source of much domestic unhappiness to Coleridge in later years. Pantisocracy foundered, dissolving among mutual recriminations between Coleridge and Southey. Coleridge now threw himself into writing, producing his first major poem, "Monody on the Death of Thomas Chatterton," and beginning to gain a reputation in London. His work rate as a lecturer, pamphleteer, and journalist during this period was prodigious. He attacked Pitt's government and the war on France in *Conciones ad Populum: or Addresses to the People* in 1795, but even at this early stage expressed his opposition to the atheism and extremism of the French Jacobins.

The journalist and poet in Coleridge combined in a series of "Sonnets on Eminent Characters" that he contributed to the *Morning Chronicle* in 1795. His newspaper *The Watchman* appeared in ten numbers the following year, with Coleridge acting as fund-raiser in chief and sole contributor. Also published in 1796 was his *Poems on Various Subjects*. Coleridge was full of confidence, and making ambitious plans to open a private school. Throughout his life he suffered from a fatal proclivity to talk up his projects rather than get on with them (his notebooks are

littered with the titles of abandoned and stillborn works), and predictably the school came to nothing. A frequent alibi when his plans fell through was the state of his health, already frail and greatly weakened over the years by the opium addiction to which he was to fall prey by the end of the 1790s. Coleridge relied heavily on the moderating influence of his friends as a check on his excesses, and had a lifelong habit of installing himself, cuckoo-like, into the protective circles of their households. The need to feel cared for was paramount: as he wrote in "The Pains of Sleep," "To be beloved is all I need, / And when I love, I love indeed." His sociability can also be seen in the early "conversation" poems (a genre he was to make his own) in which he meditates on the pantheistic interconnectedness of man and nature:

> 'Tis the sublime of man,
> Our noontide majesty, to know ourselves
> Parts and proportions of one wondrous whole!
> ("Religious Musings," ll. 127–129)

> Henceforth I shall know
> That Nature ne'er deserts the wise and pure;
> No plot so narrow, be but Nature there,
> No waste so vacant, but may well employ
> Each faculty of sense, and keep the heart
> Awake to Love and Beauty!
> ("This Lime-Tree Bower My Prison," ll. 59–64)

> O! the one life within us and abroad,
> Which meets all motion and becomes its soul,
> A light in sound, a sound-like power in light,
> Rhythm in all thought, and joyance everywhere—
> ("The Eolian Harp," ll. 26–29)

Coleridge's celebrity was by now enough to attract a stream of visitors to the West Country where he had settled, among them the essayist William Hazlitt, one of the best eyewitnesses to the compelling effect of his personality. Hazlitt was spellbound by the older man's eloquence and intellect. In time, though, his infatuation would give way to intense hostility as the two men's political paths diverged and Hazlitt, like many other younger Romantics, came to see Coleridge (with Wordsworth and Southey) as a turncoat deserter of the radical cause. A good example of the political conflict between the young and old Coleridge can be seen in the 1798 poem "Fire, Famine and Slaughter." Subtitled "A War Eclogue," it dramatizes the climate of national paranoia during the war with revolutionary France. Parodying the three witches of *Macbeth,* Coleridge imagines Fire, Famine and Slaughter gloating over "a depopulated tract in La Vendée" where a group of royalist émigrés with English backing have been defeated by the French. To Famine's question, "Who sent you here?," Slaughter answers, "Letters four do form his name," with Coleridge wisely declining to spell out the name in question (the prime minister Pitt). Antitreason laws introduced by George III had already led to a state trial of the leaders of the radical London Corresponding Society, and Coleridge's profile as a critic of the government was high enough for him to be caricatured by Joseph Gillray as a braying ass of Jacobinism. Knowing this, he disguises his hostility to Pitt's government in allegorical fantasia. Reprinting it in 1817, when his Jacobinism was well behind him, he attached an "Apologetic preface" to the poem, not apologizing for his youthful politics exactly but, rather, explaining how its imaginative form meant the poem could not possibly have any practical (i.e., treasonable) implications. "Could it be supposed, though for a moment," he writes, "that the author seriously wished what he had thus wildly imagined, even the attempt to palliate an inhumanity so monstrous would be an insult to the hearers." But the author did not, and the crisis is averted. Where imagination for the young Coleridge had been the ideal vehicle for subversive political commentary, in later life it became a guarantee that politics and literature had nothing to do with each other. As though to underline the point, Coleridge told his son Derwent that the "Apologetic preface" was the single most successful piece of prose he ever wrote.

Coleridge's growing success now presented him with a difficult choice. The radical Unitarian John Prior Estlin was urging him to enter the ministry, and the publisher Joseph Cottle offering to publish his poetry. His choice was greatly simplified by the offer of an annuity of £150 from the pottery manufacturers Tom and Josiah Wedgwood. In "On my First Acquaintance with Poets,"

Hazlitt describes Coleridge deciding while putting on his shoe one morning to accept the offer and devote himself completely to writing. It also left him free to spend more time in the company of Wordsworth, whom he had met in 1795 and with whom he had forged a deep and intense friendship: Wordsworth brought his sister Dorothy to live near Coleridge in Somerset in 1797, and in 1798 collaborated with him on the landmark volume of Romantic poetry, *Lyrical Ballads.*

LYRICAL BALLADS *AND* THE RIME OF THE ANCIENT MARINER

FOR so momentous a book, *Lyrical Ballads* had an almost spur-of-the-moment genesis. In the spring of 1798 Coleridge was working on what would become *The Rime of the Ancient Mariner* when he had the idea of a book reflecting his and Wordsworth's different styles: poems of supernatural "incidents and agents" and poems reflecting "the loveliness and the wonders of the world before us," as Wordsworth described them in his prefatory "Advertisement." Standing first and last in the volume, the *Mariner* and Wordsworth's "Tintern Abbey" exemplified these two very different poles. Although conceived jointly, the book was far from evenly divided between its authors. A late burst of creativity by Wordsworth and the nondelivery of Coleridge's *Christabel* left Wordsworth with twenty-three poems to Coleridge's four, only one of which, the *Mariner,* was a ballad (the other three were "The Foster-Mother's Tale," "The Nightingale," and "The Dungeon"). *Lyrical Ballads* was thus as much about the differences between its two authors as what they had in common, differences that became more apparent in the second and third edition (published under Wordsworth's name alone), and which would play their part in the two men's later quarrels and estrangement.

The epoch-making effect of the *Lyrical Ballads* owes much to the prefaces Wordsworth wrote for the 1800 and 1802 editions, and the new role they claim for the artist. The rejection of eighteenth-century conventions meant the rejection of "poetic diction," with its stiff rhetoric and classical allusions. Henceforth the poet would be "a man speaking to men," with "a greater knowledge of human nature, and a more comprehensive soul, than are supposed to be common among mankind." For examples of this human nature, "low and rustic life was generally chosen" since it is in this environment that "men hourly communicate with the best objects from which the best of language is originally derived." This may be true of Wordsworth but scarcely applies to the *Mariner*. It is revealing that when he came to write about *Lyrical Ballads* in chapter seventeen of *Biographia Literaria,* Coleridge singled out this claim for attack. The *Mariner* portrays a "more comprehensive soul," but without any interest in "low and rustic life." Further, the first text of the *Mariner* abounds in poetic diction ("ne" for "nor," "withouten," "eldritch"), placing the poem notably at odds with the new plain style prescribed by Wordsworth. The fact that the poem attracted the ridicule of their friend Southey in the *Critical Review* ("absurd . . . unintelligible . . . a poem of little merit") stung both men, and convinced Wordsworth of the need to remove the archaisms in the second edition of 1800. The revised text is the most commonly read today, with the addition (in 1817) of the poem's epigraph from Thomas Burnet and marginal gloss.

In the *Mariner* Coleridge drew on and synthesized his wide knowledge of maritime journals and ballads to give the Romantic age its most strange and powerful image of the sea, an image made all the more memorable for Victorian readers by Gustave Doré's celebrated illustrations of 1875. The poem is in seven parts, and is framed by the Mariner's conversations with a Wedding Guest, whom he has stopped on his way to a feast and to whom he recounts his tale. The narration is thus presented as a strange and terrifying irruption of the gothic into the normal business of social intercourse, with the Wedding Guest acting as a dramatic foil to the Mariner. From the outset Coleridge's ballad quatrains stylize the poem's mixture of the colloquial and the arcane, the realist and the uncanny, the high serious and the jinglingly playful (even in 1798 it

must have been difficult to use the word "Eftsoons" with a straight face):

It is an ancient Mariner
And he stoppeth one of three.
—"By thy long gray beard and glittering eye,
Now wherefore stopp'st thou me?

The Bridegroom's doors are opened wide,
And I am next of kin;
The guests are met, the feast is set:
May'st hear the merry din."

He holds him with his skinny hand,
"There was a ship", quoth he.
"Hold off! unhand me, graybeard loon!"
Eftsoons his hand dropped he.

(ll. 1–12)

The Mariner begins his tale with a description of the ship's progress through a theater of the elements (the sun, the sky, the sea, the fog, "the storm-blast," "the dismal sheen"). The vessel is driven south of the equator by storms and is trapped in ice until an albatross appears and is haled by the crew as a bird of good omen. Mesmerized by the tale he is hearing, the Wedding Guest interrupts to ask: " 'God save thee, ancient Mariner! / From the fiends that plague thee thus!— / Why look'st thou so?' " The Mariner answers tersely: "With my crossbow / I shot the Albatross" (ll. 79–82).

All the subsequent action turns upon this gratuitous and inexplicable killing. The Mariner's shipmates recognize that a taboo has been broken, but their fear turns to relief when the fog begins to clear. Perhaps, they think, it was right to kill the bird after all, thus supplying the basis for their punishment in part 3, which would otherwise seem like an unwarranted side effect of the Mariner's. Another effect of the killing is to accelerate the descent into phantasmagoria, as the ship is driven back to the equator and the sailors begin to suffer hallucinations. Becalmed, the vessel is "idle as a painted ship / Upon a painted ocean" (ll. 117–118), as though the Mariner were a detached observer enjoying the spectacle of it all. One reason for his detachment may be the deprivation the crew is suffering:

Water, water, everywhere,
And all the boards did shrink;

Water, water, everywhere,
Nor any drop to drink.

The very deep did rot: O Christ!
That ever this should be!
Yea, slimy things did crawl with legs
Upon the slimy sea.

(ll. 119–126)

As a reminder of his guilt, his shipmates hang the albatross around the Mariner's neck. The Mariner's punishment now begins in earnest. The west is traditionally associated with death, and from the western horizon there comes a "spectre-bark" with a crew of Death and the female Life-in-Death, who play dice for the lives of the sailors. Life-in-Death claims the victory, but while this condemns the Mariner to fresh and ever more elaborate torments, his shipmates "drop down dead." The Mariner now finds himself in a state of existential solitude and dread, though when he looks at his dead ship-mates he finds them, in another peculiar display of detachment, not terrifying but "beautiful." His separation from the rest of nature is captured in the marginal gloss: "he despiseth the creatures of the deep," since, cut off from prayer and with his heart "as dry as dust" he no longer possesses any will to live. Yet part 4 ends with a moment of reprieve when he empathizes with the water snakes, blessing them "unaware." The spontaneity of the act is an index of its purity: that "self-same moment I could pray" (l. 288), and the albatross falls from his neck.

If there is a conflict in the *Mariner* between pagan and Christian worldviews, the prospect of the Mariner winning absolution so early on provokes a violent counter-reaction in the poem. The "upper air bursts into life" and amid stormy scenes the bodies of the crew are reanimated or "inspirited" and the ship moves on, not through their efforts but the promptings of the "lonesome Spirit" from the South Pole. Reaching the equator the Mariner hears two demons discussing his fate: he has done penance, one says, "and penance more will do" (l. 409). Why exactly is his punishment so disproportionate to his crime? Had he murdered a human being it would seem much more explicable; as it is, the albatross occupies a mere five stanzas of the poem. But as an act for which no apparent motivation exists, the killing of the albatross is all the more suited to Coleridge's purposes, acting as a reminder of the ineradicable stain of human evil and original sin. The Romantic hero who places himself, in the Nietzschean phrase, beyond good and evil is one of the great nineteenth-century themes. Precisely in its gratuitousness the slaughter of the albatross allows the Mariner to come into contact with powers beyond the experience of ordinary men. On this reading his crime is not unlike the *felix culpa* ("happy fault") of Christian theology: guilty though he may be, had he not killed the bird his knowledge of good and evil would have remained naive and primitive. Among the critics to propose a religious reading of the poem is William Empson, who sees in its drama of crime and punishment a veiled account of Coleridge's problems, as a former Unitarian, with the doctrine of the Trinity. Acceptance of this doctrine was a basic distinction between Anglicans (Church of England) and the nonconforming Protestants, who, like Catholics, were still discriminated against under British law. On this reading the thought of God the Father as consubstantial (sharing one substance) with Christ yet putting him to death for the sins of mankind is the agonized subtext for the *Mariner,* with Coleridge forcing himself to accept that out of this violent sacrifice some good must come. The temptation remains, however, to look for signs of Coleridge's theological doubt and confusion underneath the drive for Christian forgiveness and release. To Camille Paglia, for instance, the *Mariner* cannot be taken seriously as a narrative of Christian guilt. The Mariner, she argues, histrionically enjoys his predicament, luxuriates in "the operatic self-dramatization of the male heroine, a prima donna who triumphs through exquisite public suffering," and shows no concern for the suffering of his crew. This reading would appear dia-metrically opposed to Coleridge's religious framework, but in reality the poem and its hero will always evade our attempts to pin them down to a simplistic moral reading. Not the least part of the poem's genius is to make us forget just how little the Mariner does: the killing of the albatross is his single decisive action. The drama of the poem lies as much and more in the interpretation of actions than in the mere actions themselves.

Having been symbolically cast out, the Mariner is brought back into the fold in part 6 when he is confronted on the deck by the accusing but dead eyes of his comrades: "All fixed on me their stony eyes, / That in the Moon did glitter" (ll. 435–436). Although "the pang, the curse, with which they died, / Had never died away," suddenly "this spell was snapped" (ll. 437–438, 441), the wind rises, and the ship begins to move towards the Mariner's native country. Once again an advance cannot be made without some immediate reverse, and as the ship comes into the bay the spirits desert the sailors' bodies, leaving their "crimson" forms to fall dead on the deck, in a final example of the rich color symbolism in which the poem abounds. Seeing a pilot boat carrying the Old Hermit, the Mariner thinks redemption is finally within his grasp. Though the Hermit does indeed absolve him, his redemption is not so complete that he escapes one final punishment: he is doomed to wander forever, accosting strangers and telling his story over and over again. The Christian analogy here is with the Wandering Jew, cursed to wander the earth forever for laughing in Christ's face as he carried the cross. The pagan elements in the poem are displaced onto the act of storytelling, allowing the Mariner and his audience to relive the gothic excitement of his crime and punishment, but under the Christian sanction of his eventual (if incomplete) forgiveness. By refusing the Mariner absolute forgiveness, the poem achieves a form of this-worldly afterlife, falling short of the absolute values of Christianity but living on as a never-ending narration. Significantly, the wedding guest is so moved by the Mariner's tale that he abandons his plans to join the feast. He too has been infected with the Mariner's existential melancholy:

> and now the Wedding-Guest
> Turned from the bridegroom's door.
>
> He went like one that hath been stunned,
> And is of sense forlorn:

> A sadder and a wiser man,
> He rose the morrow morn.

(ll. 620–625)

"KUBLA KHAN"

ONE poem not included in *Lyrical Ballads* is "Kubla Khan." Despite its standing today as one of the great Romantic masterworks, Coleridge's attitude towards the poem was curiously dismissive. The story of its composition is almost as celebrated as the text itself. According to his introductory note of 1816, Coleridge describes how on a walk in the summer of 1797 the author "retired to a lonely farm house" in the Quantocks. Falling asleep from the effects of an "anodyne" (i.e., laudanum) he began to dream of the Mogul emperor Kubla Khan, inspired by the copy of *Purchas His Pilgrimage* he had been reading. In his dream he spontaneously composed no less than two or three hundred lines of poetry, which he began to transcribe with great excitement on awakening. At this point a "person on business from Porlock" called and detained him for "above an hour," by which time all but a "vague and dim recollection" of his vision had evaporated. This improbable story prompts an obvious question: Why did Coleridge allow himself to be distracted by entertaining the busybody "Person from Porlock" at all? In her poem "Thoughts about the Person from Porlock," Stevie Smith comes up with a theory of her own:

> Coleridge received the Person from Porlock
> And ever after called him a Curse,
> Then why did he hurry to let him in?—
> He could have hid in the house.
> [. . .]
> He was weeping and wailing: I am finished, finished,
> I shall never write another word of it;
> Then along comes the person from Porlock
> And takes the blame for it.

The Person from Porlock becomes the fall guy for Coleridge's loss of nerve. The author's addition to the poem has the effect, not of shoring it up but of undermining it. No longer allowed to stand as a finished and unified object, it is presented as a mere fragment and psychological curiosity. It is easy to understand, though, how

Coleridge might have felt intimidated by the vertiginous power of what he had written. The poem begins:

In Xanadu did Kubla Khan
A stately pleasure-dome decree:
Where Alph, the sacred river, ran
Through caverns measureless to man
Down to a sunless sea.
So twice five miles of fertile ground
With walls and towers were girdled round:
And there were gardens bright with sinuous rills
Where blossomed many an incense-bearing tree;
And here were forests ancient as the hills,
Enfolding sunny spots of greenery.

(ll. 1–11)

A figure of terrifying power, Kubla can enact his every whim with a dictatorial "decree." He relates to landscape by imposing himself on it: the poem opposes the controlling bulk of the pleasure-dome to the flux of the river, the one thing to escape Kubla's mastery. The dome can only throw its shadow across the moving water, whose underground currents erupt from the earth in the second stanza with unmistakably sexual force:

But oh! that deep romantic chasm which slanted
Down the green hill athwart a cedarn cover!
A savage place! as holy and enchanted
As e'er beneath a waning moon was haunted
By woman wailing for her demon-lover!
And from this chasm, with ceaseless turmoil seething,
As if this earth in fast thick pants were breathing,
A mighty fountain momently was forced:
Amid whose swift half-intermitted burst
Huge fragments vaulted like rebounding hail,
Or chaffy grain beneath the thresher's flail:
And mid these dancing rocks at once and ever
It flung up momently the sacred river.
Five miles meandering with a mazy motion
Through wood and dale the sacred river ran,
Then reached the caverns measureless to man,
And sank in tumult to a lifeless ocean:
And 'mid this tumult Kubla heard from far
Ancestral voices prophesying war!

(ll. 12–30)

Despite initial appearances, Xanadu is no Garden of Eden. The woman, if she is present at all, is "wailing for her demon-lover," while from outside the dome come bellicose noises, announcing that the idyll will be of short duration. Will the war see Kubla achieve reconciliation between the natural and the divine, the river and the dome? This is a synthesis Coleridge had already attempted in the Pantheistic musings of "The Eolian Harp," where he reproved himself for such "unhallowed thoughts." In the short third stanza Coleridge presents nature and culture as striking an impossible balance, with either the dome or the caves of ice bound to give way:

The shadow of the dome of pleasure
Floated midway on the waves;
Where was heard the mingled measure
From the fountain and the caves.
It was a miracle of rare device,
A sunny pleasure dome with caves of ice!

(ll. 31–36)

The clearest indication that the synthesis of nature and the divine cannot last comes with the introduction of the poet's voice in the fourth and final stanza, where the tone of the poem abruptly changes to disillusionment. The "ancestral voices prophesying war" suggested that somewhere in this fantastic landscape there would be a casualty of Kubla's tyrannical imagination. In fact the casualty would appear to be the poet himself. Kubla crushes the poet just as Cain kills Abel in the contemporaneous prose fragment *The Wanderings of Cain* (projected as a collaboration with Wordsworth) and just as, in a tempting reading, the all-powerful and intimidating Wordsworth was about to crush Coleridge. Moving into first-person visionary mode, the poem lapses into the past tense. The poet identifies with Kubla, but can only hope to emulate him by recapturing a vision that has been lost. The shaman-like powers attributed to the poet in the final lines are born out of knowledge of failure rather than Kubla Khan–like brutal omnipotence:

A damsel with a dulcimer
In a vision once I saw:
It was an Abyssinian maid,
And on her dulcimer she played,
Singing of Mount Abora.
Could I revive within me
Her symphony and song,

To such a deep delight 'twould win me,
That with music loud and long,
I would build that dome in air,
That sunny dome! those caves of ice!
And all who heard should see them there,
And all should cry, Beware! Beware!
His flashing eyes, his floating hair!
Weave a circle round him thrice,
And close your eyes with holy dread,
For he on honey dew hath fed,
And drunk the milk of Paradise.

(ll. 37–54)

Mount Abora was originally Mount Amara in the manuscript, a reference to book 4 of *Paradise Lost* where the name designates a false paradise, an exotic pleasure garden of Abyssinian kings. Coleridge aspires to the omnipotent imagination of Kubla Khan but fears that he will succeed only in building himself a false paradise. As imagination pursues such absolutes of power and knowledge, the terms success and failure become relative: courting the sublime, imagination necessarily threatens to overreach itself and plunge from visionary triumph into failure. The balance Coleridge seeks is as elusive as that of the coexisting "sunny dome" and the "caves of ice"; he imagines it inspiring something like sacred awe for the poet-shaman who could carry it off. Coleridge's nervousness about the poem was not without foundation: on publication it elicited less sacred awe than incomprehension and, in a devastating review by Thomas Moore, hoots of derision ("utterly destitute of value"). Its poor critical reception is a useful reminder of the retrospective nature of a concept like Romanticism, with what we now see as one of its central documents dismissed at the time as a freakish eccentricity. As perhaps the supreme visionary poem of the Romantic tradition, there is nothing stopping us from saying that "Kubla Khan" does in fact achieve the impossible balance of nature and culture that Coleridge projects. But psychologically it was necessary for him to think of the poem as a failure, a product of the dream world that Coleridge associated with his opium taking and all that it had cost him. The daylight world may have lacked the color and excitement of "Kubla Khan," but did not reduce him to the screams of terror he describes in "The Pains of Sleep" (1803) as he wakes from yet another "fiendish dream." Weighing his options in "Kubla Khan," he chooses expulsion from its paradise rather than staying on at the cost of embracing the poem's violent, pagan vision. Standing on the visionary threshold, something in Coleridge made him draw back.

CHRISTABEL *AND LATER POEMS*

To many critics Coleridge's overdependence on Wordsworth was greatly to the detriment of his own work. His support of Wordsworth's work on *The Prelude* was crucial (cf., his poem "To William Wordsworth"), but involved an abnegation of his own epic ambitions. Craving his friend's approval in return, he was profoundly disheartened by Wordsworth's rejection of *Christabel* for the 1800 edition of *Lyrical Ballads*. Like "Kubla Khan," the poem had to wait until 1816 before being published. Nor do the similarities end there: *Christabel* too is unfinished, comes with a prose preface, and turns on an encounter between the forces of paganism and Christianity. The poem is a medieval romance written in a distinctive meter (accentual rather than syllabic) that looks forward to Christina Rossetti's "Goblin Market" and the innovations of Gerard Manley Hopkins's "sprung rhythm":

'Tis the middle of the night by the castle clock,
And the owls have awakened the crowing cock;
Tu—whit!——Tu—whoo!
And hark, again! the crowing cock,
How drowsily it crew.

(ll. 1–5)

Christabel is praying at night for her betrothed in the wood outside her family castle when she encounters Geraldine, a "damsel bright / Dressed in a silken robe of white" (ll. 58–59). Geraldine claims to have been abducted from her home by five warriors and appeals to Christabel as the daughter of Sir Roland de Vaux, the estranged friend of Christabel's father, Sir Leoline. One of the taboos on Geraldine is that she cannot pass a threshold unaided, but must be invited (in fact, carried) into the castle, where her secret malignity makes the mastiff bark and the fire flare up as she passes. Despite her innocence Christabel has connived in her corruption, however unwittingly. As in Sheridan LeFanu's 1872 novella of female vampirism *Carmilla,* there is a strong lesbian undercurrent to *Christabel.* Unlike a male vampire figure such as Dracula, Geraldine can present herself as a figure of helpless innocence, enabling her to share Christabel's chamber without arousing suspicions and to work on her victim undisturbed. As she undresses she reveals her true demonic identity. Coleridge's description is coy, as if unable to confront the unspeakable evil that Geraldine represents:

Beneath the lamp the lady bowed,
And slowly rolled her eyes around;
Then drawing in her breath aloud
Like one that shuddered, she unbound
The cincture from beneath her breast:
Her silken robe, and inner vest,
Dropped to her feet, and full in view,
Behold! her bosom and half her side——
A sight to dream of, not to tell!
O shield her! shield sweet Christabel!

(ll. 246–254)

In the morning the Bard Bracy recounts a dream in which a "bright green snake" coils around a dove. Sir Leoline equates the dove with Geraldine and the snake with her attackers, and pledges to avenge her honor. Geraldine strikes Christabel down with a serpentine glance of evil. Christabel begs her father to send their guest away, but a spell has been cast on her and she cannot say why. Sir Leoline refuses to violate the laws of hospitality, Geraldine's victory is complete, and the poem breaks off. As a figure of predatory sexuality, Geraldine spells the doom of anyone who entrusts herself to her power. Without a conclusion, the poem does not fully solve the problem of how to show Christabel taking on such absolute evil or reclaiming her violated sexuality, since this would raise the question of how far her innocence should understand or participate in Geraldine's evil in order to oppose it. Coleridge emphasizes the horror of Christabel's vision of evil while still attempting to shield her eyes from it:

a vision fell
Upon the soul of Christabel,

The vision of fear, the touch and pain!
She shrunk and shuddered, and saw again—
(Ah, woe is me! Was it for thee,
Thou gentle maid! such sights to see?)

(ll. 451–456)

That her sexuality has been violated is left in little doubt ("O Geraldine! one hour was thine— / Thou'st had thy will!"), with some degree of acquiescence and even enjoyment on Christabel's part strongly hinted at too. Her attempt to communicate her suspicions of Geraldine in part 2 of the poem come to nothing more than the pleading but powerless gaze directed at Sir Leoline as Coleridge reduces her to a cipher of victimized Christian innocence.

For Ted Hughes, Geraldine's "rape of Christabel" is the "most powerful image" in the poem, the "germinal event, in Coleridge's poetic life" (*Winter Pollen*, p. 439), since what Geraldine is raping (he argues) is Coleridge's "Christian Self" in the name of unbridled and demonic paganism. But just as in "Kubla Khan," Coleridge stares across this threshold only to draw back in alarm.

It was not just his unfinished poems that caused Coleridge problems. In his earliest translations on his return from Germany in 1799 he began a lifelong habit of silently passing off other writers' work as his own, a habit that would develop into the wholesale thefts from Gotthold Ephraim Lessing, Friedrich von Schelling, and Immanuel Kant that went into the *Biographia Literaria.* A striking example occurs in "Hymn before Sun-rise, in the Vale of Chamouni." In writing about the Alps he was metaphorically treading in Wordsworth's footsteps again (the crossing of the Simplon Pass in book 6 of *The Prelude*). It was metaphorical treading in more than just this sense, however, since Coleridge had never been to Switzerland. His contemplation of the awesome heights of an Alpine peak spurs the poet to insert God into the otherwise dangerously empty and comfortless landscape:

Motionless torrents! Silent cataracts!
Who made you glorious as the Gates of Heaven
Beneath the keen full moon? Who bade the sun
Clothe you with rainbows? Who, with living flowers
Of loveliest blue, spread garlands at your feet?

God! let the torrents, like a shout of nations,
Answer! and let the ice-plains echo, God!

(ll. 53–59)

There is another answer to his questions, albeit more mundane than God: Friederika Brun, the unacknowledged author of the German poem on which "Hymn before Sun-rise" is based. Even the remarks on Alpine botany in his prose note are derived from Brun. Writing to his friend Robert Sotheby he explained the genesis of the poem and its original inspiration by a mere English hill, which, not thinking it grand enough, Coleridge decided to change to an Alp: "I transferred myself thither, in the Spirit, & adapted my former feelings to these grander external objects." The adaptation is of *his* feelings and the "external object" is the imagined Alp, rather than the poem by someone else that he is reworking. Although this is far from the worst case of Coleridge's plagiarism, the need for concealment, perhaps even self-concealment of the full scale of what he was doing, runs morbidly through the later work.

"Later" Coleridge begins remarkably early. If the distinctive theme of later Coleridge is a feeling of loss of power, "Frost at Midnight," composed in 1798, already looks forward to the heartbroken complaints of "Dejection: An Ode" four years later. Looking into the fire while his young son Hartley sleeps, Coleridge worries that his bond with nature is no more than the projection of an "idling" mind. The flickering of the fire in the grate:

Gives it dim sympathies with me who live,
Making it a companionable form,
Whose puny flaps and freaks the idling Spirit
By its own moods interprets, everywhere
Echo or mirror seeking of itself,
And makes a toy of thought.

(ll. 18–23)

The poem ends with an address to the infant Hartley: whatever his father's disappointments, he at least will experience "The lovely shapes and sounds intelligible / Of that eternal language, which thy God / Utters" (ll. 59–61) so that even the "silent icicles / Quietly shining to the quiet Moon" (ll. 73–74) are earnests of the future bounty of nature. The prophecy was sadly unfounded (Hartley's drunkenness and squandering of early promise were one of the great sorrows of his father's last years), but other early visions of Coleridge's were unraveling around him even as he wrote. 1798 was the year of "Fire, Famine, and Slaughter" but also of "France: An Ode" and "Fears in Solitude," in which he recants his hopes for the French revolution. His fears are cast in the language of Burkean conservatism. The state is an organic entity ultimately sanctioned by God and not to be tampered with by the unruly mob. One of the most celebrated passages in Burke's *Reflections on the Revolution in France* was the description of the mob storming the Palace of Versailles and attempting to tear off Marie Antoinette's nightdress, and Coleridge too invests the image of clothing and concealment with political significance. Social malcontents behave "As if a government had been a robe, / On which our vice and wretchedness were tagged / Like fancy-points and fringes, with the robe / pulled off at pleasure" (ll. 163–166).

Thoughts of revolution are tantamount to an unholy assault on the body of the state, whose naked form propriety dictates should remain concealed. Such political impiety can only be the work of "the owlet Atheism, / Sailing on obscene wings athwart the noon" (ll. 82–83) sufficient proof in itself of the breach in nature with which the state is threatened. The coalition between political and religious radicalism in the 1790s was always a precarious thing, as can be seen in the case of Coleridge's contemporary William Blake, who was passionately prodemocratic yet disgusted by the irreligiousness of the revolutionary idols Voltaire and Rousseau. For Coleridge, unlike Blake, the question of religious orthodoxy slowly came to overrule all other considerations. When Robert Emmet led his abortive rising in Ireland in 1803, Coleridge was aghast that an upper-class Protestant could range himself against the state and wrote hysterically to his friends Sir George and Lady Beaumount of how Emmet might have been saved had he only been deported to America. America, which only a few years before Coleridge had imagined as the site of a radical anticolonial venture, was now to be a dumping ground for traitors while they relearned how to be dutiful subjects of the crown. His attempts to bring his poetry into line with the need for orthodox reassurance can make for painful reading in the later work, though as we shall see the old qualities of skepticism and doubt are never far from the surface.

Given his composition habits and haphazard publishing history, a wide gap separated the full extent of Coleridge's writing from what the public got to see of it. Another example can be seen in "A Letter to ———, April 4, 1802," much better known in the revised form of "Dejection: An Ode." The unnamed addressee of "A Letter" was Sara Hutchinson, sister of Wordsworth's fiancée Mary, the subject of Coleridge's hopeless infatuation for many years and referred to in his work as Asra. "Dejection: An Ode" is a conversation poem, but one in which the great Romantic dialogue with nature is shown to be gravely endangered. The sympathy between inner and outer has broken down as "my genial spirits fail" (l. 39; "genial" in the special Romantic sense of the adjective of "genius"). Contemplating the clouds, stars, and moon, Coleridge observes: "I see them all so excellently fair, / I see, not feel, how beautiful they are!" (ll. 37–38). The crisis is comparable to that of Wordsworth's great "Ode: Intimations of Immortality," which the poem echoes at the beginning of section six ("There was a time . . ."). The poet feels a tragic loss of power, but where Wordsworth has an epiphanic rebirth of inspiration, Coleridge manages no such thing. Instead he ends the poem with a passionate address to the woman he identifies with Joy, the "spirit and the power, / Which wedding Nature to us gives in dower" (ll. 67–68). As in the *Mariner* though, the poet has been left out of the wedding celebrations. The expressions of love that might bridge the divide cannot be pronounced in public, as we see from a comparison of "A Letter" and "Dejection: An Ode." The final stanza of "A Letter" runs:

Sister & Friend of my devoutest Choice!
Though being innocent & full of love,
And nested with the Darlings of thy Love,
And feeling in thy Soul, Heart, Lips & Arms
Even what the conjugal & mother Dove

That borrows genial Warmth from those, she warms,
Feels in her thrill'd wings, blessedly outspread—
Thou free'd awhile from Cares & human Dread
By the Immenseness of the Good & Fair
Which thou see'st every where—
Thus, thus should'st thou rejoice!
To thee would all Things live from Pole to Pole,
Their Life the Eddying of thy living Soul.
O dear! O innocent! O full of Love!
A very Friend! A Sister of my Choice—
O dear, as Light & Impulse from above,
Thus may'st thou ever, evermore rejoice!

(ll. 323–339)

The contrast with "Dejection: An Ode" is revealing—or rather concealing. Gone are the first eleven lines with their breathless, quasi-pantheist apotheosis of Asra, as though Coleridge were excluding himself from their "nest" in Dove Cottage (and symbolically or not, the poem was published in the *Morning Post* on the day of Wordsworth and Mary Hutchinson's marriage and the seventh anniversary of Coleridge's marriage to Sara Fricker). The closing lines attempt to keep her at the arm's length of the third-person pronoun, before lapsing helplessly back into the vocative:

Joy lift her spirit, joy attune her voice;
To her may all things live, from pole to pole,
Their life the eddying of her living soul!
  O simple spirit, guided from above,
Dear Lady! friend devoutest of my choice,
Thus mayest thou ever, evermore rejoice.

(ll. 134–139)

"Dejection: An Ode" announces the close of a chapter in Coleridge's life, after which he would find fewer and fewer reasons for rejoicing in his poetry. But though the years to come were plagued by chronic financial, emotional, and creative instability, they were also to witness some of the most distinctive achievements of his career.

BIOGRAPHIA LITERARIA *AND LATER LIFE*

WHEN his health collapsed in 1804, Coleridge resolved to make a break with England. Leaving his family behind he sailed to Malta, where he served as undersecretary to the British High Commissioner. Although he returned two years later, the pattern of his life was changed forever. He was now estranged from his wife, and attempts to rekindle his intimacy with Asra were not a success. A serious breach with Wordsworth in 1810 further soured him, and after a final visit to the Lakes in 1812 he made his home entirely in the South. He continued his journalistic career with the *Courier,* became a popular if not always reliable lecturer, often speaking extempore, and had an unexpected success in Drury Lane in 1813 with his play *Remorse.* In London he was taken in first by John Morgan of Hammersmith and, from 1816, Dr. James Gillman of Highgate, who did much to stabilize, if not eradicate, Coleridge's opium addiction. These were years of sudden and unpredictable turns in his fortunes, but a planned new edition of his poems under the title *Sibylline Leaves* in 1815 provided the spur for a period of heroic productivity. The preface quickly expanded to book-length proportions as Coleridge developed his defense of the *Lyrical Ballads,* a discussion of his friendship with Wordsworth, an exposition of German Idealist philosophy, and theories of the imagination into a full-scale intellectual autobiography.

Biographia Literaria is one of the great curiosities of English prose, with its expansive asides (not unlike those of Coleridge's younger friend Thomas De Quincey), thickets of quotations, many in Latin and Greek, and synthesizing of styles and genres. Coleridge defends his magpie approach by refusing to countenance any separation of literature and philosophy: "No man was ever yet a great poet, without being at the same time a great philosopher." The book begins in conventional enough fashion with an account of the formation of his taste and indebtedness to William Bowles and other early influences, but resists the temptation to develop into a memoir proper; he had, after all, described biography in one of his notebooks as "a form of stupid superstition." Instead the second chapter considers the "Supposed Irritability of genius brought to the test of facts," before leading on to a chapter on Coleridge's treatment at the hands of critics. The literary journals of the day such as the *Edin-*

burgh Review and the *Quarterly Review* and the anonymous reviewers who wrote for them wielded remarkable power to make or break reputations, and Coleridge is scathing on the literary hacks of nineteenth-century Grub Street. Their intellectual claims to "the guardianship of the Muses," he writes, are "analogous to the physical qualifications which adapt their oriental brethren for the superintendence of the Harem," or as he put it in another witty analogy: "Thus it is said, that St Nepomuc was installed the guardian of bridges, because he had fallen over one, and sunk out of sight" (*Collected Works*, vol. 7, p. 59).

Although Coleridge had always been interested in philosophy, his stay in Germany in 1799 saw his interests shift from the materialism of Locke and Hartley to the idealism of Kant and Schelling. In line with the Kantian dialectic, Coleridge set out his system in terms of paired opposites such as understanding and reason, the first narrowly mechanical and the second more broadly comprehensive. A constant feature of Coleridge's thought is the drive towards unity and integration, ironically enough in a writer so given to wandering from topic to topic and expressing himself in fragments. For Coleridge, literature was by definition a holistic pursuit: "the poet," he writes, "described in *ideal* perfection, brings the whole soul of man into activity, with the subordination of its faculties to each other, according to their relative worth and dignity." As a literary artifact, the poem resists restatement in any other form but its own ("nothing can permanently please, which does not contain in itself the reason why it is so, and not otherwise"), a verdict he turns against the prosiness of eighteenth-century verse. Another paired opposition used to make this case is that of imagination and fancy. For the most part the style of *Biographia Literaria* is generously expansive, but when it came to these key terms Coleridge opted instead for the curtest of definitions, in what became one of the book's most celebrated (and argued over) paragraphs:

The IMAGINATION then I consider either as primary or secondary. The primary IMAGINATION I hold to be the living Power and prime Agent of all human Perception, and as a repetition in the finite mind of the eternal act of creation in the infinite I AM. The secondary I consider as an echo of the former, co-existing with the conscious will, yet still as identical with the primary in the *kind* of its agency, and differing only in *degree,* and in the *mode* of its operation. It dissolves, diffuses, dissipates, in order to re-create; or where this process is rendered impossible, yet still at all events it struggles to idealize and to unify. It is essentially *vital,* even as all objects (*as* objects) are essentially fixed and dead.

Fancy, on the contrary, has no other counters to play with, but fixities and definites. The Fancy is indeed no other than a mode of Memory emancipated from the order of time and space; and blended with, and modified by the empirical phenomenon of the will, which we express by the word CHOICE. But equally with the ordinary memory it must receive all its material ready made from the law of association.

(*Collected Works*, vol. 7, pp. 304–305)

As a poet of the imagination he names Milton, while fancy is represented by the Metaphysical poet Abraham Cowley. The imagination is "esemplastic," a neologism meaning "molding into unity." The Biblical resonance of the primary imagination's "I AM" suggests divine omnipotence, but if the secondary imagination is "identical" with the first in kind there is still a crucial falling short in the "degree" and "mode" of its workings. The poet figure of "Kubla Khan" could not command the autocratic "I AM" and had to make do with dissolution and dissipation instead, but here Coleridge makes these qualities integral to the imagination's workings. The theory could not be better suited to Coleridge's practice. Through the mediating power of imagination, the poet is able to participate in the mind of God whatever his failures and shortcomings. With the imagination able to span these extremes, fancy appears as something of an afterthought, or nod in the direction of the eighteenth century. Its "fixities and definites" exclude the instability and danger of higher literary form. One form this instability might take can be seen in the discussion of the symbol in chapter 9. If Coleridge was troubled as a young man by the concept of God incarnating himself in the figure of Christ, he is troubled now by the artist-philosopher's duty to bridge the gap between contingent and the absolute:

An IDEA, in the highest sense of that word, cannot be conveyed but by a symbol; and, except in geometry, all symbols of necessity involve an apparent contradiction. . . . Veracity does not consist in saying, but in the intention of communicating truth; and the philosopher who cannot utter the whole truth without conveying falsehood and at the same time, perhaps, exciting the most malignant passions, is constrained to express himself mythically or equivocally.

Exceeding the fixed meanings of the geometrical sign, the poetic symbol may articulate truth and falsehood simultaneously. The praise for the mere "intention of communicating the truth" is generous to a fault, but Coleridge had his reasons for pleading leniency. The Banquo's ghost at the feast of the philosophical chapters, returning with a vengeance, is the question of plagiarism. With typical insecurity Coleridge himself brings up the question, describing truth as a "divine ventriloquist" indifferent to who serves as its mouthpiece. Modern copyright lawyers might take a different line: James Engell and Walter Jackson Bate calculate that 13 percent of the exclusively philosophical sections are plagiarized.

One of the attractions of writing *Biographia Literaria* was the opportunity it afforded Coleridge to have his quarrel out with Wordsworth once and for all, in a chapter devoted to the "characteristic defects" of his poetry. He softens the blow, however, by finding most of the defects not in the poems themselves but in the theory of poetry outlined in the preface to *Lyrical Ballads.* He objects strongly to Wordsworth's use of the word "real" in the description of the poems as "a selection of the real language of men." Coleridge was not a believer in the Rousseauesque Noble Savage, and cannot accept that the language of "rustics" is any more authentic than that of Milton. The usual products of a rural upbringing are "selfish, sensual, gross, and hard-headed," their vocabulary chiefly concerned with "such objects as concern their food, shelter, or safety." In any case this is not how Wordsworth writes, since he usually interposes a more cultivated narrator between his peasants and the reader to ensure the tone never slips to such a "gross" and unsophisticated level. As the case of Milton reminds us, the isolated poetic genius will always be more truly representative than the literary demagogue, deriving his authority from the pure source of imagination rather than the needs and hopes of the tribe.

If *Biographia Literaria* overshadows the rest of Coleridge's prose, many important passages can be found scattered through the little-read works of his last decades. Still worrying about the question of evil in a lecture on Shakespeare's *Othello* he coins the brilliant phrase "the motive-hunting of motiveless malignity" (*Collected Works*, vol. 5, p. 315) to describe a soliloquy by Iago. His assessment of John Donne as a religious thinker in *Notes on English Divines* (1829) is also daringly acute: "he was an orthodox Christian only because he could have been an infidel *more* easily; and therefore willed to be a Christian." The description could easily be applied to the later Coleridge's own grip on orthodoxy, religious or otherwise. Unlike Southey and Wordsworth, Coleridge's conservatism could not be put down to prosperity or official acclaim (Southey became poet laureate in 1813, and was succeeded by Wordsworth on his death in 1843). In practice this meant Coleridge was more of a maverick than an upholder of the status quo, campaigning against Malthus, laissez-faire economics, and child labor, and for radical theories of education with a foresight that would be acknowledged later in the century by John Stuart Mill and Matthew Arnold. In *On the Constitution of Church and State* (1829) he draws a pioneering distinction between "civilisation" and "cultivation": the former is little more than a "corrupting influence" unless moderated by "the harmonious development of those qualities and faculties that characterise our humanity" (*Collected Works*, vol. 10, pp. 42–43). In a passage like this the distinctive modern sense of "culture" in terms of the arts, and in opposition to more philistine values, is beginning to emerge. The guardians of culture would be a class to be known as the "Clerisy" or National Church. As a defense of enlightened elitism, Coleridge's argument can be seen as a robustly Anglican contribu-

tion to the debate on Catholic emancipation, which had finally taken place the year before *On the Constitution of the Church and State,* in 1829. For Coleridge, the presence of the Church of England in every parish in the country offered a "germ of civilisation," and a version of the organic intellectual community that he saw it as his duty to foster.

Another late work, the *Statesman's Manual,* (1816) contains an essential supplement to the discussion of symbolism in *Biographia Literaria.* Once again Coleridge chooses holism over abstraction, in terms that would be hugely influential on modern and Modernist aesthetics:

> An allegory is but a translation of abstract notions into a picture-language, which is itself nothing but an abstraction from objects of the senses. . . . On the other hand a symbol . . . is characterized by the transcendence of the special in the individual, or of the general in the especial, or of the universal in general. Above all by the translucence of the eternal through and in the temporal. It always partakes of the reality which it renders intelligible; and while it enunciates the whole, abides itself as a living part in that unity, of which it is the representative.
>
> (*Collected Works*, vol. 6, p. 30)

His table talk too, as loyally transcribed by Crabb Robinson and other admirers, sparkles with moments of casual self-revelation. To J. P. Collier in 1811, a time when his reputation was at a nadir, he sadly announced, "for my part I freely own that I have no title to the name of poet." Of Shelley, who had been a visitor to the Lakes in 1812, he told J. H. Frere: "he went to Keswick in order to see me and unfortunately fell in with Southey instead." What united Goethe and Wordsworth, he told his nephew Henry Coleridge in another dig at the preface to *Lyrical Ballads,* is their "utter non-sympathy with the subjects of their poetry." Also to Henry Coleridge, he described Jonathan Swift as "the soul of Rabelais dwelling in a dry place," a witticism only slightly marred by the raininess of Swift's Dublin.

Coleridge's later poetry often dwelt on failure and negativity. His second child Berkeley had died in infancy, prompting the elegy "On an Infant which Died before Baptism," but in the quatrain "On an Insignificant," he imagines a creature whose only reality is in nonexistence:

No doleful faces here, no sighing—
Here rots a thing that *won* by dying:
'Tis Cypher lies beneath this crust—
Whom Death *created* into dust.

In "Human Life, on the Denial of Immortality" he strenuously proclaims the absurdity of life without a belief in immortality, but his willingness to entertain the theme at all shows his susceptibility to the "viper thoughts, that coil around my mind" (l. 94) as he called them in "Dejection: An Ode." Another image of tantalizing nonexistence occurs in "Limbo," the traditional fate reserved in the Catholic Church for the souls of unbaptized infants. A state of pure extinction, it threatens (or promises):

the mere horror of blank Naught-at-all,
Whose circumambience doth these ghosts enthral.
A lurid thought is growthless, dull Privation,
Yet this is but a Purgatory curse;
Hell knows a fear far worse,
A fear—a future state;—'tis positive Negation!
(ll. 33–38)

As Samuel Beckett would write of Dr. Johnson in a letter of 1937: "He must have had the vision of *positive* annihilation." One other late poem that ranks among his best is the powerful but despairing "Work Without Hope," written in 1827 and quoted in its entirety. The separation from nature announced in "Dejection: An Ode" has here become immutable:

All Nature seems at work. Slugs leave their lair—
The bees are stirring—birds are on the wing—
And Winter slumbering in the open air,
Wears on his smiling face a dream of Spring!
And I, the while, the sole unbusy thing,
Nor honey make, nor pair, nor build, nor sing.

Yet well I ken the banks where amaranths blow,
Have traced the fount whence streams of nectar flow.
Bloom, O ye amaranths! bloom for whom ye may,
For me ye bloom not! Glide, rich streams, away!
With lips unbrightened, wreathless brow, I stroll:
And would you learn the spells that drowse my soul?
Work without hope draws nectar in a sieve,
And hope without an object cannot live.

While these moments of inspiration are rare among the mass of late verse that has been quarried from his notebooks and letters (poems of the fancy rather than the imagination, to apply Coleridgean criteria), his reputation settled into something more closely befitting his achievements in the last years of his life. He was generously taken up by Byron, the anonymous friend of the preface to "Kubla Khan" who had persuaded him to publish the poem, though of Coleridge's metaphysics Byron observed in *Don Juan*: "I wish he would explain his explanation." His reputation for philosophical prolixity made him the butt of Thomas Love Peacock's affectionate satire in three novels, most memorably as Mr. Flosky in *Nightmare Abbey,* who replies to a female character's request that he speak plainly, "I never gave a plain answer to a question in my life." After the grotesque experience of Hazlitt attacking *The Statesman's Manual* in print before the book had even been published, he had the consolation several years later of a long, adulatory article in the *Quarterly Review* by J. G. Lockhart, the notorious critical assassin of Keats's *Endymion*. Most gratifying of all would have been Wordsworth's praise, who described Coleridge in "Extempore Effusion upon the Death of James Hogg" as "the rapt One, of the golden forehead, / The heaven-eyed creature"; but sadly it took Coleridge's death in 1832 to spur his friend to the tribute.

Without the central triad of "Kubla Khan," *The Rime of Ancient Mariner,* and *Christabel*, Coleridge would scarcely feature in most readers' assessment of the great Romantic figures. The one work he published that does bear comparison with *The Prelude, Don Juan,* or *Prometheus Unbound* for its epic scope, *Biographia Literaria,* is in prose, and prose of a kind guaranteed to remain the preserve of a dedicated few rather than a large popular readership. For the reader who does take the trouble to explore Coleridge's labyrinthine oeuvre, however, the rewards to be had are as diverse as they are inexhaustible. In *The Use of Poetry and the Use of Criticism,* T. S. Eliot described him as a writer briefly "visited by the Muse" and ever afterwards "haunted" by the experience, so that "the author of *Biographia Lit-*

eraria was already a ruined man." But as he shrewdly adds: "Sometimes, however, to be a 'ruined man' is itself a vocation" (*Selected Prose*, pp. 172–173). For contemporary readers, trying to catch up with this "ruined man" remains one of the defining pleasures of Romantic literature.

SELECTED BIBLIOGRAPHY

I. COLLECTED WORKS: FIRST EDITIONS OF COLLECTED WORKS. *The Poetical Works of S. T. Coleridge* (three vols., 1828); *The Poetical Works of S. T. Coleridge* (three vols., 1829); *The Poetical Works of S. T. Coleridge* (three vols., 1834); *The Poems of S. T. Coleridge,* ed. Mrs. H. N. [Sara] Coleridge (1844); *The Poems of Samuel Taylor Coleridge,* ed. Derwent and Sara Coleridge (1852); *Poetical Works,* ed. Richard Herne Shepherd (four vols., 1877–1880); *The Poetical Works of Samuel Taylor Coleridge,* ed. James Dykes Campbell (1893); *The Complete Poetical Works of Samuel Taylor Coleridge,* ed. Ernest Hartley Coleridge (two vols., 1912).

The standard modern edition of Coleridge's works is the *Collected Works,* published for the Bollingen Foundation by Princeton University Press under the general editorship of Kathleen Coburn, as follows: Vol. 1: *Lectures, 1795: On Politics and Religion* (1971); Vol. 2: *The Watchman* (1970); Vol. 3: *Essays on His Times in* The Morning Post *and* The Courier (three vols., 1978); Vol. 4: *The Friend* (1969); Vol. 5: *Lectures 1808–1819: On Literature* (two vols., 1987); Vol. 6: *Lay Sermons* (1972); Vol. 7: *Biographia Literaria* (two vols., 1983); Vol. 8: *Lectures 1818–1819: On the History of Philosophy* (2000); Vol. 9: *Aids to Reflection* (1993); Vol. 10: *On the Constitution of the Church and State* (1976); Vol. 11: *Shorter Works and Fragments* (two vols., 1995); Vol. 12: *Marginalia* (six vols., 1980–2001); Vol. 13: *Logic* (1981); Vol. 14: *Table Talk* (two vols., 1990); Vol. 16: *Poetical Works* (three vols.: *Reading Text, Variorum Text, Plays,* 2001). Vol. 15 remains unpublished. Also: *The Notebooks of Samuel Taylor Coleridge,* ed. Kathleen Coburn (Bollingen Foundation, 1957–1990) and *Collected Letters of Samuel Taylor Coleridge,* ed. earl Leslie Griggs (Oxford, six vols., 1956–1971).

II. MAJOR PUBLICATIONS DURING COLERIDGE'S LIFETIME: POETRY. *Poems on Various Subjects* (1796); *Poems by S. T. Coleridge. Second Edition. To Which Are Now Added Poems by Charles Lamb and Charles Lloyd* (1797); *Fears in Solitude* (1798); *Lyrical Ballads* (with Wordsworth, 1798, 1800, 1802, 1805); *Poems* (1803); *Christabel; Kubla Khan; A Vision; The Pains of Sleep* (1816); *Sibylline Leaves* (1817); *The Poetical Works of S. T. Coleridge* (three vols., 1828); *The Poetical Works of S. T. Coleridge* (three vols., 1829).

PROSE. *Conciones ad Populum. Or Addresses to the People* (1795); *The Plot Discovered* (1795); *The Statesman's Manual* (1816); *Biographia Literaria* (1817); *Aids to Reflection* (1825); *On the Constitution of Church and State* (1829).

DRAMA. *The Fall of Robespierre* (with Robert Southey, 1794); *Wallenstein* (translation of Schiller, 1800); *Remorse* (1813); *Zapolya* (1817).

PERIODICALS. *The Watchman* (ten numbers, 1796); *The Friend* (twenty-seven numbers, 1809, collected in three vols., 1818).

III. BIOGRAPHIES AND BIOGRAPHICAL SKETCHES. William Hazlitt, "On My First Acquaintance with Poets" (1823); William Hazlitt, "Mr Coleridge," in *The Spirit of the Age* (1825); Thomas De Quincey, "Samuel Taylor Coleridge" (1835); Thomas De Quincey, "Southey, Wordsworth, and Coleridge" (1839); E. K. Chambers, *Samuel Taylor Coleridge* (Oxford, 1938); Walter Jackson Bate, *Coleridge* (Toronto, 1968); John Cornwell, *Coleridge: Poet and Revolutionary* (London, 1973); Richard Holmes, *Coleridge: early Visions* (London, 1989); Rosemary Ashton, *The Life of Samuel Taylor Coleridge: A Critical Biography* (Oxford, 1996); Richard Holmes, *Coleridge: Darker Reflections* (London, 1998).

IV. CRITICAL STUDIES. J. L. Lowes, *The Road to Xanadu: A Study in the Ways of the Imagination* (London, 1927); I. A. Richards, *Coleridge on Imagination* (London, 1934); Humphry House, *Coleridge* (London, 1953); John Beer, *Coleridge the Visionary* (London, 1959); John Colmer, *Coleridge: Critic of Society* (Oxford, 1959); William Empson, "The Ancient Mariner," in *Critical Quarterly* 6, no. 4 (1964); J. A. Appleyard, *Coleridge's Philosophy of Language: The Development of a Concept of Poetry 1791–1819* (Cambridge, Mass., 1965); Marshall Suther, *Visions of Xanadu* (New York, 1965); Geoffrey Yarlott, *Coleridge and the Abyssinian Maid* (London, 1967); J. R. de J. Jackson, ed. *Coleridge: The Critical Heritage* (London, 1969); Thomas McFarland, *Coleridge and the Pantheist Tradition* (Oxford, 1969); A. S. Byatt, *Unruly Times: Wordsworth and Coleridge in Their Time* (London, 1970); Stephen Prickett, *Coleridge and Wordsworth: The Poetry of Growth* (Cambridge, 1970); Norman Fruman, *Coleridge the Damaged Archangel* (New York, 1971); John Beer, *Coleridge's Poetic Intelligence* (London, 1977); Kelvin Everest, *Coleridge's Secret Ministry* (New York, 1979); Edward Kessler, *Coleridge's Metaphors of Being* (Princeton, 1979); Jerome Christensen, *Coleridge and the Blessed Machine of Language* (Ithaca, 1981); Trevor H. Lever, *Poetry Realized in Nature: Samuel Taylor Coleridge and early Nineteenth-Century Science* (Cambridge, 1981); James C. McKusick, *Coleridge's Philosophy of Language* (New Haven, 1986); Ian Wylie, *Young Coleridge and the Philosophers of Nature* (Oxford, 1989); Camille Paglia, "The Daemon as Lesbian Vampire: Coleridge," in *Sexual Personae* (New Haven, 1990); Ted Hughes, "The Snake in the Oak," in *Winter Pollen: Occasional Prose* (London, 1994); Mary Anne Perkins, *Coleridge's Philosophy* (Oxford, 1994); Morton D. Paley, *Coleridge's Later Poetry* (Oxford, 1996); Edoardo Zuccato, *Coleridge in Italy* (Cork, 1996); Seamus Perry, *Samuel Taylor Coleridge and the Uses of Division* (Oxford, 1999).

V. ARCHIVE MATERIAL. The principal collections of Coleridge manuscripts are held in the British Library, the Royal Institution, the Highgate Institution (all London), the Bodleian Library, Oxford, and Dove Cottage, Grasmere.

VI. FURTHER READING: ROMANTICISM. M. H. Abrams, *The Mirror and the Lamp: Romantic Theory and the Critical Tradition* (Oxford, 1953); Northrop Frye, *A Study of English Romanticism* (New York, 1968); Alethea Hayter, *Opium and the Romantic Imagination* (London, 1968); Marilyn Butler, *Romantics, Rebels, and Reactionaries* (Oxford, 1981); Jerome J. McGann, *The Romantic Ideology: A Critical Investi-*

gation (Chicago, 1983); Stuart Curran, *Poetic Form and British Romanticism* (Oxford, 1986); Morris Eaves and Michael Fischer, eds., *Romanticism and Contemporary Criticism* (Ithaca, 1986); Morton D. Paley, *The Apocalyptic Sublime* (New Haven, 1986); Stuart Curran, *The Cambridge Companion to British Romanticism* (Cambridge, 1993); Maurice Cranston, *The Romantic Movement* (Oxford, 1994).

POLITICAL AND HISTORICAL BACKGROUND. Raymond Wil liams, *Culture and Society 1780–1950* (London, 1958); E. J. Hobsbawm, *The Age of Revolution 1789–1848* (London, 1962); Betty T. Bennett, *British War Poetry and the Age of Romanticism: 1793–1815* (New York, 1976); Marilyn Butler, ed., *Burke, Paine, Godwin, and the Revolution Controversy* (Cambridge, 1984); H. T. Dickinson, *British Radicalism and the French Revolution 1789–1815* (Oxford, 1985); John Barrell, *Imagining the King's Death* (Oxford, 2000).

JOSEPH CONRAD

(1857–1924)

Thomas Gavin

THE SPY AND HIS SECRETS

WITH A NOVELIST'S eye for the gesture that reveals character, Joseph Conrad opens his evasive memoir, *A Personal Record* (1908), on a scene that both conceals and reveals. He introduces a mariner in his berth on "a ship frozen fast in a river" (p. 3). The mariner—Conrad himself, we soon discover—is not sleeping but writing. The third officer enters, rubbing the cold out of his hands, and asks casually what he is "always scribbling there" (p. 4). Conrad notes: "It was a fair enough question, but I did not answer him, and simply turned the pad over with a movement of instinctive secrecy" (p. 4). He goes on to confess that he had "given [him]self up to the idleness of a haunted man who looks for nothing but words wherein to capture his visions" (p. 8)—then quickly assures us that his writing was "the companion of my imagination without, I hope, impairing my ability to deal with the realities of sea life" (p. 9). The "scribbling" will become his first novel, *Almayer's Folly* (1895). This fact gives the moment its ironic point, but the movement to turn over the pad and slip it under his pillow is the revealing gesture.

Conrad brought to the English novel the temperament of a spy operating in alien territory. With a spy's instinct for secrecy he edited the facts of his life. The first generation of his biographers believed that at twenty he had been involved in a love triangle and wounded in a duel; later evidence indicates that he lost his money gambling and shot himself in the chest. A Polish exile, he took on English citizenship as if it were a disguise, living, so far as his means allowed, the life of a country gentleman. His professed devotion, he says in "A Familiar preface" to *A Personal Record,* was to "the idea of Fidelity" (p. xix)—to duty, solidarity with shipmates and compatriots, honorable conduct. Charlie Marlow, the persona he adopted to narrate some of his most effective stories, is a solid, beef-and-ale Englishman. Narrating the life of a disgraced outcast in *Lord Jim,* Marlow speaks of Jim in words that might be the benediction Conrad secretly wished for himself: "He is one of us" (p. 253). But the spy's compulsion, ultimately, is to betray himself, and beneath the disguise we make out shadowy hints of another Conrad: again and again he explores the psychology of characters hiding a shameful past, seeking redemption after conscience-scalding betrayals. He is, after all, not only Marlow but Marlow's dangerous doubles—Jim, Razumov, who betrays his friend, even (in some tortured backwater of the imagination) the abominable Kurtz. The novelist writing about imaginary people, he says (without offering particulars), "is only writing about himself" ("Familiar preface," p. xiii)—a tantalizing hint that he drew on something in his own experience to create his compelling gallery of outcasts, revolutionaries, and betrayers. Conrad's biographers find traces of that experience in his youthful flight from Poland.

Even the name we know Conrad by is a mask. He was born Jósef Teodor Konrad Korzeniowski on 3 December 1857, the only child of Apollo and Ewa Korzeniowski, fervently patriotic members of the Polish landed gentry in Russian-occupied Ukraine. Arrested for conspiracy against the czarist rule, they were exiled to Vologda, where Conrad's mother developed the tuberculosis that would kill her, as it would kill his father four years later. Orphaned at eleven, Conrad was taken in by a devoted if sometimes impatient uncle, Tadeusz Bobrowski, whose common sense contributed to Marlow's devotion to duty. As a youth, however, Conrad was more drawn to his father's self-destructive romanticism, which he expressed paradoxically, rejecting its content while remaining true to its spirit.

At fifteen he abandoned the cause for which his parents had suffered, leaving Poland for the adventurous life of a seaman. With his uncle's assistance he apprenticed himself in the French merchant marine at Marseilles. True in his fashion to his parents' revolutionary sympathies, he soon found himself smuggling guns for the Carlist revolution in Spain. Barely twenty-one years old, under the influence of two older men, he invested money his uncle had provided for his living expenses in a shipload of illegal arms. Forced to scuttle the ship to avoid capture (a tactic that would later take fictional form in *Nostromo*), Conrad and his partners spent days hiding in a cellar. For Conrad the writer this was priceless experience, but Conrad the man paid for it dearly. To recoup his loss (more than 3,000 francs) he borrowed a further 800 francs from a friend, invested it in a bout of casino gambling at Monte Carlo, and lost it all. He invited his friend to tea but apparently decided no apology would suffice. Before the friend arrived Conrad put a bullet through his chest, fortunately missing his heart. In response to a telegram that must have cost the arrogant youth his last illusion of independence ("*Conrad blessé envoyez argent—arrivez*"), Bobrowski journeyed to Marseilles, cleared Conrad's debts, and helped him make a new start in the English merchant marine.

For all his recklessness, the young Conrad was not stupid. Having attempted to end his life, he reflected on the habits of mind that brought him to the abyss. The result was a lifelong critique of the romantic ethos that had destroyed his parents and nearly destroyed him.

He served the next decade as a merchant service officer, rising through the ranks to his first command in 1888–1889. Again desperate for money, in 1890 he indulged a last seizure of romanticism, signing on as commander of a paddle-wheel steamer journeying up the Congo River in the service of a Belgian trading organization. His health broken by fever, dysentery, and gout, his spirit appalled by the horrors of colonial exploitation, he made the return journey and resigned, but continued for another four years his struggle for a seaman's life. He resigned his last commission in 1894. With the publication the following year of *Almayer's Folly* and his marriage in 1896 to Jessie George, he left behind the sea as he had left behind Poland, and began the uncertain life of a writer.

For the next three decades he drew on his years of reckless adventure to create novels that brought a new technical sophistication to the form. He developed a style of rendering action subjectively that paralleled the aesthetic aims of the Impressionist movement in painting, continued the experiments of Henry James with a limited point of view, and freed the novel from the tyranny of chronological time. With *The Secret Agent* and *Under Western Eyes* he virtually invented the novel of political intrigue later adopted by two of the twentieth century's most popular artists, Graham Greene and John Le Carré. In his themes he was equally influential. His characters struggle for integrity in a world of moral anarchy; "Heart of Darkness," his most perfectly wrought short novel, has provided a touchstone for interpretations of twentieth-century history ranging from T. S. Eliot's 1922 poem *The Waste Land* to Francis Ford Coppola's 1979 film *Apocalypse Now* and Robert Stone's 1974 novel *Dog Soldiers*.

ALMAYER'S FOLLY (1895) AND AN OUTCAST OF THE ISLANDS (1896)

CONRAD'S first novel, *Almayer's Folly*, explores the power of greed to corrupt human connections. Almayer, a clerk in the trading firm of Hudig & Co., becomes the protégé of Lingard, an English pirate and trader, who puts him in charge of a trading post in the Malay archipelago, promising a share in his schemes for wealth. As part of his agreement Almayer marries a Malay woman whom Lingard adopted in her childhood after killing her family in a raid on a privateer. Almayer enters the marriage with the cold-blooded hope that his wife "may mercifully die" (p. 17). Nevertheless, the daughter born of this union, Nina, becomes the one person he loves.

Despite Almayer's love for Nina, Lingard's promise of wealth still holds him in thrall. When

Lingard decides to have the child educated in Europe, Almayer permits the separation over his wife's objection. By the time Nina returns, the estrangement between Almayer and his wife is so thorough that he fears she will poison his food. Lingard leaves for Europe to raise money, and in his absence Almayer plans with a native trader, Dain Maroola, to recoup his fortune by selling gunpowder to the Malays for a rebellion against the Dutch (another echo of Conrad's Carlist gunrunning episode). The Dutch destroy Dain's ship and pursue him to Almayer's campong, where Dain pauses only long enough to carry away Nina, who has fallen in love with him. Almayer, seeing the ruin of his dream to return to Europe a wealthy man with Nina a princess at his side, lets her go with a twofold curse: "I will never forgive you, Nina; and tomorrow I shall forget you!" (p. 153). He erases her departing footprints from the sand and burns the house where they have lived. Till his death he haunts the decaying passages of a rooming house built when he imagined the English would make his backwater a major trading stop—a building the Dutch seamen call "Almayer's Folly" (p. 36).

In *An Outcast of the Islands,* Willems, like Almayer, begins as a clerk at Hudig & Co. He too marries to advance his career; in Willems's case the patron is Hudig himself, who bestows on Willems a favored position, even the house he lives in, where he lords it over his wife and her poor relations. Only when Willems is fired for embezzling does he learn that the wife Hudig urged him to marry is Hudig's illegitimate daughter. After a night wandering the streets, Willems is rescued by Lingard, who brings him to Sambir—to Almayer's trading post, in fact. There Willems abandons himself to a fatal passion for Aissa, the Malay daughter of Omar, a blind old pirate. When Omar's crafty lieutenant Babalatchi sees that Willems has enslaved himself to Aissa, he separates them until Willems agrees to betray Lingard's secret trading route up the river.

Just as Almayer cuts himself off from humanity by refusing to forgive Nina, Willems too isolates himself, betraying first his trusted position at Hudig's, then his fidelity to Lingard. His erotic bondage to Aissa further erodes his standing in the white community without gaining him a place in hers; he experiences "the horror of bewildered life where he could understand nothing and nobody round him; where he could guide, control, comprehend nothing and no one—not even himself" (p. 118). Lingard's revenge is to abandon Willems among the Malays, then send his wife and child to join him. When Aissa sees them, she snatches up Willems's revolver, his last vestige of power, and shoots him.

THE NIGGER OF THE "NARCISSUS" *(1897)*

WITH his third novel, *The Nigger of the "Narcissus,"* Conrad discovered in the disciplined work of sailors at sea an ethic to contain the self-destructive passions that destroyed Almayer and Willems. Like them, James Wait, the "nigger" of the title, and his foil, Donkin, isolate themselves willfully from the community. Their choice takes on even greater moral significance: by refusing to work when the rest of the crew are battling a storm, they jeopardize not only their own lives but the safety of the ship.

Both the operative words of the book's title require consideration. It is ironic that Conrad, of all writers in his generation, should need defending against the charge of racism. Although he is by no means free of the prejudice of his times, again and again he draws characters from the seamen with whom he had worked side by side, men of all nations and races. He imagines their lives with a sense of equality far more like the ideal of a pluralistic society than what we find in the writings of white Europeans for whom blacks and Asians are simply invisible. When Belfast, the crewman who will care more for Wait's comfort than any other, tells the first mate that he put his oilskins and jacket "over that half-dead nayggur," Wait responds: "You wouldn't call me nigger if I wasn't half dead, you Irish beggar!" (p. 364). The vigorous comeback Conrad gives Wait challenges the insulting word with a force that a racist untroubled by conscience would not permit. More than once, however, we see the word "nigger" in the reflections of a narrator speaking for Conrad himself. But the full range of the language describing Wait reveals an artist struggling against prejudice to achieve a truthful representation of character. Consider our first view of Wait: "a head powerful and misshapen and a tormented and flattened face . . . the tragic, the mysterious, the repulsive mask of a nigger's soul" (p. 307). It is the mask that Conrad finds repulsive, not the soul—and he is well aware that the mask has been forged in the torment of a proud man insulted and humiliated, who will achieve in the final unmasking of his soul a tragic dignity. Finally, any simple notion of Conrad as a racist must be confounded by the question why he chose to make Wait a black man. Wait's race signifies not his moral defects (which he shares with Donkin, a white man), but his isolation—a condition Conrad as a foreigner in England knew intimately. For Conrad to make Wait his hero was an act of profound identification.

"Narcissus," the second significant word of Conrad's title, was the name of a sailing ship on which he served in 1884. The name, however, also links the crew of Conrad's fictional ship with the mythic Narcissus, so rapt in love with his own reflection in a pool of water that he fell in and drowned. The crew members project onto James Wait a self-pitying love for their own comfort that lures them into relaxing their vigilance during the storm and brings the ship to the verge of mutiny.

From the moment he comes aboard Wait is both awesome and disruptive. Mr. Baker, the first mate, has already mustered the crew and dismissed them when "a deep, ringing voice" calls "Wait!" and all eyes turn to a man so tall that even when he strides into the lamplight, "his head [is] away up in the shadows" (p. 305). Mr. Baker bridles at the imperious command, and the man, who is "calm, cool, towering, superb" explains that his name is Wait and he "belongs to the ship" (p. 306).

This initial disruption foreshadows others far more threatening to the ship's discipline. Once at sea Wait, who has "a cough metallic, hollow, and tremendously loud" (p. 307), complains that the crew jabbering near his door interrupts his sleep. "Much you care for a dying man!" he says, and the crew, suspecting a sham, "hesitate[s] between pity and mistrust" (p. 323). Pity wins out with Belfast, who steals from the galley a pie meant for the officers and gives it to Wait. The officers interpret the theft as a declaration of the crew's hostility and "mutual confidence is shaken" (p. 326). This climate of suspicion delights Donkin, "the man that cannot steer, that cannot splice, that dodges the work on dark nights . . . [and] curses the sea while others work" (p. 299). He begins prodding the crew's resentment into rebellion. When the starboard watch nearly refuses to mop out their forecastle because "Jimmy object[s] to a wet floor," Baker tells the captain that Wait is "disturbing the peace of the ship" (p. 333), and the captain has him moved to a deckhouse made over as a sick bay.

A gale threatens to capsize the ship; battling it, the men and officers partially restore mutual trust until someone remembers Wait, trapped in the deckhouse of the dangerously listing ship. A party of five risk their lives to rescue him. Now Wait's importance to the crew becomes even greater. "Had we . . . undergone similar toil and trouble for an empty cask, that cask would have become as precious to us as Jimmy was" (p. 357).

The storm over and the ship once more on its way, Wait realizes that his sham sickness is real; to deny his now urgent fear of dying, he insists on returning to work. Captain Allistoun, however, refuses to permit Wait to end the isolation he once sought, ordering that he is "not to be allowed on deck to the end of the passage" (p. 402). His decision sparks the crew to outrage: " 'We've got something to say habout that,' screeche[s] Donkin from the rear. 'Never mind, Jim—we will see you righted,' cr[y] several together." The resentment culminates when Donkin, inciting the crew to overpower their officers, hurls an iron belaying pin that narrowly misses the captain. In the excitement the helmsman abandons the wheel, letting the ship drift into the wind till the sails flap against the masts. "It was as if an invisible hand had given the ship an angry shake to recall the men that peopled her decks to the sense of reality, vigilance, and duty" (p. 406).

What motivates the crew members to coddle Wait even as they resent him is a narcissistic identification of their own fear of death with his. "We understood the subtlety of his fear, sympathized with all his repulsions, shrinkings, evasions, delusions—as though we had been . . . without any knowledge of the meaning of life" (p. 420). They are, despite the warning of Singleton, the ship's wise old man, victims of the "sentimental lie" (p. 346) that Jimmy (and they) will live forever. Even Donkin, callously plotting to steal Wait's belongings as soon as he breathes his last, is not immune: "watching the end of that hateful nigger, [he] felt the anguishing grasp of a great sorrow on his heart at the thought that he himself, some day, would have to go through it all—just like this—perhaps!" (p. 434). Wait's grip on the crew is not completely broken even by his death. With the *Narcissus* becalmed off the coast of Flores, Wait's corpse is wrapped in sailcloth and laid on planks. At the end of the service the plank ends are raised to slide the corpse into the sea, but one last time Wait compels the crew to wait. The sailcloth catches on a snag, and only when Belfast shrieks, "Jimmy, be a man. . . . Go Jimmy! Jimmy, go! Go!" does the corpse "whiz off the lifted planks" (p. 441) into the sea. With that release a breeze stirs the sails and the *Narcissus* is at last free to complete her journey.

CONRAD'S ARTISTIC CREDO AND "YOUTH" (1898)

FOR *The Nigger of the "Narcissus,"* Conrad wrote a preface that defines art as "a single-minded attempt to render the highest kind of justice to the visible universe, by bringing to light the truth, manifold and one, underlying its every aspect" (p. 705). Scientist and philosopher seek the truth in the realm of facts and ideas; the artist "descends within himself, and in that lonely region of stress and strife. . . he finds the terms of his appeal" (p. 706). Because the artist's appeal is to "temperament" rather than reason, it "must be an impression conveyed through the senses," crafted to "reach the secret spring of responsive emotions" (p. 707) in the reader. If the artist seeking the truth of the visible universe descends within himself, then truth for Conrad must be not an objective reality but a relationship between the universe and a perceptive observer. Like the Impressionist painters of his time, Conrad recognized that the observer's point of view will transform the "truth" the artist records, and point of view is influenced strongly by time. A seascape appears different at noon and midnight; the "responsive emotions" it evokes in lovers on the shore are far different from those it evokes in sailors fearful of running aground.

Conrad's sense of the artist's relation to truth is central to "Youth," his first tale employing Marlow as narrator. Marlow is a middle-aged seaman looking back on his first voyage as second mate, which is also the first command of the captain, a man of sixty. The ship suffers devastating reversals; finally a smoldering fire in the hold explodes. Conrad renders the explosion through the minutely recorded perceptions of Marlow, who hears a "dull concussion" and finds himself flying through the air before he realizes that "We are being blown up" (p. 134). (This gap between perception and understanding, characteristic of many passages of subjectively rendered experience in Conrad's work, is described by Ian Watt in *Conrad in the Nineteenth Century* as "delayed decoding" [pp. 175–179].) Marlow then retells the scene as experienced by the captain, who sees "only a great hole in the floor" and "notice[s] directly the wheel deserted and his bark off her course" (p. 136). The ship must be abandoned—a delight to the young Marlow, who views the whole experience as an adventure. Telling the story as a mature man, however, Marlow understands what the youth could barely register—that his adventure was, for the captain, an old man losing his ship on his first voyage in command, a tragedy. This ironic counterpointing, shaped by the observer and by his distance in time from the events he relates, is the essence of Conrad's literary impressionism.

"HEART OF DARKNESS" (1899)

WHEN he made his trip up the Congo River as first mate of the *Roi des Belges*, Conrad was thirty years old, no longer the youth who had trusted his security to a spin of the wheel at

Monte Carlo and put a bullet through his chest to redeem his honor. His folly had taught him that a helmsman who abandons the wheel will soon experience the vigorous shake that either kills him or restores him—as it did the crew of the *Narcissus*—to reality. For Conrad reality was found in work, in his "devotion to. . .an obscure, back-breaking business" (p. 50), and "Heart of Darkness" embodies his conviction that devotion to duty is a bulwark against moral anarchy. Conrad's theme embraces not only personal depravity but the depravity threatening a civilization that allows slave labor and greed to corrupt its relation to honest work.

The tale begins with a group of friends on the deck of a cruising yawl anchored in the mouth of the Thames. The men are identified by their work—Director of Companies, Lawyer, Accountant, the anonymous writer-narrator, and Marlow, "the only man of us who still followed the sea" (p. 9). Marlow tells how, six years ago, he ended a spell of "loafing about, hindering you fellows in your work" (p. 11) by seeking a job as captain of a steamboat trading on the Congo.

Throughout his journey Marlow confronts examples of work perverted and made absurd by sloth, greed, and incompetence. On a jungle trail to the Company's Outer Station he finds "a boiler wallowing in the grass," a railway truck "with its wheels in the air," and "pieces of decaying machinery" (p. 19). His first contact with slavery implicates him in its evil: six black men linked by a chain pass him on the path, and their black guard gives Marlow "a large, white, rascally grin" that seems "to take [him] into partnership in [the guard's] exalted trust" (p. 19). In a grove where Marlow goes to rest he discovers mineworkers, slaves reduced to "black shadows of disease and starvation" (p. 20) and cast aside to die.

Once at the Central Station, Marlow finds that the steamer he is to command has sunk; his first task is "fishing [his] command out of the river" and repairing it, a job he can't accomplish without rivets—plentiful downriver but here unavailable. He meets a brickmaker idled for more than a year because he "could not make bricks without something, I don't know what—straw maybe" (p. 27). The Manager and other white men of the Central Station stroll aimlessly about, plotting, gossiping enviously about Kurtz, the mysterious head of the Inner Station, who seems to combine idealistic notions of civilizing the natives with an extraordinary ability to amass ivory. "A taint of imbecile rapacity blew through it all like a whiff from some corpse" (p. 26), Marlow says.

His only way to keep his "hold on the redeeming facts of life" (p. 26) is to turn his back on the station and go to work raising his boat from the river bottom. "I don't like work," he says, "no man does—but I like what is in the work—the chance to find yourself. Your own reality—for yourself—not for others—what no other man can ever know" (p. 31).

A virtue that parallels devotion to work in Marlow's hierarchy of values is restraint. Once the steamboat is repaired and the journey upriver to the Inner Station begins, Marlow observes that the crew are cannibals, starving because their only provision is a supply of hippo meat that has gone rotten. With no taboo against eating human flesh, what prevents them, Marlow wonders, from killing and eating the Europeans? "What possible restraint? Was it superstition, disgust, patience, fear—or some kind of primitive honour?" (p. 43). Marlow's helmsman is a black man who "steered with no end of a swagger while you were by, but if he lost sight of you he became instantly the prey of an abject funk" (p. 45). When the ship comes under attack by natives on shore, the helmsman abandons the wheel, opens the pilot-house shutter to fire a blunderbuss, and is fatally stabbed by a spear. Marlow's comment is: "Poor fool! If only he had left that shutter alone. He had no restraint, no restraint—just like Kurtz—a tree swayed by the wind" (p. 51).

At the Inner Station Marlow learns the full extent of Kurtz's lack of restraint. There he meets Kurtz's disciple, a Russian trader, in clothes so patched he looks like a harlequin, who tells him in awed admiration that the natives worship Kurtz with "unspeakable rites" (p. 50), that when his supply of trading goods dried up, Kurtz enlisted the natives to raid the countryside for ivory, that he even took the Russian's ivory at gunpoint "because there was nothing on earth to prevent him killing whom he jolly well pleased" (p. 56). The posts of the decayed fence around Kurtz's compound are decorated with shrunken human heads. The heads, Marlow observes, had nothing to do with Kurtz's remarkable energy in collecting ivory. "They only showed that Mr. Kurtz lacked restraint in the gratification of his various lusts, that there was something wanting in him" (p. 57). Marlow concludes that despite what he has learned of Kurtz's ideals—his plan to bring Western civilization to the jungle—Kurtz is "hollow at the core" (p. 58), a quality he shares with the Manager, who comments that despite the immense quantity of ivory Kurtz has collected, he has harmed the Company because his "method is unsound" (p. 61).

Marlow turns with disgust from the Manager to Kurtz, whose rapacity is at least (or at last) stripped of hypocrisy. Though wasted with fever, Kurtz, enthralled by "the memory of gratified and monstrous passions" (p. 65), has no desire to return to civilization. It was he, in fact, who ordered the attack on the steamer. When he is forcibly taken on board, the natives, led by Kurtz's "barbarous and superb" black mistress, gather on the shore, their deep murmurs "like the responses of some satanic litany" (p. 66). On the journey downriver, Kurtz dies, his last words a "judgement upon the adventures of his soul on this earth" (p. 69): "The horror! The horror!" (p. 68). Marlow understands Kurtz's final cry—his ability to discern a moral judgment where the Manager would see only unsound methods—as "an affirmation, a moral victory paid for by innumerable defeats, by abominable terrors, by abominable satisfactions" (p. 70). Back in Europe, Marlow visits Kurtz's "Intended" (p. 71), his white fiancée, whose portrait Kurtz once painted as a blindfolded woman raising a torch, surrounded by darkness; like the aunt who arranged for Marlow's appointment to the Company, she believes the Company is operated less for profit than as a kind of missionary enterprise to civilize the natives. She embodies the idealism that disguises the brutality of colonial exploitation. When she asks Marlow to repeat Kurtz's dying words, he tells a lie that encodes a secret truth: he says the last word Kurtz pronounced was her name.

LORD JIM (1900)

In *Lord Jim,* Conrad continues to explore the hazards of romantic idealism as a guide to ethical integrity. With a virtuoso mastery of narrative strategies, he shifts from ironic distance to subjective intensity, orchestrates the voices of several narrators, and juxtaposes scenes to counterpoint aspects of the story occurring over years.

Conrad introduces Jim as a dreamer whose "vocation" as a seaman "declare[s] itself" "after a course of light holiday literature" (p. 4). He develops no love for the exacting daily work of the sea, preferring to imagine himself "saving people from sinking ships, cutting away masts in a hurricane . . . always . . . as unflinching as a hero in a book" (p. 5). While still young he becomes "chief mate of a fine ship, without ever having been tested by those events of the sea that show in the light of day the inner worth of a man" (p. 7). Lamed by a falling spar, he is left to convalesce in an Eastern port and, upon recovery, takes a berth as chief mate of the *Patna,* a rusted old steamer. The ship is ferrying a human cargo of eight hundred "pilgrims" (p. 9) referred to by the German captain as "dese cattle" (p. 10). One calm night Jim is on the bridge with the captain, two Malay crewmen at the helm. They are joined by the second engineer, drunk, who complains about how unsafe the ship is, "her plates like brown paper" (p. 16). A sudden lurch of the ship staggers the men. Stunned, they hear under the hull a noise like thunder, and the ship quivers.

The next chapter—shifting to Jim's point of view—begins abruptly with his response to a question at an official inquiry in the police court of an Eastern port. "She went over whatever it was," he says, "as easy as a snake crawling over a stick" (p. 17). The magistrate and two nautical assessors want only facts, while Jim is trying to "bring out the true horror behind the appalling face of things" (p. 19). He is cut off by a direct question—a question undisclosed to the reader—and answers with "a curt 'Yes, I did' " (p. 20).

As he looks around the crowded room, his eyes meet the eyes of a white man sitting apart, someone who seems "aware of his hopeless difficulty" (p. 21).

With this, the narration shifts from Jim's anguished consciousness to the relaxed monologue of Marlow, the man Jim spotted in the crowd. From here on we learn of Jim's character and fate not as events happen but as they reveal themselves to Marlow and as he, telling the story over cigars after dinner, reveals them to his companions, including an anonymous narrator. Sometimes digressing, sometimes alluding to facts familiar to his auditors but mysterious to the reader, Marlow draws the reader along in the wake of his compelling voice—a voice that gives Conrad freedom to order revelations in a progression of dramatic effects.

For several days, Marlow says, rumors had told of a "mysterious cable message" concerning the *Patna,* which contained a fact "about as ugly and naked as a fact can be" (p. 22). Marlow was on the steps outside the harbor office as the German captain, still clad in his green-and-orange striped sleeping suit, came "pelting upstairs" with three other white men to report "in the innocence of his heart" (p. 23) that they were the sole survivors of a collision with a submerged derelict or reef that sank the *Patna.* When Marlow reveals some pages later that days before their arrival the *Patna* with its pilgrims had been found adrift by a French gunboat and towed to port, the reader's shock mimics that of the hapless captain and his officers. The captain flees, both engineers are hospitalized, and Jim alone remains to face the court of inquiry and admit that—believing the *Patna* was about to sink—he jumped from its deck to join the other ship's officers in a lifeboat, leaving the pilgrims to drown.

Marlow, at the urging of Big Brierly, one of the experienced captains sitting in judgment on Jim, offers Jim money and suggests that he avoid further shame by running away. Jim responds with his sole remaining claim to honor: "I may have jumped, but I don't run away" (p. 94).

Shortly after the inquiry Brierly—apparently haunted by a fear that in Jim's position he would have succumbed to the same temptation—hangs his gold chronometer watch by its chain from the rail of his ship and jumps overboard. Marlow's conversations with Jim give him a similar uncomfortable sense of kinship. Jim is—on the surface—a clean-cut Englishman, someone Marlow recognizes as "one of us" (p. 27). "I would have trusted the deck to that youngster on the strength of a single glance," he says, "and by Jove!—it wouldn't have been safe. There are depths of horror in that thought" (p. 28).

This horror, echoing the last words of Kurtz in "Heart of Darkness," partially explains Marlow's fascination with Jim—why he seeks Jim out and listens to his story with sympathy and revulsion. He is trying to understand the potential for such betrayal in himself:

> The commonest sort of fortitude prevents us from becoming criminals in the legal sense; it is from weakness unknown, but perhaps suspected, as in some parts of the world you suspect a deadly snake in every bush—from weakness that may lie hidden . . . repressed or maybe ignored more than half a lifetime, not one of us is safe.
>
> (p. 27)

One source of Jim's weakness, as Marlow sees it, is his imagination. Jim tells Marlow that after the collision he went below with a lantern to inspect the bulkhead: he felt it bulge under his hand and saw a flake of rust fall off the plate. "He imagined what would happen perfectly" (p. 53), Marlow says. "His confounded imagination had evoked for him all the horrors of panic, the trampling rush, the pitiful screams, boats swamped—all the appalling incidents of a disaster at sea. . . ." (p. 54). Conrad contrasts Jim's susceptible imagination with that of the two Malay helmsmen who stayed on the bridge as their white officers frantically lowered a boat to escape. One says he "thought nothing," the other that he had received no order, so "why should he leave the helm?" (p. 60). Their bland heroism echoes the matter-of-fact courage of the French lieutenant who stayed aboard the *Patna* for thirty hours while it was being towed, knowing at any minute the ship might sink and complaining only that he was given no wine with his meals.

Disgraced and deprived of his seaman's certificate, Jim works as a ship chandler's water clerk—a man who meets arriving ships and steers their captains toward his employer's firm. Whenever someone recognizes him as the *Patna's* mate, he quits his job and drifts further east.

Still trying to understand Jim's case, Marlow consults his friend Stein, a wealthy trader. Stein recognizes in Jim's dream of heroism the same imagination that betrayed him into cowardice. He cannot escape it, only use it:

> A man that is born falls into a dream like a man who falls into the sea. If he tries to climb out into the air . . . he drowns. . . . The way is to the destructive element submit yourself, and with the exertions of your hands and feet in the water make the deep, deep sea keep you up.
>
> (p. 130)

The youth's egoistic dream of heroism can become, in a mature man, a life of service to others. Stein gives Jim an opportunity to redeem his honor by making Jim manager of a trading station in a remote area of Dutch East Borneo. In Patusan, Jim—acting at last like the adventure-story hero he always longed to be—leads a battle against a warlord terrorizing the native Bugis and becomes their protector, called *Taun,* or Lord. He finds a devoted love in Jewel, the stepdaughter of Cornelius, whom he replaced as Stein's representative, and a faithful friend in Dain Waris, son of the local ruler, Doramin.

All goes well until Gentleman Brown, a pirate leading a band of desperate whites, takes his schooner's longboat up the river to pillage Patusan. With Jim away in the interior, Dain Waris directs the Bugis defense, driving Brown and his men into a narrow creek. They entrench themselves on a knoll and prepare to be attacked. Despite his success, however, Dain Waris has not Jim's "reputation of invincible, supernatural power" (p. 220), and the Bugis await Jim's return. When he comes, Jim faces Brown on the other side of the creek to find out who he is. Brown works on Jim's sympathy, making "a sickening suggestion of common guilt, of secret knowledge that was like a bond of their minds and of their hearts" (p. 235). Contrary to the will of Doramin, who wants to attack the pirates, Jim grants Brown

and his men safe passage downriver. Brown, with the aid of Cornelius, betrays him, attacking the Bugis downriver and killing Dain Waris. Jim has pledged his own life for their safety; he will not run again. Despite his promise to Jewel that he will never leave her, he presents himself "at the call of his exalted egoism" (p. 253) to Doramin, who kills him with a single shot. Jim thus "turns away from a living woman to celebrate his pitiless wedding with a shadowy ideal of conduct," and Marlow, reflecting on the egoism, betrayal, and heroism marking Jim's last act, says again that "He is one of us."

NOSTROMO *(1904)*

Nostromo is Conrad's most thorough exploration of a question that haunts both "Heart of Darkness" and *Lord Jim*: What values make a person's sense of self incorruptible? While Jim must restore a reputation dishonored by a moment of cowardice, Nostromo must live with a reputation for being incorruptible in a corrupt world. The fatal weakness of both men is that their sense of self depends less on love for the work that defines them than on the opinion of others.

Conrad dramatizes the volatility of opinion by opening the book with Captain Mitchell discussing Nostromo's reputation. Mitchell is superintendent of the steamship line transporting silver from the province of Sulaco in the South American republic of Costaguana. He tells a visitor of the country's frequent revolutions, of the recent dictator Ribiera, who "had come pelting eighty miles over mountain tracks after the lost battle of Socorro" (p. 18) and was caught by a mob when his mule collapsed under him. Ribiera was rescued by Nostromo, a "fellow in a thousand" (p. 19), the foreman of Mitchell's dock stevedores, who organized stevedores and railroad workers to repulse the mob threatening the railroad and the customhouse.

The next scene, however, questions Mitchell's view of Nostromo. Giorgio Viola, the venerable exile from Garibaldi's army of liberation, is barricaded in his railroad hotel with a shotgun, prepared to defend his family against a mob of revolutionaries. His wife Teresa, huddled with their daughters, Linda and Giselle, mutters that Nostromo has deserted them. She calls him a traitor, saying he "thinks of nobody but himself" (p. 25) and would rather "run at the heels of his English" than protect the family that has adopted him as a son. The reader, who has heard Mitchell say that Nostromo is "absolutely above reproach" (p. 19), finds it easy to dismiss Teresa's words as hysteria. Her judgment is further undercut when Nostromo rides up on his silver horse, chasing off the mob. In fact her accusations will prove literally true. Nostromo, an Italian like Viola, is Mitchell's man, and as such he serves the interests of Charles Gould, the owner of the San Tomé silver mine, whom everyone considers English.

Conrad follows this forceful opening with a tangled history of the corrupt interdependence of wealth and power in Sulaco. The efforts of Charles and Emilia Gould to restore the defunct mine provide a meandering thread through a maze of detail. Gould, inheriting the mine from his father, comes to Sulaco determined not merely to make his fortune but to end the poverty that has spawned Costaguana's long series of bloody revolutions. His wife, Emilia, is carried along by the force of Gould's idealism. With the backing of Holroyd, an American financier, Gould parcels out the necessary bribes to officials and reopens the mine. He then throws the support of Holroyd's money behind the idealistic politician Ribiera, hoping he will end government corruption. Within eighteen months, however, Ribiera is challenged by a counter-revolution claiming to represent the people against European and American financial interests—against Gould himself. Ribiera's defeat at the hands of General Montero and his brother Pedro precipitates the fat old dictator's ignominious flight on muleback.

Once Conrad has circled back to this present crisis of Costaguana's history, we soon discover that Mitchell has told only the most public facts of Nostromo's career. Nostromo's secret history, rendered in a series of tense dramatic encounters, justifies the view of many critics that *Nostromo* is among Conrad's greatest works.

As a transport ship filled with Monterist rebels steams toward the harbor of Sulaco under the command of Colonel Sotillo, Nostromo is confronted by Decoud, a journalist supporting Gould. Decoud pleads for Nostromo's help in removing from the customhouse six months' worth of the mine's silver before Sotillo can capture it. Nostromo is reluctant: the plan is risky; failure would compromise his reputation as an invincible champion. He agrees at last, because a Montero victory would subject Gould and his allies to arrest and execution. Nostromo, who has so publicly "run at the heels of his English," would be denied the strutting promenades through the streets of Sulaco that feed his vanity. In isolation from the crowd, he realizes, the sense of self his reputation confers on him is worthless.

Decoud accompanies Nostromo on the lighter in which the silver is to slip past Sotillo out of the harbor. In fog and darkness the lighter collides with Sotillo's transport, but Nostromo and Decoud evade Sotillo and beach the crippled lighter on the Great Isabel, an island in the gulf. They hide the silver, and Nostromo, promising to rescue Decoud, leaves in the lighter. Resenting the risk he has taken for Decoud and beginning to recognize the fragility of a sense of self founded on reputation, Nostromo is already plotting a betrayal. If he reaches Sulaco with an empty lighter, he knows that, whether it is Ribiera or Montero who controls the city, he must tell the location of the silver. He scuttles the lighter a mile out at sea and swims to shore, making his way to the customhouse that Sotillo has already occupied and abandoned.

There he meets Dr. Monygham, and they discover the corpse of Hirsh, a cowardly hide merchant whom Sotillo had tortured, thinking he knew the location of the silver. Monygham once more persuades Nostromo to serve the English: he must make the perilous trip to Cayta to bring back the army of General Barrios, who will drive Montero's forces from Sulaco.

Returning by sea with Barrios' army, Nostromo spots the lighter's rowboat adrift in the gulf, realizes that Decoud has perished, and decides that the silver shall be his recompense for all the years he served the English and took his pay only in praise. He resolves to "grow rich very slowly" (p. 440), stealing off to the island to lift a few bars of silver at a time. When a lighthouse is built on the Great Isabel, he arranges for old Viola to be its keeper; his friendship with the family will give him an excuse to visit the island.

Nostromo's famous ride to Cayta saved Sulaco and rescued his reputation, but the man prized for incorruptibility now knows himself a thief. He can no longer identify his sense of self with his reputation. He grows sullen, avoiding the crowds where once he loved to preen.

For Viola, too, vanity ends in isolation. As a member of Garibaldi's army he had fought for liberty. Though his honor is incorruptible, his pride in his heroic past has sealed him off from the community. When Italian workers on the railroad salute, he barely acknowledges their tribute. He has made a god of his honor, identifying it even with the virtue of his daughters. Believing that one of Giselle's unworthy suitors swims to the island for secret meetings with her, he indulges "a touch of senile vanity" (p. 478) rather than seek Nostromo's assistance. "He wanted to show that he was equal yet to the task of guarding alone the honour of his house" (p. 478).

At this point Viola's vanity and Nostromo's greed conspire to create an isolating silence that destroys the hopes of both. Viola has long assumed that Nostromo will marry his daughter Linda; when Nostromo tries to tell him he has fallen in love with her sister Giselle, a "sudden dread came upon the fearless and incorruptible Nostromo. He dared not utter the name in his mind. . . . He was afraid of being forbidden the island" (pp. 463–464)—a fear that he will lose not Giselle but the silver. Nostromo permits Viola to believe it is Linda he loves, and Viola waits in ambush for Giselle's suitor. When next Nostromo swims to the island for silver, Viola shoots by mistake the man he hoped would be his daughter's husband. Fatally wounded, Nostromo confesses his theft to Emilia Gould, abandoning reputation in a last effort to achieve integrity. The novel's other major characters endure a similar testing. In the crucible of isolation, whatever illusions sustain in them a false sense of self are burned away. Each must confront his or her es-

sential nature—and its strength or weakness either keeps them alive or works their destruction.

Decoud isolates himself through pride of intellect. In the boulevards of Paris he learned to affect the cynical views of an "exotic dandy" (p. 205). He believes he loves Antonia Avellanos, but has "no faith in anything except the truth of his own sensations" (p. 205). When she "venture[s] to treat slightingly his pose of disabused wisdom" (p. 142), he courts her approval by editing the *Porvenir,* the Ribiera party's newspaper. With Monterists threatening Sulaco, however, his political opinions endanger his life. To save himself—as well as Antonia and her father—he conceives his plan to spirit away the silver before Sotillo arrives. Joining Nostromo on the lighter will prove to Antonia that he is a man of action. His isolation on the island strips him of his easy cynicism; even his passion for Antonia—tainted by egoism—decays into despair. "On the tenth day. . .the solitude appeared like a great void, and the silence of the gulf like a tense, thin cord to which he hung suspended. . .without any sort of emotion whatever" (p. 436). He weights his pockets with bars of silver, rows into the bay, shoots himself, and rolls overboard, leaving the Placid Gulf "untroubled by the fall of his body" (p. 438).

The paradoxical idealism of Charles Gould's devotion to "material interests" is his downfall. Silver, the incorruptible metal, corrupts the man who pins to it "his faith in the triumph of order and justice" (p. 455). The triumph of Gould's material interests brings not stability but plans for a war to annex Costaguana to Sulaco (pp. 445–447). "There is no peace and no rest," comments Dr. Monygham, "in the development of material interests. . . . [T]heir law and their justice. . .is founded on expediency and is inhuman. . .without rectitude" (p. 447). Emilia sees the mine "possessing, consuming, burning up the life of the last of the Costaguana Goulds" (p. 456).

In an earlier revolution Monygham struggled for liberty as Viola did, but under torture he betrayed his friends. He suffers the isolation of shame. He lives in disgrace, crippled and indigent, until Emilia Gould makes him physician to the miners. For love of Emilia he plans to use his reputation as a traitor in a clever deception that will lure Sotillo's army away from Sulaco: He will go to the customhouse and let Sotillo capture him; threatened with torture a second time, he can believably pretend to betray the Goulds, telling Sotillo the silver has been dumped in the harbor. Monygham has no false pride and no reputation to tarnish, his shame at his previous degradation and his devotion to Emilia have burned away the last taint of egoism. As Nostromo lives on his stolen silver, Monygham lives "on the inexhaustible treasure of his devotion drawn upon in the secret of his heart like a store of unlawful wealth" (p. 441).

Emilia Gould is the one person in Sulaco whose ego has never compromised her love, but she is tested by an isolation more profound than any other. She is required to look on as the fate of the mine becomes her husband's obsession: "She had watched it. . .turning into a fetish, and now the fetish had grown into a monstrous and crushing weight. . . . He seemed to dwell alone. . . leaving her outside with her school, her hospital, the sick mothers and the feeble old men. . . ." (p. 199). Her charity work and her friendship with Dr. Monygham sustain her, but she is "as solitary as any human being had ever been, perhaps, on this earth" (p. 484).

What sustains the spirit in isolation, more important than courage or reputation, is a love untainted by egoism. Two characters attain it, Emilia Gould and Dr. Monygham—though their virtue does not make them happy.

THE SECRET AGENT (1907)

If *Nostromo* is the furthest reach of Conrad's ambition as a novelist, *The Secret Agent* is his most finely wrought accomplishment—an intricate structure of symbol and scene dramatizing his sense of the precarious balance between civilization and anarchy. The "material interests" of *Nostromo* that Charles Gould hoped would produce a stable society have been stripped of their idealistic rhetoric in *The Secret Agent* and reduced to a theory of economic cannibalism.

The wealthy, says the anarchist Karl Yundt, "nourish their greed on the quivering flesh and the warm blood of the people" (p. 53). Conrad's pessimistic assessment is that the stability of society depends not on justice and law but on keeping the greed of the powerful within limits the people will tolerate. The anarchists, with terrorist bombings as their tool, hope to goad the police to repressive acts intolerable to the people, who will then revolt.

Among the novel's many ironies is that Verloc, the secret agent of its title, is no anarchist at all, but a comfortable bourgeois in a bowler hat. He is a double agent, paid by a foreign power to gather information that will destabilize the British government and paid by the police to inform on the anarchists. As such his economic security depends on keeping both police and anarchists at bay; the triumph of either would dry up his income. His cover is a grimy pornography shop, tolerated on the fringe of society because it provides a safety valve for the release of passions that might otherwise threaten stability. Finally, Verloc is a family man, uxorious in his affection for his wife, Winnie, tolerant of the economic drain on his resources of her half-witted brother Stevie and her aged mother. This cozy triad of roles defines him: "Mr. Verloc carried on his business of a seller of shady wares, exercised his vocation of a protector of society, and cultivated his domestic virtues" (p. 19). The code symbol assigned him by the foreign power to which he reports is an equilateral triangle.

The anarchists who meet in the back room of Verloc's shop are a rogue's gallery, all but one no more committed to changing society than Verloc is. Michaelis, the paroled convict who has spent half his life in prison for trying to free prisoners from a police van, is now immobilized in his own fat; he lives on the bounty of a wealthy socialite, spicing her dinner parties with his fiery rhetoric. Karl Yundt, the theorist of economic cannibalism, is a doddering, toothless old man. Ossipon, an ex-medical student, now "scientifically" (p. 50) types people by the shape of their earlobes and waits for a chance to seduce Verloc's wife. Stevie plays with a compass, drawing countless circles that suggest "a rendering of cosmic chaos" (p. 49); he overhears the anarchists ranting and grasps a single broad idea: "Bad world for poor people" (p. 146). A cab horse beaten in the street excites his compassion to "an innocent but pitiless rage" (p. 144); he must be calmed by Winnie, whose philosophy is that "Things do not stand much looking into" (pp. 150–151). The only true anarchist is the Professor, who walks the streets ready to detonate a bomb that will "blow [him]self and everything within sixty yards of [him] to pieces" (p. 65). He strives to perfect a detonator that will eliminate the twenty-second gap between his squeezing an india-rubber ball and the explosion.

In the Verloc family, which lives by the same deceptions that govern the society around them, Winnie's reluctance to look into things has fatal consequences. When Verloc's foreign employer, Vladimir, demands that he produce a bomb, Verloc tries at bedtime to share the problem with her, but she interrupts, offering to "put the light out" (p. 153) and comfort him with "the usual remedies" (p. 58) rather than face the sordid realities that finance her comfortable life. Verloc too lives on the surface, basing his domestic happiness on the illusion that he is "loved for himself" (p. 235); in fact Winnie tolerates him solely because he protects her mother and Stevie. Since Verloc and Winnie live in secrecy, each ignorant of the other's needs, he has to solve his problem without her advice. Playing on Stevie's outrage over the suffering poor (like the anarchists who hope to stir the masses to rebellion), he sends the boy off with a bomb to blow up the Greenwich Observatory. Within yards of his target, Stevie trips over a root, blowing up only himself.

Why the observatory? Vladimir defines the bombing as an attack on science itself, "the sacrosanct fetish of to-day" (p. 38). Its significance, however, is even more specific. The observatory fixes both the standard of mean solar time and the prime meridian, locating civilization in time and space. To destroy it is, symbolically, to plunge the world into the very chaos that Stevie renders with his compass.

Verloc, with sublime egotism, explains his role in Stevie's death to Winnie, expecting that she will comfort him for the failure of his plan.

Without a word Winnie decides that her life with Verloc, "a bargain . . . which would have been infinitely shocking to Mr. Verloc's idea of love" (p. 213), is over. As he lies on the sofa calling to her in a tone "intimately known to Mrs. Verloc as the note of wooing" (p. 215), she plucks a carving knife off the table and stabs him. When she confesses her crime to Ossipon, offering herself in exchange for the security Verloc can no longer provide, he disguises his horror, then robs and abandons her, leaving Winnie to drown herself.

The society Verloc's bomb threatens is as corrupt as that of the anarchists. Sir Ethelred offers a bill in Parliament that his opponents call "a revolutionary measure" (p. 125), but his motives are deeply conservative: exploiting the poor beyond a tolerable level risks waking them from their torpor. Chief Inspector Heat has built his reputation by depending on informers, chiefly Verloc, so he steers his investigation toward Michaelis. The assistant commissioner, who takes the investigation away from Heat, is glad to link a triangle of cloth found at the bomb scene to Verloc—because the "great lady" (p. 98) whose patronage he and his wife enjoy would be dismayed to see the outrage tied to her protégé, Michaelis.

The book closes with the Professor, his hand on the rubber ball linked to his detonator, stalking the streets of London, "frail, insignificant, shabby, miserable—and terrible in the simplicity of his idea calling madness and despair to the regeneration of the world" (p. 253).

UNDER WESTERN EYES (1911)

LIKE Nostromo, the Razumov of *Under Western Eyes* lives a lie, and his ordeal climaxes with a purging confession. Razumov has none of Nostromo's swagger, though he too is concerned with reputation. He is a student, the illegitimate son of a nobleman whom he has met only once. He cares only for "his work, his studies, and his own future" (p. 7). A fellow student, Victor Haldin, confides to Razumov that he has assassinated a prominent statesman and asks Razumov's help in escaping the city. Razumov goes instead to his father, hoping that by turning Haldin over to the authorities, he can slip back into his comfortable dream of becoming "a celebrated old professor" (p. 10). The authorities keep secret his betrayal of Haldin, but it becomes known that Haldin sought refuge with Razumov, and he is celebrated as a revolutionist sympathizer. This reputation gives Razumov a perfect cover as a spy; Councillor Mikulin coerces him into infiltrating a revolutionary society in Geneva. There Razumov falls in love with Haldin's sister, Nathalie. After a period of agonizing guilt, he confesses his betrayal—first to Nathalie, then to the revolutionaries. Three men hold him while another strikes two swift blows that break his eardrums. They fling him dazed into the street and he steps in front of a tramcar. Crippled for life, he returns to Russia in the care of a compassionate servant.

The weighty theme of betrayal and redemption gives *Under Western Eyes* scenes of powerful drama, but Conrad's poetic gift has atrophied. He is no longer the artist who claimed that his task was to make us see. Where once he explored truth through patterns of imagery that made his novels vehicles for "the secret springs of emotion," he now frequently relies on ponderous abstractions. His characters once embodied ideas; now they talk about them.

SUCCESS AND ITS COST

CONRAD's artistic decline becomes more marked with each succeeding book. For all the complex juggling of narrators in *Chance* (1913), the characters are shoehorned into a ludicrous plot. When Flora de Barral's father is ruined financially and imprisoned, she comes under the influence of Mrs. Fyne, a conniving feminist. On the verge of suicide, Flora is rescued by marriage with Mrs. Fyne's brother, Roderick Anthony. Mrs. Fyne sabotages the marriage by persuading Flora that Roderick married her out of pity and persuading Roderick that Flora married him only for security. Flora's father, released from prison, attempts to poison Roderick out of jealousy, then poisons himself, bringing the lovers together. With this thin melodrama Conrad struck the popular taste at last. He followed it with another, *Victory*

(1915), in which Axel Heyst lives in misanthropic solitude on a South Seas island. Like Razumov, he is jolted from his contented isolation. Acting on a compassionate impulse, he rescues Lena, a member of a traveling orchestra, from the clutches of the lecherous hotelkeeper, Schomberg, and retreats with her to his island. To avenge himself Schomberg concocts a story of treasure on the island that sends a trio of thugs to invade the lovers' peace. Before the thugs meet violent deaths they succeed in killing Lena, and Heyst, unable to "stand his thoughts before her dead body" (p. 410), makes a funeral pyre of their bungalow and joins her in its flames.

With age Conrad became the mask he had adopted. The success of *Chance* gave him at last a bank account that would have pleased Tadeusz Bobrowski. He made a triumphant speaking tour of America. When in 1924 he had the pleasure of declining a knighthood, he must have known he was at last "one of us." On 3 August of that year he suffered a fatal heart attack. The remaining novels of his last decade—*The Arrow of Gold* (1919), *The Rescue* (1920), *The Rover* (1923), and the posthumously published *Suspense* (1925)—show occasional stretches of genius, but they are far more conventional than the tales of his great period. After years of struggle in which he discovered brilliantly convoluted solutions to the problems of narrative craft, Conrad had learned to write fast-paced, sentimental yarns for the best-seller lists. It was not of these but of "Heart of Darkness" that his old friend Ford Madox Ford wrote in *Joseph Conrad: A Personal Remembrance*, describing their passionate aesthetic arguments as though they were spies plotting revolution: "His face would light up; it was as if he whispered; as if we both whispered in a conspiracy against a sleeping world" (p. 33).

SELECTED BIBLIOGRAPHY

I. COLLECTED EDITIONS. Dent's Collected Edition of the Works of Joseph Conrad (London, 1946–1955); The Cambridge Edition of the Works of Joseph Conrad (Cambridge, 1990–).

II. WORKS. *Almayer's Folly* (1895); *An Outcast of the Islands* (1896); *The Nigger of the "Narcissus"* (1897); *Tales of Unrest,* including "The Idiots," "Karain: A Memory,"

"The Lagoon," "An Outpost of Progress," "The Return" (1898); *Lord Jim, A Tale* (1900); *The Inheritors, An Extravagant Story*, with Ford Madox Ford (1901); *Youth, A Narrative, and Two Other Stories*, including "Heart of Darkness," "The End of the Tether" (1902); *Typhoon* (1902); *Typhoon and Other Stories*, including "Amy Foster," "Typhoon," "To-morrow," "Falk" (1902); *Romance*, with Ford Madox Ford (1903); *Nostromo, A Tale of the Seaboard* (1904); *The Mirror of the Sea, Memories and Impressions* (1906); *The Secret Agent, A Simple Tale* (1907); *A Set of Six*, including "An Anarchist," "The Brute," "Gaspar Ruiz," "The Informer," "The Duel," "Il Conde" (1908); *A Personal Record* (1908); *Under Western Eyes, A Novel* (1911); *'Twixt Land and Sea: Tales*, including "The Secret Sharer," "A Smile of Fortune," "Freya of the Seven Isles" (1912); *Chance, A Tale in Two Parts* (1913); *One Day More, A Play in One Act* (1913); *Victory, An Island Tale* (1915); *Within the Tides*, including "The Partner," "The Inn of the Two Witches," "Because of the Dollars," "The Planter of Malata" (1915); *The Shadow-Line, A Confession* (1917); *The Arrow of Gold, A Story Between Two Notes* (1919); *The Rescue, A Romance of the Shallows* (1920); *Notes on Life and Letters* (1921); *The Secret Agent: Drama in Four Acts* (1921); *The Rover* (1923); *Laughing Ann: A Play* (1923); *The Nature of a Crime*, with Ford Madox Ford (1924); *Suspense, A Napoleonic Novel* (1925); *Tales of Hearsay*, including "The Black Mate," "Prince Roman," "The Tale," "The Warrior's Soul" (1925); *Last Essays* (1926); *The Sisters* (1928).

III. MODERN EDITIONS. *The Portable Conrad*, ed. by Morton Dauwen Zabel (New York, 1947; rev. ed. by Frederick R. Karl, 1969); *Nostromo, A Tale of the Seaboard*, intro. by Robert Penn Warren (New York, 1951); *The Secret Agent, A Simple Tale* (New York, 1953); *Heart of Darkness*, ed. by Robert Kimbrough (New York, 1963; 3d ed. 1988); *Under Western Eyes*, intro. by Morton Dauwen Zabel (New York, 1963); *An Outcast of the Islands*, afterword by Thomas Moser (New York, 1964); *Almayer's Folly and Other* Stories, afterword by Jocelyn Baines (New York, 1965); *Lord Jim*, ed. by Thomas Moser (New York, 1968; 2d ed. 1996); *The Secret Agent, A Simple Tale*, ed. by Norman Sherry (London, 1974); *Congo Diary and Other Uncollected Pieces*, ed. by Zdzislaw Najder (Garden City, N.Y., 1978); *The Nigger of the "Narcissus,"* ed. by Robert Kimbrough (New York, 1979); *Nostromo, A Tale of the Seaboard*, ed. by Keith Carabine (Oxford and New York, 1984); *The Shadow-Line, A Confession*, ed. by Jeremy Hawthorn (Oxford, 1985); *Victory, An Island Tale*, ed. by John Batchelor (Oxford, 1986); *Chance, A Tale in Two Parts*, ed. by Martin Ray (Oxford and New York, 1988); *The Mirror of the Sea* and *A Personal Record*, ed. by Zdzislaw Najder (Oxford, 1988); *"Heart of Darkness": A Case Study in Contemporary Criticism*, ed. by Ross C. Murfin (New York, 1989); *Almayer's Folly*, ed. by Jacques Berthoud (Oxford and New York, 1992); *The Complete Short Stories of Joseph Conrad*, 4 vols., ed. by Samuel Hynes (London and Hopewell, N. J., 1992–1993); *An Outcast of the Islands*, ed. by J. H. Stape and Hans Van Marle (Oxford and New York, 1992); *The Lagoon and Other Stories*, ed. by William Atkinson (Oxford and New York,

1997); *Nostromo, A Tale of the Seaboard*, ed. by Iain Galbraith (Cologne, Germany, 1998).

IV. LETTERS. *Joseph Conrad: Life and Letters*, ed. by Georges Jean-Aubry, 2 vols. (Garden City, N.Y., 1927); *Letters from Joseph Conrad, 1895–1924*, ed. by Edward Garnett (Indianapolis, Ind., 1928); *Joseph Conrad: Letters to William Blackwood and David S. Meldrum*, ed. by William Blackburn (Durham, N.C., 1958); *Joseph Conrad's Letters to R. B. Cunninghame Graham*, ed. by C. T. Watts (Cambridge and New York, 1969); *The Collected Letters of Joseph Conrad*, ed. by Frederick R. Karl and Laurence Davies, 8 vols. (Cambridge, 1983–).

V. BIOGRAPHIES. Jesse Conrad, *Joseph Conrad and His Circle* (London and New York, 1935); Jocelyn Baines, *Joseph Conrad: A Critical Biography* (New York, 1960); Norman Sherry, *Conrad's Eastern World* (Cambridge, 1966); Bernard C. Meyer, M.D., *Joseph Conrad: A Psychoanalytic Biography* (Princeton, N.J., 1967); Norman Sherry, *Conrad's Western World* (Cambridge, 1971); Norman Sherry, *Conrad and His World* (London, 1972); Frederick R. Karl, *Joseph Conrad: The Three Lives* (New York, 1979); Zdzislaw Najder, *Joseph Conrad: A Chronicle*, trans. by Halina Carroll Najder (New Brunswick, N.J., 1983); John Batchelor, *The Life of Joseph Conrad: A Critical Biography* (Oxford, 1994).

VI. CRITICAL STUDIES. Ford Madox Ford, *Joseph Conrad: A Personal Remembrance* (Boston, 1924); F. R. Leavis, *The Great Tradition* (London, 1948); Thomas Moser, *Joseph Conrad: Achievement and Decline* (Cambridge, Mass., 1957); Albert J. Guérard, *Conrad the Novelist* (Cambridge, Mass., 1958).

Frederick R. Karl, *A Reader's Guide to Joseph Conrad* (New York, 1960; rev. ed. 1969); Robert Wooster Stallman, ed., *The Art of Joseph Conrad: A Critical Symposium* (East Lansing, Mich., 1960; Athens, Ohio, 1982); Eloise Knapp Hay, *The Political Novels of Joseph Conrad* (Chicago, 1963; rev. ed. 1981); J. Hillis Miller, *Poets of Reality: Six Twentieth-Century Writers* (Cambridge, Mass., 1966); Marvin Mudrick, ed., *Conrad: A Collection of Critical Essays* (Englewood Cliffs, N.J., 1966); Avrom Fleishman, *Conrad's Politics: Community and Anarchy in the Fiction of Joseph Conrad* (Baltimore, 1967); Claire Rosenfield, *Paradise of Snakes: An Archetypal Analysis of Conrad's Political Novels* (Chicago, 1967); Paul Kirschner, *Conrad: The Psychologist as Artist* (Edinburgh, 1968); J. I. M. Stewart, *Joseph Conrad* (Cornwall, N.Y.: 1968).

Bruce Johnson, *Conrad's Models of Mind* (Minneapolis, 1971); Jacques Berthoud, *Joseph Conrad: The Major Phase* (Cambridge and New York, 1978); Ian Watt, *Conrad in the Nineteenth Century* (Berkeley, Calif., 1979); Harold Bloom, ed., *Joseph Conrad: Modern Critical Views* (New York and Philadelphia, 1986); Harold Bloom, ed., *Joseph Conrad's "Lord Jim"* (New York and Philadelphia, 1987); Ian Watt, *Joseph Conrad: "Nostromo"* (Cambridge and New York, 1988); Jakob Lothe, *Conrad's Narrative Method* (Oxford and New York, 1989); Cedric Watts, *Joseph Conrad, "Nostromo"* (London and New York, 1990); J. H. Stape, ed., *The Cambridge Companion to Joseph Conrad* (Cambridge and New York, 1996).

JOHN DONNE

(1573–1631)

Andrew Zawacki

LINEAGE AND EARLY LIFE

JOHN Donne was born in 1573 in the parish of St. Nicholas Olave in the city of London. Little is known of his father, John, who was born around 1530, became warden of the Company of Iron-mongers in 1574, and died when his son was three years old. Donne's mother, Elizabeth, born about 1540, was the great-granddaughter of Elizabeth More, sister of Sir Thomas More. She married a defender of Catholic doctrine against Protestant reform and shared her brother's ruin over the Act of Supremacy. Donne's mother was the daughter of John and Elizabeth Heywood. John Heywood was forced to recant at St. Paul's Cross during the reign of Henry VIII, rose again with the accession of Queen Mary, and was newly persecuted as a Catholic when Queen Elizabeth gained the throne. In earliest childhood Donne was perhaps educated by his grandfather John Heywood in Malines or Louvain. In 1584 Donne's uncle Jasper Heywood, while on a mission to England from Rome, was arraigned in Westminster Hall along with five other Catholic priests. All six were condemned, but Heywood was spared execution. Donne, then age twelve, may have visited him in prison alongside his distraught mother, before Father Heywood was sent to France under pain of death if he ever returned to his native country. "The boy may have been just able to observe and reflect when fresh persecutions fell upon his family," Edmund Gosse wrote of Donne and his beleaguered Catholic lineage (Gosse, vol. 1, p. 12).

Donne probably had five siblings, including three sisters who died in infancy, an elder sister, Anne, and younger brother, Henry. In October 1584 both the precocious Donne and his brother matriculated at Hart Hall in Oxford, where John would have been awarded a first degree except that he refused to take the oath, parts of which seemed anti-Catholic. Consequently Donne left Oxford after just six terms in 1586. He may have transferred to Cambridge, where he studied at Trinity College for three terms, until autumn 1589. During Donne's residence in Oxford the university was the center of a progressive movement favoring Spanish thought. Ever since Henry VIII's marriage to Katherine of Aragón a century earlier, England had been curious about Spanish literature and philosophy. Luis Vives, practically a personal tutor to Katherine, had been a reader at Oxford and was eventually appointed professor of humanities. By the time Donne arrived, Spanish mystics such as Saint John of the Cross and Teresa of Avila were already common, if slightly eccentric, intellectual currency, and Donne undoubtedly read Luis de Granada's *Guía de Pecadores* and "other similar works, half mystical, half heretical, in which the Spanish genius was being developed in the manner which was to prove so fascinating to Donne" (Gosse, vol. 1, p. 18). These spiritual innovators died during Donne's boyhood—Teresa in 1582, Granada in 1588, and Saint John in 1591—when he was in close family connection with Rome. In 1610 Donne would receive an honorary M.A. from Oxford and be entered as an M.A. of Cambridge.

In 1592 Donne matriculated at Lincoln's Inn in London to study law. By about age twenty-five he had read Bellarmine's *Disputationes de controversiis Christianae fidei adversus hujus temporis haereticos* and a wealth of other theological material, en route to reconsidering his staunchly anti-reformatory, pro-Roman heritage and up-bringing. His attachment to the Catholic faith gradually waned, as he became skeptical of its theoretical foundations and indifferent toward its practice. Yet, according to Gosse, "all the while he nourished a kind of dormant religiosity, ready to break forth into flame as soon as the tumult of the senses and the enraged curiosity of life had been somewhat assuaged by experience" (Gosse, vol. 1, pp. 27–28).

In the short term, tempestuous experience found its articulation in satire. Published posthumously, Donne's first four satires were written between 1593 and 1594. The last decade of the sixteenth century witnessed a general flourishing of the genre in England, among younger poets eager to naturalize Juvenal's and Persius's Latin poems into English. Its attention to social scandal and penchant for high-grounded, often heavy-handed moral assertiveness made satire attractive to aspiring poets, keen to rebel against conventions of the saccharine pastoral ode and its indulgence in naive idealism. Donne and his unofficial cohorts opted instead for a rhetorical and argumentative difficulty bordering on obscurity, and for a rugged, masculine style. "I do hate / Perfectly all this towne," Donne begins his second satire (*The Satires, Epigrams, and Verse Letters*, p. 7), directing his condescension at London elitism and entitlement in an embittered fashion that would prove prescient and personally relevant—not least because the crown soon set about burning satires, castigating their authors, and outlawing the form altogether. Nor was Donne above criticizing the slippery slopes of his own livelihood, again in Satire II: "men which chuse / Law practise for meere gaine, bold soule, repute / Worse then imbrothel'd strumpets prostitute" (*Satires*, p. 9). Underneath Donne's defiant stylistic and thematic contortions, however, runs an adamant current of uprightness. "Seeke true religion," he implores in Satire III, qualifying that "truth and falsehood bee / Neare twins," an acknowledgment of dangerous, paradoxical, and urgent complexity, to which he would be faithful throughout his life. "On a huge hill, / Cragged, and steep, Truth stands," he continues, employing the conceit of ascent,

and hee that will
Reach her, about must, and about must goe;
And what th'hills suddenness resists, winne so
. . .
To will, implyes delay, therefore now doe:

Hard deeds, the bodies paines; hard knowledge too
The mindes indeavours reach, and mysteries
Are like the Sunne, dazling, yet plaine to'all eyes
(*Satires*, pp. 12–13)

Hard knowledge came to Donne in various guises. In 1596, following what was probably a turbulent love affair with a married woman, he enlisted in the foreign service under the earl of Essex and was likely on the *Repulse* with Sir Walter Raleigh the day of the St. Barnabas the Bright victory against the Spanish armada. The following year he joined the Islands Voyage expedition to the Azores, where a tempest forced the English fleet to shelter in Falmouth. There Donne wrote "The Storm," which he sent to his chamber-fellow Christopher Brooke, likewise the recipient of its sequel, "The Calm," penned by Donne weeks later in the tropics. The former poem, in distinction to the tone of his satires, speaks of an "England to whom we'owe, what we be, and have" (*The Complete English Poems*, p. 250), while the latter considers humanity under the species of fear and trembling, claiming "wee are for nothing fit," since "Wee have no power, no will, no sense" (p. 256). It is conjectured that Donne traveled to Italy and Spain before returning to England to become private secretary to Lord Ellesmere.

Donne had been writing his *Songs and Sonnets* and the *Elegies* throughout this period. Indeed, his lifelong acquaintance Ben Jonson later told Drummond of Hawthornden that Donne had written "all his best pieces ere he was twenty-five years old" (Gosse, vol. 1, p. 59). Nevertheless, Donne refused to publish all but a handful of his poems, consistently belittling them in his letters and perhaps fearing to publicize the romantic affair that many of the poems dramatize. He could not, however, destroy his poetry, and he didn't mind its being widely circulated among friends in manuscript. This ambivalence surrounding the deprecation and dissemination of his own work was characteristic.

From 1597 to 1601 Donne served as secretary to Sir Thomas Egerton, attorney general to Queen Elizabeth. Egerton's second wife had recently adopted her niece, Anne More, daughter of Parliament representative Sir George More. When Lady Egerton died, Anne, barely sixteen, stayed at York House to help manage the lord chancellor's estate. She and Donne, who was around York House constantly on account of professional ties to Egerton, began courting secretly. When Egerton remarried in 1600, Anne removed to Loseley to help her father manage that estate, but not before she and Donne had covertly promised to wed. Three weeks before Christmas 1601, they tied the knot in secret.

When notified of his daughter's marriage to the intelligent, capable, but reputedly promiscuous Donne, George More was so angry that he implored his brother-in-law to dismiss Donne from his service, which the lord keeper did. Donne was thrown into prison for conspiracy to break both the common and canon law, which stipulated that no one could marry a girl without her father's consent. He became ill and, thanks to Egerton's intervention, was allowed to leave Fleet Prison and be confined to his chamber in the Strand. Influenced by a number of aristocratic women new to York House who felt sympathetic toward Donne, including especially Lady Derby, More eventually allowed Egerton to take the heavily indebted Donne back into his service. After careful scheming by Egerton, in April 1602 the court of the archbishop of Canterbury finally approved the marriage. "For Godsake hold your tongue, and let me love," Donne commanded soon after in "The Canonization," wondering belligerently, "Alas, alas, who's injur'd by my love?" (*Poems*, p. 57).

LOVE, LUST, AND THE ART OF LOSING

DONNE's most famous love poem is "A Valediction forbidding mourning," which Samuel Taylor Coleridge called an "admirable poem which none but Donne could have written" (quoted in *Poems*, p. 97). Donne's seminal biographer, Izaak Walton, surmised that Donne composed this poem in 1611 upon leaving for the Continent, and it depicts a passionate speaker's effort to be stoical in departing from his beloved. "So let us melt, and make no noise," he tells her, "No tearefloods, nor sigh-tempests move, / T'were prophanation of our joyes / To tell the layetie our love" (*Poems*, pp. 97–98). Poised righteously against

the undeserving "layetie," the couple here is likewise contrasted with "Dull sublunary lovers," who, he claims, "cannot admit / Absence, because it doth remove / Those things which elemented it." Donne argues that true love does not require "eyes, lips, hands" to remind lovers of their constant togetherness when apart. Instead, to be physically separated is not a "breach, but an expansion, / Like gold to ayery thinnesse beate." The poem's final third deploys the conceit of a compass, in order to describe how lovers' souls exist in constant presence and inviolable union amid actual division:

If they be two, they are two so
    As stiffe twin compasses are two,
Thy soule the fixt foot, makes no show
    To move, but doth, if the'other doe.

And though it in the center sit,
    Yet when the other far doth rome,
It leanes, and hearkens after it,
    And growes erect, as that comes home.

Such wilt thou be to mee, who must
    Like th'other foot, obliquely runne.
Thy firmnes makes my circle just,
    And makes me end, where I begunne.

(p. 98)

The speaker celebrates his lover as the stable center of a periphery he traces. Ever leaning toward him, she ensures he will never stray too far, and her fixity is such that when he comes back his return will be a kind of homecoming: not only a sexual consummation of the relationship but also the existential completion of his very self.

Another poem from the *Songs and Sonnets*, however, directly contradicts the assurance that lovers do not require each other's physical presence to certify their love. Donne was, according to critic John Carey, "the least consistent of mortals, and he never felt that an idea had been properly exploited until he had tried it out backwards as well as forwards" (Carey, p. 149). So if the optimism of the valediction is seconded by the twelfth elegy, which claims, "Rend us in sunder, thou canst not divide / Our bodies so, but that our souls are ty'd" (*Poems*, p. 163), "The

Extasie" counters it. While Donne again pursues the idea that "Love, these mixt soules, doth mixe againe, / And makes both one" (*Poems,* pp. 100–102), it is the necessity of the lovers' bodies that he emphasizes. The speaker resolves to "forbeare" neither his nor his beloved's body, claiming, "We owe them thankes, because they thus, / Did us, to us, at first convay, / Yeelded their senses force to us." He asserts that lovers' bodies are the "spheares" in which their individual identities reside, and that even if "Loves mysteries in soules doe grow, / But yet the body is his booke." Comparing the body to a book written by love figures romance in terms at once somatic and semantic, by associating tissue with text, and tacitly puns on the Latin *corpus,* which can refer to either a human body or a body of literature.

If "A Valediction forbidding mourning" demonstrates how two lovers are unified even when apart, and if "The Extasie" implies that lovers inhabit bodies that naturally separate them even when together, then "The Flea" tries to reconcile these opposed viewpoints. Participating in a long tradition of erotic flea poems that began with Ovid, Donne's conceives the commingling of lovers' souls as following from their corporal fusion. The speaker notices that a flea "suck'd me first, and now sucks thee, / And in this flea, our two bloods mingled bee" (*Poems,* pp. 47–48). This action cannot be called "sinne, nor shame, nor loss of maidenhead," since the lovers have not engaged in sexual intercourse. Instead, the flea is responsible for having drawn blood from each, which is why it "swells with one blood made of two." Their blood inside the flea, the lovers are thus "more than maryed," as the flea does not merely symbolize their conjoining but is its very site: "This flea is you and I, and this / Our marriage bed." Proceeding via metaphors taken from religious life, which dignify the poem's themes by elevating their sensual content to a spiritual plane, the speaker claims he and his beloved are now "cloystered" within the flea's "living walls of Jet." Consequently he asks her not to kill the flea, since that would amount to the "sacrilege" of murdering themselves, as Donne makes quiet recourse to the Renaissance belief that sexual climax was death in miniature.

The lovers, though joined, remain nevertheless chaste, thanks to their "mariage temple," the flea, which also remains guiltless. Meanwhile Donne cleverly gets away with insinuating sex without dramatizing it overtly, and with rendering love and lust, as Proust might put it, "real without being actual."

What is explicit in Donne's erotic poetry is that true love refuses to obey external laws of space and time, behaving instead as a "spider love" which "transubstantiates all" (*Poems,* p. 73). Just as distance means nothing to the lovers in the valediction, so "The good-morrow" asks about love and its participants, "Where can we finde two better hemispheares / Without sharpe North, without declining West?" (*Poems,* p. 49). Likewise, the close of "The Sunne Rising" proffers that, for the sun—and for everything under it, when love is invoked—"This bed," where a man and woman lazily outlast the morning, "thy center is, these walls, thy spheare" (*Poems,* p. 54). The geographical universe, not excluding the heavens, is "contracted" to the dimensions framing the pair, and within these diminished yet aggrandized parameters the lovers assume greater proportion, importance, provenance. "She'is all States, and all Princes, I," the speaker brags to the intrusive sun, "Nothing else is." Similarly, in "The Anniversarie" the speaker asserts that he and his beloved "Prince enough in one another bee" and that, more impressively, "Here upon earth, we'are Kings, and none but wee / Can be such Kings" (*Poems,* p. 69).

Chronology is also transfigured by the operations of love. "Only our love hath no decay," the voice of "The Anniversarie" observes, and "no to morrow hath, nor yesterday, / Running it never runs from us away, / But truly keepes his first, last, everlasting day." Other poems corroborate the idea—or ideal—that love inaugurates a temporal infinity. "Lovers houres be full eternity," according to "The Legacie" (*Poems,* p. 63), and in "Breake of day" the speaker wonders what ordinary time has to do with the radically gerrymandered borders of love, his tone betraying irritation at being interrupted by the world's usual schedule: "Why should we rise, because 'tis light?" (*Poems,* p. 68). "The Sunne Rising" also opens with the impulsive censure of what is "Busie," as the speaker inquires of the sun, "Must to thy motions lovers seasons run?" (*Poems*, p. 53). He sees no reason why love ought to comply by the heliocentric rules that define the quotidian. "Love, all alike, no season knowes," he argues, "nor clyme, / Nor houres, dayes, moneths, which are the rags of time." In this pleasurably distorted scenario, Donne's persona is given to a hyperbolic, possessive, disorienting ardor familiar to anyone who has been in love: "For I had rather owner bee / Of thee one houre, than all else ever" (*Poems*, p. 66).

Donne did not scoff, however, at the lascivious pastimes usually associated with—but not always indicative of—love and loyalty. The opening strains of "The Indifferent" boast, "I can love both faire and browne," before praising "Variety" as "Loves sweetest Part" and decrying constancy as "dangerous" (*Poems*, pp. 54–55). In admitting, "I can love her, and her, and you and you, / I can love any," the poem is a wry but vigorous apology for promiscuity, thinly disguised as a democratic impulse. Donne again opposes exclusivity in "Confined Love," purporting in quasi-philosophical lingo, "Good is not good, unlesse / A thousand it possesse" (*Poems*, p. 83). In the third elegy, "Change," Donne reiterates, "To live in one land, is captivitie, / To runne all countries, a wild roguery; / Waters stincke soon, if in one place they bide / And in the vast sea are more purified" (*Poems*, p. 141). A poem still more blunt, if not downright mercenary, "Communitie," mentions indifference, too, but emphasizes the "use" of women at the expense of orthodox morality. "Chang'd loves are but chang'd sorts of meat," Donne concludes with gruesome hauteur, "And when hee hath the kernell eate, / Who doth not fling away the shell?" (*Poems*, p. 78). Most fantastically, the speaker in "Loves Usury" seeks to strike a bargain with love, whereby for each hour of love he is spared now he promises to repay twenty when he is old. "Till then," he begs, "let my body raigne, and let / Mee travell, sojourne, snatch, plot, have, forget, / Resume my last yeares relict: thinke that yet / We'had never met" (*Poems*, pp. 56–57). Hoping to deceive

women of whatever social stratum into giving themselves to him, "Onely let mee love none," he wishes.

More intense than the desire to convince love to "spare mee" is the wrenching need, across Donne's poetry, to exorcise heartbreak and the betrayals effected by women he had loved—or at least made love to. The poet who demanded the right to philander was the same poet psychologically vulnerable to others' caprices and dismissals. "Womans constancy" evidences how time, quite apart from being inexhaustible or irrelevant as it is in true love, can become strictured by the worry of a brittle lover: "Now that thou hast lov'd me one whole day, / To morrow when thou leav'st, what wilt thou say?" (*Poems*, p. 51). The poem also puts into play Donne's paradoxical revolvings of fact and lie, as the speaker wonders of his lover—or former lover—whether "you / Can have no way but falsehood to be true." The upshot of Donne's more cynical songs is, "No where / Lives a woman true, and faire" (*Poems*, p. 50). It is not difficult to guess that his poetic defenses of carousing were the resentful result of real spurnings by women with whom he had been sexually acquainted.

Donne suffered enormously under "loves subliming fire." He alternately leveled and was leveled by "loves impestuous rage" and castigated himself repeatedly as a "Foole" who "didst not understand," as he complains in Elegie VII, the "mystique language of the eye nor hand" (*Poems*, pp. 75, 173, 148). He unabashedly declares in "The Funerall" that "I am / Loves martyr" (*Poems*, p. 108), and his poems are replete with images of being destroyed by love, for which his appetite remained nonetheless insatiable. In "Loves exchange" Donne asks love to "let me never know that this / Is love," ashamed that his lover "knowes my paines," and speaks of "my being cut up, and torne," before finally—in rhetoric evocative of Saint Augustine, whose theological writings Donne studied—soliciting his own destruction: "Kill, and dissect me, Love" (*Poems*, pp. 80–82). What Donne designates as "loves warfare" often seems, in the poems, not to be incited by a particular woman, despite the numerous assaults on female character, so much as waged by the "devill" love itself. "My body's a sack of bones," Donne whimpers in the fifth elegy, "broken within" (*Poems*, p. 145), and love was apparently as capable of such vandalism as the women who fell into and out of bed with Donne.

The combined weaponry of a woman and the love that she gives and retracts is most poignantly staged in "The broken heart." The speaker admits to having borne the "plague" of love for a year, a nearly impossible task insofar as "He is starke mad," according to a principle of endurance and derangement, "who ever sayes, / That he hath been in love an houre" (*Poems*, pp. 95–96). Time once again having become an index of torture, "Ah," the speaker emits, "what a trifle is a heart, / If once into loves hands it come!" Whereas all other "griefes" are intermittent and wither with the onset of subsequent woes, "Love draws, / He swallows us, and never chawes." Having elaborated a theory of "tyran" love, Donne applies the principle to a personal case. Wondering what else but love it could have been when he first saw "thee," the speaker remembers, in a pair of beautifully economic lines, "I brought a heart into the roome, / But from the roome, I carried none with mee." Elsewhere figured as an arrival, homecoming, or "anchor," love is here conceived as a divestment, not a climactic enhancement but rather diminishment. The speaker's outpouring heart never even reaches the woman, before "Love, alas" intercepts it and "At one first blow did shiver it as glasse." The poem evinces a discouraged, even exasperated tone, yet it is a hallmark of Donne's tenaciously rational temperament that the final stanza strives to anesthetize pain by understanding it. Following the scientific tenets stipulating that matter can never be entirely eliminated nor space altogether empty, Donne reaches this reasoned, but resigned, summary:

Therefore I thinke my breast hath all
  Those peeces still, though they be not unite;
And now as broken glasses show
A hundred lesser faces, so
  My ragges of heart can like, wish, and adore,
  But after one such love, can love no more.

THE SELF AND OTHER INCONSTANTS

WHILE Donne possessed an enormously concerted and imperious personality, complete with what John Carey has referred to as "power lust" (p. 108), he was also possessed by innumerable, often fragile, disparate selves. For Donne, the inconstancy of lovers might have been subconsciously bound up with a fundamental unfixity of the self: his painful experiences of romantic faithlessness undoubtedly fostered uncertainties concerning the viability of a holistic mind, heart, and body. Conversely, such intuitions regarding a de-centered, splintered self might only have reinforced his paranoia about the falsity of intimates. "Perfection is in unitie," he claims in the eighteenth elegy, applying a tirelessly rehearsed Christian theological tenet to love, where one should "preferr / One woman first" (*Poems*, p. 179). Yet in another elegy Donne proclaims, 180 degrees from valorizing "one thing," that, "Pleasure is none, if not diversifi'd" (*Poems*, p. 175). That he changes his mind so drastically and quixotically hints at a diversified self. That the subject of his deft mental reversals is the very question of singularity versus plurality only further illuminates his status as a self-proclaimed "selfe traytor" (*Poems*, p. 73). He quite confidently states in Elegy III, "Change 'is the nursery / Of musicke, joy, life, and eternity" (*Poems*, p. 141), only to turn around elsewhere and urge with equal conviction, "Be constant in some thing" (*Paradoxes and Problems*, p. 4).

Nor is each of Donne's poems internally consistent or emotionally constant in itself. The first two octaves of "The Message" oscillate between the injunction to "Send home my long strayd eyes. . . . Send home my harmlesse heart" and an imperative to "keep them still. . . . Keepe it" (*Poems*, p. 89). Addressing an absent "thee," the speaker talks himself out of his original intention and into its contrary. In the end he decides he does indeed want his heart and eyes returned, so that he might someday rejoice when the woman—whom he projects into the future as an incarnation of his own present suffering—is herself anguished by another's "lyes." Manifesting a schizophrenia less obvious and less spiteful, "The Sunne Rising" opens with the speaker commanding the sun to "goe," but after talking across twenty-eight lines, the same voice spends the final couplet ordering it to stay: "Shine here to us" (*Poems,* pp. 53–54). The abrupt change points to a recurring if faint paradigm in the emotional makeup of Donne's personae: they often begin in anger or frustration, pronouncing mantras of "breake off," "Turne thou," and "goe"—words framing Donne's first published poem, "The Expiration" (*Poems,* p. 119)—but end by begging for company or comfort. More often than not, though, such company assists in ushering the demise of Donne's selfhood, as he is severed from himself. The death that appears in Donne's poetry is not restricted to the so-called "little death" of the orgasm, or even to the emotional dissolutions of refusal and desperation, but includes a figurative dying of existential dimensions. An instance of this quasi-death is "The Will," in which Donne's speaker bequeaths his eyes, tongue, constancy, silence, money, religious faith, modesty, patience, books, and more—in short, makes "some Legacies" of his self (*Poems,* pp. 105–107). The reason for this sudden, literally self-effacing generosity is, predictably, a licentious woman he loves. The speaker finds in her behavior proof that love "disproportion[s]" his "gifts," so he resolves to "give no more; But I'll undoe / The world by dying." Hence in sighing his "last gaspe," the speaker contrives "to annihilate all three": love, his would-be lover, and himself.

This "practise" is one of enacting a metaphysical death by figuring it physically, and Donne puts it to perfection repeatedly, not least in "The Paradox." The titular enigma concerns the relationship among life, death, and love, the last of which makes living impossible and death inevitable—yet the speaker is still alive to say so. "I cannot say I lov'd," he says, in a language that, by being posed at all, undermines the rest of his claim: "for who can say / Hee was kill'd yesterday" (*Poems,* pp. 120–121). Hence Donne establishes—even as he argues to the contrary—that language is premised on a death of the self, and that such death is brought about by love. "Once I lov'd and dyed," he recalls as if posthumously, "and am now become / Mine Epitaph

and Tombe. / Here dead men speake their last, and so do I; / Love-slaine, loe, here I dye." The catch is, of course, that Donne is by no means speaking his last, for his macabre ruminations constitute this poem. The death that is purportedly making a tomb of him, then, is actually facilitating his selfhood, if not serving as its prerequisite.

So while Donne hopes to melodramatize that "Wee dye but once," his poems tell a different story, about the self's successive, finally self-*affirming* deaths. "I, by loves limbecke, am the grave / Of all, that's nothing," he writes in "A nocturnall upon *S. Lucies* day, Being the shortest day," intoning, "I am None," though clearly he is not nothing, but rather one who claims to be none (*Poems,* pp. 91–92). Again, the cause of this paradoxically enabling disability is love, which, "From dull privations, and leane emptinesse . . . ruin'd mee," so that "I am re-begot / Of absence, darknesse, death; things which are not." There is a deeply mystical thrust to this testimony of ruination and resurrection, which Donne learned from John of the Cross's meticulous itinerary of the "dark night of the soul" and the *via negativa,* or "negative way." Various critics, foremost among them Louis Martz, have likewise suggested that Donne, despite the propaganda he later aimed at Saint Ignatius of Loyola and the Catholic project of the early seventeenth century, was familiar with the Jesuit's *Spiritual Exercises,* which call for a willed anamnesis of suffering and death. In terms of the scientific discoveries of his time—Copernicus's *De revolutionibus* was published in 1543, Kepler's *Mysterium cosmographicum* in 1596, Bacon's *Advancement of Learning* in 1605, and Galileo's *Siderius Nuncius* in 1610—Donne's attitude toward death obliquely reflects Elizabethan efforts to understand the expanding universe and to account for the self's reluctant abdication from its center.

Donne's obsession with the link between death and the self, as both are consumed in love, reaches its zenith in "The Legacie," which begins from the far side of the grave, albeit a figurative grave of abandonment. Its speaker refers to when he "dyed last," implying that deaths of the self are frequent, and he qualifies that "I dye / As often as from thee I goe" (*Poems,* pp. 63–64). From the vantage of this so-called death, he speaks to his lover, and his syntactic labyrinths highlight an integral aspect of Donne's inquiry into the provisionality and revisability of the self:

I heard mee say, Tell her anon,
  That my selfe, (that's you, not I,)
  Did kill me, and when I felt mee dye,
I bid mee send my heart, when I was gone,
But I alas could there finde none.

A close reading reveals that the speaker is remembering that his lover killed him by saying a simple goodbye, but the pronouns are sufficiently confused to intimate that lover and beloved have become so entangled that they are nearly one entity. What is remarkable is the way in which this seam is figured not as a consummation that blurs the borders of lovers making love, but rather as a condition arising when one of them leaves the other for "dead." Donne's clarification, "(that's you, not I)," embedded in parentheses and necessary to sorting the poem's argument, draws attention to the difficulty in speaking at all of "I" and "thou." The speaker is first split from himself, such that he can say he hears himself speaking, as if he were no longer in the first person but the third. His selfhood is further aggravated by its indistinguishability from hers. Death again becomes a condition of language and, paradoxically, of that apartness from oneself that enables participation with the other. Hence, the lovers' being divided by "death" brings them together, as it separates each from his or her respective individuality.

A parallel self-evisceration and fusion—not to mention confusion—of one lover with another, via the operations of "death," occurs in "A Valediction of my name, in the window." The speaker writes his name on glass, as if that will "contribute my firmnesse" to it (*Poems,* pp. 70–71). Instead, the transparency of the glass, rather than solidifying his identity by "confessing" his signature, unfixes his selfhood—and hers: "Here you see me, and I am you." The intensification in verbs from "see" to "am" moves the poem from the realm of observation to the ontological plane. What is at stake is no longer what is simply witnessed, but rather what is empirically trans-

formed. Soon the speaker's name, which he'd believed to be so "hard" that it could "mock . . . diamonds," is figured as the merely "scratch'd" outline of his "ragged bony name." Moreover, this now diminished name serves to signify the "scattered body" of one who "die[s] daily," so that though the poem begins by trying to demonstrate how language "cleare reflects" speaker and addressee—according to the laws of mimesis, or representation—it quickly becomes about the dissolution of the self when language is put into operation.

To conceive lovers achieving a state in which they are one person, through sexual relation, was not new even in Donne's day. Yet Donne reinvigorated the paradigm, exhibiting that it was not only his poems about inconstancy and denial that enacted disturbances to the supposedly intact self. "The Dissolution" investigates this traditional phenomenon of how "wee were mutuall Elements to us, / And made of one another," of how "My body then doth hers involve" (*Poems,* pp. 114–115). His later epithalamion of 1613 for the marriage of Princess Elizabeth and Frederick, elector palatine, likewise celebrates the interanimation of newlyweds, for whom "one bed containes, through Thee, / Two Phoenixes, whose joyned breasts / Are unto one another mutuall nests" (*Poems,* p. 193). Critics have made endless commentary on Donne's interest in alchemy and other forms of blending, condensation and melting, calcination, evaporation and liquefying, in general what Carey calls a "fixation about unfixedness" (Carey, p. 169).

Nowhere is this dynamic of self-erasure and joining more evident than "Sapho to Philænis," the first homosexual love poem in English. Peering into a looking-glass, Sappho sees herself but imagines—since their female bodies are optically symmetrical—that she sees Philænis. Sappho expresses the quizzical way in which the self is another, while the other is practically her self:

Likenesse begets such strange selfe flatterie,
  That touching my selfe, all seemes done to thee.
My selfe I embrace, and mine owne hands I kiss,
  And amorously thanke my selfe for this.
Me, in my glasse, I call thee; But alas,

When I would kisse, teares dimme mine *eyes*, and
  glasse.
O cure this loving madnesse, and restore
  Me to mee; thee, my *halfe*, my *all*, my *more*
                                        (*Poems*, p. 191)

The poem would seem, by the fuzzing of carnal
edges it depicts, to justify Donne's contention in
"The Autumnal," that "I hate extreames" (*Poems*,
p. 154). In "The Prohibition," too, he seeks to
eschew polarities, commanding, "Yet, love and
hate mee too, / So, these extreames shall n'er
their office doe" (*Poems*, p. 118).

Yet true to Donne's inability to remain true to
himself—since his "self" was precisely what
negotiated truth, usually finding it at minimum
polyvalent—he also plied the extremes he found
perilous. So if, as he explains in "Loves Deitie,"
that "To rage, to lust, to write to, to commend, /
All is the purlewe of the God of Love" (*Poems*,
p. 103), it is equally the case that rage, lust, petition, praise, and infinite other diverse actions
comprise the precinct of the self. It was this
penchant for internal disruption that appealed to
Virginia Woolf, who admired Donne's "determination to record not the likenesses which go to
compose a rounded and seemly whole, but the
inconsistencies that break up semblances, the
power to make us feel the different emotions of
love and hate and laughter at the same time"
(quoted in Carey, p. 178). Donne was a poet
inured to both similarity and difference, because
he found in himself, no less than in the world,
striking instances of both parallels and paradoxes,
similarities and distinctions. For Donne there was
no more provocative site of contentious synthesis
and paired dissensions—hence no more suitable
space for restless examination—than his own self.
"What we know not," he says bluntly in "Negative Love," is "our selves" (*Poems*, p. 117), and
in a verse letter of 1604 to his friend Henry Wotton he spoke of "mee, (if there be such a thing as
I)" (*Poems*, p. 296).

RELIGION AND LATER LIVES

In another verse letter, Donne wrote paradoxically, "T'were too much Scisme to bee singu-
lare" (*Poems*, p. 303). In the years following his
legal training, Donne was singular in nothing
except his determination to secure a position
capable of supporting his growing family and
actualizing talents he felt had gone underutilized.
In May 1604 King James I began his legal
persecution of Catholics, and for the next several
years Donne may have been employed collecting
and composing material for Thomas Morton's
anti-Catholic maneuvers, a job that probably
entailed his going to the Continent, perhaps
covertly. The bishop of Durham asked Donne to
take holy orders, an offer that included compensa-
tion which Donne, who had five children by
1608, could certainly have used. He declined,
however, based either on shenanigans of his past
that might have brought both him and the office
dishonor, or else on theological grounds he kept
to himself.

Financial difficulties, the strain of an often sick
family, and the lack of professional affirmation
had induced in Donne a melancholy combined
with a sense of moral failure. "I have over-
fraught myself with vice," he wrote to Henry
Goodyere in 1608, explaining his irreconcilable
extremes,

> and so am riddingly subject to two contrary racks,
> sinking and oversetting, and under the iniquity of
> such a disease as inforces the patient when he is
> almost starved, not only to fast, but to purge. . . .
> [S]ometimes I thinke it easier to discharge myself
> of vice than of vanity, as one may sooner carry the
> fire out of a room than the smoke; and then I see it
> was a new vanity to thinke so. And when I think
> sometimes that vanity, because it is thin and airy,
> may be expelled with virtue or business, or substan-
> tial vice; I find that I give entrance thereby to new
> vices.
>
> (quoted in Gosse, vol. 1, pp. 185–186)

When Anne's father began assisting the family
monetarily, Donne's spirits improved, and he
could afford to reenter the society he craved. He
soon became friends with Sir Lancelot Andrewes,
the only preacher who would rival Donne in the
early seventeenth century, as well as with
Magdalen Herbert, mother of the poet George
Herbert, and with Lucy Russell, countess of Bedford, who soon became his patron.

When the daughter of another of his patrons, Sir Robert Drury, died in 1610, Donne wrote a poem for her that was published in 1611 as *An Anatomy of the World* and later titled *The First Anniversarie*. Donne refers to the late Elizabeth as "that Queene" (*Poems,* p. 327), claims she gilded the West Indies and perfumed the East, and laments that her passing inaugurated the disappearance of all virtue, harmony, and coherence from the world. As it happens Elizabeth was only fourteen when she died, and Donne had never met her. These facts, along with the hyperbole in which the poem revels, brought condescension upon Donne from his fellow literati. Jonson called the poem "profane and full of Blasphemies," saying that such overblown descriptions could only have suited the Virgin Mary, to which Donne replied that he had intended to describe the idea of Woman, not to depict a specific woman as she actually was. The poem does employ the Platonic theory of forms, as when Elizabeth is called "Shee that was best, and first originall / Of all faire copies" (*Poems,* p. 336). It is also true that Sir Philip Sidney's *Defence of Poesie*, published in 1595, had argued that "the skill of the artificer standeth in the *Idea* or foreconceit of the work, and not in the work itself" (quoted in *Poems,* p. 325). Even so, Donne's exaggerations seem egregious, and he eventually regretted the sacrifice of his personal dignity and aesthetic integrity—but not before writing a second encomium to Elizabeth.

Donne's behavior surrounding these poems betrays the obsequiousness with which he was prepared to pursue acceptance. This recklessness of ambition did not stop him from assisting the lord of Rochester in securing legal advice about the latter's intended marriage to Frances Howard, countess of Essex, who first needed to divorce her husband, Sir Thomas Overbury. Donne not only assisted in the nullity suit, but he also wrote an eclogue for the marriage of Rochester and Howard in 1613. These collusions seemed more reprehensible when the pair was condemned two years later for having murdered Overbury. In 1616 the new count and countess of Somerset were placed in the Tower under the charge of Donne's father-in-law. It is no surprise, then, to read in Donne's poem "On himselfe," his reference to "my fame which I love next my soule" (*Poems,* p. 400).

Donne was legion, not on paper alone but in real life as well, though it was to paper that he committed his most extensive treatment of transformation. *Metempsycosis: Poêma Satyricon,* composed in 1601, extends the Pythagorean doctrine of the transmigration of souls, so that, as Donne explains in his opening epistle, it "doth not onely carry one soule from man to man, nor man to beast, but indifferently to plants also" (*Poems,* p. 403). Donne traces "the progresse of a deathless soule, / Whom Fate, which God made, but doth not controule, / Plac'd in most shapes" (*Poems,* p. 405), as it travels from its origin in the apple that Eve ate, through successive incarnations, or "prisons." Its fantastical itinerary includes a mandrake, a blue shell, sparrow, brook, fish roe, swan, sea bird, whale, mouse, elephant, wolf, Abel's bitch, and an ape that, after having sex with Adam's fifth daughter Siphatecia, passes the soul to their daughter Themech, sister and wife to Cain. The poem purports to recount the genealogy of "the great soule which here amongst us now / Doth dwell, and moves the hand, and tongue, and brow" (*Poems,* p. 408), though it is not clear who exactly this ultimate personage might be. Jonson believed it to be Calvin, in part because the poem indicts Muhammad, Luther, all of Rome, and others Donne associates with the "Arguing [that] is heretiques game" (*Poems,* p. 410). Different readers, however, think Donne meant Queen Elizabeth I.

Nor is it impossible—and it may in fact be salutary—to interpret the poem as Donne's slant account of his own progress, not least because his epic pretensions seem to argue for self-definition. "O vouch thou safe to looke / And shew my story, in thy eternall booke," he writes in the fourth section: "That (if my prayer be fit) I may'understand / So much my selfe" (*Poems,* pp. 406–407). He was given to elaborating tangentially on himself throughout his work, even when he was not the apparent subject of a poem. For instance, considered from a purely formal perspective, as C. A. Patrides adroitly points out, more than four-fifths of the poems that Donne cast in stanzas employ patterns that he did not repeat. Likewise, Donne's metrics exhibit counter-movements, unparalleled until Gerard Manley Hopkins's sprung rhythms, that affirm through rhythm what the sense denies, or that use accent and syllable to subvert what the content puts forward (Patrides, pp. 20–21, 18). His inconsistency is consistent and makes a virtue of variation.

Insofar as Donne was chameleonic, he alighted finally on service to God. In a verse letter to Mr. Rowland Woodward, he states, "There is no Vertue, but Religion" (*Poems*, pp. 263–264), offering a meditation on the self and its dependence on religion. He urges, "Seeke wee then our selves in our selves," but Donne is not counseling solipsism. Instead, he encourages an appeal to virtue, so that distraction and worldly concerns will fall away, revealing the self to itself. In his expression of friendship to Woodward, an attempt to assuage his own internal rifts can be overheard: "Manure they selfe then, to thy selfe be'approv'd, / And with vaine outward things be no more mov'd, / But to know, that I love thee'and would be lov'd." Donne proffers that in order to square oneself with oneself, religion must be sought, for religion is precisely the province of virtue. Raised a Catholic but about to make formal his conversion to the Anglican Church, there is a persistent strain of religious tolerance in Donne. The various religions are "all virtual beams of one Sun," he tells Henry Goodyere in a letter of 1609, and "are co-natural pieces of one circle" (quoted in Gosse, vol. 1, p. 226).

Donne eventually heard from James I that the king believed Donne to possess "the abilities of a learned divine, and will prove a successful preacher," and that the king's "desire is to prefer him in that way" (quoted in Gosse, vol. 2, p. 60). Around December 1614 and January 1615 Donne wrote what his son John later published as the *Essays in Divinity*. These disquisitions, meditations, and prayers are, as their author put it, the record of "many debates betwixt himself, whether he were worthy, and competently learned to enter into Holy Orders" (*Essays in Divinity*, p. 2). The essays may also have been intended to demonstrate Donne's orthodoxy and erudition to the king, if not also to George Abbot, archbishop of Canterbury, who had opposed Rochester's suit. Donne harnesses an enormous range of sources, from the Scriptures and Apocrypha to the Church Fathers and their Renaissance commentators, including also Augustine, Aquinas, Scotus, Pererius, Lucretius, Juvenal, and Horace. He speaks out against unnecessary controversy, claiming that, "No garment is so neer God as his word," that Christ Jesus is the "one guide" directing not only Roman and Reformed Christianity but also "Synagogue and Church," and that, "I do zealously wish, that the whole catholick Church, were reduced to such Unity and agreement, in the form and profession Established" (*Essays in Divinity*, pp. 39, 51–52). This toleration had not always come naturally to Donne. His biting drama *Ignatius His Conclave* of 1610 or 1611 had viciously placed Pope Boniface III and Muhammad in hell, claimed papists had more frequent access to hell than Turks or any other "Innovators," condemned Saint Ignatius of Loyola and his fellow Jesuits as more evil and cunning than Satan himself, mused that the Council of Trent had purposed to "change *fables* into *Articles* of faith," and quipped that papal indulgences "do abundantly testifie the Popes liberall disposition, and that he is not so covetous in reserving sinnes to himselfe" (*Ignatius His Conclave*, pp. 13, 9, 39).

Donne was ordained around 25 January 1615, on the Feast of the Conversion of Saint Paul. "What function is so noble," he asked three years later, "as to bee / Embassadour to God and destinie?" (*Poems*, p. 471). An ambassador Donne became: in 1616 he was named rector of Sevenoaks, in Kent, as a gift of the crown. That same year he was elected divinity reader to the Benchers of Lincoln's Inn, a lucrative post requiring fifty sermons per year to a learned audience. His personal and professional angst had begun to dissipate, and he was finally financially stable. In August 1617, however, Anne died, following the birth of a stillborn child. She and Donne, who had been utterly faithful to her, had produced twelve children, only seven of whom were still alive when their mother passed away. "Since she whom I lov'd hath payd her last debt / To Nature, and to hers, and my good is dead, / And her Soule early into heaven ravished," Donne wrote in a holy sonnet, "Wholly on heavenly things my mind is set" (*Poems*, p. 445). The first sermon Donne preached after her death addressed Lamentations 3:1: "I am the man that hath seen affliction by the rod of His wrath."

Donne was, understandably, beset by a new depression, and rededicated himself to God. What vestiges of internal anxiety still lingered found their way into his *Holy Sonnets* and other divine poems, and he also translated chapters of Jeremiah's *Lamentations,* as if to exorcise his current pain and past proclivities. "Batter my heart, three person'd God," he writes repentantly in "Divine Meditations" XIV, "for, you / As yet but knock, breathe, shine, and seeke to mend; / That I may rise, and stand, o'erthrow mee,'and bend / Your force, to breake, blowe, burn and make me new" (*Poems*, p. 443). In closing he asks God to "Take me to you, imprison mee, for I / Except you'enthrall mee, never shall be free, / Nor ever chast, except you ravish mee." Such fevered but controlled sentiments had already imbued a great deal of his mature work. In the first section of "The Litanie," written while in his sickbed in 1610 or 1611, Donne prays to the Father to cancel his idolatrous ways: "O thinke mee worth thine anger, punish mee, / Burne off my rusts, and my deformity, / Restore thine Image, so much, by thy grace, / That thou may'st know me, and I'll turne my face" (*Poems*, p. 456). Yet the period following Anne's decease is striking on account of Donne's renewed productivity, especially in terms of his sermons. His formal church obligations also increased: in 1619 he accompanied the Viscount Doncaster, as his chaplain, to Germany, where the elector palatine, Frederick V, was about to be elected king, an event that troubled King James I for political reasons. Donne continued to write poetry, but his religious vocation had become his greater concern, as his sermons vilified the genre of satire that had meant so much to him when younger. In a letter to the marquis of Buckingham in 1623, Donne spoke of having made a shift from "the mistress of my youth, Poetry, to the wife of mine age, Divinity" (quoted in Gosse, vol. 2, p. 176). Four years earlier even, Donne had referred to his 1608 work *Biathanatos* as "a book written by Jack Donne, and not by Dr. Donne" (Gosse vol. 2, p. 124).

The major event of Dr. Donne's later life in the church was being elected as dean of St. Paul's on 19 November 1621. The post kept him so busy that he resigned from Lincoln's Inn the next year. As dean he was required to deliver sermons on Christmas Day, Easter Sunday, and Whitsunday. Not a few were spoken in front of James I, who rushed several into publication. Donne also became one of thirty prebendaries at St. Paul's, which meant he was assigned to recite Psalms 62 through 66 daily, as well as to preach about one of the texts on the Monday in Whitsun week. Having recently recovered from a severe sickness that he assumed would prove fatal, Donne tackled the Prebend Sermons with increased urgency, beginning with his first, in which he apologized for the entire project of preaching on the Psalms—though he was again negotiating his own spiritual condition. "[I]n the booke of Psalmes," he explicates, "every man may discern *motus animi sui*, his owne sinfull inclinations expressed, and arme himselfe against himselfe" (*Donne's Prebend Sermons*, p. 74). Later in the sermon he cautions that "no man flatters me so dangerously, as I flatter my selfe, no man wounds me so desperately, as I wound myselfe," so that everyone ought therefore to guard against "a confidence in our selves," which "makes me a lye to my selfe" (p. 88). He takes consolation in the fourth that Christians are those "to whom death is no *Consummatum est*, but an *In principio*" (p. 156).

DEATH

D<small>URING</small> a bout of depression in 1608, Donne had written *Biathanatos*, a defense of the individual's right to choose suicide over the prohibition of any institutional authority. "Whensoever any affliction assails me, methinks I have the keys of my prison in my own hand," he considers, "and no remedy presents itself so soon to my heart as mine own sword" (quoted in Gosse, vol. 1, p. 207). The self-reliance endemic to suicide undoubtedly lent it moral legitimacy in Donne's estimation, a sentiment previously expressed by Seneca, who was widely read in Donne's day. Even before he wrote *Biathanatos*, however, Donne had explored the biological causes of suicide. "To affect yea to effect their owne deaths," he writes in the first of the *Paradoxes and Problems*, a series of parodic educational episodes he composed in the early 1590s and returned to between 1603 and 1610, "all living are importun'd" (*Paradoxes and Problems*, pp. 1, 2). He proceeds to view suicide as a form of consummation in nature. "And if these things kill themselves, they do it in their best and supreme perfection," he reasons, continuing, "If then the best things kill themselves soonest (for no perfection indures) and all things labor to this perfection, all travaile to ther owne Death."

Yet as usual Donne could not let things face one direction only. As though prefiguring his admission in the final "Divine Meditation," that "to vex me, contraryes meet in one" (*Poems*, p. 447), *Paradoxes and Problems* contains internal contradictions on the issue of suicide. "What a heinous selfe murder is it, not to defend it selfe?" Donne asks (p. 1). Moreover, whereas in one paradox he claims that what "be comes naturall" is what is "therfore more full and perfect," in the next he asserts, "Nature is our worst Guide," since the mind is encumbered by the body's pain and enslaved to its pleasure. Consequently, "because no death is naturall . . . all deaths proceede of the defect of that, which nature made perfect and would preserve, and therfore are all against Nature" (*Paradoxes,* pp. 4, 6–8). The word "therefore" does double duty in these vignettes, which, if Donne was sincere in intending them as "alarums to truth to arme her then enemies" (quoted in *Paradoxes,* p. xxvi), conceal as much as they reveal.

The planned ambidexterity of the paradoxes notwithstanding, the assertion in the fifth that "to run to death importun'd, is to run into the first condemn'd desperatnes" (*Paradoxes,* p. 9) was elaborated in Donne's 1610 work *Pseudo-Martyr*. The research Donne had undertaken for Morton, especially into the arguments of the popish recusants regarding the Oath of Supremacy and Allegiance, informed this book, which was possibly commissioned by James I. Donne argues that unnecessary suffering may lead to a vain posture of martyrdom at best, that those persecuted for refusing to take the oath are not in any sense martyrs, and that the pope has no right to defend suicide in defiance of English law. In privileging the law of England over the individual conscience, Donne was taking a position antithetical to the one for which Sir Thomas More, his distant relative, had been executed. It cannot be known to what extent this genealogical apostasy, along with his switch from the Roman to the Reformed Church, agitated Donne, whose partisan zeal may be understood as overcompensation for insecurity. The note appended to the front of *Pseudo-Martyr,* in which Donne traces his spiritual development, hints at the possibility of doubt: "I was first to blot out certaine impressions of the Roman religion," he explains,

> and to wrastle both against the examples and against thr reasons, by which some hold was taken; and some anticipations early layde upon my conscience, both by Persons who by nature had a power and superiority over my will, and others who by their learning and good life, seem'd to me justly to claime an interest for the guiding, and rectifying of mine understanding in these matters
> (quoted in Carey, pp. 14–15)

In any event his exclamation in part 10 of "The Litanie," "Oh, to some / Not to be Martyrs, is a martyrdome" (*Poems,* p. 460), can be read as either a genuine lament or sardonic critique.

His own death was fast approaching. In 1623 he had an attack that exacerbated whatever chronic condition afflicted him, probably typhoid fever or gastritis. Lying in bed Donne penned what was published the following year as *Devotions upon Emergent Occasions and severall steps in my Sicknes*. Divided into meditations on the human condition, debates with God, and prayers, the *Devotions* are a graphic, fervent exploration of Donne's physical and spiritual ailments. "I fear not the hastening of my death, and yet I do fear the increase of the disease," he admits, "I should belie nature if I should deny that I feared this; and if I should say that I feared death, I should belie God" (*Devotions upon Emergent Occasions, Together with Death's Duel,*

p. 36). He devotes extended passages, in grotesque detail, to having "cut up mine own anatomy, dissected myself," though his self-surgery does not limit itself to the body: "I do nothing, I know nothing of myself" (*Devotions,* pp. 56, 138). His insistence on "how little and how impotent a piece of the world is any man alone" expands his existential investigations beyond his own self. He concludes that, "No man is an island, entire of itself," and that "any man's death diminishes me, because I am involved in mankind" (*Devotions,* pp. 108–109).

Donne recovered from his illness, but the poems of his final period exhibit a ferocious, concentrated engagement with death. "Death be not proud, though some have called thee / Mighty and dreadfull," he exclaims in the tenth of the "Divine Meditations," "for, thou are not soe, / For, those, whom thou think'st, thou dost overthrow, / Die not, poore death, nor yet canst thou kill me" (*Poems,* pp. 440–441). Not only does he claim immortality, but he also threatens death with its own cessation: "One short sleepe past, we wake eternally, / And death shall be no more, death, thou shalt die." The poem's defiant tone is markedly distinct from the humility of, say, "Goodfriday, 1613. Riding Westward," in which Donne implores, "O Father, purge away / All vicious tinctures, that new fashioned / I may rise up from death, before I'm dead" (*Poems,* p. 456). More characteristic of Donne's last poems is "A Hymne to God the Father," written following his illness, in which Donne continually puns on his surname, offering a dense refrain that goads death, admits to a host of sins, and proffers a multiplicity of selves: "When thou hast done, thou hast not done, / For, I have more" (*Poems,* p. 490).

Donne broke down again in May 1929, and rumors of his death became general. He preached for perhaps the last time in St. Paul's on Easter Day, 28 March 1630, and wrote to George Gerrard in January 1631 that it "hath been my desire (and God may be pleased to grant it me) that I might die in the pulpit" (quoted in Gosse, vol. 2, p. 268). He nearly got his wish. Despite the protestations of friends, Donne preached on 12 February, the first Friday of Lent, before King

Charles I at Whitehall, and took as his text Psalm 68:20: "To God the Lord belong the issues from death." Those in attendance said it was as if Donne had preached his own funeral service, and soon after his death on 31 March the sermon was rushed into publication as *Death's Duel; or, A Consolation to the Soul Against the Dying Life and Living Death of the Body.* In the sermon he asks "not that God will deliver us from dying, but that he will have a care of us in the hour of death" (*Devotions,* pp. 166–167). Donne also resumes some of his most poignant themes, reiterating that "all our periods and transitions in this life, are so many passages from death to death," and gathers and gives strength from the biblical promise that "this *exitus mortis* shall be *introitus in vitam,* our issue in death shall be an entrance into everlasting life."

SELECTED BIBLIOGRAPHY

I. POETRY. *The Divine Poems,* ed. by Helen Gardner (Oxford, 1952); *The Elegies and The Songs and Sonnets,* ed. by Helen Gardner (Oxford, 1965); *The Complete Poetry of John Donne,* ed. by John T. Shawcross (Garden City, N.Y., 1967); *The Satires, Epigrams, and Verse Letters,* ed. by W. Milgate (Oxford and New York, 1967); *Poems,* ed. by Frank Kermode (Cambridge, 1968; repr. 1970); *Poems,* a facsimile of the first edition of 1633 (Menston, Yorkshire, U.K., 1969); *Complete English Poems,* ed. by A. J. Smith (Harmondsworth, U.K., 1971); *The Epithalamions, Anniversaries, and Epicedes,* ed. by W. Milgate (Oxford and New York, 1978); *The Complete English Poems,* ed. by C. A. Patrides, 1985 (London, 1990); *The Variorum Edition of the Poetry of John Donne,* Gary A. Stringer, general ed. (Bloomington, Ind.,1994–).

II. PROSE. *Donne's Sermons: Selected Passages,* ed. by Logan Pearsall Smith, 1919 (Oxford, 1932); *Essays in Divinity,* ed. by Evelyn M. Simpson (Oxford, 1952); *Sermons,* ed. by George R. Potter and Evelyn M. Simpson, 10 vols. (Berkeley, Calif., 1953–1962); *Devotions upon Emergent Occasions, Together with Death's Duel* (Ann Arbor, Mich., 1959); *Selected Prose,* chosen by Evelyn Simpson and ed. by Helen Gardner and Timothy Healy (Oxford, 1967); *Ignatius His Conclave,* an edition of the Latin and English texts with an introduction and commentary by T. S. Healy (Oxford, 1969); *Donne's Prebend Sermons,* ed. by Janel M. Mueller (Cambridge, Mass., 1971); *Pseudo-Martyr,* a facsimile reproduction with an introduction by Francis Jacques Sypher (Delmar, N.Y., 1974); *Letters to Severall Persons of Honour,* ed. by M. Thomas Hester (Delmar, N.Y., 1977); *Paradoxes and Problems,* ed. by Helen Peters (Oxford and New York, 1980); *Biathanatos,* ed. by Ernest W. Sullivan 2d (London and Newark, N.J., 1984).

III. BIOGRAPHIES. Izaak Walton, *The Lives of John Donne, Sir Henry Wotton, Richard Hooker, George Herbert, and*

Robert Sanderson, 1675 (London, 1927); Edmund Gosse, *The Life and Letters of John Donne,* 2 vols., 1899 (Gloucester, Mass., 1959); R. C Bald, *John Donne: A Life,* ed. by W. Milgate (Oxford, 1970).

IV. SECONDARY STUDIES. James Smith, "On Metaphysical Poetry," in *Scrutiny* 2 (1933); Frank A. Doggett, "Donne's Platonism," in *Sewanee Review* 42 (1934); Donald R. Roberts, "The Death Wish of John Donne," in *Publications of the Modern Language Association* 62 (1947); Evelyn Simpson, *A Study of the Prose Works of John Donne* (Oxford, 1948); William Empson, "Donne and the Rhetorical Tradition," in *Kenyon Review* 11 (1949); T. S. Eliot, "The Metaphysical Poets," 1921, in *Selected Essays,* 1932 (New York, 1950); Ian Jack, "Pope and 'the Weighty Bullion of Dr. Donne's Satires,' " in *Publications of the Modern Language Association* 62 (1951); E. P. Bollier, "T. S. Eliot and John Donne: A Problem in Criticism," in *Tennessee Studies in Literature* 9 (1959); Helen Gardner, ed., *John Donne: A Collection of Critical Essays* (Englewood Cliffs, N.J., 1962); Louis Martz, *The Poetry of Meditation: A Study in English Religious Literature of the Seventeenth Century,* rev. ed. (New Haven, 1962); William R. Mueller, *John Donne: Preacher* (Princeton, N.J., 1962); Joan Webber, *Contrary Music* (Madison, Wis., 1963); Sherry Zivley, "Imagery in John Donne's *Satyres,*" in *Studies in English Literature* 6 (1966); Robert G. Collmer, "Donne and Borges," in *Revue de littérature comparée* 43 (1969); Laura G. Durand, "Sponde and Donne: Lens and Prism," in *Comparative Literature* 21 (1969); G. R. Wilson Jr., "The Interplay of Perception and Reflection: Mirror Imagery in Donne's Poetry," in *Studies in English Literature* 9 (1969).

Robert S. Jackson, *John Donne's Christian Vocation* (Evanston, Ill., 1970); Winfried Schleiner, *The Imagery of John Donne's Sermons* (Providence, 1970); William Rockett, "Donne's Libertine Rhetoric," in *English Studies* 52 (1971); Wilbur Sanders, *John Donne's Poetry* (Cambridge, 1971); Gale H. Carrithers Jr., *Donne at Sermons: A Christian Existential World* (Albany, N.Y., 1972); Barbara Everett, "Donne: A London Poet," in *Proceedings of the British Academy* 58 (1972); N. H. Keeble, "The Love Poetry of John Donne," in *Language and Literature* 1 (1972); Robert Nye, "The Body Is His Book: The Poetry of John Donne," in *Critical Quarterly* 14 (1972); H. David Brumble 3d, "John Donne's 'The Flea': Some Implications of the Encyclopedic and Poetic Flea Traditions," in *Critical Quarterly* 15 (1973); Dwight Cathcart, *Doubting Conscience: Donne and the Poetry of Moral Argument* (Ann Arbor, Mich., 1975); Barbara K. Lewalski et al., exchanges on Donne's "personae," in *Southern Quarterly* 14 (1976); Kitty Datta, "Love and Asceticism in Donne's Poetry: The Divine Analogy," in *Critical Quarterly* 19 (1977); Lynette McGrath, "John Donne's Apology for Poetry," in *Studies in English Literature* 20 (1980); John Stachniewski, "John Donne: The Despair of the *Holy Sonnets,*" in *Journal of English Literary History* 48 (1981); Gillian R. Evans, "John Donne and the Augustinian Paradox of Sin," in *Review of English Studies,* n.s., 33 (1982); John R. Roberts, "John Donne's Poetry: An Assessment of Modern Criticism," in *John Donne Journal* 1 (1982); Ilona Bell, "The Role of the Lady in Donne's *Songs and Sonnets,*" in *Studies in English Literature* 23 (1983); Terry Sherwood, *Fulfilling the Circle: A Study of John Donne's Thought* (Toronto and Buffalo, 1984); Arthur F. Marotti, *John Donne, Coterie Poet* (Madison, Wis., 1986); John Carey, *John Donne: Life, Mind, and Art,* 1981 (London and Boston, 1990); C. A. Patrides, " 'Extreme, and scattering bright': The Poetry of John Donne," in C. A. Patrides, ed., *The Complete English Poems,* 1985 (London, 1990); Dennis Flynn, *John Donne and the Ancient Catholic Nobility* (Bloomington, Ind., 1995); P. M. Oliver, *Donne's Religious Writing: A Discourse of Feigned Devotion* (London, 1997); Jeffrey Johnson, *The Theology of John Donne* (Cambridge, 1999).

V. BIBLIOGRAPHIES. Sir Geoffrey Keynes, *A Bibliography of Dr. John Donne* 3d rev. ed. (Cambridge, 1958); John R. Roberts, *John Donne: An Annotated Bibliography of Modern Criticism, 1912–1967* (Columbia, Mo., 1973); John R. Roberts, *John Donne: An Annotated Bibliography of Modern Criticism, 1968–1978* (Columbia, Mo., 1982).

GEORGE ELIOT

(1819–1880)

Tricia Welsch

THE WRITER WHO would become George Eliot was born Mary Anne (also called Mary Ann or Marian) Evans in Warwickshire on 22 November 1819, the youngest child of a rural estate manager and a farmer's daughter. From the time she was a baby her family lived at Griff House, a comfortable red brick farmhouse attached to Arbury Manor. Her childhood was a happy time for Eliot, and she would later write:

> A human life, I think, should be well rooted in some spot of a native land, where it may get the love of tender kinship for the face of the earth, for the labours men go forth to, for the sounds and accents that haunt it, for whatever will give that early home a familiar unmistakable difference amidst the future widening of knowledge.
>
> (*Daniel Deronda,* p. 50. All page references for novels refer to Penguin editions.)

A precocious child, Eliot enjoyed accompanying her father as he worked on the estate; at home, she was permitted to browse among the books in the manor library. She was educated at Mrs. Wallington's school in Nuneaton, where she was a prize-winning student. There she came under the influence of an Evangelical teacher, a follower of one of the many varieties of Dissent from traditional Anglicanism that were competing for converts during this period. Though Eliot's experiment with rigorous piety did not last, she had a lifelong interest in spiritual belief: renunciation, service, and the search for vocation would be among her great literary themes.

After her mother died in 1836, Eliot left school to keep house for her father. She continued to read widely, and to study Italian and German. When she and her father moved in 1841 to the outskirts of Coventry, the young woman became friendly with the progressive, freethinking Bray family, at whose home she met intellectuals and

artists and enjoyed wide-ranging discussions of all the important issues of the day. The enormous changes occurring during her lifetime made for heady conversation: transformations in the rural landscape brought by the coming of the railway; industrialization and its social and economic pressures; and revolutionary advances in such areas as sanitation and medicine. Of particular interest to Eliot were new developments in biblical scholarship; as she studied the history of the Bible, Eliot came to believe that Christianity was based on "mingled truth and fiction" (*Letters,* ed. Haight, p. 21). Her reluctance to go to church created tension at home that was not easily dissipated.

In these years she began her first published work: translations from the German of David Friedrich Strauss's *Life of Jesus* in 1846 and of Ludwig Andreas Feuerbach's *Essence of Christianity* in 1854. Her early extremism—both for and against dogmatic religions—would soon be replaced by a more tolerant understanding. As Eliot later wrote, "I have no longer any antagonism towards any faith in which human sorrow and human longing for purity have expressed themselves" (*Letters,* p. 236). She believed, however, that "a religion more perfect than any yet prevalent, must express less care for personal consolation, and a more deeply-awing sense of responsibility to man, springing from sympathy with that which of all things is most certainly known to us, the difficulty of the human lot" (*Letters,* p. 360).

Her father died after a long illness in 1849, leaving Eliot with a small income that had to be supplemented by additional work. Instead of moving in with her older brother Isaac or taking a position as a schoolteacher, lady's companion, or governess, however, Eliot traveled to Europe with the Bray family, staying on in Geneva on her own for the winter of 1850. Her unusual independence alienated her brother, as did Eliot's decision to move to London in 1851. There she became a part of the unconventional household of left-wing publisher John Chapman, who had just purchased the *Westminster Review.* Chapman was much impressed by the young woman's forceful intellect, and she began working as a reviewer and essayist, then became business manager and de facto editor of the journal. Her five years there (1851–1856) brought Eliot in contact with a wide social circle of the most talented and interesting minds, among whom she easily held her own. An unrequited attachment to Chapman, and another to the philosopher Herbert Spencer, did not destroy Eliot's close friendship with either man.

Independent and unmarried in her mid-thirties, Eliot was living a very odd life for a woman of her time. However, the attachment she formed to the writer, editor, and atheist George Henry Lewes would lead to her most unconventional choice. Although he no longer lived with his wife, Lewes was married without the possibility of divorce (an opportunity he had passed up when he claimed the child of his wife's extramarital union as his own, thus implicitly and legally condoning her continued liaison with the child's father). Lewes was a man of enormous and varied talents, and he and Eliot were ideally matched. When they made the momentous decision to live openly together as man and wife, however, they were breaking with the most fundamental Victorian value: the sanctity of the family. Eliot and Lewes traveled together to Germany in 1854, returning to England the next spring to a decidedly chilly reception. Eliot could not be received or visited by ladies, although gentlemen continued to come and go in the couple's new home.

Eliot insisted that she be called by her new name, Marian (or Mrs.) Lewes. The couple held themselves out as being married in every sense but the legal one, and enjoyed a devotion that was both mutual and satisfying. They acted as parents to Lewes' three sons, Eliot's income helping to support the boys and Lewes' estranged wife. To a friend who had grown cool, Eliot wrote: "Light and easily broken ties are what I neither desire theoretically nor could live for practically. Women who are satisfied with such ties do *not* act as I have done—they obtain what they desire and are still invited to dinner" (*Letters,* p. 152).

The quiet life their radical step assured them was actually preferable to the couple, who settled into a shared pattern of research, writing, and editing. They read aloud in the evenings, and were completely conversant with modern and classic literature. They were quite poor, but pinched their pennies and made occasional forays into the countryside, where Eliot's delicate constitution seemed stronger. When Eliot began to consider writing a novel, Lewes encouraged her enthusiastically. It would be difficult to overstate her husband's importance to Eliot's fictional career. He read or listened to all her work as she drafted it, often making welcome suggestions. He acted as mediator when she submitted her first manuscript for publication under her new pseudonym. He protected her from scrutiny by speaking on behalf of "George Eliot" until the author's true name finally became known in 1859, with the enormous success of her second novel. Perhaps most importantly, Lewes kept Eliot—who was unusually sensitive to even mild disparagement—insulated from all criticism of her work. He gently instructed his wife's editors in the best way of handling the author, for whom writing produced many crises of confidence.

As her fame grew, Eliot continued her lively correspondence with writers, scientists, artists, and intellectuals of all stripes. The Pre-Raphaelite painter Edward Burne-Jones, who counted her a close friend, said of Eliot, "There is no one living better to talk to. Her knowledge is really deep, and her heart one of the most sympathetic" (Haight, *George Eliot: A Biography,* p. 408). The young Henry James described her after their first meeting: "An admirable physiognomy—a delightful expression, a voice soft and rich as that of a counselling angel—a mingled sagacity and sweetness—a broad hint of a great underlying world of reserve, knowledge, pride and power—a great feminine dignity and character in these massively plain features—a hundred conflicting shades of consciousness and simpleness—shyness and frankness—graciousness and remote indifference—these are some of the more definite elements of her personality" (Haight, p. 417). Eliot and Lewes traveled throughout Europe, and enjoyed art, theater, and especially music at home and abroad. The couple came to know many of the eminent people of their era, though they preferred the quiet calm of their days at home together, writing and reading. Their companionship clearly enhanced Eliot's productivity, as her inscription to *Romola* (1863) attested: "To the Husband whose perfect Love has been the best source of her insight and strength this manuscript is given by his devoted Wife, the writer" (Haight, p. 373).

SCENES OF CLERICAL LIFE

In a part of her journal titled "How I Came to Write Fiction," Eliot confessed that writing stories "had always been a vague dream," but that she thought herself "deficient in dramatic power, both of construction and dialogue" (*Journals,* ed. Harris and Johnston, p. 289). Her fictional debut, *Scenes of Clerical Life,* proved these concerns wrong. Published in eleven installments in *Blackwood's Magazine* beginning in January 1857, its three stories were widely read and approved, and created a stir over the identity of its author. The first part to appear, "The Sad Fortunes of the Reverend Amos Barton," tells a simple story of a village clergyman not much liked by his parishioners. Neither inspired not inspiring, Barton falls into difficulty when his modest stipend is unequal to the needs of his growing family. An unwanted houseguest strains the family's financial resources beyond the breaking point, even as the visitor's demands weaken the already frail health of Barton's wife Milly. The selfish Countess Czerlaski, with her gorgeous robes, her pretty airs, and her lapdog, seems a type likely to appeal to readers of popular fiction, but Eliot insists on Barton as her hero. The cleric's unwillingness to turn the countess out, even when it excites unwelcome gossip and speculation in the parish, is a point of honor with

him. There is no big climax: the countess eventually departs; Milly dies in childbirth; and Barton's curacy is reassigned, in unrelated circumstances. But all of these events are momentous to Barton, as is the renewed goodwill of his small community.

Eliot stakes out her fictional territory early by insisting on her hero's worth despite his quiet life. Neither his character nor his predicament is unusual, as the author takes pains to say. Barton is:

> in no respect an ideal or exceptional character; and perhaps I am doing a bold thing to bespeak your sympathy on behalf of a man who was so very far from remarkable,—a man whose virtues were not heroic, and who had no undetected crime within his breast; who had not the slightest mystery hanging about him, but was palpably and unmistakably commonplace. . . . 'An utterly uninteresting character!' I think I hear a lady reader exclaim.
>
> (p. 80)

"Mr. Gilfil's Love Story," the second of the three tales, depicts another vicar who "did not shine in the more spiritual functions of his office," an aged man who would excite no apparent interest but who deserves attention nonetheless (p. 121). Here again the narrator is insistent: "I, at least, hardly ever look at a bent old man, or a wizened old woman, but I see also, with my mind's eye, that Past of which they are the shrunken remnant" (p. 128). She then tells the story of a chamber kept precisely as it was left, by Mr. Gilfil's much-loved dead wife: "a sort of visible symbol of the secret chamber in his heart, where he had long turned the key on early hopes and early sorrows, shutting up for ever all the passion and the poetry of his life" (p. 130).

This story is indeed passionate: the adopted Italian daughter of a rich man and his wife falls in love not with the curate for whom she is intended (the young Mr. Gilfil) but with the careless Captain Wybrow, who encourages Caterina's affections even though he means to marry a rich woman. Eliot is intrigued by such selfish figures, who set in motion the affections of others, often to their mutual devastation. Her clear-sighted assessment of figures like Wybrow, however, does not prevent her showing them sympathetically:

What idle man can withstand the temptation of a woman to fascinate, and another man to eclipse—especially when it is quite clear to himself that he means no mischief, and shall leave everything to come right again by-and-by? . . . Perhaps you think that Captain Wybrow . . . must have been a reckless libertine to win her affections in this manner! Not at all. . . . He really felt very kindly towards her, and would very likely have loved her—if he had been able to love any one. But nature had not endowed him with that capability.

(pp. 163–164)

When Wybrow dies unexpectedly, thwarting her passionate plan to murder him, Caterina is distraught with guilt. Gilfil finds (and conceals) her dagger, searches out her hiding place, nurses her back to health by easing her conscience, and marries her. The melodrama of these events is leavened by the acuity of Eliot's moral vision: she conveys to the reader how this drama seems to each of its players, so that their actions are (if not justifiable) wholly intelligible, the product of their varied capacities to see, to judge, to love, to forgive. Her conclusion reminds the reader that the vicar's past, unseen sorrow has shaped his character forever: "Though he had something of the knotted whimsical character of the poor lopped oak, [Gilfil] had yet been sketched out by nature as a noble tree" (p. 244).

The surprisingly modern plot of the last of the three stories, "Janet's Repentance," concerns a proud woman who will not acknowledge her husband's drunken abuse, keeping even her loving mother at a distance. Janet despairs of any comfort until she has a striking encounter with a Dissenting preacher who is vilified by the town, but who offers her genuine spiritual guidance. Janet leaves her alcoholic but respectable husband (who in a memorable scene drives her from the house in her nightgown) and puts aside her only comfort, her own drinking. The portrait of a strong woman whose life is corrupted by a poor choice of mate but who finds the moral courage to defy social norms provoked some concern from Eliot's publisher, who feared his readers would reject the portrait of a woman drinking. He advised the author to soften the story as much as possible. She replied with typical firmness:

I am unable to alter anything in relation to the delineation or development of character, as my stories always grow out of my psychological conception of the dramatis personae. . . . My artistic bent is not at all to the presentation of eminently irreproachable characters, but to the presentation of mixed human beings in such a way as to call forth tolerant judgment, pity, and sympathy. . . . If anything strikes you as untrue to human nature in my delineations, I shall be very glad if you will point it out to me, that I may reconsider the matter. But alas! inconsistencies and weaknesses are not untrue.

(*Letters*, pp. 165–166)

When she offered to withdraw the story, Blackwood, distressed, wrote back to affirm his commitment to it and to her work: "I do not fall in with George Eliots every day" (Haight, p. 237).

From the earliest, the writer's philosophy was firm: "Art must either be real and concrete, or ideal and eclectic. Both are good and true in their way, but my stories are the former kind. I undertake to exhibit nothing as it should be" (*Letters*, p. 177). Painstaking realism would be characteristic of her work; equally, Eliot consistently creates figures who espouse unpopular or controversial religious doctrines without becoming themselves unsympathetic. *Scenes of Clerical Life* was printed in two volumes in 1858, and most readers and reviewers were confident that George Eliot was not only a man but a man of the cloth, so deeply had the author penetrated the clerical world. With Lewes acting as her mediator, the new storyteller received complimentary letters from leading literary figures of the day, some of whom she knew in her life as Marian Lewes. However, no one penetrated the secret of the writer's identity.

ADAM BEDE

ELIOT told Blackwood that she was inclined to "take a large canvas" for her next work, which would be "a country story—full of the breath of cows and the scent of hay" (*Letters*, pp. 178–179). The setting of *Adam Bede* in rural Hayslope drew on Eliot's love for the landscape of her own childhood, and was partly inspired by a family story. Her Methodist aunt recalled praying with a young woman condemned for the murder of her infant child, and riding with her to the gallows after her confession. Eliot's narrative closely mirrors these events, in the tale of pretty Hetty Sorrel who delivers an illegitimate child in secret and who is brought to repent of its death by an unlikely figure: her cousin Dinah, a Methodist minister.

The two cousins are as different as possible: Dinah has her eyes fixed on the eternal, her only concern her unusual ministry. She preaches in public, in the fields, moving her listeners with the purity and obvious sincerity of her belief. Something of a puzzle to the Poysers, the solid farming family who are her closest relatives, Dinah solemnly rejects an offer of marriage, feeling led instead to minister to the poor citizens in the rough village of Snowfield some distance from Hayslope. Modesty and quiet dignity are Dinah's marked characteristics. Eliot downplays Dinah's unusual independence, as a woman preaching a controversial doctrine and moving freely through her world, in order to highlight the good Dinah's presence does. The homespun rural people who farm the Hayslope area are depicted in some detail and treated with respect and even enjoyment. (The plain-speaking Mrs. Poyser is a particularly memorable figure.) That these simple people accept Dinah—even if they do not wholeheartedly embrace her convictions—marks her worth. As one character notes, "It isn't notions sets people doing the right thing—it's feelings. . . . Religion's something else beside doctrines and notions" (pp. 181, 183). As in her earlier fiction, Eliot is more concerned with the spirit of religious belief and its effects than with the particular doctrine espoused or the personal virtues of its messenger.

Dinah's cousin Hetty has two suitors. One is Adam Bede, the strong, plain carpenter who loves her simply, as a thing of beauty whom he cannot understand. But Hetty has taken his measure: "She saw him as he was—a poor man, with old parents to keep, who would not be able, for a long while to come, to give her even such luxuries as she shared in her uncle's house. And Hetty's dreams were all of luxuries: to sit in a carpeted parlour and always wear white stock-

ings; to have some large beautiful earrings, such as were the fashion" (p. 100). Adam's affection pales in comparison to the attentions paid her by Captain Arthur Donnithorne, another handsome, self-approving, rich young man reminiscent of *Clerical Scenes's* Captain Wybrow. Heir to the local squire, Arthur's attraction to Hetty's mild beauty ensnares him as it does her: he meets with her secretly, each time vowing that it is for the last time, while Hetty naively imagines that his kisses will lead to their marriage. When Adam discovers that the couple has been meeting in the woods, his childhood friendship with Arthur ends in a fistfight. Arthur, realizing he can no longer continue his romance with Hetty, goes to join his regiment, leaving Adam to console the young woman and renew his own suit.

Eliot's characterization of Arthur as he weighs his options is typical of her approach. The narrator addresses the reader directly, warning against forming too fixed an idea of anyone's character: "Our deeds determine us, as much as we determine our deeds. . . . There is a terrible coercion in our deeds which may first turn the honest man into a deceiver, and then reconcile him to the change; for this reason—that the second wrong presents itself to him in the guise of the only practicable right" (p. 315). Arthur's transformation from beloved and upright scion of the local gentry to self-deceiving, weak seducer happens by degrees, and causes him almost as much misery as he creates. However, as Arthur's mentor Mr. Irwine tells him, "A man can never do anything at variance with his own nature. He carries within him the germ of his most exceptional action" (p. 171).

Irwine is yet another Eliot cleric who fails to do his religious duty in the approved way, and midway through the book the narrator pauses to consider why she has not given Irwine edifying sermons to deliver. "I aspire to give no more than a faithful account of men and things as they have mirrored themselves in my mind . . . as if I were in the witness-box narrating my experience on oath" (p. 177). Further, she argues, such fiction can have a higher purpose:

These fellow mortals, every one, must be accepted as they are: you can neither straighten their noses, nor brighten their wit, nor rectify their dispositions; and it is these people—amongst whom your life is passed—that it is needful you should tolerate, pity, and love: it is these more or less ugly, stupid, inconsistent people, whose movements of goodness you should be able to admire—for whom you should cherish all possible hopes, all possible patience. And I would not, even if I had the choice, be the clever novelist who could create a world so much better than this, in which we get up in the morning to do our daily work, that you would be likely to turn a harder, colder eye on the dusty streets and the common green fields—on the real breathing men and women, who can be chilled by your indifference or injured by your prejudice; who can be cheered and helped onward by your fellow-feeling, your forbearance, your outspoken, brave justice.

(p. 178)

In writing, as in much else, she concludes, "Falsehood is so easy, truth so difficult" (p. 178).

Hetty listlessly accepts Adam's offer of marriage, only to learn that she is expecting Arthur's child. Under the pretence of visiting her cousin Dinah at Snowfield, she goes off to try to find Arthur's regiment. Hetty's fruitless search for her lover finds her drifting through town and country, the rural lass who has never left home now a stranger in the world. She contemplates drowning herself, but the force of life is too strong within her. When her baby comes early, she is helpless, numbed by her own misfortunes, and the child dies of exposure. Dramatic events follow swiftly. The murder trial at which Adam stands up for Hetty; her sentence and jailhouse conversion by Dinah; Hetty's apology to Adam; Arthur's return to claim his inheritance, innocent of any of these events; and the last-minute commutation of her death sentence Arthur carries to Hetty on the scaffold: these are the stuff of Eliot's skilled and thrilling narrative. The denouement finds Dinah consoling the Poyser family, and coming slowly to feel a deep love for the worthy Adam Bede. She now believes that her religion can be practiced on the hearth as well as on the road, and their marriage creates a tender and happy ending.

Speculation about the author's real identity grew with the publication of *Adam Bede,* which appeared in February 1859. Eliot was still committed to her anonymity, believing it was the only way to get the book judged fairly. However, the secret slipped out, and soon Marian Evans Lewes was known to be the author of *Adam Bede.* "It is quite clear that people would have sniffed at it if they had known the writer to be a woman but they can't now unsay their admiration," crowed Lewes after the book had received rave reviews (Haight, p. 290). It was to be one of Eliot's greatest successes, and was reprinted and translated frequently.

THE MILL ON THE FLOSS

THE idyllic companionship of rural childhood is beautifully rendered in *The Mill on the Floss* (1860), Eliot's third novel. The headstrong Maggie Tulliver—a wild child with a lively imagination—and her stalwart brother Tom romp over the fields near their country home. Eliot gives Maggie a love for books, a quick intelligence, and a striking need for admiration and esteem—although she mostly gets criticism from her extended family for her willfulness, an attribute not valued in a Victorian girl. Maggie's misadventures testify to her independence: in one episode, she runs away from home to join a band of gypsies, whom she has a confused plan to teach and take charge of. In another, Maggie chops off her unruly mop of hair when it refuses to curl properly, shocking her staid aunts. (Her thick brown coils will be her best feature as an adult, along with her unusually bright and intelligent eyes. Maggie's is by no means, however, a conventionally pretty face.) Sadly, Maggie's brother Tom, though a close companion, frequently judges her as harshly as her elders do. He is often hard and unyielding: confident that he will never need punishment, he metes it out to Maggie unstintingly. The impulsive little girl finds it difficult to stay in her critical brother's good graces. Throughout the novel she will seek his approval, even after she recognizes that her own judgment is wiser, more sympathetic and intuitive.

Some of Eliot's best energies in the novel are devoted to the family crisis precipitated by Mr.

Tulliver's rash lawsuit against the powerful lawyer Wakem, which bankrupts the family. Mrs. Tulliver bewails the loss of her finely marked linens, her china, and her silver teapot—the small household gods whom she has served for years. Her three sisters, the former Misses Dodson, are called in to consult. Aunt Pullet, Aunt Deane, and the unforgettable Aunt Glegg believe they must not interfere with the workings of Providence, which conveniently relieves them of the burden of providing significant material assistance to their distressed sister and her imprudent family. They expect, however, to be thanked humbly for what little they do. Here we see Eliot's criticism of the religious belief that stands aside from another's misfortunes rather than entering sympathetically into them.

The crisis forces Tom to leave school, and he vows to repay his father's debts and regain the mill from the despised Wakem. The lawyer's son Philip, whose kindness to Tom when they were schoolmates Maggie cannot forget, falls victim to Tom's scorching anger with the Wakems, and their friendship ends. However, Maggie has formed a lasting bond with Philip, and the two growing children continue to meet in secret in the forest, where they share books and discuss ideas. Philip awakens Maggie's knowledge of the wider world beyond the Mill. Theirs promises to be a match of equals in every way but one: Philip is deformed, a hunchback, prone to fits of pique and depression because of his physical limitations, while Maggie grows from an awkward girlhood toward beauty as a woman. Before long they are caught in their innocent meeting place by Tom, who forces Maggie to choose between him and Philip. Though Philip rejects Maggie's talk of renunciation and selflessness, Maggie accepts Tom's ultimatum: a final break with her brother would be too painful to bear. The centrality of their relationship is seen in the novel's working title: *Sister Maggie.*

After two years working as a teacher, Maggie again meets Philip Wakem at her cousin Lucy's house. They renew their friendship and she tells him she loves no one else. Without Maggie's knowledge, Lucy hatches a plot that will both restore the Mill to the Tullivers and gain lawyer Wakem's consent to a match between Philip and Maggie. For Maggie, however, Tom's displeasure will always be the obstacle: though she does not respect his position, she consents to be governed by him. As a young woman Maggie makes a curious figure: she loves quiet ways and prizes peace of mind, but her stubborn and passionate nature are at odds with her determination to renounce whatever her brother will not approve. Disinterested in clothes and adornments, she feels rapture in music and is almost completely unable to hide her emotions. (The novel is filled with scenes in which someone reads Maggie correctly, usually to her chagrin.)

A distraction from this stalemate comes in the form of Lucy's suitor Stephen Guest. To their dismay, Maggie and Stephen are immediately smitten with each other, and slowly but inexorably drift together. Drift is literally correct here: on an afternoon boating excursion, they simply fail to stop the boat, continuing downstream until there is no hope of their returning that same day. Maggie's alarmed conscience and her sense of duty to both Philip and Lucy drive her from her lover's arms, and she returns home unwed. Eliot here meditates on how favorably "the world and the world's wife" would have received the couple had they returned, married, after a decent interval (p. 619). The reader may imagine that Eliot saw something of her own private life in Maggie's situation.

Several generations of (mostly male) critics have found Maggie's unexpected attraction to Stephen surprising (one writer famously called Stephen "a mere hairdresser's block"). Eliot's Victorian readers similarly believed the plot turn detracted from the finely tuned moral sensibility Maggie had developed, in part through her relation with (and especially her dutiful renunciation of) Philip. However, modern readers are often more in sympathy with the sexual awakening Stephen proffers. A variant on the characters of Captain Wybrow and Arthur Donnithorne, the figure of the attractive but unworthy suitor is one that recurs in Eliot's fiction.

Maggie faces her disgrace squarely, even after her brother Tom will not allow her back in the Mill, which his hard work has helped regain. Although it means living in a very modest way,

Maggie stays nearby, finding comfort in old attachments and accustomed places. Love of the familiar is always a virtue in an Eliot character, and the fear of being a wanderer in the world is particularly resonant in this novel, where so many events revolve around issues of losing or leaving—or even running away from—home. *The Mill on the Floss* also emphasizes folk tales about the river and its devastating, unpredictable floods, as well as local superstitions, among them that it is unlucky when the mill passes from hand to hand. Fittingly, in the novel's final scene Maggie is caught in a dreadful flood. She manages to steer a small rowboat across watery fields to her childhood home and rescue the brother who has repeatedly rejected her. A moment of true understanding, recognition, and forgiveness passes between them before their boat is overwhelmed and they are drowned together: "Brother and sister had gone down in an embrace never to be parted—living through again in one supreme moment, the days when they had clasped their little hands in love, and roamed the daisied fields together" (p. 655).

The Mill on the Floss was another triumph for Eliot: admired by readers and reviewers alike, it sold rapidly. Critics and biographers have long found in the novel an idealized treatment of Eliot's rural childhood, a meditation on her own awkward and unconventional looks, and a representation of her beloved childhood playmate, her older brother Isaac. The most important bond of Eliot's girlhood was undoubtedly with Isaac, who broke off relations with her over her attachment to George Henry Lewes. The siblings were estranged for more than twenty years, only renewing their ties when Eliot remarried after Lewes's death. It is heartbreaking that a novelist so inspired by scenes of forgiveness and reconciliation could imagine for Maggie and her brother only an instant of mutual recognition before death.

SILAS MARNER

The novel by which most readers know Eliot is her briefest effort, *Silas Marner, the Weaver of Raveloe* (1861), which the writer claimed "thrust itself between me and the other book I was meditating" (*Letters,* p. 253). Characteristically, the novel features two intertwined plots, in which different classes of people affect each others' lives significantly while seeming unrelated. Events will force them to recognize—and offer them the chance to value—their connections.

Silas Marner is a respectable young weaver whose life is perverted by a love of gold only after he is wrongly accused of theft and cast out from the small religious community to which he belongs. Keeping aloof from people in his new village, Silas is respected for his work but treated by his neighbors with suspicion and even superstition. In his loneliness he works long hours at his loom, taking pleasure only in the payment he receives. He examines his gold nightly: "He began to think it was conscious of him . . . , and he would on no account have exchanged those coins, which had become his familiars, for other coins with unknown faces. He handled them, he counted them, till their form and colour were like the satisfaction of a thirst to him" (p. 68). Fifteen years pass in this manner.

> His life . . . reduced itself to the functions of weaving and hoarding, without any contemplation of an end towards which the functions tended. The same sort of process has perhaps been undergone by wiser men, when they have been cut off from faith and love—only, instead of a loom and a heap of guineas, they have had some erudite research, some ingenious project, or some well-knit theory.
>
> (pp. 68–69)

The narrator first asks the reader to see in Silas a man who loves familiar faces—that is, to see a man capable of love—and then to see Silas's miserly, shrunken habits as similar to those of more respectable men who work without stint but without a purpose worthy of their labors. Love for what is near at hand and work done for a good cause are values consistently praised in Eliot's novels.

The novel's second plot features a rich local family with two sons. The eldest, Godfrey Cass, is considered a fine man; the youngest, Dunstan, is wild, lazy, and good for nothing. Dunstan, however, has learned Godfrey's secret: a marriage to an unsuitable young foreign woman about which he fears to tell his father. Always short of cash, Dunstan blackmails his brother, but fails to return home one day after a short trip. No one knows that before disappearing he had stolen Marner's heap of gold coins; Dunstan is never suspected of the theft. Years will pass before any news is gained of him. Meanwhile, Godfrey, repenting of his hasty alliance and without Dunstan to torment him, yearns to marry pretty Nancy Lammeter, daughter of a wealthy local family and a woman of some conspicuous virtue. He is tormented now by his knowledge that he cannot do so. When on New Year's Eve a young woman is found frozen in the snow, Godfrey recognizes his luckless wife and knows his unfortunate union has escaped detection forever. He is free to marry Nancy.

Conveniently for Godfrey—and miraculously for Silas Marner—the motherless child of this union has wandered across the weaver's doorstep. Silas has been inconsolable since the loss of his hoard, caring nothing for himself now that he has lost the society of his gold coins. The near-sighted weaver goes out briefly on that frigid New Year's Eve to gather firewood, leaving his cottage door open. He returns to find a child asleep by his hearth, her shiny golden curls lit up by his firelight. At first his eyes deceive him:

> Gold!—his own gold—brought back to him as mysteriously as it had been taken away! He felt his heart begin to beat violently, and for a few moments he was unable to stretch out his hand and grasp the restored treasure. The heap of gold seemed to glow and get larger beneath his agitated gaze. He leaned forward at last, and stretched forth his hand; but instead of hard coin with the familiar resisting outline, his fingers encountered soft warm curls. In utter amazement, Silas fell on his knees and bent his head low to examine the marvel: it was a sleeping child—a round, fair thing with soft yellow rings all over its head. Could this be his little sister come back to him in a dream—his little sister whom he had carried about in his arms for a year before she had died, when he was a small boy without shoes or stockings? That was the first thought that darted across Silas's ss blank wonderment. . . . [H]e had a dreamy feeling that this child was somehow a message come to him from that far-off life: it stirred fibres that had never been moved in Raveloe—old

quiverings of tenderness—old impressions of awe at the presentiment of some Power presiding over his life.
>
> (pp. 167–168)

The befuddled and lonely man adopts the child, naming her Eppie, and raising her as his daughter. Silas loves her devotedly; for Eppie's sake he reenters the community, even joining the church. The portrait of the weaver's transformation is enormously moving: the child's tenderness repays the loss of his gold many times over.

However, Eliot's moral vision demands that the Cass brothers' role in Silas's troubles and his joys must at last be revealed and judged by their community. The two stories, which cross briefly when Dunstan steals Silas's money before he disappears, intersect again when Godfrey's unacknowledged child is found. Godfrey's failure to speak up immediately and claim both the dead woman and the living child as his own makes it impossible, he feels, ever to do so. Eliot's characteristic genius is that she shows both Godfrey's irresponsibility (to the child and to his new wife) and his humanity. Who among us, the narrator asks, would not feel tempted to seek his own freedom and happiness when events conspire to make it possible?

> When events turn out so much better for a man than he has had reason to dread, is it not a proof that his conduct has been less foolish and blameworthy than it might otherwise have appeared? When we are treated well, we naturally begin to think that we are not altogether unmeritorious, and that it is only just we should treat ourselves well, and not mar our own good fortune.
>
> (p. 177)

Godfrey and his new wife have no children of their own, which grieves Nancy. When Eppie is twelve Godfrey urges his wife to consider adopting the girl. But Nancy believes that "to adopt a child, because children of your own had been denied you, was to try and choose your lot in spite of Providence," and the effort stalls (p. 216). Five years pass. Dunstan's skeleton is found, clutching the weaver's gold, in the newly drained stone pit near Silas's house, and Godfrey knows that the time has come to tell his secret. He wants to right the harm his brother has done to Silas, and to make Eppie into a lady. But Godfrey underestimates the affection between the weaver and his daughter, and Eppie refuses to leave Silas, preferring instead to marry a local boy and stay among the working people. Silas's gold is restored to him, and makes life comfortable for his small family.

What no summary can make clear is Eliot's inexhaustible fund of sympathy for even her most difficult characters. Repeatedly the narrator shows that people act the way they do because of the circumstances in which they find themselves. Silas is misanthropic and miserly because he has been chased from the society of men; Godfrey means to do well but does not want to lose what he most cherishes. When their circumstances change, so may their characters. Even for a story that Eliot herself called "a sort of legendary tale, suggested by my recollection of having once, in early childhood, seen a linen-weaver with a bag on his back," she preferred a "realistic treatment" (*Letters,* p. 258). Yet, even within this realism there is a symmetry to the novel's Providential consequences that no reader can overlook. Silas is accused of stealing as a young man, and his bitterness twists his life. In turn, his gold is stolen from him by a man who is never accused (but who doesn't live to spend the money). Silas's beloved child replaces the lost gold—first apparently and then truly, exceeding its value for him. The discovery of Dunston Cass's guilt, and of Eppie's high birth, completes the circle, even as it restores the gold.

Silas Marner, published in one volume, enjoyed critical and popular success. Admiring reviewers compared Eliot favorably to Charles Dickens and Walter Scott, singling out the "moral purpose" in the novel for special praise (Karl, p. 355). Readers were clearly relieved by *Silas Marner*'s happy ending, following as it did the tragic conclusion to *The Mill on the Floss.* Modern critics have alternately seen in the novel affirmation of patriarchal control (in which possession of a daughter is more precious than gold) and a more radical reconsideration of established social hierarchies, in which a simple weaver emerges as worthier than the landed gentry.

ROMOLA

ELIOT's next novel, *Romola* (1863), is set in Florence during the Renaissance, and shows off Eliot's considerable erudition. The subject was suggested to her by Lewes while the couple traveled in Italy, and Eliot immediately recognized that the historical novel would be "rather an ambitious project" (*Letters,* p. 247). Even by her own standards, it would demand "a great deal of study and labour" (*Letters,* p. 247). Eliot energetically immersed herself in research on Italian literature, history, politics, painting, architecture, and religion; she was "buried in musty old antiquities," said Lewes (Haight, p. 53). No detail was too small to interest her. "It is the habit of my imagination," she told one critic later, "to strive after as full a vision of the medium in which a character moves as of the character itself" (*Letters,* p. 288). *Romola* is exceptional for its lively re-creation of a world in turmoil, caught in transition between empire and republic, fascinated by the rediscovery of the classics yet uncertain how to reconcile pagan learning with Christian precepts.

The title character is the virtuous and unworldly daughter of a single-minded pedant. Romola becomes engaged to a young scholar and diplomat who appears to embrace her aged father's single purpose in life: to transmit his learning in the form of his library of antiquities to an institution that will keep the collection together. But the handsome Tito, a newcomer to Florentine society, has a secret that pursues him: he has abandoned his own aged adoptive father to almost certain slavery on a Greek isle. Tito is another Eliot character who means to be worthy of his considerable and distinguished gifts, and who would prefer to be a dutiful son if that were not such a difficult prospect under the circumstances. However, when the embittered Baldassare turns up with revenge on his mind, Tito turns his energies to maintaining the reputation he has won in Florence's edgy political climate. He must use every stratagem to keep Baldassare at bay.

Tito alienates his proud wife, Romola, by selling her father's library, and returns her anger by turning to a soft, compliant country milkmaid, with whom he eventually fathers two children. He maintains the girl, Tessa (who believes herself his wife), in secret. Tito, however, can have no secrets from Baldassare who follows his every move and eventually reveals her husband's duplicity to Romola. In the end, and by the most unlikely coincidence, Baldassare carries out his revenge, killing both Tito and himself. Much of Eliot's interest in the novel is to show how Tito's first error leads to his second, and how every subsequent move complicates and endangers his position. In an extremely complex play of cross and double cross, Tito's character shifts from hopeful and lively to cunning and destructive: his own machinations help destroy him.

Eliot, however, is equally interested in developing the character of the noble wife who realizes the great mistake she has made in her marriage. A chance encounter with the charismatic monk Savonarola persuades Romola that there can be a higher purpose for a woman's life—even superseding her father's wishes or her duty to her husband—and she longs to devote herself to a worthy cause. Romola has something like a religious conversion without consequent attachment to a specific doctrine, and may be Eliot's fullest embodiment of a character type that fascinated her throughout her career: the noble and intelligent woman who must find a pure and worthy purpose for her life. Romola finds hers in charitable efforts on behalf of Florence's poor, eventually nursing citizens stricken by the plague. Against the chaotic yet sharply drawn backdrop of Savonarola's own trial for treason and his execution at the stake, Romola finds her purpose. Her larger perspective eventually allows her to forgive Tito's second wife and to care for the children Tito's death leaves behind.

Eliot recognized that the dense historical and social fabric of the novel made *Romola* difficult. Further, she felt that the character of Romola was too ideal: "My own books scourge me," she wrote a friend (*Letters,* p. 288). The novelist expressed doubts that the book would have much commercial success, and her prediction was largely correct. Though it first appeared in the period's most distinguished literary journal (the *Cornhill Magazine*) and was almost universally acclaimed on publication, *Romola* stands in relative obscurity among her works today. However, its author also claimed proudly, "There is no book of mine about which I more thoroughly feel that I could swear by every sentence as having been written with my best blood . . . and with the most ardent care for veracity of which my nature is capable" (*Letters,* p. 481).

FELIX HOLT

WITH *Felix Holt, the Radical* (1866) Eliot returned to her native country for a complex story set during the period of the first Reform Bill. This law, passed in 1832, redrew election districts and extended voting rights to more members of the male middle classes in Britain, and a contested election is at the center of the novel. Harold Transome, heir to his family's prosperous estate, returns to England after many years abroad, and shocks the gentry with plans to run for Parliament as a member of the Radical Party. His bitter and lonely mother has longed for his return, but finds he has little affection for his birthplace and less interest in her sorrow. Because of his political aspirations, Harold is forced for a time to retain his family solicitor and estate manager, Jermyn, whom he dislikes intensely. He fails to see the hold Jermyn has over his mother, or to recognize the spite the man feels at being cast into the background. This failure will help disrupt Harold's plans.

Another son comes home to disappoint his mother as the novel opens. Felix Holt has been studying medicine, and his principles and learning lead him to end his mother's sale of the useless patent medicines that the Holt family has long dispensed. However, he also shocks her by announcing that he will learn watchmaking, an honest skill, since he no longer has any desire to be other than a working-class man. He has had what he calls a "conversion": "This world is not a very fine place for a good many of the people in it. But I've made up my mind it shan't be the worse for me, if I can help it" (p. 143). The intelligent and well-read Felix interests himself in the tumultuous political changes occurring as the county prepares for its first election.

Interest in Radical politics brings both Harold and Felix to the home of Dissenting minister Rufus Lyon, whose lovely daughter Esther attracts Harold and infuriates Felix. The workingman berates Esther for her pride in what he finds shallow and insignificant assets: a fine French accent, lovely gloves, and a nicely turned gown. He wants Esther to find some worthwhile purpose, but she rejects his rough manners and plainspoken ways. Though Felix announces that he will never marry, under his influence Esther feels a pall on her pleasures and a strange desire to secure his good opinion. She is torn between this new dissatisfaction and her glimpses of the graceful life lived at Transome Court.

When Felix learns that Jermyn and his hired men have been bribing workers to cause trouble at the polling places, he angrily brings his concern to Harold, the candidate, who promises but fails to prevent the practice. When election day comes, Felix tries to halt the drunken crowd's violence, and ends up arrested for the accidental death of a police officer. He will eventually be found guilty and narrowly escape transportation to Australia, despite the efforts of both Harold and Esther.

The outcome of Felix's trial is delayed, however, while Eliot pursues her novel's other main interest, the long-hidden secrets on which the Transomes' fortune depends. Scholars have noted Eliot's preoccupation with deception and blackmail, and this novel features both abundantly. Lyon does not tell his beloved Esther that she is the daughter of an abandoned pregnant woman he took in; unbeknownst to the preacher, Esther's parentage gives her incontestable claim to the estate Harold Transome believes is his. At the same time, Mrs. Transome has long been keeping the secret of her affair with Jermyn from their son Harold. Though Harold nobly brings Esther to Transome Court as soon as he learns of her claim, the revelation of his own illegitimacy complicates his desire to marry her (their marriage would of course renew his claim to the property). But Esther has been drawn unaccountably to Felix and his visions of a higher life. Her growing closeness to sad, faded Mrs. Transome shows Esther that worldly position does not bring happiness, and she renounces her claim on the estate to marry Felix when his sentence has been served out.

Eliot is intrigued by secrets: truths hidden by pride or fear offer endless opportunities to the unscrupulous—as well as fodder for novelistic invention. Lawyer Jermyn knows of Esther Lyon's right to Transome Court, and hides it in order to continue diverting monies from the property into his own family coffers. Jermyn's henchman Johnson knows of his duplicity and uses it to keep Jermyn on a short leash. Lyon is afraid to tell Esther about her mother because he fears she will stop loving him, and because he believes (wrongly) that her birth is ignoble. Eliot's characteristic research—this time into politics and property law—helped create *Felix Holt*'s detailed social milieu, in which each character acts and is acted upon, often with far-reaching consequences he cannot foresee. Eliot plays motive off motive in a plot that some critics have found unrewarding in its complexity, but which hints at the masterpiece soon to follow.

Her contemporaries responded to *Felix Holt* with enthusiasm. Modern audiences, however, have found the character of Felix one-dimensional, and have noted Eliot's apparent ambivalence toward her female characters. The portrayal of a woman's nobility as found through sacrifice for a worthy cause (often a marriage) has estranged some modern readers, though others have seen in the description of Esther's marriage to Felix a description of the author's own union with Lewes, which—though unsanctioned—brought Eliot untold joy. Describing the "heavy price" to be paid "for all that is greatly good," the narrator concludes:

A supreme love, a motive that gives a sublime rhythm to a woman's life, and exalts habit into partnership with the soul's highest needs, is not to be had where and how she wills: to know that high initiation, she must often tread where it is hard totread, and feel the chill air, and watch through darkness. It is not true that love makes all things easy; it makes us choose what is difficult.

(p. 591)

MIDDLEMARCH

CHOOSING the difficult and finding joy in it is one of the themes in Eliot's unquestioned masterpiece, *Middlemarch* (1872). Strikingly more ambitious than any of her earlier novels, *Middlemarch* surveys an entire community, tracing the paths by which its members are connected to one another. An enormously complex but enormously rewarding story, it follows several families and their linked fortunes. Secrets of birth concealed and revealed; deathbed vigils with wills to be made and revoked; fortunes secured by less than honest means that leave their now-respectable owners open to blackmail; lofty scientific gifts frustrated by small domestic needs; beautiful young wives repenting their marriages; scholarly reputations overshadowed by fear of the grave and very unscholarly jealousy: these are only a few of the panoramic yet human-scale dramas Eliot creates in the pages of this novel.

Many consider *Middlemarch* the greatest English novel ever written, and with good reason. The author moves effortlessly between strands of the plot, weaving the links between characters subtly tighter and showing the invisible bonds of community that egoism only reluctantly recognizes. Unlikely bonds were part of the novel's evolution: Eliot at first intended it as two stories, one called "Miss Brooke," the other an unnamed tale set in the fictional village of Middlemarch. The author quickly realized that the two efforts could be successfully combined.

Just as several of her earlier novels had considered the problem of finding one's true work, so *Middlemarch* can be considered a novel about the search for vocation, and the struggle to understand how one's choice invariably affects others. Dorothea Brooke devotes herself to her aged husband, Casaubon, acting as his patient amanuensis until she slowly and painfully realizes that his mind is narrower than hers and his scholarly project (unforgettably named "The Key to All Mythologies") is a dead end. Though she is left a wealthy widow while still very young, her dead husband's will viciously limits her freedom. It takes Dorothea some time to find satisfaction in the work that lies nearest her, but here she will find her truest freedom and her true love. Similarly, Casaubon's young cousin Will Ladislaw wants to achieve greatness, but doesn't see his path. He tries political journalism, sketching, and Byronic wandering through Europe before he accepts that his best time and place to serve may not suit his own convenience. Dorothea and Will are Romantic characters who become good Victorians by learning the value and proper place of self-sacrifice.

In keeping with suspicions about wealth evident in Eliot's earlier novels, some characters in *Middlemarch* also learn hard lessons about social ambition. Young Fred Vincy is torn between his desire to be a fine gentleman (which to him means riding good horses and being rather lazy) and his childhood love for unpretentious, hard-working farmer's daughter Mary Garth. Bereft of the fortune he expected to inherit from a rich uncle, he must earn the respect of the woman he loves—and after some trifling and backsliding, he does. Fred learns the gospel of work from Mary's father, Caleb Garth, who offers him a chance Fred ill deserves but which he seizes, hoping to be worthy of Mary. For Eliot the willingness to work hard pardons many sins.

Fred's sister Rosamund marries the new doctor in town after a brief courtship, and their household too provides an instructive look at both social and professional ambition. Tertius Lydgate fancies himself a medical innovator who will remain independent of any claims but those of science. He thinks himself a rationalist but is undone by his susceptibility to Rosamund's manipulative charms. Their marriage sinks him into debt, destroys his autonomy, and undermines his ability to be the crusading physician he once imagined himself. Lydgate does not have the luxury of starting fresh, but must wrest such meaning as he can from the work he is able to do within the limited confines of a marriage based on mutual misunderstanding; the novel makes him a tragic figure.

Lydgate's beautiful wife, Rosamund, however, presents an almost terrifyingly opaque surface. Her seamless egoism prevents her from creating a true marriage with Lydgate, one in which they share both joys and sorrows (and which the novelist depicts in the marriages of Caleb and

Susan Garth, and even in the troubled Bulstrode household). Rosamund enjoys the immovable conviction that what she wants—a spacious home full of beautiful things where she is always to be the loveliest item on display—Lydgate must provide, no matter the circumstances. Insofar as Eliot has a religion of humanity, Rosamund is spiritually bankrupt. However, Lydgate's unhappy wife provides the inspiration for Eliot's more sympathetic character Gwendolen Harleth in *Daniel Deronda*.

If Rosamund alienates the reader, we are not allowed the pleasure of seeing the novel's most importantly corrupt character as a villain. Banker Bulstrode is being blackmailed for a secret he has kept about his past, and he slowly, inch by inch, edges into moral decay. At some point the religious man has come to believe that his purposes are God's purposes, and as his self-justifications wear thin, he becomes desperate. Bulstrode's public humiliation is nearly as uncomfortable for the reader as it is for him. It is part of Eliot's genius that we see each character's perspective as though he is the only one affected by events (which, the narrator reminds us, is how we generally see events in our own lives).

What makes *Middlemarch* so rewarding, however, is the way Eliot demonstrates that events unquestionably have larger effects: they shape and change everything around them. All the characters are caught in the web that is their community, and the slightest action by one person has cumulative, unexpected, and unpredictable consequences for others in that web. The wisest characters come to see this, and this knowledge shapes their actions for the good. When Dorothea, for example, feels most humiliated because she believes her beloved has been unfaithful, she grieves, then begins to look at events differently: "Was she alone in that scene? Was it her event only?" (p. 845). After long deliberation, she begins to see a fuller and truer version of events. When after a sleepless night Dorothea at last looks out into the morning, she sees a couple with a baby trudging along the country road in the distance, and she has a revelation: "Far off in the bending sky was the pearly light; and she felt the largeness of the world and the manifold wak-ings of men to labour and endurance. She was a part of that involuntary, palpitating life, and could neither look out on it from her luxurious shelter as a mere spectator, not hide her eyes in selfish complaining" (p. 846).

Dorothea's epiphany is hard-won, entirely earned, but not entirely private or personal: it leads to both her happiness and the happiness of those around her. The novel ends with the narrator's instructive remarks about lives that seem insignificant but are anything but: "The effect of [Dorothea's] being on those around her was incalculably diffusive: for the growing good of the world is partly dependent on unhistoric acts; and that beings are not so ill with you and me as they might have been, is half owing to the number who lived faithfully a hidden life, and rest in unvisited tombs" (p. 896).

Critics unanimously hailed *Middlemarch* as Eliot's most accomplished work. It sold more copies than any of her novels, and left the writer financially secure for life; she would never again have to worry, as she had early in her career, about "writing drivel for dishonest money" (Haight, p. 271). The method of its publication, in irregularly spaced installments, first seemed a gamble but created enormous interest as enthusiastic readers waited for each new development. The novel's memorable main characters were supported by a large and varied group of skillfully drawn minor figures, and many stirring events occurred throughout the novel—political campaigns, suspicious deaths, secret meetings, gambling losses, imprudent loans, near-adulterous flirtations—all amid the characters' constant jockeying for social position and self-respect. After its publication Eliot was lionized: she received gifts from strangers, was hailed from pulpits, and got more invitations and callers than she could reasonably accept. The attention continued, and Eliot noted with pleasure that 1874 had been "crowded with proofs of affection for me and of value for what work I have been able to do" (*Journals,* p. 145). As was often the case, there was again speculation on who had served as models for the novel's striking figures, especially the withered scholar Casaubon.

DANIEL DERONDA

ELIOT chose a wider geographical scope and a modern setting for her eighth, and in some ways most ambitious, novel. *Daniel Deronda* (1876) betrays the author's familiarity with the capitals of Europe, where a good deal of its action is set. It opens at a German spa, where beautiful young Gwendolen Harleth is losing her money spectacularly. Moments later she receives a letter saying that her family has lost its fortune in a bank failure; she is to return to England immediately. Genteel poverty is a fate the high-spirited Gwendolen cannot comprehend. Her possibilities are revealed in the novel's crucial opening questions: "Was she beautiful or not beautiful?" and "Was the good or the evil genius dominant in those beams?" (p. 35). Her beauty will secure her an aristocratic husband she cannot love, and she will struggle between her good and evil impulses as she searches for meaning throughout the narrative.

The questions belong to Daniel Deronda, whose appraisal of Gwendolen at the casino attracts her irritated notice; she has "the darting sense that he [is] measuring her and looking down on her as an inferior, that he [is] of different quality from the human dross around her" (p. 38). This early encounter forms a bond between them that neither wholly comprehends. The ward of benevolent Sir Hugo Mallinger, Deronda has been educated as a gentleman and is presumed by everyone to be Sir Hugo's son. However, the pain of his unknown parentage has haunted Deronda all his young life; his journey is toward a family and a faith he can claim as his own. *Deronda* was Eliot's "Jewish novel," so called because in it she delves into the power of that faith to unite its adherents and make a strong community in exile. Eliot's travels, her research, and her own early spiritual crisis shape her portrayal of Judaism in the novel, for which she confessed an unusually didactic purpose: "Precisely because I felt that the usual attitude of Christians toward Jews is—I hardly know whether to say more impious or more stupid when viewed in the light of their professed principles, I therefore felt urged to treat Jews with such sympathy and understanding as my

nature and knowledge could attain to" (*Letters,* p. 476). However, as she also wrote in her journal, "The Jewish element seems likely to satisfy nobody" (*Journals,* p. 145).

A charitable impulse of Deronda's leads him to rescue a young woman on the brink of suicide, and he finds himself drawn to the lovely and refined Mirah, a Jewish woman who has come to London to look for her long-lost mother and brother. The despondent Mirah has run away from her rascally father, who forced her to go on the stage and kept her from practicing her religion. Deronda installs Mirah in the home of some artistic and intellectual friends, where she recovers her strength and begins giving voice lessons. Her Christian friends are surprised by Mirah's firm adherence to her Judaism, which they regard as barbaric, but Deronda is fascinated. Though he begins to love her, Deronda fears to take advantage of Mirah's gratitude toward her benefactor; in any case, Mirah proclaims that she will never marry outside her religion. Deronda quietly locates Mirah's brother Mordecai, a scholar much weakened by consumption, who is convinced that Deronda is his long-awaited disciple, the friend meant to take up the burden of Mordecai's religious learning. They slowly begin studying together, Deronda uncertain about Mordecai's ardent hopes for him.

As Deronda ponders his growing connection to both Mirah and Mordecai, Gwendolen is being wooed by the wealthy but diffident Grandcourt. When she learns that Grandcourt has been keeping a woman who left her own husband to bear him four children, she promises Lydia Glasher not to take that woman's rightful place as Grandcourt's wife. However, the crisis in her own family's fortunes overwhelms Gwendolen, and she accepts Grandcourt's offer, believing that no one else knows his secret. Persuading herself that she will exercise a salutary influence on her new husband and that the Glasher family will be better off for her intervention, she goes forward with the marriage.

Gwendolen's disillusionment with her own power begins on the evening of her wedding, when Mrs. Glasher delivers Grandcourt's family diamonds to the new bride with a curse on them. Grandcourt, interested only in exerting his power over the willful and self-confident Gwendolen, insists that she wear the jewels, and taunts her with her own good intentions. The portrait of their disastrous marriage is shattering: poor Gwendolen, a "spoiled child" with no emotional or spiritual resources of her own, cannot confess her mistake and lose the financial security her marriage has brought her mother and younger sisters. Her pride is all she has, and her demonic husband (a character whom Eliot leaves undeveloped) lives only to mortify and subdue whatever independence she shows.

In her despair, Gwendolen remembers her brief encounter with Deronda before her marriage, and she begins seeking him out, believing that only he can guide her toward some sense of meaning or purpose. Eliot's portrayal of Gwendolen in her desperation is arresting, as she sinks lower and lower in her marriage but clutches with more fervent determination at the vision of hope symbolized first by Deronda's judgment and later by his compassionate understanding. The novelist rewrites the vacuous Rosamund Vincy of *Middlemarch* here, making Gwendolen's awkward but impassioned spiritual journey one of the novel's crucial themes. The accidental drowning of the husband she has come to loathe provides the moment of crisis for Gwendolen: she is free but must acknowledge her guilty desire for Grandcourt's death, reassign his money to its rightful owners, and find a new and better path for herself. In an anguished interview, Deronda tells her:

> What makes life dreary is the want of motive; but once beginning to act with that penitential, loving purpose you have in your mind, there will be unexpected satisfactions. . . . This sorrow, which has cut down to the root, has come to you while you are so young—try to think of it, not as a spoiling of your life, but as a preparation for it. . . . You can, you will, be among the best of women, such as make others glad that they were born.
>
> (pp. 839–840)

She must do this without Deronda, who will not step into the role of Gwendolen's suitor as both families expect. He is preparing his own way, which entails both renunciation and acceptance. He has learned the secret of his birth: his Jewish mother, unwilling to give up a brilliant career on the stage, entrusted her son to Sir Hugo so that Deronda would be raised as an English gentleman and not as a Jew. The confirmation that his spiritual path is authentic comes finally as a relief to Deronda, who understands that he can embrace Mordecai as a brother. He is now free to marry Mirah, and the reunited brother and sister plan to travel with Deronda through the East to work for the cause of Jewish nationalism. Mordecai's death, however, comes before they can depart: his benediction on their shared purpose ends the novel.

Daniel Deronda is in many ways another novel about the search for vocation; again, too, Eliot here explores the significance a brief moment of recognition and understanding—such as that which passes between Deronda and Gwendolen, or between Deronda and Mordecai—can have. As Gwendolen tells Deronda when they part, "It shall be better with me because I have known you" (p. 882).

The novel appeared in eight installments and was another commercial and critical success for Eliot, who expected more resistance to its presentation of Jewish mysticism. She was instead pleased by "affectionate letters from strangers" (*Journals,* p. 199). In *Daniel Deronda* the novelist experimented with a more complex time scheme, and some readers have considered the two main plot lines, Deronda's search for his spiritual legacy and Gwendolen's unhappy marriage, a poor fit. The two stories, which intersect as the Grandcourts and Deronda meet socially in England and abroad, move flexibly back and forth in time as their characters' development demands. Thus the opening scene in the casino occurs after Gwendolen has learned of Grandcourt's first family (when she means to refuse him), but before he proposes (when her family's money is gone). Other critics approve the freedom this strategy gives Eliot to explore character psychology, and recognize an approach which anticipates the work of such writers as Virginia Woolf, herself an enthusiastic admirer of Eliot.

CONCLUSION

DANIEL Deronda was, sadly, Eliot's last novel. With the death in November 1878 of her husband George Henry Lewes, who had long been in poor health, Eliot lost her best reader, and she put down her pen. After what some viewed as a shockingly short period of mourning, in May 1880 Eliot married a longtime family friend, John Walter Cross, a man twenty years her junior. Their happiness was short-lived: a mere seven months after their wedding, on 22 December 1880, George Eliot died at her home in London. She was 61 years old. She was buried alongside Lewes in Highgate Cemetery; on the centenary of her death, she was honored by a stone memorial in Poets' Corner of London's Westminster Abbey. Before Eliot began writing fiction, she observed in an essay called "Silly Novels by Lady Novelists" that the "right elements" of a novel were "genuine observation, humour, and passion" (*Essays,* ed. Pinney, p. 324). The most celebrated woman of her day and one of the greatest of novelists, she remained true to those high ideals.

SELECTED BIBLIOGRAPHY

I. NOVELS. *Scenes of Clerical Life,* 2 vols. (Edinburgh and London, 1858; repr., ed. David Lodge, New York, 1980); *Adam Bede,* 3 vols. (Edinburgh and London, 1859; repr., ed. Stephen Gill, New York, 1985); *The Mill on the Floss,* 3 vols. (Edinburgh and London, 1860; repr., ed. A. S. Byatt, New York, 1981); *Silas Marner, the Weaver of Raveloe* (Edinburgh and London, 1861; repr., ed. Q. D. Leavis, New York, 1983); *Romola,* 3 vols. (London, 1863; repr., ed. Andrew Sanders, New York, 1980); *Felix Holt, the Radical,* 3 vols. (Edinburgh and London, 1866; repr., ed. Peter Coveney, New York, 1980); *Middlemarch, a Study of Provincial Life,* 4 vols. (Edinburgh and London, 1872; repr., ed. W. J. Harvey, New York, 1984); *Daniel Deronda,* 4 vols. (Edinburgh and London, 1876; repr., ed. Barbara Hardy, New York, 1978).

II. OTHER WORKS. "The Lifted Veil," in *Blackwood's Magazine* (July 1859), short story; "Brother Jacob," in *Cornhill Magazine* (July 1864), short story; *The Spanish Gypsy* (Edinburgh and London, 1868), poem; "Address to Working Men, by Felix Holt," in *Blackwood's Magazine* (January 1868); *The Legend of Jubal and Other Poems* (Edinburgh and London, 1874), contains all Eliot's previously written poems; *Impressions of Theophrastus Such* (London and Edinburgh, 1879), essays.

MODERN COLLECTION. *Essays of George Eliot,* ed. Thomas Pinney (London, 1963).

III. JOURNALS AND LETTERS. *The Journals of George Eliot,* ed. Margaret Harris and Judith Johnston (Cambridge, U.K., 1998); *Selections from George Eliot's Letters,* ed. Gordon S. Haight (New Haven, 1985).

IV. BIOGRAPHIES. Gordon S. Haight, *George Eliot: A Biography* (New York, 1968); Frederick Karl, *George Eliot, Voice of a Century: A Biography* (New York, 1995); Rosemary Ashton, *George Eliot: A Life* (New York, 1996).

V. CRITICAL STUDIES. Joan Bennett, *George Eliot: Her Mind and Her Art* (Cambridge, U.K., 1948); F. R Leavis, *The Great Tradition: George Eliot, Henry James, Joseph Conrad* (New York, 1948); Barbara Hardy, *The Novels of George Eliot: A Study in Form* (London, 1963); Gordon S. Haight, ed., *A Century of George Eliot Criticism* (Boston, 1965); David Carroll, ed., *George Eliot: The Critical Heritage* (New York, 1971); Elaine Showalter, *A Literature of Their Own: British Women Novelists from Brontë to Lessing* (Princeton, 1977); Sandra Gilbert and Susan Gubar, *The Madwoman in the Attic: The Woman Writer and the Nineteenth-Century Literary Imagination* (New Haven, 1979); Gillian Beer, *Darwin's Plots: Evolutionary Narratives in Darwin, George Eliot, and Nineteenth-Century Fiction* (London and Boston, 1983); Alexander Welsh, *George Eliot and Blackmail* (Cambridge, Mass., 1985); Gillian Beer, *George Eliot* (Bloomington: Ind., 1986); Dorothea Barrett, *Vocation and Desire: George Eliot's Heroines* (London and New York, 1991); Karen Chase, *George Eliot: Middlemarch* (Cambridge, U.K., 1991); Alison Booth, *Greatness Engendered: George Eliot and Virginia Woolf* (Ithaca, N.Y., 1992); David Carroll, *George Eliot and the Conflict of Interpretations: A Reading of the Novels* (Cambridge, U.K., 1992).

T. S. ELIOT

(1888–1965)

Jay Parini

T. S. ELIOT was the most influential poet-critic of his generation and one of the central figures of literary modernism. His reputation at the time of his death was unparalleled, with few doubting that he and William Butler Yeats were the leading poets of the first half of the twentieth century. He defined a period, a tone, and a manner. His major poem, *The Waste Land* (1922), was symbolic of an era. His critical essays and reviews, though never systematic in their approach, had revamped the literary past and redefined the role of the poet. Even his plays, such as *Murder in the Cathedral* (1935), attracted widespread attention. He was, in short, the complete literary artist and man of letters, and few authors in the twentieth century rival his power and influence.

Thomas Stearns Eliot was born on 26 September 1888 in St. Louis, Missouri, the son of a well-off businessman whose own family had roots deep in the upper crust of New England (one relative was president of Harvard). Eventually, in 1927, Eliot became a British subject. Working in London as a banker, then an editor, he often wore a bowler hat and conventional pin-striped suit. He adored English cheeses, belonged to several London clubs, and spoke with an accent that would not have seemed out of place in Buckingham Palace. Like Henry James, he liked all things European, and he read widely in French, Italian, and German literature. He was, in short, the model of the cosmopolitan intellectual, a man who felt equally at home in Boston, London, Paris, and Rome.

Eliot attended Milton Academy in Massachusetts before enrolling at Harvard, from which he graduated in 1909. His most influential teacher was Irving Babbitt, who crusaded against Romanticism in lectures and several books, such as *Rousseau and Romanticism* (1935). In a late essay, Eliot wrote of his old professor: "Mr. Bab-

bitt is a stout upholder of tradition and continuity, and he knows, with his immense and encyclopedic information, that the Christian religion is an essential part of the history of our race" (*Selected Essays,* p. 473). In a sense this describes Eliot as well. He was, he once declared, a classicist in literature, a royalist in politics, and an Anglo-Catholic in religion. From the first he defended the idea of tradition, believing in "the presence of the past" and meditating deeply on the subject in such famous essays as "Tradition and the Individual Talent," which appeared in his first (and finest) book of essays, *The Sacred Wood* (1919).

Eliot was a shy and diffident man, although friends attested to his wit and good humor. He studied literature extensively as an undergraduate, but he decided to pursue an academic career in philosophy and attended the Sorbonne in Paris in 1910. He also studied briefly in Munich before returning to Harvard for graduate school. Among his teachers at Harvard was Bertrand Russell, who remained a friend, and who introduced Eliot to the Bloomsbury circle, the influential group of writers and intellectuals who swirled around Lady Ottoline Morrell. (Those associated with this group included Leonard and Virginia Woolf, John Maynard Keynes, E. M. Forster, and Lytton Strachey.)

At Oxford University in 1914, Eliot finished his thesis on the philosopher F. H. Bradley. Although he sent the thesis back to Harvard, he never himself returned to collect his doctoral degree. Soon he jettisoned the academic world altogether, believing that professional philosophy was not his calling. He married Vivien Haigh-Wood in July of 1915 and began to look for work in London. After a short period of teaching in a secondary school, he took a job in the foreign-currency department of Lloyd's Bank, where he spent eight years and was often overworked. His writing career was largely an activity that occupied him during the evening hours, when he wrote poetry and reviews, the latter to supplement his income. That he managed to write as much as he did under trying circumstances is remarkable, although his nerves were badly frayed by the experience, and he eventually collapsed under the pressure.

Indeed it was during a sojourn at a sanatorium in Switzerland in the autumn of 1921 that he pulled together *The Waste Land* from a mass of poetic fragments. His poetry was little known at the time—he had published a few slim collections over the previous few years—but the effect of *The Waste Land* (published by Leonard and Virginia Woolf at the Hogarth Press) was considerable. Within a few years Eliot achieved a commanding position in the literary world and was offered an editorial position at Faber & Gwyer (later called Faber & Faber). He also became editor of an important periodical, the *Criterion,* which he continued to edit until it folded in 1939. From that base Eliot was in a position to influence contemporary opinions, and he did so with genuine relish, promoting his idea of a traditional Christian society.

Eliot's marriage collapsed in the 1920s (his wife became mentally ill and was permanently hospitalized), and he appears to have suffered from various nervous disorders. Yet he managed to publish small volumes of poetry at regular intervals, and his reputation burgeoned on both sides of the Atlantic. This was the age of the New Criticism, and Eliot was seen as a pioneer in that movement. His critical dicta, uttered in essays and reviews throughout the 1920s and 1930s, became legendary, and academics turned their attention to his work. (His numerous collections of essays included *For Lancelot Andrewes* in 1928, *Dante* in 1929, and *Essays Ancient and Modern* in 1936.) During the war Eliot published *Four Quartets* (1943), his last great work of poetry. His reputation peaked, perhaps, with the Nobel Prize in literature in 1948.

After the war Eliot wrote little poetry, turning instead to poetic drama. *Murder in the Cathedral,* a play about the twelfth-century martyr Archbishop Thomas Becket, remains the high point of his achievement as a dramatist. But his later plays, such as *The Family Reunion* (1939) and *The Cocktail Party* (1950), were surprisingly successful on the stage, although they are rarely produced nowadays.

Eliot died in 1965, a prophet with a great deal of honor. While his critical work belongs to the history of criticism, his poetry remains as fresh and vital as the day it was written. Eliot's reputation has recently, however, suffered from negative attention to his political ideas. Deeply conservative, he was a disciple of the French royalist thinker Charles Maurras, whom Irving Babbitt admired. Like Maurras, Babbitt accepted the idea that the French Revolution had set France and all of Western civilization on a downhill course. Rousseau was singled out as the source of such evil ideas as self-emancipation and mass democracy. Eliot, in Paris during the academic year of 1910–1911, responded viscerally to these ideas.

Eliot's conservatism arose at a period in history when fascism was beginning to sweep Europe, and his natural inclinations led to some dreadful moments, as when in 1933 he suggested in some lectures at the University of Virginia (published in a volume called *After Strange Gods*) that Virginia was lucky in its distance from New York, which was full of "free-thinking Jews." A degree of anti-Semitism, derived from Maurras, occurs elsewhere in Eliot, although he later regretted this prejudice.

The recent reaction against Eliot is also partly due to his position as a modernist, a movement that deconstructionist critics (such as Jacques Derrida) have condemned as "logocentric." Eliot stood for the power of the word as well as (in Christian terms) the Word. He argued for a Christian society and favored the idea of authority to ideas of individualism. In an era of multiculturalism, a time when meaning itself is regarded as inherently unstable, and when thinking about the traditional canon has tended to disrupt the usual hierarchies, Eliot's profile rubs against the grain. It is, indeed, a minor miracle that Eliot retains any respect and influence in the culture at all.

His claim to fame surely rests on the quality of the poetry, in its fundamental humanity and sheer intellectual and emotional power. Few poets have had Eliot's gift for verbal evocation. His lines are often memorable, and there is always in him a sense of gravitas, of earned authority. Having studied Sanskrit as well as Buddhism at Harvard, he brings together insights from the East as well as the West. Moreover, *The Waste Land* remains a central text of its time, embodying a feeling of dislocation and alienation that is part and parcel of the era. Its erudition is stirring, and its modernist innovations have yet to be fully assimilated. The *Four Quartets* stands as a major example of meditative poetry, a vast and moving work that attempts to recover "the timeless moment in time."

"PRUFROCK" AND THE EARLY POEMS

"The form in which I began to write, in 1908 or 1909, was drawn directly from the study of Laforgue together with the later Elizabethan drama," Eliot said, looking back on his beginnings from middle age (Kenner, p. 13). Jules Laforgue was a nineteenth-century French poet whose work reflects a bittersweet dandyism; it is satirical in approach, with moments of intense feeling embodied in sharp symbolic imagery. Eliot heard about Laforgue from *The Symbolist Movement in Literature* (1889) by Arthur Symons—a popular book at the time. What he admired was a tone of mordant satire, of emotion at once intensely felt but nevertheless despised. Thus a note of self-parody creeps in, giving his early work a tonal complexity that was unlike anything else in English verse. The Romantic impulse toward self-expression was modified by a classical impulse to hold emotion at arm's length.

Eliot's most obvious success in this mode is a poem-sequence called "Preludes," where the poet is removed from the urban landscape as "The winter evening settles down / With the smell of steak in passageways." Consider these lines closely. The personification of evening as a creature who might settle down could have occurred in any Romantic poet, but to settle down

with the smell of steak in a passageway is something else. It is unexpected and distinctly modern. It is also evocative: Eliot, here as elsewhere, often refers to smells. He appeals to the senses in most of his best poetry.

The poem goes on to summon an image of newspapers lying in vacant lots, with rain showers beating on "broken blinds and chimney-pots." This is aggressively urban imagery. Indeed, Eliot attaches his unsparing eye to many elements in urban life that unsettle and displease, finding poetry in unpoetic subjects, thus widening the circle of material that can be called poetic. The city, in Eliot's early work, became a place where lost souls wandered, finding in the imagery around them analogues to their pervasive spiritual malaise.

In the second part of "Preludes," morning arrives with the "faint smells of beer." Eliot evinces the sawdust-trampled streets, with muddy feet moving along them. In this world of "a thousand furnished rooms" the individual moves from one interaction to another without a sense of order or purpose. In the third part the speaker, referring to himself for the first time in the second person, says: "You lay upon your back, and waited." In some ways the poem is about waiting, attenuation, a lack of conclusion. That Eliot wrote this poem more or less simultaneously with "The Love Song of J. Alfred Prufrock" is not surprising. These poems share an atmosphere of sordid European urban experience, malaise, and distaste with contemporary life. In fact many of the images in "Preludes" and "Prufrock" overlap. The opening line of the fourth section of "Preludes" describes a soul "stretched tight across the skies," which is not unlike the famous opening lines of Prufrock: "Let us go then, you and I, / When the evening is spread out against the sky / Like a patient etherised upon a table."

Among the well-known early poems are "Portrait of a Lady" and the evocative "Rhapsody on a Windy Night," a masterful early example of Eliot's free verse, where repetition becomes a signature technique, as in:

Half-past one,
The street-lamp sputtered,
The street-lamp muttered,

The streetlamp said, "Regard that woman
Who hesitates toward you in the light of the door
Which opens on her like a grin."

As ever, Eliot's verse never feels entirely "free," nor would that be a good thing. Eliot has total control over his rhythms at every juncture, and he utilizes rhyme as needed. Rhythm in his verse becomes a kind of pulse, not formally tied to any particular meter, though his movement is usually iambic. His rhymes are only rarely sequential or regular, tending more toward internal rhymes and half rhymes. Rhyme, as it were, becomes an echoing device, a way of confirming certain effects. Eliot's imagery, as in the line above where the light of the door opens on her "like a grin," is perpetually surprising, risking leaps of understanding and decorum.

"The Love Song of J. Alfred Prufrock" stands as one of the finest examples of modern poetry and was a stunning achievement for a young man barely out of college. When his American friend in London, the poet Ezra Pound, read it for the first time, he wrote enthusiastically to Harriet Monroe, an editor, in the United States: "I was jolly well right about Eliot. . . . He is the only American I know of who has made what I can call adequate preparation for writing. He has actually *trained* himself and modernized himself *on his own*" (Kenner, p. 73).

One might expect the phrase "love song" to appear in a title, but for this song to emanate from a man called J. Alfred Prufrock is another matter. There was, in fact, a firm in St. Louis by the name of Prufrock-Littau, and Eliot may have gotten the name from that source. The form of the name, with the initial letter concealing something like, say, John or James, is meant to be pretentious. (Eliot himself played around in his youthful days with versions of his own name, signing poems on occasion: T. Stearns Eliot). The name J. Alfred Prufrock—by simple utterance—elicits a derisory smile. As Hugh Kenner has said, "How much of the grotesque melancholy of *Prufrock* radiates from the protagonist's name would be difficult to estimate. It was surgical economy that used the marvelous name once only, in the title, and compounded it with a fatuous 'J. Alfred.' It was a talent already finely schooled that with nice audacity weighed in a single phrase the implications of this name against those of 'Love Song' " (Kenner, p. 4).

Of course it was especially useful to Eliot as a shy young man to dissociate himself personally from the speaker by suggesting that we are listening to a man called Prufrock, who is inherently ridiculous. So Eliot does not have to keep pushing away his character-narrator, making him obviously ludicrous; instead he is able to achieve a kind of intimacy with him that is entirely fetching and ultimately produces an effect of melancholy as the narrator says, "I grow old, I grow old."

Eliot is among the most sonorous and verbal of poets, with each line gathering to itself an aphoristic wholeness. His poems are not only memorable; readers of "Prufrock" also cannot help but be mesmerized by its insistent, cumulative rhythms and trenchant asides and refrains, such as: "In the room the women come and go / Talking of Michelangelo." The repetitions are haunting, as in the third stanza, where the yellow fog becomes a creature of ominous physicality: "The yellow fog that rubs its back upon the window-panes, / The yellow smoke that rubs its muzzle on the window-panes."

Eliot's poem is set in London in the early years of the twentieth century. This cityscape becomes a soulscape, a place where streets follow upon one another "like a tedious argument / Of insidious intent." At the time Eliot wrote these lines, nothing like them had been heard in English poetry. He was, from the start, a shockingly distinctive and original poet, nailing the reader with his evocative phrases, establishing a compulsive rhythm that does not let the reader go.

The opening lines, in which the speaker urges someone to come with him, flow seamlessly from a long quotation from Dante, which might be translated as follows: "If I imagined that my words would be addressed to somebody who might get back alive, this flame would stop quivering; but since nobody ever makes it back alive from these depths (if what they tell me is true), without fear of infamy I answer you." These words, referring to hell, of course, suggest that Eliot's narrator will never return from the world of the dead, from the inferno of his own creation.

But what about the opening lines of this monologue? "Let us go then, you and I." To whom does Eliot refer? Is Prufrock talking with a friend, suggesting they go for a stroll? Is Prufrock perhaps engaging himself in dialogue? Certainly no other person emerges in the poem. Prufrock seems to indulge in self-interrogation throughout. When he says "Let us go and make our visit" he seems to be talking only to himself, encouraging himself to go and visit some woman, to whom he may wish to pose "the overwhelming question."

On a superficial level, the question might be something along the lines of "Will you marry me?" But a much graver insecurity locates in Prufrock, who is totally at a loss to seize control of his circumstances. Self-pity turns to self-hate in one powerful moment: "I should have been a pair of ragged claws / Scuttling across the floors of silent seas." His life has come to nothing but pointless rituals, such as afternoon teas, where connections with other human beings are superficial. Love is the last thing discoverable in this supposed love song. Prufrock has not been able to make contact with anyone on a deep or satisfying level. Nor can he even begin to think how he might "spit out all the butt-ends" of his "days and ways." Every decision is quickly revised: "In a minute there is time / For decisions and revisions which a minute will reverse."

Prufrock is "no prophet," he admits. He claims to have seen the moment of his greatness flicker away—as if there ever really was such a moment. In a telling phrase, he says: "It is impossible to say just what I mean!" As self-expression fails him, he resigns himself to the role of Polonius in *Hamlet,* "an attendant lord." He is "Deferential, glad to be of use." He considers himself "Politic, cautious, and meticulous." But even this would seem a form of self-inflation. He has never advised a prince on anything. Rather, he operates as a remote satellite in the social universe of London. He may have a few friends, but his connections to them are slight. Though growing old and bald, he tries to be fashionable

("I shall wear the bottoms of my trousers rolled"); but even this seems a bit ridiculous. His final dream, as he walks along a beach, is of "sea-girls wreathed with seaweed red and brown." But this dream is quickly shattered, as human voices wake and drown him.

Eliot established himself with *Prufrock and Other Observations* (1917), although his slim volume found few readers. But those readers— many of them leading intellectuals and critics, such as Pound and I. A. Richards—recognized an original and powerful voice. They could not, however, have anticipated *The Waste Land,* a literary masterwork that would revolutionize English verse.

"GERONTION"

ELIOT published another slim volume, simply entitled *Poems,* in 1920, and it contained a major poem, "Gerontion," which had appeared the previous year. While most of the poems in this collection were lightly satirical, without special originality or distinction, "Gerontion" was a leap forward of staggering proportions. The poem is a monologue, but a fragmentary one, without plot. The situation is that of an old man who sits "in a dry month" in some "decayed house" being read to by a boy.

Eliot was beginning to develop a method of sly quotation. Phrase after phrase was torn from his reading, repositioned. Scholars have identified many sources in "Gerontion," from *The Education of Henry Adams* to a biography of Edward FitzGerald. Yet readers were not genuinely expected to "get" the quotations, for the most part. Eliot was just taking what he liked, using it for effects that were wholly original; thus, it seems foolish to use the word plagiarism in this context. Eliot's allusiveness was a form of deep originality, and he never "stole" material in order to deceive. He simply evolved a method that depended on the incorporation of phrases and fragments. The overall effect was to give his poems a feeling of preexistence. One seems to overhear, not hear, his verse.

The situation of the poem is intentionally ambiguous. The speaker is a man of the present, a resident of the postwar world, where meaning is shattered and the traditional symbols no longer revive the spirit; but he appears to have evolved through many incarnations. He was not at the battle of Thermopylae—the "hot gates"—but he might well have been. He represents the European mind at large, timeless. The landscape around him is dry and barren, replete with "Rocks, moss, stonecrop, iron, merds." In a totalizing image of considerable evocative power, his world is epitomized: "A dull head among windy spaces."

History itself becomes a mirror of the old man's brain, a place full of many "cunning passages, contrived corridors." Vanity leads the old man as well as the reader forward through this maze. Then history is transformed into a whore:

> Think now
> She gives when our attention is distracted
> And what she gives, gives with such supple confusions
> That the giving famishes the craving.

Instead of satisfying her client, she makes him hungrier, more anxious. The poem descends into a morass of sensuality that is unrelieved by love—a theme that Eliot would revive and develop carefully in *The Waste Land.*

Tears come, as they must: "These tears are shaken from the wrath-bearing tree," writes Eliot, in the voice of Gerontian, the old man. One thinks of various trees here: the Cross, of course. But one also imagines the Tree of the Knowledge of Good and Evil, the Poison Tree of William Blake, or the blighted fig tree referred to in Matthew 21:19. "After such knowledge, what forgiveness?" Gerontion asks.

Eliot rather dramatically refers to a tiger who "springs in the new year." This is Christ, emblemized as devouring beast and prefiguring Eliot's conversion of 1927. But this old man does not possess salvation, in the Christian sense. "I have lost my passion," he says, but the Passion is also lost on him. The poem ends in a whirl of destruction:

> De Bailhache, Fresca, Mrs. Cammel, whirled
> Beyond the circuit of the shuddering Bear
> In fractured atoms. Gull against the wind, in the windy straits
> Of Belle Isle, or running on the Horn, . . .

This is memorable, a catalog of random souls whirling in a kind of endless purgatory.

"Gerontion" constitutes a breakthrough for Eliot and for English poetry as well. Eliot's famous obscurity, his command of rhetoric, his trenchant powers of expression, his learning, his allusiveness—these are mightily on display here. The poem leads inexorably into *The Waste Land,* a useful prelude to its vastness, ferocity, and beauty.

THE WASTE LAND

THE Waste Land, a poem in five parts, remains one of the founding texts of literary modernism. It has compelled vast critical attention, yet it remains elusive. No single reading of the poem can exhaust its mystery, which inheres in endlessly suggestive passages that cluster and resound in fresh ways on each reading.

Not a single entity, *The Waste Land* is really a sequence of loosely connected poems that, with the help of Ezra Pound, were hewn from a longer manuscript. The logic of the poem defies the usual norms of narrative progression, moving forward by association, following a kind of dream-logic as the poem zigzags from image to image. The connective tissue that might have glued a more conventional narrative together is intentionally missing.

The poem was originally called *He Do the Police in Different Voices,* a line lifted from *Little Dorrit,* where Dickens refers to a character good at impersonating various policemen. Eliot, the grand ventriloquist, becomes the impersonator in his poem, taking on different voices from many segments of society. He captures the manner of speaking of many classes in society, from the aristocratic Marie of "The Burial of the Dead" to the Cockney women in "A Game of Chess." A wide range of characters from high and low, past and present, are evoked in broad strokes, disappearing almost as quickly as they appear in the poem's phantasmagoria of association.

One of the few identified speakers is Tiresias, an "old man with wrinkled female breasts" who has "seen it all," quite literally. In classical myth, Tiresias is the blind old prophet who foretells the future. Because he contains both man and woman in one body, he has acquired the gift of clairvoyance, which he uses to survey the world of contemporary society and place against the past in haunting juxtapositions.

The poet in *The Waste Land* hides behind various masks, or personae. He winks from the corners of the poem, a controlling yet invisible presence, the poet as puppet master. Often he appears to hide behind the voices of other poets, whom he quotes literally or imitates in parodic ways, as in the eloquent opening lines of the first section:

April is the cruellest month, breeding
Lilacs out of the dead land, mixing
Memory and desire, stirring
Dull roots with spring rain.

Here Eliot parodies Chaucer's prologue to the *Canterbury Tales*, turning the medieval poet on his head. April should be a time of fecundity, a prelude to summer's fullness, and the ideal time to go on a pilgrimage, as Chaucer suggested:

Whan that Aprille with his shoures soote
The droughte of March hath perced to the roote
And bathed every veyne in swich licour
Of which vertu engendred is the flour . . .
Thanne longen folk to goon on pilgrimages.

But Eliot's April is malevolent, breeding lilacs, the most overpowering of flowers. Certainly the images culled from memory throughout the poem are mostly painful, and the desires stirred by spring rain are unwelcome, a call to appetite without the controlling discipline of love.

Toward the end of the poem's fifth section, "What the Thunder Said," Eliot writes: "These fragments I have shored against my ruins" (line 431). In a real sense this line encapsulates his method: he culls from the vast chambers of literature, both sacred and profane, dozens of quotations, giving the term "allusiveness" a whole new meaning. While nobody can hope to recognize anything but a small percentage of the works quoted, the patient reader will be rewarded in the end, as the pieces of Eliot's emotional mosaic fall into place.

The poem begins with an epigraph from *The Satyricon* of Petronius. The speaker in the quotation is Trimalchio, a wealthy and vulgar man who says: "With my own eyes I saw the Sibyl suspended in a glass bottle at Cumae—and when the boys said to her, 'Sibyl, what's the matter?' she would always respond, 'I yearn to die.'" The Sibyl of Cumae in Greek myth was a figure of dark prognostications, a version of Tiresias. She foretold the future in riddles, understanding that the unvarnished truth would be intolerable, since—as Eliot later wrote—"Human kind cannot bear very much reality."

In Switzerland, Eliot pulled various fragments together into a single poetic sequence. One can imagine him as he sits among a crowd of neurotic and bored aristocrats, listening to their idle chatter. One of those voices, summoned in "The Burial of the Dead," is Marie, the cousin of an anonymous archduke who remembers riding a sled at some mountain retreat. We hear only a snatch of the archduke's voice as he calls to his presumably younger cousin Marie, telling her to "hold on tight" as they ride a sled down the hillside. "In the mountains, there you feel free," Marie says, adding: "I read, much of the night, and go south in the winter." Nostalgically she recalls a lost world of prewar European stability and the pleasures of being a member of the upper class, where freedom—at least freedom of movement—was taken for granted.

In the second movement of the first section, Eliot assumes an almost biblical voice. "What are the roots that clutch, what branches grow / Out of this stony rubbish?" he wonders, addressing the Son of man, who is traditionally Christ. Although later a Christian, Eliot at this time was still searching, rooting in the dust, where he found only "a heap of broken images." The cross of Christ, "the dead tree," offers "no shelter." The waste land, dry and parched, emerges as the controlling image in this section, with Eliot offering no hope for restitution or recovery: "I will show you fear in a handful of dust," he writes, then quotes Wagner's opera *Tristan und Isolde* in German—a cry of unrequited sexual longing that gives way at once to one of the most lyrical moments in the poem, the evocation of the hyacinth girl:

"You gave me hyacinths first a year ago;

They called me the hyacinth girl."
—Yet when we came back, late, from the Hyacinth
 garden,
Your arms full, and your hair wet, I could not
Speak, and my eyes failed, I was neither
Living nor dead, and I knew nothing,
Looking into the heart of light, the silence.

Just as the lilacs in the first lines suggest hypersensual experience, so the hyacinth floods the senses with meaning. The hyacinth is a potent symbol, rooted in the Greek myth of Hyacinthos, one of the most beautiful boys in Greece, who was killed by Apollo when a discus the god threw hit the boy in the head. He fell to the earth, and his blood drained into the soil, emerging as the beautiful flower, the hyacinth, a symbol of unrequited love.

The third major section of "The Burial of the Dead" brings into play another prophet, though perhaps a bogus one: Madame Sosostris, a clairvoyant modeled loosely on Madame Blavatsky, a famous spiritualist who cut a broad swath through British upper-class society in Eliot's time. (Séances were especially popular in the immediate postwar period and were used by bereaved parents, wives, and children as a means of getting in touch with loved ones killed in battle.) The craze for spiritualism was such that various techniques for telling the future were employed, including the use of tarot cards. In Eliot's poem the tarot figures become convenient symbols that link to other characters and events in the poem. But as the poet carefully points out in his (largely bogus and amusingly pedantic) footnotes to *The Waste Land,* he possessed no deep knowledge of the tarot pack and used the cards to suit his own convenience.

One hears Madame Sosostris talking, calling up a vision of the walking dead: "I see crowds of people walking, walking round in a ring." A voice responds to her, "Thank you. If you see dear Mrs. Equitone, / Tell her I bring the horoscope myself: / One must be so careful these days." Her obsession with bringing her own horoscope suggests that nobody trusts anyone, and that one must control the paraphernalia of spiritualism oneself—a guard against false prophets that is obviously futile. The cards selected from the tarot pack by Eliot—the drowned Phoenician sailor,

for example—will emerge later in the poem in other contexts.

As a whole "The Burial of the Dead" refers specifically to the Anglican burial ceremony, and the final movement of the section constitutes a majestic evocation of the Unreal City, where the dead from all eras walk together in dismal consort. That city is specifically London, but it reaches beyond any geographic locale, standing in contrast to the Eternal City promised to those who believe in God. Indeed, the poet-prophet (Tiresias again?) looks out over London Bridge at the crowd and says, "I had not thought death had undone so many." These very words were uttered by Dante in *The Inferno* when he looked into the pit of hell and saw the multitude of lost souls. As ever, Eliot conflates his own voice with the Voice—the generalized voice of poetry and prophecy, as embodied by Tiresias, Dante, and others.

Eliot was, during the years just before he wrote *The Waste Land,* reading widely in a variety of fields, including anthropology. Two crucial books for him, as he suggests in his notes to the poem, were Jesse L. Weston's *From Ritual to Romance* and *The Golden Bough* by James Frazer—two pioneering works. These books alerted Eliot to certain patterns in world mythology. Primitive people, for example, found coherence and meaning in vegetation myths that followed the cycles of the seasons. These cycles informed the religions that arose in agrarian communities; in particular one found recurring versions of the myth of the dying and reviving god, which in turn were often associated with fertility myths. Eliot works much of this material into the poem, blending pagan and Christian symbols.

In the Christian tradition the search for the Holy Grail (the actual cup used by Christ during the first communion) was associated with heroic efforts to redeem the time. Eliot used aspects of these various myths to underpin *The Waste Land,* thus providing structure and coherence to a wildly disparate body of material. The overarching "story" of the poem concerns the Fisher King (a hero of the Grail legend), who inherited a dry and barren land; he can only restore fertility and prosperity to his people by finding the Grail. This search for a key to the restoration of his kingdom controls the narrative, bringing together on one plane many levels of meaning.

After a blizzard of quotations that brings the first section to a close, Eliot narrows the focus considerably in the second section, "A Game of Chess," where his satirical eye moves from the society of kings and queens to that of pawns. Like Belinda in Alexander Pope's *The Rape of the Lock,* the queen at the outset sits at her dressing table; again like Pope, Eliot uses the mock-heroic form, beginning with echoes of Shakespeare's *Antony and Cleopatra:* "The Chair she sat in, like a burnished throne, / Glowed on the marble." This parodies a famous passage in Shakespeare's play where Enobarbus depicts the royal progress of the queen on her river barge in act 2, scene 2:

The barge she sat in, like a burnished throne,
Burned on the water; the poop was beaten gold;
Purple the sails, and so perfumed that
The winds were love-sick with them; the oars were silver,
Which to the tune of flutes kept stroke, and made
The water which they beat to follow faster,
As amorous of their strokes.

By contrast, the atmosphere in Eliot's royal world is sinister. Above the queen's mantel is not a window looking out to nature but a painting of a cruel scene from classical myth: the rape of Philomel by the lascivious king Tereus. In this world of forced entry, love and lust are confused; the sound of the nightingale, which enchanted the poet John Keats, is crudely transformed. The "inviolable voice" of the bird Keats wrote about has become " 'Jug Jug' to dirty ears." Eliot in fact refers back to the version of the nightingale/Philomel myth preferred by the sixteenth-century poet-playwright John Lyly, who wrote in his play *Campaspe:*

What bird so sings yet so dos wayle?
O 'Tis the ravishd Nightingale.
Jug, Jug, Jug, tereu, shee cryes,
And still her woes at Midnight rise.

In the myth the beautiful Philomel is raped by Tereus (called tereu by Lyly) then transformed into a nightingale; the source of poetry is thus located in pain and rupture.

The first part of "A Game of Chess" bleeds into a contemporary dialogue, as the voices of a man and woman are more overheard than heard in a harrowing conversation that might well occur in a play by Harold Pinter: "My nerves are bad to-night. Yes, bad. Stay with me." There is a strange noise: "The wind under the door." Eliot's voice offers the following bizarre suggestion: "I think we are in rats' alley / Where the dead men lost their bones." The word "nothing" recurs. One does not know who is speaking or to whom; in a sense there is no such thing as dialogue in this wasted land, where human isolation is taken to the extreme. Voices merely tumble in the void, occasionally glancing off another voice or a hard object.

Soon Eliot plunges into a Cockney conversation that suggests that life at the lower end of society is just as barren as life at the top. Lil's husband, Albert, has just been "demobbed," released from the army after four years in the war. He will come home wanting "a good time," and if his wife won't give it to him, "there's others will," or so Lil's friend tells her. Albert had given her some money to buy false teeth—a symbol of artificiality and decay—but she used it for an abortion. The conversation is punctuated, with a haunting regularity, by the bartender's cry: "Hurry up please its time." (It's time to close the bar, of course, but time as well for the characters in the poem to put their house in order.) This cry is repeated with greater frequency and urgency until, in the final lines, it bleeds into the last words of Ophelia, the betrayed heroine of Shakespeare's *Hamlet*: "Good night, ladies, good night, sweet ladies, good night, good night."

In the third section, "The Fire Sermon," Eliot brings together a dizzying array of insights that refer back to and expand upon images and references already in play. The title refers to a Buddhist tradition in which the speaker warns of the fires of lust but also posits fire as a form of redemption. Eliot unites Eastern and Western traditions here, since fire plays a similar role in Christian theology, especially in the work of Saint Augustine, which Eliot summons toward the end of the section.

Past and present, as before, mingle in the Unreal City, which is the London of Eliot's day as well as some mythical metropolis where the dead still walk. The river Thames is central to the poem, a symbol of the stream of time that carries in its flow some important pieces from history as well as much irrelevant garbage. Quoting from Edmund Spenser's lovely *Prothalamion*—"Sweet Thames, run softly till I end my song"—Eliot contrasts the pristine river of the Elizabethan age with the littered banks of the London in his day, where one sees "empty bottles, sandwich papers, / Silk handkerchiefs, cardboard boxes, cigarette ends" and other "testimony of summer nights." A horrific vision of the city foreshadows death as Eliot misquotes Andrew Marvell's "To His Coy Mistress," distorting the famous lines to suit his needs: "But at my back in a cold blast I hear / The rattle of bones, and chuckle spread from ear to ear."

Eliot never stays in one place long and soon meditates again on the rape of Philomel by Tereus. Heterosexual rape is followed by a homosexual proposition as the speaker (unidentified) describes a meeting with an unshaven Smyrna merchant, Mr. Eugenides, who asks him to go away for the weekend to a well-known homosexual retreat, the Metropole. Lust again figures as a prelude to a primary scene of *The Waste Land,* the seduction of a typist at her appalling flat by a "young man carbuncular." Eliot portrays bored and lifeless sexuality with a kind of vicious, almost malicious, eye for detail, launching into a verse manner reminiscent of Pope.

The seduction of the secretary, bland and boring, by definition unfulfilling, occurs in the Unreal City, which is a version of hell or Hades, filled with the walking dead, among which are Elizabeth and Leicester, the Virgin Queen and her consort, who attempts to seduce her on the river. This section concludes with evocations of Augustine (who experienced the flames of sexual desire at Carthage, a commercial city on the North African coast that no longer exists):

To Carthage then I came

Burning burning burning burning
O Lord Thou pluckest me out
O Lord Thou pluckest

burning

This is the nadir of the poem, the pit of hell (although the next section plumbs the depths as well, underwater). Everything from this point on represents a movement toward redemption, however tentative. Not unimportantly, the notion of prayer as a redemptive move occurs to the narrator—a cry to God for help: "O Lord Thou pluckest me out."

The fourth section of the poem, "Death by Water," is a brief lyric that recollects the devastation that has gone before and prefigures the redemptive final movement of the poem. The tarot figure of the drowned sailor is tossed onto the narrative table, a man now "a fortnight dead," buried under the sea, beyond the "cry of gulls, and the deep sea swell / and the profit and loss." (Eliot's job at the bank, of course, was a world controlled by the balance sheet, and escape from it must have seemed sweet.) The underwater currents "Picked his bones in whispers." The reader is warned by the Voice of the poem to "Consider Phlebas, who was once handsome and tall as you." This reminder of our mortality comes at a crucial point in the poem. It also points to liberation: from the fires of lust, from the wheel of life. Freedom is liberation from the round of birth, copulation, and death. Water, in this section and in general, both drowns and rejuvenates.

The fifth section of the poem, "What the Thunder Said," opens in the garden of Gethsemane, then switches to the hill of Golgotha itself, then to a mountain wilderness, where one hears "dry sterile thunder without rain." There is not even the pleasure of solitude in these mountains, nothing but "red sullen faces" that seem to "sneer and snarl" from their "mudcracked houses." Moving back to an urban scene, Eliot summons the Unreal City: "Falling towers / Jerusalem Athens Alexandria / Vienna London." Here Eliot anticipates the worldwide destruction that would occur in just two decades, with bombs falling on London, Dresden, Berlin, Nagasaki, Hiroshima. His nightmarish vision borrows images from the

Dutch painter Hieronymus Bosch (1450–1516), who conjured hell in *The Garden of Earthly Delights,* in which a woman fiddles on her stretched out black hair and "bats with baby faces in the violet light / Whistled and beat their wings, / And crawled head downward down a blackened wall."

But even this vision of evil begins to fade as the narrator realizes that "Dry bones can harm no one." In a decayed hole in the mountains, seemingly in the midst of chaos and a dark night, an empty chapel appears. This is the Chapel Perilous discovered by the Fisher King. The Holy Grail is there, as perhaps suggested by the highly charged atmosphere outside the cave, a place where even "the grass is singing." In the myth, the quester who finds this chapel is shown many things; he has only to ask their meaning and it will be given. Thus in a world where everything seems like "a heap of broken images," the work of imagination involves questioning. The past remains in pieces because nobody bothers to assemble the fragments, to ask real and penetrating questions, to do the hard work of making things whole. This is the work of the artist, of course: to assemble the broken shards. He is gathering the pieces when the poem pivots dramatically: "In a flash of lightning. Then a damp gust / Bringing rain."

Now come the final movements of the poem, where Eliot meditates on the riddle of language, focusing on several related Sanskrit words: *datta, dayadhvam,* and *damyata.* They translate roughly as follows: give, sympathize, control. All have at their root the primitive syllable *da.* (This word foreshadows the Latin *dare,* to give, and survives into various English words, such as *donation.*) In the rubble of the linguistic past, Eliot has found a clue of sorts, something he can use to solve the mystery, to generate new meaning, to bring rain to the parched land. His own extraordinary learning has turned up a key.

This meditation on language leads into the final movement of the poem, a totalizing passage where many elements are brought forcefully together. Eliot reaches freely for bits and pieces of past culture, high and low, as the "I" appears, now clearly the Fisher King, who "sat upon the shore / Fishing," with the arid plain behind him. The king realizes that the time for action has come: "Shall I at least set my lands in order?" He is reminded of the vision of destruction already witnessed, embodied in a nursery rhyme that dates back to the era of the Great Plague: "London Bridge is falling down falling down falling down." But he will not let that pessimistic note stand as the conclusion. Eliot has taken us through the various forms of sympathy and giving. He can now piece together the fragments in his own way, through the use of creative imagination.

A spray of allusion follows: quotations suggesting renewal are balanced against ones suggesting despair ("Hieronymo's mad againe"). Wholeness remains an aspiration, not an accomplishment. The mere fact that Eliot quotes from so many languages suggests that the situation of the Tower of Babel remains in effect: the dream of a common language is only a dream. *The Waste Land* offers a portrait of an age, and it puts before sympathetic and questing readers a key, but the poet himself does not turn the key. He merely points in a direction that can vaguely be called positive. In the last two lines, mimicking the repetitions of liturgy, Eliot repeats the Hindu words: *Datta. Dyadhadvam. Damyata.* Then he concludes, as a liturgy might well, with the Hindu blessing of peace: *Shantih shantih shantih.*

Expressing the anxiety and malaise of postwar Britain, *The Waste Land* succeeds on many fronts, offering a complex portrait of the sophisticated European mind, one broadly familiar with a wide range of places and texts. Eliot explores ancient myth to find keys to contemporary problems. Innovative and exhilarating, the poem has justifiably become a central work of modern literature, a work that continues to attract, infuriate, intrigue, and stimulate generation after generation of readers.

TOWARD AND BEYOND FOUR QUARTETS

ELIOT achieved considerable success, on a smaller scale, with a fragment not included in *The Waste Land* called "The Hollow Men." Published in

1925, this small sequence is exquisitely musical and ends with that famous suggestion that the world will end "Not with a bang but a whimper." The poem articulates some things that Eliot in *The Waste Land* somehow missed, making a wry statement of the moral and spiritual emptiness that defines the modern condition as a living hell wherein a shadow seems to fall between every urge and its completion. Eliot evokes a "twilight kingdom," searching for the more complete kingdom of heaven.

Having become a confirmed Anglican, Eliot published *Ash-Wednesday* in 1930. This is a transitional work, taking Eliot from the despair of *The Waste Land* and the desiccated "twilight kingdom" of "The Hollow Men" into a region of hope. With its explicitly Christian title, the poem recalls Dante's *Purgatorio,* positioning Eliot on the stairs toward heaven. It is a poem of deep repentance, as the poet wishes no longer to "mourn / The vanished power of the usual reign." The poem moves toward rejoicing, although even this is phrased in Eliot's usual hesitations: "Consequently I rejoice, having to construct something / Upon which to rejoice." The poem is, finally, a petition to God. "Teach us to care and not to care," Eliot prays. "Teach us to sit still."

This six-part poem is more abstract than *The Waste Land,* and even more obscure. Eliot was clearly struggling to find an appropriate mode for his religious vision. He experimented with many forms during the 1930s, and a few of his efforts were memorable, such as "Marina," a dramatic monologue spoken by the aged king, Pericles, who contemplates the return of his dead daughter. This poem is vividly written, as in the magnificent opening:

What seas what shores what grey rocks and what
  islands
What water lapping the bow
And scent of pine and woodthrush singing through the
  fog
What images return
O my daughter.

The beautiful "Journey of the Magi" also belongs to this period—another monologue by an old man recollecting his past, contemplating its signifi-cance—in this case, the difficulties of a crucial journey, to the cradle in Bethlehem. Eliot was obviously fascinated by the idea of an old man reconsidering his life, given that so many poems adopt this dramatic situation.

The great achievement of the final years for Eliot remains *Four Quartets.* The five-part sequence was natural for him, so it comes as no surprise that the four poems written in the late 1930s and early 1940s and gathered under one rubric (in 1943) should divide into five parts. "Burnt Norton," "East Coker," "The Dry Salvages," and "Little Gidding" are each rooted in a particular place, spots where Eliot was in some ways inspired, experiencing a "timeless moment in time." While these are Eliot's most avowedly Christian poems, Eliot draws on his lifetime of reading in Eastern religious texts as well.

Various techniques relate one quartet to another. Overall the poems represent (in this order) air, earth, water, and fire—the classical four elements. (Only in the fourth quartet, in the second section, do the four elements explicitly mingle.) Part one of each quartet is usually an abstract meditation, philosophical in nature; it gives way to concrete evocations of a specific time and place, one that has meaning for Eliot personally: East Coker, for example, was an English village where Eliot's ancestors originated in the seventeenth century. The Dry Salvages refers to a stretch of seacoast in Massachusetts where Eliot, as a child, spent holidays.

The second section of each poem begins with a gnomic lyric, in tight form, then gives way to a prosaic second movement where Eliot contem-plates the symbolism of the first part. The third section usually goes the dark way of knowledge, with imagery taken from the London under-ground. There are many allusions to the wartime situation. The last three of the four quartets were, indeed, written under wartime conditions, and Eliot is explicit about this. One recalls that, in *The Waste Land,* the fourth section was a kind of death knell, a brief lyric. The fourth sections of the quartets are also brief and intense. Death permeates these sections, which serve as a prelude to the final, expansive fifth sections, which usually begin with a meditation on language or art and proceed to a religious vision. Each poem ends with a tour de force of lyric intensity as Eliot blends the various elements of each poem.

Eliot contemplates and incorporates a vast range of material in these poems, which imitate a musical form, the quartet, that Eliot admired. Throughout, Eliot draws on personal experiences, memories of his life in the United States and abroad, the London Blitz, and his struggles as a poet. From poem to poem, as from section to section, images and specific phrases are repeated—such as the symbol of the wheel, taken from Hinduism. The poems move forward in a stately manner, with various catalogues that cannot be forgotten, as when he recalls

the moment in the rose-garden,
The moment in the arbour where the rain beat,
The moment in the draughty church at smokefall.
("Burnt Norton," II)

With magisterial technique Eliot knits past and present—his own and the reader's. He sifts through the great symbols of Western and Eastern religion and literature once again, this time finding meaning. The Rose, for example, recurs—from the rose garden scenes of "Burnt Norton" through the vision of the triune Rose of Dante (Father/Son/Holy Ghost) of "Little Gidding." One cannot call this a partisan or narrowly Christian poem since Eliot finds the truth in all contemplative traditions here, although his bias, of course, is toward the Christian symbolism of the tree. (Though even here he refers frequently to other trees, including the World Tree of Norse mythology and the Bo Tree under which the Buddha found enlightenment.)

Whereas *The Waste Land* is more original and provocative, *Four Quartets* is Eliot's most satisfying work: a sequence that brings together so much of his thought in patterns that demand a lifetime of reading and contemplation. The parts where he meditates on language cannot be surpassed for beauty and even usefulness. There is a deep wisdom in this poetry that puts it into that rarefied circle of wisdom literature.

THE PLAYWRIGHT AND MAN OF LETTERS

ELIOT was primarily a poet, but he was also an important critic and accomplished playwright. He carried over into prose and drama what, in "East Coker," he described as "the intolerable wrestle / With words and meanings." While his plays now seem dated, and his criticism has long been absorbed into the history of criticism, this work still beckons to those who wish to understand Eliot as a whole.

He considered the ideal critic as one absorbed in the present problems of art but who brings the forces of the past to bear on the solution of these problems. Whether writing about *Hamlet,* Senecan tragedy, the plays of Ben Jonson, Dante, or John Donne's verse, Eliot demonstrates an easy commerce with the past. His tone is always authoritative, even mandarin. As Roger Sharrock wrote in an essay called "Eliot's 'Tone,' " "The tone of Eliot's mind . . . is fastidious and skeptical, avoiding premature dogmatic formulations. He disarmingly admits inconsistencies, but, in not subscribing to any general aesthetic theory, holds that such self-denial is a prerequisite for any honest literary perception" (in Newton–De Molina, p. 167).

Eliot revamped literary history for critics in his time, drawing attention to the poems of the seventeenth century metaphysical poets—John Donne, George Herbert, Richard Crashaw—and downgrading the eighteenth-century poets and the Romantics. He argued that a "dissociation of sensibility" occurred after the seventeenth century as thought and feeling began to move on separate tracks. He disliked Shelley intensely and had little interest in Wordsworth. While his own theories of literature owed a lot to Coleridge, he rarely mentioned him. He showed a strong interest in the Elizabethans and Jacobeans, and wrote brilliant essays on the nature of poetic drama.

In his seminal "Dialogue on Dramatic Poetry," Eliot suggests that if drama tends to poetic drama, we might expect a poet like Shakespeare to write his best poetry in his most dramatic scenes. "And this is just what we do find," he notes. What makes a scene most dramatic also makes it poetic; the poetic and dramatic are concurrent. In a general way, Eliot's many essays on drama form a blueprint for his own dramatic writing.

His best play remains *Murder in the Cathedral* (1935), which is more of a pageant than a conventional drama. This play about the assassination of the famous English archbishop could not be more dramatic, focusing as it does on a turbulent event in English history. Nevertheless, Eliot gets wonderfully inside the head of Becket, and his play is as much about his hero's inner experience as about the external political situation. As with *Four Quartets*, he writes about "the moment out of time," a flash of insight when a human being makes a connection to eternity. The whole play is built around a single choice—to die or give in—and everything in the play leads up to or away from this existential moment for Thomas Becket.

Eliot's later plays—*The Family Reunion* (1939), *The Cocktail Party* (1950), *The Confidential Clerk* (1955), and *The Elder Statesmen* (1959)—might all be seen as distant refractions of *Murder in the Cathedral*, concerning men having to make choices that will deeply affect their lives and spiritual fates. Certainly in the latter two, the urgency is missing. Eliot's life had, it seemed, come to a point of equilibrium with his second marriage, to Valerie Fletcher, a much younger woman, in 1957. He was indeed himself an elder statesman, the archbishop of poetry. He lived his life in London clubs, restaurants, committee meetings, and drawing rooms. He made elegant speeches at public functions. All signs of outward struggle were absent.

The plays vary in quality and interest, with obvious weakness of characterization in the final two, but they remain worth reading. In all of them, as Helen Gardner has noted, "the unobtrusive vigor of their language modulates from chatter, gossip, or prattle to reflection and serious self-probing, without ever losing its rhythmic vitality" (in Tate, p. 181). In each play an older man is confronted by a demanding situation. In the best of them, *The Cocktail Party*, a runaway wife, Lavinia, suddenly and unexpectedly returns to her husband, Edward. He is not pleased, but he must disguise his displeasure to perform the duties of a host at a cocktail party. He must also deal with Reilly, a badly behaved guest. To this volatile mix Eliot adds two younger people: Celia, Edward's mistress, and Peter, who was Lavinia's lover but now loves Celia. Thus Eliot is able to mix high comedy with a situation that retains certain tragic elements. He does so with elegance and wit in a play about choices. Edward must decide where his affections and duties lie. That none of Eliot's characters are the people they think they are is one of the author's many ironies in this play. Each character, finally, must choose to accept the love of another person in order to become a loving person.

Eliot's later plays are comedies of manners, a genre focused on the relation between the sexes. But Eliot lifts these comedies to a higher level of seriousness by giving his characters real and serious choices. Like Becket, his heroes are placed on the spot, forced to choose or, as in *The Confidential Clerk*, to recognize as valid certain choices made long ago. In *The Elder Statesman*, the elderly Lord Claverton is a portrait of one of Eliot's hollow men, a public figure devoid of personal texture or access to his true experience. Like Becket (who is haunted by abstract Tempters), he is haunted by figures from his past and choices he has already made. In *Four Quartets*, Eliot wrote: "The only wisdom we can hope to acquire / Is the wisdom of humility." And humility is all that is left for Lord Claverton as he approaches the point of death.

CONCLUSION

ELIOT was a protean figure, an innovative poet, an unsystematic but revolutionary critic, an accomplished playwright and social critic, and a cultural presence of considerable magnitude. Some readers will prefer one poem to another, one play or essay to another, but anyone with an objective viewpoint will see in his work an achievement with few parallels in the twentieth century. When asked to write something about Eliot after his death, Ezra Pound replied that his friend was "the true Dantescan voice" of his time. He ended his brief statement with two words that remain the best thing that can be said of this writer: "READ HIM."

T. S. ELIOT

SELECTED BIBLIOGRAPHY

I. POETRY AND PLAYS. *Collected Poems, 1909–1962* (London, 1962); *The Complete Poems and Plays* (London, 1969); *The Waste Land: A Fascimile and Transcript of the Original Drafts,* ed. Valerie Eliot (London, 1971); *Inventions of the March Hare: Poems, 1909–1917,* ed. Christopher Ricks (New York, 1996).

II. ESSAYS AND CRITICISM. *The Idea of a Christian Society* (London, 1939; New York, 1940); *Notes Toward the Definition of Culture* (London, 1948); *Selected Essays* (London, 1951); *On Poetry and Poets* (London and New York, 1957); *To Criticize the Critic* (London and New York, 1965); *The Literary Criticism of T. S. Eliot: New Essays,* ed. David Newton–De Molina (London and Atlantic Highlands, N.J., 1977); *The Varieties of Metaphysical Poetry,* ed. Richard Schuchard (London, 1993; New York, 1994).

III. LETTERS. *The Letters of T. S. Eliot,* vol. 1, 1898–1922, ed. Valerie Eliot (San Diego, Calif., 1988).

IV. BIOGRAPHIES AND CRITICAL STUDIES. Francis Otto Matthiessen, *The Achievement of T. S. Eliot* (Lndon and New York, 1935); Helen Gardner, *The Art of T. S. Eliot* (London, 1949; New York, 1950); Grover Smith, *T. S. Eliot's Poetry and Plays: A Study in Sources and Meaning* (Chicago, 1956); Hugh Kenner, *The Invisible Poet: T. S. Eliot* (New York, 1959); Allen Tate, ed., *T. S. Eliot: The Man and His Work* (London, 1965; New York, 1966); Roger Kojecký, *T. S. Eliot's Social Criticism* (London, 1971; New York, 1972); John D. Margolis, *T. S. Eliot's Intellectual Development: 1922–1939* (Chicago, 1972); James E. Miller, *Reading Eliot* (Chicago, 1978); Peter Ackroyd, *T. S. Eliot: A Life* (London and New York, 1984); James Longenbach, *Modernist Poetics of History: Pound, Eliot, and the Sense of the Past* (Princeton, N.J., 1987); John T. Mayer, *T. S. Eliot's Silent Voices* (New York, 1989); Ronald Bush, ed., *T. S. Eliot: The Modernist in History* (Cambridge and New York, 1991); A. David Moody, ed., *The Cambridge Companion to T. S. Eliot* (Cambridge and New York, 1994); Kenneth Asher, *T. S. Eliot and Ideology* (Cambridge and New York, 1995); Anthony Julius, *T. S. Eliot, Anti-Semitism, and Literary Form* (Cambridge and New York, 1995); Lyndall Gordon, *T. S. Eliot: An Imperfect Life* (London, 1998; New York, 1999).

E. M. FORSTER

(1879–1970)

Neil Powell

E. M. FORSTER would have enjoyed the suggestion—which, like much of his own writing, is not
nearly as frivolous as it seems—that he was the
reincarnation of Jane Austen. As with Austen,
there are five major novels, as well as a sixth
which stands slightly apart, and they depend for
their finest effects on social nuance, ironic humor,
and a wonderfully subtle prose style. Like Austen, too, Forster lived a very English and largely
uneventful life, though a far longer one. He
declared himself a fervent "Janeite" and in *Aspects of the Novel* the appreciative pages which
he devoted to her work might almost be self-
analysis. "All the Jane Austen characters are
ready for an extended life, for a life which the
scheme of her books seldom requires them to
lead, and that is why they lead their actual lives
so satisfactorily," he says (p. 83), perfectly
explaining the success of his own most memorable characters. A page later he gratefully
exclaims: "How Jane Austen can write!"

Edward Morgan Forster was born in London
on 1 January 1879. His father, Edward Morgan
Llewellyn Forster (1847–1880), after whom he
was accidentally named (the baby was registered
as "Henry" but baptized "Edward" by mistake),
was an architect; his mother, Alice ("Lily")
Whichelo (1855–1945), was the third child and
eldest daughter of an art teacher who died when
she was twelve years old. In that year, 1867, a
chance encounter with Marianne Thornton, the
wealthy spinster who would become the subject
of Forster's last book, assured her education and
eventually led to her marriage—for in due course
Lily was employed as a governess by friends of
Marianne Thornton at Abinger Hall in Surrey,
and it was there she met Marianne's nephew
Edward. They married in 1877, but in October
1880, before his son's second birthday, Edward
died. Lily and her various women friends were to

provide the growing boy's predominant social
context for the next decade.

A remarkably high proportion of the places
and personalities in the first thirty years of
Forster's life find their way into his fiction: he
wasted very little. Silly clergymen, sudden
deaths, the oppressive company of doting women:
all these ingredients of the novels are grounded
in his earliest years. But the event in his childhood which was to have the greatest impact on
his writing occurred in March 1883, when Lily
and her son moved to Rooksnest, Stevenage, the
house which he would later transform into
Howards End. Morgan, as Forster was known by
friends and family, grew to love the house and—
another recurrent motif—the garden boys who
were given time off to play with him. They
provided his only regular contact with children
his own age—his favorite among them was called
Ansell. This odd, idyllic life, in which he read
voraciously and behaved for the most part like a
pert little lady, came to an end in 1890 when he
was sent away to prep school in Eastbourne:
there, inevitably and for him confusingly, he
discovered sex and "smut." For the first time he
realized that he was an outsider, a loner who
stood (as he would famously say of Cavafy) "at
a slight angle to the universe."

The year 1893 was a traumatic one, again of
great significance for the future novelist: the lease
on Rooksnest ran out and it was time for Morgan
to go on to public school. Lily's solution to both
problems was ingenious and disastrous: she
would move to Tonbridge, where parents of local
day-boys paid much reduced fees. Tonbridge was
a decent second-rank public school, but Forster
hated the place: it was destined to become the
Sawston of *The Longest Journey*. Nevertheless,
he eventually did well enough to go on to King's

135

College, Cambridge, in 1897. There his most influential friend was H. O. Meredith, the dedicatee of *A Room with a View,* who proposed Forster for membership in Cambridge's most exclusive intellectual society, the Apostles—to whom in somewhat enigmatic fashion ("Fratribus") *The Longest Journey* is dedicated. Although in his Finals he missed a first (he managed an upper second), he stayed on for a fourth year, reading History; by this time, his vague intention of earning his living as a schoolmaster was fading, for he had begun to contribute to literary journals and to think of himself as a writer.

In October 1901, Forster and his mother set off for a year's traveling, mostly in Italy. This seems an extraordinary idea, but it was (as Forster's two Italian novels suggest) quite common at the time: Italian hotels turned out to be full of English women, "mostly middle aged and gushing," as he noted in a letter of 15 December 1901, some of them accompanied by more or less grown-up children. In Florence they stayed at the Pensione Simi, where there was a Cockney landlady—the name "Simi" was probably an unscrupulous Italianization of English "Sims"—and where Forster's "Lucy" novel, the book which would become *A Room with a View,* was born; elsewhere on their tour, a miserable train journey and an overheard piece of hotel gossip, about an Englishwoman's marriage to a young Italian, provided seeds for another planned novel, "Gino." On returning to England, Forster drifted between London and Cambridge—where a bitter ideological dispute between King's and Trinity provided the central conflict for *The Longest Journey*—and between hazy ideas of employment; he did, however, teach a course at the Working Men's College in Bloomsbury, the start of a long association with extramural or "extension" lecturing. By the spring of 1903, he was off again—this time to Greece, depositing his mother and a traveling companion in Florence on the way, and as usual gathering material for novels and short stories.

In 1904, having tried and disliked living in a flat in Kensington, the Forsters at last settled in a gloomy Victorian villa at Weybridge in Surrey.

Meanwhile, walking at Figsbury Rings in Wiltshire that summer, Morgan met a lame shepherd boy, a tiny encounter which was to have an enormous impact on his writing, providing among other things a key symbol and a counterbalance for the academic side of *The Longest Journey.* This book was beginning to take firm shape, alongside the two Italian novels: "Lucy" had by now been overtaken by "Gino," which was finished by the end of the year and retitled "Monteriano." Forster submitted this short novel to *Blackwood's Magazine,* possibly on the assumption that they might run it over more than one issue; instead, they offered to publish it in book form, though they understandably disliked the title. Unable to think of a better one (surprisingly, given the beautifully apt titles of his later novels), Forster consulted his friend E. J. Dent, the musicologist, who suggested "From a Sense of Duty" or "Where Angels Fear to Tread." Blackwoods chose the latter, and the book appeared in 1905.

WHERE ANGELS FEAR TO TREAD

Though not the first to be started, it is right that *Where Angels Fear to Tread* (1905) should have been Forster's first published novel, for it is certainly his *youngest* book. It begins with a brilliant and memorable scene in which the novel's entire English cast—they are all named in the opening paragraph—are assembled at Charing Cross station, where Lilia (widow of the late Charles Herriton) and her chaperone, Caroline Abbott, are setting off for Italy. The emotional chemistry of the Herriton family—Lilia's mother-in law, her prim daughter Harriet whose "education had been almost too successful" (p. 13), her cultured but naive son Philip, and her young granddaughter Irma—is one source of the novel's momentum; Forster also manages to squeeze on to the station platform two characters who will be sent offstage for the rest of the book, Lilia's troublesome mother Mrs. Theobald and her rejected suitor Mr. Kingcroft, who has escorted her down from Yorkshire (a place more distant than Italy in this imaginative world).

The opening chapter is an extraordinarily assured performance, full of the Jane Austen–like ironic touches which we have come to regard as "Forsterian." His characters continually utter speeches which are truer than they know, or which turn out to be true in unexpected ways: "Love and understand the Italians, for the people are more marvellous than the land," Philip advises Lilia (p. 5); while Mrs. Herriton, thinking of the spurned Mr. Kingcroft, complacently decides, "When a man is neither well-bred, nor well-connected, nor handsome, nor clever, nor rich, even Lilia may discard him in time," only for her son to reply, "No, I believe she would take anyone" (p. 8). Mrs. Herriton's fault is merely that of mildly endearing stupidity, but the Italophile Philip is more culpably guilty of misapplied intelligence: he knows that "this vulgar woman," his sister-in-law, may be "transfigured"—"The same had happened to the Goths"—but his own experience so far provides no inkling of the kind of transfiguration Lilia will achieve through literally following his advice to love the Italians. Meanwhile, Forster's narrative is already rich in the technique which Christopher Isherwood, whose own prose owed much to him, described as "tea-tabling": "The whole of Forster's technique is based on the tea-table," says Allen Chalmers (the novelist Edward Upward) in Isherwood's *Lions and Shadows;* "instead of trying to screw all his scenes up to the highest possible pitch, he tones them down until they sound like mothers'-meeting gossip" (p. 107). Thus, the most telling insights into the Herriton household at Sawston—the name, to be used in *The Longest Journey* for Tonbridge, probably signifies its near-neighbor, Tunbridge Wells—come from the subtlest details. "Tea was in the dining-room, with an egg for Irma, to keep up the child's spirits" (p. 7) encapsulates the Edwardian upper-middle-class family ethos in a single sentence. The letter which announces Lilia's engagement interrupts Mrs. Herriton's pleasant task of sowing peas; a good deal of panic ensues, and Philip finds that he is to go at once to Monteriano to stop the affair ("For three years he had sung the praises of the Italians, but he had never contemplated having one as a relative"

[p. 18]). Yet the chapter's final paragraph is a perfect example of the tea-tabling principle, as we return to the peas and the letter:

> Just as she [Mrs. Herriton] was going upstairs she remembered that she never covered up those peas. It upset her more than anything, and again and again she struck the banisters with vexation. Late as it was, she got a lantern from the tool-shed and went down the garden to rake the earth over them. The sparrows had taken every one. But countless fragments of the letter remained, disfiguring the tidy ground.
>
> (p. 19)

It is worth dwelling on these details from the opening pages of Forster's first published novel because they are characteristics which recur throughout his work, as does the theme of misunderstanding between social classes, a fact which partly explains the early curtailment of his career as a novelist. Although Lilia's engagement would still have seemed "unsuitable" twenty or forty years later, it would have become far less shocking than it was in 1905; later readers might reasonably feel that Lilia, being neither a blood relation of the Herritons nor much liked by them, should have been left to get on with her own life as far away from Sawston as possible. But Philip, a more conventional Edwardian than he cares to admit, sets off on his absurd mission, and the comic phase of the novel begins. Arriving at Monteriano, he eventually learns from Miss Abbott ("good, quiet, dull, and amiable, and young only because she was twenty-three" [p. 21]) that Lilia's fiancé, Gino Carella, is the twenty-one-year-old son of the local dentist, and he is appalled less by the match than by the idea of anything so prosaic as a dentist in his revered Monteriano, which is a thinly disguised San Gimignano. When Lilia tells him that "this time I marry for love," he is overwhelmed by the "coarseness and truth of her attack" (p. 33); while his attempt to bribe Gino ends in a farcical scene during which he learns that the couple are already married.

Forster inwardly understands the Herritons, for their social background is his own, but his view of both Lilia and Gino is necessarily more external. His descriptions of Italian provincial life were also, as he would later admit, based on guesswork; the guesses are good ones, however, and the portrait of Lilia's and Gino's troubled, mutually uncomprehending domesticity is largely convincing. One slightly jarring note comes from a tendency, which he would never completely overcome, to overinstruct the reader, to *tell* when he ought to *show:* "It was in this house that the brief and inevitable tragedy of Lilia's married life took place" (p. 37). Another, no less characteristic, is the tragedy's abrupt and melodramatic end: "As for Lilia, someone said to her, 'It is a beautiful boy!' But she had died in giving birth to him" (p. 60). Forster can seldom resist a sudden death, and this one is the more surprising since he has provided only the briefest and haziest hints that Lilia is indeed pregnant (a word he naturally eschews).

After Lilia's death, the novel becomes at least ostensibly about the battle for custody of the baby: one sentence about Irma from Forster's shrewd first chapter—"That curious duel which is fought over every baby was fought and decided early" (p. 10)—takes on an eerie new significance. Irma is by now nine years old and an avid collector of picture postcards: one, which the fatally unimaginative Harriet takes to be "a lot of ruined factory chimneys," is inscribed "View of the superb city of Monteriano—from your lital brother" (p. 70), and once the secret of Irma's exotic "lital brother" is out in Sawston, something has to be done. Philip is once more sent as an ambassador to retrieve the child, this time unhelpfully accompanied by Harriet. The increasingly meddlesome Caroline Abbott turns out to be there already, and it is she who will later identify the scheme's flawed moral basis: "Do you want the child to stop with his father, who loves him and will bring him up badly, or do you want him to come to Sawston, where no one loves him, but where he will be brought up well?" (p. 130). It is an expedition which can only end in disaster.

But Forster is not primarily concerned with the baby, which will eventually become, twice on successive pages (pp. 138, 139), merely a "bundle," and neither are his central characters. Philip "did not care about the baby one straw"

(p. 87) and even the unreconstructed Caroline proves forgetful: " 'The baby—?' She had forgotten it" (p. 117). None of the three visitors even bothers to ask the child's name. Instead, the author's main interest is in the growth of his two most interesting English characters, Philip and Caroline. Philip is a recurrent Forsterian type: educated and cultured, yet emotionally inexperienced and inclined to blunder—"a tall, weakly-built young man" with "a fine forehead," "a good large nose," and "observation and sympathy in his eyes." However, "below the nose and eyes all was confusion, and those people who believe that destiny resides in the mouth and chin shook their heads when they looked at him" (p. 61). Philip needs to discover the missing connection between art and life, and he does so at an amiably chaotic performance of Donizetti's *Lucia di Lammermoor,* which ends with him being hauled into Gino's box and welcomed as a long-lost brother—it is a magnificent scene, fully the equal of the more famous Beethoven concert in *Howards End.* Of course, Philip cannot be wholly transformed—he "would have a spasm of horror at the muddle he had made" (p. 107), and "muddle" is a significant and recurrent word for Forster—but from this point we sense that he will never return to the joyless life of Sawston.

For Caroline Abbott, the opera is only a partial revelation. Next morning, she visits Gino, still with the vague intention of negotiating for the baby, and ends up bathing the child and falling in love with his father. It is a scene which, in its coiled-up emotional power and domestic physicality, resembles the work of a writer whom Forster is usually thought to be wholly unlike—D. H. Lawrence—and it is not the last time that this unexpected resemblance will occur in his novels. By this point, it is plain that neither Philip nor Caroline is likely to carry out the original plan; so it is left to the inhuman Harriet to kidnap the baby and thus to precipitate the accident in which he is killed. Forster can never forgive priggishness: his ironic punishment of Harriet is to leave her untransformed and unenlightened, capable of referring to " 'this unlucky accident,' and 'the mysterious frustration of one's attempts to make things better' " (p. 155).

He does forgive Philip and Caroline, though he rightly thwarts Philip's silly proposal of marriage to her. When Caroline confesses her tearful love for Gino, Philip conventionally replies: "Rather! I love him too!" (p. 157). There is more to it than that, of course. Philip loves Gino in a way which neither he nor his author can yet acknowledge—Forster later said that when he was writing the scene in which Gino twists Philip's already broken arm (pp. 146–148), he was excited in a way which he did not fully understand—and it is this intense, subterranean sexual charge that gives the novel much of its strange power. We shall reencounter this power, and most of these themes, in Forster's subsequent novels.

Forster spent much of 1905 abroad, employed in Pomerania as tutor to the daughters of the Countess Russell—a difficult, mercurial woman who was the "Elizabeth" of a best-selling gardening book called *Elizabeth's German Garden* (1898) and a partial model for Mrs. Failing in *The Longest Journey* (Mrs. Failing's other source was his Northumbrian Uncle Willie, whose house becomes "Cadover" in the novel). He was back in England by the time *Where Angels Fear to Tread* was published, to generally favorable reviews, in October. The early months of 1906 found him extension-lecturing in the West Country; then he was back at the Working Men's College, fitting in some private coaching of a young Indian, temporarily living in Weybridge before going up to Oxford, called Syed Ross Masood. Masood was lazy and feckless; he was also attractive, charming, and uninhibitedly affectionate. He liberated Forster's emotions exactly as Gino Carella had liberated Philip Herriton's. And, meanwhile, Forster had completed his second novel, *The Longest Journey,* which appeared in April 1907.

THE LONGEST JOURNEY

THE Longest Journey was Forster's favorite among his own novels, although he was perfectly aware that it is not his best: he liked it because its ingredients are so closely related to his own youth, which also accounts for its unevenness of focus and tone. The antiheroic central character,

Rickie Elliott (properly Frederick, and thus nicknamed by his father on account of his inherited "rickety" clubfoot), owes something to Philip Herriton: he too is sensitive and educated—the opening scenes take place in the Cambridge of Forster's student days—though weak and naive. We meet him in his rooms, hosting an Apostles-like meeting in which his closest friend and chief adversary is the severely rationalist Stewart Ansell. Rickie's separateness is swiftly and emphatically established in a flashback synopsis of his childhood. First, there is the lameness: as a small child he gives the "wrong" answer to the question "Now which is your left hand?" by replying "The side my bad foot is" instead of mentioning his heart (p. 29), and at the age of twelve he wonders if he will ever have any friends, for they all walk too fast, "And a brother I shall never have" (p. 30). Then there is the fact that he is the orphaned child of an unhappy marriage: his father dies after a long illness when Rickie is a fifteen-year-old public schoolboy, and eleven days later, his mother also dies, inexplicably (evidently not from a broken heart), after hinting at a planned move to the country. Thereafter he spends his holidays with poor relations, the discouragingly named Silts.

However, he is also befriended by the Pembrokes—Herbert, a schoolmaster at Sawston, and his much younger sister, Agnes—whom he visits during the Christmas vacation near the start of the book. At Sawston he discovers to his horror that Agnes is engaged to be married to Gerald Dawes, whom he "vividly" remembers as the bully who terrorized him at school. It is a variation on a recurring Forsterian dichotomy—damaged intellectual and athletic hero—except that there is nothing admirable about Gerald, who is stupid, boorish and ugly: "Just where he began to be beautiful the clothes started" (p. 40). They have insufficient money to marry and, out of misplaced sympathy for Agnes, Rickie offers to help Gerald out financially—he is certain he will never marry and risk passing on his inherited deformity. After furiously rejecting this offer, Gerald is "broken up" in a football match and dies in the pavilion (p. 56). There have been three sudden deaths, only one of them reasonably plausible, within the first sixty pages—but this third death supplies an important motif. Instead of comforting Agnes, Rickie tells her "It's the worst thing than can ever happen to you in all your life, and you've got to mind" (p. 58); "I came to see that you mind. . . . The greatest thing is over" (p. 59). It is an almost exact echo of Caroline Abbott's moment of truth—"All the wonderful things are over" (*Where Angels Fear to Tread,* p. 156)—and we shall find its positive corollary in *A Room with a View.*

A year or so later Agnes, properly chaperoned of course, visits Rickie in Cambridge, and they fall in love. It is the wrong sort of love—English and dull rather than Mediterranean and imaginative—and it will lead to a disastrous marriage, with Rickie, who becomes a teacher at Sawston where he and his wife assist Herbert Pembroke in running a school boardinghouse called Dunwood, returning to precisely the middle-class suburbia from which he had escaped. In the meantime the engaged couple must visit Rickie's eccentric aunt, Emily Failing, at Cadover in Wiltshire (he has in fact already paid one fleeting visit while staying with the Ansells, but Forster seems to have forgotten)—this is the most powerful and the most problematic of the book's three significant locations. Living in Mrs. Failing's house, though apparently neither servant nor lodger, is a hearty, healthy young man called Stephen Wonham. He and Rickie argue almost at once, about a grotesque accident in which one of two children playing on the level-crossing had been run down by the train bringing the lovers to Cadover: "Now, now! Quarrelling already?" asks Mrs. Failing (p. 100), as if this is what she had anticipated and planned. By the end of their stay, Rickie has learnt from Mrs. Failing that Stephen (although he doesn't know this) is his younger half-brother. He reacts with prim Edwardian shock—"Then a horror leapt straight at him" (p. 136)—and, not for the last time in the novel, promptly faints.

Stephen, with some unanticipated help from Ansell, is the catalyst for almost everything else that happens in the book. He reappears soon after the birth and early death of the Elliotts' crippled daughter: a bullied boy called Varden has written

to various well-wishers and one of these letters, meant for "a man in the Church Army, living at a place called Codford" (p. 192), implausibly reaches Stephen at Cadover by mistake; he sends an honest, irreligious reply, and the contact with Sawston is shakily established. Then Agnes and the Silts begin to plot Stephen's disinheritance; when Rickie discovers this, the half-truth about his half-brother ("You see, my father went wrong" [p. 208]) is revealed to an appalled Herbert. Soon after this, Stephen is indeed sent away from Cadover and comes to Sawston with the supposedly joyful news of his newly discovered kinship. Agnes tries to buy his silence—an attempt which he, being truthful and uncomplicated, finds bizarre: "Here's a very bad mistake" (p. 225) is his response—but Ansell, who is also visiting Sawston and has already met Stephen, at last has his revenge on middle-class hypocrisy. He announces the truth at Sunday lunch in Dunwood House, adding for good measure that Stephen is Rickie's mother's son, not his father's (a fact which the astute reader might already have deduced from his able-bodiedness). Rickie, of course, faints again.

The final section of the book has an overwrought inevitability. Rickie leaves Sawston, with the vague intention of looking after Stephen, and ends up staying with the Ansells; from there he embarks on a possibly reconciliatory visit to his aunt, but Stephen insists on accompanying him, intending to stay in the village and promising not to drink. But Stephen's village friends have been evicted: he goes to the inn, gets drunk, and collapses on the level-crossing where Rickie, trying to rescue him, is run over by a train. Emily Failing supplies his epitaph—"one who has failed in everything he undertook" (p. 281)—and an epilogue briskly sketches a subsequent time in which Mrs. Failing is dead, Mr. Pembroke has become a clergyman, and his remarried sister has a son named after him. Stephen, meanwhile, has a daughter named after his (and Rickie's) mother; we leave them together in a Wiltshire field, inheriting the earth, in an image to be paralleled at the close of *Howards End.*

The Longest Journey takes its title from lines, admired and quoted by Rickie, in which Shelley challenges "that great sect" who believe that one should "With one sad friend, perhaps a jealous foe, / The dreariest and the longest journey go" (p. 133); as in his other novels, Forster tries to find ways of advocating inclusive friendship and of making connections between disparate forms of experience. Although he is right to recognize that education on its own is not enough, he is too readily trapped into romanticizing the lack of it in Stephen, just as he did in Gino. Part of the problem may be his unacknowledged sexual interest in these attractively masculine characters, but there is also a broader lack of understanding of the intuitive, natural world. Cambridge and Sawston ring true; Wiltshire, by contrast, is a place of emblems and gestures. Forster remains divided. His head is with Stewart Ansell, his heart is with Stephen Wonham; however, he is still too close to Rickie Elliott to make sense of the whole picture.

A ROOM WITH A VIEW

In Forster's third published (though first started) novel, *A Room with a View* (1908), he overcomes many of the difficulties of the two previous books, and it seems entirely appropriate that he should do so by dividing the setting between Italy and England. It is a lighter, less intense, and more optimistic novel than its two predecessors, though not for these reasons an inferior one; and there is only one sudden death, that of a nameless Italian in a brawl. This is Forster at his most Jane Austen–like—which is perhaps to say most like himself.

A Room with a View is a comedy of sincerity versus manners. We meet most of the main characters in a typically brilliant opening scene at the Pension Bertolini (with its cockney Signora) in Florence. Lucy Honeychurch and her middle-aged cousin-chaperone, Charlotte Bartlett, have north rooms without a view; Mr. Emerson and his son George have south rooms with a view, which they promptly offer to exchange. The offer, from complete and somewhat uncouth strangers, is an affront to good manners and must be declined; but the intervention of an apparently benign clergyman, Mr. Beebe (who happens to be the newly appointed vicar of Summer Street, the Honeychurches' home village in Surrey), saves the situation. When Lucy plays Beethoven on the Bertolini's piano, it is Mr. Beebe who presciently if ambiguously observes: "If Miss Honeychurch ever takes to live as she plays, it will be very exciting—both for us and for her" (p. 36). Also at the Pension Bertolini are Eleanor Lavish, a lady novelist, and two elderly spinsters, the Miss Alans.

The comedy of the early chapters stems from the fact that, despite Charlotte's ineffectual efforts to protect her, Lucy repeatedly falls into the arms of the odd and subversive Emersons, without recognizing that they are her true allies. Old Mr. Emerson rescues her when she is lost, without her Baedeker, in Santa Croce; young George Emerson catches her as she faints after seeing the Italian stabbed in the street (in a reversal of the earlier books' pessimism he realizes that "something tremendous has happened" [p. 50]); and when most of the English party take a drive into the country George not only catches but kisses her, an outrage which prompts Charlotte to take Lucy off to Rome next day. Typically, as with the Emersons' earlier blunders and with Stephen Wonham's illegitimacy and drunkenness in *The Longest Journey,* Forster makes the most of the Edwardian social mores he satirizes: as K. W. Gransden astutely points out, "the conventions against which Forster is working as a moralist, work *for* him as technician" (*E. M. Forster,* p. 32). It is, however, more para- doxical still, for Forster thoroughly enjoys the subtleties of social nuance, even though he feels he ought to mock them. His entire fictional enter- prise is founded on the knowledge that eccentricity flourishes in the nooks and crannies of con- vention, that freedom is valueless without constraint.

The action now moves to England—to Windy Corner, Summer Street. Here we meet two "pleasant people" (p. 88), Mrs. Honeychurch and her son Freddy (like the Herritons and the El- liotts, this is a fatherless family); they are indeed "pleasant"—Forster uses the word as a sort of ironic double bluff—and Mrs. Honeychurch will emerge, for all her eccentricity, as a shrewd judge of her daughter. There is also Cecil Vyse, an old friend reencountered in Rome, who now proposes for the third time to Lucy and is accepted. Freddy rightly dislikes him; his mother attempts a defense:

> "Well, *I* like him," said Mrs Honeychurch. "I know his mother; he's good, he's clever, he's rich, he's well connected—Oh, you needn't kick the piano! He's well connected—I'll say it again if you like; he's well connected." She paused, as if rehearsing her eulogy, but her face remained dissatisfied. She added: "And he has beautiful manners."
>
> (p. 91)

But we know, Forster knows, even Mrs. Honeychurch knows that this isn't enough. Cecil is another frigidly cultivated young man, a more extreme version of Philip Herriton who, like Philip, will be partially redeemed by acknowledging the error of his ways. He notes that Italy has "worked some marvel" on Lucy: it "gave her light, and—which he held more precious—it gave her shadow" (p. 95). Yet he cannot guess, and she cannot admit, that the cause of this transformation is not Italian culture but George Emerson; and he is wrong about almost everything else. When Lucy benignly arranges for the Miss Alans to rent a vacant villa at Summer Street, Cecil creates a "muddle" (p. 120), that most ominous term in Forster, by producing alternative tenants—an odd father and son called Emerson, whom he has met by chance in the National Gallery. When required to make up a tennis four with Lucy, Freddy, and George Emerson, he instead reads aloud from a novel he has picked up—*Under a Loggia* by "Joseph Emery Prank," otherwise Eleanor Lavish—which contains absurd descriptions of a view in Italy; meanwhile, Charlotte Bartlett has arrived to stay, begging "an inferior spare room—something with no view" (p. 151). Alas, Cecil chooses the wrong dreadful passage, not about the view itself but about the wordless encounter of two lovers: "No eloquence was his, nor did he suffer from the lack of it. He simply enfolded her in his manly arms" (p. 171). Almost at once, George seizes an opportunity to kiss Lucy for a second time.

With a series of shamelessly creaking coincidences, Forster has prepared the scene for his lengthy denouement. Charlotte must be scolded for breaching Lucy's confidence and react accordingly ("Never again shall Eleanor Lavish be friend of mine" [p. 175]), though we suspect she is changing sides. George, summoned to receive his dismissal from Windy Corner, bravely confronts Lucy with the truth: "You cannot live with Vyse. He's only for an acquaintance. He is for society and cultivated talk. He should know no one intimately, least of all a woman" (p. 177). This, and much else in George's speech, will be repeated almost word for word by Lucy when she breaks off her engagement, prompting Cecil's astounded (and admiring) response: "You are even greater than I thought . . . this evening you are a different person: new thoughts—even a new voice" (p. 184). After this, she plans a trip to Greece with the Miss Alans, who see through her, and it is left to old Mr. Emerson—the first of the book's truth-tellers, with his insistence that she should have a room with a view—finally to open her eyes. She is in a muddle, he tells her; "Take an old man's word: there's nothing worse than a muddle in all the world" (p. 214). And the reason is clear: "You love George! . . . You love the boy body and soul, plainly, directly, as he loves you, and no other word expresses it" (p. 215). Mr. Beebe, in whose house this exchange takes place, seems "suddenly inhuman. . . . [a] long black column." He declares himself "more grieved than I can possibly express"; George, he says, "no longer interests me" (p. 217), and Forster leaves the reader to deduce what kind of interest might have produced this reaction. The Miss Alans duly go to Greece, but Lucy and George return to a room with a view at the Pension Bertolini.

Lucy Honeychurch is a pure Jane Austen heroine: comfortably off, intelligent, and obtuse, she spends most of the novel failing to see that George Emerson is her destined match, just as Emma Woodhouse spends most of *Emma* failing to see that Mr. Knightley is hers. But the book also owes much to Shakespearean comedy: the movement from an urban opening to a rural world (where everything is scrambled and unscrambled) and back to the original scene is exactly the pattern of *A Midsummer Night's Dream;* the dark, equivocal, and eventually sidelined Mr. Beebe is a version of Jaques in *As You Like It* or Malvolio in *Twelfth Night.* To invoke these parallels is to emphasize the fact that *A Room with a View* is Forster's one true comedy. There would not be another.

HOWARDS END

By the time *A Room with a View* appeared, Forster was once again hard at work on another novel: consciously or not, he was following a variation on *Emma* with a book which, like *Mansfield Park,* takes its central values and its title from a house. *Howards End* (1910) draws on memories of his childhood home, Rooksnest, which had been nudged towards fiction when he revisited Stevenage in 1906; there he reencountered one of the Forsters' former neighbors, a wealthy retired businessman called Mr. Poston, together with his much younger and more cultivated second wife. This disparate couple were to evolve into Henry Wilcox and Margaret Schlegel, and their mysterious relationship would suggest the novel's motto: "Only connect. . . ."

Fatherless, as usual, and motherless too, the Schlegels—Margaret, Helen, and Tibby—are the most carefully thought out of all Forster's families. They are German by ancestry, in a cultural-philosophical rather than in a militaristic way; Fräulein Mosebach, their comical German cousin, is surely Forster's revenge on the milieu of gardening "Elizabeth," and there is also a ludicrous English aunt, Mrs. Munt, whose muddling interference gets the plot going. "One may as well begin with Helen's letters to her sister" (p. 5): these tell us that Helen, visiting some chance acquaintances named Wilcox at Howards End, has fallen in love with the younger son, Paul. It is the "wrong" match (he is swiftly sent to Nigeria and never seen again), and so the book appears to set off on a familiar path: well-off girl (Lucy, Helen) meets acceptable but wrong man (Cecil, Paul) and ends up with unacceptable but right man (George, Leonard). Yet *Howards End* is a far more subtle and complex novel than *A Room with a View,* for not only will this scheme be thwarted (Leonard will be dead before the book's end)—it is not even the central element of the plot, which is largely carried by Margaret Schlegel, the most ambitious characterization in all Forster's fiction.

It is Margaret who formulates the crucial difference between the Schlegels' world and the Wilcoxes': "To think that because you and a young man meet for a moment, there must be all these telegrams and anger," she tells Helen; in this other, outer world, "love means marriage settlements, death, death duties" (p. 27). Her "difficulty" is that she sees how the "grit" of the outer life—"It does breed character"—may contrast with the "sloppiness" of their own. To reinforce our sense of Margaret's intellectual independence, Forster takes the Schlegels, their German cousin, her "young man," and Mrs. Munt to a performance of Beethoven's Fifth Symphony: their eccentricities are neatly revealed in relation to the music, and Helen absentmindedly walks off with a stranger's umbrella. As its owner, a clerk called Leonard Bast, accompanies Margaret to retrieve it, she babbles happily about Monet and Debussy, and the differences between the arts: "Helen's one aim is to translate tunes into the language of painting, and pictures into the language of music" (p. 38). It is a kind of conversation to which Leonard hopelessly aspires and with which Forster would have been at ease; but, like the Cambridge chatter in *The Longest Journey,* he knows that it is not enough, that it lacks "grit." Margaret knows this too and when, by a typically Forsterian coincidence, the Wilcoxes take a London flat directly opposite their house in Wickham Place, she is quick to defend Mr. Wilcox from Mrs. Munt's slighting description of "an elderly man with a moustache and a copper-coloured face"—"He has a remarkably good complexion for a man of his age" (p. 57)— and to assert that "Money pads the edges of things. . . . God help those who have none" (p. 58). She calls on the invalid Mrs. (Ruth) Wilcox, a figure whom we shall meet again as Mrs. Moore in *A Passage to India:* unintellectual yet spiritual, she stands at a point between and beyond both the Schlegel and Wilcox worlds. Her voice only quickens when she speaks of Howards End and its wych-elm with pigs' teeth stuck into the bark (a charm against toothache);

when she lunches at Wickham Place, Margaret's clever friends are unimpressed, but Margaret—and her author, whose point of view she shares—notes that she "was not intellectual, nor even alert, and it was odd that, all the same, she should give the idea of greatness" (p. 73). Aware of Margaret's empathy, Ruth Wilcox impetuously proposes an expedition to Howards End, but this is intercepted by the rest of the Wilcox family returning from holiday.

Chapter 11 begins: "The funeral was over" (p. 83). It is a little while before we learn that it is Ruth Wilcox's funeral; the most audacious of Forster's sudden deaths has taken place offstage. She has left Howards End to Margaret in an un-witnessed pencil note, and she haunts the rest of the novel—at least, the main strand of it in which Margaret becomes the second Mrs. Wilcox. When Henry proposes marriage, "Mrs Wilcox strayed in and out, ever a welcome guest; surveying the scene, thought Margaret, without one hint of bit-terness" (p. 156); and when Margaret at last visits Howards End, Miss Avery, the eccentric old lady who is the place's unofficial guardian, says, "I took you for Ruth Wilcox," to which Margaret can only reply: "I—Mrs Wilcox—I?" (p. 189). Forster contrasts this benign, spiritual view of inheritance with the materialism of the Wilcox children—elder son Charles, his sister Evie, and his wife Dolly: to them, Margaret is "a horrid woman" (Dolly) and "a cosmopolitan" (Charles) who must not have the house. At least Henry Wilcox is more just: "If Miss Schlegel had been poor, if she had wanted a house, I could under-stand it a little. But she has a house of her own. Why should she want another? She wouldn't have any use for Howards End" (p. 95). He is unaware that the Schlegels' lease at Wickham Place is about to expire; after he discovers this, he sug-gests that they should have his London home in Ducie Street, but when Margaret arrives there he offers not his house but his hand. Charles, hear-ing of the engagement, worries that his father may be infected by the Schlegels' "artistic beast-liness" (p. 173), while Evie thinks of returning her mother's "lace and jewellery 'as a protest'" (p. 193).

But the real challenge to the marriage comes from a different direction. The idealistic though inept Helen has taken up the cause of Leonard Bast who, thanks to careless advice received secondhand from Henry Wilcox, loses first one job and then another. Leonard, the clerk who tries and fails to embrace culture, is a plausible portrait, evidently drawn from Forster's experi-ence of the Working Men's College; his ex-prostitute wife, Jacky, is less successful. She is an artless Cockney Sparrow who turns out to have had a relationship with Henry—a fact which becomes evident when Helen brings the destitute Basts to Evie's wedding at Oniton, yet another Wilcox house: this one is in Shropshire, which provides a detached third location for the novel, just as Wiltshire does in *The Longest Journey*. Quite early in the book, Forster writes: "We are not concerned with the very poor. They are unthinkable" (p. 44). But by the time the Basts reach Oniton, they have become "very poor": Jacky, hopelessly drunk, confronts her ex-lover—"If it isn't Hen!" (p. 216)—while a typically vague sexual encounter with Leonard leaves Helen pregnant and mysteriously self-exiled to Germany. It is typical, too, that the mechanism of the novel's denouement should depend on a baby (as in *Where Angels Fear to Tread*) and on illegitimacy (as in *The Longest Journey*).

The heart of this dense, inexhaustible book is Margaret's mission to join two disparate worlds: "Only connect! That was the whole of her sermon. Only connect the prose and the passion, and both will be exalted, and human love will be seen at its height" (p. 174). This connection is achieved only partially, and by unexpected means. Margaret forgives Henry his past miscon-duct, insofar as forgiveness is in her power: "For it was not her tragedy: it was Mrs. Wilcox's" (p. 218). But when the heavily pregnant Helen is lured to Howards End, to collect some of her books which are stored there, Henry cannot forgive her and idiotically sanctions the interven-tion of his son Charles. In a brief, overwrought scene, Leonard arrives, swiftly followed by Charles, who hits him with the Schlegels' ornamental sword; he stumbles against a book-case and dies beneath an avalanche of books.

Charles is convicted of manslaughter and jailed; the Wilcox world is in ruins. Meanwhile, Margaret and Henry settle at Howards End, as Miss Avery had predicted, with Helen and her child, and we leave them on a note of pastoral reconciliation: " 'The field's cut!' Helen cried excitedly—'the big meadow. We've seen to the very end, and it'll be such a crop of hay as never!' " (p. 319). But it is an imperfect reconciliation. Tibby, the unworldly brother who studies Chinese at Oxford, has no part in it. Nor do the Basts. And nor do the Wilcox children, who significantly are to be left money (which they understand) but not Howards End (which they do not): the house is to be Margaret's and, after her, her nephew's.

Howards End is a more ambitious novel than it at first seems. The tortuous relationship between the intellectual and the commercial segments of the English middle class—the tension which also underlies George Eliot's *Middlemarch*—is a vaster, trickier theme than anything Forster had previously attempted. Furthermore, he sets this in the context of a meditation on England which some readers have thought sentimental but which now looks, much more cogently, ecological. Chapter 13 opens with an extraordinary passage on the decline of London:

> And month by month the roads smelt more strongly of petrol, and were more difficult to cross, and human beings heard each other speak with greater difficulty, breathed less of the air, and saw less of the sky. Nature withdrew; the leaves were falling by midsummer; the sun shone through dirt with an admired obscurity.
>
> (p. 102)

This idea and its corollary, fulsome praise of the countryside and especially of Howards End, recur throughout the book. The passage which follows Margaret's first visit to the house—"it was English, and the wych-elm that she saw from the window was an English tree" (p. 192)—recalls Jane Austen's evocation of "English verdure, English comfort, English culture" in *Mansfield Park,* and a memorable image of London "creeping" comes at the very end: Helen "pointed over the meadow—over eight or nine meadows, but at the end of them was a red rust" (p. 316). It is an uncannily prescient moment: in 1910, even Forster could scarcely have guessed that in the 1950s Stevenage New Town would indeed be built "eight or nine meadows" away from his beloved Rooksnest.

The acclaim which greeted *Howards End* was burdensome to its author, who may have already suspected that he would have trouble following it, and it was succeeded by personal sadness: his grandmother died; his mother became acutely depressed. He published a collection of short stories, *The Celestial Omnibus* (1911), which included another example of his prescience in "The Machine Stops," a futuristic fable about a world in which humans live in identical cells (there being no point in traveling between identical cities), dependent on a universal machine so complex that it can no longer be repaired; meanwhile the natural world grows wild but holds out a hope of regeneration. During the early twentieth century this seemed fanciful; in the electronic age, it has acquired a new poignancy. Masood, meanwhile, was reading for the bar, and in 1912 Forster followed his barrister friend to India, where his travels began to provide material for an as yet unstarted novel.

When he returned to England in 1913, a visit to Edward Carpenter and his friend George Merrill in Harrogate had a momentous result. Merrill, who was fond of touching people, touched Forster on the buttocks, an experience that led Forster to immediately conceive a novel about homosexual love—and, what's more, a novel with a happy ending—something no respectable author in pre–First World War England could dream of publishing.

MAURICE

Maurice, completed in 1914 but unpublished until 1971, the year after Forster's death, is a necessary but unsatisfactory book. It is the story of Maurice Hall who, after a confused childhood, falls in love with a Cambridge contemporary, Clive Durham, who to Maurice's distress "outgrows" his homosexual phase and eventually marries. However, while visiting Penge, the Durhams' decaying ancestral home, Maurice finds himself haunted by an attractive young gamekeeper, Alec Scudder, who is shortly to emigrate to Argentina and who one night appears via a conveniently placed ladder in his room. Figures of moral authority—a pompous old doctor, a bogus hypnotherapist, a foolish vicar—make their troubling appearances; but after various misadventures, including a rendezvous at the British Museum at which Maurice also encounters his former schoolmaster, Alec misses the boat which was to take him to South America. The lovers are reunited in the boathouse at Penge, "And now we shan't be parted no more, and that's finished" (p. 225).

Although *Maurice* is a courageous book and often—in its portrayal of Edwardian Cambridge, its period details, and its sly comedy—an enjoyable one, it does not stand comparison with the other five novels. It was hastily, even urgently written, and its forty-six brief chapters lack Forster's characteristic poise and fluency: "He failed: i.e., his knowledge was incomplete, or he would have known the impossibility of vexing athletic love" (p. 101) is the kind of sentence which would not have survived in a book written for publication. Moreover, despite some fine and telling scenes about homosexuality in general— such as the one in which the Mr. Lasker Jones, the hypnotherapist, advises Maurice to emigrate since "England has always been disinclined to accept human nature" (p. 196)—whenever Forster writes more specifically about sex his prose style becomes arch and imprecise. The ending implies (as Forster specifically suggests in his later "Terminal Note") that the lovers will disappear into that pastoral England which would be destroyed by World War I: the book "belongs to the last moment of the greenwood. *The Longest Journey* belongs there too, and has similarities of atmosphere" (p. 240). But it is hard to see how Maurice Hall, any more than Rickie Elliott, could have survived there.

The war—most of which Forster enterprisingly spent working for the Red Cross in Alexandria— drastically changed the England which had been his subject. In 1921 he set off for India once more, to take up an appointment as Secretary to the Maharaja of Dews and to explore a different imaginative world.

A PASSAGE TO INDIA

In his final novel, *A Passage to India* (1924), Forster produced a book which is notably unlike its predecessors: set wholly outside England, with a large and (we would now say) multicultural cast and a mysteriously spiritual tone. Or did he? For the still more striking feature of the book is its close kinship, beneath its exotic skin, with Forster's previous novels. The whole plot pivots upon an encounter between a young Englishwoman (Adela Quested) and an attractive stranger (Dr. Aziz) in a remarkable place (the Marabar Caves)—exactly like Lilia and Gino at Monteriano or Lucy and George in Tuscany. The tripartite form—"Mosque," "Caves," "Temple"—echoes his earlier habit of using three contrasting locations: Cambridge, Sawston, Wiltshire; Howards End, London, Oniton. The characters, too, form three groups—English, Muslim, Hindu—just as they did in *Howards End* with its distinct but overlapping worlds of Schlegels, Wilcoxes, and Basts; and their fates are overseen by the benign, Ruth Wilcox–like spirit of Mrs. Moore. *A Passage to India* is an Anglo-Indian novel in a very precise sense: it is an English novel in India.

"I like mysteries but I rather dislike muddles," says Mrs. Moore (p. 68), giving memorable form to a distinction which has been implicit throughout Forster's fiction. *A Passage to India* has its share of each. The first part, "Mosque," opens with a description of Chandrapore, a city which contains "nothing extraordinary" apart from the Marabar Caves, "and they are twenty miles off" (p. 9). We will later learn that these caves are at once mysterious and featureless—identical smooth-walled cells, each reached by a short rough passage and possessing a peculiar echo which reduces all conversation, all sound, to "Boum"; it is like the disorientating "panic and emptiness" which Helen Schegel heard in the third movement of Beethoven's Fifth Symphony (*HE*, p. 33). Mrs. Moore has traveled from England to visit her son, Ronny Heaslop, the City Magistrate, bringing with her his fiancée, Adela Quested (she also has two other children, Ralph and Stella, by her second marriage, and this will become a significant complication). We encounter her in a mosque, escaping from the entertainment at the British club. Here she is surprised by the Muslim Dr. Aziz; they get into conversation and Aziz impulsively tells her, "you are an Oriental" (p. 24). Mrs. Moore's intuitive grasp of India contrasts sharply with Adela's facile wish, "I want to see the *real* India" (p. 25): this is a more intense version of the distinction which pervades the two Italian novels between those who travel by instinct and those who follow the guidebook. The parallel is emphasized when Cyril Fielding, head of the local Government College, suggests that Miss Quested should "Try seeing Indians" (p. 27), advice which, like Philip Herriton's "Love and understand the Italians," will have unexpected consequences. To amuse their guests, the leading members of the British community arrange a "bridge party" (one that bridges the racial barrier); there, Fielding invites the two ladies to tea.

There could hardly be a more striking instance of Forsterian "tea-tabling" than this. The gathering which takes place in Fielding's garden house includes Mrs. Moore, Miss Quested, Dr. Aziz, and Professor Godbole, Fielding's deeply enigmatic Hindu assistant—it is a combination rich in potential misunderstandings, which duly occur. Aziz rashly invites the assembled company to visit him but, feeling his bungalow too shabby for entertaining, changes this into a picnic at the Marabar Caves; Professor Godbole, having been persuaded to describe the caves, will only say what they are *not* like; and Ronny Heaslop blunders in tactlessly to disrupt the party. Later that evening, the Nawab Bahadur's car, in which Adela and Ronny are traveling, collides with a mysterious animal: a small, odd omen which somehow affects even Mrs. Moore, who is not physically present. "I don't want to see India now; now for my passage back," she thinks; but when her son speaks of the muddle and incompetence of the Indians she has met, she replies: "I like Aziz, Aziz is my real friend" (p. 93), an unequivocal, crucial benediction.

The expedition, which takes place in the novel's second section, "Caves," is a disaster. Fielding and Godbole, delayed by the latter's prayers, miss the train; however, Mrs. Moore comforts Aziz by saying "We shall be all Moslems together now, as you promised"; "She was perfect as always, his dear Mrs Moore" (p. 131). But when they reach the caves and Mrs. Moore enters one with an accompanying retinue, she feels claustrophobic: "For not only did the crush and stench alarm her; there was also a terrifying echo" (p. 145). Sensibly, she suggests that Adela and Aziz explore further without her, taking fewer people into each cave. What happens next seems perfectly clear, as we see it from Aziz's point of view: Adela foolishly asks him whether he has more than one wife (his wife is in fact dead); he, embarrassed, darts into a cave where he lights a cigarette; when he emerges, she is rushing downhill towards a car which has brought Fielding. But something is wrong: her field glasses are abandoned, their strap broken; and, just as Fielding reaches Aziz, the car speeds off towards Chandrapore with Adela in it. When the rest of the party returns by train, Aziz is arrested at the station, accused of attempted rape.

Despite its clear affinities with his other novels, this central section finds Forster taking new risks. Never before has his imaginative landscape been so opened out and so variously populated: the Marabar expedition is more than an alfresco tea party. Never before has he placed an insoluble mystery—one to which he would claim, perhaps playfully, to have no solution himself—at the heart of a work. The first account he provides of the "Marabar incident" is what Aziz believes to have happened: we are inclined to trust him (we shall have Fielding's authority that our trust is well-placed), so we believe him. But what of the alternative views? Unlike Turton, the Collector, and Major Callendar, the Civil Surgeon (both of whom hold violently racist views), McBryde, the Police Superintendent, is "the most reflective and best educated of the Chandrapore officials," who has "read and thought a good deal" and has "much of the cynic about him, but nothing of the bully" (p. 164). This careful endorsement lends credence to McBryde's belief in Aziz's guilt: the evidence seems compelling but one item—the photograph of a woman taken from the defendant's desk—confirms the slippery nature of reality in this novel. Fielding believes it to be of Aziz's late wife: he has already been shown the photograph—"She was my wife. You are the first Englishman she has ever come before" (p. 113)—yet this degree of intimacy between Fielding and Aziz is, to McBryde, so unthinkable as to cast even greater doubt on the story: "Wife indeed, I know those wives!" (p. 169). Professor Godbole offers another, specifically Hindu interpretation:

> "I am informed that an evil action was performed in the Marabar Hills, and that a highly esteemed English lady is now seriously ill in consequence. My answer is this: that action was performed by Dr. Aziz." He stopped and sucked in his thin cheeks. "It was performed by the guide." He stopped again. "It was performed by you." Now he had an air of daring and of coyness. "It was performed by me." He looked shyly down the sleeve of his own coat. "And by my students. It was even performed by the lady herself. When evil occurs, it expresses the whole of the universe. Similarly when good occurs."
>
> (pp. 174–175)

Godbole is, however, uncharacteristically clear that the "verdict will be in strict accordance with the evidence," and in this he is to be proved right.

The trial scene is another departure for Forster: comparable events—the inquests after the death of Gino's baby and of Leonard Bast, the trial of Charles Wilcox for manslaughter—have taken place offstage. The turning point comes when it inadvertently emerges that a key witness, Mrs. Moore, is not to be called; she has already left India and (unknown to anyone present) has died on the journey home, but her name is taken up by the crowd and transformed into "Esmiss Esmoor, a Hindu goddess" (p. 219). Shortly after this, giving evidence, Adela unconditionally withdraws her charge. In the jubilation which follows, Fielding finds himself torn between a wish to celebrate with his friend Aziz and an obligation to look after Adela, now abandoned by the British establishment. "To slink through India unlabelled was his aim" (p. 172), but he is forced to take sides, first with Aziz, then with the misguided if ultimately courageous girl. It is against this background of strained loyalties,

reinforced by rumors, that the book's final section, "Temple," takes place.

Time passes and the scene moves to the Hindu state of Mau, where Professor Godbole is now Minister of Education and Dr Aziz, despite being a Muslim, is a senior physician; the action takes place against the backdrop of a lovingly and comically described religious festival. Godbole, for all his inscrutable omniscience, remains plagued by mild absurdities: one banner, "by an unfortunate slip of the draughtsman," reads "God si Love"; "Is this," Forster asks, "the final message of India?" (p. 281). Godbole knows (but has not said) that Fielding, now an inspector of education, and his new wife are on their way, partly to visit Aziz, partly to look at an unfortunately nonexistent high school. But Aziz has destroyed Fielding's letters unread, convinced that his old friend has married his old enemy, Adela Quested (in fact, he has married Stella Moore, whose brother, Ralph, is also accompanying them). It is a muddle, though it will grow into a mystery. When they accidentally meet, Ralph is suffering from a bee sting which Aziz must treat; and after the confusion over Fielding's wife has been angrily resolved, it is Ralph who recognizes that Aziz is no longer "unkind." Surprised, Aziz asks: " 'Can you always tell whether a stranger is your friend?' 'Yes.' 'Then you are an Oriental' " (p. 306). The circle is com-completed but, as in *Howards End,* the resolution is imperfect: although Aziz and Fielding want to reestablish their friendship as they ride out together, "the horses didn't want it—they swerved apart" and "the temples, the tank, the jail, the palace, the birds, the carrion, the Guest House . . . they said in their hundred voices, 'No, not yet,' and the sky said, 'No, not there' " (p. 317).

As its closing section especially suggests, *A Passage to India* is the book in which Forster begins to pull away from the conventional idea of the novel: so much of its significance is carried by symbolism or texture that it seems to aspire to the state of poetry or of music. Its two spiritual guardians, Mrs. Moore and Professor Godbole, both withdraw from the human events they oversee—one into death and ghostly presence, the other into religious inscrutability. It is perhaps not surprising that, as far as writing novels was concerned, Forster decided to join them.

ESSAYS AND CRITICISM

APART from occasional short stories (some of which would be included in *The Life to Come,* published in 1972), Forster's main literary output during the rest of his long life consisted of reviews, critical articles, broadcasts, and lectures. In 1927 he gave the annual Clark Lectures at Trinity College, Cambridge. These were later published as *Aspects of the Novel,* a collection which is one of the twentieth century's least academic and most informative books on the novel—from its whimsical opening idea of novelists from different periods all writing simultaneously in a circular room, to its delightfully conversational treatment of fiction in its component parts, such as "The Story" ("Yes—oh dear yes—the novel tells a story" [p. 33]), "People," and "The Plot." The easy tone and civilized intelligence are also characteristic of the essays and broadcasts gathered in *Abinger Harvest* (1936), *Two Cheers for Democracy* (1951), and *The Prince's Tale and Other Uncollected Writings* (1998). At the very heart of these is the 1939 essay "What I Believe," with its faith in a particular kind of aristocracy—"Not an aristocracy of power, based upon rank and influence, but an aristocracy of the sensitive, the considerate and the plucky" (*Two Cheers for Democracy,* p. 81)— which precisely describes the moral basis of his last two novels.

Some pieces had surprising and far-reaching consequences: a talk on George Crabbe, broadcast in 1941 and published in *The Listener,* persuaded Benjamin Britten to return home from America and to compose his opera, *Peter Grimes,* based on Crabbe's poem; Forster would later provide the libretto for another Britten opera, *Billy Budd* (1951). His later book-length works are modest and affectionate, almost as if designed to avoid disrupting a reputation crowned with *A Passage to India:* biographies of his Cambridge friend Goldsworthy Lowes Dickinson (1934) and his great aunt Marianne Thornton (1956); and a notebook account of his travels in India, *The Hill of Devi* (1953).

Forster's many close literary friends included J. R. Ackerley, Christopher Isherwood, and William Plomer, and he was actively involved in such organizations at the National Council for Civil Liberties and International PEN; but his intimate relationships tended to be with bus drivers and policemen. When his Aunt Laura died in 1924, he inherited her house, West Hackhurst, at Abinger; he moved there with his mother, dividing his time between Surrey and a flat in London. After his mother's death in 1945, he accepted an honorary fellowship at King's College, Cambridge, which became his permanent home for the rest of his life. In May 1970 he suffered a fall and a stroke; he was taken at his own request to the Coventry home of the Buckinghams—his loyal policeman friend Bob and wife May— where he died on 7 June 1970.

CONCLUSION: ASPECTS OF THE NOVELIST

IN the introductory chapter to *Aspects of the Novel,* Forster amiably mocks the "pseudo-scholar," whose obsessive need is to "classify" books which he has not understood nor possibly even read. His own novels are justly troublesome to pseudo-scholarship: they defy easy classification, not least because their largest themes lurk in their smallest details, and when Forster refuses to take matters seriously he is often being very serious indeed. At the center of the five novels he published in his lifetime is a brilliantly developed contradiction: their moral drive is towards a liberal, tolerant society but their vital energy (like their comedy) springs from manners and conventions he affects to dislike. This affectionate ambiguity towards the world he describes is one reason why the Forsterian tone, for which "irony" now seems too devalued a term, is at once so hard to classify and so easy to recognize. Another is a poised yet relaxed prose style, which, some early archness apart, is always a pleasure to read, together with deftly telling dialogue: in these qualities he is, like Jane Austen before and Christopher Isherwood after him, one of the great conversational companions of English literature.

E. M. FORSTER

SELECTED BIBLIOGRAPHY

I. COLLECTED WORKS. The Abinger Edition, begun in 1972, will comprise the following volumes when complete: 1: *Where Angels Fear to Tread;* 2: *The Longest Journey;* 3: *A Room with a View;* 3a: *The Lucy Novels;* 4: *Howards End;* 4a: *The Manuscripts of* Howards End; 5: *Maurice;* 6: *A Passage to India;* 6a: *The Manuscripts of* A Passage to India; 7: *The Machine Stops,* with other stories; 8: *The Life to Come,* with other stories; 9: *Arctic Summer and Other Fiction;* 10: *Abinger Harvest* and *England's Pleasant Land;* 11: *Two Cheers for Democracy;* 12: *Aspects of the Novel;* 13: *Goldsworthy Lowes Dickinson;* 14: *The Hill of Devi,* with other Indian writings; 15: *Marianne Thornton;* 16: *Alexandria;* 17: *The Prince's Tale,* and other uncollected writings.

II. NOVELS. Page references are to the Penguin (Harmondsworth) edition where one is listed. *Where Angels Fear to Tread* (Edinburgh, 1905; repr. Harmondsworth, U.K., 1959); *The Longest Journey* (Edinburgh, 1907; repr. Harmondsworth, U.K., 1960); *A Room with a View* (London, 1908; repr. Harmondsworth, U.K., 1955); *Howards End* (London, 1910; repr. Harmondsworth, U.K., 1941); *A Passage to India* (London, 1924; repr. Harmondsworth, U.K., 1936); *Maurice* (London, 1971).

III. SHORT STORIES. *The Celestial Omnibus* (London, 1911); *The Eternal Moment* (London, 1928); *The Life to Come* (London, 1972), with other stories.

IV. ESSAYS AND CRITICISM. *Aspects of the Novel* (London, 1927; repr. Harmondsworth, U.K., 1962); *Abinger Harvest* (London, 1936; repr. Harmondsworth, U.K., 1967); *Two Cheers for Democracy* (London, 1951; repr. Harmondsworth, U.K., 1965); *The Prince's Tale* (London, 1998), with other uncollected writings.

V. BIOGRAPHY. *Goldsworthy Lowes Dickinson* (London, 1934); *Marianne Thornton* (London, 1956).

VI. OTHER WORKS. *Alexandria: A History and a Guide* (Alexandria, Egypt, 1922); *Pharos and Pharillon* (Richmond, U.K., 1923); *England's Pleasant Land: A Pageant Play* (London, 1940); *The Hill of Devi* (London, 1953).

VII. LETTERS. *Selected Letters of E. M. Forster,* ed. Mary Lago and P. N. Furbank, 2 volumes (London, 1983–1985).

VIII. BIBLIOGRAPHY. B. J. Kirkpatrick, *A Bibliography of E. M. Forster* (London, 1965).

IX. CRITICAL AND BIOGRAPHICAL STUDIES. Rose Macaulay, *The Writings of E. M. Forster* (London, 1938); Lionel Trilling, *E. M. Forster* (London, 1944); Rex Warner, *E. M. Forster* (London, 1950); K. W. Gransden, *E. M. Forster* (Edinburgh, 1962); Wilfred Stone, *The Cave and the Mountain* (Stanford, 1966); Lawrence Brander, *E. M. Forster: A Critical Study* (London, 1968); P. N. Furbank, *E. M. Forster: A Life,* 2 volumes (London, 1977–1978); Nicola Beauman, *Morgan: A Biography of E. M. Forster* (London, 1993); Mary Lago, *E. M. Forster: A Literary Life* (Basingstoke, U.K., 1994); Jeremy Tambling, ed., *E. M. Forster* (London, 1995).

GRAHAM GREENE

(1904–1991)

Cates Baldridge

GRAHAM GREENE IS a writer of far greater importance than the label "Catholic novelist"—with which he is too frequently and easily burdened—can adequately suggest. The fact is that Greene is the most significant figure in English literature between the passing of High Modernism and the present day, and his vision of life is too wide and too original to be labeled simply as "Catholic" or confined within any other ready-made category. Greene's main subject is nothing less than the endemic violence—physical, ideological, and spiritual—of the twentieth century, and his central argument is that only an active, committed engagement with modernity's dangerous political and ethical struggles can redeem the individual in both a secular and (perhaps) a religious sense. All his notions concerning God, Catholicism, and belief spring from these concerns, and not the other way around. In the course of articulating his vision of the contemporary world Greene produced not only novels but short stories, dramas, screenplays, and essays. If in what follows our focus is mainly upon his narrative fiction, it is because the novels are without question the strongest of his works from a purely artistic standpoint, and the genre in which his thought was freest, boldest, deepest, and most prophetic. Indeed, if future generations wish to understand the tone and texture of the twentieth-century world, they could hardly do better than to encounter the harrowing plots, anguished protagonists, and attenuated modes of hope and faith found within nearly all of Greene's more than two dozen novels.

Born on 2 October 1904, during an era one of his characters would later describe as "the last peace for any of us," Graham Greene's first eight years were idyllic. His father was the headmaster of an Anglican boarding school in Berkhamsted, outside London, and the village, frequented by numerous nearby relatives and shared with many brothers and sisters, was his to explore in safety and comfort. This sense of security was abruptly curtailed, however, when, in 1910, Greene became a student at his father's academy. Because of who he was, the other students assumed he was a spy and a snitch, and he soon discovered he had "left civilization behind and entered a savage country of strange customs and inexplicable cruelties: a country in which [he] was a foreigner and a suspect, quite literally a hunted creature." It was in the school dormitory—so near and yet so far from the comforts of the nursery—that the author's lifelong fascination with questions of loyalty and betrayal was forged. His chief means of escape were novels of adventure such as Rider Haggard's *King Solomon's Mines* and the equally thrilling tales of John Buchan, which had a marked influence on his own later works. However, these literary diversions did not keep young Greene from manifesting troubling symptoms of his chronic misery, and thus in 1920 his father took the unusual step of sending him for a live-in visit with a psychiatrist, a step that appeared to help, if only because it provided a respite from the terrors and humiliations of school.

Greene enrolled in Balliol College, Oxford, in 1922, where he edited the literary magazine and desultorily pursued a degree in history. It was at this time that he claims to have played Russian roulette, asserting that the hammer clicking on an empty chamber gave him "an extraordinary sense of jubilation, as if carnival lights had been switched on in a drab street." Later in life this need to counteract boredom with danger drove the author to travel to dangerous destinations in strife-torn countries, which would then become the settings of his novels. His college years also saw a brief flirtation with the Communist Party (he was to remain a man of the Left all his life), and the beginnings of his interest in Catholicism. Greene's chief reason for eventually entering the Catholic Church was his desire to marry Vivien Dayrell-Browning, a Catholic woman with whom he had fallen in love, and his relationship with Church doctrine was always characterized more by skepticism than adherence. To put it succinctly, Greene was a Catholic only in the same sense that the visionary poet William Blake was a Protestant, for Greene's religious imagination was also essentially personal and unorthodox, and he spent most of his life attempting to work out a form of Christianity compatible with the political horrors and skeptical spirit of the twentieth century.

EARLY NOVELS

GREENE published a book of poetry while at Oxford entitled *Babbling April* (1925), but his main literary ambition was to write novels, and after graduation this desire gestated as he worked to support himself and Vivien. Holding a series of jobs with provincial newspapers, he eventually worked his way around to the London *Times,* where he was a sub-editor for several years, a task at which he was competent and which gave him a good deal of satisfaction while also sharpening his writing skills and widening his experience. Still, his first published novel, *The Man Within* (1929), doesn't read much like a novel by Graham Greene, though it was a considerable public and financial success. Set on the south coast of England in the early 1800s, and centering on a group of smugglers and a doomed love affair, what really differentiates this first effort from Greene's later fictions is its relentlessly interior focus, which turns the outside world into a vague, dreamlike realm of fogs, sunsets, and moonlit foliage in which the sharp and terrible edges of the world cannot be sharply evoked. This same tendency was exaggerated in Greene's next two novels, *The Name of Action* (1930) and *Rumor at Nightfall* (1931), neither of which sold many copies and both of which Greene suppressed in later years. Downcast over a literary career that seemed to be going nowhere,

our author claimed that now "for the first time in [his] life [he] deliberately set out to write a book to please, one which with luck might be made into a film." Paradoxically it appears that this striving to match the popular taste also put Greene in touch with the wellsprings of his own original genius, for in his next novel, *Stamboul Train* (1932), he hit upon a happy combination of style, subject, and point of view that would ensure his popular and artistic success through the end of the decade: he had invented what might be called "the highbrow thriller."

Stamboul Train is very much an ensemble piece, following a group of passengers on the *Orient Express* from Ostend to Istanbul. At first they have nothing in common other than their tickets to ride. The way in which Greene gradually intertwines the lives of a weary communist revolutionary, a lesbian newspaper reporter, a workaholic businessman, a needy showgirl, and a prideful thief as the train proceeds across Europe is masterful. While the novel contains many of the standard features of the thriller such as secret codes, concealed weapons, and a daring rescue, Greene avoids the unrealistic theatricality of the genre by consistently showing that events are beyond the control of the persons involved, that actions always have unintended (and sometimes absurd) consequences, and that even central aspects of our own personalities are hidden from us. Furthermore, this tough-minded vision concerning the vanity of human aspirations is tied to a deft critique of Europe's political condition in the 1930s, for issues of economic depression and militaristic oppression are in every newspaper and on every mind, tying the timeless and the topical perspective together into a seamless whole. Finally, the writing is crisp and vivid, as if Greene's metaphors had taken on the speed and efficiency of the famous train itself: "the great blast furnaces of Liège rose along the line like ancient castles burning in a border raid" (p. 20).

Greene's next three books—*It's a Battlefield* (1934), *England Made Me* (1935), and *A Gun for Sale* (1936)—demonstrate both an expansion and a consolidation of his powers as a novelist. *It's a Battlefield* is an almost Dickensian panorama of social injustice and personal guilt, centering on the impending execution of Drover, a striker who has inadvertently killed a policeman during a labor protest. Greene's vision of 1930s Britain as the site of an endemic political contest in which isolated "regiments"—the police, the Communist Party, government bureaucrats, the newspapers—battle each other to a kind of exhausted standoff is a bleak one for the individual characters, whose dreams and even lives are trampled in the endless rounds of attack and counterattack. *England Made Me,* on the other hand, is a much more tightly focused book, concentrating as it does upon the lives of a brother and sister whose strong bonds of affection and painful responsibility for each other eventually fail to protect them from the imperatives of a ruthless international corporation, to which they have both hitched their worldly ambitions. The hero, Anthony, is an early version of a figure we meet often in Greene—a deeply flawed man who nevertheless has reservoirs of courage and decency of which he himself is unaware, but which a crisis brings to the surface. That this hidden cache of virtue is enough to perhaps save the soul but not the life of the protagonist is also a pattern we encounter elsewhere in the Greene canon. Finally, in *A Gun for Sale,* psychological and political themes again merge as the hoodlum Raven, hired by a munitions tycoon to kill a peace-loving foreign diplomat and then double-crossed by his paymaster, is shown to have been molded into the violent creature he is by a life of privation and abuse. As Raven goes in search of revenge against his plutocratic employer, Europe's armies mobilize and war hysteria grips the nation. The way in which Greene keeps the reader's focus on the inner turmoil of the surprisingly sympathetic hired gun while at the same time illustrating the symbiotic relationship between capitalism and war is quite deft, especially since the plot also deploys all the required genre elements such as manhunts, hostage-takings, and shootouts. Greene labeled *A Gun for Sale* as one of his "entertainments," but the novel shows how overly modest such a self-categorization was, for this deceptively deep book more than meets the Horatian test of grimly instructing even as it thoroughly delights.

It was around this time that Greene published the first of his travel books, *Journey Without Maps* (1936), which recounts his ramblings through the then—as now—perilous country of Liberia, a trip he undertook with alarming casualness and in the company of his equally illprepared cousin, Barbara. In the resulting narrative, the trip is as much a psychological as a geographic quest, for Greene confesses himself "impatien[t,] . . . less content to rest at the urban stage," and desirous of entering the primitive jungle in order to find "one's place in time, based on a knowledge not only of one's present but of the past from which one has emerged." This pronouncement is immediately followed by another, which some have taken as a key to his political philosophy: "There are others, of course, who prefer to look a stage ahead, for whom Intourist provides cheap tickets into a plausible future, but my journey represented a distrust of any future based on what we are" (pp. 19–20). Greene may indeed have been skeptical of all political solutions that aspire to thoroughly remake human nature, but his later writings are full of characters who gain personal redemption through their at first reluctant immersion in progressive political causes.

BRIGHTON ROCK

Brighton Rock (1938), Greene's first masterpiece, is a novel that challenges our familiar ethical categories. The protagonist is Pinkie, a vicious teenage mobster who has assumed command of a small-time gang in the seaside resort city of Brighton after the old boss, Kite—a father figure to Pinkie—is killed by rival gangsters. Pinkie directs the murder of the timid journalist Hale, who contributed to Kite's demise, but before the hunted man dies he shares a drink and a kiss or two with the good-timing Ida Arnold, who afterwards doggedly takes up the search to find his killer. Now if *Brighton Rock* were an ordinary detective thriller we would be in no quandary about how to apportion our sympathy: the robust and amorous amateur sleuth Ida would be our hero, while the sourly celibate and grimly sadistic Pinkie would be the perfect villain. As the last sentence of the following description of Ida indicates, however, things for Greene are not that simple:

> She was cheery, she was healthy, she could get a bit lit with the best of them. She liked a good time, her big breasts bore their carnality frankly down the Old Steyne, but you had only to look at her to know that you could rely on her. She wouldn't tell tales to your wife, she wouldn't remind you next morning of what you wanted to forget, she was honest, she was kindly, she belonged to the great middle law-abiding class, her amusements were their amusements, her superstitions their superstitions . . . she had no more love for anyone than they had.
>
> (p. 80)

And this is the disturbing yet exhilarating surprise at the heart of the novel: though Ida likes most everyone and engages in a lot of recreational sex, Ida will never love; Pinkie, meanwhile, despite all his hatred of the body and desire to cause pain, hovers forever on the brink of a deep and salvational passion. Thus, even though he marries the innocent teenage witness Rose only to prevent her from testifying against him, and on one level detests the act of physical love he is obliged to perform with her, his strategic intimacy with her rouses things within him that seem to promise a comprehensive change of heart. Thus, on the way to their squalid wedding, he "touched her arm with next to tenderness. As once before he had the sense of needing her" (p. 167), and after their consummation "a faint feeling of tenderness woke for his partner in the act" (p. 181). Indeed, the tenderness that stalks Pinkie may not be only of the earthly variety. As he drives toward the Channel cliffs intent upon duping Rose into killing herself in a bogus suicide pact, he finds himself under siege from a love both secular and—perhaps—divine:

> "Last night . . . the night before . . . you didn't hate me, did you, for what we did?"
>
> He said, "No, I didn't hate you."
>
> "Even though it was a mortal sin."

> It was quite true—he hadn't hated her; he hadn't even hated the act. There had been a kind of pleasure, a kind of pride, a kind of—something else. The car lurched back on to the main road; he turned the bonnet to Brighton. An enormous emotion beat on him; it was like something trying to get in; the pressure of gigantic wings against the glass. Dona nobis pacem.
>
> (p. 239)

Throughout Greene's fiction, even tawdry varieties of eros can be gateways to *caritas* and even to *agape*, for Greene's God likes to go slumming, and can be found amid the most unlikely dives and back alleys.

Ida, relentlessly on the trial of Pinkie, tries to win Rose away from her dangerous lover, bragging about her experience in the world and her healthy outlook on life, and accusing Rose of being hopelessly naive: "I know one thing you don't. I know the difference between Right and Wrong. They didn't teach you *that* at school." But Rose is unmoved, for she and Pinkie inhabit a different ethical arena altogether:

> Rose didn't answer; the woman was quite right: the two words meant nothing to her. Their taste was extinguished by stronger foods—Good and Evil. The woman could tell her nothing she didn't know about these—she knew by tests as clear as mathematics that Pinkie was evil—what did it matter in that case whether he was right or wrong?
>
> (p. 199)

Pinkie also understands that their outlook sets them apart from conventional moral categories, musing that Rose "was something that completed him," and that "what was most evil in him needed her: it couldn't get along without goodness," for "she was good . . . and he was damned: they were made for each other" (p. 126).

Pinkie and Rose's Catholicism is certainly one route to the realm of experiential and moral intensities that our author champions, but—as one finds when his oeuvre is looked at as a whole—it is by no means the only one. The characters who come in for Greene's scorn are not merely non-Catholics, but all those who reside in the easy mediocrity of a safe and "normal" routine, such as the oblivious and porcine holidaymakers of Brighton: "they followed their wives obediently into fishmongers, they carried the children's buckets to the beach, they lingered round the bars waiting for opening time, they took a penny peep on the pier at 'A Night of Love' " (p. 80). Thus Ida has "all the big battalions" (p. 221) behind her, whose mottoes are those of unthinking social conformity: "an eye for an eye, law and order, capital punishment, a bit of fun now and then, nothing nasty, nothing shady, nothing you'd be ashamed to own, nothing mysterious" (p. 77). It is this arid mélange of revenge, recreation, respectability, and rationality that Greene's heroes revolt against, some through the practice of Catholicism, some through criminality, some through taking up a gun in the cause of the downtrodden.

At the book's end, Pinkie, feeling cornered, decides he must get rid of Rose altogether, though, as we've seen, something in his heart rebels against this expedient. At any rate, Ida and the police manage to intervene and Pinkie's bottle of vitriol, with which he planned to frighten Rose, winds up being splashed in his own face, the agony of which sends him hurtling over the edge of a cliff: "It was as if he'd been withdrawn suddenly by a hand out of any existence—past or present, whipped away into zero—nothing" (p. 243). We might think that Pinkie's eternal damnation is sealed by such an exit, but the priest that a now-pregnant Rose subsequently seeks out warns her that "You can't conceive, my child, nor can I or anyone the. . .appalling. . .strangeness of the mercy of God" (p. 246). Throughout the book, Pinkie and Rose have speculated about whether a dying sinner can find mercy "between the stirrup and the ground" (p. 91), and Pinkie had a long way to fall from the top of the Channel cliffs. True, on the final page we see Rose carrying home a recording that we—unlike she—know contains a message proclaiming Pinkie's supposed hatred of her, but will it tell her anything about Pinkie that will shatter the perilous bond they share? After all, as she declares to the priest: "I'm not asking for absolution. I don't want absolution. I want to be like him—damned" (p. 245). In the end, what matters for Pinkie and Rose, as for Emily Brontë's Heathcliff and Catherine, is only that they are together, no matter the

cost in what the timid, mundane, law-abiding world labels pain and perversity.

THE CONFIDENTIAL AGENT *AND* THE POWER AND THE GLORY

GREENE wrote his next two novels simultaneously, *The Confidential Agent* (1939) hurriedly in the mornings, *The Power and the Glory* (1940) more carefully in the afternoons. Thus while it is not surprising that only the latter ranks among his highest achievements, the former is by no means without interest. The story centers around a character known only as D., a "confidential agent" sent from an unnamed country torn by civil war (it is obviously the Spanish Civil War that Greene has in mind) to buy coal in England for the communist side. Here again, *Brighton Rock*'s distinction between those who traffic in harrowing absolutes and those who enjoy the safety of good citizenship is insisted upon, but now the difference is imagined as a divide between war-weary soldiers and peace-benumbed civilians. As D. approaches England by sea, the juxtaposition of these two types strikes him as slightly absurd:

> He was filled with a sense of amazement at these people; you could never have told from their smoky good fellowship that there was a war on—not merely a war in the country from which he had come, but a war here, half a mile outside Dover breakwater. He carried the war with him. Wherever D. was, there was a war. He could never understand that people were unaware of it.
>
> (p. 9)

Indeed, there are times that D. feels closer to his enemies than to England's sleepy non-combatants, if only because the fascists too have known the baptism of fighting to the death for the sake of a cause. While the as yet unbombed buildings of London make him think of "long passages and glass doors and a spiritless routine" that can "take the heart out of a man" (p. 56), he "almost preferred the prison cell, the law of flight, the bombed house, his enemy by the door" (p. 56). In "Greeneland" there is apparently always a fellowship of the committed that binds one's

155

heart more closely to a foe's than to that of any mere bystander.

The Power and Glory emerged from a mission Greene undertook at the behest of the Catholic Church to report on religious conditions in the Mexican state of Tabasco, where the socialist government was zealously anticlerical. The trip also produced his second travel book, *The Lawless Roads* (1939), but the distaste for most things Mexican which that volume displays is magnificently transfigured by the novel into a story rich with sympathy and admiration for a suffering people. The hero is known only as the whiskey priest, an alcoholic and often cowardly cleric on the run from the secularizing government, and especially from his personal nemesis, a fanatical policeman whom Greene refers to merely as the lieutenant. It is one of the book's richest ironies that while the whiskey priest is, at least by official Church reckoning, a sinner—he has fathered a child, attempts to flee martyrdom, and desperately yearns for his next drink—the lieutenant is given many of the qualities associated with sainthood. "There was something of the priest in his intent observant walk—a theologian going back over the errors of the past to destroy them again," while his room at the police station looks "as comfortless as . . . a monastic cell." Furthermore, the lieutenant is a man possessed of a quasi-religious vision:

> It infuriated him to think that there were still people in the state who believed in a loving and merciful God. There are mystics who are said to have experienced God directly. He was a mystic, too, and what he had experienced was vacancy—a complete certainty in the existence of a dying, cooling world, of human beings who had evolved from animals for no purpose at all. He knew.
>
> (pp. 24–25)

The priest, meanwhile, is fully convinced only of his own unworthiness and exemplifies the long line of Greene's heroes who are better men than they think they are. For as the priest loses, one by one, the outward trappings of his office—altar stone, chalice, priestly credentials—he ironically becomes a better and better shepherd of souls. Back in his safe and successful youth, his spiritual influence upon his parishioners was almost nil, his days consisting of a soul-deadening routine that had nothing of the *imitatio Christi* about it. Now, hounded and nearly starving, he has come to truly sympathize and love. When, for instance, he is captured (but still not recognized) and thrown into a prison with the lowest scum of the earth—some of whom copulate in the corner of the cell—he has only Christlike sympathy in his heart. "He had a sense of companionship which he had never experienced in the old days when pious people came kissing his black cotton glove" (p. 128). Just such a pious woman attempts to get him to condemn the couple making love, but he refuses, warning her that "a saint gets a subtle taste for beauty and can look down on poor ignorant palates like theirs. But we can't" (p. 130). Indeed, it is the priest himself who is becoming saintly, though the fact that this would never occur to him is the best proof of his sanctity. Even the angry prude who accosts him evokes his sympathy:

> When you visualized a man or a woman carefully, you could always begin to feel pity—that was the quality God's image carried with it. When you saw the lines at the corners of the eyes, the shape of the mouth, how the hair grew, it was impossible to hate. Hate was just a failure of imagination.
>
> (p. 131)

Like a saint, the whiskey priest radiates Grace, for in his flight before the lieutenant he passes briefly through the lives of several people, subtly changing all of them for the better, as if his very presence gives off a benign energy that, at least temporarily, revivifies souls long abandoned to spiritual entropy. And his own religious sense deepens as well, as when he takes up with a woman carrying a dead baby to an Indian shrine in hopes of a miracle. The priest, witnessing her unorthodox gestures and prayers before a bizarre collection of rude crosses, begins to understand that salvation may most effectively take place outside the walls of a church. "Did she expect a miracle? and if she did, why should it not be granted her, the priest wondered? Faith, one was told, could move mountains, and here was faith—faith in the spittle that healed the blind man and the voice that raised the dead" (p. 154–155). It is Greene's implication that the whiskey priest himself is just such an unorthodox vessel whom God may be secretly using to effect great spiritual ends.

One of the priest's most searing encounters is with his child, who is already corrupted by worldly knowledge. In the course of his desperate attempt to reach out and redeem her we come to understand Greene's critique of the lieutenant's purely secular world view: "He said, 'I would give my life, that's nothing, my soul . . . my dear, my dear, try to understand that you are—so important.' That was the difference, he had always known, between his faith and theirs, the political leaders of the people who cared only for things like the state, the republic: this child was more important than a whole continent" (p. 82). This concern with the individual, however, does not drain Greene's view of its radical implications, as we see when the priest, trying to explain heaven to his peasant audience, pitches his address in terms of earthly political protest. "Heaven is where there is no jefe, no unjust laws, no taxes, no soldiers and no hunger. . . . You will never be afraid there—or unsafe. There are no Red Shirts" (pp. 69–70).

The priest, once he is safely across the border in another state, nevertheless turns back toward what is obviously a trap in order to give last rites to a dying American bank robber who has repeatedly murdered. Believing himself the unworthiest of God's servants, he cannot refuse his spiritual offices even to the most hardened of sinners. Captured by the lieutenant, the priest is executed, but not before he experiences a vivid dream that seems to confirm him as an unorthodox saint. On the evening after his death a new priest arrives in the town to take up the struggle, indicating that the whiskey priest has all along been a soldier in an army that, despite being outnumbered and physically unarmed, is not yet wholly defeated.

THE MINISTRY OF FEAR *AND* THE HEART OF THE MATTER

GREENE was sent back to West Africa during World War II to work for the British Secret Service, and it was there that he wrote his wartime spy novel, *The Ministry of Fear* (1943).

Here, the protagonist, Arthur Rowe, stumbles inadvertently into a Nazi fifth-column plot and is soon swept up in a drama of counterespionage. The main complication arises from Rowe's being stricken by amnesia after a bomb hits his house. Awakening a stranger to himself in an asylum run by a Nazi sympathizer, Rowe must painfully reacquire the dark memories of his life and of the violent era in which he lives. As fractured scenes of the mercy killing he inflicted upon his dying wife and of the spy ring he blundered into increasingly disturb the pleasant second childhood of his amnesia, Rowe must rouse himself to take action in order to save his own life and thwart the plot that threatens Britain's war effort. Rowe, with the help of British Counter-Intelligence, eventually prevails, but this "happy" ending is severely muted by the weight of returning adult knowledge about the evanescence of personal happiness and the tragedy of human history. Addressing his dead mother in a dream, Rowe makes reference to a popular writer of "thrillers" that his mother found absurd, but whose fictions now sound like journalism:

> I'm hiding underground, and up above the Germans are methodically smashing London to bits all round me. . .It sounds like a thriller, doesn't it, but the thrillers are like life. . .You used to laugh at the books Miss Savage read—about spies, and murders, and violence, and wild motor-car chases, but dear, that's real life: it's what we've all made of the world since you died. I'm your little Arthur who wouldn't hurt a beetle and I'm a murderer too. The world has been remade by William Le Queux.
>
> (p. 65)

Having been recalled from West Africa before the War's end, Greene still chose Sierra Leone as the setting for his next novel, *The Heart of the Matter* (1948). The protagonist is Henry Scobie, a colonial policeman serving in wartime Freetown who, unlike the lieutenant, possesses a full measure of pity for his fellow human sufferers. Scobie is married to Louise, a conventionally Catholic woman whom he has long since ceased to love, but to whom he is nevertheless still shackled by the unbreakable bonds of pity. "His wife was sitting under the mosquito-net, and for a moment he had the impression of a joint under a meat-cover. But pity trod on the heels of the cruel image and hustled it away. 'Are you feeling better, darling?' . . . He lifted the moist hand and kissed the palm: he was bound by the pathos of her unattractiveness" (pp. 23, 28). Scobie's downfall begins when, passed over once more for promotion, he borrows money from the Syrian merchant and smuggler Yusef—an act excruciating to his sense of duty and responsibility—in order to finance a rest cure for Louise in South Africa. Meanwhile the survivors from a torpedoed ship have arrived in Freetown, and it is while tending to some of the wounded that the book's most controversial theme is introduced—that of a God who is too weak to protect his human creations from intolerable suffering.

"A child like that."

"Yes. Both parents were lost. But it is all right. She will die."

Scobie watched the bearers go slowly up the hill, their bare feet very gently slapping the ground. He thought: It would need all Father Brûle's ingenuity to explain that. Not that the child would die—that needed no explanation. Even the pagans realized that the love of God might mean an early death, though the reason they ascribed was different; but that the child should have been allowed to survive the forty days and nights in the open boat—that was the mystery, to reconcile that with the love of God.

And yet he could believe in no god who was not human enough to love what He had created.

(pp. 120–121)

One of the castaways who does survive is Helen, a young widow with whom Scobie quickly falls in love and begins an affair. As with Louise, it is not Helen's beauty that attracts him so much as her helplessness, her need—as he sees it—for his protection and pity:

he watched her with sadness and affection and enormous pity because a time would come when he couldn't show her around in a world where she was at sea. When she turned and the light fell on her face she looked ugly, with the temporary ugliness of a child. The ugliness was like handcuffs on his wrists.

(p. 159)

Scobie soon finds that his loan, coupled with his desire to keep the love affair a secret, puts him increasingly under Yusef's power. As the efficient prosecution of his duty has always been Scobie's chief pride, as well as his only refuge from the personal disappointments of his life, his slide into coerced corruption takes a terrible toll on his nerves. Louise, having got wind of her husband's infidelity, now returns with the intention of using Scobie's own religious faith to force a showdown. By insisting that he accompany her to mass, she knows that as a believing Catholic he must either confess and renounce his affair before their priest, or refuse to take communion, for to do the latter without priestly absolution would constitute a mortal sin. But Scobie, unwilling to hurt either Louise or Helen, intentionally sacrifices his own soul by eating the wafer without having admitted his adultery. And whom does Scobie pity at this moment when he is (by his own lights) throwing away his eternal salvation? True to form, it is not himself, but rather the vulnerable and suffering Deity he believes he is injuring: "I am the cross" (p. 225), he thinks as he takes his unshriven communion, and the thought of further such occasions calls up "a sudden picture . . . of a bleeding face, of eyes closed by the continuous shower of blows: the punch-drunk head of God reeling sideways" (p. 237).

Since choosing finally between Louise or Helen would be to deeply hurt one or the other of them, Scobie's overdeveloped sense of responsibility leads him to believe that only his death will sufficiently insulate both from the pain of rejection. This conclusion, coupled with his own guilt and self-disgust at his connivance with Yusef, determines Scobie upon suicide. Having swallowed an overdose, the protagonist engages in a final dialogue with what might be the voice of God, an interlocutor who speaks from the "cave of his body" and who claims to be as "humble as any other beggar" and who asks a crucial question: "Can't you trust me as you'd trust a faithful dog?" Scobie's reply is forthright: "No, I don't trust you. I've never trusted you" (pp. 258–259).

This may sound blasphemous, and indeed many critics have simply seen Scobie as suffering from mental exhaustion or as being badly instructed in Catholic doctrine, or as full of a covert but monstrous pride. But a different reading of Scobie's view of God asserts that the novel strongly endorses it as a way to solve the age-old problem of reconciling an all-loving Deity with a world of terrible and chronic pain. Given such a world, an all-powerful God becomes a callous tyrant with a standard of morality below that of his suffering creatures. And thus Scobie's insistence on suicide even though he believes it will damn him is simply another way of proving that God can plead exculpatory weakness, for "thinking of what he had done and was going to do, he thought, even God is a failure" (p. 254). According to this view, Scobie—and Greene—determine to preserve that part of the Deity that is most important and attractive to them: the purely benevolent being whose all too human weakness they can pity and love. If one does view the novel in this way, one can at least formulate a clear reply to its most provocatively open question, posed by Scobie: "If one knew, he wondered, the facts, would one have to feel pity even for the planets? if one reached what they called the heart of the matter?" (p. 124). The answer, suggests Greene, is yes.

The Heart of the Matter, like almost all of Greene's novels, was made into a film, and Greene himself was an influential film reviewer for magazines such as *The Spectator* and *Night and Day* in the 1930s. By no means all of the resulting movies have done the author justice, but when he was allowed to write the screenplay himself, things usually came right. In the late 1940s Greene was asked by the studio head Alexander Korda to write an original screenplay, but Greene said that he couldn't do that without first seeing the work in novel form. The result was *The Third Man* (1950), a novelette about the "rackets" in shattered postwar Vienna, centering around the mysterious disappearance of the villainous but urbanely attractive Harry Lime. The movie, directed by Carol Reed and starring Orson Welles as Lime and Joseph Cotten as his much more naive friend, Rollo Martins, who hunts Lime down first in sympathy and then in anger, went on to great popular and critical acclaim.

THE END OF THE AFFAIR

IF by this point in his life Greene's public reputation was firmly established, his personal life was not nearly so stable. For several years he had been engaged in a passionate but often painful affair with a married American woman, Catherine Walston (he and Vivien having separated but not divorced). It is partly from this experience that *The End of the Affair* (1951) derives. The narrator is a novelist, Maurice Bendrix, who is having an illicit relationship with Sarah Miles, wife of Henry, a civil servant. The attachment between the two, though marred by Bendrix's jealousies, is deep and fulfilling, and the descriptions of their secret lovemaking are powerfully rendered.

> There was never any question in those days of who wanted whom—we were together in desire. Henry had his tray, sitting up against two pillows in his green woolen dressing-gown, and in the room below, on the hardwood floor, with a single cushion for support and the door ajar, we made love. When the moment came, I had to put my hand gently over her mouth to deaden that strange sad angry cry of abandonment, for fear Henry should hear it overhead.
>
> (p. 49)

The affair continues until one day Bendrix's house, in which he and Sarah are making love, is hit by a German bomb. Bendrix, knocked out and to all appearances dead, wakes up and surprises Sarah in a posture of prayer at their bedside. She quickly leaves and refuses to see him again, and the jealous and increasingly bitter Bendrix assumes that she has thrown him over for another lover. A year and a half later Bendrix runs into Henry, who confesses that he thinks Sarah is having an affair. Bendrix then, unbeknownst to Henry, hires a private detective—the genuinely comic Mr. Parkis—to find out whom she is seeing. It is only when the bumbling Parkis manages to steal Sarah's diary and hand it to

Bendrix that the latter finds the real reason Sarah left him. While he was unconscious from the bomb, Sarah made a deal with God—similar to the unorthodox spiritual bargains undertaken by the Whiskey Priest and Scobie—to the effect that if God allowed Bendrix to live, she would stop seeing him. Delighted at what he feels is the flimsy cause for her desertion, Bendrix again pursues her.

In the end God "wins" over Bendrix for the possession of Sarah, but nevertheless *The End of the Affair* can be seen as continuing the theme of the less than omnipotent, quasi-human God we encountered in *The Heart of the Matter,* for the novel is fueled almost exclusively by the blasphemy of Bendrix's insistence that God is nothing more than his sexual rival. Thus, before he concedes defeat, Bendrix appears to wrestle with a randy angel who might just lose, as here when he corners the fleeing Sarah in a church:

> I was cold and wet and very happy. I could even look with charity towards the altar and the figure dangling there. She loves us both, I thought, but if there is to be a conflict between an image and a man, I know who will win. I could put my hand on her thigh or my mouth on her breast: he was imprisoned behind the altar and couldn't move to plead *his* cause. . . .
>
> She shut her eyes again, and looking up at the altar I thought with triumph, almost as though he were a living rival, You see—these are the arguments that win, and gently moved my fingers across her breast.

> (pp. 128, 130)

But Bendrix does not win, for Sarah dies, and presumably it is God who now exclusively enjoys her company. Furthermore, Bendrix is troubled by three coincidences closely following her funeral that just might be interpreted as low-key miracles, including the disappearance of a birthmark on the face of Parkis's son, which Sarah once tenderly kissed. As the novel closes, what balances Bendrix's dark hatred of his divine rival is the way he and Henry have inadvertently become a sort of loving couple, sharing the nursing of Sarah during her last illness, moving in together, and supporting each other in quite touching ways. Concerning Bendrix's belief in

God, the novel ends at a moment of unstable equilibrium, with a hate-filled statement that is also, paradoxically, a prayer: "I wrote at the start that this was a record of hate, and walking there beside Henry towards the evening glass of beer, I found the one prayer that seemed to serve the winter mood: O God, You've done enough, You've robbed me of enough, I'm too tired and old to learn to love, leave me alone for ever" (p. 192). Thus, despite the fact that *The End of the Affair* might reasonably be described as the Greene novel in which God's presence is most palpably felt, it would be wrong to label it his most "Catholic" work, for the author's strikingly original—nay, heretical—view of God and his relationship to humankind is here developed to an unmistakable and unsettling degree.

Still, *The End of the Affair* marks the end of what is conventionally known as Greene's "Catholic" phase. From now on his heroes tend to be secular, middle-aged men whose most marked trait is a skepticism that encompasses God, human aspirations, and their own capacity to feel—though this last self-image is usually refuted by the novel's end. Thomas Fowler of *The Quiet American* (1955) is a case in point, asserting that "no human being will ever understand another," and speculating that "perhaps that's why men have invented God—a being capable of understanding" (p. 60). Fowler is reporting on the French war in Vietnam in the 1950s, and he prides himself on his emotional detachment from that conflict. " 'I'm not involved. Not involved,' I repeated. It had been an article of my creed. The human condition being what it was, let them fight, let them love, let them murder, I would not be involved. My fellow journalists called themselves correspondents; I preferred the title of reporter. I wrote what I saw. I took no action—even an opinion is a kind of action" (p. 28). This scrupulous detachment is challenged, however, by the arrival of Alden Pyle, a naive and idealistic young American operative who, in obedience to the abstract political theories of his beloved teacher, York Harding, is determined to organize a "Third Force" against the communists. When the unsavory general whom Pyle has decided to support explodes a bomb in a crowded square,

Fowler finds himself on hand and disgusted by the hideous suffering of the innocent, and it is at this point that he decides Pyle must be stopped, even if this means that he himself must actively intervene. As one of the communists tells him, "Sooner or later. . .one has to take sides. If one is to remain human" (p. 174).

Fowler's motives for opposing Pyle's murderous innocence, however, are not altogether pure, for the idealistic American has also stolen his young Vietnamese mistress, Phoung. Indeed, a third motive can be adduced in that Fowler seems to harbor a deep strain of anti-Americanism, which some readers have also, with some justice, attributed to Greene. What makes America the hated opposite of "Greeneland" is that it appears to be a place where it is impossible to live a life amid the perilous absolutes that Greene sees as redemptive. For instance, Fowler insists that Pyle would be better off with "a standardized American girl who subscribed to the book club" (p. 32), and wonders if Phoung will "like those bright clean little New England grocery stores where even the celery was wrapped in cellophane" (p. 156). Weeping over the loss of Phoung inside the American embassy, he complains that its air-conditioning "dried [his] tears as it dries the spit in your mouth and the seed in your body" (p. 147). America is just too safe, and thus in Greene's eyes, spiritually arid.

Fowler soon gets his revenge, however, luring Pyle to his preordained death at the hands of the communists, but like all of Greene's later heroes, he doesn't let himself off easily.

All the time that his innocence had angered me, some judge within myself had summed up in his favour, had compared his idealism, his half-baked ideas founded on the works of York Harding, with my cynicism. Oh, I was right about the facts, but wasn't he right too to be young and mistaken, and wasn't he perhaps a better man for a girl to spend her life with?

(p. 156)

Thus, although the book ends with Phoung back in his arms and Pyle's dangerous schemes forgotten, Fowler does not exit the novel at peace: "Everything had gone right with me since he had died, but how I wished there existed someone to whom I could say that I was sorry" (p. 189). Had this been one of Greene's earlier novels, there might have been a hint that Fowler's confession would catch the ear of God, but in these later fictions, the Almighty—if he exists at all—is out of earshot.

OUR MAN IN HAVANA *AND* TRAVELS WITH MY AUNT

ALL during the 1950s Greene journeyed restlessly from one Third World hot spot to another in search of invigorating danger and useful material, and after Vietnam he chose another such flash point as the setting for *Our Man in Havana* (1958), but this time the resulting story emerged as a comedy. Greene parodies the modern espionage thriller by following James Wormold—an innocuous vacuum-cleaner seller—as he inadvertently gets recruited by British Intelligence and then milks the system by providing fabricated information. As early as *The Ministry of Fear* Greene had insisted that there is something inherently adolescent about the game of spy vs. spy, and here the absurd—but ultimately dangerous—delusions and obsessions of undercover work are exposed and ridiculed. Thus while the onetime secret agent Greene consistently champions the life of danger over that of security, he nevertheless asserts that the risks of espionage confer no spiritual luster upon those who undertake them. Indeed, in his later comic novel, *Travels with My Aunt* (1969), it is a career in smuggling that eventually rescues the hero, Henry Pulling, from his life of suburban boredom. All Greene's comic works are better described as charming rather than hilarious, and the laughter is always hedged by a melancholy resignation before the hard facts of life—they consistently amuse, but they are not purely escapist by any means.

PLAYS

IT was also during the 1950s that Greene began writing plays, and his first effort for the stage—*The Living Room* (1953)—was produced in Stockholm in 1952 and toured Britain the following year. This generic departure was followed by *The Potting Shed* (1957), which enjoyed a New York premiere. Both plays have Catholic themes, but neither of them demonstrate the kind of adventurous exploration of religious ideas that the novels contain—indeed, they are blandly orthodox in comparison with the fictions—and reviews were quite mixed. Although Greene did manage alter his principles of dramatic construction in accord with the times—*Carving a Statue* (1964), for instance, clearly shows the influence of Beckett—he was never able to work the magic on stage that he commanded between covers, though he continued writing dramas well into the 1980s.

A BURNT-OUT CASE

BY the advent of the 1960s Greene's self-imposed prohibition on reading Conrad, instituted in the 1930s, had long since lapsed, and in *A Burnt-Out Case* (1961) he was able to fashion a novel that features a Conradian setting and many allusions to *Heart of Darkness* without confusing his own voice with that of his master. The story follows Querry, a famous Catholic architect who, having lost faith in God and himself, has journeyed up the Congo river to find a place of moral quarantine, there to take a sort of monastic vow of celibacy. "I can promise you. . .all of you, never again from boredom or vanity to involve another human being in my lack of love" (p. 118). What this escapee from eros finds, however, is a wider kind of love—let us call it *caritas*—when he settles in at a leper colony run by Catholic missionaries. Slowly he becomes involved in the life of the community, and in the day-to-day labor of assisting the wretched of the earth. What interrupts this spiritual recovery, however, are two people with vested interests in their own conceptions of the famous Querry: Montagu Parkinson, the tabloid journalist, who wants to publicize this celebrity-turned-"saint," and Ryker, a frustrated and self-important Catholic planter who desperately wants Querry to recognize and validate his own spiritual crises. Querry tries hard to convince both men that he has no interest in being who they want him to be—that it is only through

anonymous service that he has begun to feel human again—but they are not to be put off. He does befriend Ryker's young wife, who suffers under her husband's petty domestic tyranny, and though they do not become lovers, the chronically hysterical Ryker believes that they have, and comes gunning for the supposed seducer. Seeing the pistol pointed at him, Querry laughs at the sheer ludicrousness of the situation, but Ryker, ever the egoist, thinks he must be the butt of the joke, and pulls the trigger. Querry dies with an ambiguous, unfinished sentence on his lips, perhaps a summation of his as yet unfinished religious journey: "Absurd. . .this is absurd or else. . . ." (p. 196). When it comes to spiritual quests, Greene is always more interested in their direction than their total completion, and hence he makes his readers see victories in what the world would frequently label as defeats.

THE COMEDIANS

IF one were inclined to rank Greene's works, *The Comedians* (1966) would probably stand as the masterpiece of his later career. The novel begins on a ship bound for the "nightmare republic" of "Papa Doc" Duvalier's Haiti, bearing three men with undistinguished names: Brown, the cynical and world-weary owner of the small hotel Trianon in Port-au-Prince, who will be our narrator; Smith, an activist for vegetarianism and peace, traveling to Haiti with his wife in order to bring moral nutrition to the poor; and Jones, a small-time grifter who fabricates a military past in order to further his con games. The unpromising names are deliberate, for Greene will maneuver each of them into performing some kind of heroic act before the novel is through. In the first chapter, however, Brown gives us little reason to hope that he is capable of any great expansions of the spirit.

> When I was a boy I had faith in the Christian God. Life under his shadow was a very serious affair; I saw Him incarnated in every tragedy. He belonged to the *lacrimae rerum* like a gigantic figure looming through a Scottish mist. Now that I approached the end of life it was only my sense of humor that

enabled me sometimes to believe in Him. Life was a comedy, not the tragedy for which I had been prepared, and it seemed to me that we were all, on this boat . . . driven by an authoritative practical joker towards the extreme point of comedy.

(pp. 31–2)

As Brown asserts elsewhere, "somewhere years ago [he] had forgotten how to be involved in anything. Somehow somewhere [he] had lost completely the capacity to be concerned" (p. 182). He is, however, involved in a love affair with Martha, the wife of a diplomat in Port-au-Prince. But here too he seems focused on his—and their—distance from any heroic ideal, for while the black lover of Brown's mother killed himself after her death, Brown opines that "neither of us would ever die for love. We would grieve and separate and find another. We belonged to the world of comedy and not of tragedy" (p. 161).

In this novel the titular word "comedian" involves a vital paradox. On the one hand, a comedian is someone who has yet to risk himself for the sake of another—who has yet to take up any tragic burden—but it is Greene's point that once one exposes oneself to the tragic dangers of life to aid the downtrodden, one enters a higher comedy of redemption, for the gifts of the spirit that are there to be found more than compensate for the perils. This is what happens to our trio of men. For instance, at first the Smiths seem merely laughable and naive, but there is a dignity and sincerity about these idealists that quickly impresses even Brown.

> "Vegetarianism isn't only a question of diet, Mr. Brown. It touches life at many points. If we really eliminated acidity from the human body we would eliminate passion."
>
> "Then the world would stop.
>
> "He reproved me gently, "I didn't say love," and I felt a curious sense of shame. Cynicism is cheap—you can buy it at any Monoprix store—it's built into all poor-quality goods.

(p. 21)

Later on, by dint of sheer guts and innate moral authority, Mrs. Smith manages to drive away a squad of Tontons Macoutes who are on the brink of beating Brown to death, and in the end Brown comes to admire their courage and envy both their idealism and their genuine love for each other.

Brown and Jones are also transformed from comedians of a lower kind into those who play a part in the tragic but redemptive drama of commitment. After Jones's attempt to scam the Haitian military collapses, he holes up in the embassy of Martha's husband, where he quickly becomes a favorite, inciting Brown's jealousy. But Jones's inveterate bragging about his supposed military background allows Brown to corner him into agreeing to join and train the outnumbered rebel movement operating in the hills. Brown tells himself he is now aiding the rebels only to remove his rival from Martha's proximity, but the truth—which comes out between the lines in dozens of passages—is that Brown deeply loves Haiti and its suffering people and harbors enough outrage at their oppression to risk his life in aiding their struggle against Papa Doc. Indeed, though he features himself a permanently rootless man, he finally admits that he feels "a greater tie here, in the shabby land of terror, chosen for [him] by chance" (p. 223). Furthermore, while driving with Jones toward a dangerous rendezvous with the rebels, Brown comes to realize that the braggart has "all his devious life . . . been engaged on a secret and hopeless love-affair with virtue" (p. 267), and that this buried desire for absolutistic engagement makes himself and Jones comrades of a sort. "It was like meeting an unknown brother—Jones and Brown, the names were almost interchangeable, and so was our status. . . . [W]e had swum from very far apart to come together in a cemetery in Haiti. 'I like you, Jones,' I said" (p. 266).

Jones is eventually killed along with most of the rebel band, but not before he makes an unexpectedly heroic last stand. Brown dreams of him in a way that confirms the new, nobler meaning of "comedian," and then listens to a priest's memorial service for the fallen that again insists upon the spiritual wealth accruing to those who take up a gun in defense of the helpless.

[T]hough Christ condemned the disciple who struck off the ear of the high priest's servant, our hearts go out in sympathy to all who are moved to violence by the suffering of others. The Church condemns violence, but it condemns indifference more harshly. Violence can be the expression of love, indifference never. One is an imperfection of charity, the other the perfection of egoism. In the days of fear, doubt and confusion, the simplicity and loyalty of one apostle advocated a political solution. He was wrong, but I would rather be wrong with Saint Thomas than right with the cold and the craven. Let us go up to Jerusalem and die with him.

(p. 283)

It is altogether fitting that when Greene first entered the Catholic Church, he took as his baptismal name that of this apostle Thomas, whose name has become synonymous with doubt and who went on to write gospels deemed uncanonical, but who was willing to take up the sword out of love.

THE HONORARY CONSUL

DURING the 1970s Greene enjoyed his last decade of working at the peak of his powers. This continued strength is first evidenced by *The Honorary Consul* (1973), which, like *The Comedians,* centers upon a supposedly detached man who winds up committing to a political cause. Dr. Eduardo Plarr practices medicine in an Argentinean town on the Paraguayan border, a place where he remains in part because his father, an Englishman, was killed clandestinely resisting the Paraguayan government. Plarr, though he enjoys many sexual conquests, has ceased to believe in romantic love.

"Has no woman ever loved you, Ted?" Fortnum inquired. A kind of paternal anxiety in his voice irritated Doctor Plarr.

"Two or three have told me so, but they have had no difficulty in finding someone else after I said good-bye. Only my mother's love of sweet cakes isn't likely to change. She will love them in sickness and in health till death do them part. Perhaps that's real true love."

"You are too young to be a cynic."

"I'm not a cynic. I'm curious, that's all. I like to know the meaning which people put on the words they use."

(p. 71)

But if romantic passion is ephemeral, the novel shows Plarr moving toward a wider definition of "love" as he begins to get caught up in political events. When an amateurish band of Paraguayan guerrillas attempts to kidnap the American ambassador to Argentina but nabs merely the British honorary consul—the alcoholic Charley Fortnum—by mistake, Plarr finds himself drawn into the political drama (or farce) because he has impregnated Fortnum's young wife, the former prostitute Clara. Not quite understanding his own willingness to put himself at risk for what his intellect tells him is a noble but hopeless cause, he recalls his father's political commitment and gropes toward a new conception of love. He "sometimes recalled . . . the illicit nocturnal sounds which he had heard on the *estancia* in Paraguay—the tiny reverberations of a muffled knock, strange tiptoes on the floor below, whispers from the cellar, a gunshot which rang out an urgent warning from far across the fields—those had been the signals of a genuine tenderness, a compassion deep enough for his father to be prepared to die for it. Was that love?" (pp. 169–170).

Plarr eventually finds himself trapped within a hut where the rebels are holding Fortnum as Argentinean paratroopers close in. The leader of the guerrillas is a priest and old acquaintance of Plarr's, León Rivas, who has taken up a gun in the cause of the poor. As the noose slowly tightens, Plarr and Rivas converse about the morality of a priest who claims he is willing to kill his hostage for a political end, and through Rivas' apologia we can discern Greene's evolving thought on issues central to his vision. Here again, for instance, is the evocation of a weakened God who humanly suffers:

"I thought [says Plarr] the Church teaches that he's love?"

"Was it love [replies Rivas] which sent six million Jews to the gas ovens? You are a doctor, you must often have seen intolerable pain—a child dying of meningitis. Is that love? It was not love which cut off Aquino's fingers. The police stations where such things happen . . . He created them."

"I have never heard a priest blame God for things like that before."

"I don't blame Him. I pity Him."

(p. 219)

Rivas can pity God because if "He made us in His image" it follows that "our evil is His evil too. How could I love God if He were not like me? Divided like me. Tempted like me" (p. 225). According to Leon, "God is suffering the same evolution that we are, but perhaps with more pain" (p. 226). For the revolutionary priest, the hierarchy of the Church is corrupt and its dogmas outdated, but "sometimes the memory of that man, that carpenter, can lift a few people out of the temporary Church of these terrible years, when the Archbishop sits down to dinner with the General, into the great Church beyond our time and place, and then . . . those lucky ones . . . they have no words to describe the beauty of that Church" (p. 218).

Plarr eventually decides to risk leaving the hut in order to negotiate with the paratroopers, but he is shot down. Rivas, unable at the crucial moment to kill Fortnum as he has promised, goes instead to help Plarr and is also killed. Indeed, Charley Fortnum is the only survivor of the attack upon the hideout, but he too comes to a wider understanding of love. Having learned of Plarr's affair with Clara, but also having grown fond of Eduardo (and even his supposed executioner, Father Rivas) under the shadow of impending death, he returns to his wife but can only feel affection for her when she stops pretending and weeps openly for her dead lover. He even suggests that they name the coming baby for Plarr, so far has the honorary consul traveled beyond the clichéd jealousy of the cuckold. As Fortnum comes to realize, "There's nothing wrong with love. . . . It happens. It doesn't matter who with. We get caught up . . . we get kidnapped . . . by mistake" (p. 265). A fortunate

mistake, this, for the love Greene's late characters blunder into is less like that encountered in romance novels and more akin to that described by Saint Paul which "seeketh not itself" and thus is more durable than mere eros, and far more widely redemptive.

THE HUMAN FACTOR

GREENE's last great novel, *The Human Factor* (1978), returns to the world of espionage but merges its spy story with a poignant domestic drama. Maurice Castle, an employee of the British Secret Intelligence Service, is secretly feeding information concerning South Africa to the Russians, not because he is a communist sympathizer but because it was a communist who rescued Sarah, the black woman he is now married to, from the South African police. Maurice's love for Sarah and her son Sam (Sarah was pregnant by another man when Maurice fell in love with her) is intense, and—something of a first in Greene—his protagonist is grateful and happy in his domestic routine. As always in Greeneland, however, the price of being in love is the fear of losing your loved ones and the life you have built together, and thus Maurice's fantasies are not of escape but of homebound safety.

He didn't want to sleep until he was sure from her breathing that Sarah was asleep first. Then he allowed himself to strike, like his childhood hero Allan Quartermain, off on that long slow underground stream which bore him on toward the interior of the dark continent where he hoped that he might find a permanent home, in a city where he could be accepted as a citizen, as a citizen without any pledge of faith, not the City of God or Marx, but the city called Peace of Mind.

(p. 106)

The leak in Castle's section is discovered, but suspicion falls on his innocent colleague Davis, and because the Service has recently suffered public ridicule for security breaches, the cold-blooded director, Sir Percival, gives orders for Davis to be slowly, discreetly poisoned. Castle parries the tightening knot of official suspicion for a while but eventually concludes that he has no choice but to flee to Russia with the aid of his Soviet contact. There is some conventional spy-novel plotting here involving disguises, secret rendezvous, and coded messages, but Greene's main purpose is to show the human cost of Castle's nobly intentioned treason, and thus we are even allowed to witness the reaction of his quite conventional mother to her son's supposed political apostasy. Sarah's response to her husband's confession, however, is more in line with Greene's own feelings on the relative value of patriotism versus other forms of loyalty: " 'Who cares?' she said. She put her hand in his: it was an act more intimate than a kiss—one can kiss a stranger. She said, 'We have our own country. You and I and Sam. You've never betrayed that country, Maurice' " (p. 192). Castle does get safely to Moscow, but the novel ends on a somber note, for an enraged British government is refusing Sarah a passport, and thus it seems their reunion will be held hostage to cold war politics: "She said, 'Maurice, Maurice, please go on hoping,' but in the long unbroken silence which followed she realized that the line to Moscow was dead" (p. 276).

LATER WORK

DURING the last full decade of his life Greene more or less settled down at his villa in Antibes with his longtime mistress, Yvonne Cloetta, in part to avoid British taxes on his now consider-able wealth. He continued to publish novels through the 1980s, but there is something attenu-ated and halfhearted about them (they are all short), and it is only fair to conclude that they are the works of a writer in decline. These fic-tions include *Doctor Fischer of Geneva, or The Bomb Party* (1980), a fable about the effects of greed; *Monsignor Quixote* (1982), a rather charm-ing philosophical "buddies-hit-the-road" novel; and *The Captain and the Enemy* (1988), an ill-conceived venture into postmodern technique whose plot seems to simply peter out. There is one remarkable passage from *Monsignor Qui-xote,* however, that sums up Greene's views on the value of doubt and the dangers of certainty,

no matter what the cause or creed. The monsignor has a dream that a certain caliber of believer might consider rapturous:

> He had dreamt that Christ had been saved from the Cross by the legion of angels to which on an earlier occasion the Devil had told Him that He could ap-peal. So there was no final agony, no heavy stone which had to be rolled away, no discovery of an empty tomb. Father Quixote stood there watching on Golgotha as Christ stepped down from the Cross triumphant and acclaimed. The Roman soldiers, even the Centurion, knelt in His honor, and the people of Jerusalem poured up the hill to worship Him. The disciples clustered happily round. His mother smiled through her tears of joy.
>
> (pp. 69–70)

Rather than experiencing joy himself, however, the Monsignor "felt on waking the chill of despair" in contemplating "a kind of Saharan desert without doubt or faith, where everyone is certain that the same belief is true." And so he whispers to himself, "God save me from such a belief" (p. 70). For Greene, what makes us moral—whether we be Christians, communists, or nihilists—is the oscillation of our minds between greater and lesser burdens of doubt, for it is only certainty that allows one to kill for one's ideals, whereas doubt, once we will only admit to it, can spark solidarity between thinking people of any and all systems of belief, secular or religious.

And finally it is doubt, including self-doubt and the ability to change one's mind that self-doubt implies, that is central to Greene's concep-tion of the writer's role in society, as he affirms here in *Reflections,* his final collection of essays.

> It has always been in the interest of the State to poison the psychological wells, to encourage cat-calls, to restrict human sympathy. It makes govern-ment easier when the people shout Galilean, Papist, Fascist, Communist. Isn't it the story-teller's task to act as the devil's advocate, to elicit sympathy and a measure of understanding for those who lie outside the boundaries of State approval? The writer is driven by his own vocation to be a Protestant in a Catholic society, a Catholic in a Protestant one, to

see the virtue of the Capitalist in a Communist society, of the Communist in the Capitalist state.

(pp. 268–269)

The writer must therefore act as the devil's advocate, but unlike that office within the Catholic Church, the doctrine he ultimately serves must change with the world's changing political fortunes. For if, as Greene insists, the writer "stands for the victims, and the victims change," then this implies that no author can ever afford the moral sleep of certainty. Over the course of his long career Graham Greene sympathetically portrayed many victims of many beliefs on their way to crucifixion at the hands of the powers that be, and his novels always present us with a hard but ultimately redemptive challenge: Let us go up to Jerusalem and die with them.

SELECTED BIBLIOGRAPHY

I. Novels. *The Man Within* (London and Garden City, N.J., 1929; repr. London and New York, 1977); *The Name of Action* (London, 1930; Garden City, N.J., 1931); *Rumour at Nightfall* (London, 1931); *Stamboul Train* (London, 1932; repr. London and New York, 1975); *It's a Battlefield* (London and Garden City, N.J., 1934; repr. London and New York, 1977); *England Made Me* (London and Garden City, N.J., 1935); *Gun for Sale* (London, 1936; repr. London and New York, 1974); *Brighton Rock* (London, 1938; repr. London and New York, 1977); *The Confidential Agent* (London, 1939; repr. London and New York, 1971); *The Power and the Glory* (London, 1940; repr. London and New York, 1991); *The Ministry of Fear* (London, 1943; repr. London and New York, 1978); *The Heart of the Matter* (London and New York, 1948; repr. London and New York, 1978).

The Third Man and The Fallen Idol (London, 1950; repr. London and New York, 1976); *The End of the Affair* (London and New York, 1951; repr. London and New York, 1975); *The Quiet American* (London, 1955; New York, 1957; repr. London and New York, 1977); *Loser Takes All* (London, 1955); *Our Man in Havana* (London and New York, 1958; repr. London and New York, 1971); *A Burnt-Out Case* (London and New York, 1961; repr. London and New York, 1977); *The Comedians* (London, 1966; repr. London and New York, 1976); *Travels with My Aunt* (London and New York, 1969; repr. London and New York, 1977); *The Honorary Consul* (London and New York, 1973; repr. London and New York, 1974); *The Human Factor* (London and New York, 1978; repr. New York, 1988); *Doctor Fischer of Geneva, or The Bomb Party* (London, 1980); *Monsignor Quixote* (London and New York, 1982); *The Tenth Man* (London and New York, 1985); *The Captain and the Enemy* (London and New York, 1988).

II. Short Stories and Poetry. *Babbling April* (Oxford, 1925); *Nineteen Stories* (London, 1947; New York, 1949); *Twenty-One Stories* (London, 1954; repr. London and New York, 1981); *A Sense of Reality* (London, 1963); *May We Borrow Your Husband? and Other Comedies of the Sexual Life* (London and New York, 1967; repr. London and New York, 1973); *Collected Stories* (London, 1972; New York, 1973).

III. Plays. *The Living Room* (London, 1953; New York, 1954); *The Potting Shed* (New York, 1957; London, 1958); *The Complaisant Lover* (London, 1959; New York, 1961); *Carving A Statue* (London, 1964); *The Return of A. J. Raffles* (London and New York, 1975).

IV. Travel *Journey Without Maps* (London and Garden City, N.J., 1936; repr. London and New York, 1980); *The Lawless Roads* (London and New York, 1939; repr. London and New York, 1982); *In Search of a Character: Two African Journals* (London, 1961; New York, 1962); *Getting to Know the General* (London, 1984).

V. Essays. *Collected Essays* (London and New York, 1969); *The Pleasure Dome: Collected Film Criticism, 1935–1940* (London, 1972); *Yours Etc.: Letters to the Press, 1945–89* (London, 1989); *Reflections* (London, 1991).

VI. Autobiography. *A Sort of Life* (London and New York, 1971); *Ways of Escape* (London and New York, 1980).

VII. Critical Studies. Kenneth Allott and Miriam Farris. *The Art of Graham Greene* (London, 1951); A. A. De Vitis, *Graham Greene* (New York, 1964); Peter Wolfe, *Graham Greene the Entertainer* (Carbondale, Ill., 1972); Francis L. Kunkel, *The Labyrinthine Ways of Graham Greene*, rev. ed. (Mamaroneck, N.Y., 1973); K. C. Joseph Kurismmootil, *Heaven and Hell on Earth: An Appreciation of Five Novels of Graham Greene* (Chicago, 1982); Georg M. A. Gaston, *The Pursuit of Salvation: A Critical Guide to the Novels of Graham Greene* (Troy, N.Y., 1984); Richard Kelly, *Graham Greene* (New York, 1984); Roger Sharrock, *Saints, Sinners, and Comedians: The Novels of Graham Greene* (Notre Dame, Ind., 1984); Grahame Smith, *The Achievement of Graham Greene* (Totowa, N.J., 1986); Terry Eagleton, "Reluctant Heroes: The Novels of Graham Greene," in Harold Bloom, ed., *Graham Greene* (New York, 1987); Daphna Erdinast-Vulcan, *Graham Greene's Childless Fathers* (New York, 1988); Paul O'Prey, *A Reader's Guide to Graham Greene* (New York, 1988); Brian Thomas, *An Underground Fate: The Idiom of Romance in the Later Novels of Graham Greene* (Athens, Ga., 1988); Judith Adamson, *Graham Greene, The Dangerous Edge: Where Art and Politics Meet* (New York, 1990); R. H. Miller, *Understanding Graham Greene* (Columbia, S.C., 1990); Neil Nehring, "Revolt into Style: Graham Greene Meets the Sex Pistols," in *PMLA* 106, no. 2 (1991); Brian Diemert, *Graham Greene's Thrillers and the 1930s* (Montreal, 1996); Robert Pendleton, *Graham Greene's Conradian Masterplot: The Arabesque of Influence* (New York, 1996); Cates Baldridge, *Graham Greene's Fictions: The Virtues of Extremity* (Columbia, Mo., 2000).

VIII. Biographies. Norman Sherry, *The Life of Graham Greene*, 2 vols. (of projected 3) (New York, 1989–1995); Michael Shelden, *Graham Greene: The Enemy Within* (New York, 1994).

GEORGE HERBERT

(1593–1633)

Peter Scupham

GEORGE HERBERT'S POETRY is of a singular intensity. Its limitations are clearly defined by its unwavering dedication to one end, which is to explore man's relationship with his Maker. His life is of a comparable intensity, holding our fascinated admiration as he moves from the arrogance and accomplishment of a Renaissance aristocrat to the willed anonymity of a country priest—a movement between extremes that consciously informs the poetry. In "Affliction (I)" (*The Works of George Herbert,* ed. F. E. Hutchinson, Oxford, 1941) the dramatic contrast is made memorable:

> Whereas my birth and spirit rather took
> > The way that takes the town;
> Thou didst betray me to a lingring book,
> > And wrap me in a gown.
>
> > > > > (p. 47)

His reputation finally and now securely rests on the 164 poems that make up *The Temple: Sacred Poems and Private Ejaculations,* first published at Cambridge and dated 1633. Herbert's devotional work, *A Priest to the Temple, or, The Country Parson His Character and Rule of Holy Life,* first published in *Herbert's Remains* (1652), will, however, also always be of interest—not only to historians of the church, but as a moving exposition of that ideal of temperate, uncontentious, and good-humored sobriety which an Anglican priest should aspire to.

Herbert's poems circulated to a limited extent in manuscript during his lifetime, but none of the poems included in *The Temple* appeared in print until Herbert's friend Nicholas Ferrar arranged their posthumous publication in the year of Herbert's death. His reputation has been constantly reinterpreted in the light of the concerns of successive ages. In the turbulence and intensity of England's religious life in the seventeenth century, Herbert offered a paradigm of undemonstrative, nonsectarian thought and feeling; a life and a poetry brought into exemplary unity. When Walton's "Life" appeared in 1670 Walton, could claim that the poems had sold some twenty thousand copies since their first publication. In the eighteenth century there was little interest. A reestimation was begun by Samuel Taylor Coleridge in *Biographia Literaria* (1817) and, with the refashioning of attitudes to "metaphysical" poetry and the championship of T. S. Eliot in the twentieth century, this has now reached the point of Herbert being acknowledged as one of the finest lyricists in the English language.

THE LIFE

GEORGE Herbert was born at Montgomery Castle on 3 April 1593, the fifth son of Sir Richard and Lady Magdalen Herbert and brother to Edward, Lord Herbert of Cherbury, himself later distinguished as a poet. The family, of Norman descent, had long been established in Welsh border country. When George was only three Sir Richard died, leaving his wife with seven sons and three daughters to raise on her own. Herbert's mother was distinguished for her intelligence, charity, and care of her children, and Herbert's relationship with her was always close, as was his relationship with his stepfather, Sir John Danvers, whom she married in 1609. She was a friend of the poet John Donne, who preached her memorial sermon, and is, according to Herbert Grierson, remembered in Donne's Elegie IX, "The Autumnall," with its opening lines: "No *Spring,* nor *Summer* Beauty hath such grace, / As I have seen in one *Autumnall* face" (*The Poems of John Donne,* ed. Grierson, 1912, vol. 1, p. 92). Herbert was educated at home and at Westminster School, and then went to Trinity College, Cambridge where he proceeded through minor and major fellowships, lectured in Rhetoric, and became an excellent classicist and also an excellent musician, singing and playing the lute and viol. His literary talents went at first into the making of Latin verses, and for some seven years he held the influential post of the university's Public Orator, which brought him into contact with king and court, since the post involved all the arts of a courtier in welcoming, congratulating, and thanking the patrons and benefactors of the university. He flattered King James I by his effusive letter of thanks for the gift to the university of the king's book, *Opera Latina,* and earned the friendship and interest of Sir Francis Bacon, the Lord Chancellor. At this stage of his life Herbert could have been set on the course of worldly success expected from a young man of his background and abilities, the kind of young man who might have continued the opening stanza of "Employment (II)" by deploying further levels of arrogance and worldliness, untempered by deeper spiritual considerations:

> He that is weary, let him sit.
> My soul would stirre
> And trade in courtesies and wit,
> Quitting the furre
> To cold complexions needing it.
>
> (p. 78)

The climax of Herbert's brief worldly career was his time as a member of Parliament for Montgomery borough; he served in the session which sat between February and May 1624, but it is arguable that the deaths of two his patrons, the duke of Richmond and the marquis of Hamilton, and of King James in 1625, forced a change of direction which had temperamentally always been a possibility. At the age of seventeen he had sent two stiff sonnets to his mother from Cambridge in which he had balanced the claims of earthly and heavenly love. In his address to God in the first of these sonnets, Herbert's decision to put his own craft to the service of the divine is made explicit:

> Doth Poetry
> Wear *Venus* livery? only serve her turn?
> Why are not *sonnets* made of thee? and layes

> Upon thine altar burnt? Cannot thy love
> Heighten a spirit to sound out thy praise
> As well as any she?
>
> (p. 206)

At some time between 1624 and 1626, Herbert accepted ordination as a deacon, a step that debarred him from any civil employment. In 1626 he was installed as canon of Lincoln Cathedral and prebendary of Layton Ecclesia—which was effectively a sinecure with only one duty attached to it, that of preaching once a year in Lincoln cathedral. The property that endowed this sinecure was an estate at Leighton Bromswold, Huntingdonshire, where there was a ruined chapel. Close by was Little Gidding, the home of Nicholas Ferrar. Under Ferrar's aegis, Herbert set about raising funds to restore the church, a task that he successfully accomplished. A growing friendship between Ferrar and Herbert was largely conducted by correspondence but remained unbroken till Herbert's death.

Herbert's mother died in 1627, the year in which he resigned the Oratorship. Already in ill health from the seeds of the consumption that was to kill him, Herbert married Jane Danvers in 1629; in 1630 he was presented by Charles I with the living of Bemerton near Salisbury, Wiltshire, and was ordained a priest. At Bemerton, in less than three years, he made his name as the model of the good parish priest, repaired the church and rebuilt the parsonage. He died childless in 1633. The seventeenth-century antiquary John Aubrey recounts how "He was buryed (according to his owne desire) with the singing service for the buriall of the dead, by the singing men of Sarum" (*George Herbert: The Critical Heritage,* ed. C. A. Patrides, 1983, p. 90). His wife afterwards married Sir Robert Cook of Highnam House, Gloucestershire.

THE MYTH: EARLY HAGIOGRAPHIES BY OLEY AND WALTON

THE groundwork for the hagiographical approach to Herbert was laid down in Barnabas Oley's *A Prefatory View of the Life of Mr. Geo. Herbert,* the introduction to *Herbert's Remains* (1652), a book whose main part was the first edition of *A Priest to the Temple*. Oley, royalist and divine, had known Herbert and was concerned to establish his reputation as the model Anglican priest, a man who "afforded so unusual a Contesseration of Elegancies, and set of Rarities to the Beholder" (Patrides, p. 82).

Izaak Walton's *The Life of Mr. George Herbert* was published in 1670 and revised for a 1675 edition, when it was published with the lives of Donne, Hooker, and Wotton. Walton was not primarily concerned with Herbert's poetry. He wished to commend to his contemporaries and to posterity a pattern of Christian behavior, and his *Life* has for centuries served the double purpose of acting as a memorial put up to Herbert's position as an uncanonized saint of the Anglican communion, and as a fallible, selective guide to historical fact and the relationship of Herbert's poetry to his life. Walton's *Lives* were designed as tributes to their subjects, not as detached discussions of their vices and virtues, and a part of Walton's aim was to establish the Anglican priesthood as a suitable profession for the sons of upper-class families. Writing nearly forty years after Herbert's death, and without ever having known him, Walton used the poetry as a source of biographical information, painting a picture of such worldly temptations as Herbert's "gentile humour for cloaths, and Court-like company" (Patrides, p. 101) and his attraction for the "empty, imaginary painted pleasures" (Patrides, p. 110) of court life, then positing an agonized renunciation. Amy Charles, Herbert's definitive biographer, sees, however, a gradual and inevitable progress towards ordination beginning with his early Cambridge years (*A Life of George Herbert*, 1977, p. 89). Walton, the angler, quietist, and praiser of the Laudian emphasis on form and ceremony in worship, had viewed the ravages of the Civil War and the success of the Puritan cause with abhorrence. When Walton wrote his *Life,* he framed it with accounts of two emblematic acts of destruction from the Civil War years: the pulling down of the seat of the Herberts, Montgomery castle, and the loss of Herbert's manuscripts, destroyed when they and Highnam House were burnt. The twelve year old Herbert seems already

removed from the natural rambunctiousness of childhood by Walton's account of his years at Westminster "where the beauties of his pretty behaviour and wit, shin'd and became so eminent and lovely in this his innocent age, that he seem'd to be marked out for piety, and to become the care of Heaven, and of a particular good Angel to guard and guide him" (Patrides, p. 93). Walton's prose winds about Herbert's life, lovingly binding Herbert and his mother together by emphasizing the web "of sacred Indearments betwixt these two excellent persons" (Patrides, p. 96), and only hinting a criticism of Herbert's youth by suggesting "he kept himself too much retir'd, and at too great a distance with all his inferiours: and his cloaths seem'd to prove, that he put too great a value on his parts and Parentage" (Patrides, p. 98). The encomium reaches its height when describing Herbert's life with his wife at Bemerton. It is enlivened by strikingly beautiful phrasing, as with Walton's description of the love his wife inspired in those who knew her—a love which "followed her in all places, as inseparably, as shadows follow substances in Sunshine" (Patrides, p. 112)—or the anecdote concerning Herbert's response to being criticized by his music-making friends for appearing disheveled after helping with a fallen horse: he claimed "That the thought of what he had done, would prove Musick to him at Midnight" (Patrides, p. 121). The *Life* moves always on a double level, events in this world being seen only as a preparation for their Christian transposition to events in Heaven, and Walton's temperament leans towards fruition and promise and is not concerned with the darker themes of separation and punishment. Walton deliberately moves Herbert's life out of time into eternity. When he quotes Donne's sonnet "To the Lady Magdalen Herbert; of St. Mary Magdalen" inviting her to "Harbour these Hymns"—actually the seven sonnets of Donne's known as "La Corona," though Walton did not know this—he adds: "These *Hymns* are now lost to us, but doubtless they were such, as they now sing in Heaven" (Patrides, p. 96); The love between Herbert and his wife, he writes, "was only improvable in Heaven, where they now enjoy it" (Patrides, p. 108), and, when Herbert is described as rising from his deathbed and singing to his lute or viol, Walton adds: "Thus he sung on Earth such Hymns and Anthems, as the Angels and he. . . now sing in Heaven." The effect of Walton's *Life,* with its grave beauty, singleness of theme, and kindliness of spirit has been to bond Herbert's life and poetry to an Anglican spirituality that carries the illusion of timelessness, distanced from the moil and trouble of religious controversy. Herbert is fixed by Walton as the "Character of the Good Priest," the exemplar, almost as emblematic for us as Chaucer's fourteenth-century Catholic counterpart, the country parson who "This noble ensample to his sheep he yaf, / That first he wroghte, and afterward he taughte" (*The Works of Geoffrey Chaucer,* ed. Robinson, 1957, p. 22). Walton's legacy is ambivalent; it preserved Herbert for later generations, but deflected them from seeing the hard, sinewy intelligence that the poetry exemplifies.

HERBERT'S LATER REPUTATION

In the seventeenth century *The Temple* ran through edition after edition. By 1678 nine more editions had been added to the two that appeared in 1633. Herbert's reputation did not depend only on Barnabas Oley and Izaak Walton for its promulgation. Christopher Harvey made his debt to Herbert explicit in *The Synagogue, or, The Shadow of the Temple* (1640)—a tributary collection often published with *The Temple* itself—with the encomiastic close to its first poem, "A Stepping Stone":

In building of his Temple, Master *Herbert*
Is equally all Grace, all Wit, all Art.
 Roman and *Grecian* Muses all give way:
 One *English* Poem darkens all your day.

(Patrides, p. 64)

Many of the minor English seventeenth-century poets were influenced by the example, if not the stylistic qualities, of Herbert. Henry Vaughan, though, is notable for the extent of his acknowledged debt to Herbert. In his *preface to Silex Scintillans: Sacred Poems and Private Ejaculations* (1655), Vaughan acknowledges as his

spiritual exemplar "Mr George Herbert, whose holy life and verse gained many pious Converts, (of whom I am the least)" (*Henry Vaughan: Poetry and Selected Prose,* ed. L. C. Martin, 1963, p. 220). "Son-dayes," whose second stanza closes:

The Creatures *Jubile;* Gods parle with dust;
Heaven here; man on those hills of Myrrh, and
 flowres;
Angels descending; the Returns of Trust;
A Gleam of glory, after six-days-showres

is an exact and loving parallel, in the way it accumulates metaphor, to Herbert's sonnet "Prayer (I)," which opens:

Prayer the Churches banquet, Angels age,
Gods breath in man returning to his birth,
The soul in paraphrase, heart in pilgrimage,
The Christian plummet sounding heav'n and earth;

(p. 51)

Herbert was an Anglican, but Richard Baxter and the Puritan cause saw him as possessing a spirituality they could subsume under their banner. Composers, too, including John Blow and Henry Purcell, set some of Herbert's lyrics to music (examples of which are to be found in Patrides, Appendix I, pp. 357–373). The eighteenth century, however, saw the nadir of Herbert's reputation. Addison set the tone in his analysis of "wit" in *The Spectator* (1711), singling out Herbert's optically patterned poems as part of an outmoded "fashion of false wit" (*George Herbert, The Critical Heritage,* ed. C. A. Patrides, 1983, p. 150), and apart from Wesley's rewriting of Herbert's lyrics as hymns, Herbert was not a poet of any interest to the critics and literary lawgivers of the period.

The first serious reappraisal of Herbert's work in the nineteenth century was made by Coleridge. Coleridge skirmishes with the word "quaint" in his comments on *The Temple* in *Biographia Literaria* (1817; see Patrides, p. 166), interestingly enough not applying it to Herbert's diction, but commenting on the "too frequent quaintness of the thoughts." His considered view of Herbert's poetry as providing an example of "the most correct and natural language" was influential. Soon

Emerson became the consistent champion of Herbert in America, and, in a lecture given in 1835, he stressed the "felicity of the diction." "The thought," he said, "has so much heat as actually to fuse the words, so that language is wholly flexible in his hands, and his rhyme never stops the progress of his sense" (Patrides, p. 174). Herbert's poems appeared in numerous editions throughout the nineteenth century; his poetic admirers included Christina Rossetti and the Jesuit priest Gerard Manley Hopkins, whose intense, demanding sonnets make a correspondence with Herbert that leaps the centuries. Hopkins's "I am gall, I am heartburn. God's most deep decree / Bitter would have me taste: my taste was me," from the sonnet "I wake and feel the fell of dark, not day," finds a dramatic parallel in the first stanza of Herbert's "Affliction (IV)":

> Broken in pieces all asunder,
>> Lord, hunt me not,
>> A thing forgot,
> Once a poor creature, now a wonder,
>> A wonder tortur'd in the space
>> Betwixt this world and that of grace.
>
> (p. 90)

THE TWENTIETH CENTURY: A REVOLUTION IN HERBERT'S STATUS

In 1905 George Herbert Palmer of Harvard published the three-volume *English Works of George Herbert,* an edition that did much to elucidate the complexities of Herbert's thought and style and that was later to be an important tool in the revolutionizing of Herbert's literary place. In addition to his textual clarifications, Palmer also reordered the poems in *The Temple* to fit a psychological theory—the major themes of which he summarized in a later book, *Formative Types in English Poetry* (1918). These themes were: the dismissal of Walton's "charming romance" (Patrides, p. 290); a firm stress on Herbert the passionate Renaissance man, torn and divided between secular and spiritual worlds; a belief that the poems can be identified with four periods of Herbert's life, which Palmer defines as Education, Hesitation, Crisis, and

Consecration; an emphasis on Herbert's sophisticated command of form and structure; and a dubious psychological reading of the poetry as driving towards despondency and depression among the "illiterate rustics" (Patrides, p. 294) who were Herbert's final company in an "infirm and disappointed life" (Patrides, p. 295). There was much here for future scholars to argue about.

During the early part of the twentieth century, however, Herbert was subsumed into the so-called "metaphysical" school of poets, amongst whom John Donne was thought to be preeminent. Herbert J. C. Grierson's influential *Metaphysical Lyrics and Poems of the Seventeenth* Century (1921) had made this "metaphysical" school fashionable, but had also made Donne's position as pack-leader seemingly unassailable. The word "metaphysical," originally used pejoratively of the early seventeenth-century poets by Johnson in his *Life* of Abraham Cowley, was redefined in this context as "the peculiar blend of passion and thought, feeling and ratiocination which is their greatest achievement." Passionate thinking "is always apt to become metaphysical, probing and investigating the experience from which it takes its rise" (Grierson, p. xvi). T. S. Eliot's review of this book, published as "The Metaphysical Poets" in his *Selected Essays* (1932), is seminal, placing the writers Grierson covered "in the direct current of English poetry," no longer to be "coddled by antiquarian affection" (*Selected Essays,* p. 290). Herbert gained Eliot's special commendation and admiration, which he expressed most fully in his monograph *George Herbert,* published for the British Council in their *Writers and Their Work* (1962) series. He distinguished between the poems of Donne and those of Herbert by finding in Donne the "dominance of intellect over sensibility" and in Herbert "the dominance of sensibility over intellect" (p. 17), and even at this date, found himself having to rescue Herbert from those who wished to see *The Temple* as a "devotional handbook of meditation for the faithful." The importance of Eliot's essay is in giving his authority to an emphasis on the poetry as poetry, praising those verse forms, which, he claimed, "show a resourcefulness of invention which seems inexhaustible, and for which I know no parallel in English poetry" (p. 31). Eliot, himself an Anglican, was particularly concerned to stress the value of Herbert's poems as "a record of spiritual struggle which should touch the feeling and enlarge the understanding of those readers also who hold no religious belief and find themselves unmoved by religious emotion" (p. 19). The question Eliot raised, as to whether Herbert's singleness of theme is restrictive or a sign of "solitary greatness" (p. 19) will, he pointed out, always remain a test of the reader's own sensibility. Given such an authoritative championship, Herbert's reputation as a first-rank poet became firmly established. Freshly suggestive ways of reading Herbert were put forward, and critical controversy over readings of Herbert came to a head with Rosemond Tuve's *A Reading of George Herbert* (London, 1952); as a scholar believing in the primacy of a historical and liturgical understanding of Herbert's sources, Tuve took issue with the closely analytical, modernist reading of Herbert to be found in *William Empson's Seven Types of Ambiguity* (London, 1930). Louis Martz, Rosemary Freeman, and Joseph Summers also stressed—somewhat dauntingly—the importance for an understanding of Herbert of such neglected subjects as Emblem books, Anglican liturgies, Rhetoric, Allegory, or the traditions of Courtly Love.

THE TEMPLE

WHEN reading the following discussion of the poems in *The Temple,* it is worth bearing in mind two remarks of T. S. Eliot's. The first is from his 1932 essay for *The Spectator* (Patrides, p. 334): "But you will not get much satisfaction from George Herbert unless you can take seriously the things which he took seriously himself and which made him what he was." The second is from his lucid and affectionate 1962 monograph on Herbert:

We need not look too narrowly for a steady progress in Herbert's religious life, in an attempt to discover a chronological order. He falls, and rises again. Also, he was accustomed to working over his

poems; they may have circulated in manuscript among his intimates during his lifetime. What we can confidently believe is that every poem in the book is true to the poet's experience.

Herbert's poems are the product of a personality at home in cultural and theological worlds most of us are no longer conversant with. Though they thus will bear much patient and subtle investigation, they must, first and foremost, engage us through their language, through the twists and turns of that dialogue which some will find a heart-to-troubled-heart interior conversation, and which others will interpret, on Herbert's own terms, as the dramatic and formal record of the relationship between a man and his Maker.

An introduction to *The Temple* can hardly hope to do more than provide an enticement to become familiar with a book of poems that, by common critical assent, is notable for the fineness of Herbert's temperament and his distinction in handling his craft. The poems have been treated individually, each poem taken as an independent unity that will gain from being seen in a larger context, but what that context should be is a vexed question. Whether *The Temple* is a coherent architectural whole or a collection of internal and broken sequences is not discussed here. Amy Charles, Herbert's biographer, in her essay *The Williams Manuscript and The Temple* (*Essential Articles,* pp. 416–432), argues for a triple arrangement: the progress of the Christian year; a theological progress from sin to salvation; and that sequencing which strikes the reader most directly, a progress of moving painfully from separation to unity with God. Herbert's own description in "The Holy Scriptures II" of the relationship between verses in the Bible is suggestive of the way the poems in *The Temple* work for the reader:

This verse marks that, and both do make a motion
   Unto a third, that ten leaves off doth lie:
   Then as dispersed herbs do watch a potion,
These three make up some Christian's destinie:

      (p. 58)

According to Izaak Walton, the manuscript-book containing the poems known as *The Temple*—a title not necessarily chosen by Herbert himself, but possibly by its editor, Nicholas Ferrar—was entrusted by Herbert some three weeks before his death to Mr. Edmund Duncan, with this enjoinder:

—Sir, I pray deliver this little Book to my dear brother Ferrar, and tell him, he shall find in it a picture of the many spiritual Conflicts that have past betwixt God and my Soul, before which I could subject mine to the will of Jesus my Master: in whose service I have now found perfect freedom; desire him to read it: and then, if he can think it may turn to the advantage of any dejected poor Soul, let it be made publick: if not, let him burn it: for *I and it, are less than the least of God's mercies.*
(Patrides, p. 127)

In 1633 Herbert's collection was published posthumously under Ferrar's supervision. *The Temple* brought Herbert into that group of Anglican poets which starts historically with Donne, and includes Richard Crashaw, Henry Vaughan, and Thomas Traherne. Despite Vaughan's indebtedness to Herbert, these other poets do not share Herbert's dialectical questioning, but rather move freely into the spiritual world they are sustained by as if already citizens of that country. Though Donne's friendship with Herbert's mother and Herbert's certain knowledge of and admiration for Donne's poetry link him with the older poet, it is not necessary or helpful to read Herbert's poems as if they are written under Donne's spell or shadow. The two poets had similar interests, but Donne's drama and brilliance and his constant poetic engagement with the philosophical and scientific questions of his time are different in kind from the workings of Herbert's imagination—although Herbert also has his bravura flashes, as in "The Pearl, Matth. 13. 45.," with its masterful opening stanza:

I know the wayes of Learning; both the head
And pipes that feed the presse, and make it runne;
What reason hath from nature borrowed,
Or of it self, like a good huswife, spunne
In laws and policie; what the starres conspire,
What willing nature speakes, what forc'd by fire;
Both th'old discoveries, and the new-found seas,
The stock and surplus, cause and historie:

All these stand open, or I have the keyes:
Yet I love thee.
(p. 88)

Whereas Donne integrates "the wayes of Learning," the alchemical experiments of nature "forc'd by fire," and sixteenth and seventeenth century cartographical knowledge into his poems—he has the "keys" and will use them—Herbert's poem essentially sizes up the knowledge the world offers in order to reject it. The biblical reference to Matthew in the title leads us to the verse: "Again, the kingdom of heaven is like unto a merchant man, seeking goodly pearls," and a human soul is that "pearl of great price" which is bought at the cost of Christ's crucifixion. The poem offers a triplet of temptations: the enticements of "Learning," "Honour" and "Pleasure," those "quick returns of courtesie and wit" in the second stanza, that ravishing musical opening to the third stanza:

I know the wayes of Pleasure, the sweet strains,
The lullings and the relishes of it;
The propositions of hot bloud and brains;
What mirth and musick mean; what love and wit
Have done these twentie hundred yeares, and more.
(p. 89)

The fourth stanza shuts the book on the dubious temptations the world offers, those "labyrinths" which cannot be threaded by Herbert's "groveling wit." The means of reaching God, in an image whose beauty and lightness convey a strength greater than the summed weight of all the world's attractions, is the "silk twist" of God's freely given Grace, without which human endeavor is, for Herbert, of no account. Hitherto, each stanza has closed its decasyllabic rhyming structure with the hovering simplicity of "Yet I love thee"; the final one varies this with "To climbe to thee." The poem is, in part, a kind of running criticism of the Baconian world—that enterprising examination of the "Book of Nature," that search for scientific knowledge which so excited Donne's imagination and which Herbert was familiar with, as he was familiar with Bacon himself. That difficult "Book," Nature, whose pages have no fixed number, has to be brought into a relationship with scriptural authority, that Book of Books the

Bible, whose primacy for the Country Parson Herbert describes in *A Priest to the Temple:*

> He condescends even to the knowledge of tillage, and pastorage, and makes great use of them in teaching, because people by what they understand, are best led to what they understand not. But the chief and top of his knowledge consists in the book of books, the storehouse and magazene of life and comfort, the holy Scriptures. There he sucks and lives.
>
> (p. 228)

To bring those two "Books" into consonance has hardly proved a simple task for Herbert's or for succeeding centuries. The "silk" twist of Grace, rather than the fruits of secular study, is for Herbert the primary means of salvation. The resolution of "The Pearl" is, however, hardly simple or final. The "lullings and the relishes" of music were never rejected; they were placed at God's service. Though secular preferments were for others, we are not to imagine that mirth was debarred, any more than music, or that Herbert's patrician accomplishments were to be exchanged for a rustic uncouthness. In "The Windows" Herbert sees the Preacher, that "brittle craze glasse," in a metaphorical relationship to the stained glass of the church window:

> But when thou dost anneal in glasse thy storie,
>   Making thy life to shine within
> The holy Preachers; then the light and glorie
>   More rev'rend grows, & more doth win:
>   Which else shows warish, bleak, & thin.
>
> (p. 67)

A puritan iconoclastic distrust of beauty is hardly evident there, nor in that passage in *A Priest to the Temple* (p. 246) in which Herbert enjoins the Parson to make sure that the Church is "at great festivalls strawed, and stuck with boughs, and perfumed with incense."

The Book of Nature can and could be read in many ways. In the early seventeenth century that huge cultural conflict began which was to bring about the rejection of medieval and Tudor patterns of thought, and the decay of traditional allegorical and spiritual readings of nature. The Bestiaries of the medieval period viewed creatures emblematically as providing a series of moral lessons, to be learnt by studying the particular characteristics of the creatures themselves. The relationship between the spiritual and the physical had been developed into such elaborate image-systems as "The Great Chain of Being," the ladder which led from the inanimate through the vegetable, animal, and human realms to the "Angelic Hierarchy" and God himself; the "Cosmic Dance," which made the universe into an intricate and patterned web of movement; and the "Doctrine of Correspondences" which explored in imagery the relationships between microcosm and macrocosm. These multiple arrangements were all attempts to find an underlying unity behind disparate phenomena.

That unhelpful word "quaint," frequently employed in the nineteenth and early twentieth centuries as a patronizing term for seventeenth-century writers, was habitually used to describe the "unserious" frisson created by the jostle and juxtaposition of the actual and the fabulous, the old doctrines and the new discoveries, in books like Bacon's *Sylva Sylvarum* (1627), Sir Thomas Browne's *Pseudodoxia Epidemica* (1646), or such huge sourcebooks as Philemon Holland's translation of Pliny's *The Historie of the World* (1601).

Herbert's own nature was to be a part of the older belief system, to be at home with signs and emblems. The fallen natural world that surrounds fallen man is still part of a universe created by God's beneficence, and multifarious presences can lead the human psyche back to God, the creator. The fifth and sixth stanzas of "Man" are explicit in their praise of the arrangements of use, delight, and guidance the natural world provides:

> For us the windes do blow,
> The earth doth rest, heav'n move, and fountains flow.
> Nothing we see, but means our good,
> As our delight, or as our treasure:
> The whole is, either our cupboard of food,
>   Or cabinet of pleasure.
>
> The starres have us to bed;
> Night draws the curtain, which the sunne withdraws;
>   Musick and light attend our head.

All things unto our flesh are kinde
In their descent and being; to our minde
    In their ascent and cause.

                (p. 91)

In this poem, Herbert proclaims that "Man is one world, and hath / Another to attend him" and looks to the world's transfigured reunion with its creator. "Providence" is closely linked to "Man" in theme. In this substantial, though routine and didactic performance, Herbert makes man's relationship with nature the entire subject of the poem, nature itself being subject to "Sacred Providence," the workaday companion to Grace. Here, man is "Secretarie of thy praise" and Herbert runs the gamut of those orders in the Great Chain of Being that conspire to stock that cupboard and cabinet of use and pleasure to be found in "Man." Herbert's traditional sense of the unity of creation is delightfully, if ludicrously, expressed in these two stanzas:

Thy creatures leap not, but express a feast,
Where all the guests sit close, and nothing wants.
Frogs marry fish and flesh; bats, bird and beast;
Sponges, non-sense and sense; mines, th'earth and
  plants.

To show thou art not bound, as if thy lot
Were worse than ours, sometimes thou shiftest hands.
Most things move th' under-jaw; the Crocodile not.
Most things sleep lying; th' Elephant leans or stands.

                (p. 121)

The curious "Thy creatures leap not," according to Hutchinson (p. 519), expresses the belief that there are no sudden jumps between one created kind and another; all is a gradual, related continuum. One might almost call those last two lines "quaint."

Herbert's intuitive preference for interpreting through praise is given force by the three poems in *The Temple* with that title. The finest, "Praise (II)," with its firm simplicities, has become part of the Anglican Hymnal, its opening lines familiar to countless congregations:

King of Glorie, King of Peace,
    I will love thee:

And that love may never cease,
    will move thee.

                (p. 146)

Many of Herbert's readers want to find in him an unaffected love of the natural world, as if he were a kind of prescientific Gilbert White of Selborne, carrying lute and fishing rod over June meadows through a chorus of birdsong. It is possible that we overestimate the presence of a "natural" world in Herbert's poems because, in our own postindustrial environment, we are frequently removed from the rural life Herbert took for granted, and thus did not need to especially value. Perhaps birds and flowers can more easily become abstract poetic images when they are not labeled "protected species." The traditional sentimentalizing of Herbert may also in part be due to the subliminal effect of the word "sweet" and its derivatives, which are so constantly varied as adjectives, adverbs, and nouns in the poems that it is difficult not to transfer sweetness to the man himself and make it the basis of his temperament.

It would admittedly be foolish to imagine that Herbert's feeling for the natural world did not sometimes take the form of unaffected pleasure, as is made clear by this stanza from "The Flower":

    And now in age I bud again,
After so many deaths I live and write;
    I once more smell the dew and rain,
And relish versing: O my onely light,
        It cannot be
        That I am he
    On whom thy tempests fell all night.

                (p. 166)

Herbert, though, is not a poet of nature. He happened to live in a pastoral world in which a great stock of epithets drawn from such simple sources as houses, weathers, farms, birds, and gardens lay at hand. They served his purpose, which was to help fulfill and celebrate God's own purpose. The images in Herbert's poems are not elaborately particularized, nor are they usually extended and teased out into the conceits to be found in Donne. The correspondences between these creatures or created objects and human lives are often expressed with the directness of a simple metaphor which carries with it layer upon layer of veiled cultural meaning. In "The Flower," all flowers are contained without any flower being defined. The sense of suffering God's absence, then sensing again his presence is compared in the opening stanza to the return of:

> the flowers in spring;
> To which, beside their own demean,
> The late-past frosts tributes of pleasure bring.
> Grief melts away
> Like snow in May,
> As if there were no such cold thing.
>
> (p. 165)

Herbert's own heart had gone "Quite underground; as flowers depart / To see their mother-root, when they have blown." The poem winds about his own flower-like progress, "Offring at heav'n, growing and groning thither," and the closing stanza identifies us all, in our transitory earthly life, as "but flowers that glide," searching for that heavenly garden. Herbert's simplified diction, his formally sophisticated technique used to create the effect of common speech, his deep sense of sharing a ritual appreciation of seasonal change with the reader—all these make the poem a demonstration of his art at its finest. We can bring to such simplified imagery the ghosts of our own experiences of natural change and enter into Herbert's fluctuations of absence and presence without any particularity of image drawing attention to an experience that belongs to the poet alone. "The Flower" has something of the timeless transparency of a Shakespearean love song.

As Rosemary Freeman says, in "George Herbert and the Emblem Books" (*Essential Articles for the Study of George Herbert's Poetry,* 1979, p. 221) "Herbert's poetry remains primarily visual, and visual in the special sense that has been defined as emblematic." A distinction must be made between the emblematic and "Emblem Books." Emblem Books became popular in the sixteenth and seventeenth centuries, the most famous being Andrea Alciati's *Emblematum Liber* (1531), a collection of woodcuts, each with a motto and a poem attached. The picture in any

Emblem Book is a symbol, whether simple or complex in its delineation. The motto is a brief and suggestive interpretation of the picture; the poem explains the whole. Herbert's life is almost framed by the appearance of the first English collection, Geoffrey Whitney's *A Choice of Emblems and Other Devises* (1586), and Francis Quarles's 1635 *Emblemes*, a Jesuit work symbolizing the relationship between Amor (divine love) and Anima (the human soul). The Emblem Books gave engravers a chance to demonstrate their skill and set puzzle-solvers cunning problems; they made poets ingenious, and, perhaps, offered a meditative wisdom to the receptive. Herbert's poetry is nearest to the traditional Emblem in his patterned poems, "The Altar" (p. 26) and "Easter-wings," whose optical shape matches their subject matter. Such ingenuities fall in and out of fashion, though there is a long tradition of marrying letter- and word-forms and visual experience. Each stanza of the pair which form "Easter-wings" opens out, diminishes, and dwindles, then opens out again to make yet another consonance where meaning, movement, and pattern all come together. The lark adds its own accompaniment of song as the whole contraption soars, and lifted by the paradoxical pun on "fall" in the first stanza's last line:

> Lord, who createdst man in wealth and store,
> Though foolishly he lost the same,
> Decaying more and more,
> Till he became
> Most poore:
> With thee
> O let me rise
> As larks, harmoniously,
> And sing this day thy victories:
> Then shall the fall further the flight in me.
>
> (p. 43)

"The Church-floore" is also allied to the traditional Emblem in that its symbolism is overt, allegorical rather than possessing the freedoms of further suggestion. The first four stanzas relate the physical structure to the allegorical abstraction overtly:

Mark you the floore? that square and speckled stone,
which looks so firm and strong,
            Is *Patience:*
                        (p. 66)

Herbert often expresses his truths in those attractive devices of his time: word play, riddle, and acrostic. "Aaron" (p. 174) is a poem where many kinds of sophistication in technique fuse to create a complex and beautiful poem. It also demonstrates Herbert's fascination for a circular movement, a bringing together by bringing back. In the biblical Book of Exodus, Chapter 28 is an elaborate account of the robing of the priest, Aaron, and Herbert's poem transposes this robing into a metaphorical and spiritual "dressing" of the priest he himself is. The poem is five stanzas, and each stanza contains five lines, thus creating a double match for the number of letters in the word "Aaron." The patterning of the first two stanzas is an exact equivalence in phrasing, and so parallels the doubled "A" which begins the word "Aaron":

            Holinesse on the head,
        Light and perfections on the breast,
    Harmonious bells below, raising the dead
            To leade them unto life and rest:
                Thus are true Aarons drest.

            Profaneness in my head,
        Defects and darknesse in my breast,
    A noise of passions ringing me for dead
            Unto a place where is no rest:
                Poore priest thus am I drest.
                        (p. 174)

The central image of the poem is bell music, and Grierson suggests that the rise and fall of each stanza has the effect of the swelling and dying away of a bell note, and that the reiterated chiming of bells is indicated by the reiterated pattern of the rhymes, which remain identical in word and placing for each stanza of the poem, (Hutchinson, p. 538). A further sophistication is added by introducing a musical element into the third line of each stanza. To this texture of suggested sound, the priest robes himself. In the final stanza, the priest, clothed spiritually by Grace and robed for divine service, turns to make invitation to his congregation, and, through the well-dressed poem, to us his readers:

            So holy in my head,
        Perfect and light in my deare breast,
    My doctrine tun'd by Christ, (who is not dead,
            But lives in me while I do rest)
                Come poeple; Aaron's drest.

Such formalities of structure will always delight some temperaments, and repel those who do not see games playing as artistically elevated.

It is helpful, though, to think of Herbert's creative imagination as being more profoundly emblematic than it is formalistic. He constantly offers the reader clear images that can be caught and held in the mind's eye, then gently unpacked to reveal great depths of emotional suggestion and complexity. Sometimes there are collocations of suggestion, as in the second stanza of "Mattens":

            My God, what is a heart?
        Silver, or gold, or precious stone,
        Or starre, or rainbow, or a part
    Of all these things, or all of them in one?
                        (p. 62)

Another constellation of images, each lying beside the other, like quick-shining jewels in a box, comes in the opening stanza of "The Quidditie," a poem in which Herbert distils the essence of what poetry is to "that which while I use / I am with thee" (p. 70):

    My God, a verse is not a crown,
    No point of honour, or gay suit,
    No hawk, or banquet, or renown,
    Nor a good sword, nor yet a lute.
                        (p. 69)

Perhaps the most haunting and evocative of such constellations is the gathering of images about the nature of prayer in the last three lines of "Prayer (I)." The poetry, without strain, reaches out beyond itself and comes almost to the expression of what cannot be expressed except by silence: "The milkie way, the bird of Paradise, / Church-bels beyond the starres heard, the souls bloud, / The land of spices; something understood" (p. 51).

This same suggestive lucidity can be seen by taking another recurring Herbertian image, that of the room, chest, bottle, box, or enclosure: an emblematic image with endless suggestive power, and one that can be unpacked in many different ways. "Even-song" (pp. 63–64) brings the night, when "in thy ebony box / Thou dost inclose us," with its suggestions of the coffin. "Ungratefulnesse" (pp. 82–83) offers, more allegorically, the Trinity and the Incarnation as "two rare cabinets full of treasure," and in one of Herbert's most perfect lyrics, "Vertue" (pp. 87–88), he celebrates and mourns the beautiful and transitory nature of "Sweet spring, full of sweet dayes and roses, / A box where sweets compacted lie."

The enduring strength of Herbert's poetry, though, lies in its deep understanding of those twinned polarities, presence and absence. The poems are resilient nets and cages which catch despair, anger, and the pull away from the divine into frustration and rejection: the soul thrashes like a fish on the line to escape the patient "fisherman." The close of "The Collar" is a perfect instance:

But as I rav'd and grew more fierce and wilde
        At every word,
Me thoughts I heard one calling, *Child!*
        And I reply'd, *My Lord.*

                (pp. 153–154)

In many of the poems which home in on such troubled and troubling emotions, the imagery is stripped away and we are left in the presence of a language almost as naked as the pains it expresses. In "The Forerunners" (pp. 176–177), the forerunners being his first white hairs, Herbert deploys an awareness of his own poetic accomplishments in a poem that prepares for forsaking or being forsaken by his art. The words "Farewell sweet phrases, lovely metaphors" are followed in the next stanza by the lines "Lovely enchanting language, sugar-cane, / Hony of roses, whither wilt thou flie?" As the birds of spring leave, Herbert pleads, "let a bleak palenesse chalk the door, / So all within be livelier than before."

There is a "bleak palenesse" in Herbert's poems, too, when he turns from praise or consciousness of the presence of Grace to introspection and unanswered questions. There are five poems titled with the solitary word "Affliction"—

Herbert's titles are themselves sparse and emblematic. "Affliction (I)" (pp. 46–48) is fierce in its complaints, and God is allowed no rejoinder to the accusations thrown at him. From the harsh bravura of the opening line's "When first thou didst entice to thee my heart," through the further implications of God's perverse will and Herbert's helplessness in "Thou didst betray me to a lingering book" and "thou throwest me / Into more sicknesses," the poem takes us through the puzzled buffeting of a man in great trouble and perplexity. "Thus," Herbert writes, "doth thy power crosse-bias me, not making / Thine own gift god, yet me from my wayes taking"—the "crosse-bias" metaphor being taken from the game of bowls, in which the ball is given a bias to make it swerve from a straight (or "true") path. Without the presence of Grace, Herbert becomes powerless, incapable—as he shows himself in "Employment (I)," where his separation from the divine makes Herbert an idler among the active and fruitful:

All things are busie; onely I
  Neither bring hony with the bees,
Nor flowres to make that, nor the husbandrie
         To water these.

I am no link of thy great chain,
  But all my companie is a weed.
Lord place me in thy consort; give one strain
         To my poore reed.

                (p. 57)

In "Deniall" all the images are created by opposing to each substantive an adjective that numbs its force, a negative qualifier. That "brittle bow," "nipt blossome," and "heartlesse breast," that musical instrument, the soul, which "lay out of sight, / Untun'd, unstrung" sink the poem into shadow and absence. The opening stanza emblematically marries the broken heart with broken rhythm, as the structure of the stanza itself tips into discordance and failure, dangling into a non-rhyme:

When my devotions could not pierce
        Thy silent eares;

Then was my heart broken, as was my verse:
    My breast was full of fears
        And disorder:

(p. 79)

There is an odd potency in those "silent eares," as there is in the compressed physicality in the fourth stanza:

O that thou shouldst give dust a tongue
To crie to thee,
And then not heare it crying! all day long
My heart was in my knee,
But no hearing.

(p. 80)

The poem closes, as so many of Herbert's poems do, with a tentative solution or invocation in the final stanza. In "The Deniall" the prayer for an answer brings at least the answer of a perfect rhyme to close the poem:

O cheer and tune my heartlesse breast,
Deferre no time;
That so thy favours granting my request,
They and my minde may chime,
And mend my ryme.

(p. 80)

The formal assurance of Herbert's poetry is the one constant in the fluctuations of this ever closing, ever widening gap between the human and the divine—which leads to an important caveat. Herbert cannot but be a sophisticated pattern-maker; what has been so arduously learnt and practiced cannot be undone, and Herbert's own disclaimers are in themselves part of his art. "Plain style" is in fact a style, with its own rhetorical antecedents. As Arnold Stein says, in "George Herbert: The Art of Plainness" (*Essential Articles*, p. 167): "As for his plainness, which is not all of one kind, it is above all a rhetoric of sincerity, an art by which he may tell the truth to himself and God." In "Jordan (II)," Herbert makes his renunciation of elaboration, of a time:

That I sought out quaint words, and trim invention;
My thoughts began to burnish, sprout and swell,

Curling with metaphors a plain intention,
Decking the sense, as if it were to sell.

(p. 102)

At that time "Nothing could seem too rich to clothe the sunne," and, Herbert claims, conscious of what was due to a poet, "So did I weave my self into the sense." The conclusory self-advice comes in the italicized whisper at the end of the poem: *There is in love a sweetnesse readie penn'd / Copie out onely that, and save expense*" (p. 103).

The abnegation, the desire to subdue self and eschew the sophistications of his craft in the task of becoming God's copyist, is moving. It is an impossible task, but Herbert's disciplined limitation of exuberant possibilities makes the task seem almost achievable. Albert McHarg Hayes, in his essay "Counterpoint in Herbert" (*Essential Articles*, pp. 283–297), reminds us, however, that: "The 127 stanzaic poems in *The Temple* represent 111 stanza patterns. Of these 111 patterns, 11 are used twice, 1 three times, and 1 four times. The other 98 are unique in Herbert; most of them also, in English poetry." When one considers the apparent unforced ease of so much of Herbert's work, such invention and assurance is breathtaking, and inside those inventive forms there is a constant varying of line lengths within stringent restrictions, a subtle and unexpected placing of rhyme, and a dynamic use of through-line that rarely leaves the stanzas becalmed. Such sophistications are always present, however naked the apparent saying of the poem is.

"Mans medley" can fitly bring these comments on *The Temple* to a close. The poem expresses that duality of nature that poises man in the Great Chain of Being between beasts and angels, sense and spirit—"with th'one hand touching heav'n, with th'other earth." The duality of man's nature gives him doubled joys, those of this sensuous world and those of the spiritual world to which he is traveling; so, too, his griefs are doubled: "Both frosts and thoughts do nip." The final stanza brings us to a mature reconciliation:

Yet ev'n the greatest griefs
    May be reliefs,
Could he but take them right, and in their wayes.

181

Happie is he, whose heart
Hath found the art
To turn his double pains to double praise.

(p. 132)

CONCLUSION

ALDOUS Huxley, in *Texts and Pretexts* (1933), gives an elegant and often quoted appraisal of Herbert's quality, setting him in a natural context the poet would have understood without the sentimentalizing Walton's *Life* was taken to license:

> The climate of the mind is positively English in its variableness and instability. Frost, sunshine, hopeless drought and refreshing rains succeed one another with bewildering rapidity. Herbert is the poet of this inner weather. Accurately, in a score of lyrics unexcelled for flawless purity of diction and appositeness of imagery, he has described its changes and interpreted, in terms of a mystical philosophy, their significance. Within his limits he achieves a real perfection.

(pp. 12–13)

The drama of Herbert's comparatively brief life lies in the contrast between the polished, scholarly aristocrat he began as and the drudging parish priest he became—this makes up part of that necessary legend a distinguished life always acquires. We can speculate on the nature of that transition, remembering always that there were less than three years spent at Bemerton. It may be easier than we imagine for certain temperaments to move by opposition, rather than by gradual progression. Those last years in which *The Temple* was largely written now seem to us to carry the true weight of what Herbert means to us as poet and human being. The consumption which was to kill him must have had its impact on both the spiritual intensity with which those years were lived and, more speculatively, on the creative accomplishment of the poetry. Correspondences between a fierce creativity and consumptive disease have frequently been drawn: Keats, the Brontës, and D. H. Lawrence come immediately to mind. It is possible, too, that Herbert's physical frailty gave him a consciousness from his early years that the hurly-burly of a career in the thick of worldly affairs was not for him.

Herbert's reputation as a poet is not likely to suffer diminution. There is, perhaps, some irony in a poet so overtly concerned with the celestial achieving such high regard in our secular age. However, while Herbert's poems are built out of a Christian and specifically Anglican experience, poetry will always compel by the quality of its questioning rather than the imagined security of the answers it finds. Herbert's church built of words can be illuminated by Philip Larkin's lines on a physical church from "Church Going" (*The Less Deceived,* 1955, p. 29):

A serious house on serious earth it is,
In whose blent air all our compulsions meet,
Are recognised, and robed as destinies.

If the poetic taste of the past century has been little inclined to explore traditional religious imagery in its search for sources of absolute value, it has been attentive to internal voices— and Herbert's dialogue is of a quality and conviction that compel attention. Herbert will repay the reader who brings biblical and liturgical knowledge to a reading of the poems, but will also deeply repay the reader who brings to the poems only an instinct for the spiritual life, a sense of the depths and heights of which the human spirit is capable. Herbert is exploratory rather than didactic in tone.

Poetry, though, lives not by its philosophical depth or complexity, but through language and form, and Herbert is now recognized as a complex and supple master of his craft. There is in many of the poems an invitingly plain style, a directness, and a lucid clarity that can be breathtaking. This seeming simplicity, though, draws on hidden sophistication. The variety of Herbert's stanzaic forms, the tautness and security of his patterning, make him a poet's poet, fascinating in the way that poets such as Alfred, Lord Tennyson or W. H. Auden are. When, as in the finest poems, such skill in saying coincides with such depth in what is said, when speech and song can hardly be distinguished the one from the other, then Herbert may justly be placed in the front rank of poets.

182

It would seem unfair to Herbert not to allow him a complete poem in any introduction to his work, and so this essay closes with the final lyrical piece in *The Temple,* "Love (III)." So much of the best in Herbert comes together here, in a poem that seems to hover, psyche-like, over the experiences that inspired it. There is an almost alarming submissive sensuality in the human-divine relationship, a simultaneous courtliness and simplicity, and a great refinement and mannerliness expressed through natural speech and bare diction. After its consummation, the poem continues to unfold in the imagination, leading us on through the eucharist to the soul's reception in heaven:

Love (III)

Love bade me welcome: yet my soul drew back
    Guiltie of dust and sinne.
But quick-ey'd Love, observing me grow slack
    From my first entrance in,
Drew nearer to me, sweetly questioning,
    If I lack'd anything.

A guest, I answer'd, worthy to be here:
    Love said, You shall be he.
I, the unkinde, ungratefull? Ah my deare
    I cannot look on thee.
Love took my hand, and smiling did reply,
    Who made the eyes but I?

Truth Lord, but I have marr'd them: let my shame
    Go where it doth deserve.
And know you not, sayes Love, who bore the blame?
    My deare, then will I serve.
You must sit down, sayes Love, and taste my meat:
    So I did sit and eat.

                  (pp. 188–189)

SELECTED BIBLIOGRAPHY

I. SEVENTEENTH-CENTURY EDITIONS. *The Temple. Sacred Poems and Private Ejaculations* (Cambridge, 1633; repr. in facsimile, Menston, U.K. 1968 and 1973); *Herbert's Remains. Or, Sundry Pieces of that sweet Singer of the Temple. Mr. George Herbert* (London, 1652; repr. in facsimile, Menston, U.K., 1970), contains the first printing of *A Priest to the Temple.*

II. COLLECTED WORKS A. B. Grosart, ed., *The Complete Works of George Herbert,* 3 vols. (London, 1874), this edition, limited to 156 copies, gives English translations of the poems in Latin; George Herbert Palmer, ed., *The English Works of George Herbert,* 3 vols. (London, 1905); F. E. Hutchinson, ed., *The Works of George Herbert* (Oxford, 1941); C. A. Patrides, ed., *The English Poems of George Herbert* (London, 1974); Amy M. Charles, ed., *The Temple,* "Williams MS." *The Williams Manuscript of George Herbert's Poems,* facsimile repr. (New York, 1977); Mario A. Di Cesare, ed., *The Temple: A Diplomatic Edition of the Bodleian Manuscript (Tanner 307) with Introduction and Notes* (Binghamton, N.Y., 1995).

III. BIBLIOGRAPHIES. John. R. Roberts, *George Herbert: An Annotated Bibliography of Modern Criticism 1905–1984,* rev. ed. (Columbia, Mo., 1988); Mario A. Di Cesare and Rigo Mignani, eds., *A Concordance to the Complete Writings of George Herbert* (Ithaca, N.Y., 1977).

IV. CRITICAL AND BIOGRAPHICAL STUDIES. Izaak Walton, *The Life of Mr. George Herbert* (London, 1670), this is most conveniently found, together with Barnabas Oley's *"A Prefatory View of the Life of Mr. Geo. Herbert"* (London 1652), in C. A. Patrides, ed., *George Herbert: The Critical Heritage* (London, 1983).

William Empson, *Seven Types of Ambiguity* (London, 1930); Rosemond Tuve, *A Reading of George Herbert* (London, 1952); Joseph H. Summers, *George Herbert: His Religion and Art* (London, 1954); David Novarr, *The Making of Walton's Lives* (Ithaca, N.Y., 1958).

Louis L. Martz, *The Poetry of Meditation: A Study of English Religious Literature of the Seventeenth Century* (New Haven, 1962); Arnold Stein, *George Herbert's Lyrics* (Baltimore, 1968).

Thomas P. Roche, ed., *Essays by Rosemond Tuve* (Princeton, 1970); Stanley E. Fish, *Self-Consuming Artifacts: The Experience of Seventeenth- Century Literature* (Berkeley, 1972); Helen Vendler, *The Poetry of George Herbert* (Cambridge, Mass., 1975); Amy M. Charles, A Life of George Herbert (London and Ithaca, N.Y., 1977); Stanley E. Fish, *The Living Temple: George Herbert and Catechizing* (Berkeley, 1978); John R. Roberts, ed., *Essential Articles for the Study of George Herbert's Poetry* (Hamden, Conn., 1979).

Claude J. Summers and Ted-Larry Pebworth, ed., *"Too Riche to Clothe the Sunne": Essays on George Herbert* (Pittsburgh, 1980); Rodney Edgecombe, *"Sweetnesse Readie Penn'd": Imagery, Syntax, and Metrics in the Poetry of George Herbert* (Salzburg, 1980); Rosemary Wengen-Shute, *George Herbert and the Liturgy of the Church of England* (Leiden, 1981); Barbara Harman, *Costly Monuments: Representations of the Self in George Herbert's Poetry* (Cambridge, Mass., 1982); Diana Benet, *Secretary of Praise: The Poetic Vocation of George Herbert* (Columbia, Mo., 1984); Gene Edward Veith, *Reformation Spirituality: The Religion of George Herbert* (Lewisburg and London, 1985); Chana Bloch, *Spelling the Word: George Herbert and the Bible* (Berkeley and Los Angeles, 1985); Edmund Miller and Robert Di Yanni, eds., *Like Season'd Timber: New Essays on George Herbert* (New York, 1987).

Michael C. Schoenfeldt, *Prayer and Power: George Herbert and Renaissance Courtship* (Chicago and London, 1991); Harold Toliver, *George Herbert's Christian Narrative* (Pennsylvania, 1993); Christopher Hodgkins, *Authority, Church, and Society in George Herbert: Return to the*

Middle Way (Columbia, Mo., 1993); James Boyd White, *"The Book of Starres": Learning to Read George Herbert* (Ann Arbor, 1994).

Philip Sheldrake, *"Love Took my Hand": The Spirituality of George Herbert* (London, 2000).

V. FURTHER READING. E. M. W. Tillyard, *The Elizabethan World Picture* (London, 1943); Rosemary Freeman, *English Emblem Books* (London, 1948); L. C. Martin, ed., *The Works of Henry Vaughan* (Oxford, 1957); C. S. Lewis, *The Discarded Image* (Cambridge, U.K., 1963); John T. Shawcross, ed., *John Donne: The Complete Poetry* (Garden City, N.J., 1967); W. H. Gardner and N. H. Mackenzie, eds., *The Poems of Gerard Manley Hopkins,* rev. ed. (Oxford, London, and New York, 1970); Arthur L. Clements, *Poetry of Contemplation: John Donne, George Herbert, Henry Vaughan, and the Modern Period* (Albany, N.Y., 1990).

GERARD MANLEY HOPKINS

(1844–1889)

Jay Parini

GERARD MANLEY HOPKINS was perhaps the most original, and idiosyncratic, among the Victorian poets. A Jesuit priest and classical scholar, he died after a relatively short and frustrated life without ever gaining recognition as a poet, yet his work has been deeply influential on modern and contemporary poets, and his reputation has only gained ground since the first publication of his poems in 1918, nearly three decades after his death.

His work consists of a relatively small body of poems and poetic fragments those gathered for publication by his friend, Robert Bridges, himself a poet. With the exception of one long poem, *The Wreck of the Deutschland,* Hopkins preferred to write in short and conventional forms, although his eccentricity and originality turned even the most obvious of forms, such as the sonnet, into a highly personal vehicle. He was also a gifted prose writer, leaving behind a large quantity of writing in his journals, diaries, sermons, and letters. This work eventually made its way into print as well.

Hopkins was essentially a religious poet, his work dedicated "to the greater Glory of God" (the Jesuit motto), yet much of his work also might be called nature poetry, as he sought to discover the spiritual qualities in nature and his relationship, as part of God's creation, to the physical world around him. In this, he was not far removed from his Romantic predecessors: Blake, Wordsworth, Coleridge, Keats, and Shelley. Yet his highly eccentric way of conceiving of nature in relation to God leant to his work a remarkable freshness. His theories about his work, and poetry in general, were expressed in letters to friends such as Bridges, A. W. M. Baillie, Coventry Patmore, and R. W. Dixon, each of whom had a strong interest in his work.

What strikes the reader of Hopkins from the outset is the massive peculiarity of the style. His poems, at first glance, seem to have been written in a language related to English by some distance. In fact, Hopkins reached back to the Anglo-Saxons for sound effects: heavy alliteration and strong assonance, combined with abrupt rhythmical pauses and leaps. Being a classicist, he was also intimately familiar with the conventions of Greek and Latin poetry, yet he absorbed the classical conventions in unconventional ways, anticipating the command of Ezra Pound to all modern poets to "make it new" by nearly half a century. His work both modified and extended the traditions that underlay it.

Bridges, a conventional poet of minor talent, objected to the strangeness of his friend's work, but Hopkins defended himself in letter after letter. "Obscurity I do and will try to avoid so far as is consistent with excellences higher than clearness at first reading," he wrote to him in 1878. "As for affectation I do not believe I am guilty of it: you should point out instances, but as long as mere novelty and boldness strikes you as affectation your criticism strikes me as water of the Lower Isis."

Hopkins derived his metaphysics from the ancient Greeks, whom he read with great care. He believed that the ideal world of forms expressed itself in nature in highly individual ways, and what interested him was the way in which every object in nature was original to the point of beauty. Every tree or flower or stone was unique, as was every person. Being a Christian, he attributed all creation to God, and he suggested (in his own eccentric terminology) that God "stressed" or "instressed" each object or creature with individual beauty. Everything thus-possessed what he called "inscape" a word he commonly used in his letters, journals, and poems.

Hopkins developed an elaborate, highly personal, aesthetic theory that depended heavily on his own private notions of theology as well. In retrospect, however, there was not anything wildly original about his thinking, as one finds parallel ideas in German and English Romanticism as well as in American Transcendentalism. Shelley, for example, spoke of a spirit that swept through the world and gave all objects their particular shape and identity, a notion derived from Plato. But Hopkins developed an idiosyncratic way of writing about the same aesthetic and metaphysical reality, as in his journal entry for 19 July 1872: "Stepped into a barn of ours, a great shadowy barn, where the hay had been stacked on either side, and looking at the great rudely arched timber frames . . . I thought how sadly beauty of inscape was unknown and buried away from simply people and yet how near at hand it was if they had eyes to see it and it could be called out everywhere again" (Penguin edition, p. 126).

The poet's job, given this theory of poetry, was to become the eyes that discerned the inscape, the unique pattern, in everything that lay about in the natural and human world. Of course, Hopkins's eye tended to drift toward nature; this seems common among poets. But Hopkins had a very intensely visual as well as sensual imagination, and he was stimulated by what he found in the woods, as on 9 May 1871, when he came upon some bluebells:

> The bluebells in your hand baffle you with their inscape, made to every sense: if you draw your fingers through them they are lodged and struggle with a shock of wet heads; the long stalks rub and click and flatten to a fan on one another like your fingers themselves would when you passed the palms hard across one another, making a brittle rub and jostle like the noise of a hurdle strained by leaning against; then there is the faint honey smell and in the mouth the sweet gum when you bite them.
>
> (p. 123)

Hopkins's journals and diaries are rich with such natural descriptions as well as detailed drawings. But it was in the poems that he reached

for, and found, unique verbal representations of "inscape." He conceived of this as a duty of sorts. Thus, each poem displayed its inscape, if the poem was properly composed. In some lecture notes on poetry written in 1874, for example, he said, "Some matter or meaning is essential to [poetry] but only as an element necessary to support and employ the shape which is contemplated for its own sake. (Poetry is in fact speech employed to carry the inscape of speech for the inscape's sake and therefore the inscape must be dwelt on)" (p. xxii).

Hopkins was aware that his poetry seemed peculiar. "No doubt my poetry errs on the side of oddness," he wrote to Bridges, in 1879. Yet he considered this oddness necessary to his art, part of its essential individuality, and he likened this uniqueness to melody and design in their respective arts:

> But as air, melody, is what strikes me most of all in music and design in painting, so design, pattern or what I am in the habit of calling *inscape* is what I above all aim at in poetry. Now it is the virtue of design, pattern, or inscape to be distinctive and it is the vice of distinctiveness to become queer. This vice I cannot have escaped.

Hopkins did not escape this vice, but this was ultimately to his benefit. He was able, through close attention to the distinct and thoroughly odd voice that sounded in his poems, to establish a foothold in the history of English poetry from which he cannot easily be shaken, contributing a dozen or more lyrics that must stand among the best in the language.

THE LIFE

HOPKINS was born in Stratford, Essex, on 28 July 1844 at the beginning of Queen Victoria's long reign. His family was relatively well off, and certainly well educated. His father, Manley Hopkins, was a poet himself, although he published only one volume in his lifetime. Hopkins's mother was a widely read and cultivated woman who encouraged her son to read poems, to draw, and to appreciate music. (Two of Hopkins's younger brothers became artists of some professional reputation in their time.) Hopkins revealed an early talent for drawing and continued at it throughout his life, filling his notebooks with detailed sketches of natural scenes.

A good student at the Highgate School in London, where he won a prize for his poetry in 1860, he was admitted to Balliol College, Oxford in the autumn of 1863. Like most cultured young men of this era, he read for a degree in classics, but unlike the average student his interest in the subject was genuine, even profound. He was also interested in philosophy and aesthetics, coming under the direct influence of Walter Pater, one of the most famous aestheticians of the era. He was influenced as well by E. B. Pusey, a theologian from Christ Church College, around whom many undergraduates gathered during the middle decades of the nineteenth century. Pusey was a leader in the Oxford Movement, begun in 1833 with the purpose of reestablishing Authority and Catholicity in the Anglican Church.

Pusey's antagonist, who disliked the Romanizing attitude of the Oxford Movement, was Benjamin Jowett, the Master of Balliol, who translated Plato and other classical authors. Hopkins admired Jowett, but he preferred the ritualistic Christianity of Pusey and his followers. A crucial event for Hopkins was the conversion to Rome of John Henry Newman in 1845 a conversion that precipitated his own. Indeed, Hopkins quickly resolved to "go over" to Rome himself, rejecting the Church of England. On 17 July 1866 he wrote in his journal: "It was this night I believe but possibly the next that I saw clearly the impossibility of staying in the Church of England, but resolved to say nothing to anyone till three months are over, that is the end of the Long [Vacation], and then of course to take no step till after my Degree" (Penguin edition, p. 108). He did not wait until graduation, however; there was too much excitement and urgency in his decision, and he was received into the Catholic Church by Newman himself in October of 1866, just a year before he graduated with a First Class degree.

The influence of Oxford on his personality was considerable. It was there he became friends with Robert Bridges, the future Poet Laureate. For the

first time, he began writing poetry in a serious way. "It is a happy thing that there is no royal road to poetry," he noted in his journal in 1864, adding "The world should know by this time that one cannot reach Parnassus except by flying thither" (p. 91).

One compelling piece of prose that survives from his undergraduate years is a Platonic dialogue called "On the Origin of Beauty," which was probably written for his classics tutor, Walter Pater, an important figure at Oxford and a major voice in the aesthetic movement associated with the phrase "art for art's sake." Hopkins's dialogue is presented as between a sensitive young undergraduate called John Hanbury and "the Professor of a newly founded chair of Aesthetics" (p. 92). In the gardens of New College, they discuss the nature of beauty, concluding (on the professor's insistence) that beauty is a relation among parts of a whole, a fine if somewhat obvious notion—although the young student remains skeptical of the professor, much as Hopkins may have been skeptical of Pater, whose aestheticism seemed to lack the moral edge he craved. Pater's approach to life would also have disturbed Hopkins, whose tendencies toward asceticism and self-denial were already apparent at Oxford.

Given his success at Oxford in his studies, Hopkins would almost certainly have followed an academic career without interruption had the Church not intervened. Newman invited the young convert to teach at a school where he worked for a few months before entering the Novitiate of the Society of Jesus, the Jesuit order. On 11 May 1868, he burned his poetry (or so he believed), thinking that somehow it represented an indulgence. He resolved to write no more, unless his superiors wished for him to do so. The Jesuits were, as they remain, the most intellectual of Catholic orders, and Hopkins began a rigorous and lengthy intellectual and spiritual journey that led to his ordination in 1877. Among the philosophers and theologians he studied were Duns Scotus and Ignatius Loyola, the latter being the founder of the Society of Jesus.

Scotus, a medieval English philosopher who had taught at Oxford, was a metaphysician who believed, in contrast to Thomas Aquinas, in the force of individual things in nature. This philosophy appealed to Hopkins, who had already moved in this direction with his personal aesthetics. Scotus also attached great importance to human individuality, arguing that the difference between "a man" as a general category and "Socrates" as a distinct man was a process that he called Individuation. He praised the individual as an example of "Thisness" (a translation of the Latin term *haecceitas*). Whereas Aquinas tended to reason from the abstract to the particular, Scotus reversed the process, beginning always with the individual fact or person, then expanding outward toward the universal. He stressed the importance of imagery for knowledge, another element of his philosophy that appealed to the poet-artist in Hopkins. In a poem called "Duns Scotus's Oxford," he wrote of this thinker as the one "who of all men most sways my spirits to peace." Reading Scotus, Hopkins apparently felt sanctioned as a poet; the act of finding individual beauty in a person or thing could be justified as a theological quest for God in animate or inanimate form.

The influence of Ignatius was equally profound, especially on the shape that his poems took. The *Spiritual Exercises* of Ignatius (1536) were hugely influential in the Renaissance. They were designed by Ignatius to lead a Christian in meditation through a process that would bring him or her closer to God. Divided into four "weeks," the meditations were meant to last an hour. The idea was to bring what Ignatius considered the "powers of the soul," memory, intellect, and will, into activity. One began with a "composition of place," a concrete evocation of a specific scene. This scene was often drawn from memory. From there, one contemplated this image in metaphorical terms, bringing the intellect into play. This in turn led to an outpouring of sympathy and emotion, a fusing of intellect and feeling, and an exercise of the will in praising God. Ignatius encouraged the meditator, in the final phase of meditation, to address God as "a servant to a master" or a friend to friend.

One can see the effect of this style of meditation on many poets, including John Donne, George Herbert, and even Wordsworth, who seem to have somehow absorbed certain structures of thought from earlier poets. But Hopkins acquired his knowledge of Ignatius directly, through years of meditative practice and prayer. His poems often reflect specific Ignatian texts, as do John Donne's. His final sonnets, for example, which are called The Terrible Sonnets because they deal with a man in a state of spiritual exhaustion if not deep pain, should not be read as simple transcripts of misery, or an early form of confessional poetry. Rather, they should be seen as examples of meditative projection, a dramatization of the soul's progress from despair and negation to affirmation and praise. Hopkins, though genuinely despairing in his later years, had also learned to dramatize and objectify his emotions, and he was meditating in these sonnets in a way that would be utterly familiar to anyone who had read Ignatius closely.

Hopkins moved around a good deal, spending a crucial period in Wales during the last years of his theological training. It was there, in 1875, that he suggested to his superior that he might try to write a poem to commemorate the deaths of five nuns aboard a ship called *The Deutschland* that was fleeing Germany because of the anti-Catholic Falck Laws. The resulting long poem, now regarded as a premodern masterwork, was sent to the Jesuit magazine, *The Month,* but rejected as too difficult. Indeed, it must have seemed incomprehensible to the editor, given its astonishing originality and genuine strangeness. Nevertheless, Hopkins was encouraged to continue his work in poetry, and slowly over the next decade and a half he assembled a small body of lyrics. That he never received the encouragement of publication makes his achievement seem all the more impressive. Hopkins did, however, receive encouragement from his old schoolmaster, R. W. Dixon, who grasped the beauty and originality of his former pupil's work. He was also taken seriously by Bridges and others, and this private world of his correspondence became the only stage for his performances as poet.

Hopkins was assigned to poor parishes in London, Oxford, Liverpool, Glasgow, and Chesterfield. His parishioners liked him, and he went about his tasks with seriousness and commitment; but he never felt happy in the role of parish priest. Nevertheless, a number of poems came out of these experiences, such as "Harry Ploughman" and "Felix Randal" the latter a poem of great sympathy for a "dear and dogged man," whom Hopkins attended in the course of his clerical duties. His reaction to the brutalizing effects of industrialism in the cities where he labored among the poor also had a visible impact on his poems. One sees this mark, for example, in "God's Grandeur," one of his most inspired poems, where he complains that "all is seared with trade; bleared, smeared with toil."

Hopkins felt some relief from the difficulties of parish work when, in 1882, he was appointed to a position at Stonyhurst College, in Blackburn. He returned to an intense study of Greek and Latin poetry at this time, and now had the leisure to write more poetry himself. Unfortunately, he found himself relatively blocked and suffered periods of intense nervous exhaustion. He was, however, an excellent teacher and scholar, and this was recognized by his colleagues. In 1885 he was appointed to the Chair of Classics at University College, Dublin, a prestigious appointment that acknowledged his mastery of the field. Nevertheless, he felt "at a third removed," as he wrote, while in Ireland; that is, he felt separated from his Irish colleagues because of his nationality and political attachments as well as from his friends and family in England. Ireland proved an impossible place for him. Despite frequent trips back to England, he never acclimated himself. His letters and poems of the last four years suggest that he was frequently desperate, suffering from a lack of spiritual joy as well as a thwarted sexuality. The latter point has commonly been made by his biographers, but it rests on suppositions that have no grounding except in speculation. That Hopkins was a man of intense physicality seems obvious from his work; as a Jesuit, of course, there was no legitimate expression for this aspect of his personality. His later agonies as registered in the poems and letters seem related to feelings of sexual frustration, but this is impossible to gauge in the absence of concrete evidence.

Repeated bouts of nervous exhaustion and frequent colds left Hopkins in a vulnerable state. Although still a relatively young man, in chronological age, he was not well, and he contracted typhoid fever in the spring of 1889. This led to other complications, and his parents were summoned from England, arriving in time for his death on 8 June. His faith in God remained strong, and his last words were "I am so happy, so happy" (Penguin edition, p. xxxi).

AN ORIGINAL POETICS

HOPKINS thought long and hard about poetic technique, developing a number of theories in general and innovations in practice. Apart from his aesthetics, which have deep religious undertones, he was interested in prosody and style. He referred in his letters to what he called "Sprung Rhythm," a term always associated with his name. Hopkins understood that in English versification one does not count vowel quantity (long versus short) as one does in Latin poetry; one counts heavy and light beats. Hopkins had a peculiar ear and liked to mark his poems with stresses in manuscript; most editions of his poetry continue to include these bizarre marks on the page. They are not, however, useful to the general reader and may well confuse and disrupt readings of his work.

Hopkins explained his thoughts on rhythm to Dixon on 5 October 1878 (p. 187). He described the origins of *The Wreck of the Deutschland* and the metrical system he evolved in that work:

I had long had haunting my ear the echo of a new rhythm which now I realized on paper. To speak shortly, it consists in scanning by accents or stress alone, without any account of the number of syllables, so that a foot may be one strong syllable or it may be many light and one strong. I do not say the idea is altogether new; there are hints of it in music, in nursery rhymes and popular jingles, in the poets themselves, and, since then, I have seen it talked about as a thing possible in critics.

He gives an example from a nursery rhyme, marking the stresses thus: "Díng, dóng, béll. / Pússy's ín the ·wéll. / Whó pút her ín? Líttle

Jóhnny Thín." The traditional form is trimeter, a three-foot line; but obviously one must count the stresses in order to count the feet, especially in the first line, which has only three words, each stressed equally.

Hopkins own poetry, then, depends heavily on Sprung Rhythm. The poet leaps from stress to stress, counting only the heavy beats, letting any number (none, many) of unstressed syllables gather around the strong beats. The sonnet called "The Starlight Night," for example, begins as follows: "Look at the stars! look, look up at the skies! / O look at all the fire-folk sitting in the air!" Hopkins does not supply marks for the stresses here, but it might be scanned as follows: "Loók at the stárs! loók, look úp at the skiés! / O loók at all the fíre-fólk sítting in the aír!" This scansion does not, unfortunately, account for the second "look," or the initial "O" of the second line; it suppresses a potentially heavy beat on "all" as well. But this is most likely how Hopkins might have heard it. As one sees, there is room in Hopkins's method for interpretation.

Hopkins closely studied Anglo-Saxon poetry, learning about Sprung Rhythm there. *Beowulf,* for example, is heavily "sprung" in Hopkins's sense of the term. Yet the verse line in Anglo-Saxon depended for its effects on both assonance and alliteration, and no poet before or after Hopkins has relied so heavily on both. His poems lunge from consonant to consonant, and there is a powerful echoing of vowels. His poems are systems of linked sounds, as in the opening lines of "The Windhover":

I caught this morning morning's minion, kingdom
  of daylight's dauphin, dapple-dawn-drawn Falcon,
    in his riding
  Of the rolling level underneath him steady air, and
    striding
High there, how he rung upon the rein of a wimpling
  wing
In his ecstasy!

The abruptly sprung rhythms are evident in the second line, where unstressed syllables crowd around the stressed. The reader's eye lunges from alliterative blast to alliterative blast, from the "m"s of the first line to the "d"s of the second; all the while, the sound effects depending on the chiming vowels, as in the compound epithet "dapple-dawn-drawn." Indeed, the creation of compound epithets is another trademark effect of Hopkins, one that has its origins in Anglo-Saxon poetry just as the vowel chiming has its origins partly in Welsh poetry, a body of work Hopkins encountered during his theological training in Wales. He explained to Dixon that in his poems the "rhymes carried on from one line into another and certain chimes suggested by the Welsh poetry I had been reading (what they call *cynghanedd*)."

The heavy alliteration and assonance alone would have set Hopkins apart in his day. The most popular poets were Tennyson, Browning, and Swinburne, and Hopkins's work would have seemed a universe apart from theirs. Not surprisingly, Hopkins's literary executor, Bridges, refused to let publication of the poems occur for many years because he guessed the reading public was not ready for this work. (He may also have been jealous of Hopkins, whose originality and power were evident to the best readers at once.) Adding to the oddness of the texture was Hopkins's penchant for using peculiar or dialect words. Thus, in "Windhover," he writes that "sheer plod makes plough down sillion / Shine." The idea here is that a plough, in going through the soil, makes the dirt shimmer that it turns up in its wake. This soil, in a northern English dialect, was called "sillion," a term Hopkins had come across in his travels among farmers.

He was also drawn to a figure of speech called the "kenning," a form of periphrasis (or longer phrase employed in place of a common word) used especially by Anglo-Saxon poets. In "The Caged Skylark," Hopkins opens with this image: "As a dare-gale skylark scanted in a dull cage / Man's mounting spirit in his bone-house." He creates a kenning when he writes "bone-house" to describe a man's body. The same effect occurs in "Hurrahing in the Harvest" when he writes "Summer ends now; now, barbarous in beauty, the stooks rise / Around; up above, what wind-walks!" These "wind-walks" or sidewalks of wind that slide across the sky constitute a kenning, comparable to the *Beowulf* poet calling the sea the "whale-road." Readers familiar with

Anglo-Saxon poetry will spot the echoes quite easily, although these effects only add to the peculiar texture of Hopkins's verse. Yet in reading Hopkins consistently, one becomes familiar with his effects, and the difficulties quickly seem less formidable.

That his poetry is studded with odd words lends a distinctive and appealing flavor to the work, but his peculiar syntax can be unsettling. Consider the last lines of the opening octet of "The Windhover," where he writes "My heart in hiding / Stirred for a bird, the achieve of, the mastery of the thing!" To convey his breathlessness and the crush of emotions that he experienced the poet interrupts the normal progress of the sentence. Had he been writing in prose, he might have written "My heart, which had been hiding in my breast, stirred when I saw this bird in flight. I was amazed by its achievement, and by its mastery, of flight." That approximation is ridiculous, of course, but it suggests the kind of thinking that underlies the fiercely abbreviated and choppy syntax. Similar translations must be made, however, by the reader whenever reading Hopkins, since the usual expectations for syntactical order are frequently disrupted. In this, Hopkins once again foreshadows the modernist poets, such as Ezra Pound, Wallace Stevens, and T. S. Eliot, each of whom pushed their language and syntax to the edge of intelligibility in order to achieve certain effects.

A further syntactical effect commonly employed by Hopkins relates to his freewheeling approach to grammar. Thus, the unnamed sonnet that begins, "To seem the stranger lies my lot," ends with this stanza:

I am in Ireland now; now I am at a third
Remove. Not but in all removes I can
Kind love both give and get. Only what word
Wisest my heart breeds dark heaven's baffling ban
Bars or hell's sell thwarts. This to hoard unheard,
Heard unheeded, leave me a lonely began.

In addition to the bizarrely distorted syntax, there is the use of "began," a verb, as a noun in the last line. In fact, Hopkins often converts verbs into nouns and nouns into verbs. In "Ribblesdale," he begins "Earth, sweet Earth, sweet landscape, with leaves throng," thus transforming "throng" from a verb into an adjective. Language, for him, was a playground of effects, and he did not worry about the conventions of grammar and syntax; he considered them fair game for his inventiveness.

Hopkins was attracted to traditional forms, such as the sonnet perhaps his most frequently employed form. Yet his aggressive originality overwhelmed the conventional boundaries again and again. His sonnets, for instance, repeatedly defied the normal limitations of the form, as when he eschewed the usual iambic pentameter line, freeing his rhythms or "springing" them so that lines tumble over each other, teeming with extra syllables. He may, as in "The Windhover," break a word in two, so that "kingdom" is halved, allowing the "king-" part to end the line and rhyme with "striding" and "wing." (One often sees this effect in the poems of e. e. cummings, many decades later.)

That his poetry erred on the side of oddness, as he suggested, must be taken as a given. Hopkins was nevertheless able to achieve something of remarkable beauty by pressing the normal limits of sound and sense. His poems stay in the mind because they are so lovely in their distinctness. The oddity that plagues the poetry is generally overcome by the attractiveness of the language itself, and the sentiments that Hopkins expressed were dazzling in their unaffected purity. One never doubts the sincerity of the poet, or refuses to grant him leeway as he struggles toward expression.

THE WRECK OF THE DEUTSCHLAND

AFTER a self-imposed poetic silence of seven years, in 1875 Hopkins erupted into verse again with *The Wreck of the Deutschland.* In this massive, powerfully imagined poem, all of the notions about rhythm and poetic texture that Hopkins had been quietly contemplating for some years were put into action. The rhythms are defiantly "sprung," as the lines heave from stress to stress, and unstressed syllables scatter about in unruly ways. The diction is strange and highly personal, with nouns often working as verbs. Hopkins always preferred a strong Anglo-Saxon diction, and that is true of *The Wreck.* The poem is profoundly Christian, of course, and Ignatian in its structure and theme, depending heavily on "compositions of place," dramatic images that are meditated by analogies. The poem moves inexorably toward praise of God, whom the poet addresses in a personal way, "like a servant speaking to a master," as Ignatius suggested.

The poem is, in general, an ode a long poem on an important theme. Hopkins, being a classicist, was familiar with the Greek poet Pindar, whose odes were among the finest of the classical era. In a typical Pindaric ode, the beginning and the end of poem are personal as well as similar in tone and texture. This is certainly true of *The Wreck,* which opens with ten stanzas subtitled Part the First. This section has nothing to do with the central narrative about a German ship that sank off the coasts of Kent and drowned the five nuns whom Hopkins commemorates here. These stanzas are intensely personal and focus on the relationship between the poet and God. The last six stanzas of the poem belong to Part the Second, but they might have been called Part the Third, since they depart from the main story and return to the subject of the poet's relationship with God.

The Wreck opens with an image of the poet almost resisting God's literal and strong touch:

> Thou mastering me
> God! giver of breath and bread;
> World's strand, sway of the sea;
> Lord of the living and dead;
> Thou hast bound bones and veins in me, fastened me flesh,
> And after it almost unmade, what with dread,
> Thy doing: and dost thou touch me afresh?
> Over again I feel thy finger and find thee.

The poet addresses God directly, praising him in conventional terms as "giver of breath and bread," and "Lord of the living and dead," but the syntax is so disruptive that one is forced to think about what Hopkins wants to say in fresh ways. God is the "world's strand," which suggests he does not merely hover above the world; he infuses the world with his being. He is "sway of the sea," meaning that the mere movement of the waves in the ocean exhibits God's power.

Hopkins's universe is alive and active, in ferocious animation. There is no dead matter here.

Hopkins goes on, in a vein that anticipates modern confessional poetry, to recall the "hour and night" of his conversion. He writes about this with wild energy: "I did say yes / O at lightning and lashed rod." Christ embodies terror in this moment, and Hopkins remembers with a shudder "The swoon of a heart that the sweep and the hurl of thee trod / Hard down with a horror of height." His "midriff" or central body was "laced with fire of stress." In Ignatian fashion, he meditates upon his confrontation with God by drawing sharp visual images and metaphor, picturing himself suspended between salvation and damnation: "The frown of his face / Before me, the hurtle of hell / Behind, where, where was a, where was a place?" That last line, in its broken syntax, embodies the feeling of desperation typical of this movement between heaven and hell.

In the marvelous fourth stanza, Hopkins pictures himself as sand in an hourglass in the first lines, then shifts to an image of water in a well or rainwater coursing along a "voel," a dialect word in Welsh for hill. This meditation by analogy leads to a direct outpouring of affection for the universe: "I kiss my hand / To the stars, lovely-asunder / Starlight, wafting him out of it." In other words, he kisses his hand to the stars and "wafts" or gleans Christ from them. As usual, all things in nature, when their inscape is properly noticed, remind Hopkins of God's glory. "His mystery must be instressed, stressed," he writes, using his own terminology.

What follows in the remainder of Part the First is a meditation on the life of Christ, beginning with his birth: "Manger, maiden's knee." This gives way to "the dense and driven Passion." The breaking of the body of Christ on the cross, in the powerful but highly peculiar eighth stanza, is contemplated in terms of a berry, a sloe:

> How a lush-kept plush-capped sloe
> Will, mouthed to flesh-burst,
> Gush! flush the man, the being with it, sour or sweet,
> Brim, in a flash, full! Hither then, last or first,
> To hero of Calvary, Christ's feet

Never ask if meaning it, wanting it, warned of it men go.

That is, Hopkins imagines a berry as it is put into the mouth. If you suck on it, it will burst, "flush the man, the being with it, sour or sweet." So if we "mouth" Christ, the meaning of his sacrifice will burst upon us. The last line, however, carries a note of warning, suggesting that men go on with their lives, somewhat indifferently, unless they are willing to "mouth" the sloe of Christ.

One does not wonder that the poet's superiors in the Jesuits were baffled. Meaning virtually breaks down in the eighth stanza, although one senses Hopkins's own excitement and desire to communicate his passion for the subject. He moves into a fairly straightforward celebration of the Trinity, "three-numberéd form," in the ninth and tenth stanzas, concluding Part the First with a celebration of Christ as king: "Make mercy in all of us, out of us all / Mastery, but be adored, but be adored King."

At the core of Part the Second lies the story of the ship's sinking with five nuns aboard. "On Saturday sailed from Bremen, / American-outward-bound" a ship laden with exiles from Germany's Falck Laws, which discriminated against Catholics. There were two hundred people on board. One cannot imagine a better description of the ship as it heads into stormy waters:

> Into the snow she sweeps,
> Hurling the haven behind,
> The Deutschland, on Sunday; and so the sky keeps,
> For the infinite air is unkind,
> And the sea flint-flake, black backed in the regular blow,
> Stirring Eastnortheast, in cursed quarter, the wind;
> Wiry and white-fiery and whirlwind-swivelléd snow
> Spins to the widow-making unchilding unfathering deeps.

The massive accumulation of images is breathtaking, and the rhythms strongly embody the storm itself, heaving and groaning from stress to stress.

The ship drives into a sand bank in the fourteenth stanza as "The breakers rolled on her beam with ruinous shock." After a while, there is little hope left after the ship rocks on the sand for twelve hours, unable to free itself. In a memorable moment in the fifteenth stanza, Hopkins personifies hope itself: "Hope had grown grey hairs, / Hope had mourning on." All attempts at rescue by the crew itself are thwarted; indeed, one man is "pitched to his death" while tied to a rope. Hopkins presents a horrific image of the dead man beating against the ship while tied to the line: "They could tell him for hours, dandled the to and fro." This last phrase is typical of Hopkins: he makes "to and fro" a noun that becomes the object of the transitive "dandled" by putting "the" in front of it. It's strange, but effective.

Hopkins conjures a wild, chaotic scene on the ship, with everyone crying and shrieking, the water pouring over the ship, and a general sense of despair hanging over all. A turning point comes in the seventeenth stanza, however, when one of the five nuns steps forward, "A prophetess" who is also a "lioness." She is pictured "breasting the babble," thus overcoming the confusion of the storm and the victims of that tumult. She is "Sister, a sister calling / A master, her master and mine!" That is, she calls to God for help, the same God upon whom Hopkins himself was seen to call in the midst of his spiritual storm in Part the First.

Hopkins knew next to nothing of these nuns or what actually happened aboard the ship itself, but he imagines the characters and scene beautifully. He visualizes one nun as she steps forward to ask God for help, and likens her (in the twentieth stanza) to the German saint, Gertrude, who is compared to "a lily." Hopkins notes with irony that Germany is also the home of Luther, "beast of the waste wood," a founder of the Protestant Reformation, which Hopkins disparages. He goes so far as to compare Luther to Cain and the nun to Abel another vivid sign of his partisan feeling. He describes the nuns as people who are "Loathed for a love men knew in them." That is, they are rejected because of their love of Christ and his Church, driven from Germany and even held off by the storm from safety on English shores: "Rhine refused them. Thames would ruin them," writes Hopkins, identifying Germany and England by their famous rivers.

In the twenty-second stanza he identifies the nuns specifically, in their martyrdom, with Christ: "Five! the finding and sake / And cipher of suffering Christ. / Mark, the mark is of man's make / And the word of it Sacrificed." Note that Hopkins gravitates toward a word like "sake," meaning spirit or soul, reaching back to Anglo-Saxon for his diction and so preferring "sake" to "spirit."

The poem comes to a climax in the twenty-fourth stanza, where the one nun of the five whom Hopkins seems determined to make a heroine, reaches for Christ, calling "O Christ, Christ, come quickly." This same stanza opens in a personal way, with Hopkins "On a pastoral forehead of Wales." The reintroduction of the personal narrator here is peculiar, but it forges a connection between the poet and his subject. One must keep remembering that *The Wreck* is as much about Hopkins and his relationship to God as about the nuns who drowned. The heroic nun "christens her wild-worst Best," meaning that she seizes the worst moment of her life and declares it a triumph. Though lost at sea, she is found in Christ.

The poem rises toward a final crescendo in which the poet himself identifies with Christ. The twenty-eighth stanza is memorably written, in texture and tone related to the drama of conversion dramatized in the first few stanzas. The writing becomes breathless as Hopkins struggles for expression, using ellipses to suggest his frantic reaching for words to describe an experience that is beyond words:

> But how shall I . . . make me room there:
> Reach me a . . . Fancy, come faster
>   Strike you the sight of it? look at it loom there,
>   Thing that she . . . There then! the Master,
> *Ipse*, the only one, Christ, King, Head:
>   He was to cure the extremity where he had cast her;
>   Do, deal, lord it with living and dead;
> Let him ride, her pride, in his triumph, despatch and have done
>   with his doom there.

Hopkins continues to keep the nun who reached for Christ in mind by saying that he, Christ, would "cure the extremity where he had cast her."

But the first lines are thrilling, a dramatic portrait of the imagination at point of stress, eager for Fancy to arrive and satisfy the poet's longing for expression. The peak of inspiration comes, as it should, with the arrival of Christ, *ipse* (meaning "himself"). This is an existential moment, a moment of incarnation and poetic embodiment as well.

As in a typical Ignatian meditation, the poem moves toward adoration in the address to Christ that constitutes the thirtieth stanza, which begins with a direct petition: "Jesu, heart's light, / Jesu, Maid's son." Hopkins tries to imagine the banquet in heaven that followed the nun's death: "What was the feast followed the night / Thou hadst glory of this nun?" In the next stanza, the wreck itself is seen as "a harvest" of the five nuns, although Hopkins naturally worries about those lost souls, the "unconfessed of them" aboard the ship who may not have found salvation.

Hopkins returns to the nun in the final stanza, the heroine who showed her courage by putting herself in God's hands. Having addressed Christ, he now addresses her, as she has taken her place among the saints in heaven and is therefore somebody one can petition: "Dame, at our door / Drowned, and among our shoals, / Remember us in the roads, the heaven-haven of the Reward." As for Christ, Hopkins says "Let him easter in us." Oddly but effectively, he transforms easter into a verb to easter. In other words, let Christ rise in "us" and in "rare-dear Britain" as well, as he did on Easter Sunday.

One can hardly underestimate the cumulative power of this ode. *The Wreck of the Deutschland* is a sprawling, vivid, complex, weird, and moving poem that looks and sounds like nothing else in English poetry. Hopkins's originality is the flipside of his idiosyncrasy. His work is unmistakably branded with his style, his poetic "inscape," which is nowhere more strikingly apparent than in this ambitious poem.

THE LYRICS

THE body of work left behind by Hopkins at his death was small, consisting of five dozen or so lyrics, some of them fragments. They are largely explorations of "inscape," attempts to define in a natural scene or object or in some human form evidence of God's imprint, or stress, in the world. A typical poem celebrates the glory of creation, as in "God's Grandeur," which follows:

The world is charged with the grandeur of God.
    It will flame out, like shining from shook foil;
    It gathers to greatness like the ooze of oil
Crushed. Why do men then now not reck his rod?
Generations have trod, have trod, have trod;
    And all is seared with trade; bleared, smeared with toil;
    And wears man's smudge and shares man's smell: the soil
Is bare now, nor can foot feel, being shod.

And for all this, nature is never spent;
    There lives the dearest freshness deep down things;
And though the last lights off the black West went
    Oh, morning, at the brown brink eastward springs
Because the Holy Ghost over the bent
    World broods with warm breast and with, ah! bright wings.

As usual with Hopkins, the argument of the poem is less complicated than the texture that embodies it. In essence, Hopkins is saying that the world displays God's grandeur everywhere, but that people cannot see it because the industrial world is "seared with trade" and "bleared with toil." As a parish priest in working class areas, which in the second half of the nineteenth century were filthy and depressed beyond what anyone today can imagine, he understood what he was writing about. He also believed that the material world—shoes on the feet, for example—insulated human beings from the grass beneath them, the fresh world of nature.

In the second stanza, he breaks out in praise of nature's ability to shine through the soiled world that human beings have produced. Nature is "never spent" and flourishes despite our efforts to suppress its beauty and power. The poem ends with an astonishing image of the Holy Ghost like a great bird brooding over the world (an image taken from Milton): "with warm breast and with, ah! bright wings." The sublime aspects of this final image defy paraphrase; Hopkins manages to focus the poem with a bold stroke and to leave the reader with a feeling of awe. The Holy Ghost is dawn itself, brooding over the waking world. Nature thoroughly spiritualized, a manifestation of God. In praising nature, Hopkins celebrates the mystery of creation.

Hopkins's most famous lyric, a sonnet, is "The Windhover," a poem about a falcon. It is dedicated "To Christ our Lord," and the bird itself becomes another example of Christ making Himself manifest in various forms. The opening image of the octet, quoted earlier, is among the most eye-catching and ear-catching in all of Hopkins, couched in typically unusual, even bizarre, language: "I caught this morning morning's minion, king- / dom of daylight's dauphin, dapple-dawn-drawn Falcon." He describes the bird by comparing it to a horse that "rung upon the rein of a wimpling wing," adopting an equestrian metaphor. That is, "to ring on the rein" is what a trainer of a horse would do, holding the rein while the horse circled around the trainer. Hopkins uses another metaphor of centrifugal force by evoking an ice skater that "sweeps smooth on a bow-bend," turning a corner.

The sestet, in traditional sonnet fashion, contemplates the image already summoned. Hopkins claims that in this act of sweeping through the sky, "Brute beauty and valour and act, oh, air, pride, plume, here / Buckle!" The strong enjambment is intended, as the first line of the sestet spills over, crashing onto "Buckle!" And buckle carries a dual sense: to come together (like a belt buckle) and to collapse on itself. Once again, the falcon is addressed as a knight of heaven: "O my chevalier" echoing the opening reference to "daylight's dauphin," a dauphin being a French prince. The last three lines of the sestet constitute one of Hopkins's strangest but most effective poetic moves:

No wonder of it: sheer plod makes plough down sillion
Shine, and blue-bleak embers, ah my dear,
    Fall, gall themselves, and gash gold-vermilion.

That is, all things in the act of doing what God has fashioned them to do—a bird flying, a plough ploughing, embers in a fireplace crumbling on themselves—become a type of Christ, acquiescing to their truest nature in order to glorify God. The final image, referring to coals in a grate that seem dead ("blue-bleak") but suddenly implode, producing a "gold-vermilion" flame, inevitably recalls Christ on the cross, his body pierced and bleeding.

Hopkins adopts a lighter mode in "Pied Beauty," which could not be simpler in its theme:

Glory be to God for dappled things
  For skies of couple-colour as a brinded cow;
    For rose-moles all in stipple upon trout that swim;
Fresh-firecoal chestnut-falls; finches' wings;
  Landscape plotted and pieced fold, fallow, and
    plough;
    And all trades, their gear and tackle and trim.

Only the odd diction (dappled, brinded, stipple) makes the poem somewhat demanding. As ever, the poet is enamored of things "counter, original, spare, strange," being himself all of these. In a phrase that summarizes the poem, Hopkins concludes with a two-word sentence: "Praise him." "Him" is Christ, of course, and once again Hopkins ferrets out in all sorts of unexpected places the Christ-content that inheres there.

The same theme occurs in the splendid, untitled poem that begins "As kingfishers catch fire, dragonflies draw flame." The kingfisher is a bird often associated with Christ, and Hopkins pursues the idea that everything in nature serves God, becomes Christlike, by acting out its own nature, finding its inscape. So that, ideally, "the just man justices," becoming Christ. Indeed, "Christ plays in ten thousand places," the poet says, perhaps alluding to the Buddhist notion of the world of ten thousand things. Hopkins ends by suggesting that one finds God "through the features of men's faces."

Significantly, Hopkins includes human beings in nature. Indeed, many of his finer poems concern specific individuals all praised for their distinctness, a feature of their Godliness. He writes in praise, for example, of Duns Scotus, his favorite philosopher, in "Duns Scotus's Oxford." Henry Purcell, his favorite English composer (who died in 1695), is written about with profound sympathy in "Henry Purcell" "Have fair fallen, O fair, fair have fallen, so dear / To me,

so arch-especial a spirit as heaves in Henry Purcell." What he likes in the music is that "the rehearsal / Of own, of abrupt self there so thrusts on, so throngs the ear," in other words, that Purcell's personal inscape was so uniquely displayed. In performing himself, rehearsing his own distinctness, Purcell became Christlike. His music lifted Hopkins, thrilling him: "Let him oh! with his air of angels then lift me, lay me!" One cannot help but notice that Hopkins, in writing in his own original and self-declaring manner, is behaving like Purcell and, of course, like Christ.

Hopkins praises lesser mortals, too, as in "Harry Ploughman" or the affecting "Felix Randal." Hopkins writes as Randal's priest, having attended the subject of the poem at his deathbed. Randal was "big-boned and hardy-handsome," but illness "Fatal four disorders" undid him. He tells us how Randal resisted at first, then relaxed into his death. The poem becomes very personal, as Hopkins reflects on his priestly role: "This seeing the sick endears them to us, us too it endears." The poem concludes with a vision of the healthy Felix Randal, who worked as a farrier or blacksmith, "powerful amidst peers," a man who "Didst fettle for the great drayhorse his bright and battering sandal!"

Another poem to a person is "Spring and Fall," addressed "to a young child." The entire poem follows:

Margaret, are you grieving
Over Goldengrove unleaving?
Leaves like the things of man, you
With your fresh thoughts care for, can you?
Ah! as the heart grows older
It will come to such sights colder
By and by, nor spare a sigh
Though worlds of wanwood leafmeal lie;
And yet you will weep and know why.
Now no matter, child, the name:
Sorrow's springs are the same.
Nor mouth had, no nor mind, expressed
What heart heard of, ghost guessed:
It is the blight man was born for,
It is Margaret you mourn for.

Hopkins achieved a rare simplicity here, conjuring this child who weeps amid falling leaves in autumn the "Goldengrove unleaving." She will, Hopkins says, have more to weep about besides this "world of wanwood leafmeal," a lovely phrase (*leafmeal* is modeled on *piecemeal*). Hopkins understands that sorrows spring from the same source: mutability, the passing of lives, the fact that nothing stays. Hence, the title refers to the seasons as well as the rising and falling of life (and hope). Margaret, being human and mired in original sin (as Hopkins believed) is condemned to die like the leaves, though she can only intuit this. Her misery is universal, however. She is Everyman.

Toward the end of his life, Hopkins wrote the sonnets often referred to as the Terrible Sonnets because of their sense of life as gloom and terror. Like John Donne's Holy Sonnets, they describe the progress of the poet's soul, although Hopkins was far more despairing than Donne. A few of these poems might be considered among the bleakest in the language, which suggests that Hopkins experienced severe depression firsthand. One of these poems begins "No worst, there is none." The poet-narrator portrays himself as someone "Pitched past pitch of grief." (Note the play on "pitch," which means tar or darkness as well as the act of being hurled.) Hopkins even questions God's motives: "Comforter, where, where is your comforting?" He asks the Virgin Mother, "Mary, mother of us, where is your relief?" In a startling metaphor, he compares his cries of anguish to cattle in a road: "My cries heave, herds-log; huddle in a main." The syntax and sense of the sonnet, in the octet, break down completely as the poet is pursued by Fury itself.

The language of the concluding sestet is stunning:

O the mind, mind has mountains; cliffs of fall
Frightful, sheer, no-man-fathomed. Hold them cheap
May who ne'er hung there. Nor does our small
Durance deal with that steep or deep. Here! creep,
Wretch, under a comfort serves in a whirlwind: all
Life does end and each day dies with sleep.

The lyrical force of the first line of the sestet above can hardly be overstated, nor the fine if terrifying image of those "cliffs of fall" mental cliffs over which the spirit tumbles into an abyss of darkness. The poem's final line, saying that "each day dies with sleep," seems utterly despairing.

Christian mystics describe two paths toward God. The one path is ecstatic, the other the *via negativa* treks through a Dark Night of the Soul. Hopkins would certainly have been familiar with the tradition of the dark night, the negative path to God, but these late sonnets suggest that he personally experienced a deep anguish. He apparently plunged into turmoil and depression while in Dublin, and the fiercest expression of this state of mind occurs in the untitled sonnet that opens "I wake and feel the fell of dark, not day." The "fell of dark" suggests both dampness and depth as Hopkins alludes to the "black hours" he has spent. He depicts his prayers for relief as "dead letters sent / To dearest him that lives alas! away." The sestet must be considered one of the bleakest moments imaginable, the poet turning on himself harshly, angrily: "I am gall, I am heartburn." The only consolation he can find is to think that lost souls are like this as well, mired in despair, "but worse."

The sequence ends with two poems of recovery. The first opens "Patience, hard thing! the hard thing but to pray, / But bid for, Patience is!" (He uses the word "bid" in its Anglo-Saxon sense of meaning "to pray.") In the sestet, he says "We hear our hearts grate on themselves: it kills / To bruise them dearer." The poet begs God to give him the required patience to withstand the dark hours of his despair, noting that God himself is patient, using the metaphor of a bee's honeycomb: "Patience fills / His crisp combs, and that comes those ways we know."

The final poem begins, movingly:

My own heart let me more have pity on; let
Me live to my sad self hereafter kind,
Charitable; not live this tormented mind
With this tormented mind tormenting yet.

This is strong stuff, memorably worded. It is also tremendously simple, as though Hopkins has cut through obscurity at last. That he refers to his "sad self" suggests that he was aware of his deep malaise. Hence, in the sestet, he cries:

Soul, self; come, poor Jackself, I do advise
You, jaded, let be; call off thoughts awhile
Elsewhere; leave comfort root-room; let joy size

At Godknow when to God knows what; whose smile

'S not wrung, see you; unforeseentimes rather as skies
Betweenpie mountains lights a lovely mile.

The poem descends into a thicket once again, but the tangle of syntax is not hard to cut through. He addresses his soul and, in a very modern way, his self. Specifically, he calls to the universal in himself, the Jackself, as in Jack-of-all-trades. He seeks to call off his negative thoughts, to give comfort room to put down roots. He wishes for joy to "size" him, as a tailor might size a customer for a new suit. The oddities of the last three lines are considerable, with that possessive "'S" carried over to the penultimate line, and that phrase "Betweenpie mountains." A printer scatters his type when he "pies" it; the sunlight scatters the shadows therein lies the metaphor, somewhat obscurely. But the last phrase "lights a lovely mile" is gorgeous, referring back to God, who does the lighting of the mountain and the mind of the poet as well.

Considering the Terrible Sonnets as a dramatic sequence, apart from the poet's own personal anguish, one sees a movement from despair to hope not so different from the progress of the soul described by poets and religious thinkers in meditation. One reads the final poems of the sequence with relief and release, with a feeling of having come through something momentous, difficult, and harrowing.

CONCLUSION

HOPKINS died an obscure priest and professor. His life's work as a poet was known only to a small circle of close friends, and it would take decades for that brilliantly innovative work to emerge. When it did, in 1918, there was a certain bafflement. Gradually, however, with the help of critics such as F. R. Leavis, Hopkins gained a foothold in the pantheon of important English poets, and he has never lost his perch.

If anything, Hopkins's verse has attracted a wider following down the decades. Although meager in quantity, the poems are so original and arresting that they stay in the mind long after they have been read. Poets such as Dylan Thomas, David Jones, Robert Lowell, Sylvia Plath, and Seamus Heaney have looked to him as a source of inspiration, and his work continues to interest younger writers. The music of his poems, and their unique sensibility, speak across time and the superficial obscurity of the language.

SELECTED BIBLIOGRAPHY

I. POETRY. *The Poems of Gerard Manley Hopkins*, ed. W. H. Gardner and N. H. MacKenzie (Oxford, 1967, 1984); *Gerard Manley Hopkins*, ed. Catherine Phillips (Oxford, 1986).

II. PROSE. *The Correspondence of Gerard Manley Hopkins and Richard Watson Dixon* (London, 1955); *Gerard Manley Hopkins to Robert Bridges*, ed. C. C. Abbott (London, 1955); *Further Letters of Gerard Manley Hopkins*, ed. C. C. Abbott (London, 1956); *The Journals and Papers of Gerard Manley Hopkins*, ed. Humphrey House (London, 1959); *Selected Letters of Gerard Manley Hopkins*, ed. Catherine Phillips (Oxford, 1990).

III. CRITICAL AND BIOGRAPHICAL STUDIES. W. H. Gardner, *Gerard Manley Hopkins, 1844 1889: A Study of Poetic Idiosyncrasy in Relation to Poetic Tradition*, 2 vols. (London, 1944, 1949); Alan Heuser, *The Shaping Vision of Gerard Manley Hopkins* (London, 1958); David A. Downes, *Gerard Manley Hopkins: A Study of His Ignatian Spirit* (London, 1960); Todd K. Bender, *Gerard Manley Hopkins: The Classical Background and Critical Reception of His Work* (Baltimore, 1966); Geoffrey Hartmann, ed., *Hopkins: A Collection of Critical* Essays (Englewood Cliffs, N.J., 1966); Wendell Stacy Johnson, *Gerard Manley Hopkins: The Poet as Victorian* (Ithaca, N.Y., 1968); Alfred Thomas, S.J., *Hopkins the Jesuit: The Years of Training* (London, 1969); Paul Mariani, *Commentary on the Complete Poems of Gerard Manley Hopkins* (London, 1970); James Finn Cotter, *Inscape: The Christology and Poetry of Gerard Manley Hopkins* (Pittsburgh, 1972); Alison G. Sulloway, *Gerard Manley Hopkins and the Victorian Temper* (London, 1972); Norman H. MacKenzie, *A Reader's Guide to Gerard Manley Hopkins* (London, 1981); Michael. E. Allsopp and Michael W. Sundermeier, eds., *Gerard Manley Hopkins: New Essays on His Life, Writing, and Place in English Literature* (Lampeter, U.K., 1989); Cary H. Plotkin, *The Tenth Muse: Victorian Philology and the Genesis of the Poetic Language of Gerard Manley Hopkins* (Carbondale, Ill., 1989); Bernard Martin, *Gerard Manley Hopkins: A Very Private Life* (London, 1991); Norman White, *Hopkins: A Literary Biography* (Oxford, 1992); Eugene Hollahan, ed., *Gerard Manley Hopkins and Critical Discourse* (New York, 1993).

TED HUGHES

(1930–1998)

Gerry Cambridge

IN SOME QUARTERS, one could be forgiven for thinking that the life of Ted Hughes was synonymous with the life—and death—of Sylvia Plath. This seems to have been particularly the case in America. In the United States, Hughes has had the reputation of being primarily the poet responsible for the death of Sylvia Plath; he was lambasted and hounded accordingly for decades by feminists. Following her suicide Plath became something of a martyr in the 1970s, with the rise of feminism in American universities. As every martyr needs a persecutor, Hughes was coopted for the role. He proved an ideal candidate: over six feet tall, burly, craggy, devastatingly attractive to women—a quality he was not slow in utilizing—reputedly blunt in speech, and peremptory as some of the animals he wrote about, he was a sort of hawk in human disguise. So, at least, went the myth. ("Ted Huge" and "The Incredible Hulk," Philip Larkin called him, ambiguously.)

While it is true that the name of Hughes is irremediably linked with Plath's, like two different varieties of rock in the one stone, Hughes is by any standard a remarkable writer on his own account. He is one of the greatest nature poets found in literature, though his nature does not have the lucent naturalistic simplicities of a John Clare. The body of his work attempts to reopen a connection between alienated humanity in the West and the natural world. He began as a poet of formal control in the mid-1950s, out of which he hammered a style uniquely his own: a full-voltaged, powerful free verse that, in the best of the poems, is like an intricate machine fashioned, improbably, out of bits and pieces of scrap found to hand. A stunningly prolific writer, he has yet to be judiciously selected: the work contains large swaths of dead wood, likely to be of interest mainly for exegesis by specialists. But there is

enough that is superb to confirm Hughes as easily one of the greatest twentieth-century poets in English.

LIFE

BORN on 17 August 1930 in Mytholmroyd, in West Yorkshire, a region of England renowned for producing people of a somewhat taciturn nature, Edward James Hughes was the third and youngest child—his brother, Gerald, and sister, Olwyn, were ten and two years older respectively—of William Henry Hughes, a carpenter, and Edith Farrar Hughes. She was descended from Nicolas Ferrar, the founder in 1625 of the Anglican community of Little Gidding near Huntingdon, England. Hughes's father had narrowly survived the World War I. He was one of only seventeen men from his regiment to return, psychologically scarred, from Gallipoli.

The family's home was directly below Scout Rock, a six-hundred-foot sheer face that, for the young Hughes, had a brooding presence and made him uncomfortable about being in valleys thereafter. In his essay "The Rock," he wrote of West Yorkshire:

> [E]verything in West Yorkshire is slightly unpleasant. Nothing ever quite escapes into happiness. The people are not detached enough from the stone, as if they were only half-born from the earth, and the graves are too near the surface. A disaster seems to hang around in the air there for a long time. I can never escape the impression that the whole region is in mourning for the First World War.
> (in Summerfield, ed., p. 126)

Hughes escaped into nature. "My interest in animals began when I began," he wrote in *Poetry in the Making* (p. 15). It was an interest fostered by his brother, Gerald, a fanatical hunter. Hughes claimed that from the age of two or three, his world was entirely dominated by the hunting fanaticism of his brother. It was a fanaticism he eagerly emulated, becoming a keen hunter and later a fisherman.

When Hughes was seven years old the family moved to Mexborough, South Yorkshire, where his parents opened a newsagent business. The poet attended Mexborough Grammar School from 1943 to 1949, where among others a fine English teacher named John Fisher encouraged his interest in poetry. By age fifteen Hughes was writing poems in the style of Rudyard Kipling. At the age of eighteen he won a scholarship to Cambridge. He did not take this up until 1951, following two years of national service in East Yorkshire as a ground wireless mechanic in the Royal Air Force. Remotely stationed at Fylingdales, he read Shakespeare intensively.

As with many writers, his university years were less than happy. "In effect," he said in an interview with Ekbert Faas, "university is a prison from life in your last three or four most formative years. It's a most deadly institution unless you're aiming to be either a scholar or a gentleman" (Faas, p. 56). The essay writing requirements of the English course at Cambridge disagreed with him; one evening in his third year, following innumerable attempts to write an essay on Samuel Johnson and unable to progress beyond an opening line, he fell asleep. He had a vividly disturbing dream in which a scorched and blackened fox the size of a man entered his room on its hind legs, placed a blackened and bloody paw on the unfinished essay, and said, "Stop this, you are destroying us." Always sensitive to dreams, the poet switched courses to archaeology and anthropology. He graduated in June 1954.

A memoir by the poet and critic Philip Hobsbaum gives an account of Hughes at this time. Tall, rangy, angular-featured, shabbily dressed, somewhat peremptory, with "a kind of impressiveness." (*The Dark Horse* 8, p. 8) "He had left Cambridge without a reference from his tutor owing to an unfortunate habit of appropriating road signs such as 'No Parking' and using them

to decorate his room while he still lived in college" (p. 10).

Although he had graduated, Hughes still returned to Cambridge from London frequently, and worked variously as a rose gardener, a script reader for J. Arthur Rank, a night watchman, and a schoolteacher.

On 25 February 1956 Cambridge's *St. Botolph's Review*, a poetry journal that published four of Hughes's poems in its first and only issue, held a launch party. There Hughes met Sylvia Plath, a young American poet with a history of mental instability who was studying at Cambridge on a Fulbright scholarship. The attraction was immediate, somewhat violent, and mutual. After a passionate courtship the two were married in Bloomsbury, London, at the Church of St. George the Martyr on Bloomsday, 16 June 1956. They honeymooned in Benidorm, Spain.

The marriage seemed, for a time, a creative success. Plath's American efficiency and business sense—she often typed and sent out Hughes's poems—were a great aid to Hughes, while he provided, at least initially, a foil for her despair as well as writerly support, giving her exercises to do when she had writer's block. The couple pooled their knowledge of American and British poetry. Hughes published *The Hawk in the Rain* in 1957, which Plath had typed for him, for the first time calling him "Ted," not "Edward," Hughes on the typescript—a moniker he retained superstitiously throughout his career. Out of 287 entries, it had taken first prize in a contest judged by W. H. Auden, Marianne Moore, and Stephen Spender, sponsored by the Poetry Center of the Young Men's and Young Women's Hebrew Association in New York. The prize was publication by Harper Brothers publishers in the United States; the book was soon published too by Faber in Britain, whose poetry list was then under the editorship of T. S. Eliot. The book was received with almost unanimous praise. Three years later it was followed by *Lupercal*, which established Hughes, in the opinion of a leading critic of the time, Al Alvarez, as a major poet in the making. Following periods in America and London in the late 1950s, Hughes and Plath were living in the Devon village of North Tawton at the house they had bought, Court Green, in 1961, when the poet David Wevill and his wife, Assia Gutmann Wevill, to whom Hughes and Plath had leased a London flat, visited them on Friday, 18 May 1962 and stayed the weekend. It marked the beginning of a relationship between Gutmann and Hughes that would have permanent consequences.

Plath, psychologically vulnerable at the best of times, took this as an extreme betrayal. The couple agreed to a separation, and Hughes moved out. Plath later moved to London with their two children, Frieda, born on 1 April 1960, and Nicholas, born on 17 January 1962. Sylvia Plath was clinically depressed and living through one of the coldest British winters on record when, having written poems that would make her reputation, she laid out milk and bread for the children, then gassed herself in the kitchen oven. It was 11 February 1963.

Plath died intestate. Although divorce proceedings were pending, she was still officially married to Hughes. He inherited her literary estate and was left with the task of administering it, later helped by his sister, Olwyn. In the years following her death Hughes edited and arranged for the issue of Plath's numerous collections. He came in for major opprobrium upon admitting that he had destroyed one of Plath's journals describing her last days, not wishing her children to ever read it; another journal went missing. Feminist and other critics further accused him of restricting access to Plath's writings whenever criticism was perceived to be negative to himself. The more extreme among his antagonists regularly removed Hughes's name from Sylvia Plath's headstone—which read "Sylvia Plath Hughes"—on her grave in Heptonstall Cemetery, Yorkshire. Hughes was increasingly demonized and grew understandably touchy about his portrayal by ardent followers of Plath. (He would be embroiled in the 1970s and 1980s in numerous disputes, some involving legal action, concerning the estate, representations of Plath, and himself.)

The 1960s were darkened by further tragedy. In March 1969, Assia Gutmann Wevill, for whom the poet had left Plath, gave a drink laced with sleeping pills to Shura, the four-year-old daughter she and Hughes had had together, took sleeping pills herself, then lay down with her daughter beside the gas stove in her London home and turned on the gas, asphyxiating them both. In August 1970 Hughes married Carol Orchard, a nurse from Devon. She was twenty years younger than her husband. The couple would remain married until Hughes's death.

Throughout all this Hughes remained productive in circumstances that would have silenced other writers. He concentrated mainly on children's writing in the few years after Plath's death; in 1967 he published his third adult collection, *Wodwo*, and *Poetry in the Making*, written initially for children's programming on BBC radio; these were followed in 1970 by *Crow*, a radical departure for Hughes, and something of a cult book.

In 1972 he bought the Devon farm Moortown—later to provide the setting for some of his fine farming poems. It was farmed initially by Jack Orchard, the poet's father-in-law. It helped give the poet a new rootedness.

The 1970s continued to be a productive time: Hughes published five major adult collections—*Selected Poems, 1957–1967* (1972), along with *Season Songs, Gaudete, Remains of Elmet*, and *Moortown*. In 1974 he was awarded the Queen's Medal for Poetry; a decade later, in a Britain presided over by Prime Minister Margaret Thatcher, he was appointed poet laureate. In Britain this public honor places its bearer under the expectation, if not the obligation, to produce verse commemorating major public occasions, often royal ones. Hughes fulfilled his laureateship dutifully, if at times somewhat woodenly. His gift of highly individual vision did not transfer particularly well to the public sphere. The increasingly soap-operatic behavior of the royal family did not sit comfortably with Hughes's apparent desire to venerate them as emblematic of the nation's spiritual center. The disparity between reality and Hughes's public verse struck many readers as comic.

And that seemed to be that. Hughes continued producing new volumes of verse—*Birds and Insects, Wolfwatching*—throughout the late 1980s, but it appeared that to an extent he had lost his way. The greatness of the early and middle period animal poems had been taken over by a habitual productivity brightened by occasional successes. The poet's finest work appeared to have been written.

The 1990s, however, saw something of a Hughes renaissance. In 1994 his *Winter Pollen: Occasional Prose* appeared. This showed him as a superb, engaged critic of those writers he admired, such as Keith Douglas, Coleridge, and Emily Dickinson. His remarkable *Shakespeare and the Goddess of Complete Being* (1992), meanwhile, attempted to find the mythic blueprint behind all of the dramatist's plays. In 1997, following an initial commission from Michael Hoffman and James Lasdun, who were editing a volume of versions of Ovid, Hughes published his own widely praised *Tales from Ovid*. Lastly, in January 1998 Hughes stunned the literary world by publishing, without preamble, *Birthday Letters*, eighty-eight poems telling the story from his point of view of his relationship and marriage to Sylvia Plath. The book caused a literary sensation. The London *Times* paid ú25,000 for advance serial rights to the book and published twelve of the poems between 17 and 22 January. The book's publication date, insisted on by Hughes for astrological aptness—the date marked, astrologically, an increase in "collective awareness"—was 29 January. *Birthday Letters* became one of the biggest-selling books of poetry in history. A year after its publication it had sold more than 250,000 copies on both sides of the Atlantic. Of course, this was almost entirely for reasons outside the poetry itself.

If the publication of *Birthday Letters* had been attended by secrecy, so had the poet's private circumstances: Hughes was dying of cancer. He died in London Bridge Hospital, a private clinic, on the evening of 28 October 1998, two weeks after receiving an Order of Merit, an honor conferred by the queen and limited to twenty-four living recipients at any one time. The literary world was stunned by news of the poet's death. Hughes was a model of circumspection: few had known the poet was even ill. *Birthday Letters* thus came to be seen as a settling of emotional accounts, a rounding off of one of the most remarkable literary lives of the century. Its posthumous sales, as well, no doubt, as the sale of his archives to Emory University in Atlanta, Georgia, in February 1997, also appear to have made the poet a millionaire: his personal estate, left to his wife, Carol, was valued at over £1.4 million.

THE HAWK IN THE RAIN

By any standard, Hughes's first volume, *Hawk in the Rain* (1957), was remarkable. It appeared at a time in Britain when "The Movement" was prevalent—a literary grouping in reaction, among its poets, against the perceived excesses of Dylan Thomas. It advocated a poetry of thoughtful craft, irony, and somewhat suburban values. The English poet Philip Larkin was one of its main exemplars.

Hughes's first book appeared on the British poetry scene, to use an image from an early poem, like a hawk in a dovecote. For all its relative formality, there was a strong sense of terrific energy only just being held in check by formal control. The two main preoccupations, which were backed by outstanding poems, were: the elemental energies of the natural world, especially that of animals; and the psychic resonance of World War I and of violence generally. Read now, the best of the volume's poems have all the freshness they had then. The best are not those in which Hughes goes in for archaic language out of Shakespeare, and the contorted portentousness that could let him write: "Fair choice? The appearance of the devil! Suave / Complicity with your vacillation / To your entire undoing!" (*Hawk in the Rain*, p. 33). Nor those full of characters like "the cajoling hag," "the pretty princess," the "beggar man," the "rich man"; the stock characters of fairy tales. Nor even those like the book's title poem, overwritten and impressive as it is in its opening lines:

I drown in the drumming ploughland, I drag up
Heel after heel from the swallowing of the earth's
  mouth,

From clay that clutches my each step to the ankle
With the habit of the dogged grave. . . .

(p. 11)

Nonetheless many of Hughes's qualities are there: the strong alliteration, hammering the lines to the page, an urgency of tone, and the tension between energy and its stultification, exemplified by the narrator's dragging up his heels from the clutching clay.

The book's finest poems are a marriage of power and graceful construction. In his 1969 book *Poetry in the Making*, Hughes set out his belief at the time, developed from his own childhood activities, of poetry as a form of hunting. Animals were spirits, and a poem was a sort of spirit caught, with all the vivacity of wildness, in the lines of a verse. Some of the poems in his first book appeared to have led him to that insight. "The Thought Fox" imagines the arrival of a poem into "The dark hole of the head" as a fox; it couples poetry with Hughes's creaturely interests. Elsewhere the poet celebrates energy. Hughes's "The Jaguar" portrays a scene of animal indolence at a zoo, except for the cage containing the jaguar, at which "the crowd stands, stares, mesmerized / As a child at a dream"; there, the caged beast hurries up and down, pent with a barely contained force:

He spins from the bars, but there's no cage to him

More than to the visionary his cell:
His stride is wildernesses of freedom:
The world rolls under the long thrust of his heel.
Over the cage floor the horizons come.

(p. 12)

The poem's closure is given a certain authorial gravitas by the pacing of the lines, the last two end-stopped. The jaguar is the only vital thing in the poem's tableau. The narrator's attention is almost wholly focused on the cat's energy. Everything else is subservient to it. He perceives the jaguar as the center, the locus of power in the poem, when in fact the locus of power is the bars of the cage. The jaguar itself realizes this, as it "spins from the bars." The restraint of reality is absolute, but it is dismissed by the poem's narrator. The somewhat languid amplitude of a word

like "wildernesses" is unconvincing when used in relation to the frantic hurrying of the caged animal. Yet "The world rolls under the long thrust of his heel." The implication is that the jaguar represents the energy that turns the world.

Impressive as "The Jaguar" is, the poet's sense of elemental energies is more convincing when those energies genuinely are absolute, as in "Wind" or in the delicately written "October Dawn." This last shows Hughes's long perspective: he begins with an intimation of frost in a country garden and ends with mammoths, saber-toothed tigers, and a projected ice age. The poem begins:

October is marigold, and yet
A glass half full of wine left out

To the dark heaven all night, by dawn
Has dreamed a premonition

Of ice across its eye as if
The ice-age had begun its heave.

(p. 43)

One notes how beautifully this is fitted together. The ending of lines 1, 3, 4, and 5 set up a moment of semantic uncertainty only settled by the following line, in the reading equivalent of turning a corner onto a new scene. The technique subtly mimics the slow revelation of the advance of ice, which is the poem's subject.

Another of the volume's outstanding poems is "Six Young Men," a contemplation of a photograph of six men killed in World War I. For autobiographical reasons this was a theme of considerable resonance for Hughes. Despite rhythmical awkwardnesses, the poem has a bare documentary power. It opens with plain description before setting the scene of the photograph in the present: the narrator knows the very features of the spot where the photograph was taken, forty years earlier, "which are there yet and not changed." He contemplates the various bloody fates of the six and concludes:

That man's not more alive whom you confront
And shake by the hand, see hale, hear speak loud,

Than any of these six celluloid smiles are,
Nor prehistoric or fabulous beast more dead. . . .

                                                    (p. 57)

The narrator is shaken by photography's documentary veracity and by the paradoxes inherent in the image. The "six celluloid smiles" are certainly alive for the narrator, but their smiling is ambiguous. They live on in him as part of his obsession with World War I, a theme he would return to often.

LUPERCAL

FOR poets, second books are traditionally difficult, in particular if the first book was well received. The poet is then expected to emulate that initial success. *Lupercal*—the book's title refers to the ancient Roman fertility festival of Lupercalia—appeared in 1960. Critics including Al Alvarez and Donald Hall praised it highly. Alvarez observed: "Hughes has found his own voice, created his own artistic world and has emerged as a poet of the first importance."

Nonetheless, the faults present in the first volume—strange inverted syntaxes, an occasional oddness of diction, an attempted elevated tone unjustified by subject—were again present in *Lupercal*. Hughes was capable of writing, somewhat confusingly, "All things being done or undone / As my hands adore or abandon— / Embody a now, erect a here / A bare-backed tramp and a ditch without fire," or, in a poem such as "Dick Straightup," romanticizing almost embarrassingly an old drinker who "Sits there so full of legend and life / Quiet as a man alone."

These, however, were as nothing to the book's successes. It contains around a dozen poems, straightforward in syntax and on occasion almost peremptory in utterance; further, most were animal poems. While one could say they took the form almost of set pieces, what set pieces! They included "Esther's Tomcat," "Hawk Roosting," "The Bull Moses," "View of a Pig," "Relic," "An Otter," "Pike," and "Snowdrop"—poems of lasting significance that tended to brand Hughes as a "nature" poet. Certain patterns could be seen in the poems. At times, as in "Hawk Roosting" and

"Esther's Tomcat," they celebrate the amorality of animal vigor. "Hawk Roosting," Hughes's celebrated monologue by a sparrow hawk, was interpreted by critics as a speech by extension of a totalitarian dictator: a Hitler, say. Hughes responded that he intended the speaker—the hawk—to simply represent "nature thinking." In Britain the sparrow hawk, *Accipiter nisus*, is a hunter of small birds mainly in woods and along hedgerows, using ambush to surprise its prey. Hughes's poem utilized the convention in Anglo-Saxon poetry of having the creature itself speak; primarily straightforward in diction and syntax, the poem is convincing as hawk speech despite its mingling an at times elevated register and Latinate diction—"falsifying," "sophistry"—with monosyllabic directness. "I sit in the top of the wood, my eyes closed," it opens. "I kill where I please because it is all mine," it later tells us. The poem's closing stanza consists of four curt, end-stopped lines:

The sun is behind me.
Nothing has changed since I began.
My eye has permitted no change.
I am going to keep things like this.

                                                    (p. 26)

Such lines have a telegraphic quality. An unbroachable egotism is conveyed by the use of the first-person pronoun. The use of the "I" is fascinating. First encountered in the stanza's second line, suddenly its rhyme with "My eye" gives its repetition at the beginning of the closing line a new force. Without it one would be more inclined to place the first stress in that line on the first syllable of "going"; with it, however, the rhyme immediately grants added weight to the "I," increasing its sense of peremptory arrogance.

A masterful poem such as "An Otter" shows clearly Hughes's ability to give his animal poems a multilayered significance. Written in two sections, it begins:

Underwater eyes, an eel's
Oil of water body, neither fish nor beast is the otter:
Four-legged yet water-gifted, to outfish fish;
With webbed feet and long ruddering tail
And a round head like an old tomcat.
. . .

Of neither water nor land. Seeking
Some world lost when first he dived, that he cannot
  come at since,
Takes his changed body into the holes of lakes;
As if blind, cleaves the stream's push till he licks
The pebbles of the source; from sea

To sea crosses in three nights
Like a king in hiding.

(p. 46)

The solid craftsmanship of this is everyone on display, from the mimetic sinuousness with which the poet enjambs "an eel's / Oil of water body" to the sensual watery sibilance of a phrase such as "to outfish fish," and the robust alliteration of "ruddering" and "round" in lines 4 and 5. Hughes's otter is not only naturalistic, but can be read as symbolic of a male restiveness, "Seeking / Some world lost"; it is an otter too of the spirit. The poet handles line endings expertly. That "Seeking," for instance, poised at the line end, introduces an aural and visual significance to the verse; it is perched at the line end like an otter poised, sniffing, on a river bank. "From sea / To sea crosses" enacts with its line break the crossing it narrates.

Section 2 opens with the otter being hunted. The otter is practical:

He keeps fat in the limpid integument

Reflections live on. The heart beats thick,
Big trout muscle out of the dead cold;
Blood is the belly of logic; he will lick
The fishbone bare.

(p. 47)

This is language muscular as the otter itself. The "reflections" are both literal and conceptual. The preponderance of monosyllables, of alliteration, as in "blood," "belly," and "bare," and of "l" consonants, help reinforce the sense of the lines. The poem closes:

Yanked above hounds, reverts to nothing at all,
To this long pelt over the back of a chair.

(p. 47)

Behind the literal meaning is a ghost of another meaning: the otter is emblematic of wildness in the human spirit; overcivilized, "Yanked above hounds," that is, hierarchically above the animals, it reverts to the passiveness of a mere skin over a chair back.

Lupercal marked the close of the first stage of Hughes's work, and to some critics its best. The early work, its force notwithstanding, shared something of the lapidary brevity of the American minimalist John Crowe Ransom, whom Hughes greatly admired. His future work would differ markedly.

WODWO

Wodwo—the title refers to a strange half-human animal found in the Middle English poem *Sir Gawayn and the Green Knighte*—was the first of Hughes's books to appear (in 1967) after the death of Sylvia Plath. The title poem closes the collection. The book is divided into three sections, the middle one comprising five short stories and a play, "The Wound." The collection seemed very much a departure for Hughes: the style had been broken open; the poet is more questing, less assured. ("Wodwo" is a monologue of puzzlement at being, spoken by the creature; the last line of which has it promising "to go on looking.") Nonetheless the peculiarities of diction found in the first two books have more or less disappeared, or appear as an intrinsic component of Hughes's style. The poems' syntax has largely become that of elevated ordinary speech.

The volume opens with "Thistles," a fine poem about heroism. Hughes uses the natural history of the thistle to make a convincing comparison between them and indomitability in men:

They are like pale hair and the gutturals of dialects.
Every one manages a plume of blood.

Then they grow grey, like men.
Mown down, it is a feud. Their sons appear
Stiff with weapons, fighting back over the same ground.

(p. 17)

Hughes's achievement here is to make seemingly effortless his comparisons: his thistles are both

205

naturalistically accurate and symbolically apt.

While the poet still writes about animals in *Wodwo*, there is a change from the immaculately crafted animal poems of *Lupercal*. He begins to invent mythical composites. Some become vessels for the poet's increasingly dark vision. "Ghost-Crabs" and "The Green Wolf"—the latter the vegetable earth regarded as a predator—are statements shot through with death. Both work heavily, at the level of assertion. The Hughes of these poems sermonizes like a minister. The sermon is unremitting, and the poems are devoid of humor or any attempt to accommodate or intrigue. His "Ghost Crabs," for instance, are symbols for energy posited not as a good but a negative. They "own this world," the poet tells us:

All night, around us or through us,
They stalk each other, they fasten on to each other,
They mount each other, they tear each other to pieces,
They utterly exhaust each other.

(p. 22)

Near the poem's close "They are the turmoil of history, the convulsion / In the roots of blood, the cycles of concurrence." Hughes has moved on from the celebration of amoral energy to the consequences of that energy in the human world. As we are part, biologically, of the animal kingdom, we inherit some of those energies. One sees the poet here perhaps extrapolating from the events in his private life.

Even where Hughes's poems still celebrate animal energy, there is a new quizzicalness, as in parts of "Skylarks." The European skylark, *Alauda arvensis*, has been a frequent romantic symbol both in English verse and music. Percy Bysshe Shelley hailed it as ". . . blithe spirit! / Bird thou never wert!" The English composer Ralph Vaughan Williams commemorated it ecstatically in his beautiful composition for violin, "The Lark Ascending." Hughes's bird is a very different creature. Bird it always is (though its heart is compared to "a rotor") but one with the obsessiveness for high flight and song of an athlete perpetually trying to push him- or herself to the limit. Exemplifying Hughes's frequent

motif of energy in opposition to stasis, the lark is engaged in a "struggle / Against / Earth's centre." It is:

shot through the crested head
With the command, Not die

But climb

Climb

Sing

Obedient as to death a dead thing.

(p. 168)

Technically, at least, this is a world away from Hughes's previous animal poems. The verse form is powerfully mimetic of the ascending lark. Its blind obedience to the command "Not die," while the result is different, for Hughes emerges from the same obedience as makes a creature dead: the lark is no freer in its instincts than "a dead thing."

Wodwo, in its introduction of mythical characters and invented animals, looks forward to what would be regarded as one of Hughes's major books, *Crow*.

CROW *AND* CAVE BIRDS

HUGHES'S animals had never been simply themselves. With Crow, Hughes invented his own mythic bird. His invention came about when the artist Leonard Baskin, with whom Hughes had a lengthy collaboration, invited the poet to write some poems to accompany his crow etchings. Muscled, bristly, half-naked, stout-beaked, and huge-clawed, the crow that appeared on the cover of the 1970 book gives a first indication of Crow's character. His sheer grotesqueness has a certain charm. He is the bomb-blasted, scraggy, eye-on-the-main-chance life principle, the exemplar par excellence of the survivor in neo-Darwinism.

The revised volume of *Crow* (1972) contained sixty-nine poems that form a catalog of Crow's encounters and origins. The carrion crow, *Corvus corone cornix*, is one of the most intelligent of birds. Savage, utterly pragmatic, with all the canniness of intelligence married to the will to survive, it served as a useful starting point for the Hughesian version. Hughes's crow is altogether more cartoonish, and his adventures go far beyond the naturalistic ones of his biological model: Crow is present at the creation; God shows him the world's beauties; he survives nuclear destruction. Stylistically the poems themselves have little residual music; unlike the hammered craft of the poet's earlier work, Crow's songs don't remain in the memory. The sequence has more of a cumulative effect, though the strongest of the poems are strong precisely because of their rhythms. Hughes said of the sequence, in an interview with Ekbert Faas, "The idea was originally just to write . . . the songs that a crow would sing. In other words, songs with no music whatsoever, in a super-simple and super ugly language which would. . .shed everything except just what he wanted to say" (Faas, p. 208).

Crow was influenced by certain aspects of Native American trickster literature. In his remarkable essay "Crow on the Beach," Hughes compares and contrasts the tricksterish vision at the root of *Crow* with the nihilistic black comedy the sequence was at times accused of at its appearance. Hughes writes:

> In Black Comedy the despair and nihilism are fundamental, and the attempts to live are provisional, clownish, meaningless, 'absurd'. In Trickster literature the optimism and creative joy are fundamental, and the attempts to live, and to enlarge and intensify life, however mismanaged, fill up at every point with self-sufficient meaning.
>
> (*Winter Pollen*, p. 239)

The poet is on the side of life, no matter how finally doomed. And while critics drew some parallels between the nightmare world of *Crow* and the events in Hughes's private life, even here he celebrates vitality, not death.

The sequence's episodes take place on a mythical plane. In "Examination at the Womb Door," Crow undergoes a test. The poem takes the form of a series of interrogations, to which Crow provides monosyllabic answers, most of them "*Death*." Death is stronger than hope, the will, love, and life. "But who is stronger than death?"

is the final question. *"Me, evidently,"* Crow replies (p. 3). He passes the examination and is allowed through, an exemplar of the unphilosophical pragmatism of the life force.

In "Crow Tyrannosaurus," Crow begins to develop a conscience regarding the "cortege / of mourning and lament" comprising the creation. He looks at other creatures, able to survive only by causing death, Man ("a walking / Abattoir / of innocents") included. Crow considers whether he could "stop eating / And try to become the light?" But, seeing a grub, his animal pragmatism takes over, and he stabs at it. The poem concludes:

Weeping he walked and stabbed
Thus came the eye's
roundness
the ear's
deafness.

(p. 14)

The poem is freighted with guilt. It examines the price of being alive. Death is not "the mother of beauty" here, as in Wallace Stevens's "Sunday Morning," but the mother of harrowed and bloody life. In "A Horrible Religious Error" man and woman give up their will at the appearance of the serpent; they whisper, "Your will is our peace." The poem concludes:

But Crow only peered.
Then took a step or two forward,
Grabbed this creature by the slackskin nape,

Beat the hell out of it, and ate it.

(p. 37)

Crow's inability to be cowed by God or serpent is his strength. Utterly uncultural, he lives purely in the moment. The "hell" he beats out of the snake, one reading suggests, is the power of supposed evil—perhaps sexuality—or, perhaps, the human's fear of the power of evil. For Crow, the Christian hell is a concept which has no meaning, assuming as it does an afterlife. Crow is like "the strong" in the Robert Frost poem, who "are saying nothing until they see."

"Crow's Last Stand" posits an aspect of Crow as the everlasting principle not even the sun can render down to its component parts. This is "a final obstacle":

Limpid among the glaring furnace clinkers
The pulsing blue tongues and the red and the yellow
The green lickings of the conflagration

Limpid and black—

Crow's eye-pupil, in the tower of its scorched fort.

(p. 75)

His pupil, while "black," is also "limpid"; blackness is regarded as a lasting, irreducible absolute in comparison to the colors of the conflagration, and there's a pun on "pupil"; crow is a pupil through the eye, that is, on the evidence his eye reveals to him. This is his bastion and defense, as the noun "fort" makes plain.

Crow cannot be regarded as wholly successful, though it received considerable attention. From this point on, Hughes's development tended to have two distinct strands. One was mythical, as exemplified by *Crow,* and its somewhat obscure follow-up, *Cave Birds,* which contains two outstanding poems, "Bride and Groom Lie Hidden Together for Three Days," and "The Knight." The other was that of a far more traditional English nature and landscape poetry. His next books were exemplars of each style.

SEASON SONGS

THIS book, which appeared in 1975, emerged from the naturalistic side of Hughes's oeuvre, and perhaps reflected the more settled nature of his life at this point. The songs are a paean of sometimes-exhilarated praise to rural life throughout the seasons. The book is ostensibly for children, like a number of Hughes's other children's books, such as *What Is the Truth?* and his story *The Iron Man* (later filmed as *The Iron Giant* by Warner Brothers). But the volume transcends such categories. It contains a number of outstanding poems. "Swifts" is an astonishing performance. *Apus apus,* the common swift, is one of Britain's briefest summer visitors, arriving in the country from Africa in May. By mid-August, having bred, the birds have departed again. With their characteristic screeching cries and long, swept-back scythe-blade wings, they are perfectly adapted to airborne flight. Their feet are vestigial, for clinging only; they are even thought to sleep on the wing. Hughes's poem is a breathtakingly mimetic display. It begins:

Fifteenth of May. Cherry blossom. The swifts
Materialize at the tip of a long scream
Of needle. "Look! They're back! Look!" And they're
 gone
On a steep

Controlled scream of skid
Round the house-end and away under the cherries.
Gone.

(*New Selected Poems,* 1995, p. 134)

To anyone who knows the birds, this is virtuoso description. The two brief, almost notelike opening sentences, followed by "The swifts," which poises suspensefully at the end of the line, set up a staccato urgency for what is to come. This is reinforced by the drama of the line ends—"gone," "steep," "skid,"—lines that, with their different lengths, all help to conjure the explosive appearance of the birds out of nowhere. The one-word sentence "Gone" emphatically conjures the sudden silence left by the birds' departure. It is like the dropping of a curtain on a scene.

The poet considers what the return of the birds indicates:

The globe's still working, the Creation's
Still waking refreshed, our summer's
Still all to come—
And here they are, here they are again
Erupting across yard stones

Shrapnel-scatter terror. Frog-gapers,
Speedway goggles, international mobsters—

A bolas of three or four wire screams
Jockeying across each other
On their switchback wheel of death.
They swat past, hard-fletched,

Veer on the hard air, toss up over the roof,
And are gone again. Their mole-dark labouring,
their lunatic limber scramming frenzy
And their whirling blades

Sparkle out into blue—
Not ours any more.

(pp. 134–135)

The repetitions at the beginning of the quote— "still working," "still waking," "still all," in their alliteration on the "w" and the progression of vowels from "o" in "working" to "a" in "waking" and "all," help convey the narrator's emphatic sense of release at the return of the birds. His description of them as "international mobsters" is both apt and to an extent accurate. Swifts wheel around on the air in screaming gangs; they are "international" in their annual migrations. Hughes calls them "Frog gapers" because they have special wide froglike gapes for feeding on the wing on flies and other insects, which they scoop up by flying through the air open-beaked. The marvelous energy of a verb like "erupting" is released into "shrapnel-scatter terror": Hughes's celebration of the birds' energies is by no means unambiguous. There is an awareness in that "shrapnel" of the possible consequence of energy here. Active verbs such as "swat," "veer," and "toss" fully convey the power of the birds' flight, and the alliteration and packed syntax of lines like "their lunatic limber scramming frenzy / And their whirling blades" give the effect of tremendous energy crammed within the lineal tension of the lines. It is released into that "Sparkle out into blue": the effect is cinematographic, like a scene from a fantasy film. Hughes's poem builds from naturalistic detail into something just short of caricature. This works because the birds are so close to caricature themselves. Their energy thrums within the tension of the poem's lines: the birds are not just themselves but emblems of inspiration and its sudden redeeming arrival. "Swifts" marks one of the high points in Hughes's animal poetry.

But the poet is also open by this stage to the bleaker and sadder realities of the creaturely world. Part 1 of his three-part poem "Sheep" is a moving elegy for a runt lamb, "only half his proper size." The lamb, the narrator concludes:

was born
With everything but the will—
That can be deformed, just like a limb.
Death was more interesting to him.
Life could not get his attention.
(New Selected Poems, p. 136)

The poem has a gloomy sublimity and the verse a quietness wholly opposite to the explosive energy of "Swifts." The closing lines of the quote have an epigrammatic quality. Ostensibly about a lamb, they have great resonance.

Season Songs helped reinforce the naturalistic side of Hughes's writing; his next volume, *Gaudete,* leapt once more into myth.

GAUDETE

GAUDETE (1977) originally began life as a film script. It is a mix of prose and loose, long-lined free verse, like a strange cross between one of the longer narratives of Robinson Jeffers and a bizarre *Under Milk Wood*, without Thomas'ss wonderful humor, plangency, and life-enhancing bawdry. The story switches from character to character. The book is prefaced by the "argument": the Reverend Nicholas Lumb has been spirited away into "the other world," and a duplicate of him is made by spirits from an oak log to take his place in this world during his absence. The duplicate is a sort of Christian love god, who makes love to all the women of the parish in an attempt to father a messiah; all the women's husbands discover this via voyeuristic photographs taken by a gamekeeper, Garten. The duplicate Lumb is hunted down and shot. Soon after, the real Lumb rematerializes in the west of Ireland; there he "roams about composing hymns and psalms to a nameless female deity" (p. 9) and these compositions, somewhat obscure, serve as epilogue to the book.

Gaudete—"rejoice" in Latin—contains much fine writing: "The newly plumped grass shivers and flees. Giant wheels of light ride into the chestnuts, and the poplars lift and pour like the tails of horses," writes Hughes (p. 23). However, the plotless, arbitrary nature of the narrative and the looseness of the form mean that the incidentals have to carry the weight of the poem. Granted, these can be of interest. Here the narrator describes one of the poem's characters, Commander Estridge, listening to and watching his daughter, Jennifer, playing a Beethoven Piano Sonata:

His skull, glossy, veined, freckled, bulges
Over the small tight ferocious hawk's face
Evolved in Naval Command. Commander Estridge

Is stricken with the knowledge that his dream of
  beautiful daughters
Has become a reality.
Simply, naturally, and now inevitably, there by the
  open window.
The dream was as beautiful as the daughters.
But the reality
Is beyond him. Unmanageable and frightening,
Like leopard cubs suddenly full-grown, come into
  their adult power and burdened with it.
Primaeval frames, charged with primaeval hungers
  and primaeval beauty.
Those uncontrollable eyes, and organs of horrific
  energy, demanding satisfaction.

(pp. 41–42)

Despite its mythical framework, *Gaudete* is most interesting, as here, for its naturalistic incidentals and portrayal of primitive emotions below the settled rurality of, presumably, Hughes's adopted Devon. This is a striking portrait of a control freak unable to come to terms with the burgeoning sexuality of his daughters, though its overstatement verges on comic caricature in the last two sentences of the quote. One reading could interpret the commander as representing the male, oppressive, rational world in conflict with the female energy of the earth: a nature that is ultimately uncontrollable. Moments such as this represent the high point of the main narrative of *Gaudete*. The women, and Lumb himself, represent animal energies, the return of repressed nature, the originating principle: the men are simply respondents, controllers.

REMAINS OF ELMET

As his collaborations with Leonard Baskin show, Hughes enjoyed crossovers. This led to *Remains of Elmet* (1979), a book of poems accompanied by striking black-and-white photographs by the British landscape photographer Fay Godwin. The book is largely an elegy for the Calder Valley, where Hughes had been brought up. Formerly part of Elmet—"the last British Celtic Kingdom to fall to the Angles," as Hughes writes in a prefatory note—it was a millworking region, a curious combination of upland moorland, valleyed verdure, and industrial towns. By the time

of Hughes's volume this pattern was breaking up and the old community was dying.

Originating in a visit by Hughes's aging uncle to Devon, the book consists of sixty-one poems matched with photographs. Many of the poems represent a stage of artistry, a language unique to each poet, that Gerard Manley Hopkins called "Parnassian": that is, the achieved voice of the poet, a level below that of inspiration. In Hughes's case this meant free verse, often with staccato sentences lacking main verbs, with frequent lines consisting of one or two words and an increasing tendency to run the title of a poem into its first line. Nonetheless the volume contains a scatter of memorable poems, including "Football at Slack," "The Canal's Drowning Black," "Two," "Mount Zion," and "Cock Crows." Interestingly, "Football at Slack" and "Cock Crows," perhaps the volume's outstanding pieces, both almost escape the somber atmosphere of much of the volume. The former opens with a clowning gaiety:

Between plunging valleys, on a bareback of hill,
Men in bunting colours
Bounced, and their blown ball bounced.

The blown ball jumped, and the merry-coloured
  men
Spouted like water to head it.
The ball blew away downwind—

The rubbery men bounced after it.
The ball jumped up and out and hung on the wind
Over a gulf of treetops.
Then they all shouted together, and the ball blew
  back.

(*Remains of Elmet*, p. 68)

This has a relaxed convivial tone untypical of Hughes. The severity of the environment in the poem is later contrasted with the clownish energy of the footballers, which overcomes "the depth of Atlantic depression," with its lovely pun on state of mind as well as meteorological conditions. The alliteration on the "b"—"bareback," "bunting," "bounced," "blown," "blew," and "back"—fill the scene with movement, and the descriptions of the men has a comic exaggeration: they spout like water, they bounce like rubber, and the "Bounced," with its comma, at the opening of line 3, enacts the action of the ball itself.

"Cock Crows," a magnificent poem, opens with the narrator on "a dark summit," watching the dawn in the mist. He hears the cockerels beginning to crow on the valley farms—once an almost ubiquitous British sound. Their increasing enthusiasm and energy is described virtuosically. Their crows increase in intensity until they are

soaring harder, brighter, higher
Tearing the mist,
Bubble-glistenings flung up and bursting to light
Brightening the undercloud,
The fire-crests of the cocks, the sickle shouts,
Challenge against challenge, answer to answer,
Hooking higher, . . .

(p. 121)

The poem closes with the initial dawn flurries of the cocks subsiding; energy is replaced by the habitual everyday, which is delineated in a few lines at the poem's close. It is the energy Hughes is interested in, and the poem shows his gift for astonishing evocation. The poem presents a memory largely untampered with by Hughes's penchant for mythologizing, a tendency which would be reinforced by some of the strongest poems in his next volume.

MOORTOWN

"MOORTOWN" was the name of the ninety-five-acre farm Hughes and his wife purchased in North Devon in 1972. The sequence of that name forms, despite a number of myth-based sequences—"Prometheus on His Crag," "Adam and the Sacred Nine," among others—the centerpiece of the book, published in 1979. Here is the pastoral Hughes, writing mainly about domestic animals. There is nothing tame about the poems, however: they are full of often bloody and tragic deaths and births. In one, cattle are dehorned in stomach-churning detail. In another, a lamb stuck in the birth canal and stillborn has to be decapitated. The sequence closes with a group of elegies for Jack Orchard, Hughes's father-in-law. The sequence was later reprinted separately as *Moortown Diary* (1989), with a helpful preface

by Hughes and notes to some of the poems. Hughes makes plain in this preface that his intention was to keep a sort of verse diary of significant happenings—all of the poems with the exception of the Jack Orchard elegies carry the date of their writing—and in which rewriting was seen as tampering with the purity of the initial impulse. The poet's aim is for spontaneity and directness. The compressed energy of some of Hughes's earlier work is absent. The style, however, catches all the incidentals of farming and country life; it has a pregnant casualness.

Some poems, however, escape the diarist's tone. "Tractor" is a virtuoso account of starting a reluctant tractor on a frosty winter morning. The tendency of contemporary science has been to regard organisms as machines; in an ironic twist Hughes deftly personifies the inanimate tractor. The machine won't start. The poet writes:

I squirt commercial sure-fire
Down the black throat—it just coughs.
It ridicules me—a trap of iron stupidity
I've stepped into. I drive the battery
As if I were hammering and hammering
The frozen arrangements to pieces with a hammer
And it jabbers laughing pain-crying mockingly
Into happy life.

(*Moortown Diary*, p. 18)

By the poem's close the newly-started tractor is compared to a "demon," somewhat out of control, "streaming with sweat / Raging and trembling and rejoicing." Hughes's skill resides in the way he makes this seem by no means arbitrary.

Despite the subject matter of much of the sequence, it emanates a sense of rural contentment and near-happiness at times—exemplified in a poem like "Coming Down Through Somerset." One hot August night, the narrator glimpses in the headlights "a killed badger / Sprawled with helpless legs." He takes the animal, freshly dead, "bleeding from the nose," home with him. As the poem progresses and the badger, now laid "on the beam / Torn from a great building," starts to decay in the heat wave, it becomes apparent it is emblematic; not only is it a "Beautiful, / Beautiful, warm, secret beast;" it represents the perceived richness of the narrator's life. As the heat ushers the badger "hourly / Towards his under-worlds," the narrator says of the decaying beast:

I want him
To stay as he is. Sooty gloss-throated,
With his perfect face. Paws so tired,
Power-body relegated. I want him
To stop time. His strength staying, bulky,
Blocking time. His rankness, his bristling wildness,
His thrillingly painted face.
A badger on my moment of life.
Not years ago, like the others, but now.
I stand
Watching his stillness, like an iron nail
Driven, flush to the head,
Into a yew post. Something has to stay.

(pp. 40–41)

The poem has an air of being deeply felt. While the tractor, symbol of industrial farming, comes to demonic life at its poem's close, the badger, the emblem of old, wild, secret England, decays. Taken together the poems could be read as emblematic of that pivotal change in Devon farming, and in the rural world generally, noted by Hughes in his introduction to the *Moortown Diary* sequence: the giving way of individualistic farming to the claims of agribusiness. The air of heartfelt invocation in the closing sentence of "Coming Down Through Somerset" hovers strangely between a conviction and a hope, a belief that it would surely be inconceivable if nothing *were* to stay. The poem has an awkward yet curiously convincing notelike form in parts: "Beam waiting two years / To be built into new building. Summer coat / Not worth skinning off him. / His skeleton—for the future." In addition to the more literal meaning, the implication of the closing quote may be that the future—the future of humanity—will inherit only this symbolic badger's skeleton. Not the living animal, nor even, as with Hughes, the freshly dead one. As with the best of Hughes's animal poems, "Coming Down Through Somerset" transcends its occasion.

The "Moortown" sequence closes with a powerful group of six poems for Jack Orchard and, by extension, for an older way of life. These, with the exception of "The Day He Died," an elegy, take the form of vignettes of memories of the dead man: setting fences, at cattle auctions, shearing sheep, burning hedge-boughs. The final poem is "Hands," which marvels at the dead man's "bloody great hands!" and their toughness:

when your grasp nosed bullocks, prising their mouths
  wide,
So they dropped to their knees
I understood again
How the world of half-ton hooves, and horns,
And hides heedless as oaken-boarding, comes to be
  manageable.

(p. 59)

Here, the alliteration of "h" in the last two lines piles up like the weight of obstacles the man's hands had to deal with, before being released into the resolving clause. The form is a perfect vehicle for the sense.

RIVER

HUGHES was a keen fisherman. In an interview in the Canadian fishing journal *Wild Steelhead & Salmon,* published soon after he died, he stated his belief that his fishing helped reconnect him spiritually to the landscape. *River* is full of his fascination for rivers and the creatures, especially fish, in them. Like *Remains of Elmet*, it was a collaboration with a photographer, in this case Peter Keen. A large-format book with color photographs accompanying Hughes's poems, *River*, published in 1983, had a somewhat coffee table appearance. The volume was later reprinted, with additional and deleted poems, along with *Remains of Elmet* and *Cave Birds,* as *Three Books* (1993).

Sometimes the poet examines the creatures found in the various rivers—mink, salmon, cormorant, kingfisher, caddis fly, eel, moorhen; these are pieces full of Hughes's customary observational excellence. At other times he examines particular rivers, and there is a new polemical environmental tone in pieces such as "If" and "1984 on the Tarka Trail." The poems occasionally sink to the portentous, as in "Last Night," when he describes "the evil fish minds," and Hughes's Parnassian can be wearing to read in bulk. But there is a strand of awed, harrowed celebration in the volume that effectively engages the reader. In "Salmon Eggs," the poet examines the something "more vital than death" "going on in the river"—the development of the salmon eggs in January. The poem closes:

It is the font, brimming with touch and whisper,
Swaddling the egg.
               Only birth matters
Say the river's whorls.
                   And the river
Silences everything in a leaf-mouldering hush
Where sun rolls bare, and earth rolls,

And mind condenses on old haws.
               (*Three Books*, p. 106)

The "font" is the redd, the nest, of the salmon. It is conceivable that the whorls of the river—those spirals of current—may perhaps convey this hard-earned message, not arbitrarily but because astronomers believe that in the universe only spiral galaxies, not elliptical galaxies, are able to form new stars. Hughes reads the universal in the intimate and local. The material world constituted by the river is seen as a sort of absolute; "mind" is secondary—merely, and yet astonishingly, one reading could suggest, the dew that condenses on old hawthorn berries. "Salmon Eggs" is a paean of praise, finally, to birth.

Of course, where birth is, death must be also. "October Salmon" is an awed elegy for a salmon waiting in a pool to spawn and then die. Atlantic Salmon, *Salmo salar*, return to the rivers, and sometimes to the streams, of their births. Immediately they return to fresh water from the sea, and they stop feeding. All male salmon die after breeding. At a reading in Strathclyde University in Glasgow in autumn 1985, Hughes prefaced his reading of "October Salmon" with comments on the situation of his own father not long before he died. While the comparison between the doomed salmon and the poet's father cannot be taken too far, it would account for the emotional weight of the poem—the salmon is emblematic of fated helplessness. It is a redundant vehicle for once splendid life:

So quickly it's over!

So briefly he roamed the gallery of marvels!
Such sweet months, so richly embroidered into earth's

beauty-dress,
Her life-robe—
Now worn out with her tirelessness, her insatiable
  quest,
Hangs in the flow, a frayed scarf—
               (*Three Books*, p. 175)

While Hughes's tendency to use exclamation can become a stylistic tic in some of the later poems, here it seems justified. The "insatiable quest" of this female earth, gorgeously conjured, may be seen simply as that of evolutionary forces to which individuals are secondary. The poem mixes an elevated register with something wholly contemporary, offhand, and slangy; the latter helps ground and make more convincing the former. It also reinforces the sense of the cosmic process of death in commonplace circumstances. The salmon at sea was "the king of infinite liberty," its "Body simply the armature of energy"; it is now reduced to a "shroud in a gutter," "under the scrubby oak tree." The poem closes magnificently:

Yet this was always with him. This was inscribed in
  his egg.
This chamber of horrors is also home.
He was probably hatched in this very pool.

And this was the only mother he ever had, this uneasy
  channel of minnows
Under the mill-wall, with bicycle wheels, car-tyres,
  bottles
And sunk sheets of corrugated iron.
People walking their dogs trail their evening shadows
  across him.
If boys see him they will try to kill him.

All this, too, is stitched into the torn richness,
The epic poise
That holds him so steady in his wounds, so loyal to
  his doom, so patient
In the machinery of heaven.
               (pp. 176–177)

The salmon's death is inscribed in its DNA. The elevated phrase "chamber of horrors" transmutes to "this very pool," and the closing two stanzas operate by similar modulations of tone. The penultimate stanza is full of the clutter of industrial and commonplace life. The poem's closing stanza becomes decidedly elevated in register. This is primarily convincing because so well prepared for. There is an echo of Ginsberg's line in "Howl"—"Burning for the ancient heavenly connection to the starry dynamo in the machinery of night"—in the poem's closing line. Hughes's phrase, however, works more soundly: it utilizes in microcosm the method in the rest of the poem, twinning an industrial, mechanistic concept with a religious one. "Machinery" implies rigidity and mechanism; "heaven," in this context, is both a grave reference to the evolutionary processes that function through death, and an ironic reference to the Christian concept.

FLOWERS AND INSECTS, WOLFWATCHING, *AND* A RAIN-CHARM FOR THE DUCHY

HUGHES had been appointed as poet laureate in 1984. Almost traditionally, poet laureates have stopped producing valuable work. The poet's volumes of the late 1980s seem transitional. *Flowers and Insects* (1986) shows Hughes continuing to mine the vein of the natural world, secure in his own style of Parnassian. (Of course, Hughes's Parnassian was at times substantial.) The poems in *Flowers and Insects* are competent but mainly unsurprising, and occasionally embarrassing: a foxglove is described as "a lolling armful, and so young!" The volume was followed by *Wolfwatching* (1989), which takes its title from a long piece about an old wolf and a young one in a London zoo, echoing "Jaguar" and "Second Glance at a Jaguar." In "Wolfwatching," however, despair, not energy, forms the main focus. Its old wolf is defeated; its young wolf will be. The volume opens with a poem about "A Sparrow Hawk" and closes with "A Dove." The opening lines of the former show the fall-off in force from a piece such as "Hawk Roosting": "Slips from your eye-corner—overtaking / Your first thought" (p. 1.) There is no rhythmic power.

Wolfwatching is most interesting for the appearance of more personal poems about the poet's family. In setting, these hark back to *Remains of Elmet*. In tone they look forward to the negotiations with the shade of Sylvia Plath in the *Birthday Letters*. They include pieces like "Climbing into Heptonstall"—a sardonic look at the heritage industry in the poet's former home village—"Dust as We Are," "Source," about the poet's father's life after World War I, and "Walt," a two-part poem about Hughes's uncle. "Dust As We Are" takes its title from Wordsworth's *The Prelude*, Book I: "Dust as we are, the immortal spirit grows / Like harmony in music." Hughes's poem describes the young poet's damaged relationship with his "post-war father." Hughes describes how, combing his father's hair, he "divined" below its golden waves "the fragility of skull." The verse closes:

And I filled
With his knowledge.
After mother's milk
This was the soul's food. A soap-smell spectre
Of the massacre of innocents. So the soul grew.
A strange thing, with rickets—a hyena.
No singing—that kind of laughter.

(p. 11)

The closure could be read as a sort of *Ars Poetica* for Hughes. The growth of his soul was not the "fair seedtime" of Wordsworth's; Hughes's poem's title is sardonic. He portrays himself as warped by the legacy of World War I. The eerie, cackling cry of the hyena, with its implication of hysterical laughter, is powerfully evoked.

Rain-Charm for the Duchy (1992) gathered the eighteen of Hughes's poems written as the poet laureate. It contained one considerable poem— the book's title piece—which was really a celebration of salmon and rivers, and only tenuously linked to the christening of Prince Harry, the second son from the ill-fated marriage of Prince Charles and Princess Diana. Hughes was seen as somewhat doggedly fulfilling his obligation to produce laureate poems. The collection appended several pages of extremely detailed notes, as if in an attempt to convey respectability on the verse.

TALES FROM OVID

HUGHES had always been fascinated by myth— many of his books have mythic components. In the early 1990s the editors of *After Ovid, New Metamorphoses*, Michael Hofmann and James Lasdun, asked Hughes to contribute to their anthology. He did so with four tales. To make *Tales from Ovid* (1997) he later added another twenty from Ovid's original *Metamorphoses* of 136 episodes, originally published in fifteen books.

The stories of *Metamorphoses* feature seduction, rape, incest, sex change, plague, torture, and both gay and straight love. They are thus thoroughly contemporary. The metamorphoses of the title involve, for instance, nymphs being changed into trees to escape violation, or adolescent boys being transformed into newts or dissolved into water. The tales have a graphic brilliance. Yet as a whole they have a reputation for lightness. For all their portrayal of disaster and horror, they tend not to involve the reader emotionally; one is entertained but not implicated.

Hughes focuses on what he regards as Ovid's essence:

> Ovid was interested in passion. Or rather, in what a passion feels like to the one possessed by it. Not just ordinary passion, either, but human passion in extremis—passion where it combusts, or levitates, or mutates into an experience of the supernatural.
>
> (*Tales from Ovid*, p. ix)

The tales Hughes chooses naturally bear out this claim. While his free verse can on occasion seem flaccid and prosy when compared with, say, Robinson Jeffers's translation of *Medea*, more often he achieves a sort of electrical shorthand; he cuts away the prosier explanatory elements of the original, and one is left with the solid muscle of the text.

An example of his concision is found, for example, in "Tereus," from Book VI of the original, the tale of the king of that name's uncontrollable lust for Philomela, sister of his wife, Procne, both daughters of Pandion, the King of Athens. "Tereus" is a horror story in which Procne and Philomela, in retribution for Tereus's repeated brute rapes of Philomela, and the cutting out of her tongue, feed his own son, by Procne herself, to Tereus at a private feast. Ironically it had been Procne herself who begged for

Philomela to be allowed to visit her, sending Tereus to entreat their father, King Pandion. It is instructive to compare the standard Loeb translation with Hughes's account. Here is the moment at which Tereus first sees Philomela in her father's court. First, the Loeb:

> Philomela entered, attired in rich apparel, but richer still in beauty; such as we are wont to hear the naiads described, and dryads when they move about in the deep woods, if only one should give to them refinement and apparel like hers. The moment he saw the maiden Tereus was inflamed with love, quick as if one should set fire to ripe grain, or dry leaves, or hay stored away in the mow.
>
> (Loeb, Book VI, p. 321)

Here is Hughes's version:

> Philomela herself—arrayed
> In the wealth of a kingdom—entered:
> Still unaware that her own beauty
> Was the most astounding of her jewels.
>
> She looked like one of those elfin queens
> You hear about
> Flitting through the depths of forests.
> Tereus felt his blood alter thickly.
> Suddenly he himself was like a forest
> When a drought wind explodes it into a firestorm.
>
> (*Tales from Ovid*, p. 230)

Hughes gains in dramatic effect what he loses in adherence to the literal meaning. In place of a classical reference to dryads and naiads who would resemble Philomela if given "refinement and apparel such as hers," Hughes uses a single phrase: "one of those elfin queens," letting the reader's imagination produce the image. He also reduces the three incendiary images of Philomela's effect on Tereus in the Loeb to a single, explosive one; Tereus's passion is exploded by Philomela "into a firestorm."

As well as condensing, Hughes elaborates when necessary. He makes the most of Ovid's potential for dramatic description. This is especially noticeable in episodes such as that of Midas in Book XI. While the Loeb is plainly factual, Hughes's version is brilliantly cinematographic:

> He washed his hands under flowing water, at a fountain.

Already a hope
Told him that the gift might wash away,
As waking up will wash out a nightmare.
But the water that touched him
Coiled into the pool below as plumes
Of golden smoke, settling heavily
In a silt of gold atoms.

Suddenly his vision
Of transmuting his whole kingdom to gold
Made him sweat—
It chilled him as he sat
At the table
And reached for a roasted bird. The carcase
Toppled from his horrified fingers
Into his dish with a clunk,
As if he had picked up a table ornament.

(*Tales from Ovid*, p. 203)

The detail of the bird clunking in the dish is entirely Hughes's. So is the marvelous description of the water "settling heavily / In a silt of gold atoms." The "atoms" adds a touch of scientific credibility to the description, and the translation is heavily alliterative—"pool / plumes," "smoke / settling / silt," which has the effect of emphasizing the slow thickening of the water to gold.

Tales from Ovid was greeted admiringly by reviewers; it would be followed by the poet's most famous volume, and the last significant one of his career.

BIRTHDAY LETTERS

THIS verse account of Hughes's relationship with Sylvia Plath stunned the literary world upon publication in 1998 and received almost universal acclaim. The book's sheer documentary interest was indisputable. Hughes had remained almost completely silent about his life with his first wife since her death almost forty years earlier. In a letter Hughes made it clear what he felt his silence had cost: "If only I had done the equivalent [of making a public declaration of these secrets] I might have had a more fruitful career—certainly a freer psychological life" (*Ariel's Gift*, p. 4). The volume raises interesting questions as to how far the documentary interest of a text alters one's reading of it as poetry: Are the *Birthday Letters* good poetry, or merely intriguing or useful documentary matter—or both? Or some combination? Perhaps these questions are irrelevant: it is difficult, if not impossible, to see the volume outside its biographical context. When Thomas Hardy wrote his elegies for his wife, Emma Gifford, the "Poems of 1912–1913," the poems themselves engendered interest in their subject. Hughes, however, had a ready-made context for his own verse. Here was a major poet writing intimately about his first wife, another major poet. The story had everything: young love, brilliance, passion, ambition, adultery, tragedy, and, not least, revelation: no one but Hughes possessed such knowledge. It made for an explosive combination: small wonder the book jolted the public consciousness unlike any other book of recent poetry.

Birthday Letters consists of eighty-eight poems. They form a narrative which begins before Hughes met Plath. It ends with the poet looking back, elegiacally. Stylistically they are written in the fluent free verse Hughes had made his own. Rhythmically, in the main, the poems are undistinguished, and several critics pointed to Hughes's disconcerting penchant for using verbless sentences that give the writing at times a staccato quality. Contrasting with the documentary tone of some of the poems is the poet's persistence in seeing Plath and himself as, to an extent, helpless in the face of "fate"; the poems at times become bogged down in their mythic framework, in which Hughes attempts to delineate his former wife's psychic problems. This will be interesting to those who find Plath's own complexes interesting, but it is the sheer force of the documentary tellings that remain most fascinating to most contemporary readers, seeming, as they do, revelatory. As Edwin Morgan, writing in the Scottish-American poetry journal *The Dark Horse* commented, "[The book] shows the poet in his sixties like a dragon in its cave, opening the entrance a chink or two to let the world see its dark, coiled and twisted, intermittently flashing hoard of memories" (*The Dark Horse* 7, 1998–1999, p. 59).

The volume begins with "Fulbright Scholars," and its opening sentence sends a torch-beam of inquiry wavering uncertainly into the dark: "Where was it, in the Strand? A display / Of news items, in photographs. / For some reason I noticed it" (p. 3). Hughes ponders whether Plath was in the picture; at one level the poem is about the uncertainty of memory. When Hughes eats "the first fresh peach I had ever tasted" near the poem's close, we are made aware both of the limitations in his experience—in postwar England, the twenty-four-year-old from Yorkshire had never tasted a peach—and of his reveling in experience: the peach is "delicious." The image of the peach shimmers with suggestion: naivete and sensuality, entwined, set the stage for the unfolding story. Thereafter follows a sequence of relatively straightforward narrative poems detailing the couple's meeting, courtship, marriage, and journeys in Spain and America. The plain documentary force of these endows them with a power lacking whenever Hughes attempts psychoanalysis of Plath's psyche, or astrologizes. In "St. Botolph's," for instance, which details the couple's first encounter, Hughes's speculation regarding

That day's Sun in the Fish
Conjunct your Ascendant exactly
Opposite my Neptune and fixed
In my tenth House of good and evil fame

clarifies into his powerful account of first meeting Plath:

I see you there, clearer, more real
Than any of the years in its shadow—
As if I saw you that once, then never again.
The loose fall of hair—that floppy curtain
Over your face, over your scar. And your face
A rubbery ball of joy
Round the African-lipped, laughing, thickly
Crimson-painted mouth. And your eyes
Squeezed in your face, a crush of diamonds,
Incredibly bright, bright as a crush of tears . . .

(p. 15)

The poet may have been being deliberately ironic in contrasting his astrological speculation with the sheer force of Plath's presence, but there is nothing to suggest this.

An especially touching poem, "Fate Playing," reveals the vulnerability of Plath. She is to meet Hughes coming off "a bus from the North" which, owing to a misunderstanding, he isn't on. She panics, and wonders if he'll be on a train instead. He is, and as he steps onto the platform, Hughes is greeted by a frantic Plath, rushing down the platform to greet him

As if I had come back from the dead
Against every possibility, against
Every negative but your own prayer
To your own gods. There I knew what it was
To be a miracle.

(p. 32)

Paradoxically it is the plainness of these documentary retellings that at times transcend their connection to Plath; at one level, they could be about any young couple. Readers are likely to find aspects of their own experience summoned by the poems.

The volume, however, also has considerable intertextuality with Plath's work. In "The Rabbit Catcher," Hughes provides both a context for and a response to Plath's brilliant, acid poem of the same name. For her rabbit catcher, the "little deaths" of the rabbits in his snares have a strong sexual element. Some critics suggested Hughes was the model for the poem's central character.

Hughes provides a verse gloss to the day in question. When Plath throws away the snares with a cry of "Murderers!" Hughes sees his whole culture being misunderstood. (Cultural misunderstandings, the differences between England and America, form a background to the book as a whole.) Of Plath's action, Hughes writes:

I was aghast. Faithful
To my country gods—I saw
The sanctity of a trapline desecrated.
You saw blunt fingers, blood in the cuticles,
Clamped round a blue mug. I saw
Country poverty raising a penny,
Filling a Sunday stewpot. You saw baby-eyed
Strangled innocents, I saw sacred
Ancient custom.

(p. 145)

The to-and-fro dialectic of this, and the repetitions of "you saw" and "I saw," especially at lines' ends, sets up a lineal tension in the poem; it reinforces the argument between the two viewpoints. Both are, in their way, correct and irreconcilable. The technique also conjures the very tone of a couple arguing.

Birthday Letters closes with one of the book's strongest poems, "Red," an elegy that opens, "Red was your colour." Everything is settled here, and in retrospect. The color red, and its many manifestations in the life of the couple, is dwelt upon almost obsessively by the poet:

> When you had your way finally
> Our room was red. A judgement chamber.
> Shut casket for gems. The carpet of blood
> Patterned with darkenings, congealments.
>
> (p. 197)

Red, traditionally associated with life, vitality, danger, blood, features in the first thirty-six of the poem's forty-five lines. Red is portrayed as the color Plath used to negate white, which is symbolic of nullity in the poem. At line 37, Hughes introduces blue: "Blue was better for you. Blue was wings." The poem closes:

> In the pit of red
> You hid from the bone-clinic whiteness.
>
> But the jewel you lost was blue.
>
> (p. 198)

Red is portrayed as Plath's overcompensation for "bone-clinic whiteness," as a "pit." Blue is a "jewel," precious and durable. It is Plath who has lost the jewel. The final responsibility for what happened to her, it is implied, is her own. The poem has an air of considerable sadness.

Birthday Letters will doubtless remain an important book, not least because of the light it sheds on Sylvia Plath. While it is difficult to judge its value as poetry free of its biographical occasion, in its particulars many readers might well find echoes of their own emotional histories. It is the most personal book Ted Hughes ever wrote.

Where Hughes employs myth, the poetry can seem obscure, requiring as it does recondite knowledge extraneous to the text. It can also begin to seem subsidiary to the mythic framework, as in many of the poems in sequences such as *Cave Birds,* or the poems that conclude *Gaudete.* Ultimately, of course, it is individual poems and not entire bodies of work that are liable to survive among nonspecialist readers. The best of Hughes's poetry grows from its particulars to a wide relevance, opening up a hot line to our own instinctual energies. Among a large body of remarkable work, it seems unlikely that the animal poems such as "An Otter," "Esther's Tomcat," and "Swifts" will ever be equaled, much less surpassed, in this or any other century.

SELECTED BIBLIOGRAPHY

I. COLLECTED WORKS. *Selected Poems,* with Thom Gunn (London, 1962); *Selected Poems, 1957–1967* (London, 1972; New York, 1973); *Selected Poems, 1957–1981* (London and Boston, 1982); repub. as *New Selected Poems* (New York, 1982); *Collected Animal Poems,* 4 vols. (London and New York, 1995); *Difficulties of a Bridegroom: Collected Short Stories* (London and New York, 1995); *New Selected Poems, 1957–1994* (London, 1995); *Winter Pollen: Occasional Prose,* ed. by William Scammell (London, 1994; New York, 1995).

II. WORKS FOR ADULTS. *The Hawk in the Rain* (London and New York, 1957); *Lupercal* (London and New York, 1960); *Wodwo* (London and New York, 1967); *Crow: From the Life and Songs of the Crow* (London, 1970; New York, 1971; enl. ed., London, 1972); *Season Songs* (New York, 1975; London 1976); *Cave Birds: An Alchemical Cave Drama* (London, 1975; rev. and enl. ed., London and Boston, 1978); *Gaudete* (London and New York, 1977); *Remains of Elmet: A Pennine Sequence* (London and Boston, 1979; repub. as *Elmet* in a different edition, London and Boston, 1994); *Moortown* (London and Boston, 1979); *River* (London and Boston, 1983); *Flowers and Insects* (London and New York, 1986); *Moortown Diary* (London and Boston, 1989); *Wolfwatching* (London and Boston, 1989); *Rain-Charm for the Duchy and Other Laureate Poems* (London, 1992); *Three Books: Remains of Elmet, Cave Birds, River,* text-only versions (London, 1993); *Tales from Ovid* (London and New York, 1997); *Birthday Letters* (London and New York, 1998).

III. WORKS FOR CHILDREN. *Meet My Folks!* (London, 1961; New York, 1973); *How the Whale Became* (London, 1963; New York, 1964); *The Earth-Owl and Other Moon-People* (London, 1963); *Nessie the Mannerless Monster* (London, 1964), repub. as *Nessie the Monster* (New York, 1974); *The Iron Man: A Story in Five Nights* (London, 1968), repub. as *The Iron Giant: A Story in Five Nights* (London and New York, 1968); *The Coming of the Kings, and Other Plays* (London, 1970), enl. as *The Tiger's Bones and Other Plays for Children* (New York, 1974); *The Moon Whales and Other Moon Poems* (New York, 1976); *Moon-Bells and Other Poems* (London, 1978; exp. 2d. ed., 1986); *Under the North Star* (London and Boston, 1981); *Ffangs* the Vampire Bat and the Kiss of Truth (London, 1986); *Tales of the early World* (London, 1988; New York, 1991); *The Iron Woman* (London, 1993; New York, 1995); *The Dream-fighter and Other Creation Tales* (London, 1995); *Shaggy & Spotty* (London, 1997); *The Mermaid's Purse* (London, 1999; New York, 2000).

IV. EDITED WORKS. *Selected Poems*, Keith Douglas (London, 1964; New York, 1965); *Ariel*, Sylvia Plath (London, 1965; New York, 1966); *Poetry in the Making: An Anthology of Poems and Programmes from* Listening and Writing (London, 1967); abridged as *Poetry Is* (Garden City, N.J., 1970); *A Choice of Emily Dickinson's Verse* (London, 1968); *With Fairest Flowers While Summer Lasts: Poems from Shakespeare* (Garden City, 1971), repub. as *A Choice of Shakespeare's Verse* (London, 1971); *Crossing the Water*, Sylvia Plath (London, 1971), with different contents, London and New York, 1971); *Winter Trees*, Sylvia Plath (London, 1971; New York, 1972); *Collected Poems*, Sylvia Plath (London and Boston, 1981); *The Journals of Sylvia Plath* (New York, 1982); *The Rattle Bag*, with Seamus Heaney (London and Boston, 1982); *The School Bag*, with Seamus Heaney (London, 1997); *By Heart: 101 Poems to Remember* (London, 1997).

V. INTERVIEWS AND PROFILES. J. Richards, "An Interview with British Poet Ted Hughes, Inventor of Orghast Language," in *Drama and Theatre* 10 (1972); Blake Morrison, "Man of Mettle," in *Independent on Sunday* (5 September 1993); Drue Heinz, "Ted Hughes: The Art of Poetry," in *Paris Review* 37 (spring 1995); Eilat Negev, " 'My Life with Sylvia Plath,' by Ted Hughes," in *Daily Telegraph* (31 October 1998); Eilat Negev, " 'Poetry Is a Way of Talking to Loved Ones when It's Too Late,' " in *Daily Telegraph* (2 November 1998); Tom Pero, "So Quickly It's Over," in *Wild Steelhead & Salmon* 5 (winter 1999).

VI. CRITICAL STUDIES. Claude Rawson, "Ted Hughes: A Reappraisal," in *Essays in Criticism* 15 (January 1965); Ian Robinson and David Sims, "Ted Hughes's 'Crow,' " in *Human World* 9 (November 1972); P. E. Strauss, "The Poetry of Ted Hughes," in *Theoria* 38 (1972); Calvin Bedient, in *Eight Contemporary Poets* (London and New York, 1974); Geoffrey Summerfield, ed., *Worlds: Seven Modern Poets* (Harmondsworth, U.K., 1974); Keith Sagar, *The Art of Ted Hughes* (Cambridge, 1975; extended ed., 1978); Alan Bold, *Thom Gunn and Ted Hughes* (Edinburgh, 1976); Ekbert Faas, *Ted Hughes: The Unaccommodated Universe* (Santa Barbara, Calif., 1980); Stuart Hirschberg, *Myth in the Poetry of Ted Hughes* (Portmarnock, Ireland, and Totowa, N.J., 1981); Terry Gifford and Neil Roberts, *Ted Hughes: A Critical Study* (London and Boston, 1981); Keith Sagar, ed., *The Achievement of Ted Hughes* (Manchester, U.K., and Athens, Ga., 1983); Leonard M. Scigaj, *The Poetry of Ted Hughes: Form and Imagination* (Iowa City, Iowa, 1986); Craig Robinson, *Ted Hughes as Shepherd of Being* (London and New York, 1989); A. E. Dyson, ed., *Three Contemporary Poets: Thom Gunn, Ted Hughes, and R. S. Thomas: A Selection of Critical Essays* (Houndmills, U.K., 1990); Leonard M. Scigaj, *Ted Hughes* (Boston, 1991); Leonard M. Scigaj, ed., *Critical Essays on Ted Hughes* (New York, 1992); Keith Sagar, ed., *The Challenge of Ted Hughes* (Basingstoke, U.K., and New York, 1994); Anne Skea, *Ted Hughes: The Poetic Quest* (Armidale, NSW, 1994); Paul Bentley, *The Poetry of Ted Hughes: Language, Illusion, and Beyond.* (London and New York, 1998); Nick Gammage, ed., *The Epic Poise: A Celebration of Ted Hughes* (London, 1999); Keith Sagar, *The Laughter of Foxes: A Study of Ted Hughes* (Liverpool, 2000); Elaine Feinstein, *Ted Hughes: The Life of a Poet* (London, 2001).

VII. ARCHIVE MATERIAL. The major Ted Hughes archive is housed at the Robert W. Woodruff Library, Special Collections, Emory University, Atlanta.

D. H. LAWRENCE

(1885–1930)

John Redmond

LIFE AND BACKGROUND

D. H. LAWRENCE IS at once one of the great modernist writers and one of the most influential artists of the twentieth century. He has always been a controversial figure, and his reputation especially in the years immediately after his death, has not always been high. Through his radical views on the relations between men and women, on sexuality, race and psychology, his attacks on democracy, Christianity and scientific rationality, Lawrence challenged fundamental ideas about the individual's relationship to society. Lawrence's novels, on which his reputation mainly rests, continually seek the intensity and immediacy of experience. They show an individual responding to life with ferocious sensitivity and care. Avoiding what he considered to be dead forms, Lawrence approached all his writing as a fresh struggle—a struggle which necessarily could be messy. Hence his habits of revision—many of the novels appear in significantly altered forms. The direction of Lawrence's work was always likely to change in reaction to some new reading or landscape or experience. He remained a very open, extraordinarily enthusiastic writer. He also wrote willingly and with a puritan willingness to work hard. Hence the great range of his publications, from novels to poems, from philosophy to sociology, from travel writing to literary criticism, from short stories to drama.

Much of Lawrence's work, especially his early books, is set in the working-class area where he grew up, and for which he had great affection. In "Nottingham and the Mining Countryside" he writes:

> I was born nearly forty-four years ago, in Eastwood, a mining village of some three thousand souls, about eight miles from Nottingham, and one mile from the small stream, the Erewash, which divides Nottinghamshire from Derbyshire. It is a hilly country, looking west to Crich and towards Matlock, sixteen miles away, and east and northeast towards Mansfield and the Sherwood Forest district. To me it seemed, and still seems, an extremely beautiful countryside, just between the red sandstone and the oak-trees of Nottingham, and the cold limestone, the ash-trees, the stone fences of Derbyshire.
>
> (*Phoenix*, p. 133)

Lawrence's parents were dramatic opposites, a main source of later conflicts within his own personality. His father, Arthur John Lawrence, was a miner of great physique and remarkable charisma, fond of singing, dancing, and drinking. The pattern of his speech, which made its mark on Lawrence's sensibility, was a mixture of two dialects, Nottingham and Derbyshire. By contrast, his mother, Lydia Beardsall, was a refined former schoolteacher who felt herself to be a cut above the average members of the mining community. Her father had been a passionate Wesleyan preacher, and she in turn she was religiously pious and fond of books.

Lawrence was born on 11 September 1885. The family lived in Eastwood, bedeviled by uncertain financial circumstances. In order to supplement her husband's income, Lawrence's mother sold clothes from the front room of the house. Nevertheless, in pursuit of social improvement, the family changed houses in Eastwood several times, each time getting a little higher on the socio-topographical ladder. Arthur soon broke the pledge which he had made to his young wife to abstain completely from alcohol. Drink made him violent and unreliable, putting inevitable strains on the marriage. In the repeated struggles between the parents, Lawrence, the youngest of the three sons and the second youngest of the children, sided with his mother. The initial closeness to his mother explains much of his early outlook but towards the end of his life, his view of his father would soften. His father's job, which meant membership of an excitingly strange male community, left traces on him:

> This physical awareness and intimate *togetherness* [of miners] was at its strongest down pit. When the men came up into the light, they blinked. They had, in a measure, to change their flow. Nevertheless, they brought with them above ground the curious dark intimacy of the mine, the naked sort of contact, and if I think of my childhood, it is always as if there was a lustrous sort of inner darkness, like the gloss of coal, in which we moved and had our real being.
>
> *(Phoenix*, p. 136)

As a kind of revenge against her husband, Lydia set about making the boys as unlike him as possible (none of them would go down the mines). In this struggle, education was her trump card. Helped by this close supervision, her sons thrived, and Lawrence won a scholarship to the prestigious Nottingham High School. He was a pale, delicate child, given to a tubercular condition the seriousness of which he sought not to acknowledge, although it would eventually kill him. With the early death of his academically gifted brother, Ernest, Lawrence's mother poured ever more attention on her ailing youngest son. This probably saved his life—it certainly intensified the suffocating mother-love which became so central to his psychological development.

As a teenager Lawrence became close to a family known to his mother though chapel attendance. The Chambers family lived on a farm called 'the Haggs' where Lawrence, released from the ugliness of Eastwood, took great pleasure in basic rural tasks. He also met their daughter Jessie, two years younger than himself. With her he formed one of the closest emotional relationships of his life, a relationship which was also crucial to his intellectual development.

Lawrence would continue to emphasize the countryside surrounding Eastwood rather than the world of the miners' cottages. Escape into pastoral bliss was a constant motif in his fiction. As Anthony Burgess comments:

> If the unconscious plays so large a part in Lawrence's work, it may be because, in his youth, it had a physical counterpart in the coalmines. There was a parodic Dantesque triunity, with the purgatory of the dull rough town, enlivened by the howls of the drunks, the paradise of the fields and the farms, and the place where the coal came from.
>
> *(Flame into Being*, p. 15)

Lawrence became a pupil-teacher at the British School, Eastwood, in 1902, an assistant teacher in 1905, until becoming a student at Nottingham University in 1906. He did not enjoy being a teacher. He was uncomfortable with the then current methods of education, uncertain if he approved of the kind of people which they were designed to turn out. Education, and the necessity of reforming it, would remain a major theme in his work. His ideas for its reform were characteristically global—Lawrence did not believe in a static, compartmentalized regime. While working at this unhappy time, he began to write poems, trying them out on Jessie Chambers. He gained a scholarship to Nottingham University, embarking on a two-year teacher-training course there, before becoming a teacher at Davidson Road School, Croydon, in 1908. During this time, he began work on his first novel, *The White Peacock*. Under Jessie's name, he sent three poems and a short story called "Odour of Chrysanthemums" to *The English Review*, then under the enlightened editorship of Ford Madox Ford. Ford immediately recognized Lawrence's talent and from then on would prove to be a loyal patron to the younger man. Lawrence thus found himself, through Ford, with an entrée into the metropolitan centers of literary power, where his working-class presence was initially tolerated if not positively welcomed. Suspicious of being patronized by those who could never believe a miner's son would reach the artistic heights, his relationship with the artistic elite was prickly and defensive.

In the period just before *The White Peacock (1911)* was published, Lawrence's mother was dying of cancer. The £50 which he received for the book was spent (in vain) on her medical treatment. Her death in December 1910 had a convulsive effect on Lawrence's life. In an act of apparent desperation, he became engaged to a teacher friend, Louie Burrows. Around this time he also had a close emotional relationship with another Croydon teacher, Helen Corke.

The publication of *The White Peacock* began to open doors for Lawrence, and he had increasing contact with such luminaries of the literary establishment as William Butler Yeats and Ezra Pound. One of the influential figures he met in this period was Edward Garnett, editor for the publishing house of Gerald Duckworth. A regular and valued correspondent he would prove to be a loyal friend in the difficult period which was to follow. Lawrence had since 1910 been working on *The Trespasser* (1912), his second novel, and on *Sons and Lovers* (1913), his third, the most significant of his early phase. *The Trespasser* was not as well received as his first novel and has a low reputation today. *Sons and Lovers* was, however, a critical success and established Lawrence's early reputation.

Still too bound up with his mother, even after her death, Lawrence's relationship with Jessie Chambers eventually broke down. In April 1912, he met Frieda Richthofen Weekley, the wife of Ernest Weekley who had tutored Lawrence in French at Nottingham University. A German aristocrat who found her marriage stiflingly bourgeois, Frieda was 32 when she met Lawrence. The attraction between the pair was immediate and Lawrence proposed that they run off together. Running away with Lawrence meant that she had not only to give up a husband but also her three children. This was a sacrifice which she accepted but continued to find difficult, much to Lawrence's dismay. Beginning with a visit to her hometown of Metz, the couple embarked on an extensive round of travelling in France, Germany, Switzerland, Austria, and Italy. This would stimulate Lawrence's imagination and broaden his European sympathies. Lawrence was also starting to develop a new, more ambitious style, which would become evident in his fourth novel, *The Rainbow*. In 1912 he worked on the sequence of poems called *Look! We Have Come Through!* which was based on his relationship with Frieda and which was profoundly optimistic in tone. He started and then abandoned a novel on the life of Robert Burns and completed a play

called *The Widowing of Mrs. Holroyd* (1914). By March 1913 he had written much of *The Lost Girl* (1920), a novel he would not finish till long after the war, and which he left to one side in order to start work on what was called *The Sisters*. This book would eventually split into *The Rainbow* (1915) and *Women in Love* (1920). He also wrote a preface for *Sons and Lovers*, which although not intended for publication put forward his developing philosophy on what for him was the central problem of modern life: the relations between the sexes. As Frank Kermode has written of the preface:

> The important idea that the regeneration of the race and the individual must come from the liberation of marriage from the Mother, from the cultural and material aspirations of 'good' women, from all that makes men slaves of the Word, of the head rather than the blood, is first stated here.
>
> (*Lawrence*, pp. 35–36)

As Lawrence tried to engage with the new subject matter and new styles, he and Frieda also worked toward her securing a divorce from Weekley. Around this time, Lawrence met the critic John Middleton Murry (the model for Gerald Crich in *Women in Love*) and the New Zealand short story writer Katherine Mansield. Like Lawrence and Frieda, this pair were living together and the two couples settled into an intense, stormy friendship. Murry and Mansfield would eventually be the witnesses at the Lawrences' wedding, which took place on 13 July 1914, only weeks before the outbreak of the war. Although Lawrence had helped to break one up, he valued marriage highly; *The Sisters* on which he was working had a new title: *The Wedding-Ring*. The Lawrences were now living in Buckinghamshire and he had secured an offer of £300 for his new novel. Meanwhile he was at work on his study of the poetry of Thomas Hardy.

The experience of writing the study of Thomas Hardy bred Lawrence-the-critic, and this was a period in which there was much to criticize. Lawrence often felt that the war was a threat to his sanity. He found it hard to come to terms with the fact that supposedly civilized countries has been brought to such a pass. In his novels, Lawrence's prophetic and didactic inclinations were kept in check by the dynamics of the form, the irreducible vitality of so many of the characters. But from this point on, he began to give vent to his speculative philosophical side, now sicklied over with his experience of the war.

In 1915, this reached a new stage when Lawrence met Lady Ottoline Morrell, a rich patroness of artists, who was to be aggressively depicted in *Women in Love*. Through her, he met the philosopher Bertrand Russell with whom he entered into a frenetic intellectual exchange. At the height of his darkly prophetic stage, Lawrence's letters to Russell accuse him of an ineffectual gradualism. What was needed to save England, and by extension the world, was total combustion of the social system. This, Lawrence's most utopian phase, would lead to disappointment.

The biggest setback of his writing career was to follow when *The Rainbow*, published in September 1915, was suppressed on the grounds of obscenity. Lawrence simultaneously lost faith with the England which permitted such philistinism and with the literary community which failed to support him. Neither faith would ever be fully restored. As a kind of emotional and spiritual withdrawal, which nevertheless had utopian underpinnings, Lawrence and Frieda traveled to Cornwall and settled there in a small cottage. For a while he was happy. Reverting to the rural idyll which he had found at the Haggs farm, he identified with the locals, and consolidated his vision of the Lawrentian man. The war, however, would not leave him alone. Lawrence was called in for a medical military examination which, because of the tubercular state of his lungs, he was fortunate not to pass. The assault on his dignity, which the examination represented, was too much to bear and left a permanent scar on his character. Lawrence, though, was reacting to pressures which went beyond his immediate circumstances—the examination represented intrusion by the war, the state, and the whole machinery of industrial civilization. In the end, Lawrence who had incautiously engaged in antiwar, and hence "unpatriotic," dialogue with the local population, was driven out of Cornwall. The German background of his wife had not

helped. When the poetic sequence *Look! We Have Come Through!* (1917) was published, its optimistic tone now seemed misplaced. In 1918 the Lawrences were living in Derbyshire, and he underwent a further humiliating medical examination. By the time of armistice, he was firmly resolved to leave England and hoping to go to America. To that end, he had begun to read American authors such as Nathaniel Hawthorne, Herman Melville, Edgar Allan Poe and, above all, Whitman. This immersion would result in his most satisfying critical book, *Studies in Classic American Literature* (1923).

Lawrence left England for good in 1919 (except for three brief visits). Increasingly his audience was international, especially American, and, given the generally hostile reaction he got at home, there seemed to be no reason why he should confine himself in his novels to English subjects and English treatments. He was now an international writer, a point underlined by his lifestyle. In 1919, during a stormy period of his marriage, he traveled alone to Italy and Florence. From there he moved to Rome, Capri, and ultimately to Sicily. He was working on *Aaron's Rod* (1922) and had once again started *The Lost Girl*. During 1920, he finished *The Lost Girl* and began work in the summer on *Mr. Noon*. The latter he set aside, in order to work on his American essays, until November, whereupon he seems to have started it afresh. He worked at *Mr. Noon* on and off until 1922 although he never completed it to his own satisfaction. Frieda eventually came out to rejoin him in Taormina and from there they made a brief visit to Malta. In early 1921, they traveled to Sardinia briefly, an experience which would form the basis for *Sea and Sardinia* (1921). Then Frieda returned to Germany because her mother was ill. There followed brief visits by the pair to Germany, Austria, and Capri.

Lawrence's incessant traveling revealed the explorer aspect of his personality. In thought and action, he was not content to stay still. Even though he preached and ranted, his thinking, especially in the novels and poems, was always liable to overflow his own categories, to move on. Whatever local moments of fixity and stillness can be found in his writing are crucially secondary to his instincts as an intellectual explorer. Hating the domestic English home, the Englishman's castle of popular imagination, he identified, from his earliest days, with the open countryside roamed over by the poacher with his dog. It was a philosophy of the open road which he would later see as deeply American and identify with in Whitman. After the war, Lawrence's travels had a provisional, almost random quality. He was not sure what he would do in Australia; he just felt that something would turn up. Near Thirroul, on south coast of New South Wales, he quickly wrote most of *Kangaroo* (1923). Showing his collaborative inclinations, which had been there from the first in his relationship with Jessie Chambers, he worked on revising a novel by an Australian woman M. L. Skinner, that would eventually become *The Boy in The Bush* (1924).

Tempted by the offers of Mabel Dodge Sterne (later Luhan), a wealthy American who presided over an artists colony in New Mexico, he and Frieda then sailed for America, arriving (via San Francisco) in Taos in September 1922. Living in a provisional dwelling provided by Mabel, the famous author was a magnet for visitors, a fact he found as irritating as he found the landscape magnificent. The harsh purity of the desert and the sun exactly suited his mood. He was excited too by contact with native Americans and by traces in their culture of what he regarded as the oldest religion in the world. As he wrote in his essay "New Mexico":

> In the oldest religion, everything was alive, not supernaturally but naturally alive. There were only deeper and deeper streams of life, vibrations of life more and more vast. . . .For the whole life-effort of man was to get his life into direct contact with the elemental life of the cosmos, mountain-life, cloud-life, thunder-life, air-life, earth-life, sun-life. To come into immediate *felt* contact, and so derive energy, power and a dark sort of joy. This effort into sheer naked contact, without an intermediary or mediator, is the root meaning of religion.
>
> (*Phoenix*, pp. 146–147)

Lawrence's reaction to this revelation, at once cultural and geographic, was to set it all down in a novel, *Quetzalcoatl*, which would become *The*

Plumed Serpent (1926). He wrote it after moving from Taos to Chapala, a village by a lake thirty-five miles from Guadalajara in Mexico. Altogether Lawrence had spent six months in Taos with a brief stint in Mexico City. He would spend three years in America as a whole, following up Mexico and New Mexico with visits to Los Angeles, Chicago, and New York. Much of the later time was spent without Frieda, who had departed acrimoniously to Europe, missing her children and Germany. Lawrence felt unwell without her and traveled around obsessively in an effort to distract himself. Returning to London he was reunited with Frieda but still disliked England. He arranged a dinner party at the Café Royal, where he hoped to enlist support for his wartime dream of a utopian community called "Rananim." There he assembled his artistic friends Mark Gertler, Samuel Solomonovich Koteliansky, John Middleton Murry, and Dorothy Brett. Only the last named would be persuaded to follow the Lawrences back to Taos, where Mabel Luhan, who had some designs on the author, promised to help found the community. In the end, she generously gifted her son's ranch to Lawrence and Frieda. He was happy there, engaged in his usual round of punishing rural tasks, but his health was poor. There he wrote "The Woman Who Rode Away," "St Mawr," and "The Princess." Lawrence's father died in the autumn of 1924.

The Lawrences parted company with Brett in Taos, where she was to remain for the rest of her life, whilst they returned to Kiowa Ranch (which was seventeen miles away). In order to avoid the harsh New Mexico winter, they embarked on another round of hectic travelling. By late 1925, they were back in England, where Lawrence spent a nostalgic period revisiting his childhood landscape. This was the period in which he wrote a number of essays, including "Reflections on the Death of a Porcupine," and a play called *David* (1926). They the moved on to Baden (to visit Frieda's mother) and to Spotorno near Genoa. There he was visited by his sister with whom he went traveling to Monte Carlo and with whom he revisited Capri. Lawrence and Frieda then rented a villa at Scandicci, close to Florence, which

Lawrence used as a base to travel around the Etruscan countryside. This would form the basis of his book, *Etruscan Places* (1932). After another brief return to England and Eastwood during the General Strike, he returned to Scandicci, where he began writing the very controversial *Lady Chatterley's Lover* (1928). This was also a period in which he completed a number of oil paintings. He revised *Lady Chatterley's Lover*, wrote "The Man Who Died" and some essays about the Etruscan countryside.

Lawrence's health continued to deteriorate. When *David* was put on in London in 1927 he was too ill to attend. A visit, with Aldous Huxley and his wife, at Forte dei Marmi, where Lawrence had come to swim in the sea, worsened his condition. From there, he made his way to the Austrian Tyrol and then to Irschenhausen, a small town south of Munich. Lawrence was reluctant to be treated in a sanatorium. He rewrote *Lady Chatterley's Lover* yet again and it was ready by January 1928. He moved to Switzerland for his health and began the difficult task of finding a publisher who would take his new novel. Lawrence had begun to take painting more seriously and was considering mounting an exhibition in London. After a spell in Florence he returned to Switzerland, where he made arrangements for the private distribution of his novel, which he knew would be too risqué for an English publisher, as well as writing short stories like "Blue Moccasins." Later in the summer, the Lawrences were the guests of Richard Aldington and his wife on the island of Port Cros near Toulon. Winter was spent on the mainland, where he put together a volume of short poems called *Pansies*. Action was taken against distribution of *Lady Chatterley's Lover* in Britain and America. In fact, Lawrence was being persecuted by the British state on a number of artistic fronts. British postal officials found evidence of obscenity in *Pansies*, causing it to be withdrawn and it was only reissued in a censored form. A volume reproducing Lawrence's paintings came out simultaneously with an exhibition of his work. The police seized thirteen canvasses and several copies of the book.

In the summer of 1929 Lawrence was again in Forte dei Marmi and he went to Florence in early July. In August, he visited Baden to see Frieda's elderly mother. Although closing in on death he continued to write. He produced one of his best-known poems, "Bavarian Gentians" and a pamphlet called "Pornography and Obscenity." The winter was spent at Bandol, where he wrote "A Propos of Lady Chatterley's Lover." An introduction to the writings of Frederick Carter metamorphosed into his last prose work *Apocalypse* (1931). Lawrence had been at Bandol for four months when his condition worsened. He was moved to a sanatorium at Venice, near Nice, where he died on Sunday, 2 March 1930. His ashes were buried at Taos.

NOVELS

BEGUN in 1906 and finished in 1910, Lawrence's first novel, *The White Peacock* (1911) shows flashes of originality and maturity. Like *Women in Love*, it deals with the developing relationship between two couples. In order to satisfy the taste of the Edwardian reading public, Lawrence had his characters discussing the modish authors and listening to the modish music of the day. Instead of writing about his own class, Lawrence, reflecting his mother's yearning for social elevation, sets the novel in a social class above his own. Tellingly, the narrator of the novel bears the name of Lawrence's mother: Beardsall. Nevertheless, despite the oversupply of plot and the excessive amount of subject matter, familiar themes from his later work are perceptible: relations between men and women; unusual bonds between men; the landscape of Eastwood and Haggs Farm. Lawrence shows his persistent concern for women who spoil their men with excessive love, and with sons who spoil their wives with the wrong kind of love. In the end the book is about social climbing through marriage, and the disastrous effects of Lettice Beardsall's choosing to marry an emotionally anemic man. She flirts with but ultimately rejects the right sort of man as represented by George Saxton, who instead marries the daughter of a pub landlord and declines, like Lawrence's father, into drink.

The Trespasser (1912) is based on the experiences of Helen Corke, a woman Lawrence strenuously pursued, *The Trespasser* deals with the theme of love outside marriage. It describes the relationship between a pair of musicians: Siegmund, who is married, and Helen his former pupil. The title is an emblematic pun, referring to someone who is intruding as well as someone who is sinning. Trapped in his loveless marriage, Siegmund represents natural man. Helen is a familiar type from Lawrence's work, a woman who has refined herself out of her animal nature so that she causes ruin in her wake. Siegmund gets as far as kissing her, but when he tries to go further she is horrified and repulses him. Thus spurned, he commits suicide.

The gestation of *Sons and Lovers* (1913) clearly coincides with Lawrence's decision to end his engagement to Jessie Chambers. A few weeks later, he was engaged to Louie Burrows and his mother was dead. Therefore the book emerges from an extreme life crisis in a writer who always closely wrote his life into his work. He broke off the writing of the book in order to complete *The Trespasser* and by this time he had met Frieda. It is the first book in which Lawrence directly confronts the emotional conditions of his own family, particularly the suffocating love of a mother for her son. The mother is central to the book as it begins with her marriage and it ends with her death. Paul Morel, the main character, is torn between his love for her and his more straightforward love for Miriam Leivers. Jessie Chambers was outraged by her depiction as Miriam, shown as shying away from her animal nature, too wound up and rigid to give in to the flow of life. Jessie felt that Lawrence was guilty of projecting some of his own faults on to her.

As in *The White Peacock*, Lawrence renders in precise detail the landscape of Nottinghamshire and Derbyshire, particularly the strong contrast between the colliery and the farm. A further major contrast is between Mr. and Mrs. Morel, the bullying drunken father and narrowly refined mother. The book is in two parts. The first is stylistically more conservative, in the observational mode of Edwardian novelists like Arnold Bennett. The second is more subjective, the narrator less reliable. The first part focuses on the Morel's marriage, the second on Paul's oscillating feelings toward the mother, Miriam and a married woman, Clara Dawes. The book ends with the dereliction of Paul.

Passages in *Sons and Lovers* often advance the action, while at the same time having a symbolic strength. When Mr. and Mrs. Morel fight early in the novel, the wife retreats out of the house into a psychologized moonlit scene:

> The tall white lilies were reeling in the moonlight, and the air was charged with their perfume, as with a presence. Mrs. Morel gasped slightly in fear. She touched the big, pallid flowers on their petals, then shivered. They seemed to be stretching in the moonlight. She put her hand into one white bin; the gold scarcely showed on her fingers by moonlight. She bent down to look at the bin-ful of yellow pollen: but it only appeared dusky. Then she drank a deep draught of the scent. It almost made her dizzy.
>
> (p. 34)

The passage typically renders nonhuman life in powerful, sympathetic terms. At the same time the alien presence of the lilies can be seen to symbolize the sexual organs which Mrs. Morel would repress. The lilies, against the otherwise prevalent images of coal, represent qualities like purity and promise. Lawrence is working here with a poet's full concentration within the novel's form.

THE RAINBOW *(1915)*

On 16 December 1915, Lawrence wrote in a letter to J. B. Pinker some observations on novel construction which reveal what a radical he had become as a writer:

> Tell Arnold Bennett that all rules of construction hold good only for novels which are copies of other novels. A book which is not a copy of other books has its own construction, and what he calls faults, he being an old imitator, I call characteristics.
>
> (*Letters*, p. 479)

The Rainbow is Lawrence's first very radical novel, and if it is not a complete success it at least paves the way for what many see as his best work, *Women in Love*. The two books were originally part of one, called *The Sisters*, but then they split and evolved separately. The novel is partly a response to the outbreak of war, and Lawrence hoped (in vain, as it turned out) that the war would end in the same year —1915— that the book appeared.

The book charts three generations of a family. The original Tom Brangwen is married to a Polish widow, Lydia, who has one daughter, Anna; Tom's nephew is Will who marries Anna Lensky and the young Brangwens have two children, Ursula and Gudrun. As stated earlier, the novel was once to be called *The Wedding-Ring* and marriage is the central social ritual which it celebrates. The marriage between Tom and Anna involves a man who marries into a higher social class, to an older woman with children from a previous relationship (mirroring the situation with Frieda). The central events of the story are of births and deaths, not the plot manipulations a reader in 1916 would have expected.

The Rainbow is also unusual in that it has an optimism and brightness of a kind which Lawrence never regained after the war. The title draws attention to the book's mythical layering, with its allusion to Noah's covenant with God. Unlike other of his books, this one covers several generations, following the developing fortunes of a family, allowing one character to replace another as a focus of interest. The strong quasi-religious elements in the book, indicate Lawrence's increasingly prophetic preoccupations. Though he was no longer a believer in any orthodox sense, Lawrence's religious upbringing remained as an important framework or language through which he could develop and express his ideas about how men and women should live.

These religious elements are underpinned by the way in which book's narrative alternates in an unusual way between scenes which drive the story forward and ones which have an intense ritualistic quality. While the former link the book to the style of *Sons and Lovers*, the latter have a new quality, emphasizing the barely understood cyclical patterns which cross the human generations. In an effort to explore characters at a level deeper than the externals of social conditioning,

Lawrence detaches some of the more important scenes from the day-to-day world.

Reviewing *Women in Love* (1920) in *Nation and Athenaeum* 13 August 1921 John Middleton Murry, himself loosely depicted as Gerald Crich in the book, illustrates the difficulty readers had, and have, with reconciling the Lawrentian level of reality with the world as they encounter it. Murry sees the intensely charged sexual relationships between the characters to be as alien as the life of sea creatures:

> Mr. Lawrence believes, with all his heart and soul, that he is revealing to us the profound and naked reality of life. . . .These writhings are the only real-[sic], and these convulsive raptures, these oozy beatitudes, the only end in human life.
>
> (Coombes, p. 139)

The Gerald Crich of the book, with whom Gudrun Brangwen falls in love, is the son of a mine owner, a conduit for new methods of mining as for much else that is progressive. He represents the destructive, mechanical instinct of the west, of the white, northern races and his symbol is ice. Ursula is in love (and in hate) with Rupert Birkin, a local inspector of schools, who stands in for Lawrence himself. The fluctuating relationships of these two couples propel the book. Although the setting of the book is more modern than that of *The Rainbow*, like that work the narrative is held together by emblematic scenes. The novel reflects the new progressive milieu into which the author has been drawn, and its depiction shows what a troubled relationship Lawrence had with it. We see this principally in the person of Hermione Roddice, a portrait of Lady Ottoline Morrell, and the place of Breadalby, a Midlands version of her country house Garsington. The smart, artistic set is principally seen as decadent and dissolute.

The love relationships between the characters are as exotic. Ursula strikes Birkin with a heavy paperweight of lapis lazuli out of an excess of passion which is at once love and hatred. This is but a prelude to the onset of their love affair. Lawrence often associates love with a kind of dark surrender, an experience that is sometimes prefaced by a violent submission. A further powerful relationship in the book is the one between the men. Lawrence who admired communities of maleness such as that found in his mining community, comes close to homoeroticism in his drawing of the bond between Gerald and Birkin. Birkin proposes that they swear a bond of loyalty to one another, a type of *Blutbrüderschaft* which he associates with the old German knights. This concept is startlingly extended in the chapter 'Gladiatorial', where the two men agree to wrestle each other naked. The love is not erotic, or it lies beyond the erotic, but it takes place at a deep physical level where their instincts are profoundly satisfied.

Before that, in the 'Moony' chapter, Birkin tries to attack the female principle, the moon-goddess, in a scene which teeters on the absurd, as he hurls stones at the moon's reflection in a pool. His actions are observed by Ursula. The poetic style of this passage makes it seem like a more dynamic version of Mrs. Morel among the moonlit lilies in *Sons and Lovers*:

> the moon had exploded on the water, and flying asunder in flakes of white and dangerous fire. Rapidly, like white birds, the fires all broken rose across the pond, fleeing in clamorous confusion, battling with the flock of dark waves that were forcing their way in. . .But at the centre, the heart of all, was still a vivid, incandescent quivering of a white moon not quite destroyed, a white body of fire writhing and striving and not even now broken open, not yet violated.
>
> (*Women in Love*, p. 251)

After quitting malignant England, the two couples head to the Tyrol for one of Lawrence's unexpected conclusions. Ursula and Birkin are married and relatively content, but Gerald and Gudrun are in an unstable and painful relationship. The latter is made even more unstable by the intrusion of a rival, a German Jewish artist called Loerke, who pursues Gudrun. The relationship ruptures and Gerald dies alone, an emblematic death in the snow. The story concludes tentatively with Ursula and Birkin, attempting to come to terms with the loss of Gerald and with what it will mean for their own relationship.

The Lost Girl (1920) curiously regresses to a type of realism, but then consider that Lawrence began writing it in 1913. The book offers a very detailed account of the life of a girl born into a draper's shop in a Midland town. It is a struggle for the girl, Alvina, to avoid sinking into the materialism of the society around her—this is the seducing pressure of the mechanical death impulse which Lawrence increasingly identified and feared in western civilization. The father, James Houghton, is unable to avoid the pressure—he has too much invested in the shop. Sexually, the daughter is in danger of being left behind as she approaches age thirty and is still single. Then she falls in with a group of traveling performers and this changes her life. She meets Ciccio, an Italian, who is an example of the primitive un-English male who now features so strongly in the works of the increasingly well traveled Lawrence. The book moves towards a farewell to England, again showing the influence of the Europe-hopping elopement with Frieda.

Mr. Noon, which Lawrence worked on between 1920 and 1922, splits into two parts, the first of which was published posthumously in 1934 in *A Modern Lover*. The second part of the novel was not discovered until 1972, and the two parts were not published together as a single novel until 1984. The novel begins as a satire of lower-middle class values, particularly those associated with courtship. Lawrence's narrator often harangues the reader, although the book maintains a relatively comic tone. Gilbert Noon is a teacher, skilled in mathematics and music, who courts Emmie Bostock. Sexually, the courtship goes a stage too far, offending provincial sympathies, and Emmie's father seeks revenge by forcing Noon to resign from the school. Hearing that Emmie may be pregnant Noon escapes to Germany. In the second part of the book, Noon encounters a married woman called Johanna von Habenitz, a version of Frieda, with whom, in the teeth of familial disapproval, he eventually runs off to Italy. Lawrence uses his brilliant descriptive powers to offer us a portrait of a Germany in the grip of the mechanical death impulse. The book's geographical shift reflects Lawrence's elopement with Frieda and his penchant for restarting a book by abruptly shifting the location of the action.

The ending of *The Lost Girl*, and the shifts between parts 1 and 2 of *Mr. Noon*, indicate a geographical motif in the later novels. Of these, only *Lady Chatterley's Lover* is entirely set in England, while *Kangaroo* and *The Plumed Serpent* are drawn from his experiences in Australia and Mexico respectively. Lawrence had come increasingly to see England as a used up place, succumbing utterly to the ruinous mechanical death impulse of the industrialized west.

Aaron's Rod (1922) begins in England but soon moves to Italy. As in *Women in Love* relationships between men are a significant preoccupation of the book, nonerotic but colored with an unusual degree of intensity. Such relationships are now complicated by Lawrence's apocalyptic speculations about leadership. Aaron Sisson is a Nottinghamshire miner who leaves his wife even though he knows he loves her. His marriage stands between him and freedom, which he seeks as a musician in London. The rod of the title is his flute, but is also an obvious phallic symbol. The London bohemian set, however much it advertises its progressive ideas, turns out to be rotten to the core. The other main character is Rawdon Lilly, who represents the ideal leadership qualities which Lawrence fervently sought, both in himself and in others. One contrast between Aaron and Rawdon is that the latter stays within his marriage even though it proves to be a struggle. Nevertheless, there is a damaging lack of tension in the relationship between the two principals because both of them are Lawrence, albeit with different qualities emphasized.

Unlike *The Rainbow*, say, *Aaron's Rod* contains a great deal of dialogue, because the characters, especially Lilly are vehicles for Lawrence's ideas about race, sex, the war, education, and, characteristic of this period, the need for submission to a leader. The book ends tentatively with Aaron apparently ready to submit to Lilly as a leader.

In the person of Aaron, Lawrence shows a desire for a world outside marriage, although unclear about the shape it should take. Should this new freedom be exercised in a community of males or in solitude? Lawrence feels himself to be a type of leader but it is highly unclear if he can find anyone worth leading. Such conflicts are explored yet again in *Kangaroo* in the person of Richard Lovat Somers, another thinly disguised version of the author. Somers is an aloof, sensitive visitor to Australia, often in conflict with his wife, Harriet (a stand-in for Frieda). Somers has the chance to enter into political activity, either on behalf of the semi-fascist "Digger" movement (composed of ex-servicemen returned from the war) or else, late in the novel, on behalf of the socialist movement. The Diggers are led by Ben Cooley, the "Kangaroo" of the title. Somers, however, finds it difficult to renounce his individuality and is contemptuous of many of the colonials. While these conflicts, within and without Somers, are taking place they are significantly dwarfed by Lawrence's characteristically brilliant descriptions of the landscape. At times the magnificently empty Australian "bush" is allowed to stand as a metaphor for Somers's own personality.

> It is said that man is the chief environment of man. That, for Richard, was not true of Australia. Man was there but unnoticeable. You said a few words to a neighbour or an acquaintance, but it was merely for the sake of making a sound of some sort. Just a sound. There was really nothing to be said. The vast continent is really devoid of speech.
>
> (*Kangaroo*, p. 345)

The book was written very quickly, in a six-week period. Against Lawrence's usual practice of revision, the first draft of the book became the printed version. There is often a sense of drift. In one chapter, Lawrence transcribes material he had found in a newspaper, while another chapter, 'The Nightmare,' somewhat gratuitously dwells on the humiliation of Lawrence's wartime medical examination. Somers is skeptical about his own powers of leadership, since he finds that he cannot even control his wife as he would like to. In the end he rejects Kangaroo and leaves Australia to look for another place where he inner conflicts might be resolved.

The Boy in the Bush (1924), another product of the Australian period, shows Lawrence's fondness for collaboration, a feature of his earlier relationship with Jessie Chambers. Here he rewrites a novel by an Australian nurse, Mollie Skinner. It further extends his interest in primitivism and racial theory as the hero of the book is an isolated individual who would communicate with others through the blood. The original writer knew the facts of the region of Western Australia with which it deals. Lawrence had little in common with Skinner as a writer, and it is strange that he invested so much energy in working on a character that she created, Jack Grant. The book describes the process through which Jack has been sent to Australia at age eighteen to develop his character, adapts to the countryside and becomes an Australian. Jack eventually marries Monica Ellis who is like Jessie Chambers transposed to Australia with all of Haggs Farm. Jack becomes the true Lawrentian man, in touch with his instincts, at home in the bush.

The Plumed Serpent (1926) goes further than all his other novels in systematizing his utopian religious beliefs. Here they crystallize into an actual invented religion which forcibly establishes itself in modern Mexico. The cult of the Aztec god Quetzalcoatl overthrown long ago by the Spanish Christians is to be revived. All of this is witnessed by Kate Leslie, a forty-year-old Irishwoman, who has rejected the dissolute life which she found in the United States and Europe. Kate, a version of Frieda, is a seeker after happiness, but she is also a skeptic and carries within her some of Lawrence's own doubts about his prophetic role. She meets up with two leaders of the new cult, Don Ramon and Don Cipriano. This triangular relationship is the human element of the story, which is often distractingly concerned with the mechanics of the religious system. Lawrence goes to great imaginative lengths in order to detail the liturgy and hymns of the new cult—the hymns turn out to be apocalyptic versions of the Congregationalist hymns of his youth. As with the men in *Aaron's Rod*, it is at times difficult to distinguish between the male characters, because they bear elements of his character loosely distributed, and sometimes swapped, between them.

Politically and sexually, the book is an exercise in wish-fulfillment. Kate enters a union with Don Cipriano, the general of the movement, in which she learns to forgo the pleasures of orgasm and to submit herself utterly to the glory of male potency. Lawrence's political scheme it utopian and wildly unrealistic. Other than through violence, which he lovingly describes, it is unclear what practical measures the new religion would take to establish itself. Although his powers of description and his capacity for invention are as powerful here as elsewhere, the novel lacks all sense of proportion and, unusually for Lawrence, a sense of humor. The aspects of his doctrine which are troublingly shared with fascism are most obvious here and, together with his sexual radicalism, are what led to a decline in his reputation in the years immediately after his death. Don Ramon is united with his followers at a level "deeper" than rationality, a level of blood instinct. The structure of the cult is uncompromisingly elitist—the leader is all. And the religion makes an enemy of both Christianity and democracy, which Lawrence at the time saw as corrupting forces. At the end of the book, Kate seems to be about to leave Mexico, but there is an ambiguous possibility that she may return.

Lady Chatterley's Lover (1928) exists in three different versions. The two earlier drafts have been published as *The First Lady Chatterley* and *John Thomas and Lady Jane*. His last novel is also his best known; its notoriety and the issues surrounding its publication and suppression have, to some degree, overshadowed his other work along with a proper understanding of the work's virtues. The book has no pornographic purpose. Ironically, given the hostile reception it got, that purpose was puritan. Lawrence wanted to heal the world with a new understanding of sex; only when this impulse was understood could society be improved. Lawrence considered calling the book, *Tenderness*, after the quality which he now considered essential in all human relationships. As he wrote to Lady Ottoline Morrell on 28 December 1928:

> [Y]ou mustn't think I advocate perpetual sex. Far from it. Nothing nauseates me more than promiscuous sex in and out of season. But I want, with *Lady C.*, to make an *adjustment in consciousness* to the basic physical realities.

D. H. LAWRENCE

The book is set in a ruined England in the ruined postwar time, a stark depiction consequent on Lawrence revisiting the England of his childhood. A love affair between a titled lady, Constance Chatterley, and her gamekeeper Mellors is a symbol of how this society and landscape might be renewed. Connie's husband is Sir Clifford Chatterley, crippled below the waist, a symbol of the corruption of the industrialist class. Mellors is an educated ex-serviceman who has deliberately chosen an inferior social status. Like Lawrence, he is capable of speaking in dialect, and this capacity allows an entrance point for the supposedly obscene vocabulary which got the book into so much trouble. The landscape is Lawrence's old favorite: coal mining country. The opposition to the ruined condition of the mining town is once again greenly pastoral. In this book, Lawrence, like the Joyce of *Ulysses* (with whom he was to some degree in competition) permits himself to use words which at the time were beyond the literary pale. These words have a deliberate shock value, but at the same time their use can be unintentionally comic. From the vantage point of the early twenty-first century, it is difficult to imagine the levels of prudery and euphemism prevalent in Lawrence's day. Suffice it to say, that Lawrence's extensive use of terms like "fuck" in the book now scarcely raise an eyebrow. Like Kate Leslie in *The Plumed Serpent*, Connie enters a state of sexuality which has less to do with the pleasures of orgasm than with a kind of global biological satisfaction, a purification by means of the phallus. By the end of the book the lovers have passed beyond sex to a state of tenderness, a state of balance Lawrence had always hoped to find. As he writes in "Apropos of Lady Chatterly's Lover" (1930):

> Balance up the consciousness of the act, and the act itself. Get the two in harmony. It means having a proper reverence for sex, and a proper awe of the body's strange experience. It means being able to use so-called obscene words, because these are a natural part of the mind's consciousness of the body. Obscenity only comes in when the mind despises and fears the body, and the body hates and resists the mind.
>
> (*Phoenix II*, p. 490)

SHORTER FICTION

LAWRENCE wrote numerous short stories, many of which have a high reputation, including "Odour of Chrysanthemums," "The Rocking-horse Winner," "St Mawr" and "The Man Who Died." Lawrence's short stories usually appeared in magazines and most then appeared in the collections *The Prussian Officer* (1914); *England, My England* (1922); *The Ladybird* (1923) and *The Woman Who Rode Away* (1928). The nature of the form meant that there was less room for the sermonizing which spoils parts of the novels, while still exhibiting his powers of invention and description. Lawrence's shorter fiction tends to embrace the same themes as are found in the novels, but without adding anything new. His intellectual development is mainly worked through in his novels, where each is a new departure or thought-adventure, rather than in the shorter fiction.

"St Mawr" belongs to his Mexican period and depends heavily on geographical metaphor—the English landscape unfavorably contrasted with the burnt harshness of New Mexico (and of Lawrence's own Kiowa Ranch). Renunciation is a key feature of this novella as the heroine Lou Witt gives up one way of life for another which is grander and deeper. A representative of this superior state of being is this time a horse, an animal stand-in for Lawrence's own wild and untamed qualities. As well as renouncing her former way of life, Lou must renounce her marriage.

"Odour of Chrysanthemums" uses some of the same material as Lawrence's play *The Widowing of Mrs. Holroyd*. The story was published in *The English Review* in 1911, although Lawrence later revised it. The opening paragraph which so impressed Ford Madox Ford, quietly introduces the theme of industrialism pushing the ordinary people and the natural world to one side:

> The small locomotive engine, Number 4, came clanking, stumbling down from Selston with seven full wagons. It appeared around the corner with loud threats of speed, but the colt that it startled from among the gorse, which still flickered indistinctly in the raw afternoon, out-distanced it at a canter. A woman, walking up the railway line to

Underwood, drew back into the hedge, held her basket aside, and watched the footplate of the engine advancing.

The central character, Elizabeth Bates, is effectively Lawrence's mother, a miner's wife with pretensions to gentility. Disappointed in her marriage, she is waiting for her husband to come home from the pit. Lawrence was very knowledgeable about flowers, and the chrysanthemums of the title have numerous associations. The wife associates them with disappointment in her marriage, but by the end of the story they are associated with death. This becomes clear when the absent father, instead of being discovered in the pub is found dead at the mine. The ending of the story has a ritualistic quality, as the wife washes the dead body.

"The Man Who Died" was written in two parts, in 1927 and in 1928. In it Lawrence reconfigures the story of Christ and creates a new myth. He chooses to create a Christ who is human rather than divine. The central character is not named as Christ, which is just as well, since Lawrence would probably have drawn more scandal on to himself if he had made the identification explicit. In the story Christ is awakened from the tomb by the crowing of an escaped cock, representing the awakening of the phallic consciousness. Christ comes to appreciate the Lawrentian doctrine of the present moment, of this world, against eternity. Lawrence had been influenced by his visits to Etruscan tombs and his speculations on the civilization which had produced them. Christ discovers that his desire to love everybody is in fact a fear of death; to fully enter life he must also enter death. In a typically daring move on the author's part, Christ discovers the way to achieve this is through a physical union with the Egyptian goddess Isis. The treatment is unlike the realistic style of "Odour of Chrysanthemums" indicating Lawrence's great range within the shorter genre.

POEMS

LAWRENCE'S gifts are best shown in his novels, but his poetry also has considerable strengths. His early poetry in *Love Poems and Others* (1913) and *Amores* (1916) is written under the shadow of Hardy, but his use of staccato rhythms and conversational diction, already show a modernist departure from the stultifying style of the Georgians. Nevertheless, he still used such outmoded features as dialect and ballad-rhythms. His third collection *Look! We Have Come Through!* (1917) shows a deepening of his themes and a sharpening of his sensibility, for it is here that he charts his love affair with Frieda in a poetic sequence. Even when the poems present a commonplace situation, they have an arresting imagistic sharpness as in "Gloire de Dijon:"

She spreads the bath-cloth underneath the window
And the sunbeams catch her
Glistening white on the shoulders,
While down her sides the mellow
Golden shadow glows as
She stoops to the sponge, and her swung breasts
Sway like full-blown yellow
Gloire de Dijon roses.

(*Complete Poems*, p. 217)

Lawrence's later poetry is more controlled and varied in tone and has a more noticeable metaphysical element. The line lengths are quite varied and, as in some of his prose, he makes a great deal of use of repetition. The contemplative element is particularly strong in *Pansies* (1929), *Nettles* (1930) and *Last Poems* (1932—published posthumously) where Lawrence is aware of death approaching. Probably his best collection, is *Birds, Beasts and Flowers* (1923) which shows the influence of Whitman. It features many of his best known poems including "Snake," "The Kangaroo" and "Mosquito," in which he shows his talent for observing and describing nonhuman forms of life. "Snake" shows how effectively Lawrence could match line and rhythm to the physique and actions of a beast:

He reached down from a fissure in the earth-wall in
  the gloom
And trailed his yellow-brown slackness soft-bellied
down, over the edge of the stone trough
And rested his throat upon the stone bottom,
And where the water had dripped from the tap, in a
  small clearness,
He sipped with his straight mouth,

Softly drank through his straight gums, into his slack
  long body,
Silently.

(*Complete Poems*, p. 349.)

PROSE NONFICTION AND DRAMA

LAWRENCE's other writings are extensive and valuable even if they are much less well known than his prose fiction. His sense of place and his descriptive powers are especially evident in his travel writings, in such books as *Twilight in Italy* (1916), *Sea and Sardinia* (1921), *Mornings in Mexico* (1927), and *Etruscan Places* (1932). Most of Lawrence's plays are written before 1913 and deal with scenes from the working class life which he knew, material which the theater of the day which mostly dealt with middle-class manners found difficult to assimilate. *A Collier's Friday Night*, *The Widowing of Mrs. Holroyd*, *The Merry-Go-Round*, *The Married Man*, *The Fight for Barbara* deal with the strained relationships between man and women, and like the early novels are ways of examining struggles in his private life. He wrote two later plays, one with a public, industrial theme *Touch and Go* (1918) and one with a biblical theme, *David* (1925). Lawrence's sensitivity and prickliness made it difficult for him to operate in a world like the theater where compromises with others have to be made.

Lawrence often used his literary criticism to systematize in explicit form ideas which are worked into the texture of his novels. His *Study of Thomas Hardy* (1932) focuses on the need for self-fulfillment and the symbol which he chooses to express this is the poppy. The book, as Lawrence observed, was "mostly philosophical-ish, slightly about Hardy" (*Letters*, Vol. 2, p. 292). Here Lawrence warns against the life-suppressing mechanics of civilization. In order to realize oneself fully like the poppy, we must forgo the mainly female passion for the law, and learn to let ourselves go sexually. A more significant contribution to literary criticism was his *Studies in Classic American Literature* (1923). The book examines canonical American writers in the light of the Lawrentian values of blood-consciousness and self-realization. Benjamin Franklin, Michel-Guillaume-Jean de Crèvecoeur, James Fenimore Cooper, Edgar Allan Poe, Nathaniel Hawthorne, Herman Melville and Walt Whitman are all examined with respect to how much they allow natural man to emerge. Lawrence is particularly fascinated by the savage in American literature, by its evocations of a vast wild landscape where native peoples necessarily live close to nature. This he sees as threatened by the importation of decaying European white consciousness. The high point of American literature he identifies as the work of Whitman for in that poet he finds the values of the open road, of vagrancy, of male-to-male relationships all present on a massive scale. In *Psychoanalysis and the Unconscious* (1921) and *Fantasia of the Unconscious* (1922), Lawrence examines his philosophy in the light of Freud. Against Freud, he argues for an innocent creative unconscious which is not merely a repository of sexual neuroses, although it may be contaminated later in life by our culture's false habits of sexuality. Lawrence's thinking is mainly done in occult terms, which often results in his using strange language. This book proposes an organic cosmology which links the movement of the blood with the motions of the sun and the moon. He argues that females should submit to the rule of men, so that the relation between the sexes may be restored.

In the last of his books, *Apocalypse* (1931), Lawrence extends his attack on Christianity, which together with science and rationality, has created the false consciousness of the modern world. The book developed from an introduction which Lawrence was writing to a book by the occultist Frederick Carter. He argues that the last of the biblical books was a distortion by Christian writers of a pre-existing cosmology only dimly visible in the new version. Lawrence argues that the Jewish and Christian writers distorted the preexisting beliefs of a mystery religion that was in favor of the underdog. Lawrence's vision continues to be hierarchical and anti-democratic. The main effort of the book is to make us see that we are one with the universe—that it is the here-and-now, not the hereafter, which matters.

SELECTED BIBLIOGRAPHY

I. Novels. *The White Peacock* (1911), ed. by Andrew Robertson (Cambridge and New York, 1983); *The Trespasser* (1912), ed. by Elizabeth Mansfield (Cambridge and New York, 1981); *Sons and Lovers* (1913), (Cambridge and New York, 1992); *The Rainbow* (1915), ed. by Mark Kincaid-Weekes (Cambridge and New York, 1989); *Women in Love* (1920), ed. by David Farmer et al (Cambridge and New York, 1987); *The Lost Girl* (1920), ed. by John Worthen (Cambridge and New York, 1981); *Mr. Noon*, ed. by Lindeth Vasey, (Cambridge and New York, 1984); *Aaron's Rod* (1922), ed. by Mara Kalnins (Cambridge and New York, 1988); *Kangaroo* (1923), ed. by Bruce Steele (Cambridge and New York, 1994); *The Boy in the Bush* [with M. L. Skinner] (1924), ed. by Paul Eggert (Cambridge and New York, 1990); *The Plumed Serpent* (1926), ed. by L. D. Clark (Cambridge and New York, 1987); *Lady Chatterley's Lover* (1928), ed. by Michael Squires (Cambridge and New York, 1993), see also *The First and Second Lady Chatterley Novels*, ed. by Dieter Mehl and Christa Jansohn (Cambridge and New York, 1999).

II. Short Prose Fiction, Poems, And Plays. *The Complete Short Stories* (London, 1955); *The Complete Poems of D. H. Lawrence*, ed. by Vivian De Sola Pinto and F. Warren Roberts (London, 1964); *The Complete Short Novels* (Harmondsworth, U. K., 1990); *The Plays*, ed. by Hans-Wilhelm Schwarz and John Worther (Cambridge and New York, 1999).

III. Travel Writing. *Twilight in Italy* (1916), ed. by Paul Eggert (Cambridge and New York, 1994); *Sea and Sardinia* (1921), ed. by Mara Kalnins (Cambridge and New York, 1997); *Mornings in Mexico* (1927) and *Etruscan Places* (1932), (London, 1956).

IV. Other Prose Writings. *Phoenix: The Posthumous Papers of D. H. Lawrence*, ed. by Edward D. McDonald (London and New York, 1936); *Phoenix II: Uncollected, Unpublished and Other Prose Works by D. H. Lawrence,* ed. by Warren Roberts and Harry T. Moore (London, 1968); *Psychoanalysis and the Unconscious* (1921) and *Fantasia of the Unconscious* (1922), (London, 1961); *Studies in Classic American Literature* (1923), (London and New York, 1964); *Apocalypse and the Writings on Revelation* (1931), (Harmondsworth, U. K., 1991).

V. Letters. *The Letters of D. H. Lawrence* 7 vols., ed. by James T. Boulton (Cambridge and New York, 1979–2000).

VI. Critical Studies. Catherine Carswell, *The Savage Pilgrimage; A Narrative of D. H. Lawrence* (London and New York, 1932); Graham Hough, *The Dark Sun: A Study of D. H. Lawrence* (London, 1956; New York, 1957); F. R. Leavis, *D. H. Lawrence, Novelist* (Harmondsworth, U.K., 1955; New York 1956); H. M. Daleski, *The Forked Flame: A Study of D. H. Lawrence* (Evanston, Ill., 1965); George H. Ford, *Double Measure: A Study of the Novels and Stories of D. H. Lawrence* (New York, 1965); Keith Sagar, *The Art of D. H. Lawrence* (Cambridge, 1966); Colin Clarke, *River of Dissolution: D. H. Lawrence & English Romanticism* (London and New York, 1969); Ronald P. Draper ed., *D. H. Lawrence: The Critical Heritage* (London, 1969); H. Coombes, ed., *D. H. Lawrence: A Critical Anthology* (Harmondsworth, U.K., 1973); Frank Kermode, *Lawrence* (London, 1973); Anthony Burgess, *Flame Into Being: The Life and Work of D. H. Lawrence* (London and New York, 1985); Brenda Maddox, *The Married Man: A Life of D. H. Lawrence* (London, 1994).

SIR THOMAS MALORY

(c.1410 –1471)

Scott Ashley

ALL CRITICS WHO attempt to write on the life and works of Sir Thomas Malory must face a series of severe challenges to the assumptions underlying their discipline. Questions about the connections between a work and the life of its author, about an author's intentions, and about the underlying structural patterns in a text are familiar enough and still useful today, despite changes in critical fashion and methodology. But what happens when the identity of an author is uncertain (a not uncommon occurrence in the study of medieval literature)? More specifically, what happens when the leading candidate for writing the work under discussion here—*Le Morte Darthur,* that chivalric romance of King Arthur and the Knights of the Round Table—turns out to be a serial rapist, thief, and violent criminal? Can the life usefully be related to the work then? What can we say about intention when the author often copied directly from older works in French and English, sometimes expanding, sometimes conflating, but never working within our modern notions of originality and individual authorship? This last question is made even more difficult because the printer of the *Morte Darthur,* William Caxton, altered the text as delivered to him, certainly in terms of organization, perhaps more radically still. Was Sir Thomas Malory the sole author of the *Morte Darthur,* or should we give part of the credit to Caxton, who turned the manuscript of an author dead for fourteen years into a printed book? After a century and more of serious scholarship on Malory and the *Morte Darthur,* provisional, and occasionally more substantial, answers can be given to these difficult questions. But new historical discoveries, new perspectives, and even new technologies are constantly expanding our knowledge of the knight-prisoner, Sir Thomas Malory, and his great book, challenging modern critics and readers alike to leave behind their inherited ideas of literature and biography.

THE SEARCH FOR AN AUTHOR?

THE text of the *Morte Darthur* offers little in the way of guidance as to its author. The various prayers and authorial asides (usually placed at the end of the major tales) tell us little more than that he was called Thomas Malory, that he was a knight and a prisoner when the book was being written, and that he laid down his pen for the last time in the ninth year of the reign of King Edward IV, that is sometime in 1469–1470. William Caxton's preface to his first printed edition of 1485 does not help, merely noting he set about producing the book "after a copy unto me delivered, which copy Sir Thomas Malory did take out of certain books of French and reduced it into English" (*Works,* ed. Vinaver, p. xv).

Serious research into the identity of Sir Thomas Malory began just over a century ago, with the publication by the American scholar George Lyman Kittredge of an article identifying the author with Sir Thomas Malory of Newbold Revel, a Warwickshire knight who was active in the mid-fifteenth century and died in March 1471. At almost the same time as Kittredge, an English antiquarian, A. T. Martin, proposed an alternative candidate, Thomas Malory of Papworth St. Agnes in Cambridgeshire, a member of the local gentry who died in the autumn of 1469. Kittredge's arguments found favor in scholarly circles, however, and as a result Sir Thomas Malory of Newbold Revel "has probably attracted more attention than any other member of the fifteenth-century gentry" (Carpenter, "Sir Thomas Malory and Fifteenth-Century Local Politics," p. 31). Unfortunately, this attention proved discomforting to the traditional view of the *Morte Darthur* as the epitome of chivalric values, as it rapidly became apparent to historians that Sir Thomas of Newbold Revel was a distinctly unsavory character who had been accused of rape, attempted murder, and repeated violent attacks on property and persons through the early 1450s and who spent much of that decade in prison for his crimes. No new candidate for authorship really came on the scene to help explain away this incongruity until 1966, when William Matthews of the University of California proposed that the most likely author of the *Morte Darthur* was the little-known Thomas Malory of Hutton Conyers in North Yorkshire, a younger son of a middle-ranking landowning family active from around the 1430s to the 1470s. While Matthews's views gained some supporters, his evidence for Thomas of Hutton Conyers has proved flimsy and his influence has largely been in encouraging new attacks on Sir Thomas of Newbold Revel as the author of the *Morte Darthur.* Since Matthews's book there have been three contributions of note to the debate: in 1973 Gweneth Whitteridge suggested that Sir Thomas of Newbold Revel was a different man from Sir Thomas Malory of Fenny Newbold who is referred to in court records as the notorious criminal (though in this she does seem mistaken); in 1981 Richard R. Griffiths made an interesting new case for Thomas Malory of Papworth St. Agnes as the author; then in 1993 Peter Field, one of the most knowledgeable and eminent living Malory scholars, published the most thoroughly researched and argued case yet that Sir Thomas Malory of Newbold Revel was, after all, the only possible candidate to be the author of the *Morte Darthur.* And there the questions stands. What can be made of all this?

The fact is that after a century and more of scholarly combat Sir Thomas of Newbold Revel still seems in firm command of the field, with almost all of his challengers ultimately proving to have fatal weaknesses. All of those who have championed alternative candidates have come up against the immovable rock of the *Morte Darthur* itself, which tells us that its author was a knight-prisoner when it was being written and, most probably, completed. There is no evidence

that any of the other Thomas Malorys known to fifteenth-century history were either knights or in prison. Various stories have been concocted to try and overcome this problem, including Thomas of Hutton Conyers being a prisoner of war in Gascony (in southwestern France) in 1469 or Thomas of Papworth St. Agnes being knighted by Edward IV's brother-in-law, Anthony Woodville, while escaping from the advancing forces of his great enemy Richard Neville, earl of Warwick, better known to history as Warwick "the Kingmaker." While these scenarios are of course not impossible, there is absolutely no convincing evidence that any of them actually took place.

Problems still remain with all candidates, however, including Sir Thomas of Newbold Revel, particularly over the question of how and where any Englishman got access to the books that Malory used in writing the *Morte Darthur,* many of which were exceedingly rare. Also, it must be noted that there is absolutely no real evidence that Sir Thomas of Newbold Revel was in prison at any time after 1460. The final prayer of the *Morte Darthur* has usually been read to imply that Malory was in prison in 1469–1470: "I pray you all gentlemen and gentlewomen that read this book of Arthur and his knights from the beginning to the ending, pray for me while I am in life that God send me good deliverance" (*Works,* p. 726). Perhaps the Warwickshire knight was in jail and no record has survived; or perhaps by "deliverance" Malory means deliverance from his earthly (and probably aged) body into heaven and not from prison at all.

The seemingly straightforward issue of who wrote the *Morte Darthur* turns out to be an extremely complicated one that has resulted in millions of words and many thousands of pages, the arguments and counterarguments of which cannot be adequately summarized here. Suffice it to say, at this moment in time the knight from Newbold Revel seems most likely to be the author. Moreover, this is not just a matter of better documentation. Many scholars who argued against his authorship did so because they could not stomach the idea that the preeminent English chronicler of Arthur and the Round Table, of Lancelot of the Lake and Tristram of Lyonesse, of

Galahad and the Holy Grail, could be in life a scoundrel of the first order. Even without new historical research that has illuminated our understanding of why small local landowners like Sir Thomas were driven into a life of crime and violence in mid-fifteenth century England, at the beginning of the twenty-first century we need little reminding that culture and civilization do not always go hand in hand. We have learned to understand the disjunction between the moral work of art and the possibly immoral life that produced it.

THE UNLUCKY KNIGHT: SIR THOMAS MALORY OF NEWBOLD REVEL

THE name Malory means, in Norman French, "unlucky" and, at his death, Sir Thomas Malory of Newbold Revel may well have reflected that he had experienced his fair share of the family curse, much of it of his own making. Yet, at his birth his prospects seemed good. The Malorys of Warwickshire were a branch of a family that could trace its ancestry back to the early twelfth century and which may even had fought with William the Conqueror at Hastings in 1066. Sir Thomas's ancestors had been based in Northamptonshire and Leicestershire until 1383 when Sir John Malory inherited through marriage the manor of Newbold Revel in Warwickshire and promptly moved himself and his family there. County worthies who had risen to prominence through landowning, local office holding, and aristocratic patronage, the Malorys were by the time of Thomas's birth typical of the English provincial gentry in the early fifteenth century. They married their neighbors, sought election to Parliament, acted as sheriffs and justices of the peace, and negotiated their way through the factions of the great noblemen of the day. If we had more private documents emanating from the Malorys, they might appear very similar to the Pastons, that Norfolk family whose letters give us insight into the medieval worlds of business, local politics, and gossip. Only if, as Peter Field has argued, the Sir Robert Malory who was Prior of the Hospital of St. John of Jerusalem in England from 1432 to 1440 was an uncle or near

kinsman, was the future Sir Thomas born into a family that had any claims to real national connections.

Most biographies of Sir Thomas of Newbold Revel date his birth sometime between 1390 and 1400, on the grounds that a Thomas Malory is listed as serving in the retinue of Richard Beauchamp, the earl of Warwick, in a document dating from 1415. It has proved alluring to historians and biographers to imagine Malory seeing action in the glory days of the Hundred Years War between England and France in the year King Henry V won one of the greatest English victories at Agincourt. Unfortunately, it has also proved rather difficult for partisans of the knight from Newbold Revel as the author of the *Morte Darthur,* assuming as it does that, in an age when a man was old by the age of forty, Malory began an active life of crime and adventure in his fifties and completed his great book at the age of seventy or older. Field has argued recently that this in fact a non-problem and that there is no evidence that the Thomas Malory mentioned in the Beauchamp muster role is in fact the young Malory of Newbold Revel and has suggested a more credible birth date of c.1416—a date that also fits more neatly with the first certain reference to the Warwickshire man in 1439, when he witnessed a property settlement of his cousin Sir Philip Chetwynd.

The 1440s saw Malory living the life of the provincial English gentry and following in the footsteps of his father, John (who had died in 1433–1434), dealing in land, witnessing deeds for his neighbors, and acting as a parliamentary elector for Northamptonshire (implying he was living here at this time and not in Warwickshire), before being elected to Parliament in 1445 (and perhaps again in 1449). Malory seemed to be moving up in the world: he had been knighted by late 1441; he acted on a parliamentary commission for assessing taxes in 1445 and in 1446; he had married Elizabeth Walsh by 1448 when his son and heir, Robert, was born. During this decade he was certainly being courted by Henry Beauchamp, the duke of Warwick, (an association that continued between Malory and the Beauchamp affinity after the duke's premature death in 1446) and possibly by Humphrey Stafford, the duke of Buckingham, the two premier nobles in the west Midlands and two of the most powerful men in England. The only dark cloud, but one that foreshadowed a coming storm, gathered but did not burst in the autumn of 1443, when Malory and his brother-in-law where accused of insulting, wounding, and imprisoning a man from Northamptonshire and with stealing goods worth £40 from him. The case never came to trial and drops out of the historical record; it is worthy of note however given Malory's career a decade later.

The notorious career of Sir Thomas Malory began on 4 January 1450 when he and twenty-six other armed men allegedly lay in wait for the duke of Buckingham in the Abbot's woods at Combe in Warwickshire. What provoked him to this act against a man that previously seems to have been well-disposed towards Malory is not known for certain, although the labyrinthine struggles for local power and influence between the various noble "affinities" (groups of men tied to aristocratic patrons to provide political and, if necessary, military support) provides the immediate context. By early 1450 the reign of the weak King Henry VI was sending ripples of instability coursing through the state and the country, allowing private feuds and factions to proliferate. Malory seems to have taken full advantage of the illicit opportunities offered. The charges come thick and fast: the rape of Joan Smith of Coventry in May 1450; extortion of money from monks in the same month; a second rape of Joan in August 1450 followed by the theft of goods from her husband and further extortion from locals around Newbold Revel (a spree that was just possibly interrupted by Malory's election to Parliament); the rustling of cows, calves, and sheep in June 1451; deer-stealing and destruction at the duke of Buckingham's park in July 1451; escape from prison, by swimming the moat of his jail, two days after his imprisonment by Buckingham; and the robbing of Coombe abbey of money and ornaments (twice) immediately after his daring escape. Then his luck seems to have run out, for Buckingham and the law closed in on him, and

by early 1452 at the very latest he was firmly held in Ludgate prison in London.

The next eight years of Malory's life were spent in and out of (but largely in) London's prisons, as he was moved between Ludgate, the King's Bench, the Tower, and Newgate. He was bailed out three times, all but the last with disastrous consequences. In October 1452 he was released on bail by what seems to be a group representing the power brokers of Warwickshire, but he swiftly abused their trust, since it was most probably at this time that he allegedly raided Lady Katherine Peyto's manor and stole her oxen; by the spring of 1453 the call had gone out for Malory's arrest and he was soon back in prison. He was bailed for a second time in May 1454, this time backed by the major noblemen of Warwickshire, including Buckingham, clearly in an attempt to reintegrate the wayward knight back into county society. Again, Malory rejected their conciliatory gestures, exporting his criminal dealings to Essex, where he sheltered his servant, John Allen, who had been busy stealing horses, while the two plotted to rob various innocent citizens. When the plot went wrong and Malory was captured and imprisoned in Colchester prison the bold streak he had shown in escaping from prison in 1451 surfaced again and he broke out a second time on 30 October 1454. He was not on the run for long however, and by November he was behind bars in the King's Bench prison in London.

A more determined effort to keep Malory safely locked up appears to mark the next few years. Record penalties were threatened against any jailer who allowed him to escape, and when he tried to take advantage of the general pardon issued by the Lord Protector, the duke of York, (Henry VI having descended into incapacity and madness) the court refused to recognize either the pardon or Malory's securities for bail, a sure sign that the powerful had run out of patience at last and abandoned him to his fate. He was transferred to the Tower of London and then, "for more secure custody," to Newgate jail. During all this time his case never came to trial, whether through the failings of the fifteenth century judicial system or through political machination we do not know. In any case, there were certainly some who thought it better for him to remain in prison indefinitely. For by this time the political tension in England between the weak Lancastrian government of Henry VI and his ministers and the Yorkist faction led by Richard, duke of York, his son, Edward, earl of March, and Richard Neville, earl of Warwick, had broken out into violence. In May 1455 the two sides had clashed at St. Albans, in a minor scuffle only remembered because it became known as the first battle of the Wars of the Roses. As someone who had links of patronage with York and the Neville family, and who was seen as an enemy of Buckingham (who remained loyal to Henry VI), Malory may well have been thought of as a potentially dangerous ally of the Yorkists. Apart from October 1457 when the Nevilles managed to bail him out of jail for two months, and a short spell in 1459 when he seems to have been in Warwickshire, he remained in prison probably until July 1460. In that month the Yorkist lords won a major victory over the Lancastrians at Northampton, killing Buckingham and capturing King Henry. The Tower surrendered to them, and the prisoners, including Malory, were freed. In 1462 he was fully pardoned for his crimes by the new king and his government. For in March 1461, after nine months of fighting that had seen alternate Yorkist and Lancastrian successes, the earls of March and Warwick defeated the Lancastrians at the Battle of Towton; Henry VI fled and March was crowned as the first king of the House of York, Edward IV. Unfortunately, we have no evidence to say whether Malory was involved in this most active phase of the Wars of the Roses.

The last decade of Sir Thomas's life is a curious mixture of a return to the ordinary, gaps in the record, and mysterious reversals of fortune. When Malory went back to Warwickshire after his long, enforced absence he seems to have reconnected himself to the routines of landowning society without too much trouble. We see him once again dealing in land, arranging the marriage of his eldest son, Robert, begetting another son, Nicholas, and witnessing the marriage settlements of his kinsmen and neighbors.

The only excitement may have been in 1462 when a Thomas Malory is recorded as having taken part in the expedition by Edward IV and Warwick to capture the last remaining Lancastrian castles in northern England. Matthews argued that this was more likely to have been Thomas of Hutton Conyers than his namesake of Newbold Revel; however, Field has recently vigorously restated the case for the latter on a wider study of the evidence than that undertaken by Matthews. On a balance of probabilities, it looks as if the new Yorkist government was cashing in on the favors owed by Malory of Newbold Revel.

If it is the case that he was actively engaged in Edward IV's successful northern campaign in 1462, then the last major documents to name him become all the more surprising. For in July 1468 and again in February 1470 Malory was excluded by name from the general pardon of Edward IV. Here was a man whose political sympathies (such as they were) had always seemed to veer towards the Yorkists, suddenly placed among a list of the most diehard Lancastrians. Perhaps Malory had a change of heart—Peter Field talks of "a bad conscience" (*Life and Times of Sir Thomas Malory,* p. 173)—or he may have been implicated, rightly or wrongly, in a Lancastrian plot, or been an innocent victim of the rapidly worsening relations between his patron, the earl of Warwick, and Edward IV (which would cause Edward to be toppled from his throne in 1470 and Henry VI to be momentarily restored as king). Whatever the truth may be, if we accept Sir Thomas of Newbold Revel as the author of the *Morte Darthur,* then we probably have to accept that he was imprisoned again in 1468 or 1469, probably in the Tower, even though there is no record of it. It was during this period, in "the ninth year of the reign of King Edward the Fourth" (*Works,* p. 726), that the *Morte Darthur* was written, or more likely completed—indirect testimony to the fact that Malory cannot have been kept in harsh circumstances and may even have been comfortable. He was probably freed again after the Warwick-led Lancastrian victory in October 1470 and died on 14 March 1471. Malory seems to have prospered under the short-lived Lancastrian regime, since he was buried in Greyfriars, Newgate, in London, one of the richest and most fashionable churches of the time. The very day of his death Edward IV returned to England and within two months he had killed Warwick and destroyed the hopes of the House of Lancaster. Sir Thomas Malory of Newbold Revel, the unlucky knight, had found the smallest piece of good fortune only in the hour of his end.

CAXTON'S MALORY

FOR four and half centuries after William Caxton first printed his edition of the *Morte Darthur* in 1485 very little for certain was known about the actual processes of composition of Malory's great book. Then, amazingly, in 1934 a manuscript was discovered in the library of Winchester College, now housed in the British Library. Although clearly not Malory's original (it is now thought to date to about 1480), it suggested that Caxton's printed version may well have differed significantly from what the author had written. Through a brilliant piece of scholarly detective work, helped by advances in photographic technology, Lotte Hellinga has been able to prove by analyzing tiny smudges of printer's ink on the pages of the Winchester manuscript that it was actually in Caxton's workshop from c.1480–c.1489. It may even have been there until 1498, though, surprisingly, neither Caxton nor his successor, Wynkyn de Worde, seems to have printed directly from it. Perhaps Caxton used the Winchester manuscript as a backup to the manuscript he was using for his own edition. Whatever may be the truth of this, it needs to be stressed that neither the Winchester manuscript nor Caxton's book can be said to contain the more exact version of what Malory actually wrote. There are several errors and omissions made by the two scribes of the manuscript that only a reading of Caxton can correct. In addition, the opening and closing pages of the Winchester manuscript are missing. We are always at least one remove from Sir Thomas's actual words.

In his preface Caxton had made it plain that he had divided Malory's original work into twenty-one books with each book subdivided into chapters. Comparison with the Winchester manuscript now demonstrated that the Caxton *Morte Darthur* had significant differences, especially in the Roman war section, and that several of the *explicits* (the formal endings to each section of the manuscript) naming Sir Thomas Malory, a knight-prisoner, as the author had been dropped, along with innumerable smaller changes. The looser format of the Winchester manuscript and the existence of the *explicits* led the most influential Malory scholar of the twentieth century, Eugène Vinaver, to argue that we should stop thinking of the *Morte Darthur* as a "whole book" (as the final *explicit* calls it—because of the missing leaves at the beginning and end of the manuscript we do not know if this is original or Caxton's). Instead, he argued that Malory had written eight separate Arthurian tales that had been yoked together by Caxton into a single book; he even went so far as to drop the famous title, *Morte Darthur,* from his standard editions and replace it with the more neutral and plural *Works.*

Few scholars today would take such a radical position as Vinaver. There are various examples of interconnectedness between the several parts of the book, where Malory refers forward or back to other stories, evidence that if he was not always consistent in his structuring, he at least did have an overarching vision for the work. The title, *Morte Darthur,* has also proved resilient to Vinaver's assaults, and not just because of its familiarity. The defensiveness with which Caxton introduces the title at the very end of his edition, where he admits that the book actually includes many other things than just the death of Arthur, suggests that the unsuitable title was in the manuscript he had in front of him and was not of his invention. Recently, scholars have suggested that the abbreviated version of the Roman War episode in Caxton's edition may have been taken from a revision of his original text by Malory himself and that the Winchester manuscript merely preserves the earlier version. There can be no certainty about any of these interpretations, but scholarly consensus seems to be moving toward the position that while the finding of the

Winchester manuscript has enriched and complicated our understanding of Malory's work, it has not completely overthrown it.

Yet the role of William Caxton in creating the text we know today remains important, not least because in his preface of 1485 he set out the earliest critical responses to Malory's work. The addition of that preface to nearly all modern editions of the *Morte Darthur* means that first-time readers continue to approach the book through Caxton's understanding of it. There are two major aspects to this that can prove an obstacle to those readers' full appreciation of Malory's achievement: firstly, Caxton underestimated Malory's originality as an author; secondly, he interpreted the *Morte Darthur* as an essentially moral book with a didactic purpose.

Malory must never be judged by the standards of originality we are familiar with today. In the mid-fifteenth century innovation and invention were not the prime qualities expected of an author, but rather fidelity to older, authoritative accounts and the drawing out of their true significance. To be "original" in 1470 did not mean to be new; it meant respect for, and use of, the "original" texts that had been circulating for centuries. Perhaps this distinction passed Caxton by in 1485, however, for he was keen to stress that Malory's role was *merely* as an abbreviator and translator of French Arthurian romances. This obscured the fact that Malory had indeed significantly changed the intent and character of his originals as well as introducing new episodes into the cycle, particularly the *Tale of Sir Gareth* (though some critics perceive a lost source behind this story) and the healing of Sir Urry by Lancelot in the *Tale of Sir Lancelot and Queen Guinevere.* Together with the suppression of Malory's name in the *explicits,* this may have been a deliberate ploy by Caxton to avoid mentioning the name of a notorious enemy of the House of York while a member of that dynasty still, albeit just, sat on the throne in the person of Richard III. Alternatively, it may have been part of Caxton's self-fashioning as the premier arbiter of vernacular literary taste in the 1480s: he presents himself as actively presenting, organizing, and printing the work; Malory has merely, and rather passively, "reduced" his French material into English.

Without knowing he was doing so, Caxton also set up one of the big problems for Malory scholars in the twentieth century. If the *Morte Darthur* is a book concerned with "noble acts, feats of arms of chivalry, prowess, hardiness, humanity, love, courtesy, and very gentleness" (*Works,* p. xv), then how could it have been written by Sir Thomas of Newbold Revel, a man who had signally failed to show such qualities in life? As we have seen, several scholars have sought to evade the question by denying that the Warwickshire knight was the author. Others have tried to answer it by arguing that the *Morte Darthur* is not really a noble book at all, but a violent and barbaric one in which chivalry is constantly compromised. Caxton was simply misreading his text when he recommended it to his readers on the ground that if they took the correct lessons from it "it shall bring you to good fame and renown" (*Works,* p. xv). While such stark views have not gained much general acceptance, it is undoubtedly the case that Caxton's "moral" reading downplays the darker aspects of Malory's vision. The *Morte Darthur* presents less a series of stories telling of the rewarding of the virtuous and the punishing of the sinful, as Caxton seems to suggest, than an analysis of the undermining and gradual unraveling of the chivalric ideal under the pressures of its own internal contradictions. It is not, as some have claimed, a glorious rejection of the dirty politics of mid-fifteenth century England, or a conduct book to help Caxton's "noble princes, lords and ladies, gentlemen and gentlewomen" (*Works,* p. xv) escape the moral ambiguity of their times; rather, it provides a mirror in which that ambiguity and corruption can be seen more clearly. There are many original and powerful insights in Caxton's preface, not least his recognition of the historical quality to Malory's imagination and an intuitive sense of how his early readers would respond to the book. Nevertheless, it is clear that the knight-author and the merchant-printer had very different agendas and priorities in their presentations of the stories of King Arthur and the Round Table.

SIR THOMAS MALORY

THE SOURCES OF THE MORTE DARTHUR

IF Malory had a more creative response to his sources than Caxton (and sometimes Malory himself) suggests, it is still the case that the *Morte Darthur* refers to a wide array of both English and French sources and, at times, is directly reliant upon them. Malory calls upon his "French book" consistently, both as a direct source and as an authority for his statements. While there is, and most probably never was, a single French manuscript collection from which Malory worked, painstaking scholarship has re-created something of the library he must have had access to at some point (or perhaps at different points) in his turbulent career. It is not known for certain where he found the manuscripts he used, or even what particular form those manuscripts took, so much has been lost in the intervening centuries. Yet it has been shown that he certainly knew the French romances the *Suite de Merlin,* the *Prose Lancelot, La Queste del Saint Graal,* and *La Mort le roi Artu,* all part of the so-called Vulgate Cycle of Arthurian legends dating from the first quarter of the thirteenth century. He also knew the massive *Prose Tristan,* another French romance dating from the years around 1240. These were his main sources, but Malory supplemented and, on occasion, replaced these continental works with native English Arthurian material, specifically with two poems titled the *Morte Arthure* or *Morte Arthur,* one dating from around 1390 and written using northern dialect and metrical form (alliterative meter), the other dating from about a decade later and having a more southern provenance, being in stanzaic meter. In addition, he may well have used the English *Chronicle* of John Hardyng, a historical account of the early history of Britain dating from Malory's own times. These English works were mainly used by Malory in section 2 of the *Morte Darthur,* referred to in Vinaver's edition as *The Noble Tale of King Arthur and the Emperor Lucius,* and in the final section, *The Most Piteous Tale of the Morte Arthur Saunz Guerdon.*

Malory used his sources in three main ways. Sometimes he does what Caxton claimed he was doing: he translated and abbreviated his French sources into English and his English sources from verse into prose in a literal way, sometimes word for word. But he could also use his sources merely as the starting point for his own imagination. Much of the *Morte Darthur* follows the basic outline provided by the Vulgate Cycle romances while changing the entire narrative thrust of the stories, particularly by stripping away the spiritual, supernatural, and ethical concerns of the French authors for a more plain, historical approach. Some of these changes were the result of Malory's occasionally brutal abridgement of his sources, but in many cases was clearly intentional, part of his desire to emphasize the more heroic, political, and social aspects of the Arthurian world. Finally, on more than one occasion Malory claims that he is relying on his French book when there is no evidence of any such stories in the surviving romances. When he wrote at the end of the *Tale of Sir Lancelot and Queen Guinevere* that "because I have lost the very matter of le Chevalier de Chariot I depart from the tale of Sir Lancelot" (*Works,* p. 669), it is difficult to know if Malory really had lost an existing source or whether he simply invented it to give the story he had told authority. If these various and occasionally disingenuous responses to his sources make the *Morte Darthur* look something like the first novel in the English language, it needs to be clearly stated again that Malory would not have identified with the inventive, creative, self-aware literary personality the modern novelist presents. Yet he undoubtedly would have understood the practice of Daniel Defoe and Jonathan Swift in using invented sources as the basis of their novelistic writings. Even some contemporary works, such as Umberto Eco's historical novel *The Name of the Rose,* remind us that that tradition has never died. While undeniably different from most twentieth century novels the *Morte Darthur* stands in some kind of genealogical relationship to them.

When Caxton wrote that Malory had "reduced" his French sources into English he was noting a very literal truth: the *Morte Darthur* is only a fraction of the vast length of the Vulgate Cycle and the English poems on which he drew. This can sometimes lead to narrative confusion, for Malory had a tendency to abbreviate his sources too drastically on occasion. For example, he mechanically conflated similar characters who fulfilled very different functions in the French romances, producing a narrative where "good" characters become "bad" in a matter of pages and for no apparent reason. A well-known example of this is the Lady of the Lake, the magical fairy woman who gives Arthur his sword, Excalibur, at the beginning of his reign, and to whom the sword is apparently returned by Sir Bedivere at the king's death. Yet several hundred pages before this the Lady of the Lake has been beheaded by Balin le Savage with the words, "this same lady was the untruest lady living, and by enchantment and by sorcery she hath been the destroyer of many good knights" (*Works,* p. 41). The contradictions can be resolved by turning to the French Vulgate Cycle which shows that, in fact, there were several Ladies of the Lake, some of impeccable and some of dubious virtue, and Malory has failed to differentiate between them.

Yet do we, as readers, lose something by referring all the ambiguities, mysteries, and downright strangeness in Malory to the judgment of the Vulgate Cycle, as if it were some ideal telling of the Arthurian story that the *Morte Darthur* fails to live up to? There has always been a tendency among some readers, the seeds of which were sown by Caxton himself, to see Malory as something of a literary innocent, an unsophisticated Englishman adrift among the complexities of the French books. Many years ago C. S. Lewis called Malory the last of the misunderstanders of the Arthurian tradition; but at the heart of Lewis's sense of the *Morte Darthur* was the insight that misunderstanding had been enormously productive of new interpretations, new visions. He noted the "deep suggestiveness" of Malory's treatment of Morgan le Fay and Queen Morgause, representatives of that dark family of Tintagel that entangle Arthur as their mother, Igrayne, obsessed his father, Uther Pendragon (Lewis, "The English Prose *Morte,*" in Bennett, ed., *Essays on Malory,* p. 25). What could be more mysterious and yet more apt than the king's half sister and sworn enemy, Morgan, appearing, as if from nowhere, at the last battle of the Round Table to take her brother away to Avalon?

Then Sir Bedivere took the king upon his back and so went with him to the water's side. And when they were there, even fast by the bank hoved a little barge with many fair ladies in it, and among them all was a queen, and all they had black hoods. And all they wept and shrieked when they saw King Arthur. . . . And so they set him down, and in one of their laps King Arthur laid his head. And then the queen said, "Ah, my dear brother! Why have ye tarried so long from me?"

(*Works,* p. 716)

If we are content merely to note that the *Morte Darthur* carelessly conflates two narrative traditions of Morgan, one positive, one negative, then we miss the fact that in Malory's world moral clarity is as rare as the Questing Beast pursued by King Pellinore and Sir Palomides. By thinking Malory has merely made a mistake, that this is not deliberate, then the mysterious bonds of love and hate, kinship and sexuality that bring Morgan le Fay and Arthur together throughout their lives are severed, the "deep suggestiveness" is lost.

Looked at on its own terms, as a text independent of the French romances that inspired it, Malory's work achieves a unique and disquieting effect that continues to excite the general reader while the Vulgate Cycle lies in libraries undisturbed, except by the historian and the professional critic. Because his characters never fully emerge from the half-light, are never assessed, as their French counterparts are, in the harsh glare of Christian ethics, it is not Arthur but mystery that truly rules in Malory's Camelot. He created a world in which it is perfectly possible that for reasons mere mortals cannot fathom the Lady of the Lake might well give Arthur Excalibur while also being the killer of Balin's mother, or in which Morgan le Fay seeks to both destroy and save the king. Just as in the Greek myths, in the Anglo-Saxon epic *Beowulf,* and the Icelandic sagas of the thirteenth and fourteenth centuries, the supernatural is not outside the world, but talking, walking, feuding, and feasting in the same spheres frequented by human beings. But since it is *super*-natural, we should not expect it to obey human rules. Equally, the human characters operate not within a world realistically represented but one in which that reality is heightened;

Arthur's England resembles, but most definitely is not, the kingdom ruled by Edward IV and cannot be judged as if it were. Malory may have misrepresented his French sources, but he also saw things they did not, imbuing the Arthurian stories with an uncanny, subterranean power lurking just beneath their bright, ordered surfaces.

READING THE MORTE DARTHUR

IF he is to be judged by the standards current for the last two centuries, then Malory was no historian. If, however, we are to assess the *Morte Darthur* within its own context as part of the Arthurian tradition of the European Middle Ages then his great work has some claim to be legitimately called a history. Caxton read it as such in his preface (despite some personal doubts as to the literal truth of the tales), setting Arthur alongside such undeniably real figures as Alexander the Great, Julius Caesar, Charlemagne, and Godfrey of Bouillon. But it is for its form and style rather than its degree of truthfulness that the *Morte Darthur* can most justly be classified as an historical work. For Malory was the first author since Geoffrey of Monmouth in the 1130s to attempt to give, in the space of a single book, a connected account of the birth, life, and death of King Arthur and the adventures that occurred during his reign.

The great French Arthurian authors, Chrétien de Troyes and the creators of the Vulgate Cycle, had left a series of interwoven and beautifully crafted individual works, but they had not brought them together into a single whole. The English tradition had concerned itself with episodes from the Arthurian story, either from the king's life, such as his Roman war in the alliterative *Mort Arthure,* or from the lives of his greatest knights, as in the famous fourteenth century poem, *Sir Gawain and the Green Knight.* This is, of course, to reject the weighty authority of Eugène Vinaver and accept that Malory actually did write a single *Morte Darthur* and not another collection of "works." Yet, as we have already noted, there is considerable evidence to suggest that if Malory did not quite succeed in resolving all the internal problems between the individual

parts of his book (and may never have wished to), he was working towards a unified whole. Indeed, Vinaver, a medieval French scholar before he began work on Malory, may have been influenced by the fragmentary nature of the French romances into seeing the same multiplicity at work in the *Morte Darthur.*

While the more mythicizing narrators of the Arthurian story, such as Geoffrey of Monmouth or the anonymous English *Gawain*-poet, sought to provide Arthur with a pseudo-historical ancient past—as with the story of the Trojan Brutus's journey to Britain and the founding of the royal line—Malory begins at the beginning: King Uther Pendragon's illicit tryst with Igrayne of Cornwall and the conception of Arthur. There is not even any firm sense of the century in which events start. Instead, he plunges us right into the middle of Uther's war with the duke of Tintagel and the king's sexual obsession with his enemy's wife, Igrayne. Working largely from the thirteenth century French *Suite du Merlin* and the Middle English alliterative *Morte Arthure,* Malory shows an historian's mind as he takes the reader on a rapid journey through the early days of Arthur's kingship, while laying down the foundations for future adventure and tragedy in telling of the king's incestuous fathering of Mordred with his half sister, Morgause of Orkney, and the wounding of King Pellam by Balin le Savage. In these opening pages of the *Morte Darthur,* magic coexists with the real and the everyday, public wars and conquests sit alongside personal and private concerns, and the individual is seen as part of a larger whole. Despite chronological vagueness, Malory's desire to blend all the elements of his story and his unwillingness to let the magical and spiritual dominate the quotidian and secular, results in something approaching a "total history" of an imaginary Britain in the early years of Arthur's reign.

Yet Malory also shows in these early "tales" his ability to ruthlessly alter the sources to suit his own purposes. In almost all of the English versions of the Arthurian story, from Geoffrey of Monmouth onwards, Arthur had been engaged in a European war with the Roman emperor, Lucius, when rebellion by his nephew (or illegitimate son), Mordred, forced him to return to Britain and the last apocalyptic encounter. This is the version of the story Malory would have encountered in the alliterative *Morte Arthure* which he follows very closely, except that the entire Roman campaign is dragged to the beginning of Arthur's reign, where it functions as the final stamp on his rise to power, not as a hubristic enterprise leading to ultimate catastrophe. Although debate still rages about whether the Winchester or Caxtonian versions of the Roman war are more authentically Malorian, there is no doubt that this episode unequivocally demonstrates Malory's ability to manipulate his sources in pursuit of his independent narrative aims. If Malory had the essentially secular and various sensibility of the historian, he also had the skills necessary to rework his sources and make them serve his own ends.

The first parts of the *Morte Darthur* are concerned largely, but not exclusively, with King Arthur himself. Having got the historical introductions out of the way, Malory throws himself into the adventures and characters of his favorite knights, Gareth, Tristram, and, preeminently, Lancelot. The problems of finding an exact source for *The Tale of Sir Gareth of Orkney* have already been alluded to, but we know that Malory used the Vulgate Cycle *Prose Lancelot* (severely abridged) and the French *Prose Tristan* when composing *A Noble Tale of Sir Lancelot du Lake* and *The Book of Sir Tristram de Lyonesse*. These texts allow Malory to open out his Arthurian world and the king and his court fade into the background, the focus of the narrative now being on the exploits and adventures of individual knights and the nature of their heroic virtue. The tales of Lancelot and Gareth seem particularly paired together in this glad morning of Camelot, both telling how young men leave the court to find "worship" (meaning honor or glory), a term that recurs again and again throughout the *Morte Darthur,* being one of the highest aims of earthly knights. Both undergo various adventures on an outward trajectory away from the civilized world of Arthur's court into the wilderness of forest and plain, only to complete their geographical and personal orbits by returning to fame and honor. And at the end of *The Tale of Sir Gareth of Orkney* the two knights are brought together in a smiling snapshot of chivalric harmony such as the Round Table was inaugurated to encourage: "Lord, the great cheer that Sir Lancelot made of Sir Gareth and he of him! For there was no knight that Sir Gareth loved so well as he did Sir Lancelot; and ever for the most part he would ever be in Sir Lancelot's company" (*Works*, p. 224).

Yet in a typically Malorian touch, this moment of knightly fraternity is immediately undermined by the possibility of discord, for as Gareth moves to Lancelot, so he moves away from his own eldest brother, Gawain: "he withdrew himself from his brother Sir Gawain's fellowship, for he was ever vengeable, and where he hated he would be avenged with murder; and that hated Sir Gareth" (*Works,* p. 224). With loyalty to kin, even unto the spilling of blood, one of the great binding forces in Malory's Camelot, such boldness on Gareth's part already seems to augur dissension. And, indeed, Malory may well have been able to assume that his readers know the tragic and ironic outcome of this placing of chivalric above family loyalty. For many years later it is Lancelot himself who is accidentally to kill Gareth while rescuing Queen Guinevere from being burned alive as punishment for her adultery. Gawain and his brothers demand vengeance, as is their right, and Arthur is drawn unwillingly into a war that begins the unraveling and eventual destruction of the fellowship of the Round Table. "And for Gareth," says Lancelot to Arthur and Gawain, "I loved no kinsman I had more than I loved him" (*Works,* p. 695): the irony, that neither Gareth nor Lancelot recognize, is that despite all the ideals of the Round Table, biological brotherhood always remains more powerful than chivalric brotherhood. Lancelot and Gareth may have loved each other *like* kinsmen, but because they were not kinsmen, they are naturally drawn into opposing camps in life and in death. Throughout the *Morte Darthur* older forms of social organization repeatedly break through and corrupt the new chivalric codes of conduct that Arthur has tried to impose. When infected by clannishness, knightly loyalty can turn into faction; when infused with the spirit of blood-vengeance, abstract justice can lead to blood feud. It is Malory's great grim theme: that which we think makes us civilized, and raises us above our primitive ancestors, leads only to our eventual destruction.

The issues raised in these early "tales" continue to run through the massive central section of the *Morte Darthur,* the *Book of Tristram de Lyonesse*—which in the Winchester manuscript occupies almost 200 of the surviving 480 folios—and appear in the *Tale of the Sankgrail,* the greatest of the Arthurian adventures, if not quite the climax in Malory's telling. The story of Tristram follows Malory's style of magical, or heightened, realism, with plenty of knights-errant in forest clearings, jousting, disguises, spells, and the like. It takes in a wide, almost epic, sweep, from Tristram's birth, through his illicit love with Queen Isolde of Cornwall (after their accidental drinking of a love potion) and his banishment by her husband, King Mark of Cornwall, to his lone adventures and joining of the Round Table. Looking to the future and the next "tale" of the *Morte Darthur,* the story also interweaves Lancelot's fateful wooing of Elaine of Corbin and the birth of Galahad, the perfect knight who will achieve the quest for the Holy Grail.

Yet Malory the historian and Malory the social analyst are as much in evidence as Malory the romancer. For if the story of Tristram does give the supernatural an important role, it also limits it to a handful of episodes. Instead, the motivating force behind the actions of the characters becomes personal (and often transient) allegiance, which may begin with the medieval virtues of loyalty and "worship" (as in Tristram and Mark's original relationship as subject and lord) but which degrades into hatred and envy. As in the earlier Lancelot and Gareth episodes, abstract values of fellowship or fraternity prove unable to withstand the stresses placed upon them by family-based affinities. In the story of Tristram it is once again that most clannish of all Malory's kin groups, the Orkney family led by Gawain, who scrape away the veneer from the Round Table by murdering Sir Lamorak, whose father had killed their father. While Arthur is presented by Malory as furious at such internal feuding, he

is powerless to prevent it; the king is himself bound to Gawain's clan through the female line. Malory offers a secular, historical analysis of the forces undermining Arthur's rule from within, and in doing so he also took his text into an engagement with the outside world. For as Helen Cooper has argued, "in so far as the *Morte Darthur* is a book about the state of England, the *Tristram* offers one of the closest analogies to the troubled fifteenth century. . . . [T]he Wars of the Roses were fuelled by just such local faction-fighting and private vendettas as the *Tristram* shows getting increasingly out of hand" (Archibald and Edwards, eds., *A Companion to Malory,* p. 198).

This essentially secular and historical vision is maintained in what might appear to be the most obviously spiritual part of the entire Arthurian corpus, the *Tale of the Sankgrail.* The Holy Grail, the cup or bowl used by Christ at the Last Supper and brought into England by Joseph of Arimathea, had been first introduced into the story of Arthur by Chrétien de Troyes in the twelfth century and had been gradually turned into a spiritual, otherworldly aspect of the legends in France from the early thirteenth century. Although Malory follows rather closely the French *Queste del Saint Graal,* he changes almost the whole meaning of the Grail Quest to fit it more closely with the social and cultural conditions of Lancastrian and Yorkist England.

Unlike in the French romances, Malory's quest is not one that seeks to criticize the secular ambitions of worldly chivalry by juxtaposing the tainted knight, Lancelot, with his son, the virgin knight Galahad. Malory is notably unanxious about the effects of sexuality and of the desire for "worship" among his knights. In the *Morte Darthur* the Grail quest is not really the point at which the heroes of earthly chivalry, exemplified by Lancelot, find their limitations and are surpassed by the pure, innocent knights, Galahad, Perceval, and Bors. The kind of chivalry set up by Arthur, himself a man tainted by incest and child murder, is not shown as simply inferior to a divine chivalry available only in heaven. Malory's vision is subtler, in that he is again concerned with dissecting and assessing the nature of chivalry on this earth, its contradictions and its glories. His favorite knight, Lancelot, becomes in many ways the true hero of the quest, for, despite the fact that his love for Queen Guinevere means he cannot succeed, he will never give up seeking. He may be unable and unwilling to convert his undoubted physical preeminence into a spiritual preeminence, but his persistence is nevertheless rewarded with a fleeting sight of the Grail: " 'I have seen,' said he, 'great marvels that no tongue may tell, and more than any heart can think. And had not my sin been beforetime, else I had seen much more' " (*Works,* p. 597).

Malory's interest is in how near earthly chivalry can reach spiritual perfection, not how far distant it remains. The Round Table is doomed to be broken up and is already fragmenting before the search for the Grail is even begun. The oath sworn by Gawain to begin the quest marks in Arthur's eyes the beginning of the end:

> "Alas!" said King Arthur unto Sir Gawain, "ye have nigh slain me for the vow that ye have made, for through you ye have bereft me the fairest and the truest of knighthood that ever was seen together in any realm of the world. For when they depart from hence I am sure they all shall never meet more together in this world, for they shall die many in the quest."
>
> (*Works,* p. 522)

Gawain has already amply demonstrated that knightly fellowship is a weaker force for cohesion than blood. Now he unwittingly begins the destruction of the unity of the Round Table by his desire for "worship" (the double meaning, religious and secular, is apposite in the Grail quest). But Malory's Lancelot proves that even if doomed to failure, even if exemplified by sinful human beings, the chivalric values of the Round Table are worth striving for and will be rewarded. The Grail symbolizes the apogee of Arthurian chivalry, not its ultimate failure. In the context of mid-fifteenth century England, with its political instability, treachery, and open bloodshed, this is a plea to keep faith with the forces of secular knighthood, never to forget that peace, loyalty, and unity are worthy ideals. And for Sir Thomas of Newbold Revel, knight-prisoner, it was perhaps an apology for his actions, an assertion that even sinful, criminal men could achieve redemption.

If the Grail quest marks the high-water mark of Arthur's kingdom, the flood of optimism occasioned by Lancelot's noble failure rapidly ebbs away. The final two books of the *Morte Darthur,* the *Book of Sir Lancelot and Queen Guinevere* and the *Morte Darthur* proper, follow the narrative outline provided by the French *La Mort le roi Artu* and the English stanzaic *Morte Arthur,* but Malory so consistently reshapes these sources that in practice they provide little more than starting points for his imagination. The reader is presented with a wholly Malorian picture of the destruction from within of the honorable society created by Arthur, with the final unleashing of the forces barely held in check earlier in the work. Rumbles of future disaster sound almost from the moment the remnants of the Round Table reassemble after the end of the quest for the Grail, with the return of Lancelot and Guinevere to their adulterous affair and the beginning of faction-led gossip. And it is this combination of rumor, distrust, and faction that begins to unravel not only the Arthurian fellowship, but also an entire world order.

If the adultery of Lancelot and Queen Guinevere provides the occasion for the final tragedy of the *Morte Darthur,* deep forces over which they have no control find an outlet through their behavior. Blood feud rears its ugly head almost immediately when the queen organizes a banquet for the Round Table knights at which one of the company is murdered by a poisoned apple, planted for Sir Gawain by a knight seeking to revenge his kinsman, Sir Lamorak, killed by the Orkney brothers in the *Book of Tristram de Lyonesse.* Suspicion immediately falls on the head of the queen, from both Gawain and Sir Mador de la Porte, the poisoned knight's cousin, who demands justice from the king. Arthur is forced to admit that he must be a rightful judge in the matter and is therefore compelled to condemn the queen's case to a trial by battle. She is vindicated in this by a disguised Lancelot, but the seeds have been sown. Justice is demanded in increasingly strident and bloodthirsty terms and in pursuit of private vendettas, not as the abstract resolution desired by a civilized society. Rather than rescuing Arthurian England from its own violent impulses, the rule of law becomes part of the corrosion eating away at the social fabric.

The self-destructive aspect of chivalric society finally boils to the surface when Lancelot is discovered in the queen's chamber by the Orkney brothers, led by Agravain and Mordred (in reality Arthur's son), acting as the king's close kinsmen and defenders of his honor. In the ensuing melee Agravain and twelve other Round Table knights are killed by Lancelot, and Mordred is seriously wounded. In the aftermath Arthur admits to his court the bind he is in: " 'And now it is fallen so,' said the king, 'that I may not with my worship but my queen must suffer death,' and was sore moved" (*Works,* p. 682). The commitment to "worship" pulls the king and the entire Round Table in two opposite directions. On the one hand they are sworn to act in an honorable way to each other, and to the poor and defenseless. On the other hand they are constantly forced to defend their personal "worship" when insulted by others. The system works when the threat comes from outside the inner circle of the Round Table, from foreign kings or false knights. But now, at last, the court is turned against itself, the enemy is perceived to be within Camelot, and all the latent contradictions of the honorable society are revealed. When Gareth is killed by Lancelot while attempting to rescue Guinevere from execution the Round Table splits into two warring factions, each committed to preserving their honor and maintaining justice. There is, however, no longer any consensus about what these terms might mean in an abstract or universalist sense. What Gawain believes to be just is no longer what Lancelot believes to be just; the social values of the Round Table have become labels to legitimate the private desires of its individual members.

Some kind of resolution to this civil war is achieved when a new and greater threat to the very survival of Arthur's kingdom is announced. Mordred has seized the queen and the kingdom and has made himself ruler of England. Abandoning the war against Lancelot in France, the king and Gawain return home to meet Mordred in a series of apocalyptic battles, at which the last tattered remnants of the Round Table are destroyed. A kind of cyclical closure is achieved: Arthur kills Mordred but is himself mortally wounded, ending the rhythm of illicit reproduction that has haunted the *Morte Darthur* from its opening pages; Excalibur is returned to the lake from which it came; and the king disappears with Morgan le Fay into a magical haze of uncertainty and mystery analogous to that from which he first emerged. The kingship is passed on to Constantine of Cornwall, but it is a kingship without a future, and therefore without a history, symbolized by the retreat of Lancelot and Guinevere into the celibate worlds of the hermitage and nunnery and by the abandonment of England for the Holy Land by the remaining knights of Lancelot's kin. The gilded bubble of Arthur's kingdom, seemingly existing outside real historical forces, poverty, plagues, taxes, and the quotidian necessities of living, has been punctured. The chivalric dream of a world of endless tournaments, questing, feasting, and courtly love is exposed as no more than a pretence when the real world finally breaks in. As he lies dying on the battlefield Arthur hears the crying of many people in the darkness. The king sends the mortally wounded Sir Lucan to investigate:

> And so as he yode, he saw and hearkened by the moonlight how that pillagers and robbers were come into the field to pillage and to rob many a full noble knight of brooches and bees and of many a good ring and many a rich jewel. And who that were not dead all out, there they slew them for their harness and their riches.
>
> (*Works,* p. 714)

The people may finish the honorable society off, but Malory shows us how, in their heartlessness, their selfishness, their love of personal gain, they were only emulating their self-styled betters.

CONCLUSION

WE began this essay by asking how Sir Thomas Malory of Newbold Revel could be related to Sir Thomas Malory, author of the *Morte Darthur.* If his great book now looks less like a chivalric romance—clean, heroic, and virtuous—and more like a pessimistic analysis of a flawed and contradictory society, then we do indeed have a point of contact between the man and his work. Not perhaps on a personal or psychological level, but in his relationship with the context of mid-fifteenth century English political life, Sir Thomas of Newbold Revel can be glimpsed lurking behind his stories. Maurice Keen has pointed out the very same irony built into late Lancastrian England as Malory had explored in the *Morte Darthur:* "The social threat came rather from the violence of the least deprived sectors of society, lords, landowners and gentlemen; that is to say, ironically, from those with whom the principal responsibility for law enforcement and the maintenance of order locally lay" (Keen, *English Society in the Later Middle Ages,* p. 189). The men expected to uphold the civilized values of loyalty, justice, and chivalry, whether they be Sir Thomas or Sir Gawain, were those doing the most to undermine them.

In the context of an England in the midst of the Wars of the Roses there is no paradox in Sir Thomas of Newbold Revel being the author of the *Morte Darthur.* One of the reasons the book is worth reading is that Malory faithfully analyzes those treacherous and violent years, while simultaneously, like Lancelot in the Grail quest, hoping and longing to catch even a fleeting glimpse of a better world. As Queen Guinevere is put on trial as an unwitting participant in the long simmering blood feud between the families of Orkney and King Pellinore, Malory notes, "such custom was used in those days, for favour, love, nor affinity there should be none other but righteous judgement" (*Works,* p. 618). Idealistic indeed, yet it is precisely because the Orkney affinity is so strong and so close to the king himself that justice is enacted the way it is. And, almost at the end of the *Morte Darthur,* as the opposing armies of Arthur and Mordred close in on each other, Malory gives a much-quoted criticism of contemporary society:

Lo ye all Englishmen, see ye not what a mischief here was? For he that was the most kind and noblest knight of the world, and most loved the fellowship of noble knights, and by him they all were upheld, and yet might not these Englishmen hold them content with him. Lo thus was the old custom and usages of this land, and men say that we of this land have not yet lost that custom. Alas! this is a great default of us Englishmen, for there may nothing us please no term.

(*Works,* p. 708)

If this is a sign that towards the end of his life Malory began to doubt his earlier allegiance to the House of York and began to see the deposition of Henry VI as a betrayal of the rightful king, it is an interpretation perhaps inspired by his writing of the *Morte Darthur.* In one of the most moving speeches in the entire book, the dying Arthur looks out over the battlefield, his gaze finding only two of the Round Table left alive: " 'Jesu Mercy!' said the king, 'where are all my noble knights become?' " (*Works,* p. 713). Within the reality of the story they are, of course, all dead; in the reality of fifteenth-century England they have realized that being a noble knight has become meaningless. They either have taken up a more selfish code of conduct, or spend their time wondering where it all went wrong. Or in the case of Sir Thomas Malory of Newbold Revel, both.

SELECTED BIBLIOGRAPHY

I. Manuscript And First Edition Facsimiles. *The Winchester Malory: A Facsimile,* ed. N. R. Ker, (London, 1976); *Le Morte Darthur: Printed by William Caxton, 1485,* intro. Paul Needham (London, 1976); *Caxton's Malory: A New Edition of Sir Thomas Malory's "Le Morte Darthur" Based on the Pierpont Morgan Copy of William Caxton's Edition of 1485,* ed. James W. Spisak (Berkeley, 1985).

II. Collected Works. *The Works of Sir Thomas Malory,* 3d ed., 3 vols., ed. by Eugène Vinaver, rev. by P. J. C. Field (Oxford, 1990).

III. Selected And Moder-Spelling Editiions. *The Morte Darthur: Parts Seven and Eight,* ed. D. S. Brewer (London, 1968); *Le Morte D'Arthur,* ed. Janet Cowan, intro. John Lawlor, 2 vols. (Harmondsworth, U.K., 1969); *The Morte Darthur: The Seventh and Eighth Tales,* ed. P. J. C. Field (London, 1978); *Le Morte D'Arthur: The Winchester Manuscript,* ed. Helen Cooper (Oxford, 1998).

IV. BIBLIOGRAPHY AND REFERENCE. Tomomi Kato, ed., *A Concordance to the Works of Sir Thomas Malory* (Tokyo, 1974); Bert Dillon, *A Malory Handbook* (London, 1978); Page West Life, *Sir Thomas Malory and the "Morte Darthur": A Survey of Scholarship and Annotated Bibliography* (Charlottesville, N.C., 1980).

V. Biographical Studies. Edward Hicks, *Sir Thomas Malory: His Turbulent Career* (Cambridge, Mass, 1928); A. C. Baugh, "Documenting Sir Thomas Malory," in *Speculum* 8 (1933); William Matthews, *The Ill-framed Knight: A Skeptical Enquiry into the Identity of Sir Thomas Malory* (Berkeley, 1966); Gweneth Whitteridge, "The Identity of Sir Thomas Malory, Knight-Prisoner," in *Review of English Studies,* new series, 24 (1973); Christine Carpenter, "Sir Thomas Malory and Fifteenth-Century Local Politics," in *Bulletin of the Institute of Historical Research* 53 (1980); Richard R. Griffiths, "The Authorship Question Reconsidered: A Case for Thomas Malory of Papworth St. Agnes, Cambridgeshire," in Takamiya and Brewer, eds., *Aspects of Malory* (Cambridge, U.K., 1981); P. J. C. Field, *The Life and Times of Sir Thomas Malory* (Cambridge, 1993).

VI. Critical Studies. Eugène Vinaver, *Malory* (Oxford, 1929); Roger Sherman Loomis, ed., *Arthurian Literature in the Middle Ages* (Oxford, 1959).

J. A. W. Bennett, ed., *Essays on Malory* (Oxford, 1963); R. M. Lumiansky, ed., *Malory's Originality: The Unity of Malory's "Morte Darthur"* (Univ. of Kentucky, 1965); Charles Moorman, *The Book of Kyng Arthur: The Unity of Malory's "Morte Darthur"* (Lexington, 1965); Edmund Reiss, *Sir Thomas Malory* (New York, 1966); Stephen Knight, *The Structure of Sir Thomas Malory's Arthuriad* (Sydney, 1969).

P. J. C. Field, *Romance and Chronicle: A Study of Malory's Prose Style* (London, 1971); Elizabeth T. Pochada, *Arthurian Propaganda: "Le Morte Darthur" as an Historical Ideal of Life* (Chapel Hill, 1971); R. R. Griffith, "The Political Bias of Malory's *Morte Darthur,*" in *Viator* 5 (1974); Mark Lambert, *Malory: Style and Vision in "Le Morte Darthur"* (New Haven, 1975); Larry D. Benson, *Malory's "Morte Darthur"* (Cambridge, Mass, 1976).

Toshiyuki Takamiya and Derek Brewer, eds., *Aspects of Malory* (Cambridge, 1981); Muriel Whitaker, *Arthur's Kingdom of Adventure: The World of Malory's "Morte Darthur"* (Cambridge, 1984); James W. Spisak, ed., *Studies in Malory* (Kalamazoo, Mich., 1985); R. M. Lumiansky, "Sir Thomas Malory's *Le Morte Darthur,* 1947–1987: Author, Title, Text," in *Speculum* 62 (1987); Felicity Riddy, *Sir Thomas Malory* (Leiden, 1987); Marylyn Jackson Parins, ed., *Malory: The Critical Heritage* (London, 1988).

Terence McCarthy, *Reading the "Morte Darthur"* (Cambridge, 1988), repr. as *An Introduction to Malory* (Cambridge, 1991); Jill Mann, *The Narrative of Distance, the Distance of Narrative in Malory's "Morte Darthur"* (London, 1991); Elizabeth Archibald and A. S. G. Edwards, eds., *A Companion to Malory* (Cambridge, 1996); P. J. C. Field, *Malory: Texts and Sources* (Cambridge, 1998). D. Thomas Hanks, Jr., and Jessica Gentry Brogdon, eds., *The Social and Literary Contexts of Malory's "Morte Darthur"* (Cambridge, U.K., 2000); Catherine Batt, *Malory's "Morte Darthur": Remaking Arthurian Tradition* (Basingstoke, U.K., 2001).

VII. Further Reading: Introductory Surveys. J. A. Burrow, *Medieval Writers and Their Work: Middle English Literature and Its Background, 1100–1500* (Oxford, 1982); Derek Brewer, *English Gothic Literature* (London, 1983); Boris Ford, ed., *Medieval Literature, Part One: Chaucer and the Alliterative Tradition* (Harmondsworth, U. K., 1983); David Wallace, ed., *Cambridge History of Medieval English Literature* (Cambridge, U.K., 1999).

Historical Context. H. S. Bennett, *The Pastons and Their England* (Cambridge, U.K., 1922); R. L. Storey, *The End of the House of Lancaster* (London, 1966); N. F. Blake, *Caxton and His World* (London, 1969); J. R. Lander, *Conflict and Stability in Fifteenth-Century England* (London, 1969); Charles Ross, *Edward IV* (London, 1974); N. F. Blake, *Caxton: England's First Publisher* (London, 1976); George D. Painter, *William Caxton: A Quincentenary Biography of England's First Printer* (London, 1976); Charles Ross, *The Wars of the Roses* (London, 1976); Anthony Goodman, *The Wars of the Roses: Military Activity and English Society, 1452–1497* (London, 1981); Ralph A. Griffiths, *The Reign of Henry VI: The Exercise of Royal Authority, 1422–1461* (London, 1981); K. B. McFarlane, *England in the Fifteenth Century,* intro. by G. L. Harriss (1981); Bertram Wolffe, *Henry VI* (London, 1981); Norman Davis, ed., *The Paston Letters: A Selection in Modern Spelling,* 2d ed. (Oxford, 1983); Maurice Keen, *Chivalry* (New Haven, 1984); Maurice Keen, *English Society in the Later Middle Ages, 1348–1500* (Harmondsworth, U.K., 1990); Christine Carpenter, *Locality and Polity: A Study of Warwickshire Landed Society, 1401–1499* (Cambridge, U.K., 1992); Rosemary Horrox, ed., *Fifteenth-Century Attitudes: Perceptions of Society in Late Medieval England* (Cambridge, U.K., 1994); Christine Carpenter, *The Wars of the Roses: Politics and the Constitution in England, c.1437–1509* (Cambridge, U.K., 1997).

ANDREW MARVELL

(1621–1678)

Sandie Byrne

THE TITLE OF Pierre Legouis's scholarly 1928 study—*Andrew Marvell: "Poet, Puritan, Patriot"*—is made all the more apt on the title page of its revised and translated 1965 edition by the typographer's decision to separate the subtitle's three terms not with commas but with full points. Writers have found endless fascination in pondering the ways in which the roles these terms refer to may have intersected, interacted, and conflicted in Marvell's life, and the ways in which we construct, and rank, the personae from readings of the poems and prose. It is difficult to obtain a whole and coherent view from this distance in time—and the facts about his life that are known make the many uncertainties even more provoking. However, the fascination with Marvell's complex character continues. The works of Marvell's that are most admired today are the poems that exhibit wit and urbanity, while also presenting serious matters and complex ideas. We should not overlook his prose, however, nor attempt to divide the political writing from the rest or the poet from the politician and patriot. Marvell was an orator or rhetorician in the Classical style. Like Cicero, he saw his role as that of public legislator and defender of civil liberties, a mediator between the intellectual and individual life and the life of the state.

Very few anthologies of the major English poets have been without examples of Marvell's work, and his *carpe diem* ("seize the day") poem "To His Coy Mistress" is one of the best known in the language, but his reputation has undergone dramatic alteration over the years. To his contemporaries he was known as a satirist, scholar, traveler, linguist, anti-clericalist, anti-Catholic, and outspoken opponent of arbitrary government. During his lifetime, Marvell's fame was based largely on prose and lampoon, and on several poems written in an official or semi-official capacity. Few would have read his lyric poems, which were unpublished until after his death, when his housekeeper, Mary Palmer, claiming to have married the poet secretly in 1667, took his papers to a bookseller.

During the eighteenth century there was considerable interest in Marvell, but he was venerated as a forefather of the Whig movement rather than as a poet. His poems were republished only twice during the century, in editions by Thomas Cooke in 1726 and by Edward Thompson in 1776, the latter also including several poems published from papers found in Marvell's rooms and attributed to him, but probably copies of other poets' work. The favored subject for poetry by then had become the public rather than the personal life; its predominant tone was confident and didactic, rather than complex and polyvalent. Marvell, of course, wrote on topics both private and public, but the Metaphysical mode, centered on the conceit, was out of fashion; Dr. Johnson's "Life of Cowley," in his *Lives of the English Poets* (1779–1781), had disparaged it as primarily designed to show off the poets' learning.

During the early nineteenth century the greater part of Marvell's work was neglected; only a few of the poems (primarily "An Horatian Ode," "The Garden" and "Bermudas," and "The Nymph Complaining for the Death of her Faun") were anthologized, but he was known to Romantic essayists such as Charles Lamb and William Hazlitt and the poets Leigh Hunt and John Clare. The rehabilitation had begun, however. A short critical biography appeared in the *Retrospective View* (1824–1825) and was followed in 1832 by two lives, by John Dove and Hartley Coleridge (son of the poet Samuel Taylor Coleridge). The admiration of critics and poets in the Victorian period (Alfred, Lord Tennyson admired "To His

Coy Mistress" and Gerard Manley Hopkins considered Marvell to be "a most rich and nervous poet") created a demand for an accessible edition that was fulfilled by Alexander Grosart in 1872. Edmund Gosse recognized Marvell's Metaphysical quality, bracketing him with "the school of Donne," and one of the most important critical analyses of the nineteenth century was E. K. Chambers's, which asserted that the conceit, central to Marvell's art, was "of the very essence of poetic imagination." By the end of the century, Marvell was established in the canon of English poetry, but almost exclusively as a pastoral and lyric poet, an inversion of the former bias.

In the twentieth century, the stock of Marvell and the Metaphysicals soared after four scholars laid the foundations for future critical study of Marvell's writing. Sir Herbert Grierson's *Metaphysical Poetry: Donne to Butler* (1921) established Marvell as both a Metaphysical and a major poet; T. S. Eliot's *Times Literary Supplement* article (31 March 1921) and his essay "The Metaphysical Poets" of a year later provided an endorsement of lasting influence; H. M. Margoliouth's two-volume *Poems and Letters* of 1927 made the poet's often guarded, but fascinating, correspondence more widely available; and Pierre Legouis's *Andre Marvell: poète, puritain, patriote* supplied the first important full-scale critical study. Much important Marvell scholarship was produced between the tercentenaries of his birth (celebrated by T. S. Eliot's *TLS* piece and, in Hull, by the painting of the city trams in Marvellian livery) and of his death (marked in 1978 by an exhibition at the British Library in London and the publication of a collection of essays edited by C. A. Patrides, *Approaches to Marvell: The York Tercentenary Lectures*). Since then, growing interest in the relationship between the complex society and art of the seventeenth century has generated a range of studies that locate Marvell in his political, cultural, and literary contexts. The twenty-first-century reader can approach Marvell's writing with the benefit of both contextual and close textual analyses by leading critics such as John Carey, David Norbrook, and Thomas Healy.

LIFE

ANDREW Marvell's father was born in the village of Meldreth in Cambridgeshire, c.1586, and after education at Cambridge University took orders and became a curate at Flamborough, in Yorkshire. He was presented with the living of Winestead in Holderness, a large peninsula in the East Riding of Yorkshire. There his wife, Anne Pease, gave birth to five children, including Andrew, the fourth child and only surviving son, who was born on 31 March 1621. In 1624 the family moved to the city of Hull, where the Reverend Andrew Marvell had been appointed lecturer (assistant preacher) at Holy Trinity Church and Master of the Charterhouse (an almshouse). Andrew Marvell Jr., attended Hull Grammar School, where he studied Latin, Greek, and Hebrew, and became steeped in the Bible and Anglican doctrine. The Reverend Andrew Marvell had attended Emmanuel, the most Puritan of the Cambridge colleges, but he sent his son to the more moderate, middle-of-the road Trinity College. Andrew Marvell Jr., matriculated at the age of twelve, in 1633, and in 1638 was elected to a scholarship. Cambridge at the time was staunchly Protestant, but there were increasing influences from Platonism and Latitudinarianism and, it seems, an underground network of Jesuits (priests of the Catholic Society of Jesus). According to his first editor, Marvell was converted by the Jesuits to the old faith and ran away from Cambridge but was found by his father in a London bookseller's. He was prevailed upon to return to college, but may have missed some months of study, since he supplicated for his B.A. degree later than was customary, in 1639. The story may be apocryphal, but to this assumed "brainwashing" episode has been attributed Marvell's implacable and virulent anti-Catholicism, which to a modern reader seems incongruous in a man of an otherwise liberal and tolerant nature.

We know little of Marvell's life at Cambridge, but we do have the verses in Latin and Greek which he contributed to one of the collections traditionally presented by the universities on the occasion of royal births, marriages, and other occasions, in this case the birth of the fifth child of

King Charles and his Queen, Princess Anne, in 1637. The following year, the poet's mother, Anne Marvell, died and her husband remarried seven months later. In 1640 the Reverend Andrew Marvell was drowned whilst crossing the Humber River, soon after which his son left Cambridge without completing his M.A., perhaps from lack of funds, perhaps to pursue larger ambitions. His activities between 1642 and 1647 are unclear, but when in 1653 John Milton recommended Marvell as qualified for the post of Assistant Latin Secretary, it was on the basis of his language skills gained, Milton's letter suggests, from four years spent in Holland, France, Italy, and Spain. Whether Marvell was making the Grand Tour, or acting as a tutor, or on business for one of his brothers-in-law is unclear, but for whatever reason, it is likely that while the Civil War raged Marvell wandered Europe. After the Restoration, he was to declare that "the Cause was too good to have been fought for" (*The Rehearsal Transpros'd and the Rehearsal Transpros'd: The Second Part,* ed. D. I. B. Smith, 1971, p. 135), and to insist (not entirely truthfully) that he "never had any, not the remotest relation to publick matters, nor correspondence with the persons then predominant, until the year 1657" (p. 203). He certainly reached Rome, probably in 1646, and met there the English priest and poetaster Richard Flecknoe, the subject of one of his earliest English verses, a deft and sophisticated satire. Marvell returned to an England about to be plunged into the second phase of the Civil War. Charles I had escaped from Hampton Court, where he had been kept as the puppet head of a luxurious court, to Carisbrooke Castle on the Isle of Wight. His capture, arrest, and trial were imminent, and he was to be executed on 30 January 1649.

Having disposed of the small estate he had inherited in Cambridgeshire, Marvell settled in fashionable, Cavalier circles in London, and composed at least two verses in memory of men with Royalist sympathies, Richard Lovelace and Henry, Lord Hastings, son of the earl of Huntingdon. "To his Noble Friend Mr Richard Lovelace, upon his Poems," was affixed to Lovelace's collection *Lucasta* (1649), and "Upon the Death of

the Lord Hastings" was thought worthy of inclusion in *Lacrymae Musarum* (1649) together with verses by the established poets John Denham, John Dryden, and Robert Herrick. Though he was moving among Royalist sympathizers, these are tributes to individuals rather than expressions of a generalized sympathy for the Royalist cause. The poem to Lovelace is a respectful panegyric to the Cavalier poet and an attack on the censorship by the Presbyterian element in Parliament that was silencing his fellow poets' right to objectivity. The politics of the time were complex and ambivalent; it was perfectly possible to be a monarchist yet deplore tyranny, or to acknowledge the justness of the Parliamentarian cause whilst deploring its methods and some of its adherents. Marvell's more famous poem of the following year, "An Horation Ode upon Cromwell's Return from Ireland" (1650), displays a political stance of moderate Parliamentarianism, yet may not represent an about-face.

Shortly after writing "An Horatian Ode," Marvell joined the service of the man whom Cromwell had replaced as commander-in-chief of the Parliamentary armies, General Fairfax. Thomas, third baron Fairfax of Cameron (a Scottish title), came from an old Yorkshire family to whose estates he returned when, disapproving of the coming war against the Scots, he resigned his commission in 1650. He was a cultured man, and when ill health forced him to give up hunting, he turned to his collections, his writing, and his library. Marvell was appointed language tutor to the Fairfaxes' only child, Mary, then twelve years old. He remained with the household until the end of 1652, his only prolonged sojourn in rural surroundings since his infancy. We do not know the exact dates of composition of any of Marvell's work, but it is assumed that in the grounds of the Fairfax houses of York, Denton, Bilborough, and Nun Appleton, Marvell found the inspiration for some of his best-known poems, such as "The Garden," "Upon Nun Appleton House," and "The Mower."

The poems that bracket Marvell's rural retreat seem contradictory on a first reading. If "An Horatian Ode" expresses a modified Parliamentarianism, then "Tom May's Death" appears to express a modified Royalism. Thomas May, playwright, translator, and court poet to Charles I, changed sides to become the historian of the Long Parliament (which inaugurated moves against the despotism of Charles I). When he died in November 1650, May was satirized by Marvell (possibly unfairly) as a drunken mercenary. Yet three months later, a Latin poem praises one of the most hated Parliamentarians, Oliver St. John, Chief Justice of the Common Pleas, and the next English poem, "The Character of Holland," is surprisingly belligerent; endorsing the Commonwealth policy of waging war against its fellow Republic, where many exiled Royalists had found refuge. Perhaps Marvell swayed towards the Royalist cause but was reconverted to the Commonwealth just as he had (allegedly) swayed towards Catholicism but returned to Protestantism; more likely, he was a consistent opponent of tyranny in all its forms, and though not blind to the brutal consequences of Cromwell's policies, saw him as the strong leader England required. David Norbrook, in *Writing the English Republic: Poetry, Rhetoric, and Politics 1627–1660* (1999), finds Marvell's poetry inconsistent, but argues that his changes in ideology do not represent his "real," private, versus assumed, "public," opinions. Norbrook sees Marvell as trying out different voices, keeping his options open, and while responding to the republicanism of respected friends such as Milton, also remaining engaged with the courtly (pp. 244–245).While Marvell's writings may be full of ambiguities, he ultimately became firmly aligned to Cromwell's Protectorate. He may have wavered in 1647–1648 between the dynamism of the party of energy, modernity, and change ("forwardness") and the languid ornamental beauty of Cavaliers like Villiers, with their connections to England's ancient rights and the monarchy, but in the end he chose "forward youth."

That Marvell's allegiance to the Parliamentary cause was genuine, if not unalloyed, is suggested by the testimonial provided for him by John Milton. Milton's failing eyesight made his duties as Latin Secretary difficult, and he wrote to Bradshaw, the president of the Council of State, recommending Marvell as a suitable assistant. Soon after, the Council of State was dissolved and civil power was invested in Cromwell, so Marvell did not obtain the post; however he did meet Cromwell at about this time, and was appointed by him as tutor to a protégé of Cromwell's, William Dutton. (Dutton was lodged in the Eton household of the Puritan John Oxenbridge, a governor of the Bermudas, who may have been a source of the detail in Marvell's poem "Bermudas.") Other poems from this time support Cromwell's home and foreign policies, and Marvell celebrated the first anniversary of Cromwell's election to the Protectorate on 16 December 1654 with a long poem, "The First Anniversary of the Government under O. C." (published 1655). In 1656 Marvell and his pupil spent several months in Saumur, in the Loire district of France, but were back in England before September 1657, when Marvell at last obtained the post of Assistant Latin Secretary, under John Thurloe and Milton, with a salary of £200 per annum. This, Marvell's first public office, was roughly equivalent to the post of translator in the civil service, since Latin was the language of diplomacy, and Marvell would have been required to draft and translate documents relating to affairs of state.

The tutorship had brought Marvell closer to Cromwell, since William Dutton was not only Cromwell's protégé (and eventually his ward) but also promised in marriage to the Protector's youngest daughter (though the marriage never took place). The Latin Secretaryship, while not an executive position, gave Marvell numerous opportunities to see how the machinery of government, and the Protector, worked. Marvell seems to have become genuinely attached to Cromwell. He composed a number of poems celebrating marriage and other events in the family and on Cromwell's death the following year (1658), took part in the funeral procession and wrote one of the most personal of his "official" poems, "Upon the Death of His Late Highness the Lord Protector."

Marvell continued to serve as Latin Secretary during the government of Cromwell's son Richard and for a short time after it, but seems to have decided to exchange civil service for a parliamentary career. In 1659 he became the Member of Parliament for Hull, which position he retained—after an early hiatus—through three Parliaments until his death. Although there were occasional complaints of his absence from the House of Commons, and a belligerent episode with Thomas Clifford in 1662 that nearly resulted in Marvell's expulsion, Marvell was an active M.P., sitting on a number of committees during Richard Cromwell's Parliament and the "Convention" Parliament that followed. His was the lone voice raised in opposition to the renewal of the Conventicles Act that prevented Nonconformists from holding religious meetings.

The Restoration of 1660 left Marvell relatively unscathed, but the life of his friend and mentor Milton was in danger. Marvell intervened on his behalf, speaking in Parliament in Milton's defense in December 1660 and helping to secure his release from prison without the imposition of the crippling fine exacted by the Sergeant at Arms. In celebration, the second edition of Milton's *Paradise Lost* (1674) appeared with a congratulatory poem by Marvell, "On Mr Milton's *Paradise Lost.*"

Though less outspoken a Parliamentarian than Milton, Marvell must have felt himself under suspicion—and if his political and religious allegiances were as ambivalent as we now believe, he may well have found equivocation increasingly prudent. As Annabel Patterson points out in the introduction to her *Marvell and the Civic Crown* (1978), irony and detachment characterized his attitude to himself no less than to his contemporaries, and allowed him to distance himself from his own activities. In some of his letters he even writes about himself in the third person. Writing to Sir Edward Harlay on 1 July 1676, he remarks:

> the book said to be Marvels [his satire *Mr Smirke*] makes what shift it can in the world but the Author walks negligently up & down as unconcerned. The Divines of our Church say it is not in the merry part so good as the Rehearsall Transpros'd, that it runns dreggs: the Essay they confesse is writ well enough to the purpose he intended it but that was a

very ill purpose. . . . Marvell, if it be he, has much staggerd me.

> (*The Poems and Letters of Andrew Marvell,* p. 346).

A letter to William Popple of June 1678 is either playful or extremely circumspect:

> There came out, about Christmass last, here a large Book concerning *the Growth of Popery and Arbitrary Government*. There have been great Rewards offered in private, and considerable in the Gazette, to any who could inform of the Author or Printer, but not yet discovered. Three or four printed Books since have described, as near as it was proper to go, the Man being a Member of Parliament, Mr *Marvell* to have been the Author; but if he had, surely he should not have escaped being questioned in Parliament, or some other Place.

> (p. 357)

In 1663 Marvell joined Charles II's newly appointed ambassador on an expedition to Russia, Sweden, and Denmark. The embassy was intended to restore trading and diplomatic relations with Russia (known as Muscovy), then under the rule of Tsar Alexis (father of Peter the Great), but failed in all its objectives. Marvell returned to the House shortly before the declaration of the Second Dutch War, a few months before an outbreak of the plague that swept Britain, and one year before the Great Fire of London swept away many of the narrow streets through which the infection had run. Marvell sat on a committee appointed to examine miscarriages of justice during the war and another that looked into the causes of the fire. The verses which can be dated to this time are satires on public affairs and public men, some published openly, such as those on the Secretary of State, Arlington, and the Lord Chancellor, the earl of Clarendon, others anonymously—such as the "Advices to the Painter" (c.1667), followed by "Further Advices to a Painter" (1670), which use the convention of verse giving instructions to a painter to tie together satires on a number of figures in church, court, and Parliament.

In 1672 Marvell published the first part of the pamphlet for which he was most famous in his lifetime, *The Rehearsal Transpros'd* (the title comes from *The Rehearsal,* a play by the duke of Buckingham which satirizes plagiaristic and bombastic playwrights). The pamphlet was a defense of freedom of conscience, in particular an apology for Charles II's "Declaration of Indulgence" (which suspended penal laws against Catholics and Nonconformists), and an anticlerical gauntlet thrown down to Samuel Parker, bishop of Oxford, later archdeacon of Canterbury, who violently opposed tolerance of Nonconformism. Parker, among others, replied with lampoons of his own, which Marvell flattened with *The Rehearsal Transpros'd: The Second Part,* published under his own name in 1673. Besides Parker, another target for the pamphlets was John Dryden, Marvell's opposite in politics, religion, and literary style, who had been satirized as Bayes, a poor dramatist, in the play from which Marvell took his title. "On Mr Milton's *Paradise Lost*" (1674) added insult to injury by comparing Milton's magisterial blank verse to the "tinkling Rime" of Dryden's opera.

Soon, though, Marvell's hopes for the continuance of a policy of religious tolerance were dashed, and his loyalty to Charles II rapidly eroded. The Declaration had been voted down by Parliament; the Conventicles Act put forward by the Presbyterian majority in Parliament forbade the meeting of more than five people for any act of religion other than the rites of the established Church of England; and the Test Act both required holders of public office to swear that they rejected the Catholic doctrine of transubstantiation and compelled them to provide a certificate proving that they had recently taken communion in the Anglican rite. Charles's refusal to repudiate his Catholic queen; the feared accession to the throne of the Catholic duke of York, brother of the king and heir presumptive; and the threat to the survival of Puritanism, made the king, from Marvell's patriotic Protestant point of view, no longer a true defender of the realm. Scandal had followed scandal and strife strife: the king's conduct with his drinking friends and his mistresses; his willingness to bleed the populace dry to finance his extravagances; the duke of Monmouth's assault on Sir John Coventry (who had criticized the king in Parliament); the at-

tempt by Colonel Thomas Blood to steal the Crown of England from the Tower of London as a political protest; the defection of a group of leading country M.P.s to the government side; the closing of the Exchequer against the king's creditors. Marvell had been able to justify his transferal of allegiance from Cromwell to Charles II as a switch from one strong leader and defender of English, and Protestant, interests to another. Now he may have contemplated another transferal.

In 1673–1674 Marvell may have been the British agent known as "Mr George" or "Mr Thomas" involved in secret negotiations with William, duke of Orange, toward whom Parliament was beginning to look as the next king. Any such negotiations would have been considered espionage, and treasonable, since England was still technically at war with Holland until February 1674, and allied to France, from which Charles received a large pension. During the last years of his life Marvell was also a frequent visitor to the duke of Monmouth, Charles II's favorite illegitimate son, and a possible pretender to the throne. Although none of the exciting Metaphysical poems nor the pastoral or other lyric verse seems to come from this period, Marvell did continue to write. His last known work, *Account of the Growth of Popery and Arbitrary Government,* was published anonymously in 1677.

After a rare visit to Hull in July, Marvell returned to the house he rented in Great Russell Street in London, where he died on 16 August 1678. He had made enemies enough for rumors of poisoning to circulate, but the cause appears to have been an old-fashioned treatment for a "tertian ague" (fever)—bleeding and sweating—that brought about a coma, and death.

THE POETRY

EDITORS of Marvell's poems have proposed an order of composition for them, and thus a history of Marvell's development as a writer, but any such chronology can only be speculative. We know that *"Ad Regem Carolum Parodia,"* the Latin and Greek verses written while he was an undergraduate, are the earliest available to us; we know that the pastoral dialogue "A Dialogue Between Thyrsis and Dorinda" is of relatively early composition (since it was set to music by William Lawes, who died in 1645); we can date quite accurately the composition of occasional poems, such as those commemorating landmarks in the life of Cromwell, and date within a short period satires directed at Marvell's religious and political opponents, but many of the pastoral and lyric poems remain undateable, and others, as with some of the prose, though attributed to Marvell cannot definitively be assigned to him.

Much of Marvell's poetry is today classed as Metaphysical, though he would not have used that term; that is, it is inventive and witty, its wordplay is ingenious, and it uses stylistic devices such as the extended or exaggerated metaphor in which the thing substituted for the original is often unexpected and incongruous. William Drummond wrote of poets who used "Metaphysical Ideas and Scholastical Quiddities," but John Dryden was probably the first to apply the term to poetry in his *A Discourse Concerning the Original and Progress of Satire* (1693), in which he complained that John Donne: "affects the metaphysics . . . in his amorous verses where nature only should reign; and perplexes the minds of the fair sex with nice speculations of philosophy, when he should engage their hearts." Metaphysical poetry uses the techniques and diction of philosophical speculation and logical argument to explore humankind and the world, but in no passively objective spirit; it is opinionated, forceful, and witty. Eliot admired it for its fusion of passion and intellectual curiosity and argument; he argued that reason and feeling were united in poets such as Donne, but in poetry since Dryden have been divided; there has been a "dissociation of sensibility." Marvell's work lacks the tender tone that Donne's often employs (as well as Donne's polarized libidinal and religious motivations), and in fact few of Marvell's poems are love poems. Some of the poems are private, but none seems truly personal. While Marvell's poetry shares the dialectal character of Donne's and Herbert's, his

interest in nature brings him closer to Thomas Vaughan, and his colorful visual descriptions to Milton.

Metaphysical poetry is rarely humble or soothing in tone, but more often energetic, vigorous, and even haranguing. Much of the energy of Marvell's verse comes from his masterly handling of the iambic tetrameter couplet, that is, lines of eight syllables in four "feet" consisting of an unstressed followed by a stressed syllable, rhyming in pairs:

u / u / u / u /
Had we but world enough and time
u / u / u / u /
This coyness, lady, were no crime.
("To His Coy Mistress" ll. 1–2)

The rhymed couplets give an epigrammatic neatness to the lines, but simple, even colloquial, diction prevents the neatness from becoming pompously assertive, while enjambment (in which the end of the poetic line is not the same as the end of the grammatical sentence, so when read aloud, the rhymes are not at the ends of lines) gives an impetus to the form, and some variation in stress and line length prevents monotony:

What wondrous life is this I lead!
Ripe apples drop about my head;
The luscious clusters of the vine
Upon my mouth do crush their wine;
The nectarene, and curious peach,
Into my hands themselves do reach;
Stumbling on melons, as I pass,
Ensnared with flowers, I fall on grass.
("The Garden" ll. 33–40)

Many Metaphysical poems are rhetorical; they seek to convince us of an argument. The narrative "I" of Donne's poems frequently tries to convince us that all women are fickle, and that he is a true and constant lover. The narrator of Marvell's poem "To His Coy Mistress" uses the form of a syllogism to convince his girlfriend to sleep with him. That is, it argues from the general to the specific in the form "All type As have the quality B; you are A therefore you must be B." Its argument is that if the lover and his mistress were immortal she could be as coy as she chose, and their dalliance could continue for eons, but since they are mortal, and able to enjoy earthly pleasures (of the flesh) for only a brief time, they should enjoy each other without delay. Two persuasive lines read like a gauntlet thrown down to Marvell's poetic predecessor, John Donne. Donne's "The Relique" (1633) makes the coffin almost a bed for undying lovers, envisaging a gravedigger planning to reuse the grave finding the narrator's body with a "bracelet of bright air about the bone," and thinks:

> that there a loving couple lies,
> Who thought that this device might be some way
> To make their souls, at the last busy day,
> Meet at this grave, and make a little stay.

Marvell, however, asserts:

> The grave's a fine and private place,
> But none, I think, do there embrace.
>
> (ll. 31–32)

Although the ostensible aim of the poem is a seduction, the tone is not erotic but, though fierily energetic, detached and intellectual, just as the power of the "Horatian Ode" comes from the detached, dispassionate representation of Cromwell's secular power (he is a force of nature; God's arrowhead) and of the king's tragic dignity in death rather than from any attempt at involving the reader in vicarious emotions. The visceral satisfaction of "To His Coy Mistress" is not in the imagining of sexual pleasure following conquest, but in its rhetorical tropes, its forceful persuasive power. If the poetry is not precisely erotic, neither is it sentimental, and it has an extraordinary range of reference, far wider than the conventional lexicon of seduction poetry. The image of amorous birds of prey at "sport," who "devour" time suggests a compelling sexuality, but not necessarily tenderness (ll. 37–38).

Similarly, the lines "Let us roll all our strength, and all / Our sweetness, up into one ball / And tear our pleasures with rough strife, / Thorough the iron gates of life" (ll. 43–44) powerfully evoke the impetus of an unstoppable desire which sweeps aside any obstacle—but the emotion is entirely solipsistic—turned-in exclusively to the male desire, with the woman's "coyness" (virtue, lack of desire, prudence) merely an obstacle to be reasoned or cajoled away. The poem's register is diverse, and sets up a complex matrix of associations. T. S. Eliot praised its "concentrated images," but, as J. V. Cunningham points out (in "Logic and Lyric: 'To his Coy Mistress' " in *Andrew Marvell: Poems,* ed. Arthur Pollard, 1980), the central poetic device of the poem conjures not vivid images but abstract concepts; its play is intellectual rather than visual. Cunningham gives the example of "my vegetable love," suggesting that, reading this, Eliot and subsequent readers envisage a monstrous, expanding cabbage, but explaining that, for the educated seventeenth-century reader, "vegetable" was an abstract philosophical term. The doctrine of the three souls defines three types: the rational soul, which in man subsumes the other two; the sensitive soul, which men and animals have in common and which is the principle of motion and perception; and the vegetable soul, which is the only one that plants possess and which is the principle of generation and corruption, of augmentation and decay. Marvell's narrator's use of the term implies that his love, denied the exercise of sense, but possessed of the power of augmentation, will increase "vaster than empires." This is not a visual but an intellectual image, and thus not really an image but a conceit, a piece of wit (pp. 170–171).

A conceit involves the presentation of a proposition referring to one field of experience (or discourse) in terms of an intellectual structure derived from another, often a field of learning. Donne and the earlier Metaphysical poets had made themselves masters of the conceit, but by Marvell's time it could operate as the organizing principle of entire poems. The technique of proposing an equivalence of concepts (preferably wildly implausible) whose supposed identicality is reiterated with variations through an entire poem that expands, seemingly ad infinitum, in rhyming couplets which themselves echo the doubling of the comparison, was known as "Clevelandizing," after the poet John Cleveland. The conceit does not add to the force of the poem's proposition by a new and convincing element of the argument, but only by the bludgeoning effect of repetition.

Metaphysical wit is largely based on contradiction, but whereas Donne and George Herbert show us paradoxes (often religious or spiritual in nature) that are ultimately resolved, Marvell's oppositions remain antithetical. An opposition that pervades Marvell's verse is between the material, transitory world and the spiritual and eternal, and several of his lyrics articulate a dialogue in which the latter is shown as desirable and the former, while tempting, deeply flawed. Perhaps the rough images of "To His Coy Mistress" hint at the transitory and ultimately unsatisfactory nature of the pleasures the poem's narrator demands. In "Bermudas," the pilgrims escape both storms and "Prelat's rage" to find a new world of tranquility and religious freedom; in "The Coronet" and "On a Drop of Dew," the trappings of materiality are rejected in favor of consummation with the "glories of th'Almighty Sun." Earthbound baseness is personified in the idealized pastoral world of "The Nymph Complaining for the Death of Her Fawn" by "wanton troopers" who have shot the nymph's fawn, and in "The Mower Against Gardens" by gardeners who, not content with the natural shape and color of indigenous plants, cultivate strange graftings and hybrids, and pay fortunes for exotic specimens.

"The Garden" depicts the narrator finding a kind of transcendental state through meditation in a rural retreat:

Meanwhile the mind, from pleasures less,
Withdraws into its happiness:
The mind, that ocean where each kind
Does straight its own resemblance find,
Yet it creates, transcending these,
Far other worlds, and other seas,
Annihilating all that's made
To a green thought in a green shade.

Here at the fountain's sliding foot,
Or at some fruit-trees mossy root,
Casting the body's vest aside,
My soul into the boughs does glide:
There like a bird it sits and sings,
Then whets, and combs its silver wings;

And, till prepared for longer flight,
Waves in its plumes the various light.

(ll. 41–56)

In retired contemplation the soul can shed its outer husk of flesh, and retirement, it seems, requires solitude: "Two paradises 'twere in one / To live in paradise alone" (ll. 63–64).

Again, much of the pleasure of reading this poem comes from its ambiguities. "A green thought in a green shade" in literal terms is nonsense, since we cannot think greenly, and shadows are generally gray, but the reader understands the associations and connotations of the adjective, and infers that the narrator is under the shade of green leaves, or perhaps looking at the dappled green of a tree canopy, and that in this retired arbor the mind is soothed to contemplation of the pastoral. The bar to this pleasant image of a rural sanctuary is, however, the word that precedes it. The world outside is not kept at bay by the garden walls, or simply far away—it is "annihilated." Annihilated means reduced to nothing; what is annihilated is not just the outside world, whose once-important affairs have retreated into insignificance for the poet, but the world itself, "all that's made." The green shade is not cast by any tree, but is a world of the mind, an imaginative and intellectual projection, and it comes at the cost of the destruction of the mind's projections of the material world. The relationship between the external, phenomenological world and the mind was a preoccupation of seventeenth-century philosophy. Thomas Hobbes, in *Leviathan* (1651), stated that all knowledge is gained through sensory impressions that, like the mind, are nothing but matter in motion. Our perceptions of things are equivalent to those things.

"Upon Appleton House" celebrates a specific rather than generic private life of retirement, and again depicts the poet as a contemplative, yet the poem which was (probably) composed immediately afterwards, the "Horatian Ode" is diametrically opposed in theme and tone, and celebrates the man of action. There may be no contradiction here; Marvell may be suggesting that a life of rural contemplation is the ideal, but is impermissible in the current situation—history demands that the man of destiny take action. The garden is made a microcosm of which England is the macrocosm:

Oh thou, that dear and happy isle
The garden of the world ere while,
Thou paradise of Four seas,
Which heaven planted is to please,
But, to exclude the world, did guard
With watery if not flaming sword;
What luckless apple did we taste,
To make us mortal, and thee waste?
("Upon Appleton House," ll. 321–328)

The virtues of the garden preserved at Appleton House are the virtues enshrined in English culture. Yet public events are intruding upon the private world, at least in the imagination of the poet. Much of the register of the poem is martial, and the narrator's meditative contemplation produces a series of visions in which the constantly changing vistas of grass enact the history of mankind, including the horrors of war. The mowers:

With whistling scythe, and elbow strong,
These massacre the grass along:
While one, unknowing, carves the rail,
Whose yet unfeathered quills her fail.
The edge all bloody from its breast
He draws, and does his stroke detest,
Fearing the flesh untimely mowed
To him a fate as black forebode.
[. . . .]
The mower now commands the field,
In whose new traverse seemeth wrought
A camp of battle newly fought:
Where, as the meads with hay, the plain
Lies quilted o'er with bodies slain:
The women that with forks it fling,
Do represent the pillaging.
(ll. 393–424)

The narrator suggests that men such as Fairfax and Cromwell are impelled by duty to leave their rural retreats in order to defend the ideals and the very way of life that their country estates represent. There is a sense of regret in Marvell's description of Fairfax's diminution from commander of armies and arbiter of men's destinies to layer-out of flower beds (which he arranges in the shape of forts):

there walks one on the Sod
Who, had it pleasèd him and God,
Might once have made our Gardens spring
Fresh as his own and flourishing.
But he preferr'd to the Cinque Ports
These five imaginary Forts:
And, in those half-dry Trenches, spann'd
Pow'r which the Ocean might command.
(ll. 345–352)

The poem celebrates the rustic retreat, and the narrator glories in the sanctuary it affords him, alike from the temptations and the trials of the world:

Where Beauty, aiming at the Heart,
Bends in some tree its useless Dart;
And where the World no certain Shot
Can make, or me it toucheth not.
(ll. 601–606)

Its culmination, however, suggests that this retreat is only a preparation, a nursery for the rearing of the new hope of the Fairfax dynasty, and thus England—"the young Maria," Marvell's pupil. Perhaps also a preparation for the entry into public life of Mary Fairfax's tutor, since he too has "read in Natures mystick Book" (l. 584) and gained the wisdom and virtue that make him fit for service of the nation.

This theme is continued in Marvell's Cromwell poems. In "The First Anniversary" the Protector is depicted as someone who has sacrificed a retired life for one of (violent) service for the national good:

For all delights of life thou then didst lose
When to Command thou didst thy self Depose;
Resigning up thy Privacy so dear,
To turn the headstrong People Charioteer.
(ll. 221–224)

Now he is urged, in the natural imagery that pervades many of the public as well as private poems, to make a final sacrifice, to accept the role of king:

Thou with the same strength, and an Heart as plain,
Didst (like thine Olive) still refuse to Reign;
Though why should others all thy Labour spoil,
And brambles be anointed with thine Oyl,

Whose climbing Flame, without a timely stop,
Had quickly Levell'd every Cedar's top.

(ll. 257–262)

Marvell reinforces his representation of Cromwell as an agent of fate, or divine providence:

. . .indefatigable Cromwell hyes,
And cuts his way still nearer to the Skyes,
Learning a Musique in the Region clear,
To tune this lower to that higher Sphere.

(ll. 45–48)

Cromwell did not accept the crown, but his son did, briefly, inherit the Protectorship. "Upon the Death of His Late Highness the Lord Protector," ladens Richard Cromwell with rich, monarchical images as though he were a royal Prince inheriting the throne:

How he becomes that seat, how strongly strains,
How gently winds at once the ruling reins?
Heaven to this choice prepared a diadem,
Richer than any Eastern silk or gem;
A pearly rainbow, where the sun enchased
His brows, like an imperial jewel graced.

(ll. 313–318)

Marvell places Richard Cromwell in the same light as his father and Fairfax, in the line of leaders prepared for their public roles by a secluded upbringing:

He, as his father, long was kept from sight
In private, to be view'd by better light;
But open'd once, what splendour does he throw? A
Cromwell in an hour a prince will grow.

(ll. 309–312)

Finally, he is hailed as the direct continuation of Cromwell's rule, and thus of all-important stability:

We find already what these omens mean,
Earth ne'er more glad, nor heaven more serene.
Cease now our griefs, calm peace succeeds a war,
Rainbows to storms, Richard to Oliver.
Tempt not his clemency to try his power,
He threats no deluge, yet foretells a shower.

(ll. 319–324)

That so many of Marvell's poems were composed in iambic tetrameter couplets might suggest a consistency of tone and voice, but deft touches to the visual and aural framework of each poem match form to theme and mood. "The Garden"—arranged in octets of regular line length and unobtrusive rhyme, many containing only one or two grammatical sentences, end-stopped at the last line—presents us with a series of complete thoughts in linked poetic paragraphs which convey a sense of expansiveness. Assonance adds internal coherence, and in seventy-two lines we feel that thematically we haven't traveled very far. The "Horatian Ode" contains a simple variation: the octosyllabic couplets are alternated with six-syllable couplets. There are no stanzas—the 120 lines are a whole—but from ll. 1–24 each octosyllabic couplet followed by a six-syllable couplet contains an entire grammatical sentence. The effect is to curtail the expansiveness of the form of "The Garden" and to inject a note of urgency, but an urgency that seesaws: two steps forward and one step back. In the first twenty-four lines, which are regularly punctuated, the poet makes a series of points (it's time to act; Cromwell did, and look what he achieved). After l. 24, many of the sentences are spread across several couplets, in which the poet describes past events (Cromwell's Irish episode, the Regicide) and draws a parallel or lesson to be learned from them, and thus develops his argument. Variation in the length of the sentences, and units of sense, which range from two to eight poetic lines, prevents the meter from becoming monotonous. Listening to the poem, we would not be sure whether a pause marking the end of line were coming, so the enjambed (run-on) lines' rhymes would be heard as internal, and we would not be distracted by anticipating the coming rhyme.

Marvell was well-informed, well read, and proficient in a number of languages. His education, at the Grammar School, Hull, and at Cambridge, would have included reading, translation, and imitation of the classical authors. He produced a number of companion poems in Latin for his English verses, and used both classical conventions and classical models for many of his English poems. "An Horatian Ode upon Cromwell's Return from Ireland" (May 1650) appropriates the traditional poem of return commemorating a sovereign's triumphal campaign or similar event. Its ostensible models are the *Odes* of the Latin poet Horace (Quintus Horatius Flaccus, 65–8 B.C.), themselves imitations of earlier, Greek forms—though critics have suggested that the poem is in some ways closer to Lucan's *Pharsalia,* which narrates the struggle between Pompey and Caesar for the Roman Empire. Lucan (Marcus Annaeus Lucanus, 39–65 A.D.) lost the friendship of the Emperor Nero by defeating him in a public contest. Nero was a bad loser, and Lucan replied with such biting satire that he was forbidden to publish or recite verse. He joined a conspiracy against Nero, and was ordered to kill himself. Close parallels could be drawn between the power struggles of the English Civil War and of the Roman Republic and Empire.

Whereas Horace celebrates the end of war and a restoration of peace and stability brought about by the imperial armies' defeat of the Republicans, Marvell heralds the beginning of a new period of conflict, initiated by the Republican General, Cromwell. His subject is the recall of Cromwell from his campaigns of slaughter in Drogheda and Wexford, by the Long Parliament, who feared threat of an invasion from Scotland under Charles II. The tone is unsentimental, the attitude coolly detached, but it is difficult not to believe that at one point at least the poem is bitterly ironic. Marvell employs the convention, common in "epideictic" texts that ceremonially praise, of a defeated enemy lauding its conqueror; thus, the dispossessed and decimated population of Ireland is described as the most fitted to praise the perpetrator of the atrocities:

And now the Irish are ashamed
To see themselves in one year tamed:
  So much one man can do,
  That does both act and know.
They can affirm his praises best,
And have, though overcome, confessed
  How good he is, how just,
  And fit for highest trust

While admirers of Cromwell found the praise faint and the reservations many, and cite the stanzas about the executed Charles I as the most

lyrical, Cromwell is the admired subject of the poem. Yet though the hero, he is not invested with all the heroic virtues; he is a man of action chosen to be the agent of God, or Fate, and he will cut a swathe through outworn institutions and corruption, but he is duly warned that having taken up the sword he will find it impossible to put it down. Nor does Marvell's admiration of Cromwell mitigate his regret for the murder of Charles I; the two are not incompatible. The suggestion in the later poem, "The First Anniversary," that Cromwell legitimize his rule and secure future stability by reestablishing the monarchy, with himself as king and his son Richard as heir, perhaps indicates that Marvell never ceased to be a monarchist, but simply sought a monarchic dynasty strong enough to protect England and liberal enough to countenance religious tolerance. Marvell's lines present lofty ideals of right and justice, but they are generally swiftly brought down to earth by a clear-sighted pragmatism. Justice and Rights "do hold or break / As Men are strong or weak" (ll. 39–40). He praises Charles I's dignified bearing on the scaffold in terms of the appropriate demeanor of the central actor in a ritual of ceremonial stages and long preordained outcome:

That thence the Royal Actor born
The Tragick Scaffold might adorn:
  While round the armed Bands
  Did clap their bloody hands.
He nothing common did or mean
Upon that memorable Scene:
  But with his keener Eye
  The Axes edge did try:
Nor call'd the Gods with vulgar spight
To vindicate his helpless Right,
  But bow'd his comely Head,
  Down, as upon a Bed.

(ll. 53–64)

SATIRES AND POLEMIC

MARVELL'S reputation in his lifetime was largely made by the two parts of *The Rehearsal Transpros'd,* which admirers and detractors alike acknowledged as establishing Marvell as one of the most leading political satirists of the time.

Gilbert Burnet called them "the wittiest books that have appeared in this age" (in *History of My Own Time,* ed., O. Airy, 1897, p. 1); Anthony à Wood (in *Athenae Oxonienses,* 1691, p. 620) called Marvell "a very celebrated wit among the Fanaticks, and the only one truly so"; John Dryden referred to him in the preface to his *Religio Laici* (1682) as "the Martin Marprelate of our times, the first Presbyterian Scribbler who sanctifi'd Libels and Scurrility to the use of the Good Old Cause." (The Puritan "Martin Marprelate" pamphlets of the 1580s were hyperbolic, abusive attacks on the Elizabethan compromise on the issue of church vestments.)

Annabel Patterson, in *Marvell and the Civic Crown,* points out an important difference between the verse and the prose satires. While the verse satires focus on public figures and affairs of state, the prose satires and pamphlets debate ideological issues and long-standing controversies of church policy and doctrine. They reveal Marvell's extensive knowledge of church history and the intricacies of doctrinal disputes. Patterson suggests that exposure to the style and methods of Archdeacon Parker led Marvell to see that Juvenilian satire (i.e., vituperative attack) was a form of aggression, and of the very intolerance he despised and had attempted to refute. He therefore gradually developed a new style of polemic, not without the leaven of wit but less personal, and more compatible with an ideal of moderation (pp. 176–178). Marvell may have come to see a contradiction in *The Rehearsal Transpros'd:* in mocking Parker for his immodesty, lack of restraint, and abusiveness, he writes in an equally unrestrained style and does not scruple to make scurrilous and sometimes crude jokes at his subject's expense. Patterson detects unease in the last paragraph of the first part of *The Rehearsal,* in which Marvell says that he will be recompensed for his effort "if" the reader judges his polemical methods to be suited to the task—if, that is, "any one that hath been formerly of another mind, shall learn by this Example, that it is not impossible to be merry and angry . . . without profaning and violating those things which are and ought to be most sacred" (*The Rehearsal Transpros'd,* in A. B.

Grosart, ed., *Andrew Marvell, Complete Works,* 1966, p. 145).

For Patterson, the negative syntax of this appeal is more suggestive of anxiety than confidence, and she points out that it leads directly into the *Second Part* of the *Rehearsal Transpros'd,* in which the tensions in Marvell's polemical theory are made explicit (p. 192). The *Second Part* begins with a defense of Marvell's methods, which had been attacked as disrespectful to the church and to the gravity of Parker's position in the church. Marvell appears to acknowledge that satire is a double-edged weapon: "How can the Author of an Invective, though never so truly founded, expect approbation . . . who, in a world all furnished with subjects of praise, instruction and learned inquiry, shall studiously chuse and set himself apart to comment upon the blemishes and imperfections of some particular person?" (*Complete Works,* p. 161).

Characteristically, however, he states the objection only to overrule it: "And yet nevertheless, and all that has been said before being granted, it may so chance that to write, and that Satyrically, and . . . this too even against a Clergyman, may be not only excusable but necessary" (p. 163), since any clergyman who has entered the public arena "is laid open to the Pen of any one that knows how to manage it; and every person who has either Wit, Learning or Sobriety is licensed, if debauch'd to curb him, if erroneous to catechize him, and if foul-mouth'd and biting, to muzzle him" (p. 164). The satirist should not be assumed to be setting himself up as an arbiter of morality beyond criticism: "For I am too conscious of mine own imperfections to rake into and dilate upon the failings of other men; and though I carry always some ill Nature about me, yet it is I hope no more than is in this world necessary for a Preservative" (p. 165). Nor does he necessarily take pleasure in the discomfiture satire imposes on its object:

It hath been thus far the odiousest task that ever I undertook, and has look't to be all the while like the cruelty of a Living Dissection, which, however it may tend to publick instruction, and though I have pick'd out the most noxious Creature to be anatomiz'd, yet doth scarce excuse or recompense the offensiveness of the scent and fouling of my fingers.

(p. 185)

The two works which followed *The Rehearsal* were not primarily attacks but defenses: *Mr Smirke: Or, The Divine in Mode* (1676, published with *A Short Historical Essay touching General Councils, Creeds, and Imposition in Religion*) was written in support of Herbert Croft, Bishop of Hereford, while *Remarks upon a Late Disingenuous Discourse Writ by one T. D.* (1678) defended John Howe. Both, like much of Marvell's writing, reflect on the nature and function of writing, and each defends the art of satire, if it is modest, informed, and true. The tone is more moderate than either of the *Rehearsals,* and without their boisterousness and sexual innuendo. His choice of a pseudonym for *Mr Smirke* underlines Marvell's call for a simple, undecorated, and tolerant style of worship and writing: "Andreas Rivetus" is an anagram of *Res nuda veritas,* the naked truth. "*Mr Smirke,*" a character in Etherege's *The Man of Mode,* was Francis Turner, Master of St. John's College, Cambridge, who had attacked Croft's pamphlet *The Naked Truth: Or, the True State of the Primitive Church,* a call for tolerance of differences between different factions in the church. Since Turner was also chaplain to the duke of York, Marvell was dangerously close to identifying the duke with "Sir Fopling Flutter," whom Smirke serves as chaplain. Marvell denigrates Turner's learning and style, deplores his broadcasting of scurrilous lies and his want of charity, caps his Biblical quotation, and uses his own examples against him. "Calumny is like London-dirt, with which though a man may be spatter'd in an instant, yet it requires much time, pains, and Fullers-earth to scour it out again" (*Complete Works,* p. 18).

The "Disengenuous Discourse" was the attack on Howe by another Nonconformist, Thomas Danson. His Discourse had been published under his initials, which Marvell undertakes to interpret as standing for "The Discourse," thus keeping his case dispassionate and making his target, albeit with tongue in cheek, the text rather than the man: "heartily wishing that there were some way

of finding it guilty, without reflecting upon the Author; which I shall accordingly indeavour, that I may both preserve his, whatsoever, former reputation, and leave him a door open to ingenuity for the future" (*Complete Works,* vol. 4, p. 174).

The text is accordingly personified and mocked; though it offers itself as a defense of the faith, championing the cause of God, its braggadocio is inappropriate:

The cause of God! Turn, I beseech you, Its whole book over, and show me anything of that decorum with which that should have been managed. What is there to be found of that gravity, humility, meekness, piety or charity requisite to so glorious a presence? (graces with which God usually assists those that undertake His quarrel?)

(vol. 4, p. 234)

The character of the book is depicted as a kind of militant pedant: "dreadfully accoutred and armed cap-a-pie in logic, categorical and hypothetical syllogisms, majors, minors, enthymems, antecedents, consequents, distinctions, definitions," all of which are said to be "terms that good Mr Howe as a meer novice is presum'd to be unacquainted with, and so far from being able to endure the ratling of The Discourse's armour, that as those Roman legions once bragg'd, even the sweaty smell of Its armpits would be sufficient to rout him" (vol. 4 p. 198). The author is reminded that "[t]hey that take the sword, shall perish by the sword . . . and the taking of the pen hath seldom better success, if handled in the same manner" (vol. 4, p. 174).

Published under a false "Amsterdam" imprint in 1678, *The Account of the Growth of Popery and Arbitrary Government* should be bracketed with the *Essay* attached to *Mr Smirke,* as a new departure for Marvell, into revisionist history. The works are not satirical but polemical, and documentary; Marvell's professed intention is "only to write a naked narrative" which will be a précis and interpretation of events for the public. "I shall summarily, as short as so copious and redundant a matter will admit, deduce the order of affairs both at home and abroad" (vol. 4, pp. 263–264). Rather than individual officials or their books, as with the *Advices to Painter* and earlier prose pamphlets, the *Account* takes on large targets, and purports to uncover a widespread, well-organized, and dangerous conspiracy. "There has been now for divers years a design been carried on to change the lawful Government of England into an absolute Tyranny, and to convert the established Protestant Religion into downright Popery"(*Complete Works,* vol. 4, p. 248).

Marvell warns of the dangers inherent in Charles II's alliance with the French king, Louis XIV, but his main focus is the erosion of the powers of Parliament and the constitution by a corrupt and repressive regime. In a political climate of mistrust and pessimism, in which those who ought to offer models of rectitude were providing models of venality, corruption, and self-interest, a vituperative satire was no longer appropriate. Marvell needed to adopt a style that would identify both author and arguments as of the party of decorum, principle, and reason. *An Account* repeatedly emphasizes its author's modesty and disinterestedness:

> Thus far hath the conspiracy against our Religion and Government been laid open, which if true, it was more than time that it should be discovered, but if anything therein have been falsely suggested, the disproving of it in any particular will be a courtesie both to the publick and to the relator; who would be glad to have the world convinced of the contrary, though to the prejudice of his own reputation.
>
> (vol. 4, p. 411)

He refuses to identify individuals, asserting that though some people will expect "that the very persons should have been named; whereas he only gives evidence to the fact, and leaves the malefactors to those who have the power of inquiry. It was his design indeed to give information, but not to turn informer"(vol. 4, p. 413). The language is largely moderate and open-minded, making the few deviations into the brutality of satire all the more shocking. The "relator"piously hopes that the malefactors will repent and expiate their misdeeds, yet if they do not, readers who want to bring them to justice will have in the pamphlet sufficient clues for their identification: "if any one delight in the chase, he is an ill woodman that knows not . . . the beast

by the proportion of his excrement"(vol. 4, p. 413). The chief miscreant is protected not only by anonymity but by the fiction that he was beyond reproach. *An Account* begins with a statement about the government of England, described as an enviable, unique state in which the commoner's rights are as enshrined in law as the king's, and the king rules by virtue of the same law that protects the commoner. It could read like a paean to Charles's enlightened rule, but it is also an inventory of the restraints upon him:

> His very prerogative is no more than what the Law hath determined. His Broad Seal, which is the legitimate stamp of his pleasure, yet is no longer currant, than upon the trial it is found to be legal. He cannot commit any person by is particular warrant. He cannot himself be witness in any cause. . . . Nothing is left to the King's will, but all is subjected to is authority; by which means it follows that he can do no wrong, nor can he receive wrong; and a King of England keeping to these measures, may without arrogance, be said to remain the onely intelligent Ruler over a rational People.
>
> (vol. 4, pp. 248–249)

Throughout the pamphlet, the "relator"avoids any direct reproach. The king has been ill-advised and is surrounded by iniquitous flatterers; *An Account* is offered as honest, unembellished advice, free of ill will towards the monarch: "so far is the relator himself from any sinister surmise of his Majesty . . . that he acknowledges, if it were fit for Caesar's wife to be free, much more is Caesar himself from all crime and suspicion." It is unlikely that any of the pamphlet's readers would have considered either Charles II or his Catholic wife beyond suspicion, and the opening vision of a Utopian England would serve as a reminder of how reality fell short of the ideal, and of the possibility of recourse.

Marvell found Howe an unfit champion of the cause of God. We cannot tell whether his own cause was that of God, England, Protestantism, or parliament; whether he was sincere and unwavering or inconstant and expedient; but he does seem to have had an ideal of justice, and a sense of the poet's role:

When the Sword glitters ore the Judges head,
And fear has Coward Churchmen silenced

Then is the Poets time, 'tis then he drawes
And single fights forsaken Vertues cause.

("Tom May's Death," ll. 62–66)

The climate in which he lived required circumspection, concealment, and compromise; the poet could rarely fight, and write openly, but Marvell did write, and not with a "servil' wit and mercenary pen."

SELECTED BIBLIOGRAPHY

I. POEMS PUBLISHED OR CIRCULATED DURING MARVELL'S LIFETIME. "Ad Regem Carolum Parodia," in sive Musarum Cantabrigiensium Concentus et Congratulatio (1636–1637); "An Elegy upon the Death of My Lord Francis Villiers" (1648); "To His Noble Friend Mr Richard Lovelace," in Richard Lovelace, *Lucasta* (1649); "Upon the Death of the Lord Hastings," in Richard Brome, ed., *Lachrymae Musarum* (1649); "An Horatian Ode upon Cromwell's Return from Ireland" (1650); "Tom May's Death" (1650); "*In Legationem Domini Oliveri St John*" (1651); "To His Worthy Friend Doctor Witty" ("*Dignissimo Suo Amico Doctori Witty*"), in Robert Witty, ed. and trans., *Popular Error or the Errors of the People in the Matter of Physic* (1651); "The First Anniversary of the Government under His Highness the Lord Protector" (1655); "The Character of Holland" (1665); "On the Victory Obtained by Blake over the Spaniards," publ. in part in John Bulteel, ed., *A New Collection of Poems and Songs* (1674); "Two Songs at the Marriage of the Lord Fauconberg and the Lady Mary Cromwell" (1657); "The Loyal Scott" (1669–1670); *The Rehearsal Transpros'd* (1672); *The Rehearsal Transpros'd, The Second Part* (1673); "On Mr Milton's *Paradise Lost*" (1674); *Mr Smirk: Or the Divine in Mode with A Short Historical Essay Concerning General Councils, Creeds, and Imposition in Religion* (1676), published under the name "Andreas Rivetus, Jr."; *An Account of the Growth of Popery and Arbitrary Government* (1677); *Remarks upon a Late Disengenuous Discourse Writ by One T. D. . . .By a Protestant* (1678).

II. EARLY EDITIONS. *A Short Historical Essay Concerning General Councils, Creeds, and Imposition in Religion* (1680, rev. repr. 1687, 1703, 1709), without *Mr Smirke; Miscellaneous Poems by Andrew Marvell, Esq; Late Member of the Honorable House of Commons* (London, 1681); Richard Baldwin, ed., *Mr Andrew Marvell's Character of Popery* (1689); *Poems on Affairs of State* (1689); *The Works of Andrew Marvell*, 2 vols., ed. Thomas Cooke (London, 1726); *The Works of Andrew Marvell*, 3 vols., ed. Captain Edward Thompson (London, 1776).

III. MODERN COLLECTED EDITIONS. *The Complete Works of Andrew Marvell*, 4 vols., ed. the Reverend Alexander B. Grosart (1872–1875, repr. New York, 1966), contains just the prose works; *The Poems and Letters of Andrew Marvell*, 2 vols., ed. H. M. Margoliouth (Oxford, 1927, rev. ed. 1952, 1971), 1952 ed. revd. by Pierre Legouis with E. E. Duncan-Jones; *The Poems of Andrew Marvell*, ed. Hugh MacDonald (London, 1956); *Poems on Affairs of State: Augustan Satirical Verse, 1660–1674*, vol. I: 1660–1678, ed. George de Forest Lord (New Haven, 1963); *The Latin Poetry of Andrew Marvell*, eds. William A. McQueen and Kiffin A. Rockwell (Chapel Hill, N.C., 1964); *The Selected Poetry of Marvell*, ed. Frank Kermode (New York, 1967); *Andrew Marvell: Complete Poetry*, ed. George de Forest Lord (New York, 1968); *Andrew Marvell, The Rehearsal Transpros'd and The Rehearsal Transpros'd, The Second Part*, ed. D. I. B. Smith (Oxford, 1971); *Andrew Marvell: The Complete Poems*, ed. Elizabeth Story Dunno (Harmondsworth, U.K., 1972; repr. 1985), includes a list of poems attributed to Marvell.

IV. CRITICAL AND BIOGRAPHICAL STUDIES. M. C. Bradbrook and M. G. Lloyd Thomas, *Andrew Marvell* (Cambridge, 1961); Pierre Legouis, *Andrew Marvell: Poet, Puritan, Patriot* (Oxford, 1965), abridged trans. of 1928 French original; Harold E. Toliver, *Marvell's Ironic Vision* (New Haven, 1965); J. B. Leishman, *The Art of Marvell's Poetry* (London, 1966); George de Forest Lord, ed., *Andrew Marvell: A Collection of Critical Essays* (Englewood Cliffs, N.J., 1968); John Wallace, *Destiny His Choice: The Loyalism of Andrew Marvell* (Cambridge, 1968); John Carey, ed., *Andrew Marvell: A Critical Anthology* (Harmondsworth, U.K., 1969).

Rosalie Colie, *"My Ecchoing Song"* (Princeton. N.J., 1970); Donald M. Friedman, *Marvell's Pastoral Art* (London, 1970); Elizabeth Story Dunno, ed., *Andrew Marvell: The Critical Heritage* (London, 1978); W. Kelliher, ed., *Andrew Marvell: Poet and Politician, 1621–1678. An Exhibition to Commemorate the Tercentenary of His Death* (London, 1978); C. A. Patrides, ed., *Approaches to Marvell: The York Tercentenary Lectures* (London, 1978); Annabel M. Patterson, *Marvell and the Civic Crown* (Princeton, N.J., 1978).

Arthur Pollard, ed., *Andrew Marvell: Poems* (London, 1980); Warren Chernaik, *The Poet's Time: Politics and Religion in the Work of Andrew Marvell* (Cambridge, 1983); David Norbrook, *Poetry and Politics in the English Renaissance* (Oxford, 1984); Kevin Sharpe and Steven N. Zwicker, eds., *Politics of Discourse: The Literature and History of Seventeenth-Century England* (Berkeley and London, 1987); Graham Parry, *The Seventeenth Century: The Intellectual and Cultural Context of English Literature, 1603–1700* (Harlow, 1989).

Thomas Healy, *Literature of the English Civil War* (Cambridge, 1990); Judith Haber, *Pastoral and the Poetics of Self-Contradiction: Theocritus to Marvell* (Cambridge, 1994); Thomas Healy, ed., *Andrew Marvell* (Harlow, 1998); Robert H. Ray, ed., *An Andrew Marvell Companion* (New York, 1998); Warren Chernaik and Martin Dzelzainis, eds., *Marvell and Liberty* (New York, 1999); Nicholas Murray, *Andrew Marvell: World Enough and Time* (London, 1999); David Norbrook, *Writing the English Republic: Poetry, Rhetoric, and Politics, 1627–1660* (Cambridge, 1999).

Robert Ellrodt, *Seven Metaphysical Poets: A Structural Study of the Unchanging Self* (Oxford, 2000); Annabel M. Patterson, *Marvell: The Writer in Public Life* (Harlow, 2000).

JOHN MILTON

(1608–1674)

Robert Faggen

JOHN MILTON PURSUED a grand and heroic conception of the poet's vocation. Condemning the authority of the English Church and its priests, Milton argued that the spiritual guidance of humanity demanded

> such a one as is as a true knower of himself, and himself in whom contemplation, practice and wit, prudence fortitude, and eloquence must be rarely met, both to comprehend the hidden causes of things and span in his thoughts all the various effects that passion or complexion can work in man's nature; and hereto must his hand be at defiance with gain, and his heart in all virtues heroic.
>
> ("The Reason of Church Government" 1642, p. 643)

Milton aspired to those ideals of learning and virtue and considered himself unfit to write of them until he had embodied them:

> I was confirmed in this opinion that he who would not be frustrate of his hope to write well hereafter in laudable things ought himself to be a true poem, that is a composition and pattern of the best and honorablest things—not presuming to sing high praises of heroic men, or famous cities, unless he have in himself the experience and the practice of all that which is praiseworthy.
>
> ("Apology for Smectymnuus,"1642, p. 694)

Yet Milton also came to regard virtue as hollow and possibly evil unless directed by an illumined spirit in service of an ultimate good. His life and poetry became a search for the heroic and virtuous existence in a fallen, embattled world.

If Milton's means was poetry, his end was prophecy. Like Moses, Milton sought to forge a new covenant between God and men, with neither political nor ecclesiastical oversight: "For now the time seems come, wherein Moses, the great prophet, may sit in heaven rejoicing to see that memorable and glorious wish of his fulfilled, when not only our seventy elders, but all the Lord's people, are become prophets" ("Areopagitica," 1644, p. 744). Milton sought to teach a true vision of the Christian life, liberated from arcane theology and the need for priests. Though he strove "to justify the ways of God to men," he may not have meant "mankind" but only those men of good will, the "fit though few" capable of reason and reformation. Milton's thought maintains a tension between the possibilities of effort and the mystery of grace; he believed both necessary "to repair the ruins of our first parents by regaining to know God aright, and out of that knowledge to love him, to imitate him, to be like him, as we may the nearest by possessing our souls of true virtue, which being united to the heavenly grace of faith makes up the highest perfection" ("Of Education," 1644, p. 631). This perfection, Milton believed, could only be realized by separating ecclesiastical from political authority, purging the former from any control over the individual conscience. He insisted that individual conscience should remain unmediated in its relation to God and that man's service to God should be based on "humane reason."

Milton's work has become synonymous with freedom, the freedom of individuals to will and to will the good. By freedom, Milton meant not only freedom *from* tyranny but freedom *for* service to God. Liberty in Milton was held in constant relation with obedience and self-government. The hazards of liberty could be tempered by strict government but only from within—from the reason and conscience of the just and virtuous in service of charity. Though one of the greatest apologists for the power of poetry to educate and liberate the human spirit, Milton also often somberly recognized and depicted the failure of human endeavors to know and to reform. Though Milton shifted throughout his life between periods of intense study and of political activism, he wavered little from his ambition to write poetry worthy of the ages and of his God. Milton's career, if that pedestrian word can be used for such a life, can be seen in three parts: 1608–1639, 1640–1658, and 1658–1674. Born in London on 9 December 1608, he was educated at Saint Paul's School and Christ's College, Cambridge. At Cambridge, he prepared for the clergy, a choice not at odds with his literary ambitions if one considers that his contemporaries John Donne and George Herbert had blended lives as priests and poets. However, Milton's objections to the political authority and practices of the clergy were ultimately to keep him devoted to poetry and to his own personal study of matters divine. After leaving Cambridge, he spent five years of private study on his father's estate in Horton, Buckinghamshire. His father, though a successful businessman, was also a talented musician and composer who encouraged his son's study of music, religion, and literature. On leaving Horton, Milton went on a fifteen-month tour of Italy ending in 1639. The years that made up this first phase of Milton's life produced the great early pastoral poems, "On the Morning of Christ's Nativity," "Comus: A Masque," and "Lycidas."

When Milton returned to England in 1639, he felt the need to enter the political fray of those revolutionary years, and turned from study and lyric poetry to a public existence as an ecclesiastical and political reformer:

> As soon as I was able, I hired a spacious house in the city for myself and my books; where I again with rapture renewed my literary pursuits, and where I calmly awaited the issue of the contest, which I trusted to the wise conduct of Providence, and to the courage of the people. The vigor of the parliament had begun to humble the pride of the bishops.
>
> As long as the liberty of speech was no longer subject to control, all mouths began to be opened against the bishops; some complained of the vices of the individuals, others of those of the order. They said that it was unjust that they alone should differ from the model of other reformed churches, that the government of the church should be according to the pattern of other churches, and particularly the word of God. This awakened all my attention and my zeal. I saw that a way was opening for the establishment of real liberty; that the foundation was laying for the deliverance of man from the yoke of slavery and superstition; that the principles of religion, which were the first objects of our care, would exert a salutary influence on the manners and constitution of the republic; and as I had from my youth studied the distinctions between religious and civil rights, I perceived that if I ever wished to be of use, I ought at least not to be wanting to my country, to the church, and to so many of my fellow-Christians, in a crisis of so much danger.
>
> I therefore determined to relinquish the other pursuits in which I was engaged, and to transfer the whole force of my talents and my industry to this one important object.
>
> ("Second Defense of the English People," 1652, p. 830)

From 1640 to 1658, the second period of his life, Milton served as Oliver Cromwell's Latin Secretary and penned his great and daring political tracts, including *The Areopagitica, Eikonoklastes,* and *The Tenure of Kings and Magistrates,* in which he justified the execution of King Charles I for being a "lawless tyrant."

Milton made religious freedom his primary concern during those years, working to break the bond between religious and political authority. Milton sided early with the Presbyterians against the tenure of Anglican William Laud, archbishop of Canterbury. The Presbyterians held that the Episcopal church should be replaced by a synod of Presbyters. But after the Civil War (1639–1642), it became apparent to Milton that the Presbyterians were not the revolutionaries he had hoped, but were becoming as notorious in their authority as the Anglicans before them. Milton sided with the Independents; though some of them were traditional Calvinists, they were united in opposition to the need for any establishment church. Independents composed most of Cromwell's New Model Army, eventually defeating the Presbyterians and the Presbyterian Parliament negotiating with Charles I, whom they tried and executed. The revolution eventually failed after defeating both the Anglicans and the Presbyterians because the new government would have to assume the role of tyrant or let the country drift into anarchy. In his sonnets to Henry Vane and to Cromwell, Milton urged against setting up any state religion: "Help us save free Conscience from the paw / Of hireling wolves whose Gospel is their maw."

Milton never abandoned his republicanism, and continued to produce strident political pamphlets, even at great risk to his life. Just before the restoration of Charles II in 1660, Milton argued strenuously against heredity Kingship or any other form of monarchy:

> Certainly then that people must needs be mad or strangely infatuated that build the chief hope of their common happiness or safety on a single person; who, if he happen to be good, can do no more than another man; if to be bad, hath in his hands to do more evil without check than millions of other men. The happiness of a nation must needs be firmest and certainest in a full and free council of their own electing, where no single person, but reason only, sways. . . . .All protestants hold that Christ in his church hath left no vicegerence of his power; but himself, without deputy, is the only head thereof, governing it from heaven.
>
> ("The Readie and Easie Way," 1660, p. 887)

Only the intercession of his more influential contemporaries, including fellow poet Andrew Marvell, prevented Milton's beheading with the advent of the Restoration.

In 1642 Milton married the first of his three wives, Mary Powell, with whom he had three daughters, Anne (b. 1646), Mary (b. 1648), and Deborah (b.1652), as well as a son, John (b. 1651), who died in infancy. Powell left Milton after a month of marriage and did not return to him until 1645. The difficulties of their marriage led, in part, to his pamphlet "The Doctrine of Discipline and Divorce" (1643). The pamphlet made Milton famous as "the divorcer" because he argued that marriage was based on mutual compatibility; compatibility or the lack of it was alone the grounds for marriage and divorce, not carnal attachment or carnal failings. With ingenious exegetical strategy, Milton argued around the Christian prohibition of divorce except foradultery (Matthew 19: 3–9) and the Mosaic permission for divorce only on the basis of "uncleanness" (Deuteronomy 24:1–2) by redefining the term to mean obstinacy. Mary Powell died in 1652. In 1656 he married Katherine Woodcock who died in 1658.

During the third and final period of his life, 1658–1674, Milton witnessed the failure of the English Revolution, and the restoration of Charles II. Completely blind, he dictated his great epic *Paradise Lost,* the briefer epic *Paradise Regained,* and the tragedy *Samson Agonistes.* In his last years, suffering from gout but cared for by Elizabeth Minshull, his third wife, Milton completed one of his most cherished works, *On Christian Doctrine.* An elaborate study in scriptural exegesis, this represents Milton's return at the end of his life to the intellectual effort of establishing the meaning of Christianity. Milton died on 8 November 1674, and this last work was not published until 1825.

Anyone who could claim to "assert Eternal Providence / And justify the ways of God to men" against all prevailing religious authority while simultaneously asserting man's fallen condition, risked being accused of epistemological and moral presumption, if not hopeless contradiction. Milton's erudition, wit, and poetic skill and daring made his case for the power of individual conscience a strong one. Critics of Milton have ranged among those who have seen him less as an advocate of Christian charity than as a rebel whose true allegiances consciously or unconsciously were with Satan and with ruining the sacred truths that he appeared committed to saving. Others have seen the compelling seductions and temptations present in Milton's work as his successful attempt to present the power of evil but not to advocate it. Milton could never accept that Augustinian view that evil was merely the absence of good, though he often seemed to welcome it as the force against and by which our virtue is tested. The heroic Christian life, to which Milton himself aspired, is always "trial by what is contrary," almost to the point of making contradiction and conflict the path of transcendence.

"ODE ON THE MORNING OF CHRIST'S NATIVITY" AND OTHER EARLY WORKS

"Trial by what is contrary" forms the dramatic basis of Milton's earliest work, in which he attempts to reconcile the poet's vocation and ideals of Christian charity. In *Ad Patrem* (?1634), Milton pays tribute to the classical traditions of poetry as well as to his father: "You should not despise the poet's task, divine song, which preserves some spark of Promethean fire and is the unrivalled glory of the heaven-born human mind and an evidence of our ethereal origin and celestial descent" (p. 85). Milton's idea of divine poetry is not mere music but song worthy of the religious cult of Orpheus, "who by his song—not by his cithara—restrained rivers and gave ears to the oaks, and by his singing stirred the ghosts of the dead to tears. That fame he owes to his song" (p. 84). Milton's father allowed his son five years of unburdened study on his estate, study that enabled him to enjoy a pastoral existence of contemplation:

> You may pretend to hate the delicate Muses, but I do not believe in your hatred. For you would not bid me go where the broad way lies wide open, where the field of lucre is easier and the golden hope of amassing money is glittering and sure; neither do you force me into the law and the evil administration of the national statutes. You do not condemn my ears to noisy impertinence. But rather, because you wish to enrich the mind which you have carefully cultivated, you lead me far away from the uproar of cities into these high retreats of delightful leisure beside the Aonian stream, and permit me to walk there by Phoebus's side, his blessed companion.
>
> (p. 84)

For all Milton's praise of the power of the Orphic cult of poetry in opposition to base lucre, "evil administration," or other worldly pursuits, Milton's early poetry also conveys his skepticism of pastoral and poetic contemplation. In "Ode on the Morning of Christ's Nativity" (1629), he depicts shepherds tending to their flocks ignorant of the advent of Pan, who had been praised in Virgil's first Georgic and in the Orphic *Hymn to Pan,* but had also become associated in the Renaissance with Christ:

> The Shepherds on the Lawn,
> Or ere the point of dawn,
>   Sat simply chatting in a rustic row;
> Full little thought they then,
> That the mighty *Pan*
>   Was kindly come to live with them below;
> Perhaps their loves, or else their sheep,
> Was all that did their silly thoughts so busy keep.
>
> (VIII: 85–92, p. 45)

Milton then announces the diminishment of the pagan gods and idols altogether as the advent of Christ approaches:

> The Oracles are dumb,
> No voice or hideous hum
>   Runs through the arched roof in words deceiving.
> *Apollo* from his shrine
> Can no more divine
>   With hollow shriek the steep of *Delphos* leaving.
> No nightly trance, or breathed spell,
> Inspires the pale-eyed Priest from the prophetic spell.
>
> (XIX: 173–180, p. 48)

Milton concludes, as he often does in his early poems, with a diminished view of his own "tedious Song," and points to the waiting readiness of the angels who are "serviceable." He aspires to the prophetic mode, a kind of poetry distinguishable by the grandeur of its music. The sweet music of God involves the harmonies of the golden age reformed in the Christian one:

> Ring out ye Crystal spheres,
> Once bless our human ears,
>   (If you have power to touch our sense so)
> And let your silver chime
> Move in melodious time;
>   And let the Bass of Heav'n's deep Organ blow,
> And with your ninefold harmony
> Make up full consort to th'Angelic symphony.
>
> (XIII: 125–132, p. 46)

This invocation presages a similar one two years later in *Il Penseroso* (?1631, printed 1645), his hymn to serious, if not melancholic study and contemplation. In contrast to the more pagan and pastoral *L'Allegro,* written during the same year, Milton here invokes the virtues of study and the cloister to achieve the prophetic, angelic strain:

But let my due feet never fail
To walk the studious Cloister's pale,
And love the high embowed Roof,
With antic Pillars massy proof,
And storied Windows richly dight,
Casting a dim religious light.
There let the pealing Organ blow
To the full voiced Choir below,
In Service high and Anthems clear,
As may with sweetness, through mine ear,
Dissolve me into ecstasies,
And bring all Heav'n before mine eyes.

(I. 155–166, p. 76)

As his thought developed, Milton struggled between the power of classical traditions of pastoral poetry and the need to create a new poetry embodying a vision of faith and devotion to the Christian God.

"COMUS"

"Comus: A Masque" (written 1634, printed 1637) works within the traditions of pastoral poetry, in this case specifically the Renaissance pageant, to explore the conflicts between a life of sensuality and one of chaste virtue. This symbolic pageant portrays the journey of a fifteen year-old Lady accompanied by her two brothers as they cross a dark wood. Separated from her brothers, the Lady becomes a captive of the rustic Comus, a son of Circe whose name in Latin means "revelry," and his temptations. The biblical-pastoral stories of the Fall and of Jesus' temptation in the wilderness inform this masque's symbolism as does Homer's account of Odysseus's need to resist Circe in order to return home. Milton reverses the gender roles of the Homeric story by portraying the wanderer as a woman and the tempter as a man. Traditionally, the pastoral mode was characterized not only by the presence of shepherds and other rustics, who are opposed to the world of heroic action, but also by the conflict between moral and social hierarchies. Milton's *Comus* expresses the perennial concern with nature and Arcadia, a mythic land of plentitude and an idealized contrast to the corruptions of the city and the power struggles that exist even among shepherds. This poem marks the beginning of Milton's preoccupation with the possibility of recovering a perfect world—rather than expressing hopes for a New Jerusalem, Milton tends to meditate on restoring an Eden that has been lost. Nature and its uses becomes an important part of the poem's symbolic labyrinth. Milton's depiction of nature in the poem is hardly pure, and often ambiguous. The ambiguity is stressed right from the beginning of the poem as the character of the Spirit speaks first of a divine, heavenly world:

Above the smoke and stir of this dim spot,
Which men call earth, and with low-thoughted care
Confined and pestered in this pinfold here,
Strive to keep up a frail and Feverish being,
Unmindful of the crown that Virtue gives
After this mortal change, to her true Servants
Amongst the enthroned gods on Sainted seats.

(I. 5–11, p. 90)

The heavenly world is set off sharply against the sublunary one that remains at best "pinfold" earth, a place of "Sin-worn mold."

On the other hand, the estate to which the Lady and her brothers are traveling is somehow gemlike, noble, and worthy of salvation. If earth is itself "pinfold," within it there appears to be a nearly utopian isle saved from the dross of the rest of the planet. Indeed, Milton here as elsewhere relies heavily on the ancient idea of paradise as being a placed "walled-in," which must be made safe from the rest of nature through disciplined labor.

The tension between the state of the "Sin-worn" world and the possibility of paradise is never resolved. Comus's successful masquerade makes it clear that no worldly paradise can remain entirely safe from seductions that no enclosure is ever perfect enough to protect from evil. The Lady makes her virtue meaningful by being able to maintain it against the seductions of Comus's rhetoric, even though her purity and her chastity make her world unapproachably inhuman and cold and a rejection rather than affirmation of God's creation. Her elder brother gives voice to the inviolable realm of virtue:

> against the threats
> Of malice or of sorcery, or that power
> Which erring men call chance, this I hold firm,
> Virtue may be assailed, but never hurt,
> Surprised by unjust force, but not enthralled,
> Yea even that which mischief meant most harm
> Shall in the happy trial prove most glory.
>
> (I. 587–592, p. 103–104)

If nature and the world suffer from hopeless corruption, can there be any discourse with the classical view that did not regard it as fallen? The Lady's elder brother expresses a Manichean vision of the conflict of good and evil. Providential history must ultimately allow good to transcend evil or become meaningless:

> But evil on itself shall back recoil
> And mix no more with goodness, when at last
> Gathered like scum, and settled to itself
> It shall be in eternal restless change
> Self-fed, and self-consumed. If this fail,
> The pillared firmament is rottenness,
> And earth's base built on stubble.
>
> (I. 593–599, p. 104)

To justify Creation, the brother asserts, there must be a process of historical progress by which good is purified from evil and materiality. He envisions the latter as an ouroboros, a snake feeding on itself and sinking into Lucretian flux. Milton had expressed this apocalyptic hope for the purification of the soul and the triumph over time and earthly grossness in the stunning one-sentence lyric "On Time":

> And joy shall overtake us as a flood,
> When every thing is sincerely good
> And perfectly divine,
> And truth, and peace, and love shall ever shine
> About the supreme throne
> Of him, to whose happy-making sight alone,
> When once our heavenly-guided soul shall climb,
> Then all this earthly grossness quit,
> Attired with stars, we shall for ever sit,
> Triumphing over Death, and Chance, and thee O Time.
>
> (I. 13–22, p. 80)

The sheer force of the poetry is the greatest evidence of Milton's faith. But Milton does seem at least tempted by the sensuous, if not the sensual, world, as well as by the need to live a virtuous life within the world as it stands. Comus makes a compelling moral rebuke to the Lady's claims of chastity, arguing that she is ungrateful for what nature has given and too arrogant to accept the "unexempt condition" of "mortal frailty":

> But you invert the covenants of her trust,
> And harshly deal like an ill borrower
> With that which you received on other terms,
> Scorning the unexempt condition
> By which all mortal frailty must subsist,
> Refreshment after toil, ease after pain,
> That have been tired all day without repast,
> And timely rest have wanted, but fair virgin
> This will restore all soon
>
> (I. 682–689, p. 106)

The Lady's response goes beyond pointing out Comus's duplicity. She asserts her "taste," the inward goodness of her appetites, which makes her free from corrupting external forces. Milton here first introduces this metaphorical use of the word "taste" (which figures prominently in *Paradise Lost,* where the failure of "taste" leads to the plucking of the forbidden tree's fruit). For the Lady (and Milton) it is crucial to the soul's transcendence:

> And wouldst thou seek again to trap me here
> With liquorish baits fit to ensnare a brute?
> . . . none
> But such as are good men can give good things,
> And that which is not good, is not delicious
> To a well-governed and wise appetite.
>
> (I. 699–701; 703–705, p. 106)

The phrase "well-governed" places emphasis on self-determination and self-discipline over any external moral or political authority.

Comus's rejoinder to the Lady's response plays on the idea of divine service, underscoring the ingratitude of temperance as it scorns the lavish provisions of the "all-giver," and repudiates the responsibilities of the dutiful shepherd. Here, as elsewhere, echoes of the prelapsarian commandments to be fruitful and multiply will make strong claims against unworldly purity:

> . . . if all the world
> Should in a pet of temperance feed on pulse,

Drink the clear stream, and nothing wear but frieze,
The all-giver would be unthanked, would be
  unpraised,
Not half his riches known, and yet despised,
And we should serve him as a grudging master,
As a penurious niggard of his wealth,
And live like nature's bastards, not her sons,
Who would be quite surcharged with her own weight,
And strangled with her waste fertility;
The earth cumbered, and the winged air darked with
  plumes.

(I. 720–730, p. 707)

Milton will continue to consider arguments about what kind of thanks God needs, what it means to serve, and to praise. The Lady's final response argues for the fair distribution of wealth instead of the covetousness and greed to which Comus's view, encouraging bounty "upon some few with vast excess," may tend. In the end, the Lady refuses to argue at all on the grounds that it is impossible to teach anyone who "has nor ear, nor soul to apprehend / the sublime notion, and high mystery / That must be uttered to unfold the sage / And serious doctrine of Virginity" (I. 784–757, p. 108). The "sage and serious doctrine of virginity" is never explained, though it suggests the inwardness and spiritual integrity of the citadel of the self. As Milton wrote in *The Apology for Smectymnuus,* virtue begins and ends with the soul. Virtue is a quality often associated with masculinity (from the root, *vir,* meaning man), but here becomes embodied in the Lady. Lust and profligacy are here embodied in Comus who is Circe's son. Milton confounds accepted concepts of moral and gender hierarchy.

Despite the fact that Comus has confined her to a chair, the Lady's otherworldly allegiances seem to keep her from further harm. The Spirit, a figure of the classical and pagan world, comes to her rescue and enlists the skills of a shepherd lad and a strange flower, Haemony, "a small unsightly root, / But of divine effect," which in "another Country . . . Bore a bright golden flow'r" (I. 629–630; 633, p. 104). Nature, embodied in this flower, holds the possibility of rescue. The Spirit later learns from Meliboeus, a figure from Virgil's eclogues, to call upon Sabrina, a nymph, who uses the cleansing waters of the river Severn and the power of song to liberate the Lady in her

hour of need. The dances and songs that conclude the poem, after her rescue, attempt to bring together the sensuousness that Milton loved and the simplicity and purity appropriate to the elevation and transcendence of chastity. The presence of dance at the conclusion of the poem unites the physical and metaphysical and affirms the union of pagan and Christian worlds.

"LYCIDAS"

THE worldly temptations of fame and sensuality become the object of meditation in Milton's greatest short lyric, "Lycidas" (1638), a pastoral elegy written in memory of Cambridge classmate Edward King, who was drowned in a shipwreck at sea in 1637. The impossibility of accounting for a world that would so unfairly take the life of a young man forces Milton to question his own poetic vocation: "What boots it with incessant care / To tend the homely slighted Shepherd's trade, / And strictly meditate the thankless Muse?" (I. 64–66, p. 122). The nagging question for Milton is both how and whom one serves. The "Shepherd's Trade" could have either the classical sense of the poet or the more modern sense of the Christian pastor, the keeper of the flock—or, perhaps, both. The muse may be either indifferent to gratitude or unwilling to show it. The poem's classicism has raised questions among critics about the attitude expressed toward Christianity, particularly in light of the narrator's attack on the Anglican clergy. Why would Milton choose classical conventions to speak of Christianity? Samuel Johnson saw Milton's classicism as blasphemous:

Among the flocks, and copses, and flowers, appear the heathen deities. . . . With these trifling fictions are mingled the most awful and sacred truths, such as ought never to be polluted with such irreverent combinations. The shepherd likewise is now a feeder of sheep, and afterwards an ecclesiastical pastor, a superintendent of a Christian flock. Such equivocations are always unskillful; but here they are indecent, and at least approach to impiety, of which, however, I believe the writer not to have been conscious.

Johnson may have been right that there was something irreverent about Milton's classicism but it hardly appears unconscious.

If Comus was the child of Circe, Milton turns Lycidas, a Virgilian Shepherd, into a figure related to Orpheus, the divinely inspired singer. Church fathers had already suggested that Orpheus in his descent into the underworld and return to life was symbolic of Christ's saving of the soul and of his church. In "Lycidas," Milton calls attention to Ovid's description of Orpheus's fate of being torn apart by Bacchic revelers: "What could the Muse herself that Orpheus bore, / The Muse herself, for her enchanting son / Whom universal nature did lament, / When by the rout that made the hideous roar, / His gory visage down the stream was sent, / Down the swift Hebrus to the Lesbian shore?" (I. 58–63, p. 122). Orpheus' death becomes an inexplicable martyrdom for sweet "enchantments" against the "hideous roar" of change and brutality. Throughout his life, Milton regarded his vision of poetry and the poet as dangerous to the vulgarity of the world. His praise of this heroic martyrdom was in large part an opposition to the corrupt authority of the clergy.

The poet, as Milton conceived him, is best suited to transform the sensuous world of classical antiquity, the material of poets, into the matter of Christian virtue. Milton, no doubt, intended to be irreverent toward an ecclesiastical authority he had come to hate and whose language and ways he believed needed to be purified. Milton's rage informs the most political and most controversial parts of the poem in which St. Peter, "The pilot of the Galilean lake," attacks the contemporary clergy:

'How well could I have spared for thee, young swain,
enow of such as for their bellies' sake
creep, and intrude, and climb into the fold!
Of other care they little reckoning make,
Than how to scramble at the shearers' feast
And shove away the worthy bidden guest.
Blind mouths! that scarce themselves know how to
   hold
A sheep-hoook, or have learned aught else the least
That to the faithful herdman's art belongs.
What recks it them? What need they? They are sped;
And when they list, their lean and flashy songs

Grate on their scrannel pipes of wretched straw;
The hungry sheep look up and are not fed,
But swoln with wind and the rank mist they draw
Rot inwardly, and foul contagion spread;
Besides what the grim wolf with privy paw
Daily devours apace, and nothing said.'
                              (I. 1113–1129, p. 123)

Milton hated religion turned organizational, hieratic, and professional. His puritanical desire to have individuals aspire freely to the divine fueled his attack most particularly on the lack of spiritual depth in the professional clergy, a lack evident in their "lean and flashy songs." Their language and their music gives them away, and Milton himself is wary of speaking before he is ready to provide a new language that might actually express the power God's ways. Several years after "Lycidas," Milton wrote "The Reason of Church Government" (1641), a prose tract in which he attacks the clergy while providing his own justification for ranking the vocation of the poet alongside the office of the ministry. Milton praises King David's psalms as worthy "beside the office of the pulpit" for spiritual education:

But those frequent songs throughout the law and prophets beyond all these, not in their divine argument alone, but in the very critical art of composition, may be easily made appear over all the kinds of lyric poesy to be incomparable. These abilities, wheresoever they be found, are the inspired gift of God rarely bestowed, but yet to some (though most abuse) in every nation; and are of power beside the office of a pulpit, to inbreed and cherish in a great people the seeds of virtue and public civility, to allay the perturbations of the mind and set the affections in right tune, to celebrate in glorious and lofty hymns the throne and equipage of God's almightiness, and what he works and what he suffers to be wrought with high providence in his church, to sing the victorious agonies of martyrs and saints, the deeds and triumphs of just and pious nations doing valiantly through faith against the enemies of Christ, to deplore the general relapses of kingdoms and states from justice and God's true worship.
                              (p. 699–670)

This level of poetry can be achieved, in Milton's view, outside "this impertinent yoke of prelaty, under whose inquisitorious and tyrannical duncery no free and splendid wit can flourish" (p.

670). To the hot coal of divine and prophetic inspiration "must be added industrious and select reading, steady observation, insight into all seemly and generous arts and affairs." Milton's commitment to poetry—but of a particular kind, free from the flawed work of vulgar amorists—is the subject of hope in "Lycidas." What poetic trappings and forms are suitable for divine poetry? How can classical literature be used in service of Christian context? If the creation of such a high art involves long and arduous study, the death of a young friend, Edward King, threatened him with doubts about committing to such a task, given the fragility of life and the chance that he might never live to see himself prepared.

The poem's ultimate answer may be a triumphant vision of Lycidas purified in a death by water and resurrected by "the dear might of him that walked the waves," an epiphany of Christ's power. The poem begins and ends, however, with Milton's self-doubt about his readiness to write the kind of poetry to which he aspires. If at the outset he saw this classical elegy as plucking with "forced fingers rude" the unripe fruit of poetry, in his conclusion, he retreats from Christian epiphany and presents himself as an "uncouth Swain," one still working in classical language and pastoral conventions. He concludes with the hope of "fresh Woods and Pastures new," (I. 193, p. 125) presumably a transformation of the figurative world of pagan pastoral convention into the true one of Genesis.

Milton's belief that a life of great preparation was necessary before the writing of great poetry fuels at least part of the agony of "Lycidas." How long could he wait and would life allow him to wait before he would write the poetry he felt destined to create? As Milton became engaged in the struggles of political revolution, he wrote less poetry and more political tracts ("with the left hand"). Intensifying his pain was the gradual loss of his sight. By 1652, his blindness was nearly total. The sonnet written at the time, "When I consider how my light is spent," (Sonnet XIX) conveys the agony of his desire to serve his God, and his failure, as yet, to have produced poetry worthy of his goal. Like Job, he begins to question why God would so afflict one so committed to service and, therefore, the intent of the Creator. The voice of patience responds to the questioning in the octave. The concluding sestet undercuts, though in a more muted way than God's answer to Job, the speaker's assumption that his desire or need to serve matters at all to a God who governs a multitude of servants in a vast world:

. . . God doth not need
Either man's work or his own gifts; who best
Bear his mild yoke, they serve him best; his State
Is Kingly. Thousands at his bidding speed
And post o'er Land and Ocean without rest:
They also serve who also only stand and wait.
(I. 9–14, p. 168)

Poignant, too, is the recognition that any of man's gifts are ultimately "his own," not man's but God's. Milton does not abandon the possibility that he will serve by acting through poetry, but accepts that service may also demand the continued suffering of patience.

"AREOPAGITICA"

WHILE waiting, Milton produced prose tracts of immense power against monarchy and against the Anglican Church. The ascendancy of reforming Presbyterians in 1641 did little to appease those like Milton who had committed themselves to the abolition of all national ecclesiastical authority. One sign of progress was the dissolving in 1641 of the crown's Star Chamber, which had been charged with the approving or licensing of all books. But the Long Parliament, supported by the Presbyters who feared the outpouring of unorthodox publications, reestablished licensing in 1643. Nothing could be printed without the approval of the official licenser, and it could only be printed at one of the approved presses of the Stationer's Company, a state monopoly. Violations were punishable by imprisonment. Milton reacted with his greatest and most memorable, though fundamentally undeliverable speech, "Areopagitica" (1644), in which he argued strenuously not only against licensing but for the importance of allowing differing views to combat each other in public. Not so much a defense of freedom of speech as of the freedom of the will to test its power of choice, it became the prose precursor to the moral and theological vision of *Paradise Lost.*

In "Areopagitica," Milton's defense of books becomes a passionate defense of the sanctity of reason. He turns the fears expressed by the Commonwealth and the Church about the demeaning effect of books against them. Books are, indeed, more powerful than their creators, which is precisely what censors fear. He goes so far as to argue that the destruction of a good book is the murder of reason itself:

> I deny not but that it is of greatest concernment in the Church and Commonwealth to have a vigilant eye how books demean themselves as well as men; and thereafter to confine, imprison, and do sharpest justice on them as malefactors. For books are not absolutely dead things, but do contain a potency of life in them to be as active as that soul was whose progeny they are; nay they do preserve as in a vial the purest efficacy and extraction of that living intellect that bred them. I know they are as lively, and as vigorously productive, as those fabulous dragon's teeth; and being sown up and down, may chance to spring up armed men. And yet, on the other hand unless wariness be used, as good almost kill a man as kill a good book; who kills a man kills a reasonable creature, God's image; but he who destroys a good book, kills reason itself, kills the image of God, as it were, in the eye. . . . We should be wary, therefore, what persecution we raise against the living labours of public men, how we spill that seasoned life of man, preserved and stored up in books; since we see a kind of homicide may be thus committed, sometimes a martyrdom; and if it extend to the whole impression, a kind of massacre, whereof the execution ends not in the slaying of an elemental life, but strikes at that ethereal and fift essence, the breath of reason itself, slays an immortality rather than a life.
>
> (p. 720)

This view appears to go against the general iconoclasm and hatred of idolatry in Milton's work and in Puritanism in general. Milton comes dangerously close to turning the book into an idol or graven image. On the other hand, Milton sees books not as dead life but as sowing the seeds of further action that will unsettle entrenched authority. Milton does not argue that all books or views are of equal value or that all kinds of thought are worthy. However, if there were a choice between permissiveness in what is published and censorship by a central authority of dubious judgment, Milton would choose the former.

The deeper part of Milton's argument veers away from the praise of books as embodiments of reason or even of free speech itself. No book, including the Bible, can be guaranteed in Milton's mind to cause a soul to become or to do either good or evil. But no conscience can maintain its goodness without exercising its will to choose between good and evil:

> Good and evil we know in the field of this world grow up together almost inseparably; and the knowledge of good is so involved and interwoven with the knowledge of evil, and in so many cunning resemblances hardly to be discerned, that those confused seeds which were imposed on Psyche as an incessant labor to cull out and sort asunder, were not more intermixed. It was from out the rind of one apple tasted, that the knowledge of good and evil, as two twins cleaving together, leaped forth into the world. And perhaps this is the doom which Adam fell into of knowing good and evil, that is to say, of knowing good by evil.
>
> (p. 728)

Milton here outlines the fact and the psychology of the Fall and, to an extent, the doctrine of *felix culpa,* that we know good by knowing bad and struggling to transcend it. Evil cannot be banished from consciousness but its presence is part of the continual challenge to exercise our freedom to will and to choose:

> As therefore the state of man now is, what wisdom can there be to choose, what continence to forbear without the knowledge of evil? He that can apprehend and consider vice with all her baits and seeming pleasures, and yet abstain, and yet distinguish, and yet prefer that which is truly better, he is the true warfaring Christian.
>
> (p. 728)

Milton then extols, in one of the most memorable passages in English letters, the virtue of exercising choice in a purifying trial by contraries:

> I cannot praise a fugitive and cloistered virtue, un-exercised and unbreathed, that never sallies out and sees her adversary, but slinks out of the race where that immortal garland is to be run for, not without dust and heat. Assuredly we bring not innocence into the world, we bring impurity much rather: that which purifies us is trial, and trial is by what is contrary.
>
> (p. 728)

Milton concludes this line of argument with the example of Spenser's Knight of Temperance who is tested by the cave of Mammon and the bower of bliss. The example has rhetorical force beyond being illustrative. He holds the work of a poet to be of greater instructive importance than that of scholastics and theologians, and he condemns those who would ban or diminish poetical works as mere fancy:

> That virtue therefore which is but a youngling in the contemplation of evil, and knows not the utmost that vice promises to her followers, and rejects it, is but a blank virtue, not a pure; her whiteness is but an excremental whiteness; which was the reason why our sage and serious poet Spenser, whom I dare be known to think a better teacher than Scotus or Aquinas, describing true temperance under the person of Guion, brings him in with his palmer through the cave of Mammon and the bower of earthly bliss, that he might see and know, and yet abstain.
>
> (p. 728–729)

The possibility of teaching how we can see and know evil and yet still abstain from it persists as the crucial poetic challenge of Milton's late work, *Paradise Lost, Paradise Regained,* and *Samson Agonistes.*

PARADISE LOST

DESPITE its immense complexity, the subject of *Paradise Lost* (1667) is stated compactly in its first two lines: "Of man's first disobedience and the fruit / Of that forbidden tree" (I. 1–2, p. 211). Neither God nor Satan is of as great importance as man's responsibility for his fall and the need to understand self-government in light of the temptations of knowledge, sensuality, and nature. The subject leads to Milton's object, which he proclaimed at the conclusion of the poem's invocation: "to justify the ways of God to men" (I. 25, p. 212). Milton will attempt to make the Judeo-Christian God worthy of reasonable men's devotion and service. Though he once considered King Arthur as the subject for his epic, he regarded only a universal, transnational topic worthy of his epic. Arthur was historical conjecture but Genesis was truth. Around the story, Milton wove an intricate cosmology that attempts to demystify the grounds of faith and to explain in a rational way the existence of evil.

As an epic poem composed, in part, on Homeric and Virgilian models, *Paradise Lost* presents the cunning and power of heroic figures, a terrifying vision of the underworld, and the expectation of a triumphant search for home and establishment of an empire. Milton draws heavily on the power of classical literary traditions. Justifying, for example, the poem's lack of rhyme, he praises "the ancient liberty recovered to Heroic Poem from the troublesome and modern bondage of riming" (p. 210). But Milton underscores the sadness and loss in ancient epic and supplants national triumph with the primordial world of a prenational God. It may be true that the failure of the English revolution to produce any adequate alternative to the potential tyranny of the monarchy drove Milton to abandon a vision of a political utopia. The precarious balance between chaos and totalitarianism in the political life of his country may have inspired Milton to focus in *Paradise Lost,* as well as *Paradise Regained* and *Samson Agonistes,* solely on the agency and uncertainty of the individual conscience. Yet Milton also makes brilliant use of the dialogic mode of Virgil's *Eclogues,* as well as his *Georgics,* to describe the vigilant thought and labor necessary to manage life in a precarious world.

Milton dramatized the problem of achieving a balance between liberty and obedience; violation of that balance by the individual will leads to the fall of the angels and of man. Rather than assume evil only to be the absence of good, Milton renders it a manifestation of intractable pride born of unbridled freedom and irrepressible ego. Heroic grandeur in the poem often dissipates and becomes less important than contemplative dialogue. Satan, the tragic and Shakespearean hero of the poem, suffers almost comic deflation by the end of the fourth book. Some have regarded Satan as an allegory for either the papacy, the English monarchy, or the excesses of revolutionary individualism. No doubt his character embodies some of all three. The poem's central books—IV, V, and VI—focus on the less heroic pastoral life in Eden, in which careful education and cultivation may be the only defenses against evil. It is also true that the recounting of the warfare in Heaven occupies the formal center of the book. The futility of the war may attest to Satan's courage and integrity in the face of God's trickery and brutality; or it may reveal only his obstinacy and foolishness.

Satan's arguments for his own rebellion are among the most controversial and memorable episodes of the poem; readers have been compelled by his nobility and surprised by his crippling irony. Satan first appears in the poem as a revolutionary hero who has defied a brutal tyrant. But his revolutionary grandeur becomes compromised by his sclerotic pride, relentless ambition, and degrading hatred and envy. He himself becomes a charismatic tyrant who ultimately fails in his leadership and succeeds only in helping the innocent bring about their ruin. Satan's iconic worship of his own mind becomes a misapprehension of the puritan ideal of reason in the service of God. Celebrating his mind's ability to remake the world in its own image, Satan gradually becomes a willing prisoner of his own mental icons:

. . . Be it so, since he
Who now is Sovran can dispose and bid
What shall be right: fardest from him is best
Whom reason hath equalled, force hath made supreme
Above his equals. Farewell happy Fields
Where Joy forever dwells: Hail horrors, hail
Infernal world, and thou profoundest Hell
Receive thy new Possessor: One who brings
A mind not to be changed by Place or Time.
The mind is its own place, and in itself
Can make a Heav'n of Hell, a Hell of Heav'n.
What matter where, if I be still the same,

And what I should be, all but less than hee
Whom Thunder hath made greater? Here at least
We shall be free: th'Almighty hath not built
Here for his envy, will not drive us hence:
Here we may reign secure, and in my choice
To reign is worth ambition though in Hell:
Better to reign in Hell, than serve in Heav'n.
(I: 217–218, p. 245–263)

Satan praises rebellion to justify to his fellow travelers the pains of Hell; their goal was never to serve, only to reign. But if in the beginning of the poem he boasts of his independence of time and place and his ability to make "a Heav'n of Hell, / a Hell of Heav'n," later, in Book IV, Satan admits he cannot fly from "the Hell within him," "no more than from himself can fly / By change of place" (IV: 74, p. 279). Subverting the ideal of service, Satan praises only the importance of sovereignty. Heaven and Hell in both mirror each other as part of Satan's solipsistic world. Though he argues that it was his choice to "reign" in Hell, he joins the rebel angels in complaining that "Fate" their "Free Virtue" "enthralled." Milton casts them as bad theologians, wandering in a maze of philosophical discourse about "Providence, Foreknowledge, Will, and Fate, / Fix't Fate, Free will, Foreknowledge absolute" (II: 559–560, p. 245).

As Satan undertakes his putatively heroic mission to the newly created Earth, he feels only the intensity of his helplessness and despair. Though he claims to feel love for the newly created couple in Eden, the insatiability of his desire can only lead to harm:

O Hell! What do mine eyes with grief behold,
Into our room of bliss thus high advanc't
Creatures of other mold, earth-born perhaps,
Not Spirits, yet to heav'nly Spirits bright
Little inferior; whom my thoughts pursue
With wonder, and could love, so lively shines
In them Divine resemblance, and such high grace
That hand that formed them on thir shape hat poured.
(IV: 358–365, p. 287)

So taken is Satan with Adam and Eve's beauty that he claims bondage to his desire. And he confuses his love for them with the need for their bondage:

. . . League with you I seek,
And mutual amity so strait, so close,
That I with you must dwell, or you with me
Henceforth; my dwelling haply may not please
Like this fair Paradise, your sense, yet such
Accept your Maker's work; he gave it me,
Which I as freely give; Hell shall unfold,
To entertain you two, her widest Gates,
And send forth all her Kings; there will be room,
Not like these narrow limits, to receive
Your numerous offspring; if no better place,
Thank him who puts me loath to this revenge
On you who wrong me not for him who wronged.
And should I at your harmless innocence
Melt, as I do, yet public reason just,
Honor and Empire with revenge enlarged,
By conquering this new World, compels me now
To do what else though damned I should abhor.

(IV: 375–392, p. 287)

Satan contradicts his assertions of "public reason just" and the freedom of his actions by simultaneously asserting the necessity and compulsion of his deeds. Satan's goal of "Empire" "enlarg'ed," contradicts the ideals of freedom from servitude that he claims to champion.

Milton has God speak to justify himself in a way unprecedented in the Hebrew Bible; his clarity becomes a foil to theological mysticism and to Satan's tortured logic. Rather than providing laws, offering covenant, or expressing the wrath of his judgment or the promise of covenant, Milton's God explains that the abiding principle of his justice is freedom, and insists that the rebel angels chose their predicament. Freedom to will becomes God's operative principle without which service would be meaningless servitude. God also insists that his foreknowledge of rebellion does not constitute determinism:

Such I created all th'ethereal Powers
And Spirits, both them who stood and them who failed;
Freely they stood who stood, and fell who fell.
Not free, what proof could they have giv'n sincere
Of true allegiance, constant Faith or Love,
Where only what they needs must do, appeared,
Not what they would? What praise could they receive,
What pleasure I from such obedience paid,
When Will and Reason (Reason also is choice)
Useless and vain, of freedom both despoiled,

Made passive both, had served necessity,
Not me. They therefore as to right belonged,
So were created, nor can justly accuse
Thir maker, or their making, or thir Fate;
As if Predestination over ruled
Their will, disposed by absolute Decree
Or high foreknowledge; they themselves decreed
Their own revolt, not I: if I foreknew,
Foreknowledge had not influence on their fault,
Which had no less proved certain unforeknown.

(III: 100–119, p. 260)

Original sin becomes a matter of conscious choice and reason, not something preordained by either God or matter. Milton here gives full vent to his adherence to the Arminian heresy that challenged Calvin's doctrine of predestination. God argues that he abides by his own rules in a way that is neither arbitrary nor personal:

. . . for so
I formed them free, and free they must remain,
Till they enthrall themselves: I else must change
Their nature, and revoke the high Decree
Unchangeable, Eternal, which ordained
Their freedom; they themselves ordained their fall.

(III: 123–128, p. 261)

However free the angels may have been to choose, God certainly does not provide a haven for dissenters. Despite the claim that he does not foreordain, his foreknowledge and the ultimate arbitrariness of his authority, particularly in the seemingly nepotistic creation of his Son, trouble both Satan and critics of Milton. God's monarchy appears to be difficult to reconcile with perfect freedom and reason, and he announces a plan of abdication by which he would become an immanent part of a self-governing realm. At the end of time, there will be a new heaven and earth, and eventually even the Son his "regal Sceptre shalt lay by, / For regal Sceptre then no more shall need, / God shall be All in All" (III: 339–341, p. 266). Later, in Book VI, Raphael describes the Son declaring his abdication to his Father: "Sceptre and power, thy givings, I assume, / And gladlier shall resign, when in the end / Thou shalt be All in All, and I in thee / For ever, and in me all whom though lov'st" (IV: 730–732, p. 340). Milton strives for a vision in which no sovereign is necessary in the government of the universe. Satan's unforgiving hatred ("For never can true reconcilement grow / Where wounds of deadly hate have pierceed so deep" [IV: 98–99, p. 279]) becomes the force that precludes this pantheism. He becomes wedded to his eternal and relentless individuality.

The fall of thousands of angels provides a purpose, one not given in Genesis, for God's creation of earth and of Adam and Eve: the eventual repopulation of heaven. The first couple must learn how to grow to God's service without being seduced by ambition or knowledge. The angel Raphael must explain to Adam and Eve the contradictions that intrude on their innocence without ruining that innocence. The problem ultimately involves understanding nature, man's relation to it, and the government of the small world of Eden. Though permitting the possibilities of growth and perfection, Raphael must warn the couple not to dream of other worlds. Eden demands cultivation and Adam and Eve's perfection does not preclude development and change—though this change could be either for better or worse. The exercise of choice, taste, and judgment must have consequences to make their freedom meaningful. How can any knowledge be sufficiently circumscribed to prevent the desire and rebellion that produced the fall of the angels? Milton's monism and materialism undermines notions of transcendence from a sensuous world; he sees them as desire for an impossible purity that does violence to creation.

Milton draws not only on the Hebrew Bible but on classical and modern scientific sources—from Lucretius to Copernicus—for his cosmology. Fixity and change vie for cosmological mastery in Milton's universe. It becomes impossible in Milton to separate creation into simple poles of good and evil. To describe Satan's massiveness, Milton uses the simile of a whale and leads us through an epic labyrinth of ancient analogies ending in the Leviathian of Genesis and Job:

Thus Satan talking to his nearest Mate
With Head up-lift above the wave, and Eyes
That sparkling blazed, his other Parts besides
Prone on the Flood, extended long and large
Lay floating many a rood, in bulk as huge
As whom the Fables name of monstrous size,
Titanian, or Earth-born, that warred on Jove,
Briareos, or Typhon, whom the Den
By ancient Tarsus held, or that Sea-beast
Leviathan, which God of all his works
Created hugest that swim th'Ocean stream:
                              (I. 192–202, p. 216)

The classical similes, mostly from Hesiod's account of creation, evoke the war between the Titans and the Olympian Gods, a foreshadowing of Satan's revolt in Heaven. However, Leviathan in the Bible is one of God's creations and an example of God's awful power. The analogies suggests, therefore, that Satan is a part of God's creation, making his presence and even his revolt an inextricable part of the scheme of things.

Nature itself emanates from warring factions and tends toward the disruption of fixity and proscribed hierarchies. For his science, Milton draws on Lucretius' atomic and material conception of the world to challenge the theological mysticism that suggests God created the world ex nihilo, from nothing:

. . . where eldest Night
And Chaos, Ancestors of Nature, hold
Eternal Anarchy, amidst the noise
Of endless wars, and by confusion stand.
For hot, cold, moist, and dry, four champions fierce
Strive here for Mastery, and to Battle bring
Thir embryon Atoms; they around the flag
Of each his Faction, In their several Clans,
Light-armed or heavy, sharp, smooth, swift or slow . . .
Swarm populous, unnumbered as the sands of Barca, or
Cyrenes torrid soil,
Levied to side with warring winds, and poise
Their lighter wings
. . . To whom these most adhere,
Hee rules a moment; Chaos Umpire sits,
And by the decision more imbroils the fray
By which he Reigns; next him high Arbiter
Chance governs all. Into this wild Abyss,
The Womb of nature and perhaps her Grave,
Of neither Sea, nor Shore, nor Air, nor Fire,
But all these in their pregnant causes mixt
Confusedly, and which thus must ever fight
                              (II: 894–914, p. 253)

The metaphors of political warfare here underscore Milton's general focus on the need for some kind of just order and hierarchy to provide "Maistry" lest the womb of nature become its own grave. The angels themselves, we are reminded, turn out to be matter, capable of gentle and amorous interpenetration, who can "either Sex assume, or both; so soft / And uncompounded is thir Essence pure, / Nor tied or manacled with joint or limb, / Nor founded on the brittle strength of bones, / Like cumbrous flesh" (II: 423–424, p. 222). Liberty then is grounded in the refinement of matter's fluidity, not in the abandonment of matter altogether.

Adam and Eve must learn to live within the demands of the material world that gives them form and provides the potential for their growth. Raphael's own corporeal pleasure in regard to the consumption of food underscores the need for "taste," one of Milton's metaphors for choice, in the realm of domestic governance and agriculture. Pastoral contemplation must be balanced by an understanding of the necessity and limits of effort and control, both aspects of the Georgic poetic tradition of work and knowledge. Adam and Eve can aspire but only within bounds. Raphael, the "Hierarch," insists on hierarchy and order as an exercise of will against chaos and confusion:

O *Adam,* one Almighty is, from whom
All things proceed, and up to him return,
If not depraved from good, created all
Such to perfection, one first matter all,
Endued with various forms, various degrees
Of substance, and in things that live, of life;
But more refined, more spiritous, and pure,
As nearer to him placed or nearer tending
Each in their several active Spheres assigned,
Till body up to spirit work, in bounds
Proportioned to each kind.
                              (V: 469–479, p. 313)

"Almighty" in this speech resonates with "all" in a way that indicates a kind of pantheism. Spheres and kinds exits not fixed but "tending," and potential is here dangled subtly before Adam. Being is a growing plant, not a fixed ladder, scale, or chain of being. If man is only different in "degree" and not "kind" from other creatures, including angels, then all creation can be honored and man may aspire to divinity:

So from the root
Springs lighter the green stalk, from thence the leaves
More airy, last the bright consummate flow'r
Spirits odorous breathes: flow'rs and their fruit
Man's nourishment, by gradual scale sublimed
To vital spirits aspire, to animal,
To intellectual, give both life and sense,
Fancy and understanding, whence the Soul
Reason receives, and reason is her being,
Discursive, or Intuitive; discourse
Is oftest yours, the latter most is ours,
Differing but in degree, of kind the same.
                              (V: 479–490, p. 313)

Raphael announces again the possibility that refinement of spirit and body will go hand in hand to making man one with the angels. In keeping with an ethos of choice and freedom, man may at that point choose whether to dwell in earth or in heaven:

. . . time may come when men
With Angels may participate, and find
No inconvenient Diet, nor too light Fare:
And from these corporal nutriments perhaps
Your bodies may at last turn all to spirit,
Improved by tract of time, and winged ascend
Ethereal as we, or may at choice
Here or in Heav'nly Paradises dwell;
If ye be found obedient, and retain
Unalterably firm his love entire
Whose progeny you are. Meanwhile enjoy
Your fill what happiness this happy state
Can comprehend, incapable of more.
                              (V: 493–505, p. 313–314)

What Raphael reveals to Adam and Eve of future possibilities in relation to taste may be as seductive, if not as dangerous as Satan's offering of the fruit of forbidden knowledge. Disguising himself as a serpent, he becomes evidence for the possibilities of transformation already suggested by Raphael. But Raphael stresses that growth is a gradual process, dependent on discipline and self-government, and his gradualism contradicts the leaps and violence of revolutionary change. Crippling mutability of the will becomes the risk of a world of freedom.

Eve's susceptibility to the possibilities offered by Satan attests as much to her power as to her weakness. Her intelligence, perception, and strangely Platonic and unworldly aspirations make it difficult to ascribe a simple gender hierarchy to Milton's representation of the first man and woman. Milton's Eve is a feminine transformation of Narcissus, one who becomes obsessed with the extraordinary beauty of her own reflection. Yet it becomes difficult to blame her for recognizing in herself a beauty at least as compelling as Adam's. The fact of difference, so necessary for independence, initiates desire and longing. Blame becomes impossible to fix in the complex labyrinth of conflicting desires, and Milton succeeds in making it difficult to ascribe blame to any one figure, much less God.

After the exile from Paradise, it is fair to wonder whether Milton believed in any kind of redemption in this world and whether the future could be anything more than mankind's living out repeated cycles of tyranny and violence until the end of the world. Milton's eschatology hardly provides a vision of utopia. He allows Gabriel, however, to redefine perfection as entirely internal. The poem concludes with a paean to wisdom to compensate for the tragedy of knowledge. Gabriel presents the power of the inner world to make up for the loss of Paradise. Unlike Satan's extolling the virtues of the mind to compensate for loss of Heaven, the inner world Gabriel describes must be one ruled not by self-interest but by the virtue of Charity:

> . . . thou hast attained the sum
> Of wisdom; hope no higher, though all the stars
> Thou knew'st by name, and all the ethereal powers,
> All secrets of the deep, all nature's works,
> Or works of God in heaven, air, earth, or sea,
> And all the riches of this world enjoy,
> And all the rule, one empire; only add
> Deeds to the knowledge answerable, add faith,
> Add virtue, patience, temperance, add love,
> By name to some called Charity, the soul
> Of all the rest: then wilt thou not be loath
> To leave this Paradise, but shalt possess
> A paradise within thee, happier far.
>
> (XII: 575–587, p. 467)

PARADISE REGAINED

THE ideal of attaining the "paradise within" forms the basis for Milton's brief epic *Paradise Regained* (1671), which is almost unnervingly simple in relation to *Paradise Lost*. The drama is based on the accounts of Christ's temptation in the wilderness. The Jesus of Milton's poem is decidedly human; he must suffer as a man and with great uncertainty in order to make his resistance to Satan and his own virtue meaningful. Following the Aryan heresy, Milton dissented from the doctrine of the Trinity and believed Christ to have been created after God and therefore a willing and free servant of his glory. Milton's Jesus becomes tested in a trial against Satan with nothing upon which to base his actions other than the power of his own faith. Christ's spiritual development, as he recounts it, seems to echo Milton's own development from a serious childhood of books and learning:

> When I was yet a child, no childish play
> To me was pleasing, all my mind was set
> Serious to learn and know, and thence to do
> What might be public good; myself I thought
> Born to that end, born to promote all truth,
> All righteous things: therefore above my years,
> The Law of God I read, and found it sweet,
> Made it my whole delight . . .
>
> (IV: 201–208, p. 487)

But Milton's Jesus, of course, renounces even the Hebrew law as lesser than the understanding of the spirit. Heroic action becomes the renunciation of almost every worldly form of law and public action. Satan recognizes what appears Jesus' indifference to "worldly Crown," seeing him as "addicted more / To contemplation and profound dispute." He therefore offers Jesus the "Olive Grove of Academe" where the "famous Orators repair," where Jesus can learn the greatest rules of classical rhetoric, which he claims, "will render thee a King complete / Within thyself, much more with Empire joined." The severity of Jesus' response has stunned many, not only because of its renunciation of classical oratory but of the life contemplation and disputation. Philosophy and learning become superfluous:

> Alas! what can they teach, and not mislead;
> Ignorant of themselves, of God much more,
> And how the world began, and how man fell
> Degraded by himself, on grace depending?

Much of the Soul they talk, but all awry,
And in themselves seek virtue, and to themselves
All glory arrogate, to God give none,
Rather accuse him under usual names,
Fortune and Fate, as one regardless quite
Of mortal things. Who therefore seeks in these
True wisdom, finds her not, or by delusion
Far worse, her false resemblance only meets,
An empty cloud. However, many books
Wise men have said are wearisome; who reads
Incessantly, and to his reading brings not
A spirit and judgment equal or superior
(And what he brings, what needs he elsewhere seek)
Uncertain and unsettled still remains,
Deep versed in books and shallow in himself,
Crude or intoxicate, collecting toys,
And trifles for choice matters, worth a sponge;
As Children gathering pebbles on the shore.

(IV: 309–330, p. 577–523)

Jesus reduces the seeking of wisdom in books to one of those childish things that needs to be put away. "Spirit and judgment" are far more important than knowledge. Jesus does not argue so much that books in themselves are bad but that the need to seek anything outside of the self is troubling to the perfection of the charitable spirit. To elevate books remains a form of idolatry, though Jesus reserves praise for the "plainest" of the Hebrew prophets over "Oratory of *Greece* and *Rome*."

All three of Satan's temptations represent significant styles of life—the contemplative, the active, and the sensuous. Jesus refuses each without turning any one into an icon of evil; he rejects less the inherent evil of the temptations dangled before him than the argument that any one could be *necessary* for salvation of the soul. Nothing external could provide that salvation.

SAMSON AGONISTES

IN *Paradise Regained* almost nothing happens, and Jesus is reminiscent of the Lady of Comus in his austere, detached rejections of Satan. In contrast, *Samson Agonistes* portrays the problem of how one might do good in an ambiguous and corrupt world and represents the redemptive power of the warrior hero of classical tragedy and of the Old Testament.

Drawing on the form of Greek tragedy, Milton transforms the Israelite Samson into a blind Oedipus whose every action risks bringing further grief upon him. The parallel to Milton's own suffering as a blind captive of the Restoration regime is unmistakable. How can one of such great strength go on when his cause and his heroic aspirations have ended in ruins and entrapment? Meditating on his captivity, weakness, and above all his blindness, Samson's opening soliloquy remains one of Milton's greatest poetic achievements, and a great experiment in the possibilities of free verse:

Light the prime work of God to me is extinct,
And all her various objects of delight
Annulled, which might in part my grief have eased,
Inferior to the vilest now become
Of man or worm; the vilest here excel me,
They creep, yet see; I dark in light exposed
To daily fraud, contempt, abuse and wrong,
Within doors, or without, still as a fool,
In power of others, never in my own;
Scarce half I seem to live, dead more than half.
O dark, dark, dark, amid the blaze of noon,
Irrecoverably dark, total Eclipse
Without all hope of day!
O first created Beam, and thou great Word,
"Let there be light, and light was over all";
Why am I thus bereaved thy prime decree?
The Sun to me is dark
And silent as the Moon,
When she deserts the night,
Hid in her vacant interlunar cave.
Since light is so necessary to life,
And almost life itself, if it be true
That light is in the Soul,
She all in every part; why was the sight
To such a tender ball as th'eye confined?
So obvious and so easy to be quenched,
And not as feeling through all parts diffused,
That she might look at will through every pore?

(I. 70–97, p. 553)

Samson reasons because he suffers, and his reasoning reanimates the questions of theodicy that have haunted Milton's poetry since "Lycidas." Why would the Creator entrust the body's conductor of light to an object so vulnerable and delicate as the eye? *Samson Agonistes,* not unlike *Paradise Regained,* is a series of Job-like dialogues that veer precariously between weakening and strengthening Samson's ability to accept responsibility for his predicament and maintain faith in his ability to do God's bidding. Samson's agony is whether, in spite of his failings, he must live degraded in Philistine captivity or find some way still to sacrifice himself in service to a God and a nation whom he believes he has failed. Through the three major dialogues of the poem, Samson reveals the extent to which self-pity, blame, and even action seem vain attempts to assuage his failure. His dialogue with his father represents, in part, the temptations of self-pity and suicide, which express "self-offense" more than they offend God. Samson makes a strong argument for suicide, and his words echo the questions put in "Lycidas" and "Sonnet XIX" about the worth of attempting to serve God given the world's treachery and the weaknesses of the flesh. If Samson abstained from wild drink, he nevertheless allowed himself to be "effeminately vanquished," referring both to his own weakness and to the power of Dalila:

But what availed this temperance, not complete
Against another object more enticing?
What boots it at one gate to make defense,
And at another to let in the foe,
Effeminately vanquished? by which means,
Now blind, disheart'ned, shamed, dishonored, quelled,
To what can I be useful, wherein serve
My nation, and the work from Heav'n imposed,
But to sit idle on the household hearth,
A burdenous drone; to visitants a gaze,
Or pitied object, these redundant locks
Robustious to no purpose clust'ring down,
Vain monument of strength.
(I. 559–570, p. 565)

Samson fears that God has become indifferent to his gifts, and he cannot bear being wasted and cast away indifferently among Philistines.

Samson's dialogue with Dalila reveals the inadequacy of blaming his own weakness, much less Dalila's: "She was not the prime cause, but I myself, / Who vanquished with a peal of words (O weakness!) / Gave up my fort of silence to a Woman." Samson's search for "the prime cause" leads only to himself. His "peal of words" is little more than the conduit that had carried away the

secret of his strength; here, his words merely diminish the depths of his responsibility. If Samson has attempted to explain his failure by his own weakness, Dalila's own explanation of her actions appears only to mimic and, thereby, mock his own:

I may, if possible, thy pardon find
The easier toward me, or thy hatred less.
First granting, as I do, it was a weakness
In me, but incident to all our sex,
Curiosity, inquisitive, importune
Of secrets, then with like infirmity
To publish them, both common female faults:
Was it not weakness also to make known
For importunity, that is for naught,
Wherein consisted all thy strength and safety?
To what I did thou showst me first the way.
(I. 771–781, p. 570)

Samson recognizes that she torments him more by revealing the extent to which he is neither far different from nor superior to her. Samson must shed his own plea of weakness, finally recognizing that it is an excuse for evil so universal as to be meaningless:

. . . Weakness is thy excuse,
And I believe it, weakness to resist
Philistian gold; if weakness may excuse,
What Murderer, what Traitor, Parricide,
Incestuous, Sacriligeous, but may plead it?
All wickedness is weakness: that plea therefore
With God or Man will gain thee no remission.
(I. 829–835, p. 571)

In this crucial exchange with Dalila, Samson comes face to face with a worthy antagonist, one capable of showing him how almost any expressible foundation of pride or goodness can be undermined with a little relativistic logic. Dalila argues that she was serving the worthy cause of her nation and their gods, and that her actions represented the heroic virtue of service. Samson struggles to distinguish the worthiness of his public service to a nation from hers, but senses the trap of her argument. He dismisses her with cold forgiveness but adds, facetiously, that she can cherish her treachery by comparison with the famous deeds of good, maritally faithful women:

At distance I forgive thee, go with that;
Bewail thy falsehood, and the pious works

It hath brought forth to make thee memorable
Among illustrious women, faithful wives:
Cherish thy hastened widowhood with the gold
Of matrimonial treason: so farewell.

(I. 954–959, p. 574)

Samson has, once again, said too much, and leaves himself open to Dalila's parting shot, one of the most disturbing, if not devastating rejoinders in all of Milton's work. She proclaims her fame as a national hero and does so with near lethal rhetorical brilliance:

But in my country where I most desire,
In *Ekron, Gaza, Asdod,* and in *Gath*
I shall be named among the famousest
Of Women, sung at solemn festivals,
Living and dead recorded, who to save
Her country from a fierce destroyer, chose
Above the faith of wedlock bands, my tomb
With odors visited and annual flowers.
Not less renowned than in Mount *Ephraim,*
Jael, who with inhospitable guile
Smote *Sisera* sleeping through the Temples nailed.

(I. 980–990, p. 574–75)

Jael appears earlier than Samson in Judges, but her story is recounted in "The Song of Deborah," long considered one of the oldest of Biblical texts. Deborah was a prophetess and leader of Israel before there were Kings. She calls on a soldier named Barak to lead the Israelites against the Canaanites under the command of a fierce general named Sisera. Sisera flees from the victorious Israelite army and seeks refuge at the tent of Jael, a married woman whom he believes to be of a neutral tribe (she is not, in fact, an Israelite). Jael offers Sisera refuge, seduces him, and then hides him; Sisera falls asleep, thinking he has nothing to fear from his enemies. While he sleeps, Jael drives a tent peg through his head, killing him. When Barak shows up looking for him, Jael proudly reveals the dead general, his head nailed to the ground. Like Dalila, Jael is a woman who violated the code of hospitality and the boundaries of her marriage, and who, through seduction and treachery, destroyed an enemy general once thought invincible. Along with Rebekah, Tamar, Rahab, and Ruth, she becomes a trickster heroine of the Israelites. Jael has placed herself brilliantly in this pantheon and eviscerated Samson's moralizing conceptions of national service and of womanly servility.

The possibilities left for Samson to redeem himself in service to his God have become remote. Very little that he could do would necessarily make much difference; yet, as he says to Harapha, he insists that he is destined for public good: "I was no private but a person raised / With strength sufficient and command from Heav'n / To free my Country" (I. 1211–1213, p. 580). Anxious for that redemption, he wishes a fight with the monstrous Philistine:

All these indignities, for such they are
From thine, these evils I deserve and more,
Acknowledge them from God inflicted on me
Justly, yet despair not of his final pardon
Whose ear is ever open; and his eye
Gracious to re-admit the suppliant;
In confidence whereof I once again
Defy thee to the trial of mortal fight
By combat to decide whose god is God,
Thine or whom I with Israel's Sons adore.

(I. 1168–1177, p. 574)

Harapha remains too shrewd for such a deal, and Samson must remain frustrated in his desire. When he is called upon to participate in a Philistine festival as a kind of circus act, Samson debates with the chorus about maintaining private integrity while participating, no matter if under force, in the festivals of his captors and their false gods. When the chorus suggests that one can maintain inner virtue and faith no matter what the outward acts—"[w]here the heart joins not, outward acts defile not" (I. 1368, p. 584)— Samson maintains that any such masquerade is intolerable. Arguing for the freedom of the will, he maintains that Philistine commands are no excuse for servile behavior: "Commands are no constraints. If I obey them, / I do it freely; venturing to displease / God for the fear of Man, and Man prefer, / Set God behind: which in his jealousy / Shall never, unrepented, find forgiveness" (I. 1372–1376, p. 584). How, under such circumstances, can the blind captive redeem himself? As he is led away, we wonder how he will escape this trap, and Samson only gives us hints of possibilities of which he himself remains unclear: "Be of good courage, I begin to feel /

Some rousing motions in me which dispose / To something extraordinary my thoughts" (I. 1381–83, p. 584) and "Happen what may, of me expect to hear / Nothing dishonorable, impure, unworthy / Our God, our Law, my Nation, or myself; / The last of me or no. I cannot warrant" (I. 1423–1426, p. 586).

Having failed once before by revealing his secrets, Samson succeeds in death by keeping them. Just before pulling down the pillars and roof of the theater, he can be described only "as one who prayed, / Or some great matter in his mind revolved." Samson becomes a holy fool who traps, destroys, and kills the unsuspecting Philistines but also brings the same destruction upon himself. Heroic sacrifice for his God comes with the ultimate—though we cannot be quite sure deliberate—sacrifice of his own life. Samson no longer lives to suffer the agonies of guilt, and his success may only be measured after him. The chorus echoes the Bible in pointing out that Samson has in death slain more of the enemy than he ever did in life. True to the ways of Biblical tricksters, Samson embodies another instance of God performing his greatest tasks often through the marginal, the outcast, and the degraded:

O dearly bought revenge, yet glorious!
Living or dying thou hast fulfilled
The work for which thou wast foretold
To *Israel,* and now li'st victorious
Among thy slain self-killed
Not willingly, but tangled in the fold
Of dire necessity, whose law in death conjoined
Thee with thy slaughtered foes in number more
Than all thy life had slain before.
                    (I. 1660–1669, p. 591)

Perhaps Samson knew his act would destroy him; it was a way of relieving a shame and agony that could never be assuaged while attempting one more time to fulfill his heroic calling, a choice made freely and to some extent in service of his own freedom. Samson's greatness, though, rests in the uncertainty with which his final act was conceived and the dire constraints in which it was enacted. "All is best, though we oft doubt," (I. 1745, p. 593) could be taken as the pat pronouncement of a moralizing chorus or a recogni-

tion of faith in the midst of all possible sadness about a God who achieves his ends through suffering—and also a recognition of personal blindness. Nonetheless, Milton maintained his belief—whether in peace or war, with restraint or action—in the possibility of heroic service to God.

SELECTED BIBLIOGRAPHY

I. COLLECTED WORKS. Frank Allen Patterson, gen. ed., *The Columbia Edition of the Works of John Milton*, 18 vols. (New York, 1931–1938); Merritt Y. Hughes, ed., *John Milton: Complete Poems and Major Prose* (New York, 1957); Douglas Bush, ed., *The Complete Poetical Works of John Milton* (Boston, 1965); John Carey and Alastair Fowler, eds., *The Poems of John Milton,* rev. ed. (London, 1980); Don M. Wolfe, gen. ed., *The Complete Prose Works of John Milton,* 8 vols. (New Haven, 1953–1982); John Carey, ed., *Complete Shorter Poems,* 2d ed. (London, 1997).

II. BIOGRAPHIES. E. M. W. Tillyard, *Milton*, rev. ed. (London, 1967); A. N. Wilson, *The Life of John Milton* (Oxford, 1983); Cedric Brown, *John Milton: A Literary Life* (New York, 1995); William R. Parker, *Milton: A Biography*, 2 vols., 2d ed., rev. Gordon Campbell (Oxford, 1996); Barbara Lewalski, *The Life of John Milton* (Oxford, 2000).

III. CRITICAL STUDIES. John Diekhoff, *Milton on Himself* (New York, 1939); Arthur E. Barker, *Milton and the Puritan Dilemma, 1641–1660* (Toronto, 1942); C. S. Lewis, *A preface to "Paradise Lost"* (Oxford, 1942; rev. ed. 1974); Balachandra Rajan, *"Paradise Lost" and the Seventeenth-Century Reader* (London, 1947); Kester Svendsen, *Milton and Science* (Cambridge, Mass., 1956).

Frank Kermode, ed., *The Living Milton* (London, 1960); Christopher Ricks, *Milton's Grand Style* (Oxford, 1963); William Empson, *Milton's God*, rev. ed. (London, 1965); Scott Elledge, *Milton's "Lycidas"* (New York, 1966); Barbara Lewalski, *Milton's Brief Epics: The Genre, Meaning, and Art of "Paradise Regained"* (Providence, R.I., 1966); Louis Martz, *Milton: A Collection of Critical Essays* (Englewood Cliffs, N.J., 1966), repub. as *Milton, "Paradise Lost": A Collection of Critical Essays* (Englewood Cliffs, N. J., 1986); Stanley Fish, *Surprised by Sin: The Reader in "Paradise Lost"* (London, 1967); William G. Madsen, *From Shadowy Types to Truth: Studies in Milton's Symbolism* (New Haven, 1968); John Carey, *Milton* (London, 1969).

Michael Lieb, *The Dialectics of Creation: Patterns of Birth and Regeneration in "Paradise Lost"* (Amherst, Mass., 1970); Joseph A. Wittreich, *The Romantics on Milton* (Cleveland, Ohio, 1970); Angus Fletcher, *The Transcendental Masque: An Essay on Milton's "Comus"* (Ithaca, N.Y., 1971); William B. Hunter, C. A. Patrides, and J. H. Adamson, *Bright Essence: Studies in Milton's Theology* (Salt Lake City, 1971); John R. Knott, *Milton's Pastoral Vision* (Chicago, 1971); John Broadbent, *John Milton: Introductions* (Cambridge, U.K., 1973); William W. Kerrigan, *The Prophetic Milton* (Charlottesville, N.C., 1974); Michael Lieb and John Shawcross, eds., *Achievements of the Left Hand: Essays on the Prose of John Milton* (Amherst, Mass.,

1974); Anthony Low, *The Blaze of Noon: A Reading of "Samson Agonistes"* (New York, 1974); Christopher Hill, *Milton and the English Revolution* (London, 1977); Roland Frye, *Milton's Imagery and the Visual Arts: Iconographic Tradition in the Epic Poems* (Princeton, 1978); Mary Ann Radzinowicz, *Towards "Samson Agonistes": The Growth of Milton's Mind* (Princeton, 1978).

Louis Martz, *Poet of Exile: A Study of Milton's Poetry* (New Haven, 1980); Michael Lieb, *Poetics of the Holy: A Reading of "Paradise Lost"* (Chapel Hill, N.C., 1981); Christopher Hill, *The Experience of Defeat: Milton and Some Contemporaries* (New York, 1984); Barbara Lewalski, *"Paradise Lost" and the Rhetoric of Literary Forms* (Princeton, 1985); Joseph A. Wittreich, *Feminist Milton* (Ithaca, N.Y., 1987); Julia M. Walker, ed., *Milton and the Idea of Woman* (Urbana,Ill., 1988); Mary Ann Radzinowicz, *Milton's Epics and the Book of Psalms* (Princeton, 1989).

Laura Lunger Knoppers, *Historicizing Milton: Spectacle, Power, and Poetry in Restoration England* (Athens, Ga., 1994); Michael Lieb, *Milton and the Culture of Violence* (Ithaca, N.Y., 1994); Linda Gregerson, *The Reformation of the Subject: Spenser, Milton, and the English Protestant Epic* (Cambridge, U.K., 1995); William R. Parker, *Milton: A Biography*, 2 vols., 2d ed., rev. Gordon Campbell, (Oxford, 1996); William Kolbrenner, *Milton's Warring Angels* (Cambridge, Mass., 1997); John Rogers, *The Matter of Revolution* (Ithaca, N.Y., 1998); Dennis Danielson, *The Cambridge Companion to John Milton* (Cambridge, U.K., 1999); Barbara Lewalski, *The Life of John Milton* (Oxford, 2000); Stanley Fish, *How Milton Works* (Cambridge, Mass, 2001).

OLD ENGLISH LITERATURE

Paul Bibire

OLD ENGLISH (OCCASIONALLY known as "Anglo-Saxon") is the earliest recorded form of English, surviving in texts written between the late seventh and the early twelfth century A.D. The language is very different from any variety of modern or even later-medieval English, and is not intelligible to any modern speaker without study. It is known from some 412 surviving manuscripts (handwritten books) and from a large number of single-sheet legal documents, "charters," which were either written during the Old English period or are later copies of documents originally written then. During the Old and Middle English periods, most Old English manuscripts were produced and preserved in the libraries of medieval ecclesiastical institutions, mostly monasteries and nunneries. The survival of Old English texts was therefore dependent upon the survival of these libraries through the vagaries of dissolution, war, and fire. A few such libraries have survived to the present day: mostly cathedral libraries such as those of Exeter, Worcester, and Vercelli. Warfare destroyed many monasteries during the Old English period, and presumably also destroyed most of their books. Many medieval libraries are also known to have been destroyed by fire, and many existing manuscripts show fire damage. After the Dissolution of the English monasteries (1536–1539) during the reign of King Henry VIII, manuscripts from monastic libraries survived only when collected by individual scholar-antiquarians. Most Old English manuscripts now survive in three large collections in England. Archbishop Matthew Parker (b. 1504, consecrated archbishop of Canterbury 1559, d. 1575) and his scholarly associates collected the manuscripts now held in trust by Corpus Christi College, Cambridge; the antiquarian book collector Sir Robert Cotton (1571–1631) collected many manuscripts now held in the British Library in London; and the Franco-Dutch scholar Franciscus Junius (1589–1677) collected manuscripts now held in Bodleian Library, Oxford. Cotton's library was badly damaged by fire in 1731.

During most of the Middle English period, Old English seems to have been largely unintelligible, and its texts mostly unread. It was rediscovered by the group of scholars gathered by Archbishop Parker, in their quest to find the origins of the English church. These scholars learned to read the language, mostly using bilingual texts in Latin and Old English, and compiled early dictionaries. Further scholarly work followed in the seventeenth and eighteenth century: for instance, Humphrey Wanley (1672–1726) cataloged all the then-known surviving manuscripts, and George Hickes (1642–1715) published a grammar of the language (1689) and printed some texts. Nineteenth-century scholars, largely German, produced accurate editions of all the major texts and a detailed understanding of the language. Study of the literature, as such, was mostly undertaken by twentieth-century British and American scholars, led by figures such as W. P. Ker (1855–1923) and J. R. R. Tolkien (1892–1973), who were trained in the nineteenth-century German philological tradition, but who brought to it the cultural and literary sensibilities that had developed in classical studies and in English literary criticism.

CULTURAL HISTORY OF THE OLD ENGLISH PERIOD

THE English were formed from a conglomeration of Germanic peoples who had invaded Britain in the fifth and sixth centuries A.D. They had their own writing system, the runic alphabet (the *futhorc*), before they were converted to Christianity in the seventh century A.D. Runes seem to have been intended for incising on wood, metal, or stone, rather than writing. Very few runic inscriptions survive from the pre-Christian period; these are mostly unintelligible and may never have been intended to be meaningful. Runic inscriptions are much more frequent in the early Christian period, but these seem to reflect uses of the Roman alphabet. In the seventh century A.D. the English learned to write the Roman alphabet; their teachers were the Irish missionaries from St. Columba's monastery of Iona, who largely converted them to Christianity. These missionaries were led by figures such as St. Aidan (d. 651), based at the monastery on the island of Lindisfarne (founded 635) off the Northumbrian coast. The English learned to write an Irish script, often called Insular minuscule, and this script continued to be used in English manuscripts until the eleventh century. Augustine (d. 604/5), under the instruction of Pope Gregory the Great, had founded the older, Roman mission at Canterbury in 597; this had apparently aimed for political effect and seems to have had small impact on the English people and culture. However, after the Synod of Whitby (663/4), when the Northumbrian church decided to follow Roman rather than Irish custom, Pope Vitalian sent two Greek-speaking clerics to reform the English church. These were Theodore, from Tarsus in Asia Minor (b. about 602, consecrated archbishop of Canterbury 668, d. 690), and Hadrian (d. 710), a North African, previously abbot of Nerida near Naples, and then abbot of the monastery of S.S. Peter and Paul, later St. Augustine's, Canterbury. They set up a major school at Canterbury, and together with Benedict "biscop" (c. 628–689/90), founder and abbot of the double monastery of Wearmouth-Jarrow in Northumbria, they created the educational environment for the "Golden Age" of early Old English culture: the period encompassing Aldhelm of Malmesbury (c. 639–709), the Venerable Bede (672/3–735), and Alcuin of York (c. 732–804). Surviving physical evidence of this cultural achievement includes the *Codex Amiatinus,* now in Florence, which was written at Wearmouth-Jarrow before 716 and is the most important surviving manuscript of the Latin Bible, and the *Lindisfarne Gospels,* now in the British Library, written at Lindisfarne probably before 698 and arguably the most beautiful book ever produced in the British Isles.

Although most surviving writings from this period are in Latin, there is indirect evidence for written Old English, and conventions for writing Old English seem to have developed before 700. These conventions show much innovative intelligence in the use of redundant letters or letter groups in the Latin alphabet, and in the cases of *æ, oe, h,* and *y* must show knowledge of the earlier Latin grammarians, and probably also of Greek. A letter was also borrowed from the runic *futhorc,* the letter þ, named "thorn," used for the *th* sounds not found in classical Latin; the letter ð ("eth"), a crossed *d,* was also invented, or borrowed from cursive Greek scripts, for the *th* sounds. The letter þ endured in English into the early modern period, by which time its written form had become very similar to *y:* hence early modern spellings such as *ye* for "the." These conventions for writing English must have been developed at a major educational center, with access to grammatical literature; the possible input from Greek strongly suggests Canterbury, though some knowledge of Greek was also available in Northumbria. The evidence of early Latin-English glossaries strongly suggests that advanced study of difficult Latin texts took place in the medium of written English before 700, probably at Canterbury.

Writing in England seems at this early period to have been entirely limited to the Church, and only those who received a clerical education could read or write: priests, monks, and nuns. The eighth-century renaissance seems already to have been in decline towards the end of that century, and fairly early in the ninth century came the first major raids from pagan Scandinavia, the Viking invasions, which developed into general warfare lasting most of that century. The Vikings invaded, conquered, and settled the northeastern half of England, creating the Danelaw, of which the boundary ran roughly from London northwest to Chester. Only one of the earlier English kingdoms, Wessex, survived as a political entity by the end of the ninth century, and although the organization of the Church partly survived in the Danelaw, monastic activity was for the most part disrupted. Very few manuscripts survive from the period 830–890, and even legal documents largely vanish. Even at Canterbury, the surviving mid-century charters for the cathedral are all written by the same scribe, and his handwriting gets progressively shakier and more inaccurate: he could not see what he was writing. When he stops, about 867, the documents stop for several decades, suggesting that there was no one left at Canterbury who could write.

The survival of Wessex, and perhaps even the survival of the English language, were largely dependent upon one man: King Alfred the Great of Wessex (b. 849, king 871, d. 899). He was almost unique among military leaders in northwestern Europe in withstanding, converting, and even befriending the ninth-century Scandinavian invaders. He also set in place an almost wholly new urbanization of his kingdom, establishing fortified garrison towns as economic and political as well as military centers of power, the "Alfredian Boroughs," to exploit the new and vastly extended trade routes established by the Vikings. These "boroughs" correspond to the new Viking urban trading-centers such as Dublin and Wexford in Ireland, Hedeby in Denmark, Novgorod and Kiev in Russia, and York in England. Many of Alfred's "boroughs" survive as important centers to the present, including Oxford. He was also the first to claim the kingship of all the English: England as a political entity owes its conception to him. And, having learned to read and write, he set in place a program of primary education not merely for churchmen but for all free-born children. This program was intended to produce general literacy amongst laypeople: an ideal not achieved in England until nearly a millennium later. In pursuit of this, he caused a number of educational works to be translated or even composed in English, and himself undertook some translation. King Alfred's educational reforms established English, not Latin, as the primary written language of the kingdom of England, the first such association in Western Europe of a national language and literature with an incipient nation-state.

Alfred's work was continued throughout the tenth century by his descendants and successors, who gradually conquered the Danelaw, so that by the end of that century the kingdom of England with roughly its present boundaries was a political reality. A reform of the monastic movement, the Benedictine Revival, also inspired educational reforms during the last third or so of the tenth century, led by figures such as St. Dunstan (b. 924, archbishop of Canterbury 959, d. 988) and Æþelwold of Abingdon (b. 909, bishop of Winchester 963, d. 984). The form of written English which they used, "late West Saxon," became a standard schoolbook language and was used across the whole of England in more or less fixed form for nearly two centuries: it was the Standard English of that time. Associated with the Benedictine Reform was a large outpouring of English prose writing, and also the collection and copying of English poetry. These activities do not seem to have been significantly disrupted by the so-called "Second Viking Age," a systematic and successful military campaign by the Christian Danish king Sveinn Forkbeard to conquer England. His son Cnut (Norse Knútr, modern Canute; reigned 1016–1035) ruled a North Sea empire of England, Denmark, Norway, and parts of Sweden. Cnut moved the center of political power from Winchester in Wessex to London, partly because of its economic importance and access to the North Sea trade routes; thereafter London English became dominant. The native dynasty was briefly restored after Cnut's reign, but other descendants of Vikings, king Haraldr Sigurðarson of Norway, and William the Bastard, duke of the Viking duchy of Normandy, both invaded in the early autumn of 1066. The last native king, Harold, defeated Haraldr of Norway, but himself then fell in battle against William of Normandy. William, now the Conqueror, took power and founded a new dynasty. Although initially he seems to have tried to act, like Cnut, as an English monarch, he soon imposed Norman French as his official language. Old English seems to have vanished from the schoolroom, and, with some few exceptions (at Peterborough and probably Worcester), it ceased to be written within fifty years of the Norman Conquest. When manuscripts in English appear again, late in the twelfth century, written English was presented so differently that it seems a different language: Middle English.

THE OLD ENGLISH LANGUAGE

MOST Old English survives in manuscripts of the Alfredian period and of the Benedictine Revival, from the late ninth to the eleventh centuries, and is in the dialect of the kingdom of Wessex: "West Saxon." Other attested dialects are Kentish, Mercian, and Northumbrian. Kentish is known from ninth-century charters and tenth-century glosses (English written above Latin to translate it) and two poems in mixed dialect. Mercian (the dialects of the kingdom of Mercia, based in the west Midlands of England) is known from glosses of the early ninth century and late tenth century. Northumbrian (the dialects spoken in the north of England between the Humber and the Forth) is known from some short eighth-century texts and inscriptions and some large late-tenth-century glosses. Other Old English dialects, including those of East Anglia and most of the east Midlands, are not represented in writing, and can only be reconstructed from Middle English evidence. Modern Standard English is derived mostly from east Midland dialects, and so is not derived from any attested form of Old English. The dialects were already different from each other when first attested, to such an extent that West Saxon and Northumbrian may not fully have been mutually intelligible. Northumbrian, in particular, shows many developments that were to spread southwards in Middle English and are important for Modern English.

The vowel system of Old English was on balance simpler than that of modern English, but made a few important distinctions no longer wholly functional in the modern language. It possessed "rounded" ("labialized") vowels like modern German *ü*, a sound represented by *y*; it also distinguished short and long vowels from each other. In the earlier forms of the language, unstressed vowels were distinguished from each other, and this is still partly shown in late West Saxon spelling, although by the end of the tenth century they had probably all been reduced in

pronunciation to the "grunt" vowel of modern English unstressed "the."

The language was inflected, like Latin, so that words showed their sentence function by their forms, particularly their endings, rather than by their position as in modern English. Nouns, adjectives, and pronouns were declined, with separate case endings for four cases: nominative, accusative, genitive, and dative, in both singular and plural—traces of this survive in modern pronouns (for example, "I, me, my; we, us, our"). Verbs were conjugated in two tenses, present and past, and in two main moods, indicative and subjunctive, with separate forms for first, second, and third persons in the singular indicative, and one for the plural in each tense and mood—traces of this survive in archaic modern English (for example, "I do, thou dost, he doth; we, you, they do"). Compound verb forms, using the verb "to be" for the passive, and the verb "to have" for the perfect, were used as in modern English's "it was done," "he has done." Futurity was shown by using adverbs of future time, as is still possible in modern English (for example, "He goes home tomorrow"). The language seems to have had nothing that corresponds to the modern English "progressive" (continuous) tenses ("I am doing," and so on).

Old English word order was much more variable than the very strict word order of modern English, though it shared with modern German a strong tendency for the verb to stand no later than second position in main clauses, but to go to or towards the end of subordinate clauses.

The vocabulary of Old English was still fairly purely Germanic, with only a small number of Latin loanwords, usually for specifically Roman or ecclesiastical things: for instance *stræt* ("street, paved [Roman] road"), *celc* ("chalice"), *mynstre* ("monastery; minster"). It contained very few attested Norse or French loanwords; these do not generally appear in English until the Middle English period.

NON-LITERARY TEXTS

MANY Old English texts survive which would not normally be considered "literary." Glossed texts are frequent, particularly in manuscripts of the Latin Psalter and Gospels, with an interlinear English translation written over each Latin word. Several glossaries survive; these are collections of glosses roughly alphabetized to form early Latin-English dictionaries. These are important for literary purposes, in that they show which Latin texts were being studied, and the very varying knowledge of literary Latin. Genealogies and lists of benefactors are little more than catalogs of personal names, though sometimes they have historical or legal importance, and they show the basis for the genealogies and name lists in some literary texts. Some 1,602 charters survive, usually because they document landownership. Many of these are bilingual in English and Latin, sometimes just with names in English, sometimes the estate boundaries, sometimes the entire text. Although estate boundaries are of little literary interest, charters often give direct insights into personal life; further, their preambles are sometimes ornate rhetorical exercises and are stylistically important. Many law codes survive, mostly in English, including codes attributed to the earliest Christian kings, but by far the largest are those of later kings such as Alfred, Æþelræd (Ethelred), and Cnut (Canute). These later codes often show rhetorical ornament and are not without stylistic interest; they are also important because they do not merely show practical lawmaking, but demonstrate and discuss the ethical framework within which society was meant to work. Scientific and medical texts also survive from the late period: for instance, a book of medical recipes, *Bald's Leechbook,* or a manual for horse doctors, *Medicina de quadrupedibus;* these show little literary ambition, but demonstrate the flexibility and range of written Old English.

ALFREDIAN PROSE

SURVIVING Old English prose dates mostly from two periods about a century apart: the Alfredian period at the end of the ninth century, and the Benedictine Revival at the end of the tenth. Most of it is translated from Latin, or at least based upon Latin models. Alfredian prose is associated with the king himself. prefaces to each text claim that he produced the Old English translations of Pope Gregory the Great's *Pastoral Care,* Boethius's *Consolation of Philosophy,* and St. Augustine's *Soliloquies,* and these claims are supported by stylistic and linguistic analysis that shows that they probably share a common translator. Alfred may also have translated the first fifty psalms into prose; he may also be responsible for part of the Old English version of Orosius' universal history and geography, as stated some centuries later by William of Malmesbury. William's other attribution to Alfred, of the Old English translation of Bede's *Ecclesiastical History of the English People,* is now not generally accepted, but the translation is of the Alfredian period and may well have been commissioned by the king. The earliest part of the *Anglo-Saxon Chronicle,* up to the year 891, is also Alfredian, though not composed by the king himself.

Alfred's preface to his translation of the *Pastoral Care* is of great importance. Writing mostly in the first person, the king describes the disastrous state of learning in England. He claims that, when he came to power, there were very few priests south of the Humber who knew how to make sense of the Latin liturgy, or translate a letter from Latin into English, and he thinks that there were not many beyond the Humber either. So he presents the need for educational reform, and his own techniques of translation, "sometimes word beside word, sometimes sense from sense" under the guidance of his own named teachers. This preface itself is stylistically ambitious; it is mostly successful in its detailed discussion, but is occasionally bewildered by the complexity of its own syntax, and in a couple of instances Alfred is only able to rescue an awkward sentence with some clumsiness. He attempts one developed metaphor with considerable success. The *Pastoral Care* itself was an obvious choice for educational purposes: Gregory had intended it as a handbook for training priests, and it inculcated moral truths through brief, exemplary anecdotes; it is very simply written and rather entertaining. Alfred preserves these characteristics, and the text comes across with pleasingly naive charm.

Educational intention can equally be seen behind the Old English translation of Orosius's *Historiae adversum paganos,* which gives the entire geographic and historic context for early medieval culture and history. Although Alfred probably did not produce the whole of this translation, it is remarkable for the interpolation of two linked passages, quite possibly composed by Alfred himself, in which two travelers give geographic and ethnographic accounts of northern Europe in the late ninth century. One of these informants is Ohthere, a Norwegian from Halogaland in northern Norway, who told "his lord King Alfred" of a northward voyage round North Cape into the White Sea, together with many hardheaded details of peoples, produce, and goods traded. Ohthere (Norse *Óttarr*) must therefore have been a Viking who had sworn allegiance to the English king, and the passage shows both his and Alfred's detailed and practical interest in trade even in the remote north of Europe. This shows a relationship between King Alfred and the Vikings completely different from the military conflicts recorded in the *Anglo-Saxon Chronicle.* The other interpolated account is that of an English merchant, Wulfstan, of a voyage to Estonia in the Baltic, giving rather picturesque, if not always credible, ethnographic information. The style of these interpolated passages shows considerable skill in presenting detailed narrative with great clarity; it is considerably more lively and complex than that of the translated text.

A historical context for the kingdom of the English is also provided by the Old English translation of Bede's *Ecclesiastical History of the English People.* On stylistic and linguistic grounds this cannot now be attributed to Alfred himself, and is likely to be of west Midland origin: it may be associated with the circle of Bishop Wærferþ of Worcester, with whom Alfred corresponded as a participant in his educational program, and to whom Alfred's biographer, Asser, attributes the Old English translation of Gregory the Great's *Dialogues;* this has an Alfredian preface in which the king attributes the translation to "his friends." The style of these two translations is Latinate and slightly stiff, but usually succeeds in reproducing the originals' lucidity of mind and style.

The history of Alfred's own reign, and of his immediate predecessors, is provided in the first section (to 891) of the *Anglo-Saxon Chronicle,* which appears in all surviving versions of the *Chronicle.* This must be seen as a self-conscious literary and scholarly creation of Alfred's court; it was probably modeled on Frankish chronicles, and was not itself based on earlier English annals. It derives early material from Orosius and Bede; after this runs out, the chronicler clearly has very little information for the second half of the eighth century and the beginning of the ninth: a king-list, and a list of bishops, both of which establish chronologies, and some few fragments of apparently archaic narrative (for example, the annal entry for 755). With Alfred's father and elder brother, however, the *Chronicle* begins to present coherent and fairly full narratives, and its account of Alfred's own reign is detailed and well-organized. It is far from mere flattery of the king: Alfred's defeats are recorded with the same impartial detail as his successes. He is always, however, the central figure, and other events are recounted only if they impinge on him, his reign, and his realm. The style chosen is simple, impersonal, and direct, but the chronicler's mastery of complex narrative is complete. This is the more striking, since apart from Alfred's own prefaces, and the interpolated passages in the *Orosius,* this is the only Alfredian prose that is not translated from Latin.

Alfred's other translations fit less easily into his program of elementary education. Boethius's *Consolation of Philosophy,* a fairly large Neoplatonic work produced in the fifth century A.D., was the only work of classical philosophy that survived into the knowledge of the early Middle Ages in Western Europe. It was a major philosophical work, and also had great literary importance, since after each section of prose discussion the argument is then summarized in metaphysical poetry of very high quality, the so-called "Metres of Boethius." This provided a spur to philosophical poetry throughout the western Middle Ages, not least in Old English. Alfred seems to have translated all the text—prose and poetry—into prose; this prose is usually effective but sometimes awkward, especially when wrestling with abstractions, though it can rise to nobility in translating some of the "Metres." At some later date this prose translation of the "Metres" was versified into very uninspired Old English poetry. Alfred's translation involved substantial modification of the content of the work. Boethius's abstract discussion is usually made concrete; it is given an explicitly Christian framework, and is consistently applied to kingship. Alfred uses Boethius as a starting point for discussing the ethical problems facing a Christian king. In such modification he was effectively incorporating a commentary upon Boethius's text into his translation: many such commentaries were available, and Alfred may have used some of them. But he goes beyond known commentaries. In Book IV of the *Consolation,* Boethius discusses the nature of time, and predestination within time, and their relation to Platonic eternity; he uses for this the geometric image of the infinite number of points on the circumference of a circle relative to the single point at its center. Alfred translates this into elaborate and explicitly Christian terms: God is at the center. The abstraction of the geometric circle is made concrete: it is now a cartwheel, with spokes. This enables him to introduce the concept of the Christian, who stands on the wheel-rim of recurrent time, but reaches upwards and in, to the still center of the turning world, towards God. This reinterpretation seems to be peculiar to the Old English translation, and shows a creative mind, that grasps Boethius's abstraction and makes a conceptual leap beyond it to a new and powerful understanding. If this is Alfred's own work, as seems likely, it shows a mind of very unusual ability.

Alfred's other known translation, the *Soliloquies* of St. Augustine, also addresses philosophical issues, and also applies them to problems of kingship; there also are, as well, many verbal echoes between the two translations, and some of Alfred's additions to the *Soliloquies* correspond to passages of Boethius; this may indicate that the *Soliloquies* were translated at a time when he was already familiar with Boethius. Although it is not preserved intact, and only in a twelfth-century manuscript, Alfred's skills clearly reach new heights in this work, and the surviving fragment of his first-person preface is among the finest known Old English prose. Here he is able to sustain large-scale and complex imagery with ease and grace; his rhetorical ornaments always support and never overwhelm the sense, and his syntax, although complicated, never seems strained.

Neither the *Consolation of Philosophy* nor the *Soliloquies* of St. Augustine is at all an elementary work; neither could be considered suitable for teaching children to read or write, or even for the training of priests. King Alfred's intellectual ability and his range of interest go far further than his program of elementary education.

TENTH- AND ELEVENTH-CENTURY PROSE

APART from the increasingly separate continuations of the different versions of the *Anglo-Saxon Chronicle,* and, debatably, some homilies, not much prose survives that can be securely dated to the earlier parts of the tenth century. Chronicle prose continues to develop in discursive fullness, and in particular the account of the last years of Alfred's reign shows an easy ability to control complex narratives with great clarity and some passion. With the Benedictine Revival of the last decades of the century, however, prose writing is resumed with great vigor, and continues until after the Norman Conquest. The bulk of prose produced at this period was religious, and its main literary form was the homily or sermon. Although apparently earlier homilies survive, particularly in the Blickling and Vercelli collections, this literature is largely associated with two writers, Abbot Ælfric of Eynsham (c. 955–c. 1010), and Archbishop Wulfstan of Worcester and York (bishop of London 996–1002, archbishop of York 1002–1023, and bishop of Worcester 1002–1016, d. 1023). These were contemporaries at the end of the century, and Wulfstan was acquainted with Ælfric's work. Ælfric produced two entire series of "Catholic Homilies," sermons for most Sundays of the church year, as well as some not assigned to specific occasions: at least

116 of these sermons survive. He also composed a cycle of some 34 surviving Saints' Lives for most major saints' days of the year. These were not in any modern sense original compositions. Ælfric, like most other sermon writers, consulted earlier texts, always in Latin, and reworked their material, sometimes with acknowledgement, in a chain of authority that leads back to the Fathers of the Church such as St. Augustine or Pope Gregory the Great. His merits do not lie in original thought, but in skills of presentation and style. In these he shows a great range, from detailed and complex theological argument, supported by comparably complex imagery and style, to a simple and touching directness. The Saints' Lives are mostly composed in so-called "rhythmical prose," almost loose alliterative verse; they make few demands on their audience and even when recounting brutal martyrdom are mostly lighthearted entertainment literature, clerical adventure stories. They were presumably intended for performance in contexts such as the monastic refectory, as edifying entertainment to forestall idle talk. Ælfric also produced educational works, such as the first known Latin grammar written in English, and a short astronomical treatise, *De temporibus.*

Archbishop Wulfstan was also a fairly prolific writer, and was apparently responsible for drafting Cnut's law code, as well as the so-called *Canons of Edgar.* Some twenty-one sermons and related pieces survive which are fairly certainly by Wulfstan. Although he redrafted one homily originally composed by Ælfric, his content and style are very different. He rarely presents reasoned argument, but instead makes an emotional appeal to his audience, sometimes with great passion. His prose is very strongly alliterative, but does not approach verse; instead, he builds up cumulative paragraphs of sharply defined paratactic rhythmic phrases; these are held together internally by alliteration and assonance, but are mostly linked by symmetry. The effect is impressive, but can become repetitive, even rather mechanical.

Most other surviving prose is likely to date from this period. The late *Chronicle* continuations generally become fuller and more circum-

stantial, and more partisan. The accounts of the reigns of Æþelræd (Ethelred the Unready) or of Edward the Confessor and William the Conqueror contain particularly fine historical narrative. Most other prose is translation from Latin. One remarkable oddity is the fragmentary translation of *Apollonius of Tyre,* originally a Hellenistic Greek novella; the story was widely known throughout Europe during the later Middle Ages, and was used by Gower, and then by Shakespeare for *Pericles.* The Old English version shows a quite unexpected elegance and delicacy, presented in a supple and subtle prose style. From the same postclassical Greek background are the translations of *Alexander's Letter to Aristotle,* and of the *Wonders of the East,* though these are more useful in showing the range of inputs into late Old English culture than for any inherent merit. Most of the technical prose is also likely to date from this period, above all *Byrhtferþ's Manual.*

Nothing in Old English prose reaches the stature of *Ancrene Wisse* at the end of the twelfth century, of Malory in the fifteenth century, or of Bunyan in the seventeenth century. But at their best, prose writers such as King Alfred or Abbot Ælfric are completely in command of their medium, and can still touch, move, sometimes persuade even the skeptical and world-weary modern reader.

POETRY

Most Old English poetry is known only from four surviving manuscripts. These are often known as the Junius (or Cædmon) Manuscript (MS Bodley Junius 11), the Vercelli Book (MS Biblioteca Capitolare cxvii), the Exeter Book (MS Exeter Dean and Chapter 3501), and the *Beowulf* Manuscript (or Nowell Codex) (MS BL Cotton Vitellius A.xv). These all date from the Benedictine Revival, and were probably written within about thirty years of each other: the Exeter Book could have been written as early as the 970s, while the *Beowulf* Manuscript might have been written just after 1000. The Junius Manuscript is probably a Canterbury book; the places of origin of the others are uncertain. They are all carefully written and have been checked and corrected by their own scribes; the Junius Manuscript is also illustrated with ink drawings. None gives evidence of subsequent medieval use. They are all more or less systematic collections of poetry, with a strong leaning towards religious poems, and may have been produced as part of a scholarly revival of interest in Old English poetry. The Exeter Book might represent a collection of all or most of the poetry in a particular library or group of libraries; the Junius Manuscript, the Vercelli Book, and the *Beowulf* Manuscript seem to have collected their content on a thematic basis. Even though only these four major poetic manuscripts exist, they may therefore give a fairly good sample of Old English poetry surviving at the end of the tenth century.

Other manuscripts contain some verse: the Paris Psalter contains a probably Alfredian prose translation of the first fifty psalms, followed by a wholly uninspired versification of the remaining hundred psalms. Equally uninspired versifications of the "Metres of Boethius" also survive. Later parts of the *Anglo-Saxon Chronicle* preserve occasional poems, mostly royal praise-poems or memorial lays: these are of interest in that they can be dated, but only *The Battle of Brunanburh* is of any small literary merit. Apart from these, there is a random scattering of short texts, a few of which are preserved in eighth-century versions (*Cædmon's Hymn, Bede's Death Song*, the *Leiden Riddle*) and can accordingly be used to try to reconstruct the literary history of Old English poetry; a few inscriptions, mostly early, also seem to be poetic, most importantly that on the Ruthwell Cross in Dumfriesshire. Some texts survive only in modern transcripts of manuscripts now lost: of these the most important are *The Battle of Maldon* and the *Finnesburh Fragment,* both incomplete. The total corpus of all surviving Old English poetry amounts to approximately 30,000 lines.

Almost all Old English poetry is of anonymous authorship, apart from the two very short poems attributed to Cædmon and Bede respectively, and the four poems which contain Cynewulf's runic signature as an acrostic at their ends. The names of all Old English poems are modern; the usage of the *Anglo-Saxon Poetic Records* is generally followed here.

METER AND DICTION

ALL surviving Old English poetry is composed in effectively a single alliterative, rhythmical meter; the modern description of this is based almost entirely upon statistical analysis of the corpus. The poetry was written continuously in the surviving manuscripts, but modern editors usually print it in verse-lines. Each line consists of two separate half-lines with a rhythmic and often syntactic pause between them, marked in modern editions by spacing; the half-lines seem to be the basic metrical unit. The two half-lines are tied together only by alliteration on their first accented (stressed) syllables; a second accented syllable in the first half-line can also sometimes participate in the alliteration, but never a second accented syllable in the second half-line. The half-line is apparently based on the two-accent phrase that seems to be fundamental to English speech rhythm, and much modern English can be scanned as if it were Old English verse. The only fundamental differences between Old English and the modern language in this respect are that all vowels could alliterate with each other, that long and short accented syllables functioned differently from each other, and that the accent (stress) always fell on the root-syllable of a word (usually its first syllable). Much variation is possible in half-line structure: it could contain more or fewer syllables, down to a minimum of four; the number and organization of the accented syllables also varied; these variations seem to be subject to fairly strict rules, though these rules seem to change during the period.

Regularity of syllable numbers or of rhythm seems to be irrelevant to this meter. End rhyme is rare and seems almost always to be an ornament borrowed from Latin, rather than having any inherent metrical function. The poetry is not strophic and can only rarely be divided into anything resembling stanzas.

Two modern English verse-lines that exactly reflect Old English verse-patterns are Milton's "while other animals inactive range" and Pope's "by force to ravish or by fraud betray." This meter is in all essentials identical with that of Old Saxon and Old High German poetry, and is very closely related to that of Old Norse Eddaic poetry. It was probably, therefore, inherited from the common Germanic past of these poetic traditions, and may be very ancient.

The diction of Old English poetry differed substantially from that of prose, and was largely shared by the Old Saxon and Old High German poetic traditions. Poetry used a different and more archaic noun-vocabulary, which was very rich in near-synonyms for common concepts. The range of available words usually gave a range of different implications and overtones, and sometimes even shifts of meaning. So words that must be translated as "warrior" include *cempa*, originally a loanword derived from Latin *campus* ("battle-field") and so ultimately related to modern English "champion" (it was a rather lofty word, and was often used in Christian contexts); *beorn*, a native word, ultimately related to terms for "bear," which may have implied the pre-Christian warrior enraged in a berserk frenzy; *wiga*, a lower-status word meaning "striker;" *secg*, which may have meant "companion, fellow-fighter" but was probably specifically associated with swords; and *gesiþ*, which also meant "companion" but more "traveling companion," "companion on a (military) expedition." Similarly, words that have to be translated roughly as "mind" include *hyge*, perhaps meaning the capacity for rational thought; *mod*, the capacity for emotional experience; *geþonc*, perhaps "consideration"; and *geþoht*, "considered opinion." Old English could freely produce compounds, where the first element modified the second, and this allowed far more delicate exploration of sense (for example, *modgeþonc*, perhaps "consideration of the heart," "reflection drawing conclusions from emotional experience").

Old English poetic syntax also differed from that of prose. It often exploited parallelism and verbal variation, where the key concepts of a sentence were repeated, usually by apposition, in different wording and contexts, so turning them around in the mind's eye and seeing different aspects of them from different angles almost simultaneously. The Old English poetic sentence thus tends to progress in a spiral around its central concepts rather than by the progression of Aristotelian logic. This creates a multidimensional poetic perception, both analytic and holistic at the same time.

Much Old English poetic phraseology was repeated or varied, sometimes within a single poem, sometimes across the entire corpus. These semi-stable, repeated phrases are known as "formulae." Some attested poetic traditions of oral improvisation, for example Serbian epic, use formulae, apparently so that illiterate poets could use traditional phrases while planning ahead. So, for instance, in the *Iliad* Agamemnon is usually described as *anax andron* "king of men," where the poetic tradition, not merely the poet, supplies the wording. Such poems may have been composed and performed in oral improvisation, so each performance was not a reproduction of a memorized text but was improvised anew and so was different from every other performance, and there were no stable texts until the poetry was recorded in writing. This "oral-formulaic" theory was applied to Old English poetry by F. P. Magoun Jr., and his many disciples. These scholars largely disregarded the distinctions between different poetic traditions concerning formulae and their uses: formulae are used in fundamentally different ways in Homeric Greek and Old English poetry. Oral improvisation may, in some instances, use formulaic diction, but this is not universal: other poetic traditions of illiterate oral composition, closely related to Old English, avoid any use of formulae, for example early Old Norse skaldic poetry. Further, formulaic diction does not prove oral improvisation. In other literary traditions much formulaic poetry was demonstrably composed in writing, for example eighteenth-century English pastoral poetry. Even in the Old English period, Latin poetry, certainly composed in writing by highly literate poets such as Aldhelm, can be highly formulaic, as has been shown by Andy Orchard. There is no direct nor circumstantial evidence that any surviving Old English poetry, apart from *Cædmon's Hymn*, was composed and transmitted other than in writing.

OLD ENGLISH LITERATURE

THE JUNIUS MANUSCRIPT

THE Junius Manuscript contains only four fairly long religious poems: three verse-paraphrases of books of the Old Testament, *Genesis, Exodus,* and *Daniel,* are followed by *Christ and Satan.* They all treat their Biblical subject matter very freely. *Genesis* stays the closest to its source, and is for the most part a fairly simple retelling of the Biblical stories. It has a sober, restrained dignity, not instantly appealing but compelling ultimate respect. Within the main text, however, there is a large interpolation, usually known as *Genesis B.* This tells in dramatic and largely apocryphal detail the accounts of the Fall of Satan and the Fall of Man. It is metrically distinct from most other Old English poetry, and also has some unusual word-usage; this led Eduard Sievers to suggest in 1875 that it was translated from another Germanic language, Old Saxon, and this was confirmed when in 1894 large fragments of the Old Saxon *Genesis* were discovered in the Vatican Library. The brief section of overlap between the passages of Old Saxon and Old English shows that the Old English text is a close translation of the Old Saxon. *Genesis B* shows remarkable freedom, dramatic power, and skill of characterization, particularly of Satan. Junius owned this manuscript, and was a friend of John Milton. Milton had some knowledge of Old English, possibly acquired through Junius, and so he could have known this text: this would give an explanation of the striking correspondences in the characterization of Satan between *Genesis B* and *Paradise Lost.*

Exodus is a very free retelling of the first part of the Biblical book, dealing with the escape of the Israelites from Egypt and the crossing of the Red Sea. It is a vigorous and colorful poem, full of wildly metaphysical imagery, perhaps derived from patristic allegorical interpretations. It is passionate and exciting, but may not always seem fully in control of its material.

Daniel tells the story of Nebuchadnezzar and the Burning Fiery Furnace, and culminates in a gloriously expansive paraphrase of the hymn of the three Hebrew boys, taken into Christian liturgy as the *Benedicite.*

Christ and Satan is a poetic meditation upon the doctrinal issues that arise from various encounters between Christ and the devil, in the Temptation, at the Harrowing of Hell, and at Judgment. It is restrained in its treatment of its rather colorful subject matter, and seems a text perhaps intended for personal devotion. It provides the thematic key to this collection of poems, all of which deal with literal and allegorical images of Hell and the Harrowing of Hell, from damnation to redemption.

THE VERCELLI BOOK

THE Vercelli Book is so named because it survives in the cathedral library at Vercelli, in north Italy, where it has probably been since the twelfth century, as it contains an annotation in Italian handwriting from about 1100. It seems to be almost complete, but has been damaged by chemicals—applied by its first transcriber in the late nineteenth century to make the writing clearer to read. It is a mixed manuscript of twenty-three prose homilies and six poems. These are *Andreas, Fates of the Apostles, Soul and Body I, Homiletic Fragment I, The Dream of the Rood,* and *Elene.*

Andreas is a fairly long verse life of St. Andrew, based ultimately on a Greek life that in style and content is more nearly a novella, full of extravagant description of fantastic events. The Old English poem matches these well, with great excitement and a driving momentum; it also deepens the text and gives it a more serious undertow without diminishing its entertainment value. The quality of poetry is variable but usually high, and often seems to echo *Beowulf.*

Fates of the Apostles is a short apostolic martyrology of little interest other than that it has an epilogue containing Cynewulf's signature as a runic acrostic. *Soul and Body I,* incomplete at its end, is one of two short verse debates in Old English between the soul and dead body, in which the soul berates the decaying body for causing its damnation. It is entirely conventional and has little literary merit other than vigor. *Homiletic Fragment I* has lost its beginning, but as it stands is a fairly conventional ending to an elegiac poem: it uses motifs deriving from the biblical Book of Proverbs to lament the transience of this world and to urge its reader to look to eternal truths beyond it.

In contrast, *The Dream of the Rood* is one of the finest and most unusual English poems to survive from the Dark or Middle Ages. The poem is short, at 156 lines, but compresses religious revelation and theological interpretation into its two symmetrical halves. It uses the convention of the dream vision, and its outer narrator is a Dreamer, as in William Langland's *Piers Plowman* or the anonymous fourteenth-century poem *Pearl*. The Dreamer sees a vision of the Cross in majesty, towering above the world, clad in garments, gold, and gems, gazed upon by angels, men, and all creation. He is terrified by the sight, aware of his own mortal wounds of sin, and in his fear he sees the Cross change, so that through the gold he sees flowing blood. Then the Cross itself speaks: as the inner narrator of the poem, it gives an account of the Passion of Christ. This owes rather little to the biblical account, but employs motifs of alarmingly disparate origins to portray the animate Cross. In order to obey Christ in spiritual warfare, the Cross must slay him, and yet is slain with him. "All Creation wept." United with Christ by the nails that pierce them both, it undergoes its own passion, burial, resurrection, and ascension. At this point (l. 78), the arithmetical center of the poem, the inner narrative ends. As often in shorter Old English religious poems, the second half of the poem is homiletic, and expounds the significance of the content of its first half. The Cross addresses the Dreamer, and tells him to recount his vision to all men; the poem is therefore internally self-justifying. The Cross looks forward to Judgment at the Second Coming, but this Judgment is no conventional bookkeeping of good and evil: Christ will ask "where the man may be who for the Lord's name would wish to taste bitter death, as He did before on the tree." The Cross itself is Judgment; it is the test of man's love for God as it is the proof of God's love for man. Finally, the Dreamer himself expresses his own devotion in an upward-straining association of man's redemption with Christ's Ascension.

This poem shows extraordinary intellectual boldness and originality. It reorganizes elements of biblical narrative, combined with themes from heroic poetry and even possibly from paganism, in order to present its portrait of the animate, speaking Cross, apparently unique to this poem in early medieval Christian sources. It is also bold nearly to the point of heresy in its doctrinal interpretation. The union of Christ with the Cross allows the Cross to share in Christ's Passion. Its mortal wood is animated by union with Christ's divinity, while at the same time it is the anguished instrument of Christ's death. Thus the Cross shares not only Christ's nature in crucifixion, but it also shares man's nature, an earthly being animated with a God-given soul, the agent of Christ's death but thereby enabled to share Christ's Resurrection and Ascension. Similarly the Cross becomes not merely a sign of the Second Coming, but the very means of Judgment. Such a theological interpretation appears to be unique to this poem. It is matched by poetry of equal quality, powerful and economical, unified in local paradox and by large-scale symmetries across the poem.

The Dream of the Rood may be much older than its late tenth-century manuscript. The Ruthwell Cross in Dumfriesshire, a large and elaborate free-standing carved stone cross dated on art-historical grounds to the late seventh or early eighth century, bears a damaged runic inscription that must be related to the poem. The language of this inscription is likely to be rather later than the Ruthwell Cross itself, and it was probably carved after the cross was erected; it may be of the mid to late eighth century. Possibly the runic inscription inspired the poem, but alternatively it may quote from the poem. Quotation seems more probable, since although the inscription is certainly poetic, it is not quite metrical, and so seems to be a quotation from existing poetry rather than an actual poem itself. If so, then the poem itself must be older than the runic inscription on the Ruthwell Cross, and was probably composed in the first half of the eighth century.

Elene is a fairly long verse life of St. Helena, the reputedly British mother of Emperor Constantine the Great, who converted the Roman

Empire to Christianity soon after 312 A.D.; she is credited with the "Invention" (finding) of the relics of the True Cross in 326 A.D. when on pilgrimage to the Holy Land. The poem contains another instance of Cynewulf's runic signature; it is otherwise competent but of little literary merit. Its association of pilgrimage with devotion to the Cross, however, may again define the purpose of the entire manuscript: a vade mecum of devotional literature for an English pilgrim to the sanctuaries of apostolic martyrdom, whose book has remained in Italy to the present day.

THE EXETER BOOK

THE Exeter Book contains by far the largest number of surviving Old English poems, without prose or illustration; it is defective in that leaves have fallen out of it in probably at least seven places; it has also suffered fairly serious fire damage, especially affecting *The Ruin*. Its contents are not organized by any obvious overall plan, though local groupings are clear. Five fairly large texts stand at the beginning of the manuscript: *Crist, Guthlac, Azarias, The Phoenix,* and *Juliana*. The remainder of the manuscript is occupied by several large groups of fairly short poems: *The Wanderer, Gifts of Men, Precepts, The Seafarer, Vainglory, Widsith, The Fortunes of Men, Maxims I, The Order of the World,* and *The Riming Poem; The Panther, The Whale,* and *The Partridge;* and *Soul and Body II, Deor,* and *Wulf and Eadwacer.* These are followed by a group of fifty-nine riddles. The manuscript ends with *The Wife's Lament, Judgement Day I, Resignation, Descent into Hell, Alms-Giving, Pharaoh, The Lord's Prayer I, Homiletic Fragment II,* two riddles, *The Husband's Message, The Ruin,* and a further group of thirty-four riddles.

Crist is actually a group of three poems: *Crist I,* also known as the *Advent Lyrics; Crist II,* also known as *The Ascension;* and *Crist III,* also known as *Christ in Judgement.* They are organized thematically, and are figurative meditations upon different aspects of their subject, rather than narrative or literal exposition. The first two, in particular, glory in the exultant yet controlled metaphoric power of their figurative techniques,

expressed in equally controlled yet powerful poetry. *Crist II* contains another of Cynewulf's runic acrostic signatures. *Guthlac* is also a group of two verse lives of the Anglo-Saxon hermit saint, each organized loosely around a narrative framework, but both quietly meditative rather than strictly narrative in presentation. *Azarias* is probably related to *Daniel* in the Junius Manuscript, and likewise is an elaboration of the *Benedicite. The Phoenix* is a bestiary poem in the tradition of the *Physiologus,* which describes animals and then places an allegorical interpretation upon their description; in this case, the poem is a free translation, enlargement, and elaboration of a Latin poem by Lactantius. It is complex and ornate, and is something of a rhetorical tour-de-force in its successful combination of classical and native poetic techniques. *Juliana,* in contrast, is a verse life of the Roman virgin-martyr, and apart from a pleasingly comic devil is rather conventional; it contains Cynewulf's fourth surviving runic acrostic signature.

The Exeter Book contains several short poems which have been classified as "elegies," but which would be better seen as employing the "elegiac mode" found widely elsewhere in Old English poetry: expressions of human grief, often given metaphysical significance, and sometimes but not always followed by divine consolation. *The Wanderer* and *The Seafarer* are usually considered the prime examples of this genre or mode, and are often grouped together by modern critics; they share possible verbal and thematic links supporting this association. The text of *The Seafarer* is now partly corrupt: a section towards its end does not make sense or meter, and cannot be safely reconstructed. In the first half of the poem, the speaker tells of his longing for seafaring and his fear of it, of the perils and attractions of the great waters, in increasingly figurative terms. In its second half, the poem gives an allegorical interpretation of this, signifying the soul's quest for God. At the transition from metaphor to allegory, the poem achieves an intensity matching the paradoxical emotions that tear at the awareness of its speaker. It has often, probably correctly, been associated with the early Irish traditions of seafaring hermits that in part had led to the conversion of the English; on this basis it might be a relatively early poem. *The Wanderer* may be modeled upon something similar to *The Seafarer;* its speaker recounts his exile from past human happiness, and his grim and grievous perception of universal transience; in darkness and despair at the passing of all things beneath the skies, he turns to God as the only permanence. The poem is Boethian in its philosophical understanding of emotional experience; some of its themes and vocabulary may point towards composition late in the tenth century. The elegiac mode appears in many other poems in the Exeter Book, for instance *Resignation* and *Deor.*

Some of the poems in the Exeter Book, the so-called "Wisdom Literature," consist of little more than collections of vaguely ethical propositions. These poems, including *The Gifts of Men, Precepts, Vainglory, The Fortunes of Men, Maxims,* and *The Order of the World,* look back to texts such as the biblical Book of Proverbs or the Latin *Disticha Catonis,* and are paralleled in other ancient Germanic literatures, such as the Old Norse *Hávamál.* The Old English examples are not of much inherent literary interest, but they give a context in which to understand similar exempla, proverbs, or maxims that occur in other poems.

The Exeter Book contains a few other bestiary poems beside *The Phoenix: The Panther, The Whale,* and *The Partridge* are fairly short and picturesque poems, which bring out the riddling aspect of the Physiologus tradition. The physical animal, whose characteristics are described in the first section of each poem, is presented as a metaphysical riddle, to represent Christ or the Devil, as expounded in the second part of the poem. The whale as "type" of the Devil is an image that was still available to Milton.

Widsith and *Deor,* although they incorporate elegiac elements and consist of lists of exempla, are distinguished from all other poems in the manuscript in that their content is that of the legends available to the early English. *Widsith* is not very much more than an annotated encyclopedic catalog, or rather three such catalogs, of available legendary names of persons and peoples,

sometimes with brief fragments of narrative attached to the name. The range is mostly native Germanic legend, but some classical and biblical names have also been incorporated; to judge from the name-forms, these have reached the poem through oral transmission. This is presented in a perfunctory narrative frame: a wandering minstrel called Widsiþ ("Wide-farer") tells that he has performed for all these people. Although the poem has little literary merit of its own, it is invaluable as an index of known legend, and most of its material can be corroborated elsewhere, either in Old English or sometimes in other early Germanic literatures. *Deor* also presents its material within the narrative frame of a wandering minstrel, and the material itself is a short sequence of juxtaposed narrative exempla derived from Germanic legend, on the theme of transience. Not all its material is easily understood, but at least in one instance, its initial reference to the legend of Wayland Smith, it has close verbal links to the Norse poem on that subject, *Völundarkviða,* which must indicate some textual relationship. It is almost unique in Old English poetry in being composed in irregular stanzas, rather than continuously, and in having a quasi-proverbial refrain, *Þæs ofereode, þisses swa mæg,* perhaps "it came to an end of that; so it can of this." The effect is of a multifaceted consideration with some emotional power, as its ambivalent refrain is applied to successive legendary examples of sorrow and joy, and then finally to the speaker of the poem himself.

The Riming Poem is also metrically unusual, in that it attempts to make consistent use of end rhyme, which elsewhere appears only ornamentally in Old English poetry. The poem is otherwise unremarkable.

Several poems are simply homiletic: *Soul and Body II* is another diatribe by the soul against the dead body for the fleshly sins which have damned it; *Alms Giving* and *Homiletic Fragment II* are very brief sets of injunctions to Christians. A small group of poems deals with quasi-biblical material: *The Descent into Hell, Pharaoh,* and *The Lord's Prayer I.* Of these only *The Descent into Hell* is of literary interest, and it seems to function as an appendix to *Crist* at the beginning of the manuscript.

Three remarkable and powerful poems deal, apparently or actually, with the relationship between men and women: *Wulf and Eadwacer, The Wife's Lament,* and *The Husband's Message. Wulf and Eadwacer* is a short but powerful lament (19 lines) by a female speaker for her lover, Wulf, and against Eadwacer (literally "wealth-watcher," the English form of the historical name *Odoacer*), who restrains her against her will. It does not make full sense as it stands, and is also metrically very irregular, as if it had been excerpted from a larger text. Its conclusion is one of the most haunting and evocative fragments of Old English: *Þæt mon eaþe tosliteð þætte næfre gesomnad wæs uncer giedd geador* "that is easily torn apart that was never put together, the song of us two together." *The Wife's Lament* is a rather longer lament (53 lines), again by a female speaker, for her "lord." She is exiled because of his exile. Again the maxim that ends the poem is powerful: *Wa bið þam þe sceal of langoþe leofes abidan* "woe shall be to that one who must from longing await a loved one." The poem is full of internal self-inconsistencies and even self-contradictions, which make reconstruction of any implied, external narrative nearly impossible, but its imagery is so precise and powerful that this merely reinforces its impact: the poem nags at the mind like an unsolved riddle. *The Husband's Message* is, as its modern title implies, a message from a man to his exiled wife, asking her to come and be reunited with him; although widely separated in the manuscript, it is difficult not to see this poem as an answer to the anguished exile of *The Wife's Lament;* both poems give the impression that they might have been excerpted from a larger text giving an explanatory narrative context.

The Ruin stands by itself. Although the text is seriously defective due to fire damage, it seems to be an Old English description of Roman remains, given some light elegiac interpretation reminiscent of *The Wanderer's* description of storm-swept ruins. This poem, however, is remarkable in that the ruins are almost certainly specific: it describes a hot spring, unique in Britain to Bath, and the structures through which the hot water flows, all of which have been corroborated by archaeological investigation of the Roman baths at Bath. The poem describes specific features which cannot have been visible later than the eighth century: peat, which were already deep enough by the tenth century for a cemetery to be dug in it, was subsequently deposited over them. The poem must therefore have been composed early in the Old English period. It largely lacks the melancholy of the elegiac mode, but concentrates instead upon structural details of the ruined buildings, and the glitter and glory of those who once had inhabited them.

Lastly, the Exeter Book contains two large collections of vernacular riddles. These owe relatively little to the Latin collections of riddles by Symphosius or Aldhelm: each riddle presents a brief vignette of its unnamed subject, and often ends with "Say what am I called." Sometimes the glimpses into everyday life are very vivid; some of the riddles indulge in double meanings, and are occasionally lightheartedly improper. These vernacular riddles are certainly entertainment literature, and they have nothing of Aldhelm's metaphysical concerns, where the reader looks through the meaning of the physical world to the hand of God. However, these riddles reflect a general concern with interpretation of the literal world, found throughout the Exeter Book, whether a matter of the events of the life of Christ, or of animals such as the phoenix or panther in the bestiary poems, or of events from Germanic legend in *Deor,* or of the experience of human transience in *The Wanderer.* Things in this world have meaning, and they can be interpreted to gain wisdom. In short, the riddles show a means of metaphorical understanding explored more fully and powerfully in the major poems of this manuscript.

THE BEOWULF *MANUSCRIPT*

THE *Beowulf* Manuscript, as it presently stands, contains only two poems: *Beowulf* and the headless fragment of *Judith.* Although *Judith* was written by the second scribe of *Beowulf,* it seems only to have been bound with it in modern times. *Beowulf* is the last of a group of otherwise prose texts: a fragmentary Life of St. Christopher, *The Wonders of the East,* and *Alexander's Letter to Aristotle.* Little obvious seems to unite these texts other than a naive interest in exotic marvels: the manuscript may have been meant as a Book of Monsters. *Beowulf* itself is the longest surviving poem in Old English, at 3,182 lines. It is also the only Old English poem that may justly be compared with the classical epics of Homer or Vergil. It is epic in intellectual, emotional, and narrative scale, if only barely in physical length, but it shares much of its rhapsodic melancholy not only with Vergil but also with the Old English elegiac poems. Its authorship and date of composition are unknown: plausible cases can be made for composition at any time between the early eighth century and the late tenth. The poem tells of the slaying, by beheading, of three supernatural monsters—two troll-like beings and a dragon—and of the death of its hero, who dies as a consequence of a wound inflicted by the dragon. The hero, Beowulf, does nothing else reported at first-hand in the poem. His three narratives are set against a mosaic of Germanic legend and legendary history, usually recounted in detailed but incomplete allusion. Both the monster-slayings and the legendary background are known from a large range of other texts in Old English and other early languages, and much of this material is likely to have been inherited from ancient legendary tradition. Although the narratives of the poem might seem to be fantasy, they are presented as the vehicle of constant ethical analysis, darkening towards the endless despair of Germanic heroic legend. In modes of narrative presentation, and also in some aspects of verbal technique, the poem has no known models and no successors: it is unique both within English and more widely within classical or medieval literature. Beowulf may stand beside Odysseus, the wise and long-suffering, or pious Æneas—and he does not suffer in such comparison—but the northern hero inhabits a world far darker than either Homer's or Vergil's. Christian hope is available within the poem, but is only known to its poet and audience; the pre-Christian past that it depicts permitted no such knowledge. This story matter is presented in poetry of richness, passion, and great density, and with a long-breathed inevitability of pace that develops a huge, slow momentum. It is as unstoppable as a lava flow, and as astonishing.

Judith tells the story, derived from the biblical Apocrypha, of a Jewish prostitute who murders an Assyrian general by beheading him during a tryst. The Old English poem almost succeeds in presenting this vicious tale as if of a woman warrior-saint; it is vigorous and not without some subtlety of both narrative and expression.

FURTHER POEMS

SOME Old English poems survive outside the main poetic manuscripts. Apart from those already mentioned, these fall into a number of categories. Some are paraphrases of biblical or liturgical texts: the Paris Psalter with its metrical versions of psalms 51–150, various isolated psalms, the *Lord's Prayer II* and *III,* the *Creed,* the *Gloria.* Some are religious exhortation: *An Exhortation to Christian Living, A Summons to Prayer, The Seasons for Fasting.* A few are further collections of proverbs or maxims. There are a few loosely metrical charms. Metrical prefaces or epilogues to a few texts, mostly Alfredian, also survive, as well as the metrical version of the "Metres of Boethius." Unclassifiable items include the Old English *Rune Poem,* with its parallels from later medieval Norway and Iceland; the *Menologium,* a poetic interpretation of the church's calendar; *Durham,* a poem in praise of the shrine of St. Cuthbert; and the two poetic fragments of *Solomon and Saturn,* difficult and obscure debates between figures representing Christian and secular wisdom (also represented in Old English prose). Two fragmentary texts survive dealing with legendary subjects: the *Finnesburh Fragment,* recounting part of a story also known from *Beowulf,* and two short fragments of *Waldere,* an epic retelling of the legend of Walter of Aquitaine, otherwise unknown from early English, but known most importantly from a continental Latin epic, the *Waltharius,* sometimes attributed to Ekkehard of St. Gallen (*fl.* early tenth century).

Waldere is the only direct evidence other than *Beowulf* for a secular epic tradition in Old English.

A number of poems deal with historical events during the late Old English period. Most of these survive embedded within the *Anglo-Saxon Chronicle,* and of these only *The Battle of Brunanburh* can stand by itself; it is a vigorous if rather conventional encomium of the West-Saxon king Æþelstan (Athelstan) and his victory in 937, at an unidentified location, against an alliance of Vikings, Strathclyde British, and Picts. Others celebrate the capture of the Five Boroughs in 942 and the coronation of Eadgar in 973; others are memorial lays for Eadgar (d. 975), Ælfred "se æþeling" (d. 1036), and Edward the Confessor (d. 1065). These are of little literary interest other than in the much freer meter that they sometimes employ, apparently anticipating the meters of Middle English alliterative poetry. The only historical poem that survives outside the *Anglo-Saxon Chronicle* is *The Battle of Maldon,* known only from an early-modern transcript. It is a substantial fragment (325 lines) of a poetic account of a battle in August 991 between an English earl of Essex, Byrhtnoþ, and a Viking army, in which Byrhtnoþ was defeated and fell; the poem seems to be a much-elaborated memorial lay for him, but provides a lot of detail about the English participants and their actions. It is economical, vigorous, and powerful, above all in its presentation of the hopeless heroism of Byrhtnoþ's followers, who after his fall fight on to their inevitable defeat and death. The poem does not lack subtlety, but is memorable for its immediacy and impact. It forms a fitting end to this survey of Old English poetry, as indeed it marks nearly the end of Old English poetic culture.

CONCLUSION

THE surviving Old English poetic corpus contains many texts which are unremarkably conventional, and some which are simply mediocre, though very few which can be dismissed as incompetent. The conventional texts have their uses: they demonstrate the available literary conventions that other, more individual texts manipulate for particular effect. Beyond these, much Old English poetry is by any external standards good: poems such as *Crist II* or *Deor* or *The Seafarer* or *The Battle of Maldon,* each of their kind, may stand unashamed beside most later English poetry. Two texts, however, stand out beyond these, and of themselves justify the study of Old English. *The Dream of the Rood* can be set beside *Pearl* or *Piers Plowman,* or the finest of seventeenth-century English metaphysical religious poetry. In its intensity and intellectual power, it is the match for *Pearl* or Donne; in its humanity for Langland; and in its depth and freedom of doctrinal understanding it is arguably supreme. *Beowulf* is unique, not only in English, but in the Germanic and classical worlds. It may be claimed, perhaps beside *Troilus and Criseyde,* the *Faerie Queene,* and *Paradise Lost,* as one of the most important long poems that English has contributed to world literature.

Not much Old English literature survives, and much may well have been lost. The existing texts, however, do far more than simply give glimpses into thought-worlds of the past. In presenting alternative modes of perception and understanding, different from those available in classical, or high medieval, or modern conceptual frameworks, they enrich us. They look beyond our own weary and limited preconceptions. Old English, at its best, extends our own self-awareness.

SELECTED BIBLIOGRAPHY

I. COLLECTIONS OF OLD ENGLISH POETRY. R. K. Gordon, ed. and trans., *Anglo-Saxon Poetry* (London, 1926); A. H. Smith, ed., *Three Northumbrian Poems* (London, 1933), contains *Cædmon's Hymn, Bede's Death Song,* and *The Leiden Riddle;* G. P. Krapp and E. V. K. Dobbie, eds., *The Anglo-Saxon Poetic Records,* 4 vols. (New York and London, 1931–1942); R. F. Leslie, ed., *Three Old English Elegies* (Manchester, 1961), contains *The Wife's Lament, The Husband's Message, The Ruin;* M. Swanton, ed. and trans., *Anglo-Saxon Prose* (London, 1975); T. A. Shippey, ed., *Poems of Wisdom and Learning in Old English* (Cambridge, 1976), contains *Precepts, Vainglory, The Fortunes of Men, Maxims I and II, The Rune Poem, Solomon and Saturn, Soul and Body I, Descent into Hell,* and *Judgement Day I;* S. A. J. Bradley, ed. and trans., *Anglo-Saxon Poetry* (London, 1982); O. D. Macrae-Gibson, ed., *The Old English Riming Poem* (Cambridge, 1983); A. Squires, ed., *The Old English Physiologus* (Durham, 1988), contains *The Panther, The Whale,* and *The Partridge;* A. L. Klinck, ed., *The Old English Elegies: A Critical Edition and Genre Study* (Montreal, 1992); B. J. Muir, ed., *The Exeter Anthology of Old English Poetry,* 2 vols. (Exeter, U.K. 1994).

II. MAJOR EDITIONS OF INDIVIDUAL POEMS. *Andreas* and *The Fates of the Apostles,* ed. K. R. Brooks (Oxford, 1961); *The Battle of Brunanburh,* ed. A. Campbell (London, 1938); *The Battle of Maldon,* ed. D. G. Scragg (Manchester, 1981); *Beowulf,* ed. F. Klaeber (Boston, Mass., 1922, 3d ed. 1950); *Beowulf,* ed. G. B. Jack (Oxford, 1994); *Christ and Satan,* ed. M. D. Clubb (New Haven, Conn., 1925); *The Christ of Cynewulf,* ed. A. S. Cook (Boston, Mass, 1909); *Daniel and Azarias,* ed. R. T. Farrell (London, 1974); *Deor,* ed. K. Malone (London, 1933); *The Dream of the Rood,* ed. M. Swanton (Manchester, 1970); *Elene,* ed. P. O. E. Gradon (London, 1958); *Exodus,* ed. P. J. Lucas (London, 1977); *Finnsburh Fragment and Episode,* ed. D. K. Fry (London, 1974); *Genesis A,* ed. A. N. Doane (Madison, Wis., and London, 1978); *The Later Genesis [Genesis B],* ed. B. J. Timmer (Oxford, 1948); *The Guthlac Poems of the Exeter Book,* ed. J. Roberts (Oxford, 1979); *Judith,* ed. B. J. Timmer (London, 1952); *Juliana,* ed. R. Woolf (London, 1955); *The Phoenix,* ed. N. F. Blake (Manchester, 1964); *Resignation,* ed. L. Malmberg (Durham, N.C., 1979); *The Riddles of the Exeter Book,* ed. F. Tupper (Boston, Mass., 1910); *The Riddles of the Exeter Book,* ed. C. Williamson (Chapel Hill, N.C.,1977); *The Seafarer,* ed. I. L. Gordon (London, 1960); *Waldere,* ed. A. Zettersten (Manchester, 1979); *The Wanderer,* ed. T. P. Dunning and A. J. Bliss (London, 1969); *Widsith,* ed. R. W. Chambers (Cambridge, U.K., 1912); *Widsith,* ed. K. Malone (Copenhagen, 1936, rev. ed. 1962).

III. MAJOR EDITIONS OF THE PROSE TEXTS. B. Thorpe, ed., *Aelfric Sermones Catholici* [Ælfric's Catholic Homilies], 2 vols. (London, 1844–1846), supplemented by *Homilies of Ælfric,* 2 vols., ed. J. C. Pope (London, 1967–1968), and *Ælfric's Catholic Homilies, the Second Series,* ed. M. Godden (London, 1979); T. O. Cockayne, ed., *Leechdoms, Wortcunning, and Starcraft of early England,* 3 vols. (London, 1864–1866), contains *Bald's Leechbook;* H. Sweet, ed., *King Alfred's West-Saxon Version of Gregory's Pastoral Care,* 2 vols. (London 1871); R. Morris, ed., *The Blickling Homilies,* 3 vols. (London, 1874–1880); J. Zupitza, ed., *Aelfric Grammatik und Glossar* [Ælfric's Grammar] (Berlin, 1880); T. Miller, ed., *The Old English Version of Bede's Ecclesiastical History of the English People,* 4 vols. (London, 1890–

1898); J. earle and C. Plummer, eds., *Anglo-Saxon Chronicle* (Oxford, 1892–1899); W. J. Sedgefield, ed., *King Alfred's Old English Version of Boethius's De consolatione philosophiae* (Oxford, 1899); W. W. Skeat, ed., *Ælfric's Lives of Saints,* 4 vols. (London, 1881–1900); H. Hecht, ed., *Bischof Wærferths von Worcester Übersetzung der Dialoge Gregors des Grossen,* (Leipzig, 1900); F. Liebermann, ed., *Die Gesetze der Angelsachsen* [Old English Laws], 3 vols. (Halle, 1903–1916); S. Rypins, ed., *Three Old English Prose Texts* (London, 1924), contains *Alexander's Letter to Aristotle* and *The Wonders of the East;* H. Henel, ed., *Ælfric's De temporibus anni* (London, 1942); P. Goulden, ed., *The Old English "Apollonius of Tyre"* (London, 1958); D. Bethurum, ed., *The Homilies of Wulfstan,* (Oxford, 1957); T. A. Carnicelli, ed., *King Alfred's Version of St. Augustine's Soliloquies* (Cambridge Mass., 1969); J. Bately, ed., *The Old English Orosius* (London, 1980); J. E. Cross and T. D. Hill, eds., *The Prose Solomon and Saturn and Adrian and Ritheus* (Toronto, 1982); D. G. Scragg, ed., *The Vercelli Homilies and Related Texts,* (London, 1992); P. S. Baker and M. Lapidge, eds., *Byrhtferth's Enchiridion* [*Byrhtferþ's Manual*] (London, 1996).

IV. BIBLIOGRAPHIES AND CATALOGS. N. R. Ker, *Catalogue of Manuscripts Containing Anglo-Saxon* (Oxford, 1957); P. H. Sawyer, *Anglo-Saxon Charters: An Annotated List and Bibliography* (London, 1968); *Anglo-Saxon England* (Cambridge, U.K., 1972–), includes annual bibliographies; S. B. Greenfield and F. C. Robinson, *A Bibliography of Publications on Old English Literature to the end of 1972* (Toronto and Manchester, 1980).

V. CRITICAL STUDIES. W. P. Ker, *Epic and Romance* (London, 1897); J. R. R. Tolkien, *Beowulf: The Monsters and the Critics* (London, 1936); F. P. Magoun, Jr., "The Oral-Formulaic Character of Anglo-Saxon Narrative Poetry," in *Speculum* 28 (1953); A. J. Bliss, "The Appreciation of Old English Metre," in N. Davis and C. L. Wrenn, eds., *English and Medieval Studies Presented to J. R. R. Tolkien* (London, 1962); A. P. McD. Orchard, "Some Aspects of Seventh-Century Hiberno-Latin Syntax: A Statistical Approach," in *Peritia* 6–7 (1987–1988) B. Cassidy, ed., *The Ruthwell Cross* (Princeton, 1992).

VI. GENERAL BACKGROUND. *The Cambridge Companion to Old English Literature,* ed. M. Godden and M. Lapidge (Cambridge, 1991); *The Blackwell Encyclopaedia of Anglo-Saxon England,* ed. M. Lapidge, J. Blair, S. Keynes, and D. G. Scragg (Oxford, 1999).

GEORGE BERNARD SHAW

(1856–1950)

John A. Bertolini

ALTHOUGH BERNARD SHAW was many things—an Irishman in England, an autodidact, a novelist, a political representative, an art critic, a music critic, a drama critic, a socialist who helped to found the Fabian Society (1884) yet married an Irish millionairess, a commentator on world affairs, a public gadfly, a thinker, a man of letters, an indefatigable letter writer, an atheist with profound religious instincts, an evolutionist but not a Darwinian—he was primarily a playwright. And his reputation, controversial as it is at present, rests on the achievement of his plays as dramatic art. In 1925 the world testified to the worth of Shaw's body of work—the largest number of English-language plays to be regularly revived worldwide since Shakespeare—by awarding him the Nobel Prize (Shaw gave away the money). But his characteristic contribution to dramatic literature does not stand out in sharp relief; nor does it lend itself readily to definition by school or style.

Shakespeare, Molière, and Ibsen are the dramatists who most influenced him, though the conventions of nineteenth-century theater and of opera—Mozart, Wagner, and Italian opera, especially—played an unusually lively role in forming the style of his plays. Shaw patterned his characters after the stage types familiar to him from his youth, and often arranged their encounters with one another onstage as ensembles, from duets to nonets, and gave their personalities expressive power through arialike set speeches. Shaw knew that no one would ever write better plays than Shakespeare because he did it as well as it could be done. Nevertheless, throughout his playwriting career Shaw felt a sense of specific competition with his mighty predecessor. Indeed, in Shaw's last play, *Shakes Versus Shav* (1949), puppet alter-egos of the two playwrights compare speeches, argue, and box

over which of them is the greater dramatist. With Molière, Shaw shares two characteristics: infinite comic inventiveness and geniality. There is no nastiness or hatred in Shaw's comedies. From Ibsen, Shaw learned that the drama could be a forum to address the large social, political, and philosophical problems of the day.

But Shaw also learned from Ibsen that the dramatist's business was not to present a partisan view of such problems but rather to represent fairly the different sides of any particular issue, giving full, vigorous expression to points of view with which he himself did not particularly agree. Referring to the opinions of his various characters, Shaw puts it this way in the "Epistle Dedicatory" to *Man and Superman*:

> They are all right from their several points of view; and their points of view are, for the dramatic moment, mine also. This may puzzle the people who believe that there is such a thing as an absolutely right point of view, usually their own. It may seem to them that nobody who doubts this can be in a state of grace. However that may be, it is certainly true that nobody who agrees with them can possibly be a dramatist.
>
> (*Collected Plays*, vol. 2, p. 517)

Shaw did not find his true métier as a playwright until he was in his forties, his first play, *Widowers' Houses*, having been written and produced in 1892, when he was thirty-six years old. Before that Shaw's family history was unpromising. He was born a Protestant Irishman on 26 July 1856 into a family with pretensions to status but without the means to sustain the pretense. His mother was Lucinda Gurly, who passed on her love of music to her son; his father, George Carr Shaw, passed on his sense of humor to his son but not his alcoholism. Quite the contrary, his example made Shaw a lifetime teetotaler. Eventually his mother, tired of her husband's failings, followed her music teacher, Vandeleur Lee, to London in 1874, bringing her daughters—but not her son—with her. Two years later Shaw joined his mother in London, where he tried very hard to be a novelist. At first he was unemployed and supported by his mother (as he himself said, "When I came to London, I did not throw myself into the struggle for life, I threw my mother into it"). He was employed briefly by the Edison Phone Company and eventually worked as a book reviewer, an art critic, a music critic, and lastly as a drama critic. In all Shaw wrote five novels, one a year from 1879 to 1883: *Immaturity*; *The Irrational Knot*; *Love Among the Artists*; *Cashel Byron's Profession*, and *An Unsocial Socialist*. Every single one of these novels was rejected by every single publisher to whom Shaw submitted them (though the last four were serialized in periodicals edited by friends of Shaw). A lesser man would have taken these rejections to heart, but not Shaw, who believed in himself wholeheartedly.

The importance of Shaw's theater reviews (mostly belonging to the 1890s) extends beyond their immediate cultural and historical sphere, not only because of the quality of Shaw's prose—the wit and humor on display, the incisive articulation of a consistent critical point of view—but also because they reveal Shaw's determined campaign to get audiences of the time to be receptive to the plays of Henrik Ibsen. For Shaw, Ibsen was writing the kind of play Shaw wanted to see (and later which he himself would want to write)—plays that were designed to reflect seriously the true nature of life, society, and the world, and to project a vision of humankind's potential for improvement. He wanted to see the theater freed from all thought that was merely fashionable or conventional. Consequently he ridiculed the plays of his contemporaries, including such major dramatists as Henry Arthur Jones and Arthur Wing Pinero, when their plays seemed to him an automatic or false response to complex moral issues.

PLAYS UNPLEASANT

SHAW wrote his first play, *Widowers' Houses,* in 1892. He based it in part on some plot ideas furnished to him several years earlier by his friend and fellow critic William Archer, Ibsen's primary translator for the English-speaking world during the next two decades. This was no accidental collaboration; Shaw's first play is in several respects modeled after the pattern of Ibsen's drama, in which a social evil is gradually revealed to have a deadly grip on the lives of the play's central characters. The action turns on young Harry Trench's discovery that the income he lives on derives from slum-landlordism. Previously he had broken off his engagement to Blanche when he learned that her father, Mr. Sartorius, was a slum landlord. He comes to understand that all who live in a capitalist system are tainted by the drive to acquire wealth and by its attendant cruelties and corruption. The lesson the play seeks to inculcate is that all who participate in capitalism are morally culpable for its abuses, and further that there is no use pointing fingers at the supposedly guilty parties; the system itself needs to be changed, or better, abolished, and replaced by something better, namely socialism (in Shaw's view).

When William Archer first made Shaw's acquaintance in the reading room of the British Museum, he observed Shaw to be studying "alternately, if not simultaneously," a French translation of Karl Marx's *Das Kapital* and the orchestral score of Wagner's *Tristan und Isolde*. These two works might be said to symbolize in stark form the two sides—in some ways the warring sides—of Shaw's literary project. On the one hand, Shaw studied economics and politics intensely in order to show how such forces affect the lives and destinies of his characters; on the other hand, he was powerfully susceptible to the expressive power of art and sought to make his plays as directly appealing to the emotions as opera. But since he felt temperamentally and philosophically most at home in the genre of comedy, the emotions his plays express are exuberance, hope, joy, vitality, and buoyancy, not in ignorance of life's darker abysses but in spite of them.

At the climax of *Widowers' Houses*, when Harry Trench and Blanche Sartorius confront one another over the question of whether or not they will get married, Shaw presents their encounter thus (please note that Shaw does not use apostrophes in contractions and uses spaced letters rather than italics for emphasis):

BLANCHE: [*shrewishly*] Well? So you have come back here. You have had the m e a n n e s s to come into this house again. [*He flushes and retreats a step. She follows him up remorselessly*]. What a poor spirited creature you must be! Why don't you go? [*Red and wincing, he starts huffily to get his hat from the table; but when he turns to the door with it she deliberately stands in his way; so that he has to stop*]. I don't want you to stay. [*For a moment they stand face to face, quite close to one another, she is provocative, taunting, half defying, half inviting him to advance, in a flush of undisguised animal excitement. It suddenly flashes on him that all this ferocity is erotic: that she is making love to him. His eye lights up: a cunning expression comes into the corners of his mouth: with a heavy assumption of indifference he walks straight back to his chair, and plants himself in it with his arms folded. She comes down the room after him*]. But I forgot: you have found there is some money to be made here.

(vol. 1, p. 119)

Blanche and Harry here display Shaw's characteristic high-pitched struggle for dominance between male and female, where the couple always seems on the verge of physical violence ("*Shrewishly*" alerts the reader to Shaw's model in this regard, Shakespeare's *Taming of the Shrew*). Such brinkmanship between the man and the woman embodies the emotional intensity of the relationship but also partakes of the farcical elements that are fundamental to comedy. The larger subtext of animal sexuality is the bass line to the dialogue's melody: they block one another, chase one another, provoke one another, always with an erotic energy that charms the audience as well as excites it. Shaw's language in the stage directions strongly states that they are behaving in accord with their natural instincts ("*animal excitement*," "*ferocity*," "*cunning*," "*plants*").

When Harry's "*eye lights up*," we know that he now sees a way to get around her pose of anger and contempt, and we anticipate with pleasure their union. Simultaneously, however, Shaw presents us with a second meaning for this union, namely Harry's resignation to his role within capitalist society. The mixture of this unpleasant truth with the sexual charm of the two leading characters leaves the audience with no convenient villains to blame for the evils of capitalism; indeed, the audience is implicated and is not allowed to stand aloof or to take its pleasure unalloyed. One might call it the mixture of Marx's *Das Kapital* with Wagner's *Tristan und Isolde*, a denunciation of capitalism's exploitation of the poor combined with the exultation of sexual passion. If this mixture discomfited the audience, so much the better from Shaw's point of view.

Several characteristics of Shaw's style of playwriting stand out in this passage: the elaborate detail of the stage directions, both as to the psychological states and the physical movements of the characters; and the histrionic nature of the characters' behavior. Shaw wrote extensive stage directions for two reasons. It was his habit to rehearse his own plays with the actors from manuscript copies, then to have the play printed after he had worked out the stage directions with the actors for production. He did so to insure that future directors of his plays would not distort the meanings he intended his characters and stories to have. He also wanted his plays to be thought of as serious literature on a par with fiction and poetry, not just as descriptions of stage spectacles with dialogue added. Toward that end he assiduously removed all traces of the technical stage directions commonly found in "acting editions" of plays, directions such as "crosses from down stage right to up stage left." Notwithstanding the absence of such technical stage directions, Shaw's characters behave as if they are aware of being onstage. Their poses and movements are statements, and their statements are poses and movements. This is what Shaw meant when he observed of his own characters that they are "of the stage stagey" (vol. 4, p. 900).

Widowers' Houses did not have a conventional stage run. Rather it was presented for two performances only by a semiprivate group, the Independent Theatre. Likewise Shaw's two subsequent plays, *The Philanderer* and *Mrs. Warren's Profession* (both written in 1893), did not receive professional commercial productions until a decade or more later. But all three were published, first separately then together as the unpleasant plays in *Plays Pleasant and Unpleasant* (1898). Both works show Shaw breathing Ibsen's influence but also breaking free of that influence to become himself, that is, establishing a distinctive style that expresses his personality and the individuality of his imagination.

In *The Philanderer*, Shaw signals Ibsen's presence by inventing an Ibsen Club for the main characters to frequent, the club being a place for people of advanced social and political views. The play has serious objects of satire—the authority and prestige of doctors, the outmoded mores governing courtship and marriage, and the evil of animal vivisection, among them—which mark the play as a product of Ibsen's transformation of the theater into a forum for examining social problems. But *The Philanderer* also unleashes Shaw's penchant for extravagant comedy and the realm of the fantastic. As one critic has pointed out, the Ibsen Club, where women smoke cigars and supposed discoveries of fatal liver diseases turn out to be mistakes, is really "a fantastical state of mind, like Cloud-Cuckoo-Land in *The Birds*" (Frederick Marker, "Shaw's Early Plays", in Innes, ed., *Cambridge Companion,* p. 113). The comparison to Aristophanes' protagonists, who get the birds to set up a utopian society in the clouds, is apt because it suggests how easily would-be social reformers detach themselves from reality and imagine a perfect world so different from their own. Neither Shaw's admiration for Ibsen nor his adherence to causes like the campaign against using animals in medical tests prevents him from making fun of people like himself who identify themselves as followers of Ibsen and therefore as persons of advanced views.

The play concludes with a return to reality from the rarefied atmosphere of the Ibsen Club, as indicated by the play's final stage direction regarding the main female character, Julia

Craven: *"The rest look at Julia with concern, and even a little awe, feeling for the first time, the presence of a keen sorrow"* (vol. 1, p. 227). Julia's sorrow stems from the frustration of her love for Leonard Charteris, a man who is simply unsuited to marriage, and the play ends with their not marrying. The endings of *Widowers' Houses* and *The Philanderer,* Shaw's first two plays, set a pattern for the rest of his comedies, where the leading male and female characters either do marry after a lengthy psychological (and frequently physical) struggle, or, almost as often, do not marry.

The last of Shaw's Ibsenite "unpleasant plays," *Mrs. Warren's Profession* (1893), like *The Philanderer*, ends with a keen sorrow for its heroine, Vivie, because she breaks off her engagement to Frank Gardner as well as her relationship with her mother, Mrs. Warren. The latter refuses to give up her profession as manager of a string of brothels, 'a secret from the past that, as in Ibsen's plays, poisons the lives of the main characters until it is revealed and addressed. The play seems to endorse Vivie's independent womanhood and choice of her own occupation (doing actuarial calculations) as a higher good than either her romance with Frank or filial closeness with her mother. But Shaw's final stage direction, after Vivie has rejected her mother and would-be lover—[*she goes at her work with a plunge, and soon becomes absorbed in its figures*] (vol. 1, p. 356)—suggests a certain bracing satisfaction in Vivie's achievement of independence but also a real human loss. Has Vivie dived into her future with pride? Or has she turned herself into one of the unfeeling ciphers of her actuarial calculations? Although the play treats prostitution tamely by current standards, it was a taboo subject when Shaw put it on the stage, and his courage in doing so was considerable, for he had to fight censorship attempts and faced possible prosecution on several occasions. What remains current in the play is the depth and ambiguity with which Shaw represents Vivie's choice of professional over personal success. As always in Shaw's plays, the cause he seems to support, here women's independence, is not proffered to the audience in

GEORGE BERNARD SHAW

the manner of propagandistic plays, but rather presented in all its complicated human dimensions.

PLAYS PLEASANT

ARMS *and the Man* (1894) belongs with two immediately subsequent plays, *Candida* and *You Never Can Tell*, that Shaw grouped as "Pleasant Plays" and published in *Plays Pleasant and Unpleasant* (1898), thus dividing them from the three preceding Ibsenite "unpleasant plays." The "pleasant plays" distinguish themselves from their predecessors by what Shaw would call "smiling comedy with some hope in it" (vol. 7, p. 311). Although such comedy would remain Shaw's generic, philosophical, and temperamental preference throughout his long career, he revisits the tragic sense of life with some regularity, if only to reaffirm his rejection of it. Since *Arms and the Man* ostensibly attacks and satirizes battle glee and the glorification of war, two susceptibilities the current age is not much vulnerable to, the play would seem to have dated. And yet Shaw insured the play's lasting appeal by making the play a contest between authentic romantic feeling and sexual love on one side, and on the other, forces inimical to such love, such as the idealized view of war and the idolization of the military hero. The play shows how easily such forces lend themselves to fraud while, as a counter-statement to war, it makes palpable onstage the cozy warmth of burgeoning romantic attachment and sexual love between a man and a woman, in this instance, a fleeing mercenary soldier, Captain Bluntschli (the name itself mocks the conventional image of the military hero), and Raina Petkoff, a believer in "the higher love."

In accord with the conventions of comedy (and especially of Shakespearean comedy, always Shaw's principal model), which require a second couple to highlight the relationship of the primary couple, Shaw provides an ambitious servant girl, Louka, whose realistic approach to love contradicts Raina's, and Raina's officer fiancé, Sergius Saranoff, who conforms perfectly to the image of the dashing military man. Both Sergius and Raina suffer from romantic illusions about love, but

both also suffer doubts about their beliefs. To Sergius, however, Shaw allots a tragic cast by making him acutely self-aware of his own inconsistencies, hypocrisies, and insincerities, and by making him agonize over the irony of his various selves contradicting one another. Shaw called Sergius his Hamlet, by which he meant that he shared Shakespeare's sense that Hamlet's tragedy was the unbearable discovery that he was not the unified personality he thought himself to be. Shaw takes this tragic condition of being a divided self and turns it to comic purposes by having Sergius finally abandon his pretensions to the higher love and accept his sexual attraction to Louka, the servant girl.

Arms and the Man was Shaw's first play to achieve success on stage in the conventional sense; it ran for fifty performances in 1894 (in rotation with W. B. Yeats's *The Land of Heart's Desire*) and brought Shaw much public attention. Here the public became aware of Shaw as a wit and humorist: at the opening night's author's call, it was reported that while the audience was applauding the play loudly, one lone voice from the gallery persistently booed, to which Shaw responded, "My dear fellow, I quite agree with you, but what are we two against so many?"

In Shaw's next "pleasant play," *Candida* (1894), first produced in 1897 then again in 1900, Shaw continued two preoccupations from *Arms and the Man*. The figure of Hamlet, first assayed in Sergius, becomes Eugene Marchbanks, the poet. Only here Shaw focuses on the oedipal dimension of Hamlet's obsession with his mother by making Eugene try to win an older married woman (and a mother), Candida, away from her husband, the Christian socialist Reverend James Morell. Once again, however, Shaw converts tragic material into comedy by having Eugene overcome his emotional dependency on the young mother, Candida, as the first step toward his becoming a true poet. But again, not without cost, for he makes his final exit from the stage with full awareness that he is forever excluded from the intimacy of family love, that his poet's destiny is aloneness. But Shaw also affirms the husband and wife's love as a rival, if not entirely equal, value, for though, as the final stage direction has it, *"They do not know the secret in the poet's heart"* (vol. 1, p. 594), they do come to a better understanding of one another and of their own good marriage. The departure of Eugene can also be seen as the exorcism of a force inimical to marriage, in the same way that in *Arms and the Man* war itself and romantic illusions about war are forces antithetical to love and therefore to be excluded.

Shaw asserted that the end of *Candida* imitated the end of Ibsen's *A Doll's House,* the play in which a wife leaves her husband and children because the conditions of her marriage had reduced her to the position of a child in her own household. The imitation takes two forms. First, instead of Ibsen's heroine, Nora, ending the play—and her marriage—by walking out the door of the house, Shaw's Eugene walks out but leaves an intact marriage in spite of the husband's discovery that he was the child in the relationship, leaving all domestic cares to his wife so that he might pursue his socialist ideals without worry. Second, Shaw imitated Ibsen's practice of resolving the conflict between the husband and wife not with a melodramatic action such as suicide or public humiliation but through a discussion of the problem. Shaw referred to Ibsen's introduction of this strategy in *A Doll's House* as his technical innovation in play construction. And from *Candida* on, Shaw made this technical innovation a keystone of his own style of playwriting, unfortunately giving critics a versatile tool of complaint against his "discussion plays," which were supposedly all talk, not really plays at all.

Shaw's next play, *You Never Can Tell* (1896), was to be the last of the three full-length "pleasant plays." He had written a one-act play in the same genial comic spirit the year before, called *The Man of Destiny* (1895), in the hope of its being produced by the leading actor-manager of the day, Sir Henry Irving, whom Shaw had criticized frequently in his theater reviews. Irving, however, did not accept it for production. Napoleon was the subject of this short play, the first of a series of one-act plays in which Shaw dramatized the power of laughter and humor to turn the wrath of

the politically powerful into tolerance and forgiveness. *You Never Can Tell* differed from its predecessors in two important ways. It was Shaw's first ensemble play, written for a large cast of major characters, with almost equal parts for each of the required nine actors. It was also the play by means of which Shaw tried to distinguish himself from his greatest living rival upon the London stage in the art of comedy, Oscar Wilde.

Shaw had started to write *You Never Can Tell* in July 1895 but then abandoned the attempt. He took it up again in December and completed it in May 1896. He had reviewed Wilde's masterpiece, *The Importance of Being Earnest,* in February 1895 and had criticized it in very particular ways. All of Wilde's previous plays that Shaw had reviewed he had praised highly. Indeed the two were friends, and Wilde, though he was much better known at the time and had more literary achievements to his name, treated Shaw as an equal, exchanging presentation copies of his plays with Shaw and referring to Shaw and himself as the cofounders of the Hibernian School of Drama. Shaw recognized the comic power of Wilde's final play but also recognized that he must write a very different kind of comedy, for Wilde's *Importance of Being Earnest* is so stylized and exists so purely in the realm of absurdity that his characters and his plot hardly ever touch reality except in glancing blows. Shaw's way of dealing with this perceived challenge to his determination to make theater a laboratory for social and political thought was to assert that *Earnest* must be an earlier play penned by Wilde in emulation of the drama of Henry Arthur Jones and the humor of W. S. Gilbert before he found his own superior comic style. Shaw wrote of Wilde's comedy:

> It amused me, of course; but unless comedy touches me as well as amuses me, it leaves me with a sense of having wasted my evening. I go to the theatre to be moved to laughter, not to be tickled or bustled into it; and that is why, though I laugh as much as anybody at a farcical comedy, I am out of spirits by the end of the second act, and out of temper by the end of the third, my miserable mechanical laughter

intensifying these symptoms at every outburst.

(In Dukore, ed., *Drama Observed*,
vol. 1, p. 268)

Shaw's insistence that *Earnest* was an early play (a view that offended Wilde) expresses Shaw's own anxiety that he might follow that same road to the same endpoint, where style itself becomes the protagonist of the play, as it is in *Earnest*. Therefore, Shaw concludes, *Earnest* must be something Wilde as an artist has outgrown. From *The Philanderer* on, there is a tension in Shaw's plays between style and content, between the fantastic and the real. Likewise Shaw's assertion that the laughter in *Earnest* is mechanical rather than human is his way of defining his own style of playwriting, one in which characters try to behave mechanically but keep getting tripped by reality and feeling. *You Never Can Tell* responds to *Earnest* by adapting several of the latter's characters and situations but transforms them into Shavian comedy. The firm matron, Lady Bracknell, becomes Mrs. Clandon, feminist author of numerous books prescribing behavior for the twentieth century. Jack Worthing's discovery of his true identity and family becomes Fergus Crampton's quest to be reunited with his children, but where the former discovery provokes only laughter, the latter's quest provokes both amusement and compassion. The absurd ability of Wilde's pairs of young lovers to speak and move in unison without prior rehearsal or agreement becomes the complementarity between the twins, Phil and Dolly, who usually speak antiphonally or finish one another's sentences.

Shaw's stylization of his characters and dialogue differs from Wilde's in that Shaw stops just short of the boundary between reality and absurdity, whereas Wilde constantly leads his audience to the boundary and then pushes them delightfully across, as when Gwendolyn tells Jack that even before she knew him she was far from indifferent to him. Shaw's instinct takes him to that same boundary but then makes him withdraw to an area of recognizable human emotion, so that the artificial and the real dance together, as in the following exchange between Valentine and Gloria:

VAL: Do you expect me to believe that you are the most beautiful woman in the world?

GLOR: That is ridiculous, and rather personal.

VAL: Of course it's ridiculous. Well that's what my eyes tell me. [*Gloria makes a movement of contemptuous protest*]. No: I'm not flattering. I tell you I don't believe it. [*She is ashamed to find that this does not quite please her either*].

(vol. 1, pp. 738–739)

The artifice here, Valentine's wonderfully contrived strategy to let Gloria know how attractive he finds her while claiming that he knows her beauty has no objective reality but is only an illusion created by his sexual instincts, is designed to get around her feminist principles (which scorn attraction based on mere physical beauty). However, the contrivance collides with Gloria's human side, the reality that she is disappointed to know that he does not think her beautiful. Gloria's rejection of her father, a situation to which Gloria feels her mother has contributed, impedes her ability to respond to Valentine's love. Only after she is reconciled to being her father's daughter does she grow out of her "*freezing coldness of manner*" (vol. 1, p. 680) and become able to love Valentine in return. No such real family conflicts trouble the calm waters of Wilde's immaculately artificial comedy, where one can discover one's father's name by consulting the army lists of the period. Wilde's death in 1900 would revive Shaw's sense of competition with his great Anglo-Irish rival, and he created a character to argue Wilde's art-for-art's-sake aesthetic, the Devil in *Man and Superman* (written in 1901–1903). But before that Shaw wrote three major plays on the theme of justice and vengeance.

THREE PLAYS FOR PURITANS

SHAW's habit of grouping his plays under headings, such as "plays pleasant," when he came to publish them, arose from his tendency to explore a family of themes in successive plays until he felt he had treated them sufficiently. Such is the case with his subsequent *Three Plays for Puritans*

(1901), which included *The Devil's Disciple* (1896), *Caesar and Cleopatra* (1898), and *Captain Brassbound's Conversion* (1899). These plays at once recapitulate themes and situations from the "pleasant" plays while defining their own areas of concern (most notably the judicial distinction between justice and vengeance), which weave in and out of the trilogy. All three plays offer imperial-colonial contexts: the American War for Independence; the Roman occupation of Egypt; and the British presence in Moorish Africa. And each play culminates in a trial where justice and vengeance are at issue.

Although Shaw makes ironic points about the self-justifying policies of imperial forces, he also treats the colonials' maneuvers with an almost equally ironic humor. These plays do not approve of imperialism, but neither do they sentimentalize the contexts into tales of evil oppressors and pure victims. Beyond the ironic political points, Shaw uses the imperial-colonial context as a metaphor for the battleground between instinctual drives and the demands of morality, which for Shaw means the struggle to grow into a sense of responsibility for oneself. Hence *The Devil's Disciple* draws a parallel between the American victory over the British and Minister Anthony Anderson's recognition of his true vocation to be a man of action, a fighter rather than a man of peace. In doing so Shaw also prevents what would otherwise be an oedipal triumph for Dick Dudgeon, who wins the affections of the minister's beautiful young wife, Judith. Clearly this play repeats the basic triangle of *Candida,* with Dick functioning in place of Eugene Marchbanks as the intruder on the marital hearth, threatening family happiness. However, Shaw varies the triangular form by changing the relationship of the rivals from a merely oedipal one to that of psychological doubles. The double initials of Anthony Anderson and Dick Dudgeon imitate the exchange of identities they undergo, for each one discovers that the other is his true inner self. The trial of Dick Dudgeon is precipitated by his impromptu impersonation of the minister, when British soldiers come to arrest Anderson for treason. Dick does so by putting on the minister's coat. Later, when Anderson leaves

to find the revolutionists to rescue Dick, the minister puts on Dick's coat. Shaw is here appropriating the melodramatic plot device from *A Tale of Two Cities* (Dickens, along with Shakespeare, Sir Walter Scott, Alexandre Dumas, and John Bunyan were the writers Shaw read most in his youth), where Sidney Carton exchanges coats with Charles Darnay in order to take his place on the scaffold.

The Devil's Disciple is Shaw's first play openly to make conversion its main preoccupation—conversion of one kind or another being henceforth a central motif of Shavian drama. *Caesar and Cleopatra* is no exception in this regard, for Cleopatra attempts to convert from her old-fashioned ethic of vengeance to Caesar's new ethic of forgiveness, but fails. The play, however, does not simply endorse Caesar's superior ethic. To be sure, in Caesar, Shaw replaces the conventional melodramatic conception of the hero as a handsome, self-sacrificing, truthful young man with a character who systematically does not embody such traits. As well as being a brave and brilliant general, a wise and tolerant ruler, Caesar is also vain, pettily deceptive, physically unimpressive, old, and sometimes careless with the safety of those who support him. The characteristics for which Shaw exalts him are his abjuration of vengeance and his promulgation of an ethic of forgiveness.

But Shaw also demonstrates that sometimes Caesar's forgiveness of his enemies can endanger the lives of his friends and allies, as in the episode when Caesar is presented with a list of all his enemies, and instead of making use of it insists that it be hurled into the sea. Immediately afterwards it is reported by Apollodorus that "some fool threw a great leathern bag into the sea" (vol. 2, pp. 242–243) which broke the nose of his boat and caused it to sink. Shaw undercuts Caesar's posture here because he is not writing propaganda for the ethic of forgiveness. He is making the audience think hard about the question of whether justice requires commensurate punishment, about the costs of forgiving one's enemies. Thus the audience is not permitted to applaud Caesar's renunciation of vengeance in a complacent way; rather, viewers must accept the principle as they may, in full awareness of the difficulties, dangers, and consequences of such an ethic.

Captain Brassbound's Conversion returns to the wise maternal figure that Candida represented in the person of Lady Cicely Waynflete (modeled on the formidable women explorers of Victoria's empire in Africa). Like Caesar, she stands for the ideal of repudiating vengeance but more fittingly and less problematically than Caesar does. The conversion Captain Brassbound undergoes consists of his outgrowing and renouncing his obsession with avenging his mother. The play culminates in a trial scene where, through the magic of her personal charm and humane forgiveness, Lady Cicely prevents vengeance from disguising itself as judicial process and from achieving its ends by calling itself justice. Like *Candida,* also, the play does not allow the son figure, Captain Brassbound, to win the mother figure, Lady Cicely, though full scope is given to the potent attraction they feel toward one another.

Certain images connected to particular ideas recur regularly within groups of Shaw's plays, for it was his habit to make his plays versions of one another until he felt he had allowed all sides of a given issue to be dramatized for the audience. In *The Devil's Disciple,* Shaw used the exchange of coats between Dick and Anderson to create a striking visual embodiment in stage action of the conversion of each to the other's views. In *Caesar and Cleopatra,* Shaw had ended the first act with Caesar's helping to attire Cleopatra as a queen, and then in the second act he had Cleopatra help Caesar put on his armor. In both cases, each character is trying to dress the other in their particular ideas more than in different clothes. But Shaw's most successful staging of this clothing conversion motif comes in the great central scene of Captain Brassbound's conversion, where Lady Cicely, by deftly combining her personal charm with gentle reasoning, skillfully defuses Brassbound's desire for vengeance. Her sewing and fitting his coat upon him make palpable for the audience what she is really doing: repairing his divided self and clothing him

with a whole, new self, free of the past's weight of guilt. In the comic vision of life, such renewal is possible.

MAN AND SUPERMAN

BEFORE 1900, all the plays Shaw wrote had achieved mostly short-lived productions by small independent theater companies that were mainly known for producing controversial or avant-garde literary playwrights like Ibsen or Yeats (as opposed to popular professional playwrights whose goal was to entertain the public and make a handsome living). Shaw's plays were, of course, being published simultaneously, along with his extensive stage directions, commentaries on his characters, and elaborate descriptions of settings, furnishings, dress, and grooming. Since Shaw usually directed the first productions of his plays, his additions to the dialogue derived in no small measure from the experience of staging the plays. Moreover, Shaw deliberately strove to make the reading of his plays more like the reading of novels—an important conception because he did not think of his plays as only coming to life on the stage but rather as living in the text. The staging and action, and the interpretation of character, were important as Shaw the author conceived them and recorded that conception in the published editions of the plays, not as a director might reconceive the action in opposition to the author's expressed intent. Shaw's advice to directors who wanted to alter the meaning of his plays was that they should write their own plays to say what they wanted to say.

In May of 1898 Shaw wrote his last column as drama critic for the *Saturday Review* and resigned his position to the "incomparable" (as Shaw dubbed him) Max Beerbohm. From that point Shaw would be thought of as a playwright, though it should be borne in mind that he continued to juggle several other spheres of professional activity. He remained an active member of the socialist Fabian Society along with his friends H. G. Wells and Sidney and Beatrice Webb. In 1897 he became a vestryman for the borough of St. Pancras (that is, he was part of a local governing board for a section of

London), and served for about six years. Among other projects he campaigned for an increased number of public lavatories for women.

In his private life, after a series of romantic relationships (some sexual, some not, with, among others, Jenny Patterson and the actresses Florence Farr and Ellen Terry), Shaw married in 1898 an Irish millionairess named Charlotte Payne-Townsend, whom he had met in the Fabian Society. Their feelings for one another greatly increased during a period of convalescence for Shaw from a broken leg when Charlotte took it upon herself to nurse him. The marriage was mostly happy until her death in 1943, except on occasion when one or the other formed deep emotional attachments to others, most notably his to Mrs. Patrick Campbell (who created the role of Eliza Doolittle in *Pygmalion*), and she, maternally, with T. E. Lawrence. Shaw and Charlotte maintained a childless marriage, apparently by agreement.

In 1901 Shaw started to write what was to become a big play that not only epitomized his contribution to stage comedy but also marked him as the most original playwright in Britain: *Man and Superman*. It took Shaw a year to complete the play, and it was first published in 1903, though not performed until 1905 (without the third act, or the "Don Juan in Hell" scene, as it came to be known when performed separately in 1907). Shaw prefaced his new play with a long essay explaining its genesis, both immediate and long-range. The addressee of the "Epistle Dedicatory" (as Shaw called his preface in acknowledgment of the play's inheritance from Restoration comedy), Arthur Bingham Walkley, a friend and former colleague in journalism, had once suggested that Shaw write a Don Juan play. Shaw's compliance with that suggestion produced a play about a woman, Ann Whitefield, who pursues a man, John ("Jack") Tanner, until he agrees to marry her.

That is the basic story of the play, but Shaw called it a comedy and a philosophy, and he meant it. As a comedy it exhibits Shaw's particular talent for representing the sexual attractiveness of men and women, with the variation that in this case the man resists the woman's determi-

nation, and consequently their courtship becomes a battle of the sexes. In that sense Shaw's central couple, Jack and Ann, descend from a long line of "gay," or witty, battling couples: from Shakespeare's Kate and Petrucchio to Rosalind and Orlando and especially Beatrice and Benedick, through Congreve's Millamant and Mirabell in *The Way of the World*. It is a line that survives into Noël Coward's Amanda and Elyot in *Private Lives*. As a comedy, also, the play repeats Shaw's preoccupation with the oedipal struggle. During the course of the action Jack confronts a series of mock, weak, and deficient fathers (Mr. Whitefield, Roebuck Ramsden, the Statue of the Commander, Hector Malone Sr.), until he finally understands that he must supply the lack created by their absences and deficiencies, that his destiny is to become a father through his marriage to Ann.

The philosophy of the play and its originality of form manifest themselves most clearly in the long third act, which is a dream sequence and a four-handed discussion of humankind's destiny. There, Jack's spiritual ancestor, Don Juan, argues against the Devil's assertion that the death instinct rules mankind, that man is essentially destructive. Shaw, however, following Milton's treatment of Satan in *Paradise Lost*, gives the Devil magnificently impressive rhetoric with which to argue his case:

> [T]he power that governs the earth is not the power of Life, but of Death; and the inner need that has nerved Life to the effort of organizing itself into the human being is not the need for higher life but for a more efficient engine of destruction. The plague, the famine, the earthquake, the tempest were too spasmodic in their action; the tiger and crocodile were too easily satiated and not cruel enough: something more constantly, more ruthlessly, more ingeniously destructive was needed; and that something was Man, the inventor of the rack, the stake, the gallows, the electric chair; of sword and gun and poison gas.
>
> (vol. 2, p. 656)

The Devil's humane tone here is beguiling; he enacts his knowing indignation at the potential for cruelty in humanity calmly, musically, and suspensefully in the set of rising adverbs—"constantly, ruthlessly, ingeniously"—the first two thickened to a seeming weightiness by pairs of triple consonants, the third by two additional syllables that also allow him to draw out the effect of the accent falling on the second syllable (in-*gen*-iously). He seems to be praising man's cleverness while he also seems to be damning his cruelty. When he comes to name the actual inventions, he shifts to monosyllabic words ending in a hard consonant ("rack," "stake") that jar the auditor with their fixedness. Calling man the "inventor" of such implements of death rather than, say, the "deviser," parallels these devices with beneficial inventions, as if both sprang from the same amoral impulse. It is for passages such as this that T. S. Eliot identified *Man and Superman* as Shaw's greatest work (though Eliot disagreed vehemently with Shaw's socialist politics) and praised Shaw as the finest prose stylist in British drama since Congreve.

Of course, the Devil himself is the first destroyer (as Goethe portrayed him in *Faust*), and by persuading humanity that it is essentially destructive, he is accomplishing his goal of destroying humanity. Don Juan resists this temptation volubly. He argues that humankind, under the guidance of the "life force"—Shaw's name for the animating will to live—constantly evolves toward a higher form of existence. Although regularly diverted from its course by blunders and blindness, the life force nevertheless always returns to its upward struggle. For Don Juan the direction and goal of this evolutionary struggle is real:

> DON JUAN: I tell you that as long as I can conceive something better than myself I cannot be easy unless I am striving to bring it into existence or clearing the way for it. That is the law of my life. That is the working within me of Life's incessant aspiration to higher organization, wider, deeper, intenser self-consciousness, and clearer self-understanding.
>
> (vol. 2, pp. 679–680)

Shaw was not a Darwinian evolutionist, for he believed Darwin's theory of natural selection made evolution random and directionless and left no room for the individual human will to play a role. He preferred the theories of Lamarck (since discredited by evolutionary biologists), who proposed that will determined the way creatures evolved. (In the classic example, giraffes evolved longer necks in order to reach the tenderest leaves at the tops of trees.) Shaw transferred this theory to social and spiritual development and produced his "religion" of creative evolution. Hence Don Juan decides to move from hell to heaven in order to help life in its evolutionary quest to understand itself. Shaw distinguishes hell from heaven in this way: Hell is the realm of art for art's sake, of artifice and fantasy, of the unreal, whereas heaven is the home of reality and the contemplation of the real. Shaw makes the Devil expound ideas that echo Wilde's view of art and life. For example, the Devil expresses his preference for beauty over suffering in a speech that is clearly imitated from *The Picture of Dorian Gray,* where Lord Henry Wotton (Wilde's spokesman in the novel) says: "There is something terribly morbid in the modern sympathy with pain. One should sympathize with the colour, the beauty, the joy of life" (chapter 3). And here is the Devil: "[The world's] sympathies are all with misery, with poverty, with starvation of the body and the heart. I call on it to sympathize with joy, with love, with happiness, with beauty. . . ." (vol. 2, p.644). Even though Shaw assigns Wilde's views to the Devil and he himself prefers Don Juan's, Shaw feels the pull of those views within himself sufficiently to make a real drama out of the debate between the Devil and Don Juan. It is really a quarrel Shaw is having with himself—the kind of quarrel from which Yeats said poetry is made.

Before Don Juan leaves to go to heaven, Shaw gives the Devil one more devastating counter to Don Juan's fervent belief in the evolutionary ascent of humanity. The Devil warns Don Juan that his faith is an illusion:

> Where you now see reform, progress, fulfillment of upward tendency, continual ascent by Man on the stepping stones of his dead selves to higher things, you will see nothing but an infinite comedy of illusion. You will discover the profound truth of the saying of my friend Koheleth, that there is nothing new under the sun.
>
> (vol. 2, p. 683)

Don Juan dismisses the warning and insists that life and nature have purpose and that he must serve that purpose. And there the debate ends; but not the play, for in the frame play, Jack Tanner awakens from his dream and finally consents to let Ann marry him. Jack's dream allows him to face all the fears and anxieties attendant upon marriage: Why marry and produce children, when life may be purposeless? But Jack comes to understand that Ann, as Everywoman, embodies all the vitality of the life force (Shaw describes her as a "vital genius"—p. 549), and that he himself has a "father's heart" (p. 729). Marrying her *is* serving the life force in its upward evolutionary course, because every child is an experiment by the life force to develop a more understanding kind of human being. Thus Shaw makes Don Juan's departure from hell to find his way to heaven, the metaphor for Jack's decision to leave the single state and become a husband and father.

Like Goethe's *Faust,* Milton's *Paradise Lost,* and Dante's *Divine Comedy, Man and Superman* is a literary work of epic size and scope. Like those works it attempts to account for humanity's purpose and destiny, its place in the cosmos. Although Shaw did not publish *Man and Superman* with the two plays that follow it, *John Bull's Other Island* (1904) and *Major Barbara* (1905), all three plays share an extensive use of heaven/ hell imagery—in the case of *Man and Superman* literally, since the third act is set in hell, while the two subsequent plays use the images metaphorically.

JOHN BULL'S OTHER ISLAND AND MAJOR BARBARA

John Bull's Other Island was Shaw's first play to be performed successfully and achieve a substantial run in the same year it was written (1904). It was written at the request of W. B. Yeats for the Abbey Theatre, but Yeats rejected it, saying it was beyond the Abbey's financial means to produce. (Actually it was because he found it too rhetorical and insufficiently poetic.) Consequently *John Bull's Other Island* was produced instead at the Royal Court in November. It was preceded by a successful revival of *Candida* in April, which led to a series of Shaw's plays, both revivals and productions of new plays, being put on at the Royal Court under the management of Harley Granville-Barker and J. E. Vedrenne for the next two years. It was this series of productions and the availability of Shaw's plays in print that established his reputation with the public. From this time on Shaw could count on his plays being translated into foreign languages, receiving productions (sometimes premieres) in New York, Dublin, Berlin, or other foreign capitols, especially in eastern Europe.

John Bull's Other Island tells the tale of an Irishman and an Englishman, Larry Doyle and Tom Broadbent, both civil engineers, who travel to Ireland on behalf of a land development syndicate and get involved with the lives of various locals, including Nora Reilly, an old flame of Larry's, and Father Keegan, a defrocked Catholic priest with mystical tendencies. For Larry this voyage represents a homecoming after a long absence. Shaw puts into the play much of his feeling for his native land, partly emphasizing the allure of its natural beauty but mostly the despair and destruction he sees as the consequence of his countrymen's tormenting imaginations, which never allow them to face reality seriously. While his Irish protagonist, Doyle, falls into the kind of paralytic inaction that James Joyce in the next decade would ascribe to his fellow Dubliners as the national disease of Ireland, Shaw's Englishman thrives by winning Nora Reilly and by getting himself to be the parliamentary nominee for the region. While all this ironic comedy is going on, Father Keegan confides to a cricket his conviction that Ireland must really be hell, and at the end of the play he offers a vision of what heaven on earth would be, not unlike Don Juan's conception of heaven:

> In my dreams [Heaven] is a country where the State is the Church and the Church the people: three in one and one in three. It is a commonwealth in which work is play and play is life: three in one and one in three. It is a temple in which the priest is the worshipper and the worshipper the worshipped: three in one and one in three. It is a godhead in which all life is human and all humanity divine:

three in one and one in three. It is, in short, the dream of a madman. [*He goes away across the hill*].
(vol. 2, p. 1,021)

Yeats late in his life listed this speech as one of a few pieces of writing that had most moved him (even though when he first read the play, he thought it too discursive). In Keegan's vision of community (which is Shaw's as well), there are no divisions because everything is in harmony, everything is a part of everything else, the spiritual, the political, and the material work together. Shaw's impulse to marry contraries to one another derives mainly from William Blake, a poet whom Shaw listed as one of the primary influences on his thought. In *The Marriage of Heaven and Hell,* Blake writes: "Without Contraries is no progression. Attraction and repulsion, Reason and Energy, Love and Hate are necessary to human existence." As Jonathan Wisenthal has amply demonstrated, that principle dominates the plays of Shaw's middle period, from *Man and Superman* to *Saint Joan*, but most especially Shaw's next play, *Major Barbara* (1905) which ends with a tripartite marriage between the Greek professor, Adolphus Cusins, the Salvation Army Major, Barbara Undershaft, and her father, the munitions millionaire, Andrew Undershaft, each of whom might be said to represent a different kind of power—intellectual, spiritual, and material respectively. The vision of a new heaven with which the play ends depends on these three people's having formed an alliance. Barbara and Adolphus agree to marry and to take control of the munitions factory and the model town in which it is built and which supplies its labor force. But the dramatic power of the play comes from Barbara's quest to find a place in life for herself and a home for her spiritual yearnings.

Like its two immediate predecessors, *Major Barbara* represents hell and heaven metaphorically to its audience, the former in the West Ham Salvation Army shelter where all is pretense, deception, and irony, and the latter in Perivale St. Andrews, where the Undershaft munitions factory and model town lie. However, Shaw connects the factory to enough hellish images—courtesy of all the gunpowder, fire, and explosive devices associated with the running of the place—to impart to it a distinct ambiguity. It seems just another kind of hell, yet it is joined inextricably to the heavenly model town. Undershaft continually suggests to Cusins and Barbara, as he tempts them to take it over, that it is up to them whether they make a heaven or a hell out of it. By implication, Shaw says to the audience, material life is like the raw energy that runs a factory; it can be used for different purposes. As Undershaft says (in the 1941 film version scripted by Shaw), nitrates can be used to make explosives or fertilizers. Later Cusins justifies his acceptance of the factory to Barbara by recognizing that the power gives them a choice: "You cannot have power for good without having power for evil too" (vol. 3, p. 181).

After *Major Barbara*, Shaw was a playwright much in demand, and he went on to write a group of heterogeneous plays that addressed an astonishing range of themes and issues both topical, such as England's marriage laws in *Getting Married* (1908), and perennial, such as relations between parents and children in *Misalliance* (1910). Both plays experimented with dramatic form by being made up almost entirely of discussion and by treating what action there was whimsically. For example, in the middle of *Misalliance*, an aeroplane piloted by a Polish aviatrix crash lands in the garden of a wealthy underwear manufacturer. Shaw had always had to rein in his propensity for fantastic humor; the latter part of his playwriting career saw him loosening the reins considerably.

PYGMALION *AND OTHER PLAYS*

ALTERNATING with such experimental plays were more traditionally conceived plays such as *The Doctor's Dilemma* (1906), which Shaw called a tragedy, and *Pygmalion* (1912), his greatest commercial success. Both plays deal with the social responsibilities of the scientist and the artist as well as the conflicts between the two. The doctor's dilemma is ethical: should Sir Colenso Ridgeon, who has developed an expensive, difficult, and dangerous treatment for tuberculosis, save the life of a great but amoral artist, Louis Dubedat, or the life of a mediocre physician but good man, Blenkinsop? Ridgeon falls in love with the wife of the artist, Jennifer, thereby complicating his dilemma. The symmetry of the dilemma allows Shaw to return to his interest in the psychological relationship of doubles, here between the scientist and the artist. In "killing" Dubedat, which Ridgeon effects by turning him over to an incompetent physician, Ridgeon turns himself into Dubedat, the individual who believes his creative power places him above morality. Ridgeon's tragedy is to remain isolated at the end of the play, for he has murdered to no purpose: the artist's wife not only rejects him, she marries another man.

In *Pygmalion*, Shaw combines the scientist and the artist into one figure, Henry Higgins, a professor of phonetics, who takes it upon himself to pass off a flower girl as a duchess by teaching her to speak better English. Shaw identifies Higgins as a Miltonist, and the identification is purposeful, for the peculiarity of his project of helping people change their original accents, that is, to master language in such a way that they erase the evidence of their origins, connects Higgins to Milton's greatest character, Satan, in *Paradise Lost*. Satan has a fantasy of autonomy; he denies that he was created by God. Likewise Higgins wants to see himself as the only one with the power to create and therefore as the author of himself. Milton, living in the shadow of Shakespeare, the looming predecessor, felt a similar need to deny his descent as a writer, to see himself as an original, not as an imitator of Shakespeare. Shaw as a playwright felt the same anxiety over Shakespeare's influence that Milton felt, hence Shaw's lifelong sense of rivalry with Shakespeare and his strong personal identification with Higgins, possessor of a "Miltonic mind" (vol. 4, p. 776). Shaw identified so strongly with Higgins that when he writes a letter (11 August 1913) to denounce Mrs. Patrick Campbell (the actress then about to play Eliza in London) for rejecting his romantic advances (*Collected Letters,* vol. 3, pp. 194–195), he echoes the speeches in which Higgins denounces Eliza for rejecting *him.* (vol. 4, pp. 776, 779).

However, Shaw also strongly identifies with his heroine, Eliza, and at the end of the play she liberates herself from Higgins' tyranny by leaving, like Ibsen's Nora at the end of *A Doll's House.* Eliza, not Higgins, embodies Shaw's successful artistic self. From the first hugely successful London production of the play in 1914, through the 1938 film version directed by Anthony Asquith and Leslie Howard, to the 1956 musical version of the play *My Fair Lady,* the actors or adapters have contrived some way to imply an eventual romantic union between Higgins and Eliza, but Shaw intended the issue to be unresolved.

Shaw wrote one other major play before World War One, and that was *Androcles and the Lion* (1912). It uses the legend to explore varieties of religious sensibility from the kindly feeling toward all fellow creatures felt by Androcles to Lavinia's intense commitment to her chosen faith as a symbol of individual integrity and dignity. It is among Shaw's funniest plays in spite of its subject and theme, largely due to Shaw's demonstration that there is not one Christianity to which all Christians conform but as many different Christianities as there are Christians, with each person's interpreting it to reflect their particular temperaments and attitudes. The comic triumph of Lavinia, Androcles, and his lion friend over Roman imperial politics at the end of the play echoes the combination of spiritual power and brute strength that concluded *Major Barbara.*

HEARTBREAK HOUSE

ALTHOUGH *Heartbreak House* was written during the First World War, Shaw did not publish it until 1919 because he did not want its view of current European civilization in chaos to add to the weight of demoralization produced by the war. It was not performed until 1920, and even then in New York. A pamphlet written by Shaw in 1914, "Common Sense About the War" had severely damaged his reputation and led to poisonous personal attacks on him in the press and elsewhere. The Dramatists' Club expelled him, and the Society of Authors attempted to do the same. All this reaction mattered little to Shaw, whose political and moral courage often led him to espouse unpopular causes. He maintained an almost superhuman good humor about all the hostility launched in his direction. For example, when the Dramatists' Club expelled him, they had no constitutional procedures to effect such an expulsion of one of their members, so Shaw kindly wrote to them explaining how they must proceed in order to be rid of him.

Though Shaw did not fear such attacks, he did fear the destruction of civilization by stupidity, and Heartbreak House, the residence of the rum-drinking Captain Shotover built to resemble a ship, symbolically represented Europe in the process of self-destructing. Shaw warns in the play that humanity must seize direction of its own destiny (or, in the play's metaphor, to steer the ship of state to avoid going on the rocks). The young but disillusioned Ellie Dunne's spiritual marriage to the ancient Shotover suggests a transcending of the mindless, mundane pursuit of leisure and excitement that occupies the other inhabitants of Heartbreak House, but the play ends ambiguously with a bombing attack from zeppelins that nearly destroys the house. Ellie is so thrilled by the sheer energy of the bombers, the aesthetic appeal of the powerful sound they produce, that she longs for them to return the next night. Shaw makes palpable the attraction of the apocalypse, of the world's ending not with a whimper but with a bang and the pleasurable anticipation of finally being done with it all. Such an ambiguous statement was too dangerous for Shaw's optimism, and he combated the threat by writing two plays that not only provide more encouraging and less ambiguous visions, but which offer the imagination as a stay against despair and death.

BACK TO METHUSELAH AND SAINT JOAN

BACK to Methuselah (1920), which Shaw subtitled "a Metabiological Pentateuch," comprises a cycle of five plays of varying lengths and takes several evenings to perform. It begins in the Garden of Eden with the Serpent's teaching Eve how to procreate by means of imagination and will: "You imagine what you desire; you will what you imagine; and at last you create what you will" (vol. 5, p. 348). It ends in the year 31,930 A.D.

with Lilith warning humankind to "dread, of all things, stagnation" (vol. 5, p. 630), and with her visionary hope that spirit will master matter finally. The knowledge that there is a future must suffice for human beings. Between Shaw's rewriting of Genesis and his futuristic ending, the action is Aristophanic science fiction. Shaw fantasizes that humankind has learned to overcome death by imagining and then willing longevity into infinity. No one dies any longer except by accident. Death itself remains, but its power is diminished. All comedy imparts the view that love and procreation have far more importance and power than evil and death: Back to Methuselah tries to imagine that view into scientific reality.

Imagination then is the saving human faculty for Shaw, and he makes the eponymous heroine of his next play, Saint Joan (1923), herself embody imagination. Although Joan uses common sense, she achieves the nationhood of France chiefly by the power of her free imagination, which gives her a self-assurance that makes others want to do her will. The play climaxes with her trial, where she asserts that the value of imagination is equal to the value of life itself. When Joan faces the alternatives of life imprisonment or death by fire, she chooses the latter because imprisonment for her would mean her separation from nature, the source of her imagination and therefore her connection to God. Shaw makes Joan's tragedy more than personal by imagining an epilogue in which Joan confronts her allies and enemies after her death, only to be rejected by them once again when she offers to return to life. One by one they demur, excuse themselves, and leave the stage, so that at the play's final moment Joan's tragedy is double: she has been rejected and killed in her own person but then is rejected and isolated, as all saints are, by an uncomprehending and cowardly humanity. The epilogue caused much controversy at the play's premiere for its seeming violation of tragedy's requisite gravity of tone, but then was imitated by T. S. Eliot in Murder in the Cathedral a decade later. Joan's last line is a haunting question: "O God that madest this beautiful earth, when will it be ready to receive Thy saints? How long, O Lord, how long?" (vol. 6, p. 208).

Saint Joan went on from its controversial premiere to have a worldwide success. This cannot be said of any of Shaw's subsequent major plays—some nine of them, written between 1928, the year of *The Apple Cart*, and 1950, the year of Shaw's last full-length play, *Farfetched Fables*, and his death at age ninety-four. His last group of plays are generically homogenous: most of them are versions of Shakespearean romance, characterized by a largeness and generosity of vision. There are two exceptions, *On the Rocks* (1933) and *Geneva* (1938), which show a Shaw preoccupied with world politics: in the former, the worldwide economic depression and the institution of communism in Soviet Russia; in the latter, the rise of totalitarian dictators and the threat of war. The limitations of their topicality yield before Shaw's comic inventiveness.

FINAL PLAYS

THE other plays of Shaw's last two decades have in common exotic or fantastic locales, the leisurely unfolding of whimsical action, characters who are more often emblems or types than individuals, and extravagant farce that alternates with episodes of discussion. These plays are *Too True To Be Good* (1931), *The Simpleton of the Unexpected Isles* (1934), *The Millionairess* (1935), *In Good King Charles's Golden Days* (1939), and *Buoyant Billions* (1947). Not so comic are the prefaces to some of these plays in which Shaw seems to justify whatever exterminations need to be carried out to ensure the success of communism, and where he seems to admire the three totalitarian dictators of the era, Hitler, Mussolini, and Stalin. There was a good deal of the provocateur in Shaw, and he sometimes lauded dictators in order to get people's attention by taking an obviously outrageous viewpoint. Although Shaw was always a most humane socialist in his public advocacy of various causes, a civilized disputant in any disagreement, an almost saintly man in his generosity, and always honorable in his private dealings, in the case of the Soviet Union he was culpable for his blindness to what was really happening there: Lenin's murder of the property-owning classes and Stalin's starvation and murder of innocent millions of his own people. As we recognize now, Shaw had plenty of company in his blindness. And perhaps a man in his eighties may not see as clearly as someone younger. Also, his frustration at the West's failure to adopt socialist practices made him want to offer an example of the success of socialism. Nevertheless, he who saw so clearly social and political abuses wrought by the capitalist system became blind—whether through will or impatience or the failing intellectual powers of old age—when it came to the much greater abuses by the communist system in the Soviet Union.

Notwithstanding this failing, his legacy as a critic, man of letters, and most importantly as a dramatic artist, remains a formidable achievement. It has been observed rightly that the gift for comedy is much more rare in literary history than that for tragedy. It became more rare still on 2 November 1950, when the ninety-four-year-old Shaw died, after a fall in his own garden.

SELECTED BIBLIOGRAPHY

I. COLLECTED WORKS. *The Works of Bernard Shaw: Standard Edition*, 37 vols. (London, 1931–1951); *Collected Plays with Their Prefaces,* 7 vols., ed. by Dan H. Laurence (New York, 1975); *The Collected Screenplays of Bernard Shaw,* ed. by Bernard Dukore (Athens, Ga., 1980); *Complete Prefaces,* 3 vols., ed. by Dan H. Laurence and Daniel J. Leary (London, 1993–1997).

II. CRITICISM. *Shaw's Music,* 3 vols., ed. by Dan H. Laurence (New York, 1981); *Bernard Shaw on the London Art Scene: 1885–1950,* ed. by Stanley Weintraub (University Park, Penn., and London, 1989); *Bernard Shaw's Book Reviews,* vol. 1, *1885–1888,* ed. by Brian Tyson, vol. 2, *1884–1950,* ed. by Brian Tyson (University Park, Penn., and London, 1991–1996); *The Drama Observed,* 3 vols., ed. by Bernard F. Dukore (University Park, Penn., 1993).

III. LETTERS. *Bernard Shaw's Letters to Siegfried Trebitsch,* ed. by Samuel A. Weiss (Stanford, Calif., 1986); *Collected. Letters,* 4 vols., ed. by Dan H. Laurence (New York, 1988).

IV. DIARIES AND INTERVIEWS. *Bernard Shaw: The Diaries, 1885–1897,* 2 vols., ed. by Stanley Weintraub (University Park, Penn., and London, 1986); *Interviews and Recollections,* ed. by A. M. Gibbs. (Iowa City, Iowa, 1990).

V. BIOGRAPHICAL STUDIES. St. John Ervine, *Bernard Shaw: His Life, Work, and Friends* (New York, 1956); Archibald Henderson, *George Bernard Shaw: Man of the Century* (New York, 1956); Michael Holroyd, *Bernard Shaw,* 4 vols. (New

York, 1988–1992); A. M. Gibbs, *A Bernard Shaw Chronology and Who's Who* (New York, 2001).

VI. CRITICAL STUDIES. Eric Bentley, *Bernard Shaw* (New York, 1947); Richard M. Ohmann, *Shaw: The Style and the Man* (Middletown, Conn., 1962); Martin Meisel, *Shaw and the Nineteenth-Century Theater* (Princeton, N.J., 1963); R. J. Kaufman, ed., *G B. Shaw: A Collection of Critical Essays* (Englewood Cliffs, N.J., 1965); Louis Crompton, *Shaw the Dramatist* (Lincoln, Neb., 1969); Bernard F. Dukore, *Bernard Shaw, Director* (London and Seattle, 1971); Stanley Weintraub, *Journey to Heartbreak* (New York, 1971); Margery M. Morgan, *The Shavian Playground* (London, 1972); Barbara Bellow Watson, *A Shavian Guide to the Intelligent Woman* (New York, 1972); Charles A. Berst, *Bernard Shaw and the Art of Drama* (Urbana, Ill., 1973); Bernard F. Dukore, *Bernard Shaw, Playwright: Aspects of Shavian Drama* (Columbia, Mo., 1973); Maurice Valency, *The Cart and the Trumpet* (New York, 1973); Stanley Weintraub, ed., *Saint Joan: Fifty Years After* (Baton Rouge, La., 1973); J. L. Wisenthal, *The Marriage of Contraries* (Cambridge, Mass., 1974); T. F. Evans, ed., *Shaw: The Critical Heritage* (London and Boston, 1976); Alfred Turco Jr., *Shaw's Moral Vision* (Ithaca, N.Y., 1976); Rodelle Weintraub, ed., *Fabian Feminist: Bernard Shaw and Woman* (University Park, Penn., 1977); Robert F. Whitman, *Shaw and the Play of Ideas* (Ithaca, N.Y., 1977); Michael Holroyd, ed., *The Genius of Shaw* (New York, 1979); J. L. Wisenthal, ed., *Shaw and Ibsen* (Toronto and Buffalo, N.Y., 1979); A. M. Gibbs, *The Art and Mind of Shaw* (New York, 1983); David J. Gordon, *Bernard Shaw and the Comic Sublime* (New York, 1990); John A. Bertolini, *The Playwrighting Self of Bernard Shaw* (Carbondale, Ill., 1991); Richard F. Dietrich, *Bernard Shaw's Novels* (Gainesville, Fla., 1996); Christopher Innes, ed., *The Cambridge Companion to George Bernard Shaw* (Cambridge and New York, 1998); Leon Hugo, *Edwardian Shaw: The Writer and His Age* (Houndmills, U.K., and New York, 1999); Michel W. Pharand, *Bernard Shaw and the French* (Gainesville, Fla., 2000).

VII. PERIODICAL. Stanley Weintraub and Fred D. Crawford, eds., *SHAW: The Annual of Bernard Shaw Studies* (University Park, Penn., 1981–).

VIII. BIBLIOGRAPHIES. Dan H. Laurence, *Bernard Shaw: A Bibliography*, 2 vols. (Oxford and New York, 1983); Supplemented by Dan H. Laurence and Fred D. Crawford, eds., *SHAW: The Annual of Bernard Shaw Studies, Vol. 20, Bibliographical Shaw* (University Park, Penn., 2000).

SIR PHILIP SIDNEY

(1554–1586)

Diana E. Henderson

IN HIS SHORT but eventful life, Sir Philip Sidney managed to produce literary works that would provide the standard for the English Renaissance. Even as he failed to realize his own political and personal ambitions, he became a figure of heroic myth and courtly perfection. Although he would hardly have seen himself as primarily a writer, he was a model for those who aspired to that profession in his wake, and the remarkable quality of his works belies the label of courtly amateur. He wrote the first real treatise on aesthetic theory and literary criticism in English, *An Apology for Poetry;* the first English sonnet sequence of great merit and influence, *Astrophil and Stella*; and the most popular English prose romance for over a century to follow, the *Arcadia*. Additionally, he participated in the jousts and festivals of Elizabeth I's court, writing a short entertainment, *The Lady of May;* and through his travels and friendships with continental humanists as well as his translations, he reduced the distance between his northern isle and the energetic, combative world of European culture. In inventiveness, range, and poetic craft Sidney had only one peer during his lifetime: the other great English writer born in the 1550s, Edmund Spenser. But in his combination of roles—as cultural model as well as author—Sidney stood alone, bringing European sophistication and stature to English letters.

LIFE

SIDNEY was an aristocrat of his day, however, and would have hoped to be remembered differently—or at least not for his artistic achievements alone. He was groomed from childhood for statesmanship. As befit his station, he was deeply loyal to his family, which was a mixed blessing: despite his being the focus of high expectations and talents, his family history illustrated the precariousness and frustrations that attended of the life of a Tudor courtier. His mother, Mary Dudley, was the daughter of John, duke of Northumberland, at one time Protector to King Edward VI but executed for treason. Her brother Guilford Dudley had married Lady Jane Gray; for his part in attempting to install her on the throne after Edward's death, this would-be king likewise accompanied his consort to the chopping block. Mary's surviving brother Robert was the frustrating favorite of Queen Elizabeth whose combination of arrogance and talent brought him great power and great danger, repeatedly. His nephew would both benefit and suffer from his association with this charismatic, erratic uncle.

Sidney's paternal line was less tempestuous, but also reveals the mixed blessings of loyalty to the Tudors. Philip's father, Sir Henry Sidney, was thrice Lord Deputy Governor of Ireland, a position that carried great risk and worry as well as responsibility: despite his dedication to the crown and his relative competence in a no-win job (the Irish being understandably and violently resistant to English colonization), Henry was not particularly well rewarded. Moreover, his wife, Mary, suffered physically for her devotion to Queen Elizabeth: nursing her during the smallpox epidemic of the early 1560s, it was Mary rather than the Queen who ended up disfigured and afterwards shunned public view. This led to the expense of her sustaining a separate household away from court, despite her husband's continued devotion. The smallpox also left its mark on young Philip.

Before that unhappy turn, however, Mary and Henry Sidney conceived several children; Philip, the eldest, was born on 30 November 1554 at Penshurst Place, Kent. (This country home was later memorialized in Ben Jonson's famous poem "To Penshurst.") The child was named after King Philip II of Spain, consort of the Catholic Queen Mary Tudor, known (un)popularly as "Bloody Mary" for her persecution of Protestants. She died young, and so from the age of four until his premature death at age thirty-one, Philip Sidney was a subject of Elizabeth Tudor—a monarch he, like his uncle Robert, often found too cautious and politic for his own good. No doubt this is also one reason she outlived them both by many years.

Philip was most likely educated by his mother until 1564, when he left for Shrewsbury School, in Shropshire. Sidney seems to have been preternaturally serious and studious—at least if we believe his classmate, lifetime friend, fellow poet, and laudatory biographer, Fulke Greville. Greville writes, "Though I lived with him, and knew him from a child, yet I never knew him other than a man: with such staidnesse of mind, lovely, and familiar gravity, as carried grace, and reverence above greater years. His talk ever of knowledge, and his very play tending to enrich his mind" (*Life*, p. 6, cited in Robinson, p. ix). Of course the philosophical statesman Greville was enshrining his friend for posterity, but his comments do accord with (and did help shape) Sidney's reputation. At Shrewsbury, young Philip would have received the basis of a solid classical education under Headmaster Thomas Ashton, who was also a Calvinist; although subsequent generations may associate radical Protestantism with forms of anti-intellectualism, quite the opposite was true during Sidney's formative years. Balancing the stern discipline at school, Sidney enjoyed exceptionally exciting holidays. In 1566, he went to visit his uncle Robert Dudley (by now the earl of Leicester and also the newly installed chancellor of Oxford University), first at his home, Kenilworth Castle, and then at Oxford, where the queen's visit prompted an elaborate spectacle replete with drama and oratory.

Two years later, Sidney went on to attend Christ Church, Oxford, in the company of future historians and writers such as William Camden and Richard Hakluyt. As testimony to his diplomatic skills, it seems he also got along well with Sir William Cecil (later Lord Burghley), his uncle Robert's political rival and sometime nemesis: in 1569 there was even a settlement assuming that Philip would marry William's daughter Anne. (It was subsequently cancelled.) Sidney seems to have been a good student but left without a degree in 1571; the reason is unknown but the behavior was not unusual for aristocrats. He may have gone to Cambridge as well, where he would quite likely have met some of the many writers who later looked to him for patronage, including Gabriel Harvey and Edmund Spenser.

In 1572, Sidney left for the continent in the train of the earl of Lincoln, and spent three years there studying and socializing with major Protestant thinkers. In addition to providing an unusual early model for the European "grand tour," Sidney was received as something of an intellectual prodigy, and his European encounters would shape his thought and political attitudes throughout his adulthood. Arriving in Paris for the summer, he met the French Huguenot Admiral Coligny shortly before Coligny was assassinated, and then on 24 August Philip witnessed the horror of the St. Bartholomew's Day Massacre, when the Catholic faction led by Queen Mother Catherine de Medici encouraged the wholesale slaughter of French Protestants. Those who died included the logician Petrus Ramus, also a brief acquaintance of Sidney; indubitably, the carnage that horrified Englishmen from across the channel must have been a traumatic event for a young eyewitness, solidifying his antagonism towards the Catholic powers and his desire to find common cause with continental Protestants. Equally important for Sidney was his friendship with the elderly scholar and diplomat Hubert Languet, who "adopted" him as a protégé and with whom he corresponded until Languet's death in 1581. His further travels in Europe were in part shaped by Languet, with whom he wintered in Frankfurt and later visited in Vienna at the Imperial court. Sidney also displayed his strong will and artistic desires, however, by going to Catholic Italy despite his mentor's worries: he spent time in Padua, Venice, and Florence, and was painted by Veronese (a portrait, alas, lost). Having also visited Hungary, Poland, and the Netherlands by the time he arrived back in England, Sidney was an exceptionally cultivated gentleman who appeared also to have great expectations as heir to two wealthy and powerful uncles.

Sidney's promise was only to be fulfilled artistically, however. Although he participated in royal entertainments and exchanged gifts with the queen, Sidney's close association with Robert Dudley often cost him politically, while that uncle's remarriage and new offspring cost him financially. In 1576 Sidney was made royal cup-bearer, in 1577 he was sent as an ambassador to Vienna, and eventually in 1582 he was knighted: however, this last was for reasons of protocol as he was escorting the French Prince Alençon (later Anjou) back to the Netherlands, and was really the least reward Queen Elizabeth could accord him given his talents and associations. His advocacy for his uncle (including a published *Defense of the earl of Leicester*), his letter of opposition to Elizabeth's courtship with the duke of Alençon, and his idealistic scheme to involve England militarily in a Protestant League on the continent—all found a chilly reception from a ruler sensibly reluctant to upset the tenuous balance of powers or to undermine her own diplomatic efforts. Adding to his personal disappointments was the 1581 marriage of Lord Rich and Sidney's would-be beloved, Penelope Devereux, who was soon to be immortalized as "Stella" in his sonnet sequence. In 1583 Sidney married Frances, daughter of the Secretary of State (and famous spymaster) Sir Francis Walsingham; they would have one daughter, but no sons. Two years later, Sir Philip tried to sail with Sir Francis Drake to the West Indies but was recalled by the queen while en route to Plymouth, and appointed governor of the Dutch port of Flushing instead. Having become involved in the Netherlanders' attempts to throw off Spanish rule, on 22 September 1586 he was shot in the thigh in a battle near Zutphen; romantically but stupidly, he seems to have given away his leg armor. After weeks of infection and pain, Sidney died at Arnhem, on 17 October. His body was returned to England where, on 16 February 1587, he was buried in St. Paul's Cathedral. The grand funeral procession, paid for by Walsingham, testified to his symbolic importance as a figure of both great and dashed hopes.

Over the following decade, Sidney's major works, written for a coterie and circulated in manuscript, were gradually published and even translated into numerous European languages. His goal of bringing England into the European mainstream was finally being realized. But Sir Philip Sidney's posthumous elevation into the status of a courtly and poetic ideal carried obvious irony. It was solely as an author that he would gain an important place in history, but it had been the enforced stretches of "idleness" between his involvement in courtly and continental affairs—so frustrating for him—that allowed him to produce enough poetry and prose to shape Elizabethan literature and win him devoted readers for centuries to come.

COURTLY CULTURE AND THE ARCADIA

SIDNEY'S two performance scripts designed to entertain (and perhaps instruct) the queen situate him most obviously within the Elizabethan court culture. *The Lady of May* (1578) and *The Triumph of the Four Foster Children of Desire* (1581) continue to attract those interested in Elizabethan politics, spectacle, and the development of the masque; they are nevertheless occasional pieces in the narrowest sense. The latter was an elaborate festivity including a joust, in which Fulke Greville and Sidney—known as an expert rider and tilter—along with two other "foster children" sought to storm the fortress of perfect beauty, symbolizing the queen. Failing in the attempt because of her absolute chastity, they apologize to Elizabeth for their violence, caused by her desirability. Given that the French delegation was also in attendance, one may plausibly infer that this was a slap at Alençon's proposal to go where the foster children could not, as well as a chance to express frustration in a way acceptable to the queen (under the guise of compliment to her much-vaunted virginity). One imagines the effect of such lavish spectacles on those who attended and heard of them; Spenser's description of Meleager's siege in book 2 and the Castle of

Busyrane episode in book 3 of *The Faerie Queene* hint at ways in which such memories seeped into the literary imagination as well.

Likewise, Master Rombus's parodic oration in the outdoor entertainment *The Lady of May* provides an inspiration for Shakespeare's schoolmaster Holofernes in *Love's Labours Lost.* Rombus proudly spouts pseudo-learned malapropisms of the sort that will repeatedly well up in the mouths of Shakespeare's comic characters. Getting the last words, the pedantic Rombus also displays Sidney's delight in the fluidity of languages, mixing Latin and the emergent vernacular in preposterous ways:

> *Videte* these obscure barbarons, *perfidem perfide,* you were well served to be vapilated, relinquishing my dignity before I have valedixed this nymph's serenity. Well, *alias* I will be vindicated. But to you Juno, Venus, Pallas *et profecto plus,* I have to ostend a mellifluous fruit of my fidelity.
>
> (Duncan-Jones, ed., 1994, p. 10)

Let him be set down an ass, indeed. The old shepherd Dorcas suggests the title of Shakespeare's *Love's Labours* as well, when he describes how frustrated courtiers retreat into the pastoral world to complain of their mistresses: "some of the extremity of her beauty mixed with extreme cruelty; some of her too much wit, which made all their loving labors folly . . . so that with long lost labor, finding their thoughts bear no other wool but despair, of young courtiers they grew old shepherds" (Duncan-Jones, 1994, p. 7). And the echoes of Sidney's sonnets in *Love's Labours Lost* further attest that the earlier writer was on Shakespeare's mind, as an object of tribute and mockery mixed, when he created his drama of Navarrese courtier-poets in their own (preposterous) pastoral retreat. Sidney's courtly entertainments have otherwise made little lasting impact on literary history.

They do reveal, however, some characteristic concerns that would be more fully developed in Sidney's major works: the tension between the active and contemplative lives; the possibilities of the pastoral as a form of social commentary; a love of debate and self-dramatization; and the intertwined personal and political frustrations of thwarted desire. Moreover, these shows convey some sense of the power relations being played out through lyric and spectacle at the time, as the sovereign mistress vies with her male "suitors" (amatory and political) for control over state affairs. In semi-fantastical, rustic landscapes, Sidney found veiled—and sometimes inadequately veiled—ways to comment on matters of ethics, policy, and amour. In *The Lady of May* in particular, frustration about the queen's marital and foreign policies are played out in verse. Sidney constructs a rivalry for the hand of the Lady of May between the active forester Therion and the more passive, meditative shepherd, Espilus, with the choice to be made by the queen herself. Scholars such as Steven May have questioned whether we should automatically assume Sidney's partisanship in favor of Therion (given that woodsman's wildness). Nevertheless, Therion does seem fairly clearly aligned with the party of political action—that is, with the kind of interventionist continental policy that Sidney and his uncle Leicester advocated. No wonder, then, that the more cautious Elizabeth chose to make narrative hash of the ending by favoring the shepherd instead. Ultimately the queen, not Rombus or Sidney, gets the final say at her court entertainments.

Sometime in the late 1570s, Sidney began his first major work, a prose romance containing poetic eclogues called *Arcadia.* Sharing its title with Jacopo Sannazaro's *Arcadia* (1504), which also alternated between prose and verse, Sidney's creation draws on a wide array of classical and Renaissance continental models, including Heliodorus's *Ethiopica,* and (especially in Sidney's revised draft) Ariosto's *Orlando Furioso,* the immensely popular *Amadis de Gaul,* and the Spaniard Montemayor's prose *Diana.* Yet this *Arcadia* also has a distinct sense of intimacy and of Sidney's personality, beginning with the dedication to his sister Mary, countess of Pembroke, as its original cause and audience. First composed in pieces (some of which were read to Mary at her house at Wilton, near Salisbury, others sent to her when Sidney was away), *Arcadia* mixes Sidney's own obsessions and delights with a conventional form then in vogue. Like Roman comedy, the *Arcadia* has five "Acts" or books. It records the exploits of the knight-adventurers Pyrocles and Musidorus in a pastoral landscape that nevertheless contains amorous and political dangers aplenty. Indeed, a cautionary political tale provides the basic frame: in order to avoid the seemingly horrible truths told by an oracle whom he should not have consulted in the first place, the ruler Basilius retreats into the countryside with his wife, Gynecia, and daughters Pamela and Philoclea, attended only by the shepherd Dametas and his family. In ways sometimes comic and sometimes pathetic, the oracle's prophecies are of course fulfilled. Had Basilius instead heeded the good counselor Philanax, he would not have led his country into disruption and his family into danger. For Sidney, the pastoral landscape is never far from the political state, nor the amorous dilemma from the ethical. Because Sidney would later return to this story and recast it as an (incomplete) epic, this first version is now known as the *Old Arcadia*. It would, though, have been the only *Arcadia* in manuscript circulation during Sidney's lifetime and, judging from the nine surviving copies and comments by Fulke Greville, seems to have been quite widely disseminated.

Frequently addressing an imagined audience of "fair ladies," Sidney's romance shows unusual empathy with female characters, and presents its "heroes" in a decidedly ambiguous light. While motivated by love and youthful energies, they are not always gentlemen. Pyrocles disguises himself as an Amazon woman, in order to get near his desired Philoclea: the cross-dressed confusions that follow (involving the unfortunately deluded queen Gynecia as well as her daughter) raise questions about his sense of honor. Musidorus (who adopts a shepherd's guise) almost attempts the rape of his desired, unsuspecting Pamela—when he is fortuitously interrupted by bandits. (Thoughts of Shakespeare's *Two Gentlemen of Verona*, written a decade later, would not be amiss here.) By the fifth book, both men are on trial for the apparent murder of king Basilius. While some readers find these developments inappropriate when mixed with pastoral and comical intrigues, Katherine Duncan-Jones argues that Sidney is exploring the "ever-widening

discrepancies between [the heroes'] idealized pretensions and their actual self-interest" (*Old Arcadia*, p. xv). In other words, Sidney takes a form of literary entertainment, highly popular among the privileged classes, and deepens its psychological and ethical complexity. His Arcadia is an alternative landscape but not an escape from the problems of his own.

In his *Arcadia*, Sidney also produced some of the clearest, most readable prose in English at the time, far less mannered and more elegant than most contemporary fiction with literary pretensions (of which there was not very much, though a few proto-novels such as *Euphues* were best sellers). Likewise, the poetry within *Arcadia* shows a mastery of metrics new in English, and an understanding of classical quantitative versification as well as the accentual-syllabic system that would become normative in the vernacular. While earlier poets such as Sir Thomas Wyatt, Henry Howard Surrey, and George Gascoigne had begun to show the possibilities of English poetry, none had the command of form and the sheer range of talent displayed here. Sidney composes a virtual encyclopedia of complex forms and metrical structures, including classical anacreontics, hexameters, and the difficult and obscure "phaleuciacs" (derived from Catullus); among the rhymed verses appear madrigals, rime royal stanzas, elegies, sestinas, pastoral debates, an epithalamium, and an entire sonnet with but a single rhyme sound. What is more remarkable, some of these poems do not read as mere exercises or displays of craft: the famed double sestina beginning "Ye goat-herd gods, that love the grassy mountains" manages, for all its rhetorical formality, to convey the shepherds' sense of loss at the departure of the goddess Urania from their once delightful landscape (an explicit announcement that the golden age has already ended in this Arcadia).

In 1584, Sidney began revising—or rather, rewriting—his romance. He expanded it greatly, and in doing so changed not only the tone but major aspects of the story as well. Much of the poetry was removed. Sidney's surrogate character Philisides, who had been a shepherd-poet before, was now a knight. The interweaving of multiple narratives made the work more intricate. New characters were added, and Arcadia—never a simple pastoral retreat—was now at war. Princesses were tortured, princes imprisoned, and the forces of darkness and confusion were far more powerful than before. Erotic desire was even more troubling, and the representation of marriage more cynical and threatened. It is hard to avoid inferring that some of the changes in tone stemmed from Sidney's own disappointments in love and politics. Fulke Greville, who felt the unfinished revision, now called the *New Arcadia,* was "fitter to be printed than that first" (letter to Walsingham, November 1586), divided the later manuscript into chapters and published it in 1590 as *The Countess of Pembroke's Arcadia.* Three years later, a book published with the same title removed the chapter divisions from the *New Arcadia* but appended to it books 3–5 of the *Old Arcadia,* to complete the story. Sidney's sister, Lady Mary, the eponymous countess of Pembroke, seems to have taken the lead in revising parts she found less palatable, such as Musidorus's attempted rape; whether at Sidney's bequest or of her own initiative, it was removed, and other lascivious parts were likewise tamed or edited out. The protagonists, in other words, looked more like heroes. This "literary centaur," as Duncan-Jones calls it (*Old Arcadia,* p. ix), became and remained remarkably popular for centuries and across Europe in a way rare for works written originally in English. As King Charles I stood on the Whitehall scaffold in 1649, about to be beheaded, he quoted (so the story goes) its heroine Pamela's prayer. His enemy John Milton, no fan of the book's morality and genre, still acknowledged that Sidney's romance was "full of worth and wit." Samuel Richardson would name a novel after one of its heroines. And yet, *The Countess of Pembroke's Arcadia* is also a volume whose printed form was never imagined by its author.

Sidney's romance provided fertile territory for other writers in search of a plot or two. Most famously, the story of the king of Paphlagonia reappears in the Gloucester plot of Shakespeare's *King Lear. Mucedorus,* a play hardly read now but possibly the most popular of all presentations on the Elizabethan stage, derived its title character and many incidents from Sidney's copious work—though the unremarkable quality of its dramatic verse and the patchwork quality of its episodes nearly hides its ancestry. More edifying was Spenser's extensive use of the *Arcadia* in composing the adventures of Sir Calidore, the knight of Courtesy, in book 6 of the *Faerie Queene.* Only in the latter half of the eighteenth century did *Arcadia* wane in popularity. Its aristocrats, shepherds, and clowns—lascivious and noble, involved in unlikely intricacies and affairs of state—were not the right stuff for the age of bourgeois revolutions: the critic William Hazlitt, in his *Lectures on the Age of Elizabeth* (1820), called it "one of the greatest monuments of the abuse of intellectual power upon record" (Evans, p. 13). Nevertheless, and unlike most other works of Elizabethan prose, the *Arcadia* is still available in popular paperback form, now supplemented for the first time by the *Old Arcadia* as written: readers still pick these books up to wander for pleasure's sake amidst their fantastic mixtures of archaic chivalry, psychological confusions, ethical lapses, and social commentary. And as a form of storytelling that—despite the pastoral trappings—stressed the imperfections of the world Sidney knew and presented the gradual education of flawed protagonists, the *Arcadia* signaled the direction of fiction after the Renaissance: toward the "low" mimetic realism of the novel.

THE THEORIST

AROUND 1581, Sidney composed his treatise on literary creativity, published posthumously in nearly identical forms by two different printers under the still-dueling titles, *The Defence of Poetry* (William Posonby) and *An Apology for Poetry* (Henry Olney). The stimulus for its composition was the ill-judged dedication to Sidney of an anti-theatrical tract, *The School of Abuse,* by Stephen Gosson. As a onetime playwright who had seen the light of radical Protestantism, Gosson thought Sir Philip would appreciate his attack on the ungodly and crass practices in the newly developing commercial theaters. While

Sidney would indeed take issue with the tragicomic mixtures and undistinguished style of the plays of his day, the bulk of his essay instead defends the practice of fiction-making and the ideals and excellence of "right poets." As ever, Sidney combines extensive knowledge of classical and biblical authorities with a fresh, lighthearted immediacy, and in the process creates one of the most important works of literary criticism and theory of the Renaissance.

Unlike metrical or rhetorical handbooks of the time, Sidney's piece establishes his personal voice immediately, as he begins by recalling a speech in praise of horsemanship given by his riding instructor at the Imperial court. He professes that "if I had not been a piece of a logician before I came to him, I think he would have persuaded me to have wished myself a horse" (Robinson, ed., pp. 4–5). As a preface and parallel to his defense of his own "unelected vocation," the witty, self-deprecating tone here announces an aristocrat's alternative to dry pedantry, and captures that quality so valued in the Renaissance—*sprezzatura,* the ability to make something difficult look easy. For Sidney's was a difficult task: he was in a sense creating his own form in this prose piece, despite its debt to the structure of a classical oration and a few shorter precedents such as George Gascoigne's *Certain Notes of Instruction.* He was also trying to balance Protestant ethical concerns with a sweeping defense of that worrisome faculty, the imagination. Combining classical philosophy with idiomatic English, grand claims with comic asides and tongue-in-cheek concessions, Sidney created a stylish argument that, like his romance, can still be read with pleasure.

For the Renaissance, poetry encompassed not only verse but the whole enterprise of fiction-making, and as such was vulnerable to attack for being both frivolous and dangerous. Sidney's first strategy is to employ the traditional form of defense through precedents and classical examples. Even Plato—who famously banished the poets from his ideal Republic—is enlisted (quite plausibly) as a creator of feigned dialogues and poetic images. The Greeks, the Turks, the Welsh, and the Romans all recognized that the verse of a poet "did seem to have some divine force in it" (Robinson, p. 11). This is heady stuff, and leads Sidney to make bolder claims than most of his classical authorities for the special powers of the "maker": he draws as well on Renaissance Neoplatonic thought in arguing that the poet is not simply an imitator of nature or mimetic artist. Rather, "the poet, disdaining to be tied to any such subjection, lifted up with the vigor of his own invention, doth grow in effect another nature, in making things either better than nature bringeth forth, or quite anew . . . so as he goeth hand in hand with nature, not enclosed within the narrow warrant of her gifts, but freely ranging only within the zodiac of his own wit" (Robinson, p. 14). Here Sidney brings together the two Renaissance senses of "originality": on the one hand, a return to origins and mythic sources; and on the other, the meaning we now recognize, a sense of the new, a form of "inspiration" taken seriously as an alternative to mere imitation of external models. Always one to end a paragraph with a pithy phrase, Sidney concludes that Nature's "world is brazen, the poets only deliver a golden" (Robinson, p. 15).

Having risen to the skies, Sidney soon returns to earth with more familiar ethical and psychological arguments. The poet creates what we would call role models for ethical study, who carry, in Sidney's evocative phrase, "an apparent shining" (Robinson, p. 29). In this regard poetry is indeed, as Aristotle said, an art of imitation; it provides a "speaking picture" whose end, following Horace, is "to teach and delight" (Robinson, p. 18). Furthermore, poetry is the superior discipline for teaching because it provides the proper balance between the ideal and real, the general and the particular. In contrast, history is bound by the world as it is and remains mired in specifics which are often unedifying as moral examples, while philosophy is too general and idealizing. Poetry bridges the two, showing "what may be and what should be" through vivid, memorable images that meld knowledge derived from sensory perception with abstract reasoning (Robinson, pp. 20 ff.). It is truly a "medicine of cherries," its pleasures moving our "infected wills" in the service of "erected wit" (Robinson, pp. 40, 17). Nor is the goal of poetry mere appreciation of the beautiful or contemplation of the good. As a Protestant courtier as well as humanist, Sidney stresses that the end of learning is "praxis," or virtuous action; he argues for "the end of well doing and not of well knowing only" (Robinson, p. 23). At the same time, the more homely side of Sidney never forgets the basic appeal of the storyteller, who "cometh unto you, with a tale which holdeth children from play and old men from the chimney corner" (Robinson, p. 38).

Some might counter that his emphasis on the conceptual "foreconceit" or "Idea" of a fiction has the danger of saving art at the expense of actual practice, and indeed Sidney is frequently critical of English writers as abusers of their art. On the other hand, even here he shows sympathy for those who are perhaps misled from more elevated topics by beauty, and confesses his enjoyment of works he acknowledges to be flawed or crude, such as *Amadis de Gaul* and the ballad *Chevy Chase.* One should keep in mind the polemical attack that prompted Sidney's rebuttal, and his desire to improve rather than simply denigrate contemporary practice. Taken out of context, some of his comments about playwriting may seem uncharitable and stiffly neoclassical—but then, few readers have spent time perusing the pre-Shakespearean romances such as *Sir Clyomon and Sir Clamydes,* the kind of disorganized, doggerel stuff dominating the stage when Sidney was alive. He can hardly be faulted for not foreseeing what Marlowe and Shakespeare would soon manage to do with mixed genres and locations, after his death. More questionable is Sidney's attempt to shield fiction-makers from ethical reproach by arguing that "the poet, he nothing affirms, and therefore never lieth" (Robinson, p. 57)—a bit of a literalist's quibble from one who has made such major claims for poetry as a form of instruction.

The *Apology* (or *Defence*) remains a masterpiece of polished, playful prose that vigorously upholds humanist idealism. While the latter sections focus on specifics of different genres and languages (including praise for the possibilities of versification in English), much of its aesthetic theory pertains to other art forms as well. Ideas that might seem at odds are united here in the "syncretic" method of the Renaissance: classical and Biblical traditions, precept and example, utility and idealism, action and contemplation—all these dyads might seem logical contraries to some. But for Sidney and the fiction-makers he inspired and defended, contraries could be true: the art of poetry was to transform exclusive oppositions into a paradoxical fantasy, with images and wit moving their audience toward greater understanding.

ASTROPHIL AND STELLA

When one turns from Sidney the theorist to Sidney the love poet, one can hardly avoid asking: How do his high ideals inform his own literary practice in *Astrophil and Stella*? How does the upright humanist defend a sonnet sequence in which the author's persona tries to persuade his beloved to commit adultery, and knowingly pursues lust and desire? Is Sidney a poet who "coldly" makes "fiery speeches" in the voice of Astrophil, or is he distinguishable from those unimpassioned love poets whom his *Apology* disparages for just such behavior (Robinson, p. 81)? The sequence concludes with Astrophil located far from realms of gold, with iron doors blocking his way to happiness (sonnet 108); should his descent into lust and frustration be read as a negative exemplum showing how an infected will can thwart erected wit? It soon becomes clear that if these two works are connected beyond being written at about the same time (the early 1580s), it is no simple relationship. The *Apology* does not serve as a key or obvious explanatory guide to *Astrophil and Stella*. Nor should the experienced reader of Sidney expect it to do so: as ever, Sidney delights in the play of wit and discernment, enjoying the paradox and the puzzle rather than the easy solution.

Written in the wake of Penelope Devereux's marriage to Lord Rich, and filled with teasing biographical reminders of that connection (most obvious when the poet mocks "Rich fools"), *Astrophil and Stella* is an artful fiction that defies a

New Critical method of reading that would exclude biography and historical context as "off limits" for artistic analysis. At the same time, however, it announces itself as allegorical (its titular figures being a star and star-lover) and "conventional"—not in our modern sense of uninteresting, but rather, as a work alluding to and translating a continental literary tradition. To find single meanings in this duplicitous set of songs and sonnets is to undo its artistry and reduce its achievement.

Astrophil and Stella builds on the poetic contributions of earlier Tudor sonneteers such as Wyatt, Surrey, Turberville, Whitney, and Gascoigne, but takes that tradition to an entirely new level with its range of ambition, craft, and accomplishment. Not only was it a longer, more sustained narrative and lyric sequence than had previously been attempted in English; it also first established, as Hallett Smith observes, "the vitality (as distinguished from the mere 'manner') of the Petrarchan tradition" (*Elizabethan Poetry,* 1952, p. 143). Almost single-handedly it induced the "sonnet craze" of the 1590s, which led to hundreds of less distinguished sequences but also to Spenser's *Amoretti,* Shakespeare's *Sonnets,* and Donne's *Songs and Sonnets.* Thomas Watson's *Hekatompathia* may officially be the first extensive love sonnet sequence published in English (1582) and certainly other poets were trying their hand at the form, but it wasn't until Sidney's sonnets were printed posthumously in 1591 that masses of other sonnet sequences were printed and sold. The apex of "courtly" writing, *Astrophil and Stella* thus moved out beyond the selective coterie allowed to see such revealing poems during Sidney's lifetime, to exert its considerable powers upon a more "general" reading public.

The sonnet sequence itself dated back to Dante and especially Petrarch, but by the time Sidney was writing the fashion had spread across Western Europe. Sidney was influenced by the French poets called the Pléiades, including Ronsard and Marot: the inclusion of a series of "baiser" poems, focusing on Astrophil's desire for and response to Stella's kiss, is a case in point. For a modern reader, such a clear set of conventions and even the sonnet stanza itself may initially seem limiting, but on closer examination the sonnet turns out to be an extremely useful tool for shaping deeply emotional material; the predictable form becomes an essential framework within which the lyric poet can use subtle variations of style and attitude to convey a particular version of a self—a "voice," a "subjectivity." By recognizing Sidney's participation in, but also his departures from, the continental tradition, one can better appreciate his ingenious achievement.

Whereas others had worshipped unavailable ladies from afar, Sidney's Astrophil pursues a married woman vigorously and physically: he kisses her when she is sleeping and later receives a voluntary embrace as well. Even more focally, in his inner struggles and torments, bodily desire is never successfully subordinated to heavenly adoration: unlike Dante or Petrarch, Astrophil cannot move up the "ladder of love" to a heavenly Beatrice or the Virgin Mary. Part of this difference from the Catholic Italian sonneteers may be attributed to Sidney's Calvinism, since worship of saints or Mary would be seen as idolatry; then again, his contemporary Spenser, equally protestant, managed to play with precisely this representational problem rather than reject the possibility of sublimation. But Sidney was also stymied by particulars derived from his own biographical dilemma: because he had loved "not at first sight" when he might have attained the hand of young Penelope Devereux, but rather gradually, "by degrees" (sonnet 2), he found himself implicated in his own distress. It was not a mystical separation but a matter of bad timing. He remained all too aware that the lady in question was also earthbound, sexually available (to someone else), and nearby. They moved in the same political and familial circles, making her difficult to recast as an Idea. Even the half-hearted attempt in the sequence's penultimate sonnet to make her an inspiration to duty, when Stella is imagined "as a queen" who will send her servant away on a mission, Astrophil's "great cause" remains murky. Nor does the poet resort to the most obvious displacement in any explicit or sustained way, by substituting Queen Elizabeth for his beloved—as both royal entertainments and other poets had taught him would be wise.

Clearly, Sidney chose to keep his focus on earthly love within a courtly context, finding in its contradiction to the Protestant marriage ethic a stage for combustible drama. The tendency towards satire that emerges as a result (against the speaker, against the court) is juxtaposed with a philosophical debate within Astrophil. While the oxymoronic nature of love is a staple of Petrarchan poetry, with its "icy flames" and "dear wounds," here the nature of the conflict is not (only) emotional but ethical: Sidney defies Aristotle by knowing the better while doing the worse. And whenever Astrophil tries to escape his difficulties, "ah, desire still cries: Give me some food" (sonnet 71). Whereas other poets would see love happening "to" them for the most part, Sidney mixes that externalized language of Cupid with a more modern sense of the subject's self-construction as the site of crisis: he is aware of the gaps between words and things, thought and action, social behavior and internal attitudes. Such a breakdown in correspondences between microcosm and macrocosm makes these love poems something more: before Shakespeare's sonnets, they hint at the breakdown of the semiotic systems that sustained the premodern world, and capture the struggles of incipiently modern selfhood. No wonder here, then, that desire still and always will cry for more "food."

In addition to creating a sustained psychodramatic conflict and a meditation on the nature of love and subjectivity, Sidney is of course also writing verse: by turn exquisite, ornate, comical, quirky, and elegant. As the play between convention and biography shapes interpretation of the "story," so too does it raise questions about the speaker's verse: Are the "bad" lines and unfortunate images Astrophil's or Sidney's? Are we to believe that the self-professed anti-Petrarchan poet who says he "never drank of Aganippe well," the Greek font of inspiration from the Muses (sonnet 74), is Sidney, the author of classical hexameters? What are the boundaries between lyric and drama, character and confessional? Seen one way, formality, wordplay, rhetorical shaping, and mockery can signal just

how raw and extreme are the poet's subjective states: the feelings seem so intense that they force him to find tight structures and ironic strategies to gain control. Conversely, if one emphasizes the distinction between the actual poet and his fictive star-loving "speaker," the tendency is to see Astrophil as the one out of control and meant to be perceived as such, while the sophisticated author hovers above—if not exactly paring his fingernails, perhaps sharpening his quill—as he shapes a lover's torments to tragicomic effect. Here Sidney the theorist may begin to merge with Sidney the love poet: if these contrary positions are both true, we are left with a paradoxical fiction that both simultaneously imitates nature and ranges in the "zodiac of his own wit," both delights with lively images and forces us to contemplate their meaning. And while poetry is more than versifying, here the verse has gone beyond the exquisite craft of the *Arcadia* eclogues in shedding signs of effort and artifice: it has become the kind of fluent speech that echoes the character's state of mind—a use of iambic pentameter (in most of the poems) that will provide Shakespeare with a model for lyrical drama on the stage. Indeed, in the preface to the 1591 edition of *Astrophil and Stella*, the writer Thomas Nashe praised it as a "theater of pleasure" in which "the tragicomedy of love is performed by starlight," with the muse Melpomene as "chief actor," the "argument cruel chastity, the prologue hope, the epilogue dispair" (Rollins and Baker, eds., p. 324). Whether one agrees with the particulars of Nashe's dramatic interpretation, the analogies with theater are prescient.

Like many sequences, *Astrophil and Stella* begins with a "programmatic" sonnet, announcing the poetic as well as amatory intentions of the lyricist. It illustrates Sidney's talents as a rhetorician, and the comic touch that makes his sonnets seem fresh across centuries. "Loving in truth, and fain in verse my love to show," he begins, playing with the pun on fain (wishing) and feign (pretending—or, less kindly, lying) to make his first oxymoron. Rather than the typical reflection of the lover's torment (though tormented with love he is), this verbal paradox aims directly at the status of poetic truth—and so again, we discern the mark of the author of the *Apology for Poetry*. The following three lines likewise use the poet's tools to raise the central thematic problems sketched above. Through a sequence of parallel half lines in which key words are reiterated (a rhetorical figure known as *gradatio* or the "ladder"), the speaker imagines how his verses will win his lady's favor: "Pleasure might make her read, reading might make her know; / Knowledge might pity win, and pity grace obtain." Already, the ironies are multiple: this ladder leads not to heaven but to an earthly love, one that would make the lady stoop and would lead neither person to spiritual "grace." In the second quatrain, in an effort "to paint" his own pain, the poet studies others' "inventions fine"—that is, he follows the traditional method of learning to write by imitation, "turning others' leaves." But with the mention of "leaves" (a favorite English Renaissance pun uniting nature and art), the imagery goes haywire: he looks there for "showers" to flow "upon my sunburnt brain." Even before the ninth-line turn (the conventional moment in a Petrarchan sonnet, between octet and sestet), we know that a poet seeking rain from leaves is in trouble. This will indeed be the point of the poem's conclusion, after another quatrain using comic personification and hyperbole to dramatize his plight: "Biting my truant pen, beating myself for spite, / 'Fool,' said my muse to me; 'look in thy heart, and write.'"

Rather than more study and literary imitation, he needs "Invention, nature's child" found in his own heart: the kind of "inspiration" that he praised in poets as Neoplatonic "makers." Or at least as imitators of nature rather than art, one might say as a supplement, just as the *Apology* adds a second argument for the mimetic artistry of the poet; for in his "heart" he will find (as the Renaissance psychophysiology of love would have it, and as later poems in the sequence will confirm) the lively image of the beloved, Stella herself.

"Others' feet" may seem to Astrophil "strangers in my way," and throughout the work, he professes his "anti-Petrarchan" defiance of literary convention and clichéd expressions in favor of his own "truth." Yet Sidney also mocks that defiance, here making a formal joke out of those "feet" (another nice art-and-nature pun). The traditional fourteen lines of sonnet 1 are knit even tighter by its rhyme scheme (using only two basic sounds for the first twelve end-rhymes), but it is precisely an extra "foot" that Sidney adds to make this sonnet unconventional by English standards: it is written in iambic hexameter. Moreover, it is notoriously difficult to make long lines sound like a single unit in English, since we tend to hear them in pieces (as trimeter or tetrameter). Through artful and (for his time) unusual variation of caesura, Sidney makes the lines sound short when he's being funny, but sustains them when he wishes. Some would say he is showing off. But as a poetic introduction, this is a tour de force of wit and substance.

Whereas Shakespeare uses the comparatively loose English sonnet form, Sidney manages the much tighter Italianate rhyme scheme in *Astrophil and Stella*. At the same time, he varies the formal details, and intersperses "songs" to advance the story and provide alternative perspectives. The eighth song, for example, describes Astrophil in a third-person narrative written in tetrameter quatrains. Sidney thus sends a typically double message: he will both use and adapt forms, be ultra-Petrarchan and anti-Petrarchan, play the fool and demonstrate his artistic command simultaneously. Furthermore, he creates a romance with many moods, rather than just the abjection of a disconsolate, frustrated lover: Astrophil is that, but he is also energetic, preoccupied, surly, belligerent, witty, proud, aggressive, and meditative. Stella too is a more human, changing beloved than in most sequences, causing a range of reactions from Astrophil. She chastises, relents, kisses, rejects, ignores, and inspires: her black eyes flash, her lapdog and pet bird annoy, and her passion for theater inspires absurd jealousy. Since she likes shows, Astrophil ridiculously advises, pretend he is a fiction and pay attention to him: in one of those richly debated lines that keeps scholars arguing and readers guessing, he concludes sonnet 45 by proclaiming "I am not I; pity the tale of me." As in so many of these sonnets, this fourteenth and last line provides a punch line of sorts. But is it a joke or "truth"? Bathos or a psychological meltdown? A poetic commentary or a bawdy "ending"? A Satanic flash of bad faith or a comment on the impossibility of authentic self-fashioning? Or all of the above?

Here as elsewhere, there is more than a little room for interpretation. Sidney clearly signals his interest in text as performance, making explicit gestures at himself as an autobiographical subject but always teasing the relationship between life and fiction. In sonnet 27, it is hard to distinguish between Sidney and Astrophil as he acknowledges that others interpret his abstraction as "that poison foul of bubbling pride"; in fact, he says, it is "ambition, I confess, / That makes me oft my best friends overpass"—but with yet another fourteenth-line twist, his thoughts of "highest place" refer not to public office but "Stella's grace." A poem like this to some extent relies on the in-joke of Sidney's great expectations, without which the final line loses its zing and seems mere sentimentality. One can of course still enjoy its masterful use of sound repetitions to express the way words become slippery gossip: "They deem, and of that doom the rumour flies." But the ambiguous and playful treatment of the lyric speaker additionally allows Sidney to be the butt of his own jokes, and tempers the potential ostentation of his poetic control. In some cases, distance disappears entirely: when, in sonnet 30 ("Whether the Turkish new moon minded be"), he catalogs current political debates, he also includes a reference to his father Henry Sidney's position in Ireland: "How Ulster likes of that same golden bit / Wherewith my father once made it half tame." Again, poetic technique artfully reinforces the matter, as he concludes this public recitation by remarking: "These questions busy wits to me do frame. / I, cumbered with good manners, answer do, / But know not how, for still I think of you." The simplicity of this turn, and the direct address of "you"—rather than she, or Stella—stands out all the more in context, and heightens the contrast between courtly politics and private intimacy.

Many intrusions and problems recur in the sequence, but surprisingly little resentment is aimed at Stella herself—or at least in comparison with what is often called the anti-idealizing or anti-Petrarchan tendency of much English sonneteering. There is still the occasional misogynist outburst (most notable in the fifth song, adapted from an eclogue of Philisides in the *Old Arcadia*). But as in the *Arcadia,* it is the larger courtly milieu, with its backbiting rivalries of "envious wits" and suffocating surveillance, which seems the real culprit. This, and of course Stella's husband, the "rich fool" who stands for Lord Rich. It comes as little surprise, then, that these sonnets were seen as potentially more personal and damaging than the *Arcadia*'s veiled eclogues, and were kept close, whereas the *Arcadia* poems to Mira were widely circulated (see Steven May, pp. 99ff). Likewise, one hears less about posterity than in the poems of professional writers such as Shakespeare and Drayton: much of the energy of Astrophil's complaints comes from this full engagement in the present time and place, with the immediacy of his desire and the inadequacy of any form of deferral or sublimation. But the court's external constraints prove more recalcitrant than Stella's virtue, with the result that, near the end of the sequence, the adulterous duo start to sound a bit like Romeo and Juliet. The eleventh song begins with a balcony scene, and the unusual inclusion of direct speech emanating from the beloved's mouth: "Who is it that this dark night / Underneath my window plaineth?'" Stella inquires. After seven stanzas of a lover's dialogue regarding constancy, their bantering debate is trumped by the debasing, inevitable social frame:

'Peace, I think that some give ear;
Come no more, lest I get anger.'
Bliss, I will my bliss forbear,
Fearing, sweet, you to endanger,
But my soul shall harbour there.

'Well, be gone, be gone, I say,
Lest that Argus' eyes perceive you.'
O, unjust is fortune's sway,
Which can make me thus to leave you,
And from louts to run away.

Given Astrophil's refusal to perceive the authority of such "louts," and the physicality of his desire, it is little surprise that the sequence ends without a sense of real resolution: Astrophil continues to pine for Stella's "absent presence" (sonnet 106). Nor is it difficult to discern how and why Sidney could become the dashing, doomed icon of Renaissance courtship, a proto-Byronic figure struggling with competing forms of authority and originality.

The story would be told that, on his deathbed, Sidney wished his profane sonnets burnt. Likewise, some see his sonnet "Leave me O Love which reachest but to dust" (from *Certain Sonnets*) as a form of rebuttal to *Astrophil and Stella,* or the true resolution and ending of the sequence. Its attempt to shift to "higher things" and God's eternal light rather than temporal earthly love certainly allows an imagined end to the restless struggles of Astrophil. Moreover, in 1585 Sidney did begin translating Duplessis-Mornay's *De la verité de la religion chrestienne,* and perhaps also Du Bartas's *Semaine,* works of Christian faith. He also started working on verse translations of the biblical Psalms, which he praised as the highest of all poetry in his *Apology.* And yet, to think of *Astrophil and Stella* as abandoned or superseded remains a bit too neat, a bit pat, and a good bit unlikely—rather like saying John Donne put aside all his fleshly desires and intensity when he took up orders in the Anglican Church. Even in the sonnet "Leave me," one discerns not just artful metrics when the rhythm of line 9 stresses the holy light as *that* light, but also the ongoing sense of effort and a remembered alternative: "O take fast hold, let that light be thy guide" (Duncan-Jones, ed., 1973, p. 114). If one must specify "that" light, that pesky *other* light remains as well, and leads us back, full circle, to Sidney's comments on love poetry in the *Apology:*

> But grant love of beauty to be a beastly fault (although it be very hard, sith only man, and no beast, hath that gift to discern beauty); grant that lovely name of love to deserve all hateful reproaches (although even some of my masters the philosophers spent a good deal of their lamp-oil in setting forth the excellency of it); grant, I say, whatsoever they will have granted, that not only love, but lust, but vanity, but (if they list) scurrility, possesseth many

> leaves of the poet's books; yet think I, when this is granted, they will find their sentence may with good manners put the last words foremost, and not say that poetry abuseth man's wit, but that man's wit abuseth poetry.
>
> (Robinson, p. 59)

Even if we grant that Sidney turned to holy writings, those modifying, qualifying, playfully undermining parentheses still remain. And "it be very hard" to ignore them. Not to mention that, among a slew of unfinished works, *Astrophil and Stella* was one of the very few he saw fit to complete. When the countess of Pembroke collected together Philip's works for an "authorized" edition (which, given the siblings' closeness in life, was not so inaccurate a title), it included not only the *Defence of Poetry, Certain Sonnets* and the *Arcadia,* but also *Astrophil and Stella.*

THE LEGACY

FROM the moment of Sidney's death, the process of mythmaking began in earnest. Fulke Greville's letter to Walsingham regarding which *Arcadia* to publish was sent months before the body was buried in Saint Paul's, and Edmund Molyneux managed to get his account of Sidney ready in time for publication in the second edition of Holinshed's *Chronicles* (1587). Later, Fulke Greville's *Life* (1652) would become a classic, all the rarer and more remarkable for the paucity of biographies in the Renaissance; if not always reliable given its aim as tribute and exemplary life, it nevertheless allows us to know more about Sidney the man than we do about almost any other writer of his day. Elegies were composed—not only by those who knew him well (Fulke Greville's "An epitaph upon the Right Honorable Sir Philip Sidney"; a pastoral elegy, "The Dolefull Lay of Clorinda," usually attributed to Mary Sidney Herbert) but also by any writer worth his salt. Most notable in this enterprise as in much else was Edmund Spenser, whose volume of pastoral elegies, *Astrophel,* appeared in print in 1595 and helped shift the memorial emphasis from Sidney the soldier and courtier to Sidney the poet. Still, Spenser's friend and patron Sir Walter Ralegh wrote an epitaph that illustrates the continuing usefulness of the figure of Sidney as a forerunner for courtiers interested in advancing their social stature. After acknowledging their rivalry in life, Ralegh soon resorts to familiar conceits and ornate rhetoric in his effort to advance his own position. Penelope Devereux's brother, the earl of Essex, tried to assume the mantle of his friend (Sir Philip had bequeathed him his "best sword," and Essex went on to marry Philip's widow Frances as well). But like Sidney, Essex had an energetic willfulness that on occasion went too far—certainly too far from Queen Elizabeth's perspective—and, lacking Philip's other talents and intelligence, he ended up a rebel and a traitor.

Lasting longer than the elegy-writing in Sir Philip's honor was Sidney's writing, a model and inspiration for both intimates and strangers. The "Sidney circle," the large group of friends and relations and the writers they patronized, took it upon themselves to carry the torch for a dead hero. Carrying on her brother's legacy gave Lady Mary, countess of Pembroke, a particular license to write, despite her gender. She not only supervised "authorized" editions of his works but also continued the project of translating the Psalms, with great success. She also translated French drama, something her brother never had tried. Robert Sidney, the younger brother who grew up in a powerful shadow, would write his own sonnet sequence, which in turn would be a model (along with Philip's) for his remarkable writing daughter, Lady Mary Sidney Wroth. Lady Wroth, unhappily married and carrying on an affair with her first cousin William Herbert (son of the countess of Pembroke, and dedicatee of Shakespeare's First Folio), would mimic her uncle in writing a full-length prose romance, the *Urania*, with an appended sonnet sequence written from the female lover's perspective, *Pamphilia to Amphilanthus*. Whereas Sir Philip had been content to circulate his work in manuscript, Lady Wroth boldly published the first volume of her romance in 1621—only to become embroiled in courtly accusations of slander that reinforced the wisdom of her uncle's comparative reticence.

The 1591 publication of *Astrophil and Stella* provided similar incentive for others outside the male aristocracy to circulate and publish their sonnets. From the *Delia* of Samuel Daniel (who spent time at Wilton House) to Barnabe Barnes's *Pathenophil and Parthenope,* from Fulke Greville's *Caelica* to Michael Drayton's *Idea*—and of course from Spenser's *Amoretti* to Shakespeare's *Sonnets*—it seemed that everyone who could write managed to produce a sonnet sequence during the 1590s, and the best of those remain at the heart of the English lyric tradition. Thus Sidney also serves as a pivotal figure for considering the historical shifts in who wrote and how their work was distributed—including the movement from immediacy and performance at court to the wider social circulation of poetry as published text, and from an historically embedded moment to a transcendent idea of literature.

Likewise, his prose romance encouraged the circulation of that genre (already becoming quite popular through the efforts of Lodge, Greene, and others) and the creation of shorter "chapbooks" for the growing number of readers with less leisure and less money than the aristocrats. *The Countess of Pembroke's Arcadia* went through thirteen editions in the next century. Sir William Alexander made additions to the 1613 edition, and Gervase Markham produced a sequel, *The English Arcadia, Alluding His Beginning from Sir Philip Sidney's Ending* (quite literally "son of *Arcadia*," published in 1607 and 1613). Richard Beling in the 1620s and Anna Weamys in the 1650s wrote other *Arcadia* "spinoffs," and many more wrote pastoral romances of their own.

Nor did Sidney's specific poetic influence end with the Renaissance. To cite only two recent examples from opposite sides of the Atlantic, John Berryman famously turned to Sir Philip in composing his Dream Songs, and Philip Larkin produced a marvelous response to sonnet 31 of *Astrophil and Stella* ("With how sad steps, O moon, thou climb'st the skies") in his poem "Sad Steps." Recollecting the energy and vigor of youth, and of a more youthful time in the history of English poetry, Larkin laments his own belated, aged position but also briefly recalls the rapture ("Lozenge of love! Medallion of art! / O wolves of memory! Immensements! No,"), in a fittingly comic yet metrically tight form that might well have pleased Sir Philip. For the late twentieth-century writer, the moon "Is a reminder of the strength and pain / Of being young; that it can't come again, / But is for others undiminished somewhere" (Larkin, p. 169).

Sidney's sonnet ends with questions (only partially rhetorical) concerning the correspondence between sublunary love and cosmic order:

Then even of fellowship, O moon, tell me,
Is constant love deemed there but want of wit?
Are beauties there as proud as here they be?
Do they above love to be loved, and yet
Those lovers scorn whom that love doth possess?
Do they call virtue there ungratefulness?

For Larkin, the gap between the old world and the new has widened into an abyss, and yet he finds quiet acceptance through his knowledge that there remain "others undiminished": the young, and the still-remembered sonnet.

While poets allude, scholars debate—and here too Sir Philip Sidney lives on. John Thompson argues that Sidney's artistry misleads us to look at his writings as if they were biographical; Richard McCoy argues that we can only understand Sidney's "rebellion in Arcadia" if we consider the life. Some neo-Aristotelians and scholars of religion see in Astrophil's decline a moral exemplum testifying to love's corrupting power, while Alan Sinfield declares, "It is difficult to overestimate the impact on the love tradition of Astrophil's explicit rejection of virtue" ("Sidney and Astrophil," in *SEL* 20, no. 1, winter 1980, p. 29). Given that more than four hundred books, articles, and dissertations about Sidney have been published during the past twenty years, interest in him shows no signs of abating. We must hope that students too will find the dazzle and polish, the intensity and comedy, the ambition and the contemplation of Sir Philip Sidney an ongoing delight in an age of so many distractions. If so, the soldier-scholar who helped make writing in English rather than Latin a highly respectable literary choice, who struggled to make his nation part of Europe, and whose work fostered the expansion of the reading audience for poetry and romance, will yet again bridge boundaries posthumously—sallying forth from the world of manuscript and print out across the digital divide.

BIBLIOGRAPHY

I. COLLECTED WORKS: FIRST EDITION. *The Countess of Pembroke's Arcadia* (1598), includes *Astrophil and Stella* and *Certain Sonnets*. MODERN EDITIONS. Albert Feuillerat, ed., *The Complete Works of Sir Philip Sidney* (Cambridge, U.K., 1912–1926, rpt. 1962); W. A. Ringler, ed., *The Poems of Sir Philip Sidney* (Oxford, 1962), includes *Astrophil and Stella;* J. C. Rathmell, ed., *The Psalms of Sir Philip Sidney and the Countess of Pembroke* (New York, 1963); Katherine Duncan-Jones, ed., *Selected Poems* (Oxford, 1973); Katherine Duncan-Jones and J. van Dorsten, eds., *Miscellaneous Prose of Sir Philip Sidney* (Oxford, 1973); Katherine Duncan-Jones, ed., *The Oxford Authors: Sir Philip Sidney* (Oxford, 1989); Katherine Duncan-Jones, ed., *Sir Philip Sidney* (Oxford, 1994).

II. FIRST EDITIONS OF INDIVIDUAL WORKS. *Old Arcadia,* in Albert Feuillerat, ed., *The Complete Works of Sir Philip Sidney,* Vol. 4. (1926), only circulated in manuscript during the 1580s; *The Countess of Pembroke's Arcadia* [The *New Arcadia*] (London, 1590); *The Countess of Pembroke's Arcadia* [*New Arcadia* plus *Old Arcadia,* Books 3–5] (London, 1593); *Astrophil and Stella* (London, 1591), first edition pirated by Thomas Newman; *The Defense of Poetry,* published by William Posonby (London 1595); *An Apology for Poetry,* published by Henry Olney (London, 1595).

III. MODERN EDITIONS OF INDIVIDUAL WORKS. *The Countess of Pembroke's Arcadia* [*The Old Arcadia*], ed. Jean Robertson (Oxford, 1973); *The Old Arcadia,* ed. Katherine Duncan-Jones (Oxford, 1985); *The Countess of Pembroke's Arcadia,* ed. Maurice Evans (New York, 1977). *Apology/Defence of Poetry: An Apology for Poetry,* ed. Forrest G. Robinson (New York, 1985).

IV. BIOGRAPHIES. Fulke Greville, *Life of Sir Philip Sidney* (1652), ed. by Nowell Smith in 1907 and also appears in *The Prose Works of Fulke Greville, Lord Brooke,* ed. John Gouws (Oxford, 1986); Malcolm William Wallace, *The Life of Sir Philip Sidney* (Cambridge, U.K., 1915); Roger Howell, *Sir Philip Sidney, The Shepherd Knight* (Boston, 1968); James M. Osborn, *Young Philip Sidney: 1572–1577* (New Haven, 1972); Katherine Duncan-Jones, *Sir Philip Sidney, Courtier Poet* (New Haven, 1991).

V. CRITICAL STUDIES. Hallett Smith, *Elizabethan Poetry* (Cambridge, Mass., 1952); Hyder E. Rollins and Herschel Baker, eds. *The Renaissance in England.* (Lexington, Mass., 1954). John Buxton, *Sir Philip Sidney and the English Renaissance* (London, 1964); David Kalstone, *Sidney's Poetry: Contexts and Interpretations* (Cambridge, Mass., 1965). John G. Nichols, *The Poetry of Sir Philip Sidney* (Liverpool, 1974); Dorothy Connell, *Sir Philip Sidney: The Maker's Mind* (Oxford 1977); A. C. Hamilton, *Sir Philip Sidney: A Study of his Life and Works* (Cambridge, U.K., 1977); Louis Adrian Montrose, "Celebration and Insinuation: Sir Philip Sidney and the Motives of Elizabethan Courtship," in *Renaissance Drama* 8 (1977); Ronald Levao, "Sidney's Feigned *Apology,"* in *PMLA* 94, no. 2 (March 1979); Richard C. McCoy, *Rebellion in Arcadia* (New Brunswick, N.J., 1979). Alan Sinfield, "Sidney and Astrophil," in *SEL: Studies in English Literature, 1500–1800* 20, no. 1 (winter 1980); Ann Rosalind Jones and Peter Stallybrass, "The Politics of Astrophil and Stella," in *SEL* 24, no. 1 (winter 1984); Gary F. Waller and Michael Moore, eds., *Sir Philip Sidney and the Interpretation of Renaissance Culture: The Poet in His Time and in Ours* (Totowa, N.J., 1984); Jan van Dorsten, Dominic Baker-Smith, and Arthur F. Kinney eds. *Sir Philip Sidney: 1586 and the Creation of a Legend* (Leiden, 1986); Arthur F. Kinney, ed., *Essential Articles for the Study of Sir Philip Sidney* (Hamden, Conn., 1986); Dennis Kay, ed., *Sir Philip Sidney: An Anthology of Modern Criticism* (Oxford, 1987); Arthur F. Kinney, ed., *Sidney in Retrospect: Selections from English Literary Renaissance* (Amherst, 1988); Michael McCanles, *The Text of Sidney's Arcadian World* (Durham, 1989). M. J. B. Allen, Dominic Baker-Smith, Arthur F. Kinney, and Margaret Sullivan, eds., *Sir Philip Sydney's Achievements* (New York, 1990); Mary Ellen Lamb, *Gender and Authorship in the Sidney Circle* (Madison, 1990); M. J. Doherty, *The Mistress-Knowledge: Sir Philip Sidney's Defence of Poesie and Literary Architectonics in the English Renaissance* (Nashville, 1991); Steven W. May, *The Elizabethan Courtier Poets: The Poems and Their Contexts* (Columbia, Mo. 1991); William Craft, *Labyrinth of Desire: Invention and Culture in the Work of Sir Philip Sidney* (Newark, Del., 1994); Martin Garrett, ed., *Sidney: The Critical Heritage* (London, 1996); Blair Worden, *The Sound of Virtue: Philip Sidney's Arcadia and Elizabethan Politics* (New Haven, 1996); Edward Berry, *The Making of Sir Philip Sidney* (Toronto, 1998).

TOM STOPPARD

(1937–)

John Wilders

TOM STOPPARD WAS born Tomas Straussler on 3 July 1937 in Zlin, Czechoslovakia, the second son of Eugene Straussler, a medical officer for the Bata shoe company. With the approach of the German army two years later this Jewish family was transferred to Singapore, and in 1942, as the Japanese advanced toward Malaya, the Strausslers were again forced to flee. Dr. Straussler himself was killed when the Japanese sank the ship in which he was escaping to Australia, but Tom's mother and the children found their way to Darjeeling in northern India where she married Kenneth Stoppard, a major in the British army. At the age of five Tom went to an American school where English became his first language. When he was eight the family moved to England and settled in Bristol. Tom was sent as a boarder to a prep school, which he says he loved, and then to Pocklington School, a boarding school for boys in Yorkshire.

He left Pocklington at the age of seventeen and became a journalist with a Bristol newspaper, the *Western Daily Press,* where he was a news reporter, feature writer, and film and theater critic. Although he regrets not going to college, he regards his experience on the newspaper as valuable in a different way. "When you go to a boarding school," he says, "you don't get to know very much about anything else. Being a journalist is a very good way of getting into the deep end of things" (Gussow, p. 70). He did not wish to spend his life as a journalist, however, and during his last years on the newspaper began to write short stories and plays, including *A Walk on Water,* which was shown on television in 1963. He revised the play several times and it was produced at the St. Martin's theater in London in March 1968 under the title *Enter a Free Man.* Meanwhile, in 1965, Stoppard married Jose Ingle; they would have two sons. The couple later divorced,

and in 1972 Stoppard married Dr. Miriam Moore-Robinson, with whom he also had two sons.

During the period when Stoppard was a young man, the English theater was undergoing a renaissance, with first performances of John Osborne's *Look Back in Anger,* Samuel Beckett's *Waiting for Godot,* and the plays of Harold Pinter, Arnold Wesker, and John Arden. Indeed, in an interview Stoppard later said that "after 1956 everybody of my age who wanted to write, wanted to write plays." And in Bristol there was plenty of drama to be seen. There were three professional theaters, the Hippodrome, which was big enough to accommodate musicals, opera, and ballet; the Little Theatre, which had a permanent repertory company; and the Bristol Old Vic, the oldest theater in England still in use, where a number of distinguished actors played early in their careers and both classical and modern plays were staged. As a theater critic Stoppard had plenty of opportunities to see plays in performance, and when, after moving to London, he became the theater critic of a new but short-lived magazine called *Scene,* he saw 132 plays in seven months.

In 1966 the play that established his reputation, *Rosencrantz and Guildenstern Are Dead,* was given its first production. Its beginnings were not auspicious. Initially Stoppard sent it to the Royal Shakespeare Company, which took an option on it, but the option expired and the play was performed by a group of Oxford students as part of the "Fringe" at the Edinburgh Festival. He describes the conditions under which it opened: "The play was done in a church hall on a flat floor so that people couldn't actually see it. There was no scenery, student actors. The director didn't show up. Someone else filled in. I turned up for thirty-six hours and tried to put a few things right. It went on in some kind of state or other." (Jenkins, *Theatre,* p. 37). A great many productions were shown on the "Fringe," and most of them were not even seen by the critics, but the theater critic of the *Observer*, Ronald Bryden, to his great credit, did see it and praised it as "an erudite comedy, punning, far-fetched, leaping from depth to dizziness. . . . It's the most brilliant debut by a young playwright since John Arden's" (Jenkins, *Theatre*, p. 37). Within a week of the publication of his review, the National Theatre had acquired the rights to the play, which opened to great acclaim in April 1967.

The play is a version of Shakespeare's *Hamlet* as seen by two of its minor characters, Rosencrantz and Guildenstern, who have been student friends of Hamlet's at the university and have been summoned by the king in order to discover what troubles the prince. Shakespeare's play is assumed to be taking place offstage, so that when the characters make an exit from Stoppard's play, they automatically enter *Hamlet* and vice-versa, to the extent that some characters—the king, the queen, Polonius—enter in the middle of a conversation that occurs in *Hamlet*. Rosencrantz and Guildenstern are unaware of what is happening off the stage—unaware of *Hamlet*—and spend much of their time trying to reconstruct that play's events from the fragments of information they can glean. It is assumed that the audience, unlike the two principal characters, is familiar with *Hamlet*, however sketchily, and can recognize how little Rosencrantz and Guildenstern understand. More fundamentally, the two do not know where they are, why they have been summoned, or even who they are; they have, literally, no sense of direction and no idea what their own roles might be:

GUIL: Then what are we doing here, I ask myself.

ROS: You might well ask.

GUIL: We better get on.

ROS: You might well think.

GUIL: We better get on.

ROS: (*actively*) Right! (*Pause.*) On where?

GUIL: Forward.

ROS: Ah. (*Hesitates*) Which way do we—Which way did we—?

1967, p. 14)

In creating characters who are less well informed than the audience, Stoppard creates a dramatic irony that extends throughout the play and thereby makes them seem absurd while at the same time drawing the audience into their predicament.

Many people have noticed that Stoppard was much influenced by Samuel Beckett's *Waiting for Godot,* and while he was working as a theater critic for the Bristol newspaper, both *Hamlet* and *Godot* were produced at the Bristol Old Vic theater in the same season, with Stoppard's friend Peter O'Toole playing Shakespeare's hero and one of Beckett's tramps. Both Stoppard's and Beckett's plays take place on a practically empty stage, "a place without any visible character," which gives no indication where it might be, and the dialogue in both consists largely of short, single sentences. Like Beckett's tramps, Rosencrantz and Guildenstern, having no notion what their purpose might be, devise ways of passing the time—playing language games, tossing coins. The language game reflects their situation because the rule is that it must consist of a series of questions to which no answers are allowed to be given (a game regularly played by children), and tossing the coins disturbs them because every coin that Guildenstern spins falls with the head uppermost. This worries them because it goes against the law of probability, which, like most people, they have taken for granted and which they try (and fail) to explain. They are "kept intrigued without ever being quite enlightened." They are actors in search of a script.

A company of actors enters during the course of the play—traveling players—who suffer none of these anxieties because they do have scripts and are well acquainted with them: "For a jingle of a coin we can do you a selection of gory romances, full of fine cadence and corpses," says the Player, who later explains that their specialty is deaths: "It's what the actors do best. They have to exploit whatever talent is given to them and their talent is dying. They can die heroically, comically, ironically, slowly, suddenly, disgustingly, charmingly, or from a great height." But, he points out, an actual, literal death is not nearly as convincing as a feigned one, because real death is not necessarily spectacular, it is a mere termination of life: "The *fact* of [death] is nothing to do with seeing it happen—it's not gasps and blood and falling about—that isn't what makes it death. It's just a man failing to reappear, that's all—now you see him, now you don't. That is the only thing that's real: here one minute and gone the next and never coming back . . . a disappearance gathering weight as it goes along, until, finally, it's heavy with death."

Rosencrantz and Guildenstern continue to discuss the topic when they are on the boat going to England where, as we know and they do not, they will be executed, but such is Stoppard's wit that they talk about death in the same lively, quick-witted way that they have talked about everything else:

> GUIL: Death is the ultimate negative. Not-being. You can't not be on a boat.
>
> ROS: I've frequently not been on boats.
>
> GUILD: No, no, no—what you've been is not on boats.

The play almost inevitably gives rise to a number of philosophical questions: Is the inevitability of their deaths the effect of chance or fate or choice or divine will? But such questions are not explored very fully. Stoppard simply raises them and allows his characters to discuss them in their usual quick, humorous way. When he wrote this play, he says, "I didn't start off with certain abstract ideas and then look around for a vessel to contain them. [This] stopped being applicable round about the time I started writing *Jumpers*. There the play was the end product of an idea as much as the converse." When he was given his own column on the newspaper in Bristol, he admits, "I was indefatigably facetious," and this inclination to write amusingly about serious subjects continued throughout his early work (*Gambit*, p. 10).

Academic critics tend to interpret Stoppard's plays in terms of their ideas and themes, but he insists that he had no desire to teach anything. In writing *Rosencrantz and Guildenstern* he did not set out to examine questions of destiny and free will but was intrigued by the situation: "The real beginning . . . had much to do with having these two outsiders knocking about the court and not understanding what was happening. Goodness knows why I thought that" (Gussow, p. 90). His later plays similarly grew out of dramatic situations. *Every Good Boy Deserves Favour* began with an idea suggested by the conductor André Previn, who invited him to write a play in which a full symphony orchestra appears in the cast, and *Jumpers* grew out of the desire to create a play in which a troupe of acrobats forms a pyramid and one of them is shot. "Some writers write because they burn with a cause which they further by writing about it. I burn with no causes. I cannot say that I write with any social objective. One writes because one loves writing, really" (*Gambit*, p. 20).

Neither of Stoppard's next two plays, *The Real Inspector Hound* (1968) and *After Magritte* (1970) is, he has claimed, "anything more than entertainment. A friendly critic described *Hound* as being as useful as an ivory Mickey Mouse" (*Plays 1*, p. viii). Both are short and are often played in tandem as a double bill.

The Real Inspector Hound begins as two theater critics, Birdboot and Moon, wait in the audience to see a play. The whole play consists of conversations between the two critics and excerpts from the performance they are watching. Both are parodies—parodies of the conventional language of theater criticism and of popular murder mysteries in the style of Agatha Christie's *The Mousetrap*, which had been showing in London for decades. Moon, assuming his critic's voice, tells Birdboot:

> If we examine this more closely, and I think close examination is the least tribute that this play deserves, I think we will find that within the austere framework of what is seen to be on one level a country house week-end, and what a useful symbol that is, the author has given us—yes, I will go so far—he has given us the human condition. . . . An uncanny ear that might have belonged to a Van Gogh.

The play they are watching is a parody of its conventional form and begins, characteristically, with the telephone ringing and being answered by the charwoman who repeats the words usually found in the opening stage directions: "Hello, the drawing room of Lady Muldoon's country residence one morning in early spring?" The situation is crudely set up to prepare us for the murder. There are "treacherous swamps that surround the strangely inaccessible house"; at high tide it is "cut off from the outside world"; and a fog "rolls off the sea without warning, shrouding the cliffs in a deadly blind man's buff." To add to the suspense, Stoppard introduces another conventional feature of the genre, the radio announcement: "The search still goes on for the escaped madman who is on the run in Essex. . . . County police led by Inspector Hound have received a report that the man has been seen in the desolate marshes around Muldoon Manor" (*Plays One*, p. 9). What Mrs. Drudge (and the other characters when they appear) fails to see is that there is a body lying on the floor. It is not noticed until the play is almost over.

There is an unexpected development when the telephone rings during a pause in the performance and Moon steps onto the stage, answers it, and calls to Birdboot, "It's for you." From then onwards, the two critics become caught up in the action of the play, just as Rosencrantz and Guildenstern are caught up in the action of *Hamlet*. In the denouement, Moon, who is the second-string critic for his newspaper, is killed on the stage by the third-string critic who, posing as an actor in the play, has previously killed the first-string critic (whose corpse has been lying in the floor throughout) and rigged the evidence to frame Moon.

There was a retrospective exhibition of the paintings of René Magritte at the Tate Gallery in 1969 and, since *After Magritte* was first performed in April 1970, it seems likely that the play was inspired by the exhibition. It opens with a bizarre tableau. In a living room, most of the furniture, including an old gramophone with a horn, has been stacked up against the door to the street as though forming a barricade. One of the characters, Mother, is almost completely covered by a white towel; she wears a black rubber bathing cap, and a black bowler hat sits on her stomach. Thelma, her daughter, wearing a long evening gown, is kneeling on her hands and knees gazing at the floor. Reginald, Thelma's husband, is standing on a wooden chair, blowing at a hanging lamp. His torso is bare, and he wears black evening dress trousers and green, thigh-high rubber fishing boots. Through a window at the back of the stage Police Constable Holmes, in his helmet, looks in on the scene. For several seconds the tableau is held to allow the audience to take in the scene. Reginald removes the bulb from the overhead light, and it becomes apparent that it has been held in place by a counterweight, a basket of fruit, so that when Reginald removes the bulb, the basket of fruit begins to move downwards until he takes an apple from it and the lampshade descends. He takes a bite out of the apple and replaces it, thus restoring the equilibrium.

Within this situation, we are told of another bizarre sight. When Reginald and Thelma were returning in their car from a Magritte exhibition, they encountered an unusual figure that each of them describes and accounts for in a different way. Thelma believes he was a footballer with only one leg who was wearing a West Bromwich Albion shirt and carrying a football. Reginald insists that he was an old man with one leg and a white beard, dressed in pajamas, hopping along with a tortoise under his arm, and brandishing a white stick. Inspector Foot now enters with a totally different explanation based on an eyewitness report that the man was a member of the Happy Minstrel Troupe with a black face who went into the theater box office, broke his crutch over the heads of the box-office staff, and ran off with the money which he carried in a crocodile boot.

During the play it transpires that Reginald and Thelma are dressed formally because they are about to go dancing and that the furniture has been cleared away to give them room to practice. Reginald is bare to the waist because his shirt needs ironing, and he wears rubber boots because he has been replacing a lightbulb in the bathroom and the bath is full of water. Thelma is on her hands and knees because she is looking for her shoes, and Mother is lying on the ironing board because she is about to be given a massage.

It is gradually revealed that the one-legged footballer or white-bearded man in pajamas was actually Inspector Foot himself who, while shaving, had hurriedly come outside to move his parked car and, in his haste, had left his face half-covered with lather and put both his feet into the same leg of his pajamas. He was carrying not a football or a tortoise but his wife's handbag. The play ends with a final tableau involving all the characters, all of them in positions as bizarre as they were at the opening.

According to Stoppard, *Jumpers* (1972) grew out of a theatrical image: a pyramid of acrobats and a rifle shot "and one member of the pyramid just being blown out of it and the others imploding in the hole as he leaves" (Hayman, p. 4). At the same time, he knew he wanted to write a play about of a professor of moral philosophy, "and it's the work of a moment to think that there was a metaphor at work in the play already between acrobats, mental acrobats and so on" (Hayman, p. 5). The human pyramid and the shooting of one of the acrobats occurs early in the play together with several apparently unrelated events. It begins with the entrance of the "much-loved star of the musical stage, Dorothy Moore" who attempts to sing "Shine on Harvest Moon" but is unable to continue and makes an embarrassed exit. She is followed by a woman who enters on a swing and performs a striptease. At this point the human pyramid is formed, one member of it is shot dead, and Dorothy Moore is left holding the body. Some explanation is given of these events, though the identity of the murdered man is delayed for some time and the identity of the murderer is never disclosed. They are part of an entertainment held to celebrate the election victory of the Radical Liberal Party, also known as the Jumpers, the leader of which is Sir Archibald Jumper, "doctor of medicine, philosophy, literature and law, with diplomas in psychological medicine and P.T., including gym," and vice chancellor of the University. With the victory of the Radical Liberals a political regime has taken over that denies the existence of any absolute moral values and regards ethical principles as a purely human, social creation that can be altered at will, like the rules of tennis. The effect of this denial of absolute good and evil is demonstrated by the behavior of two astronauts whose presence on the moon is shown on a television screen in Dorothy's bedroom, from which we learn that the space capsule has been damaged and has the power to bring only one of the astronauts back to earth. The two men struggle at the foot of the ladder until Captain Scott knocks down his colleague, Oates, pulls up the ladder, and closes the hatch with the words, "I am going up now. I may be gone for some time," leaving Oates "a tiny receding figure waving forlornly from the featureless wastes of the lunar landscape." Stoppard clearly invites us to compare the two men with Captain Scott, who led an Antarctic expedition in 1910, and his colleague Oates who, injured by frostbite and unwilling to hamper his colleagues, walked out into the snow. The historical Oates performed a celebrated act of self-sacrifice, an expression of that innate sense of loyalty and fellow-feeling that is denied by Archie Jumper and his logical positivist political party. The Scott who betrayed his colleague on the moon demonstrates how a formerly held belief in right and wrong has been replaced by pragmatic self-interest. Dorothy is profoundly distressed by what has happened:

Man is on the Moon, his feet on solid ground, and he has seen us whole, all in one go, *little, local . . .* and all our absolutes, the thou-shalts and the thou-shalt-nots that seemed to be the very condition of our existence, how did *they* look to two moonmen with a single neck to save between them? Like the local customs of another place.

She can no longer sing the songs about the moon for which she was formerly celebrated.

The conduct of the astronauts and Dorothy's breakdown are, however, only two of the many changes that are taking place under the influence of the new philosophy. The parliamentary election has been rigged, the archbishop of Canterbury has been replaced by the Radical Liberal spokesman for agriculture, the university chapel has been turned into a gymnasium, the party has taken over the broadcasting system, and Archie Jumper is planning to thin out the police force and retain it only as "a ceremonial front for the peace-keeping activities of the army."

It is in reaction against this philosophy and its consequences that Professor George Moore, Dorothy's husband, is dictating to his secretary a lecture on the existence of God and his manifestation in the absolute, unchanging principles of good and evil. The dictation of the lecture actually occupies the bulk of the play, which is extraordinary because it consists of a series of complex philosophical arguments and is at the same time very funny. Nowhere is Stoppard's gift for combining the serious with the comic more apparent. Professor Moore's lecture is composed in the style of contemporary philosophers such as A. J. Ayer and is so like the original that it is scarcely recognizable as a parody:

> To say that this is a good bacon sandwich is only to say that by the criteria applied by like-minded lovers of bacon sandwiches, this one is worthy of approbation. The word good is reducible to other properties such as crisp, lean and unadulterated by tomato sauce. You will have seen at once that to a man who likes his bacon sandwiches underdone, fatty and smothered in ketchup, this would be a rather *poor* bacon sandwich. . . . But when we say that the Good Samaritan acted well, we are surely expressing more than a circular prejudice about behaviour. We mean he acted kindly, selflessly—*well.*
> 1972, p. 66)

George is so deeply absorbed in his lecture that he is unaware of the events going on around him. He has not noticed that a murder has taken place in his own house. He describes the Greek philosopher Zeno's argument that "since an arrow shot towards a target first had to cover half the distance, then half the remainder, and then half the remainder after that, and so on *ad infinitum,* the result was . . . that though an arrow is always approaching its target, it never quite gets there." "Saint Sebastian," he adds, "died of fright." He then takes a bow and arrow and sends the arrow over the top of a cupboard, accidentally

killing his pet rabbit. Then, as he steps down from the cupboard, he steps fatally on Pat, his pet tortoise.

For all his absent-mindedness and self-absorption, however, George is more than a figure of fun. He was devoted to the animals he accidentally killed and, when he has time to be aware of her, he genuinely loves his wife. And though his attempt to establish the permanence of good and evil leads him through a series of circuitous, unfinished arguments, nevertheless his convictions are preferable to the ruthless self-interest practiced by his opponents. Stoppard has himself said, "I absolutely firmly believe that what are quite coincidentally known as Christian values are good in themselves and don't need rationalization. I don't believe that telling the truth and not stealing are mechanistic human conventions which we have evolved by living in groups. Some behaviour is good in itself and some is bad in itself" (Gussow, pp. 5–6). Stoppard, privately, agrees with Moore, but Moore is so scatterbrained that he is by no means idealized. Conversely, though the principles of the Radical Liberal Democrats are logical, they are shown to be inhuman in practice.

The identity of the acrobat who is shot dead is not revealed until the end of the first act, when it emerges that he was a philosophy professor named McPhee who followed the logical positivist line of Archie Jumper and his supporters but had recently abandoned their beliefs and "decided that he was Saint Paul to Moore's Messiah," a betrayal that, according to Archie, deserved "an ice-pick in the back of the skull." It may be, then, that Archie was the murderer, but Dorothy was seen with the body, which she hides in her bedroom. With the arrival of Inspector Bones the play becomes a whodunit, but Archie disposes of the body, and Dorothy lures Bones into dropping the charges against her. We never do discover who killed McPhee, nor does George ever finish his lecture, and some critics have connected this to Archie's remark, "The truth to us philosophers . . . is always an interim judgement. We will never know for certain who did kill McPhee. Unlike mystery novels life does not guarantee a denouement; and if it came, how would one know whether to believe it?" Archie has good reason to say this, however, because he himself may be the murderer. But George's belief in absolute moral standards cannot be proved either and must, of necessity, be "an interim judgement." In any case the question of McPhee's murder is of secondary importance. Much more central is the debate between George and Archie.

Jumpers is clearly not a naturalistic play, nor is it consistently a satire, though George's lecture is a parody of a certain kind of philosophical argument. Kenneth Tynan called it "a farce whose main purpose is to affirm the existence of God . . . a farcical defense of transcendental moral values." It is essentially a play of ideas.

Between *Jumpers* (1972) and his next full-length play, *Travesties* (1974), Stoppard wrote several shorter works for radio, including *Artist Descending a Staircase* (1972), commissioned by a consortium of European broadcasting companies. It has a complex time scheme. It begins in the present, moves back in five stages to 1914 and then gradually returns to the present, so the play is divided in the time sequence ABCDE-FEDCBA. The structure makes it possible for Stoppard to create a number of effects: the contrast between the old men in the present and their former selves; the experiences that shaped them and their relationships over the course of time, and the difference between the way they saw things when they actually happened and their imperfect recollections of them. The play was conceived for radio, and its effects could not be created on the stage. The listener hears what is happening but, unable to see it, can interpret it in different ways. This is apparent in the opening when we hear "an irregular droning noise" followed by a series of footsteps and a voice saying, "Ah! There you are," a cry as someone crashes through a balustrade, the sound of a body falling downstairs, and a crash as it hits the bottom, followed by a silence. This series of events is then discussed by two of the characters, Martello and Beauchamp, who are artists and from whom we learn that the falling body was that of Donner, with whom they share a studio on the top floor of a house. The droning, which like the other sounds was recorded on a tape recorder,

appears to have been created by Donner snoring, and the other two accuse each other of causing his death. The mystery is unresolved until the end of the play when it is revealed that the droning sound was that of a fly, the footsteps those of Donner himself as he strode over to swat it, and "Ah! There you are" was spoken by him to the fly. His death was an accident.

Each of the men is a different kind of artist. Beauchamp works with a tape recorder, creating what he calls "a masterwork of accumulated silence" that Donner dismisses as "rubbish." In the scenes set in the past Donner is also an avant-garde artist, creating an edible Venus de Milo: "Think of pizza pies raised to the level of Van Gogh sunflowers!—a whole new range of pigments from salt to liquorice. . . . Edible art is what we've all been looking for." More recently, however, Donner has adopted a much more traditional manner and is painting a portrait in the style of the Pre-Raphaelites. He has come to the conclusion that originality is not in itself sufficient to create genuine art: "An artist is someone who is gifted in some way which enables him to do something more or less well which can only be done badly or not at all by someone who is not thus gifted." On the other hand, "skill without imagination is craftsmanship and gives us many useful objects such as wickerwork picnic baskets. Imagination without skill gives us modern art." In painting a portrait in a traditional style, Donner is making use of both skill and imagination.

Discussions, often impassioned, about the nature and purpose of art are much more central to Stoppard's next play for the theater, *Travesties*, first performed by the Royal Shakespeare Company in June 1974. In a program note for the production, Stoppard explains:

Travesties is a work of fiction which makes use and misuse of history. Scenes which are self-evidently documentary mingle with others which are just as self-evidently fantastical. People who were hardly aware of each others' existence are made to collide; real people and imaginary people are brought together without ceremony, and events which took place months, even years, apart are presented as synchronous.

(in Hodgson, p. 75)

The "real" people are principally the novelist James Joyce, the Dadaist Tristan Tzara, and Lenin, all of whom lived in Zurich in 1917. But the play is also "fantastical" in the sense that there is no evidence that they knew one another and certainly no evidence that they discussed the questions about which they argue in the play. The neutrality of Switzerland allows the three men to pursue their own interests without being affected by the military and political situation in the rest of Europe; as one character says, "To be an artist *at all* is like living in Switzerland during a world war. To be an artist *in Zurich in 1917* implies a degree of self-absorption that would have glazed over the eyes of Narcissus."

In order to link the three men Stoppard presents the action as it is remembered by Henry Carr, an official at the British consulate, but Carr's memory is failing and he tends to repeat himself. Stoppard learned about Henry Carr from Richard Ellmann's biography of Joyce, which he presumably read in preparation for writing the play. Carr was a real person who played the leading role of Algernon Moncrieff in a production of Oscar Wilde's *The Importance of Being Earnest* by a newly formed theater group called the English Players, of which Joyce was the business manager. *Travesties* is full of allusions to and quotations from *Earnest* and the characters frequently speak in Wilde's epigrammatic style, as when Carr declares (in the manner of Lady Bracknell), "Unrelieved truthfulness can give a girl a reputation for insincerity. I have known plain girls with nothing to hide captivate the London season purely by discriminate mendacity." But *Earnest* is not nearly as central to *Travesties* as *Hamlet* is to *Rosencrantz and Guildenstern*. It gives rise to a good deal of humor but does not provide the structural foundation of the play. The main connection between Joyce, Tzara, and Lenin is in their views of literature. Tzara is committed to Dada, or anti-art as a reaction against the sophistries of those for waging wars of expansion and self-interest. Lenin, on the other hand, sees art as a means of changing society and overthrowing the tyranny of the capitalist system. "Literature," he declares, "must become a part of the common cause of the proletariat, a cog in the

Social Democratic system." In complete contrast, Joyce attaches no importance to "the swings and roundabouts of political history" and regards his own work as a striving for aesthetic perfection, a way of conferring immortality on transient events:

> If there is any meaning in any of it, it is in what survives as art, yes even in the celebration of tyrants, yes even in the celebration of nonentities. What now of the Trojan war if it had been passed over by the artist's touch? Dust. A forgotten expedition prompted by Greek merchants looking for new markets. A minor redistribution of broken pots. But it is we who stand enriched by a tale of heroes, of a golden apple, a wooden horse, a face that launched a thousand ships—and above all, Ulysses the wanderer, the most human, the most complete of all heroes—husband, father, son, lover, farmer, soldier, pacifist, politician, inventor and adventurer.
>
> (1975, p. 62)

All three characters are allowed their say, and their opinions are expressed accurately, but Stoppard does not obviously favor any of them. "I don't write plays with heroes who express my point of view," he explains, "I write argument plays." Elsewhere he says, "I write plays because writing dialogue is the only respectable way of contradicting yourself. . . . I put a position, rebut it, refute the rebuttal and rebut the refutation" (Gussow, p. 3). Nevertheless James Joyce's defense of literature is more eloquently expressed than the beliefs of the other two, and it is not difficult to see that Stoppard favors him, if only by implication. "And what did you do in the Great War?" asks Carr, an ex-soldier, of Joyce. "I wrote *Ulysses*," he said. "What did you do? Bloody nerve."

Hitherto Stoppard had expressed no political opinions in his plays, apart from his disapproval of the Radical Liberals in *Jumpers,* and they, of course, were purely fictitious. In fact Stoppard was a member of the Committee Against Psychiatric Abuse, addressed a rally in Trafalgar Square in 1976 on the violation of human rights in eastern Europe and, together with others, delivered a petition at the Soviet embassy. In the following year he visited Moscow and Leningrad with an assistant director of Amnesty International and began to consider writing a play about Russian dissidents. At about the same time, André Previn, the conductor of the London Symphony Orchestra, proposed that he should write a play for a group of actors and a full symphony orchestra, and he was very taken by the idea. "I just loved the idea of having a hundred musicians in a play." At the same time, he was reading about "people locked away in insane asylums for political reasons . . . Suddenly the two things came together. The subject matter seemed appropriate to the form: the dissident is a discordant note in a highly orchestrated society."

The resulting play was *Every Good Boy Deserves Favour*, in which two men—Alexander, a political prisoner, and Ivanov, a mental patient—are imprisoned in the same cell. Both men are at odds with their society—Alexander, who has protested against the imprisonment of men for their political views, and Ivanov, who thinks he has a symphony orchestra that plays intermittently when he imagines it. Both are examined from time to time by a doctor who expresses the official point of view. The doctor tries to persuade Ivanov that he has no orchestra and to convince Alexander that sane people are not put into mental hospitals. At the same time, Sasha, Alexander's son, keeps sabotaging the performances given by the school band by playing the triangle continuously and beating a snare drum so violently that it is punctured. Sasha has a teacher, another authority figure, who tries to persuade him to behave himself and play his part in the band. A parallel is drawn between abiding by the rules of society and playing in the orchestra. When Sasha has deliberately punctured his drum, the teacher points out the parallel: "Is this how it began with your father? First he smashes school property. Later he keeps bad company. Finally slanderous letters. Lies. To his superiors. To the Party. To the newspapers."

Eventually Sasha is sent to his father in prison and attempts to persuade him to lie to the authorities and say they have cured him. This places Alexander in an impossible dilemma. He is forced to choose between his devotion to his son and his devotion to truth. Fortunately his imprisonment has been reported in the newspapers and he

has become an embarrassment to the authorities, who finally work out a formula for releasing him. Sasha assures his father, "Everything can be all right," and the characters join the orchestra, which brings the play to a conclusion. *Every Good Boy* was the most purely serious play Stoppard had yet written. The dialogue is not particularly witty, there are no literary references, and Alexander's extended account of the two months he spent on hunger strike could scarcely be treated lightly. The orchestra plays an integral part in the play and Previn's music underlines the situations and expresses the feelings of the characters.

Every Good Boy was produced at the Royal Festival Hall in 1977, and in the same year a television play, *Professional Foul*, was shown by the BBC on television. It is again a play about political dissidents, but it also has much in common with *Jumpers*. As Stoppard has observed, both plays are about "a moral philosopher preoccupied with the true nature of absolute morality, trying to separate absolute values from local ones and local situations. That description would apply to either play, yet one is a rampant farce and the other is a piece of naturalistic TV drama" (*Gambit*, p. 7). The difference between the two is created by the situation, which in *Jumpers* is palpably fictitious, and by the character of the philosopher. Whereas George Moore is a confused, ridiculous man, vainly trying to put his ideas in order, Anderson in *Professional Foul* is highly intelligent, clearheaded, and civilized.

Anderson and his fellow philosophers are attending a professional congress in Prague, and staying at the same hotel are the members of the England soccer team, who are playing against Czechoslovakia in a World Cup qualifying game. There is a comic episode in which the footballers are mistaken for the philosophers, and Anderson's half-hearted commitment to his subject is shown by his plan to miss one of the philosophy lectures in order to watch the soccer game. The paper he plans to give at the conference is on "Ethical Fictions as Ethical Foundations" and sounds as if it was purely academic and theoretical, but a situation for which he is unprepared radically alters his attitude towards ethics.

He is visited in his hotel room by a brilliant former student of his, Pavel Hollar, who is now reduced to cleaning toilets at the bus station. Hollar asks Anderson to take his doctoral thesis, which is written in Czech, to a friend in England who will translate it into English and try to have it published. Anderson is unwilling to take the typescript because, he says, he is a guest of the government and it would be "bad manners," but this may simply be an excuse. Anderson's real motive may be a fear of being caught with a subversive document. Chatting to the soccer players in the elevator, he warns them that the Czech team may commit a "professional foul" and score goals to which they are not entitled. He then goes to Hollar's apartment to find that Hollar has been arrested, his wife is in tears, and the apartment is full of plainclothes policemen. The police search the place exhaustively but, unable to find anything incriminating, produce a bundle of American dollars. During this episode the radio is broadcasting a commentary on the soccer game, from which we hear that a member of the British team has committed a "professional foul" as, indeed, the police have done by claiming to have discovered the dollars.

That evening Anderson meets Hollar's wife and son, who reveal that, unable to find anything incriminating, the police planted the money and have arrested Hollar for currency offences. The boy bursts into tears. As a result of these experiences Anderson learns firsthand what it is like to live under an unjust regime, and he writes a new lecture which he starts to deliver instead of the one he had announced. "There is a sense of right and wrong," he says, "[which] is individually experienced and it concerns one person's dealings with another person. From this experience we have built a system of ethics which is the sum of individual acts of recognition of individual right." He goes on to describe the effects of this right on the state, "which finds itself in conflict with individual rights, and seeks, in the name of the people, to impose its values on the very individuals who comprise the State. The illogic of this manoeuvre is an embarrassment to totalitarian systems." At his point the chairman, realizing the subversive nature of Anderson's lecture, arranges for the fire bell to sound and orders the audience to leave the hall. Perhaps this could also be seen as a professional foul.

In the final episode Anderson and two other British members of the congress, Chetwyn and McKendrick, are being searched as they make their way to the plane home. In one of their suitcases, Chetwyn's, the official finds some typewritten papers, and Chetwyn's face turns white. McKendrick's suitcase is searched cursorily and he moves on. Anderson is searched very thoroughly but nothing incriminating is found. On the plane home Anderson and McKendrick sit together:

MCKEN: Why did they search you?

AND: They thought I might have something. . . .

MCKEN: What was it?

AND: A thesis. Apparently rather slanderous from the State's point of view.

MCKEN: Where did you hide it?

AND: In your briefcase. . . .

MCKEN: You utter bastard.

AND: I thought you would approve.

MCKEN: Don't get clever with me. Jesus. It's not quite playing the game is it?

AND: No, I suppose not. But they were very unlikely to search you.

MCKEN: That's not the bloody point.

AND: I thought it was. But you could be right. Ethics is a very complicated business. That's why they have these congresses.

At this point the plane takes off. Anderson has committed a professional foul and has gotten away with it.

Professional Foul is about freedom of expression and freedom of information. When Anderson departs from his prepared script he is immediately silenced by the authorities. *Night and Day* (1978) is also about freedom of expression but this time in relation to the press. As Guthrie,a journalist himself, explains, "People do awful things to each other. But it's worse in places where everybody is kept in the dark. It really is. Information is light. Information, in itself, about anything, is light. That's all you can say, really."

Night and Day takes place at the home of Geoffrey Carson in an imaginary African state, formerly a British colony, where a war of secession is about to break out. Three British journalists have arrived there in order to cover the war for their newspapers, and each of them has a different attitude toward his profession. Milne, the youngest of the three, is described as "definitely attractive in a way which has been called 'boyish.'" Having lost his job on an English provincial newspaper, the *Grimsby Evening Messenger*, he has come independently to Africa in the hope of picking up a story. He has a passionately idealistic belief in the importance of a free press. "A free press," he insists, "free expression—it's the last line of defense for all the other freedoms. . . . No matter how imperfect things are, if you've got a free press everything is correctable, and without it everything is concealable." He is treated sneeringly by Wagner, an experienced journalist from Australia, especially when he discovers that Milne went on working after the rest of the staff had gone on strike. "The Grimsby scab," Wagner calls him. Wagner is a great believer in trade unions but Milne regards them with contempt.

The discussion is complicated by the fact that newspapers are full of trivial, sensational stories of a kind Milne quotes from a collection of papers in front of him: " 'Exposed! The Ouija Board Widow Who's Writing Hitler's Memoirs' . . . 'Sally Smith is a tea lady in a Blackpool engineering works, but it was the way she filled those C-cups which got our cameraman all stirred up.' It's *crap*. And it's written by grown men earning maybe ten thousand a year" (*Plays Five*, p. 289). Ruth, Geoffrey Carson's wife, also despises journalists, having been pursued by some of them after her divorce and before marrying Geoffrey. It is not simply their intrusion into her private life that she ob-

jects to, but the style in which the story was written up, "or rather snapped together in that Lego-set language they have. . . . The populace and the popular press. What a grubby symbiosis it is" (*Plays Five*, p. 302).

Whereas Stoppard's view of the characters in *Professional Foul* is clear enough, his attitude in *Night and Day* is more complicated, as appears from the conflicting opinions that are expressed during the course of the play. He himself explained his view of the press during the course of an interview: "The press is a *real thing*, you know, papers are *real things* which you can *read*. And you like some of it and feel that it's important, and some of it you think is despicable but it's the price you pay for the part that matters. And that's all there is to it" (Gambit, p. 15).

When he sets out to write a play, Stoppard is sometimes attracted by an odd or extraordinary dramatic situation, such as a pyramid of acrobats, one of whom is shot, or the combination of a group of actors and a symphony orchestra, and out of the situation the play grows. His starting point for *The Real Thing* was the idea of "a play in which the first scene was written by a character in the second scene" (Gussow, p. 40).

In the first scene Max is married to Charlotte who, as the play opens, arrives home supposedly from a trip to Switzerland. In her absence Max discovers that she did not take her passport and has therefore never left the country. He assumes, rightly, that she has been with another man, but far from being angry with her, he relapses into witticisms and remains entirely calm: "You can slap me if you like. I won't slap you back. I abhor cliché. It's one of the things that has kept me faithful." Charlotte walks out of the house. At the beginning of the second scene Henry is sorting through a collection of records and Charlotte enters barefoot, wearing Henry's bathrobe. We assume that Henry is the man to whom she went when she left her husband, Max, at the end of the first scene, but it transpires that she is actually married to Henry and that the first scene was a performance of a scene from a play written by Henry in which Charlotte played the wife and Max played her husband. According to Charlotte, her real husband, Henry, would never be merely calm and witty if he found she had been unfaithful: "Like hell he would. He'd come apart like pick-a-sticks."

In scene three Max is with his real wife, Annie, also an actress, whom he confronts with Henry's handkerchief, which he found in the car, and accuses her of having an affair with Henry. But his reaction is totally different from Max's in the play. He becomes almost inarticulate:

> It looks filthy. It's dried filthy.
>
> You're filthy.
>
> You filthy cow.
>
> You rotten filthy—*He starts to cry, barely audible, immobile.*

(*Plays Five*, p. 183)

In the next scene we are back in Henry's house, but it transpires that Henry has married Annie. Annie is on the Justice for Brodie committee, a group of people who are attempting to bring about the release of Brodie, a man she met on a train who set fire to a wreath on The Cenotaph, a monument in London commemorating people killed in the two world wars, and then resisted arrest. He has written a play about his experiences, which Annie believes should be put on but which is badly written. As Henry says, "He's got something to say. It happens to be something extremely silly and bigoted. But leaving that aside, there is still the problem that he can't write." Nevertheless, for Annie's sake, Henry agrees to revise and polish Brodie's script, part of which we see when it is shown on television.

Twice in *The Real Thing* Stoppard shows us two different versions of the same experience: Max the actor's response to his wife's infidelity and Max's own response to her infidelity. Similarly we see Annie's meeting with Brodie on the train and the same episode in the play written by Brodie and polished by Henry. "The idea," Stoppard has said, "is that you have a man on stage going through a situation. It turns out he's written it. Then you have the actor in the scene going through the same situation, except he reacts differently. Then you have the guy who wrote it going through the exact situation and he reacts dif-

ferently too. It's quite a schematic idea" (Gussow, p. 40). This idea is repeated in the case of Brodie's play. He himself underwent the experiences depicted in his play, and Henry polishes the dialogue. Donner in *Artist Descending a Staircase* makes a similar distinction: "Skill without imagination is craftsmanship and gives us many useful objects such as wickerwork baskets. Imagination without skill gives us modern art."

The distinction is between "art" and "life," and the main difference between the two is that art is more articulate. Henry is a professional playwright and is preoccupied with words. "Words," he says, "if you look after them, can build bridges across incomprehension and chaos. But when they get their corners knocked off, they're no good any more, and Brodie knocks corners off without knowing he's doing it. So everything he builds is jerry-built. It's rubbish. An intelligent child could push it over. I don't think writers are sacred but words are. They deserve respect. If you get the right ones in the right order, you can nudge the world a little or make a poem which children will speak for you when you're dead." Henry here seems to speak for the playwright who created him.

At about this time Stoppard wrote a play for radio, *The Dog It Was That Died* (1982) and a television play, *Squaring the Circle* (1984). He also adapted two comedies by the Viennese dramatist Arthur Schnitzler, *Undiscovered Country* (1979) and *Dalliance* (1986), and two farces, Johann Nestroy's *On the Razzle* (1981) and the Hungarian dramatist Ferenc Molnar's *Rough Crossing* (1984). "For someone like me," he admits, "who enjoys writing dialogue but has a terrible time writing plays, adaptation is joy time. . . . I really enjoy doing film scripts because you can have someone like Graham Greene invent the story and character, parts I don't enjoy" (Gussow, p. 36).

His next original play, *Hapgood*, opened in March 1988. In his interviews with Mel Gussow he explains how it originated. Gussow reminds him that he once said, "If there's a central idea in the play, it is the proposition that in each of our characters is the working majority of a dual personality, part of which is always there in a submerged state," with which Stoppard agrees "that was the hypothesis which generated the play" (Gussow, p. 78). It is a play about international espionage in the manner of John Le Carré. The central character, Elizabeth Hapgood, works in intelligence, and together with her colleagues Blair and Wates attempts to unmask one of their agents, who is passing secrets to the Soviet Union. In fact the espionage world of agents and double agents is a very suitable vehicle in which to depict dual personalities. The characters have their own private identity and the one they show to others. For example, Hapgood has a son at a boarding school, which she visits to watch him playing rugby, but she is also in charge of a counter-spy investigation and arrives for a meeting carrying some new rugby boots for her son. She is generally known as "Mother."

Stoppard includes a number of references to the behavior of electrons, which serve as a recurring metaphor for the dual personality. Kerner, originally Russian but now working for the British, explains how electrons behave: "An electron can be here or there at the same moment. You can choose. It can go from here to there without being in between; it can pass through two doors at the same time, or from one to another by a path which is there for all to see until someone looks and then the act of looking has made it take a different path. It defeats surveillance because when you know what it's doing you can't be certain where it is, and when you know where it is you can't be certain what it's doing."

Kerner's explanation of the behavior of electrons is a metaphor for the opening sequence in which a series of men, one after another, enter the cubicles of a swimming pool, leaving and retrieving briefcases. This attempt secretly to pass information goes wrong, however, in a way that Hapgood and her colleagues cannot understand until they realize that two of the men are twins. Only in this way can people appear to behave like electrons.

Hapgood resembles Stoppard's earlier plays to the extent that an absorbing plot encloses a philosophical discussion. The spy story is integrated into an account of the world of nuclear physics. Similarly *Jumpers* begins with a murder but develops into a debate about the existence of God, and *Travesties,* which is superficially about an amateur production of *The Importance of Being Earnest,* is more centrally about the responsibility of the artist. *Hapgood,* however, has none of the comedy and wit of the earlier plays, and both elements are extremely complex. Some audiences were simply baffled by it.

Five years after the first performance of *Hapgood,* Stoppard's next play, *Arcadia,* thought by many people to be his best, opened at the Royal National Theatre (1993). It is set throughout in a spacious room in a large country house, Sidley Park, but it shifts in time between 1809 and the present day. These time shifts enable Stoppard to create several effects: the modern characters are carrying out research into the history and occupants of the house, but, having seen what actually happened there, we know the extent to which their findings are correct. Conversely we know what will become of the nineteenth-century characters from the researchers of the following century. Stoppard takes care to document the earlier period with references to the writers of the time, Byron, Scott, Mrs. Radcliffe, Southey, and Horace Walpole, and to the changes in taste in landscape gardening from the classical, formal style to the irregular, "gothick" style inspired by the paintings of Salvator Rosa. Each of the two periods has its own conversational style. The earlier characters address each other in a restrained, decorous manner, but the modern characters lose their tempers, call each other "bastard" and tell each other to "piss off."

What connects the people from the two different periods is their eagerness for knowledge. They lead quiet, leisured lives, pursuing their intellectual interests. Thomasina, the brilliantly gifted thirteen-year-old, establishes herself as an observant child with a natural curiosity when, early in the play, she questions her tutor, Septimus, about the behavior of jam in rice pudding: "When you stir your rice pudding, Septimus, the spoonful of jam spreads itself round making red trails like the picture of a meteor in my astronomical atlas. But if you stir backward, the jam will not come together again. Indeed the pudding does not notice and continues to turn pink just as before. Do you think this is odd?" Septimus explains that since time can not run backwards, "we must stir our way onward, mixing as we go, disorder out of disorder into disorder, until pink is complete, unchanging and unchangeable, and we are done with it for ever." This idea of the irrecoverable nature of the past recurs in the play and surrounds the early characters with a pathos because they have all died, notably Thomasina who, we learn, was burned to death in a fire.

Two of the modern characters are historians. Bernard is researching into the life of Byron, who was a guest at Sidley Park, and Hannah is writing a history of the garden. Among the documents in the library they discover Thomasina's school exercise book where she wrote her mathematical calculations and are astonished at how far ahead of her time she is. The time shifts convey the sense of the irrecoverable nature of the past. During the interim between the two periods the garden has changed beyond recognition, game is continually shot, Thomasina is burned to death, all the other characters have vanished, and their lives can be reconstructed only with difficulty. The title of the play, *Arcadia,* has two implications. On the one hand the people of Sidley Park lead quiet, untroubled lives in beautiful surroundings. But on the other hand the play recalls the well-known Latin inscription, *Et in Arcadia ego* ("And I, too, am in Arcadia"). The inscription is usually found on tombs where the "I" refers to death. The transience of the characters' lives, however, is partially redeemed by their creativity. As Hannah says, "It's wanting to know that makes us matter. Otherwise we're going out the way we came in."

Indian Ink (1995) has close resemblances to *Arcadia.* In both there are time shifts. *Indian Ink* alternates between 1930 and the mid 1980s, with the early scenes set in a bungalow in Jummapur, a small Indian town, and the later ones in a house in the suburbs of London. The pivotal character is Flora Crewe, a poetess who has gone to India in the hope that the warm climate will restore her precarious health, and who, by the time of the English scenes, has died of consumption, but is remembered and discussed. As in *Arcadia* the time shift allows Stoppard to create ironies when the characters look forward to events we know will not happen or try to reconstruct the past but misinterpret it. Research into Flora's life is carried out by Eldon Pike, an American professor from the University of Maryland who is editing her letters and collecting material for a biography. Flora writes copious letters from which we hear long extracts as she writes them in India and further extracts as they are read by her sister Mrs. Swan, to whom they were addressed, and who is helping Pike with his edition. For example, Pike is baffled by Flora's remark that she had "a funny dream" about The Queen's Elm, and he wonders why she should dream about a tree. Mrs. Swan is able to explain that The Queen's Elm is "a pub in the Fulham Road."

Stoppard creates in great detail the India just before independence and especially the minds of the Indians and the extent to which they are influenced by British culture. Flora tells Nirad Das, who is painting her portrait, that she lives in Chelsea, which Das says is his favorite part of London: "The Chelsea of Turner and the pre-Raphaelite brotherhood!—Rossetti lived in Cheen [*sic*] Walk! Holman Hunt lived in Old Church Street! *The Hireling Shepherd* was *painted* in Old Church Street! What an inspiration it would be to me to visit Chelsea!" Yet for all his knowledge of London, Das has never left India. He uses oil paints from Winsor and Newton and reads aloud from Browning, Tennyson, Macaulay's *Lays of Ancient Rome,* and Dickens. He was educated at Elphinstone College in Bombay and, as his son later says, "You only have to look at Elphinstone College to see that it was built to give us a proper English education." Yet Das has also been imprisoned for "taking part in some actions against the Raj during the Empire Day celebrations." Das also reminds Flora that Indian civilization is far older than the European: "We had the Bhagavata Purana, and the Rasik-priya which was written exactly when Shakespeare had his first play. And long before Chaucer we had the Chaurapanchasika from Kashmir." Stoppard says that he wanted to "write about the empire, and more particularly the ethics of empire." He does so not by writing political speeches but by portraying in remarkable detail the minds of the Indians. These include the rajah who has a collection of more than eighty European cars.

Stoppard also creates for Flora the kind of literary background she would have had in the 1920s. She is given a walk-on part in Beerbohm Tree's original production of Shaw's *Pygmalion,* and it was this connection that "brought her into the orbit of Tree's daughter, Iris, and her friend Nancy Cunard, and thence to the Sitwells, and arguably to the writing of poetry." She was offended by an article by J. C. Squire, the editor of the *London Mercury,* and poured a pint of beer over his head in the Fitzroy Tavern. These copious details give the characters substance and authenticity.

Das paints a portrait of Flora as she sits writing a poem, and both are dissatisfied with what they have done. "My painting has no *rasa* today," says Das, and he explains that "*Rasa* is juice. Its taste. Its essence. A painting must have its *rasa,* which is not *in* the painting exactly. *Rasa* is what you must feel when you see a painting, or hear music; it is the emotion which the artist must arouse in you." "And poetry?" asks Flora. "Does a poem have its *rasa?*" "Oh yes," he replies, "poetry is a sentence whose soul is *rasa.*" He tells her he is painting the portrait as a gift to please her. Flora believes he should paint like an Indian, to express himself. Perhaps then it would have *rasa.*

Having created the world of pre-independence India, Stoppard then went on to create an entirely different world, the world of late-nineteenth-century Oxford in *The Invention of Love.* The central character is A. E. Housman who, as well as being a poet, was also a distinguished classical scholar. When the play opens Housman is dying and, appropriately for a classical scholar, finds himself beside the river Styx waiting to be taken by Charon the ferryman to the next world. During the course of the play he recalls episodes from his life as an undergraduate at Oxford and as a young man working for the Patent Office. Another actor plays the role of the young Housman, and this shift in time, not unlike the shifts Stoppard had used in *Arcadia* and *Indian Ink,* allows the old Housman to look back on the experiences of his youth. As in those two other plays, Stoppard re-creates the past in extraordinary detail. Several people from the period—Benjamin Jowett, the Master of Balliol College; Mark Pattison, the rector of Lincoln College; the art critic John Ruskin; the textual scholar A. W. Pollard; the essayist and Fellow of Brasenose Walter Pater; and Oscar Wilde—all appear in person and express their own characteristic ideas. The scholars lament the destruction of the city by the introduction of the railway, the young men enthuse over the production of the Gilbert and Sullivan operas at the Savoy Theatre (the first to be lit by electricity), and we hear of the introduction of a bill in Parliament to make homosexual acts a crime, as a result of which Oscar Wilde is sent to jail.

During an interview Stoppard confessed that he couldn't read Latin but had studied Latin at school, "so it's not gibberish to me. But I read it with cribs." His Oxford scholars appear to be so knowledgeable about Latin literature, especially the poetry of Horace, that he gives the impression that he was a Latin scholar himself. This is particularly the case with the older Housman, who quotes difficult passages and explains where the text may be incorrect. As a textual scholar Housman devoted many years to producing the definitive edition of the poet Manilius, and as a young man he explains what textual scholarship consists of:

> By taking out a comma and putting it back in a different place, sense is made out of nonsense in a poem that has been read continuously since it was first misprinted four hundred years ago. A small victory over ignorance and error. A scrap of knowledge to add to our stock. . . . Reason and common sense, a congenial intimacy with the author, a comprehensive familiarity with the language, a knowledge of ancient scripts for those fallible fingers, concentration, integrity, mother wit and repression of self-will—these are a good start for a textual critic. In other words, almost anybody can be a botanist or a zoologist. Textual criticism is the crown and summit of scholarship.
>
> (1997, p. 38)

There is much talk of Oscar Wilde, his preaching of aestheticism and his flamboyant dress and behavior. Ruskin recalls that when he first came to Oxford in 1836 the word "aesthete" was unknown, though in Germany aesthetics was regarded as a branch of philosophy. But, says Ruskin, "there was no suggestion that it involved dressing up, as it might be the London Fire Brigade; nor was it connected in some way with that excessive admiration for male physical beauty which conduced to the fall of Greece." Wilde's homosexuality is condemned by men like Ruskin, but Housman explains that in classical literature love between men was celebrated as a virtue: "Theseus was never so happy as when he was with his friend. They weren't sweet on each other. They loved each other, as men loved each other in the heroic age, in virtue, paired together in legend and poetry as the pattern of comradeship, the chivalric ideal of virtue in the ancient world." Housman speaks with enthusiasm about the love between men because he was himself a homosexual and loved a fellow student, Moses Jackson, who appears in the play as a likeable young man and a gifted athlete who is fond of Housman but has no sexual feelings towards him. It was in classical times, according to Housman and Pollard, that the love poem was invented: "After millenniums of sex and centuries of poetry, the love poem as understood by Shakespeare and Donne, and by Oxford undergraduates—the true-life confessions of the poet in love, immortalizing the mistress, who is actually *the cause of the poem*—that was invented in Rome in the first century before Christ."

In the year in which *The Invention of Love* appeared, Stoppard received the public recognition of a knighthood. In 2000 he was given the even greater distinction of being made a member of the Order of Merit by Queen Elizabeth II.

SELECTED BIBLIOGRAPHY

I. COLLECTIONS. *The Plays for Radio, 1964–1991,* containing *Plays 2, Artist Descending a Staircase, The Dog It Was That Died, In the Native State* (London, 1994); *Plays 1: The Real Inspector Hound, After Magritte, Dirty Linen, New-Found-Land, Dogg's Hamlet; Cahoot's Macbeth* (London, 1996); *Plays 2: The Dissolution of Dominic Boot, "M" Is for Moon Among Other Things, If You're Glad I'll Be Frank, Albert's Bridge, Where Are They Now?* (London, 1996); *Plays 3: A Separate Peace, Teeth, Another Moon Called Earth, Neutral Ground, Professional Foul, Squaring the Circle* (London, 1998); *Plays 4: Dalliance, Undiscovered Country, Rough Crossing, On the Razzle, The Seagull* (London, 1999); *Plays 5: Arcadia, Hapgood, Indian Ink, Night and Day, The Real Thing* (London, 1999).

II. PLAYS. *Rosencrantz and Guildenstern Are Dead* (London, 1967); *Enter a Free Man* (London, 1968; *The Real Inspector Hound* (London, 1968); *Albert's Bridge* and *If You're Glad I'll Be Frank* (London, 1969); *After Magritte* (London, 1971); *Jumpers* (London, 1972); *Artist Descending a Staircase* and *Where Are They Now?* (London, 1973); *Travesties* (London, 1975); *Dirty Linen* and *New-Found-Land* (London, 1976); *Every Good Boy Deserves Favour* and *Professional Foul* (London, 1978); *Night and Day* (London, 1978); *Dogg's Hamlet, Cahoot's Macbeth* (London, 1979); *The Real Thing* (London, 1982); *The Dog It Was That Died and Other Plays* (London, 1983); *Squaring the Circle, Every Good Boy Deserves Favour,* and *Professional Foul* (London, 1984); *Hapgood* (London, 1988); *In the Native State* (London, 1991); *Arcadia* (London, 1993); *Indian Ink* (London, 1995); *The Invention of Love* (London, 1997).

III. ADAPTATIONS. *Dalliance* and *Undiscovered Country* by Arthur Schnitzler (London, 1986); *Rough Crossing* by Ferenc Molnar and *On the Razzle* by Johann Nestroy (London, 1991).

IV. FICTION. *Lord Malquist and Mr. Moon* (London, 1966, 1974).

V. INTERVIEWS. *Gambit International Theatre Review* 10, no. 37 (1981); Paul Delaney, ed., *Stoppard in Conversation* (Ann Arbor, Mich., 1994); Mel Gussow, *Conversations with Stoppard* (New York, 1995).

VI. CRITICAL STUDIES. C. W. E. Bigsby, *Tom Stoppard* (Harlow, U.K., 1976); Ronald Hayman, *Tom Stoppard*, 3d ed. (London and Totowa, N.J., 1979); Jim Hunter, *Tom Stoppard's Plays* (London and New York, 1982); Thomas R. Whitaker, *Tom Stoppard* (New York, 1983); Tim Brassell, *Tom Stoppard: An Assessment* (New York, 1985); Harold Bloom, ed., *Tom Stoppard* (New York, 1986); Malcolm Page, *File on Stoppard* (London and New York, 1986); John Harty 3d, ed., *Tom Stoppard: A Casebook* (New York, 1988); Roger Sales, *Rosencrantz and Guildenstern Are Dead* (London, 1988); Anthony Jenkins, *The Theatre of Tom Stoppard*, 2d ed., (Cambridge, 1989); T. Bareham, ed., *Tom Stoppard: Rosencrantz and Guildenstern Are Dead, Jumpers and Travesties* (London, 1990); Anthony Jenkins, ed., *Critical Essays on Tom Stoppard* (London, 1990); Jim Hunter, *Tom Stoppard* (London, 2000); Terry Hodgson, *The Plays of Tom Stoppard* (Cambridge, 2001).

VII. BIBLIOGRAPHY. David Bratt, *Tom Stoppard: A Reference Guide* (London, 1982).

OSCAR WILDE

(1854–1900)

Thomas Wright

THE LIFE OF Oscar Wilde continues to exercise a powerful fascination over us. The story of his rise to fame, his imprisonment, and his final years in Paris has achieved the status of a modern myth. Wilde himself viewed his biography in exactly these terms, and so have his biographers. We are also fascinated by Wilde's attempt to transform his life into a work of art and to dramatize his philosophy within it. He was, to use his own phrase, an "artist in life" who tried to envelop every single aspect of his existence, such as clothes and his conversation, in poetry.

Wilde was, in other words, one of the last Romantics. Like Byron, to whom he compared himself, an important part of his work was the creation of his own biographical legend and the fashioning of his marvelous personality. That personality was dazzlingly multifaceted: Wilde was a complex, multiform creature who effortlessly invented and then discarded various identities.

Wilde was thoroughly Romantic too in the way he used his art to explore and express his personality. In his writings he seems to continually weave and unweave various aspects of his character. His protean nature found expression in inherently ambiguous and indeterminate forms such as the paradox, the drama, the parable, and the dialogue, and in criticism that recognized no position as final. The relationship between his life and art, which is complex and symbiotic, accounts in large part for his enormous popularity. In his writings Wilde was able to transcribe his remarkable personality; he also provided us with a biographical context in which to read them.

There are many other reasons why Wilde's name remains "musical in the mouth of fame." His humor acts as an agent of preservation, as does the simplicity of his style, which, despite his fondness for purple prose, is characterized by a fluency and a lucidity that make it a delight to read and relatively easy to translate. It is largely because of his style that Wilde appeals to the general public as well to scholars: it is difficult to think of another author who has inspired as many pop songs as Ph.D. dissertations. Wilde also continues to fascinate artists and writers such as Alan Bun and Peter Ackroyd. He has, in other words, become a living literary and artistic presence and part of the landscape of our imaginations.

The complexity and the ultimate unknowability of Wilde's personality and writings have also ensured his posthumous survival, as every generation has felt the need to re-create him in its own image. Our image, or rather images, of Wilde are appropriately contradictory. To the public at large Wilde is a dandified "prince of paradox" and a gay martyr. To Wilde scholars he is a serious and radical writer who can be compared to Friedrich Nietzsche in his transvaluation of late-nineteenth-century values. The rise of gay and postcolonial studies in particular has had a great effect on Wilde criticism, which recently has tended to emphasize Wilde's homosexuality and his Irishness. Wilde has also been seen as a precursor of various forms of twentieth-century literary theory and as an industrious professional writer who skillfully manipulated late-Victorian markets of readers and theatergoers.

The sheer quantity of recent Wilde criticism suggests that his life and work have a particular resonance in our so-called postmodern period. His interest in surfaces and irony, and his criticism of fixed ideological positions, may give him a special contemporary relevance. This was confirmed in 2000 by the numerous events with which the centenary of his death was commemorated. Wilde would surely be gratified to know that, a hundred years on, he would still cause a great sensation.

EARLY LIFE

OSCAR Fingal O'Flahertie Wills Wilde was born at 21 Westland Row, Dublin, on 16 October 1854. "Fingal" and "Oscar" were the apellations of the father and son of Ossian, the great hero of Celtic mythology—fitting names for a man who would himself become a legend. Wilde's father, Sir William, was a great eye and ear surgeon, a leading Irish antiquarian, and one of the country's first folklorists. Wilde's mother, Jane Francesca Elgee, was a passionate, patriotic, and somewhat theatrical woman. Wilde inherited her dissatisfaction with the everyday world, her hatred of bourgeois respectability, her exhibitionism, and her fondness for improving on nature and reality (she frequently lied about her age and her ancestry). She had two other children: Oscar's younger sister, Isola, whose death at the age of nine inspired his poem *Requiescat*, and Willie, his indolent and rather wicked elder brother.

Wilde was educated at home by a German governess. As a child he explored his father's vast and eclectic library, so that by the time he went to Portora Royal, a boarding school in Enniskillen, at the age of nine, he had already acquired a wide culture and extraordinary skills as a reader. (He could apparently devour a three-volume novel in a half hour and then recount the plot.) At Portora he also became something of a public performer. He told fantastic tales to his classmates and announced his determination to become either famous or notorious: his ambition, he declared prophetically, was to go down in posterity as the defendant in such a case as "The Queen versus Wilde."

Wilde also developed his love of the classics, a passion that he explored further at Trinity College, Dublin, which he entered in 1871. In his four years there, under the tutelage of J. P. Mahaffy, he established himself as a brilliant classicist. During his time there we also find the first significant evidence of Wilde's aesthetic tastes. In 1874 Wilde won a scholarship to study at Magdalen College, Oxford.

As critics such as Davis Coakley have demonstrated, Wilde's years of study in Ireland were extremely important. Notebooks that survive from his Trinity years display an impressive breadth of culture. The education Wilde received at home in Merrion Square, the fashionable quarter of Dublin that his family had moved to in 1855, was also significant. There, at dinners and at the family's "at homes" on Saturday afternoons, he would meet and converse with the intellectual elite of Dublin and continental Europe. This was, he later remarked, the best possible education he could have received.

At a more general level Wilde's Irishness also has been the subject of much critical comment. Scholars such as Declan Kiberd have argued that Wilde was a recalcitrant patriot who delighted in exposing the truths of the English as convenient fictions and who subverted their language with his paradoxes. His entire life and work, Kiberd suggests, can be seen as an extravagant Celtic crusade against beer, the English Bible, and the unimaginative Anglo-Saxon intellect. Although there are certain difficulties with this argument (it is, for example, impossible to define "Irishness"), it has certainly enriched our understanding of Wilde's life and work. Critics have noted the influence of Irish folktales on Wilde's fairy stories, for instance. His Irishness and his social background (he hailed from an Irish Protestant class that was patriotic yet dependent on England for its social power) may also help us to understand his protean personality and his ambiguous relationship with the English.

Wilde always spoke fondly of his four years at Oxford (1874–1878). The university provided him with the perfect background: he wrote much of his verse there and won the Newdigate poetry prize with his poem *Ravenna*; he also fashioned himself as an aesthetic personality. He attended social events in spectacular outfits, entertained in his lavishly furnished rooms, and uttered phrases (such as, "I find it harder and harder every day to live up to my blue china") that were quoted throughout the university.

As well as cultivating his genius for self-publicity, Wilde also developed intellectually. "Greats" (*Literae Humaniores*), the subject in which he achieved a double first, comprised courses in classical literature, ancient history, and philosophy. The notebook and "commonplace book" Wilde kept at Oxford testify to his boundless intellectual curiosity and to a degree of industriousness that he tried hard to conceal from his contemporaries. They contain notes written in a number of languages concerning writers as diverse as Hegel, Baudelaire, and Saint Augustine. Like a scholar of the Renaissance, Wilde makes connections between such authors and effortlessly moves between science, philology, literature, and philosophy. The accessibility of Wilde's oeuvre makes it easy to forget his vast culture; a glance at an annotated edition of any of his works however, shows that that culture informs all of his writing.

At Oxford, Wilde encountered John Ruskin and Walter Pater, two writers who have been regarded as formative influences on him. From Ruskin, Wilde learned that art has a social and a moral dimension, while Pater taught him a less ethical, public, and utilitarian idea of art. In the latter's famous conclusion to *The Renaissance,* which Wilde referred to as his "golden book," Pater propounded a doctrine of enlightened hedonism that Wilde found seductive.

1878–1883

THE influence of Ruskin and Pater is evident throughout Wilde's oeuvre; sometimes it is even possible to hear a dialogue going on between the two Oxford professors within his writings. As Richard Ellmann has suggested, it was typical of Wilde to express, rather than attempt to resolve, opposing doctrines in his work. This is certainly true of the poems Wilde wrote at Oxford and during the three years after his final examination in 1878, and which he published in a single volume in 1881.

Reviewers of Wilde's *Poems* (1881) typically accused him of insincerity and inconsistency. One critic was, for instance, bewildered by the irregular pulsations of a sympathy that embraced in turn Roman Catholicism, puritanism, paganism, Christianity, republicanism, and despotism. Perhaps to warn readers of what was in store for

them, at the head of the book he placed the poem "Hélas!" which opens with the lines: "To drift with every passion till my soul / Is a stringed lute on which all winds can play" (*Collins Complete Works,* p. 864).

Poems also demonstrates the breadth of Wilde's reading. He alludes to so many authors that the act of poetic creation for him seems to have consisted of moving between the shelves of his library and selecting lines to paraphrase from his favorite books. All of Wilde's work has this polyphonic or anthological quality: he was a writer who needed to continually draw upon and echo other authors. In this respect he can be compared to a premodern author such as Geoffrey Chaucer, or to modern writers such as Coleridge or Jorge Luis Borges, who are renowned for being "rotten" with literature. A contemporary at Oxford described Wilde's habit of reciting endless streams of poetry (his own blended with that of other poets), and this, along with Aubrey Beardsley's famous picture of Wilde writing in his study surrounded by open books, might serve as an image of his authorship.

While it is possible for us to appreciate the intertextual quality of Wilde's poetry, his contemporaries used other criteria to judge verse and charged him with outright plagiarism. Such accusations are rarely leveled at Wilde today, but his poetry is still regarded as weak, and Harold Bloom's famous judgment that he lacked the strength to overcome his anxiety of influence is still generally accepted.

At the end of his life Wilde is reported to have remarked that true artists first create themselves, then create their public, and then and only then do they begin to create their work. In *Poems,* and in the various public pronouncements he made at this time, Wilde was fashioning himself as an aesthetic personality and attempting to become popular in this guise. A measure of his success is the amount of satire he inspired in the press and in the theaters.

Poems was thus part of a social campaign in a city that was for Wilde the ultimate stage. He also set about conquering London by dressing in a highly idiosyncratic and dandified manner (he wore a velvet jacket and knee breeches) and by making flamboyant public gestures. He was, however, running short of money. Perhaps this is why, having failed to find employment, he decided to write a play, *Vera; or, The Nihilists* (c. 1879–1880). Although it went into rehearsal in London, *Vera* never opened, probably because of lack of funds. It was eventually produced in 1883 in New York, where it ran only for a single week.

Vera, which concerns a group of Russian conspirators who plan to assassinate the newly crowned czar, is both a political play and a romantic melodrama. Wilde also added a dash of comedy, particularly in the speeches of the prime minister, Prince Paul, who utters epigrams that Wilde would recycle, such as, "Life is too important a thing ever to talk seriously about" (*Collins*, p. 698).

Wilde explained in a letter why he had chosen to blend these diverse dramatic elements. "Never be afraid that by raising a laugh you destroy tragedy," he wrote; "on the contrary you intensify it" (*Complete Letters,* p. 204). This principle of heterogeneity (Dickens called it the "streaky-bacon effect") informs other writings by Wilde. But while on other occasions the mixture is a potent one, in *Vera* the various elements seem altogether incongruous. Prince Paul's urbane aphorisms are followed by Vera's high-flown rhetoric, and the New York audience, unsure of whether to cry or laugh, ended up yawning.

Wilde's failure to have *Vera* produced in London must have contributed to his sensation that he had as yet hardly set the world on fire. It may also have encouraged him to accept an offer for an American lecture tour from the producer of Gilbert and Sullivan's *Patience,* a comic opera in which he was caricatured and which, it was hoped, his tour would help to promote. At the end of 1881 Wilde sailed to America for a year-long tour that would include 140 lectures. On arrival in New York, Wilde is reported to have remarked at the customs, "I have nothing to declare except my genius."

Aestheticism, the subject of his lectures, was a reaction against the ugliness of industrial society. One of its tenets was that art was autonomous; another, inspired by Plato, was that external beauty could purify man's inner being. Using oracular phrases and mellifluous cadences inspired by the Bible, Wilde, the self-styled "professor of aesthetics," propounded such doctrines in his lectures. In "The English Renaissance," a lecture that drew heavily upon on Pater, the Pre-Raphaelite Brotherhood, and Théophile Gautier, he discussed aestheticism in theoretical and historical terms. In other lectures, such as "The House Beautiful," he drew upon Ruskin and William Morris in his consideration of aestheticism's practical application to dress and interior decoration. There was nothing original about Wilde's aestheticism: he was merely popularizing or, according to some, vulgarizing, the opinions of others. What was new, however, was his attempt to combine so many diverse and apparently contradictory sources, and his endeavor to become a living embodiment of the doctrine by, for example, wearing extravagant aesthetic costumes.

Wilde's lecture tour was an immense success. It established him as a household name in America and England, and he sailed back to England in December 1882 with large bags of his beloved "Red and Yellow gold (around $6,000)." He spent some of this financing a three-month stay in Paris, where he decided to reinvent himself. "The Oscar of the first period," he announced, "is dead." Wilde's new persona was that of the assiduous writer who dedicated himself to putting "black upon white." In order to ease himself into the part he dressed in a long, white dressing gown in imitation of his great hero Balzac.

In Paris, Wilde wrote his second play, *The Duchess of Padua*, a five-act blank verse tragedy commissioned by the American actress Mary Anderson. In it, the young Guido Ferranti seeks to revenge his father's death by killing his murderer, the duke of Padua. On meeting the duke's wife, however, Guido falls in love and decides against his plan. The denouement of the play, which involves a double suicide and a game of dice, is rather histrionic. As Wilde said of Little Nell's death scene in Dickens' *Old Curiosity Shop*: you would have to have a heart of stone to watch it without laughing.

The Duchess contains countless echoes from the works of Elizabethan dramatists. Its grandiloquent style is punctuated with the kind of low comic passages we find in Shakespeare. At about this time Wilde is reported to have devoured numerous Renaissance dramas and to have recounted their plots to his friends, conflating different plays and adding his own interpolations as he did so. This may serve as an apt symbol of *The Duchess*, which reads like a compilation of several Elizabethan dramas.

Wilde believed that the play would make him immortal in a night, but Mary Anderson did not share his confidence and rejected it. It was not produced on the stage in New York until 1891, when it ran for only three weeks. Once again Wilde's confection of tragedy and comedy seems to have bewildered and bored the public. At the end of his life Wilde said that *The Duchess* was the only one of his works that was unfit for publication.

1883–1891 (LECTURES, JOURNALISM, AND STORIES)

BETWEEN 1883 and the end of the 1880s Wilde established himself domestically, socially, and professionally. In 1884 he married Constance Lloyd, an intelligent and independent-minded woman, with whom he had two sons, Cyril and Vyvyan. During the early years of his marriage Wilde seems to have been happy; he cared for his wife and delighted in the company of his two children. After awhile, however, married life bored him. In around 1886 he also discovered, or at any rate started to explore, his physical attraction to men. It is widely believed that it was in this year that a young man called Robert Ross, who was later to be Wilde's muse, amanuensis, and literary executor, "seduced" him.

At this late date it is difficult for us to understand Wilde's sexual identity, as terms such as "gay" or even "homosexual" are anachronistic. Critics such as Alan Sinfield have in fact argued that the modern idea of the "homosexual" was developed in order to explain and classify Wilde's tastes and identity. Wilde did not, therefore, think of himself as a "gay" man: when discussing his relationships he invariably alluded to ancient Neo-Platonic types of male friendship. As a result, the numerous attempts to discover specifically "homosexual" subtexts in Wilde's works seem to be of limited value. As Sinfield has commented with regard to Dorian Gray's mysterious "vices," "[they] should be viewed not as the cunning masking of an already-known queerness, but as reaching out towards formulations of same-sex experience that were . . . as yet nameless" (pp. 102–103).

And yet it is patently obvious that, however we choose to define it, Wilde's sexuality exercised a powerful influence over his life and writing. Whether or not, as Ellmann has suggested, it "fired" his mind or gave him the consciousness that he was an outsider and an "artist criminal" is an open question. What is undeniable, however, is that some of his works, such as "The Portrait of Mr. W. H." (1889), do contain those "formulations of same-sex experience" Sinfield speaks of; they were also in part written with a "homosexual" audience in mind.

Now that Wilde had a family, his need to make money was even more pressing. Having learned through his experiences in the early 1880s that it was impossible for him to live on pure literary work, he decided to earn money by lecturing and writing journalism. Between 1883 and 1888 Wilde lectured in towns and cities throughout England. He attempted to "civilize the provinces" by speaking on practical subjects such as "Beauty, Taste and Ugliness in Dress." In addition, he delivered an anecdotal talk entitled "Personal Impressions of America," spoke about theoretical topics to the students of the Royal Academy, and gave a lecture on the life and work of the forger and poet Thomas Chatterton that was, fittingly enough, entirely made up of paragraphs he had stolen from other books. As well as providing Wilde with a fairly regular income, these lectures helped to establish him as something of an arbiter in matters of art, taste, and style.

Between 1884 and 1890 Wilde published numerous articles in periodicals such as the *Dramatic Review*; he also wrote more than eighty unsigned book reviews for the *Pall Mall Gazette,* a one-penny daily newspaper aimed at a middle-class readership. Wilde's journalism is varied in content, style, and quality. It includes chatty pieces on "society" topics, witty discussions of art exhibitions, and caustic and incisive book reviews. Although he was often inconsistent, many of his reviews are informed by his distinctive critical attitudes. In his criticism of novels, for example, he frequently took an anti-realist position. He also repeatedly suggested that earnestness and good moral intentions are not the true basis of art.

Our sense of the overall coherence of Wilde's journalism is heightened by his idiosyncratic style, which was entertaining and imperious. Of one novel he remarked that it can be read without any trouble and was probably written "without any trouble also"; even former mentors, such as Pater, were sometimes found wanting. Other stylistic traits included a remarkable gift for summing up the chief quality of a writer in an evocative phrase and a tendency to imitate the color and tone of the author he happened to be discussing. By adopting a definite theoretical standpoint and by using a style that was essentially a signature, Wilde transformed his journalism into a kind of personal performance.

In May 1887 Wilde became the editor of a women's magazine called *The Lady's World*. He set about transforming a production that he found "vulgar" into "the recognized organ for the expression of women's opinions on all subjects of literature, art, and modern life" (*Complete Letters*, p. 297). He attempted to do this by changing the magazine's cover, its name (to *The Woman's World*), and its content. He commissioned articles on literary and cultural matters rather than pieces on fashion, from interesting writers such as Olive Schreiner, the novelist Ouida (Marie Louise de la Ramée), his own mother, and his wife. He also contributed several long articles on literary matters himself. After awhile, however, his interest waned, and in October 1889 he resigned.

Toward the end of the 1880s Wilde started to write short stories. These were published first in periodicals, then in three anthologies between 1888 and 1891. Having been brought up on Irish folktales and fantastic Gothic stories, Wilde was instinctively drawn in maturity to writers who had a mastery of narrative, such as Edgar Allan Poe. He was also fond of philosophers, such as Socrates or Christ, who expressed their ideas through myth and parable. The evidence of his writings and surviving accounts of his conversation suggest that Wilde's mind characteristically moved from idea to metaphor and then from metaphor to story. To one friend Wilde remarked that his ideas never came "naked" into the world: "I can *think*," he said, "in no other way save in stories."

Wilde had an inexhaustible fund of tales and was without doubt the greatest storyteller of his age. At dinner parties he would tell tale after tale, sometimes for several hours at a time. So famous did his performances become that hosts and hostesses would write "To meet Oscar Wilde and to listen to him tell a new story" on their invitation cards. It is hardly surprising then that most, indeed perhaps all, of Wilde's short stories began life as spoken tales. He also told literally hundreds of stories that he did not set down. Fortunately some of these were transcribed by those who heard them and survive as a rich body of oral work.

Wilde's stories bear the stylistic birthmark of their oral origins. His fondness for repetition and long, colorful descriptive passages, as well as his extensive use of dialogue, are typical of an oral artist. Scholars also have identified many of the sources of Wilde's stories in the narratives his parents published in their two anthologies of Irish folktales and superstitions. Of course, Wilde's short stories have specifically literary sources, such as the writings of Hans Christian Andersen, Gustave Flaubert, and the King James Bible. He was also consciously working within, and in some instances subverting, popular genres such as those of the fairy tale, the ghost story, and the detective story. This ability to blend oral and written elements is characteristic of Wilde. As Pater commented, there is always something of the "excellent talker" about his writings, in spite of the fact that they are also incredibly bookish. Wilde's critical works offer us a striking image of this particular quality of his writing: in them men sit and talk in libraries.

Wilde's collection of five fairy stories, *The Happy Prince and Other Tales*, was published in 1888. Although these stories are extremely popular with children, Wilde also intended them for an adult readership. He described them as attempts to mirror modern life in a form that was remote from reality; to deal with social issues in a style that aimed at delicacy and imaginative treatment. In the story "The Happy Prince" the problem of urban poverty is discussed; throughout the volume Wilde also explores different forms of aestheticism.

The stories are not, however, Aesopian morality tales. Wilde "did not" he explained, "start with an idea and clothe it in form, but began with a form and strove to make it beautiful enough to have many secrets and many answers" (*Complete Letters*, p. 354). He was referring here to "The Nightingale and the Rose," a story which, along with "The Selfish Giant," is, as Pater remarked, perfect of its kind. In these tales Wilde displays an absolute mastery of form and commands a wide range of emotional effects. Stories such as "The Devoted Friend" and "The Remarkable Rocket," for example, contain elements of satire and comedy. Although it has attracted little scholarly interest, the collection has become a classic with the reading public. It was issued in a relatively inexpensive white volume that contained simple and illustrative pictures and designs.

In contrast, Wilde's second collection of fairy tales, *A House of Pomegranates* (1891), is an expensive and lavish aesthetic production. It contains beautiful and largely decorative illustrations, and pictures that were reproduced by an entirely new method of printing. It was, in other words, aimed not at children but at wealthy readers with "aesthetic" tastes and an interest in the book as a total artistic object.

Wilde's style is of a piece with the book's physical attributes. He employs numerous passages of decorative purple prose and long catalogs of heavily jeweled description. The rhythms and cadences of his elaborate sentences echo the King James Bible. "Vermillion-finned and with eyes of bossy gold," reads a typical sentence, "the tunnies went by in shoals, but he

heeded them not" (*Collins*, p. 237). Wilde continued to use the fairy-tale genre to explore contemporary issues. "The Young King" might be described as a parable concerning hedonistic and altruistic forms of aestheticism, while "The Birthday of Infanta" can be read as a meditation on the relationship between art and life.

In 1891 Wilde also published *Lord Arthur Savile's Crime and Other Stories*, a cheaply priced collection of comic tales. These stories are mainly set in aristocratic society, the context in which Wilde originally told them. The story "Lord Arthur Savile's Crime" combines elements of Gothic fiction, the detective story, and the society comedy. At the same time, it parodies the first two of these genres. In the looking-glass world of this darkly comic tale, decency and common sense are close to madness and the maintenance of social harmony and order depend on a hideous crime. "The Canterville Ghost," another story in the collection, also mixes social comedy with elements of Gothic or ghost fiction.

CRITICAL WORKS, 1888–1891

BETWEEN 1889 and 1891 Wilde published in monthly magazines several prose writings that are usually classified as critical works. They are, however, generically diverse, and within individual pieces Wilde also blends elements of different genres. "The Portrait of Mr. W.H.," which was published in *Blackwood's Magazine* in July 1889, is, for example, both an exciting literary detective story and an essay in which a theory regarding the identity of Mr. W.H., the mysterious dedicatee of Shakespeare's sonnets, is put forward. Mr. W.H., it is suggested, was Willie Hughes, a boy actor who played the women's parts of Shakespeare's dramas and who became the bard's great love and muse.

Wilde rescued the theory from an eighteenth-century scholar named Thomas Tyrwhitt, and in Wilde's story this theory is by turns dismissed, presented, developed, praised, and then refuted. Finally the narrator reflects that there might be something in it after all. This kind of game of ambiguity and indeterminacy is typical of Wilde's works, which tend to suggest several, frequently contradictory, conclusions at the same time. Where a conventional mode of criticism would have forced Wilde to adopt a single position, the fictional form of "Mr. W. H." allowed him to have it every way he wanted.

Wilde demonstrated the limitations of conventional criticism in more explicit ways. The subjective nature of any response to literature is emphasized by the fact that Wilde's characters develop the Willie Hughes theory because it is resonant with their personal lives. Likewise Wilde suggests that all theories ultimately depend on faith and a kind of "spiritual and artistic" sense rather than on empirical evidence. Literary criticism is thus seen not as an objective science but as a kind of fiction. This is, of course, another reason why Wilde's theory takes the form of a story.

After its publication Wilde produced a longer version of "Mr. W. H." that was never published in his lifetime. This version is more transparently "homosexual," but even in its original form the allusions were obvious to reviewers who spoke of its "unpleasantness." Wilde was suggesting that Platonic love was the mainspring of the art of a writer the English regarded as a national hero and as a source of moral authority second only to the Bible, so it is hardly surprising that the critics were not amused.

"Mr. W. H." is a bravura performance that, in its imaginative and intellectual playfulness, prefigures the work of Borges. In a way that is also thoroughly Borgesian, it had a mysterious life beyond the page, as it prefigured Wilde's relationship (or at least his idealized conception of it) with Alfred Douglas. Douglas in turn later published his own theory of the sonnets and, most incredibly of all, discovered the first piece of evidence that confirmed the historical existence of Willie Hughes. This is an uncanny case of life imitating art, an idea that Wilde propounded in "The Decay of Lying," a dialogue that was published in the *Nineteenth Century* in January 1889.

Wilde was drawn to the dialogue because it enabled him, as Gilbert put it in *The Critic as Artist*, to both "reveal and conceal himself," to explore an idea from every point of view and to preserve the oral flavor of his inventions. It also suited Wilde's particular cast of mind, as he was, to use Coleridge's distinction, a dramatic rather than a metaphysical thinker. In other words, instead of trying to arrive at conclusions, Wilde was more interested in the process by which thought moved. In a dialogue he could trace the movement and graceful development of a particular thought.

"The Decay" is a conversation set in a library between two men who are mischievously named after Wilde's young children. The precocious Vivian reads out an article he has written called "The Decay of Lying" to the intellectually inferior Cyril, who acts as his straight man. Vivian attacks realism, a literary style then in vogue. The ideal of verisimilitude has, he argues, debased literature, and writers have lost sight of the important truth that art soars above sordid reality and "never expresses anything but itself."

Vivian's aestheticism is, however, not of the ivory tower variety practiced by Wilde's "Young King." He goes on to argue that life and art are intimately related because art contaminates, and might even be said to create, the "real" world. After all, people often emulate their heroes from literature, and the way in which they view nature is influenced by art. Thus, concludes Vivian, "Life imitates Art far more than Art imitates Life" (*Collins*, p. 1,091).

Wilde's position, expressed here by the flippant and audacious Vivian, can be traced back to Romanticism and to more ancient attitudes toward literature. The Celtic race (of which Wilde considered himself a member) believed that the word was a magical agency that created rather than reflected reality. Vivian's creed is also part of the socially radical and fundamentally optimistic element of Wilde's philosophy, in which the real world is presented as a cultural construct rather than as something organic. It is the duty of artists to expose reality as the invention of the powers that be and to encourage people to dream up their own world. It would be wrong, however, to reduce "The Decay" to a set of tenets, as its witty and inherently ambiguous style denies us precisely this kind of simplistic reading. In that sense, its form embodies its argument: like the kind of art it advocates, it is rich and imaginative and difficult to analyze in terms of "content."

Wilde called the dialogue his "trumpet against the gate of dullness," by which he was probably referring to conventional criticism as well as to literary realism. Along with his other critical works, it has been seen as Wilde's attempt to create a space for himself away from both journalistic and academic criticism. During the late Victorian period the former became increasingly vulgar, while the latter became more professional and specialized. It has been suggested by the scholar Ian Small that Wilde was trying to revive a much older tradition of criticism in which an amateur sagelike figure, such as Pater or Matthew Arnold, ranged over a number of intellectual disciplines. The authority of such figures derived not from the institutions they represented but from the depth of their culture and the magnificence of their style. A contemporary example of such a figure is the defiantly amateur man of letters, Gore Vidal.

Characteristically, Wilde went beyond his precursors by declaring that the critic was not only a sage but also an artist. This was the subject of his next dialogue, "The True Function and Value of Criticism," published in two parts in the *Nineteenth Century* in 1890 and later republished as "The Critic as Artist."

Aptly enough "The Critic" might be described as a dialogue with Arnold and Pater. Its original title echoes Arnold's "The True Function of Criticism at the Present Time," an essay in which he defined the aim of criticism as seeing "the object as in itself it really is." Pater qualified this with his argument that before being able to see the object the critic had to first fully understand his or her impression of it. In "The Critic," Wilde took this idea and exploded it: the end of criticism, he said, is to see the object as it "really is not." What Wilde meant by this was that criticism ought to be entirely independent of the art "object" it happened to be discussing. That object, as Gilbert, Wilde's spokesman in the dialogue, explains (and as Wilde himself had previously demonstrated in "Mr. W.H.") is to serve as the starting point for the critic's own creation.

The dialogue consists of a discussion between the remarkable Gilbert and his foil, Ernest. Wilde develops his thesis to such an extent that he renders it absurd. According to Gilbert, by teaching man that no intellectual position is absolute, criticism will destroy racial prejudice and ensure world peace. And yet, while there is a kind of baroque playfulness and self-parody at work throughout "The Critic," it does evince Wilde's genuine awareness that "aestheticism" could and indeed should have a social dimension. Wilde explored this dimension in "The Soul of Man Under Socialism," an essay that was published in the *Fortnightly Review* in 1891 and republished as "The Soul of Man" in a limited-edition pamphlet in 1895.

Here he argues that "Socialism, Communism, or whatever one chooses to call it" (*Collins*, p. 1,175) was both necessary and welcome, for it would create a society in which everyone would be able to cultivate and express their individuality. Under capitalism only certain people, such as aristocrats, artists, and saints, had been able to develop their personalities, and even they had been forced to do so in partial and limited ways.

Wilde's socialist (or, given that he wanted to abolish all forms of government, anarchist) utopia is utterly pagan. In it one imagines Greek and gracious men and women lying around discussing art and eating ortolans. Aesthetics have taken the place of ethics, and the sense of beauty has become the dominant law of life. It is necessary to imagine Wilde's utopia because he never describes it directly. This may be because, as Lawrence Danson has suggested, Wilde was the Socratic gadfly of his age who generally needed to be in opposition to something in order to write. His art was essentially a disturbing and disintegrating force rather than a creative one.

In 1891 Wilde published an anthology of criticism under the title *Intentions*, which included "The Decay," "The Critic," and two other essays, "Pen, Pencil and Poison" and "The Truth of Masks," both of which had previously been published in the periodical press.

"Pen, Pencil, and Poison" is a biographical essay concerning the early-nineteenth-century painter, art critic, forger, and poisoner Thomas Griffiths Wainewright. Wilde uses Wainewright to demonstrate the notion that there is no "essential incompatibility" between culture and crime. He goes on to suggest that Wainewright's insincerity, duplicity, and criminal tendencies actually helped him to become an artist. Of course Wilde may have been joking, but then again he may have been serious. The deadpan tone of his prose, which recalls that of Thomas De Quincey's *Murder Considered as One of the Fine Arts*, gives nothing away. Like Wainewright himself, Wilde hides behind a number of disguises such as those of the biographer, the dandy, and the storyteller. His detachment is also a conscious attempt to treat his subject in the spirit of art. Wainewright, he suggests, is now a historical figure who has "passed into the sphere of art and science" (*Collins*, p. 1,107). To exercise moral judgment in an essay concerning him would therefore be inappropriate.

"The Truth of Masks" was Wilde's contribution to a debate of the mid-1880s concerning the archeological accuracy of costume and stage scenery in the production of Shakespeare's plays. Unfortunately the essay fails to transcend the specific context of its origins and is chiefly remembered today for the conclusion that Wilde appended to it for its republication. "Not that I agree," he wrote, "with everything I have said in this essay. . . . The essay simply represents an artistic standpoint. . . . For in art there is no such thing as a universal truth. A truth in art is that whose contradictory is also true" (*Collins*, p. 1,173). This is an appropriate ending to a volume that is irresponsible, flamboyant, and inconsistent.

Largely dismissed at the time of its publication as showy and vulgar, *Intentions* has since been hailed as the work of a prophet who anticipated various branches of twentieth-century literary theory such as poststructuralism. Terry Eagleton, for example, has persuasively argued that in Wilde's idea of "Language as self-referential, truth as convenient fiction, the human subject as contradictory and 'deconstructed' . . . [he] looms up for us more and more as the Irish Roland Barthes" (*Saint Oscar*, p. vii).

1890–1895

IF, in the words of one reviewer, Wilde's criticism made him "quite newly significant," the publication of *The Picture of Dorian Gray* made him notorious. Like so many of his works it began as a spoken story, which Wilde told in a number of ways before its composition and original publication in the July 1890 issue of *Lippincott's Magazine*.

The origin of *Dorian Gray* is thus similar to that of Wilde's fairy tales. Like those earlier fictions it also draws upon folktales for its central narrative. The hero, Dorian Gray, expresses the wish that his portrait will grow old while he himself remains young. In return for his soul, his wish is granted. This fantastic plot is enough to keep the reader's interest throughout the long short story. In 1891 Wilde added a preface and six new chapters to it and published it as a novel.

Dorian Gray is a typically imitative and multifarious production. Wilde draws upon French literature, the Gothic tradition, the decadent novel, and social satire as well as popular subgenres such as the detective story, the magic picture story, and the melodrama. It is also a characteristically intimate and egotistical work. "Basil Hallward," Wilde famously commented, "is what I think I am: Lord Henry [Dorian's witty corrupter] what the world thinks me: Dorian what I would like to be—in other ages, perhaps" (*Complete Letters*, p. 585).

Perhaps dissatisfaction with the money that he received from the publication of *Dorian Gray* prompted Wilde to turn to the popular drama, the most lucrative genre available to him. In retrospect it seems perfectly logical that Wilde, the greatest conversationalist of his age, a master of the dialogue form, and a man who had been in love with theater all of his adult life, should have done so.

Wilde adopted and combined a number of theatrical conventions and dramatic traditions such as the melodrama, the farce, the burlesque, Restoration comedy, and the French well-made play. His characters are all drawn from the aristocratic English society in which he moved, and the time is always "The Present." Wilde saw English society with the clear-sightedness of an outsider. As Bernard Shaw wrote: "to the Irishman . . . there is nothing in the world quite so exquisitely comic as an Englishman's seriousness. . . . the Englishman [is] utterly unconscious of his real self, [and] Mr. Wilde [is] keenly observant of it" (Beckson, ed., *Critical Heritage,* p. 177). Wilde's representative on the stage is the dandy, a modern version of the Shakespearean fool, who comments on society from its margins. The extent to which Wilde was critical of English society, and the extent to which he subverted the conventions he drew upon, have been matters of great scholarly debate. Recent studies of the theatrical institutions of the 1890s have placed this debate in a broader context by emphasizing the fact that Wilde was not an entirely independent artist.

Wilde's mature plays contain a number of elements that are idiosyncratic. Like his earlier plays they are distinguished by their heterogeneity, as they typically combine melodrama, wit and farce, and sentimental tragedy. They are also dominated by Wilde's personality, in particular by his epigrammatic wit. Wilde's claim to have taken "the drama, the most objective form known to art, and made it as personal a mode of expression as the lyric or the sonnet" (*Complete Letters,* p. 729) thus contains an element of truth.

The actor-manager George Alexander commissioned Wilde's first society comedy in 1890. It opened in February 1892 as *Lady Windermere's Fan,* ran for almost two hundred performances and was published in 1893. The play uses a conventional plot from nineteenth-century French and English drama: that of a mother (Mrs. Erlynne) who has abandoned her child (Lady Windermere) and who in later years seeks her out. The play concerns their relationship and Mrs. Erlynne's attempt to re-enter London society. It is punctuated by a several brilliant interludes in which ridiculous society figures and Wildean dandies enter and utter marvelous aphorisms before exiting again. The following exchange between Cecil Graham and Lord Augustus (Tuppy) gives a taste of Wilde's epigrammatic quality:

> GRAH: [W]henever people agree with me, I always feel I must be wrong.

> AUG: My dear boy, when I was your age—

> GRAH: But you never were, Tuppy, and you never will be.

> (*Collins,* p. 451)

The scene in which their conversation takes place goes on for several minutes and contains no action whatsoever. As one reviewer put it, Wilde thus created a kind of unrealistic "cloud-cuckoo land" out of words and wit.

Wilde was involved at every stage and with every aspect of the play's production. Despite the fact that, when asked to revise one of his earlier works, he had declared himself "unfit to tamper with such a masterpiece," he also altered the play in accordance with George Alexander's wishes. This displays his essential pragmatism as a writer and also his lack of a proprietorial attitude to his work. At the curtain on the first night Wilde made a mischievous speech in which he congratulated the audience on the success of *their* performance.

Wilde's second society comedy, *A Woman of No Importance,* opened at the Haymarket Theatre on 19 April 1893 and was published in 1894. Its plot, like that of its predecessor, was unoriginal. A virtuous woman (Mrs. Arbuthnot) who has been seduced and abandoned by a wicked aristocrat (Lord Illingworth) dedicates her life to bringing up the child of her "shame." That child (Gerald) later meets and is dazzled by his urbane and witty father, who offers him a position as his secretary.

The characters of the play can be divided into dowagers, dandies, and puritans. The latter dress in black and frequently employ biblical rhetoric: "Leave me," Mrs. Arbuthnot pleads to Lord Illingworth, "the ewe-lamb God sent me, in pity or wrath, oh . . ." (*Collins,* p. 491). The dandies, represented by Lord Illingworth and Mrs. Allonby, are given a number of witty exchanges. "The Book of Life begins with a man and a woman in a garden," remarks the former; Mrs. Allonby replies: "It ends with Revelations" (*Collins,* p. 477). It is generally agreed that *A Woman of No Importance* is the weakest of Wilde's comedies. As W. B. Yeats remarked, Wilde seems to rely too heavily on popular conventions.

Wilde's next comedy, *An Ideal Husband*, opened on 3 January 1895 but was not published until 1899. Its plot, which was derived from the masters of the "well-made play," concerns an attempt to blackmail a politician, Sir Robert Chiltern, who at the start of his career made a great deal of money by selling a cabinet secret. In the course of the play Lord Goring, one of Wilde's most entertaining dandies, rescues Sir Robert. Everything thus ends happily, but only after Wilde has exposed the hypocrisy and corruption at the heart of the English establishment. This radical element was recognized by Bernard Shaw and has been commented upon by modern critics such as Regina Gagnier.

Wilde's fourth comedy, *The Importance of Being Earnest*, is widely regarded as his masterpiece. It was performed on 14 February 1895 and published in 1899. Wilde's sources range from long-since-forgotten popular comedies and farces of the 1890s to Menander and Shakespeare. The plot concerns two brothers who discover their true relationship and succeed in marrying the women they love.

Earnest is an incisive satire of Victorian society in which Wilde mocks religion, education, marriage, the family, private property, and every society ritual dear to the upper classes. In a way that prefigures the theater of the absurd, he also demonstrates the insanity of rational and putatively normal behavior. Yet Wilde's satire is tempered by his hilarious wit and by the fact that *Earnest* is at heart an optimistic play. Its universe is an enchanted place in which words such as truth and falsehood can be easily interchanged and in which reality can be banished with a few epigrams. The characters treat all the trivial things of life very seriously, and all the serious things of life with sincere and studied triviality; they also effortlessly invent and reinvent their personalities. It is, in other words, Wilde's Eden or Utopia.

The play makes no concession to reality in stylistic terms. It is a brilliant and burnished globe of artifice entirely built out of marvelous words. As W. H. Auden noted, it has a distinctly musical quality. After awhile the voices of the characters begin to resemble the different instruments of an orchestra, and their exquisitely trivial utterances, entirely divested of signifying force, start to sound like music. Pater once wrote that all the arts aspire to the condition of music: a form in which style and substance are one. *Earnest* actually achieves that status: in its lightness, playfulness, and iridescent humor Wilde's delicate bubble of fancy is reminiscent of a Mozart opera.

Writing in the *World,* William Archer declared himself charmed and bewildered by Wilde's musical extravaganza. "What can a poor critic do," he asked, "with a play which . . . imitates nothing, represents nothing, means nothing [and is] nothing . . . but an absolutely willful expression of an irrepressibly witty personality?" (*Critical Heritage,* p. 190). Subsequent critics have taken up his challenge by teasing out a number of political and homosexual meanings from the play. *Earnest* is now generally regarded as the finest, and certainly the funniest, comedy of the nineteenth century.

In 1891, when Wilde was embarking on his career as a popular dramatist, he also wrote *Salomé,* a symbolist play in French. In it he blends biblical elements with effects from the various writers and artists who had been inspired by the legend such as Flaubert, Joris-Karl Huysmans, and Gustave Moreau. The result is a drama that reads like a cross between a mystery play, a decadent French poem, and a critical essay on Wilde's sources.

At the time of its composition Wilde did not envisage producing the play, but when the actress Sarah Bernhardt expressed interest in taking the lead, it went into rehearsal in London. To Wilde's outrage the Lord Chamberlain refused the production a license on the grounds that it dealt with a biblical subject. In the event, it was never produced in England in Wilde's lifetime, although it was premiered in Paris in 1896. After having been corrected by a number of Wilde's French friends, the play was published in London and Paris in 1893. Alfred Douglas's less than satisfactory English translation was published in 1894 in a beautiful volume illustrated by Aubrey Beardsley. Like *Earnest, Salomé* has been described as a musical drama, and it is thus entirely fitting that Richard Strauss should have used it as the basis of his famous opera. It contains refrains and recurring phrases that, as Wilde remarked, bind it together like a piece of music; it also moves toward its terrible climax with the inevitability of a musical theme. On its publication in 1893 the play repulsed certain reviewers; others dismissed it as slight and derivative. Recent scholarly attention and a number of brilliant productions have, however, revived interest in the play.

Salomé was clearly aimed at a more avant-garde audience than the one that flocked to Wilde's social comedies. Wilde referred to this audience of fellow artists and forward-thinking critics as the "elect." Between 1890 and 1895 Wilde wrote a number of other works with the "elect" in mind. Some of these, such as *La Sainte Courtisane*, a play written in the style of *Salomé*, and *A Florentine Tragedy,* a Renaissance drama, survive only in fragmentary form.

Wilde did manage to complete other coterie writings, however, and to publish them in exclusive limited editions or in magazines. His decadent poem *The Sphinx*, which is written in his lush, ornamental manner, was issued in 1894 in a handsome edition of 225 copies illustrated by Charles Ricketts. In 1895 Arthur Humphreys published *Oscariana*, a limited edition of Wilde's epigrams. It was the first of many such publications which have had the unfortunate effect of establishing Wilde's popular reputation as a witty but intellectually lightweight epigrammatist.

In 1893 and 1894 Wilde published several *Poems in Prose*. These works, which are among his most interesting and most neglected, are written versions of the kind of parable or philosophical short story that Wilde used to narrate in company. Composed in a luxurious biblical style and generally dealing with religious subjects, they can be read as part of Wilde's audacious attempt to rewrite the King James Bible. "The Master," for instance, is Wilde's interpolation to the story of the Passion. These short works, which are essentially epigrams extended to the length of anecdotes, are thus, along with *Salomé*, fragments of Wilde's apocryphal gospel. One, as it were, genuinely apocryphal work, can be mentioned in passing. *Teleny* (1893) is a homo-erotic novel that Wilde is said to have contributed to, but which few scholars regard as part of the Wilde canon.

1895–1900

FOLLOWING the succès de scandale of *Dorian Gray* and the popularity of his social comedies, Wilde became one of the first great mass-media personalities. He was frequently caricatured on the stage and in newspapers and fictional works, such as Robert Hichens's witty *The Green Carnation* (1894), a thinly veiled fictional evocation of Wilde's relationship with Alfred Douglas ("Bosie").

Wilde was to pay an enormous price for his association with Bosie when he became involved in a quarrel between him and his father, the marquess of Queensberry. Queensberry publicly insulted Wilde by leaving a card at Wilde's club with the words "To Oscar Wilde posing Somdomite [sic]." Egged on by Bosie, Wilde decided to prosecute Queensberry for libel.

As Queensberry had amassed a great deal of evidence that leant credence to his accusation (he had rounded up a number of the "rent boys" [young male prostitutes] with whom Wilde and Bosie had associated), Wilde lost his case. He was then arrested, found guilty of acts of "gross indecency," and sentenced to two years' hard labor on 25 May 1895. Wilde's sufferings in prison were terrible. With little contact with the outside world and, for most of his sentence, without books or writing materials, both Wilde and his friends feared that he was becoming insane.

In Reading Gaol toward the end of his sentence in 1897, Wilde was allowed to write his longest and most famous letter. It was posthumously published in an abridged form in 1905 under the title *De Profundis* by Wilde's literary executor, Robert Ross. The letter has an ambiguous status within the Wilde canon, as it is at once a private communication to Bosie and a highly wrought work of art. There can be no doubt, however, that Wilde regarded it as something more than a personal letter; all the evidence suggests that he also envisaged its posthumous publication.

The letter is roughly divided into three main sections. The first and third read like one side of an impassioned conversation between Wilde and Bosie. Wilde gives a partial account of their "ill-fated and most lamentable friendship" and accuses Bosie of bringing him to a state of ethical, physical, and financial ruin. The second part is a philosophical meditation on the nature of suffering, and in particular the character and teachings of Christ.

Unsurprisingly Wilde's idea of Christ is extremely unconventional. His Christ is a man whose life was the most "wonderful of poems" and who, with sublime paradoxes and subtle parables not unlike Wilde's own, preached a creed of individualism, tolerance, and joy. An antinomian in the sphere of ethics, and a marvelous artist in life, Christ is for Wilde a precursor of the Romantics. Wilde takes a more orthodox Christian position, however, when he embraces suffering as a means of self-realization.

It is impossible to read the letter without imagining the terrible school, as Wilde put it, in which he was sitting at his task. In its concentration on the past, its frequent references to delicious food and drink, and in the very luxuriance of its purple prose, the letter is typical of prison literature. And yet, even though Wilde necessarily cannot transcend the conditions in which he writes, his letter represents a heroic and quintessentially Wildean victory of art over life.

Wilde succeeds in shaping his life into a coherent and resonant legend. Borrowing thematic elements from Greek tragedy, folklore, and his own fairy tales, and using stylistic effects from his prose poems and fictions, he presents his biography as a wonderful myth. He emerges from the letter as a kind of composite of mythical figures such as Christ, Socrates, Faust, and Hamlet. In this way Wilde transformed his biography into what Max Beerbohm called "one of the tragedies that will live always in romantic history" (*Critical Heritage,* p. 251) and effectively fixed his image for all time.

In a passage in his great prison letter Wilde expresses the hope that he will be able to write after his release in May 1897. Wilde did succeed in writing one more long poem, *The Ballad of Reading Gaol* (1898), in which he describes an execution that had taken place during his incarceration. The condemned man was a soldier who in a fit of jealousy had murdered his wife. For Wilde his crime is symbolic of the crime committed by all men: that of "killing the thing" they love. This phrase has many possible meanings but most obviously refers to the way in which people murder their own souls. The idea is expressed in one of the poem's most famous stanzas:

Yet each man kills the thing he loves,
By each let this be heard,
Some do it with a bitter look,
Some with a flattering word,
The coward does it with a kiss,
The Brave man with a sword!

(*Collins*, p. 884)

As Wilde commented, the poem "suffers under the difficulty of a divided aim in style. Some is realistic, some is romantic: some poetry, some propaganda" (*Complete Letters*, p 956). The realistic parts of the poem concern prison life and the condemned man's experiences; the romantic stanzas contrast man's "grim justice" with Christ's forgiveness. The propagandist sections, in which Wilde condemns the prison system, can be compared to the two letters concerning prison reform he wrote to the newspapers in 1897 and 1898.

In its didacticism and in its realistic flavor *The Ballad* is an uncharacteristic work. Wilde remarked that the poem constituted a denial of his philosophy of art. Certain elements of the poem are, however, typically Wildean. In its composition he imitated—some would say plagiarized—a number of poets such as Coleridge and A. E. Housman. In spite of the fact that it was published pseudonymously as the work of "C.3.3" (Wilde's cell number at Reading), Wilde's personality permeates the poem and indeed lends it coherence. It also has a typically oral quality and, like many traditional ballads, it demands to be read aloud.

At its best *The Ballad* is a remarkably powerful poem. It was very favorably reviewed and went through countless editions. Unfortunately its success did not inspire Wilde to further literary efforts. Although he did revise two of his plays, *An Ideal Husband* and *Earnest*, for publication in 1899, he effectively ceased to write after the composition of his poem. There are a number of reasons for this, the most obvious of which is the fact that Wilde had been broken physically and mentally by his imprisonment.

Wilde spent the last three years of life journeying through the boulevards of Paris and further afield, paying strangers for the drinks they bought him with the only currency he had left—his jokes and his marvelous tales. He also wrote countless letters, some of which are addressed to his friends and some of which are addressed to posterity. On 30 November 1900 nature finally got her revenge on the man who had mocked her so mercilessly, and Wilde died in his hotel on the Left Bank in Paris. Right up to the end he laughed and joked with his friends, and at the very last moment converted to Catholicism.

CONCLUSION

In its obituary, the *Pall Mall Gazette* dismissed Wilde as an insubstantial figure and predicted that nothing he wrote would have the strength to endure. Curiously enough many of Wilde's friends agreed. They regarded his writings as a pale reflection of his conversation and thought that they were not great enough to stand by themselves without his remarkable personality behind them.

They were of course completely mistaken in their evaluation of writings that are now firmly established within the literary canon. They were also wrong to suppose that Wilde's charismatic personality would not survive the death of his body. For Wilde is almost as immediate to us as he was to his contemporaries. The posthumous survival of Wilde's personality has been ensured by the countless memoirs and biographies that have been written about him, and most of all by the publication of *The Letters of Oscar Wilde* (1962). Like the letters of Keats, Wilde's give us the illusion that we actually know their author; in terms of style and occasionally theme, they resemble and sometimes even equal his "creative" works.

At the beginning of this essay Wilde's particular relevance to our time was mentioned. When the great sensation that he has recently caused dies down and when he is no longer so fashionable in academia, Wilde will doubtless become a less prominent figure. It is, however, unlikely that his ghost will ever return to the obscure shades that it occupied, for example, in the period 1920–1950, when he was still regarded as a pervert and a superficial writer. This is because attitudes toward homosexuality have changed and because he is now established as a versatile and serious, or at least seriously trivial, author. In addition, it is due to the fact that his greatest works, the interest in his personality, and the fascination of the relationship between them, will endure. Finally, it also has something to do with the fact that Wilde remains something of an enigma. Wilde himself would no doubt have been delighted by this, as he knew that, as far as posterity was concerned, "To be great is to be misunderstood."

SELECTED BIBLIOGRAPHY

I. Collected Works. *Collected Works of Oscar Wilde,* 14 vols., ed. by Robert Ross (London, 1908); *The Artist as Critic: Critical Writings of Oscar Wilde*, ed. by Richard Ellmann (New York, 1969); *Oscar Wilde: The Complete Shorter Fiction*, ed. by I. Murray (Oxford, 1979); *The Writings of Oscar Wilde*, ed. by I. Murray (Oxford, 1989); *Collins Complete Works of Oscar Wilde, Centenary Edition* (London, 1999); *Oscar Wilde: Complete Poetry*, ed. by I. Murray (Oxford, 1997); *Poems and Poems in Prose,* ed. by Karl Beckson and Bobby Fong (Oxford, 2000), vol. 1 of *The Complete Works of Oscar Wilde,* general eds. Russell Jackson and Ian Small, with other volumes forthcoming.

II. Individual Works. *Ravenna* (Oxford, 1878); *Vera; or, The Nihilists* (London, 1880); *Poems* (London, 1881; Boston, 1882); *The Duchess of Padua* (London?, 1883); *The Happy Prince and Other Tales* (London, 1888); *The Picture of Dorian Gray* (London and New York, 1891), ed. by Donald L. Lawler (London and New York, 1988); *Intentions* (London, 1891; New York, 1894); *Lord Arthur Savile's Crime and Other Stories* (London and New York, 1891); *A House of Pomegranates* (London, 1891; New York 1892); *Salomé* (London and Paris, 1893), ed. by P. Aquien (French and English versions, Paris, 1993); *Lady Windermere's Fan* (London, 1893), ed. by Ian Small (London, 1980; rev. ed., 1999); *Salome,* English trans. (London, 1894); *The Sphinx* (London, 1894); *A Woman of No Importance* (London,

1894), ed. by Ian Small (London, 1983; rev. ed. 1993); *The Soul of Man* (London, 1895); *Oscariana* (London, 1895); *The Ballad of Reading Gaol* (London, 1898; New York, 1899); *The Importance of Being Earnest* (London, 1899), ed. by Russell Jackson (London, 1980); *An Ideal Husband* (London, 1899), ed. by Russell Jackson (London, 1983; rev. ed., 1993); *De Profundis* (London, 1905), in *The Complete Letters of Oscar Wilde*, ed. by Merlin Holland and Rupert Hart-Davis (London, 2000).

III. Letters. *The Complete Letters of Oscar Wilde*, ed. by Merlin Holland and Rupert Hart-Davis (London, 2000); *Selected Letters of Oscar Wilde*, ed. by Rupert Hart-Davis (Oxford and New York, 1979).

IV. Biographies. Frank Harris, *Oscar Wilde: His Life and Confessions* (New York, 1916); Vincent O'Sullivan, *Aspects of Wilde* (London and New York, 1936); Hesketh Pearson, *The Life of Oscar Wilde* (London, 1946); H. M. Hyde, *The Trials of Oscar Wilde* (London, 1948); E. H. Mikhail, ed., *Oscar Wilde: Interviews and Recollections* (London and New York, 1979); Richard Ellmann, *Oscar Wilde* (London, 1987; New York, 1988); Norman Page, *An Oscar Wilde Chronology* (London and Boston, 1991); Davis Coakley, *Oscar Wilde: The Importance of Being Irish* (Dublin, 1994); Merlin Holland, *The Wilde Album* (London, 1997; New York, 1998); Simon Callow, *Oscar Wilde and His Circle* (London, 2000).

V. Critical Studies. Arthur Ransome, *Oscar Wilde. A Critical Study* (London, 1912); Holbrook Jackson, *The Eighteen Nineties: A Review of Art and Ideas at the Close of the Nineteenth Century* (London and New York, 1913); Richard Ellmann, ed., *Oscar Wilde: A Collection of Critical Essays* (Englewood Cliffs, N.J., 1969); Karl Beckson, ed. *Oscar Wilde: The Critical Heritage* (London and New York, 1970); Rodney Shewan, *Oscar Wilde: Art and Egotism* (London and New York, 1977); Reginia Gagnier, *Idylls of the Marketplace: Oscar Wilde and the Victorian Public* (Stanford, Calif., 1986); Peter Raby, *Oscar Wilde* (Cambridge and New York, 1988); Norbert Kohl, *Oscar Wilde: The Works of a Conformist Rebel* (Cambridge and New York, 1989); Philip E. Smith 2d and Michael S. Helfand, *Oscar Wilde's Oxford Notebooks: A Portrait of a Mind in the Making* (Oxford and New York, 1989).

Margery Morgan, ed., *File on Wilde* (London and Portsmouth, N.H., 1990); Kerry Powell, *Oscar Wilde and the Theatre of the 1890s* (Cambridge and New York, 1990); Ian Small, *Conditions for Criticism: Authority, Knowledge, and Literature in the Late Nineteenth Century* (Oxford, 1991); Donald Mead, ed., *The Wildean: The Journal of The Oscar Wilde Society* (1992–); Ian Small, *Oscar Wilde: Recent Research* (Greensboro, N.C., 1993, 2000); Ian Small, *Oscar Wilde Revalued* (Greensboro, N.C., 1993); C. George Sandulescu, ed., *Rediscovering Oscar Wilde* (Gerrards Cross, U.K., 1994). Alan Sinfield, *The Wilde Century* (London and New York, 1994); Sos Eltis, *Revising Wilde: Society and Subversion in the Plays of Oscar Wilde* (Oxford, 1996); Jonathan Freedman, ed., *Oscar Wilde: A Collection of Critical Essays* (Upper Saddle River, N.J., 1996); J. Stokes, *Myths, Miracles, and Imitations* (Cambridge, 1996). Lawrence Danson, *Wilde's Intentions: The Artist in His Criticism* (Oxford and New York, 1997); Peter Raby, ed., *The Cambridge Companion to Oscar Wilde* (Cambridge and New York, 1997); Karl Beckson, *The Oscar Wilde Encyclopedia* (New York, 1998); Jerusha McCormack, ed., *Wilde the Irishman* (London and New Haven, Conn., 1998); Nicholas Frankel, *Oscar Wilde's Decorated Books*. (Michigan, 2000); Josephine M. Guy and Ian Small, *Oscar Wilde's Profession: Writing and the Culture Industry in the Late Nineteenth Century* (Oxford and New York, 2000); Thomas Wright, ed., *Table Talk / Oscar Wilde: Wilde's spoken stories* (London, 2000).

VI. Fictional Works Relating To Wilde. Robert Smythe Hichens, *The Green Carnation* (London and New York, 1894); Laurence Housman, *Echo de Paris* (London, 1923; New York, 1924); Micheál Mac Liammóir, *The Importance of Being Oscar* (Dublin, 1963); Tom Stoppard, *Travesties* (London and New York, 1975); Peter Ackroyd, *The Last Testament of Oscar Wilde* (London and New York, 1983); Terry Eagleton, *Saint Oscar* (Derry, 1989); C. Robert Holloway, *The Unauthorized Letters of Oscar Wilde* (New York, 1997); David Hare, *The Judas Kiss* (London and New York, 1998).

VII. Bibliography. E. H. Mikhail, *Oscar Wilde: An Annotated Bibliography of Criticism* (London and Totowa, N.J., 1978).

MASTER INDEX

The following index covers the entire British Writers series through Retrospective Supplement II. All references include volume numbers in boldface Roman numerals followed by page numbers within that volume. Subjects of articles are indicated by boldface type.

A. *Couleii Plantarum Libri Duo* (Cowley), **II:** 202

A la recherche du temps perdu (Proust), **Supp. IV:** 126, 136

A Laodicean (Hardy), **Retro. Supp. I:** 112, 114

"A Propos of Lady Chatterley's Lover" (Lawrence), **IV:** 106; **VII:** 91

"Aaron" (Herbert), **Retro. Supp. II:** 179

Aaron's Rod (Lawrence), **VII:** 90, 94, 106–107; **Retro. Supp. II:** 230

Abaft the Funnel (Kipling), **VI:** 204

"Abasement of the Northmores, The" (James), **VI:** 69

"Abbé Delille and Walter Landor, The" (Landor), **IV:** 88*n*, 92–93

Abbess of Crewe, The (Spark), **Supp. I:** 200, 201, 210

"Abbey Mason, The" (Hardy), **Retro. Supp. I:** 119

Abbey Theatre, **VI:** 212, 218, 307, 309, 316; **VII:** 3, 6, 11

Abbey Walk, The (Henryson), **Supp. VII:** 146, 147

Abbot, The (Scott), **IV:** 39

Abbott, C. C., **V:** 379, 381

ABC Murders, The (Christie), **Supp. II:** 128, 130, 135

"ABC of a Naval Trainee" (Fuller), **Supp. VII:** 69

"Abomination, The" (Murray), **Supp. VII:** 273

Abyssophone (Redgrove), **Supp. VI:** 236

Abdelazer; or, The Moor's Revenge (Behn), **Supp. III:** 27, 36

Abercrombie, Lascelles, **II:** 247

"Abiding Vision, The" (West), **Supp. III:** 442

Abinger Harvest (Forster), **VI:** 411, 412; **Supp. II:** 199, 223

"Abject Misery" (Kelman), **Supp. V:** 244

Ableman, Paul, **Supp. IV:** 354

Abolition of Man, The (Lewis), **Supp. III:** 248, 255, 257

Abortive (Churchill), **Supp. IV:** 181

About the House (Auden), **Retro. Supp. I:** 13

"About Two Colmars" (Berger), **Supp. IV:** 85

"Above the Dock" (Hulme), **Supp. VI:** 134, 136

Abridgement of the History of England, An (Goldsmith), **III:** 191

Abridgement of the Light of Nature Pursued, An (Hazlitt), **IV:** 139

Abroad; British Literary Traveling Between the Wars (Fussell), **Supp. IV:** 22

Absalom and Achitophel (Dryden), **II:** 292, 298–299, 304

"Absalom, My Son" (Warner), **Supp. VII:** 380

"Absence" (Jennings), **Supp. V:** 218

"Absence" (Thompson), **V:** 444

"Absence, The" (Warner), **Supp. VII:** 373

Absence of War, The (Hare), **Supp. IV:** 282, 294, 297–298

"Absences" (Larkin), **Supp. I:** 277

Absent Friends (Ayckbourn), **Supp. V:** 2–3, 10, 13, 14

Absent in the Spring (Christie), **Supp. II:** 133

Absentee, The (Edgeworth), **Supp. III:** 154, **160–161,** 165

"Absent–Minded Beggar, The" (Kipling), **VI:** 203

"Absent–Mindedness in a Parish Choir" (Hardy), **VI:** 22

Abstract of a Book Lately Published, A: A Treatise of Human Nature . . . (Hume), **Supp. III:** 230–231

Absurd Person Singular (Ayckbourn), **Supp. V:** 2, 5–6, 9

"Abt Vogler" (Browning), **IV:** 365, 366, 370

Abuses of Conscience, The (Sterne), **III:** 135

Academy (periodical), **VI:** 249

"Academy, The" (Reid), **Supp. VII:** 331

Academy Notes (Ruskin), **V:** 178

Acceptable Sacrifice, The (Bunyan), **II:** 253

Acceptance World, The (Powell), **VII:** 347, 348, 350

"Access to the Children" (Trevor), **Supp. IV:** 504

Accident (Bennett), **VI:** 250

Accident (Pinter), **Supp. I:** 374, 375; **Retro. Supp. I:** 226

Accidental Man, An (Murdoch), **Supp. I:** 227

"Accompanist, The" (Desai), **Supp. V:** 65

"According to His Lights" (Galsworthy), **VI:** 276–277

"Account, The" (Cowley), **II:** 197

Account of Corsica, An (Boswell), **III:** 236, 239, 243, 247

Account of the European Settlements in America, An (Burke), **III:** 205

Account of the Growth of Popery and Arbitrary Government, An (Marvell), **I:** 207–208, 219; **Retro. Supp. II:** 266–268

Account of the Life of Dr. Samuel Johnson . . . by Himself, An (Johnson), **III:** 122

Account of the Life of Mr. Richard Savage, An (Johnson), **Retro. Supp. I:** 142

Account of the Settlement at Port Jackson, An **Supp. IV:** 348

Ace of Clubs (Coward), **Supp. II:** 155

Achilles (Gay), **III:** 55, 66, 67

Achilles in Scyros (Bridges), **VI:** 83

Ackroyd, Peter, **Supp. VI: 1–15**

"Acid" (Kelman), **Supp. V:** 245

Acis and Galatea (Gay), **III:** 55, 67

"Across the Estuary" (Nicholson), **Supp. VI:** 216

Across the Plains (Stevenson), **V:** 389, 396

"Act, The" (Harrison), **Supp. V:** 161–162

Act of Creation, The (Koestler), **Supp. I:** 37, 38

Act of Grace (Keneally), **Supp. IV:** 347

"Act of Reparation, An" (Warner), **Supp. VII:** 380

Act of Terror, An (Brink), **Supp. VI: 55–56,** 57

Act Without Words I (Beckett), **Supp. I:** 46, 55, 57

Act Without Words II (Beckett), **Supp. I:** 46, 55, 57

Actaeon and Diana (Johnson), **I:** 286

Acte (Durrell), **Supp. I:** 126, 127

Actions and Reactions (Kipling), **VI:** 204

Acton, John, **IV:** 289, 290; **VI:** 385

"Ad Amicam" sonnets (Thompson), **V:** 441

Ad Patrem (Milton), **Retro. Supp. II:** 272

Adam and the Sacred Nine (Hughes), **Supp. I:** 357, 363

Adam Bede (Eliot), **V:** xxii, 2, 191–192, 194, 200; **Retro. Supp. II:** 104–106

Adams, Henry, **VI:** 65

Adam's Breed (Hall), **Supp. VI:** 120, 122, 128

"Adam's Curse" (Yeats), **III:** 184; **VI:** 213

"Adam's Dream" (Muir), **Supp. VI:** 207–208

"Adapting *Nice Work* for Television" (Lodge), **Supp. IV:** 373, 381

Addison, Joseph, **II:** 195, 200; **III:** 1, 18, 19, **38–53,** 74, 198; **IV:** 278, 281, 282

"Additional Poems" (Housman), **VI:** 161

Address to the Deil (Burns), **III:** 315, 317
Address to the Irish People, An (Shelley), **IV:** 208; **Retro. Supp. I:** 245
"Address to the Unco Guid" (Burns), **III:** 319
"Adina" (James), **VI:** 69
Administrator, The (MacNeice), **VII:** 401
Admirable Bashville, The (Barker), **VI:** 113
Admiral Crichton, The (Barrie), **Supp. III:** 6, 9, **14–15**
Admiral Guinea (Stevenson), **V:** 396
Adolphe (Constant), **Supp. IV:** 125, 126, 136
Adonais (Shelley), **I:** 160; **VI:** 73; **IV:** xviii, 179, 196, 205–206, 207, 208; **Retro. Supp. I:** 255
Adonis and the Alphabet (Huxley), **VII:** 206–207
Adonis, Attis, Osiris: Studies in the History of Oriental Religion (Frazer), **Supp. III:** 175, 180
Adored One, The (Barrie), **Supp. III:** 5, 9
Adorno, Theodor, **Supp. IV:** 29, 82
"Adrian and Bardus" (Gower), **I:** 54
"Advanced Lady, The" (Mansfield), **VII:** 172
Advancement of Learning, The (Bacon), **I:** 261–265; **II:** 149; **IV:** 279
Advantages Proposed by Repealing the Sacramental Test, The (Swift), **III:** 36
"Adventure of Charles Augustus Milverton, The" (Doyle), **Supp. II:** 173
"Adventure of Charles Wentworth" (Brontë), **V:** 118–119
"Adventure of the Abbey Grange, The" (Doyle), **Supp. II:** 168, 173, 176
"Adventure of the Blanched Soldier, The" (Doyle), **Supp. II:** 168
"Adventure of the Blue Carbuncle, The" (Doyle), **Supp. II:** 173
"Adventure of the Bruce–Partington Plans, The" (Doyle), **Supp. II:** 170, 175
"Adventure of the Copper Beeches, The" (Doyle), **Supp. II:** 168
"Adventure of the Creeping Man, The" (Doyle), **Supp. II:** 165
"Adventure of the Devil's Foot, The" (Doyle), **Supp. II:** 167, 176
"Adventure of the Empty House, The" (Doyle), **Supp. II:** 160
"Adventure of the Engineer's Thumb, The" (Doyle), **Supp. II:** 170
"Adventure of the Golden Pince–Nez, The" (Doyle), **Supp. II:** 175
"Adventure of the Illustrious Client, The" (Doyle), **Supp. II:** 169
"Adventure of the Lion's Mane, The" (Doyle), **Supp. II:** 168–169
"Adventure of the Missing Three–Quarter, The" (Doyle), **Supp. II:** 165, 171
"Adventure of the Norwood Builder, The" (Doyle), **Supp. II:** 169, 170, 173
"Adventure of the Retired Colourman, The" (Doyle), **Supp. II:** 172
"Adventure of the Second Stain, The" (Doyle), **Supp. II:** 175, 176

"Adventure of the Six Napoleons, The" (Doyle), **Supp. II:** 170–171, 174–175
"Adventure of the Speckled Band, The" (Doyle), **Supp. II:** 165–166
"Adventure of the Sussex Vampire, The" (Doyle), **Supp. II:** 169
"Adventure of the Three Garridebs, The" (Doyle), **Supp. II:** 165
"Adventure of Wisteria Lodge, The" (Doyle), **Supp. II:** 168
Adventure Story (Rattigan), **Supp. VII:** 316–317
Adventures in the Skin Trade (Thomas), **Supp. I:** 182
Adventures of Caleb Williams, The (Godwin), **III:** 332, 345; **IV:** 173
Adventures of Covent Garden, The (Farquhar), **II:** 352, 354, 364
Adventures of Ferdinand Count Fathom, The (Smollett), *see* Ferdinand Count Fathom
Adventures of Harry Richmond, The (Meredith), **V:** xxiii, 228, 234
Adventures of Peregrine Pickle, The (Smollett), *see* Peregrine Pickle
Adventures of Philip on His Way Through the World, The (Thackeray), **V:** 19, 29, 35, 38
Adventures of Roderick Random, The (Smollett), *see* Roderick Random
Adventures of Sir Launcelot Greaves, The (Smollett), *see* Sir Launcelot Greaves
Adventures of the Black Girl in Her Search for God, The (Shaw), **VI:** 124, 127, 129
Adventures of Ulysses, The (Lamb), **IV:** 85
"Adventurous Exploit of the Cave of Ali Baba, The" (Sayers), **Supp. III:** 340
Advice: A Satire (Smollett), **III:** 152n, 158
Advice to a Daughter (Halifax), **III:** 40
Advice to a Son (Osborne), **II:** 145
Advocateship of Jesus Christ, The (Bunyan), *II:* 253
A. E. Housman (Gow), **VI:** 164
A. E. Housman: A Divided Life (Watson), **VI:** 164
A. E. Housman: An Annotated Handlist (Sparrow), **VI:** 164
Ælfric of Eynsham, Abbot, **Retro. Supp. II:** 297–298
Aeneid (tr. Douglas), **III:** 311
Aeneid (tr. Surrey), **I:** 116–119
Aeneid of Virgil, The (tr. Day Lewis), **Supp. III:** 118
Aeneids of Virgil, Done into English Verse, The (Morris), **V:** 306
Aeneis (Dryden), **II:** 290, 293, 297, 301
Aeschylus, **IV:** 199
"Aesculapian Notes" (Redgrove), **Supp. VI:** 234
Aesop (Vanbrugh), **II:** 324, 332, 336
"Aesop and Rhodopè" (Landor), **IV:** 94
Aesop's Fables (Behn), **Supp. III:** 37
"Aesthetic Apologia, An" (Betjeman), **VII:** 357–358
"Aesthetic Poetry" (Pater), **V:** 356, 357
Aethiopian History (Heliodorus), **I:** 164

Affair, The (Snow), **VII:** xxi, 324, 329–330
"Affliction" (Herbert), **II:** 125, 127; **Retro. Supp. II:** 179
"Affliction" (Vaughan), **II:** 187–188
Affliction (Weldon), **Supp. IV:** 531, 532–533
"Affliction of Childhood, The" (De Quincey), **IV:** 152–153, 154
African Elegy, An (Okri), **Supp. V:** 359
African Stories (Lessing), **Supp. I:** 240, 243
African Witch, The (Cary), **VII:** 186
"After a Childhood away from Ireland" (Boland), **Supp. V:** 36
"After a Death" (Stevenson), **Supp. VI:** 254
"After a Journey" (Hardy), **VI:** 18; **Retro. Supp. I:** 118
"After an Operation" (Jennings), **Supp. V:** 214
"After a Romantic Day" (Hardy), **Retro. Supp. I:** 118
After Bakhtin (The Art of Fiction: Illustrated from Classic and Modern Texts) (Lodge), **Supp. IV:** 366–367
"After Dunkirk" (Lewis), **VII:** 445
"After Eden" (MacCaig), **Supp. VI:** 187
After Hannibal (Unsworth), **Supp. VII:** 357, 365–366
"After Her Death" (Stevenson), **Supp. VI:** 254
After Leaving Mr. Mackenzie (Rhys), **Supp. III:** 388, **392–394, 400**
"After Long Silence" (Yeats), **VI:** 212
After Magritte (Stoppard), **Supp. I:** 443, 444–445, 447, 451; **Retro. Supp. II:** 346–347
After Many a Summer (Huxley), **VII:** xviii, 205
"After Rain" (Thomas), **Supp. III:** 406
After Rain (Trevor), **Supp. IV:** 505
After Strange Gods (Eliot), **VI:** 207; **VII:** 153
After the Ark (Jennings), **Supp. V:** 217
After the Ball (Coward), **Supp. II:** 155
After the Dance (Rattigan), **Supp. VII:** 310–311, 312, 318
After the Death of Don Juan (Warner), **Supp. VII:** 376, 377
"After the funeral" (Thomas), **Supp. I:** 176, 177
"After the Irish of Aodghan O'Rathaille" (Boland), **Supp. V:** 36
After–Dinner Joke, The (Churchill), **Supp. IV:** 181
"Afterflu Afterlife, The" (Ewart), **Supp. VII:** 42–43
Aftermath, The (Churchill), **VI:** 359
"Afternoon Dancing" (Trevor), **Supp. IV:** 503–504
"Afternoon in Florence" (Jennings), **Supp. V:** 210
Afternoon Men (Powell), **VII:** 343–345
"Afternoons" (Larkin), **Supp. I:** 281
"Afterthought, An" (Rossetti), **V:** 258
"Afterwards" (Hardy), **VI:** 13, 19; **Retro. Supp. I:** 119
"Against Absence" (Suckling), **II:** 227

"Against Dryness" (Murdoch), **Supp. I:** 216, 218, 219, 221

Against Entropy (Frayn), see *Towards the End of Morning*

"Against Fruition" (Cowley), **II:** 197

"Against Fruition" (Suckling), **II:** 227

Against Hasty Credence (Henryson), **Supp. VII:** 146, 147

Against Religion (Wilson), **Supp. VI:** 297, **305–306,** 309

"Against Romanticism" (Amis), **Supp. II:** 3

Against Venomous Tongues (Skelton), **I:** 90

Agamemnon (Seneca), **II:** 71

Agamemnon (Thomson), **Supp. III:** 411, 424

Agamemnon, a Tragedy Taken from Aeschylus (FitzGerald), **IV:** 349, 353

Agamemnon of Aeschylus, The (tr. Browning), **IV:** 358–359, 374

Agamemnon of Aeschylus, The (tr. MacNeice), **VII:** 408–409

Agate, James, **Supp. II:** 143, 147

Age of Anxiety, The (Auden), **VII:** 379, 388, 389–390; **Supp. IV:** 100; **Retro. Supp. I:** 11

Age of Bronze, The (Byron), **IV:** xviii, 193

Age of Indiscretion, The (Davis), **V:** 394

Age of Iron (Coetzee), **Supp. VI:** 76, **85**

Age of Longing, The (Koestler), **Supp. I:** 25, 27, 28, 31–32, 35

Age of Reason, The (Hope), **Supp. VII:** 164

Age of Shakespeare, The (Swinburne), **V:** 333

Age of the Rainmakers, The (Harris), **Supp. V:** 132

Agents and Patients (Powell), **VII:** 345–346

Aglaura (Suckling), **II:** 226, 238

Agnes Grey (Brontë), **V:** xx, 129–130, 132, 134–135, 140–141, 153; **Supp. IV:** 239; **Retro. Supp. I:** 52, 54–55

"Agnes Lahens" (Moore), **VI:** 98

Agnostic's Apology, An (Stephen), **VI:** 289

"Agonies of Writing a Musical Comedy" (Wodehouse), **Supp. III:** 451

Ah, But Your Land Is Beautiful (Paton), **Supp. II: 353–355**

"Ah, what avails the sceptred race" (Landor), **IV:** 88

Aids to Reflection (Coleridge), **IV:** 53, 56

Aiken, Conrad, **VII:** 149, 179; **Supp. III:** 270

Aimed at Nobody (Graham), **Supp. VII:** 106

Ainger, Alfred, **IV:** 254, 267

"Air and Angels" (MacCaig), **Supp. VI:** 185

Ainsworth, Harrison, **IV:** 311; **V:** 47

"Air Disaster, The" (Ballard), **Supp. V:** 33

"Aire and Angels" (Donne), **II:** 197

"Aisling" (Muldoon), **Supp. IV:** 418–419

"Aisling Hat, The" (McGuckian), **Supp. V:** 286, 288, 289

Aissa Saved (Cary), **VII:** 185

"Akbar's Bridge" (Kipling), **VI:** 201

Akerman, Rudolph, **V:** 111

Akhmatova, Anna, **Supp. IV:** 480, 494

"Al Som de l'Escalina" (Eliot), **VII:** 152

Alamanni, Luigi, **I:** 110–111

Alamein to Zem–Zem (Douglas), **VII:** xxii, 441

Alarcos (Disraeli), **IV:** 306, 308

Alaric at Rome (Arnold), **V:** 216

Alastair Reid Reader, An: Selected Poetry and Prose (Reid), **Supp. VII:** 333, 336

Alastor (Shelley), **III:** 330, 338; **IV:** xvii, 195, 198, 208, 217; **Retro. Supp. I:** 247

"Albergo Empedocle" (Forster), **VI:** 399, 412

Albert's Bridge (Stoppard), **Supp. I:** 439, 445

"Albinus and Rosemund" (Gower), **I:** 53–54

"Albion & Marina" (Brontë), **V:** 110

Albion and Albanius (Dryden), **II:** 305

Album Verses (Lamb), **IV:** 83, 85

Alcazar (Peele), *see Battle of Alcazar, The*

Alcestis (Euripides), **IV:** 358

Alchemist, The (Jonson), **I:** 304–341, 342; **II:** 4, 48; **Retro. Supp. I:** 163

"Alchemist in the City, The" (Hopkins), **V:** 362

Alcott, Louisa May, **Supp. IV:** 255

Aldington, Richard, **VI:** 416; **VII:** xvi, 36, 121

Aldiss, Brian, **III:** 341, 345; **Supp. V:** 22

Aldous Huxley (Brander), **VII:** 208

Alexander, Peter, **I:** 300*n*, 326

Alexander, William (earl of Stirling), **I:** 218; **II:** 80

"Alexander and Zenobia" (Brontë), **V:** 115

Alexander Pope (Sitwell), **VII:** 138–139

Alexander Pope (Stephen), **V:** 289

Alexander Pope as Critic and Humanist (Warren), **II:** 332*n*

Alexander's Feast; or, The Power of Musique (Dryden), **II:** 200, 300, 304

Alexandria: A History and Guide (Forster), **VI:** 408, 412

Alexandria Quartet (Durrell), **Supp. I:** 94, 96, 97, 98, 100, 101, **104–110,** 113, 122

"Alfieri and Salomon the Florentine Jew" (Landor), **IV:** 91

Alfred (Thomson and Mallet), **Supp. III:** 412, 424–425

Alfred Lord Tennyson: A Memoir (Tennyson), **IV:** 324, 338

Alfred the Great of Wessex, King, **Retro. Supp. II:** 293, 295–297

Algernon Charles Swinburne (Thomas), **VI:** 424

Alice in Wonderland (Carroll), *see Alice's Adventures in Wonderland*

Alice Sit-by-the-Fire (Barrie), **Supp. III:** 8, 9

Alice's Adventures in Wonderland (Carroll), **V:** xxiii, 261–265, **266–269,** 270–273

Alice's Adventures Under Ground (Carroll), **V:** 266, 273; *see Alice's Adventures in Wonderland*

"Alicia's Diary" (Hardy), **VI:** 22

Alien (Foster), **III:** 345

"Alien Corn, The" (Maugham), **VI:** 370, 374

Alien Sky, The (Scott), **Supp. I:** 261–263

"Alien Soil" (Kincaid), **Supp. VII:** 221, 229

All About Mr. Hatterr (Desani), **Supp. IV:** 445

"All blue and bright, in glorious light" (Brontë), **V:** 115

"All Day It Has Rained" (Lewis), **VII:** 445

"All Flesh" (Thompson), **V:** 442

All Fools (Chapman), **I:** 235, 238, 244

All for Love (Dryden), **II:** 295–296, 305

All for Love (Southey), **IV:** 71

All My Eyes See: The Visual World of G. M. Hopkins (ed. Thornton), **V:** 377*n*, 379*n*, 382

All My Little Ones (Ewart), **Supp. VII:** 36

All Ovid's Elegies (Marlowe), **I:** 280, 291, 293

"All philosophers, who find" (Swift), **IV:** 160

All Quiet on the Western Front (Remarque), **VII:** xvi

All Religions Are One (Blake), **III:** 292, 307; **Retro. Supp. I:** 35

"All Saints: Martyrs" (Rossetti), **V:** 255

All That Fall (Beckett), **Supp. I:** 58, 62; **Retro. Supp. I:** 25

All the Conspirators (Isherwood), **VII:** 310

"All the hills and vales along" (Sorley), **VI:** 421–422

All the Usual Hours of Sleeping (Redgrove), **Supp. VI:** 230

All the Year Round (periodical), **V:** 42

All Trivia (Connolly), **Supp. III:** 98

All What Jazz: A Record Diary, 1961–1968 (Larkin), **Supp. I:** 286, 287–288

Allan Quatermain (Haggard), **Supp. III:** 213, 218

Allegory of Love: A Study in Medieval Tradition (Lewis), **Supp. III:** 248, 249–250, 265

Allen, John, **IV:** 341, 349–350, 352

Allen, Walter Ernest, **V:** 219; **VI:** 257; **VII:** xvii, xxxvii, 71, 343

Allestree, Richard, **III:** 82

Allott, Kenneth, **IV:** 236; **VI:** xi, xxvii, 218

Allott, Miriam, **IV:** x, xxiv, 223*n*, 224, 234, 236; **V:** x, 218

All's Well That Ends Well (Shakespeare), **I:** 313, 318

"Allusion to the Tenth Satire of the Second Book of Horace" (Rochester), **II:** 259

Almayer's Folly (Conrad), **VI:** 135–136, 148; **Retro. Supp. II:** 70–71

Almeria (Edgeworth), **Supp. III:** 158

"Aloe, The" (Mansfield), **VII:** 173–174

Alone (Douglas), **VI:** 293, 294, 297, 304, 305

Alpers, Antony, **VII:** 176

"Alphabetical Catalogue of Names . . . and Other Material Things Mentioned in These Pastorals, An" (Gay), **III:** 56

Alphabetical Order (Frayn), **Supp. VII:** 60

"Alphabets" (Heaney), **Retro. Supp. I:** 131

Alps and Sanctuaries (Butler), **Supp. II:** 114

"Alps in Winter, The" (Stephen), **V:** 282

Alroy (Disraeli), **IV:** 296, 297, 308

"Altar, The" (Herbert), **II:** 128

"Altar of the Dead, The" (James), **VI:** 69

"Altarwise by owl–light" (Thomas), **Supp. I: 174–176**

Alteration, The (Amis), **Supp. II:** 12–13

"Alternative to Despair, An" (Koestler), **Supp. I:** 39

Althusser, Louis, **Supp. IV:** 90

Alton, R. E., **I:** 285

Alton Locke (Kingsley), **V:** vii, xxi, 2, 4; **VI:** 240

Alvarez, A., **II:** 125n

Amadeus (Shaffer), **Supp. I:** 326–327

Amadis of Gaul (tr. Southey), **IV:** 71

Amado, Jorge, **Supp. IV:** 440

Amalgamemnon (Brooke–Rose), **Supp. IV:** 99, 110–111, 112

Amateur Emigrant, The (Stevenson), **V:** 389, 396

"Amateur Film–Making" (Fuller), **Supp. VII:** 73

Amazing Marriage, The (Meredith), **V:** 227, 232, 233, 234

Ambarvalia: Poems by T. Burbidge and A. H. Clough, **V:** 159–160, 161, 170

Ambassadors, The (James), **VI:** 55, 57–59; **Supp. IV:** 371

"Amber Bead, The" (Herrick), **II:** 106

Amberley, Lady, **V:** 129

"Ambiguities" (Fuller), **Supp. VII:** 73

Ambler, Eric, **Supp. IV: 1–24**

Amboyna (Dryden), **II:** 305

Amelia (Fielding), **III:** 102–103, 105; **Retro. Supp. I:** 81, 89–90

"Amen" (Rossetti), **V:** 256

Amendments of Mr. Collier's False and Imperfect Citations (Congreve), **II:** 339, 340, 350

America. A Prophecy (Blake), **III:** 300, 302, 307; **Retro. Supp. I:** 39, 40–41

America I Presume (Lewis), **VII:** 77

American, The (James), **VI:** 24, 28–29, 39, 67

American Ghosts and Other World Wonders (Carter), **Supp. III:** 91

American Notes (Dickens), **V:** 42, 54, 55, 71

American Scene, The (James), **VI: 54, 62–64,** 67

American Senator, The (Trollope), **V:** 100, 102

American Visitor, An (Cary), **VII:** 186

"Americans in My Mind, The" (Pritchett), **Supp. III:** 316

"Ametas and Thestylis Making Hay–Ropes" (Marvell), **II:** 211

Aminta (Tasso), **II:** 49

"Amir's Homily, The" (Kipling), **VI:** 201

Amis, Kingsley, **Supp. II: 1–19; Supp. IV:** 25, 26, 27, 29, 377; **Supp. V:** 206

Amis, Martin, **Supp. IV: 25–44,** 65, 75, 437, 445

"Among All Lovely Things My Love Had Been" (Wordsworth), **IV:** 21

"Among School Children" (Yeats), **VI:** 211, 217

Among the Believers: An Islamic Journey (Naipaul), **Supp. I:** 399, 400–401, 402

Amores (tr. Marlowe), **I:** 276, 290

Amoretti and Epithalamion (Spenser), **I:** 124, 128–131

Amorous Prince, The; or, The Curious Husband (Behn), **Supp. III:** 26

"Amos Barton" (Eliot), **V:** 190

Amours de Voyage (Clough), **V:** xxii, 155, 156, 158, 159, 161–163, 165, 166–168, 170

Amphytrion; or, The Two Sosias (Dryden), **II:** 296, 305

"Ample Garden, The" (Graves), **VII:** 269

Amrita (Jhabvala), **Supp. V:** 224–226

"Amsterdam" (Murphy), **Supp. V:** 326

Amusements Serious and Comical (Brown), **III:** 41

"Amy Foster" (Conrad), **VI:** 134, 148

An Duanaire: An Irish Anthology, Poems of the Dispossessed, 1600–1900 (Kinsella), **Supp. V:** 266

An Giall (Behan), **Supp. II:** 71–73

Anacreontiques (Johnson), **II:** 198

"Anactoria" (Swinburne), **V:** 319–320, 321

"Anahorish" (Heaney), **Retro. Supp. I:** 125, 128

Anand, Mulk Raj, **Supp. IV:** 440

"Anarchist, An" (Conrad), **VI:** 148

Anathemata, The (Jones), **Supp. VII:** 167, 168, 169, 170, 175–178

Anatomy of Exchange–Alley, The (Defoe), **III:** 13

Anatomy of Frustration, The (Wells), **VI:** 228

Anatomy of Melancholy (Burton), **II:** 88, 106, 108; **IV:** 219

Anatomy of Oxford (eds. Day Lewis and Fenby), **Supp. III:** 118

Anatomy of Restlessness: Selected Writings, 1969–1989 (Chatwin), **Supp. IV:** 157, 160

"Ancestor" (Kinsella), **Supp. V:** 274

Ancient Allan, The (Haggard), **Supp. III:** 222

Ancient and English Versions of the Bible (Isaacs), **I:** 385

"Ancient Ballet, An" (Kinsella), **Supp. V:** 261

Ancient Lights (Ford), **VI:** 319, 320

"Ancient Mariner, The" (Coleridge), **III:** 330, 338; **IV:** viii, ix, 42, 44–48, 54, 55; **Retro. Supp. II:** 53–56

"Ancient Sage, The" (Tennyson), **IV:** 329

"Ancient to Ancients, An" (Hardy), **VI:** 13

"And country life I praise" (Bridges), **VI:** 75

"And death shall have no dominion" (Thomas), **Supp. I:** 174

And Our Faces, My Heart, Brief as Photos (Berger), **Supp. IV:** 94, 95

And Then There Were None (Christie), *see* Ten Little Niggers

And What if the Pretender Should Come? (Defoe), **III:** 13

Anderson, Lindsay, **Supp. IV:** 78

Anderson, Sherwood, **VII:** 75

Anderton, Basil, **II:** 154, 157

"Andrea del Sarto" (Browning), **IV:** 357, 361, 366; **Retro. Supp. II:** 27–28

Andrea of Hungary, and Giovanna of Naples (Landor), **IV:** 100

Andreas, **Retro. Supp. II:** 301

"Andrey Satchel and the Parson and Clerk" (Hardy), **VI:** 22

Androcles and the Lion (Shaw), **VI:** 116, 124, 129; **Retro. Supp. II:** 322

"Andromeda" (Hopkins), **V:** 370, 376

Andromeda Liberata (Chapman), **I:** 235, 254

Ane Prayer for the Pest (Henryson), **Supp. VII:** 146, 148

Anecdotes (Spence), **II:** 261

"Anecdotes, The" (Durrell), **Supp. I:** 124

Anecdotes of Johnson (Piozzi), **III:** 246

Anecdotes . . . of Mr. Pope . . . by the Rev. Joseph Spence (ed. Singer), **III:** 69, 78

Angel at the Gate, The (Harris), **Supp. V:** 137, 139

Angel Pavement (Priestley), **VII:** xviii, 211, 216–217

Angels and Insects (Byatt), **Supp. IV:** 139, 151, 153–154

Angels and Insects (film), **Supp. IV:** 153

"Angels at the Ritz" (Trevor), **Supp. IV:** 503

Angels at the Ritz (Trevor), **Supp. IV:** 504

"Angle–Land" (Jones), **Supp. VII:** 176

Anglo–Italian Review (periodical) **VI:** 294

"Anglo–Saxon, The" (Golding), **Supp. I:** 78

Anglo–Saxon Attitudes (Wilson), **Supp. I:** 154, 155, 156, 159–160, 161, 162, 163

Anglo–Saxon Chronicle, **Retro. Supp. II:** 296, 297, 298, 307

Angrian chronicles (Brontë), **V:** 110–111, 120–121, 122, 124–125, 126, 135

"Anima and Animus" (Jung), **Supp. IV:** 10–11

Anima Poetae: From the Unpublished Notebooks (Coleridge), **IV:** 56

Animadversions upon the Remonstrants Defense Against Smectymnuus (Milton), **II:** 175

Animal Farm (Orwell), **VII:** xx, 273, 278, 283–284; **Supp. I:** 28n, 29; **Supp. IV:** 31

Animal Lover's Book of Beastly Murder, The (Highsmith), **Supp. V:** 179

Animal's Arrival, The (Jennings), **Supp. V:** 208

Animated Nature (Goldsmith), *see History of the Earth . . .*

Ann Lee's (Bowen), **Supp. II:** 81

Ann Veronica: A Modern Love Story (Wells), **VI**: 227, 238

"Anna, Lady Braxby" (Hardy), **VI**: 22

Anna of the Five Towns (Bennett), **VI**: xiii, 248, 249, 252, 253, 266

Annals of Chile, The (Muldoon), **Supp. IV**: 428–432

Annan, Gabriele, **Supp. IV**: 302

Annan, Noel, **V**: 284, 290

Anne Brontë (Gérin), **V**: 153

"Anne Killigrew" (Dryden), **II**: 303

Anne of Geierstein (Scott), **IV**: 39

Annie, Gwen, Lily, Pam, and Tulip (Kincaid), **Supp. VII**: 222

Annie John (Kincaid), **Supp. VII**: 217, 223–225, 229, 230

Anniversaries (Donne), **I**: 361–362, 364, 367; **Retro. Supp. II**: 88

Annotations of Scottish Songs by Burns (Cook), **III**: 322

Annual Register (periodical), **III**: 194, 205

Annunciation, The (Henryson), **Supp. VII**: 146, 148

"Annunciation, The" (Jennings), **Supp. V**: 212

"Annunciation, The" (Muir), **Supp. VI**: 207

Annunciation in a Welsh Hill Setting (Jones), **Supp. VII**: 180

Annus Domini (Rossetti), **V**: 260

"Annus Mirabilis" (Larkin), **Supp. I**: 284

Annus Mirabilis: The Year of Wonder (Dryden), **II**: 292, 304

"Anorexic" (Boland), **Supp. V**: 49

"Another Grace for a Child" (Herrick), **II**: 114

Another Mexico (Greene), *see* Lawless Roads, The

Another Part of the Wood (Bainbridge), **Supp. VI**: 17–19

Another September (Kinsella), **Supp. V**: 260

"Another September" (Kinsella), **Supp. V**: 260

"Ansell" (Forster), **VI**: 398

Anstey, Christopher, **III**: 155

"Answer, The" (Wycherley), **II**: 322

"Answer to a Paper Called 'A Memorial of true Poor Inhabitants'" (Swift), **III**: 35

Answer to a Poisoned Book (More), **Supp. VII**: 245

Answer to a Question That No Body Thinks of, An (Defoe), **III**: 13

"Answer to Davenant" (Hobbes), **II**: 256n

"Answers" (Jennings), **Supp. V**: 206

"Ant, The" (Lovelace), **II**: 231

Ant and the Nightingale or Father Hubburd's Tales, The (Middleton), **II**: 3

"Ant-Lion, The" (Pritchett), **Supp. III**: 105–106

Antal, Frederick, **Supp. IV**: 80

Antechinus: Poems 1975–1980 (Hope), **Supp. VII**: 159

"Antheap, The" (Lessing), **Supp. I**: 242

"Anthem for Doomed Youth" (Owen), **VI**: 443, 447, 448, 452; **Supp. IV**: 58

"Anthem of Earth, An" (Thompson), **V**: 448

Anthology of War Poetry, An (ed. Nichols), **VI**: 419

Anthony Trollope: A Critical Study (Cockshut), **V**: 98, 103

Antic Hay (Huxley), **VII**: 198, 201–202

"Anti–Christ; or, The Reunion of Christendom" (Chesterton), **VI**: 340–341

Anticipations of the Reaction of Mechanical and Scientific Progress upon Human Life and Thought (Wells), **VI**: 227, 240

Anti–Coningsby (Disraeli), **IV**: 308

Anti–Death League, The (Amis), **Supp. II**: 14–15

Antigua, Penny, Puce (Graves), **VII**: 259

"Antigua Crossings" (Kincaid), **Supp. VII**: 220, 221

Antiquarian Prejudice (Betjeman), **VII**: 358, 359

Antiquary, The (Scott), **IV**: xvii 28, 32–33, 37, 39

Anti–Thelyphthora (Cowper), **III**: 220

Antonina; or, The Fall of Rome (Collins), **Supp. VI**: 92, 95

Antonio and Mellida (Marston), **II**: 27–28, 40

Antonio's Revenge (Marston), **II**: 27–29, 36, 40

Antonioni, Michelangelo, **Supp. IV**: 434

Antony and Cleopatra (Sedley), **II**: 263, 271

Antony and Cleopatra (Shakespeare), **I**: 318, 319–320; **II**: 70; **III**: 22; **Supp. IV**: 263

Antony and Octavus. Scenes for the Study (Landor), **IV**: 100

Ants, The (Churchill), **Supp. IV**: 180–181

"Antwerp" (Ford), **VI**: 323, 416

"Anxious in Dreamland" (Menand), **Supp. IV**: 305

"Any Saint" (Thompson), **V**: **444**

Anything for a Quiet Life (Middleton and Webster), **II**: 21, 69, 83, 85

Apartheid and the Archbishop: The Life and Times of Geoffrey Clayton, Archbishop of Cape Town (Paton), **Supp. II**: 343, 356, 357–358

"Apartheid in Its Death Throes" (Paton), **Supp. II**: 342

"Ape, The" (Pritchett), **Supp. III**: 325

Apes of God, The (Lewis), **VII**: xv, 35, 71, 73, 74, 77, 79

Aphorisms on Man (Lavater), **III**: 298

Aphrodite in Aulis (Moore), **VI**: 88, 95, 99

Apocalypse (Lawrence), **VII**: 91; **Retro. Supp. II**: 234

"Apollo and the Fates" (Browning), **IV**: 366

"Apollo in Picardy" (Pater), **V**: 355, 356

"Apollonius of Tyre" (Gower), **I**: 53

"Apologia pro Poemate Meo" (Owen), **VI**: 452

Apologia pro Vita Sua (Newman), **Supp. VII**: 289, 290, 291, 294, 295, 296, 298, 299–300

Apologie for Poetry (Sidney), *see Defence of Poesie, The Apologie for the Royal Party, An . . . By a Lover of Peace and of His Country* (Evelyn), **II**: 287

Apology Against a Pamphlet Call'd A Modest Confutation of the Animadversions upon the Remonstrant Against Smectymnuus, An (Milton), **II**: 175

"Apology for Plainspeaking, An" (Stephen), **V**: 284

Apology for Poetry, An (Sidney), **Retro. Supp. I**: 157

"Apology for Smectymnuus" (Milton), **Retro. Supp. II**: 269

Apology for the Bible (Watson), **III**: 301

Apology for the Life of Mrs. Shamela Andrews, An (Fielding), *see Shamela*

"Apology for the Revival of Christian Architecture in England, A" (Hill), **Supp. V**: 189, 191–192

Apology for the Voyage to Guiana (Ralegh), **I**: 153

Apophthegms (Bacon), **I**: 264, 273

"Apostasy, The" (Traherne), **II**: 191

Apostles, The (Moore), **VI**: 88, 96, 99

Apostes, The (Cambridge Society), **IV**: 331; **V**: 278; **VI**: 399

"Apotheosis of Tins, The" (Mahon), **Supp. VI**: 172

"Apparition of His Mistresse Calling Him to Elizium, The" (Herrick), **II**: 113

Appeal from the New to the Old Whigs, An (Burke), **III**: 205

Appeal to England, An (Swinburne), **V**: 332

Appeal to Honour and Justice, An (Defoe), **III**: 4, 13; **Retro. Supp. I**: 66, 67

Appeal to the Clergy of the Church of Scotland, An (Stevenson), **V**: 395

"Appius and Virginia" (Gower), **I**: 55

Appius and Virginia (R. B.), **I**: 216

Appius and Virginia (Webster), **II**: 68, 83, 85

Apple Broadcast, The (Redgrove), **Supp. VI**: 235

Apple Cart, The: A Political Extravaganza (Shaw), **VI**: 118, 120, 125–126, 127, 129

"Apple Tragedy" (Hughes), **Supp. I**: 351, 353

"Apple Tree, The" (du Maurier), **Supp. III**: 138

"Apple Tree, The" (Galsworthy), **VI**: 276

"Apple Tree, The" (Mansfield), **VII**: 173

Applebee, John, **III**: 7

Appley Dapply's Nursery Rhymes (Potter), **Supp. III**: 291

Apollonius of Tyre, **Retro. Supp. II**: 298

Apology for Poetry, An (Sidney), **Retro. Supp. II**: 332–334, 339

"Appraisal, An" (Compton–Burnett), **VII**: 59

Appreciations (Pater), **V**: 338, 339, 341, 351–352, 353–356

"Apprentice" (Warner), **Supp. VII**: 380

"April" (Kavanagh), **Supp. VII**: 188

"April Epithalamium, An" (Stevenson), **Supp. VI**: 263

April Love (Hughes), **V**: 294

"Apron of Flowers, The" (Herrick), **II:** 110

Apropos of Dolores (Wells), **VI:** 240

"Aquae Sulis" (Hardy), **Retro. Supp. I:** 121

"Arab Love Song" (Thompson), **V:** 442, 445, 449

"Arabella" (Thackeray), **V:** 24

Arabian Nights, The, **III:** 327, 335, 336; **Supp. IV:** 434

"Araby" (Joyce), **Retro. Supp. I:** 172

Aragon, Louis, **Supp. IV:** 466

"Aramantha" (Lovelace), **II:** 230, 231

Aran Islands, The (Synge), **VI:** 308–309; **Retro. Supp. I:** 291–294

Ararat (Thomas), **Supp. IV:** 484

Aratra Pentelici (Ruskin), **V:** 184

Arbuthnot, John, **III:** 19, 34, 60

"Arcades" (Milton), **II:** 159

Arcadia (Sidney), **I:** 161, 163–169, 173, 317; **II:** 48, 53–54; **III:** 95; **Retro. Supp. II:** 330–332, 340

Arcadia (Stoppard), **Retro. Supp. II:** 355–356

Arcadian Rhetorike (Fraunce), **I:** 164

Archeology of Love, The (Murphy), **Supp. V:** 317

Archer, William, **II:** 79, 358, 363, 364; **V:** 103, 104, 113

Architectural Review (periodical), **VII:** 356, 358

Architecture in Britain: 1530–1830 (Reynolds), **II:** 336

Architecture, Industry and Wealth (Morris), **V:** 306

"Arctic Summer" (Forster), **VI:** 406

Arden of Feversham (Kyd), **I:** 212, 213, 218–219

Arden, John, **Supp. II: 21–42**

"Ardour and Memory" (Rossetti), **V:** 243

Ardours and Endurances (Nichols), **VI:** 423

"Are You Lonely in the Restaurant" (O'Nolan), **Supp. II:** 323

Area of Darkness, An (Naipaul), **Supp.I,** 383, 384, 387, 389, 390, 391–392, 394, 395, 399, 402

Arendt, Hannah, **Supp. IV:** 306

Areopagitica (Milton), **II:** 163, 164, 169, 174, 175; **IV:** 279; **Retro. Supp. II:** 277–279

Aretina (Mackenzie), **III:** 95

"Argonauts of the Air, The" (Wells), **VI:** 244

Argonauts of the Pacific (Malinowski), **Supp. III:** 186

Argufying (Empson), **Supp. II:** 180, 181

Argument . . . that the Abolishing of Christianity . . . May . . . be Attended with some Inconveniences, An (Swift), **III:** 26, 35

"Argument of His Book, The" (Herrick), **II:** 110

Argument Shewing that a Standing Army . . . Is Not Inconsistent with a Free Government, An (Defoe), **III,** 12

Ariadne Florentina (Ruskin), **V:** 184

Ariel Poems (Eliot), **VII:** 152

Arians of the Fourth Century, The (Newman), **Supp. VII:** 291

Aristocrats (Friel), **Supp. V:** 122

Aristophanes, **V:** 227

Aristophanes' Apology (Browning), **IV:** 358, 367, 370, 374; **Retro. Supp. II:** 30

Aristos, The: A Self-Portrait in Ideas (Fowles), **Supp. I:** 293–294, 295, 296

"Armada, The" (Macaulay), **IV:** 283, 291

Armadale (Collins), **Supp. VI:** 91, 93–94, **98–100,** 101, 103

Arms and the Covenant (Churchill), **VI:** 356

Arms and the Man (Shaw), **VI:** 104, 110, 120; **Retro. Supp. II:** 313

Armstrong, Isobel Mair, **V:** xi, xxvii, 339, 375

Armstrong, William, **V:** xviii, xxxvii

Armstrong's Last Goodnight (Arden), **Supp. II:** 29, 30

Arnold, Matthew, **IV:** 359; **V:** viii–xi, 14, 156–158, 160, **203–218,** 283, 285, 289, 342, 352–353; works, **III:** 23, 174, 277; **V:** 206–215; literary criticism, **I:** 423; **III:** 68, 277; **IV:** 220, 234, 323, 371; **V:** 160, 165–169, 352, 408; **Supp. II:** 44, 57; **Retro. Supp. I:** 59

Arnold, Thomas, **V:** 155–156, 157, 165, 207, 208, 277, 284, 349

Arnold Bennett (Lafourcade), **VI:** 268

Arnold Bennett (Pound), **VI:** 247, 268

Arnold Bennett (Swinnerton), **VI:** 268

Arnold Bennett: A Biography (Drabble), **VI:** 247, 253, 268; **Supp. IV:** 203

Arnold Bennett: A Last Word (Swinnerton), **VI:** 268

Arnold Bennett and H. G. Wells: A Record of a Personal and Literary Friendship (ed. Wilson), **VI:** 246, 267

Arnold Bennett in Love (ed. and tr. Beardmore and Beardmore), **VI:** 251, 268

Arnold Bennett: The AEvening Standard-"Years (ed. Mylett), **VI:** 265n, 266

Arouet, Françoise Marie, *see* Voltaire

Around Theatres (Beerbohm), **Supp. II:** 54, 55

"Aromatherapy" (Redgrove), **Supp. VI:** 236

Arraignment of London, The (Daborne and Tourneur), **II:** 37

Arraignment of Paris (Peele), **I:** 197–200

"Arrest of Oscar Wilde at the Cadogan Hotel, The" (Betjeman), **VII:** 356, 365–366

Arrival and Departure (Koestler), **Supp. I:** 27, 28, 30–31

Arrow in the Blue (Koestler), **Supp. I:** 22, 25, 31, 34, 36

Arrow of Gold, A (Conrad), **VI:** 134, 144, 147

Ars Longa, Vita Brevis (Arden and D'Arcy), **Supp. II:** 29

Ars Poetica (Horace), **Retro. Supp. I:** 166

"Arsonist" (Murphy), **Supp. V:** 326

"Art and Criticism" (Harris), **Supp. V:** 140

"Art and Extinction" (Harrison), **Supp. V:** 156

Art & Lies: A Piece for Three Voices and a Bawd (Winterson), **Supp. IV:** 542, 547, 552–553, 554–555, 556, 557

"Art and Morality" (Stephen), **V:** 286

Art and Reality (Cary), **VII:** 186

Art and Revolution: Ernst Neizvestny and the Role of the Artist in the U.S.S.R. (Berger), **Supp. IV:** 79, 88

"Art and Science" (Richards), **Supp. II:** 408–409

Art History and Class Consciousness (Hadjinicolaou), **Supp. IV:** 90

"Art McCooey" (Kavanagh), **Supp. VII:** 190

Art Objects: Essays on Ecstasy and Effrontery (Winterson), **Supp. IV:** 541, 542, 544, 557

Art of Angling, The (Barker), **II:** 131

Art of Being Ruled, The (Lewis), **VII:** 72, 75, 76

Art of English Poetry, The (Puttenham), **I:** 94, 146, 214

Art of Fiction, The (James), **VI:** 46, 67

Art of Fiction, The (Kipling), **VI:** 204

Art of Fiction, The (Lodge), **Supp. IV:** 381

"Art of Fiction, The" (Woolf), **VII:** 21, 22

Art of Love, The (Ovid), **I:** 237–238

Art of Sinking in Poetry, The (Pope), **IV:** 187

Art of the Big Bass Drum, The (Kelman), **Supp. V:** 256

Art of the Novel, The (James), **VI:** 67

"Art Work" (Byatt), **Supp. IV:** 155

"Arthur Snatchfold" (Forster), **VI:** 411

Article of Charge Against Hastings (Burke), **III:** 205

"Articles of Inquiry Concerning Heavy and Light" (Bacon), **I:** 261

Articulate Energy (Davie), **Supp. VI:** 114

"Artifice of Versification, An" (Fuller), **Supp. VII:** 77

Artificial Princess, The (Firbank), **Supp. II:** 199, 205, 207–208

Artist Descending a Staircase (Stoppard), **Retro. Supp. II:** 349

Artist of the Floating World, An (Ishiguro), **Supp. IV:** 301, 304, 306, 309–311

"Artist to His Blind Love, The" (Redgrove), **Supp. VI:** 234

"Artistic Career of Corky, The" (Wodehouse), **Supp. III:** 459

"Artistic Temperament of Stephen Carey, The" (Maugham), **VI:** 373

"Artists, The" (Thackeray), **V:** 22, 37

"Artists and Value" (Kelman), **Supp. V:** 257

Arts and Crafts Movement, The (Naylor), **VI:** 168

"Arundel Tomb, An" (Larkin), **Supp. I:** 280

As If By Magic (Wilson), **Supp. I: 163–165,** 166

"As It Should Be" (Mahon), **Supp. VI:** 170

"As kingfishers catch fire" (Hopkins), **V:** 371

"As the Team's Head–Brass" (Thomas), **VI:** 425; **Supp. III:** 405

As You Like It (Shakespeare), **I:** 278, 312; **III:** 117; **Supp. IV:** 179

"Ascent into Hell" (Hope), **Supp. VII:** 153

Ascent of F6, The (Auden and Isherwood), **VII:** 312, 380, 383, 385; **Retro. Supp. I:** 7

Ascent to Omai (Harris), **Supp. V:** 135, 136, 138

"Ash Grove, The" (Thomas), **Supp. III:** 402

Ashenden (Maugham), **VI:** 371; **Supp. IV:** 9–10

Ashford, Daisy, **V:** 111, 262

Ashley, Lord, *see* Shaftesbury, seventh earl of

Ash–Wednesday (Eliot), **VII:** 144, 150, 151–152

Ashworth, Elizabeth, **Supp. IV:** 480

Asimov, Isaac, **III:** 341

"Ask Me No More" (Tennyson), **IV:** 334

"Askam Unvisited" (Nicholson), **Supp. VI:** 214

"Askam Visited" (Nicholson), **Supp. VI:** 214

Asking Around (Hare), **Supp. IV:** 282, 298

"Asleep" (Owen), **VI:** 455

Asolando (Browning), **IV:** 359, 365, 374; **Retro. Supp. II:** 31

"Aspects" (MacCaig), **Supp. VI:** 188

Aspects of E. M. Forster (Stallybrass), **VI:** 413

Aspects of the Novel (Forster), **V:** 229; **VI:** 397, 411, 412; **VII:** 21, 22; **Retro. Supp. II:** 149

"Aspens" (Thomas), **Supp. III:** 406

Aspern Papers, The (James), **VI:** 38, **46–48**

Asquith, Herbert, **VI:** 417

Asquith, Raymond, **VI:** 417, 428

"Ass, The" (Vaughan), **II:** 186

"Assassination of John Fitzgerald Kennedy Considered as a Downhill Motor Race" (Ballard), **Supp. V:** 21

Assassins, The (Shelley), **Retro. Supp. I:** 247

Assignation, The; or, Love in a Nunnery (Dryden), **II:** 305

"Assisi" (MacCaig), **Supp. VI:** 189–190, 194–195

"Assunta 2" (Chatwin), **Supp. IV:** 173

"Astarte Syriaca"(Rossetti), **V:** 238, 240

Astonished Heart, The (Coward), **Supp. II:** 152

Astonishing the Gods (Okri), **Supp. V:** 347, 349, 353, 359, 360–361

"Assault, The" (Nichols), **VI:** 419

Assembling a Ghost (Redgrove), **Supp. VI:** 236

"Assumption" (Beckett), **Retro. Supp. I:** 17

Astraea Redux. A Poem on the Happy Restoration . . . of . . . Charles the Second (Dryden), **II:** 292, 304

Astride the Two Cultures (Koestler), **Supp. I:** 36

"Astronomy" (Housman), **VI:** 161

Astrophel (collection), **I:** 160

Astrophel. A Pastoral Elegy (Spenser), **I:** 126; **IV:** 205

Astrophel and Other Poems (Swinburne), **V:** 333

Astrophel and Stella (Sidney), **I:** 161, 169–173; **Retro. Supp. II:** 334–339, 340–341

Asylum Piece and Other Stories (Kavan), **Supp. VII:** 210–211, 212, 214

"At a Calvary near the Ancre" (Owen), **VI:** 450, 451

"At a Potato Digging" (Heaney), **Supp. II:** 270

"At a Warwickshire Mansion" (Fuller), **Supp. VII:** 73

"At Castle Boterel" (Hardy), **VI:** 18

"At East Coker" (Day Lewis), **Supp. III:** 130

"At First Sight" (Reid), **Supp. VII:** 328

At Freddie's (Fitzgerald), **Supp. V:** 96, 98, 101, 103–104

"At Grass" (Larkin), **Supp. I:** 277

"At Isella" (James), **VI:** 69

At Lady Molly's (Powell), **VII:** 348

"At Last" (Kincaid), **Supp. VII:** 220–221

"At Lehmann's" (Mansfield), **VII:** 172, 173

"At Senlis Once" (Blunden), **VI:** 428

At Swim–Two–Birds (O'Nolan), **Supp. II:** **323–326**, 332, 336, 338

"At the Ball" (Fuller), **Supp. VII:** 80

"At the Bay" (Mansfield), **VII:** 175, 177, 179, 180

At the Bottom of the River (Kincaid), **Supp. VII:** 217, 221, 222, 223, 224, 225

"At the British War Cemetery, Bayeux" (Causley), **VII:** 448

"At the Centre" (Gunn), **Supp. IV:** 267

"At the Crossroads" (Kinsella), **Supp. V:** 267

"At the Edge of the Wood" (Redgrove), **Supp. VI:** 228

"At the End of the Passage" (Kipling), **VI:** 173–175, 183, 184, 193

"At the Grave of Henry James" (Auden), **VII:** 380; **Retro. Supp. I:** 2

"At the Great Wall of China" (Blunden), **VI:** 429

"At the 'Mermaid'" (Browning), **IV:** 35

"At the Head Table" (Kinsella), **Supp. V:** 273

"At the Musical Festival" (Nicholson), **Supp. VI:** 219

"At the White Monument" (Redgrove), **Supp. VI:** 228–229, 237

Atalanta in Calydon (Swinburne), **IV:** 90; **V:** xxiii, 309, 313, 318, **321–324**, 331, 332; **VII:** 134

"Atheism" (Bacon), **III:** 39

Atheist's Tragedy, The (Tourneur), **II:** 29, 33, 36, 37, **38–40**, 41, 70

Athenaeum (periodical), **IV:** 252, 254, 262, 310, 315; **V:** 32, 134; **VI:** 167, 234, 374; **VII:** 32

"Athene's Song" (Boland), **Supp. V:** 39

Athenian Mercury (newspaper), **III:** 41

Atlantic Monthly (periodical), **VI:** 29, 33

"Atlantis" (Auden), **Retro. Supp. I:** 10

Atlas (periodical), **V:** 144

Atrocity Exhibition, The (Ballard), **Supp. V:** 19, 21, 25

"Attack" (Sassoon), **VI:** 431

Attempt to Describe Hafod, An (Cumberland), **IV:** 47

Attenborough, Richard, **Supp. IV:** 455

Atterbury, Francis, **III:** 23

"Attic, The" (Mahon), **Supp. VI:** 175

Attlee, Clement, **VI:** 358

"Attracta" (Trevor), **Supp. IV:** 502

Atwood, Margaret, **Supp. IV:** 233

"Aubade" (Empson), **Supp. II:** 191

"Aubade" (Larkin), **Supp. I:** 284

"Aubade" (Sitwell), **VII:** 131

Aubrey, John, **I:** 260; **II:** 45, 46, 205–206, 226, 233

"Auction" (Murphy), **Supp. V:** 317

"Auction of the Ruby Slippers, The" (Rushdie), **Supp. IV:** 443

Auden, W. H., **I:** 92, **IV:** 106, 208; **V:** 46; **VI:** 160, 208; **VII:** xii, xviii, xix–xx, 153, **379–399**, 403, **407; Supp. II:** 143–144, 190, 200, 213, 267, 481–482, 485, 486, 493, 494; **Supp. III:** 60, 100, 117, 119, 123, 131; **Supp. IV:** 100, 256, 411, 422, 423; **Retro. Supp. I: 1–15**

"Audenesque for an Initiation" (Ewart), **Supp. VII:** 37

"Auditors In" (Kavanagh), **Supp. VII:** 195–196

"Audley Court" (Tennyson), **IV:** 326n

"Auguries of Innocence" (Blake), **III:** 300

"August for the People" (Auden), **Retro. Supp. I:** 7

August Is a Wicked Month (O'Brien), **Supp. V:** 339

"August Midnight, An" (Hardy), **Retro. Supp. I:** 119

"August 1914" (Rosenberg), **VI:** 434

Augusta Triumphans; or, The Way to Make London the Most Flourishing City . . . (Defoe), **III:** 14

Augustan Ages, The (Elton), **III:** 51n

Augustan Lyric (Davie), **Supp. VI:** 115

Augustans and Romantics (Butt and Dyson), **III:** 51n

Augustus Does His Bit (Shaw), **VI:** 120

"Auld Lang Syne" (Burns), **III:** 321

Auld Licht Idylls, When a Man's Single (Barrie), **Supp. III:** 2, 3

Ault, Norman, **III:** 69, 78

"Aunt and the Sluggard, The" (Wodehouse), **Supp. III:** 447–448, 455, 457

Aunt Judy's (periodical), **V:** 271

Aunts Aren't Gentlemen (Wodehouse), **Supp. III:** 455

Aunt's Story, The (White), **Supp. I:** 131, **134–136**, 148

Aureng–Zebe (Dryden), **II:** 295, 305

Aurora Leigh (Browning), **IV:** xxi, 311, 312, 314–315, 316–318, 321

Aus dem Zweiten Reich [From the Second Reich] (Bunting), **Supp. VII:** 4

Ausonius, **II:** 108, 185

Austen, Alfred, **V:** 439

Austen, Cassandra, **Retro. Supp. II:** 13–14

Austen, Jane, **III:** 90, 283, 335–336, 345; **IV:** xi, xiv, xvii, 30, **101–124; V:** 51; **Supp. II:** 384; **Supp. IV:** 154, 230, 233, 236, 237, 319; **Retro. Supp. II: 1–16,** 135

Austen–Leigh, J. E., **III:** 90

Austin, J. L., **Supp. IV:** 115

"Australia" (Hope), **Supp. VII:** 153

Australia and New Zealand (Trollope), **V:** 102

"Author of 'Beltraffio,' The," (James), **VI:** 69

"Author Upon Himself, The" (Swift), **III:** 19, 32

Authoress of the Odyssey, The (Butler), **Supp. II:** 114–116

Authorized Version of the Bible, *see* King James Version

Author's Apology, The (Bunyan), **II:** 246n

Author's Farce, The (Fielding), **III:** 105

Autobiographical Writings (Newman), **Supp. VII:** 289, 290

Autobiographies (Yeats), **V:** 301, 304, 306, 404; **VI:** 317

"Autobiographies, The" (James), **VI:** 65

"Autobiography" (Gunn), **Supp. IV:** 270

"Autobiography" (MacNeice), **VII:** 401

"Autobiography" (Reid), **Supp. VII:** 325

Autobiography (Russell), **VII:** 90

Autobiography, An (Muir), **Supp. VI:** 197, **198–200,** 201, 205

Autobiography, An (Trollope), **V:** 89, 90–93, 96, 101, 102

Autobiography and Other Essays, An (Trevelyan), **VI:** 383, 386, 388

Autobiography of a Supertramp (Davies), **Supp. III:** 398

Autobiography of Alice B. Toklas, The (Stein), **Supp. IV:** 557

Autobiography of Edward Gibbon, The (ed. Smeaton), **III:** 229n

Autobiography of My Mother, The (Kincaid), **Supp. VII:** 217, 229–230

"Autumn" (Hulme), **Supp. VI:** 134, 136, 142

Autumn (Thomson), **Supp. III:** 414–415, 416, 417, 420

Autumn Journal (MacNeice), **VII:** 412

"Autumn 1939" (Fuller), **Supp. VII:** 69

"Autumn 1942" (Fuller), **VII:** 430–431

"Autumn on Nan–Yueh" (Empson), **Supp. II:** 191–192

Autumn Sequel (MacNeice), **VII:** 407, 412, 415

"Autumn Sunshine" (Trevor), **Supp. IV:** 504

"Autumnall, The" (Donne), **II:** 118

Available for Dreams (Fuller), **Supp. VII:** 68, 79, 80, 81

Ave (Moore), **VI:** 99

"Ave Atque Vale" (Swinburne), **V:** 314, 327

"Ave Imperatrix" (Kipling), **VI:** 201

Aveling, Edward, **VI:** 102

Avignon Quintet (Durrell), **Supp. I:** 100, 101, **118–121**

"Avising the bright beams of those fair eyes" (Wyatt), **I:** 110

Avowals (Moore), **VI:** 97–98, 99

"Awake, my heart, to be loved" (Bridges), **VI:** 74, 77

Awakened Conscience, The (Dixon Hunt), **VI:** 167

Awakening Conscience, The (Holman Hunt), **V:** 45, 51, 240

Awfully Big Adventure, An (Bainbridge), **Supp. VI:** 18, **23–24**

Awkward Age, The (James), **VI:** 45, 56, 67

"Axel's Castle" (Mahon), **Supp. VI:** 177

Ayala's Angel (Trollope), **V:** 100, 102

Ayckbourn, Alan, **Supp. V: 1–17**

Ayesha: The Return of She (Haggard), **Supp. III:** 214, 222

Aylott & Jones (publishers), **V:** 131

"Baa, Baa Black Sheep" (Kipling), **VI:** 166

Babees Book, The (Early English Poems and Treatises on Manners and Meals in Olden Time) (ed. Furnival), **I:** 22, 26

Babel Tower (Byatt), **Supp. IV:** 139, 141, 149–151

Babes in the Darkling Wood (Wells), **VI:** 228

"Baby's cradle with no baby in it, A" (Rossetti), **V:** 255

Babylon Hotel (Bennett), *see Grand Babylon Hotel, The*

Bachelors, The (Spark), **Supp. I:** 203, 204

Back (Green), **Supp. II:** 254, 258–260

"Back of Affluence" (Davie), **Supp. VI:** 110

"Back to Cambo" (Hartley), **Supp. VII:** 124

Back to Methuselah (Shaw), **VI: 121–122,** 124; **Retro. Supp. II:** 323

"Background Material" (Harrison), **Supp. V:** 155

Background to Danger (Ambler), **Supp. IV:** 7–8

Backward Place, A (Jhabvala), **Supp. V:** 229

Backward Son, The (Spender), **Supp. II:** 484, 489

Bacon, Francis, **I:** 257–274; **II:** 149, 196; **III:** 39; **IV:** 138, 278, 279; annotated list of works, **I:** 271–273; **Supp. III:** 361

Bad Boy (McEwan), **Supp. IV:** 400

"Bad Five Minutes in the Alps, A" (Stephen), **V:** 283

"Bad Night, A" (Auden), **Retro. Supp. I:** 14

Bagehot, Walter, **IV:** 289, 291; **V:** xxiii, 156, 165, 170, 205, 212

"Baggot Street Deserta" (Kinsella), **Supp. V:** 259–260

Bagman, The; or, The Impromptu of Muswell Hill (Arden), **Supp. II:** 31, 32, 35

"Bagpipe Music" (MacNeice), **VII:** 413

Bailey, Benjamin, **IV:** 224, 229, 230, 232–233

Bailey, Paul, **Supp. IV:** 304

Baillie, Alexander, **V:** 368, 374, 375, 379

Bainbridge, Beryl, **Supp. VI:** 17–27

Baines, Jocelyn, **VI:** 133–134

Baird, Julian, **V:** 316, 317, 318, 335

"Baite, The" (Donne), **IV:** 327

Bakerman, Jane S., **Supp. IV:** 336

"Baker's Dozen, The" (Saki), **Supp. VI:** 243

Bakhtin, Mikhail, **Supp. IV:** 114

"Balakhana" (McGuckian), **Supp. V:** 284

"Balance, The" (Waugh), **Supp. VI:** 271

Balance of Terror (Shaffer), **Supp. I:** 314

Balaustion's Adventure (Browning), **IV:** 358, 374; **Retro. Supp. II:** 30

"Balder Dead" (Arnold), **V:** 209, 216

Baldwin, Stanley, **VI:** 353, 355

Bale, John, **I:** 1, 3

Balfour, Arthur, **VI:** 226, 241, 353

Balfour, Graham, **V:** 393, 397

Balin; or, The Knight with Two Swords (Malory), **I:** 79

Ball and the Cross, The (Chesterton), **VI:** 338

Ballad at Dead Men's Bay, The (Swinburne), **V:** 332

"Ballad of Bouillabaisse" (Thackeray), **V:** 19

"Ballad of Death, A" (Swinburne), **V:** 316, 317–318

Ballad of Jan Van Hunks, The (Rossetti), **V:** 238, 244, 245

"Ballad of Life, A" (Swinburne), **V:** 317, 318

Ballad of Peckham Rye, The (Spark), **Supp. I:** 201, 203–204

Ballad of Reading Gaol, The (Wilde), **V:** xxvi, 417–418, 419; **Retro. Supp. II:** 372–373

"Ballad of the Investiture 1969, A" (Betjeman), **VII:** 372

"Ballad of the Long–legged Bait" (Thomas), **Supp. I:** 177

"Ballad of the Three Spectres" (Gurney), **VI:** 426

"Ballad of the White Horse, The" (Chesterton), **VI:** 338–339, 341

"Ballad of Villon and Fat Madge, The" (tr. Swinburne), **V:** 327

"Ballad upon a Wedding, A" (Suckling), **II:** 228–229

Ballade du temps jadis (Villon), **VI:** 254

Ballade of Truthful Charles, The, and Other Poems (Swinburne), **V:** 333

Ballade on an Ale–Seller (Lydgate), **I:** 92

Ballads (Stevenson), **V:** 396

Ballads (Thackeray), **V:** 38

Ballads and Lyrical Pieces (Scott), **IV:** 38

Ballads and Other Poems (Tennyson), **IV:** 338

Ballads and Poems of Tragic Life (Meredith), **V:** 224, 234

Ballads and Sonnets (Rossetti), **V:** xxiv, 238, 244, 245

Ballads of the English Border (Swinburne), **V:** 333

Ballard, J. G., **III:** 341; **Supp. V: 19–34**

Ballast to the White Sea (Lowry), **Supp. III:** 273, 279

Balliols, The (Waugh), **Supp. VI:** 273

Ballot (Smith), **Supp. VII:** 351

"Ballroom of Romance, The" (Trevor), **Supp. IV:** 503

"Bally *Power Play*" (Gunn), **Supp. IV:** 272

Ballygombeen Bequest, The (Arden and D'Arcy), **Supp. II:** 32, 35

Balthazar (Durrell), **Supp. I:** 104–105, 106, 107

Balzac, Honoré de, **III:** 334, 339, 345; **IV:** 153n; **V:** xvi, xviii, xix–xxi, 17, 429; **Supp. IV:** 123, 136, 238, 459

Bamborough, J. B., **Retro. Supp. I:** 152

Bancroft, John, **II:** 305

"Bangor Requiem" (Mahon), **Supp. VI:** 177

"Banim Creek" (Harris), **Supp. V:** 132

Banks, John, **II:** 305

"Bann Valley Eclogue" (Heaney), **Retro. Supp. I:** 134

"Barbara of the House of Grebe" (Hardy), **VI:** 22; **Retro. Supp. I:** 117

Barbara, pseud. of Arnold Bennett

Barbauld, Anna Laetitia, **III:** 88, 93

"Barber Cox and the Cutting of His Comb" (Thackeray), **V:** 21, 37

Barcellona; or, The Spanish Expedition under . . . Charles, Earl of Peterborough (Farquhar), **II:** 353, 355, 364

Barchester Towers (Trollope), **V:** xxii, 93, 101

"Bard, The" (Gray), **III:** 140–141

Bardic Tales (O'Grady), **Supp. V:** 36

"Bards of Passion . . ." (Keats), **IV:** 221

Barker, Granville, *see* Granville Barker, Harley

Barker, Sir Ernest, **III:** 196

Barker, Pat, **Supp. IV: 45–63**

Barker, Thomas, **II:** 131

Barker's Delight (Barker), *see Art of Angling, The*

Barksted, William, **II:** 31

"Barley" (Hughes), **Supp. I:** 358–359

Barnaby Rudge (Dickens), **V:** 42, 54, 55, 66, 71

Barnes, William, **VI:** 2

Barnes, Julian, **Supp. IV: 65–76**, 445, 542

"Barney Game, The" (Friel), **Supp. V:** 113

"Barnfloor and Winepress" (Hopkins), **V:** 381

"Barnsley Cricket Club" (Davie), **Supp. VI:** 109

Barrack–Room Ballads (Kipling), **VI:** 203, 204

Barreca, Regina, **Supp. IV:** 531

Barren Fig Tree, The; or, The Doom . . . of the Fruitless Professor (Bunyan), **II:** 253

Barrett, Eaton Stannard, **III:** 335

Barrie, James M., **V:** 388, 392; **VI:** 265, 273, 280; **Supp. III: 1–17**, 138, 142

Barry Lyndon (Thackeray), **V:** 24, 28, 32, 38

Barrytown Trilogy, The (Doyle), **Supp. V:** 78, 80–87, 88, 89

Barsetshire novels (Trollope), **V:** 92–96, 98, 101

Bartas, Guillaume du, **II:** 138

Bartered Bride, The (Harrison), **Supp. V:** 150

Barth, John, **Supp. IV:** 116

Barthes, Roland, **Supp. IV:** 45, 115

Bartholomew Fair (Jonson), **I:** 228, 243, 324, 340, 342–343; **II:** 3; **Retro. Supp. I:** 164

Bartlett, Phyllis, **V:** x, xxvii

Barton, Bernard, **IV:** 341, 342, 343, 350

Barton, Eustace, **Supp. III:** 342

"Base Details" (Sassoon), **VI:** 430

Basement, The (Pinter), **Supp. I:** 371, 373, 374; **Retro. Supp. I:** 216

"Basement Room, The" (Greene), **Supp. I:** 2

Basic Rules of Reason (Richards), **Supp. II:** 422

Basil: A Story of Modern Life (Collins), **Supp. VI:** 92, 95

Basil Seal Rides Again (Waugh), **VII:** 290

"Basking Shark" (MacCaig), **Supp. VI:** 192

Bate, Walter Jackson, **Retro. Supp. I:** 185

Bateman, Colin, **Supp. V:** 88

Bateson, F. W., **IV:** 217, 323n, 339

Bath (Sitwell), **VII:** 127

Bath Chronicle (periodical), **III:** 262

"Bath House, The" (Gunn), **Supp. IV:** 268–269

Bathurst, Lord, **III:** 33

"Bats' Ultrasound" (Murray), **Supp. VII:** 281

Batsford Book of Light Verse for Children (Ewart), **Supp. VII:** 47

Batsford Book of Verse for Children (Ewart), **Supp. VII:** 47

Battenhouse, Roy, **I:** 282

"*Batter my heart, three person'd God*" (Donne), **I:** 367–368; **II:** 122

Battiscombe, Georgina, **V:** xii, xxvii, 260

"Battle Hill Revisited" (Murphy), **Supp. V:** 323

Battle of Alcazar, The (Peele), **I:** 205, 206

Battle of Aughrim, The (Murphy), **Supp. V:** 321–324

"Battle of Aughrim, The" (Murphy), **Supp. V:** 317, 321–322

"Battle of Blenheim, The" (Southey), **IV:** 58, 67–68

Battle of Brunanburh, The, **Retro. Supp. II:** 307

Battle of Life, The (Dickens), **V:** 71

Battle of Maldon, The, **Retro. Supp. II:** 307

Battle of Marathon, The (Browning), **IV:** 310, 321

Battle of Shrivings, The (Shaffer), **Supp. I:** 323–324

Battle of the Books, The (Swift), **III:** 17, 23, 35; **Retro. Supp. I:** 276, 277

Baucis and Philemon (Swift), **III:** 35

Baudelaire, Charles **III:** 337, 338; **IV:** 153; **V:** xiii, xviii, xxii–xxiii, 310–318, 327, 329, 404, 405, 409, 411; **Supp. IV:** 163

Baum, L. Frank, **Supp. IV:** 450

Baumann, Paul, **Supp. IV:** 360

Baumgartner's Bombay (Desai), **Supp. V:** 53, 55, 66, 71–72

Bay (Lawrence), **VII:** 118

Bay at Nice, The (Hare), **Supp. IV:** 282, 293

Bayley, John, **Supp. I:** 222

Bayly, Lewis, **II:** 241

"Baymount" (Murphy), **Supp. V:** 328

"Be It Cosiness" (Beerbohm), **Supp. II:** 46

Be my Guest! (Ewart), **Supp. VII:** 41

"Be still, my soul" (Housman), **VI:** 162

Beach, J. W., **V:** 221n, 234

"Beach of Fales, The" (Stevenson), **V:** 396; **Retro. Supp. I:** 270

Beachcroft, T. O., **VII:** xxii

Beaconsfield, Lord, *see* Disraeli, Benjamin

Beardsley, Aubrey, **V:** 318n, 412, 413

"Beast in the Jungle, The" (James), **VI:** 55, 64, 69

Beasts and Super–Beasts (Saki), **Supp. VI:** 245, 251

Beasts' Confession to the Priest, The (Swift), **III:** 36

Beatrice (Haggard), **Supp. III:** 213

Beattie, James, **IV:** 198

Beatty, David, **VI:** 351

Beau Austin (Stevenson), **V:** 396

Beauchamp's Career (Meredith), **V:** xxiv, 225, 228–230, 231, 234

Beaumont, Francis, **II: 42–67**, 79, 82, 87

Beaumont, Joseph, **II:** 180

Beaumont, Sir George, **IV:** 3, 12, 21, 22

Beauties and Furies, The (Stead), **Supp. IV:** 463–464

Beauties of English Poesy, The (ed. Goldsmith), **III:** 191

"Beautiful Lofty Things" (Yeats), **VI:** 216; **Retro. Supp. I:** 337

"Beautiful Young Nymph Going to Bed, A" (Swift), **III:** 32, 36; **VI:** 256

"Beauty" (Thomas), **Supp. III:** 401–402

Beauty and the Beast (Hughes), **Supp. I:** 347

Beauty in a Trance, **II:** 100

Beauvoir, Simone de, **Supp. IV:** 232

Beaux' Stratagem, The (Farquhar), **II:** 334, 353, 359–360, 362, 364

"Because of the Dollars" (Conrad), **VI:** 148

"Because the pleasure–bird whistles" (Thomas), **Supp. I:** 176

Becket (Tennyson), **IV:** 328, 338

Beckett, Samuel, **Supp. I: 43–64; Supp. IV:** 99, 106, 116, 180, 281, 284, 412, 429; **Retro. Supp. I: 17–32**

Beckford, William, **III:** 327–329, 345; **IV:** xv, 230

"Bedbug, The" (Harrison), **Supp. V:** 151

Beddoes, Thomas, **V:** 330

Bedford–Row Conspiracy, The (Thackeray), **V:** 21, 37

"Bedroom Eyes of Mrs. Vansittart, The" (Trevor), **Supp. IV:** 500

Bedroom Farce (Ayckbourn), **Supp. V:** 3, 12, 13, 14

Beds in the East (Burgess), **Supp. I:** 187

Bedtime Story (O'Casey), **VII:** 12

"Bedtime Story for my Son" (Redgrove), **Supp. VI: 227–228,** 236

Bee (periodical), **III:** 40, 179

"Bee Orchd at Hodbarrow" (Nicholson), **Supp. VI:** 218

"Beechen Vigil" (Day Lewis), **Supp. III:** 121

Beechen Vigil and Other Poems (Day Lewis), **Supp. III:** 117, 120–121

"Beehive Cell" (Murphy), **Supp. V:** 329

Beekeepers, The (Redgrove), **Supp. VI:** 231

"Beeny Cliff" (Hardy), **Retro. Supp. I:** 118

Beerbohm, Max, **V:** 252, 390; **VI:** 365, 366; **Supp. II: 43–59,** 156

"Before Action" (Hodgson), **VI:** 422

Before Dawn (Rattigan), **Supp. VII:** 315

"Before Her Portrait in Youth" (Thompson), **V:** 442

"Before I knocked" (Thomas), **Supp. I:** 175

Before She Met Me (Barnes), **Supp. IV:** 65, 67–68

"Before Sleep" (Kinsella), **Supp. V:** 263

"Before the Mirror" (Swinburne), **V:** 320

"Before the Party" (Maugham), **VI:** 370

Beggar's Bush (Beaumont, Fletcher, Massinger), **II:** 66

Beggar's Opera, The (Gay), **III:** 54, 55, **61–64,** 65–67; **Supp. III:** 195; **Retro. Supp. I:** 80

"Beggar's Soliloquy, The" (Meredith), **V:** 220

Begin Here: A War–Time Essay (Sayers), **Supp. III:** 336

"Beginning, The" (Brooke), **Supp. III:** 52

Beginning of Spring, The (Fitzgerald), **Supp. V:** 98, 106

Behan, Brendan, **Supp. II: 61–76**

Behind the Green Curtains (O'Casey), **VII:** 11

Behn, Aphra, **Supp. III: 19–33**

"Behold, Love, thy power how she despiseth" (Wyatt), **I:** 109

"Being Stolen From" (Trevor), **Supp. IV:** 504

"Being Treated, to Ellinda" (Lovelace), **II:** 231–232

"Beldonald Holbein, The" (James), **VI:** 69

"Belfast vs. Dublin" (Boland), **Supp. V:** 36

Belief and Creativity (Golding), **Supp. I:** 88

Belief in Immortality and Worship of the Dead, The (Frazer), **Supp. III:** 176

Belin, Mrs., **II:** 305

Belinda (Edgeworth), **Supp. III: 157– 158,** 162

Belinda, An April Folly (Milne), **Supp. V:** 298–299

Bell, Acton, pseud. of Anne Brontë

Bell, Clive, **V:** 345

Bell, Currer, pseud. of Charlotte Brontë

Bell, Ellis, pseud. of Emily Brontë

Bell, Julian, **Supp. III:** 120

Bell, Quentin, **VII:** 35; **Retro. Supp. I:** 305

Bell, Robert, **I:** 98

Bell, Vanessa, **VI:** 118

Bell, The (Murdoch), **Supp. I:** 222, 223– 224, 226, 228–229

"Bell of Aragon, The" (Collins), **III:** 163

"Bell Ringer, The" (Jennings), **Supp. V:** 218

Bellamira; or, The Mistress (Sedley), **II:** 263

"Belle Heaulmière" (tr. Swinburne), **V:** 327

"Belle of the Ball–Room" (Praed), **V:** 14

Belloc, Hilaire, **VI:** 246, 320, 335, 337, 340, 447; **VII:** xiii; **Supp. IV:** 201

Belloc, Mrs. Lowndes, **Supp. II:** 135

Bellow, Saul, **Supp. IV:** 26, 27, 42, 234

Bells and Pomegranates (Browning), **IV:** 356, 373–374

Belmonte, Thomas, **Supp. IV:** 15

Belsey, Catherine, **Supp. IV:** 164

Belton Estate, The (Trollope), **V:** 100, 101

"Bench of Desolation, The" (James), **VI:** 69

Bend in the River, A (Naipaul), **Supp. I:** 393, **397–399,** 401

Bender, T. K., **V:** 364–365, 382

Bending of the Bough, The (Moore), **VI:** 87, 95–96, 98

Benedict, Ruth, **Supp. III:** 186

Benjamin, Walter, **Supp. IV:** 82, 87, 88, 91

Benlowes, Edward, **II:** 123

Benn, Gotfried, **Supp. IV:** 411

Bennett, Arnold, **VI:** xi, xii, xiii, 226, 233n, **247–268,** 275; **VII:** xiv, xxi; **Supp. III:** 324, 325; **Supp. IV:** 229, 230–231, 233, 239, 241, 249, 252; **Retro. Supp. I:** 318

Bennett, Joan, **II:** 181, 187, 201, 202; **V:** 199, 201

Benson, A. C., **V:** 133, 151; **Supp. II:** 406, 418

Benstock, Bernard, **Supp. IV:** 320

Bentham, Jeremy, **IV:** xii, xv, 50, 130– 133, 278, 295; **V:** viii

Bentley, Clerihew, **IV:** 101

Bentley, E. C., **VI:** 335

Bentley, G. E., Jr., **III:** 289n, 307

Bentley, Richard, **III:** 23

Bentley's Miscellany (periodical), **V:** 42

Benveniste, Émile, **Supp. IV:** 115

"Benvolio" (James), **VI:** 69

Beowulf, **I:** 69; **Supp. VI: 29–44; Retro. Supp. II:** 298, 299, 305–306, 307

"Beowulf: The Monsters and the Critics" (Tolkien), **Supp. II:** 521

Beppo (Byron), **IV:** xvii, 172, 177, **182– 184,** 186, 188, 192

Bequest to the Nation, A (Rattigan), **Supp. VII:** 320

Berdoe, Edward, **IV:** 371

Bérénice (Racine), **II:** 98

Bergerac, Cyrano de, *see* Cyrano de Bergerac

Bergonzi, Bernard, **VII:** xxi, xxxvii; **Supp. IV:** 233, 364

"Berkeley and 'Philosophic Words'" (Davie), **Supp. VI:** 107

Berkeley, George, **III:** 50

Berlin stories (Isherwood), **VII:** 309, 311–312

"Bermudas" (Marvell), **II:** 208, 210, 211, 217

Bernard, Charles de, **V:** 21

Bernard, Richard, **II:** 246

Bernard Shaw and Mrs. Patrick Campbell: Their Correspondence (ed. Dent), **VI:** 130

Bernard Shaw's Letters to Granville Barker (ed. Purdom), **VI:** 115n, 129

Bernard Shaw's Rhyming Picture Guide . . . (Shaw), **VI:** 130

"Bertie Changes His Mind" (Wodehouse), **Supp. III:** 458

Bertrams, The (Trollope), **V:** 101

Besant, Annie, **VI:** 103, 249

Beside the Ocean of Time (Brown), **Supp. VI:** 64, **67–68**

Best of Defoe's Review, The (ed. Payne), **III:** 41

Best of Enemies, The (Fry), **Supp. III:** 195

Best of Roald Dahl, The (Dahl), **Supp. IV:** 209

"Best of the Young British Novelists, The" (Granta special issue), **Supp. IV:** 304

Best Wine Last: An Autobiography through the Years 1932–1969, The (Waugh), **Supp. VI:** 268, **271–272,** 273, 275–276

"Bestre" (Lewis), **VII:** 77

Bethell, Augusta, **V:** 84

Betjeman, John, **VII:** xxi–xxii, **355–377**

Betrayal (Pinter), **Supp. I:** 377

Betrayal, The (Hartley), **Supp. VII:** 121, 131, 132

Betrayal of the Left, The (Orwell), **VII:** 284

Betrothed, The (Scott), **IV:** 39

Better Class of Person, A (Osborne), **Supp. I:** 329

Better Dead (Barrie), **Supp. III:** 2

"Better Resurrection, A" (Rossetti), **V:** 254

Between (Brooke–Rose), **Supp. IV:** 98, 99, 104, 105, 108–109, 112

"Between Mouthfuls" (Ayckbourn), **Supp. V:** 11

Between the Acts (Woolf), **VII:** 18, 19, 22, 24, 26; **Retro. Supp. I:** 308, 321

"Between the Conceits" (Self), **Supp. V:** 402–403

Between the Iceberg and the Ship (Stevenson), **Supp. VI:** 257, 259, 264

"Between the Lotus and the Robot" (Koestler), **Supp. I:** 34n

Between These Four Walls (Lodge and Bradbury), **Supp. IV:** 365

"Between Two Nowheres" (MacCaig), **Supp. VI:** 192

Between Us Girls (Orton), **Supp. V:** 363, 366–367, 372

"Bevel, The" (Kelman), **Supp. V:** 245

"Beware of Doubleness" (Lydgate), **I:** 64

"Beware of the Dog" (Dahl), **Supp. IV:** 209

Beyle, Marie Henri, *see* Stendhal

Beyond (Richards), **Supp. II:** 421, 426, **428–429**

Beyond Good and Evil (Nietzsche), **IV:** 121; **V:** xxv; **Supp. IV:** 50

"Beyond Howth Head" (Mahon), **Supp. VI:** 170, 175

Beyond Personality (Lewis), **Supp. III:** 248

Beyond Reductionism: New Perspectives in the Life Sciences (Koestler), **Supp. I:** 37, 38

Beyond the Mexique Bay (Huxley), **VII:** 201

"Beyond the Pale" (Kipling), **VI:** 178–180

"Beyond the Pale" (Trevor), **Supp. IV:** 502

"Beyond Words" (Okri), **Supp. V:** 360

BFG, The (Dahl), **Supp. IV:** 204, 207, 225

Bhutto, Benazir, **Supp. IV:** 444, 455

Bhutto, Zulfikar Ali, **Supp. IV:** 444

Biala, Janice, **VI:** 324

"Bianca Among the Nightingales" (Browning), **IV:** 315

Biathanatos (Donne), **I:** 370; **Retro. Supp. II:** 96–97

Bible, *see* English Bible

Bibliography of Henry James, A (Edel and Laurence), **VI:** 66

Bickerstaff, Isaac, pseud. of Sir Richard Steele and Joseph Addison

Big Day, The (Unsworth), **Supp. VII:** 354, 357

"Big Deaths, Little Deaths" (Thomas), **Supp. IV:** 492

Big H, The (Harrison), **Supp. V:** 150, 164

Big House, The (Behan), **Supp. II:** 70–71

Big Toys (White), **Supp. I:** 131, 151

Bill for the Better Promotion of Oppression on the Sabbath Day, A (Peacock), **IV:** 170

Bingo (Bond), **Supp. I:** 423, 433–434

"Binsey Poplars" (Hopkins), **V:** 370, 371

Binyon, Laurence, **VI:** 416, 439

Biographia Literaria (Coleridge), **IV:** xvii, **4,** 6, 18, 25, 41, **44–45,** 50, 51, 52–53, 56; **Retro. Supp. II:** 62–64

"Biographical Notice of Ellis and Acton Bell" (Brontë), **V:** 131, 134, 152, 153

"Bird and Beast" (Rossetti), **V:** 258

"Bird Auction, The" (McGuckian), **Supp. V:** 284

"Bird in the House" (Jennings), **Supp. V:** (Jennings), **Supp. V:** 218

Bird of Paradise (Drabble), **Supp. IV:** 230

"Bird Poised to Fly, The" (Highsmith), **Supp. V:** 180

"Bird Study" (Jennings), **Supp. V:** 218

"Birds, The" (du Maurier), **Supp. III:** 143, 147, 148

Birds, The (film), **III:** 343; **Supp. III:** 143

"Birds at Winter Nightfall" (Hardy), **Retro. Supp. I:** 119

Birds, Beasts and Flowers (Lawrence), **VII:** 90, 118, 119; **Retro. Supp. II:** 233–234

Birds Fall Down, The (West), **Supp. III:** 440, 444

Birds of Heaven (Okri), **Supp. V:** 359, 360

"Birds of Paradise" (Rossetti), **V:** 255

Birds of Paradise, The (Scott), **Supp. I:** 259, **263–266,** 268

Birthday Letters (Hughes), **Retro. Supp. II:** 202, 216–218

Birkenhead, Lord (F. E. Smith), **VI:** 340–341

Birmingham Colony, **VI:** 167

Birney, Earle, **Supp. III:** 282

Birrell, A., **II:** 216

Birth by Drowning (Nicholson), **Supp. VI:** **222–223**

Birth of Manly Virtue, The (Swift), **III:** 35

"Birth of the Squire, The" (Gay), **III:** 58

Birth of Tragedy, The (Nietsche), **Supp. IV:** 3, 9

"Birth Place" (Murphy), **Supp. V:** 328

"Birth–Bond, The" (Rossetti), **V:** 242

Birthday (Frayn), **Supp. VII:** 57

"Birthday, A" (Mansfield), **VII:** 172, 173

"Birthday, A" (Muir), **Supp. VI:** 207

"Birthday, A" (Rossetti), **V:** 252

Birthday Boys, The (Bainbridge), **Supp. VI:** **24–25,** 26

Birthday Party (Milne), **Supp. V:** 309

Birthday Party, The (Pinter), **Supp. I:** 367, 369–370, 373, 380; **Retro. Supp. I:** 216–217, 224

"Birthdays" (MacCaig), **Supp. VI:** 192

"Birthplace, The" (James), **VI:** 69

Birthstone (Thomas), **Supp. IV:** 479, 480–481, 492

"Bishop Blougram's Apology" (Browning), **IV:** 357, 361, 363

"Bishop Burnet and Humphrey Hardcastle" (Landor), **IV:** 91

"Bishop Orders His Tomb at St. Praxed's Church, The" (Browning), **IV:** 356, 370, 372

Bishop's Bonfire, The (O'Casey), **VII:** xvii 10

"Bishop's Fool, The" (Lewis), **VII:** 80

Bishton, John, **Supp. IV:** 445

Bit o' Love, A (Galsworthy), **VI:** 280

"Bit of Young Life, A" (Gordimer), **Supp. II:** 232

Bit Off the Map, A (Wilson), **Supp. I:** 155

"Bit Off the Map, A" (Wilson), **Supp. I:** 155, 157, 161

"Bitch" (Dahl), **Supp. IV:** 220

Bitter Fame (Stevenson), **Supp. VI:** **263**

Bitter Lemons (Durrell), **Supp. I:** 104, 111–113

Bitter Sweet (Coward), **Supp. II:** 142, 146, 147

Black and Silver (Frayn), **Supp. VII:** 57

"Black and Tans,"**VII:** 2

Black and White (Collins), **Supp. VI:** 102

Black Arrow, The (Stevenson), **V:** 396

Black Book, The (Durrell), **Supp. I:** 93, 94, 96, **97–100,** 118, 122, 123

Black Book, The (Middleton), **II:** 3

Black Comedy (Shaffer), **Supp. I:** 317, 318, 321–322, 324

Black Daisies for the Bride (Harrison), **Supp. V:** 164

Black Dogs (McEwan), **Supp. IV:** 389, 390, 398, 404–406

Black Dwarf, The (Scott), **IV:** 39

"Black Goddess, The" (Graves), **VII:** 261, 270

"Black Guillemot, The" (Nicholson), **Supp. VI:** **218**

Black House, The (Highsmith), **Supp. V:** 180

Black Knight, The (Lydgate), *see Complaint of the Black Knight, The Black Lamb and Grey Falcon* (West), **Supp. III:** 434, 438–439, 445

"Black Lace Fan My Mother Gave Me, The" (Boland), **Supp. V:** 46–47

"Black Madonna, The" (Lessing), **Supp. I:** 242–243

"Black March" (Smith), **Supp. II:** 469

Black Marsden (Harris), **Supp. V:** 138–139

Black Mass (Bond), **Supp. I:** 423, 429

"Black Mass, The" (Ewart), **Supp. VII:** 45

"Black Mate, The" (Conrad), **VI:** 135, 148

Black Mischief (Waugh), **VII:** 290, 294–295

"Black Mountain Poets: Charles Olson and Edward Dorn, The" (Davie), **Supp. VI:** 116

Black Prince, The (Murdoch), **Supp. I:** 226, 228, 229–230

Black Robe, The (Collins), **Supp. VI:** 102–103

Black Goddess and the Sixth Sense, The (Redgrove), **Supp. VI:** 234–235

"Black Takes White" (Cameron), **VII:** 426

Black Tower, The (James), **Supp. IV:** 319, 320, 325, 327–328

"Black Virgin" (McGuckian), **Supp. V:** 288

"Blackberry-Picking" (Heaney), **Retro. Supp. I:** 123

"Blackbird in a Sunset Bush" (MacCaig), **Supp. VI:** 192

Black–out in Gretley (Priestley), **VII:** 212, 217

"Blackness" (Kincaid), **Supp. VII:** 221, 223, 229

Blackstone, Bernard, **VII:** xiv, xxxvii

Blackstone, Sir William, **III:** 199

Blackwood's (periodical), **IV:** xvii, 129, 145, 269–270, 274; **V:** 108–109, 111, 137, 142, 190, 191

Blair, Robert, **III:** 336

Blair, Tony, **Supp. IV:** 74

Blake (Ackroyd), **Supp. VI:** 10, **11**

Blake, Nicholas (pseud.), *see* Day Lewis, Cecil

Blake, Robert, **IV:** 296, 304, 306–308

Blake, William, **II:** 102, 115, 258; **III:** 174, **288–309,** 336; **IV:** 178; **V:** xiv–xvi, xviii, **244,** 316–317, 325, 329–330, 403; **V:** viii, 163; **VI:** viii; **VII:** 23–24; **Supp. II:** 523, 531; **Supp. IV:** 188, 410, 448; **Retro. Supp. I:** 33–47

Blake, William (neé Blech), **Supp. IV:** 459, 461

Blake's Chaucer: The Canterbury Pilgrims (Blake), **III:** 307

"Blakesmoor in H—shire" (Lamb), **IV:** 76–77

Blandings Castle (Wodehouse), **Supp. III:** 453

"Blank, A" (Gunn), **Supp. IV:** 278

Blank Cheque, The (Carroll), **V:** 274

Blank Verse (Lloyd and Lamb), **IV:** 78, 85

Blasphemers' Banquet, The (Harrison), **Supp. V:** 164

Blast (periodical), **VII:** xiii, 72

Blasting and Bombardiering (Lewis), **VII:** 72, 76, 77

Blather (periodical), **Supp. II:** 323, 338

Blatty, William Peter, **III:** 343, 345

Bleak House (Dickens), **IV:** 88; **V:** 4, 42, 47, 53, 54, 55, 59, 62–66, 68, 69, 70, 71; **Supp. IV:** 513

Blenheim (Trevelyan), **VI:** 392–393

"Blessed Among Women" (Swinburne), **V:** 325

"Blessed Are Ye That Sow Beside All Waters: A Lay Sermon" (Coleridge), **IV:** 56

Blessed Body (More), **Supp. VII:** 245

"Blessed Damozel, The" (Rossetti), **V:** 236, 239, 315

"Blighters" (Sassoon), **VI:** 430

Blind Beggar of Alexandria, The (Chapman), **I:** 234, 243

Blind Date (film; Ambler), **Supp. IV:** 3

Blind Fireworks (MacNeice), **VII:** 411

Blind Love (Collins), **Supp. VI:** 103

"Blind Love" (Pritchett), **Supp. III:** 325–327

Blind Love and Other Stories (Pritchett), **Supp. III:** 313, 325

Blind Mice, The (Friel), **Supp. V:** 115

"Blinded Bird, The" (Hardy), **Retro. Supp. I:** 119

Blindness (Green), **Supp. II:** 249–251

"Bliss" (Mansfield), **VII:** 174

Blithe Spirit (Coward), **Supp. II:** 154–155, 156

"Blizzard Song" (Thomas), **Supp. IV:** 494

Bloch, Robert, **III:** 342

Blomberg, Sven, **Supp. IV:** 88

"Blood" (Murray), **Supp. VII:** 273, 281, 282

Blood and Family (Kinsella), **Supp. V:** 270, 271

"Blood–feud of Toad–Water, The" (Saki), **Supp. VI:** 246

Blood of the Bambergs, The (Osborne), **Supp. I:** 335

Blood Red, Sister Rose (Keneally), **Supp. IV:** 346

Blood, Sweat and Tears (Churchill), **VI:** 349, 361

Blood Will Tell (Christie), *see Mrs. McGinty's Dead*

"Bloodlines" (Motion), **Supp. VII:** 263

"Bloody Chamber, The" (Carter), **Supp. III:** 88

Bloody Chamber and Other Stories, The (Carter), **Supp. III:** 79, 87, 88–89

"Bloody Cranesbill, The" (Nicholson), **Supp. VI:** 219

"Bloody Son, The" (Swinburne), **V:** 321

Bloom, Harold, **III:** 289n, 307; **V:** 309, 316, 329, 402

Bloomfield, Paul, **IV:** xii, xxiv, 306

Bloomsbury: A House of Lions (Edel), **VII:** 39

Bloomsbury Group, The (Johnstone), **VI:** 413

Blot in the Scutcheon, A (Browning), **IV:** 374

"Blow, The" (Hardy), **VI:** 17

Blow Your House Down (retitled *Liza's England;* Barker), **Supp. IV:** 45, 46, 50–53, 57

"Blucher and Sandt" (Landor), **IV:** 92

Bludy Serk, The (Henryson), **Supp. VII:** 146, 148

"Blue bell is the sweetest Flower, The" (Brontë), **V:** 134

"Blue Closet, The" (Morris), **IV:** 313

"Blue Dress, The" (Trevor), **Supp. IV:** 501

"Blue Eyes" (Warner), **Supp. VII:** 371

Blue Flower, The (Fitzgerald), **Supp. V:** 95, 96, 98, 99, 100, 107–108

"Blue Lenses, The" (du Maurier), **Supp. III:** 147

"Bluebeard's Ghost" (Thackeray), **V:** 24, 38

Blunden, Edmund, **IV:** xi, xxiv, 86, 210, 254, 267, 316; **VI:** 416, **427–429,** 439, 454; **VII:** xvi

Blunderer, The (Highsmith), **Supp. V:** 170

Blyton, Enid, **Supp. IV:** 434

Boarding House, The (Trevor), **Supp. IV:** 501, 506–507, 511

Boas, F. S., **I:** 218, 275

Boat, The (Hartley), **Supp. VII:** 123, 127, 128

"Boat House, Bank Ground, Coniston, The" (Nicholson), **Supp. VI:** 216

Boat That Mooed, The (Fry), **Supp. III:** 195

Boating for Beginners (Winterson), **Supp. IV:** 541, 542, 545–547, 555

"Bob Hope Classic Show (ITV) and 'Shelley Among the Ruins,' Lecture by Professor Timothy Webb—both Saturday evening, 26.9.81" (Ewart), **Supp. VII:** 45

"Bob Robinson's First Love" (Thackeray), **V:** 24, 38

"Bob's Lane" (Thomas), **Supp. III:** 394, 405

Boccaccio, Giovanni, **II:** 292, 304; **Supp. IV:** 461

Body Below (film; Ambler), **Supp. IV:** 3

Body in the Library (Christie), **Supp. II:** 131, 132

Body Language (Ayckbourn), **Supp. V:** 3, 10, 11

Body Snatcher, The (Stevenson), **V:** 396

"Body's Beauty" (Rossetti), **V:** 237

Boehme, Jacob, **IV:** 45

"Boeotian Count, The" (Murray), **Supp. VII:** 275

Boethius, **I:** 31, 32; **II:** 185

Bog of Allen, The (Hall), **Supp. II:** 322

Bog People, The (Glob), **Retro. Supp. I:** 128

"Bogland" (Heaney), **Supp. II:** 271–272

"Bohemians, The" (Gurney), **VI:** 427

Boiardo, Matteo, **IV:** 231

Boileau, Nicolas, **IV:** 92, 93

Boke of Eneydos, The (Skelton), **I:** 82

Boklund, Gunnar, **II:** 73

Boland, Eavan, **Supp. V:** **35–52**

Bold, Alan, **Supp. IV:** 256

Böll, Heinrich, **Supp. IV:** 440

"Bombers" (Day Lewis), **Supp. III:** 127

"Bombing Practice" (Nicholson), **Supp. VI:** 214

Bond, Edward, **Supp. I:** **421–436; Supp. IV:** 182

Bond Honoured, A (Osborne), **Supp. I:** 335–336, 337–338

Bonduca (Fletcher), **II:** 45, 58, 60, 65

"Bone Elephant, The" (Motion), **Supp. VII:** 262

"Bonfire Under a Black Sun" (O'Casey), **VII:** 13

Bonnefon, Jean de, **II:** 108

Boodle, Adelaide, **V:** 391, 393, 397

"Book, The" (Vaughan), **II:** 187

"Book Ends" (Harrison), **Supp. V:** 153–154

Book for Boys and Girls, A; or, Country Rhimes for Children (Bunyan), **II:** 253

Book of Ahania, The (Blake), **III:** 307; **Retro. Supp. I:** 44

Book of Answers, A (Hope), **Supp. VII:** 164

Book of Balaam's Ass, The (Jones), **Supp. VII:** 170

Book of Common Praise, The (Newman), **Supp. VII:** 291

Book of Los, The (Blake), **III:** 307

Book of Nonsense, A (Lear), **V:** xx, 76, 82–83, 87

Book of Sir Lancelot and Queen Guinevere, The (Malory), **I:** 70–71, 77; **Retro. Supp. II:** 249–250

Book of Snobs, The (Thackeray), **V:** 24–25, 28, 38

Book of the Church, The (Southey), **IV:** 71

Book of the Duchess, The (Chaucer), **I:** 29, 31, 43, 54; **Retro. Supp. II:** 36–38

Book of Thel, The (Blake), **III:** 302, 307; **Retro. Supp. I:** 35–36

Book of Tristram de Lyonesse (Malory), **Retro. Supp. II:** 248

Book of Urizen, The (Blake), *see First Book of Urizen, The*

Booke of Balettes, A (Wyatt), **I:** 97

Books and Persons: Being Comments on a Past Epoch (Bennett), **VI:** 265, 267

Books Do Furnish a Room (Powell), **VII:** 352

Books of Bale (Arden), **Supp. II:** 41

"Books of the Ocean's Love to Cynthia, The" (Ralegh), **I:** 147, 148, 149

Bookshop, The (Fitzgerald), **Supp. V:** 95, 97, 100, 101–102

Boon (Wells), **VI:** 227, 239–240, 333

Border Antiquities (Scott), **IV:** 38

Border Ballads (Swinburne), **V:** 333

"Border Campaign, The" (Heaney), **Retro. Supp. I:** 134

Borderers, The (Wordsworth), **III:** 338; **IV:** 3, 5–6, 25

Borges, Jorge Luis, **Supp. IV:** 558

Borges: A Reader (tr. Reid), **Supp. VII:** 332

"Borgia, thou once wert almost too august" (Landor), **IV:** 98

"Boris Is Buying Horses" (Berger), **Supp. IV:** 93

"Born 1912" (Fuller), **Supp. VII:** 80

Born in Exile (Gissing), **V:** 425, 428, 429–430, 437

"Born Yesterday" (Larkin), **Supp. I:** 278

Borough, The (Crabbe), **III:** 273–274, 275, 280, 281, 283–285, 286

Borstal Boy (Behan), **Supp. II: 61–63,** 64, 69, 70, 72, 73

Bosch, Hieronymus, **Supp. IV:** 199, 249

"Boscombe Valley Mystery, The" (Doyle), **Supp. II:** 171

Bostock, Anya, **Supp. IV:** 87

Bostonians, The (James), **VI: 39–41,** 67

Boswell, James, **III:** 54, 107, 110–115, 117, 119–122, **234–251; IV:** xv, xvi, 27, 88n, 280; **Retro. Supp. I:** 145–149

"Boswell and Rousseau" (Leigh), **III:** 246n

Boswell for the Defence 1769–1774 (ed. Pottle and Wimsatt), **III:** 249

Boswell in Extremis 1776–1778 (ed. Pottle and Weis), **III:** 249

Boswell in Holland 1763–1764 (ed. Pottle), **III:** 249

Boswell in Search of a Wife 1766–1769 (ed. Brady and Pottle), **III:** 249

Boswell: Lord of Auchinleck 1778–1782 (ed. Pottle and Reed), **III:** 249

Boswell on the Grand Tour: Germany and Switzerland 1764 (ed. Pottle), **III:** 249

Boswell on the Grand Tour: Italy . . . 1765–1766 (ed. Brady and Pottle), **III:** 249

Boswell: The Ominous Years 1774–1776 (ed. Pottle and Ryskamp), **III:** 249

Boswelliana . . . Memoir and Annotations by the Rev. Charles Rogers (Rogers), **III:** 249

Boswell's Book of Bad Verse (ed. Werner), **III:** 249

Boswell's London Journal 1762–1763 (ed. Pottle), **III:** 249

Boswell's Notebook, 1776–1777 (Boswell), **III:** 244, 249

"Botany Bay Eclogues" (Southey), **IV:** 60

Bothie of Tober–na–Vuolich, The (Clough), **V:** 155, 156, 158, 159, 161–164, 166, 167, 169, 170

Bothie of Toper–na–Fuosich, The (Clough), **V:** 170

Bothwell (Swinburne), **V:** 314, 330, 331, 332

Botticelli, Sandro, **V:** 345

Bottle Factory Outing, The (Bainbridge), **Supp. VI:**18–20, 24, 27

"Bottle Imp, The" (Stevenson), **V:** 396

Bottle in the Smoke, A (Wilson), **Supp. VI:** 304, 307

Boucicault, Dion, **V:** 415; **VII:** 2

Bouge of Court, The (Skelton), **I:** 83, 84–85

Boughner, D. C., **I:** 186

Boursault, Edme, **II:** 324, 332

Bow Down (Harrison), **Supp. V:** 164

"Bow in the Cloud, The" (Nicholson), **Supp. VI:** 215

Bowen, Elizabeth, **Supp. II: 77–95; Supp. V:** 151, 500, 514

Bowen, Stella, **VI:** 324

Bowen's Court (Bowen), **Supp. II:** 78, 84, 91

Bowers, Fredson, **II:** 44

Bowles, Caroline, **IV:** 62, 63

"Bowling Alley and the Sun, or, How I Learned to Stop Worrying and Love America, The" (Lodge), **Supp. IV:** 373

Bowra, C. M., **VI:** 153

Bowra, Maurice, **V:** 252–256, 260

Boy and the Magic, The (tr. Fry), **Supp. III:** 195

Boy Comes Home, The (Milne), **Supp. V:** 299

Boy Hairdresser, The (Orton), **Supp. V:** 363, 364, 367

Boy in the Bush, The (Lawrence), **VII:** 114; **Retro. Supp. II:** 230–231

Boy: Tales of Childhood (Dahl), **Supp. IV:** 204, 205, 206, 208, 225

Boy Who Followed Ripley, The (Highsmith), **Supp. V:** 171

"Boy Who Talked with Animals, The" (Dahl), **Supp. IV:** 223, 224

Boy with a Cart, The; Cuthman, Saint of Sussex (Fry), **Supp. III:** 191, 194, 195, 196

Boyd, H. S., **IV:** 312

Boyer, Abel, **II:** 352

Boyhood: Scenes from Provincial Life (Coetzee), **Supp. VI:** 77–78

Boyle, Robert, **III:** 23, 95

Boys Who Stole the Funeral, The: A Novel Sequence (Murray), **Supp. VII:** 270, 284–286

"Boys' Weeklies" (Orwell), **Supp. III:** 107

Bradbrook, M. C., **I:** xi, 292, 329; **II:** 42, 78; **VII:** xiii–xiv, xxxvii, 234

Bradbury, Ray, **III:** 341

Bradbury, Malcolm, **Supp. IV:** 303, 365

Braddon, Mary Elizabeth, **V:** 327

Bradley, A. C., **IV:** 106, 123, 216, 235, 236

Bradley, F. H., **V:** xxi, 212, 217

Bradley, Henry, **VI:** 76

Brady, F., **III:** 249

Braine, John, **Supp. IV:** 238

Brand (Hill), **Supp. V:** 199, 200–201

Brander, Laurence, **IV:** xxiv; **VII:** xxii

Brantley, Ben, **Supp. IV:** 197–198

Branwell Brontë (Gerin), **V:** 153

Branwell's Blackwood's (periodical), **V:** 109, 123

Branwell's Young Men's (periodical), *see Branwell's Blackwood's*

Brass Butterfly, The (Golding), **Supp. I:** 65, 75

Brassneck (Hare and Brenton), **Supp. IV:** 281, 282, 283, 284–285, 289

Brave New World (Huxley), **III:** 341; **VII:** xviii, 200, 204

Brave New World Revisited (Huxley), **VII:** 207

"Bravest Boat, The" (Lowry), **Supp. III:** 281

Brawne, Fanny, **IV:** 211, 216–220, 222, 226, 234

Bray, Charles, **V:** 188

Bray, William, **II:** 275, 276, 286

Brazil (Gilliam), **Supp. IV:** 442, 455

"Breach, The" (Murray), **Supp. VII:** 276

"Bréagh San Réilg, La" (Behan), **Supp. II:** 73

"Break My Heart" (Golding), **Supp. I:** 79

Break of Day in the Trenches (Rosenberg), **VI:** 433, 434

"Breake of day" (Donne), **Retro. Supp. II:** 88

"Breaking Ground" (Gunn), **Supp. IV:** 271

"Breaking the Blue" (McGuckian), **Supp. V:** 287

Breath (Beckett), **Supp. I:** 60; **Retro. Supp. I:** 26

Brecht, Bertolt, **II:** 359; **IV:** 183; **VI:** 109, 123; **Supp. II:** 23, 25, 28; **Supp. IV:** 82, 87, 180, 194, 198, 281, 298

"Bredon Hill" (Housman), **VI:** 158

Brendan (O'Connor), **Supp. II:** 63, 76

Brendan Behan's Island (Behan), **Supp. II:** 64, 66, 71, 73, 75

Brendan Behan's New York (Behan), **Supp. II:** 75

Brennoralt (Suckling), *see Discontented Colonel, The*

Brenton, Howard, **Supp. IV:** 281, 283, 284, 285

Brethren, The (Haggard), **Supp. III:** 214

"Breton Walks" (Mahon), **Supp. VI:** 168, 172

Brett, Raymond Laurence, **IV:** x, xi, xxiv, 57

Brickfield, The (Hartley), **Supp. VII:** 131–132

Bricks to Babel (Koestler), **Supp. I:** 37

Bridal of Triermain, The (Scott), **IV:** 38

"Bride and Groom" (Hughes), **Supp. I:** 356

"Bride in the 30's, A" (Auden), **Retro. Supp. I:** 8

Bride of Abydos, The (Byron), **IV:** xvii, 172, 174–175, 192

Bride of Frankenstein (film), **III:** 342

Bride of Lammermoor, The (Scott), **IV:** xviii, 30, 36, 39

Brides of Reason (Davie), **Supp. VI:** 106–107

"Brides, The" (Hope), **Supp. VII:** 154

"Bride's Prelude, The" (Rossetti), **V:** 239, 240

Brideshead Revisited (Waugh), **VII:** xx–xxi, 290, 299–300; **Supp. IV:** 285

"Bridge, The" (Thomas), **Supp. III:** 401

"Bridge for the Living" (Larkin), **Supp. I:** 284

"Bridge of Sighs, The" (Hood), **IV:** 252, 261, 264–265

Bridges, Robert, **II:** 160; **V:** xx, 205, 362–368, 370–372, 374, 376–381; **VI:** xv, **71–83,** 203

Brief History of Moscovia . . . , A (Milton), **II:** 176

Brief Lives (Aubrey), **I:** 260

Brief Lives (Brookner), **Supp. IV:** 131–133

Brief Notes upon a Late Sermon . . . (Milton), **II:** 176

Briefing for a Descent into Hell (Lessing), **Supp. I:** 248–249

Briggflatts (Bunting), **Supp. VII:** 1, 2, 5, 7, 9–13

Bright, A. H., **I:** 3

"Bright Building, The" (Graham), **Supp. VII:** 109, 110–111

"Bright–Cut Irish Silver" (Boland), **Supp. V:** 49–50

Bright Day (Priestley), **VII:** 209, 218–219

"Bright Star!" (Keats), **IV:** 221

Brighton Rock (Greene), **Supp. I:** 2, 3, **7–9,** 11, 19; **Retro. Supp. II:** 153–155

"Brigid's Girdle, A" (Heaney), **Retro. Supp. I:** 132

"Brilliance" (Davie), **Supp. VI:** 113

"Brilliant Career, A" (Joyce), **Retro. Supp. I:** 170

Bring Larks and Heroes (Keneally), **Supp. IV:** 345, 347, 348–350

"Bringing to Light" (Gunn), **Supp. IV:** 269–270

Brink, Andre, **Supp. VI: 45–59**

Brinkmanship of Galahad Threepwood, The (Wodehouse), *see Galahad at Blandings*

Brissenden, R. F., **III:** 86n

Bristow Merchant, The (Dekker and Ford), **II:** 89, 100

Britain and West Africa (Cary), **VII:** 186

Britannia (periodical), **V:** 144

Britannia (Thomson), **Supp. III:** 409, 411, 420

Britannia Rediviva: A Poem on the Birth of the Prince (Dryden), **II:** 304

"Britannia Victrix" (Bridges), **VI:** 81

"British Church, The" (Herbert), **I:** 189

British Dramatists (Greene), **Supp. I:** 6, 11

"British Guiana" (Ewart), **Supp. VII:** 38

British History in the Nineteenth Century (Trevelyan), **VI:** 390

British Magazine (periodical), **III:** 149, 179, 188

British Museum Is Falling Down, The (Lodge), **Supp. IV:** 363, 365, 367, 369–370, 371

British Women Go to War (Priestley), **VII:** 212

Briton (Smollett), **III:** 149

Brittain, Vera, **II:** 246

Britten, Benjamin, **Supp. IV:** 424

"Broad Bean Sermon, The" (Murray), **Supp. VII:** 275

"Broad Church, The" (Stephen), **V:** 283

Broadbent, J. B., **II:** 102, 116

Broadcast Talks (Lewis), **Supp. III:** 248

"Broagh" (Heaney), **Retro. Supp. I:** 128

"Brodgar Poems" (Brown), **Supp. VI:** 71

Broken Chariot, The (Sillitoe), **Supp. V:** 411, 421

Broken Cistern, The (Dobrée), **V:** 221, 234

"Broken heart, The" (Donne), **Retro. Supp. II:** 90

Broken Heart, The (Ford), **II:** 89, 92, 93–98, 99, 100

"Broken Wings, The" (James), **VI:** 69

Brome, Richard, **II:** 87

Brontë, Anne, **IV:** 30; **V:** xviii, xx, xxi, 105, 106, 108, 110, 112–119, 122, 126, **128–130,** 131, 132, **134–135, 140–141, 145, 150, 153; Supp. III:** 195; **Supp. IV:** 239; **Retro. Supp. I:** 55–56

Brontë, Branwell, **V:** xvii, 13, 105, 106, 108–112, 117–119, 121–124, 126, 130, 131, 135, 141, 145, 150, 153

Brontë, Charlotte, **III:** 338, 344, 345; **IV:** 30, 106, 120; **V:** xvii, xx–xxii, 3, 13–14, 20, 68, 105–107, **108–112,** 113–118, **119–126,** 127, 129, 130–140, 144, 145–150, 152, 286; **Supp. III:** 144, 146; **Supp. IV:** 146, 471; **Retro. Supp. I:** 58–61

Brontë, Emily, **III:** 333, 338, 344, 345; **IV:** ix, xvii, xx–xxi, 13, 14, 105, 106, 108, 110, **112–117,** 118, 122, 130, 131, **132–135, 141–145,** 147, 150, 152–153, 254; **Supp. III:** 144; **Supp. IV:** 462, 513; **Retro. Supp. I:** 56–58

Brontë, Patrick, **V:** 105–108, 109, 122, 146, 151

Brontë Poems (ed. Benson), **V:** 133, 151

Brontë Sisters, **Retro. Supp. I: 49–62**

Brontë Story, The: A Reconsideration of Mrs. Gaskell's "Life of Charlotte Brontë" (Lane), **V:** 13n, 16

Brontës, The, Their Lives, Friendships and Correspondence (ed. Wise and Symington), **V:** 117, 118, 151

Brontës of Haworth, The (Fry), **Supp. III:** 195

Brontës' Web of Childhood, The (Ratchford), **V:** 151

"Bronze Head, The" (Yeats), **VI:** 217

Bronze Horseman: Selected Poems of Alexander Pushkin (tr. Thomas), **Supp. IV:** 495

Brooke, Arthur, **I:** 305

Brooke, Jocelyn, **VII:** xviii, xxxvii; **Supp. II:** 202, 203

Brooke, Rupert, **VI:** xvi, 416, **419–420,** 439; **VII:** 35; **Supp. II:** 310; **Supp. III: 45–61**

Brooke Kerith, The. A Syrian Story (Moore), **VI:** xii, 88, 89, **93–94,** 99

Brooke–Rose, Christine, **Supp. IV: 97–118**

Brookner, Anita, **Supp. IV: 119–137**

Brooks, C., **IV:** 323n, 339

"Brooksmith" (James), **VI:** 48, 69

Brophy, Brigid, **IV:** 101

"Brother Fire" (MacNeice), **VII:** 414

Brotherly Love: A Sermon (Swift), **III:** 36

"Brothers" (Hopkins), **V:** 368–369

Brothers and Sisters (Compton–Burnett), **VII:** 61, 66, 67, 69

Brown, Charles, **IV:** 211, 221, 231–233

Brown, E. K., **V:** 211–212, 217

Brown, Ford Madox, **V:** 248

Brown, George Mackay, **Supp. VI: 61–73**

Brown, John, **II:** 245, 253, 254

Brown, Tom, **III:** 41

Brown Owl, The (Ford), **VI:** 320

Brownbread (Doyle), **Supp. V:** 77, 87–88

Browne, Moses, **II:** 142

Browne, Sir Thomas, **II: 145–157,** 185, 345n; **III:** 40

"Brownie" (Gissing), **V:** 437

Browning, Elizabeth Barrett, **IV:** xvi, xix–xxii, **310–322,** 356, 357; **Retro. Supp. II:** 23–24

Browning, Robert, **IV:** viii, xii, xiii, xix–xxiii, 240, 248, 252, 254, 311–312, 314, 318–319, 352, **354–375; V:** xxv, 209, 287, 315, 330; **VI:** 336; **Supp. IV:** 139; **Retro. Supp. II: 17–32**

Browning: "Men and Women" and Other Poems: A Casebook (ed. Watson), **IV:** 375

Browning Version, The (Rattigan), **Supp. VII:** 307, 315–316

Browning's Essay on Chatterton (ed. Smalley), **IV:** 374

Browning's Major Poetry (Jack), **IV:** 375

"Bruno" (Warner), **Supp. VII:** 381

"Bruno's Revenge" (Carroll), **V:** 270

"Brute, The" (Conrad), **VI:** 148

Brutus (Pope), **III:** 71–72

Brutus's Orchard (Fuller), **Supp. VII: 73–74**

Bryce, James, **IV:** 289

Brydon, Diana, **Supp. IV:** 459, 462

Bryskett, Lodowick, **I:** 124

Bubble, The (Swift), **III:** 35

Bucer, Martin, **I:** 177

Buchan, John, **Supp. II:** 299, 306; **Supp. IV:** 7

Buchanan, Robert, **V:** 238, 245

Buckhurst, Lord, *see* Dorset, earl of (Charles Sackville)

Buckingham, duke of (George Villiers), **II:** 206, 255, 294

Buckle, G. E., **IV:** 306–308

"Buckles of Superior Dosset, The" (Galsworthy), **VI:** 270

Bucolic Comedies (Sitwell), **VII:** 131, 132

"Bucolics" (Auden), **Retro. Supp. I:** 13

Budgell, Eustace, **III:** 48

Buffon, Georges–Louis, **Supp. II:** 106, 107, 108; **III:** 189

Buff (Fuller), **Supp. VII:** 74

"Bugle Call" (Thomas), **Supp. III:** 404

"Bugler's First Communion, The" (Hopkins), **V:** 368–369

"Building, The" (Larkin), **Supp. I:** 280, 282, 283

"Build–Up" (Ballard), **Supp. V:** 21

"Bujak and the Strong Force" (Amis), **Supp. IV:** 40

"Buladelah–Taree Song Cycle, The" (Murray), **Supp. VII:** 276–277

Bulgakov, Mikhail, **Supp. IV:** 445

"Bull" (MacCaig), **Supp. VI:** 188

"Bull: A Farce" (Self), **Supp. V:** 405–406

"Bull That Thought, The" (Kipling), **VI:** 189, 190

"Bulldog"Drummond series (Sapper), **Supp. IV:** 500

Bullett, Gerald, **V:** 196, 199, 200

Bulwer–Lytton, Edward, **III:** 340, 345; **IV:** 256, 295, 311; **V:** 22, 47

Bundle, The (Bond), **Supp. I:** 423

Bundle of Letters, A (James), **VI:** 67, 69

Bunting, Basil, **Supp. VII: 1–15**

Bunyan, John, **I:** 16; **II: 240–254; III:** 82; **V:** 27

Buoyant Billions: A Comedy of No Manners in Prose (Shaw), **VI:** 127, 129

Burbidge, Thomas, **V:** 159

Burckhardt, Jakob, **V:** 342

"Burden of Itys, The" (Wilde), **V:** 401

"Burden of Ninevah, The" (Rossetti), **V:** 240, 241

Bürger, Gottfried August, **IV: 44, 48**

Burger's Daughter (Gordimer), **Supp. II:** 225, 228, 230, 231, 232, **234–237,** 241, 242, 243

Burgess, Anthony, **Supp. I: 185–198; Supp. IV:** 4, 13, 234, 449

"Burghers, The" (Hardy), **Retro. Supp. I:** 120

"Burial of the Dead, The" (Eliot), **Retro. Supp. II:** 126

"Burial of the Rats, The" (Stoker), **Supp. III:** 382

Buried Alive (Bennett), **VI:** 250, 252, 257, 266

Buried Day, The (Day Lewis), **Supp. III:** 116, 128

"Buried Life, The" (Arnold), **V:** 210

Burke, Edmund, **III:** 185, **193–206,** 274; **IV:** xii–xvi, 54, 127, 130, 133, 136–138, 271, 275; **VI:** 356; **Supp. III:** 371, 467, 468, 470

Burke, Kenneth, **Supp. IV:** 114

Burke and Bristol, 1774–1780 (Barker), **III:** 196

"Burleigh" (Macaulay), **IV:** 279

Burlington Magazine, **Supp. IV:** 121

"Burma Casualty" (Lewis), **VII:** 447

Burmann, Peter, **III:** 96

Burmese Days (Orwell), **VII:** 276, 278

Burn, The (Kelman), **Supp. V:** 243, 249, 250–251

Burne–Jones, Edward, **IV:** 346; **V:** 236, 293–296, 302, 318n, 355; **VI:** 166; **Supp. V:** 98, 99

Burney, Charles, Supp. III: 65–67

Burney, Frances, **Supp. III: 63–78**

Burning Cactus, The (Spender), **Supp. II:** 488

Burning of the Brothel, The (Hughes), **Supp. I:** 348

"Burning Want" (Murray), **Supp. VII:** 283–284

Burning World, The (Ballard), **Supp. V:** 24

Burnshaw, Stanley, **Supp. IV:** 460, 473

Burnt Ones, The (White), **Supp. I:** 131, 136, 143

Burnt-Out Case, A (Greene), **Supp. I:** 7, 13, 15, 16, 18; **Retro. Supp. II:** 162

Burroughs, William S., **Supp. V:** 26

Busconductor Hines, The (Kelman), **Supp. V:** 242, 246–247

Business of Good Government, The (Arden), **Supp. II:** 29

Busker, The (Kelman), **Supp. V:** 256

Busman's Honeymoon (Sayers), **Supp. III:** 335, 336, 347–348

"Busted Scotch" (Kelman), **Supp. V:** 249

"Busy" (Milne), **Supp. V:** 302

"But at the Stroke of Midnight" (Warner), **Supp. VII:** 381

...but the Clouds (Beckett), **Retro. Supp. I:** 29

Butcher's Dozen (Kinsella), **Supp. V:** 267

Butler, Samuel, **Supp. II: 97–119**

Butor, Michel, **Supp. IV:** 115

"Butterflies" (McEwan), **Supp. IV:** 391

"Buzzard and Alder" (Stevenson), **Supp. VI:** 261

"By Achmelrich Bridge" (MacCaig), **Supp. VI:** 182

"By the burn" (Kelman), **Supp. V:** 250–251

By Jeeves (Ayckbourn and Webber), **Supp. V:** 3

By Night Unstarred (Kavanagh), **Supp. VII:** 189

"By the Fire-Side" (Browning), **Retro. Supp. II:** 23–24

By the Line (Keneally), **Supp. IV:** 345

By Way of Introduction (Milne), **Supp. V:** 300

Byatt, A. S.(neé Antonia Drabble), **Supp. IV: 139–156,** 229

Bye–Bye, Blackbird (Desai), **Supp. V:** 55, 60–62

"Byre" (MacCaig), **Supp. VI:** 188, 190, 194

Byron, George Gordon, Lord, **III:** 329; **IV:** x, xi, 46, 61, 91, 129, 132, 168, **171–194,** 198–199, 202, 206, 215, 281, 299; **V:** 111–112, 247, 324; **Supp. III:** 356, 365; and Coleridge, **IV:** 46, 48; and Hazlitt, **IV:** 129; and Shelley, **IV:** 159, 172, 176–177, 179, 181, 182, 198–199, 202, 206; **Retro. Supp. I:** 250–251; and Southey, **IV:** 61, 184–187; literary style, **III:** 336, 337–338; **IV:** viii, ix, xi, 129, 281; **V:** 17, 116; **VII:** xix

"Byron" (Durrell), **Supp. I:** 126

"Byron" (Macaulay), **IV:** 281

Byron, Robert, **Supp. IV:** 157

Byron and the Ruins of Paradise (Gleckner), **IV:** 173, 194

Byron in Italy (Quennell), **IV:** 194

Byron: The Years of Fame (Quennell), **IV:** 194

Byronic Hero, The Types and Prototypes (Thorslev), **IV:** 173, 194

Byron's Conspiracy (Chapman), **I:** 249–251

Byron's Tragedy (Chapman), *see Tragedy of Byron, The*

"Byzantium" (Yeats), **VI:** 215; **Retro. Supp. I:** 336–337

"C. G. Jung's First Years" (Kinsella), **Supp. V:** 269*Cab at the Door, A* (Pritchett), Supp. III: 311, 312

Cabinet of Dr. Caligari, The (film), **III:** 342

Cadenus and Vanessa (Swift), **III:** 18, 31, 35; **Retro. Supp. I:** 283–284

"Caedmon" (Nicholson), **Supp. VI:** 216

Caesar and Cleopatra (Shaw), **VI:** 112; **Retro. Supp. II:** 316–317

Caesar and Pompey (Chapman), **I:** 252–253

Caesar Borgia (Lee), **II:** 305

Caesar's Fall (Drayton, Middleton, Munday, Webster, et al.), **II:** 68, 85

Caesar's Wife (Maugham), **VI:** 369

"Cage of Sand" (Ballard), **Supp. V:** 24

Cage Without Grievance (Graham), **Supp. VII:** 105, 107–109, 112

"Caged Skylark, The" (Hopkins), **Retro. Supp. II:** 190

Cagliostro, Alessandro di, **III:** 332

Cahier d'un retour au pays natal (Césaire), **Supp. IV:** 77

Cain (Byron), **IV:** xviii, 173, 177, **178–182,** 193

Cakes and Ale (Maugham), **VI:** 367, 371, 374, 377

Calderón de la Barca, Pedro, **II:** 312n, 313n; **IV:** 206, 342, 349

Caleb Williams (Godwin), *see Adventures of Caleb Williams, The*

Caledonia (Defoe), **III:** 13

Calendar of Love, A (Brown), **Supp. VI:** 64

Calendar of Modern Letters (periodical), **VII:** 233

"Calenture" (Reid), **Supp. VII:** 328

"Caliban upon Setebos" (Browning), **IV:** 358, 364, 370, 372; **Retro. Supp. II:** 26

"Calidore" (Keats), **IV:** 214

Caliph's Design, The (Lewis), VII: 72, 75n

Call for the Dead (le Carré), **Supp. II:** 299, **305–307,** 308, 311

Called to Be Saints (Rossetti), **V:** 260

Call–Girls, The (Koestler), **Supp. I:** 28n, 32

Callista: A Tale of the Third Century (Newman), **Supp. VII:** 299

"Calm, The" (Donne), **Retro. Supp. II:** 86

"Calmative, The" (Beckett), **Supp. I:** 50, 59; **Retro. Supp. I:** 21

Calvin, John, **I:** 241

Calvino, Italo, **Supp. IV:** 558

"Camberwell Beauty, The" (Pritchett), **Supp. III:** 312, **327–328,** 329

Camberwell Beauty and Other Stories, The (Pritchett), **Supp. III:** 313, 327

Cambises (Preston), **I:** 122, 213–214

"Cambridge" (Ewart), **Supp. VII:** 36

Cambridge (Phillips), **Supp. V:** 380, 386, 388–390

Cambridge Bibliography of English Literature, **III:** 51, 52

Cambyses (Preston), *see Cambises*

Camden, William, **Retro. Supp. I:** 152–153

Cameron, Norman, **VII:** 421, 422, 426

Camilla; or, A Picture of Youth (Burney), **Supp. III:** 64, 65, 68, 72, 73–75, 76

Cammaerts, Emile, **V:** 262, 274

Camp, The (Sheridan), **III:** 253, 264

Campaign, The (Addison), **III:** 46

Campaspe (Lyly), **I:** 198, 199–200

Campbell, Ian, **IV:** xii, xxiv, 250

Campbell, Joseph, **VII:** 53

Campbell, Roy, **IV:** 320; **VII:** 422, 428; **Supp. III:** 119

Campbell, Sue Ellen, **Supp. IV:** 336

Campbell's Kingdom (film, Ambler), **Supp. IV:** 3

Campensis, Joannes, **I:** 119

Camus, Albert, **Supp. IV:** 259

Can You Find Me: A Family History (Fry), **Supp. III:** 192, 193

Can You Forgive Her? (Trollope), **V:** 96, 101

Canaan (Hill), **Supp. V:** 192–194

"Canacee" (Gower), **I:** 53–54, 55

"Canal Bank Walk" (Kavanagh), **Supp. VII:** 197

Canavans, The (Gregory), **VI:** 315

"Canberra Remnant" (Murray), **Supp. VII:** 273

"Cancer Hospital, The" (Fuller), **Supp. VII:** 80

Candida (Shaw), **III:** 263; **VI:** 108, 110–111, 113; **Retro. Supp. II:** 313–314

Candidate, The (Crabbe), III: 286

"Candidate, The" (Gray), **III:** 142

Candide (Voltaire), **IV:** 295; **Supp. IV:** 221

"Candle Indoors, The" (Hopkins), **V:** 370

Candy Floss Tree, The (Nicholson), **Supp. VI:** 218–219

Canning, George, **IV:** 132, 164

Canon of Thomas Middleton's Plays, The (Lake), **II:** 1, 21

Canopus in Argos, Archives (Lessing), **Supp. I:** 250–253

"Canterbury Cathedral" (Murphy), **Supp. V:** 328

Canterbury Tales, The (Chaucer), **I:** 1, 2, **20–47; Retro. Supp. I:** 45; **Retro. Supp. II:** 45–49, 125

Canticle of the Rose, The (Sitwell), **VII:** xvii, 130, 137

"Canto 45" (Pound), **Supp. IV:** 114, 115

Cantos (Pound), **V:** 317n; **Supp. IV:** 100, 115

Cantos of Mutability (Spenser), **I:** 140

Cap, The, and, The Falcon (Tennyson), **IV:** 338

"Cap and Bells, The" (Keats), **IV:** 217

Cape of Storms: The First Life of Adamastor (Brink), **Supp. VI: 54–55,** 57

Capell, Edward, **I:** 326

Caprice (Firbank), **Supp. II:** 201, 204, 205, **211–213**

Captain, The (Beaumont and Fletcher), **II:** 65

Captain Brassbound's Conversion (Shaw), **VI:** 110; **Retro. Supp. II:** 317

"Captain Henry Hastings" (Brontë), **V:** 122, 123–124, 135, 138, 151

Captain Lavender (McGuckian), **Supp. V:** 280, 287–289

"Captain Lavender" (McGuckian), **Supp. V:** 289

"Captain Parry" (Hood), **IV:** 267

"Captain Rook and Mr. Pigeon" (Thackeray), **V:** 21, 37

Captain Singleton (Defoe), **III:** 8, 13; **Retro. Supp. I:** 72

Captains Courageous (Kipling), **VI:** 204

"Captain's Doll, The" (Lawrence), **VII:** 90

Captives, The (Gay), **III:** 60–61, 67

Car, Thomas, **II:** 181

Caravaggio, Michelangelo Merisi da, **Supp. IV:** 95, 262

Carceri d'invenzione (Piranesi), **III:** 325

Card, The (Bennett), **VI:** 250, 258–259, 266; **Supp. III:** 324, 325

Card, The (film, Ambler), **Supp. IV:** 3

Card Castle (Waugh), **Supp. VI:** 270

Cardenio (Fletcher and Shakespeare), **II:** 43, 66, 87

Cards on the Table (Christie), **Supp. II:** 131, 135

"Care" (Murphy), **Supp. V:** 327

"Careless Lover, The" (Suckling), **II:** 227

"Careless Talk" (Bowen), **Supp. II:** 93

Careless Widow and Other Stories, A (Pritchett), **Supp. III:** 328, 329

Caretaker, The (Pinter), **Supp. I:** 367, 368, 369, **372–374,** 379, 380, 381; **Retro. Supp. I:** 224–225

Carew, Thomas, **I:** 354; **II: 222–225,** 237

Carey, John, **V:** ix, xxvii, 39, 62, 73

Carlingford, Lord, *see* Fortescue, Chichester

"Carlow Village Schoolhouse" (Murphy), **Supp. V:** 328

Carlyle, A. J., **III:** 272n

Carlyle, Jane, **IV:** 239, 240

Carlyle, R. M., **III:** 272n

Carlyle, Thomas, **IV:** xii, 38, 41–42, 70, 231, **238–250,** 266n, 273, 289, 295, 301–302, 311, 324, 341–342; **V:** vii, ix, xii, 3, 5, 165, 182, 213n, 285, 319

"Carlyon Bay Hotel" (Murphy), **Supp. V:** 328

"Carmen Becceriense, Cum Prolegomenis et Commentario Critico, Edidit H. M. B."(Beerbohm), **Supp. II: 44**

Carmen Deo Nostro, Te Decet Hymnus, Sacred Poems, Collected (Crashaw), **II:** 180, 181, 184, 201

Carmen Triumphale, for the Commencement of the Year 1814 (Southey), **IV:** 71

"Carmilla" (Le Fanu), **III:** 340, 345; **Supp. III:** 385–836

Carmina V (Herrick), **II:** 108

Carnal Island, The (Fuller), **Supp. VII:** 77–78, 81

"Carnal Knowledge" (Gunn), **Supp. IV:** 258

Carnall, Geoffrey Douglas, **IV:** xxiv, 72, 156

Carnival Trilogy, The (Harris), **Supp. V:** 135, 136, 138, 140–141

"Carol" (Nicholson), **Supp. VI:** 214–215

"Carol on Corfu" (Durrell), **Supp. I:** 123–124, 126

Caroline (Maugham), **VI:** 369

"Caroline Vernon" (Brontë), **V:** 112, 122, 123, 124, 125, 138, 151

Carpenter, Edward, **VI:** 407, 408

Carr, John Dickson, **Supp. IV:** 285

"Carrickfergus" (MacNeice), **VI:** 401

Carrington, Charles, **VI:** 166

"Carrion Comfort" (Hopkins), **V:** 374

Carroll, Lewis, **V:** xi, xix, xxii, xxvi, 86, 87, **261–275; Supp. IV:** 199, 201

Carry On, Jeeves (Wodehouse), **Supp. III:** 455, 461, 462

Carter, Angela, **III:** 341, 345; **Supp. III: 79–93; Supp. IV:** 46, 303, 459, 549, 558

Carter, Frederick, **VII:** 114

Cartoons: The Second Childhood of John Bull (Beerbohm), **Supp. II:** 51

Cartwright, John, **IV:** 103

Cartwright, William, **II:** 134, 185, 222, 237, 238

Cary, Joyce, **VII:** xvii, **185–196**

Caryl Churchill, A Casebook (King), **Supp. IV:** 194–195

"Casa d'Amunt" (Reid), **Supp. VII:** 329

Casa Guidi Windows (Browning), **IV:** 311, 314, 318, 321

"Casadh Súgaín Eile" (Behan), **Supp. II:** 68

Casanova's Chinese Restaurant (Powell), **VII:** 348–349

Cascando (play, Beckett), **Supp. I:** 60

"Cascando" (poem, Beckett), **Supp. I: 44**

Case, A. E., **III:** 25, 36

Case for African Freedom, The (Cary), **VII:** 186

"Case for Equality, The" (Drabble), **Supp. IV:** 31, 233

Case is Alter'd, The (Jonson), **Retro. Supp. I:** 156–157

"Case of Bill Williams, The" (Kavan), **Supp. VII:** 210

Case of Conscience Resolved, A (Bunyan), **II:** 253

Case of Elijah, The (Sterne), **III:** 135

Case of General Ople and Lady Camper, The (Meredith), **V:** 230–231, 234

"Case of Identity, A" (Doyle), **Supp. II:** 171

Case of Ireland . . . Stated, The (Molyneux), **III:** 27

Case of the Abominable Snowman, The (Day Lewis), **Supp. III:** 130

Case of the Midwife Toad, The (Koestler), **Supp. I:** 38

Cashel Byron's Profession (Shaw), **VI:** 102, 103, 105–106, 109–110, 113, 129

"Cask of Amontillado, The" (Poe), **III:** 339

Cassinus and Peter (Swift), **Retro. Supp. I:** 284

"Castalian Spring" (Heaney), **Retro. Supp. I:** 134

"Castaway, The" (Cowper), **III:** 218–219

Castle, The (Kafka), **III:** 340, 345; **Supp. IV:** 439

Castle Corner (Cary), **VII:** 186

Castle Dangerous (Scott), **IV:** 39

Castle of Indolence, The (Thomson), **III:** 162, 163, 171, 172; **Supp. III:** 412, **425–428**

Castle of Otranto, The (Walpole), **III:** 324, **325–327**, 336, 345; **IV:** 30; **Supp. III:** 383–384

Castle Rackrent (Edgeworth), **Supp. III:** 154–155; **Supp. IV:** 502

Castle Richmond (Trollope), **V:** 101

Castle–Croquet (Carroll), **V:** 274

Castles of Athlin and Dunbayne, The (Radcliffe), **IV:** 35

Casualties of Peace (O'Brien), **Supp. V:** 339

"Casualty" (Heaney), **Retro. Supp. I:** 130

Casuarina Tree, The (Maugham), **VI:** 370, 371

"Cat–Faith" (Reid), **Supp. VII:** 328

Cat Nappers, The (Wodehouse), *see Aunts Aren't Gentlemen*

Cat on a Houseboat (Desai), **Supp. V:** 55, 62

"Catarina to Camoens" (Browning), **IV:** 314

Catcher in the Rye, The (Salinger), **Supp. IV:** 28

Catepillar Stew (Ewart), **Supp. VII:** 47

Catharine and Petruchio, **I:** 327; *see also Taming of the Shrew, The*

Cather, Willa, **Supp. IV:** 151

Catherine (Thackeray), **V:** 22, 24, 28, 37

Cathleen ni Houlihan (Yeats and Gregory), **VI:** 218, 222, 309; **VII:** 4

Catholic Church, The (Newman), **Supp. VII:** 292

"Catholic Church and Cultural Life, The" (Lodge), **Supp. IV:** 376

"Catholic Homilies" (Ælfric of Eynsham), **Retro. Supp. II:** 297–298

"Catholic Novel in England from the Oxford Movement to the Present Day, The" (Lodge), **Supp. IV:** 364

Catiline (Jonson), **I:** 345–346; **Retro. Supp. I:** 161, 164

Cato (Addison), **III:** 46

Catriona (Stevenson), **V:** 387, 396; **Retro. Supp. I:** 267

Cat's Cradle Book, The (Warner), **Supp. VII:** 369, 381–382

Catullus, **II:** 108; **IV:** 327; **Supp. IV:** 491

Caudwell, Christopher, **Supp. III:** 120

Caught (Green), **Supp. II:** **254–256**

Cause Célèbre (Rattigan), **Supp. VII:** 318, 321

Cause For Alarm (Ambler), **Supp. IV:** 8–9

Causeries du lundi (Sainte–Beuve), **III:** 226

Causley, Charles, **VII:** 422, 434–435

"Caught in a Hurry" (Redgrove), **Supp. VI:** 231

Caution to Stir up to Watch Against Sin (Bunyan), **II:** 253

Cavafy, C. P., **VI:** 408

Cavalcade (Coward), **VI:** 264; **Supp. II:** 147, 149, 150–151

Cave, Edward, **III:** 107

Cave and the Spring, The: Essays in Poetry (Hope), **Supp. VII:** 155, 163

Cave Birds (Hughes), **Supp. I:** 351, 356–357, 363

Cavendish, George, **I:** 114

"Caverns of the Grave I've Seen, The" (Blake), **III:** 305

Cawelti, John, **Supp. IV:** 7

Caxton, William, **I:** 67, 82; **Retro. Supp. II:** 242–2

Cayley, Charles Bagot, **V:** 250–251, 253, 259

Ceausescu, Nicolae, **Supp. IV:** 195, 196

Cecilia; or, Memoirs of an Heiress (Burney), **Supp. III:** 63, 64, 67, 70, 71, 72

Cefalû (Durrell), **Supp. I:** 100, 101

"Ceix and Alceone" (Gower), **I:** 53–54

Celan, Paul, **Supp. V:** 189–190, 199–200

Celebrations and Elegies (Jennings), **Supp. V:** 217

"Celestial Omnibus" (Forster), **Supp. I** 153

Celestial Omnibus, The (Forster), **VI:** 399

Celestials, **Supp. IV:** 344–345

Celibate Lives (Moore), **VI:** 95

Celibates (Moore), **VI:** 87, 91, 95

Cellular Pathologie (Virchow), **V:** 348

Celt and Saxon (Meredith), **V:** 234

"Celtic Twilight" (MacCaig), **Supp. VI:** 187

Celtic Twilight, The, Men and Women, Ghouls and Faeries (Yeats), **VI:** 221

Cement Garden, The (McEwan), **Supp. IV:** 390, 392–393, 400, 407

Cenci, The (Shelley), **III:** 338; **IV:** xviii, 202, 208; **Supp. IV:** 468; **Retro. Supp. I:** 254

"Censored, Banned, Gagged" (Gordimer), **Supp. II:** 237

"Censors and Unconfessed History" (Gordimer), **Supp. II:** 237

"Centenary of Charles Dickens, The" (Joyce), **V:** 41

Centlivres, Susanna, **Supp. III:** 70

Centuries of Meditations (Traherne), **II:** 189n, 190, 192–193, 202

Century of Roundels, A (Swinburne), **V:** 332

Century Was Young, The (Aragon), **Supp. IV:** 466

Century's Daughter, The (retitled *Liza's England*, Barker), **Supp. IV:** 45, 46, 53–56

"Ceremony after a fire raid" (Thomas), **Supp. I:** 178

"Certain Mercies" (Graves), **VII:** 265

Certain Noble Plays of Japan (Yeats), **VI:** 218

Certain Satires (Marston), **II:** 25

Cervantes, Miguel de, **IV:** 190

Césaire, Aimé, **Supp. IV:** 77

Cestus of Aglaia, The (Ruskin), **V:** 180–181, 184

Cetywayo and His White Neighbours (Haggard), **Supp. III:** 213, 214, 216–217

Chabot, Admiral of France (Chapman), **I:** 252–253

Chadourne, Marc, **III:** 329

"Chair that Will sat in, I sat in the best, The" (FitzGerald), **IV:** 341

Chain of Voices, A (Brink), **Supp. VI:** **51–52**, 57

"Chalet" (Murphy), **Supp. V:** 329

Chalkhill, John, **II:** 133

Chamber Music (Joyce), **VII:** 41, 42; **Retro. Supp. I:** 171

Chamberlain, Neville, **VI:** 353, 355–356

"Chambermaid's Second Song, The" (Yeats), **VI:** 215

Chambers, E. K., **I:** 299; **II:** 187; **IV:** 41, 57

Chambers, R. W., **I:** 3; **Retro. Supp. I:** 143

"Chamois, The" (du Maurier), **Supp. III:** 143, 147

Champion (periodical), **III:** 97–98, 105

"Champion of the World, The" (Dahl), **Supp. IV:** 214, 223

Chance (Conrad), **VI:** 144, 146; **Supp. IV:** 250; **Retro. Supp. II:** 82

Chance Encounters (Hope), **Supp. VII:** 152

Chancer, A (Kelman), **Supp. V:** 242, 247–249

Chances, The (Fletcher), **II:** 65

Chandler, Edmund, **V:** 354, 359

Chandler, Raymond, **Supp. II:** 130, 135

"Chanel" (Durrell), **Supp. I:** 125

"Change" (Donne), **Retro. Supp. II:** 89

"Change of Policy, A" (Pritchett), **Supp. III:** 329

Change the Name (Kavan), **Supp. VII:** 212

"Changed Man, A" (Hardy), **VI:** 22

Changed Man, A, The Waiting Supper, and Other Tales (Hardy), **VI:** 20, 22

"Changeling, The" (Byatt), **Supp. IV:** 140

Changeling, The (Middleton and Rowley), **II:** 1, 3, 8, **14–18**, 21, 93

"Changing Face of Fiction, The" (Weldon), **Supp. IV:** 522, 533

Changing Places: A Tale of Two Campuses (Lodge), **Supp. IV:** 363, 365, 371, 372–375, 376, 377, 385

Changing Room, The (Storey), **Supp. I:** 408, 416–417

"Channel Passage, A" (Brooke), **Supp. III:** 53

Channel Passage, A, and Other Poems (Swinburne), **V:** 333

Chant of Jimmie Blacksmith, The (Keneally), **Supp. IV:** 345, 347–348, 350–352, 360

Chant of the Celestial Sailors, The (Pater), **V:** 357

"Chant–Pagan" (Kipling), **VI:** 203

Chants for Socialists (Morris), **V:** 306

Chaos and Night (Montherlant), **II:** 99n

"Chapel Organist, The" (Hardy), **Retro. Supp. I:** 120

"Chaperon, The" (James), **VI:** 69

Chapman, George, **I:** **232–256**, 278, 288; **II:** 30, 37, 47, 55, 70, 71, 85; **IV:** 215, 255–256

Chapman, John, **V:** 189

Chapman, R. W., **III:** 249

Chappell, E., **II:** 288

Character and Opinions of Dr. Johnson, The (Swinburne), **V:** 333

Character of a Trimmer (Halifax), **III:** 40

"Character of a Virtuous Widow" (Webster), **II:** 77

Character of England, A, as It Was Lately Presented . . . (Evelyn), **II:** 287

"Character of Holland, The" (Marvell), **II:** 211, 219

"Character of Mr. Burke" (Hazlitt), **IV:** 136

Character of Robert Earl of Salisbury, The (Tourneur), **II:** 37, 41

Characterismes of Vertues and Vice (Hall), **II:** 81

Characteristicks (Shaftesbury), **III:** 44

"Characteristics" (Carlyle), **IV:** 241

Characteristics: In the Manner of Rochefoucault's Maxims (Hazlitt), **IV:** 132, 139

"Characters" (Dickens), **V:** 46

Characters (Theophrastus), **III:** 50

Characters (Webster), **II:** 68, 81

"Characters of Dramatic Writers Contemporary with Shakespeare" (Lamb), **IV:** 79, 80

Characters of Love, The: A Study in the Literature of Personality (Bayley), **Supp. I:** 222, 224

Characters of Shakespeare's Plays (Hazlitt), **I:** 329; **IV:** xvii, 129, 139

"Characters of the First Fifteen" (Ewart), **Supp. VII:** 36

Charge Delivered to the Grand Jury, A (Fielding), **III:** 105

"Charge of the Light Brigade, The" (Tennyson), **IV:** xxi, 325

"Charity" (Cowper), **III:** 212

Charles, Amy, **Retro. Supp. II:** 174

"Charles Augustus Milverton" (Ewart), **Supp. VII:** 42

Charles Dickens (Swinburne), **V:** 333

Charles Dickens: A Critical Study (Gissing), **V:** 424, 435, 437

Charles I (Shelley), **IV:** 206

"Charles Lamb" (De Quincey), **IV:** 148

Charles Lamb and His Contemporaries (Blunden), **IV:** 86

"Charles Lamb, to those who know thee justly dear" (Southey), **IV:** 85

Charley Is My Darling (Cary), **VII:** 186, 188, 189, 190–191

Charlie and the Chocolate Factory (Dahl), **Supp. IV:** 202–203, 207, 222–223

Charlie and the Great Glass Elevator (Dahl), **Supp. IV:** 207

"Charlotte Brontë as a Critic of *Wuthering Heights*" (Drew), **V:** 153

Charlotte Brontë, 1816–1916: A Centenary Memorial (ed. Wood), **V:** 152

"Charlotte Brontë in Brussels" (Spielman), **V:** 137n

Charlotte Brontë: The Evolution of Genius (Gérin), **V:** 111, 152

Charlotte Mew and Her Friends (Fitzgerald), **Supp. V:** 98–99

Charmed Circle, A (Kavan), **Supp. VII:** 203, 205, 206–207

Chartism (Carlyle), **IV:** xix, 240, 244–245, 249, 250; **V:** viii

Chase, The, and William and Helen (Scott), **IV:** 29, 38

Chaste Maid in Cheapside, A (Middleton), **II:** 1, 3, **6–8**, 10, 21

Chastelard (Swinburne), **V:** 313, 330, 331, 332

Chatterton (Ackroyd), **Supp. VI: 7–8**

Chatterton, Thomas, **IV:** iv, 228; **V:** 405; **Supp. IV:** 344

Chatwin, Bruce, **Supp. IV: 157–177**

Chaucer, Geoffrey, **I:** 2, 15, 16, **19–47,** 49, 60, 67, 126; **II:** 70, 292, 302, 304; **IV:** 189; **V:** 298, 303; **Supp. IV:** 190; **Retro. Supp. II: 33–50,** 125

Châtiments, Les (Hugo), **V:** 324

"Cheap in August" (Greene), **Supp. I:** 16

"Chearfulness" (Vaughan), **II:** 186

"Cheek, The" (Hope), **Supp. VII:** 157–158

Cheery Soul, A (White), **Supp. I:** 131, 150

"Cheery Soul, A" (White), **Supp. I:** 143

Chekhov, Anton, **VI:** 372

"Chekhov and Zulu" (Rushdie), **Supp. IV:** 445

Cherry Orchard, The (tr. Frayn), **Supp. VII:** 61

"Cherry-ripe" (Herrick), **II:** 115

"Cherry Stones" (Milne), **Supp. V:** 302–303

"Cherry Tree, The" (Gunn), **Supp. IV:** 271

"Chest" (Self), **Supp. V:** 403

Chester Nimmo trilogy (Cary), **VII:** 186, 191, 194–195; *see also Prisoner of Grace, Except the Lord, Not Honour More*

Chester, Robert, **I:** 313

Chesterton, G. K., **IV:** 107; **V:** xxiv, 60, 262, 296, 383, 391, 393, 397; **VI:** 200, 241, 248, **335–345; VII:** xiii

Chettle, Henry, **I:** 276, 296; **II:** 47, 68

Chief of Staff (Keneally), **Supp. IV:** 347

"Chief Petty Officer" (Causley), **VII:** 434

"Child, The" (Friel), **Supp. V:** 113

"Child and the Shadow, The" (Jennings), **Supp. V:** 210

Child Christopher and Goldilind the Fair (Morris), **V:** 306

"Child Dying, The" (Muir), **Supp. VI:** 207

"Child in the House, The" (Pater), **V:** 337, 357

Child in Time, The (McEwan), **Supp. IV:** 389, 390, 400–402, 404, 406, 407

Child of Misfortune (Day Lewis), **Supp. III:** 118, 130–131

Child of Storm (Haggard), **Supp. III:** 214

Child of the Jago, The (Morrison), **VI:** 365–366

Childe Harold's Pilgrimage (Byron), **III:** 337, 338; **IV:** x, xvii, 172, **175–178,** 180, 181, 188, 192; **V:** 329

"Childe Roland to the Dark Tower Came" (Browning), **IV:** 357; **VI:** 16

"Childe-hood" (Vaughan), **II:** 188, 189, 190

Childermass (Lewis), **VII:** 71, 79, 80–81

"Childhood" (Muir), **Supp. VI:** 204–205

Childhood of Edward Thomas, The (Thomas), **Supp. III:** 393

"Childish Prank, A" (Hughes), **Supp. I:** 353

Children of Dynmouth, The (Trevor), **Supp. IV:** 501, 510–511

Children of Men, The (James), **Supp. IV:** 320, 338–339, 340

Children of the Chapel (Gordon), **V:** 313

"Children of the Zodiac, The" (Kipling), **VI:** 169, 189, 191–193

Children of Violence (Lessing), **Supp. I:** 238, **243–246**

Children's Encyclopedia (Mee), **Supp. IV:** 256

"Child's Christmas in Wales, A" (Thomas), **Supp. I:** 183

"Child's Calendar, A" (Brown), **Supp. VI:** 71

Child's Garden of Verses, A (Stevenson), **V:** 385, 387, 395; **Retro. Supp. I:** 264

Child's History of England, A (Dickens), **V:** 71

Chimeras, The (Mahon), **Supp. VI:** 173

Chimes, The (Dickens), **V:** 42, 64, 71

"Chimney Sweeper" (Blake), **III:** 297; **Retro. Supp. I:** 36, 42

China. A Revised Reprint of Articles from Titan . . . (DeQuincey), **IV:** 155

China Diary (Spender), **Supp. II:** 493

Chinamen (Frayn), **Supp. VII:** 57–58

"Chinese Button, The" (Brooke–Rose), **Supp. IV:** 103

"Chinese Letters" (Goldsmith), *see Citizen of the World, The*

"Chinese Lobster, The" (Byatt), **Supp. IV:** 155

Chinese Love Pavilion, The (Scott), **Supp. I:** 259, 263

"Chip of Glass Ruby, A" (Gordimer), **Supp. II:** 232

Chit–chat (periodical), **III:** 50

Chitty Chitty Bang Bang (film, Dahl), **Supp. IV:** 213

Chitty Chitty Bang Bang (Fleming), **Supp. IV:** 212–213

Chivers, Thomas Holley, **V:** 313

Chloe (Meredith), **V:** 231n, 234

Chloe Marr (Milne), **Supp. V:** 310

Choice of Kipling's Prose, A (Maugham), **VI:** 200, 204

"Choir School" (Murphy), **Supp. V:** 328

Chomei at Toyama (Bunting), **Supp. VII:** 4, 6–7

Chomsky, Noam, **Supp. IV:** 113–114

"Chorale" (Hope), **Supp. VII:** 158

Chorus of Disapproval, A (Ayckbourn), **Supp. V:** 3, 9–10, 14

Christ a Compleat Saviour in His Intercession (Bunyan), **II:** 253

Christ and Satan, **Retro. Supp. II:** 301

Christ Stopped at Eboli (Levi), **VI:** 299

"Christ Surprised" (Jennings), **Supp. V:** 217

"Christ upon the Waters" (Newman), **Supp. VII:** 298

Christabel (Coleridge), **II:** 179; **III:** 338; **IV:** ix, xvii, 29, 44, 48–49, 56, 218, 313; **Retro. Supp. II:** 58–59

Christe's Bloody Sweat (Ford), **II:** 88, 100

"Christening" (Murphy), **Supp. V:** 322

Christian Behaviour (Lewis), **Supp. III:** 248

Christian Behaviour . . . (Bunyan), **II:** 253

Christian Captives, The (Bridges), **VI:** 83

Christian Dialogue, A (Bunyan), **II:** 253

Christian Ethicks (Traherne), **II:** 190, 191, 201

Christian Hero, The (Steele), **III: 43, 44,** 53

Christian Morals (Browne), **II:** 149, 153, 154, 156; **III:** 40

Christie, Agatha, **III:** 341; **Supp. II: 123– 135; Supp. III:** 334; **Supp. IV:** 500

Christina Alberta's Father (Wells), **VI:** 227

Christina Rossetti (Packer), **V:** 251, 252– 253, 260

Christina Rossetti: A Divided Life (Battiscombe), **V:** 260

Christina Stead (Brydon), **Supp. IV:** 463

Christina Stead: A Biography (Rowley), **Supp. IV:** 459

"Christmas Antiphones" (Swinburne), **V:** 325

"Christmas at Sea" (Stevenson), **V:** 396

Christmas at Thompson Hall (Trollope), **V:** 102

Christmas Books (Dickens), **V:** 71

Christmas Carol, A (Dickens), **V:** xx, 42, 56–57, 71

"Christmas Carol, A" (Swinburne), **V:** 315

"Christmas Childhood, A" (Kavanagh), **Supp. VII:** 194

Christmas Comes But Once a Year (Chettle, Dekker, Heywood, Webster), **II:** 68, 85

"Christmas Day in the Workhouse" (Wilson), **Supp. I:** 153, 157

Christmas Eve and Easter Day (Browning), **Retro. Supp. II:** 25–26

"Christmas Garland Woven by Max Beerbohm, A" (Beerbohm), **Supp. II:** 45

Christmas Garland, A (Beerbohm), **Supp. II:** 45, 49

Christmas His Masque (Jonson), **Retro. Supp. I:** 165

Christmas Holiday (Maugham), **VI:** 377

"Christmas Oratorio, A" (Auden), **Retro. Supp. I:** 10–11

"Christmas Storms and Sunshine" (Gaskell), **V:** 15

Christmas–Eve and Easter–Day (Browning), **IV:** 357, 363, 370, 372, 374

Christopher, John, **Supp. V:** 22

Christopher and His Kind (Isherwood), **VII:** 318

Christopher Columbus (MacNeice), **VII:** 406

"Christopher Columbus and Queen Isabella of Spain Consummate Their Relationship" (Rushdie), **Supp. IV:** 452

"Christopher Marlowe" (Swinburne), **V:** 332

Christopher Marlowe in Relation to Greene, Peele and Lodge (Swinburne), **V:** 333

Christ's Hospital, A Retrospect (Blunden), **IV:** 86

"Christ's Hospital Five–and–Thirty Years Ago"(Lamb), **IV:** 42, 76

"Chronicle, The" (Cowley), **II:** 198

Chronicle Historie of Perkin Warbeck, The (Ford), *see Perkin Warbeck*

chronicle history, **I:** 73

Chronicle of Carlingford series (ed. Fitzgerald), **Supp. V:** 98

Chronicle of Friendships, A, 1873–1900 (Low), **V:** 393, 397

Chronicle of Queen Fredegond, The (Swinburne), **V:** 333

Chronicle of the Cid (tr. Southey), **IV:** 71

"Chronicle of the Drum, The" (Thackeray), **V:** 17, 38

Chronicles (Hall), **II:** 43

Chronicles of Barset (Trollope), **Supp. IV:** 231

Chronicles of Clovis, The (Saki), **Supp. VI:** 240–243, 245, 249

Chronicles of Narnia, The (Lewis), **Supp. III:** 247, 248, **259–261**

Chronicles of the Canongate (Scott), **IV:** 39

Chroniques (Froissart), **I:** 21

"Chronopolis" (Ballard), **Supp. V:** 22

"Chrysalides" (Kinsella), **Supp. V:** 262

Chrysaor (Landor), **IV:** 96

Church, Dean R. W., **I:** 186

Church and Queen. Five Speeches, 1860– 1864 (Disraeli), **IV:** 308

"Church-floore, The" (Herbert), **Retro. Supp. II:** 178–179

"Church Going" (Larkin), **Supp. I:** 277, 279, 280, 285

"Church Service" (Vaughan), **II:** 187

"Church Windows, The" (Herbert), **II:** 127

"Churche–Floore, The" (Herbert), **II:** 126

Church in Crisis, The (Wilson), **Supp. VI:** 305

"Churches of Northern France, The" (Morris), **V:** 293, 306

Churchill, Caryl, **Supp. IV: 179–200**

Churchill, Lady Randolph, **VI:** 349

Churchill, Winston, **III:** 27; **VI:** xv, 261, 274, **347–362,** 369, 385, 392; **Supp. III:** 58–59; speeches, **VI:** 361

Churchill by His Contemporaries (ed. Eade), **VI:** 351*n*, 361

"Church–monuments" (Herbert), **II:** 127

"Church–warden and the Curate, The" (Tennyson), **IV:** 327

"Churl and the Bird, The" (Lydgate), **I:** 57

Chymist's Key, The (tr. Vaughan), **II:** 185, 201

Cibber, Colley, **I:** 327; **II:** 314, 324–326, 331, 334, 337

Cicadas, The (Huxley), **VII:** 199

"Cicero and His Brother" (Landor), **IV:** 90, 91

Ciceronianus (Harvey), **I:** 122

"Cinders" (Hulme), **Supp. VI:** 133, 135– 136, 140, **141,** 146

Cinkante balades (Gower), **I:** 56

Cinque Ports, The (Ford), **VI:** 238, 332

Cinthio, Giraldi, **I:** 316; **II:** 71

Circe (Davenant), **II:** 305

Circle, The (Maugham), **VI:** 369

"Circle of Deception" (Waugh), **Supp. VI:** 275

Circular Billiards for Two Players (Carroll), **V:** 273

"Circus Animals' Desertion, The" (Yeats), **V:** 349; **VI:** 215; **Supp. III:** 102; **Retro. Supp. I:** 338

"Circus Wheel" (Redgrove), **Supp. VI:** 236

Citation and Examination of William Shakespeare . . . (Landor), **IV:** 100

Cities, Plains and People (Durrell), **Supp. I:** 126

Citizen of the World, The; or, Letters from a Chinese Philosopher . . . (Goldsmith), **III:** 177, 179, 185, 188–189, 191

"City of Brass, The" (Kipling), **VI:** 203

"City Sunset, A" (Hulme), **Supp. VI:** 136

"City Ways" (Amis), **Supp. II:** 2

City Wives' Confederacy, The (Vanbrugh), *see Confederacy, The*

"Civilised, The," (Galsworthy), **VI:** 273, 274, 276

Civilization in the United States (Arnold), **V:** 216

Civilization of the Renaissance in Italy, The (Burckhardt), **V:** 342

Civitatis Amor (Middleton), **II:** 3

Cixous, Hélène, **Supp. IV:** 99, 117, 232, 547, 558

"Clachtoll" (MacCaig), **Supp. VI:** 186

Clancy, Laurie, **Supp. IV:** 348

Clapp, Susannah, **Supp. IV:** 164

Clara Florise (Moore), **VI:** 96

Clare, John, **IV:** 260

Clare Drummer (Pritchett), **Supp. III:** 313

Clarel (Melville), **V:** 211

"Clarence Mangan" (Kinsella), **Supp. V:** 260

"Clarice of the Autumn Concerts" (Bennett), **VI:** 266

Clarissa (Richardson), **III:** 80–81, **85– 89,** 91, 92, 95; **VI:** 266; **Supp. III:** 30–31; **Supp. IV:** 150; **Retro. Supp. I:** 81

"Clarissa": Preface, Hints of Prefaces and Postscripts (ed. Brissenden), **III:** 86*n*

"Clarissa Harlowe Poem, The" (Ewart), **Supp. VII:** 41

Clark, Kenneth, **III:** 325, 346

Clark, Sir George, **IV:** 290

Clarke, Charles Cowden, **IV:** 214, 215

Clarke, Herbert E., **V:** 318*n*

Clarke, Samuel, **II:** 251

Clarkson, Catherine, **IV:** 49

Classic Irish Drama (Armstrong), **VII:** 14

Classical Tradition, The: Greek and Roman Influence on Western Literature (Highet), **II:** 199*n*

Classics and Commercials (Wilson), **Supp. II:** 57

Claude Lorrain's House on the Tiber (Lear), **V:** 77

Claudius novels (Graves), **VII:** xviii, 259

Claudius the God and His Wife Messalina (Graves), **VII:** 259

"Claud's Dog" (Dahl), **Supp. IV:** 214

Claverings, The (Trollope), **V:** 99–100, 101

Clayhanger (Bennett), **VI:** 248, 250, 251, 257–258

Clayhanger series(Bennett), **VI:** xiii, 247, 248, 250, 251, 257–258

Clea (Durrell), **Supp. I:** 103, 104, 106, 107

"Clean Bill, A" (Redgrove), **Supp. VI:** 234

"Cleaned Out" (Motion), **Supp. VII:** 263

"Cleaning Out the Workhouse" (McGuckian), **Supp. V:** 291

Cleanness (Gawain–Poet), **Supp. VII:** 83, 84, 98–99

Clear Light of Day (Desai), **Supp. V:** 53, 55, 62, 65–67, 68, 73

Clear State of the Case of Elizabeth Canning, A (Fielding), **III:** 105

"Clearances" (Heaney), **Supp. II:** 279–280; **Retro. Supp. I:** 131

"Cleator Moor" (Nicholson), **Supp. VI:** 214

"Cleggan Disaster, The" (Murphy), **Supp. V:** 313, 319–320

Cleomenes, The Spartan Hero (Dryden), **II:** 296, 305

"Cleon" (Browning), **IV:** 357, 360, 363

Cleopatra (Daniel), **I:** 162

Cleopatra (Haggard), **Supp. III:** 213, 222

"Cleopatra" (Swinburne), **V:** 332

"Clergy, The" (Wilson), **Supp. VI:** 305

Clergyman's Daughter, A (Orwell), **VII:** 274, 278

"Clergyman's Doubts, A" (Butler), **Supp. II:** 117

Clergymen of the Church of England (Trollope), **V:** 101

"Cleric, The" (Heaney), **Supp. II:** 279

Clerk, N. W., *see* Lewis, C. S.

Clerk's Prologue, The (Chaucer), **I:** 29

Clerk's Tale, The (Chaucer), **I:** 34; **Supp. IV:** 190

Cleveland, John, **II:** 123

"Clicking of Cuthbert, The" (Wodehouse), **Supp. III:** 462

Clifford, J. L., **III:** 244n

Clifford, W. K., **V:** 409n

"Clinical World of P. D. James, The" (Benstock), **Supp. IV:** 320

Clio: A Muse (Trevelyan), **VI:** 383–384

Clishbotham, Jedidiah, pseud. of Sir Walter Scott

"Clive" (Browning), **IV:** 367

"Clock Ticks at Christmas, A" (Highsmith), **Supp. V:** 180

"Clocks, The" (Christie), **Supp. II:** 135

Clockwork Orange, A (Burgess), **Supp. I:** 190–191

Clockwork Testament, The; or, Enderby's End (Burgess), **Supp. I:** 189

Clodd, Edward, **V:** 429

Cloning of Joanna May, The (Weldon), **Supp. IV:** 535, 536

"Clopton Hall" (Gaskell), **V:** 3

"Clorinda and Damon" (Marvell), **II:** 210, 211

Close Quarters (Golding), **Retro. Supp. I:** 104

Closed Eye, A (Brookner), **Supp. IV:** 120, 133

Closing the Ring (Churchill), **VI:** 361

"Cloud, The" (Fowles), **Supp. I:** 304

"Cloud, The" (Shelley), **IV:** 196, 204

Cloud Nine (Churchill), **Supp. IV:** 179, 180, 188–189, 198

"Clouds" (Brooke), **VI:** 420

Clouds (Frayn), **Supp. VII:** 61

"Cloud–Sculptors of Coral–D, The" (Ballard), **Supp. V:** 26

Clouds of Witness (Sayers), **Supp. III:** 338, 339

"Cloud's Swan Song, The" (Thompson), **V:** 443

Clough, Arthur Hugh, **IV:** 371; **V:** ix, xi, xviii, xxii, 7, **155–171,** 207, 208n, 209, 211, 212

"Club in an Uproar, A" (Thackeray), **V:** 25

Clune, Frank, **Supp. IV:** 350

Cnut, King, **Retro. Supp. II:** 293

Coakley, Thomas P., **Supp. IV:** 350

Coal Face (Auden), **Retro. Supp. I:** 7

"Coast, The" (Fuller), **VII:** 431

"Coat, A" (Yeats), **Retro. Supp. I:** 330

"Coat of Many Colors, A" (Desai), **Supp. V:** 53

Cobbett, William, **VI:** 337

Cobra Verde (film), **Supp. IV:** 168

Coburn, Kathleen, **IV:** 52, 55–57

Cocaine Nights (Ballard), **Supp. V:** 31–32, 34

"Cock: A Novelette" (Self), **Supp. V:** 404–405

Cock and Bull (Self), **Supp. V:** 404–406

Cock and the Fox, The (Henryson), **Supp. VII:** 136, 137–138, 147

Cock and the Jasp, The (Henryson), **Supp. VII:** 136, 137

"Cock Crows" (Hughes), **Retro. Supp. II:** 211

Cock–a–Doodle Dandy (O'Casey), **VII:** xviii, 9–10

Cockatoos, The (White), **Supp. I:** 132, 147

Cockburn, Alexander, **Supp. IV:** 449

"Cockcrow" (Herrick), **II:** 114

"Cock–crowing" (Vaughan), **II:** 185

Cockrill, Maurice, **Supp. IV:** 231

Cockshut, A. O. J., **V:** 98, 100–101, 103

Cocktail Party, The (Eliot), **VII:** 158, 159, 160–161; **Retro. Supp. II:** 132

"Coda" (Kinsella), **Supp. V:** 271

Code of the Woosters, The (Wodehouse), **Supp. III:** 459–460

"Codham, Cockridden, and Childerditch" (Thomas), **Supp. III:** 401

Coelum Britannicum . . . (Carew), **II:** 222

Coetzee, J(ohn) M(ichael), **Supp. VI:** 75–90

Coffin for Dimitrios, A (Ambler), **Supp. IV:** 9–11, 12

Coggan, Donald, archbishop of Canterbury, **I:** vi

Cohen, Francis, **IV:** 190

Cohn, Ruby, **Retro. Supp. I:** 215

Colasterion: A Reply to a Nameless Answer Against the Doctrine and Discipline of Divorce (Milton), **II:** 175

Colburn, Henry, **IV:** 254, 293; **V:** 135

"Cold, The" (Warner), **Supp. VII:** 380

"Cold, clear, and blue, The morning heaven" (Brontë), **V:** 115

Cold Coming, A (Harrison), **Supp. V:** 150

"Cold Coming, A" (Harrison), **Supp. V:** 161–163

"Cold in the earth" (Brontë), **V:** 114, 133, 134

Colenso, Bishop John William, **V:** 283

Coleridge, Derwent, **IV:** 48–49, 52

Coleridge, Hartley, **IV:** 44; **V:** 105, 125

Coleridge, Samuel Taylor, **III:** 338; **IV:** viii–xii, **41–57,** 59, 75–78, 82, 84, 115, 204, 253, 257, 281; **V:** 244; **Retro. Supp. II: 51–67;** and De Quincey, **IV:** 143, 144, 150; and Hazlitt, **IV:** 125–130, 133–134, 137, 138; and Peacock, **IV:** 161–162, 167; and Wordsworth, **IV:** 3–4, 6, 15, 128; at Christ's Hospital, **IV:** 75–78, 82; critical works, **II:** 42, 119n, 155, 179, 249–250, 298; **III:** 174, 281, 286; **IV:** 4, 6, 18, 96, 253, 257; **Retro. Supp. II:** 172; literary style, **II:** 154; **III:** 336, 338; **IV:** viii, xi, 18, 180; **V:** 62, 361, 447; Pater's essay in *Appreciations,* **V:** 244, 340–341; **Supp. IV:** 425, 426–427

"Coleridge" (Mill), **IV:** 50, 56

"Coleridge" (Pater), **V:** 338, 340–341, 403

Coleridge on Imagination (Richards), **Supp. II:** 422–423, 429

Coleridge's Miscellaneous Criticism (ed. Raysor), **IV:** 46

Coleridge's Shakespearean Criticism (ed. Raysor), **IV:** 51, 52, 56

Colette, **Supp. III:** 86; **Supp. IV:** 136

"Coleum; or, The Origin of Things" (Bacon), **I:** 267

Colin Clout (Skelton), **I:** 84, 86, 87, 91–92

Colin Clout's Come Home Again (Spenser), **I:** 124, 127–128, 146–147

"Collaboration" (James), **VI:** 48, 69

"Collar, The" (Herbert), **II:** 120–121, 216; **Retro. Supp. II:** 180

Collected Essays (Greene), **Supp. I:** 9

Collected Essays, Papers, etc. (Bridges), **VI:** 83

Collected Ewart 1933–1980, The (Ewart), **VII:** 423, **Supp. VII:** 35, 36, 37, 38, 41, 43

Collected Impressions (Bowen), **Supp. II:** 78, 82

Collected Letters (Cowen), **VI:** 448

Collected Papers on Analytical Psychology (Jung), **Supp. IV:** 3, 4

Collected Plays (Maugham), **VI:** 367

Collected Plays (Rattigan), **Supp. VII:** 311, 312, 318

Collected Poems (Amis), **Supp. II:** 15

Collected Poems (Brooke), **Supp. III:** 55–56

Collected Poems (Bunting), **Supp. VII:** 6, 13–14

Collected Poems (Durrell), **Supp. I: 124–126**

Collected Poems (Empson), **Supp. II:** 179, 181, 192

Collected Poems (Ford), **VI:** 323, 332

Collected Poems (Jennings), **Supp. V:** 216

Collected Poems (MacCaig), **Supp. VI:** 185, 187, 192

Collected Poems (Mahon), **Supp. VI:** 165–167, 169–170, 172–177

Collected Poems (Muir), **Supp. VI:** 201, 204–205, 208

Collected Poems (Murray), **Supp. VII:** 271, 273, 275, 277, 278, 279, 281, 283, 284

Collected Poems (Nicholson), **Supp. VI:** 213–214, 217–219

Collected Poems (Sillitoe), **Supp. V:** 424

Collected Poems (Smith), **Supp. II:** 464

Collected Poems (Thomas), **Supp. I:** 169, 170, 171, 175, 179, 184; **Supp. III:** 393

Collected Poems (Warner), **Supp. VII:** 371, 372, 373

Collected Poems (Yeats), **Retro. Supp. I:** 330

Collected Poems 1909–1962 (Muir), **Supp. VI:** 205

Collected Poems 1928–1985 (Spender), **Supp. II:** 486, 493

Collected Poems 1930–1965 (Hope), **Supp. VII:** 153, 155, 156, 157, 159, 162, 164, 165

Collected Poems 1950–1970 (Davie), **Supp. VI:** 105–106, 108, 110, 114

Collected Poems, 1953–1985 (Jennings), **Supp. V:** 211, 216, 218

Collected Poems 1955–1995 (Stevenson), **Supp. VI:** 254, 256–257, 260–262, 264–265

Collected Poems, 1956–1994 (Kinsella), **Supp. V:** 273, 274

Collected Poems 1980–1990 (Ewart), **Supp. VII:** 35, 43, 44, 46

Collected Poems of Robert Louis Stevenson (ed. Smith), **V:** 393

Collected Poetry of Malcolm Lowry, The (ed. Scherf), **Supp. III:** 283

Collected Stories (Maugham), **VI:** 370

Collected Stories (Thomas), **Supp. I:** 180, 181–182, 183

Collected Verse, The (Carroll), **V:** 270, 273

Collected Works (Smith), **Supp. VII:** 340

Collected Works of Izaak Walton (Keynes), **II:** 134

Collected Writings of T. E. Hulme (Hulme), **Supp. VI:** 134–136, 139–146

Collection, The (Pinter), **Supp. I:** 373, 374, 375

"Collection, The" (Pritchett), **Supp. III:** 315

Collection of Meditations and Devotions in Three Parts, A (Traherne), **II:** 191, 201

Collection of Original Poems, A (Boswell), **III:** 247

Collector, The (Fowles), **Supp. I:** 291, 292, 293, 294–295, 297, 307, 310

Collector, The (Redgrove), **Supp. VI:** 227–228

"Collector Cleans His Picture, The" (Hardy), **Retro. Supp. I:** 120

"College Garden, The" (Bridges), **VI:** 82

"College in the Reservoir, The" (Redgrove), **Supp. VI:** 235–236

"College Magazine, A" (Stevenson), **Retro. Supp. I:** 261

Collier, Jeremy, **II:** 303, 325, 331–332, 338, 340, 356; **III: 44**

Collier, John Payne, **I:** 285; **IV:** 52, 56

Collier's Friday Night, A (Lawrence), **VII:** 89, 121

Collingwood, R. G., **VI:** 203

Collingwood, S. D., **V:** 270, 273, 274

Collins, Michael, **VI:** 353

Collins, Phillip, **V:** 46, 73

Collins, Wilkie, **III:** 334, 338, 340, 345; **V:** xxii–xxiii, 42, 62; **Supp. III:** 341; **Supp. VI: 91–104**

Collins, William, **II:** 68, 323n; **III: 160–176,** 336; **IV:** 227

Collinson, James, **V:** 249

Colloquies on the Progress and Prospects of Society (Southey), *see* Sir Thomas More; or, Colloquies on the Progress . . .

Colman, George, **IV:** 271

Colombe's Birthday (Browning), **IV:** 374

"Colonel Fantock" (Sitwell), **VII:** 133

Colonel Jack (Defoe), **III:** 5, 6, 7, 8, 13

Colonel Quaritch, V. C. (Haggard), **Supp. III:** 213

Colonel Sun (Markham), **Supp. II:** 12

"Colonel's Lady, The" (Maugham), **VI:** 370

"Color of Herring, The" (Reid), **Supp. VII:** 331

"Colour Machine, The" (Gunn), **Supp. IV:** 267

Coloured Countries, The (Waugh), **Supp. VI:** 272

"Colours of Good and Evil" (Bacon), *see* "Examples of the Colours of Good and Evil"

"Colubriad, The" (Cowper), **III:** 217–218

"Columbus in Chains" (Kincaid), **Supp. VII:** 223, 224

Colvin, Sidney, **V:** 386, **389–396**

"Coma Berenices" (Thomas), **Supp. IV:** 491

"Combat, The" (Muir), **Supp. VI:** 200, 207

Come and Go (Beckett), **Supp. I:** 60

Come and Welcome, to Jesus Christ (Bunyan), **II:** 253

Come Dance with Kitty Stobling and Other Poems (Kavanagh), **Supp. VII:** 193

Comedians, The (Greene), **Supp. I:** 10, 13, 15–16; **Retro. Supp. II:** 162–164

"Comedy" (Fry), **Supp. III:** 201

Comedy of Dante Alighieri, The (tr. Sayers), **Supp. III:** 333, 336, 350

Comedy of Errors, The (Shakespeare), **I:** 302, 303, 312, 321

Comfort of Strangers, The (McEwan), **Supp. IV:** 390, 396–398, 400, 402

Comforters, The (Spark), **Supp. I:** 199, 200, 201–202, 213

Comic Annual, The (Hood), **IV:** 251, 252, 253–254, 258, 259, 266

"Comic Cuts" (Kelman), **Supp. V:** 256

Comic Romance of Monsieur Scarron, The (tr. Goldsmith), **III:** 191

Comical Revenge, The (Etherege), **II:** 266, 267–268, 271

Comicall Satyre of Every Man Out of His Humour, The (Jonson), **Retro. Supp. I:** 158, 159–160

"Coming" (Larkin), **Supp. I:** 285

"Coming Down Through Somerset" (Hughes), **Retro. Supp. II:** 211–212

"Coming Home" (Bowen), **Supp. II:** 81, 82

Coming of Gabrielle, The (Moore), **VI:** 96, 99

"Coming of the Anglo–Saxons, The" (Trevelyan), **VI:** 393

Coming of the Kings, The (Hughes), **Supp. I:** 347

"Coming to Visit" (Motion), **Supp. VII:** 256

Coming Up for Air (Orwell), **VII:** 281–282

"Commemoration of King Charles the I, martyr'd on that day (King), **Supp. VI:**162

Commendatory Verses Prefixed to Heywood's Apology for Actors (Webster), **II:** 85

Commendatory Verses Prefixed to . . . Munday's Translation of Palmerin . . . (Webster), **II:** 85

"Comment on Christmas, A" (Arnold), **V:** 216

Commentaries of Caesar, The (Trollope), **V:** 102

Commentarius solutus (Bacon), **I:** 263, 272

"Commentary" (Auden), **Retro. Supp. I:** 9

Commentary on Macaulay's History of England, A (Firth), **IV:** 290, 291

Commentary on the "Memoirs of Mr. Fox" (Landor), **IV:** 100

Commentary on the Collected Plays of W. B. Yeats (Jeffares and Knowland), **VI:** 224; **VI:** 224

Commentary on the Complete Poems of Gerard Manley Hopkins, A (Mariani), **V:** 373n, 378n 382

Comming of Good Luck, The (Herrick), **II:** 107

Commitments, The (Doyle), **Supp. V:** 77, 80–82, 93

"Committee Man of 'The Terror,' The" (Hardy), **VI:** 22

Common Asphodel, The (Graves), **VII:** 261

Common Chorus, The (Harrison), **Supp. V:** 164

"Common Entry" (Warner), **Supp. VII:** 371

Common Grace, A (MacCaig), **Supp. VI: 187,** 194

Common Pursuit (Leavis), **VII:** 234, 246

Common Reader, The (Woolf), **VII:** 22, 28, 32–33

Common Sense of War and Peace, The: World Revolution or War Unending (Wells), **VI:** 245

Commonplace and Other Short Stories (Rossetti), **V:** 260

Commonplace Book of Robert Herrick, **II:** 103

"Commonsense About the War" (Shaw), **VI:** 119, 129

Commonweal (periodical), **V:** 302

Commonweal, The: A Song for Unionists (Swinburne), **V:** 332

"Commonwealth Literature Does Not Exist" (Rushdie), **Supp. IV:** 454–455

Communication Cord, The (Friel), **Supp. V:** 124–125

Communicating Doors (Ayckbourn), **Supp. V:** 3, 9, 11, 12

Communication to My Friends, A (Moore), **VI:** 89, 99

"Communist to Others, A" (Auden), **Retro. Supp. I:** 8

"Communitie" (Donne), **Retro. Supp. II:** 89

Companions of the Day (Harris), **Supp. V:** 136, 138

Company (Beckett), **Supp. I:** 62; **Retro. Supp. I:** 29

"Company of Laughing Faces, A" (Gordimer), **Supp. II:** 232

"Company of Wolves, The" (Carter), **Supp. III:** 88

Compassion: An Ode (Hardy), **VI:** 20

Compendium of Authentic and Entertaining Voyages, A (Smollett), **IV:** 158

Complaint of Chaucer to His Purse (Chaucer), **I:** 31

Complaint of the Black Knight, The (Lydgate), **I:** 57, 60, 61, 65

Complaint of Venus, The (Chaucer), **I:** 31

Complaints (Spenser), **I:** 124

Compleat Angler, The (Walton), **II:** 131–136, **137–139,** 141–143

Compleat English Gentleman, The (Defoe), **III:** 5, 14

Compleat Gard'ner, The; or, Directions for . . . Fruit–Gardens and Kitchen–Gardens . . . (tr. Evelyn), **II:** 287

Compleat Tradesman, The (Defoe), **Retro. Supp. I:** 63

Compleat Vindication of the Licensers of the Stage, A (Johnson), **III:** 121; **Retro. Supp. I:** 141–142

"Complement, The" (Carew), **II:** 223–224

Complete Clerihews of Edward Clerihew Bentley (Ewart), **Supp. VII:** 43, 46

Complete Collected Essays (Pritchett), **Supp. III:** 313, 315

Complete Collected Stories (Pritchett), **Supp. III:** 312

Complete Collection of Genteel and Ingenious Conversation, A (Swift), **III:** 29, 36

Complete English Tradesman, The (Defoe), **III:** 5, 14

Complete History of England . . . (Smollett), **III:** 148, 149, 158

Complete Little Ones (Ewart), **Supp. VII:** 45

Complete Plays, The (Behan), **Supp. II:** 67, 68, 69, 70, 73, 74

Complete Plays of Frances Burney, The (ed. Sabor), **Supp. III:** 64

Complete Poems (Muir), **Supp. VI:** 204

Complete Poems (Day Lewis), **Supp. III:** 130

Complete Poems and Fragments of Wilfred Owen, The (Stallworthy), **VI:** 458, 459

Complete Poems of Emily Brontë, The (ed. Hatfield), **V:** 133, 152

"Complete Poetical Works of T.E. Hulme" (Hulme), **Supp. VI:** 136

Complete Saki, The (Saki), **Supp. VI:** 240

Complete Short Stories (Pritchett), **Supp. III:** 313

Complete Works of John Webster, The (ed. Lucas), **II:** 70n

"Complicated Nature, A" (Trevor), **Supp. IV:** 500

Compton–Burnett, Ivy, **VII:** xvii, **59–70; Supp. IV:** 506

Comte, Auguste, **V:** 428–429

Comus (Milton), **II:** 50, 159–160, 166, 175; **Retro. Supp. II:** 273–275

"Concealment, The" (Cowley), **II:** 196

"Conceit Begotten by the Eyes" (Ralegh), **I:** 148, 149

Concept of Nature in Nineteenth–Century Poetry, The (Beach), **V:** 221n

"Concentration City, The" (Ballard), **Supp. V:** 21

"Concerning Geffray Teste Noir" (Morris), **V:** 293

Concerning Humour in Comedy (Congreve), **II:** 338, 341, 346, 350

"Concerning the Beautiful" (tr. Taylor), **III:** 291

Concerning the Eccentricities of Cardinal Pirelli (Firbank), **Supp. II:** 202, **220–222**

"Concerning the regal power" (King), **Supp. VII:** 158

Concerning the Relations of Great Britain, Spain, and Portugal . . . (Wordsworth), **IV:** 24

"Concert Party: Busseboom" (Blunden), **VI:** 428

Conciones ad Populum (Coleridge), **IV:** 56

Concluding (Green), **Supp. II: 260–263**

Concordance to the Poems of Robert Browning, A (Broughton and Stelter), **IV:** 373

Concrete Island (Ballard), **Supp. V:** 27, 28

Condemned Playground, The: Essays 1927–1944 (Connolly), **Supp. III: 107–108**

"Condition of England, The" (Masterman), **VI:** viii, 273

Condition of the Working Class in England in 1844, The (Engels), **IV:** 249

Conduct of the Allies, The (Swift), **III:** 19, 26–27, 35; **Retro. Supp. I:** 274, 275

"Coney, The" (Muldoon), **Supp. IV:** 422

Confederacy, The (Vanbrugh), **II:** 325, 336

Confederates, The (Keneally), **Supp. IV:** 346, 348

Conference of Pleasure, A (Bacon), **I:** 265, 271

Confessio amantis (Gower), **I:** 48, 49, 50–56, 58, 321

Confession of My Faith, A, . . . (Bunyan), **II:** 253

"Confessional Poetry" (Harrison), **Supp. V:** 153

Confessions (St. Augustine), **Supp. III:** 433

"Confessions of a Kept Ape" (McEwan), **Supp. IV:** 394

Confessions of a Young Man (Moore), **VI:** 85–86, 87, 89, 91, 96

Confessions of an English Opium–Eater (De Quincey), **III:** 338; **IV:** xviii, 141, 143, 148–149, 150–153, 154, 155

Confessions of an Inquiring Spirit (Coleridge), **IV:** 53, 56

Confessions of an Irish Rebel (Behan), **Supp. II:** 63, 64–65, 71, 75, 76

Confidence (James), **VI:** 67

Confidence Man, The (Melville), **Supp. IV:** 444

Confidential Agent, The (Greene), **Supp. I:** 3, 4, 7, 10; **Retro. Supp. II:** 155–156

Confidential Clerk, The (Eliot), **VII:** 161–162; **Retro. Supp. II:** 132

"Confined Love" (Donne), **Retro. Supp. II:** 89

Confines of Criticism, The (Housman), **VI:** 164

"Confirmation, The" (Muir), **Supp. VI:** 206

"Confirmation Suit, The" (Behan), **Supp. II:** 66–67

"Conflict, The" (Day Lewis), **Supp. III:** 120, 126

Confusions (Ayckbourn), **Supp. V:** 3, 11

Confutation of Tyndale's Answer (More), **Supp. VII:** 245

Congreve, William, **II:** 269, 289, 302, 304, 325, 336, **338–350,** 352; **III:** 45, 62

Coningsby (Disraeli), **IV:** xii, xx, 294, 300–303, 305, 307, 308; **V:** 4, 22

Conjugal Lewdness; or, Matrimonial Whoredom (Defoe), **III:** 14

"Conjugial Angel, The" (Byatt), **Supp. IV:** 153

Connell, John, **VI:** xv, xxxiii

"Connoisseur" (MacCaig), **Supp. VI:** 192–193

Connolly, Cyril, **VI:** 363, 371; **VII:** xvi, 37, 138, 310; **Supp. II:** 156, 199, 489, 493; **Supp. III: 95–113**

Connolly, T. L., **V:** 442n, 445, 447, 450, 451

"Connor Girls, The" (O'Brien), **Supp. V:** 339–340

Conquest, Robert, **Supp. IV:** 256

Conquest of Granada by the Spaniards, The (Dryden), **II:** 294, 305
"Conquest of Syria, The: If Complete" (Lawrence), **Supp. II:** 287
Conrad, Joseph, **VI:** xi, **133–150,** 170, 193, 242, 270, 279–280, 321; **VII:** 122; **Retro. Supp. II: 69–83;** list of short stories, **VI:** 149–150; **Supp. I:** 397–398; **Supp. II:** 290; **Supp. IV:** 5, 163, 233, 250, 251, 302, 403
Conrad in the Nineteenth Century (Watt), **VI:** 149
"Conrad's Darkness" (Naipaul), **Supp. I:** 397, 402, 403
Conrad's Prefaces to His Works (Garnett), **VI:** 149
"Conquistador" (Hope), **Supp. VII:** 158
Conscience of the Rich, The (Snow), **VII:** 324, 326–327
"Conscious" (Owen), **VI:** 451
Conscious and Verbal (Murray), **Supp. VII:** 271, 286–287
"Conscious Mind's Intelligible Structure, The: A Debate" (Hill), **Supp. V:** 183
"Conscript" (Larkin), **Supp. I:** 277
Consequently I Rejoice (Jennings), **Supp. V:** 217
Conservationist, The (Gordimer), **Supp. II:** 230–231, 232, 239
"Consider" (Auden), **Retro. Supp. I:** 5
Consider (Rossetti), **V:** 260
Considerations Touching the Likeliest Means to Remove Hirelings out of the Church (Milton), **II:** 176
"Considering the Snail" (Gunn), **Supp. IV:** 262–263
Consolation of Philosophy (Boethius), **I:** 31; **Retro. Supp. II:** 36, 296–297
Consolations (Fuller), **Supp. VII:** 79, 80, 81
Consolidator, The (Defoe), **III:** 4, 13
Constance (Durrell), **Supp. I:** 119, 120
Constant, Benjamin, **Supp. IV:** 125, 126, 136
Constant Couple, The; or, A Trip to the Jubilee (Farquhar), **II:** 352, 356–357, 364
Constant Wife, The (Maugham), **VI:** 369
"Constantine and Silvester" (Gower), **I:** 53–54
Constantine the Great (Lee), **II:** 305
"Constellation" (Kelman), **Supp. V:** 255
"Constellation, The" (Vaughan), **II:** 186, 189
Constitutional (periodical), **V:** 19
Constitutional History of England, The (Hallam), **IV:** 283
Constructing Postmodernism (McHale), **Supp. IV:** 112
Constructions (Frayn), **Supp. VII:** 51, 53, 58, 64
"Contemplation" (Thompson), **V:** 442, 443
"Contemporary Film of Lancasters in Action, A" (Ewart), **Supp. VII:** 44
Contemporaries of Shakespeare (Swinburne), **V:** 333
Continual Dew (Betjeman), **VII:** 365
Continuation of the Complete History, A (Smollett), **III:** 148, 149, 158

Continuous: 50 Sonnets from "The School of Elegance" (Harrison), **Supp. V:** 150
Contractor, The (Storey), **Supp. I:** 408, 416–417, 418
Contrarini Fleming (Disraeli), **IV:** xix, 292–293, 294, 296–297, 299, 308
Contrary Experience, The (Read), **VI:** 416
Contre–Machiavel (Gentillet), **I:** 283
"Convenience" (Murphy), **Supp. V:** 328
"Convergence of the Twain, The" (Hardy), **II:** 69; **VI:** 16; **Retro. Supp. I:** 119–120
"Conversation of prayer, The" (Thomas), **Supp. I:** 178
"Conversation, The" (Gunn), **Supp. IV:** 272; **Supp. IV:** 273
"Conversation with a Cupboard Man" (McEwan), **Supp. IV:** 392
"Conversation with Calliope" (Hope), **Supp. VII:** 162–163
Conversations in Ebury Street (Moore), **V:** 129, 153; **VI:** 89, 98, 99
Conversations of James Northcote, Esq., R. A. (Hazlitt), **IV:** 134, 140
"Conversations with Goethe" (Lowry), **Supp. III:** 286
"Conversion" (Hulme), **Supp. VI:** 136
"Convict and the Fiddler, The" (Hardy), **Retro. Supp. I:** 121
Convivio (Dante), **I:** 27
Cook, D., **III:** 322
Cook, Eliza, **IV:** 259, 320
Cook, J. D., **V:** 279
Cooke, W., **III:** 184n
"Cool Web, The" (Graves), **VII:** 266
"Coole Park" (Yeats), **VI:** 212; **Retro. Supp. I:** 336
"Coole Park and Ballylee" (Yeats), **VI:** 215; **Retro. Supp. I:** 336
Cooper, Lettice Ulpha, **V:** x, xxvii, 397, 398
Cooper, William, **VII:** xxi, xxxvii
"Co–ordination" (Forster), **VI:** 399
Coover, Robert, **Supp. IV:** 116
Copeland, T. W., **III:** 245n, 250
Copenhagen (Frayn), **Supp. VII:** 63–64
"Coppersmith" (Murphy), **Supp. V:** 325
Coppy of a Letter Written to . . . Parliament, A (Suckling), **II:** 238
Coral Island, The (Ballantyne), **Supp. I:** 68; **Retro. Supp. I:** 96
Corbett, Sir Julian, **I:** 146
Cordelia Gray novels (James) **Supp. IV:** 335–337
"Corinna's Going a–Maying" (Herrick), **II:** 109–110
"Coriolan" (Eliot), **VII:** 152–153, 158
Coriolanus (Shakespeare), **I:** 318; **II:** 70
Coriolanus (Thomson), **Supp. III:** 411, 423
Corke, Helen, **VII:** 93
Corker's Freedom (Berger), **Supp. IV:** 79, 84, 85
Corkery, Daniel, **Supp. V:** 37, 41
"Cornac and His Wife, The" (Lewis), **VII:** 77, 78
Corneille, Pierre, **II:** 261, 270, 271
Cornelia (Kyd), **I:** 162, 220
Cornélie (Garaier), **I:** 220

Cornelius: A Business Affair in Three Transactions (Priestley), **VII:** 224
Corner That Held Them, The (Warner), **Supp. VII:** 376, 377–378
"Cornet Love" (McGuckian), **Supp. V:** 291
Cornhill (periodical), **V:** xxii, 1, 20, 279; **VI:** 31
Corno di Bassetto, pseud. of George Bernard Shaw
Cornwall, Barry, **IV:** 311
Cornwall, David John Moore, *see* le Carré, John
Cornwallis, Sir William, **III:** 39–40
"Coronet, The" (Marvell), **II:** 113, 211, 216
Coronet for His Mistress Philosophy, A (Chapman), **I:** 234
"Corposant" (Redgrove), **Supp. VI:** 228
"Corregidor" (Nicholson), **Supp. VI:** 214
Correspondence (Flaubert), **V:** 353
Correspondence (Swift), **III:** 24
Correspondence of James Boswell and John Johnston . . . (ed. Walker), **III:** 249
Correspondence . . . of James Boswell Relating to the "Life of Johnson,"The (ed. Waingrow), **III:** 249
Correspondence of James Boswell with . . . the Club, The (ed. Fifer), **III:** 249
Corrida at San Feliu, The (Scott), **Supp. I:** 259, 263, 266
Correspondences (Stevenson), **Supp. VI:** 254, 256, **257–260,** 261
Corridors of Power (Snow), **VII:** xxvi, 324, 330–331
"Corruption" (Vaughan), **II:** 185, 186, 189
Corsair, The (Byron), **IV:** xvii, 172, 173, 175, 192; *see also* Turkish tales
Corson, James C., **IV:** 27, 38–40
"Corymbus for Autumn" (Thompson), **V:** 442
Cosmopolitans (Maugham), **VI:** 370
"Cost of Life" (Motion), **Supp. VII:** 265, 266
"Cottage Hospital, The" (Betjeman), **VII:** 375
Cotter's England (Stead), **Supp. IV:** 473–476
"Cotter's Saturday Night, The" (Burns), **III:** 311, 313, 315, 318
Cottle, Joseph, **IV:** 44, 45, 52, 56, 59
Cotton, Charles, **II:** 131 134, 137
Coué, Emile, **VI:** 264
"Council of the Seven Deadly Sins, The" (Nicholson), **Supp. VI:** 214–215
Count Belisarius (Graves), **VII:** xviii, 258
Count Julian (Landor), **IV:** 89, 96, 100
Count Robert of Paris (Scott), **IV:** 39
"Countdown" (Ayckbourn), **Supp. V:** 2, 4, 11
Counter–Attack (Sassoon), **VI:** 430, 431
Counterblast (McLuhan), **VII:** 71n
Counterclock World (Dick), **Supp. IV:** 41
Counterparts (Fuller), **Supp. VII:** 72, 74
"Counterpoint in Herbert" (Hayes), **Retro. Supp. II:** 181
Countess Cathleen, The (Yeats), **VI:** 87; **Retro. Supp. I:** 326

Countess Cathleen and Various Legends and Lyrics, The (Yeats), **VI:** 211, 309

Countess of Pembroke, **I:** 161, 163–169, 218

Countess of Pembroke's Arcadia, The (Sidney), *see Arcadia*

"Countess of Pembroke's Dream" (Hope), **Supp. VII:** 158

"Country Bedroom" (MacCaig), **Supp. VI:** 187

Country Comets (Day Lewis), **Supp. III:** 117, 120–121

"Country Dance" (MacCaig), **Supp. VI:** 192

Country Girls, The (O'Brien), **Supp. V:** 333–336

Country Girls Trilogy and Epilogue, The (O'Brien), **Supp. V:** 338

"Country House" (MacCaig), **Supp. VI:** 185–186, 194

Country House, The (Galsworthy), **VI:** 271, 272, 273, 275, 278, 282

Country House, The (Vanbrugh), **II:** 325, 333, 336

Country Life, (Ackroyd), **Supp. VI:** 3

"Country Measures" (Warner), **Supp. VII:** 371

"Country of the Blind, The" (Wells), **VI:** 234

Country of the Blind, The, and Other Stories (Wells), **VI:** 228, 244

"Country Walk, A" (Kinsella), **Supp. V:** 262

Country–Wife, The (Wycherley), **I:** 243; **II:** 307, 308, **314–318,** 321, 360

"Coup: A Story, A" (Chatwin), **Supp. IV:** 167

"Courage Means Running" (Empson), **Supp. II:** 191

Courier (periodical), **IV:** 50

Course of Lectures on the English Law, A: Delivered at the University of Oxford 1767-1773 (Johnson), **Retro. Supp. I:** 143

Court and the Castle, The (West), **Supp. III:** 438

"Court of Cupid, The" (Spenser), **I:** 123

"Court Revolt, The" (Gunn), **Supp. IV:** 257

Courte of Venus, The (Wyatt), **I:** 97

"Courter, The" (Rushdie), **Supp. IV:** 438

"Courtesies of the Interregnum" (Gunn), **Supp. IV:** 277

Courtyards in Delft (Mahon), **Supp. VI:** 173

"Courtyards in Delft" (Mahon), **Supp. VI:** 174

Cousin Henry (Trollope), **V:** 102

"Cousin Maria" (James), **VI:** 69

Cousin Phillis (Gaskell), **V:** 1, 2, 4, 8, 11, 15

Cousin Rosamund: A Saga of the Century (West), **Supp. III:** 443

Cousine Bette (Balzac), **V:** xx, 17

"Cousins, The" (Burne–Jones), **VI:** 167, 169

Covent Garden Drolery, The (Behn), **Supp. III:** 36

Covent Garden Journal, The (periodical), **III:** 103–104; **Retro. Supp. I:** 81

Covent Garden Tragedy, The (Fielding), **III:** 97, 105

Cover Her Face (James), **Supp. II:** 127; **Supp. IV:** 321–323

Coverdale, Myles, **I:** 377

"Covering End" (James), **VI:** 52, 69

Coward, Noël, **Supp. II:** **139–158**

Cowasjee, S., **VII:** 4

Cowell, Edward, **IV:** 342–346

Cowley, Abraham, **II:** 123, 179, **194–200,** 202, 236, 256, 259, 275, 347; **III:** 40, 118; **Retro. Supp. I:** 144

Cowper, William, **II:** 119n, 196, 240; **III:** 173, **207–220,** 282; **IV:** xiv–xvi, 93, 184, 281

"Cowper's Grave" (Browning), **IV:** 312, 313

"Cows on Killing Day, The" (Murray), **Supp. VII:** 282

"Cowyard Gates" (Murray), **Supp. VII:** 276

Cox, Charles Brian, **VI:** xi, xxxiii

"Cox's Diary" (Thackeray), *see* "Barber Cox and the Cutting of His Comb"

Coxcomb, The (Beaumont, Fletcher, Massinger), **II:** 66

Coxhead, Elizabeth, **VI:** xiv, xxxiii

"Coxon Fund, The" (James), **VI:** 69

Coyle, William, pseud. of Thomas Keneally

C. P. Snow (Karl), **VII:** 341

Crabbe, George, **III:** **272–287,** 338; **IV:** xv, xvii, 103, 326; **V:** 6; **VI:** 378

Cracking India (Sidhwa), **Supp. V:** 62

Craig, Hardin, **I:** 187, 326

Craig, W. J., **I:** 326

Craigie, Mrs., **VI:** 87

"Craigvara House" (Mahon), **Supp. VI:** 174

Crampton Hodnet (Pym), **Supp. II:** **364–366,** 370

Crane, Stephen, **VI:** 320; **Supp. IV:** 116

Cranford (Gaskell), **V:** xxi, 1–4, 8–10, 11, 14, 15

"Crankshaft" (Murray), **Supp. VII:** 283

"Crapy Cornelia" (James), **VI:** 69

Crash (Ballard), **Supp. V:** 19, 27, 28, 33–34

Crashaw, Richard, **II:** 90–91, 113, 122, 123, 126, **179–184, 200–201;** **V:** 325

"Craving for Spring" (Lawrence), **VII:** 118

"Crawford's Consistency" (James), **VI:** 69

Creative Element, The (Spender), **Supp. II:** 491

"Creative Writing: Can It/Should It Be Taught?" (Lodge), **Supp. IV:** 381

"Creator in Vienna" (Jennings), **Supp. V:** 218

Creators of Wonderland (Mespoulet), **V:** 266

Crediting Poetry (Heaney), **Retro. Supp. I:** 125

Creed or Chaos? and Other Essays in Popular Theology (Sayers), **Supp. III:** 336

Creighton, Joan, **Supp. IV:** 244

Cricket on the Hearth, The (Dickens), **V:** 71

Crime of the Century, The (Amis), **Supp. II:** 12

Crime Omnibus (Fuller), **Supp. VII:** 70

Crime Times Three (James), **Supp. IV:** 323, 324, 325

Crimes (Churchill), **Supp. IV:** 181

"Criminal Ballad"(Hughes), **Supp. I:** 354

Criminal Case, A (Swinburne), **V:** 333

Crimson in the Tricolour, The (O'Casey), **VII:** 12

"Crinoline" (Thackeray), **V:** 22

Crisis, The, a Sermon (Fielding), **III:** 105

Crisis Examined, The (Disraeli), **IV:** 308

Crist, **Retro. Supp. II:** 303

Criterion (periodical), **VI:** 248; **VII:** xv 143, 165

Critic (periodical), **V:** 134

Critic, The (Sheridan), **III:** 253, **263–266,** 270

"Critic, The" (Wilde), **Retro. Supp. II:** 367

"Critic as Artist, The" (Wilde), **V:** 407, 408, 409

Critical and Historical Essays (Macaulay), **IV:** xx, 272, 277, **278–282,** 291

Critical Bibliography of Katherine Mansfield, The (Mantz), **VII:** 182

Critical Essays (Orwell), **VII:** 282

Critical Essays of the Seventeenth Century (Spingarn), **II:** 256n

Critical Essays on George Eliot (Hardy), **V:** 201

Critical Essays on the Poetry of Tennyson (ed. Killham), **IV:** 323n, 338, 339

Critical Observations on the Sixth Book of the Aeneid (Gibbon), **III:** 233

Critical Review (periodical), **III:** 147–148, 149, 179, 188

Critical Strictures on the New Tragedy of Elvira . . . (Boswell, Dempster, Erskine), **III:** 246

Critical Studies of the Works of Charles Dickens (Gissing), **V:** 437

Criticism on Art: And Sketches of the Picture Galleries of England (Hazlitt), **IV:** 140

Crito (Plato), **Supp. IV:** 13

Croker, J. W., **IV:** 280

Crome Yellow (Huxley), **VII:** 197, 200

Cromwell (Carlyle), *see Oliver Cromwell's Letters and Speeches*

Cromwell (Storey), **Supp. I:** 418

Cromwell's Army (Firth), **II:** 241

Cronica tripertita (Gower), **I:** 50

Crook, Arthur, **Supp. IV:** 25

Crooked House (Christie), **Supp. II:** 125

Croquet Castles (Carroll), **V:** 274

Cross, John Walter, **V:** 13, 198, 200

Cross, Wilbur L, **III:** 125, 126, 135

Cross Channel (Barnes), **Supp. IV:** 65, 67, 75–76

"Crossing alone the nighted ferry" (Housman), **VI:** 161

Crossing the River (Phillips), **Supp. V:** 380, 386, 390–391

Crotchet Castle (Peacock), **IV:** xix, 165–166, 169, 170

Crow (Hughes), **Supp. I:** **350–354,** 363; **Retro. Supp. II:** 206–208

"Crow Alights" (Hughes), **Supp. I:** 352

"Crow Blacker than Ever" (Hughes), **Supp. I:** 353

"Crow Hears Fate Knock on the Door" (Hughes), **Supp. I:** 350

"Crow on the Beach" (Hughes), **Supp. I:** 352; **Retro. Supp. II:** 207

"Crow Tyrannosaurus" (Hughes), **Supp. I:** 352

"Crow's Account of the Battle" (Hughes), **Supp. I:** 353

"Crow's Last Stand" (Hughes), **Retro. Supp. II:** 207–208

"Crow's Song of Himself" (Hughes), **Supp. I:** 353

"Crowd of Birds and Children, The" (Graham), **Supp. VII:** 110

Crowley, Aleister, **VI:** 374; **Supp. II:** 204

Crowley, Robert, **I:** 1, 3

Crown of All Homer's Works, The (Chapman), **I:** 236

Crown of Life, The (Gissing), **V:** 437

Crown of the Year (Fry), **Supp. III:** 195

Crown of Wild Olive, The (Ruskin), **V:** 184

"Crowning of Offa, The" (Hill), **Supp. V:** 195

Crowning Privilege, The (Graves), **VII:** 260, 268

Cruel Sea, The (film, Ambler), **Supp. IV:** 3

"Cruelty and Love" (Lawrence), **VII:** 118

Cruelty of a Stepmother, The, **I:** 218

"Cruiskeen Lawn" (O'Nolan), **Supp. II:** 323, **329–333,** 336

Crusader Castles (Lawrence), **Supp. II:** 283, 284

Crux Ansata: An Indictment of the Roman Catholic Church (Wells), **VI:** 242, 244

"Cry Hope, Cry Fury!" (Ballard), **Supp. V:** 26

"Cry of the Children, The" (Browning), **IV:** xx 313

"Cry of the Human, The" (Browning), **IV:** 313

Cry of the Owl, The (Highsmith), **Supp. V:** 173

Cry, The Beloved Country (Paton), **Supp. II:** 341, 342, 343, 344, **345–350,** 351, 354

Cry, the Peacock (Desai), **Supp. V:** 54, 58–59, 75

"Cryptics, The" (Ewart), **Supp. VII:** 39

Crystal and Fox (Friel), **Supp. V:** 118–119

Crystal World, The (Ballard), **Supp. V:** 24, 25–26, 34

C. S. Lewis (Wilson), **Supp. VI:** 304, **305**

Cuala Press, **VI:** 221

Cub, at Newmarket, The (Boswell), **III:** 247

Cuckold in Conceit, The (Vanbrugh), **II:** 337

"Cuckoo, The" (Thomas), **Supp. III:** 399–400

Cuirassiers of the Frontier, The (Graves), **VII:** 267

Culture and Anarchy (Arnold), **III:** 23; **V:** 203, 206, 213, 215, 216

Culture and Society (Williams), **Supp. IV:** 380

Cumberland, George, **IV:** 47

Cumberland, Richard, **II:** 363; **III:** 257

Cumberland and Westmoreland (Nicholson), **Supp. VI:** 223

Cunningham, William, **VI:** 385

"Cup Too Low, A" (Ewart), **Supp. VII:** 39–40

"Cupid and Psyche" (tr. Pater), **V:** 351

"Cupid; or, The Atom" (Bacon), **I:** 267

Cupid's Revenge (Beaumont and Fletcher), **II:** 46, 65

"Curate's Friend, The" (Forster), **VI:** 399

"Curate's Walk; The," (Thackeray), **V:** 25

Cure at Troy, The (Heaney), **Retro. Supp. I:** 131

Cure for a Cuckold, A (Rowley and Webster), **II:** 69, 83, 85

Curiosissima Curatoria (Carroll), **V:** 274

Curious Fragments (Lamb), **IV:** 79

"Curious if True" (Gaskell), **V:** 15

"Curiosity" (Reid), **Supp. VII:** 330

Curse of Kehama, The (Southey), **IV:** 65, 66, 71, 217

Curse of Minerva, The (Byron), **IV:** 192

Curtain (Christie), **Supp. II:** 124, 125, 134

Curtis, Anthony, **VI:** xiii, xxxiii, 372

Curtis, L. P., **III:** 124n, 127n

Curtmantle (Fry), **Supp. III:** 195, **206–207,** 208

Custom of the Country, The (Fletcher [and Massinger]), **II:** 66, 340

"Custom–House, The" (Hawthorne), **Supp. IV:** 116

"Cut Grass" (Larkin), **Supp. I:** 285

Cut–Rate Kingdom, The (Keneally), **Supp. IV:** 346

Cyclopean Mistress, The (Redgrove), **Supp. VI:** 231

"Cygnus A." (Thomas), **Supp. IV:** 490, 491

Cymbeline (Shakespeare), **I:** 322

Cymbeline Refinished (Shaw), **VI:** 129

"Cynic at Kilmainham Jail, A" (Boland), **Supp. V:** 36

Cynthia's Revels (Jonson), **I:** 346; **Retro. Supp. I:** 158, 160

"Cypress and Cedar" (Harrison), **Supp. V:** 161

Cyrano de Bergerac, **III:** 24

Cyrano de Bergerac (tr.. Fry), **Supp. III:** 195

Cyril Connolly: Journal and Memoirs (ed. Pryce–Jones), **Supp. III:** 96, 97, 112

"Cyril Tourneur" (Swinburne), **V:** 332

D. G. Rossetti: A Critical Essay (Ford), **VI:** 332

"D. G. Rossetti as a Translator" (Doughty), **V:** 246

D. H. Lawrence: A Calendar of His Works (Sugar), **VII:** 104, 115, 123

D. H. Lawrence: Novelist (Leavis), **VII:** 101, 234–235, 252–253

Da Silva da Silva's Cultivated Wilderness (Harris), **Supp. V:** 139, 140

Daborne, Robert, **II:** 37, 45

Dad's Tale (Ayckbourn), **Supp. V:** 2

"Daedalus" (Reid), **Supp. VII:** 331

"Daedalus; or, The Mechanic" (Bacon), **I:** 267

Daemon of the World, The (Shelley), **IV:** 209

Daffodil Murderer, The (Sassoon), **VI:** 429

"Daffodil Time" (Brown), **Supp. VI:** 72

Dahl, Roald, Supp. **IV: 201–227,** 449

Daiches, David, **V:** ix

Daily Graphic (periodical), **VI:** 350

Daily News (periodical), **VI:** 335

Daily Worker (periodical), **VI:** 242

Daisy Miller (James), **VI:** 31–32, 69

Dale, Colin (pseud., Lawrence), **Supp. II:** 295

Dali, Salvador, **Supp. IV:** 424

Dalkey Archive, The (O'Nolan), **Supp. II:** 322, **337–338**

Dallas, Eneas Sweetland, **V:** 207

Damage (film, Hare), **Supp. IV:** 282, 292

Damage (play, Hare), **Supp. IV:** 282, 292

"Damnation of Byron, The" (Hope), **Supp. VII:** 159

Dampier, William, **III:** 7, 24

"Danac" (Galsworthy), *see Country House, The*

Danae (Rembrandt), **Supp. IV:** 89

Dan Leno and the Limehouse Golem (Ackroyd), **Supp. VI:** 10–13

Danby, J. F., **II:** 46, 53, 64

"Dance, The" (Kinsella), **Supp. V:** 271

Dance of Death, The, **I:** 15

Dance of Death, The (Strindberg), **Supp. I:** 57

"Dance the Putrefact" (Redgrove), **Supp. VI:** 234

Dance to the Music of Time, A (Powell), **VII:** xxi, 343, **347–353; Supp. II: 4**

"Dancing Hippo, The" (Motion), **Supp. VII:** 257

Dancourt, Carton, **II:** 325, 336

"Dandies and Dandies" (Beerbohm), **Supp. II:** 46

Dangerous Corner (Priestley), **VII:** 223

Dangerous Love (Okri), **Supp. V:** 349, 359, 360

Dangerous Play: Poems 1974–1984 (Motion), **Supp. VII:** 251, 254, 255, 256–257, 264

Daniel, **Retro. Supp. II:** 301

Daniel, Samuel, **I:** 162

Daniel Deronda (Eliot), **V:** xxiv, 190, 197–198, 200; **Retro. Supp. II:** 115–116

Daniel Martin (Fowles), **Supp. I:** 291, 292, 293, **304–308,** 310

D'Annunzio, Gabriele, **V:** 310

"Danny Deever" (Kipling), **VI:** 203

Danny, the Champion of the World (Dahl), **Supp. IV:** 214, 223

"Dans un Omnibus de Londre" (Fuller), **Supp. VII:** 80

Dante Alighieri, **II:** 75, 148; **III:** 306; **IV:** 93, 187; **Supp. IV:** 439, 493; **Retro. Supp. I:** 123–124

Dante and His Circle (Rossetti), **V:** 245

"Dante and the Lobster" (Beckett), **Retro. Supp. I:** 19

"Dante at Verona" (Rossetti), **V:** 239, 240

"Dante . . . Bruno. Vico . . . Joyce" (Beckett), **Retro. Supp. I:** 17

"Dantis Tenebrae" (Rossetti), **V:** 243

Danvers, Charles, **IV:** 60

Daphnaida (Spenser), **I:** 124

"Daphne" (Sitwell), **VII:** 133

"'Daphne with Her Thighs in Bark' [Ezra Pound]" (Boland), **Supp. V:** 39

"Daphnis, an Elegiac Eclogue" (Vaughan), **II:** 185

"Daphnis and Chloe" (Marvell), **II:** 209, 211, 212

"Daphnis and Chloe" (tr. Moore), **VI:** 89

D'Arcy, Margaretta, **Supp. II:** 21, 29, 30, 31, 32–38, 39, 40–41

Darcy's Utopia (Weldon), **Supp. IV:** 528–529, 531

Dark Angel, The," (Johnson), **VI:** 211

Dark As the Grave Wherein My Friend Is Laid (Lowry), **Supp. III:** 274–275, 279, 280, **283–284**

"Dark Dialogues, The" (Graham), **Supp. VII:** 114

Dark Flower, The (Galsworthy), **VI:** 274

Dark Frontier, The (Ambler), **Supp. IV:** 1, 3, 5–7

Dark Is Light Enough, The (Fry), **Supp. III:** 195, 203–204, 207

Dark Labyrinth (Durrell), *see Cefalû*

Dark Lady of the Sonnets, The (Shaw), **VI:** 115, 129

Dark Night's Work, A (Gaskell), **V:** 15

Dark Places of the Heart (Stead), *see Cotter's England*

Dark Side of the Moon, The (anon.), **Supp. IV:** 100

Dark Sisters, The (Kavan), **Supp. VII:** 205, 207

"Dark Times" (Harrison), **Supp. V:** 156–157

Day of Creation, The (Ballard), **Supp. V:** 29

"Day of the Ox" (Brown), **Supp. VI:** 69

Dark Tower, The (MacNeice), **VII:** 407, 408

"Darkling Thrush, The" (Hardy), **VI:** 16; **Retro. Supp. I:** 119

Darkness at Noon (Koestler), **V:** 49; **Supp. I:** 22, 24, 27, 28, 29–30, 32, 33; **Supp IV:** 74

Darkness Visible (Golding), **Supp. I: 83–86; Retro. Supp. I:** 101–102

Darwin, Charles, **Supp. II:** 98, 100, 105–107, 119; **Supp. IV:** 6, 11, 460; **Supp. VII: 17–31**

Darwin, Erasmus, **Supp. II:** 106, 107; **Supp. III:** 360

"Darwin Among the Machines" (Butler), **Supp. II:** 98, 99

Darwin and Butler: Two Versions of Evolution (Willey), **Supp. II:** 103

"Darwin and Divinity" (Stephen), **V:** 284

Das Leben Jesu (tr. Eliot), **V:** 189, 200

Daughter of the East (Bhutto), **Supp. IV:** 455

Daughter–in–Law, The (Lawrence), **VII:** 119, 121

Daughters and Sons (Compton–Burnett), **VII:** 60, 63, 64–65

"Daughters of the Late Colonel, The" (Mansfield), **VII:** 175, 177, 178

"Daughters of the Vicar" (Lawrence), **VII:** 114

"Daughters of War" (Rosenberg), **VI:** 434

Davenant, Charles, **II:** 305

Davenant, Sir William, **I:** 327; **II:** 87, 185, 196, 259

Davenport, Arnold, **IV:** 227

David, Jacques–Louis, **Supp. IV:** 122

David and Bethsabe (Peele), **I:** 198, 206–207

"David Balfour" (Stevenson), *see Catriona*

David Copperfield (Dickens), **V:** xxi, 7, 41, 42, 44, 59–62, 63, 67, 71

David Lodge (Bergonzi), **Supp. IV:** 364

Davideis (Cowley), **II:** 195, 198, 202

Davidson, John, **V:** 318n

Davie, Donald, **VI:** 220; **Supp. IV:** 256; **Supp. VI: 105–118**

Davies, W. H., **Supp. III:** 398

Davis, Clyde Brion, **V:** 394

Davis, H., **III:** 15n, 35

Davy, Sir Humphry, **IV:** 200; **Supp. III:** 359–360

Dawkins, R. M., **VI:** 295, 303–304

"Dawn" (Brooke), **Supp. III:** 53

Dawn (Haggard), **Supp. III:** 213, 222

"Dawn at St. Patrick" (Mahon), **Supp. VI:** 174

"Dawn on the Somme" (Nichols), **VI:** 419

Dawson, Christopher, **III:** 227

Dawson, W. J., **IV:** 289, 291

"Day Dream, A" (Brontë), **V:** 142

Day Lewis, Cecil, **V:** 220, 234; **VI:** x, xxxiii, 454, **VII:** 382, 410; **Supp. III: 115–132**

Day of Creation, The (Ballard), **Supp. V:** 29

"Day of Days, At" (James), **VI:** 69

"Day of Forever, The" (Ballard), **Supp. V:** 26

"Day of the Rabblement, The" (Joyce), **Retro. Supp. I:** 170

Day of the Scorpion, The (Scott), **Supp. I:** 260, 267

"Day They Burned the Books, The" (Rhys), **Supp. II:** 401

"Day We Got Drunk on Cake, The" (Trevor), **Supp. IV:** 500

Day Will Dawn, The (Rattigan), **Supp. VII:** 311

Daydreamer, The (McEwan), **Supp. IV:** 390, 406–407

Daylight Moon and Other Poems, The (Murray), **Supp. VII:** 270, 271, 279–280, 281

Daylight on Saturday (Priestley), **VII:** 212, 217–218

Day's Work, The (Kipling), **VI:** 204

De arte graphica (tr. Dryden), **II:** 305

De augmentis scientiarum (Bacon), **I:** 260–261, 264; *see also Advancement of Learning, The*

de Beer, E. S., **II:** 276n, 287

De casibus virorum illustrium (Boccaccio), **I:** 57, 214

De doctrina christiana (Milton), **II:** 176

De genealogia deorum (Boccaccio), **I:** 266

"De Grey: A Romance" (James), **VI:** 25–26, 69

De Guiana Carmen Epicum (Chapman), **I:** 234

"'De Gustibus—'" (Browning), **IV:** 356–357

De inventione (Cicero), **I:** 38–39

"De Jure Belli ac Pacis" (Hill), **Supp. V:** 192

de la Mare, Walter, **III:** 340, 345; **V:** 268, 274; **VII:** xiii; **Supp. III:** 398, 406

de Man, Paul, **Supp. IV:** 114, 115

De Profundis (Wilde), **V:** 416–417, 418, 419; **Retro. Supp. II:** 371–372

De Quincey, Thomas, **III:** 338; **IV:** ix, xi–xii, xv, xviii, xxii, 49, 51, 137, **141–156**, 260, 261, 278; **V:** 353

De Quincey Memorials (ed. Japp), **IV:** 144, 155

"De Quincey on 'The Knocking at the Gate'" (Carnall), **IV:** 156

De re publica (Cicero), **Retro. Supp. II:** 36

De rerum natura (tr. Evelyn), **II:** 275, 287

De sapientia veterum (Bacon), **I:** 235, 266–267, 272

de Selincourt, E., **IV:** 25

De tranquillitate animi (tr. Wyatt), **I:** 99

De tristitia Christi (More), **Supp. VII:** 245, 246

"De Wets Come to Kloof Grange, The" (Lessing), **Supp. I:** 240–241

Deacon Brodie (Stevenson), **V:** 396; **Retro. Supp. I:** 260

"Dead, The" (Brooke), **VI:** 420; **Supp. III:** 57–58, 59; **Retro. Supp. I:** 19, 172

"Dead, The" (Joyce), **VII:** xiv, 44–45; **Supp. II:** 88; **Supp. IV:** 395, 396

"Dead and Alive" (Gissing), **V:** 437

Dead Babies (Amis), **Supp. IV:** 26, 29–31

"Dead Bride, The" (Hill), **Supp. V:** 189

"Dead Love" (Swinburne), **V:** 325, 331, 332

Dead Man Leading (Pritchett), **Supp. III:** 311, 312, 313, 314

"Dead Man's Dump" (Rosenberg), **VI:** 432, 434

"Dead on Arrival" (Kinsella), **Supp. V:** 261

Dead Secret, The (Collins), **Supp. VI:** 92, 95

"Dead–Beat, The" (Owen), **VI:** 451, 452

"Deadlock in Darwinism, The" (Butler), **Supp. II:** 108

Dealings with the Firm of Dombey and Son . . . (Dickens), *see Dombey and Son*

Dean, L. F., **I:** 269

"Dean Swift Watches Some Cows" (Ewart), **Supp. VII:** 40

Deane, Seamus, **Supp. IV:** 424

Dear Brutus (Barrie), **Supp. III:** 5, 6, 8, 9, **11–14**, 138

"Dear Bryan Wynter" (Graham), **Supp. VII:** 115

Dear Deceit, The (Brooke–Rose), **Supp. IV:** 98, 99, 102–103

Dearest Emmie (Hardy), **VI:** 20

"Death and Doctor Hornbook" (Burns), **III:** 319

"Death and Dying Words of Poor Mailie, The" (Burns), **IV:** 314, 315

"Death and the Professor" (Kinsella), **Supp. V:** 260

"Death Bed" (Kinsella), **Supp. V:** 267

"Death by Water" (Eliot), **VII:** 144–145; **Retro. Supp. II:** 128

"Death Clock, The" (Gissing), **V:** 437

Death Comes as the End (Christie), **Supp. II:** 132–133

"Death in Bangor" (Mahon), **Supp. VI:** 177

"Death in Ilium" (Kinsella), **Supp. V:** 263

Death in the Clouds (Christie; U.S. title, *Death in the Air*), **Supp. II:** 131

"Death in the Desert, A" (Browning), **IV:** 358, 364, 367, 372; **Retro. Supp. II:** 26

Death in Venice (Mann), **Supp. IV:** 397

Death of a Naturalist (Heaney), **Supp. II:** 268, **269–270**, 271; **Supp. IV:** 412; **Retro. Supp. I:** 123, 124, 126–127

Death of a Salesman (Miller), **VI:** 286

"Death of a Scientific Humanist, The" (Friel), **Supp. V:** 114

"Death of a Tsotsi" (Paton), **Supp. II:** 345

"Death of a Tyrant" (Kinsella), **Supp. V:** 261

Death of an Expert Witness (James), **Supp. IV:** 319, 328–330

"Death of an Old Lady" (MacNeice), **VII:** 401

"Death of an Old Old Man" (Dahl), **Supp. IV:** 210

"Death of Bernard Barton" (FitzGerald), **IV:** 353

Death of Christopher Marlowe, The (Hotson), **I:** 275

Death of Cuchulain, The (Yeats), **VI:** 215, 222

"Death of King George, The" (Betjeman), **VII:** 367

Death of Oenone, The, Akbar's Dream, and Other Poems (Tennyson), **IV:** 338

"Death of Simon Fuge, The" (Bennett), **VI:** 254

Death of Sir John Franklin, The (Swinburne), **V:** 333

"Death of the Duchess, The" (Eliot), **VII:** 150

Death of the Heart, The (Bowen), **Supp. II:** 77, 78, 79, 82, 84, **90–91**

"Death of the Lion, The" (James), **VI:** 69

"Death of the Rev. George Crabbe" (FitzGerald), **IV:** 353

Death of Wallenstein, The (Coleridge), **IV:** 56

Death of William Posters, The (Sillitoe), **Supp. V:** 409, 410, 414, 421–422, 423

"Death stands above me, whispering low" (Landor), **IV:** 98

"Death the Drummer" (Lewis), **VII:** 79

Death–Trap, The (Saki), **Supp. VI:** 250

Death Under Sail (Snow), **VII:** 323

"Deathbeds" (Ewart), **Supp. VII:** 45

Deaths and Entrances (Thomas), **Supp. I:** 177–178

"Death's Chill Between" (Rossetti), **V:** 252

Death's Duel (Donne), **Retro. Supp. II:** 98

"Deathshead" (Hare), **Supp. IV:** 283

Debates in Parliament (Johnson), **III:** 108, 122

Debits and Credits (Kipling), **VI:** 173, 204

"Debt, The" (Kipling), **VI:** 201

Debut, The (Brookner; first published as *A Start in Life*), **Supp. IV:** 122, 123–124, 131

Decameron (Boccaccio), **I:** 313; **Supp. IV:** 461; **Retro. Supp. II:** 45–46

"Decay of Lying, The" (Wilde), **V:** 407–408; **Retro. Supp. II:** 366–367

"Deceased, The" (Douglas), **VII:** 440

Deceptive Grin of the Gravel Porters, The (Ewart), **Supp. VII:** 39–40

Declaration (Maschler), **Supp. I:** 237, 238

Declaration of Rights (Shelley), **IV:** 208

Decline and Fall (Waugh), **VII:** 289–290, 291; **Supp. II:** 218

Decline and Fall of the Roman Empire, The (Gibbon), **III:** 109, 221, **225–233**

"Decline of the Novel, The" (Muir), **Supp. VI:** 202

Decline of the West, The (Spengler), **Supp. IV:** 12

Decolonising the Mind: The Politics of Language in African Literature (Thiong'o), **Supp. V:** 56

"Décor" (MacCaig), **Supp. VI:** 185

Decorative Art in America: A Lecture (Wilde), **V:** 419

"Dedication" (Motion), **Supp. VII:** 260

"Dedicatory Letter" (Ford), **VI:** 331

Deep Blue Sea, The (Rattigan), **Supp. VII:** 309, 315, 317–318

Deep Water (Highsmith), **Supp. V:** 171–172

"Deepe Groane, fetch'd at the Funerall of that incomparable and Glorious Monarch, Charles the First, King of Great Britaine, France, and Ireland, &c., A" (King), **Supp. VI:** 159–161

Defeat of Youth, The (Huxley), **VII:** 199

"Defence of an Essay of 'Dramatick Poesie'" (Dryden), **II:** 297, 305

Defence of English Commodities, A (Swift), **III:** 35

Defence of Guenevere, The (Morris), **V:** xxii, 293, 305–306, 312

Defence of Poesie, The (Sidney), **I:** 161–163, 169, 170, 173; **Retro. Supp. II:** 332–334, 339

"Defence of Poetry, A" (Shelley), **IV:** 168–169, 204, 208, 209; **Retro. Supp. I:** 250

Defence of the Doctrine of Justification, A, . . . (Bunyan), **II:** 253

"Defense of Cosmetics, A" (Beerbohm), **Supp. II:** 45, 53

"Deathbeds" (Ewart), **Supp. VII:** 45

"Definition of Love, The" (Marvell), **II:** 208, 211, 215

Defoe, Daniel, **II:** 325; **III:** **1–14**, 24, 39, 41–42, 50–53, 62, 82; **V:** 288; **Supp. III:** 22, 31; **Retro. Supp. I:** **63–77**

"Deformed Mistress, The" (Suckling), **II:** 227

Deformed Transformed, The (Byron), **IV:** 193

"Degas's Laundresses" (Boland), **Supp. V:** 39–40

Degeneration (Nordau), **VI:** 107

Degrees of Freedom: The Novels of Iris Murdoch (Byatt), **Supp. IV:** 145

Deighton, Len, **Supp. IV:** 5, 13

Deirdre (Yeats), **VI:** 218

Deirdre of the Sorrows (Synge), **Retro. Supp. I:** 301–302

"Dejection" (Coleridge), **IV:** 41, 49, 50; **Retro. Supp. II:** 61

Déjuner sur l'herbe (Manet), **Supp. IV:** 480

Dekker, Thomas, **I:** 68, 69; **II:** 3, 21, 47, 71, 89, 100; **Retro. Supp. I:** 160

"Delay" (Jennings), **Supp. V:** 208

"Delay Has Danger" (Crabbe), **III:** 285

Delight (Priestley), **VII:** 212

"Delight in Disorder" (Herrick), **II:** 104

Delillo, Don, **Supp. IV:** 487

"Demephon and Phillis" (Gower), **I:** 53–54

Demeter, and Other Poems (Tennyson), **IV:** 338

"Demeter and Persephone" (Tennyson), **IV:** 328

"Demo" (Murray), **Supp. VII:** 284

"Democracy" (Lawrence), **VII:** 87–88

Demon Lover, The (Bowen; U.S. title, *Ivy Gripped the Steps*), **Supp. II:** 77, 92, 93

Demon of Progress in the Arts, The (Lewis), **VII:** 74

Demos (Gissing), **V:** 432–433, 437

Denham, Sir John, **II:** 236, 238

"Deniall" (Herbert), **II:** 127, 128; **Retro. Supp. II:** 180–181

Denis Duval (Thackeray), **V:** 27, 34, 36, 38

Dennis, John, **II:** 69, 310, 338, 340

Dennis, Nigel, **III:** 23, 37

"Dennis Haggarty's Wife" (Thackeray), **V:** 23–24

"Dennis Shand" (Rossetti), **V:** 239

Denry the Audacious (Bennett), *see Card, The*

Dent, Arthur, **II:** 241, 246

Denzil Quarrier (Gissing), **V:** 437

Deor, **Retro. Supp. II:** 304

Departmental Ditties (Kipling), **VI:** 168, 204

"Depression, A" (Jennings), **Supp. V:** 214

Der Rosenkavalier (Strauss), **Supp. IV:** 556

Derham, William, **III:** 49

Derrida, Jacques, **Supp. IV:** 115

Derry Down Derry, pseud. of Edward Lear

Dervorgilla (Gregory), **VI:** 315

Des Imagistes: An Anthology (ed. Pound), **Supp. III:** 397

Desai, Anita, **Supp. IV:** 440; **Supp. V:** **53–76**

Desani, G. V., **Supp. IV:** 443, 445

Descartes, René, **Supp. I:** 43–44

"Descent into the Maelstrom, The" (Poe), **III:** 339

Descent of Man and Selection in Relation to Sex, On the (Darwin), **Supp. VII:** 17, 19, 25–28

"Descent of Odin, The" (Gray), **III:** 141

"Description of a City Shower, A" (Swift), **III:** 30

"Description of an Author's Bedchamber" (Goldsmith), **III:** 184

Description of Antichrist and His Ruin, A (Bunyan), **II:** 253

"Description of the Morning, A" (Swift), **III:** 30; **Retro. Supp. I:** 282–283

Description of the Scenery of the Lakes in the North of England, A (Wordsworth), **IV:** 25

Description of the Western Islands (Martin), **III:** 117

Descriptive Catalogue of Pictures . . . , A (Blake), **III:** 305, 307

Descriptive Sketches (Wordsworth), **IV:** xv, 1, 2, 4–5, 24

"Desecration" (Jhabvala), **Supp. V:** 236

Desert Highway (Priestley), **VII:** 227–228

"Deserted Garden, The" (Browning), **IV:** 312

Deserted Parks, The (Carroll), **V:** 274

Deserted Village, The (Goldsmith), **III:** 177, 180, 185, 186–187, 191, 277

Design for Living (Coward), **Supp. II:** 151–152, 156

Desperate Remedies (Hardy), **VI:** 2, 19–20; **Retro. Supp. I:** 111–112

"Despite and Still" (Graves), **VII:** 268

"Despondency, an Ode" (Burns), **III:** 315

"Destinie" (Cowley), **II:** 194, 195, 198

"Destiny and a Blue Cloak" (Hardy), **VI:** 20

"Destroyers in the Arctic" (Ross), **VII:** 433

Destructive Element, The (Spender), **Supp. II:** 487–488, 489, 491

"Development" (Browning), **IV:** 365

Development of Christian Doctrine, The (Newman), **V:** 340

"Development of Genius, The" (Browning), **IV:** 310

Devices and Desires (James), **Supp. IV:** 320, 331–333

"Devil, The" (Murray), **Supp. VII:** 284

Devil and the Lady, The (Tennyson), **IV:** 338

Devil Is an Ass, The: A Comedie (Jonson), **Retro. Supp. I:** 165

Devil of a State (Burgess), **Supp. I:** 187

Devil of Dowgate, The (Fletcher), **II:** 67

Devil, The World and the Flesh, The (Lodge), **Supp. IV:** 364

Devil to Pay, The (Sayers), **Supp. III:** 336, 349

"Devil's Advice to Story–tellers, The" (Graves), **VII:** 259, 263

Devil's Disciple, The (Shaw), **VI:** 104, 105, 110, 112; **Retro. Supp. II:** 316

"Devil's Due, The" (Swinburne), **V:** 332

Devil's Elixir, The (Hoffmann), **III:** 334, 345

Devil's Law–Case, The (Webster), **II:** 68, 82–83, 85

Devils of Loudon, The (Huxley), **VII:** 205–206

Devil's Walk, The (Coleridge and Southey), **IV:** 56, 208

Devil's Walk, The (Shelley), **IV:** 208

Devlin, Christopher, **V:** 372, 373, 381

"Devoted Friend, The" (Wilde), **Retro. Supp. II:** 365

Devotions upon Emergent Occasions and severall steps in my Sicknes (Donne), **Retro. Supp. II:** 97–98

Devout Trental for Old John Clarke (Skelton), **I:** 86

Dhomhnaill, Nuala Ní, **Supp. V:** 40–41

Diabolical Principle and the Dithyrambic Spectator (Lewis), **VII:** 72, 76, 83

Dialectic of the Enlightenment (Adorno), **Supp. IV:** 29

Dialogue Between the Devil, The Pope, and the Pretender, The (Fielding), **III:** 105

"Dialogue Between the Resolved Soul and Created Pleasure, A" (Marvell), **II:** 208, 211, 216

"Dialogue Between the Soul and Body, A" (Marvell), **II:** 208, 211, 216

"Dialogue Between the Two Horses, The" (Marvell), **II:** 218

"Dialogue Between Thyrsis and Dorinda, A" (Marvell), **II:** 211

Dialogue Concerning Heresies, The (More), **Supp. VII:** 244

Dialogue of Comfort against Tribulation, A (More), **Supp. VII:** 245, 247–248

"Dialogue of Self and Soul" (Kavanagh), **Supp. VII:** 191

"Dialogue of Self and Soul, A" (Yeats), **Retro. Supp. I:** 336

"Dialogue on Dramatic Poetry" (Eliot), **VII:** 157; **Retro. Supp. II:** 131–132

Dialogue with Death (Koestler), **Supp. I:** 23–24

Dialogues Concerning Natural Religion (Hume), **Supp. III:** 240, 242–243

Diana (Montemayor), **I:** 164, 302

Diana of the Crossways (Meredith), **V:** xxv, 227, 232–233, 234

"Diaphanéité" (Pater), **V:** 345, 348, 356

Diaries (Warner), **Supp. VII:** 382

Diaries of Jane Somers, The (Lessing), **Supp. I: 253–255**

Diaries of Lewis Carroll, The (ed. Green), **V:** 264, 274

Diaries, Prayers, and Annals (Johnson), **Retro. Supp. I:** 143

Diarmuid and Grania (Moore and Yeats), **VI:** 87, 96, 99

Diary (Evelyn), **II: 274–280, 286–287**

Diary (Pepys), **II: 274, 280–286, 288,** 310

Diary and Letters of Madame D'Arblay (ed. Barrett), **Supp. III:** 63

"Diary from the Trenches" (Hulme), **Supp. VI: 139–141**

Diary of a Dead Officer (West), **VI:** 423

Diary of a Good Neighbour, The (Lessing), **Supp. I:** 253

[am.2]*Diary of a Journey into North Wales . . . , A* (Johnson), **III:** 122

Diary of a Madman, The (Gogol), **III:** 345

Diary of a Man of Fifty, The (James), **VI:** 67, 69

Diary of Fanny Burney (Burney), **III:** 243

Diary, Reminiscences and Correspondence of H. Crabb Robinson, The, **IV:** 52, 56, 81

Dibb, Michael, **Supp. IV:** 88

Dick, Philip K., **Supp. IV:** 41

"Dick King" (Kinsella), **Supp. V:** 261

Dick Willoughby (Day Lewis), **Supp. III:** 117

Dickens, Charles, **II:** 42; **III:** 151, 157, 340; **IV:** 27, 34, 38, 88, 240, 241, 247, 251, 252, 259, 295, 306; **V:** viii, ix, 3, 5, 6, 9, 14, 20, 22, 41–74, 148, 182, 191, 424, 435; **VI:** viii; **Supp. I:** 166–167; **Supp. IV:** 120, 202–203, 229, 379, 460, 505, 513, 514

Dickens (Ackroyd), **Supp. VI: 8–9**

Dickens and Daughter (Storey), **V:** 72

Dickens and the Twentieth Century (ed. Cross and Pearson), **V:** 63, 73

Dickens from Pickwick to Dombey (Marcus), **V:** 46

"Dickens in Memory" (Gissing), **V:** 437

Dickens: Interviews and Recollections (ed. Collins), **V:** 46

Dickens the Novelist (Leavis), **VII:** 250–251

Dickens Theatre, The (Garis), **V:** 70, 73

Dickinson, Goldsworthy Lowes, **VI:** 398, 399

Dickinson, Emily, **Supp. IV:** 139, 480

Dickson, Lovat, **VI:** 239

Dictionary of Madame de Sévigné (FitzGerald and Kerrich), **IV:** 349, 353

Dictionary of National Biography (ed. Stephen and Lee), **V:** xxv, 280–281, 290

Dictionary of the English Language, A (Johnson), **III:** 113–114, 115, 121; **Retro. Supp. I:** 137, 141, 142

Dictionary of the Khazars: A Lexicon Novel in 100,000 Words (Pavic), **Supp. IV:** 116

"Did any Punishment attend" (Sedley), **II:** 265

Did He Steal It? (Trollope), **V:** 102

Diderot, Denis, **Supp. IV:** 122, 136

Didion, Joan, **Supp. IV:** 163

Dido, Queen of Carthage (Marlowe), **I:** 278–279, **280–281,** 292; **Retro. Supp. I:** 211

Die Ambassador (Brink), **Supp. VI: 46–47**

Die Eerste lewe van Adamastor (Brink), **Supp. VI:** 54

Die muur van die pes (Brink), **Supp. VI:** 52

Die Räuber (Schiller), **IV:** xiv, 173

Die Spanier in Peru (Kotzebue), **III:** 254, 268

Dierdre of the Sorrows (Synge), **VI:** 310, 313

"Dietary" (Lydgate), **I:** 58

Differences in Judgement about Water Baptism . . . (Bunyan), **II:** 253

"Difficulties of a Bridegroom" (Hughes), **Supp. I:** 346

"Difficulties of a Statesman" (Eliot), **VII:** 152–153

Difficulties with Girls (Amis), **Supp. II:** 18

"Diffugere Nives" (Housman), **VI:** 155

"Digging" (Heaney), **Supp. II:** 270; **Retro. Supp. I:** 124, 126–127

"Digging for Pictures" (Golding), **Supp. I:** 65

"Digging Up Scotland" (Reid), **Supp. VII:** 336

Dilecta (Ruskin), **V:** 184

Dilke, Charles, **IV:** 254, 262, 306

"Dill Pickle, A" (Mansfield), **VII:** 174

"Dining Room Tea" (Brooke), **Supp. III:** 49, 52

"Dinner at Poplar, A" (Dickens), **V:** 41, 47n

"Dinner in the City, A" (Thackeray), **V:** 25

Diodorus Siculus (tr. Skelton), **I:** 82

"Diogenes and Plato" (Landor), **IV:** 91

"Dip in the Pool" (Dahl), **Supp. IV:** 217

Dipsychus (Clough), **V:** 156, 159, 161, 163–165, 167, 211

"Dirce" (Landor), **IV:** 96–97

Directions to Servants (Swift), **III:** 36

"Dirge" (Eliot), **VII:** 150

"Dirge for the New Sunrise" (Sitwell), **VII:** 137

"Dirge of Jephthah's Daughter, The: Sung by the Virgins" (Herrick), **II:** 113

Dirty Beasts (Dahl), **Supp. IV:** 226

Dirty Story (Ambler), **Supp. IV:** 16

"Dis aliter visum; or, Le Byron de nos jours" (Browning), **IV:** 366, 369

"Disabled" (Owen), **VI:** 447, 451, 452

"Disabused, The" (Day Lewis), **Supp. III:** 130

"Disappointmnt, The" (Behn), **Supp. III:** 39

Disappointment, The (Southern), **II:** 305

"Disc's Defects, A" (Fuller), **Supp. VII:** 80

Discarded Image, The: An Introduction to Medieval and Renaissance Literature (Lewis), **Supp. III:** 249, 264

"Discharge, The" (Herbert), **II:** 127

Discontented Colonel, The (Suckling), **II:** 238

Discourse, Introductory to a Course of Lectures on Chemistry, A (Davy), **Supp. III:** 359–360

"Discourse from the Deck" (Gunn), **Supp. IV:** 269

"Discourse of a Lady Standing a Dinner to a Down–and–Out Friend" (Rhys), **Supp. II:** 390

Discourse of Civil Life (Bryskett), **I:** 124

Discourse of the Building of the House of God, A (Bunyan), **II:** 253

Discourse of the Contests and Dissensions between the Nobles and the Commons in Athens and Rome (Swift), **III:** 17, 35

Discourse on Pastoral Poetry, A (Pope), **III:** 56

Discourse on Satire (Dryden), **II:** 297

Discourse on the Love of Our Country (Price), **IV:** 126

Discourse on the Pindarique Ode, A (Congreve), **II:** 346–347

Discourse on 2 Corinthians, i, 9 . . . , A (Crabbe), **III:** 286

Discourse upon Comedy, A (Farquhar), **II:** 332, 355

Discourse upon the Pharisee and the Publican, A (Bunyan), **II:** 253

Discourses Addressed to Mixed Congregations (Newman), **Supp. VII:** 297

Discourses by Way of Essays (Cowley), **III:** 40

Discourses in America (Arnold), **V:** 216

Discoveries (Jonson), **I:** 270; **Retro. Supp. I:** 166

Discovery of Guiana, The (Ralegh), **I:** 145, 146, 149, 151–153

Discovery of the Future, The (Wells), **VI:** 244

"Disdaine Returned" (Carew), **II:** 225

Disenchantment (Montague), **VII:** 421

Disgrace (Coetzee), **Supp. VI:** 76, **86–88**

"Disguises" (McEwan), **Supp. IV:** 391–392

"Disinheritance" (Jhabvala), **Supp. V:** 223–224, 228, 230, 232

"Disinherited, The" (Bowen), **Supp. II:** 77, 87–88

Disney, Walt, **Supp. IV:** 202, 211

"Disobedience" (Milne), **Supp. V:** 301

"Disorderly, The" (Murray), **Supp. VII:** 287

"Displaced Person" (Murphy), **Supp. V:** 326

Disraeli, Benjamin, **IV:** xii, xvi, xviii, xix, xx, xxiv, 271, 288, **292–309; V:** viii, x, xxiv, 2, 22; **VII:** xxi; **Supp. IV:** 379

Disraeli (Blake), **IV:** 307, 308

"Dissatisfaction" (Traherne), **II:** 192

"Dissolution, The" (Donne), **Retro. Supp. II:** 92

"Distant Fury of Battle, The" (Hill), **Supp. V:** 186

Disaffection, A (Kelman), **Supp. V:** 243, 249, 251–252

"Distant Past, The" (Trevor), **Supp. IV:** 504

"Distracted Preacher, The" (Hardy), **VI:** 22; **Retro. Supp. I:** 116

"Distraction" (Vaughan), **II:** 188

"Distress of Plenty" (Connolly), **Supp. III:** 108

Distress'd Wife, The (Gay), **III:** 67

"Disturber of the Traffic, The" (Kipling), **VI:** 169, **170–172**

"Disused Shed in County Wexford, A" (Mahon) **Supp. VI:** 169–170, 173

Diversions of Purley and Other Poems, The (Ackroyd), **Supp. VI:** 3Diversions of Purley and Other Poems, The (Ackroyd), Supp. VI: 3

"Diversity and Depth" (Wilson), **Supp. I:** 167

"Divided Life Re–Lived, The" (Fuller), **Supp. VII:** 72

Divine and Moral Songs for Children (Watts), **III:** 299

Divine Comedy, The (Dante), **II:** 148; **III:** 306; **IV:** 93, 187, 229; **Supp. I:** 76; Supp. IV: 439

"Divine Judgments" (Blake), **III:** 300

"Divine Meditations" (Donne), **Retro. Supp. II:** 98

Divine Poems (Waller), **II:** 238

"Divine Wrath and Mercy" (Blake), **III:** 300

Diviner, The (Friel), **Supp. V:** 113

"Diviner, The" (Friel), **Supp. V:** 115

"Diviner, The" (Heaney), **Supp. II:** 269–270

"Division, The" (Hardy), **VI:** 17

Division of the Spoils, A (Scott), **Supp. I:** 268, 271

Dixon, Richard Watson, **V:** 362–365, 371, 372, 377, 379; **VI:** 76, 83, 167

Dixon Hunt, John, **VI:** 167

"Dizzy" (Strachey), **IV:** 292

"Do not go gentle into that good night" (Thomas), **Supp. I:** 178

"Do Take Muriel Out" (Smith), **Supp. II:** 471, 472

Do What You Will (Huxley), **VII:** 201

"Do you remember me? or are you proud?" (Landor), **IV:** 99

Dobell, Sydney, **IV:** 310; **V:** 144–145

Dobrée, Bonamy, **II:** 362, 364; **III:** 33, 51, 53; **V:** 221, 234; **VI:** xi, 200–203; **V:** xxii

"Dockery and Son" (Larkin), **Supp. I:** 281, 285

Doctor, The (Southey), **IV:** 67n, 71

Doctor Birch and His Young Friends (Thackeray), **V:** 38

Dr. Faust's Sea–Spiral Spirit (Redgrove), **Supp. VI:** 231, 233–234

Doctor Faustus (film), **III:** 344

Doctor Faustus (Marlowe), **I:** 212, 279–280, **287–290; Supp. IV:** 197

Doctor Fischer of Geneva; or, The Bomb Party (Greene), **Supp. I:** 1, 17–18

Doctor Is Sick, The (Burgess), **Supp. I:** 186, 189, 195

Doctor Therne (Haggard), **Supp. III:** 214

Doctor Thorne (Trollope), **V:** xxii, 93, 101

Doctors' Delusions, Crude Criminology, and Sham Education (Shaw), **VI:** 129

Doctor's Dilemma, The (Shaw), **VI:** xv 116, 129; **Retro. Supp. II:** 321–322

"Doctor's Legend, The" (Hardy), **VI:** 20

Doctors of Philosophy (Spark), **Supp. I:** 206

Doctrine and Discipline of Divorce . . . , The (Milton), **II:** 175; **Retro. Supp. II:** 271

"Doctrine of Scattered Occasions, The" (Bacon), **I:** 261

Doctrine of the Law and Grace Unfolded, The (Bunyan), **II:** 253

Documents in the Case, The (Sayers and Eustace), **Supp. III:** 335, 342–343

Documents Relating to the Sentimental Agents in the Volyen Empire (Lessing), **Supp. I:** 252–253
Dodge, Mabel, **VII:** 109
Dodgson, Charles Lutwidge, *see* Carroll, Lewis
"Does It Matter?" (Sassoon), **VI:** 430
"Does That Hurt?" (Motion), **Supp. VII:** 263–264
"Dog and the Waterlily, The" (Cowper), **III:** 220
Dog Beneath the Skin, The (Auden and Isherwood), **VII:** 312, 380, 385; **Retro. Supp. I:** 7
Dog Fox Field (Murray), **Supp. VII:** 280–281, 282
"Dogged" (Saki), **Supp. VI:** 239
Dog's Ransom, A (Highsmith), **Supp. V:** 176–177
"Dogs" (Hughes), **Supp. I:** 346
"Doing Research for Historical Novels" (Keneally), **Supp. IV:** 344
Doktor Faustus (Mann), **III:** 344
Dolben, Digby Mackworth, **VI:** 72, 75
"Doldrums, The" (Kinsella), **Supp. V:** 261
"Doll, The" (O'Brien), **Supp. V:** 340
Doll's House, A (Ibsen), **IV:** xxiii, 118–119; **V:** xxiv; **VI:** ix, 111
"Doll's House, The" (Mansfield), **VII:** 175
"Doll's House on the Dal Lake, A" (Naipaul), **Supp. I:** 399
"Dollfuss Day, 1935" (Ewart), **Supp. VII:** 36
Dolly (Brookner), **Supp. IV:** 134–135, 136–137
Dolores (Compton–Burnett), **VII:** 59, 68
"Dolores" (Swinburne), **V:** 313, 320–321
"Dolorida" (Swinburne), **V:** 332
Dolphin, The (Lowell), **Supp. IV:** 423
Dombey and Son (Dickens), **IV:** 34; **V:** xxi, 42, 44, 47, 53, 57–59, 70, 71
"Domestic Interior" (Boland), **Supp. V:** 50
"Domicilium" (Hardy), **VI:** 14
Don Fernando (Maugham), **VI:** 371
Don Juan (Byron), **I:** 291; **II:** 102n; **IV:** xvii, 171, 172, 173, 178, 183, 184, 185, **187–191,** 192
Don Quixote (Cervantes), **II:** 49; **IV:** 190; **V:** 46; **Retro. Supp. I:** 84
Don Quixote in England (Fielding), **III:** 105
Don Sebastian, King of Portugal (Dryden), **II:** 305
"Dong with a Luminous Nose, The" (Lear), **V:** 85
"Donkey, The" (Smith), **Supp. II:** 468
Donkeys' Years (Frayn), **Supp. VII:** 60–61
Donne, John, **I:** 352–369; **II:** 102, 113, 114, 118, 121–124, 126–128, 132, 134–138, 140–143, 147, 185, 196, 197, 209, 215, 221, 222, 226; **IV:** 327; **Supp. II:** 181, 182; **Supp. III:** 51, 57; **Retro. Supp. II:** 85–99, 173, 175, 259, 260
Donne, William Bodham, **IV:** 340, 344, 351

Donnelly, M. C., **V:** 427, 438
Donohue, J. W., **III:** 268
Don't Look Now (du Maurier), **Supp. III:** 148
"Doodle Bugs" (Harrison), **Supp. V:** 151
"Doom of the Griffiths, The" (Gaskell), **V:** 15
Doom of Youth, The (Lewis), **VII:** 72
"Door in the Wall, The" (Wells), **VI:** 235, 244
Door Into the Dark (Heaney), **Supp. II:** 268, **271–272; Retro. Supp. I:** 127
Dorando, A Spanish Tale (Boswell), **III:** 247
Dorian Gray (Wilde), *see Picture of Dorian Gray, The*
"Dorinda's sparkling Wit, and Eyes" (Dorset), **II:** 262
Dorothy Wordsworth (Selincourt), **IV:** 143
Dorset, earl of (Charles Sackville), **II:** 255, **261–263,** 266, 268, 270–271
Dorset Farm Laborer Past and Present, The, (Hardy), **VI:** 20
Dostoyevsky, Fyodor, **Supp. IV:** 1, 139
Dostoevsky: The Making of a Novelist (Simmons), **V:** 46
Doting (Green), **Supp. II:** 263, 264
Double Falsehood, The (Theobald), **II:** 66, 87
"Double Life" (MacCaig), **Supp. VI:** 186
"Double Looking Glass, The" (Hope), **Supp. VII:** 159
Double Man, The (Auden), **Retro. Supp. I:** 10
Double Marriage, The (Fletcher and Massinger), **II:** 66
"Double Rock, The" (King), **Supp. VI:** 151
Double Tongue, The (Golding), **Retro. Supp. I:** 106–107
"Double Vision of Michael Robartes, The" (Yeats), **VI:** 217
Double–Dealer, The (Congreve), **II:** 338, 341–342, 350
Doublets: A Word–Puzzle (Carroll), **V:** 273
Doubtful Paradise (Friel), **Supp. V:** 115
Doughty, Charles, **Supp. II:** 294–295
Doughty, Oswald, **V:** xi, xxvii, 246, 297n, 307
Douglas, Gavin, **I:** 116–118; **III:** 311
Douglas, Keith, **VII:** xxii, 422, **440–444**
Douglas, Lord Alfred, **V:** 411, 416–417, 420
Douglas, Norman, **VI: 293–305**
Douglas Cause, The (Boswell), **III:** 247
Douglas Jerrold's Weekly (periodical), **V:** 144
"Dovecote" (McGuckian), **Supp. V:** 280
"Dover" (Auden), **VII:** 379
Dover Road, The (Milne), **Supp. V:** 299
"Down" (Graves), **VII:** 264
Down Among the Women (Weldon), **Supp. IV:** 524–525
Down and Out in Paris and London (Orwell), **VII:** xx, 275, 277; **Supp. IV:** 17
"Down at the Dump" (White), **Supp. I:** 143

Down by the River (O'Brien), **Supp. V:** 344–345
"Down by the Sally–Garden" (Yeats), **VII:** 368
Down from the Hill (Sillitoe), **Supp. V:** 411
"Down Kaunda Street" (Fuller), **Supp. VII:** 80
Down There on a Visit (Isherwood), **VII:** 315–316
Downfall and Death of King Oedipus, The (FitzGerald), **IV:** 353
Downs, Brian, **III:** 84, 93
"Downs, The" (Bridges), **VI:** 78
Downstairs (Churchill), **Supp. IV:** 180
Downstream (Kinsella), **Supp. V:** 259, 260, 261–262
"Downstream" (Kinsella), **Supp. V:** 262
Dowson, Ernest, **V:** 441; **VI:** 210
Doyle, Arthur Conan, **III:** 341, 345; **Supp. II:** 126, 127, **159–176**
Doyle, Roddy, **Supp. V: 77–93**
Dr. Goldsmith's Roman History Abridged by Himself . . . (Goldsmith), **III:** 191
Dr. Jekyll and Mr. Hyde (Stevenson), *see Strange Case of Dr. Jekyll and Mr. Hyde, The*
"Dr. Woolacott" (Forster), **VI:** 406
Dr. Wortle's School (Trollope), **V:** 100, 102
Drabble, Antonia, *see* Byatt, A. S.
Drabble, Margaret, **VI:** 247, 253, 268; **Supp. IV:** 141, **229–254**
Dracula (Stoker), **III:** 334, 342, 345; **Supp. III: 375–377,** 381, 382, 383, **386–390**
Dracula (films), **III:** 342; **Supp. III:** 375–377
"Dracula's Guest" (Stoker), **Supp. III:** 383, 385
"Draff" (Beckett), **Retro. Supp. I:** 19
Drafts and Fragments of Verse (Collins), **II:** 323n
Dragon of the Apocalypse (Carter), **VII:** 114
Drake, Nathan, **III:** 51
"Drama and Life" (Joyce), **Retro. Supp. I:** 170
Drama in Muslin, A (Moore), **VI:** 86, 89, **90–91,** 98
"Drama of Exile, A" (Browning), **IV:** 313
Dramatic Character in the English Romantic Age (Donohue), **III:** 268n
Dramatic Idyls (Browning), **IV:** xxiii, 358, 374; **V:** xxiv
Dramatic Lyrics (Browning), **IV:** xx, 374
Dramatic Romances and Lyrics (Browning), **IV:** 374
Dramatic Works of Richard Brinsley Sheridan, The (ed. Price), **III:** 258
Dramatis Personae (Browning), **IV:** xxii, 358, 364, 374; **Retro. Supp. II:** 26–27
Dramatis Personae (Yeats), **VI:** 317
Drapier's Letters, The (Swift), **III:** 20n 28, 31, 35; **Retro. Supp. I:** 274
"Drawing you, heavy with sleep" (Warner), **Supp. VII:** 373
Drayton, Michael, **I:** 196, 278; **II:** 68 134, 138

"Dread of Height, The" (Thompson), **V: 444**

Dreadful Pleasures (Twitchell), **Supp. III:** 383

"Dream" (Heaney), **Supp. II:** 271

"Dream" (Kinsella), **Supp. V:** 273

"Dream, The" (Galsworthy), **VI:** 280

"Dream, The" (MacCaig), **Supp. VI:** 185

"Dream, The. A Song" (Behn), **Supp. III:** 37–38

Dream and Thing (Muir), **Supp. VI:** 208

Dream Children (Wilson), **Supp. VI: 308–309**

"Dream in Three Colours, A" (McGuckian), **Supp. V:** 285

Dream of Destiny, A (Bennett), **VI:** 262

"Dream of Eugene Aram, The Murderer, The" (Hood), **IV:** 256, 261–262, 264, 267; **Supp. III:** 378

Dream of Fair to Middling Women, A (Beckett), **Retro. Supp. I:** 17

Dream of Gerontius, The (Newman), **Supp. VII:** 293, 300, 301

Dream of John Ball, A (Morris), **V:** 301, 302–303, 305, 306

"Dream of Nourishment" (Smith), **Supp. II:** 466

"Dream of Private Clitus, The" (Jones), **Supp. VII:** 175

Dream of Scipio, The (Cicero), **IV:** 189

Dream of the Rood, The, **I:** 11; **Retro. Supp. II:** 302, 307

"Dream Play" (Mahon), **Supp. VI:** 178

"Dream Work" (Hope), **Supp. VII:** 155

"Dream–Fugue" (De Quincey), **IV:** 153–154

"Dream–Language of Fergus, The" (McGuckian), **Supp. V:** 285–286

Dreaming in Bronze (Thomas), **Supp. IV:** 490

"Dreaming Spires" (Campbell), **VII:** 430

"Dreams" (Spenser), **I:** 123

Dreams of Leaving (Hare), **Supp. IV:** 282, 289

"Dreams Old and Nascent" (Lawrence), **VII:** 118

"Dream–Tryst" (Thompson), **V:** 444

Drebbel, Cornelius, **I:** 268

Dressed as for a Tarot Pack (Redgrove), **Supp. VI:** 236

"Dressing" (Vaughan), **II:** 186

Dressing Up—Transvestism and Drag: The History of an Obsession (Ackroyd), **Supp. VI:** 3–4, 12

Dressmaker, The (Bainbridge), **Supp. VI:** 19–20, 24

Drew, Philip, **IV:** xiii, xxiv, 375

"Drink to Me Only with Thine Eyes" (Jonson), **I:** 346; **VI:** 16

Drinkers of Infinity (Koestler), **Supp. I:** 34, 34n

"Drinking" (Cowley), **II:** 198

Driver's Seat, The (Spark), **Supp. I:** 200, 209–210, 218n

"Driving Through Sawmill Towns" (Murray), **Supp. VII:** 271

Droe wit seisoen, 'n (Brink), **Supp. VI: 50–51**

"Droit de Seigneur: 1820" (Murphy), **Supp. V:** 321

Drought, The (Ballard), **Supp. V:** 24–25, 34

"Drowned Giant, The" (Ballard), **Supp. V:** 23

Drowned World, The (Ballard), **Supp. V:** 22–23, 24, 34

"Drummer Hodge" (Housman), **VI:** 161; **Retro. Supp. I:** 120

Drummond of Hawthornden, William, **I:** 328, 349

Drums of Father Ned, The (O'Casey), **VII:** 10–11

Drums under the Windows (O'Casey), **VII:** 9, 12

Drunken Sailor, The (Cary), **VII:** 186, 191

"Dry Point" (Larkin), **Supp. I:** 277

Dry Salvages, The (Eliot), **V:** 241; **VII:** 143, 144, 152, 154, 155

Dry, White Season, A (Brink), **Supp. VI: 50–51**

Dryden, John, **I:** 176, 327, 328, 341, 349; **II:** 166–167, 195, 198, 200, **289–306**, 325, 338, 340, 348, 350, 352, 354–355; **III:** 40, 47, 68, 73–74, 118; **IV:** 93, 196, 287; **V:** 376; **Supp. III:** 19, 24, 27, 36, 37, 40; **Supp. V:** 201–202

Dryden, John, The younger, **II:** 305

"Dryden's Prize–Song" (Hill), **Supp. V:** 201–202

Du Bellay, Joachim, **I:** 126; **V:** 345

Du Bois, W. E. B., **Supp. IV:** 86

du Maurier, Daphne, **III:** 343; **Supp. III: 133–149**

du Maurier, George, **V:** 403; **Supp. III:** 133–137, 141

du Maurier, Guy, **Supp. III:** 147, 148

Du Mauriers, The (du Maurier), **Supp. III:** 135–136, 137, 139

Dual Tradition: An Essay on Poetry and Politics in Ireland (Kinsella), **Supp. V:** 272, 273–274

Dubliners (Joyce), **VII:** xiv, 41, 43–45, 47–52; critical studies, **VII:** 57; **Supp. I:** 45; **Supp. IV:** 395; **Retro. Supp. I:** 171–173

"Duchess of Hamptonshire, The" (Hardy), **VI:** 22

Duchess of Malfi, The (Webster), **II:** 68, 70–73, **76–78**, 79, 81, 82, 84, 85

Duchess of Padua, The (Wilde), **V:** 419; **Retro. Supp. II:** 362–363

"Duddon Estuary, The" (Nicholson), **Supp. VI:** 214

Due Preparations for the Plague (Defoe), **III:** 13

"Duel, The" (Conrad), **VI:** 148

Duel of Angels (Fry), **Supp. III:** 195

"Duel of the Crabs, The" (Dorset), **II:** 271

Duenna, The (Sheridan), **III:** 253, 257, 259–261, 270

"Duffy's Circus" (Muldoon), **Supp. IV:** 415

Dufy, Raoul, **Supp. IV:** 81

Dugdale, Florence Emily, **VI:** 17n

Dugdale, Sir William, **II:** 274

Dugmore, C. W., **I:** 177n

Dujardin, Edouard, **VI:** 87

Duke of Gandia, The (Swinburne), **V:** 333

Duke of Guise, The (Dryden), **II:** 305

Duke's Children, The (Trollope), **V:** 96, 99, 101, 102

"Duke's Reappearance, The" (Hardy), **VI:** 22

"Dulce et Decorum Est" (Owen), **VI:** 448, 451

"Dull London" (Lawrence), **VII:** 94, 116, 121

"Dulwich Gallery, The" (Hazlitt), **IV:** 135–136

Dumas père, Alexandre, **III:** 332, 334, 339

Dumb Virgin, The; or, The Force of Imagination (Behn), **Supp. III:** 31

Dumb Waiter, The (Pinter), **Supp. I:** 369, 370–371, 381; **Retro. Supp. I:** 222

"Dumnesse" (Traherne), **II:** 189

Dun Cow, The (Landor), **IV:** 100

Dun Emer Press, **VI:** 221

Dunbar, William, **I:** 23

Duncan, Robert, **Supp. IV:** 269

Dunciad, The (Pope), **II:** 259, 311; **III:** 73, 77, 95; **IV:** 187; **Supp. III:** 421–422; **Retro. Supp. I:** 76, 231, 235, 238–240

"Dunciad Minimus" (Hope), **Supp. VII:** 161

Dunciad Minor: A Heroick Poem (Hope), **Supp. VII:** 161–163

Dunciad of Today, The; and, The Modern Aesop (Disraeli), **IV:** 308

Dunciad Variorum, The (Pope), **Retro. Supp. I:** 238

Dunn, Nell, **VI:** 271

Dunne, John William, **VII:** 209, 210

Duns Scotus, John, **V:** 363, 370, 371; **Retro. Supp. II:** 187–188

"Duns Scotus's Oxford" (Hopkins), **V:** 363, 367, 370

Dunsany, Lord Edward, **III:** 340

Dunton, John, **III:** 41

Dupee, F. W., **VI:** 31, 45

"Dura Mater" (Kinsella), **Supp. V:** 272

Dürer, Albrecht, **Supp. IV:** 125

"Duriesdyke" (Swinburne), **V:** 333

"During Wind and Rain" (Hardy), **VI:** 17

Durrell, Lawrence, **Supp. I: 93–128**

Dusklands (Coetzee), **Supp. VI: 78–80,** 81

"Dust" (Brooke), **Supp. III:** 52

"Dust, The" (Redgrove), **Supp. VI:** 228

"Dust As We Are" (Hughes), **Retro. Supp. II:** 214

Dutch Courtesan, The (Marston), **II:** 30, 40

Dutch Love, The (Behn), **Supp. III:** 26–27, 40

Duties of Clerks of Petty Sessions in Ireland, The (Stoker), **Supp. III:** 379

Dutiful Daughter, A (Keneally), **Supp. IV:** 345

"Duty—that's to say complying" (Clough), **V:** 160

Dwarfs, The (play, Pinter), **Supp. I:** 373

"Dwarfs, The" (unpublished novel, Pinter), **Supp. I:** 367

Dyer, John, **IV:** 199

Dyer, Sir Edward, **I:** 123

Dyer's Hand, The, and Other Essays (Auden), **V:** 46; **VII:** 394, 395

Dyet of Poland, The (Defoe), **III:** 13

Dying Gaul and Other Writings, The (Jones), **Supp. VII:** 171, 180

Dying Paralytic (Greuze), **Supp. IV:** 122

"Dying Race, A" (Motion), **Supp. VII:** 254

"Dying Swan, The" (Tennyson), **IV:** 329

"Dykes, The" (Kipling), **VI:** 203

Dymer (Lewis), **Supp. III:** 250

Dynamics of a Particle, The (Carroll), **V:** 274

Dynasts, The: A Drama of the Napoleonic Wars (Hardy), **VI:** 6–7, **10–12**; **Retro. Supp. I:** 121

Dyson, A. E., **III:** 51

"Dyvers thy death doo dyverslye bemone" (Surrey), **I:** 115

E. M. Forster: A Study (Trilling), **VI:** 413

E. M. Forster: A Tribute, with Selections from His Writings on India (Natwar–Singh), **VI:** 413

E. M. Forster: The Critical Heritage (ed. Gardner), **VI:** 413

"Eagle Pair" (Murray), **Supp. VII:** 283

Eagles' Nest (Kavan), **Supp. VII:** 213–214

Eagle's Nest, The (Ruskin), **V:** 184

Eagleton, Terry, **Supp. IV:** 164, 365, 380

Eames, Hugh, **Supp. IV:** 3

"Earl Robert" (Swinburne), **V:** 333

Earle, John, **IV:** 286

Early Days (Storey), **Supp. I:** 419

Early Diary of Frances Burney, The (eds. Troide et al.), **Supp. III:** 64

Early Essays (Eliot), **V:** 200

Early Italian Poets, The (Rossetti), **V:** 245

Early Kings of Norway, The (Carlyle), **IV:** 250

Early Lessons (Edgeworth), **Supp. III:** 152

"Early Life of Ben Jonson, The" (Bamborough), **Retro. Supp. I:** 152

Early Morning (Bond), **Supp. I:** 422, 423, 426–428, 430

"Early One Morning" (Warner), **Supp. VII:** 379

Early Plays, The (Hare), **Supp. IV:** 283

Early Years of Alec Waugh, The (Waugh), **Supp. VI:** 267–270, 272, 274

Earnest Atheist, The (Muggeridge), **Supp. II:** 118, 119

"Ears in the turrets hear" (Thomas), **Supp. I:** 174

Earth Owl, The (Hughes), **Supp. I:** 348

Earthly Paradise, The (Morris), **V:** xxiii, **296–299,** 302, 304, 306

Earthly Powers (Burgess), **Supp. I:** 193

Earths in Our Solar System (Swedenborg), **III:** 297

Earthworks (Harrison), **Supp. V:** 149, 150

"East Coker" (Eliot), **II:** 173; **VII:** 154, 155

East into Upper East: Plain Tales from New York and Delhi (Jhabvala), **Supp. V:** 235

"East London" (Arnold), **V:** 209

East of Suez (Maugham), **VI:** 369

East, West: Stories (Rushdie), **Supp. IV:** 438, 443, 452

Eastaway, Edward (pseud.), *see* Thomas, Edward

"Easter 1916" (Yeats), **VI:** 219, 220; **Retro. Supp. I:** 332

"Easter Day" (Crashaw), **II:** 183

"Easter Day, Naples, 1849" (Clough), **V:** 165

"Easter Day II" (Clough), **V:** 159

Easter Greeting for Every Child Who Loves AAlice,"An (Carroll), **V:** 273

"Easter Hymn" (Housman), **VI:** 161

"Easter 1916" (Yeats), **VI:** 219, 220

Easter Rebellion of 1916, **VI:** 212; **VII:** 3

"Easter Wings" (Herbert), **II:** 128; **Retro. Supp. II:** 178

Eastern Front, The (Churchill), **VI:** 359

Eastern Tales (Voltaire), **III:** 327

Eastlake, Lady Elizabeth, **Retro. Supp. I:** 59

Eastward Ho! (Chapman, Jonson, Marston), **I:** 234, 254 **II:** 30, 40; **Retro. Supp. I:** 162

Easy Death (Churchill), **Supp. IV:** 180

Easy Virtue (Coward), **Supp. II:** 145, 146, 148

Eating Pavlova (Thomas), **Supp. IV:** 488–489

Eaton, H. A., **IV:** 142*n*, 155, 156

Ebb–Tide, The (Stevenson), **V:** 384, 387, 390, 396

Ebony Tower, The (Fowles), **Supp. I:** **303–304**

"Ebony Tower, The" (Fowles), **Supp. I:** 303

Ecce Ancilla Domini! (Rossetti), **V:** 236, 248

"Ecchoing Green, The" (Blake), **Retro. Supp. I:** 37, 42

Ecclesiastical History of the English People (Bede), **Retro. Supp. II:** 296

Ecclesiastical Polity (Hooker), **II:** 147

Ecclesiastical Sonnets (Wordsworth), **IV:** **22, 25**

"Echo from Willowwood, An" (Rossetti), **V:** 259

Echo's Bones (Beckett), **Supp. I:** 44, 60–61

"Eclogue for Christmas, An" (MacNeice), **VII:** 416

Eclogues (Vergil), **III:** 222*n*

Eclogues of Virgil, The (tr. Day Lewis), **Supp. III:** 118

Eco, Umberto, **Supp. IV:** 116

"Economies or Dispensations of the Eternal" (Newman), **Supp. VII:** 291

Ecstasy, The (Donne), **I:** 238, 355, 358

Edel, Leon, **VI:** 49, 55

"Eden" (Traherne), **II:** 189

Eden End (Priestley), **VII:** 224

Edge of Being, The (Spender), **Supp. II:** 486, 491

Edge of the Unknown (Doyle), **Supp. II:** 163–164

Edgeworth, Maria, **Supp. III: 151–168; Supp. IV:** 502

Edgeworth, Richard Lovell, **Supp. III:** 151–153, 163

"Edinburgh Court" (MacCaig), **Supp. VI:** 194

Edinburgh: Picturesque Notes (Stevenson), **V:** 395; **Retro. Supp. I:** 261

Edinburgh Review (periodical), **III:** 276, 285; **IV:** xvi, 129, 145, 269–270, 272, 278

"Edinburgh Spring" (MacCaig), **Supp. VI:** 194

Edith Sitwell (Bowra), **VII:** 141

Edith's Diary (Highsmith), **Supp. V:** 177–178, 180

Editor's Tales, An (Trollope), **V:** 102

Edmonds, Helen, *see* Kavan, Anna

Education and the University (Leavis), **VII:** 238, 241

"Education of Otis Yeere, The" (Kipling), **VI:** 183, 184

Edward I (Peele), **I:** 205–206, 208

Edward II (Marlowe), **I:** 278, **286–287**; **Retro. Supp. I:** 201–202, 209–211

Edward III (anon.), **V:** 328

Edward and Eleonora (Thomson), **Supp. III:** 411, 424

Edward Burne–Jones (Fitzgerald), **Supp. V:** 98

"Edward Dorn and the Treasures of Comedy" (Davie), **Supp. VI:** 116

Edward Lear in Greece (Lear), **V:** 87

Edward Lear's Indian Journal (ed. Murphy), **V:** 78, 79, 87

"Edward the Conqueror" (Dahl), **Supp. IV:** 215

Edwards, H. L. R., **I:** 87

"Edwin and Angelina: A Ballad" (Goldsmith), **III:** 185, 191

Edwin Drood (Dickens), **V:** xxiii, 42, 69, 72

"Edwin Morris" (Tennyson), **IV:** 326*n*

Edwy and Elgiva (Burney), **Supp. III:** 67, 71

Egan, Pierce, **IV:** 260*n*

"Egg–Head" (Hughes), **Supp. I:** 348–349

Egoist, The (Meredith), **V:** x, xxiv, 227, 230–232, 234

"Egremont" (Nicholson), **Supp. VI:** 214

"Egypt" (Fraser), **VII:** 425

"Egypt from My Inside" (Golding), **Supp. I:** 65, 83, 84, 89

"Egypt from My Outside" (Golding), **Supp. I:** 84, 89

Egyptian Journal, An (Golding), **Supp. I:** 89–90; **Retro. Supp. I:** 103

"Egyptian Nights" (Pushkin), **Supp. IV:** 484

Eh Joe (Beckett), **Supp. I:** 59–60

Eichmann in Jerusalem (Arendt), **Supp. IV:** 306

"Eight Awful Animals" (Ewart), **Supp. VII:** 39

Eight Dramas of Calderón (tr. Fitz-Gerald), **IV:** 353

"Eight o'clock" (Housman), **VI:** 160

Eight or Nine Wise Words about Letter–Writing (Carroll), **V:** 273

Eight Short Stories (Waugh), **Supp. VI:** 273

"Eight Suits, The" (Ewart), **Supp. VII:** 39

Eighteen Poems (Thomas), **Supp. I:** 170, 171, 172

Eighteen–Eighties, The (ed. de la Mare), **V:** 268, 274

85 Poems (Ewart), **Supp. VII:** 34–35, 46

ΕΙΚΟΝΟΚΛΑΣΤΗΣ: . . . (Milton), **II:** 175

Einstein's Monsters (Amis), **Supp. IV:** 40, 42

Ekblad, Inga Stina, **II:** 77, 86

El maestro de danzar (Calderón), **II:** 313*n*

Elder Brother, The (Fletcher and Massinger), **II:** 66

Elder Statesman, The (Eliot), **VII:** 161, 162; **Retro. Supp. II:** 132

Elders and Betters (Compton–Burnett), **VII:** 63, 66

Eldest Son, The (Galsworthy), **VI:** 269, 287

"Eldorado" (Lessing), **Supp. I:** 240

Election, An (Swinburne), **V:** 332

"Election in Ajmer, The" (Naipaul), **Supp. I:** 395

Elections to the Hebdomadal Council, The (Carroll), **V:** 274

Electric Light (Heaney), **Retro. Supp. I:** 133–135

"Electric Orchard, The" (Muldoon), **Supp. IV:** 413

"Elegiac Stanzas, Suggested by a Picture of Peele Castle . . . A (Wordsworth), **IV:** 21–22

"Elegie. Princesse Katherine, An" (Lovelace), **II:** 230

"Elegie upon the Death of . . . Dr. John Donne" (Carew), **II:** 223

Elegies (Donne), **I:** 360–361; **Retro. Supp. II:** 89–90

Elegies (Johannes Secundus), **II:** 108

Elegies for the Dead in Cyrenaica (Henderson), **VII:** 425

"Elegy" (Gunn), **Supp. IV:** 271–272, 274

"Elegy Before Death" (Day Lewis), **Supp. III:** 129

"Elegy for an Irish Speaker" (McGuckian), **Supp. V:** 285, 290

"Elegy for Margaret" (Spender), **Supp. II:** 490

"Elegy for W. H. Auden" (Jennings), **Supp. V:** 217

"Elegy in April and September" (Owen), **VI:** 453

"Elegy on Dead Fashion" (Sitwell), **VII:** 133

Elegy on Dicky and Dolly, An (Swift), **III:** 36

Elegy on Dr. Donne, An (Walton), **II:** 136

"Elegy on Marlowe's Untimely Death" (Nashe), **I:** 278

"Elegy on the Death of a Mad Dog" (Goldsmith), **III:** 184

Elegy on the Death of an Amiable Young Lady . . ., An (Boswell), **III:** 247

"Elegy on the Dust" (Gunn), **Supp. IV:** 264

Elegy on the Usurper O. C., An (Dryden), **II:** 304

"Elegy to the Memory of an Unfortunate Lady" (Pope), **III:** 70, 288

Elegy upon the Death of My Lord Francis Villiers, An (Marvell), **II:** 219

"Elegy upon the most Incomparable King Charls the First, An" (King), **Supp. VI:** 159

"Elegy Written in a Country Church-yard" (Gray), **III:** 119, 137, **138–139,** 144–145; **Retro. Supp. I:** 144

"Elementary Sketches of Moral Philosophy" (Smith), **Supp. VII:** 342

Elementary, The (Mulcaster), **I:** 122

Elements of Drawing, The (Ruskin), **V:** 184

Elements of Perspective, The (Ruskin), **V:** 184

Elene, Retro. Supp. II: 302–303

Eleonora: A Panegyrical Poem (Dryden), **II:** 304

"Elephant and Colosseum" (Lowry), **Supp. III:** 281

Elephants Can Remember (Christie), **Supp. II:** 135

Eleutheria (Beckett), **Retro. Supp. I:** 23

Elia, pseud. of Charles Lamb

"Eliduc" (Fowles), **Supp. I:** 303

"Elinor Barley" (Warner), **Supp. VII:** 379

"Elinor and Marianne" (Austen), *see Sense and Sensibility*

Eliot, George, **III:** 157; **IV:** 238, 323; **V:** ix–x, xviii, xxii–xxiv, 2, 6, 7, 14, 45, 52, 56, 57, 63, 66, 67, **187–201,** 212, **VI:** 23; **Supp. IV:** 146, 169, 230, 233, 239–240, 243, 379, 471, 513; **Retro. Supp. II:** 101–117

Eliot T. S., **II:** 148; **IV:** 271; **V:** xxv, 241 309 402; **VII:** xii–xiii, xv, 34, **143–170**; **Retro. Supp. II:** 119–133; and Matthew Arnold, **V:** 204, 205–206, 210, 215; and Yeats, **VI:** 207, 208; influence on modern literature, **I:** 98; **VII:** xii–xiii, xv, 34 143–144, 153–154, 165–166; **Retro. Supp. I:** 3; list of collected essays, **VII:** 169–170; literary criticism, **I:** 232, 275, 280; **II:** 16, 42, 83, 179, 196, 204, 208, 219; **III:** 51, 305; **IV:** 195, 234; **V:** 204–206, 210, 215, 310, 367; **VI:** 207, 226; **VII:** 162–165; **Retro. Supp. I:** 166; **Retro. Supp. II:** 173–174; style, **II:** 173; **IV:** 323, 329; in drama, **VII:** 157–162; in poetry, **VII:** 144–157; **Supp. I:** 122–123; **Supp. II:** 151, 181, 420, 428, 487; **Supp. III:** 122; **Supp. IV:** 58, 100, 139, 142, 180, 249, 260, 330, 377, 558

"Elixir" (Murphy), **Supp. V:** 326

"Ella Wheeler Wilcox Woo, The" (Ewart), **Supp. VII:** 41

"Elvers, The" (Nicholson), **Supp. VI:** 214

"Ely Place" (Kinsella), **Supp. V:** 267

Elizabeth Alone (Trevor), **Supp. IV:** 509–510

Elizabeth and Essex (Strachey), **Supp. II:** 514–517

Elizabeth and Her German Garden (Forster), **VI:** 406

Elizabeth Cooper (Moore), **VI:** 96, 99

Elizabeth I, Queen of England, **Supp. IV:** 146

Elizabethan Drama and Shakespeare's Early Plays (Talbert), **I:** 224

"Elizas, The" (Gurney), **VI:** 425

"Ellen Orford" (Crabbe), **III:** 281

Ellen Terry and Bernard Shaw, a Correspondence (ed. St. John), **VI:** 130

Ellis, Annie Raine, **Supp. III:** 63, 65

Ellis, Havelock, **I:** 281

Ellis–Fermor, U. M., **I:** 284, 292

"Elm Tree, The" (Hood), **IV:** 261–262, 264

"Eloisa to Abelard" (Pope), **III:** 70, 75–76, 77; **V:** 319, 321

Elopement into Exile (Pritchett), *see Shirley Sanz*

Eloquence of the British Senate, The (Hazlitt), **IV:** 130, 139

Elton, Oliver, **III:** 51

Emancipated, The (Gissing), **V:** 437

"Embankment, The" (Hulme), **Supp. VI:** 134, 136

Embarrassments (James), **VI:** 49, 67

Embers (Beckett), **Supp. I:** 58

Emblem Hurlstone (Hall), **Supp. VI:** 129–130

"Emerald Dove, The" (Murray), **Supp. VII:** 281

Emerson, Ralph Waldo, **IV:** xx, 54, 81, 240; **V:** xxv

Emigrant Ship, The (Stevenson), **Retro. Supp. I:** 262

Emigrant Train, The (Stevenson), **Retro. Supp. I:** 262

Emigrants, The (Lamming), **Supp. IV:** 445

Emilia in England (Meredith), *see Sandra Belloni*

Emilie de Coulanges (Edgeworth), **Supp. III:** 158

Emily Brontë: A Biography (Gérin), **V:** 153

Eminent Victorians (Wilson), **Supp. VI:** 305

Eminent Victorians (Strachey), **V:** 13, 157, 170; **Supp. II:** 498, 499, **503–511**

Emma (Austen), **IV:** xvii, 108, 109, 111, 112, 113, 114, 115, 117, 119, 120, 122; **VI:** 106; **Supp. IV:** 154, 236; **Retro. Supp. II:** 11–12

Empedocles on Etna (Arnold), **IV:** 231; **V:** xxi, 206, 207, 209, 210, 211, 216

"Emperor Alexander and Capo d'Istria" (Landor), **IV:** 92

"Emperor and the Little Girl, The" (Shaw), **VI:** 120

Emperor Constantine, The (Sayers), **Supp. III:** 336, 350

"Emperor's Tomb Found in China" (Fuller), **Supp. VII:** 80

Empire of the Sun (Ballard), **Supp. V:** 19, 29–30, 31, 35

Empire State (Bateman), **Supp. V:** 88

"Employment (I)" (Herbert), **Retro. Supp. II:** 180

Empson, William, **I:** 282; **II:** 124, 130; **V:** 367, 381; **Supp. II: 179–197**

"Empty Birdhouse, The" (Highsmith), **Supp. V:** 180

Empty Purse, The (Meredith), V: 223, 234

"Enallos and Cymodameia" (Landor), **IV:** 96

Enchafèd Flood, The (Auden), **VII:** 380, 394

Enchanted Isle, The (Dryden), **I:** 327

"Enchantment of Islands" (Brown), **Supp. VI:** 61

Enchantress, The, and Other Poems (Browning), **IV:** 321

Encounter, **Supp. II:** 491

Encounters (Bowen), **Supp. II:** 79, 81

Encyclopaedia Britannica, **Supp. III:** 171

"End, The" (Beckett), **Supp. I:** 50; **Retro. Supp. I:** 21

"End, The" (Milne), **Supp. V:** 303

"End, The" (Owen), **VI:** 449

"End of a Journey" (Hope), **Supp. VII:** 156–157

End of a War, The (Read), **VI:** 436, 437

End of the Affair, The (Greene), **Supp. I:** 2, 8, 12–13, 14; **Retro. Supp. II:** 159–160

End of the Beginning, The (O'Casey), **VII:** 12

End of the Chapter (Galsworthy), **VI:** 275, 282

"End of the City" (Fuller), **Supp. VII:** 69

"End of the Relationship, The" (Self), **Supp. V:** 403

"End of the Tether, The" (Conrad), **VI:** 148

Enderby Outside (Burgess), **Supp. I:** 189, 194–195

Enderby's Dark Lady; or, No End to Enderby (Burgess), **Supp. I:** 189

Endgame (Beckett), **Supp. I:** 49, 51, 52, 53, 56–57, 62; **Retro. Supp. I:** 24–25

Ending in Earnest (West), **Supp. III:** 438

Ending Up (Amis), **Supp. II:** 18

Endiomion (Lyly), **I:** 202

Endless Night (Christie), **Supp. II:** 125, 130, 132, 135

Ends and Means (Huxley), **VII:** xvii 205

Endymion (Disraeli), **IV:** xxiii, 294, 295, 296, 306, 307, 308; **V:** xxiv

"Endymion" (Keats), **III:** 174, 338; **IV:** x, xvii, 205, 211, 214, 216–217, 218, 222–224, 227, 229, 230, 233, 235; **Retro. Supp. I:** 184, 189–192

"Enemies, The" (Jennings), **Supp. V:** 211

Enemies of Promise (Connolly), **VI:** 363; **Supp. III:** 95, 96, 97, 98, **100–102**

"Enemy, The" (Naipaul), **Supp. I:** 386n

"Enemy Dead, The" (Gutteridge), **VII:** 433

Enemy in the Blanket, The (Burgess), **Supp. I:** 187–188

"Enemy Interlude" (Lewis), **VII:** 71

Enemy of the People, An (Ibsen), **VI:** ix

Enemy of the Stars, The (Lewis), **VII:** 72, 73, 74–75

Enemy Within, The (Friel), **Supp. V:** 115–116

Enemy's Country, The: Word, Contexture, and Other Circumstances of Language (Hill), **Supp. V:** 196, 201

England (Davie), **Supp. VI:** 111–112

"England" (Stevenson), **Supp. VI:** 255–256, 264

"England" (Thomas), **Supp. III:** 404

England and the Italian Question (Arnold), **V:** 216

England in the Age of Wycliffe (Trevelyan), **VI:** 385–386

England Made Me (Greene; U.S. title, *The Shipwrecked*), **Supp. I:** 6, 7

"England, My England" (Lawrence) **VII:** xv, 114; **Retro. Supp. II:** 153

England, My England, and Other Stories (Lawrence), **VII:** 114

England Under Queen Anne (Trevelyan), **VI: 391–393**

England Under the Stuarts (Trevelyan), **VI:** 386

England Your England (Orwell), **VII:** 282

"England's Answer" (Kipling), **VI:** 192

England's Helicon, **I:** 291

"England's Ireland" (Hare), **Supp. IV:** 281

England's Pleasant Land (Forster), **VI:** 411

"English and the Afrikaans Writer" (Brink), **Supp. VI:** 48–49

English, David, **Supp. IV:** 348

English Bards and Scotch Reviewers (Byron), **IV:** x, xvi, 129, 171, 192

English Bible, **I: 370–388;** list of versions, **I:** 387

"English Climate" (Warner), **Supp. VII:** 380

English Comic Characters, The (Priestley), **VII:** 211

English Eccentrics, The (Sitwell), **VII:** 127

English Folk–Songs (ed. Barrett), **V:** 263n

English Grammar (Jonson), **Retro. Supp. I:** 166

English Historical Review, **VI:** 387

English Hours (James), **VI:** 46, 67

English Humour (Priestley), **VII:** 213

English Humourists of the Eighteenth Century, The (Thackeray), **III:** 124, 146n; **V:** 20, 31, 38

English Journey (Bainbridge), **Supp. VI:** 22–23

English Journey (Priestley), **VII:** 212, 213–214

English Literature: A Survey for Students (Burgess), **Supp. I:** 189

English Literature and Society in the Eighteenth Century (Stephen), **III:** 41; **V:** 290

"English Literature and the Small Coterie" (Kelman), **Supp. V:** 257

English Literature, 1815–1832 (ed. Jack), **IV: 40, 140**

English Literature in Our Time and the University (Leavis), **VII:** 169, 235, 236–237, 253

English Literature in the Sixteenth Century, Excluding Drama (Lewis), **Supp. III:** 249, 264

"English Mail–Coach, The" (De Quincey), **IV:** 149, 153, 155

English Mirror, The (Whetstone), **I:** 282

English Music (Ackroyd), **Supp. VI: 9–10,** 11, 12

English Novel, The (Ford), **VI:** 322, 332

English Novel, The: A Short Critical History (Allen), **V:** 219

English Novelists (Bowen), **Supp. II:** 91–92

English Pastoral Poetry (Empson), *see Some Versions of Pastoral*

English People, The (Orwell), **VII:** 282

English Poems (Blunden), **VI:** 429

"English Poet, An" (Pater), **V:** 356, 357

English Poetry (Bateson), **IV:** 217, 323n, 339

English Poetry and the English Language (Leavis), **VII:** 234

English Poetry of the First World War (Owen), **VI:** 453

English Poets (Browning), **IV:** 321

English Prisons under Local Government (Webb), **VI:** 129

English Protestant's Plea, The (King), **Supp. VI:** 152

"English Renaissance of Art, The" (Wilde), **V:** 403–404

English Review (periodical), **VI:** xi–xii, 294, 323–324; **VII:** 89

English Revolution, 1688–1689 (Trevelyan), **VI:** 391

"English School, An" (Kipling), **VI:** 201

English Seamen (Southey and Bell), **IV:** 71

English Social History: A Survey of Six Centuries (Trevelyan), **VI:** xv, 393–394

English Songs of Italian Freedom (Trevelyan), **V:** 227

English South African's View of the Situation, An (Schreiner), **Supp. II:** 453

English Through Pictures (Richards), **Supp. II:** 425, 430

English Town in the Last Hundred Years (Betjeman), **VII:** 360

English Traits (Emerson), **IV:** 54

English Utilitarians, The (Stephen), **V:** 279, 288–289

"English Wife, The" (Ewart), **Supp. VII:** 36

English Without Tears (Rattigan), **Supp. VII:** 311

English Works of George Herbert (Palmer), **Retro. Supp. II:** 173

Englishman (periodical), **III:** 7, 50, 53

"Englishman in Italy, The" (Browning), **IV:** 368

Englishman in Patagonia, An (Pilkington), **Supp. IV:** 164

Englishman Looks at the World, An (Wells), **VI:** 244

Englishman's Home, An (du Maurier), **Supp. III:** 147, 148

"Englishmen and Italians" (Trevelyan), **V:** 227; **VI:** 388n

Englishness of English Literature, The (Ackroyd), **Supp. VI:** 12

"Enigma, The" (Fowles), **Supp. I:** 303–304

Ennui (Edgeworth), **Supp. III:** 154, 156, **158–160**

Enoch Arden (Tennyson), **IV:** xxii, 388; **V:** 6n

"Enoch Soames" (Beerbohm), **Supp. II:** 56

Enormous Crocodile, The (Dahl), **Supp. IV:** 207

"Enormous Space, The" (Ballard), **Supp. V:** 33

Enough Is as Good as a Feast (Wager), **I:** 213

Enough of Green, (Stevenson), **Supp. VI:** 260

Enquiry Concerning Human Understanding, An (Hume), **Supp. III:** 231, 238, 243–244

Enquiry Concerning Political Justice, An (Godwin), **IV:** xv, 181; **Supp. III:** 370; **Retro. Supp. I:** 245

Enquiry Concerning the Principles of Morals, An (Hume), **Supp. III:** 231, 238, 244

Enquiry into the Causes of the Late Increase of Robbers (Fielding), **III:** 104; **Retro. Supp. I:** 81

Enquiry into the Occasional Conformity of Dissenters . . . . An (Defoe), **III:** 12

Enquiry into the Present State of Polite Learning in Europe, An (Goldsmith), **III:** 179, 191

Enright, D. J., **Supp. IV:** 256, 354

"Enter a Cloud" (Graham), **Supp. VII:** 103

"Enter a Dragoon" (Hardy), **VI:** 22

Enter a Free Man (Stoppard), **Supp. I:** 437, 439–440, 445

"Enter One in Sumptuous Armour" (Lowry), **Supp. III:** 285

Entertainer, The (Osborne), **Supp. I:** 332–333, 336–337, 339

Entertaining Mr. Sloane (Orton), **Supp. V:** 364, 367, 370–371, 372, 373–374

Entertainment (Middleton), **II:** 3

"Entertainment for David Wright on His Being Sixty, An" (Graham), **Supp. VII:** 116

"Entertainment of the Queen and Prince at Althorpe (Jonson), **Retro. Supp. I:** 161

"Entire Fabric, The" (Kinsella), **Supp. V:** 268

"Entrance" (Kinsella), **Supp. V:** 271

"Entreating of Sorrow" (Ralegh), **I:** 147–148

"Envoy Extraordinary" (Golding), **Supp. I:** 75, 82, 83

"Eolian Harp, The" (Coleridge), **IV:** 46; **Retro. Supp. II:** 52

Epicoene (Johnson), **I:** 339, 341; **Retro. Supp. I:** 163

"Epicure, The" (Cowley), **II:** 198

"Epicurus, Leontion and Ternissa" (Landor), **IV:** 94, 96–97

Epigram CXX (Jonson), **I:** 347

"Epigram to My Muse, the Lady Digby, on Her Husband, Sir Kenelm Digby" (Jonson), **Retro. Supp. I:** 151

Epigrammata (More), **Supp. VII:** 234, 236–237

Epigrammatum sacrorum liber (Crashaw), **II:** 179, 201

Epigrams (Jonson), **Retro. Supp. I:** 164

Epilogue (Graves), **VII:** 261

Epilogue to the Satires (Pope), **III:** 74, 78

"Epipsychidion" (Shelley), **IV:** xviii, 204, 208; **VI:** 401; **Retro. Supp. I:** 254–255

"Epistle, An: Edward Sackville to Venetia Digby" (Hope), **Supp. VII:** 159

"Epistle from Holofernes, An" (Hope), **Supp. VII:** 157

Epistle to a Canary (Browning), **IV:** 321

Epistle to a Lady . . . , An (Swift), **III:** 36

Epistle to Augustus (Pope), **II:** 196

Epistle to Cobham, An (Pope), *see Moral Essays*

"Epistle to Davie" (Burns), **III:** 316

Epistle to Dr. Arbuthnot (Pope), **III:** 71, 74–75, 78; **Retro. Supp. I:** 229

"Epistle to Henry Reynolds" (Drayton), **I:** 196

Epistle to Her Grace Henrietta . . . , An (Gay), **III:** 67

"Epistle to John Hamilton Reynolds" (Keats), **IV:** 221

Epistle to . . . Lord Carteret, An (Swift), **III:** 35

"Epistle to Mr. Dryden, An, . . ." (Wycherley), **II:** 322

Epistle to the . . . Earl of Burlington, An (Pope), *see Moral Essays*

Epistle upon an Epistle, An (Swift), **III:** 35

Epistles to the King and Duke (Wycherley), **II:** 321

Epistola adversus Jovinianum (St. Jerome), **I:** 35

Epitaph For A Spy (Ambler), **Supp. IV:** 8

"Epitaph for Anton Schmidt" (Gunn), **Supp. IV:** 264

Epitaph for George Dillon (Osborne), **Supp. I:** 329–330, 333

"Epitaph on a Fir–Tree" (Murphy), **Supp. V:** 317–318

"Epitaph on a Jacobite" (Macaulay), **IV:** 283

"Epitaph on an Army of Mercenaries" (Housman), **VI:** 161, 415–416

Epitaph on George Moore (Morgan), **VI:** 86

"Epitaph on the Admirable Dramaticke Poet, W. Shakespeare, An" (Milton), **II:** 175

"Epitaph on the Lady Mary Villers" (Carew), **II:** 224

"Epitaphs" (Warner), **Supp. VII:** 371

Epitaphs and Occasions (Fuller), **Supp. VII:** 72

"Epitaphs for Soldiers" (Fuller), **Supp. VII:** 72

Epitaphium Damonis (Milton), **II:** 175

"Epithalamion" (Hopkins), **V:** 376, 377

Epithalamion (Spenser), **I:** 130–131; *see also Amoretti and Epithalamion*

"Epithalamion for Gloucester" (Lydgate), **I:** 58

"Epithalamion Thamesis" (Spenser), **I:** 123

"Epithalamium" (Motion), **Supp. VII:** 266

Epoch and Artist (Jones), **Supp. VII:** 168, 170, 171

Epping Hunt, The (Hood), **IV:** 256, 257, 267

Equal Skies, The (MacCaig), **Supp. VI:** 193

Equus (Shaffer), **Supp. I:** 318, 323, **324–326,** 327

Erdman, D. V., **III:** 289n, 307

Erechtheus (Swinburne), **V:** 314, 331, 332

Erewhon (Butler), **Supp. II:** 99–101

Erewhon Revisited (Butler), **Supp. II:** 99, 111, 116–117

Eric Ambler (Lewis), **Supp. IV:** 13

Eric Brighteyes (Haggard), **Supp. III:** 214

Eridanus (Lowry), **Supp. III:** 280

Ernie's Incredible Illucinations (Ayckbourn), **Supp. V:** 2

Eros and Psyche (Bridges), **VI:** 83

"Erotion" (Swinburne), **V:** 320

Erpingham Camp, The (Orton), **Supp. V:** 367, 371, 375–376

"Errata" (Rushdie), **Supp. IV:** 442

Erskine, Andrew, **III:** 247

Escape (Galsworthy), **VI:** 275, 287

"Escaped Cock, The" (Lawrence), **VII:** 91, 115

"Escapement" (Ballard), **Supp. V:** 21

"Escapist, The" (Day Lewis), **Supp. III:** 127–128

"Escorial, The" (Hopkins), **V:** 361

Esio Trot (Dahl), **Supp. IV:** 225

Esmond in India (Jhabvala), **Supp. V:** 226–227

Espalier, The (Warner), **Supp. VII:** 370, 371

"Especially when the October Wind" (Thomas), **Supp. I:** 173

Esprit de Corps (Durrell), **Supp. I:** 113

Essai sur l'étude de la littérature (Gibbon), **III:** 222, 223

Essais (Montaigne), **III:** 39

Essay Concerning Human Understanding (Locke), **III:** 22; **Supp. III:** 233

"Essay Concerning Humour in Comedy, An" (Congreve), *see Concerning Humour in Comedy*

Essay of Dramatick Poesy (Dryden), **I:** 328, 349; **II:** 301, 302, 305; **III:** 40

"Essay on Burmese Days" (Orwell), **VII:** 276

"Essay on Christianity, An" (Shelley), **IV:** 199, 209

Essay on Comedy and the Uses of the Comic Spirit, An (Meredith), **V:** 224–225, 234

Essay on Criticism, An (Pope), **II:** 197; **III:** 68, 72, 77; **Retro. Supp. I:** 230, 231, 233

Essay on Irish Bulls (Edgeworth), **Supp. III:** 155–156

Essay on Man, An (Pope), **III:** 72, 76, 77–78, 280; **Retro. Supp. I:** 229–231, 235

Essay on Mind, An (Browning), **IV:** 310, 316, 321

"Essay on Percy Bysshe Shelley, An" (Browning), **IV:** 357, 366, 374

Essay on the Development of Christian Doctrine, An (Newman), **Supp. VII:** 296–297, 301

Essay on the Dramatic Poetry of the Last Age (Dryden), **I:** 328

Essay on the External use of Water . . ., An (Smollett), **III:** 158

Essay on the First Book of T. Lucretius Carus de Rerum Natura, An (Evelyn), *see De rerum natura*

Essay on the Genius and Writings of Pope (Warton), **III:** 170*n*

Essay on the Genius of George Cruikshank, An (Thackeray), **V:** 37

Essay on the History and Reality of Apparitions, An (Defoe), **III:** 14

Essay on the Idea of Comedy (Meredith), **I:** 201–202

Essay on the Lives and Works of Our Uneducated Poets (Southey), **IV:** 71

Essay on the Principle of Population (Malthus), **IV:** xvi, 127

Essay on the Principles of Human Action, An (Hazlitt), **IV:** 128, 139

Essay on the Theatre; Or, A Comparison Between the Laughing and Sentimental Comedy (Goldsmith), **III:** 187, 256

Essay on the Theory of the Earth (Cuvier), **IV:** 181

Essay to Revive the Antient Education of Gentlewomen, An (Makin), **Supp. III:** 21

Essay Towards an Abridgement of the English History, An (Burke), **III:** 205

Essay upon Projects, An (Defoe), **III:** 12; **Retro. Supp. I:** 64, 75

Essayes (Cornwallis), **III:** 39

Essays (Bacon), **I:** 258, 259, 260, 271; **III:** 39

Essays (Goldsmith), **III:** 180

Essays and Leaves from a Note–book (Eliot), **V:** 200

Essays and Reviews (Newman), **V:** 340

Essays and Studies (Swinburne), **V:** 298, 332

Essays and Treatises on Several Subjects (Hume), **Supp. III:** 238

Essays from "The Guardian" (Pater), **V:** 357

Essays Illustrative of the Tatler (Drake), **III:** 51

Essays in Criticism (Arnold), **III:** 277; **V:** xxiii, 203, 204–205, 212, 213, 214, 215, 216

Essays in Divinity (Donne), **I:** 353, 360, 363; **Retro. Supp. II:** 95

Essays in London and Elsewhere (James), **VI:** 49, 67

Essays in Verse and Prose (Cowley), **II:** 195

Essays, Moral and Political (Hume), **Supp. III:** 231, 237

Essays, Moral and Political (Southey), **IV:** 71

Essays of Elia (Lamb), **IV:** xviii, 73, 74, 75, 76, 82–83, 85

Essays of Five Decades (Priestley), **VII:** 212

Essays on Freethinking and Plainspeaking (Stephen), **V:** 283, 289

Essays on His Own Times (Coleridge), **IV:** 56

Essays on Literature and Society (Muir), **Supp. VI:** 202

Essays on Shakespeare (Empson), **Supp. II:** 180, 193

Essays, Theological and Literary (Hutton), **V:** 157, 170

Essence of Christianity, The (tr. Eliot), **V:** 200

Essence of the Douglas Cause, The (Boswell), **III:** 247

"Essential Beauty" (Larkin), **Supp. I:** 279

Essential Gesture (Gordimer), **Supp. II:** 226, 237, 239, 242, 243

"Essential Gesture, The" (Gordimer), **Supp. II:** 225

Essex Poems (Davie), **Supp. VI: 109–111**

Esslin, Martin, **Supp. IV:** 181; **Retro. Supp. I:** 218–219

Estate of Poetry, The (Muir), **Supp. VI:** 197–198, 202, **203**, 209

Esther Waters (Moore), **VI:** ix, xii, 87, 89, 91–92, 96, 98

"Et Dona Ferentes" (Wilson), **Supp. I:** 157

"Et Tu, Healy" (Joyce), **Retro. Supp. I:** 169

"Eternal Contemporaries" (Durrell), **Supp. I:** 124

Eternal Moment, The (Forster), **VI:** 399, 400

Eternity to Season: Poems of Separation and Reunion (Harris), **Supp. V:** 132, 136

Etherege, Sir George, **II:** 255, 256, **266–269, 271,** 305

Etherege and the Seventeenth–Century Comedy of Manners (Underwood), **II:** 256*n*

Ethical Characters (Theophrastus), **II:** 68

Ethics of the Dust, The (Ruskin), **V:** 180, 184

Ethnic Radio (Murray), **Supp. VII:** 270, 276–277

Etruscan Places (Lawrence), **VII:** 116, 117

Euclid and His Modern Rivals (Carroll), **V:** 264, 274

Eugene Aram (Bulwer–Lytton), **IV:** 256; **V:** 22, 46

"Eugene Aram" (Hood), *see* "Dream of Eugene Aram, The Murderer, The"

Eugene Onegin (Pushkin), **Supp. IV:** 485

"Eugene Pickering" (James), **VI:** 69

Eugenia (Chapman), **I:** 236, 240

Eugénie Grandet (Balzac), **Supp. IV:** 124

Eugenius Philalethes, pseud. of Thomas Vaughan

Euphranor: A Dialogue on Youth (FitzGerald), **IV:** 344, 353

Euphues and His England (Lyly), **I:** 194, 195–196

Euphues, The Anatomy of Wit (Lyly), **I:** 165, 193–196

Euripides, **IV:** 358; **V:** 321–324

"Europe" (James), **VI:** 69

Europe. A Prophecy (Blake), **III:** 302, 307; **Retro. Supp. I:** 39, 41–42

European Tribe, The (Phillips), **Supp. V:** 380, 384–385

European Witness (Spender), **Supp. II:** 489–490

Europeans, The (James), **VI:** 29–31

"Eurydice" (Sitwell), **VII:** 136–137

Eurydice, a Farce (Fielding), **III:** 105

"Eurydice to Orpheus" (Browning), **Retro. Supp. II:** 28

Eustace and Hilda: A Trilogy (Hartley), **Supp. VII:** 119, 120, 122, 123–124, 127, 131, 132

Eustace Diamonds, The (Fuller), **Supp. VII:** 72

Eustace Diamonds, The (Trollope), **V:** xxiv, 96, 98, 101, 102

Eustace, Robert, *see* Barton, Eustace

Eva Trout (Bowen), **Supp. II:** 82, 94

"Evacuees, The" (Nicholson), **Supp. VI:** 214

Evan Harrington (Meredith), **V:** xxii, 227, 234

Evans, Abel, **II:** 335

Evans, G. Blakemore, **I:** 326

Evans, Marian, *see* Eliot, George

"Eve" (Rossetti), **V:** 258

"Eve of St. Agnes, The" (Keats), **III:** 338; **IV:** viii, xviii, 212, **216–219,** 231, 235; **V:** 352; **Retro. Supp. I:** 193

Eve of Saint John, The (Scott), **IV:** 38

"Eve of St. Mark, The" (Hill), **Supp. V:** 191

"Eve of St. Mark, The" (Keats), **IV:** 212, 216, 218, 220, 226

"Eveline" (Joyce), **Retro. Supp. I:** 172

"Evening Alone at Bunyah" (Murray), **Supp. VII:** 272

Eve's Ransom (Gissing), **V:** 437

Evelina (Burney), **III:** 90, 91; **IV:** 279; **Supp. III:** 64, 67, 68, 69, 70, 71–72, 75–76

"Eveline" (Joyce), **VII: 44**

Evelyn, John, **II:** 194, 196, **273–280, 286–287**

Evelyn Innes (Moore), **VI:** 87, 92

Evelyn Waugh (Lodge), **Supp. IV:** 365

"Even So" (Rossetti), **V:** 242

"Even Such Is Time" (Ralegh), **I:** 148–149

Evening (Macaulay), **IV:** 290

Evening Colonnade, The (Connolly), **Supp. III:** 98, 110, 111

Evening Standard (periodical), **VI:** 247, 252, 265

Evening Walk, An (Wordsworth), **IV:** xv 2, 4–5, 24

Evening's Love, An; or, The Mock Astrologer (Dryden), **II:** 305

Events and Wisdom (Davie), **Supp. VI:** 109

"Events at Drimaghleen" (Trevor), **Supp. IV:** 505

"Events in your life" (Kelman), **Supp. V:** 251

Ever After (Swift), **Supp. V:** 438–440

"Ever drifting down the stream" (Carroll), **V:** 270

"Ever Fixed Mark, An" (Amis), **Supp. II:** 3

"Ever mine hap is slack and slow in coming" (Wyatt), **I:** 110

"Everlasting Gospel" (Blake), **III:** 304

Everlasting Man, The (Chesterton), **VI:** 341–342

Everlasting Spell, The: A Study of Keats and His Friends (Richardson), **IV:** 236

"Evermore" (Barnes), Supp. IV: 75–76

Every Changing Shape (Jennings), **Supp. V:** 207, 213, 215

Every Day of the Week (Sillitoe), **Supp. V:** 423

Every Good Boy Deserves Favour (Stoppard), **Supp. I:** 450, 451, 453; **Retro. Supp. II:** 351

Every Man for Himself (Bainbridge), **Supp. VI: 25–26,** 27

Every Man out of His Humor (Jonson), **I:** 336–337, 338–340; **II:** 24, 27

Every–Body's Business, Is No–Body's Business (Defoe), **III:** 13–14

Everybody's Political What's What? (Shaw), **VI:** 125, 129

Everyman, **II:** 70

Everyman in His Humor (Jonson), **I:** 336–337; **Retro. Supp. I:** 154, 157–159, 166

"Everything that is born must die" (Rossetti), **V:** 254

Evidence for the Resurrection of Jesus Christ as Given by the Four Evangelists, Critically Examined (Butler), **Supp. II:** 99, 102

Evidences of Christianity (Paley), **IV:** 144

Evil Genius: A Domestic Story, The (Collins), **Supp. VI:** 103

Evolution and Poetic Belief (Roppen), **V:** 221n

Evolution Old and New (Butler), **Supp. II:** 106, 107

Ewart, Gavin, **VII:** 422, 423–424, **Supp. VII: 33–49**

Ewart Quarto, The (Ewart), **Supp. VII:** 44

Ex Voto (Butler), **Supp. II:** 114

Examen Poeticum (ed. Dryden), **II:** 290, 291, 301, 305

Examination, The (Pinter), **Supp. I:** 371

"Examination at the Womb Door" (Hughes), **Supp. I:** 352; **Retro. Supp. II:** 207

Examination of Certain Abuses, An (Swift), **III:** 36

Examiner (periodical), **III:** 19, 26, 35, 39; **IV:** 129

"Example of a Treatise on Universal Justice; or, The Fountains of Equity" (Bacon), **I:** 261

"Examples of Antitheses" (Bacon), **I:** 261

"Examples of the Colours of Good and Evil" (Bacon), **I:** 261, 264

Examples of the Interposition of Providence in . . . Murder (Fielding), **III:** 105

"Excellent New Ballad, An" (Montrose), **II:** 236–237

Excellent Women (Pym), **Supp. II: 367–370**

Except the Lord (Cary), **VII:** 186, 194–195

Excursion, The (Wordsworth), **IV:** xvii, 5, 22–24, 95, 129, 214, 230, 233

Excursions in the Real World (Trevor), **Supp. IV:** 499

"Execration Upon Vulcan, An" (Jonson), **Retro. Supp. I:** 165

"Execution of Cornelius Vane, The" (Read), **VI:** 436

"Exequy To his Matchlesse never to be forgotten Friend, An" (King), **Supp. VI:** 153

"Exequy, The" (King), **Supp. VI: 153–155,** 159, 161

Exeter Book, The, **Retro. Supp. II:** 303–305

"Exhortation" (Shelley), **IV:** 196

Exiles (Joyce), **VII:** 42–43; **Supp. II:** 74; **Retro. Supp. I:** 175–176

"Existentialists and Mystics" (Murdoch), **Supp. I:** 216–217, 219, 220

"Exit" (Kinsella), **Supp. V:** 271

Exorcist, The (film), **III:** 343, 345

Exodus, **Retro. Supp. II:** 301

"Expanding Universe, The" (Nicholson), **Supp. VI:** 217

Expedition of Humphrey Clinker, The (Smollett), *see Humphrey Clinker*

Expedition of Orsua and the Crimes of Aquirre, The (Southey), **IV:** 71

"Expelled, The" (Beckett), **Supp. I:** 49–50; **Retro. Supp. I:** 21

Experience of India, An (Jhabvala), **Supp. V:** 235

"Experience with Images" (MacNeice), **VII:** 401, 414, 419

Experiment, The (Defoe), **III:** 13

Experiment in Autobiography (Wells), **V:** 426–427, 429, 438; **VI:** xi, 225, 320, 333

Experiment in Criticism, An (Lewis), **Supp. III:** 249, 264

Experimental Drama (Armstrong), **VII:** 14

Experiments (Douglas), **VI:** 296, 305

"Expiation" (Jhabvala), **Supp. V:** 236

"Explained" (Milne), **Supp. V:** 303

"Explaining France" (Motion), **Supp. VII:** 256

Explorations (Knights), **II:** 123

"Explorers, The" (Hope), **Supp. VII:** 154

"Explosion, The" (Larkin), **Supp. I:** 285–286

Exposition of the First Ten Chapters of Genesis, An (Bunyan), **II:** 253

Expostulation (Jonson), **I:** 243

"Expostulation and Inadequate Reply" (Fuller), **Supp. VII:** 73

"Expostulation and Reply" (Wordsworth), **IV:** 7

"Exposure" (Heaney), **Supp. II:** 275

"Exposure" (Owen), **VI:** 446, 450, 452, 455, 457

Exposure of Luxury, The: Radical Themes in Thackeray (Hardy), **V:** 39

Expression of the Emotions in Man and Animals, The (Darwin), **Supp. VII:** 26–28

"Exstasie, The" (Donne), **II:** 197; **Retro. Supp. II:** 88

"Extempore Effusion on the Death of the Ettrick Shepherd" (Wordsworth), **IV:** 73

Extending the Territory (Jennings), **Supp. V:** 216

Extravagant Strangers: A Literature of Belonging (ed. Phillips), **Supp. V:** 380

Extravagaria (tr. Reid), **Supp. VII:** 332

Exultations (Pound), **Supp. III:** 398

Eye for an Eye, An (Trollope), **V:** 102

Eye in the Door, The (Barker), **Supp. IV:** 45, 46, 57, 59–61

"Eye of Allah, The" (Kipling), **VI:** 169, 190–191

Eye of the Scarecrow, The (Harris), **Supp. V:** 136–137, 139, 140

Eye of the Storm, The (White), **Supp. I:** 132, 146–147

Eyeless in Gaza (Huxley), **II:** 173; **VII:** 204–205

"Eyes and Tears" (Marvell), **II:** 209, 211

Eyes of Asia, The (Kipling), **VI:** 204

Ezra Pound and His Work (Ackroyd), **Supp. VI:** 4

"Ezra Pound in Pisa" (Davie), **Supp. VI:** 110, 113

Ezra Pound: Poet as Sculptor (Davie), **Supp. VI:** 115

Flint Anchor, The (Warner), **Supp. VII:** 376, 378–379

"Foregone Conclusion, The" (Warner), **Supp. VII:** 380

Faber Book of Contemporary Irish Poetry, The (ed. Muldoon), **Supp. IV:** 409, 410–411, 422, 424

Fabian Essays in Socialism (Shaw), **VI:** 129

Fabian Freeway (Martin), **VI:** 242

Fabian Society, **Supp. IV:** 233

"Fable" (Golding), **Supp. I:** 67, 83

"Fable of the Widow and Her Cat, A" (Swift), **III:** 27, 31

Fables (Dryden), **II:** 293, 301, 304; **III:** 40; **IV:** 287

Fables (Gay), **III:** 59, 67

Fables (Stevenson), **V:** 396

Façade (Sitwell and Walton), **VII:** xv, xvii, 128, 130, 131n, 132

Face of the Deep, The (Rossetti), **V:** 260

Face to Face: Short Stories (Gordimer), **Supp. II:** 226

"Faces, The" (James), **VI:** 69

Facial Justice (Hartley), **Supp. VII:** 131

Facilitators, The (Redgrove), **Supp. VI:** 231

Fadiman, Clifton, **Supp. IV:** 460

Faerie Queene, The (Spenser), **I:** 121, 123, 124, **131–141,** 266; **II:** 50; **IV:** 59, 198, 213; **V:** 142

"Faery Song, A" (Yeats), **VI:** 211

"Faeth Fiadha: The Breastplate of Saint Patrick" (Kinsella), **Supp. V:** 264

"Fafaia" (Brooke), **Supp. III:** 55–56

"Failed Mystic" (MacCaig), **Supp. VI:** 188, 194

"Failure, A" (Thackeray), **V:** 18

Fair Haven, The (Butler), **Supp. II:** 99, **101–103,** 104, 117

"Fair Ines" (Hood), **IV:** 255

Fair Jilt, The; or, The Amours of Prince Tarquin and Miranda (Behn), **Supp. III:** 29, 31–32

Fair Maid of the Inn, The (Ford, Massinger, Webster), **II:** 66, 69, 83, 85

Fair Margaret (Haggard), **Supp. III:** 214

Fair Quarrel, A (Middleton and Rowley), **II:** 1, 3, 21

"Fair Singer, The" (Marvell), **II:** 211

Fairfield, Cicely, *see* West, Rebecca

Fairly Honourable Defeat, A (Murdoch), **Supp. I:** 226, 227, 228, 232–233

Fairy and Folk Tales of the Irish Peasantry (ed. Yeats), **VI:** 222

Fairy Caravan, The (Potter), **Supp. III:** 291, 303–304, 305, 306, 307

Fairy Knight, The (Dekker and Ford), **II:** 89, 100

"Faith" (Herbert), **II:** 127

Faith Healer (Friel), **Supp. V:** 123

"Faith Healing" (Larkin), **Supp. I:** 280–281, 282, 285

"Faith on Trial, A" (Meredith), **V:** 222

Faithful Fictions: The Catholic Novel in British Literature (Woodman), **Supp. IV:** 364

Faithful Friends, The, **II:** 67

Faithful Narrative of . . . Habbakkuk Hilding, A (Smollett), **III:** 158

Faithful Shepherdess, The (Fletcher), **II:** 45, 46, 49–52, 53, 62, 65, 82

"Faithfulness of GOD in the Promises, The" (Blake), **III:** 300

"Faithless Nelly Gray" (Hood), **IV:** 257

"Faithless Sally Brown" (Hood), **IV:** 257

Faiz, Faiz Ahmad, **Supp. IV:** 434

"Falk" (Conrad), **VI:** 148

Falkner (Shelley), **Supp. III:** 371

Falling Out of Love and Other Poems, A (Sillitoe), **Supp. V:** 424

Fall of Hyperion, The (Keats), **IV:** xi, 211–213, 220, **227–231,** 234, 235

Fall of Princes, The (Lydgate), **I:** 57, 58, 59, 64

Fall of Robespierre, The (Coleridge and Southey), **IV:** 55

"Fall of Rome, The" (Auden), **Retro. Supp. I:** 11

"Fall of the House of Usher, The" (Poe), **III:** 339

Fallen Angels (Coward), **Supp. II:** 141, 145

Fallen Leaves, The (Collins), **Supp. VI:** 93, 102

"Fallen Majesty" (Yeats), **VI:** 216

"Fallen Yew, A" (Thompson), **V:** 442

"Fallow Deer at the Lonely House, The" (Hardy), **Retro. Supp. I:** 119

Fallowell, Duncan, **Supp. IV:** 173

"Falls" (Ewart), **Supp. VII:** 39

False Alarm, The (Johnson), **III:** 121

False Friend, The (Vanbrugh), **II:** 325, 333, 336

"False Morality of the Lady Novelists, The" (Greg), **V:** 7

False One, The (Fletcher and Massinger), **II:** 43, 66

"False though she be to me and love" (Congreve), **II:** 269

Fame's Memoriall; or, The Earle of Devonshire Deceased (Ford), **II:** 100

Familiar and Courtly Letters Written by Monsieur Voiture (ed. Boyer), **II:** 352, 364

Familiar Letters (Richardson), **III:** 81, 83, 92

Familiar Letters (Rochester), **II:** 270

Familiar Studies of Men and Books (Stevenson), **V:** 395; **Retro. Supp. I:** 262–263

Family (Doyle), **Supp. V:** 78, 91

Family Album (Coward), **Supp. II:** 153

Family and a Fortune, A (Compton-Burnett), **VII:** 60, 61, 62, 63, 66

Family and Friends (Brookner), **Supp. IV:** 127–129

Family Instructor, The (Defoe), **III:** 13, 82; **Retro. Supp. I:** 68

Family Madness, A (Keneally), **Supp. IV:** 346

Family Memories (West), **Supp. III:** 431, 432, 433, 434

Family of Love, The (Dekker and Middleton), **II:** 3, 21

Family of Swift, The (Swift), **Retro. Supp. I:** 274

Family Prayers (Butler), **Supp. II:** 103

Family Reunion, The (Eliot), **VII:** 146, 151, 154, 158, 160; **Retro. Supp. II:** 132

Family Romance, A (Brookner), *see Dolly*

"Family Seat" (Murphy), **Supp. V:** 328

Family Sins (Trevor), **Supp. IV:** 505

"Family Supper, A" (Ishiguro), **Supp. IV:** 304

Family Voices (Pinter), **Supp. I:** 378

Famished Road, The (Okri), **Supp. V:** 347, 348, 349, 350, 351, 352–353, 357–359

Famous for the Creatures (Motion), **Supp. VII:** 252

"Famous Ghost of St. Ives, The" (Redgrove), **Supp. VI:** 235–237

Famous History of Sir Thomas Wyat, The (Webster), **II:** 85

Famous Tragedy of the Queen of Cornwall . . . , The (Hardy), **VI:** 20

Famous Victoria of Henry V, The, **I:** 308–309

Fan, The: A Poem (Gay), **III:** 67

Fanatic Heart, A (O'Brien), **Supp. V:** 339

Fancies, Chaste and Noble, The (Ford), **II:** 89, 91–92, 99, 100

"Fancy" (Keats), **IV:** 221

Fancy and Imagination (Brett), **IV:** 57

Fanfare for Elizabeth (Sitwell), **VII:** 127

"Fanny and Annie" (Lawrence), **VII:** 90, 114, 115

Fanny Brawne: A Biography (Richardson), **IV:** 236

Fanny's First Play (Shaw), **VI:** 115, 116, 117, 129

Fanon, Frantz, **Supp. IV:** 105

Fanshawe, Sir Richard, **II:** 49, 222, 237

Fanshen (Hare), **Supp. IV:** 282, 284

Fanshen (Hinton), **Supp. IV:** 284

"Fantasia" (Redgrove), **Supp. VI:** 231

Fantasia of the Unconscious (Lawrence), **VII:** 122; **Retro. Supp. II:** 234

"Fantasia on 'Horbury'" (Hill), **Supp. V:** 187

Fantastic Mr. Fox (Dahl), **Supp. IV:** 203, 223

fantasy fiction, **VI:** 228–235, 338, 399

Fantasy and Fugue (Fuller), **Supp. VII:** 71–72

Far Cry (MacCaig), **Supp. VI:** 184–185

"Far—Far—Away" (Tennyson), **IV:** 330

Far from the Madding Crowd (Hardy), **VI:** 1, 5–6; **Retro. Supp. I:** 113–114

Far Journey of Oudin, The (Harris), **Supp. V:** 132, 134, 135

Far Journeys (Chatwin), **Supp. IV:** 157

"Fare Thee Well" (Byron), **IV:** 192

"Farewell, A" (Arnold), **V:** 216

"Farewell to Angria" (Brontë), **V:** 125

"Farewell to Essay–Writing, A" (Hazlitt), **IV:** 135

Farewell to Military Profession (Rich), **I:** 312

"Farewell to Tobacco" (Lamb), **IV:** 81

Farfetched Fables (Shaw), **VI:** 125, 126

Farina (Meredith), **V:** 225, 234

Farm, The (Storey), **Supp. I:** 408, 411, 412, 414

Farmer Giles of Ham (Tolkien), **Supp. II:** 521

"Farmer's Ingle, The" (Fergusson), **III:** 318

Farmer's Year, A (Haggard), **Supp. III:** 214

Farnham, William, **I:** 214

Farquhar, George, **II:** 334–335, 351–365

Farrell, Barry, **Supp. IV:** 223

Farther Adventures of Robinson Crusoe, The (Defoe), **III:** 13; **Retro. Supp. I:** 71

Farthing Hall (Walpole and Priestley), **VII:** 211

Fascinating Foundling, The (Shaw), **VI:** 129

"Fashionable Authoress, The" (Thackeray), **V:** 22, 37

Fashionable Lover, The (Cumberland), **III:** 257

Fasti (Ovid), **II:** 110n

"Fat Contributor Papers, The" (Thackeray), **V:** 25, 38

Fat Woman's Joke, The (Weldon), **Supp. IV:** 521, 522–524, 525

"Fatal Boots, The" (Thackeray), **V:** 21, 37

Fatal Gift, The (Waugh), **Supp. VI:** 276

"Fatal Sisters, The" (Gray), **III:** 141

Fate of Homo Sapiens, The (Wells), **VI:** 228

"Fate Playing" (Hughes), **Retro. Supp. II:** 217

"Fates, The" (Owen), **VI:** 449

Fates of the Apostles, **Retro. Supp. II:** 301

Father and His Fate, A (Compton–Burnett), **VII:** 61, 63

"Father and Lover" (Rossetti), **V:** 260

"Father and Son" (Butler), **Supp. II:** 97

Father Brown stories (Chesterton), **VI:** 338

Father Damien (Stevenson), **V:** 383, 390, 396

"Father Mat" (Kavanagh), **Supp. VII:** 194

Fathers and Sons (tr. Friel), **Supp. V:** 124

Father's Comedy, The (Fuller), **Supp. VII:** 74, 75–76, 77, 81

"Fathers, Sons and Lovers" (Thomas), **Supp. IV:** 493

Fathers, The; or, The Good–Natur'd Man (Fielding), **III:** 98, 105

"Fatigue, The" (Jones), **Supp. VII:** 175

Faulkner, Charles, **VI:** 167

Faust (Goethe), **III:** 344; **IV:** xvi, xix, 179

"Faustine" (Swinburne), **V:** 320

Faustus and the Censor (Empson), **Supp. II:** 180, **196–197**

Faustus Kelly (O'Nolan), **Supp. II:** 323, **335–337**

Fawkes, F., **III:** 170*n*

Fawn, The (Marston), **II:** 30, 40

Fay Weldon's Wicked Fictions (Weldon), **Supp. IV:** 522, 531

"Fear" (Collins), **III:** 166, 171, 336

"Fear, A" (Jennings), **Supp. V:** 214

Fear, The (Keneally), **Supp. IV:** 345

Fears in Solitude . . . (Coleridge), **IV:** 55

Feast of Bacchus, The (Bridges), **VI:** 83

"Feast of Famine, The" (Stevenson), **V:** 396

"Feastday of Peace, The" (McGuckian), **Supp. V:** 291

"February" (Hughes), **Supp. I:** 342

"Feeding Ducks" (MacCaig), **Supp. VI:** 187

Feeding the Mind (Carroll), **V:** 274

"Feeling into Words" (Heaney), **Supp. II:** 272, 273

Felicia's Journey (Trevor), **Supp. IV:** 505, 517

"Félise" (Swinburne), **V:** 321

Felix Holt, The Radical (Eliot), **V:** xxiii, 195–196, 199, 200; **Retro. Supp. II:** 111–112

"Felix Randal" (Hopkins), **V:** 368–369, 371; **Retro. Supp. II:** 196

"Fellow–Townsmen" (Hardy), **VI:** 22

Fellowship of the Ring (Tolkien), **Supp. II:** 519

Female Friends (Weldon), **Supp. IV:** 534–535

"Female God, The" (Rosenberg), **VI:** 432

"Female Vagrant, The" (Wordsworth), **IV:** 5

"Feminine Christs, The" (McGuckian), **Supp. V:** 290

Feminine Mystique, The (Freidan), **Supp. IV:** 232

Fen (Churchill), **Supp. IV:** 179, 188, 191–192, 198

Fénelon, François, **III:** 95, 99

Fenton, James, **Supp. IV:** 450

Fenwick, Isabella, **IV:** 2

Ferdinand Count Fathom (Smollett), **III:** 153, 158

Ferguson, Helen, *see* Kavan, Anna

Fergusson, Robert, **III:** 312–313, 316, 317, 318

Ferishtah's Fancies (Browning), **IV:** 359, 374

Fermor, Patrick Leigh, **Supp. IV:** 160

"Fern Hill" (Thomas), **Supp. I:** 177, 178, 179

Fernandez, Ramon, **V:** 225–226

Ferrex and Porrex (Norton and Sackville), *see* Gorboduc

Festival at Farbridge (Priestley), **VII:** 219–210

"Festubert: The Old German Line" (Blunden), **VI:** 428

"Fetching Cows" (MacCaig), **Supp. VI:** 188

"Fetish" (Harris), **Supp. V:** 138

Feuerbach, Ludwig, **IV:** 364

"Feuille d'Album" (Mansfield), **VII:** 364

"Few Crusted Characters, A" (Hardy), **VI:** 20, 22

Few Green Leaves, A (Pym), **Supp. II:** 370, **382–384**

Few Late Chrysanthemums, A (Betjeman), **VII:** 369–371

Few Sighs from Hell, A (Bunyan), **II:** 253

Fichte, Johann Gottlieb, **V:** 348

Ficino (philosopher), **I:** 237

Fiction and the Reading Public (Leavis), **VII:** 233, 234

Fiction–Makers, The (Stevenson), **Supp. VI: 262–263**

"Fiction: The House Party" (Ewart), **Supp. VII:** 42

"Fictions" (Reid), **Supp. VII:** 334

"Fiddler of the Reels, The" (Hardy), **VI:** 22

Field, Isobel, **V:** 393, 397

Field, Nathaniel, **II:** 45, 66, 67

"Field of Vision" (Heaney), **Retro. Supp. I:** 132

Field of Waterloo, The (Scott), **IV:** 38

Field Work (Heaney), **Supp. II:** 268, **275–277**; **Retro. Supp. I:** 124, 130

Fielding, Henry, **II:** 273; **III:** 62, 84, **94–106**, 148, 150; **IV:** 106, 189; **V:** 52, 287; **Supp. II:** 57, 194, 195; **Supp. IV:** 244; **Retro. Supp. I: 79–92**

Fielding, K. J., **V:** 43, 72

Fifer, C. N., **III:** 249

Fifine at the Fair (Browning), **IV:** 358, 367, 374; **Retro. Supp. II:**25

Fifteen Dead (Kinsella), **Supp. V:** 267

"Fifth Philosopher's Song" (Huxley), **VII:** 199

Fifth, Queen, The (Ford), **VI:** 324

Fifth Queen Crowned, The (Ford), **VI:** 325, 326

"Fifties, The" (Fuller), **Supp. VII:** 73

"Fifty Faggots" (Thomas), **Supp. III:** 403

Fifty Years of English Literature, 1900–1950 (Scott–James), **VI:** 21

"Fight, The" (Thomas), **Supp. I:** 181

Fight for Barbara, The (Lawrence), **VII:** 120

"Fight to a Finish" (Sassoon), **VI:** 430

Fighting Terms (Gunn), **Supp. IV:** 256, 257–259

"Figure in the Carpet, The" (James), **VI:** 69

"Figures on the Freize" (Reid), **Supp. VII:** 330

File on a Diplomat (Brink), **Supp. VI:** 46

Filibusters in Barbary (Lewis), **VII:** 83

Fille du Policeman (Swinburne), **V:** 325, 333

Film (Beckett), **Supp. I:** 51, 59, 60

Filostrato (Boccaccio), **I:** 30

Filthy Lucre (Bainbridge), **Supp. VI:** 23

Final Passage, The (Phillips), **Supp. V:** 380–383

"Final Problem, The" (Doyle), **Supp. II:** 160, 172–173

Finden's Byron Beauties (Finden), **V:** 111

Findlater, Richard, **VII:** 8

Finer Grain, The (James), **VI:** 67

Finished (Haggard), **Supp. III:** 214

"Finistére" (Kinsella), **Supp. V:** 268

Finnegans Wake (Joyce), **VII:** 42, 46, 52–54; critical studies, **VII:** 58; **Supp. III:** 108; **Retro. Supp. I:** 169, 179–181

Firbank, Ronald, **VII:** 132, 200; **Supp. II: 199–223**

"Fire and Ice" (Kinsella), **Supp. V:** 261

Fire and the Sun, The: Why Plato Banished the Artists (Murdoch), **Supp. I:** 230, 232

"Fire and the Tide" (Stevenson), **Supp. VI:** 260

Fire Down Below (Golding), **Retro. Supp. I:** 104–105

"Fire, Famine and Slaughter" (Coleridge), **Retro. Supp. II:** 53

Fire of the Lord, The (Nicholson), **Supp. VI: 219**

Fire on the Mountain (Desai), **Supp. V:** 53, 55, 64–65, 73

"Fire Sermon, The" (Eliot), **Retro. Supp. II:** 127–128

"Firing Practice" (Motion), **Supp. VII:** 251, 254, 257, 260

First and Last Loves (Betjeman), **VII:** 357, 358, 359

First & Last Things (Wells), **VI:** 244

First Anniversary, The (Donne), **I:** 188, 356; **Retro. Supp. II:** 94

"First Anniversary of the Government under O. C., The" (Marvell), **II:** 210, 211; **Retro. Supp. II:** 262–263

First Book of Odes (Bunting), **Supp. VII:** 5, 13

First Book of Urizen, The (Blake), **III:** 299, 300, 306, 307; **Retro. Supp. I:** 43–44

"First Countess of Wessex, The" (Hardy), **VI:** 22

First Earthquake, The (Redgrove), **Supp. VI: 236**

First Eleven, The (Ewart), **Supp. VII:** 41

First Episode (Rattigan), **Supp. VII:** 308

First Flight, The (Heaney), **Supp. II:** 278

First Folio (Shakespeare), **I:** 299, 324, 325

First Hundred Years of Thomas Hardy, The (Weber), **VI:** 19

"First Hymn to Lenin" (MacDiarmid), **Supp. III:** 119

"First Impressions" (Austen), *see Pride and Prejudice*

"First Journey, The" (Graham), **Supp. VII:** 109

First Lady Chatterley, The (Lawrence), **VII:** 111–112

First Light (Ackroyd), **Supp. VI:** 1, 8

"First Light" (Kinsella), **Supp. V:** 263

First Life of Adamastor, The (Brink), **Supp. VI: 54–55,** 57

"First Love" (Beckett), **Retro. Supp. I:** 21

First Love, Last Rites (McEwan), **Supp. IV:** 390–392

"First Man, The" (Gunn), **Supp. IV:** 264–265

First Men in the Moon, The, (Wells), **VI:** 229, 234, 244

First Ode of the Second Book of Horace Paraphras'd, The (Swift), **III:** 35

First Poems (Muir), **Supp. VI:** 198, **204–205**

First Satire (Wyatt), **I:** 111

First Satire of the Second Book of Horace, Imitated, The (Pope), **III:** 234

First Steps in Reading English (Richards), **Supp. II:** 425

"First Winter of War" (Fuller), **Supp. VII:** 69

First World War, see World War I

First Year in Canterbury Settlement, A (Butler), **Supp. II:** 98, 112

Firstborn, The (Fry), **Supp. III:** 195, 196, 198–199, 207

Firth, Sir Charles Harding, **II:** 241; **III:** 25, 36; **IV:** 289, 290, 291

Fischer, Ernst, **Supp. II:** 228

"Fish" (Lawrence), **VII:** 119

"Fish, The" (Brooke), **Supp. III:** 53, 56, 60

Fish Preferred (Wodehouse), **Supp. III:** 460

"Fisherman, The" (Yeats), **VI:** 214; **Retro. Supp. I:** 331

"Fishermen with Ploughs: A Poem Cycle (Brown), **Supp. VI:** 63

"Fishy Waters" (Rhys), **Supp. II:** 401

Fit for the Future: The Guide for Women Who Want to Live Well (Winterson), **Supp. IV:** 542

"Fitz–Boodle Papers, The" (Thackeray), **V:** 38

FitzGerald, Edward, **IV:** xvii, xxii, xxiii, 310, **340–353; V:** xxv

Fitzgerald, Penelope, **Supp. V: 95–109**

Fitzgerald, Percy, **III:** 125, 135

Five (Lessing), **Supp. I:** 239, 240, 241, 242

Five Autumn Songs for Children's Voices (Hughes), **Supp. I:** 357

Five Finger Exercise (Shaffer), **Supp. I:** 313, **314–317,** 319, 322, 323, 327

Five Looks at Elizabeth Bishop (Stevenson), **Supp. VI:** 264–265

"Five Minutes" (Nicholson), **Supp. VI:** 216

Five Metaphysical Poets (Bennett), **II:** 181, 202

Five Nations, The (Kipling), **VI:** 204

Five Novelettes by Charlotte Brontë (ed. Gérin), **V:** 151

"Five Orange Pips, The" (Doyle), **Supp. II:** 174

Five Red Herrings, The (Sayers), **Supp. III:** 334, 343–344

Five Rivers (Nicholson), **Supp. VI: 213–215,** 216

"Five Songs" (Auden), **Retro. Supp. I:** 11–12

"Five Students, The" (Hardy), **VI:** 17

Five Tales (Galsworthy), **VI:** 276

Five Uncollected Essays of Matthew Arnold (ed. Allott), **V:** 216

Fixed Period, The (Trollope), **V:** 102

Flag on the Island, A (Naipaul), **Supp. I:** 394

Flame of Life, The (Sillitoe), **Supp. V:** 410, 421, 424

"Flaming Heart Upon the Book and Picture of the Seraphicall Saint Teresa, The" (Crashaw), **II:** 182

"Flaming sighs that boil within my breast, The" (Wyatt), **I:** 109–110

Flare Path (Rattigan), **Supp. VII:** 311–312, 313, 314

Flatman, Thomas, **II:** 133

Flaubert, Gustave, **V:** xviii–xxiv, 340, 353, 429; **Supp. IV:** 68, 69, 136, 157, 163, 167

Flaubert's Parrot (Barnes), **Supp. IV:** 65, 67, 68–70, 72, 73

Flaws in the Glass: A Self–Portrait (White), **Supp. I:** 129, 130, 132, 149

Flea, The (Donne), **I:** 355; **Retro. Supp. II:** 88

"Fleckno, an English Priest at Rome" (Marvell), **II:** 211

Fleming, Ian, **Supp. IV:** 212

Fleshly School of Poetry, The (Buchanan), **V:** 238, 245

Fletcher, Ian, **V:** xii, xiii, xxvii, 359

Fletcher, Ifan Kyrle, **Supp. II:** 201, 202, 203

Fletcher, John, **II: 42–67,** 79, 82, 87–88, 90, 91, 93, 185, 305, 340, 357, 359

Fletcher, Phineas, **II:** 138

Fletcher, Thomas, **II:** 21

Fleurs du Mal (Baudelaire), **V:** xxii, 316, 329, 411

Fleurs du Mal (Swinburne), **V:** 329, 331, 333

"Flickerbridge" (James), **VI:** 69

Flight from the Enchanter, The (Murdoch), **Supp. I: 220–222**

Flight into Camden (Storey), **Supp. I:** 408, 410–411, 414, 415, 419

"Flight of the Duchess, The" (Browning), **IV:** 356, 361, 368; **Retro. Supp. II:** 24

"Flight of the Earls, The" (Boland), **Supp. V:** 36

Flight of the Falcon, The (du Maurier), **Supp. III:** 139, 141

Flint Anchor, The (Warner), **Supp. VII:** 376, 378–379

"Flitting, The" (McGuckian), **Supp. V:** 281

Flood, A (Moore), **VI:** 99

"Flooded Meadows" (Gunn), **Supp. IV:** 267

Floor Games (Wells), **VI:** 227

Flora Selbornesis (White), **Supp. VI:** 282–283

"Florent" (Gower), **I:** 55

Florentine Painting and Its Social Background (Antal), **Supp. IV:** 80

Flores Solitudinis (Vaughan), **II:** 185, 201

Floud, Peter, **V:** 296, 307

"Flower, The" (Herbert), **II:** 119n 125; **Retro. Supp. II:** 177–178

Flower Beneath the Foot, The (Firbank), **Supp. II:** 202, 205, **216–218**

Flower Master, The (McGuckian), **Supp. V:** 277, 278, 281–282

"Flower Master, The" (McGuckian), **Supp. V:** 281

Flower Master and Other Poems, The (McGuckian), **Supp. V:** 281

"Flower Poem" (Hope), **Supp. VII:** 154

Flowers and Shadows (Okri), **Supp. V:** 347–348, 350, 352, 354–355

Flower of Courtesy (Lydgate), **I:** 57, 60, 62

Flowering Death of a Salesman (Stoppard), **Supp. I:** 439

Flowers and Insects (Hughes), **Retro. Supp. II:** 214

"Flowers of Empire, The" (Kincaid), **Supp. VII:** 229

"Flowers of Evil" (Kincaid), **Supp. VII:** 219

Flowering Rifle (Campbell), **VII:** 428

Flowering Wilderness (Galsworthy), **VI:** 275, 282

Flowers of Passion (Moore), **VI:** 85, 98

Flurried Years, The (Hunt), **VI:** 333

Flush: A Biography (Woolf), **Retro. Supp. I:** 308, 320–321

Flute–Player, The (Thomas), **Supp. IV:** 479–480, 481

"Fly, The" (Blake), **III:** 295–296

"Fly, The" (Chatwin), **Supp. IV:** 158

"Fly, The" (Mansfield), **VII:** 176

"Flying Above California" (Gunn), **Supp. IV:** 263

"Flying Ace, The" (Redgrove), **Supp. VI:** 236

Flying Hero Class (Keneally), **Supp. IV:** 347

Flying in to Love (Thomas), **Supp. IV:** 486–487

Flying Inn, The (Chesterton), **VI:** 340

Foe (Coetzee), **Supp. VI:** 75–76, **83–84**

Foe–Farrell (Quiller–Couch), **V:** 384

"Folk Wisdom" (Kinsella), **Supp. V:** 263

"Folklore" (Murray), **Supp. VII:** 276

Folk–Lore in the Old Testament (Frazer), **Supp. III:** 176

Follow My Leader (Rattigan), **Supp. VII:** 310

"Follower" (Heaney), **Supp. IV:** 410

"Followers, The" (Thomas), **Supp. I:** 183

Following a Lark (Brown), **Supp. VI:** 72

"Folly" (Murphy), **Supp. V:** 327

Folly of Industry, The (Wycherley), **II:** 322

"Fond Memory" (Boland), **Supp. V:** 35

Fontaine amoureuse, **I:** 33

"Food of the Dead" (Graves), **VII:** 269

Fool, The (Bond), **Supp. I:** 423, 434, 435

Fools of Fortune (Trevor), **Supp. IV:** 502, 503, 512–514, 517

Foot of Clive, The (Berger), **Supp. IV:** 79, 84–85

"Football at Slack" (Hughes), **Retro. Supp. II:** 210–211

Foote, Samuel, **III:** 253; **V:** 261

Footfalls (Beckett), **Retro. Supp. I:** 28

Footnote to History, A: Eight Years of Trouble in Samoa (Stevenson), **V:** 396

"For a Greeting" (MacCaig), **Supp. VI:** 185

"For a Young Matron" (McGuckian), **Supp. V:** 284–285

"For All We Have and Are" (Kipling), **VI:** 415

"For Ann Scott–Moncrieff" (Muir), **Supp. VI:** 207

For Children: The Gates of Paradise (Blake), **III:** 307

"For Conscience' Sake" (Hardy), **VI:** 22

"For John Heath–Stubbs" (Graham), **Supp. VII:** 116

For Love Alone (Stead), **Supp. IV:** 470–473

For Queen and Country: Britain in the Victorian Age (ed. Drabble), **Supp. IV:** 230

"For Ring–Givers" (Reid), **Supp. VII:** 329

For Services Rendered (Maugham), **VI:** 368

"For St. James" (Nicholson), **Supp. VI:** 214

"For the Fallen" (Binyon), **VI:** 416; **VII:** 448

For the Islands I sing (Brown), **Supp. VI:** 61–66, 68–69

"For the Previous Owner" (McGuckian), **Supp. V:** 283

For the Sexes: The Gates of Paradise (Blake), **III:** 307

For the Time Being (Auden), **VII:** 379; **Retro. Supp. I:** 10–11

For the Unfallen: Poems (Hill), **Supp. V:** 184–186

"For to Admire" (Kipling), **VI:** 203

"Force, The" (Redgrove), **Supp. VI:** 231

Force, The (Redgrove), **Supp. VI:** 231

"Force that through the green fuse drives the flower, The" (Thomas), **II:** 156; **Supp. I:** 171–173, 177

Forc'd Marriage, The; or, The Jealous Bridegroom (Behn), **Supp. III:** 22, 24, 25–26

Ford, Charles, **III:** 33, 34

Ford, Ford Madox, **VI:** 145–146, 238, **319–333**, 416, 439; **VII:** xi, xv, xxi, 89

Ford, John, **II:** 57, 69, 83, 85, **87–101**

Ford Madox Ford (Rhys), **Supp. II:** 388, 390, 391

Ford Madox Ford: Letters (ed. Ludwig), **VI:** 332

"Fordham Castle" (James), **VI:** 69

Foreigners, The (Tutchin), **III:** 3

"Foregone Conclusion, The" (Warner), **Supp. VII:** 380

"Forerunners, The" (Herbert), **Retro. Supp. II:** 180

Forest, The (Galsworthy), **VI:** 276, 287

Forest, The (Jonson), **Retro. Supp. I:** 164

"Forest Path to the Spring, The" (Lowry), **Supp. III:** 270, 282

Forester, C. S., **Supp. IV:** 207, 208

"Foresterhill" (Brown), **Supp. VI:** 59

Foresters, The (Tennyson), **IV:** 328, 338

Forests of Lithuania, The (Davie), **Supp. VI:** 108, 115

Forewords and Afterwords (Auden), **VII:** 394; **Retro. Supp. I:** 1, 6

Forge, The (Hall), **Supp. VI:** 120–121, 124–125

"Forge, The" (Heaney), **Supp. II:** 271; **Retro. Supp. I:** 128

"Forget about me" (tr. Reid), **Supp. VII:** 332

"Forget not yet" (Wyatt), **I:** 106

"Forgiveness" (Jennings), **Supp. V:** 217–218

"Forgiveness, A" (Browning), **IV:** 360

"Forgotten" (Milne), **Supp. V:** 303

"Forgotten of the Foot" (Stevenson), **Supp. VI:** 262

"Form and Realism in the West Indian Artist" (Harris), **Supp. V:** 145

Forrest, James F., **II:** 245n

Fors Clavigera (Ruskin), **V:** 174, 181, 184

"Forsaken Garden, A" (Swinburne), **V:** 314, 327

Forster, E. M., **IV:** 302, 306; **V:** xxiv, 208, 229, 230; **VI:** xii, 365, **397–413**; **VII:** xi, xv, 18, 21, 34, 35, 122, 144; **Supp. I:** 260; **Supp. II:** 199, 205, 210, 223, 227, 289, 293; **Supp. III:** 49; **Supp. IV:** 440, 489; **Retro. Supp. II:** 135–150

Forster, John, **IV:** 87, 89, 95, 99, 100, 240; **V:** 47, 72

Forsyte Saga, The (Galsworthy), **VI:** xiii, 269, 272, 274; *see also Man of Property, The;* "Indian Summer of a Forsyte"; *In Chancery; To Let*

Fortescue, Chichester, **V:** 76–83, 85

Fortnightly Review (periodical), **V:** 279, 338

Fortunate Isles, and Their Union, The (Jonson), **Retro. Supp. I:** 165

Fortunate Mistress, The: or, A History of . . . Mademoiselle de Beleau . . . (Defoe), **III:** 13

Fortunes and Misfortunes of the Famous Moll Flanders, The (Defoe), *see Moll Flanders*

Fortunes of Falstaff, The (Wilson), **III:** 116n

Fortunes of Nigel, The (Scott), **IV:** 30, 35, 37, 39

"Forty–seventh Saturday, The" (Trevor), **Supp. IV:** 501

Forward from Liberalism (Spender), **Supp. II:** 488

Foster, A. D., **III:** 345

Foucault, Michel, **Supp. IV:** 442

Foucault's Pendulum (Eco), **Supp. IV:** 116

"Found" (Rossetti), **V:** 240

Found in the Street (Highsmith), **Supp. V:** 171, 178–179

"Foundation of the Kingdom of Angria" (Brontë), **V:** 110–111

Foundations of Aesthetics, The (Richards and Ogden), **Supp. II:** 408, **409–410**

"Fountain" (Jennings), **Supp. V:** 210, 212

Fountain of Self-love, The (Jonson), **Retro. Supp. I:** 158, 160

Fountain Overflows, The (West), **Supp. III:** 431–432, 443

Fountains in the Sand (Douglas), **VI:** 294, 297, 299, 300, 305

Four Ages of Poetry, The (Peacock), **IV:** 168–169, 170

Four and a Half Dancing Men (Stevenson), **Supp. VI: 264**

Four Banks of the River of Space, The (Harris), **Supp. V:** 137, 140, 142–144

Four Day's Wonder (Milne), **Supp. V:** 310

Four–Dimensional Nightmare, The (Ballard), **Supp. V:** 23

Four Dissertations (Hume), **Supp. III:** 231, 238

4.50 from Paddington (Christie; U.S. title, *What Mrs. McGillicuddy Saw*), **Supp. II:** 132

Four Georges, The (Thackeray), **V:** 20, 34–35, 38

Four Hymns (Spenser), **I:** 124

Four Last Things (More), **Supp. VII:** 234, 246–247

Four Lectures (Trollope), **V:** 102

Four Loves, The (Lewis), **Supp. III:** 249, 264–265

"Four Meetings" (James), **VI:** 69

Four Plays (Stevenson and Henley), **V:** 396

Four Plays (White), **Supp. I:** 131

Four Plays for Dancers (Yeats), **VI:** 218

Four Prentices of London with the Conquest of Jerusalem (Heywood), **II:** 48

Four Quartets (Eliot), **VII:** 143, 148, 153–157; **Retro. Supp. II:** 121, 130–131; *see also* "The Dry Salvages," "East Coker," "Little Gidding"

"Four Walks in the Country near Saint Brieuc" (Mahon) **Supp. VI:** 168

Four Zoas, The (Blake), **III:** 300, 302–303, 307; **Retro. Supp. I:** 44

Four-Gated City, The (Lessing), **Supp. I:** 245, 248, 250, 251, 255

Foure-footed Beastes (Topsel), **II:** 137

"14 November 1973" (Betjeman), **VII:** 372

Fourteenth Century Verse and Prose (Sisam), **I:** 20, 21

"Fourth of May, The" (Ewart), **Supp. VII:** 36

Fowler, Alastair, **I:** 237

Fowler, H. W., **VI:** 76

Fowles, John, **Supp. I: 291–311**

Foxe, The (Jonson), **Retro. Supp. I:** 163, 164

Fox and the Wolf, The (Henryson), **Supp. VII:** 136, 138, 140

Fox, Caroline, **IV:** 54

Fox, Chris, **Supp. IV:** 88

Fox, George, **IV:** 45

Fox, Ralph, **Supp. IV:** 464, 466

"Fox, The" (Lawrence), **VII:** 90, 91

Fox, the Wolf, and the Cadger, The (Henryson), **Supp. VII:** 136, 140

Fox, the Wolf, and the Husbandman, The (Henryson), **Supp. VII:** 136, 140

"Fox Trot" (Sitwell), **VII:** 131

Foxe, that begylit the Wolf, in the Schadow of the Mone, The (Henryson), see *Fox, the Wolf, and the Husbandman, The*

"Fra Lippo Lippi" (Browning), **IV:** 357, 361, 369; **Retro. Supp. II:** 27

Fra Rupert: The Last Part of a Trilogy (Landor), **IV:** 100

"Fragment" (Brooke), **VI:** 421

"Fragment of a Greek Tragedy" (Housman), **VI:** 156

Fragmenta Aurea (Suckling), **II:** 238

"Fragments" (Hulme), **Supp. VI:** 137–138

"Fragoletta" (Swinburne), **V:** 320

"Frail as thy love, The flowers were dead" (Peacock), **IV:** 157

Framley Parsonage (Trollope), **V:** xxii, 93, 101

"France, an Ode" (Coleridge), **IV:** 55

"France, December 1870" (Meredith), **V:** 223

"Frances" (Brontë), **V:** 132

Francophile, The (Friel), **Supp. V:** 115

Francillon, R. E., **V:** 83

Francis, Dick, **Supp. IV:** 285

Francis, G. H., **IV:** 270

Francis, P., **III:** 249

"Francis Beaumont" (Swinburne), **V:** 332

Franck, Richard, **II:** 131–132

"Frank Fane: A Ballad" (Swinburne), **V:** 332

Frankenstein; or, The Modern Prometheus (Shelley), **III:** **329–331**, 341, 342, 345; **Supp. III:** 355, **356–363**, 369, 372, 385; **Retro. Supp. I:** 247

Frankenstein Un–bound (Aldiss), **III:** 341, 345

Franklin's Tale, The (Chaucer), **I:** 23

Fraser, Antonia, **Supp. V:** 20

Fraser, G. S., **VI:** xiv, xxxiii; **VII:** xviii, 422, 425, 443

Fraser's (periodical), **IV:** 259; **V:** 19, 22, 111, 142

"Frater Ave atque Vale" (Tennyson), **IV:** 327, 336

Fraternity (Galsworthy), **VI:** 274, 278, 279–280, 285

"Frau Brechenmacher Attends a Wedding" (Mansfield), **VII:** 172

"Frau Fischer" (Mansfield), **VII:** 172

Fraud (Brookner), **Supp. IV:** 134

Fraunce, Abraham, **I:** 122, 164

Frayn, Michael, **Supp. VII: 51–65**

Frazer, Sir James George, **V:** 204; **Supp. III: 169–190; Supp. IV:** 11, 19

Fred and Madge (Orton), **Supp. V:** 363, 366–367, 372

Fredy Neptune (Murray), **Supp. VII:** 271, 284–286

"Freddy" (Smith), Supp. **II:** 462

Free and Offenceless Justification of a Lately Published and Most Maliciously Misinterpreted Poem Entitled "Andromeda Liberata, A" (Chapman), **I:** 254

Free Fall (Golding), **Supp. I: 75–78,** 81, 83, 85; **Retro. Supp. I:** 98

Free Inquiry into the Nature and Origin of Evil (Jenyns), **Retro. Supp. I:** 148

"Free Radio, The" (Rushdie), **Supp. IV:** 438

Free Thoughts on Public Affairs (Hazlitt), **IV:** 139

"Free Verse: A Post Mortem" (Hope), **Supp. VII:** 155

"Free Women" (Lessing), **Supp. I:** 246–247

Freedom of the City, The (Friel), **Supp. V:** 111, 112, 120–121

Free–Holder (periodical), **III:** 51, 53

Free–Holders Plea against . . . Elections of Parliament–Men, The (Defoe), **III:** 12

Freelands, The (Galsworthy), **VI:** 279

Freeman, Rosemary, **Retro. Supp. II:** 178

Freidan, Betty, **Supp. IV:** 232

French, Sean, **Supp. IV:** 173

French Eton, A (Arnold), **V:** 206, 216

"French Flu, The" (Koestler), **Supp. I:** 35

French Gardiner, The: Instructing How to Cultivate All Sorts of Fruit–Trees . . . (tr. Evelyn), **II:** 287

French Lieutenant's Woman, The (Fowles), **Supp. I:** 291, **300–303**

French Lyrics (Swinburne), **V:** 333

French Poets and Novelists (James), **VI:** 67

French Revolution, The (Blake), **III:** 307; **Retro. Supp. I:** 37

French Revolution, The (Carlyle), **IV:** xii, xix, 240, 243, 245, 249, 250

French Without Tears (Rattigan), **Supp. VII:** 308–310, 311

Frenchman's Creek (du Maurier), **Supp. III:** 144

Frere, John Hookham, **IV:** 182–183

"Fresh Water" (Motion), **Supp. VII:** 259, 262, 263, 264

Freud, Sigmund, **Supp. IV:** 6, 87, 331, 481, 482, 488, 489, 493

"Freya of the Seven Isles" (Conrad), **VI:** 148

Friar Bacon and Friar Bungay (Greene), **II:** 3

Friar's Tale, The (Chaucer), **I:** 30

"Friary" (Murphy), **Supp. V:** 329

"Friday; or, The Dirge" (Gay), **III:** 56

Friedman, A., **III:** 178, 190

Friel, Brian, **Supp. V: 111–129**

Friend (periodical), **IV:** 50, 55, 56

"Friend, The" (Milne), **Supp. V:** 303

Friend from England, A (Brookner), **Supp. IV:** 129–130

"Friendly Epistle to Mrs. Fry, A" (Hood), **IV:** 257, 267

Friendly Tree, The (Day Lewis), **Supp. III:** 118, 130–131

Friends and Relations (Bowen), **Supp. II:** 84, **86–87**

"Friends of the Friends, The" (James), **VI:** 69

Friendship's Garland (Arnold), **V:** 206, 213n, 215, 216

Fringe of Leaves, A (White), **Supp. I:** 132, 147–148

Frog He Would A–Fishing Go, A (Potter), **Supp. III:** 298

Frog Prince and Other Poems (Smith), **Supp. II:** 463

Froissart, Jean, **I:** 21

Frolic and the Gentle, The (Ward), **IV:** 86

"From a Brother's Standpoint" (Beerbohm), **Supp. II:** 53–54

From a View to a Death (Powell), **VII:** 345, 353

"From an Unfinished Poem" (Stevenson), **Supp. VI:** 262–263

From Centre City (Kinsella), **Supp. V:** 272

From Every Chink of the Ark (Redgrove), **Supp. VI:** 234, 236

From Feathers to Iron (Day Lewis), **Supp. III:** 118, 122, 123–124

From Man to Man (Schreiner), **Supp. II:** 439, 440, 441, 442, **450–452**

"From My Diary. July 1914" (Owen), **VI:** 446

"From my sad Retirement" (King), **Supp. VI:** 159

"From My Study" (Stevenson), **Supp. VI:** 264

"From Sorrow Sorrow Yet Is Born" (Tennyson), **IV:** 329

"From the Answers to Job" (Redgrove), **Supp. VI:** 235

From the Four Winds (Galsworthy), **VI:** 276

"From the Frontier of Writing" (Heaney), **Supp. II:** 280

"From the Greek" (Landor), **IV:** 98

From the Joke Shop (Fuller), **Supp. VII:** 79

"From the Life of a Dowser" (Redgrove), **Supp. VI:** 235, 237

"From the New World" (Davie), **Supp. VI:** 110

"From the Night of Forebeing" (Thompson), **V:** 443, 448

"From the Painting *Back from Market* by Chardin" (Boland), **Supp. V:** 40

From "The School of Eloquence" (Harrison), **Supp. V:** 150

"From the Wave" (Gunn), **Supp. IV:** 267

"From Tuscan cam my ladies worthi race" (Surrey), **I:** 114

Frost, Robert, **VI:** 424; **Supp. III:** 394–395; **Supp. IV:** 413, 420, 423, 480, 487

"Frost at Midnight" (Coleridge), **IV:** 41, 44, 55; **Retro. Supp. II:** 60

Frost in the Flower, The (O'Casey), **VII:** 12

Froude, James Anthony, **IV:** 238, 240, 250, 324; **V:** 278, 287

Frozen Deep, The (Collins), **V:** 42; **Supp. VI:** 92, 95

"Fruit" (Betjeman), **VII:** 373

Fry, Christopher, **IV:** 318; **Supp. III:** 191–210

Fry, Roger, **VII:** xii, 34

Fuel for the Flame (Waugh), **Supp. VI:** 276

Fuentes, Carlos, **Supp. IV:** 116, 440

Fugitive, The (Galsworthy), **VI:** 283

Fugitive Pieces (Byron), **IV:** 192

Fulbecke, William, **I:** 218

"Fulbright Scholars" (Hughes), **Retro. Supp. II:** 217

Fulford, William, **VI:** 167

"Full Measures" (Redgrove), **Supp. VI:** 235

Full Moon (Wodehouse), **Supp. III:** 459

"Full Moon and Little Frieda" (Hughes), **Supp. I:** 349–350

Full Moon in March, A (Yeats), **VI:** 222

Fuller, Roy, **VII:** 422, 428–431, **Supp. VII:** 67–82

Fuller, Thomas, **I:** 178; **II:** 45; **Retro. Supp. I:** 152

Fully Empowered (tr. Reid), **Supp. VII:** 332

Fumed Oak (Coward), **Supp. II:** 153

Fumifugium; or, The Inconvenience of Aer and Smoak . . . (Evelyn), **II:** 287

"Function of Criticism at the Present Time, The" (Arnold), **V:** 204–205, 212, 213

"Funeral, The" (Redgrove), **Supp. VI:** 235

Funeral, The (Steele), **II:** 359

"Funeral Blues" (Auden), **Retro. Supp. I:** 6

Funeral Games (Orton), **Supp. V:** 367, 372, 376–377

"Funeral Music" (Hill), **Supp. V:** 187–188

"Funeral of Youth, The: Threnody" (Brooke), **Supp. III:** 55

"Funeral Poem Upon the Death of . . . Sir Francis Vere, A," **II:** 37, 41

"Funerall, The" (Donne), **Retro. Supp. II:** 89–90

"Fungi" (Stevenson), **Supp. VI:** 256

Furbank, P. N., **VI:** 397; **Supp. II:** 109, 119

Furetière, Antoine, **II:** 354

"Furnace, The" (Kinsella), **Supp. V:** 271

Furness, H. H., **I:** 326

Furnivall, F. J., **VI:** 102

Fussell, Paul, **Supp. IV:** 22, 57

"Fust and His Friends" (Browning), **IV:** 366

"Futility" (Owen), **VI:** 453, 455

"Future, The" (Arnold), **V:** 210

"Future, The" (Murray), **Supp. VII:** 277

Future in America, The: A Search After Reality (Wells), **VI:** 244

"Futurity" (Browning), **IV:** 313

Fyvel, T. R., **VII:** 284

G. (Berger), **Supp. IV:** 79, 85–88, 94

G. B. Shaw (Chesterton), **VI:** 130

G. M. Trevelyan (Moorman), **VI:** 396

"Gabor" (Swift), **Supp. V:** 432

"Gabriel–Ernest" (Saki), **Supp. VI:** 244

"Gabrielle de Bergerac" (James), **VI:** 67, 69

Gadfly, The (Voynich), **VI:** 107

Gager, William, **I:** 193

"Gala Programme: An Unrecorded Episode in Roman History, The" (Saki), **Supp. VI:** 242

Galahad at Blandings (Wodehouse), **Supp. III:** 460

Galile (Brecht), **IV:** 182

Galland, Antoine, **III:** 327

Gallathea (Lyly), **I:** 200–202

"Gallery, The" (Marvell), **II:** 211

Galsworthy, Ada, **VI:** 271, 272, 273, 274, 282

Galsworthy, John, **V:** xxii, 270n; **VI:** ix, xiii, 133, 260, **269–291**; **VII:** xii, xiv; **Supp. I:** 163; **Supp. IV:** 229

Galsworthy the Man (Sauter), **VI:** 284

Galt, John, **IV:** 35

"Game, The" (Boland), **Supp. V:** 35

Game, The (Byatt), **Supp. IV:** 139, 141, 143–145, 154

"Game, The" (Motion), **Supp. VII:** 265

Game at Chess, A (Middleton), **II:** 1, 2, 3, **18–21**

Game for the Living, A (Highsmith), **Supp. V:** 172

"Game of Chess, A" (Eliot), **Retro. Supp. II:** 127

Game of Cricket, A (Ayckbourn), **Supp. V:** 3

"Game of Glass, A" (Reid), **Supp. VII:** 327

Game of Logic, The (Carroll), **V:** 273

"Games at Twilight" (Desai), **Supp. V:** 65

Games at Twilight and Other Stories (Desai), **Supp. V:** 55, 65

Gandhi (film), **Supp. IV:** 455

Gandhi, Indira, **Supp. IV:** 165, 231

"Ganymede" (du Maurier), **Supp. III:** 135, 148

Gaol Gate, The (Gregory), **VI:** 315

García Márquez, Gabriel, **Supp. IV:** 93, 116, 440, 441, 454, 558

Garden Kalendar (White), **Supp. VI:** 279, 282

"Garden, The" (Cowley), **II:** 194

"Garden, The" (Marvell), **II:** 208, 210, 211, 212, 213–214; **Supp. IV:** 271; **Retro. Supp. II:** 261, 263

"Garden in September, The" (Bridges), **VI:** 78

Garden of Cyrus, The (Browne), **II:** 148, **150–153**, 154, 155, 156

"Garden of Eros, The" (Wilde), **V:** 401, 402

"Garden of Love, The" (Blake), **Retro. Supp. I:** 42

"Garden of Proserpine, The" (Swinburne), **V:** 320, 321

"Garden of Remembrance" (Kinsella), **Supp. V:** 261

"Garden of the Innocent" (Nicholson), **Supp. VI:** 215

"Garden of Time, The" (Ballard), **Supp. V:** 22

"Garden on the Point, A" (Kinsella), **Supp. V:** 261

Garden Party, A (Behan), **Supp. II:** 67, 68

"Garden Party, The" (Davie), **Supp. VI:** 106

Garden Party, The (Mansfield), **VII:** xv, 171, 177

"Gardener, The" (Kipling), **VI:** 197

Gardeners and Astronomers (Sitwell), **VII:** 138

"Gardener's Daughter, The" (Tennyson), **IV:** 326

Gardener's Year, A (Haggard), **Supp. III:** 214

"Gardens go on forever" (Kelman), **Supp. V:** 256

Gardiner, S. R., **I:** 146

Gardiner, Judith Kegan, **Supp. IV:** 459

Gardner, Helen, **II:** 121, 129

Gardner, Philip, **VI:** xii, xxxiii

Gareth and Lynette (Tennyson), **IV:** 338

Gargantua and Pantagruel (Rabelais), **Supp. IV:** 464

Garibaldi and the Making of Italy (Trevelyan), **VI:** 388–389

Garibaldi and the Thousand (Trevelyan), **VI:** 388–389

Garibaldi, Giuseppe, **Supp. IV:** 86

Garibaldi's Defence of the Roman Republic (Trevelyan), **VI:** xv, **387–389,** 394

Garis, Robert, **V:** 49–50, 70, 73

Garland of Laurel, The (Skelton), **I:** 81, 82, 90, 93–94

Garmont of Gud Ladeis, The (Henryson), **Supp. VII:** 146, 148

Garner, Ross, **II:** 186

Garnered Sheaves: Essays, Addresses, and Reviews (Frazer), **Supp. III:** 172

Garnett, Edward, **VI:** 135, 149, 273, 277, 278, 283, 366, 373; **VII:** xiv, 89

Garnier, Robert, **I:** 218

Garrett, John, **Supp. IV:** 256

Garrick, David, **I:** 327

Garrick Year, The (Drabble), **Supp. IV:** 230, 236–237

"Garrison, The" (Auden), **Retro. Supp. I:** 13

Garrod, H. W., **III:** 170n, 176

Gascoigne, George, **I:** 215–216, 298

Gaskell, Elizabeth, **IV:** 241, 248; **V:** viii, x, xvi, xxi–xxiii, **1–16,** 108, 116, 122, 137, 147–150; **VI:** viii; **Supp. IV;** 119, 379

Gaskill, William, **II:** 6

"Gaspar Ruiz" (Conrad), **VI:** 148

Gaston de Latour (Pater), **V:** 318n, 357

Gate, The (Day Lewis), **Supp. III:** 118, 129–130

Gate of Angels, The (Fitzgerald), **Supp. V:** 96, 98, 106–107

Gates of Ivory, The (Drabble), **Supp. IV:** 231, 250–252

Gates of Paradise, The (Blake), *see For Children: The Gates of Paradise; For the Sexes: The Gates of Paradise*

Gates of Wrath, The (Bennett), **VI:** 249

"Gathered Church, A" (Davie), **Supp. VI:** 107

Gathered Church, The (Davie), **Supp. VI:** 105, 115

"Gathering Mushrooms" (Muldoon), **Supp. IV:** 420

"Gathering Sticks on Sunday" (Nicholson), **Supp. VI:** 217

Gathering Storm, The (Churchill), **VI:** 361

Gathering Storm, The (Empson), **Supp. II:** 179, 184, 190

Gatty, Margaret, **V:** 270

Gaudete (Hughes), **Supp. I: 359–363; Retro. Supp. II:** 209–210

Gaudy Night (Sayers), **Supp. III:** 334, 341, 343, 346–347

Gaunt, William, **VI:** 169

Gautier, Théophile, **IV:** 153*n*; **V:** 320*n*, 346, 404, 410–411; **Supp. IV:** 490

Gavin Ewart Show, The (Ewart), **Supp. VII:** 40

Gawain–Poet, The, **Supp. VII:** 83–101

Gay, John, **II:** 348; **III:** 19, 24, 44, **54–67,** 74

Gayton, Edward, **I:** 279

Gaze of the Gorgon, The (Harrison), **Supp. V:** 160, 164

Gebir (Landor), **IV:** xvi, 88, 95, 99, 100, 217

Gebirus, poema (Landor), **IV:** 99–100

Gem (periodical), **IV:** 252

"Gemini" (Kipling), **VI:** 184

"General, The" (Sassoon), **VI:** 430

General, The (Sillitoe), **Supp. V:** 410, 415

"General Election, A" (Rushdie), **Supp. IV:** 456

General Grant: An Estimate (Arnold), **V:** 216

General History of Discoveries . . . in Useful Arts, A (Defoe), **III:** 14

General History of Music (Burney), **Supp. III:** 66

General History of the Robberies and Murders of . . . Pyrates, A (Defoe), **III:** 13

General History of the Turkes (Knolles), **III:** 108

General Inventorie of the History of France (Brimeston), **I:** 249

General Prologue, The (Chaucer), **I:** 23, 26, 27–28, 38–40

"Generations" (Stevenson), **Supp. VI:** 257

Generous Days, The (Spender), **Supp. II:** 493

Genesis, **Retro. Supp. II:** 301

"Genesis" (Hill), **Supp. V:** 184–185

"Genesis" (Swinburne), **V:** 325

"Genesis and Catastrophe" (Dahl), **Supp. IV:** 221

Genesis B, **Retro. Supp. II:** 301

Geneva (Shaw), **VI:** 125, 127–128, 129; **Retro. Supp. II:** 324

Genius of the Future: Studies in French Art Criticism, The (Brookner), **Supp. IV:** 122–123

Genius of the Thames, The (Peacock), **IV:** 169

Genius of Thomas Hardy, The (ed. Drabble), **Supp. IV:** 230

"Gentians" (McGuckian), **Supp. V:** 281

Gentle Island, The (Friel), **Supp. V:** 119–120

"Gentle Sex, The" (Ewart), **Supp. VII:** 42

Gentleman Dancing–Master, The (Wycherley), **II:** 308, 309, **313–314,** 321

Gentleman in the Parlour, The (Maugham), **VI:** 371

Gentleman Usher, The (Chapman), **I:** 244–245

Gentleman's Magazine (periodical), **III:** 107

Gentlemen in England (Wilson), **Supp. VI:** 302–303, 305

Gentlewomen's Companion, The (Woolley), **Supp. III:** 21

Geoffrey de Vinsauf, **I:** 23 39–40, 59

Geography and History of England, The (Goldsmith), **III:** 191

George, Henry, **VI:** 102

"George and the Seraph" (Brooke–Rose), **Supp. IV:** 103

George Bernard Shaw (Chesterton), **VI:** 344

George Crabbe and His Times (Huchon), **III:** 273*n*

George Eliot (Stephen), **V:** 289

George Eliot: Her Life and Books (Bullet), **V:** 196, 200–201

George Eliot, Selected Essays, Poems and Other Writings (Byatt), **Supp. IV:** 151

George Eliot's Life as Related in Her Letters and Journals (ed. Cross), **V:** 13, 200

George Gissing: Grave Comedian (Donnelly), **V:** 427*n,* 438

"George Herbert: The Art of Plainness" (Stein), **Retro. Supp. II:** 181

George Moore: L'homme et l'oeuvre (Noel), **VI:** 98, 99

George Orwell (Fyvel), **VII:** 287

George Passant (Snow), **VII:** 324, 325–326

George Silverman's Explanation (Dickens), **V:** 72

George's Ghosts (Maddox), **Retro. Supp. I:** 327, 328

George's Marvellous Medicine (Dahl), **Supp. IV:** 204–205

"Georgian Boyhood, A" (Connolly), **Supp. III:** 1–2

Georgian Poetry 1911–1912 (ed. Marsh), **VI:** 416, 419, 420, 453; **VII:** xvi; **Supp. III:** 45, 53–54, 397

Georgics of Virgil, The (tr. Day Lewis), **Supp. III:** 118

"Georgina's Reasons" (James), **VI:** 69

Gerald: A Portrait (du Maurier), **Supp. III:** 134–135, 138–139

Gerard Manley Hopkins: A Critical Symposium (Kenyon Critics), **V:** 382

Gerard Manley Hopkins: The Classical Background . . . (Bender), **V:** 364–365, 382

Géricault, Théodore, **Supp. IV:** 71–72, 73

Gérin, Winifred, **V:** x, xxvii, 111, 151, 152, 153

Germ (periodical), **V:** xxi, 235–236, 249

"German Chronicle" (Hulme), **Supp. VI:** 139

"Gerontion" (Eliot), **VII:** 144, 146, 147, 152; **Retro. Supp. II:** 123–124

Gerugte van Reen (Brink), **Supp. VI:** 49

Gesta Romanorum, **I:** 52 53

"Gethsemane" (Nicholson), **Supp. VI:** 214

Get Ready for Battle (Jhabvala), **Supp. V:** 228–229

Getting Married (Shaw), **VI:** 115, 117–118

"Getting Off the Altitude" (Lessing), **Supp. I:** 240

"Getting Poisoned" (Ishiguro), **Supp. IV:** 303

"Getting there" (Kelman), **Supp. V:** 249

Getting to Know the General (Greene), **Supp. I:** 1, 13, 14, 17

Geulincx, Arnold, **Supp. I: 44**

"Geve place ye lovers" (Surrey), **I:** 120

"Geysers, The" (Gunn), **Supp. IV:** 268, 269, 276

Ghastly Good Taste (Betjeman), **VII:** 357, 361

Ghost in the Machine, The (Koestler), **Supp. I:** 37, 38

Ghost of Lucrece, The (Middleton), **II:** 3

Ghost Road, The (Barker), **Supp. IV:** 45, 46, 57, 61–63

Ghost Trio (Beckett), **Retro. Supp. I:** 29

"Ghost–Crabs" (Hughes), **Supp. I:** 349, 350; **Retro. Supp. II:** 206

"Ghostkeeper" (Lowry), **Supp. III:** 285

"Ghostly Father, The" (Redgrove), **Supp. VI:** 228

"Ghosts" (Redgrove), **Supp. VI:** 228, 236

"Ghosts" (Reid), **Supp. VII:** 327

Giants' Bread (Christie), **Supp. II:** 133

Giaour, The (Byron), **III:** 338; **IV:** xvii, 172, 173–174, 180, 192

Gibbon, Edward, **III:** 109, **221–233; IV:** xiv, xvi, 93, 284; **V:** 425; **VI:** 347, 353, 383, 390*n*

Gibbons, Brian, **I:** 281

Gibson, W. W., **VI:** 416

Gide, André, **V:** xxiii, 402

Gidez, Richard B., **Supp. IV:** 326, 339–340

Gifford, William, **II:** 96; **IV:** 133

"Gigolo and Gigolette" (Maugham), **VI:** 370

Gil Blas (tr. Smollett), **III:** 150

Gil Perez, The Gallician (tr. FitzGerald), **IV:** 344

Gilbert, Elliott, **VI:** 194

"Gilbert" (Brontë), **V:** 131–132

Gilbert, Peter, **Supp. IV:** 354

Gilbert, Sandra, **Retro. Supp. I:** 59–60

"Gilbert's Mother" (Trevor), **Supp. IV:** 505

Gilchrist, Andrew, **Retro. Supp. I:** 46

Gilfillan, George, **I:** 98

"Gilles de Retz" (Keyes), **VII:** 437

Gilliam, Terry, **Supp. IV:** 455

Gillman, James, **IV:** 48–49, 50, 56

Gilman, Charlotte Perkins, **Supp. III:** 147

Gilpin, William, **IV:** 36, 37

Gilson, Étienne, **VI:** 341

"Gin and Goldenrod" (Lowry), **Supp. III:** 282

"Ginger Hero" (Friel), **Supp. V:** 113

Ginger, You're Barmy (Lodge), **Supp. IV:** 364–365, 368–369, 371

Giorgione da Castelfranco, **V:** 345, 348

"Giorgione" (Pater), **V:** 345, 348, 353

"Gipsy Vans" (Kipling), **VI:** 193, 196

"Giraffes, The" (Fuller), **VII:** 430, **Supp. VII:** 70

"Girl" (Kincaid), **Supp. VII:** 220, 221, 223

"Girl at the Seaside" (Murphy), **Supp. V:** 313, 318

Girl in Winter, A (Larkin), **Supp. I:** 286, 287

Girl, 20 (Amis), **Supp. II:** 15–16; **Supp. IV:** 29

Girl Weeping for the Death of Her Canary (Greuze), **Supp. IV:** 122

"Girl Who Loved Graveyards, The" (James), **Supp. IV:** 340

Girlhood of Mary Virgin, The (Rossetti), **V:** 236, 248, 249

Girls in Their Married Bliss (O'Brien), **Supp. V:** 334, 337–338

"Girls in Their Season" (Mahon), **Supp. VI:** 167

Girls of Slender Means, The (Spark), **Supp. I:** 200, 204, 206

"Girls on a Bridge" (Mahon), **Supp. VI:** 174

Gisborne, John, **IV:** 206

Gismond of Salerne (Wilmot), **I:** 216

Gissing, George, **V:** xiii, xxii, xxv–xxvi, 69, **423–438; VI:** 365; **Supp. IV:** 7–8

Gittings, Robert, **Supp. III:** 194

"Give Her A Pattern" (Lawrence), **II:** 330n

Give Me Your Answer, Do! (Friel), **Supp. V:** 127–128

"Given Heart, The" (Cowley), **II:** 197

Giving Alms No Charity . . . (Defoe), **III:** 13

Gladiators, The (Koestler), **Supp. I:** 27, 28, 29n

"Glanmore Revisited" (Heaney), **Retro. Supp. I:** 132

"Glanmore Sonnets" (Heaney), **Supp. II:** 276

Glanvill, Joseph, **II:** 275

Glass–Blowers, The (du Maurier), **Supp. III:** 136, 138

Glass Cell, The (Highsmith), **Supp. V:** 174

Glass Cottage, A Nautical Romance, The (Redgrove), **Supp. VI:** 230–231

Glass of Blessings, A (Pym), **Supp. II:** **377–378**

Glass Town chronicles (Brontës), **V:** 110–111

Gleanings from the Menagerie and Aviary at Knowsley Hall (Lear), **V:** 76, 87

Gleckner, R. F., **IV:** 173, 194

Glen, Heather, **III:** 297

Glendinning, Victoria, **Supp. II:** 78, 80, 90, 95

Glimpse of America, A (Stoker), **Supp. III:** 380

Glimpse of Reality, The (Shaw), **VI:** 129

Gloag, Julian, **Supp. IV:** 390

"Globe in North Carolina, The" (Mahon), **Supp. VI:** 174

"Gloire de Dijon" (Lawrence), **Retro. Supp. II:** 233

Glorious First of June, The, **III:** 266

"Glory of Women" (Sassoon), **VI:** 430

"Gnomes" (Ewart), **Supp. VII:** 39

gnomic moralizing poem, **I:** 57

"Go for" (Thomas), **Supp. III:** 399

"Go, Lovely Rose!" (Waller), **II:** 234

Go, Piteous Heart (Skelton), **I:** 83

Go When You See the Green Man Walking (Brooke–Rose), **Supp. IV:** 103–104

"Goal of Valerius" (Bacon), **I:** 263

Go–Between, The (Hartley), **Supp. VII:** 119, 120, 121, 127–129, 131, 132; **Retro. Supp. I:** 227

"Goblin Market" (Rossetti), **V:** 250, 256–258

Goblin Market and Other Poems (Rossetti), **V:** xxii, 250, 260

Goblins, The (Suckling), **II:** 226

God and His Gifts, A (Compton–Burnett), **VII:** 60, 64, 65

God and the Bible (Arnold), **V:** 216

"God! How I Hate You, You Young Cheerful Men" (West), **VI:** 423

"God Moves in a Mysterious Way" (Cowper), **III:** 210

God of Glass, The (Redgrove), **Supp. VI:** 231

God of Small Things (Roy), **Supp. V:** 67, 75

God that Failed, The (Crossman), **Supp. I:** 25

"God the Eater" (Smith), **Supp. II:** 468

God the Invisible King (Wells), **VI:** 227

"God Who Eats Corn, The" (Murphy), **Supp. V:** 313, 323–324

"God's Eternity" (Blake), **III:** 300

"God's Funeral" (Hardy), **Retro. Supp. I:** 121

God's Funeral (Wilson), **Supp. VI:** 298, 306, 308, **309**

"God's Grandeur" (Hopkins), **V:** 366; **Retro. Supp. II:** 195

"God's Judgement on a Wicked Bishop" (Southey), **IV:** 67

"Gods of the Copybook Heading, The" (Ewart), **Supp. VII:** 41

God's Revenge Against Murder (Reynolds), **II:** 14

Godber, Joyce, **II:** 243, 254

"Goddess, The" (Gunn), **Supp. IV:** 266, 271

Godman, Stanley, **V:** 271, 274

Godolphin, Sidney, **II:** 237, 238, 271

Godwin, E. W., **IV:** 404

Godwin, Mary Wollstonecraft, *see* Shelley, Mary Wollstonecraft

Godwin, William, **III:** 329, 330, 332, 340, 345; **IV:** xv, 3, 43, 127, 173, 181, 195–197; **Supp. III:** 355, 363, 370, 474, 476, 480

Goethe, Johann Wolfgang von, **III:** 344; **IV:** xiv–xix, 179, 240, 245, 249; **V:** 214, 343, 344, 402; **Supp. IV:** 28, 479

Goethe's Faust (MacNeice), **VII:** 408–410

Gogh, Vincent van, **Supp. IV:** 148, 154

Gogol, Nikolai, **III:** 340, 345; **Supp. III:** 17

"Going, The" (Hardy), **VI:** 18; **Retro. Supp. I:** 118

"Going Back" (Stevenson), **Supp. VI:** 265

"Going, Going" (Larkin), **Supp. I:** 283

Going Home (Lessing), **Supp. I:** 237

"Going Home" (Mahon), **Supp. VI:** 172

Going Solo (Dahl), **Supp. IV:** 206, 208, 210, 211, 222, 225

Going Their Own Ways (Waugh), **Supp. VI:** 273

"Going to Italy" (Davie), **Supp. VI:** 107

"Going to See a Man Hanged" (Thackeray), **V:** 23, 37

Gold, Mike, **Supp. IV:** 464

Gold: A Poem (Brooke–Rose), **Supp. IV:** 99, 100

Gold Coast Customs (Sitwell), **VII:** xvii, 132, 133–134

Gold in the Sea, The (Friel), **Supp. V:** 113

"Gold in the Sea, The" (Friel), **Supp. V:** 114

"Golden Age, The" (Behn), **Supp. III:** 39–40

Golden Ass (Apulius), **Supp. IV:** 414

Golden Bird, The (Brown), **Supp. VI:** 64

Golden Book of St. John Chrysostom, The, Concerning the Education of Children (tr. Evelyn), **II:** 275, 287

Golden Bough, The (Frazer), **V:** 204; **Supp. III:** 170, 172, 173, 174, 175, 176–182, 184, 185, 186, 187; **Supp. IV:** 12

Golden Bowl, The (James), **VI:** 53, 55, 60–62, 67; **Supp. IV:** 243

"Golden Calf" (MacCaig), **Supp. VI:** 186

Golden Child, The (Fitzgerald), **Supp. V:** 98, 100–101

Golden Echo, The (Garnett), **VI:** 333

"Golden Hair" (Owen), **VI:** 449

Golden Labyrinth, The (Knight), **IV:** 328n, 339

Golden Lads: Sir Francis Bacon, Anthony Bacon, and Their Friends (du Maurier), **Supp. III:** 139

Golden Lion of Granpère, The (Trollope), **V:** 102

Golden Mean, The (Ford), **II:** 88, 100

Golden Notebook, The (Lessing), **Supp. I:** 238, **246–248,** 254, 256; **Supp. IV:** 473

Golden Targe, The (Dunbar), **I:** 23

Golden Treasury, The (Palgrave), **II:** 208; **IV:** xxii, 196, 337

Golding, Arthur, **I:** 161

Golding, William, **Supp. I:** **65–91; Supp. IV:** 392–393; **Retro. Supp. I:** **93–107**

Goldring, Douglas, **VI:** 324, 419

Goldsmith, Oliver, **II:** 362, 363; **III:** 40, 110, 149, 165, 173, **177–192,** 256, 277, 278; **Retro. Supp. I:** 149

Goldsworthy Lowes Dickinson (Forster), **VI:** 411

Gollancz, Victor, **VII:** xix, 279, 381

Gondal literature (Brontë), **V:** 113–117, 133, 142

Gondal Poems (Brontë), **V:** 152

Gondal's Queen (Ratchford), **V:** 133, 152

Gondibert (Davenant), **II:** 196, 259

Gonne, Maud, **VI:** 207, 210, 211, 212

Good and Faithful Servant, The (Orton), **Supp. V:** 364, 367, 370, 371, 372, 374–375

Good Apprentice, The (Murdoch), **Supp. I:** 231, 232, 233

"Good Aunt, The" (Edgeworth), **Supp. III:** 162

"Good Climate, Friendly Inhabitants" (Gordimer), **Supp. II:** 232

Good Companions, The (Priestley), **VII:** xviii, 209, 211, 215–216

"Good Counsel to a Young Maid" (Carew), **II:** 224

Good Fight, The (Kinsella), **Supp. V:** 267

"Good Friday" (Herbert), **II:** 128

"Good Friday: Rex Tragicus; or, Christ Going to His Crosse" (Herrick), **II:** 114

"Good Friday, 1613" (Donne), **I:** 368

Good Kipling, The (Gilbert), **VI:** 194

"Good ladies ye that have" (Sumy), **I:** 120

Good Morning. Midnight (Rhys), **Supp. II:** 388, **396–398**

"Good Morrow, The" (MacCaig), **Supp. VI:** 185

Good Natur'd Man, The (Goldsmith), **III:** 111, 180, 187, 191

Good News for the Vilest of Men; or, A Help for Despairing Souls (Bunyan), **II:** 253

"Good Night" (Kinsella), **Supp. V:** 267

Good Soldier, The (Ford), **VI:** 49; **VI:** 319, 323, **327–328**, 329

Good Son, The (film), **Supp. IV:** 390, 400

Good Terrorist, The (Lessing), **Supp. I:** 255–256

Good Time Was Had by All, A (Smith), **Supp. II:** 462

Good Times, The (Kelman), **Supp. V:** 243, 254–256

"Good Town, The" (Muir), **Supp. VI:** 207

Goodbye Earth and Other Poems (Richards), **Supp. II:** 427, 428

"Good–bye in fear, good–bye in sorrow" (Rossetti), **V:** 255

"Goodbye Marcus, Goodbye Rose" (Rhys), **Supp. II:** 401

Goodbye to All That (Graves), **VI:** xvi; **VII:** xviii, 257, 258

Goodbye to Berlin (Isherwood), **VII:** xx

Goodbye to Berlin (Wilson), **Supp. I:** 156

"Good–Bye to the Mezzogiorno" (Auden), **Retro. Supp. I:** 13

"Goodbye to the USA" (Davie), **Supp. VI:** 113

"Good–Morrow, The" (Donne), **II:** 197

"Goodness—the American Neurosis" (Rushdie), **Supp. IV:** 455–456

"Good–night" (Thomas), **Supp. III:** 400

Goopy Gyne Bagha Byne (film), **Supp. IV:** 450

Goose Cross (Kavan), **Supp. VII:** 208

"Goose Fair" (Lawrence), **VII:** 114

"Goose to Donkey" (Murray), **Supp. VII:** 282

Gorboduc (Norton and Sackville), **I:** 161–162, 214–216

Gordimer, Nadine, **Supp. II:** **225–243**

Gordon, D. J., **I:** 237, 239

Gordon, Ian Alistair, **VII:** xvii, xxxvii

Gorgon's Head and Other Literary Pieces, The (Frazer), **Supp. III:** 176

Gorton, Mary, **V:** 312, 313, 315–316, 330

Gosse, Edmund, **II:** 354, 361, 363, 364; **V:** 311, 313, 334, 392, 395

Gossip from the Forest (Keneally), **Supp. IV:** 346

Gosson, Stephen, **I:** 161

Gothic Architecture (Morris), **V:** 306

Gothic fiction, **III:** **324–346; IV:** 110, 111; **V:** 142–143

Gothic Revival, The (Clark), **III:** 325, 346

"Gourmet, The" (Ishiguro), **Supp. IV:** 304, 306

Government of the Tongue: The 1986 T. S. Eliot Memorial Lectures and Other Critical Writings (Heaney), **Supp. II:** 268, 269; **Retro. Supp. I:** 131

Gower, John, **I:** 20, 41, **48–56**, 57, 321

Goya, Francisco de, **Supp. IV:** 125

Grace Abounding to the Chief of Sinners (Bunyan), **II:** 240, 241, 243–245, 250, 253; **Supp. IV:** 242

Grace Darling (Swinburne), **V:** 333

"Grace of the Way" (Thompson), **V:** 442

Graffigny, Mme de, **Supp. III:** 75

Graham Greene (Lodge), **Supp. IV:** 365

Graham, James, *see* Montrose, marquess of

Graham, W. S., **Supp. VII:** **103–117**

Grammar of Assent, An Essay in Aid of a (Newman), **V:** 340, **Supp. VII:** 301–302

Grammar of Metaphor, A (Brooke–Rose), **Supp. IV:** 98, 113

"Grammarian's Funeral, A" (Browning), **IV:** 357, 361, 366

Grand Alliance, The (Churchill), **VI:** 361

Grand Babylon Hotel, The (Bennett), **VI:** 249, 253, 262, 266

Grand Meaulnes, Le (Alain–Fournier), **Supp. I:** 299

"Grandmother's Story, The" (Murray), **Supp. VII:** 280

"Grandparent's" (Spender), **Supp. II:** 494

Grania (Gregory), **VI:** 316

Granny Scarecrow (Stevenson), **Supp. VI:** **265**

Grant, Duncan, **VI:** 118

Granta (publication), **Supp. IV:** 304

"Grantchester" (Brooke), **Supp. III:** 52, 60

Granville Barker, Harley, **I:** 329; **VI:** ix, 104, 113, 273

Grass, Günter, **Supp. IV:** 440

Grass Is Singing, The (Lessing), **Supp. I:** 237, 239, 243, 248

"Grass Widows, The" (Trevor), **Supp. IV:** 503

"Gratiana Dancing and Singing" (Lovelace), **II:** 230

Grave, The (Blair), **Retro. Supp. I:** 45

"Grave by the Handpost, The" (Hardy), **VI:** 22

"Gravel Walks, The" (Heaney), **Retro. Supp. I:** 133

Graves, Robert, **II:** 94; **VI:** xvi, 207, 211, 219, 419; **VII:** xvi, xviii–xx, **257–272; Supp. II:** 185; **Supp. III:** 60; **Supp. IV:** 558; **Retro. Supp. I:** 144

Gravity's Rainbow (Pynchon), **Supp. IV:** 116

Gray, Thomas, **II:** 200; **III:** 118, 119, **136–145**, 173, 294, 325

Great Adventure, The (Bennett), **VI:** 250, 266; *see also Buried Alive*

Great Apes (Self), **Supp. V:** 398–400

"Great Automatic Grammatisator, The" (Dahl), **Supp. IV:** 216–217

Great Boer War, The (Doyle), **Supp. II:** 160

Great Broxopp, The (Milne), **Supp. V:** 299

Great Catherine (Shaw), **VI:** 119

Great Contemporaries (Churchill), **VI:** 354, 356

Great Depression, **VII:** xix

Great Divorce, The (Lewis), **Supp. III:** 56

Great Exhibition, The (Hare), **Supp. IV:** 281

Great Expectations (Dickens), **V:** xxii, 42, 60, 63, 66–68, 72

Great Favourite, The; or, The Duke of Lerma (Howard), **II:** 100

Great Fire of London, The (Ackroyd), **Supp. VI:** 4–5, 10

"Great Good Place, The" (James), **VI:** 69

Great Hoggarty Diamond, The (Thackeray), **V:** 21, 38

Great Hunger, The (Kavanagh), **Supp. VII:** 187, 190–192, 193, 194, 199

Great Instauration, The (Bacon), **I:** 259, 272

Great Law of Subordination Consider'd, The (Defoe), **III:** 13

"Great Lover, The" (Brooke), **Supp. III:** 556

"Great Man, The" (Motion), **Supp. VII:** 256

"Great men have been among us" (Wordsworth), **II:** 208

Great Moments in Aviation (film), **Supp. IV:** 542

Great Short Stories of Detection, Mystery and Horror (ed. Sayers), **III:** 341; **Supp. III:** 340, 341

"Great Spirits Now on Earth Are Sojourning . . . A (Keats), **IV:** 214

Great Trade Route (Ford), **VI:** 324

Great Tradition, The (Leavis), **VI:** 68, 149; **VII:** 234, **248–251; Retro. Supp. I:** 90

"Great Unknown, The" (Hood), **IV:** 267

Great War and Modern Memory, The (Fussell), **Supp. IV:** 57

Greater Lakeland (Nicholson), **Supp. VI:** 223

"Greater Love" (Owen), **VI:** 450

"Greatest TV Show on Earth, The" (Ballard), **Supp. V:** 28

Greatness of the Soul, A, . . . (Bunyan), **II**: 253

Greber, Giacomo, **II**: 325

Grecian History, The (Goldsmith), **III**: 181, 191

Greek Christian Poets, The, and the English Poets (Browning), **IV**: 321

"Greek Interpreter, The" (Doyle), **Supp. II**: 167

Greek Islands, The (Durrell), **Supp. I**: 102

Greek Studies (Pater), **V**: 355, 357

Greeks have a word for it, The (Unsworth), **Supp. VII**: 354, 355–356, 357, 359

Green Fool, The (Kavanagh), **Supp. VII**: 183, 186, 187, 188, 194, 199

Green, Henry, **Supp. II**: 247–264

"Green Hills of Africa, The" (Fuller), **Supp. VII**: 69

Green, Joseph Henry, **IV**: 57

Green, Roger Lancelyn, **V**: 265n, 273, 274

Green Crow, The (O'Casey), **VII**: 13

"Green Geese" (Sitwell), **VII**: 131

"Green, Green Is Aghir" (Cameron), **VII**: 426

Green Helmet, The (Yeats), **VI**: 222

"Green Hills of Africa" (Fuller), **VII**: 429, 432

Green Man, The (Amis), **Supp. II**: 13–14

"Green Mountain, Black Mountain" (Stevenson), **Supp. VI**: 256–257, 261–262, 266

Green Shore, The (Nicholson), **Supp. VI**: 219–220

Green Song (Sitwell), **VII**: 132, 135, 136

"Green Tea" (Le Fanu), **III**: 340, 345

Greene, Graham, **VI**: 329, 370; **VII**: xii; **Supp. I**: 1–20; **Supp. II**: 311, 324; **Supp. IV**: 4, 10, 13, 17, 21, 157, 365, 369, 373–374, 505; **Supp. V**: 26; **Retro. Supp. II**: 151–167

Greene, Robert, **I**: 165, 220, 275, 286, 296, 322; **II**: 3

Greenlees, Ian Gordon, **VI**: xxxiii

"Greenshank" (MacCaig), **Supp. VI**: 192

Greenvoe (Brown), **Supp. VI**: 64, 65–66

"Greenwich—Whitebait" (Thackeray), **V**: 38

Greenwood, Edward Baker, **VII**: xix, xxxvii

Greenwood, Frederick, **V**: 1

Greer, Germaine, **Supp. IV**: 436

Greg, W. R., **V**: 5, 7, 15

Greg, W. W., **I**: 279

Gregory, Lady Augusta, **VI**: 210, 218, **307–312, 314–316**, 317–318; **VII**: 1, 3, 42

Gregory, Sir Richard, **VI**: 233

Greiffenhagen, Maurice, **VI**: 91

Gremlins, The (Dahl), **Supp. IV**: 202, 211–212

"Grenadier" (Housman), **VI**: 160

Grenfell, Julian, **VI**: xvi, 417–418, 420

"Gretchen" (Gissing), **V**: 437

"Gretna Green" (Behan), **Supp. II**: 64

Greuze, Jean–Baptiste, **Supp. IV**: 122

Greuze: The Rise and Fall of an Eighteenth Century Phenomenon (Brookner), **Supp. IV**: 122

Greville, Fulke, **I**: 160, 164; **Supp. IV**: 256

Grey Area (Self), **Supp. V**: 402–404

Grey Eminence (Huxley), **VII**: 205

Grey of Fallodon (Trevelyan), **VI**: 383, 391

"Grey Woman, The" (Gaskell), **V**: 15

Greybeards at Play (Chesterton), **VI**: 336

Greyhound for Breakfast (Kelman), **Supp. V**: 242, 249–250

"Greyhound for Breakfast" (Kelman), **Supp. V**: 250

"Grief" (Browning), **IV**: 313, 318

Grief Observed, A (Lewis), **Supp. III**: 249

"Grief on the Death of Prince Henry, A" (Tourneur), **II**: 37, 41

Grierson, Herbert J. C., **II**: 121, 130, 196, 200, 202, 258; **Retro. Supp. II**: 173

Grigson, Geoffrey, **IV**: 47; **VII**: xvi

Grim Smile of the Five Towns, The (Bennett), **VI**: 250, 253–254

Grimus (Rushdie), **Supp. IV**: 435, 438–439, 443, 450

Gris, Juan, **Supp. IV**: 81

"Grisly Folk, The" (Wells), **Retro. Supp. I**: 96

Groatsworth of Wit, A (Greene), **I**: 275, 276

Grosskurth, Phyllis, **V**: xxvii

Grote, George, **IV**: 289

Group of Noble Dames, A (Hardy), **VI**: 20, 22

"Grove, The" (Muir), **Supp. VI**: 206

"Growing, Flying, Happening" (Reid), **Supp. VII**: 328

"Growing Old" (Arnold), **V**: 203

Growing Pains: The Shaping of a Writer (du Maurier), **Supp. III**: 135, 142, 144

Growing Points (Jennings), **Supp. V**: 217

Growing Rich (Weldon), **Supp. IV**: 531, 533

Growth of Love, The (Bridges), **VI**: 81, 83

Growth of Plato's Ideal Theory, The (Frazer), **Supp. III**: 170–171

"Grub First, Then Ethics" (Auden), **Retro. Supp. I**: 7, 13

Grünewald, Mathias, **Supp. IV**: 85

Gryffydh, Jane, **IV**: 159

Gryll Grange (Peacock), **IV**: xxii, 166–167, 170

Grylls, R. Glynn, **V**: 247, 260; **VII**: xvii, xxxviii

Guardian (periodical), **III**: 46, 49, 50

Guardian, The (Cowley), **II**: 194, 202

Guarini, Guarino, **II**: 49–50

Gubar, Susan, **Retro. Supp. I**: 59–60

Guerrillas (Naipaul), **Supp. I**: 396–397

Guest of Honour, A (Gordimer), **Supp. II**: 229–230, 231

Guide Through the District of the Lakes in the North of England, A (Wordsworth), **IV**: 25

Guide to Kulchur (Pound), **VI**: 333

Guido della Colonna, **I**: 57

Guild of St. George, The, **V**: 182

Guillaume de Deguilleville, **I**: 57

Guillaume de Lorris, **I**: 71

"Guilt and Sorrow" (Wordsworth), **IV**: 5, 45

"Guinevere" (Tennyson), **IV**: 336–337, 338

Guise, The (Marlowe), *see Massacre at Paris, The*

Guise, The (Webster), **II**: 68, 85

Gulliver's Travels (Swift), **II**: 261; **III**: 11, 20, **23–26**, 28, 35; **VI**: 121–122; **Supp. IV**: 502; **Retro. Supp. I**: 274, 275, 276–277, 279–282

Gun for Sale, A (Greene; U.S. title, *This Gun for Hire*), **Supp. I**: 3, 6–7, 10; **Retro. Supp. II**: 153

Gunn, Ander, **Supp. IV**: 265

Gunn, Thom, **Supp. IV**: **255–279**

Guns of Navarone, The (film, Ambler), **Supp. IV**: 3

Gurdjieff, Georges I., **Supp. IV**: 1, 5

Gurney, Ivor, **VI**: 416, **425–427**

Gussow, Mel, **Retro. Supp. I**: 217–218

Gutch, J. M., **IV**: 78, 81

Guthlac, **Retro. Supp. II**: 303

Gutteridge, Bernard, **VII**: 422, 432–433

Guy Domville (James), **VI**: 39

Guy Mannering (Scott), **IV**: xvii, 31–32, 38

Guy of Warwick (Lydgate), **I**: 58

Guy Renton (Waugh), **Supp. VI**: 274–275

Guyana Quartet (Harris), **Supp. V**: 132, 133, 135

Guzman Go Home and Other Stories (Sillitoe), **Supp. V**: 410

"Gym" (Murphy), **Supp. V**: 328

Gypsies Metamorphos'd (Jonson), **II**: 111n

"Gyrtt in my giltetesse gowne" (Surrey), **I**: 115

"Healthy Landscape with Dormouse" (Warner), **Supp. VII**: 380

"Hee–Haw" (Warner), **Supp. VII**: 380

"House Grown Silent, The" (Warner), **Supp. VII**: 371

H. G. Wells and His Critics (Raknem), **VI**: 228, 245, 246

H. G. Wells: His Turbulent Life and Times (Dickson), **VI**: 246

H. G. Wells: The Critical Heritage (ed. Parrinder), **VI**: 246

Ha! Ha! Among the Trumpets (Lewis), **VII**: 447, 448

Habermas, Jürgen, **Supp. IV**: 112

Habington, William, **II**: 222, 237, 238

Habit of Loving, The (Lessing), **Supp. I**: 244

"Habit of Perfection, The" (Hopkins), **V**: 362, 381

Hadjinicolaou, Nicos, **Supp. IV**: 90

"Hag, The" (Herrick), **II**: 111

Haggard, H. Rider, **Supp. III**: **211–228**; **Supp. IV**: 201, 484

Haight, Gordon, **V**: 199, 200, 201

Hail and Farewell (Moore), **VI**: xii, 85, 88, 97, 99

"Hailstones" (Heaney), **Supp. II**: 280

Hakluyt, Richard, **I**: 150, 267; **III**: 7

Hale, Kathleen, **Supp. IV:** 231
"Half–a–Crown's Worth of Cheap Knowledge" (Thackeray), **V:** 22, 37
Halidon Hill (Scott), **IV:** 39
Halifax, marquess of, **III:** 38, 39, 40, 46
Hall, Donald, **Supp. IV:** 256
Hall, Edward, **II:** 43
Hall, Joseph, **II:** 25–26, 81; **IV:** 286
Hall, Radclyffe, **VI:** 411; **Supp. VI: 119–132**
Hall, Samuel (pseud., O'Nolan), **Supp. II:** 322
Hall of Healing (O'Casey), **VII:** 11–12
Hall of the Saurians (Redgrove), **Supp. VI:** 236
Hallam, Arthur, **IV:** 234, 235, 328–336, 338
Hallam, Henry, **IV:** 283
Haller, Albrecht von, **III:** 88
Halloran's Little Boat (Keneally), **Supp. IV:** 348
"Hallowe'en" (Burns), **III:** 315
Hallowe'en Party (Christie), **Supp. II:** 125, 134
Ham Funeral, The (White), **Supp. I:** 131, 134, 149, 150
"Hamadryad, The" (Landor), **IV:** 96
Hamburger, Michael, **Supp. V:** 199
Hamilton, Sir George Rostrevor, **IV:** xxiv
Hamlet (early version), **I:** 212, 221, 315
Hamlet (Shakespeare), **I:** 188, 280, 313, 315–316; **II:** 29, 36, 71, 75, 84; **III:** 170, 234; **V:** 328; **Supp. IV:** 63, 149, 283, 295
"Hamlet, Princess of Denmark" (Beerbohm), **Supp. II:** 55
Hammerton, Sir John, **V:** 393, 397
Hammett, Dashiell, **Supp. II:** 130, 132
Hampden, John, **V:** 393, 395
"Hampstead: the Horse Chestnut Trees" (Gunn), **Supp. IV:** 270–271
Hampton, Christopher, **Supp. IV:** 281
"Hand, The" (Highsmith), **Supp. V:** 179–180
"Hand and Soul" (Rossetti), **V:** 236, 320
Hand of Ethelberta, The: A Comedy in Chapters (Hardy), **VI:** 4, 6, 20; **Retro. Supp. I:** 114
"Hand of Solo, A" (Kinsella), **Supp. V:** 267, 274
"Hand that signed the paper, The" (Thomas), **Supp. I:** 174
Handful of Dust, A (Waugh), **VII:** xx, 294, 295–297
"Handful of People, A" (Ewart), **Supp. VII:** 39
"Hands" (Ewart), **Supp. VII:** 39
"Hands" (Hughes), **Retro. Supp. II:** 212
Hands Across the Sea (Coward), **Supp. II:** 153
"Handsome Heart, The" (Hopkins), **V:** 368–369
Handsworth Songs (film), **Supp. IV:** 445
Hanged by the Neck (Koestler), **Supp. I:** 36
"Hanging, A" (Powell), **VII:** 276
Hanging Judge, The (Stevenson), **V:** 396
"Hangover Square" (Mahon), **Supp. VI:** 177

Hapgood (Stoppard), **Retro. Supp. II:** 354–355
"Happily Ever After" (Huxley), **VII:** 199–200
"Happiness" (Owen), **VI:** 449, 458
"Happinesse to Hospitalitie; or, A Hearty Wish to Good House–keeping" (Herrick), **II:** 111
Happy Days (Beckett), **Supp. I:** 46, 52, 54, 56, 57, 60; **Retro. Supp. I:** 26–27
"Happy Family, A" (Trevor), **Supp. IV:** 503
Happy Haven, The (Arden), **Supp. II:** 29
Happy Hypocrite: A Fairy Tale for Tired Men, The (Beerbohm), **Supp. II:** 45, 46
"Happy Man, The" (Thomson), **Supp. III:** 417
"Happy old man, whose worth all mankind knows" (Flatman), **II:** 133
Happy Pair, The (Sedley), **II:** 266, 271
"Happy Prince, The" (Wilde), **V:** 406, 419; **Retro. Supp. II:** 365; **Retro. Supp. II:** 365
Happy Valley (White), **Supp. I:** 130, 132–133, 136
Haq, Zia ul–, **Supp. IV:** 444
Hard Life, The (O'Nolan), **Supp. II: 336–337**
Hard Times (Dickens), **IV:** 247; **V:** viii, xxi, 4, 42, 47, 59, 63–64, 68, 70, 71
Hardie and Baird: The Last Days (Kelman), **Supp. V:** 256–257
Hardie and Baird and Other Plays (Kelman), **Supp. V:** 256–257
"Hardness of Light, The" (Davie), **Supp. VI:** 109
Hardy, Barbara, **V:** ix, xxviii, 39, 73, 201
Hardy, G. H., **VII:** 239–240
Hardy, Thomas, **II:** 69; **III:** 278; **V:** xx–xxvi, 144, 279, 429; **VI:** x, **1–22**, 253, 377; **VII:** xvi; list of short stories, **VI:** 22; **Supp. IV:** 94, 116, 146, 471, 493; **Retro. Supp. I: 109–122**
"Hardy and the Hag" (Fowles), **Supp. I:** 302, 305
Hardy of Wessex (Weber), **VI:** 21
Hare, J. C., **IV:** 54
Hare, David, **Supp. IV:** 182, **281–300**
"Harem Trousers" (McGuckian), **Supp. V:** 286
Harington, Sir John, **I:** 131
"Hark, My Soul! It Is the Lord" (Cowper), **III:** 210
"Hark! the Dog's Howl" (Tennyson), **IV:** 332
Harlequinade (Rattigan), **Supp. VII:** 315–316
Harlot's House, The (Wilde), **V:** 410, 418, 419
"Harmonies" (Kinsella), **Supp. V:** 271
"Harmony, The" (Redgrove), **Supp. VI:** 236
"Harmony of the Spheres, The" (Rushdie), **Supp. IV:** 445
Harness Room, The (Hartley), **Supp. VII:** 132
Harold (Tennyson), **IV:** 328, 338
Harold Muggins Is a Martyr (Arden and D'Arcy), **Supp. II:** 31

Harold the Dauntless (Scott), **IV:** 39
Harold's Leap (Smith), **Supp. II:** 462
Haroun and the Sea of Stories (Rushdie), **Supp. IV:** 433, 438, 450–451
Harriet Hume: A London Fantasy (West), **Supp. III:** 441–442
Harrington (Edgeworth), **Supp. III: 161–163**
Harriet Said? (Bainbridge), **Supp. VI:** 17, **19**
Harriot, Thomas, **I:** 277, 278
Harris, Frank, **VI:** 102
Harris, Joseph, **II:** 305
Harris, Wilson, **Supp. V: 131–147**
"Harris East End" (MacCaig), **Supp. VI:** 182
Harrison, Frederic, **V:** 428–429
Harrison, Tony, **Supp. V: 149–165**
Harry Heathcote of Gangoil (Trollope), **V:** 102
"Harry Ploughman" (Hopkins), **V:** 376–377
Harsh Voice, The (West), **Supp. III:** 442
Hartley, David, **IV:** 43, 45, 50, 165
Hartley, L. P., **Supp. VII: 119–133**
Hartmann, Edward von, **Supp. II:** 108
"Harvest Bow, The" (Heaney), **Supp. II:** 276–277
Harvest Festival, The (O'Casey), **VII:** 12
"Harvesting, The" (Hughes), **Supp. II:** 348
Harvey, Christopher, **II:** 138; **Retro. Supp. II:** 172
Harvey, Gabriel, **I:** 122–123, 125; **II:** 25
Harvey, T. W. J., **V:** 63, 199, 201
Harvey, William, **I:** 264
"Has Your Soul Slipped" (Owen), **VI:** 446
Hastings, Warren, **IV:** xv–xvi, 271, 278
Hatfield, C. W., **V:** 133, 151, 152, 153
Haunch of Venison, The (Goldsmith), **III:** 191
Haunted and the Haunters, The (Bulwer–Lytton), **III:** 340, 345
"Haunted House, The" (Graves), **VII:** 263
"Haunted House, The" (Hood), **IV:** 261, 262
Haunted Man and the Ghost's Bargain, The (Dickens), **V:** 71
"Haunter, The" (Hardy), **VI:** 18; **Retro. Supp. I:** 117
Haunter of the Dark, The . . . (Lovecraft), **III:** 345
Have His Carcase (Sayers), **Supp. III:** 345–346
Having a Wonderful Time (Churchill), **Supp. IV:** 180, 181
Haw Lantern, The (Heaney), **Supp. II:** 268, **279–281**; **Retro. Supp. I:** 131–132
Hawes, Stephen, **I:** 49, 81
"Hawk, The" (Brown), **Supp. VI: 71**
Hawk in the Rain, The (Hughes), **Supp. I:** 343, 345, 363
"Hawk in the Rain, The" (Hughes), **Supp. I:** 345; **Retro. Supp. II:** 200, 202–204
"Hawk Roosting" (Hughes), **Retro. Supp. II:** 204

Hawkfall (Brown), **Supp. VI:** 69

Hawkins, Lewis Weldon, **VI:** 85

Hawkins, Sir John, **II:** 143

Hawksmoor (Ackroyd), **Supp. VI:** 6–7, 10–11

Hawthorne, Nathaniel, **III:** 339, 345; **VI:** 27, 33–34; **Supp. IV:** 116

Hawthorne (James), **VI:** 33–34, 67

Haxton, Gerald, **VI:** 369

Hay Fever (Coward), **Supp. II:** 139, 141, **143–145,** 148, 156

Haydon, Benjamin, **IV:** 214, 227, 312

Hayes, Albert McHarg, **Retro. Supp. II:** 181

"Haymaking" (Thomas), **Supp. III:** 399, 405

"Haystack in the Floods, The" (Morris), **V:** 293

Hayter, Alethea, **III:** 338, 346; **IV:** xxiv–xxv, 57, 322

Hazard, Paul, **III:** 72

Hazlitt, William, **I:** 121, 164; **II:** 153, 332, 333, 337, 343, 346, 349, 354, 361, 363, 364; **III:** 68, 70, 76, 78, 165, 276–277; **IV:** ix, xi, xiv, xvii–xix, 38, 39, 41, 50, **125–140,** 217; **Retro. Supp. I:** 147; **Retro. Supp. II:** 51, 52

"He" (Lessing), **Supp. I:** 244

He Knew He Was Right (Trollope), **V:** 98, 99, 102

"He Revisits His First School" (Hardy), **VI:** 17

"He saw my heart's woe" (Brontë), **V:** 132

"He Thinks of His Past Greatness . . . When a Part of the Constellations of Heaven" (Yeats), **VI:** 211

"He thought he saw a Banker's Clerk" (Carroll), **V:** 270

"He Wonders Whether to Praise or to Blame Her" (Brooke), **Supp. III:** 55

Head to Toe (Orton), **Supp. V:** 363, 365–366

"Head Spider, The" (Murray), **Supp. VII:** 283, 284

Heading Home (Hare), **Supp. IV:** 288, 290–291

Headlong (Frayn), **Supp. VII:** 64, 65

Headlong Hall (Peacock), **IV:** xvii, **160–163,** 164, 165, 168, 169

Healing Art, The (Wilson), **Supp. VI:** **299–300,** 301, 303, 308

Health and Holiness (Thompson), **V:** 450, 451

"Healthy Landscape with Dormouse" (Warner), **Supp. VII:** 380

Heaney, Seamus, **Supp. II: 267–281;** **Supp. IV:** 410, 412, 416, 420–421, 427, 428; **Retro. Supp. I: 123–135**

Hear Us O Lord from Heaven Thy Dwelling Place (Lowry), **Supp. III: 281–282**

Hearing Secret Harmonies (Powell), **VII:** 352, 353

"Hears not my Phillis, how the Birds" (Sedley), **II:** 264

Heart and Science (Collins), **Supp. VI:** 102–103

"Heart, II, The" (Thompson), **V:** 443

"Heart Knoweth Its Own Bitterness, The" (Rossetti), **V:** 253–254

Heart of Darkness (Conrad), **VI:** 135, **136–139,** 172; **Supp. IV:** 189, 250, 403; **Retro. Supp. II:** 73–75

"Heart of John Middleton, The" (Gaskell), **V:** 15

Heart of Mid–Lothian, The (Scott), **IV:** xvii, 30, 31, 33–34, 35, 36, 39; **V:** 5

Heart of the Country, The (Weldon), **Supp. IV:** 526–528

Heart of the Matter, The (Greene), **Supp. I:** 2, 8, 11–12, 13; **Retro. Supp. II:** 157–159

Heart to Heart (Rattigan), **Supp. VII:** 320

Heartbreak House (Shaw), **V:** 423; **VI:** viii, xv, 118, **120–121,** 127, 129; **Retro. Supp. II:** 322–323

Heartland (Harris), **Supp. V:** 135, 136

Hearts and Lives of Men, The (Weldon), **Supp. IV:** 536

"Heart's Chill Between" (Rossetti), **V:** 249, 252

Heat and Dust (Jhabvala), **Supp. V:** 224, 230, 231–232, 238

Heat of the Day, The (Bowen), **Supp. II:** 77, 78, 79, 93, 95

"Heather Ale" (Stevenson), **V:** 396

Heather Field, The (Martyn), **IV:** 87, 95

"Heaven" (Brooke), **Supp. III:** 56, 60

Heaven and Earth (Byron), **IV:** 178, 193

Heaven and Its Wonders, and Hell (Swedenborg), **Retro. Supp. I:** 38

Heavenly Foot–man, The (Bunyan), **II:** 246, 253

"Heber" (Smith), **Supp. II:** 466

Hebert, Ann Marie, **Supp. IV:** 523

Hebrew Melodies, Ancient and Modern . . . (Byron), **IV:** 192

Hecatommitthi (Cinthio), **I:** 316

Hedda Gabler (Ibsen), **Supp. IV:** 163, 286

"Hedgehog" (Muldoon), **Supp. IV:** 414

"Hee–Haw" (Warner), **Supp. VII:** 380

Heel of Achilles, The (Koestler), **Supp. I:** 36

Hegel, Georg Wilhelm Friedrich, **Supp. II:** 22

"Height–ho on a Winter Afternoon" (Davie), **Supp. VI:** 107–108

Heilbrun, Carolyn G., **Supp. IV:** 336

Heine, Heinrich, **IV:** xviii, 296

Heinemann, William, **VII:** 91

"Heiress, The" (McGuckian), **Supp. V:** 282

Heit, S. Mark, **Supp. IV:** 339

"Hélas" (Wilde), **V:** 401

Helen (Scott), **Supp. III:** 151, **165–166**

Helena (Waugh), **VII:** 292, 293–294, 301

Hélène Fourment in a Fur Coat (Rubens), **Supp. IV:** 89

Hellas (Shelley), **IV:** xviii, 206, 208; **Retro. Supp. I:** 255

Hellenics, The (Landor), **IV:** 96, 100

Héloïse and Abélard (Moore), **VI:** xii, 88, 89, **94–95,** 99

Hemans, Felicia, **IV:** 311

Hemingway, Ernest, **Supp. III:** 105; **Supp. IV:** 163, 209, 500

Hemlock and After (Wilson), **Supp. I:** 155–156, 157, 158–159, 160, 161, 164

Hello, America (Ballard), **Supp. V:** 29

"Hen Woman" (Kinsella), **Supp. V:** 266–267

Henceforward (Ayckbourn), **Supp. V:** 3, 10, 11, 13

"Hendecasyllabics" (Swinburne), **V:** 321

"Hendecasyllabics" (Tennyson), **IV:** 327–328

Henderson, Hamish, **VII:** 422, 425–426

Henderson, Hubert, **VII:** 35

Henderson, Philip, **V:** xii, xviii, 335

Henderson, T. F., **IV:** 290n

Hengist, King of Kent; or, The Mayor of Quinborough (Middleton), **II:** 3, 21

Henley, William Ernest, **V:** 386, 389, 391–392; **VI:** 159; **Retro. Supp. I:** 260, 264

Henn, T. R., **VI:** 220

"Henrietta Marr" (Moore), **VI:** 87

Henrietta Temple (Disraeli), **IV:** xix, 293, 298–299, 307, 308

"Henrik Ibsen" (James), **VI:** 49

Henry Esmond (Thackeray), *see History of Henry Esmond, Esq. . . ., The*

Henry for Hugh (Ford), **VI:** 331

Henry James (ed. Tanner), **VI:** 68

Henry James (West), **Supp. III:** 437

"Henry James: The Religious Aspect" (Greene), **Supp. I:** 8

"Henry Purcell" (Hopkins), **V:** 370–371; **Retro. Supp. II:** 196

Henry II (Bancroft), **II:** 305

Henry IV (Shakespeare), **I:** 308–309, 320

Henry V (Shakespeare), **I:** 309; **V:** 383; **Supp. IV:** 258

Henry VI trilogy (Shakespeare), **I:** 286, 299–300, 309

Henry VI's Triumphal Entry into London (Lydgate), **I:** 58

Henry VIII (Shakespeare), **I:** 324; **II:** 43, 66, 87; **V:** 328

"Henry VIII and Ann Boleyn" (Landor), **IV:** 92

Henry Vaughan: Experience and the Tradition (Garner), **II:** 186n

Henry's Past (Churchill), **Supp. IV:** 181

Henryson, Robert, **Supp. VII: 135–149**

Henslowe, Philip, **I:** 228, 235, 284; **II:** 3 25, 68

Henty, G. A., **Supp. IV:** 201

"Her Second Husband Hears Her Story" (Hardy), **Retro. Supp. I:** 120

Her Triumph (Johnson), **I:** 347

Her Vertical Smile (Kinsella), **Supp. V:** 270–271

Her Victory (Sillitoe), **Supp. V:** 411, 415, 422, 425

Herakles (Euripides), **IV:** 358

Herbert, Edward, pseud. of John Hamilton Reynolds

Herbert, Edward, *see* Herbert of Cherbury, Lord

Herbert, George, **II:** 113, **117–130,** 133, 134, 137, 138, 140–142, 184, 187, 216, 221; **Retro. Supp. II: 169–184**

Herbert of Cherbury, Lord, **II:** 117–118, 222, 237, 238

Herbert's Remains (Oley), **Retro. Supp. II:** 170–171

Hercule Poirot's Last Case (Christie), **Supp. II:** 125

"Hercules and Antaeus" (Heaney), **Supp. II:** 274–275

Hercules Oetaeus (Seneca), **I:** 248

"Here" (Larkin), **Supp. I:** 279, 285

Here Comes Everybody: An Introduction to James Joyce for the Ordinary Reader (Burgess), **Supp. I:** 194, 196–197

Here Lies: An Autobiography (Ambler), **Supp. IV:** 1, 2, 3, 4

"Heredity" (Harrison), **Supp. V:** 152

Heretics (Chesterton), **VI:** 204, 336–337

Hering, Carl Ewald, **Supp. II:** 107–108

Heritage and Its History, A (Compton–Burnett), **VII:** 60, 61, 65

Hermaphrodite Album, The (Redgrove), **Supp. VI:** 230

"Hermaphroditus" (Swinburne), **V:** 320

Hermetical Physick . . . Englished (tr. Vaughan), **II:** 185, 201

Hermit of Marlow, The, pseud. of Percy Bysshe Shelley

"Hero" (Rossetti), **V:** 260

"Hero and Leander" (Hood), **IV:** 255–256, 267

Hero and Leander (Marlowe), **I:** 234, 237–240, 276, 278, 280, 288, **290–291,** 292; **Retro. Supp. I:** 211

Hero and Leander, in Burlesque (Wycherley), **II:** 321

"Hero as King, The" (Carlyle), **IV:** 245, 246

Hero Rises Up, The (Arden and D'Arcy), **Supp. II:** 31

"Heroine, The" (Highsmith), **Supp. V:** 180

Herodotus, **Supp. IV:** 110

Heroes and Hero–Worship (Carlyle), **IV:** xx, 240, 244–246, 249, 250, 341

Heroes and Villains (Carter), **Supp. III:** 81, 84

Heroic Idylls, with Additional Poems (Landor), **IV:** 100

"Heroic Stanzas" (Dryden), **II:** 292

Heroine, The; or, The Adventures of Cherubina (Barrett), **III:** 335

Herrick, Robert, **II: 102–116,** 121

Herself Surprised (Cary), **VII:** 186, 188, 191–192

"Hertha" (Swinburne), **V:** 325

"Hervé Riel" (Browning), **IV:** 367

Herzog, Werner, **IV:** 180

"Hesperia" (Swinburne), **V:** 320, 321

Hesperides, The (Herrick), **II:** 102, 103, 104, 106, 110, 112, 115, 116

Heyday of Sir Walter Scott, The (Davie), **Supp. VI:** 114–115

Heylyn, Peter, **I:** 169

Heywood, Jasper, **I:** 215

Heywood, Thomas, **II:** 19, 47, 48, 68, 83

"Hexagon" (Murphy), **Supp. V:** 328

Hibberd, Dominic, **VI:** xvi, xxxiii

Hide, The (Unsworth), **Supp. VII:** 354, 356

"Hide and Seek" (Gunn), **Supp. IV:** 272

Hide and Seek (Collins), **Supp. VI:** 92, 95

Hide and Seek (Swinburne), **V:** 334

"Hidden History, A" (Okri), **Supp. V:** 352

Hidden Ireland, The (Corkery), **Supp. V:** 41

"Hidden Law" (MacCaig), **Supp. VI:** 186

Higden, Ranulf, **I:** 22

Higgins, F. R., **Supp. IV:** 411, 413

High Island: New and Selected Poems (Murphy), **Supp. V:** 313, 315, 316, 324–325

"High Life in Verdopolis" (Brontë), **V:** 135

"High wavering heather . . . " (Brontë), **V:** 113

High Windows (Larkin), **Supp. I:** 277, 280, **281–284,** 285, 286

Higher Ground (Phillips), **Supp. V:** 380, 386–388

Higher Schools and Universities in Germany (Arnold), **V:** 216

"Higher Standards" (Wilson), **Supp. I:** 155

Highet, Gilbert, **II:** 199

"Highland Funeral" (MacCaig), **Supp. VI:** 193

Highland Widow, The (Scott), **IV:** 39

Highly Dangerous (Ambler), **Supp. IV:** 3

High–Rise (Ballard), **Supp. V:** 27

High Summer (Rattigan), **Supp. VII:** 315

Highsmith, Patricia, **Supp. IV:** 285; **Supp. V: 167–182**

"Highwayman and the Saint, The" (Friel), **Supp. V:** 118

Hilaire Belloc (Wilson), **Supp. VI:** 301–302

Hilda Lessways (Bennett), **VI:** 258; **Supp. IV:** 238

Hill, G. B., **III:** 233, 234n

Hill, Geoffrey, **Supp. V: 183–203**

"Hill, The" (Brooke), **Supp. III:** 51

Hill of Devi, The (Forster), **VI:** 397, 408, 411

Hill of Venus, The (Morris), **V:** 298

Hilton, Walter, **Supp. I:** 74

Hind, The, and the Panther (Dryden), **II:** 291, 292, 299–300, 304

Hinge of Faith, The (Churchill), **VI:** 361

Hinman, Charlton, **I:** 326–327

Hinton, William, **Supp. IV:** 284

Hints Towards the Formation of a More Comprehensive Theory of Life (Coleridge), **IV:** 56

Hippolytus (Euripides), **V:** 322, 324

Hireling, The (Hartley), **Supp. VII:** 129–131

"His Age, Dedicated to his Peculiar Friend, M. John Wickes" (Herrick), **II:** 112

His Arraignment (Jonson), **Retro. Supp. I:** 158

"His Chosen Calling" (Naipaul), **Supp. I:** 385

"His Country" (Hardy), **Retro. Supp. I:** 120–121

"His Fare–well to Sack" (Herrick), **II:** 111

"His Father's Hands" (Kinsella), **Supp. V:** 268

"His Last Bow" (Doyle), **Supp. II:** 175

"His Letanie, to the Holy Spirit" (Herrick), **II:** 114

His Majesties Declaration Defended (Dryden), **II:** 305

His Majesty Preserved . . . Dictated to Samuel Pepys by the King . . . (ed. Rees–Mogg), **II:** 288

His Noble Numbers (Herrick), **II:** 102, 103, 112, 114, 115, 116

"His Returne to London" (Herrick), **II:** 103

His Second War (Waugh), **Supp. VI:** 274

Historia naturalis et experimentalis (Bacon), **I:** 259, 273

Historia regis Henrici Septimi (André), **I:** 270

Historiae adversum paganos (Orosius), **Retro. Supp. II:** 296

"Historian, The" (Fuller), **Supp. VII:** 74

Historical Account of the Theatre in Europe, An (Riccoboni), **II:** 348

Historical Register, The (Fielding), **III:** 97, 98, 105; **Retro. Supp. I:** 82

Historical Relation of the Island of Ceylon, An (Knox), **III:** 7

"Historical Society" (Murphy), **Supp. V:** 322

"History" (Macaulay), **IV:** 284

History and Adventures of an Atom, The (Smollett), **III:** 149–150, 158

History and Adventures of Joseph Andrews and of His Friend Mr. Abraham Adams (Fielding), **Retro. Supp. I:** 80, 83–86

History and Remarkable Life of . . . Col. Jack (Defoe), *see* Colonel Jack

History of a Good Warm Watch–Coat, The (Sterne), *see* Political Romance, A

History of a Six Weeks' Tour Through a Part of France . . . (Shelley and Shelley), **IV:** 208; **Supp. III:** 355

"History of Angria" (Brontë), **V:** 110–111, 118

History of Antonio and Mellida, The (Marston), *see* Antonio and Mellida

History of Brazil (Southey), **IV:** 68, 71

History of Britain . . . , The (Milton), **II:** 176

History of British India, The, (Mill), **V:** 288

History of England (Hume), **II:** 148; **IV:** 273; **Supp. III:** 229, 238–239

History of England, An (Goldsmith), **III:** 180, 181, 189, 191

History of England, The (Trevelyan), **VI:** xv, 390–391, 393

History of England from the Accession of James II, The (Macaulay), **II:** 255; **IV:** xx, 272, 273, 280, 282, **283–290,** 291

History of England in the Eighteenth Century (Lecky), **Supp. V:** 41

History of English Thought in the Eighteenth Century (Stephen), **V:** 280, 288, 289

History of Frederick the Great, The (Carlyle), **IV:** xxi, 240, 246, 249, 250

History of Friar Francis, The, **I:** 218

History of Henry Esmond, Esq. . . , The (Thackeray), **V:** xxi, 20, **31–33**, 38

History of King Richard III, The (More), **Supp. VII:** 234, 237–238, 246

History of Madan, The (Beaumont), **II:** 67

History of Mr. Polly, The (Wells), **VI:** xii, 225, 238–239

History of My Own Times (Burnet), **III:** 39

History of Pendennis, The (Thackeray), **V:** xxi, **28–31**, 33, 35, 38; **VI:** 354

History of Rasselas Prince of Abyssina, The (Johnson), **III:** 112–113, 121; **IV:** 47; **Retro. Supp. I:** 139–140, 148

History of Samuel Titmarsh and the Great Hoggarty Diamond, The (Thackeray), *see Great Hoggarty Diamond, The*

History of Shikasta (Lessing), **Supp. I:** 251

History of Sir Charles Grandison, The (Richardson), *see Sir Charles Grandison*

History of the Adventures of Joseph Andrews . . . , The (Fielding), *see Joseph Andrews*

"History of the Boswell Papers" (Pottle), **III:** 240*n*

History of the Church of Scotland (Spottiswoode), **II:** 142

History of the Earth, and Animated Nature, An (Goldsmith), **III:** 180, 181, 189–190, 191

History of the English–Speaking Peoples, A (Churchill), **VI:** 356

History of the Four Last Years of Queen Anne, The (Swift), **III:** 27, 36

"History of the Hardcomes, The" (Hardy), **VI:** 22

History of the Italian Renaissance (Symonds), **V:** 83

History of the Kentish Petition, The (Defoe), **III:** 12

History of the League, The (tr. Dryden), **II:** 305

"History of the Next French Revolution, The" (Thackeray), **V:** 38

History of the Nun, The; or, The Fair Vow–Breaker (Behn), **Supp. III:** 32

History of the Peninsular War (Southey), **IV:** 58, 63, 71; **V:** 109

History of the Plague Year, A (Defoe), **Retro. Supp. I:** 68

History of the Pyrates, The (Defoe), **III:** 13

History of the Reign of Henry the Seventh, The (Bacon), **I:** 259, 269, 270, 272

History of the Royal Society of London (Sprat), **II:** 196; **III:** 29

History of the Union of Great Britain, The (Defoe), **III:** 4, 13; **Retro. Supp. I:** 65

History of the Wars of . . . Charles XII . . ., The (Defoe), **III:** 13

"History of the Winds" (Bacon), **I:** 263

History of the World in 10 Chapters, A (Barnes), **Supp. IV:** 65, 67, 71–72, 73

History of the World, The (Ralegh), **I:** 145, 146, 149, 153–157

History of Titus Andronicus, The, **I:** 305

History of Tom Jones, a Foundling, The (Fielding), *see Tom Jones*

History of Van's House, The, **II:** 335

History Plays, The (Hare), **Supp. IV:** 283

Histriomastix (Prynne), **II:** 339; **Supp. III:** 23

Histriomastix; or, The Player Whipt (Marston), **II:** 27, 28, 40

Hitchcock, Alfred, **III:** 342–343; **Supp. III:** 147, 148, 149

"Hitchhiker, The" (Dahl), **Supp. IV:** 201

Hitherto unpublished Poems and Stories . . . (Browning), **IV:** 321

Hoare, D.M., **V:** 299, 306

Hobbes, John Oliver, pseud. of Mrs. Craigie

Hobbes, Thomas, **II:** 190, 196, 256, 294; **III:** 22; **IV:** 121, 138

Hobbit, The (Tolkien), **Supp. II:** 520, 521, 525, 527–528, 529, 530, 531–532

Hobsbaum, Philip, **Retro. Supp. I:** 126; **Retro. Supp. II:** 200

Hoccleve, Thomas, **I:** 49

"Hock–Cart; or, Harvest Home, The" (Herrick), **II:** 110–111

Hockney's Alphabet (McEwan), **Supp. IV:** 389

Hodder, E., **IV:** 62*n*

Hodgkins, Howard, **Supp. IV:** 170

Hodgson, W. N., **VI:** 422, 423

Hoff, Benjamin, **Supp. V:** 311

Hoffman, Calvin, **I:** 277

Hoffman, Heinrich, **I:** 25; **Supp. III:** 296

Hoffmann, E. T. A., **III:** 333, 334, 345

"Hoffmeier's Antelope" (Swift), **Supp. V:** 432

Hofmeyr (Paton; U.S. title, *South African Tragedy: The Life and Times of Jan Hofmeyr*), **Supp. II: 356–357**, 358

Hogarth Press, **VII:** xv, 17, 34

Hogg, James, **IV:** xvii, 73

Hogg, Thomas Jefferson, **IV:** 196, 198, 209

Hoggart, Richard, **VII:** xx, xxxviii; **Supp. IV:** 473

Hold Your Hour and Have Another (Behan), **Supp. II:** 65–66, 70

Holiday, The (Smith), **Supp. II:** 462, 474, **476–478**

Holiday Romance (Dickens), **V:** 72

Holiday Round, The (Milne), **Supp. V:** 298

"Holidays" (Kincaid), **Supp. VII:** 220

Hollington, Michael, **Supp. IV:** 357

Hollis, Maurice Christopher, **VI:** xxxiii

Hollis, Richard, **Supp. IV:** 88

"Hollow Men, The" (Eliot), **VII:** 150–151, 158; **Retro. Supp. II:** 129–130

Hollow's Mill (Brontë), *see Shirley*

Holloway, John, **VII:** 82

Holroyd, Michael, **Supp. IV:** 231

"Holy Baptisme I" (Herbert), **II:** 128

Holy City, The; or, The New Jerusalem (Bunyan), **II:** 253

"Holy Fair, The" (Burns), **III:** 311, 315, 317

Holy Grail, The, and Other Poems (Tennyson), **IV:** 338

Holy Life, The Beauty of Christianity, A (Bunyan), **II:** 253

"Holy Mountain, The" (Nicholson), **Supp. VI:** 215

"Holy Scriptures" (Vaughan), **II:** 187

"Holy Scriptures II, The" (Herbert), **Retro. Supp. II:** 174

Holy Sinner, The (Mann), **II:** 97n

Holy Sonnets (Donne), **I:** 362, 366, 367; **Retro. Supp. II:** 96

Holy War, The: Made by Shaddai . . . (Bunyan), **II:** 246, 250, 251–252, 253

"Holy Willie's Prayer" (Burns), **III:** 311, 313, 319

"Holy–Cross Day" (Browning), **IV:** 367

"Holyhead, September 25, 1717" (Swift), **III:** 32

"Homage to a Government" (Larkin), **Supp. I:** 284

Homage to Catalonia (Orwell), **VII:** 275, 280–281

Homage to Clio (Auden), **VII:** 392

"Homage to Burns" (Brown), **Supp. VI:** 72

"Homage to the British Museum" (Empson), **Supp. II:** 182

"Homage to William Cowper" (Davie), **Supp. VI:** 106

Homans, Margaret, **Retro. Supp. I:** 189

"Home" (Ewart), **Supp. VII:** 37

Home (Storey), **Supp. I:** 408, 413, 417

Home and Beauty (Maugham), **VI:** 368–369

Home and Dry (Fuller), **Supp. VII:** 70, 81

"Home at Grasmere" (Wordsworth), **IV:** 3, 23–24

Home Chat (Coward), **Supp. II:** 146

"Home for a couple of days" (Kelman), **Supp. V:** 250

"Home for the Highland Cattle, A" (Lessing), **Supp. I:** 241–242

Home Front (Bishton and Reardon), **Supp. IV:** 445

Home Letters (Disraeli) **IV:** 296, 308

Home Letters of T. E. Lawrence and His Brothers, The (Lawrence), **Supp. II:** 286

"Home Thoughts from Abroad" (Browning), **IV:** 356

"Home Thoughts Abroad" (Newman), **Supp. VII:** 293

"Home [2]" (Thomas), **Supp. III:** 405

"Home [3]" (Thomas), **Supp. III:** 404

Home University Library, **VI:** 337, 391

Homebush Boy (Keneally), **Supp. IV:** 344, 347

Homecoming, The (Pinter), **Supp. I:** 375, 380, 381; **Retro. Supp. I:** 225–226

Homecomings (Snow), **VII:** xxi, 324, 329, 335

"Homemade" (McEwan), **Supp. IV:** 389, 391, 396

"Homemaking" (Kincaid), **Supp. VII:** 229

Homer, **I:** 236; **II:** 304, 347; **III:** 217, 220; **IV:** 204, 215

Homeric Hymns (tr. Chapman), **I:** 236

"Homesick in Old Age" (Kinsella), **Supp. V:** 263

"Homeward Prospect, The" (Day Lewis), **Supp. III:** 129

Homiletic Fragment I, **Retro. Supp. II:** 301–302

Hone, Joseph, **VI:** 88

Hone, William, **IV:** 255

Honest Man's Fortune, The (Field, Fletcher, Massinger), **II:** 66

Honest Whore, The (Dekker and Middleton), **II:** 3, 21, 89

Honey for the Bears (Burgess), **Supp. I:** 191

Honeybuzzard (Carter), *see Shadow Dance*

Honeymoon Voyage, The (Thomas), **Supp. IV:** 490

Honorary Consul, The (Greene), **Supp. I:** 7, 10, 13, 16; **Retro. Supp. II:** 164–165

Honour of the Garter, The (Peele), **I:** 205

Honour Triumphant; or, The Peeres Challenge (Ford), **II:** 88, 100

"Honourable Laura, The" (Hardy), **VI:** 22

Honourable Schoolboy, The (le Carré), **Supp. II:** 301, **313–314,** 315

Hood, Thomas, **IV:** xvi, xx, **251–267,** 311

Hood's (periodical), **IV:** 252, 261, 263, 264

"Hood's Literary Reminiscences" (Blunden), **IV:** 267

Hood's Own (Hood), **IV:** 251–252, 253, 254, 266

Hook, Theodore, **IV:** 254

Hooker, Richard, **I:** **176–190,** 362; **II:** 133, 137, 140–142, 147

"Hope" (Cowper), **III:** 212

Hope, A. D., **Supp. VII: 151–166**

Hope for Poetry, A (Day Lewis), **Supp. III:** 117, 119

Hopes and Fears for Art (Morris), **V:** 301, 306

Hopkins, Gerard Manley, **II:** 123, 181; **IV:** xx; **V:** ix, xi, xxv, 53, 205, 210, 261, 309–310, 338, **361–382; VI:** 75, 83; **Supp. II:** 269; **Supp. IV:** 344, 345; **Retro. Supp. II:** 173, **185–198**

Hopkins (MacKenzie), **V:** 375n 382

Hopkinson, Sir Tom, **V:** xx, xxxviii

Horace, **II:** 108, 112, 199, 200, 265, 292, 300, 309, 347; **IV:** 327

"Horae Canonicae" (Auden), **Retro. Supp. I:** 12–13

Horae Solitariae (Thomas), **Supp. III:** 394

"Horatian Ode . . . , An" (Marvell), **II:** 204, 208, 209, 210, 211, 216–217; **Retro. Supp. II:** 263–264

"Horatius" (Macaulay), **IV:** 282

Horestes (Pickering), **I:** 213, 216–218

Horizon (periodical), **Supp. II:** 489; **Supp. III: 102–103,** 105, 106–107, 108–109

Horne, Richard Hengist, **IV:** 312, 321, 322

Hornet (periodical), **VI:** 102

Horniman, Annie, **VI:** 309; **VII:** 1

"Horns Away" (Lydgate), **I:** 64

Horse and His Boy, The (Lewis), **Supp. III:** 248, 260

"Horse Dealer's Daughter, The" (Lawrence), **VII:** 114

"Horse–Drawn Caravan" (Murphy), **Supp. V:** 329

"Horse, Goose and Sheep, The" (Lydgate), **I:** 57

"Horses" (Muir), **Supp. VI:** 204–205

"Horses" (Muir), Supp. VI: 204–205

Horse's Mouth, The (Cary), **VII:** 186, 188, 191, 192, 193–194

Hoskins, John, **I:** 165–166, 167

"Hospital Barge" (Owen), **VI:** 454

Hostage, The (Behan), **Supp. II:** 70, **72–73,** 74

Hot Anger Soon Cold (Jonson), **Retro. Supp. I:** 157

Hot Countries, The (Waugh), **Supp. VI:** 272, 274

Hot Gates, The (Golding), **Supp. I:** 81; **Retro. Supp. I:** 93

Hotel, The (Bowen), **Supp. II: 82–83**

Hotel du Lac (Brookner), **Supp. IV:** 120, 121, 126–127, 136

Hotel in Amsterdam, The (Osborne), **Supp. I:** 338–339

"Hotel of the Idle Moon, The" (Trevor), **Supp. IV:** 501

"Hotel Room in Chartres" (Lowry), **Supp. III:** 272

Hothouse, The (Pinter), **Supp. I:** 377–378

Hothouse by the East River, The (Spark), **Supp. I:** 210

Hotson, Leslie, **I:** 275, 276

Houd–den–bek (Brink), **Supp. VI:** 51

Hough, Graham, **IV:** 323n, 339; **V:** 355, 359

Houghton, Lord, *see Monckton Milnes, Richard*

Hound of Death, The (Christie), **III:** 341

"Hound of Heaven, The" (Thompson), **V:** 445–447, 449, 450

Hound of the Baskervilles, The (Doyle), **III:** 341, 342, 345; **Supp. II:** 161, 163, 164, 170, 171, 172

"Hour and the Ghost, The" (Rossetti), **V:** 256

Hours in a Library (Stephen), **V:** 279, 285, 286, 287, 289

Hours of Idleness (Byron), **IV:** xvi 192

House, Humphry, **IV:** 167

"House" (Browning), **IV:** 359; **Retro. Supp. II:** 29

House and Its Head, A (Compton-Burnett), **VII:** 61

"House and Man" (Thomas), **Supp. III:** 403, 404

House at Pooh Corner, The (Milne), **Supp. V:** 295, 305, 306, 307, 308–309

House by the Churchyard, The (Le Fanu), **III:** 340, 345

House for Mr Biswas, A (Naipaul), **Supp. I:** 383, 386, **387–389**

"House Grown Silent, The" (Warner), **Supp. VII:** 371

House in Paris, The (Bowen), **Supp. II:** 77, 82, 84, 89–90

"House in the Acorn, The" (Redgrove), **Supp. VI:** 236

House of All Nations (Stead), **Supp. IV:** 464–467

"House of Aries, The" (Hughes), **Supp. I:** 346

"House of Beauty, The" (Christie), **Supp. II:** 124

House of Children, A (Cary), **VII:** 186, 187, 189

"House of Christmas, The" (Chesterton), **VI:** 344

House of Cobwebs, The (Gissing), **V:** 437

House of Doctor Dee (Ackroyd), **Supp. VI:** 4, 10

"House of Dreams, The" (Thomas), **Supp. IV:** 493

House of Fame, The (Chaucer), **I:** 23, 30; **Retro. Supp. II:** 38–39

House of Life, The (Rossetti), **V:** 237, 238, 241, 242, 243, 244, 245

House of Pomegranates, A (Wilde), **V:** 419; **Retro. Supp. II:** 365

House of Seven Gables, The (Hawthorne), **III:** 339, 345

House of Sleep, The (Kavan), **Supp. VII:** 212–213

House of Splendid Isolation (O'Brien), **Supp. V:** 341–344

House on the Beach, The (Meredith), **V:** 230–231, 234

House on the Strand, The (du Maurier), **Supp. III:** 138, 139, 140, 141, 147

"Household Spirits" (Kinsella), **Supp. V:** 272

Household Words (periodical), **V:** xxi, 3, 42

Householder, The (Jhabvala), **Supp. V:** 227–228, 237

Housman, A. E., **III:** 68, 70; **V:** xxii, xxvi, 311; **VI:** ix, xv–xvi, **151–164,** 415

Housman, Laurence, **V:** 402, 420

Housman: 1897–1936 (Richards), **VI:** 164

How About Europe? (Douglas), **VI:** 295, 305

"How Are the Children Robin" (Graham), **Supp. VII:** 115

How Brophy Made Good (Hare), **Supp. IV:** 281

How Can We Know? (Wilson), **Supp. VI:** 305

"How Distant" (Larkin), **Supp. I:** 284

"How Do You See" (Smith), **Supp. II:** 467

How Far Can You Go? (Lodge; U.S. title, *Souls and Bodies*), **Supp. IV:** 366, 368, 371, 372, 375–376, 381, 408

How He Lied to Her Husband (Shaw), **VI:** 129

How I Became a Holy Mother and Other Stories (Jhabvala), **Supp. V:** 235

"How I Became a Socialist" (Orwell), **VII:** 276–277

How It Is (Beckett), **Supp. I:** 43, 50, 52, 54–55, 58

"How It Strikes a Contemporary" (Browning), **IV:** 354, 367, 373

How Late It Was, How Late (Kelman), **Supp. V:** 243, 252–254

How Lisa Loved the King (Eliot), **V:** 200

"How Many Bards" (Keats), **IV:** 215

"How Pillingshot Scored" (Wodehouse), **Supp. III:** 449–450

How Right You Are, Jeeves (Wodehouse), **Supp. III:** 460, 461, 462

"How Sleep the Brave" (Collins), **III:** 166

"How soon the servant sun" (Thomas), **Supp. I:** 174

"How Sweet the Name of Jesus Sounds" (Newton), **III:** 210

How the "Mastiffs" Went to Iceland (Trollope), **V:** 102

How the Other Half Lives (Ayckbourn), **Supp. V:** 2, 4, 9, 11, 12

How the Whale Became (Hughes), **Supp. I:** 346

"How They Brought the Good News from Ghent to Aix (16—)" (Browning), **IV:** 356, 361

How this foirsaid Tod maid his Confession to Freir Wolf Waitskaith (Henryson), see *Fox and the Wolf, The*

"How to Accomplish It" (Newman), **Supp. VII:** 293

How to Become an Author (Bennett), **VI:** 264

"How to Kill" (Douglas), **VII: 443**

How to Live on 24 Hours a Day (Bennett), **VI:** 264

How to Read (Pound), **VII:** 235

How to Read a Page (Richards), **Supp. II:** 426

How to Settle the Irish Question (Shaw), **VI:** 119, 129

"How to Teach Reading" (Leavis), **VII:** 235, 248

"How would the ogling sparks despise" (Etherege), **II:** 268

Howard, Henry, earl of Surrey, *see* Surrey, Henry Howard, earl of

Howard, R., **V:** 418

Howard, Sir Robert, **II:** 100

Howards End (Forster), **VI:** viii, xii, 397, 398, 401, **404–406,** 407; **Supp. I:** 161; **Retro. Supp. II:** 143–145

Howarth, R. G., **II:** 69

Howe, Irving, **VI:** 41

Howells, William Dean, **VI:** 23, 29, 33

Howitt, William, **IV:** 212

Hubert De Vere (Burney), **Supp. III:** 71

Huchon, René, **III:** 273n

Hudibras (Butler), **II:** 145

Hudson, Derek, **V:** xi, xxviii, 263, 274

Hudson, W. H., **V:** 429

Hudson Letter, The (Mahon), **Supp. VI:** 175–176

Hueffer, Ford Madox, *see* Ford, Ford Madox

"Hug, The" (Gunn), **Supp. IV:** 274–275, 276, 277

Huggan, Graham, **Supp. IV:** 170

Hugh Selwyn Mauberley (Pound), **VI:** 417; **VII:** xvi

Hughes, Arthur, **V:** 294

Hughes, John, **I:** 121, 122; **III:** 40

Hughes, Ted, **Supp. I: 341–366; Supp. IV:** 257; **Supp. V:** xxx; **Retro. Supp. I:** 126; **Retro. Supp. II: 199–219**

Hughes, Thomas, **I:** 218; **V:** xxii, 170; **Supp. IV:** 506

Hughes, Willie, **V:** 405

Hugo, Victor, **III:** 334; **V:** xxii, xxv, 22, 320; **Supp. IV:** 86

Hugo (Bennett), **VI:** 249

Huis clos (Sartre), **Supp. IV:** 39

Hulme, T. E., **VI:** 416; **Supp. VI: 133–147**

Hulse, Michael, **Supp. IV:** 354

"Human Abstract, The" (Blake), **III:** 296

Human Age, The (Lewis), **VII:** 80

Human Factor, The (Greene), **Supp. I:** 2, 11, 16–17; **Retro. Supp. II:** 165–166

"Human Life, on the Denial of Immortality" (Coleridge), **Retro. Supp. II:** 65

Human Machine, The (Bennett), **VI:** 250

Human Odds and Ends (Gissing), **V:** 437

"Human Seasons, The" (Keats), **IV:** 232

Human Shows, Far Phantasies, Songs and Trifles (Hardy), **VI:** 20

Human Voices (Fitzgerald), **Supp. V:** 95, 100, 103

"Humanism and the Religious Attitude" (Hulme), **Supp. VI:** 135, 140

"Humanitad" (Wilde), **V:** 401–402

"Humble Petition of Frances Harris" (Swift), **III:** 30–31

Humboldt's Gift (Bellow), **Supp. IV:** 27, 33, 42

Hume, David, **III:** 148; **IV:** xiv, 138, 145, 273, 288; **V:** 288, 343; **Supp. III: 220–245**

Humorous Day's Mirth, A (Chapman), **I:** 243, 244

Humorous Lieutenant, The (Fletcher), **II:** 45, 60–61, 65, 359

Humours of the Court (Bridges), **VI:** 83

Humphrey Clinker (Smollett), **III:** 147, 150, **155–157,** 158

"Hunchback in the Park, The" (Thomas), **Supp. I:** 177, 178

"Hundred Years, A" (Motion), **Supp. VII:** 266

"Hunger" (Lessing), **Supp. I:** 240

Hungry Hill (du Maurier), **Supp. III:** 144

Hunt, John, **IV:** 129, 132

Hunt, Leigh, **II:** 332, 355, 357, 359, 363; **IV:** ix, 80, 104, 129, 132, 163, 172, 198, 202, 205–206, 209, 212–217, 230, 306; **Retro. Supp. I:** 183, 248

Hunt, Violet, **VI:** 324

Hunt, William Holman, **V:** 45, 77–78, 235, 236, 240

Hunt by Night, The (Mahon), **Supp. VI:** 173–174, 177

"Hunt by Night, The" (Mahon), **Supp. VI:** 174

Hunted Down (Dickens), **VI:** 66, 72

Hunter, G. K., **I:** 165; **II:** 29, 41

Hunting of Cupid, The (Peele), **I:** 205

Hunting of the Snark, The (Carroll), **V:** 270, 272, 273

Hunting Sketches (Trollope), **V:** 101

Huntley, F. L, **II:** 152, 157

"Huntsman, The" (Lowbury), **VII:** 431–432

Hurd, Michael, **VI:** 427

Hurd, Richard, **I:** 122

"Hurrahing in Harvest" (Hopkins), **V:** 366, 367, 368

"Husband and Wife" (Rossetti), **V:** 259

Husband His Own Cuckold, The (Dryden the younger), **II:** 305

Husband's Message, The, **Retro. Supp. II:** 305

Hussey, Maurice, **II:** 250, 254

Hutcheon, Linda, **Supp. IV:** 162

Hutchinson, F. E., **II:** 121, 123, 126, 129

Hutchinson, Sara, **IV:** 15, 49, 50, 54

Hutton, James, **IV:** 200

Hutton, R. H., **V:** 157–158, 168, 170

Huxley, Aldous, **II:** 105, 173; **III:** 341; **IV:** 303; **V:** xxii, 53; **VII:** xii, xvii–xviii, 79, **197–208; Retro. Supp. II:** 182

Huxley, Thomas, **V:** xxii, 182, 284

Hyacinth Halvey (Gregory), **VI:** 315, 316

Hyde, Douglas, **VI:** 307; **VII:** 1

Hyde–Lees, George, **VI:** 213

Hydriotaphia (Browne), **II: 150–153,** 154, 155, 156

Hygiasticon (Lessius), **II:** 181n

Hymenaei (Jonson), **I:** 239

"Hymn before Sun-rise, in the Vale of Chamouni" (Coleridge), **Retro. Supp. II:** 59–60

"Hymn of Apollo" (Shelley), **II:** 200; **IV:** 203

Hymn of Nature, A (Bridges), **VI:** 81

"Hymn to Adversity" (Gray), **III:** 137

Hymn to Christ on the Cross (Chapman), **I:** 241–242

"Hymn to Colour" (Meredith), **V:** 222

Hymn to Diana (Jonson), **I:** 346; **Retro. Supp. I:** 162

"Hymn to God, my God, in my sickness" (Donne), **I:** 368; **II:** 114

Hymn to Harmony, A (Congreve), **II:** 350

"Hymn to Intellectual Beauty" (Shelley), **IV:** 198

"Hymn. To Light" (Cowley), **II:** 198, 200, 259

"Hymn to Mercury" (Shelley), **IV:** 196, 204

"Hymn to Pan" (Keats), **IV:** 216, 217, 222

"Hymn to Proust" (Ewart), **Supp. VII:** 38

"Hymn to the Name and Honor of the Admirable Sainte Teresa, A" (Crashaw), **II:** 179, 182

Hymn to the Pillory, A (Defoe), **III:** 13; **Retro. Supp. I:** 65, 67–68

"Hymn to the Sun" (Hood), **IV:** 255

"Hymn to the Winds" (du Bellay), **V:** 345

"Hymn to Venus" (Shelley), **IV:** 209

"Hymne of the Nativity, A" (Crashaw), **II:** 180, 183

"Hymne to God the Father, A" (Donne), **Retro. Supp. II:** 98

Hymns (Spenser), **I:** 131

Hymns Ancient and Modern (Betjeman), **VII:** 363–364

Hymnus in Cynthiam (Chapman), **I:** 240

Hyperion (Keats), **IV:** 95, 204, 211, 212, 213, **227–231,** 235; **VI:** 455; **Retro. Supp. I:** 194

Hypnerstomachia (Colonna), **I:** 134

Hypochondriack, The (Boswell), **III:** 237, 240, 243, 248

"Hypogram and Inscription" (de Man), **Supp. IV:** 115

Hysterical Disorders of Warfare (Yealland), **Supp. IV:** 58

"I abide and abide and better abide" (Wyatt), **I:** 108, 109

I Am a Camera (Isherwood), **VII:** 311

I Am Lazarus: Short Stories (Kavan), **Supp. VII:** 210–211

"I am Raftery" (Mahon), **Supp. VI:** 170

"I Bring Her a Flower" (Warner), **Supp. VII:** 371

I Can Remember Robert Louis Stevenson (ed. Masson), **V:** 393, 397

"I care not if I live" (Bridges), **VI:** 81

I, Claudius (Graves), **VII:** 259

I Crossed the Minch (MacNeice), **VII:** 403, 411

"I dined with a Jew" (Macaulay), **IV:** 283

"I Do, You Do" (Motion), **Supp. VII:** 260

"I find no peace and all my war is done" (Wyatt), **I:** 110

"I go night–shopping like Frank O'Hara I go bopping" (Mahon), **Supp. VI:** 175

"I Have Been Taught" (Muir), **Supp. VI:** 208

"I have longed to move away" (Thomas), **Supp. I:** 174

"I have loved and so doth she" (Wyatt), **I:** 102

"I heard an Angel singing" (Blake), **III:** 296

"I, in my intricate image" (Thomas), **Supp. I:** 174

I Knock at the Door (O'Casey), **VII:** 12

"I know a Bank Whereon the Wild Thyme Grows" (Shakespeare), **IV:** 222

"I lead a life unpleasant"(Wyatt), **I:** 104

I Like It Here (Amis), **Supp. II:** 8–10, 12

I Live under a Black Sun (Sitwell), **VII:** 127, 135, 139

"I Look into My Glass" (Hardy), **VI:** 16

I Lost My Memory, The Case As the Patient Saw It (Anon.), **Supp. IV:** 5

"I love all beauteous things" (Bridges), **VI:** 72

"I never shall love the snow again" (Bridges), **VI:** 77

I promessi sposi (Manzoni), **III:** 334

"I Remember" (Hood), **IV:** 255

"I Remember, I Remember" (Larkin), **Supp. I:** 275, 277

"I Say No" (Collins), **Supp. VI:** 93, 103

"I see the boys of summer" (Thomas), **Supp. I:** 173

"I Stood Tip–toe" (Keats), **IV:** 214, 216

"I strove with none" (Landor), **IV:** 98

"I took my heart in my hand" (Rossetti), **V:** 252

"I wake and feel the fell of dark" (Hopkins), **V:** 374*n*, 375

"I Wandered Lonely as a Cloud" (Wordsworth), **IV:** 22

I Want It Now (Amis), **Supp. II:** 15

"I Will Lend You Malcolm" (Graham), **Supp. VII:** 116

"I will not let thee go" (Bridges), **VI:** 74, 77

I Will Pray with the Spirit (Bunyan), **II:** 253

"I will write" (Graves), **VII:** 269

"I would be a bird" (Bridges), **VI:** 81–82

Ian Hamilton's March (Churchill), **VI:** 351

"Ianthe"poems (Landor), **IV:** 88, 89, 92, 99

Ibrahim (Scudéry), **III:** 95

Ibsen, Henrik, **IV:** 118; **V:** xxiii–xxvi, 414; **VI:** viii–ix, 104, 110, 269; **Supp. III:** 4, 12; **Supp. IV:** 1, 286; **Retro. Supp. I:** 170; **Retro. Supp. II:** 309

Ibsen's Ghost; or, Toole Up to Date (Barrie), **Supp. III:** 4, 9

Ice (Kavan), **Supp. VII:** 201, 208, 214–215

Ice Age, The (Drabble), **Supp. IV:** 230, 245–246, 247

Ice in the Bedroom (Wodehouse), **Supp. III:** 460

Icelandic journals (Morris), **V:** 299, 300–301, 307

"Icy Road" (MacCaig), **Supp. VI:** 188–189

Idea of a University, The (Newman), **Supp. VII:** 294, 296, 298–299

Idea of Christian Society, The (Eliot), **VII:** 153

Idea of Comedy, The, and the Uses of the Comic Spirit (Meredith), *see Essay on Comedy and the Uses of the Comic Spirit*

"Idea of Entropy at Maenporth Beach, The" (Redgrove), **Supp. VI: 233–234,** 237

"Idea of Perfection, The" (Murdoch), **Supp. I:** 217, 220

Idea of the Perfection of Painting, An (tr. Evelyn), **II:** 287

Ideal Husband, An (Wilde), **V:** 414–415, 419

Ideals in Ireland (ed. Lady Gregory), **VI:** 98

Ideas and Places (Connolly), **Supp. III:** 110

Ideas of Good and Evil (Yeats), **V:** 301, 306

"Idenborough" (Warner), **Supp. VII:** 380

Identical Twins (Churchill), **Supp. IV:** 181

"Identities" (Muldoon), **Supp. IV:** 414, 424

"Ides of March, The" (Fuller), **Supp. VII:** 73

Idiocy of Idealism, The (Levy), **VI:** 303

"Idiot Boy, The" (Wordsworth), **IV:** 7, 11

"Idiots, The" (Conrad), **VI:** 148

Idleness of Business, The, A Satyr . . . (Wycherley), *see Folly of Industry, The*

Idler (periodical), **III:** 111–112, 121; **Retro. Supp. I:** 145

Idol Hunter, The (Unsworth) see *Pascali's Island*

Idyllia heroica decem (Landor), **IV:** 100

"Idylls of the King" (Hill), **Supp. V:** 191

Idylls of the King (Tennyson), **IV:** xxii, 328, 336–337, 338

"If by Dull Rhymes Our English Must be Chained . . ." (Keats), **IV:** 221

"If I Could Tell You" (Auden), **Retro. Supp. I:** 10

If I Were Four and Twenty: Swedenborg, Mediums and Desolate Places (Yeats), **VI:** 222

"If I were tickled by the rub of lover" (Thomas), **Supp. I:** 172

"If in the world there be more woes"(Wyatt), **I:** 104

"If, My Darling" (Larkin), **Supp. I:** 277, 285

"If my head hurt a hair's foot" (Thomas), **Supp. I:** 176–177

If the Old Could . . . (Lessing), **Supp. I:** 253, 254

"If This Were Faith" (Stevenson), **V:** 385

If You're Glad I'll Be Frank (Stoppard), **Supp. I:** 439, 445

Ignatius His Conclave (Donne), **Retro. Supp. I:** 95

"Ikey" (Brown), **Supp. VI:** 68

Ikons, The (Durrell), **Supp. I:** 121

"Il Conde" (Conrad), **VI: 148**

Il cortegiano (Castiglione), **I:** 265

Il Filostrato (Boccaccio), **Retro. Supp. II:** 40–42

Il pastor fido (Guarini), **II:** 49–50

Il pecorone (Fiorentino), **I:** 310

"Il Penseroso" (Milton), **II:** 158–159; **III:** 211*n*; **IV:** 14–15

Ilex Tree, The (Murray), **Supp. VII:** 270, 271–272

Iliad, The (tr. Cowper), **III:** 220

Iliad, The (tr. Pope), **III:** 77

Ill Beginning Has a Good End, An, and a Bad Beginning May Have a Good End (Ford), **II:** 89, 100

"I'll come when thou art saddest" (Brontë), **V:** 127

I'll Leave It To You (Coward), **Supp. II:** 141

I'll Never Be Young Again (du Maurier), **Supp. III:** 139–140, 144

Ill Seen Ill Said (Beckett), **Retro. Supp. I:** 29

I'll Stand by You (Warner), **Supp. VII:** 370, 382

"Illiterations" (Brooke–Rose), **Supp. IV:** 97

"Illuminated Man, The" (Ballard), **Supp. V:** 24

Illusion and Reality (Caudwell), **Supp. III:** 120

"Illusions of Anti–Realism" (Brooke–Rose), **Supp. IV:** 116

Illustrated Excursions in Italy (Lear), **V:** 77, 79, 87

Illustrated London News (periodical), **VI:** 337

Illustrations of Latin Lyrical Metres (Clough), **V:** 170

Illustrations of the Family of Psittacidae, or Parrots (Lear), **V:** 76, 79, 87

I'm Dying Laughing (Stead), **Supp. IV:** 473, 476

"I'm happiest when most away" (Brontë), **V:** 116

"Image, The" (Day Lewis), **Supp. III:** 115–116

"Image, The" (Fuller), **Supp. VII:** 73

"Image, The" (Warner), **Supp. VII:** 371

"Image from Beckett, An" (Mahon), **Supp. VI:** 169, 172

Image Men, The (Priestley), **VII:** 209, 210, 218, 221–223

Image of a Society (Fuller), **Supp. VII:** 68, 74–75

"Images" (Fuller), **Supp. VII:** 80

Imaginary Conversations (Landor), **IV:** xviii, 87, 88, 89, **90–94,** 96–97, 99, 100

Imaginary Conversations of Greeks and Romans (Landor), **IV:** 100

Imaginary Homelands: Essays and Criticism (Rushdie), **Supp. IV:** 171, 434

Imaginary Love Affair, An (Ewart), **Supp. VII:** 41

Imaginary Portraits (Pater), **V:** 339, 340, 348–349, 355, 356

Imagination Dead Imagine (Beckett), **Supp. I:** 53, 61; **Retro. Supp. I:** 29

Imagination in the Modern World, The (Spender), **Supp. II:** 492

"Imaginative Woman, An" (Hardy), **VI:** 22

Imaginings of Sand (Brink), **Supp. VI:** 57

Imitation Game, The (McEwan), **Supp. IV:** 390, 398–399

"Imitation of Spenser" (Keats), **IV:** 213; **Retro. Supp. I:** 187

Imitations of English Poets (Pope), **Retro. Supp. I:** 231–232

Imitation of the Sixth Satire of the Second Book of Horace, An (Swift), **III:** 36

Imitations of Horace (Pope), **II:** 298; **III:** 77; **Retro. Supp. I:** 230, 235–238

Immaturity (Shaw), **VI:** 105

Immorality and Profaneness of the English Stage, A (Collier), *see Short View of the Immorality . . . , A*

Immorality, Debauchery and Prophaneness (Meriton), **II:** 340

Immortal Dickens, The (Gissing), **V:** 437

"Immortals, The" (Amis), **Supp. IV:** 40

"Immram" (Muldoon), **Supp. IV:** 415–418, 420, 421, 425

"Impercipient, The" (Hardy), **Retro. Supp. I:** 121

"Imperial Adam" (Hope), **Supp. VII:** 158

"Imperial Elegy, An" (Owen), **VI:** 448

Imperial Palace (Bennett), **VI:** xiii, 247, 250, 251, 262–263

Implements in Their Places (Graham), **Supp. VII:** 103, 115–116

Importance of Being Earnest, The (Wilde), **V:** xxvi, 415, 416, 419; **Supp. II:** 50, 143, 148; **Retro. Supp. II:** 350, 370, 314–315

"Importance of Glasgow in My Work, The" (Kelman), **Supp. V:** 257

Importance of the Guardian Considered, The (Swift), **III:** 35

Impossible Thing, An: A Tale (Congreve), **II:** 350

Impressions and Opinions (Moore), **VI:** 87

Impressions of America (Wilde), **V:** 419

Impressions of Theophrastus Such (Eliot), **V:** 198, 200

Imprisonment (Shaw), **VI:** 129

"Improvisation" (Gunn), **Supp. IV:** 276

In a Free State (Naipaul), **VII:** xx; **Supp. I:** 383, 390, 393, **394–396,** 397

"In a Free State"(Naipaul), **Supp. I:** 395, 396

In a German Pension (Mansfield), **VII:** 171, 172–173

In a Glass Darkly (Le Fanu), **III:** 345

"In a Shaken House" (Warner), **Supp. VII:** 380

In a Time of Violence (Boland), **Supp. V:** 43

"In an Artist's Studio" (Rossetti), **V:** 249

"In Another Country" (Ewart), **Supp. VII:** 45

In Between the Sheets (McEwan), **Supp. IV:** 390, 394–396

"In Broken Images"(Graves), **VII:** 267

"In California" (Davie), **Supp. VI:** 109

"In Carrowdore Churchyard" (Mahon), **Supp. VI:** 167–168

In Celebration (Storey), **Supp. I:** 408, 411, 412, 413–414

In Chancery (Galsworthy), **VI:** 274

In Custody (Desai), **Supp. V:** 53, 55, 65, 68, 69–71

"In Deep and Solemn Dreams" (Tennyson), **IV:** 329

"In Defence of Milton" (Leavis), **VII:** 246

"In Defense of Astigmatism" (Wodehouse), **Supp. III:** 454

"In Defense of the Novel, Yet Again" (Rushdie), **Supp. IV:** 455

"In dungeons dark I cannot sing"(Brontë), **V:** 115–116

In Excited Reverie: A Centenary Tribute to William Butler Yeats, 1865–1939 (ed. Jeffares and Cross), **VI:** 224

"In Flanders Fields" (McCrae), **VI:** 434

"In God We Trust" (Rushdie), **Supp. IV:** 434, 456

"In Good Faith" (Rushdie), **Supp. IV:** 437, 450

In Good King Charles's Golden Days (Shaw), **VI:** 125, 127, 129

In Her Own Image (Boland), **Supp. V:** 48

"In Her Own Image" (Boland), **Supp. V:** 48, 49

"In His Own Image" (Boland), **Supp. V:** 48–49

"In Lambeth Palace Road" (Fuller), **Supp. VII:** 76

"In Love for Long" (Muir), **Supp. VI:** 206–207

"In Me Two Worlds" (Day Lewis), **Supp. III:** 126

In Memoriam (Tennyson), **IV:** xxi, 234, 248, 292, 310, 313, 323, 325–328, 330, 333–338, 371; **V:** 285, 455

"In Memoriam, Amada" (Reid), **Supp. VII:** 333

"In Memoriam (Easter, 1915)" (Thomas), **VI:** 424–425; **Supp. III:** 403, 404

"In Memory of Ernst Toller" (Auden), **Retro. Supp. I:** 9

"In Memory of Eva Gore–Booth and Con Markiewicz" (Yeats), **VI:** 217

"In Memory of Major Robert Gregory" (Yeats), **Retro. Supp. I:** 331

"In Memory of my Cat, Domino" (Fuller), **Supp. VII:** 77

"In Memory of My Mother" (Kavanagh), **Supp. VII:** 198

"In Memory of Sigmund Freud" (Auden), **VII:** 379; **Retro. Supp. I:** 1

"In Memory of W. B. Yeats" (Auden), **VI:** 208; **Retro. Supp. I:** 1, 9

"In Memory of Zoe Yalland" (Motion), **Supp. VII:** 264

"In my craft or sullen art"(Thomas), **Supp. I:** 178

"In My Dreams" (Smith), **Supp. II:** 466

In My Good Books (Pritchett), **Supp. III:** 313

"In My Own Album" (Lamb), **IV:** 83

In Our Infancy (Corke), **VII:** 93

In Our Time (Hemingway), **Supp. IV:** 163

In Parenthesis (Jones), **VI:** xvi, 437–438, **Supp. VII:** 167, 168, 169, 170, 171–175, 177

In Patagonia (Chatwin), **Supp. IV:** 157, 159, 161, 163–165, 173

"In Praise of Lessius His Rule of Health" (Crashaw), **II:** 181n

"In Praise of Limestone"(Auden), **VII:** 390, 391; **Retro. Supp. I:** 12

In Praise of Love (Rattigan), **Supp. VII:** 320–321

"In Procession" (Graves), **VII:** 264

In Pursuit of the English (Lessing), **Supp. I:** 237–238

"In Santa Maria del Popolo" (Gunn), **Supp. IV:** 262

In Search of Love and Beauty (Jhabvala), **Supp. V:** 223, 233

"In Sickness and in Health" (Auden), **Retro. Supp. I:** 10

In Single Strictness (Moore), **VI:** 87, 95, 99

"In Such a Poise Is Love" (Reid), **Supp. VII:** 328–329

"In Tenebris II" (Hardy), **VI:** 14

In the Beginning (Douglas), **VI:** 303, 304, 305

In the Cage (James), **VI:** 67, 69

"In the City of Red Dust" (Okri), **Supp. V:** 352

In the Country of the Skin (Redgrove), **Supp. VI: 230**

In the Days of the Comet (Wells), **VI:** 227, 237, 244

"In the Garden at Swainston" (Tennyson), **IV:** 336

"In the Great Metropolis" (Clough), **V:** 164

In the Green Tree (Lewis), **VII:** 447

In the Heart of the Country (Coetzee), **Supp. VI:** 76, **80–81**

"In the House of Suddhoo" (Kipling), **VI:** 170

In the Labyrinth (Robbe–Grillet), **Supp. IV:** 116

In the Meantime (Jennings), **Supp. V:** 219

In the Night (Kelman), **Supp. V:** 256

"In the Night" (Jennings), **Supp. V:** 211–212

"In the Night" (Kincaid), **Supp. VII:** 220

"In the Nursery" (Stevenson), **Supp. VI:** 264

"In the Ringwood" (Kinsella), **Supp. V:** 260

"In the rude age when science was not so rife" (Surrey), **I:** 115–116

"In the Same Boat" (Kipling), **VI:** 193

In the Scales of Fate (Pietrkiewicz), **Supp. IV:** 98

In the Seven Woods (Yeats), **VI:** 213, 222

In the Shadow of the Glen (Synge), **Retro. Supp. I:** 295–296

In the South Seas (Stevenson), **V:** 396

In the Stopping Train (Davie), **Supp. VI:** 112

"In the Stopping Train" (Davie), **Supp. VI:** 112

In the Twilight (Swinburne), **V:** 333

"In the Vermilion Cathedral" (Redgrove), **Supp. VI:** 234

In the Year of Jubilee (Gissing), **V:** 437

"In This Time" (Jennings), **Supp. V:** 214

"In Time of Absence" (Graves), **VII:** 270

"In Time of 'The Breaking of Nations'" (Hardy), **Retro. Supp. I:** 120

"In Time of War" (Auden), **Retro. Supp. I:** 9

In Touch with the Infinite (Betjeman), **VII:** 365

In Which We Serve (Coward), **Supp. II:** 154

In Wicklow, West Kerry, and Connemara (Synge), **VI:** 309, 317

Inadmissible Evidence (Osborne), **Supp. I:** 330, 333, 336–337

"Inarticulates" (MacCaig), **Supp. VI:** 191

Inca of Perusalem, The (Shaw), **VI:** 120

"Incarnate One, The" (Muir), **Supp. VI:** 208

"Incantata" (Muldoon), **Supp. IV:** 428–429, 430, 431–432

"Incendiary Method, The" (Murray), **Supp. VII:** 273

"Inchcape Rock, The" (Southey), **IV:** 58

"Incident in the Life of Mr. George Crookhill" (Hardy), **VI:** 22

"Incident on a Journey" (Gunn), **Supp. IV:** 256, 258–259

Incidents at the Shrine (Okri), **Supp. V:** 347, 348, 352, 355–356

"Incidents at the Shrine" (Okri), **Supp. V:** 356–357

Incidents in the Rue Laugier (Brookner), **Supp. IV:** 135–136

Inclinations (Firbank), **Supp. II:** 201, 202, 209–211

Inclinations (Sackville–West), **VII:** 70

Incline Our Hearts (Wilson), **Supp. VI:** 307

Incognita; or, Love and Duty Reconcil'd (Congreve), **II:** 338, 346

Inconstant, The; or, The Way to Win Him (Farquhar), **II:** 352–353, 357, 362, 364

Incredulity of Father Brown, The (Chesterton), **VI:** 338

"Incubus, or the Impossibility of Self-Determination as to Desire (Self), **Supp. V:** 402

"Indaba Without Fear" (Paton), **Supp. II:** 360

"Independence" (Motion), **Supp. VII:** 255

Independent Labour Party, **VII:** 280

Independent Review (periodical), **VI:** 399

Independent Theatre Society, **VI:** 104

Index to AIn Memoriam,"An (ed. Carroll), **V:** 274

Index to the Private Papers of James Boswell . . . (ed. Pottle et al.), **III:** 249

India: A Wounded Civilization (Naipaul), **Supp. I:** 385, 399, 401

Indian Education Minutes . . . , The (Macaulay), **IV:** 291

Indian Emperour, The; or, The Conquest of Mexico . . . , Being the Sequel to the Indian Queen (Dryden), **II:** 290, 294, 305

"Indian Fiction Today" (Desai), **Supp. V:** 67

Indian Ink (Stoppard), **Retro. Supp. II:** 356–357

Indian Journal (Lear), *see Edward Lear's Indian Journal*

Indian Queen, The (Dryden), **II:** 305

"Indian Serenade, The" (Shelley), **IV:** 195, 203

"Indian Summer of a Forsyte" (Galsworthy), **VI:** 274, 276, 283

"Indian Summer, Vermont" (Stevenson), **Supp. VI:** 255

"Indifferent, The" (Donne), **Retro. Supp. II:** 89

Indiscretion in the Life of an Heiress, An (Hardy), **VI:** 20

"Induction" (Sackville), **I:** 169

Induction, The (Field), **II:** 66

Inebriety (Crabbe), **III:** 274, 278–279, 286

"Infancy" (Crabbe), **III:** 273, 281

"Inferior Religions" (Lewis), **VII:** 77

Infernal Desire Machine of Dr. Hoffman, The (Carter), **III:** 345; **Supp. III:** 84–85, 89

Infernal Marriage, The (Disraeli), **IV:** 297, 299, 308

Infernal World of Branwell Brontë, The (Carter), **Supp. III:** 139

Inferno (Dante), **Retro. Supp. II:** 36

Infinite Rehearsal, The (Harris), **Supp. V:** 140, 141–142, 144

Information, The (Amis), **Supp. IV:** 26, 37–39, 42

"Informer, The" (Conrad), **VI:** 148

Infuence of the Roman Censorship on the Morals of the People, The (Swinburne), **V:** 333

Ingannati: The Deceived . . . and Aelia Laelia Crispis (Peacock), **IV:** 170

Inge, William Ralph, **VI:** 344

Ingelow, Jean, **Supp. IV:** 256

"Inheritance" (Murphy), **Supp. V:** 322

Inheritors, The (Golding), **Supp. I:** 67, **70–72,** 75, 84; **Retro. Supp. I:** 96–97

Inheritors, The: An Extravagant Story (Conrad and Ford), **VI:** 146, 148, 321, 332

Inishfallen, Fare Thee Well (O'Casey), **VII:** 4, 12

Injury Time (Bainbridge), **Supp. VI:** 21

"Inland" (Motion), **Supp. VII:** 254, 255

Inland Voyage, An (Stevenson), **V:** 386, 395; **Retro. Supp. I:** 261

Inn Album, The (Browning), **IV:** 358, 367, 369–370, 374; **Retro. Supp. II:** 30

"Inn of the Two Witches, The" (Conrad), **VI:** 148

"Inniskeen Road: July Evening" (Kavanagh), **Supp. VII:** 188

Innocence (Fitzgerald), **Supp. V:** 100, 104–106

"Innocence" (Gunn), **Supp. IV:** 262

Innocence of Father Brown, The (Chesterton), **VI:** 338

Innocent, The (McEwan), **Supp. IV:** 390, 399, 402–404, 405, 406

Innocent and the Guilty, The (Warner), **Supp. VII:** 381

Innocent Blood (James), **Supp. IV:** 337–338, 340

Inquiry into the Nature & Causes of the Wealth of Nations (Smith), **IV:** xiv, 145

Insatiate Countess, The (Barsted and Marston), **II:** 31, 40

"Insect World, The" (Rhys), **Supp. II:** 402

"Insensibility" (Owen), **VI:** 453, 455

Inside a Pyramid (Golding), **Supp. I:** 82

Inside Mr Enderby (Burgess), **Supp. I:** 185, 186, 189, 194

Inside the Whale (Orwell), **VII:** 282

"Inside the Whale" (Orwell), **Supp. IV:** 110, 455

Insight and Outlook: An Enquiry into the Common Foundations of Science, Art and Social Ethics (Koestler), **Supp. I:** 37

"Insight at Flame Lake" (Amis), **Supp. IV:** 40

"Installation Ode" (Gray), **III:** 142

"Instance, An" (Reid), **Supp. VII:** 328

"Instant, The" (Redgrove), **Supp. VI:** 231

Instant in the Wind, An (Brink), **Supp. VI:** 49

Instead of Trees (Priestley), **VII:** 209–210

Instructions Concerning Erecting of a Liberty (tr. Evelyn), **II:** 287

Instructions for the Ignorant (Bunyan), **II:** 253

"Instructions to a Painter . . . A (Waller), **II:** 233

Instrument of Thy Peace (Paton), **Supp. II: 358–359**

Inteendeel (Brink), **Supp. VI:** 56

"Intellectual Felicity" (Boswell), **III:** 237

Intelligence (journal), **III:** 35

Intelligent Woman's Guide to Socialism and Capitalism, The (Shaw), **VI:** 116, 125

"Intensive Care Unit, The" (Ballard), **Supp. V:** 28

Intentions (Wilde), **V:** 407, 419; **Retro. Supp. II:** 367–368

Intercom Conspiracy, The (Ambler), **Supp. IV:** 4, 16, 18, 20–21

"Intercom Quartet, The" (Brooke–Rose), **Supp. IV:** 110–113
"Interference" (Barnes), **Supp. IV:** 75
"Interior Mountaineer" (Redgrove), **Supp. VI:** 236
"Interloper, The" (Hardy), **VI:** 17
"Interlopers at the Knapp" (Hardy), **VI:** 22
"Interlude, An" (Swinburne), **V:** 321
"Intermediate Sex, The" (Carpenter), **VI:** 407
"Intermezzo" (Kinsella), **Supp. V:** 271
"International Episode, An" (James), **VI:** 69
International Guerrillas (film), **Supp. IV:** 438
internationalism, **VI:** 241n; **VII:** 229
Interpretation in Teaching (Richards), **Supp. II:** 423, 430
"Interrogator, The" (Jennings), **Supp. V:** 215
"Interruption" (Gunn), **Supp. IV:** 273, 274
Interview, The (Sillitoe), **Supp. V:** 411
Intimate Exchanges (Ayckbourn), **Supp. V:** 3, 6, 12, 14
"Intimate Supper" (Redgrove), **Supp. VI:** 234
"Intimate World of Ivy Compton–Burnett, The" (Karl), **VII:** 70
"Intimations of Immortality . . . A (Wordsworth), *see* AOde. Intimations of Immortality from Recollections of Early Childhood"
"Into Arcadia" (Heaney), **Retro. Supp. I:** 134
Into Battle (Churchill), **VI:** 356
"Into Battle" (Grenfell), **VI:** 418
"Into her Lying Down Head" (Thomas), **Supp. I:** 178
Into Their Labours (Berger), **Supp. IV:** 80, 90–95
Intriguing Chambermaid, The (Fielding), **III:** 105
"Introduction" (Blake), **Retro. Supp. I:** 37
Introduction 7: Stories by New Writers (Faber & Faber), **Supp. IV:** 303
Introductory Lecture (Housman), **VI:** 164
"Introductory Rhymes" (Yeats), **Retro. Supp. I:** 330
Intruder, The (Hardy), **VI:** 20
Invasion of the Space Invaders (Amis), **Supp. IV:** 42
Invective against Jonson, The (Chapman), **I:** 243
Invention of Love, The (Stoppard), **Retro. Supp. II:** 357–358
"Inversnaid" (Hopkins), **V:** 368, 372
Invisible Friends (Ayckbourn), **Supp. V:** 3, 12, 14–15
Invisible Man, The: A Grotesque Romance (Wells), **VI:** 226, 232–233, 244
Invisible Writing, The (Koestler), **Supp. I:** 22, 23, 24, 32, 37
"Invitation, The" (Shelley), **IV:** 196
"Invocation" (Hope), **Supp. VII:** 154
"Invocation" (Sitwell), **VII:** 136
"Inward Bound" (MacCaig), **Supp. VI:** 192

Inward Eye, The (MacCaig), **Supp. VI:** 184–185
Ion (Plato), **IV:** 48
"Iowa" (Davie), **Supp. VI:** 110
Iphigenia (Peele), **I:** 198
"Iphis and Araxarathen" (Gower), **I:** 53–54
Iqbal, Muhammad, **Supp. IV:** 448
"Ireland" (Swift), **III:** 31
Ireland Since the Rising (Coogan), **VII:** 9
Ireland's Abbey Theatre (Robinson), **VI:** 317
Ireland's Literary Renaissance (Boyd), **VI:** 316
Irene: A Tragedy (Fielding), **III:** 109, 121
Irene: A Tragedy (Johnson), **Retro. Supp. I:** 138–139
Irigaray, Luce, **Supp. IV:** 232
"Irish Airman Foresees His Death, An" (Yeats), **Retro. Supp. I:** 331
"Irish Child in England" (Boland), **Supp. V:** 35
Irish Drama, The (Malone), **VI:** 316
Irish Dramatic Movement, The (Ellis–Fermor), **VI:** 317
Irish dramatic revival, **VI:** xiv, 207, 218, 307–310; **VII:** 3
Irish Essays and Others (Arnold), **V:** 216
Irish Faust, An (Durrell), **Supp. I:** 126, 127
Irish Impressions (Chesterton), **VI:** 345
"Irish Revel" (O'Brien), **Supp. V:** 340
Irish Sketch Book, The (Thackeray), **V:** 25, 38
Iron, Ralph (pseud., Schreiner), **Supp. II:** 448–449
Iron Man, The (Hughes), **Supp. I:** 346
Ironhand (Arden), **Supp. II:** 29
Irrational Knot, The (Shaw), **VI:** 102, 103, 105, 129
Irving, Washington, **III:** 54
Is He Popenjoy? (Trollope), **V:** 100, 102
"Is Nothing Sacred?" (Rushdie), **Supp. IV:** 437, 442–443
Isabel Clarendon (Gissing), **V:** 437
"Isabella" (Keats), **IV:** xviii, 216, 217–218, 235; **Retro. Supp. I:** 193–194
"Isba Song" (McGuckian), **Supp. V:** 283
"Ischia" (Auden), **Retro. Supp. I:** 12
Isenheim Altar (Grünewald), **Supp. IV:** 85
Isherwood, Christopher, **VII:** xx, 309–320; **Supp. II:** 408, 485, 486; **Retro. Supp. I:** 3, 7, 9
Ishiguro, Kazuo, **Supp. IV:** 75, **301–317**
Island (Huxley), **VII:** xviii, 206
Island, The (Byron), **IV:** xviii 173, 193
"Island, The" (Jennings), **Supp. V:** 209
Island in the Moon, An (Blake), **III:** 290, 292; **Retro. Supp. I:** 34
Island in the Sun (Waugh), **Supp. VI:** 267, 274, **275**
Island Nights' Entertainments (Stevenson), **V:** 387, 396
Island of Dr. Moreau, The (Wells), **VI:** 230–231
Island of Statues, The (Yeats), **Retro. Supp. I:** 325

Island of Terrible Friends (Strutton), **Supp. IV:** 346
Island of the Mighty, The (Arden and D'Arcy), **Supp. II:** 30, **32–35,** 39
Island Pharisees, The (Galsworthy), **VI:** 271, 273, 274, 277, 281
Island Princess, The (Fletcher), **II:** 45, 60, 65
"Islanders, The" (Kipling), **VI:** 169, 203
Isle of Dogs, The (Jonson/Nashe), **Retro. Supp. I:** 156
Isle of Man, The (Bernard), **II:** 246
"Isle of Voices, The" (Stevenson), **V:** 396
"Isobel" (Golding), **Supp. I:** 66
"Isobel's Child" (Browning), **IV:** 313
"Isopes Fabules" (Lydgate), **I:** 57
Israel: Poems on a Hebrew Theme (Sillitoe), **Supp. V:** 411
Israel's Hope Encouraged (Bunyan), **II:** 253
"It Happened in 1936" (Waugh), **Supp. VI:** 273
"It is a beauteous evening, calm and free" (Wordsworth), **IV:** 22
"It May Never Happen" (Pritchett), **Supp. III:** 315
It May Never Happen and Other Stories (Pritchett), **Supp. III:** **318–319**
"It Was Upon a Lammas Night" (Burns), **III:** 315
It's a Battlefield (Greene), **Supp. I:** 2, 5–6; **Retro. Supp. II:** 152–153
"It's a Long, Long Way" (Thomas), **Supp. III:** 404
"It's a Woman's World" (Boland), **Supp. V:** 41
It's an Old Country (Priestley), **VII:** 211
"It's Hopeless" (MacCaig), **Supp. VI:** 191
"It's No Pain" (Redgrove), **Supp. VI:** 234
Italian, The (Radcliffe), **III:** 331–332, 335, 337, 345; **IV:** 173; **Supp. III:** 384
Italian Hours (James), **VI:** 43, 67
Italian Mother, The, and Other Poems (Swinburne), **V:** 333
Italian Visit, An (Day Lewis), **Supp. III:** 118, 122, 129
Italics of Walter Savage Landor, The (Landor), **IV:** 100
"Italio, Io Ti Saluto" (Rossetti), **V:** 250
"Italy and the World" (Browning), **IV:** 318
"Itylus" (Swinburne), **V:** 319
Ivanhoe (Scott), **IV:** xviii, 31, 34, 39
"I've Thirty Months" (Synge), **VI:** 314
Ivory Door, The (Milne), **Supp. V:** 300–301
Ivory Tower, The (James), **VI:** 64, 65
"Ivry: A Song of the Huguenots" (Macaulay), **IV:** 283, 291
Ivy Compton–Burnett (Iprigg), **VII:** 70
"Ivy Day in the Committee Room" (Joyce), **VII:** 44, 45
Ivy Gripped the Steps (Bowen), *see Demon Lover, The*
Ixion in Heaven (Disraeli), **IV:** 297, 299, 308.

J. B. Priestley, The Dramatist (Lloyd–Evans), **VII:** 223, 231

J. M. Synge and the Irish Dramatic Movement (Bickley), **VI:** 317
"J. W. 51B A Convoy" (Ross), **VII:** 434
"Jabberwocky" (Carroll), **V:** 265
Jack, Ian Robert James, **II:** 298; **III:** 125n; **IV:** xi, xxv, 40, 140, 236, 373, 375
Jack Drum's Entertainment (Marston), **II:** 27, 40
Jack Flea's Birthday Celebration (McEwan), **Supp. IV:** 390, 398
Jack Straw (Maugham), **VI:** 368
Jack Straw's Castle (Gunn), **Supp. IV:** 257, 268–271
"Jack Straw's Castle" (Gunn), **Supp. IV:** 270
Jackdaw, The (Gregory), **VI:** 315
Jacko: The Great Intruder (Keneally), **Supp. IV:** 347
Jackson, T. A., **V:** 51
Jacob, Giles, **II:** 348
Jacob's Room (Woolf), **VII:** 18, 20, 26–27, 38; **Retro. Supp. I:** 307, 316
Jacobite's Journal, The (Fielding), **III:** 105; **Retro. Supp. I:** 81
Jacques–Louis David: A Personal Interpretation (Brookner), **Supp. IV:** 122
Jacta Alea Est (Wilde), **V:** 400
Jaggard, William, **I:** 307
"Jaguar, The" (Hughes), **Retro. Supp. II:** 203
Jaguar Smile: A Nicaraguan Journey, The (Rushdie), **Supp. IV:** 436, 454
Jake's Thing (Amis), **Supp. II:** 16–17; **Supp. IV:** 29
Jakobson, Roman, **Supp. IV:** 115
"Jam Tart" (Auden), **Retro. Supp. I:** 6
Jamaica Inn (du Maurier), **Supp. III:** 139, 144, 145, 147
James, Henry, **I:** 42; **III:** 334, 340, 345; **IV:** 35, 107, 319, 323, 369, 371, 372; **V:** x, xx, xiv–xxvi, 2, 48, 51, 70, 95, 97, 98, 102, 191, 199, 205, 210, 295, 384, 390–392; **VI:** x–xi, 5, 23–69, 227, 236, 239, 266, 320, 322; list of short stories and novellas, **VI:** 69; **Supp. II:** 80–81, 89, 487–488, 492; **Supp. III:** 47–48, 60, 217, 437; **Supp. IV:** 97, 116, 133, 153, 233, 243, 371, 503, 511
James, M. R., **III:** 340
James, P. D., **Supp. II:** 127; **Supp. IV:** 319–341
James, Richard, **II:** 102
James, William, **V:** xxv, 272; **VI:** 24
James and the Giant Peach (Dahl), **Supp. IV:** 202, 213, 222
James and the Giant Peach (film), **Supp. IV:** 203
"James Honeyman" (Auden), **Retro. Supp. I:** 8
James Joyce and the Making of "Ulysses" (Budgen) **VII:** 56
"James Lee's Wife" (Browning), **IV:** 367, 369
Jamie on a Flying Visit (Frayn), **Supp. VII:** 56–57
Jane and Prudence (Pym), **Supp. II:** 370–372

Jane Austen: The Critical Heritage (ed. Southam), **IV:** 122, 124
Jane Austen's Literary Manuscripts (ed. Southam), **IV:** 124
Jane Eyre (Brontë), **III:** 338, 344, 345; **V:** xx, 106, 108, 112, 124, 135, **137–140,** 145, 147, 148, 152; **VII:** 101; **Supp. III:** 146; **Supp. IV:** 236, 452, 471; **Retro. Supp. I:** 50, 52, 53–55, 56, 58–60
"Janeites, The" (Kipling), **IV:** 106
"Jane's Marriage" (Kipling), **IV:** 106, 109
"Janet's Repentance" (Eliot), **V:** 190–191; **Retro. Supp. II:** 104
Janowitz, Haas, **III:** 342
Janus: A Summing Up (Koestler), **Supp. I:** 35, 37, 38–39
Japp, A. H., **IV:** 144n, 155
Jarrell, Randall, **VI:** 165, 194, 200; **Supp. IV:** 460
"Jars, The" (Brown), **Supp. VI:** 71–72
"Jasmine" (Naipaul), **Supp. I:** 383
"Jason and Medea" (Gower), **I:** 54, 56
"Je est un autre" (Durrell), **Supp. I:** 126
"Je ne parle pas Français" (Mansfield), **VII:** 174, 177
"Je t'adore" (Kinsella), **Supp. V:** 263
"Jealousy" (Brooke), **Supp. III:** 52
Jeames's Diary; or, Sudden Wealth (Thackeray), **V:** 38
Jean de Meung, **I:** 49
Jeeves (Ayckbourn and Webber), **Supp. V:** 3
"Jeeves and the Hard–Boiled Egg" (Wodehouse), **Supp. III:** 455, 458
Jeeves and the Tie That Binds (Wodehouse), *see Much Obliged*
"Jeeves Takes Charge" (Wodehouse), **Supp. III:** 456, 457–458
Jeffares, Alexander Norman, **VI:** xxxiii–xxxiv, 98, 221
Jefferson, D. W., **III:** 182, 183
Jeffrey, Francis, **III:** 276, 285; **IV:** 31, 39, 60, 72, 129, 269
Jeffrey, Sara, **IV:** 225
Jenkin, Fleeming, **V:** 386
Jenkyn, D., **Supp. IV:** 346
Jennings, Elizabeth, **Supp. IV:** 256; **Supp. V:** **205–221**
"Jenny" (Rossetti), **V:** 240
Jenyns, Soame, **Retro. Supp. I:** 148
Jerrold, Douglas, **V:** 19
Jerrold, W. C., **IV:** 252, 254, 267
"Jersey Villas" (James), **III:** 69
Jerusalem (Blake), **III:** 303, 304–305, 307; **V:** xvi, 330; **Retro. Supp. I:** 45–46
Jerusalem Sinner Saved (Bunyan), *see Good News for the Vilest of Men*
Jerusalem the Golden (Drabble), **Supp. IV:** 230, 231, 238–239, 241, 243, 248, 251
Jesus (Wilson), **Supp. VI:** 306
Jess (Haggard), **Supp. III:** 213
Jesting Pilate (Huxley), **VII:** 201
Jew of Malta, The (Marlowe), **I:** 212, 280, **282–285, 310**; **Retro. Supp. I:** 208–209
Jew Süss (Feuchtwanger), **VI:** 265

Jewel in the Crown, The (Scott), **Supp. I:** 266–267, 269–270
Jeweller of Amsterdam, The (Field, Fletcher, Massinger), **II:** 67
"Jews, The" (Vaughan), **II:** 189
Jhabvala, Ruth Prawer, **Supp. V:** **223–239**
Jill (Larkin), **Supp. I:** 276, 286–287
Jill Somerset (Waugh), **Supp. VI:** 273
Jimmy Governor (Clune), **Supp. IV:** 350
Jitta's Atonement (Shaw), **VI:** 129
"Joachim du Bellay" (Pater), **V:** 344
Joan and Peter (Wells), **VI:** 240
Joan of Arc (Southey), **IV:** 59, 60, 63–64, 71
Joannis Miltonii Pro se defensio . . . (Milton), **II:** 176
Job (biblical book), **III:** 307
Jocasta (Gascoigne), **I:** 215–216
Jocelyn (Galsworthy), **VI:** 277
"Jochanan Hakkadosh" (Browning), **IV:** 365
Jocoseria (Browning), **IV:** 359, 374
"Joe Soap" (Motion), **Supp. VII:** 260–261, 262
"Johann Joachim Quantz's Five Lessons" (Graham), **Supp. VII:** 116
"Johannes Agricola in Meditation" (Browning), **IV:** 360
Johannes Secundus, **II:** 108
"John Betjeman's Brighton" (Ewart), **Supp. VII:** 37
John Bull's Other Island (Shaw), **VI:** 112, **113–115**; **Retro. Supp. II:** 320–321
John Caldigate (Trollope), **V:** 102
"John Fletcher" (Swinburne), **V:** 332
John Gabriel Borkman (Ibsen), **VI:** 110
"John Galsworthy" (Lawrence), **VI:** 275–276, 290
John Galsworthy (Mottram), **VI:** 271, 275, 290
"John Galsworthy, An Appreciation" (Conrad), **VI:** 290
"John Gilpin" (Cowper), **III:** 212, 220
John Keats: A Reassessment (ed. Muir), **IV:** 219, 227, 236
John Keats: His Like and Writings (Bush), **IV:** 224, 236
John Knox (Muir), **Supp. VI:** 198
John M. Synge (Masefield), **VI:** 317
"John Norton" (Moore), **VI:** 98
"John of the Cross" (Jennings), **Supp. V:** 207
"John Ruskin" (Proust), **V:** 183
John Ruskin: The Portrait of a Prophet (Quennell), **V:** 185
John Sherman and Dhoya (Yeats), **VI:** 221
John Thomas and Lady Jane (Lawrence), **VII:** 111–112
John Woodvil (Lamb), **IV:** 78–79, 85
Johnnie Sahib (Scott), **Supp. I:** 259, 261
Johnny I Hardly Knew You (O'Brien), **Supp. V:** 338, 339
Johnny in the Clouds (Rattigan), *see Way to the Stars, The*
Johnson, Edgar, **IV:** 27, 40; **V:** 60, 72
Johnson, James, **III:** 320, 322
Johnson, Joseph, **Retro. Supp. I:** 37
Johnson, Lionel, **VI:** 3, 210, 211

Johnson, Samuel, **III:** 54, 96, **107–123,** 127, 151, 275; **IV:** xiv, xv, 27, 31, 34, 88n, 101, 138, 268, 299; **V:** 9, 281, 287; **VI:** 363; **Retro. Supp. I: 137–150;** and Boswell, **III:** 234, 235, 238, 239, 243–249; and Collins, **III:** 160, 163, 164, 171, 173; and Crabbe, **III:** 280–282; and Goldsmith, **III:** 177, 180, 181, 189; dictionary, **III:** 113–116; **V:** 281, 434; literary criticism, **I:** 326; **II:** 123, 173, 197, 200, 259, 263, 293, 301, 347; **III:** 11, 88, 94, 139, 257, 275; **IV:** 101; on Addison and Steele, **III:** 39, 42, 44, 49, 51; **Supp. IV:** 271

Johnson, W. E., **Supp. II:** 406

Johnson over Jordan (Priestley), **VII:** 226–227

"Joker as Told" (Murray), **Supp. VII:** 279

Joking Apart (Ayckbourn), **Supp. V:** 3, 9, 13, 14

Jolly Beggars, The (Burns), **III:** 319–320

"Jolly Corner, The" (James), **Retro. Supp. I:** 2

Jonah Who Will Be 25 in the Year 2000 (film), **Supp. IV:** 79

Jonathan Swift (Stephen), **V:** 289

Jonathan Wild (Fielding), **III:** 99, 103, 105, 150; **Retro. Supp. I:** 80–81, 90

Jones, David, **VI:** xvi, 436, 437–439, **Supp. VII: 167–182**

Jones, Henry Arthur, **VI:** 367, 376

Jones, Henry Festing, **Supp. II:** 103–104, 112, 114, 117, 118

Jonestown (Harris), **Supp. V:** 144–145

Jonson, Ben, **I:** 228, 234–235, 270, **335–351; II:** 3, 4, 24, 25, 27, 28, 30, 45, 47, 48, 55, 65, 79, 87, 104, 108, 110, 111n, 115, 118, 141, 199, 221–223; **IV:** 35, 327; **V:** 46, 56; **Supp. IV:** 256; **Retro. Supp. I: 151–167**

Jonsonus Virbius (Digby), **Retro. Supp. I:** 166

Jonsonus Virbius (King), **Supp. VI:** 157

Joseph Andrews (Fielding), **III:** 94, 95, 96, 99–100, 101, 105; **Retro. Supp. I:** 80, 83–86

Joseph Conrad (Baines), **VI:** 133–134

Joseph Conrad (Ford), **VI:** 321, 322

Joseph Conrad (Walpole), **VI:** 149

Joseph Conrad: A Personal Reminiscence (Ford), **VI:** 149

Joseph Conrad: The Modern Imagination (Cox), **VI:** 149

"Joseph Grimaldi" (Hood), **IV:** 267

"Joseph Yates' Temptation" (Gissing), **V:** 437

Journal (Mansfield), **VII:** 181, 182

Journal, 1825–32 (Scott), **IV:** 39

Journal and Letters of Fanny Burney, The (eds. Hemlow et al.), **Supp. III:** 63

Journal of Bridget Hitler, The (Bainbridge), **Supp. VI:** 22

Journal of a Dublin Lady, The (Swift), **III:** 35

Journal of a Landscape Painter in Corsica (Lear), **V:** 87

Journal of a Tour in Scotland in 1819 (Southey), **IV:** 71

Journal of a Tour in the Netherlands in the Autumn of 1815 (Southey), **IV:** 71

Journal of a Tour to the Hebrides, The (Boswell), **III:** 117, 234n, 235, 243, 245, 248, 249

Journal of a Voyage to Lisbon, The (Fielding), **III:** 104, 105

Journal of Beatrix Potter from 1881 to 1897, The (ed. Linder), **Supp. III: 292–295**

"Journal of My Jaunt, Harvest 1762" (Boswell), **III:** 241–242

Journal of Researches into the Geology and Natural History of the various countries visited by HMS Beagle (Darwin), **Supp. VII:** 18–19

Journal of the Plague Year, A (Defoe), **III:** 5–6, 8, 13; **Retro. Supp. I:** 63, 73–74

Journal to Eliza, The (Sterne), **III:** 125, 126, 132, 135

Journal to Stella (Swift), **II:** 335; **III:** 32–33, 34; **Retro. Supp. I:** 274

Journalism (Mahon), **Supp. VI:** 166

Journalism for Women: A Practical Guide (Bennett), **VI:** 264, 266

Journals and Papers of Gerard Manley Hopkins, The (ed. House and Storey), **V:** 362, 363, 371, 378–379, 381

Journals 1939–1983 (Spender), **Supp. II:** 481, 487, 490, 493

Journals of a Landscape Painter in Albania etc. (Lear), **V:** 77, 79–80, 87

Journals of a Landscape Painter in Southern Calabria . . . (Lear), **V:** 77, 79, 87

Journals of a Residence in Portugal, 1800–1801, and a Visit to France, 1838 (Southey), **IV:** 71

Journals of Arnold Bennett (Bennett), **VI:** 265, 267

"Journals of Progress" (Durrell), **Supp. I:** 124

"Journey, The" (Boland), **Supp. V:** 41

"Journey Back, The" (Muir), **Supp. VI:** 207

Journey Continued (Paton), **Supp. II:** 356, 359

Journey from Cornhill to Grand Cairo, A (Thackeray), *see Notes of a Journey from Cornhill to Grand Cairo*

Journey from This World to the Next (Fielding), **Retro. Supp. I:** 80

Journey into Fear (Ambler), **Supp. IV:** 11–12

"Journey of John Gilpin, The" (Cowper), *see "John Gilpin"*

"Journey of the Magi, The" (Eliot), **VII:** 152

Journey Through France (Piozzi), **III:** 134

Journey to a War (Auden and Isherwood), **VII:** 312; **Retro. Supp. I:** 9

Journey to Armenia (Mandelstam), **Supp. IV:** 163, 170

"Journey to Bruges, The" (Mansfield), **VII:** 172

Journey to Ithaca (Desai), **Supp. V:** 56, 66, 73–74

Journey to London, A (Vanbrugh), **II:** 326, 333–334, 336

Journey to Oxiana (Byron), **Supp. IV:** 157, 170

Journey to the Hebrides (Johnson), **IV:** 281

Journey to the Western Islands of Scotland, A (Johnson), **III:** 117, 121; **Retro. Supp. I:** 143

Journey Without Maps (Greene), **Supp. I:** 9; **Retro. Supp. II:** 153

Journeys and Places (Muir), **Supp. VI:** 204, **205–206**

Jowett, Benjamin, **V:** 278, 284, 285, 312, 338, 400

Joy (Galsworthy), **VI:** 269, 285

"Joy Gordon" (Redgrove), **Supp. VI:** 236

Joyce, James, **IV:** 189; **V:** xxv, 41; **VII:** xii, xiv, 18, **41–58; VII:** 54–58; **Supp. I:** 43, 196–197; **Supp. II:** 74, 88, 327, 332, 338, 420, 525; **Supp. III:** 108; **Supp. IV:** 27, 233, 234, 363, 364, 365, 371, 390, 395, 396, 407, 411, 424, 426, 427, 500, 514; **Retro. Supp. I:** 18, 19, **169–182**

Joyce, Jeremiah, **V:** 174n

"Jubilate Matteo" (Ewart), **Supp. VII:** 44

Jude the Obscure (Hardy), **VI:** 4, 5, 7, 8, 9; **Supp. IV:** 116; **Retro. Supp. I:** 110, 116

Judge, The (West), **Supp. III:** 441, 442

"Judge's House, The" (Stoker), **Supp. III:** 382

Judgement of Martin Bucer . . . , The (Milton), **II:** 175

Judgement of Paris, The (Congreve), **II:** 347, 350

Judge's Wife, The (Churchill), **Supp. IV:** 181

"Judging Distances" (Reed), **VII:** 422

Judgment on Deltchev (Ambler), **Supp. IV:** 4, 12–13, 21

Judith, **Supp. VI:** 29; **Retro. Supp. II:** 305, 306

Judith (Bennett), **VI:** 267

Judith (Giraudoux), **Supp. III:** 195

"Judkin of the Parcels" (Saki), **Supp. VI:** 245

Jugement du roi de Behaingne, **I:** 32

"Juggling Jerry" (Meredith), **V:** 220

"Julia" (Brontë), **V:** 122, 151

Julia and the Bazooka and Other Stories (Kavan), **Supp. VII:** 202, 205, 214

"Julia Bride" (James), **VI:** 67, 69

"Julia's Churching; or, Purification" (Herrick), **II:** 112

"Julian and Maddalo" (Shelley), **IV:** 182, 201–202; **Retro. Supp. I:** 251

"Julian M. & A. G. Rochelle" (Brontë), **V:** 133

Juliana of Norwich, **I:** 20; **Retro. Supp. II:** 303

Julius Caesar (Shakespeare), **I:** 313, 314–315

"July Evening" (MacCaig), **Supp. VI:** 187, 194

July's People (Gordimer), **Supp. II:** 231, 238–239, 241

Jumpers (Stoppard), **Supp. I:** 438, 444, 445–447, 451; **Retro. Supp. II:** 347–349

Jump–to–Glory Jane (Meredith), **V:** 234

"June Bracken and Heather" (Tennyson), **IV:** 336

"June the 30th, 1934" (Lowry), **Supp. III:** 285

Jung, Carl, **Supp. IV:** 1, 4–5, 6, 10–11, 12, 19, 493

"Jungle, The" (Lewis), **VII:** 447

Jungle Books, The (Kipling), **VI:** 188, 199

Junius Manuscript, **Retro. Supp. II:** 298–299, 301

Junk Mail (Self), **Supp. V:** 406–407

Juno and the Paycock (O'Casey), **VII:** xviii, 4–5, 6, 11

Jure Divino (Defoe), **III:** 4, 13

Jusserand, Jean, **I:** 98

Just Between Ourselves (Ayckbourn), **Supp. V:** 3, 13

Just So Stories for Little Children (Kipling), **VI:** 188, 204

Just Vengeance, The (Sayers), **Supp. III:** 336, 350

Justice (Galsworthy), **VI:** xiii, 269, 273–274, 286–287

Justine (Durrell), **Supp. I:** 104, 105, 106

Juvenal, **II:** 30, 292, 347, 348; **III:** 42; **IV:** 188

Kafka, Franz, **III:** 340, 345; **Supp. IV:** 1, 199, 407, 439

Kain, Saul, pseud. of Siegfried Sassoon

Kaisers of Carnuntum, The (Harrison), **Supp. V:** 164

Kakutani, Michiko, **Supp. IV:** 304

Kalendarium Hortense (Evelyn), **II:** 287

Kallman, Chester, **IV:** 422, 424; **Retro. Supp. I:** 9–10, 13

Kama Sutra, **Supp. IV:** 493

Kangaroo (Lawrence), **VII:** 90, **107–109,** 119

Kant, Immanuel, **IV:** xiv, 50, 52, 145

Kanthapura (Rao), **Supp. V:** 56

"Karain: A Memory" (Conrad), **VI:** 148

Karl, Frederick R., **VI:** 135, 149

Karl–Ludwig's Window, (Saki), **Supp. VI:** 250

"Karshish" (Browning), **IV:** 357, 360, 363

Katchen's Caprices (Trollope), **V:** 101

"Kathe Kollwitz" (Rukeyser), **Supp. V:** 261

Katherine Mansfield (Alpers), **VII:** 183

Kathleen and Frank (Isherwood), **VII:** 316–317

Kathleen Listens In (O'Casey), **VII:** 12

"Katina" (Dahl), **Supp. IV:** 210

Kavan, Anna, **Supp. VII: 201–215**

Kavanagh, Julia, **IV:** 108, 122

Kavanagh, Dan, pseud. of Julian Barnes

Kavanagh, Patrick, **Supp. IV:** 409, 410, 412, 428, 542; **Supp. VII: 183–199; Retro. Supp. I:** 126

Kazin, Alfred, **Supp. IV:** 460

Keats, John, **II:** 102, 122, 192, 200; **III:** 174, 337, 338; **IV:** viii–xii, 81, 95, 129, 178, 196, 198, 204–205, **211–**

237, 255, 284, 316, 323, 332, 349, 355; **V:** 173, 361, 401, 403; **Supp. I:** 218; **Supp. V:** 38; **Retro. Supp. I: 183–197**

Keats and the Mirror of Art (Jack), **IV:** 236

Keats Circle, The: Letters and Papers . . . (Rollins), **IV:** 231, 232, 235

Keats: The Critical Heritage (ed. Matthews), **IV:** 237

Keats's Publisher: A Memoir of John Taylor (Blunden), **IV:** 236

Keble, John, **V:** xix, 252

"Keel, Ram, Stauros" (Jones), **Supp. VII:** 177

"Keen, Fitful Gusts" (Keats), **IV:** 215

Keep the Aspidistra Flying (Orwell), **VII:** 275, 278–279

"Keep the Home Fires Burning" (Novello), **VI:** 435

Keeton, G. W., **IV:** 286

Kell, Joseph, *see* Burgess, Anthony

Kellys and the O'Kellys, The (Trollope), **V:** 101

Kelman, James, **Supp. V: 241–258**

Kelmscott Press, publishers, **V:** xxv, 302

Kelsall, Malcolm Miles, **IV:** x, xxv

Kelvin, Norman, **V:** 221, 234

Kemble, Fanny, **IV:** 340, 350–351

Kemp, Harry, **Supp. III:** 120

Keneally, Thomas, **Supp. IV: 343–362**

Kenilworth (Scott), **IV:** xviii, 39

Kennedy, John F., **Supp. IV:** 486

Kenner, Hugh, **V:** 323

Kennis van die aand (Brink), **Supp. VI: 47–48,** 49

Kenyon, Frederic, **IV:** 312, 321

Kenyon, John, **IV:** 311, 356

Kept (Waugh), **Supp. VI:** 270

Kept in the Dark (Trollope), **V:** 102

Kermode, Frank, **I:** 237; **V:** 344, 355, 359, 412, 420; **VI:** 147, 208

Kettle, Thomas, **VI:** 336

Key to Modern Poetry, A (Durrell), **Supp. I:** 100, **121–123,** 125, 126, 127

Key to My Heart, The (Pritchett), **Supp. III: 324–325**

"Key to My Heart, The" (Pritchett), **Supp. III:** 324

Key to the Door (Sillitoe), **Supp. V:** 410, 415

Keyes, Sidney, **VII:** xxii, 422, **433–440**

Keynes, G. L., **II:** 134; **III:** 289n, 307, 308, 309

Kickleburys on the Rhine, The (Thackeray), **V:** 38

Kidnapped (Stevenson), **V:** 383, 384, 387, 395; **Retro. Supp. I:** 266–267

Kierkegaard, Sören, **Supp. I:** 79

"Kill, A" (Hughes), **Supp. I:** 352

"Killary Hostel" (Murphy), **Supp. V:** 328

Killham, John, **IV:** 323n, 338, 339; **VII: 248–249**

Killing Bottle, The (Hartley), **Supp. VII:** 123

"Killing Time" (Harrison), **Supp. V:** 156

Kiltartan History Book, The (Gregory), **VI:** 318

Kiltartan Molière, The (Gregory), **VI:** 316, 318

Kiltartan Poetry Book, The (Gregory), **VI:** 318

Kilvert, Francis, **V:** 269; **Supp. IV:** 169

Kim (Kipling), **VI:** 166, 168, 169, **185–189; Supp. IV:** 443

Kincaid, Jamaica, **Supp. VII: 217–232**

"Kind Ghosts, The" (Owen), **VI:** 447, 455, 457

Kind Keeper, The; or, Mr Limberham (Dryden), **II:** 294305

Kind of Alaska, A (Pinter), **Supp. I:** 378

Kind of Anger, A (Ambler), **Supp. IV:** 16, 18–20

"Kind of Business: The Academic Critic in America, A" (Lodge), **Supp. IV:** 374

Kind of Scar, A (Boland), **Supp. V:** 35

Kindness of Women, The (Ballard), **Supp. V:** 24, 28, 31, 33

Kindly Light (Wilson), **Supp. VI:** 299, 308

Kindly Ones, The (Powell), **VII:** 344, 347, 348, 349, 350

King, Francis Henry, **VII:** xx, xxxviii; **Supp. IV:** 302

King, Bishop Henry, **II:** 121, 221; **Supp. VI: 149–163**

King, Kimball, **Supp. IV:** 194–195

King, S., **III:** 345

King, T., **II:** 336

King and No King, A (Beaumont and Fletcher), **II:** 43, 45, 52, 54, 57–58, 65

King Arthur; or, The British Worthy (Dryden), **II:** 294, 296, 305

"King Arthur's Tomb" (Morris), **V:** 293

"King Duffus" (Warner), **Supp. VII:** 373

"King James I and Isaac Casaubon" (Landor), **IV:** 92

King James Version of the Bible, **I:** 370, 377–380

King John (Shakespeare), **I:** 286, 301

King Lear (Shakespeare), **I:** 316–317; **II:** 69; **III:** 116, 295; **IV:** 232; **Supp. II:** 194; **Supp. IV:** 149, 171, 282, 283, 294, 335; **Retro. Supp. I:** 34–35

"King of Beasts" (MacCaig), **Supp. VI:** 189

King of Hearts, The (Golding), **Supp. I:** 82

King of Pirates, The . . . (Defoe), **III:** 13

King of the Golden River, The; or, The Black Brothers (Ruskin), **V:** 184

King Solomon's Mines (Haggard), **Supp. III:** 211, 213, **215–217, 218–219,** 227; **Supp. IV:** 484

King Stephen (Keats), **IV:** 231

King Victor and King Charles (Browning), **IV:** 373

"Kingdom of God, The" (Thompson), **V:** 449–450

Kingdom of the Wicked, The (Burgess), **Supp. I:** 186, 193

Kingdoms of Elfin (Warner), **Supp. VII:** 369, 371, 381

King's General, The (du Maurier), **Supp. III:** 146

"King's Tragedy, The" (Rossetti), **V:** 238, 244

"King John's Castle" (Kinsella), **Supp. V:** 260

King Log (Hill), **Supp. V:** 186–189

"Kings" (Jennings), **Supp. V:** 211, 218

Kingsland, W. G., **IV:** 371

Kingsley, Charles, **IV:** 195; **V:** viii, xxi, 2, 4, 283; **VI:** 266; **Supp. IV:** 256

Kinsayder, W., pseud. of John Marston

Kinsella, Thomas, **VI:** 220; **Supp. V:** **259–275**

Kinsley, James, **III:** 310n 322

Kipling, Rudyard, **IV:** 106, 109; **V:** xxiii–xxvi; **VI:** ix, xi, xv, **165–206,** 415; **VII:** 33; poetry, **VI:** 200–203; list of short stories, **VI:** 205–206; **Supp. I:** 167, 261; **Supp. IV:** 17, 201, 394, 440, 506

Kipling and the Critics (Gilbert), **VI:** 195n

Kipling: Realist and Fabulist (Dobrée), **VI:** xi, 200–203, 205

Kipps: The Story of a Simple Soul (Wells), **VI:** xii, 225, 236–237

Kirk, Russell, **IV:** 276

Kirkpatrick, T. P. C. **III:** 180*n*

"Kiss, The" (Sassoon), **VI:** 429

Kiss for Cinderalla, A (Barrie), **Supp. III:** 8, 9

Kiss Kiss (Dahl), **Supp. IV:** 214, 215, 218

"Kiss Me Again, Stranger" (du Maurier), **Supp. III:** 134

Kitaj, R. B., **Supp. IV:** 119

Kitay, Mike, **Supp. IV:** 256, 257

"Kitchen Sonnets" (Fuller), **Supp. VII:** 80

Kitchener, Field Marshall Lord, **VI:** 351

Kittredge, G. L., **I:** 326

Klee, Paul, **Supp. IV:** 80

Klosterheim (De Quincey), **IV:** 149, 155

"Kneeshaw Goes to War" (Read), **VI:** 437

Knife, The (Hare), **Supp. IV:** 282

Knight, G. W., **IV:** 328*n*, 339

"Knight, The" (Hughes), **Supp. I:** 356

Knight of the Burning Pestle, The (Beaumont), **II:** 45, 46, 48–49, 62, 65

"Knight of the Cart, The" (Malory), **I:** 70

Knight with the Two Swords, The (Malory), **I:** 73

Knights, L. C., **II:** 123, 126, 130

Knights of Malta, The (Field, Fletcher, Massinger), **II:** 66

Knight's Tale, The (Chaucer), **I:** 21, 23, 30, 31, 40

Knoblock, Edward, **VI:** 263, 267; **VII:** 223

"Knockbrack" (Murphy), **Supp. V:** 327

"Knole" (Fuller), **Supp. VII:** 72

Knolles, Richard, **III:** 108

Knowles, Sheridan, **IV:** 311

Knox, Robert, **III:** 7

Knox, Ronald, **Supp. II:** 124, 126

Knox Brothers, The (Fitzgerald), **Supp. V:** 95, 96, 98

Knuckle (Hare), **Supp. IV:** 282, 285–286

Koestler, Arthur, **V:** 49; **Supp. I:** **21–41;** **Supp. III:** 107; **Supp. IV:** 68

Kokoschka, Oskar, **Supp. IV:** 81

Kontakian for You Departed (Paton), **Supp. II:** 343, 359

"Kosciusko and Poniatowski" (Landor), **IV:** 92

Kostakis, George, **Supp. IV:** 174

Kotzebue, August von, **III:** 254, 268

"Kraken, The" (Tennyson), **IV:** 329; **VI:** 16

Krapp's Last Tape (Beckett), **Supp. I:** 46, 55, 58, 61; **Retro. Supp. I:** 25–26

Krause, Ernest, **Supp. II:** 107

"Kristbjorg's Story: In the Black Hills" (Lowry), **Supp. III:** 285

Kristeva, Julia, **Supp. IV:** 115, 232

Krutch, J. W., **III:** 246

"Kubla Khan" (Coleridge), **IV:** ix, xvii, 44, 46–48, 56; **V:** 272, 447; **Supp. IV:** 425; **Retro. Supp. II:** 56–58

Kullus (Pinter), **Supp. I:** 368, 371

Kumar, Gobind, **Supp. IV:** 449

"Kumquat for John Keats, A" (Harrison), **Supp. V:** 160

Kundera, Milan, **Supp. IV:** 440

Kurosawa, Akira, **Supp. IV:** 434

Kyd, Thomas, **I:** 162, **212–231,** 277, 278, 291; **II:** 25, 28, 74

"La Belle Dame Sans Merci" (Keats), **IV:** 216, 219, 235, 313

La Bete Humaine (Zola), **Supp. IV:** 249

La Chapelle, Jean de, **II:** 358

La Die de Fénelon (Ramsay), **III:** 99

La Fayette, Madame de, **Supp. IV:** 136

"La Fontaine and La Rochefoucault" (Landor), **IV:** 91

"La Grosse Fifi" (Rhys), **Supp. II:** 390

La maison de campagne (Dancourt), **II:** 325

La Mordida (Lowry), **Supp. III:** 280

"La Nuit Blanche" (Kipling), **VI:** 193

La parisienne (Becque), **VI:** 369

La Princesse de Clèves (La Fayette), **Supp. IV:** 136

"La Rochefoucauld" (Durrell), **Supp. I:** 126

La Saisiaz (Browning), **IV:** 359, 364–365, 374

La Soeur de la Reine (Swinburne), **V:** 325, 333

La strage degli innocenti (Marino), **II:** 183

La traicion busca el castigo (Roias Zorilla), **II:** 325

La Vendée: An Historical Romance (Trollope), **V:** 101

La vida de la Santa Madre Teresa de Jesus, **II:** 182

La vida es sueño (Calderón), **IV:** 349

La vie de Fénelon (Ramsay), **III:** 99

Labels (Waugh), **VII:** 292–293

Laborators, The (Redgrove), **Supp. VI:** 236

Labours of Hercules, The (Christie), **Supp. II:** 135

Laburnum Grove (Priestley), **VII:** 224

Labyrinth, The (Muir), **Supp. VI:** 204, **207**

Labyrinthine Ways, The (Greene), *see Power and the Glory, The*

Lacan, Jacques, **Supp. IV:** 99, 115

"Lachrimae, or Seven Tears Figured in Seven Passionate Pavanas" (Hill), **Supp. V:** 189, 190

"Lachrimae Amantis" (Hill), **Supp. V:** 191

"Lachrimae Verae" (Hill), **Supp. V:** 190

"Laconics: The Forty Acres" (Murray), **Supp. VII:** 276

"Ladder and the Tree, The" (Golding), **Supp. I:** 65

Ladder of Perfection (Hilton), **Supp. I:** 74

Ladies from the Sea (Hope), **Supp. VII:** 160

Ladies Triall, The (Ford), *see Lady's Trial, The*

Ladies Whose Bright Eyes (Ford), **VI:** 327

"Ladle" (Berger), **Supp. IV:** 93

Lady Anna (Trollope), **V:** 102

"Lady Appledore's Mesalliance" (Firbank), **Supp. II:** 207

Lady Athlyne (Stoker), **Supp. III:** 381

"Lady Barbarina" (James), **VI:** 69

Lady Chatterley's Lover (Lawrence), **VII:** 87, 88, 91, **110–113; Supp. IV:** 149, 234, 369; **Retro. Supp. II:** 226, 231–232

"Lady Delavoy" (James), **VI:** 69

Lady Frederick (Maugham), **VI:** 367–368

"Lady Geraldine's Courtship" (Browning), **IV:** 311

Lady Gregory, **VI:** xiv

Lady Gregory: A Literary Portrait (Coxhead), **VI:** 318

"Lady Icenway, The" (Hardy), **VI:** 22

Lady Jane (Chettle, Dekker, Heywood, Webster), **II:** 68

Lady Lisa Lyon (Mapplethorpe photography collection), **Supp. IV:** 170

Lady Maisie's Bairn and Other Poems (Swinburne), **V:** 333

"Lady Mottisfont" (Hardy), **VI:** 22

Lady of Launay, The (Trollope), **V:** 102

Lady of May, The (Sidney), **I:** 161; **Retro. Supp. II:** 330

"Lady of Quality, A" (Kinsella), **Supp. V:** 260

"Lady of Shalott, The" (Tennyson), **IV:** xix, 231, 313, 329, 331–332

Lady of the Lake, The (Scott), **IV:** xvii, 29, 38

"Lady of the Pool, The" (Jones), **Supp. VII:** 176, 177, 178

Lady of the Shroud, The (Stoker), **Supp. III:** 381

"Lady Penelope, The" (Hardy), **VI:** 22

"Lady Rogue Singleton" (Smith), **Supp. II:** 466–467, 470

Lady Susan (Austen), **IV:** 108, 109, 122; **Supp. IV:** 230

Lady Windermere's Fan (Wilde), **V:** xxvi, 412, 413–414, 419; **Retro. Supp. II:** 369

Lady with a Laptop (Thomas), **Supp. IV:** 489–490

"Lady with the Dog, The" (Chekhov), **V:** 241

"Ladybird, The" (Lawrence), **VII:** 115

"Lady's Dream, The" (Hood), **IV:** 261, 264

"Lady's Dressing Room, The" (Swift), **III:** 32

Lady's Magazine (periodical), **III:** 179

"Lady's Maid, The" (Mansfield), **VII:** 174–175

Lady's Not for Burning (Fry), **Supp. III:** 195, 202

Lady's Pictorial (periodical), **VI:** 87, 91

Lady's Trial, The (Ford), **II:** 89, 91, 99, 100

Lady's World, The (periodical), **Retro. Supp. II:** 364

Lafourcade, Georges, **VI:** 247, 256, 259, 260, 262, 263, 268

"Lagoon, The" (Conrad), **VI:** 136, 148

Lair of the White Worm, The (Stoker), **Supp. III:** 381–311

Laird of Abbotsford: A View of Sirt Walter Scott, The (Wilson), **Supp. VI:** 301

Lake, David J., **II:** 1, 2, 21

Lake, The (Moore), **VI:** xii, 88, 89, 92–93, 98

"Lake Isle of Innisfree, The" (Yeats), **VI:** 207, 211; **Retro. Supp. I:** 329

Lakers, The (Nicholson), **Supp. VI:** 223

"L'Allegro" (Milton), **II:** 158–159; **IV:** 199

Lamarck, Jean–Baptiste, **Supp. II:** 105–106, 107, 118, 119

Lamb, Charles, **II:** 80, 86, 119*n*, 143, 153, 256, 340, 361, 363, 364; **IV:** xi, xiv, xvi xviii, xix, 41, 42, **73–86,** 128, 135, 137, 148, 252–253, 255, 257, 259, 260, 320, 341, 349; **V:** 328

Lamb, John, **IV:** 74, 77, 84

Lamb, Mary, **IV:** xvi, 77–78, 80, 83–84, 128, 135

"Lamb to the Slaughter" (Dahl), **Supp. IV:** 215, 219

Lambert, Gavin, **Supp. IV:** 3, 8

"Lament" (Gunn), **Supp. IV:** 277–278

Lament for a Lover (Highsmith), **Supp. V:** 170

Lament of Tasso, The (Byron), **IV:** 192

"Lament of the Images" (Okri), **Supp. V:** 359

Lamia (Keats), **III:** 338; **IV:** xviii, 216, 217, 219–220, 231, 235; **Retro. Supp. I:** 192–193

Lamia, Isabella, The Eve of St. Agnes, and Other Poems (Keats), **IV:** xviii, 211, 235; **Retro. Supp. I:** 184, 192–196

Lamming, George, **Supp. IV:** 445

"Lamp and the Jar, The" (Hope), **Supp. VII:** 158

Lamp and the Lute, The (Dobrée), **VI:** 204

Lampitt Papers, The (Wilson), **Supp. VI:** 297, 304, **306–307**

Lancelot and Guinevere (Malory), **I:** 70–71, 77

Lancelot du Laik, **I:** 73

Lancelot, The Death of Rudel, and Other Poems (Swinburne), **V:** 333

"Lancer" (Housman), **VI:** 160

"Land of Counterpane, The" (Stevenson), **Retro. Supp. I:** 260

Land of Heart's Desire, The (Yeats), **VI:** 221; **Retro. Supp. I:** 326

"Land of Loss, The" (Kinsella), **Supp. V:** 271

Land of Promise, The (Maugham), **VI:** 369

"Land under the Ice, The" (Nicholson), **Supp. VI:** 216

Landing on the Sun, A (Frayn), **Supp. VII:** 62–63

"Landlady, The" (Behan), **Supp. II:** 63–64

"Landlady, The" (Dahl), **Supp. IV:** 215–216, 217

Landleaguers, The (Trollope), **V:** 102

Landlocked (Lessing), **Supp. I:** 245, 248

Landmarks in French Literature (Strachey), **Supp. II:** **502–503**

Landon, Letitia, **IV:** 311

Landor, Walter Savage, **II:** 293; **III:** 139; **IV:** xiv, xvi, xviii, xix, xxii, **87–100,** 252, 254, 356; **V:** 320

Landscape (Pinter), **Supp. I:** 375–376

"Landscape Painter, A" (James), **VI:** 69

Landscapes Within, The (Okri), **Supp. V:** 347, 348, 350, 352, 353–354, 360

Landseer, Edwin, **V:** 175

Lane, Margaret, **V:** 13*n*, 16

Lang, Andrew, **V:** 392–393, 395; **VI:** 158; **Supp. II:** 115

Lang, C. Y., **V:** 334, 335

Langland, William, **I:** vii, **1–18**

"Language Ah Now You Have Me" (Graham), **Supp. VII:** 115

Language Made Plain (Burgess), **Supp. I:** 197

Language of Fiction: Essays in Criticism and Verbal Analysis of the English Novel (Lodge), **Supp. II:** 9; **Supp. IV:** 365, 366

Language, Truth and Logic (Ayer), **VII:** 240

Languages of Love, The (Brooke–Rose), **Supp. IV:** 99, 100–101

Lannering, Jan, **III:** 52

"Lantern Bearers, The" (Stevenson), **V:** 385

"Lantern out of Doors, The," (Hopkins), **V:** 380

Lantern Slides (O'Brien), **Supp. V:** 341

Laodicean, A; or, The Castle of the De Stancys (Hardy), **VI:** 4–5, 20

Laon and Cynthia (Shelley), **IV:** 195, 196, 198, 208; **Retro. Supp. I:** 249–250; *see also Revolt of Islam, The*

"Lapis Lazuli" (Yeats), **Retro. Supp. I:** 337

Lara (Byron), **IV:** xvii, 172, 173, 175, 192; *see also* Turkish tales

"Large Cool Store, The" (Larkin), **Supp. I:** 279

Lark, The (Fry), **Supp. III:** 195

"Lark Ascending, The" (Meredith), **V:** 221, 223

"Larkin Automatic Car Wash, The" (Ewart), **Supp. VII:** 41

Larkin, Philip, **Supp. I:** 275–290; **Supp. II:** 2, 3, 375; **Supp. IV:** 256, 431

"Lars Porsena of Clusium" (Macaulay), **IV:** 282

Lars Porsena; or, The Future of Swearing and Improper Language (Graves), **VII:** 259–260

"Last Address, The" (Lowry), **Supp. III:** 272

Last and the First, The (Compton–Burnett), **VII:** 59, 61, 67

"Last Ark, The" (Tolkien), **Supp. II:** 522

Last Battle, The (Lewis), **Supp. III:** 248, 261

Last Chronicle of Barset, The (Trollope), **II:** 173; **V:** xxiii, 93–95, 101

"Last Confession, A" (Rossetti), **V:** 240–241

"Last Day of Summer, The" (McEwan), **Supp. IV:** 390

Last Days of Lord Byron, The (Parry), **IV:** 191, 193

Last Days of Sodom, The (Orton), **Supp. V:** 364

"Last Duchess" (Hardy), **Retro. Supp. I:** 120

Last Essay (Conrad), **VI:** 148

Last Essays of Elia, The (Lamb), **IV:** xix, 76–77, 82–83, 85

Last Essays on Church and Religion (Arnold), **V:** 212, 216

Last Fight of the Revenge at Sea, The (Ralegh), **I:** 145, 149–150

Last Fruit off the Old Tree, The (Landor), **IV:** 100

"Last Galway Hooker, The" (Murphy), **Supp. V:** 313, 316, 319

"Last Hellos, The" (Murray), **Supp. VII:** 283

"Last Instructions to a Painter, The" (Marvell), **II:** 217–218

Last Loves (Sillitoe), **Supp. V:** 411, 414, 415–416, 425

"Last Man, The" (Gunn), **Supp. IV:** 264

Last Man, The (Shelley), **Supp. III:** **364–371**

"Last of the Fire Kings" (Mahon), **Supp. VI:** 172

Last Orders (Swift), **Supp. V:** 440–441

Last Poems (Browning), **IV:** 312, 315, 357

Last Poems (Fuller), **Supp. VII:** 79

Last Poems (Housman), **VI:** 157, 158, 160, 161, 162, 164

Last Poems (Meredith), **V:** 234

Last Poems (Yeats), **VI:** 214

Last Poems and Two Plays (Yeats), **VI:** 213

Last Post (Ford), **VI:** 319, 330–331

Last Pre–Raphaelite, The: A Record of the Life and Writings of Ford Madox Ford (Goldring), **VI:** 333

Last September, The (Bowen), **Supp. II:** 77, 78, 79, 83–86, 89

Last Testament of Oscar Wilde, The (Ackroyd), **Supp. VI:** 5

Last Thing (Snow), **VII:** xxi, 324, 332–333

"Last Things, The" (Ewart), **Supp. VII:** 40

"Last to Go" (Pinter), **Retro. Supp. I:** 217

"Last Tournament, The" (Tennyson), **V:** 327

"Last Will and Testament" (Auden), **Retro. Supp. I:** 7

Last Words of Thomas Carlyle, The (Carlyle), **IV:** 250

Late Augustans, The (Davie), **Supp. VI:** 115

Late Bourgeois World, The (Gordimer), **Supp. II:** 228, 229, 231, 233, 234, 236, 238

Late Call (Wilson), **Supp. I:** 156, 161–162, 163

Late Harvest (Douglas), **VI:** 300, 302–303, 305, 333

Late Murder in Whitechapel, The; or, *Keep the Widow Waking, see Late Murder of the Son . . .*

Late Murder of the Son Upon the Mother, A; or, Keep the Widow Waking (Dekker, Ford, Rowley, Webster), **II:** 85–86, 89, 100

"Late Period" (Fuller), **Supp. VII:** 78

Late Picking, A: Poems 1965–1974 (Hope), **Supp. VII:** 157, 158

Late Pickings (Ewart), **Supp. VII:** 45

Latecomers (Brookner), **Supp. IV:** 130–131, 136

"Later Poems" (Bridges), **VI:** 78, 83

"Later Decalogue, The," (Clough), **V:** 155

Later and Italian Poems of Milton (tr. Cowper), **III:** 220

Latter–Day Pamphlets (Carlyle), **IV:** xxi, 240, 247–248, 249, 250

"Laud and Praise made for our Sovereign Lord The King" (Skelton), **I:** 88–89

Laugh and Lie Down (Swinburne), **V:** 312, 332

Laugh and Lie Down; or, The World's Folly (Tourneur), **II:** 37

Laughable Lyrics (Lear), **V:** 78, 85, 87

Laughing Anne (Conrad), **VI:** 148

"Laughter" (Beerbohm), **Supp. II:** 47–48

"Laughter Beneath the Bridge" (Okri), **Supp. V:** 355

Laughter in the Next Room (Sitwell), **VII:** 130, 135

"Laundon, City of the Moon" (Redgrove), **Supp. VI:** 234

"Laundress, The" (Kinsella), **Supp. V:** 261

"Laus Veneris" (Swinburne), **IV:** 346; **V:** 316, 318, 320, 327, 346

L'Autre monde ou les états et empires de la lune (Cyrano de Bergerac), **III:** 24

Lavater, J. C., **III:** 298

Law, William, **IV:** 45

Law and the Lady, The (Collins), **Supp. VI:** 102

Law Against Lovers, The (Davenant), **I:** 327

Law Hill poems (Brontë), **V:** 126–128

Lawless Roads, The (Greene; U.S. title, "nother Mexico*), **Supp. I:** 9, 10

Lawrence, D. H., **II:** 330; **IV:** 106, 119, 120, 195; **V:** xxv, 6, 47; **VI:** 235, 243, 248, 259, 275–276, 283, 363, 409, 416; **VI:** xii, xiv–xvi, 18, 75, **87–126,** 201, 203–204, 215; **Supp. II:** 492; **Supp. III:** 86, 91, 397–398; **Supp. IV:** 5, 94, 139, 233, 241, 369; **Retro. Supp. II:** **221–235**

Lawrence, Frieda, **VII:** 90, 111

Lawrence, T. E., **VI:** 207, 408; **Supp. II:** 147, **283–297**; **Supp. IV:** 160

"Lawrence, of virtuous father virtuous son" (Milton), **II:** 163

Laws of Candy, The, **II:** 67

Lawson, Henry, **Supp. IV:** 460

"Lay By" (Hare), **Supp. IV:** 281, 283

"Lay for New Lovers" (Reid), **Supp. VII:** 325

Lay Morals and Other Papers (Stevenson), **V:** 396

Lay of Lilies, A, and Other Poems (Swinburne), **V:** 333

"Lay of the Brown Rosary, The" (Browning), **IV:** 313

"Lay of the Labourer, The" (Hood), **IV:** 252, 261, 265–266

Lay of The Last Minstrel, The (Scott), **IV:** xvi, 29, 38, 48, 218

"Lay of the Laureate" (Southey), **IV:** 61, 71

Layamon, **I:** 72

Lays of Ancient Rome (Macaulay), **IV:** xx, 272, 282–283, 290–291

"Lazarus and the Sea" (Redgrove), **Supp. VI: 225–227,** 231

"Lazarus Not Raised" (Gunn), **Supp. IV:** 259

Lazy Tour of Two Idle Apprentices, The (Collins), **Supp. VI:** 92

Lazy Tour of Two Idle Apprentices, The (Dickens), **V:** 72

Le Carré, John, **Supp. II: 299–319; Supp. IV:** 4, 5, 9, 13, 14, 15, 17, 22, 445, 449

"Le christianisme" (Owen), **VI:** 445, 450

Le dépit amoureux (Molière), **II:** 325, 336

Le Fanu, Sheridan, **III:** 333, 340, 342, 343, 345; **Supp. II:** 78–79, 81; **Supp. III:** 385–386

Le Gallienne, Richard, **V:** 412, 413

Le Jugement du Roy de Behaingne (Machaut), **Retro. Supp. II:** 37

Le misanthrope (Molière), **II:** 318

Le roman bourgeois (Furetière), **II:** 354

Le Roman de la Rose (Guillaurne), **Retro. Supp. II:** 36

Le Sage, Alain René, **II:** 325; **III:** 150

"Lead" (Kinsella), **Supp. V:** 260

"Lead, Kindly Light" (Newman), **Supp. VII:** 291

"Leaden Echo and the Golden Echo, The" (Hopkins), **V:** 371

Leader (periodical), **V:** 189

"Leaf by Niggle" (Tolkien), **Supp. II:** 521

Leak in the Universe, A (Richards), **Supp. II:** 426–427

Lean Tales (Kelman, Owens, and Gray), **Supp. V:** 249

"Leaning Tower, The" (Woolf), **VII:** 26; **Retro. Supp. I:** 310

Lear (Bond), **Supp. I:** 423, 427, **430–432,** 433, 435

Lear, Edward, **V:** xi, xvii, xv, xxv, **75–87,** 262; **Supp. IV:** 201

Lear Coloured Bird Book for Children, The (Lear), **V:** 86, 87

Lear in Sicily (ed. Proby), **V:** 87

Lear in the Original (ed. Liebert), **V:** 87

Learned Comment upon Dr. Hare's Excellent Sermon, A (Swift), **III:** 35

Learned Hippopotamus, The (Ewart), **Supp. VII:** 47

Learning Human: Selected Prose (Murray), **Supp. VII:** 271

Learning Laughter (Spender), **Supp. II:** 491

"Learning to Swim" (Swift), **Supp. V:** 431–432

Learning to Swim and Other Stories (Swift), **Supp. V:** 431–434

"Learning's Little Tribute" (Wilson), **Supp. I:** 157

Lease of Life (film, Ambler), **Supp. IV:** 3

"Leather Goods" (Redgrove), **Supp. VI:** 236

"Leave–Taking, A" (Swinburne), **V:** 319

"Leaving Barra" (MacNeice), **VI:** 411–412

"Leaving Belfast" (Motion), **Supp. VII:** 254, 262

Leavis, F. R., **II:** 254, 258, 271; **III:** 68, 78; **IV:** 227, 323, 338, 339; **V:** 195, 199, 201, 237, 309, 355, 375, 381, 382; **VI:** 13; **V:** xvi, xix, 72–73, 88, 101, 102, **233–256; Supp. II:** 2, 179, 429; **Supp. III:** 60; **Supp. IV:** 142, 229–230, 233, 256; **Retro. Supp. I:** 90

Leavis, Q. D., **II:** 250; **V:** 286, 290; **VI:** 377; **VII:** 233, 238, 250

Leben des Galilei (Brecht), **Supp. IV:** 298

"Lecknavarna" (Murphy), **Supp. V:** 328

Lecky, William, **IV:** 289

Lecky, William E. H., **Supp. V:** 41

L'école des femmes (Molière), **II:** 314

L'école des maris (Molière), **II:** 314

"Lecture on Modern Poetry, A" (Hulme), **Supp. VI:** 135–136, 138, 142–144

Lectures Chiefly on the Dramatic Literature of the Age of Elizabeth (Hazlitt), **IV:** xviii, 125, 129–130, 139

Lectures on Architecture and Paintings (Ruskin), **V:** 184

Lectures on Art (Ruskin), **V:** 184

Lectures on Certain Difficulties Felt by Anglicans in Submitting to the Catholic Church (Newman), **Supp. VII:** 297–298

Lectures on Justification (Newman), **II:** 243n; **Supp. VII:** 294, 301

Lectures on Shakespeare (Coleridge), **IV:** xvii, 52, 56

Lectures on the Early History of the Kingship (Frazer), **Supp. III:** 175

Lectures on the English Comic Writers (Hazlitt), **IV:** xviii, 129–130, 131, 136, 139

Lectures on the English Poets (Hazlitt), **IV:** xvii, 41, 129–130, 139; **Retro. Supp. II:** 51

Lectures on the Present Position of Catholics in England (Newman), **Supp. VII:** 298

Lectures on the Prophetical Office of the Church Viewed Relatively to Romanism and Popular Protestantism (Newman), **Supp. VII:** 293–294, 301, 302

"Leda and the Swan" (Yeats), **V:** 345

Lee, George John Vandeleur, **VI:** 101

Lee, Gypsy Rose, **Supp. IV:** 422, 423, 424

Lee, Hermione, **Retro. Supp. I:** 305

Lee, J., **II:** 336

Lee, Nathaniel, **II:** 305

Lee, Sidney, **V:** 280

Leech, Clifford, **II:** 44, 49, 52, 60, 62, 64, 70, 86, 90*n*, 100

Leech, John, **IV:** 258

Left Bank and Other Stories, The (Rhys), **Supp. II:** 388, **389–390**

Left-Handed Liberty (Arden), **Supp. II:** 29, 30

Left Heresy in Literature and Art, The (Kemp and Riding), **Supp. III:** 120

"Left, Right, Left, Right: The Arrival of Tony Blair" (Barnes), **Supp. IV:** 74

"Legacie, The" (Donne), **Retro. Supp. II:** 88, 91–92

"Legacy, The" (King), **Supp. VI:** 152–153

"Legacy, The" (Motion), **Supp. VII:** 261

Legacy of Cain, The (Collins), **Supp. VI:** 103

Legend of Good Women, The (Chaucer), **I:** 24–31, 38; **Retro. Supp. II:** 40

Legend of Juba;, The, and Other Poems (Eliot), **V:** 200

Legend of Montrose, A (Scott), **IV:** xviii, 35, 39

Legend of the Rhine, A (Thackeray), **V:** 38

"Legacy on My Fiftieth Birthday, A" (Stevenson), **Supp. VI:** 262

Legendre's Elements of Geometry (Carlyle), **IV:** 250

Legends of Angria (ed. Ratchford), **V:** 112

Léger, Fernand, **Supp. IV:** 81

"Legion Club, The" (Swift), **III:** 21, 31

Legion Hall Bombing, The (Churchill), **Supp. IV:** 181

Legion's Memorial to the House of Commons (Defoe), **III:** 12; **Retro. Supp. I:** 67

Legislation (Ruskin), **V:** 178

Legouis, Pierre, **II:** 207, 209, 218, 219, 220

Lehmann, John Frederick, **VII:** xvii, xxxviii

Leigh, R. A., **III:** 246*n*

Leigh Hunt's Examiner Examined (Blunden), **IV:** 236

Leila, A Tale (Browning), **IV:** 321

"Leisure" (Lamb), **IV:** 83

"Leith Races" (Fergusson), **III:** 317

Leland, John, **I:** 113

Lemon, Mark, **IV:** 263

"Lenten Offering, The" (Warner), **Supp. VII:** 371

Leonard's War: A Love Story (Sillitoe), **Supp. V:** 411

"Leonardo Da Vinci" (Pater), **V:** 345–347, 348

Leonora (Edgeworth), **Supp. III:** 158

"'Leopard' George" (Lessing), **Supp. I:** 242

"Lepanto" (Chesterton), **VI:** 340

"Leper, The" (Swinburne), **V:** 315

LeQueux, William, **Supp. II:** 299

"Lerici" (Gunn), **Supp. IV:** 259

Les aventures de Télémaque (Fénelon), **III:** 95, 99

Les bourgeoises à la mode (Dancourt), **II:** 325, 336

Les carrosses d'Orleans (La Chapelle), **II:** 358

"Les Chats" (Baudelaire), **Supp. IV:** 115

Les Damnés de la terre (Fanon), **Supp. IV:** 105

Les fables d'Ésope (Boursault), **II:** 324

Les Misérables (Hugo), **Supp. IV:** 86

"Les Noyades" (Swinburne), **V:** 319, 320

"Les Vaches" (Clough), **V:** 168

Lesbia Brandon (Swinburne), **V:** 313, 325, 326–327, 332

Leslie Stephen (MacCarthy), **V:** 284, 290

Leslie Stephen and Matthew Arnold as Critics of Wordsworth (Wilson), **V:** 287, 290

Leslie Stephen: Cambridge Critic (Leavis), **VII:** 238

Leslie Stephen: His Thought and Character in Relation to His Time (Annan), **V:** 284–285, 290

Less Deceived, The (Larkin), **Supp. I:** 275, 277, 278, 279, 285

Less Than Angels (Pym), **Supp. II: 372–374**

"Lesser Arts, The" (Morris), **V:** 291, 301

Lessing, Doris, **Supp. I: 237–257; Supp. IV:** 78, 233, 234, 473

Lessing, Gotthold Ephraim, **IV:** 53

Lessius, **II:** 181*n*

Lessness (Beckett), **Supp. I:** 52, 61

"Lesson in Music, A" (Reid), **Supp. VII:** 324–325

"Lesson of the Master, The" (James), **VI:** 48, 67, 69

"Lessons of the Summer" (Fuller), **Supp. VII:** 80

Lessons of the War (Reed), **VII:** 422

L'Estrange, Sir Robert, **III:** 41

"Let It Go" (Empson), **Supp. II:** 180, 194

Let Me Alone (Kavan), **Supp. VII:** 202–204, 205, 206, 207, 214

"Let that be a Lesson" (Kelman), **Supp. V:** 249

"Let the Brothels of Paris be opened" (Blake), **III:** 299

Let the People Sing (Priestley), **VII:** 217

"Let Them Call It Jazz" (Rhys), **Supp. II:** 402

Let's Have Some Poetry! (Jennings), **Supp. V:** 206, 214

Lethaby, W. R., **V:** 291, 296, 306

"Letter, The" (Brontë), **V:** 132

Letter, The (Maugham), **VI:** 369

Letter Addressed to His Grace the Duke of Norfolk (Newman), **Supp. VII:** 302

Letter and Spirit: Notes on the Commandments (Rossetti), **V:** 260

Letter . . . oncerning the Sacramental Test, A (Swift), **III:** 35

Letter from a Member . . . in Ireland to a Member in England, A (Defoe), **III:** 18

Letter from Amsterdam to a Friend in England, A, **II:** 206

"Letter from Armenia, A" (Hill), **Supp. V:** 189

"Letter from Artemiza . . . to Chloë, A" (Rochester), **II;** 260, 270; **Supp. III:** 70

"Letter from Hamnovoe" (Brown), **Supp. VI:** 64

"Letter from Home, The" (Kincaid), **Supp. VII:** 221

Letter . . . in Vindication of His Conduct with Regard to the Affairs of Ireland, A (Burke), **III:** 205

Letter of Advice to a Young Poet, A (Swift), **III:** 35

Letter of Thanks . . . to the . . . Bishop of S. Asaph, A (Swift), **III:** 35

Letter . . . on the Conduct of the Minority in Parliament, A (Burke), **III:** 205

"Letter to —, April 4, 1802, A" (Coleridge), **Retro. Supp. II:** 61

"Letter to a Brother of the Pen in Tribulation, A" (Behn), **Supp. III:** 40

Letter . . . to a Country Gentleman . . . , A (Swift), **III:** 35

Letter to a Friend, A (Browne), **II:** 153, 156

Letter . . . to a Gentleman Designing for Holy Orders, A (Swift), **III:** 35

Letter to a Member of the National Assembly, A (Burke), **III:** 205

Letter to a Monk (More), **Supp. VII:** 240, 241–242

Letter to a Noble Lord (Burke), **IV:** 127

Letter to a Peer of Ireland on the Penal Laws (Burke), **III:** 205

"Letter to an Exile" (Motion), **Supp. VII:** 254, 257

Letter to Brixius (More), **Supp. VII:** 241

"Letter to Curtis Bradford, A" (Davie), **Supp. VI:** 109

Letter to Dorp (More), **Supp. VII:** 240–241

Letter to Edward Lee (More), **Supp. VII:** 240

Letter to John Murray, Esq., "Touching"Lord Nugent (Southey), **IV:** 71

"Letter to Lord Byron" (Auden), **IV:** 106; **Supp. II:** 200; **Retro. Supp. I:** 7

Letter to Lord Ellenborough, A (Shelley), **IV:** 208

"Letter to Maria Gisborne" (Shelley), **IV:** 204

"Letter to Mr. Creech at Oxford, A" (Behn), **Supp. III:** 41

Letter to Mr. Harding the Printer, A (Swift), **III:** 35

Letter to Oxford (More), **Supp. VII:** 240–241

Letter to Robert MacQueen Lord Braxfield . . . , A (Boswell), **III:** 248

Letter to Samuel Whitbread (Malthus), **IV:** 127

"Letter to Sara Hutchinson" (Coleridge), **IV:** 15

Letter to Sir Hercules Langrishe on . . . the Roman Catholics . . . , *A* (Burke), **III:** 205

"Letter to Sylvia Plath" (Stevenson), **Supp. VI:** 263–264

"Letter to the Bishop of Llandaff" (Wordsworth), **IV:** 2

Letter to the Noble Lord on the Attacks Made upon Him . . . in the House of Lords, A (Burke), **III:** 205

Letter to the People of Scotland, on . . . the Articles of the Union, A (Boswell), **III:** 248

Letter to the People of Scotland, on the Present State of the Nation, A (Boswell), **III:** 248

Letter to the Shop–Keepers . . . of Ireland, A (Swift), **III:** 28, 35

Letter to the Whole People of Ireland, A (Swift), **III:** 35

Letter to Viscount Cobham, A (Congreve), **II:** 350

Letter to . . . Viscount Molesworth, A (Swift), **III:** 35

"Letter to William Coldstream" (Auden), **Retro. Supp. I:** 7

Letter to William Gifford, Esq., A (Hazlitt), **IV:** 139

Letter to William Smith, Esq., MP, A (Southey), **IV:** 71

Letter Writers, The (Fielding), **III:** 97, 105

Letter Written to a Gentleman in the Country, A . . . (Milton), **II:** 176

Letterbook of Sir George Etherege, The (ed. Rosenfeld), **II:** 271

"Letterfrack Industrial School" (Murphy), **Supp. V:** 316

Letters (Coleridge), **II:** 119*n*

Letters (Warner), **Supp. VII:** 377, 382

Letters Addressed to Lord Liverpool, and the Parliament . . . (Landor), **IV:** 100

Letters and Diaries (Newman), **Supp. VII:** 293, 297

Letters and Journals (Byron), **IV:** 185, 193

Letters and Journals of Lord Byron, with Notices of His Life, by T. Moore (Moore), **IV:** 193, 281; **V:** 116

Letters and Passages from . . . Clarissa (Richardson), **III:** 92

Letters and Private Papers of W. M. Thackeray (ed. Ray), **V:** 37, 140

Letters and Works of Lady Mary Wortley Montagu, The (ed. Ray), **III:** 326*n*

Letters for Literary Ladies (Edgeworth), **Supp. III:** 153

Letters from a Citizen of the World (Goldsmith), *see Citizen of the World, The*

Letters from America (Brooke), **Supp. III:** 47, 50, 54–55, 59–60

Letters from England: By Don Manuel Alvarez Espriella (Southey), **IV:** 60, 68–69, 71

Letters from Iceland (Auden and MacNeice), **VII:** 403; **Retro. Supp. I:** 7

Letters from John Galsworthy (ed. Garnett), **VI:** 290

Letters from London (Barnes), **Supp. IV:** 65, 74–75

Letters from the Lake Poets to D. Stuart (ed. Coleridge), **IV:** 144

Letters from W. S. Landor to R. W. Emerson (Landor), **IV:** 100

Letters of a Conservative, The (Landor), **IV:** 100

"Letters of an Englishman" (Brontë), **V:** lll

Letters of an Old Playgoer (Arnold), **V:** 216

Letters of Charles Lamb . . . , The (ed. Lucas), **II:** 119*n*, **IV:** 84, 86

Letters of Elizabeth Barrett Browning (ed. Kenyon), **IV:** 312, 321

Letters of G. M. Hopkins to Robert Bridges (ed. Abbott), **VI:** 83

Letters of James Boswell . . . (ed. Francis), **III:** 249

Letters of James Boswell (ed. Tinker), **III:** 234*n*, 249

Letters of John Keats to Fanny Browne, **Retro. Supp. I:** 185

Letters of Laurence Sterne (ed. Curtis), **III:** 124*n*

Letters of Matthew Arnold, 1848–1888 (ed. Russell), **V:** 205, 206, 208, 211, 216

Letters of Mrs. Gaskell, The (ed. Chapell and Pollard), **V:** 108, 137, 151

Letters of Robert Browning and Elizabeth Barrett, 1845–46, **IV:** 318–319, 320, 321

Letters of Runnymede (Disraeli), **IV:** 298, 308

Letters of State, Written by Mr. John Milton . . . (Milton), **II:** 176

Letters of T. E. Lawrence, The (Lawrence), **Supp. II:** 287, 290

Letters of W. B. Yeats (ed. Wade), **VII:** 134

Letters of Walter Savage Landor, Private and Public (ed. Wheeler), **IV:** 89, 98, 100

Letters of William and Dorothy Wordsworth (ed. Selincourt), **IV:** 11, 25

Letters of Wit, Politicks and Morality, **II:** 352, 364

Letters on Several Occasions (Dennis), **II:** 338

Letters on the Subject of the Catholics, to my brother Abraham, who lives in the Country (Smith), **Supp. VII:** 343

Letters to a Young Gentleman . . . (Swift), **III:** 29

"Letters to a Young Man" (De Quincey), **IV:** 146

Letters to Alice on First Reading Jane Austen (Weldon), **Supp. IV:** 521–522, 536

Letters to Archdeacon Singleton (Smith), **Supp. VII:** 349–350

Letters to Malcolm: Chiefly on Prayer (Lewis), **Supp. III:** 249, 264, 265

Letters to T. E. Lawrence (Lawrence), **Supp. II:** 293

Letters to the Sheriffs of Bristol . . . (Burke), **III:** 205

"Letters to the Winner" (Murray), **Supp. VII:** 279

Letters with a Chapter of Biography, The (Sorley), **VI:** 421

Letters Written During a Short Residence in Spain and Portugal (Southey), **IV:** 71

Letters Written During a Short Residence in Sweden, Norway, and Denmark (Wollstonecraft), **Supp. III:** 473–475, 479

Letters Written to and for Particular Friends (Richardson), *see Familiar Letters*

Lettres d'une péruvienne (Graffigny), **Supp. III:** 75

Letty Fox: Her Luck (Stead), **Supp. IV:** 473

Levanter, The (Ambler), **Supp. IV:** 16

"Level–Crossing, The" (Warner), **Supp. VII:** 380

Levi, Peter, **Supp. IV:** 159

Leviathan (Hobbes), **II:** 190; **III:** 22; **IV:** 138

Levin, Harry, **I:** 288, 292

Levin, Ira, **III:** 343

Levin, Richard, **II:** 4, 23

Lévi–Strauss, Claude, **Supp. IV:** 115

Levitt, Morton, **Supp. IV:** 233

Levy, Paul, **Supp. IV:** 145

Lewes, George Henry, **IV:** 10l, 122; **V:** 137, 189–190, 192, 198; **Retro. Supp. II:** 102–103

Lewis, Alun, **VII:** xxii, 422, **444–448**

Lewis, C. Day, *see* Day Lewis, Cecil

Lewis, C. S., **I:** 81, 95, 117; **III:** 51; **V:** 301, 306; **VII:** 356; **Supp. I:** 71, 72; **Supp. III:** **247–268**

Lewis, Matthew, **III:** 331, 332–333, 336, 340, 343, 345; **Supp. III:** 384

Lewis, Peter, **Supp. IV:** 13

Lewis, Wyndham, **VI:** 118, 216, 247, 322; **VII:** xii, xv, 35, 41, 45, 49, 50, **71–85; Supp. IV:** 5

"Lewis Carroll" (de la Mare), **V:** 268, 274

Lewis Carroll (Hudson), **V:** 262–263, 274

Lewis Eliot stories (Snow), **VII:** 322; *see Strangers and Brothers* cycle

Lewis Seymour and Some Women (Moore), **VI:** 86, 89–90, 98, 99

"Lexicography" (Ewart), **Supp. VII:** 45

"Liar, The" (James), **VI:** 69

"Libbie Marsh's Three Eras" (Gaskell), **V:** 15

Libel on D[octor] Delany, A (Swift), **III:** 35

Liber Amoris (Hazlitt), **IV:** 128, 131–132, 133, 139

Liber niger (Edward IV), **I:** 25, 44

Liberal (periodical), **IV:** 132, 172

"Liberty" (Collins), **III:** 166, 172

Liberty (Thomson), **Supp. III:** 411–412, **419–422**

Libra (Delillo), **Supp. IV:** 487

Library, The (Crabbe), **III:** 274, 280, 286

Licking Hitler (Hare), **Supp. IV:** 282, 287–288

"Licorice Fields at Pontefract, The" (Betjeman), **VII:** 368

Lidoff, Joan, **Supp. IV:** 459

"Lie, The" (Ralegh), **I:** 148

"Lieutenant Bligh and Two Midshipmen" (Brown), **Supp. VI:** 70

"Life, The" (Ewart), **Supp. VII:** 39

Life, Adventures, and Pyracies of . . . Captain Singleton, The (Defoe), *see Captain Singleton*

Life After Death (Toynbee), **Supp. I:** 40

Life and Adventures of Martin Chuzzlewit, The (Dickens), *see Martin Chuzzlewit*

Life and Adventures of Nicholas Nickleby, The (Dickens), *see Nicholas Nickleby*

Life and Art (Hardy), **VI:** 20

"Life and Character of Dean Swift, The" (Swift), **III:** 23, 32, 36

Life and Correspondence of Robert Southey, The (Southey), **IV:** 62, 72

Life and Correspondence of Thomas Arnold, The (Stanley), **V:** 13

"Life and Death of God, The" (Ballard), **Supp. V:** 28

Life and Death of Jason, The (Morris), **V:** 296, 297, 298, 304, 306

Life and Death of Mr. Badman, The (Bunyan), **II:** 242, 248, 250–251, 253

Life and Death of Tom Thumb, the Great, The (Fielding), **Retro. Supp. I:** 82

"Life and Fame" (Cowley), **II:** 196

Life and Habit (Butler), **Supp. II,** 102, 104–105, 106, 107, 111

Life and Labours of Blessed John Baptist De La Salle, The (Thompson), **V:** 450, 451

Life and Letters of John Galsworthy, The (Marrot), **V:** 270; **VI:** 287

Life and Letters of Leslie Stephen, The (Maitland), **V:** 277, 290

Life and Letters, The (Macaulay), **IV:** 270–271, 284, 291

Life and Loves of a She–Devil, The (Weldon), **Supp. IV:** 537–538

Life and Opinions of Tristram Shandy, Gentleman, The (Sterne), *see Tristram Shandy*

"Life and Poetry of Keats, The" (Masson), **IV:** 212, 235

Life and Strange Surprizing Adventures of Robinson Crusoe . . . , The (Defoe), *see Robinson Crusoe*

Life and the Poet (Spender), **Supp. II:** 489

Life and Times of Laurence Sterne, The (Cross), **III:** 125

Life and Times of Michael K (Coetzee), **Supp. VI:** 76, **82–83**

Life and Work of Harold Pinter, The (Billington), **Retro. Supp. I:** 216

Life as We Have Known It (Woolf), **Retro. Supp. I:** 314

"Life and Writings of Addison" (Macaulay), **IV:** 282

Life Goes On (Sillitoe), **Supp. V:** 411

"Life in a Love" (Browning), **IV:** 365

Life in Greece from Homer to Menander (Mahafty), **V:** 400

"Life in London" (Egan), **IV:** 260

Life in Manchester (Gaskell), **V:** 15

Life, Letters, and Literary Remains of John Keats (Milnes), **IV:** 211, 235, 351; **Retro. Supp. I:** 185–186

Life of Addison (Johnson), **III:** 42

Life of Alexander Pope (Ruffhead), **III:** 69n, 71

Life of Algernon Charles Swinburne, The (Gosse), **V:** 311, 334

Life of Benjamin Disraeli, Earl of Beaconsfield, The (Monypenny and Buckle), **IV:** 292, 295, 300, 307, 308

Life of . . . Bolingbroke, The (Goldsmith), **III:** 189, 191

Life of Charlotte Brontë, The (Gaskell), **V:** xii, 1–2, 3, 13–14, 15, 108, 122

Life of Christina Rossetti, The (Sanders), **V:** 250, 260

Life of Cicero, The (Trollope), **V:** 102

Life of Collins (Johnson), **III:** 164, 171

Life of Crabbe (Crabbe), **III:** 272

Life of Dr. Donne, The (Walton), **II:** 132, 136, 140, 141, 142

Life of Dr. Robert Sanderson, The (Walton), **II:** 133, 135, 136–137, 140, 142

Life of Dryden, The (Scott), **IV:** 38

Life of George Moore, The (Horne), **VI:** 87, 96, 99

Life of Henry Fawcett, The (Stephen), **V:** 289

Life of John Bright, The (Trevelyan), **VI:** 389

Life of John Hales, The (Walton), **II:** 136

Life of John Milton, The (Wilson), **Supp. VI:** 301–302

Life of John Sterling (Carlyle), **IV:** 41–42, 240, 249, 250

Life of Johnson, The (Boswell), **I:** 30; **III:** 58, 114n, 115, 120, 234, 238, 239, 243–248; **IV:** xv, 280; **Retro. Supp. I:** 145–148

Life of Katherine Mansfield, The (Mantz and Murry), **VII:** 183

"Life of Ma Parker" (Mansfield), **VII:** 175, 177

Life of Man, The (Arden), **Supp. II:** 28

Life of Mr. George Herbert, The (Walton), **II:** 119–120, 133, 140, 142, 143; **Retro. Supp. II:** 171–172

Life of Mr. Jonathan Wild the Great, The (Fielding), *see Jonathan Wild*

Life of Mr. Richard Hooker, The (Walton), **II:** 133, 134, 135, 140–143

Life of Mr. Richard Savage (Johnson), **III:** 108, 121

Life of Mrs. Godolphin, The (Evelyn), **II:** 275, 287

"Life of Mrs. Radcliffe" (Scott), **IV:** 35

Life of Mrs. Robert Louis Stevenson, The (Sanchez), **V:** 393, 397

Life of Napoleon, The (Scott), **IV:** 38

Life of Napoleon Bonaparte, The (Hazlitt), **IV:** 135, 140

Life of Nelson, The (Southey), **IV:** xvii, 58, 69, 71, 280

Life of Our Lady, The (Lydgate), **I:** 22, 57, 65–66

Life of Pico (More), **Supp. VII:** 233, 234, 238

Life of Pope (Johnson), **Retro. Supp. I:** 144–145

Life of Richard Nash, The (Goldsmith), **III:** 189, 191

Life of Robert Louis Stevenson, The (Balfour), **V:** 393, 397

Life of Robert Louis Stevenson, The (Masson), **V:** 393, 397

Life of Rudyard Kipling, The (Carrington), **VI:** 166

Life of Saint Albion, The (Lydgate), **I:** 57

Life of Saint Cecilia, The (Chaucer), **I:** 31

Life of Saint Edmund, The (Lydgate), **I:** 57

Life of Saint Francis Xavier, The (tr. Dryden), **II:** 305

Life of Samuel Johnson, The (Boswell), *see Life of Johnson, The*

Life of Schiller (Carlyle), **IV:** 241, 249, 250

Life of Sir Henry Wotton, The (Walton), **II:** 133, 141, 142, 143

Life of Sir James Fitzjames Stephen, The (Stephen), **V:** 289

Life of Sterling (Carlyle), *see Life of John Sterling*

"Life of the Emperor Julius" (Brontë), **V:** 113

"Life of the Imagination, The" (Gordimer), **Supp. II:** 233–234

Life of the Rev. Andrew Bell, The (Southey and Southey), **IV:** 71

Life of the Seventh Earl of Shaftesbury (Hodder), **IV:** 62

Life of Thomas Hardy (Hardy), **VI:** 14–15

Life of Thomas More, The (Ackroyd), **Supp. VI:** **12,** 13

"Life of Thomas Parnell" (Goldsmith), **III:** 189

Life of Wesley, The (Southey), **IV:** 68, 71

Life of William Blake (Gilchrist), **Retro. Supp. I:** 46

Life of William Morris, The (Mackail), **V:** 294, 297, 306

"Life Sentence" (West), **Supp. III:** 442

"Life to Come, The" (Forster), **VI:** 411

"Life with a Hole in It, The" (Larkin), **Supp. I:** 284

Life's Handicap (Kipling), **VI:** 204

Life's Little Ironies (Hardy), **VI:** 20, 22

Life's Morning, A (Gissing), **V:** 437

"Liffey Hill, The" (Kinsella), **Supp. V:** 267

"Lifted Veil, The" (Eliot), **V:** 198

Light and the Dark, The (Snow), **VII:** 324, 327

"Light breaks where no sun shines" (Thomas), **Supp. I:** 172

Light for Them That Sit in Darkness . . . (Bunyan), **II:** 253

Light Garden of the Angel King: Journeys in Afghanistan, The (Levi), **Supp. IV:** 159

Light Heart, The (Jonson), **Retro. Supp. I:** 165

"Light Man, A" (James), **VI:** 25, 69

Light Music, (Mahon), **Supp. VI:** 173

Light of Day, The (Ambler), **Supp. IV:** 4, 16–17

Light Shining in Buckinghamshire (Churchill), **Supp. IV:** 180, 186–188

"Light Shining Out of Darkness" (Cowper), **III:** 211

Light That Failed, The (Kipling), **VI:** 166, 169, 189–190, 204

"Light Woman, A" (Browning), **IV:** 369

Lighthouse, The (Collins), **Supp. VI:** 95

"Lighthouse Invites the Storm, The" (Lowry), **Supp. III:** 282

Lighthouse Invites the Storm, The (Lowry), **Supp. III:** 282

"Lights Among Redwood" (Gunn), **Supp. IV:** 263

"Lights Out" (Thomas), **Supp. III:** 401

"Like a Vocation" (Auden), **Retro. Supp. I:** 9

Like Birds, Like Fishes and Other Stories (Jhabvala), **Supp. V:** 235

Like It Or Not (Ewart), **Supp. VII:** 47

Lilac and Flag: An Old Wives' Tale of a City (Berger), **Supp. IV:** 93–95

Lilian (Bennett), **VI:** 250, 259–260

"Lilly in a Christal, The" (Herrick), **II:** 104

"Lily Adair" (Chivers), **V:** 313

Limbo (Huxley), **VII:** 199, 200

Lincolnshire poems (Tennyson), **IV:** 327, 336

Linda Tressel (Trollope), **V:** 102

Linden Tree, The (Priestley), **VII:** 209, 228–229

Line of Life, A (Ford), **II:** 88, 100

"Lines Composed a Few Miles Above Tintern Abbey" (Wordsworth), **IV:** ix, 3, 7, 8, 9–10, 11, 44, 198, 215, 233

"Lines Composed in a Wood on a Windy Day" (Brontë), **V:** 132

"Lines Composed While Climbing the Left Ascent of Brockley Combe" (Coleridge), **IV: 43–44**

"Lines for a Book" (Gunn), **Supp. IV:** 260, 261

"Lines for Cuscuscaraway . . . " (Elliot), **VII:** 163

"Lines for Thanksgiving" (McGuckian), **Supp. V:** 289

"Lines of Desire" (Motion), **Supp. VII:** 254, 260–261

"Lines on a Young Lady's Photograph Album" (Larkin), **Supp. I:** 285

"Lines on the Loss of the *Titanic*" (Hardy), **VI:** 16

"Lines Written Among the Euganean Hills" (Shelley), **IV:** 199; **Retro. Supp. I:** 250–251

"Lines Written in the Bay of Lerici" (Shelley), **IV:** 206

"Lines Written on a Seat" (Kavanagh), **Supp. VII:** 198

"Lingam and the Yoni, The" (Hope), **Supp. VII:** 154

"Linnet in the rocky dells, The" (Brontë), **V:** 115

Lion and the Fox, The (Lewis), **VII:** 72, 74, 82

Lion and the Mouse, The (Henryson), **Supp. VII:** 136, 139

Lion and the Ostrich, The (Koestler), **Supp. I:** 35

Lion and the Unicorn, The (Orwell), **VII:** 282

Lion, The Witch, and the Wardrobe, The (Lewis), **Supp. III:** 248, 260

Lions and Shadows (Isherwood), **VII:** 310, 312

Lipton Story: A Centennial Biography, A (Waugh), **Supp. VI:** 275

"Litanie, The" (Donne), **Retro. Supp. II:** 96

Litanies de Satan (Baudelaire), **V:** 310

"Litany, A" (Swinburne), **V:** 320

"Literary Criticism and Philosophy: A Reply" (Leavis), **VII:** 241–242

Literary Criticisms by Francis Thompson (ed. Connolly), **V:** 450, 451

Literary Reminiscences (Hood), **IV:** 252, 253, 254, 259–260, 266

Literary Studies (Bagehot), **V:** 156, 170

Literary Taste: How to Form It (Bennett), **VI:** 266

"Literature and Dogma" (Arnold), **V:** xxiv, 203, 212, 216

"Literature and Offence" (Brink), **Supp. VI:** 47

"Literature and the Irish Language" (Moore), **VI:** 98

Literature and Western Man (Priestley), **VII:** 209, 214–215

Literature at Nurse; or, Circulating Morals (Moore), **VI:** 90, 98

Lithuania (Brooke), **Supp. III:** 47, 54

"Little and a lone green lane" (Brontë), **V:** 112–113

"Little Black Boy, The" (Blake), **Supp. IV:** 188; **Retro. Supp. I:** 36

"Little Boy Lost, The" (Blake), **III:** 292

Little Dinner at Timmins's, A (Thackeray), **V:** 24, 38

Little Dorrit (Dickens), **V:** xxii, 41, 42, 47, 55, 63, 64–66, 68, 69, 70, 72

Little Dream, The (Galsworthy), **VI:** 274

Little Drummer Girl, The (le Carré), **Supp. II:** 305, 306, 307, 311, 313, **315–318**

Little French Lawyer, The (Fletcher and Massinger), **II:** 66

"Little Ghost Who Died for Love, The" (Sitwell), **VII:** 133

"Little Gidding" (Eliot), **VII:** 154, 155, 156

Little Girl, The (Mansfield), **VII:** 171

Little Girls, The (Bowen), **Supp. II:** 77, 82, 84, 94

Little Gray Home in the West (Arden and D'Arcy), **Supp. II:** 32, 35

Little Hotel, The (Stead), **Supp. IV:** 473, 476

Little Learning, A (Waugh), **Supp. VI:** 271

Little Men (Alcott), **Supp. IV:** 255

Little Minister, The (Barrie), **Supp. III:** 1, 3, 8

"Little Paul and the Sea" (Stevenson), **Supp. VI:** 264

"Little Photographer, The" (du Maurier), **Supp. III:** 135

"Little Puppy That Could, The" (Amis), **Supp. IV:** 40

"Little Red Twin" (Hughes), **Supp. I:** 359

Little Tales of Misogyny (Highsmith), **Supp. V:** 177, 180

Little Tea, a Little Chat, A (Stead), **Supp. IV:** 462, 473

"Little Tembi" (Lessing), **Supp. I:** 241

Little Tour in France, A (James), **VI:** 45–46, 67

"Little Travels and Roadside Sketches" (Thackeray), **V:** 38

Little Wars: A Game for Boys (Wells), **VI:** 227, 244

"Little While, A" (Rossetti), **V:** 242

"Little while, a little while, A," (Brontë), **V:** 127–128

Littlewood, Joan, **Supp. II:** 68, 70, 73, 74

Live Like Pigs (Arden), **Supp. II:** 24–25, 29

Lively, Penelope, **Supp. IV:** 304

"Lively sparks that issue from those eyes, The" (Wyatt), **I:** 109

"Liverpool Address, A" (Arnold), **V:** 213, 216

Lives, (Mahon), **Supp. VI: 168–171,** 172

"Lives" (Mahon), **Supp. VI:** 169

Lives, The (Walton), **II:** 131, 134–137, 139, **140–143;** *see also* individual works: *Life of Dr. Donne; Life of Dr. Robert Sanderson; Life of Mr. George Herbert; Life of Mr. Richard Hooker; Life of Sir Henry Wotton*

Lives of the British Admirals (Southey and Bell), **IV:** 71

Lives of the English Poets, The (Johnson), **II:** 259; **III:** 118–119, 122, 160, 173, 189; **Retro. Supp. I:** 143–145, 274

Lives of the Hunted (Seton), **Supp. IV:** 158

Lives of the 'Lustrious: A Dictionary of Irrational Biography (Stephen and Lee), **V:** 290

Lives of the Novelists (Scott), **III:** 146n; **IV:** 38, 39

Lives of the Poets, The (Johnson), *see Lives of the English Poets, The*

Lives of the English Saints (Newman), **Supp. VII:** 296

Livia (Durrell), **Supp. I:** 118, 119

Living (Green), **Supp. II:** 251–253

Living and the Dead, The (White), **Supp. I:** 129, 130, 134

Living in America (Stevenson), **Supp. VI: 254–256**

"Living in Time" (Reid), **Supp. VII:** 329

Living Novel, The (Pritchett), **IV:** 306

Living Principle, The (Leaves), **VII:** 237

Living Quarters (Friel), **Supp. V:** 122

Living Room, The (Greene), **Supp. I:** 13; **Retro. Supp. II:** 161–162

Living Together (Ayckbourn), **Supp. V:** 2, 5

"Livings" (Larkin), **Supp. I:** 277, 282

Livingstone's Companions (Gordimer), **Supp. II:** 229, 233

Liza of Lambeth (Maugham), **VI:** 364–365

Liza's England (Barker), *see Century's Daughter, The*

"Lizbie Brown" (Hardy), **Retro. Supp. I:** 110

"Lizzie Leigh" (Gaskell), **V:** 3, 15
Lloyd, Charles, **IV:** 78
Lloyd George, David, **VI:** 264, 340, 352, 353; **VII:** 2
Loaves and Fishes (Brown), **Supp. VI:** 65, 71
"Lob" (Thomas), **Supp. III:** 394, 405
Lobo, Jeronimo, **III:** 107, 112
Local Habitation (Nicholson), **Supp. VI:** 213, **217–218**
"Loch Roe" (MacCaig), **Supp. VI:** 182
"Loch Sionascaig" (MacCaig), **Supp. VI:** 195
"Lock up, fair lids, The treasure of my heart" (Sidney), **I:** 169
Locke, John, **III:** 22; **IV:** 169; **Supp. III:** 33, 233
Lockhart, J. G., **IV:** 27, 30, 34, 36, 38, 39, 294; **V:** 140
"Locksley Hall" (Tennyson), **IV:** 325, 333, 334–335
"Locksley Hall Sixty Years After" (Tennyson), **IV:** 328, 338
"Locust Songs" (Hill), **Supp. V:** 187
Lodge, David, **Supp. II:** 9, 10; **Supp. IV:** 102, 139, **363–387**, 546; **Retro. Supp. I:** 217
Lodge, Thomas, **I:** 306, 312
"Lodging for the Night, A" (Stevenson), **V:** 384, 395
Lodore (Shelley), **Supp. III:** 371, 372
Loftis, John, **III:** 255, 271
"Lofty in the Palais de Danse" (Gunn), **Supp. IV:** 258
"Lofty Sky, The" (Thomas), **Supp. III:** 401
Logan, Annie R. M., **VI:** 23
Logan Stone (Thomas), **Supp. IV:** 490
"Logan Stone" (Thomas), **Supp. IV:** 491, 492
"Logic of Dreams" (Fuller), **Supp. VII:** 74
Logic of Political Economy, The (De Quincey), **IV:** 155
"Logical Ballad of Home Rule, A" (Swinburne), **V:** 332
"Logos" (Hughes), **Supp. I:** 350
Loiners, The (Harrison), **Supp. V:** 149, 150–151
"Lois the Witch" (Gaskell), **V:** 15
Loitering with Intent (Spark), **Supp. I:** 204, 212, 213
Lolita (Nabokov), **Supp. IV:** 26, 30
Lolly Willowes (Warner), **Supp. VII:** 370, 373–374, 375, 381
Lombroso, Cesare, **V:** 272
Londinium Redivivum (Evelyn), **II:** 287
"London" (Blake), **III:** 294, 295
"London" (Johnson), **III:** 57, 108, 114, 121; **Retro. Supp. I:** 137
London (Russell), **Supp. IV:** 126
London Assurance (Boucicault), **V:** 415
"London by Lamplight" (Meredith), **V:** 219
London Fields (Amis), **Supp. IV:** 26, 27, 35–37
"London hast thou accusèd me" (Surrey), **I:** 113, 116
London Journal 1762–1763 (Boswell), **III:** 239, 240, 242

London Lickpenny (Ackroyd), **Supp. VI:** 3
London Life, A (James), **VI:** 67, 69
London Magazine (periodical), **III:** 263; **IV:** xviii, 252, 253, 257, 260; **V:** 386
London Mercury (periodical), **VII:** 211
London Review of Books, **Supp. IV:** 121
"London Revisited" (Beerbohm), **Supp. II:** 52
"London Snow" (Bridges), **VI:** 78
London Spy (periodical), **III:** 41
London Street Games (Douglas), **VI:** 304, 305
London: The Biography (Ackroyd), **Supp. VI:** 13
London to Ladysmith via Pretoria (Churchill), **VI:** 351
London Tradesmen (Trollope), **V:** 102
Londoners (Ewart), **Supp. VII:** 38
"Lone Voices" (Amis), **Supp. II:** 11
"Loneliness" (Auden), **Retro. Supp. I:** 13
"Loneliness" (Behan), **Supp. II:** 64
"Loneliness of the Long–Distance Runner, The" (Sillitoe), **Supp. V:** 409, 410, 413, 419–421
Lonely Girl, The (O'Brien), **Supp. V:** 334, 336–337
Lonely Londoners, The (Selvon), **Supp. IV:** 445
Lonely Unicorn, The (Waugh), **Supp. VI:** 270
"Long ages past" (Owen), **VI:** 448
Long Day Wanes, The (Burgess), *see Malayan trilogy*
"Long Story, A" (Gray), **III:** 140
"Longes MACnUSNIG: The Exile of the Sons of Usnech and The Exile of Fergus and The Death of the Sons of Usnech and of Deidre" (Kinsella), **Supp. V:** 264
Longest Day, The (Clough), **V:** 170
Longest Journey, The (Forster), **VI:** 398, **401–403**, 407; **Retro. Supp. II:** 136, 139–141
"Long–Legged Fly" (Yeats), **Retro. Supp. I:** 337
Longley, Michael, **Supp. IV:** 412
"Longstaff's Marriage" (James), **VI:** 69
Lonsdale, R., **III:** 142*n*, 144
"Look" (Motion), **Supp. VII:** 259
Look After Lulu (Coward), **Supp. II:** 155
Look at All Those Roses (Bowen), **Supp. II:** 92–93
Look at Me (Brookner), **Supp. IV:** 125–126
"Look at the Children" (Graham), **Supp. VII:** 116
"Look at the Cloud His Evening Playing Cards" (Graham), **Supp. VII:** 116
Look Back in Anger (Osborne), **Supp. I:** 329, **330–332**, 338; **Supp. II:** 4, 70, 155; **Supp. III:** 191; **Supp. IV:** 282, 283
Look Look (Frayn), **Supp. VII:** 61
Look, Stranger! (Auden), **VII:** xix, 384
Look! We Have Come Through! (Lawrence), **VII:** 127; **Retro. Supp. II:** 233
Looking Back (Douglas), **VI:** 304, 305
Looking Back (Maugham), **VI:** 365

"Looking Back" (Vaughan), **II:** 185, 188
Looking for a Language (Fry), **Supp. III:** 191
Looking Glass War, The (le Carré), **Supp. II:** 308, 309–310; **Supp. IV:** 22
Looking on Darkness (Brink), **Supp. VI:** 48
Loom of Youth, The (Waugh), **Supp. VI:** 267, **268–269**
"Loose Saraband, A" (Lovelace), **II:** 232
Loot (Orton), **Supp. V:** 363, 367, 371, 375
Lopez, Bernard, **VI:** 85
Loquituri (Bunting), **Supp. VII:** 5
"Lorca" (Thomas), **Supp. IV:** 493
"Lord Arthur Savile's Crime" (Wilde), **V:** 405, 419; **Retro. Supp. II:** 365
"Lord Beaupre" (James), **VI:** 69
"Lord Carlisle on Pope" (De Quincey), **IV:** 146
Lord Chancellor Jeffreys and the Stuart Cause (Keeton), **IV:** 286
Lord Cucumber (Orton), **Supp. V:** 363
Lord George Bentinck (Disraeli), **IV:** 303, 308
Lord Grey of the Reform Bill (Trevelyan), **VI:** 389–390
Lord Jim (Conrad), **VII:** 34, **139–140**, 148; **Supp. II:** 290; **Retro. Supp. II:** 69, 75–77
Lord Malquist and Mr Moon (Stoppard), **Supp. I:** 438
"Lord of Ennerdale, The" (Scott), **IV:** 31
Lords of Limit, The: Essays on Literature and Ideas (Hill), **Supp. V:** 201
"Lord of the Dynamos" (Wells), **VI:** 235
Lord of the Flies (Golding), **Supp. I:** 67, 68–70, 71, 72, 75, 83; **Supp. IV:** 393; **Retro. Supp. I:** 94–97
Lord of the Isles, The (Scott), **IV:** 39
Lord of the Rings, The (Tolkien), **Supp. II:** 519, 520, 521, 524, 525, 527, 528, 529–530, 531, 532–534; **Supp. IV:** 116
Lord Ormont and His Aminta (Meredith), **V:** 226, 232, 233, 234
Lord Palmerston (Trollope), **V:** 102
Lord Peter Views the Body (Sayers), **Supp. III:** 340
Lord Raingo (Bennett), **VI:** 250, 252, 261–262
Lord Randolph Churchill (Churchill), **VI:** 352
Lord Soulis (Swinburne), **V:** 333
"Lords of Hell and the Word, The" (Brown), **Supp. VI:** 72
Lorenz, Konrad, **Supp. IV:** 162
Losing Nelson (Unsworth), **Supp. VII:** 365, 366–367
Loss and Gain (Newman), **Supp. VII:** 293, 297, 299
Loss of El Dorado, The (Naipaul), **Supp. I:** 390, 392–393
"Loss of the Eurydice, The" (Hopkins), **V:** 369–370, 379
Lost Childhood, and Other Essays, The (Greene), **VI:** 333; **Supp. I:** 2
"Lost Days" (Rossetti), **V:** 243
Lost Empires (Priestley), **VII:** 220–221

Lost Flying Boat, The (Sillitoe), **Supp. V:** 411

Lost Girl, The (Lawrence), **VII:** 90, 104–106; **Retro. Supp. II:** 229

"Lost Leader, The" (Browning), **IV:** 356

"Lost Legion, The" (Kipling), **VI:** 193

"Lost Mistress, The" (Browning), **IV:** 369

Lost Ones, The (Beckett), **Supp. I:** 47, 55, 61–62

Lost Season, A (Fuller), **Supp. VII:** 69–70

Lost World, The (Doyle), **Supp. II:** 159

"Lot and His Daughters" (Hope), **Supp. VII:** 158

Lothair (Disraeli), **IV:** xxiii, 294, 296, 304, 306, 307, 308

Loti, Pierre, **Retro. Supp. I:** 291

Lotta Schmidt (Trollope), **V:** 101

Lottery, The (Fielding), **III:** 105

"Lotus, The" (Rhys), **Supp. II:** 402

Lotus and the Robot, The (Koestler), **Supp. I:** 34*n*

"Lotus–Eaters, The" (Tennyson), **IV:** xix; **V:** ix

"Loud without the wind was roaring" (Brontë), **V:** 127

"Loudest Lay, The" (Warner), **Supp. VII:** 371–372

Lough Derg (Kavanagh), **Supp. VII:** 192–193, 199

Louis Percy (Brookner), **Supp. IV:** 131

"Louisa in the Lane" (Hardy), **Retro. Supp. I:** 110

"Louisa Pallant" (James), **VI:** 69

"Love" (Brooke), **Supp. III:** 55

Love (Carter), **Supp. III:** 79, 81, 82, 83

Love After All (Ayckbourn), **Supp. V:** 2

Love All (Sayers), **Supp. III:** 348

Love Among the Artists (Shaw), **VI:** 103, 105, 106, 129

Love Among the Chickens (Wodehouse), **Supp. III:** 450

"Love Among the Haystacks" (Lawrence), **VII:** 115

"Love Among the Ruins" (Browning), **IV:** 357, 369

Love Among the Ruins (Waugh), **VII:** 302

Love and a Bottle (Farquhar), **II:** 352, 356, 364

Love and Business (Farquhar), **II:** 352, 355, 364

"Love and Debt Alike Troublesome" (Suckling), **II:** 227

Love and Fashion (Burney), **Supp. III:** 64

Love and Freindship [sic] and Other Early Works (Austen), **IV:** 122

"Love and Life" (Cowley), **II:** 197, 198

"Love and Life" (Rochester), **II:** 258

Love and Mr. Lewisham (Wells), **VI:** 235–236, 244

Love and Napalm: Export U.S.A (Ballard), **Supp. V:** 26

Love and other Deaths (Thomas), **Supp. IV:** 490

Love and Truth (Walton), **II:** 134, 143

"Love Arm'd" (Behn), **Supp. III:** 36, 37

"Love Declared" (Thompson), **V:** 442

Love Department, The (Trevor), **Supp. IV:** 501, 507–508

Love for Love (Congreve), **II:** 324, 338, 342–343, 350

"Love from the North" (Rossetti), **V:** 259

"Love in a Colder Climate" (Ballard), **Supp. V:** 33

Love in a Life (Motion), **Supp. VII:** 253, 254, 257, 258–260, 261, 263

"Love in a Valley" (Betjeman), **VII:** 366

Love in a Wood; or, St. James's Park (Wycherley), **II:** 308, 309, **311–313,** 321

"Love in Dian's Lap" (Thompson), **V:** 441

Love in Idleness (Nicholls), **IV:** 98*n*

Love in Idleness (Rattigan), **Supp. VII:** 313

Love in Several Masques (Fielding), **III:** 96, 105; **Retro. Supp. I:** 79–80, 81–82

"Love in the Environs of Voronezh" (Sillitoe), **Supp. V:** 424

Love in the Environs of Voronezh and Other Poems (Sillitoe), **Supp. V:** 424

"Love in the Valley" (Meredith), **V:** 219–220

"Love Is Dead" (Betjeman), **VII:** 359–360

Love Is Enough (Morris), **V:** 299*n*, 306

Love–Letters Between a Nobleman and His Sister (Behn), **Supp. III:** 30–31, 37, 39

"Love Match, A" (Warner), **Supp. VII:** 380

Love Object, The (O'Brien), **Supp. V:** 339

"Love Song of Har Dyal, The" (Swift), **VI:** 202

"Love Song of J. Alfred Prufrock, The" (Eliot), **V:** 163; **VII:** 144; **Supp. IV:** 260; **Retro. Supp. II:** 121, 122–123

"Love Songs in Age" (Larkin), **Supp. I:** 281

"Love still has something of the Sea" (Sedley); **II:** 264

"Love that doth raine and live within my thought" (Surrey), **I:** 115

"Love III" (Herbert), **II:** 129; **Retro. Supp. II:** 183

Love Triumphant; or, Nature Will Prevail (Dryden), **II:** 305

Love Unknown (Wilson) **Supp. VI:** 302, **303–304**

Lovecraft, H. P., **II:** 340, 343, 345

Loved One, The (Waugh), **VII:** 301

Love–Hate Relations (Spender), **Supp. II:** 492

Lovel the Widower (Thackeray), **V:** 35, 37, 38

Lovelace, Richard, **II:** 222, **229–232**

Lover (periodical), **III:** 50, 53

Lover, The (Pinter), **Supp. I:** 373, 374, 375; **Retro. Supp. I:** 223–224

"Lover of Things, The" (Hall), **Supp. VI:** 121

Lover's Assistant, The (Fielding), *see Ovid's Art of Love Paraphrased*

"Lover's Complaint, A, "**I:** 307

Lovers (Friel), **Supp. V:** 118

"Lovers How They Come and Part" (Herrick), **II:** 107

"Lovers in Pairs" (Ewart), **Supp. VII:** 46

"Lover's Journey, The" (Crabbe), **III:** 282–283

Lover's Melancholy, The (Ford), **II:** 88–91, 100

Lovers in London (Milne), **Supp. V:** 297, 298

"Lovers of Orelay, The" (Moore), **VI:** 96

"Lovers of Their Time" (Trevor), **Supp. IV:** 504

Lover's Progress, The (Fletcher and Massinger), **II:** 66

"Lover's Quarrel, A" (Browning), **Retro. Supp. I:**25

Lovers' Quarrels . . . (King), **II:** 336

"Lovers' Rock, The" (Southey), **IV:** 66

Lover's Tale, The (Tennyson), **IV:** 338

Love's Catechism Compiled by the Author of The Recruiting Officer (Farquhar), **II:** 364

Love's Cross Currents (Swinburne), **V:** 313, 323, 325–326, 330, 333

Love's Cure (Beaumont, Fletcher, Massinger), **II:** 66

"Loves Deitie" (Donne), **Retro. Supp. II:** 93

"Love's Journeys" (Redgrove), **Supp. VI:** 234

Love's Labour's Lost (Shakespeare), **I:** 303–304; **Retro. Supp. II:** 330

Love's Last Shift (Cibber), **II:** 324, 326

Love's Martyr (Chester), **I:** 313

Love's Metamorphosis (Lyly), **I:** 202

"Love's Nocturn" (Rossetti), **V:** 241

Loves of Amos and Laura, The (S.P.), **II:** 132

Loves of Cass McGuire, The (Friel), **Supp. V:** 118

Loves of Ergasto, The (Greber), **II:** 325

"Love's Philosophy" (Shelley), **IV:** 203

Love's Pilgrimage (Beaumont and Fletcher), **II:** 65

Love's Riddle (Cowley), **II:** 194, 202

Love's Sacrifice (Ford), **II:** 88, 89, 92, 96, 97, 99, 100

"Love's Siege" (Suckling), **II:** 226–227

"Loves Usury" (Donne), **Retro. Supp. II:** 89

Lovesick (Churchill), **Supp. IV:** 181

Loving (Green), **Supp. II:** 247, 254, **256–258**

Loving Memory (Harrison), **Supp. V:** 164

Loving Spirit, The (du Maurier), **Supp. III:** 133, 141, 144–145

Low, Will, **V:** 393, 397

"Low Barometer" (Bridges), **VI:** 80

Lowbury, Edward, **VII:** 422, 431–432

Lowell, Amy, **Supp. III:** 397

Lowell, James Russell, **I:** 121

Lowell, Robert, **Supp. II:** 276; **Supp. IV:** 423; **Retro. Supp. I:** 129, 130

Lowes, J. L., **IV:** 47, 57

Lowry, Malcolm, **Supp. III: 269–286**

Loyal Brother, The (Southern), **II:** 305

Loyal General, The (Tate), **II:** 305

"Loyal Mother, The" (Hughes), **Supp. I:** 356

Loyal Subject, The (Fletcher), **II:** 45, 65

Loyalties (Galsworthy), **VI:** xiii, 275, 287

Lucas, E. V., **IV:** 74, 76*n*, 84, 85, 86

Lucas, F. L., **II:** 69, 70*n*, 80, 83, 85

Lucasta (Lovelace), **II:** 238
Lucian, **III:** 24
Lucie–Smith, Edward, **IV:** 372, 373
Luck of Barry Lyndon, The (Thackeray), *see Barry Lyndon*
Luck, or Cunning (Butler), **Supp. II:** 106, 107, 108, 113
"Lucky Break—How I Became a Writer" (Dahl), **Supp. IV:** 209, 211
Lucky Chance, The; or, An Alderman's Bargain (Behn), **Supp. III:** 26, 29
Lucky Jim (Amis), **Supp. II:** 2, 3, 4, 5–6, 7; **Supp. IV:** 25, 27, 28, 377
"Lucky Jim's Politics" (Amis), **Supp. II:** 11–12
"Lucrece" (Gower), **I:** 54
Lucretia Borgia: The Chronicle of Tebaldeo Tebaldei (Swinburne), **V:** 325, 333
Lucretius, **II:** 275, 292, 300, 301; **IV:** 316
"Lucubratio Ebria" (Butler), **Supp. II:** 98, 99
Lucubrationes (More), **Supp. VII:** 240
Lucy (Kincaid), **Supp. VII:** 217, 219, 227–229
"Lucy Grange" (Lessing), **Supp. I:** 240
"Lucy"poems (Wordsworth), **IV:** 3, 18; **V:** 11
"Lui et Elles" (Moore), **VI:** 87
Lukács, György, **Supp. IV:** 81, 82, 87
"Lullaby" (Auden), **VII:** 383, 398; **Retro. Supp. I:** 6
"Lullaby" (Sitwell), **VII:** 135
"Lullaby for Jumbo" (Sitwell), **VII:** 132
"Lumber Room, The" (Saki), **Supp. VI:** 245
Lunar Caustic (Lowry), **Supp. III:** 269, 270, **271–273**, 280, 283
Lunch and Counter Lunch (Murray), **Supp. VII:** 270, 275–276
"Lunch with Pancho Villa" (Muldoon), **Supp. IV:** 414–415
Lupercal (Hughes), **Supp. I:** 343, 345, 363; **Retro. Supp. I:** 126; **Retro. Supp. II:** 204–205
Luria: and a Soul's Tragedy (Browning), **IV:** 374
"Lust" (Brooke), **Supp. III:** 53
Luther (Osborne), **Supp. I:** 334–335, 338
"Lux Perpetua" (Brown), **Supp. VI:** 72
"Lycidas" (Milton), **II:** 160–161, 164, 165, 168, 169, 175; **III:** 118–119, 120; **IV:** 205; **VI:** 73; **Retro. Supp. II:** 275–277
Lycidus; or, The Lover in Fashion (Behn), **Supp. III:** 37
"Lycus, The Centaur" (Hood), **IV:** 256, 267
Lydgate, John, **I:** 22, 49, **57–66**
Lyell, Sir Charles, **IV:** 325
Lyfe of Johan Picus Erle of Myrandula (More), **Supp. VII:** 246
Lying Days, The (Gordimer), **Supp. II:** 226–227
Lying Together (Thomas), **Supp. IV:** 485–486
Lyly, John, **I: 191–211**, 303
Lyric Impulse, The (Day Lewis), **Supp. III:** 118, 131

"Lyrical Ballad, A" (Motion), **Supp. VII:** 256–257
Lyrical Ballads (Wordsworth and Coleridge), **III:** 174, 336; **IV:** ix, viii, x, xvi, 3, 4, 5, **6–11**, 18, 24, **44–45**, 55, 77, 111, 138–139, 142; **Retro. Supp. II:** 53–54
Lyttelton, George, **III:** 118
Lyttleton, Dame Edith, **VII:** 32

Mabinogion, **I:** 73
"Mabinog's Liturgy" (Jones), **Supp. VII:** 177
Mac (Pinter), **Supp. I:** 367
Mac Flecknoe; or, A Satyre Upon the . . . Poet, T. S. (Dryden), **II:** 299, 304
"McAndrew's Hymn" (Kipling), **VI:** 202
Macaulay, Rose, **VII:** 37
Macaulay, Thomas Babington, **II:** 240, 241, 254, 255, 307; **III:** 51, 53, 72; **IV:** xii, xvi, xx, xxii, 101, 122, **268–291**, 295; **V:** viii; **VI:** 347, 353, 383, 392
Macbeth (Shakespeare), **I:** 317–318, 327; **II:** 97, 281; **IV:** 79–80, 188; **V:** 375; **Supp. IV:** 283
MacCaig, Norman, **Supp. VI: 181–195**
MacCarthy, Desmond, **V:** 284, 286, 290; **VI:** 363, 385; **VII:** 32; **Supp. III:** 98
McCarthy, Mary, **Supp. IV:** 234
McCartney, Colum, **Retro. Supp. I:** 131
McClintock, Anne, **Supp. IV:** 167
McClure, John, **Supp. IV:** 163
McCullers, Carson, **Supp. IV:** 422, 424
McCullough, Colleen, **Supp. IV:** 343
MacDermots of Ballycloran, The (Trollope), **V:** 101
MacDiarmid, Hugh, **III:** 310; **Supp. III:** 119
Macdonald, George, **V:** 266; **Supp. IV:** 201
Macdonald, Mary, **V:** 266, 272
McElroy, Joseph, **Supp. IV:** 116
McEwan, Ian, **Supp. IV:** 65, 75, **389–408; Supp. V:** xxx
McGann, Jerome J., **V:** 314, 335
McGuckian, Medbh, **Supp. V: 277–293**
McHale, Brian, **Supp. IV:** 112
Machiavelli, Niccolò, **II:** 71, 72; **IV:** 279; **Retro. Supp. I:** 204
"Machine Stops, The" (Forster), **VI:** 399
McInherny, Frances, **Supp. IV:** 347, 353
Mack, Maynard, **Retro. Supp. I:** 229
Mackail, J. W., **V:** 294, 296, 297, 306
McKane, Richard, **Supp. IV:** 494–495
Mackay, M. E., **V:** 223, 234
Mackenzie, Compton, **VII:** 278
Mackenzie, Henry, **III:** 87; **IV:** 79
MacKenzie, Jean, **VI:** 227, 243
MacKenzie, Norman, **V:** 374n, 375n, 381, 382; **VI:** 227, 243
McKenney, Ruth, **Supp. IV:** 476
Mackenzie, Sir George, **III:** 95
"Mackery End, in Hertfordshire" (Lamb), **IV:** 83
MacLaren, Moray, **V:** 393, 398
McLeehan, Marshall, **IV:** 323n, 338, 339
Maclure, Millar, **I:** 291
Macmillan's (periodical), **VI:** 351

MacNeice, Louis, **VII:** 153, 382, 385, **401–418; Supp. III:** 119; **Supp. IV:** 423, 424
Macpherson, James, **III:** 336; **Supp. II:** 523
Macready, William Charles, **I:** 327
McTaggart, J. M. E., **Supp. II:** 406
Mad Forest: A Play from Romania (Churchill), **Supp. IV:** 179, 188, 195–196, 198, 199
Mad Islands, The (MacNeice), **VII:** 405, 407
Mad Lover, The (Fletcher), **II:** 45, 55, 65
"Mad Maids Song, The" (Herrick), **II:** 112
"Mad Mullinix and Timothy" (Swift), **III:** 31
Mad Soldier's Song (Hardy), **VI:** 11
Mad World, My Masters, A (Middleton), **II:** 3, 4, 21
Madagascar; or, Robert Drury's Journal (Defoe), **III:** 14
Madame Bovary (Flaubert), **V:** xxii, 429; **Supp. IV:** 68, 69
"Madame de Mauves" (James), **VI:** 69; **Supp. IV:** 133
"Madame Rosette" (Dahl), **Supp. IV:** 209–210
Madan, Falconer, **V:** 264, 274
Maddox, Brenda, **Retro. Supp. I:** 327, 328
"Mademoiselle" (Stevenson), **Supp. VI:** 255
Mademoiselle de Maupin (Gautier), **V:** 320n
Madge, Charles, **VII:** xix
Madoc (Muldoon), **Supp. IV:** 420, 424–427, 428
"Madoc" (Muldoon), **Supp. IV:** 422, 425–427, 430
Madoc (Southey), **IV:** 63, 64–65, 71
"Madoc" (Southey), **Supp. IV:** 425
"Madonna" (Kinsella), **Supp. V:** 273
Madonna and Other Poems (Kinsella), **Supp. V:** 272–273
Madonna of the Future and Other Tales, The (James), **VI:** 67, 69
"Madonna of the Trenches, A" (Kipling), **VI:** 193, **194–196**
Madras House, The (Shaw), **VI:** 118
Madwoman in the Attic, The (Gilbert/Gubar), **Retro. Supp. I:** 59–60
Maggot, A (Fowles), **Supp. I:** 309–310
"Magi" (Brown), **Supp. VI:** 71
Magic (Chesterton), **VI:** 340
Magic Box, The (Ambler), **Supp. IV:** 3
Magic Finger, The (Dahl), **Supp. IV:** 201
"Magic Finger, The" (Dahl), **Supp. IV:** 223–224
Magic Toyshop, The (Carter), **III:** 345; **Supp. III:** 80, 81, 82
Magic Wheel, The (eds. Swift and Profumo), **Supp. V:** 427
Magician, The (Maugham), **VI:** 374
Magician's Nephew, The (Lewis), **Supp. III:** 248
Maginn, William, **V:** 19
"Magna Est Veritas" (Smith), **Supp. II:** 471, 472
"Magnanimity" (Kinsella), **Supp. V:** 263

Magnetic Mountain, The (Day Lewis), **Supp. III:** 117, 122, 124–126

Magnetick Lady, The (Jonson), **Retro. Supp. I:** 165

Magnificence (Skelton), **I:** 90

"Magnolia" (Fuller), **Supp. VII:** 78

Magnus (Brown), **Supp. VI: 66–67**

Magnusson, Erika, **V:** 299, 300, 306

Magus, The (Fowles), **Supp. I:** 291, 292, 293, **295–299**, 310

Mahafty, John Pentland, **V:** 400, 401

Mahon, Derek, **Supp. IV:** 412; **Supp. VI: 165–180**

"Mahratta Ghats, The" (Lewis), **VII:** 446–447

Maid in the Mill, The (Fletcher and Rowley), **II:** 66

Maid in Waiting (Galsworthy), **VI:** 275

Maid Marian (Peacock), **IV:** xviii, 167–168, 170

Maid of Bath, The (Foote), **III:** 253

"Maiden Name" (Larkin), **Supp. I:** 277

Maid's Tragedy, The (Beaumont and Fletcher), **II:** 44, 45, **54–57**, 58, 60, 65

Maid's Tragedy, Alter'd, The (Waller), **II:** 238

Mailer, Norman, **Supp. IV:** 17–18

"Maim'd Debauchee, The" (Rochester), **II:** 259–260

"Main Road" (Pritchett), **Supp. III:** 316–317

Mainly on the Air (Beerbohm), **Supp. II:** 52

Maitland, F. W., **V:** 277, 290; **VI:** 385

Maitland, Thomas, pseud. of Algernon Charles Swinburne

Maiwa's Revenge (Haggard), **Supp. III:** 213

Majeske, Penelope, **Supp. IV:** 330

Major, John, **Supp. IV:** 437–438

Major Barbara (Shaw), **VII:** xv, 102, 108, **113–115**, 124; **Retro. Supp. II:** 321

Major Political Essays (Shaw), **VI:** 129

Major Victorian Poets, The: Reconsiderations (Armstrong), **IV:** 339

Makin, Bathsua, **Supp. III:** 21

Making History (Friel), **Supp. V:** 125

Making of a Poem, The (Spender), **Supp. II:** 481, 492

Making of an Immortal, The (Moore), **VI:** 96, 99

"Making of an Irish Goddess, The" (Boland), **Supp. V:** 44–45

Making of the English Working Class, The (Thompson), **Supp. IV:** 473

Making of the Representative for Planet 8, The (Lessing), **Supp. I:** 252, 254

"Making Poetry" (Stevenson), **Supp. VI:** 262

Mal vu, mal dit (Beckett), **Supp. I:** 62

Malayan trilogy (Burgess), **Supp. I:** 187

Malcolm Lowry: Psalms and Songs (Lowry), **Supp. III:** 285

Malcolm Mooney's Land (Graham), **Supp. VII:** 104, 106, 109, 113–115, 116

Malcontent, The (Marston), **II:** 27, 30, **31–33**, 36, 40, 68

Malcontents, The (Snow), **VII:** 336–337

Male Child, A (Scott), **Supp. I:** 263

Malign Fiesta (Lewis), **VII:** 72, 80

Malinowski, Bronislaw, **Supp. III:** 186

Mallet, David, **Supp. III:** 412, 424–425

Malone, Edmond, **I:** 326

Malone Dies (Beckett), **Supp. I:** 50, 51, 52–53, 63; **Supp. IV:** 106; **Retro. Supp. I:** 18, 22–23

Malory, Sir Thomas, **I: 67–80;** **IV:** 336, 337; **Retro. Supp. II: 237–252**

Malraux, André, **VI:** 240

"Maltese Cat, The" (Kipling), **VI:** 200

Malthus, Thomas, **IV:** xvi, 127, 133

"Man" (Herbert), **Retro. Supp. II:** 176–177

"Man" (Vaughan), **II:** 186, 188

Man, The (Stoker), **Supp. III:** 381

Man Above Men (Hare), **Supp. IV:** 282, 289

"Man and Bird" (Mahon), **Supp. VI:** 168

"Man and Boy" (Heaney), **Retro. Supp. I:** 132

Man and Boy (Rattigan), **Supp. VII:** 318, 320

"Man and Dog" (Thomas), **Supp. III:** 394, 403, 405

Man and Literature (Nicholson), **Supp. VI:** 213, 223

Man and Superman: A Comedy and a Philosophy (Shaw), **IV:** 161; **VI: 112–113**, 114, 127, 129; **Retro. Supp. II:** 309, 317–320

Man and Time (Priestley), **VII:** 213

Man and Two Women, A (Lessing), **Supp. I:** 244, 248

Man and Wife (Collins), **Supp. VI:** 102

Man Born to Be King, The (Sayers), **Supp. III:** 336, 349–350

"Man Called East, The" (Redgrove), **Supp. VI:** 236

Man Could Stand Up, A (Ford), **VI:** 319, 329

Man Does, Woman Is (Graves), **VII:** 268

"Man Friday" (Hope), **Supp. VII:** 164–165

Man from the North, A (Bennett), **VI:** 248, 253

"Man from the South" (Dahl), **Supp. IV:** 215, 217–218

"Man I Killed, The" (Hardy), **Retro. Supp. I:** 120

"Man in Assynt, A" (MacCaig), **Supp. VI:** 191

Man in My Position, A (MacCaig), **Supp. VI: 191–192**

Man Named East, The (Redgrove), **Supp. VI:** 235–236

Man of Destiny, The (Shaw), **VI:** 112

Man of Devon, A (Galsworthy), **VI:** 277

Man of Honour, A (Maugham), **VI:** 367, 368

Man of Law's Tale, The (Chaucer), **I:** 24, 34, 43, 51, 57

Man of Mode, The; or, Sir Fopling Flutter (Etherege), **II:** 256, 266, 271, 305

Man of Nazareth, The (Burgess), **Supp. I:** 193

Man of Property, A (Galsworthy), **VI:** 271, 272, 273, 274, 275, 276, 278, 282–283

Man of Quality, A (Lee), **II:** 336

Man of the Moment (Ayckbourn), **Supp. V:** 3, 7–8, 10

"Man Was Made to Mourn, a Dirge" (Burns), **III:** 315

"Man Who Changes His Mind, The" (Ambler), **Supp. IV:** 5

"Man Who Could Work Miracles, The" (Wells), **VI:** 235

"Man Who Died, The" (Lawrence), **VII:** 115; **Retro. Supp. II:** 233

Man Who Loved Children, The (Stead), **Supp. IV:** 460, 467–470, 473

"Man Who Loved Islands, The" (Lawrence), **VII:** 115

"Man Who Walked on the Moon, The" (Ballard), **Supp. V:** 33

Man Who Was Thursday, The (Chesterton), **VI:** 338

Man Who Wasn't There, The (Barker), **Supp. IV:** 45, 46, 56–57

"Man with a Past, The" (Hardy), **VI:** 17

"Man with Night Sweats, The" (Gunn), **Supp. IV:** 276–277

Man with Night Sweats, The (Gunn), **Supp. IV:** 255, 257, 274–278

"Man with the Dog, The" (Jhabvala), **Supp. V:** 236

"Man with the Twisted Lip, The" (Doyle), **Supp. II:** 171

Man Within, The (Greene), **Supp. I:** 2; **Retro. Supp. II:** 152

"Man Without a Temperament, The" (Mansfield), **VII:** 174, 177

"Mana Aboda" (Hulme), **Supp. VI:** 136

Manalive (Chesterton), **VI:** 340

Mañanas de abril y mayo (Calderón), **II:** 312n

Manchester Enthusiasts, The (Arden and D'Arcy), **Supp. II:** 39

"Manchester Marriage, The" (Gaskell), **V:** 6n, 14, 15

Manciple's Prologue, The (Chaucer), **I:** 24

Manciple's Tale, The (Chaucer), **I:** 55

"Mandela" (Motion), **Supp. VII:** 266

Mandelbaum Gate, The (Spark), **Supp. I: 206–208**, 213

Mandelstam, Osip, **Supp. IV:** 163, 493

Manet, Edouard, **Supp. IV:** 480

Manfred (Byron), **III:** 338; **IV:** xvii, 172, 173, 177, **178–182**, 192

"Manhole 69" (Ballard), **Supp. V:** 21

Manifold, John, **VII:** 422, 426–427

Manin and the Venetian Revolution of 1848 (Trevelyan), **VI:** 389

Mankind in the Making (Wells), **VI:** 227, 236

Manly, J. M., **I:** 1

"Man–Man" (Naipaul), **Supp. I:** 385

Mann, Thomas, **II:** 97; **III:** 344; **Supp. IV:** 397

Manner of the World Nowadays, The (Skelton), **I:** 89

Mannerly Margery Milk and Ale (Skelton), **I:** 83

Manners, Mrs. Horace, pseud. of Algernon Charles Swinburne

"Manners, The" (Collins), **III:** 161, 162, 166, 171

Manning, Cardinal, **V:** 181

Manoeuvring (Edgeworth), **Supp. III:** 158

"Manor Farm, The" (Thomas), **Supp. III:** 399, 405

"Mans medley" (Herbert), **Retro. Supp. II:** 181–182

Manservant and Maidservant (Compton–Burnett), **VII:** 62, 63, 67

Mansfield, Katherine, **IV:** 106; **VI:** 375; **VII:** xv, xvii, **171–184**, 314; list of short stories, **VII:** 183–184

Mansfield Park (Austen), **IV:** xvii, 102–103, 108, 109, 111, 112, 115–119, 122; **Retro. Supp. II:** 9–11

Mantissa (Fowles), **Supp. I:** 308–309, 310

Manto, Saadat Hasan, **Supp. IV:** 440

Mantz, Ruth, **VII:** 176

"Manus Animam Pinxit" (Thompson), **V:** 442

Manzoni, Alessandro, **III:** 334

Map, Walter, **I:** 35

Map of Love, The (Thomas), **Supp. I:** 176–177, 180

"Map of the City, A" (Gunn), **Supp. IV:** 262, 274

Map of the World, A (Hare), **Supp. IV:** 282, 288–289, 293

Map of Verona, A (Reed), **VII:** 423

Mapp Showing . . . Salvation and Damnation, A (Bunyan), **II:** 253

Mapplethorpe, Robert, **Supp. IV:** 170, 273

Marble Faun, The (Hawthorne), **VI:** 27

March of Literature, The (Ford), **VI:** 321, 322, 324

"Marchese Pallavicini and Walter Landor" (Landor), **IV:** 90

Marching Soldier (Cary), **VII:** 186

"Marchioness of Stonehenge, The" (Hardy), **VI:** 22

Marconi's Cottage (McGuckian), **Supp. V:** 284, 286–287

Marcus, Jane, **Retro. Supp. I:** 306

Marcus, S., **V:** 46, 73

Margaret Drabble: Puritanism and Permissiveness (Myer), **Supp. IV:** 233

Margaret Ogilvy (Barrie), **Supp. III:** 3

Margin Released (Priestley), **VII:** 209, 210, 211

Margoliouth, H. M., **II:** 214n, 219

Mari Magno (Clough), **V:** 159, 168

Maria; or, The Wrongs of Woman (Wollstonecraft), **Supp. III:** 466, **476–480**

"Mariana" (Tennyson), **IV:** 329, 331

"Mariana in the South" (Tennyson), **IV:** 329, 331

Mariani, Paul L., **V:** 373n, 378, 382

Marianne Thornton (Forster), **VI:** 397, 411

Marie (Haggard), **Supp. III:** 214

Marinetti, Filippo T., **Supp. III:** 396

"Marina" (Eliot), **Retro. Supp. II:** 130

Marino, Giambattista, **II:** 180, 183

Marino Faliero (Swinburne), **V:** 332

Marino Faliero, Doge of Venice (Byron), **IV:** xviii, 178–179, 193

Marion Fay (Trollope), **V:** 102

Marionette, The (Muir), **Supp. VI:** 198, **203–204**

Marius the Epicurean (Pater), **V:** xxv, 339, 348, **349–351**, 354, 355, 356, 411

Marjorie, **VI:** 249; pseud. of Arnold Bennett

"Mark of the Beast, The" (Kipling), **VI:** 183, 193

Mark of the Warrior, The (Scott), **Supp. I:** 263

Markandaya, Kamala, **Supp. IV:** 440

"Market at Turk" (Gunn), **Supp. IV:** 260–261

"Market Square" (Milne), **Supp. V:** 302

Markey, Constance, **Supp. IV:** 347, 360

Markham, Robert, **Supp. II:** 12; pseud. of Kingsley Amis

"Markheim" (Stevenson), **V:** 395; **Retro. Supp. I:** 267

"Mark–2 Wife, The" (Trevor), **Supp. IV:** 503

Marlborough: His Life and Times (Churchill), **VI:** 354–355

Marlowe, Christopher, **I:** 212, 228–229, **275–294**, 336; **II:** 69, 138; **III:** 344; **IV:** 255, 327; **Supp. IV:** 197; **Retro. Supp. I:** **199–213**

Marlowe and His Circle (Boas), **I:** 275, 293

Marlowe and the Early Shakespeare (Wilson), **I:** 286

Marmion (Scott), **IV:** xvi, 29, 30, 38, 129

Marmor Norfolciense (Johnson), **III:** 121; **Retro. Supp. I:** 141

Marquise, The (Coward), **Supp. II:** 146

Marriage A–la–Mode (Dryden), **II:** 293, 296, 305

Marriage of Heaven and Hell, The (Blake), **III:** 289, 297–298, 304, 307; **V:** xv, 329–330, 331; **Supp. IV:** 448; **Retro. Supp. I:** 38–39

Marriage of Mona Lisa, The (Swinburne), **V:** 333

"Marriage of Tirzah and Ahirad, The" (Macaulay), **IV:** 283

Marriages Between Zones Three, Four and Five, The (Lessing), **Supp. I:** 251

Married Life (Bennett), *see Plain Man and His Wife, The*

Married Man, The (Lawrence), **VII:** 120

"Married Man's Story, A" (Mansfield), **VII:** 174

Married to a Spy (Waugh), **Supp. VI:** 276

Marryat, Captain Frederick, **Supp. IV:** 201

Marsh, Charles, **Supp. IV:** 214, 218

Marsh, Edward, **VI:** 416, 419, 420, 425, 430, 432, 452; **VII:** xvi; **Supp. III:** 47, 48, 53, 54, 60, 397

Marshall, William, **II:** 141

Marston, John, **I:** 234, 238, 340; **II:** 4, 24–33, 34–37, 40–41, 47, 68, 72; **Retro. Supp. I:** 160

Marston, Philip, **V:** 245

Marston, R. B., **II:** 131

Martha Quest (Lessing), **Supp. I:** 237, 239, 243–244; **Supp. IV:** 238

Martial, **II:** 104, 265

Martian, The (du Maurier), **Supp. III:** 134, 151

Martin, John, **V:** 110

Martin, L. C., **II:** 183, 184n, 200

Martin, Martin, **III:** 117

Martin Chuzzlewit (Dickens), **V:** xx, 42, 47, 54–56, 58, 59, 68, 71; **Supp. IV:** 366, 381

Martin Chuzzlewit (teleplay, Lodge), **Supp. IV:** 366, 381

Martin Luther (Lopez and Moore), **VI:** 85, 95, 98

Martineau, Harriet, **IV:** 311; **V:** 125–126, 146

Martyn, Edward, **VI:** 309

Martyrdom of Man (Reade), **Supp. IV:** 2

"Martyrs' Song" (Rossetti), **V:** 256

Martz, Louis, **V:** 366, 382

Marvell, Andrew, **II:** 113, 121, 123, 166, 195–199, **204–220**, 255, 261; **Supp. III:** 51, 56; **Supp. IV:** 271; **Retro. Supp. II:** **253–268**

Marvell and the Civic Crown (Patterson), **Retro. Supp. II:** 265

Marwick, A., **IV:** 290, 291

Marwood, Arthur, **VI:** 323, 331

Marxism, **Supp. I:** 24–25, 26, 30, 31, 238

Mary, A Fiction (Wollstonecraft), **Supp. III:** 466, 476

"Mary and Gabriel" (Brooke), **Supp. III:** 55

Mary Anne (du Maurier), **Supp. III:** 137

Mary Barton (Gaskell), **V:** viii, x, xxi, 1, 2, 4–5, 6, 15

"'Mary Gloster', The," (Kipling), **VI:** 202

Mary Gresley (Trollope), **V:** 101

"Mary Postgate" (Kipling), **VI:** 197, 206

"Mary Queen of Scots" (Swinburne), **V:** 332

Mary Rose (Barrie), **Supp. III:** 8, 9

Mary Stuart (Swinburne), **V:** 330, 332

"Mary the Cook–Maid's Letter . . . " (Swift), **III:** 31

"Mary's Magnificat" (Jennings), **Supp. V:** 217

"Masculine Birth of Time, The" (Bacon), **I:** 263

Masefield, John, **VI:** 429; **VII:** xii, xiii

Mask of Dimitrios, The (Ambler), **Supp. IV:** 21

"Mask of Love" (Kinsella), **Supp. V:** 262

Mason, William, **III:** 141, 142, 145

"Masque, The" (Auden), **Retro. Supp. I:** 11

"Masque of Anarchy, The" (Shelley), **IV:** xviii, 202–203, 206, 208; **Retro. Supp. I:** 253–254

Masque of Blackness, The (Jonson), **Retro. Supp. I:** 161–162

Masque of Queenes (Jonson), **II:** 111n; **Retro. Supp. I:** 162

Mass and the English Reformers, The (Dugmore), **I:** 177n

Massacre at Paris, The (Marlowe), **I:** 249, 276, 279–280, **285–286**; **Retro. Supp. I:** 211

Massinger, Philip, **II:** 44, 45, 50, 66–67, 69, 83, 87

Masson, David, **IV:** 212, 235

Masson, Rosaline, **V:** 393, 397

"Mastectomy" (Boland), **Supp. V:** (Boland), **Supp. V:** 49

Master, The (Brontë), *see Professor, The*

"Master, The" (Wilde), **Retro. Supp. II:** 371

Master and Margarita, The (Bulgakov), **Supp. IV:** 448

Master Georgie (Bainbridge), **Supp. VI:** 26–27

Master Humphrey's Clock (Dickens), **V:** 42, 53–54, 71

"Master John Horseleigh, Knight" (Hardy), **VI:** 22

Master of Ballantrae, The (Stevenson), **V:** 383–384, 387, 396; **Retro. Supp. I:** 268–269

Master of Petersburg, The (Coetzee), **Supp. VI:** 75–76, **85–86,** 88

Master of the House, The (Hall), **Supp. VI:** 120, 122, 128

Masterman, C. F. G., **VI:** viii, 320

Masters, John, **Supp. IV:** 440

Masters, The (Snow), **VII:** xxi, 327–328, 330

"Match, The" (Marvell), **II:** 211

Match for the Devil, A (Nicholson), **Supp. VI: 222**

"Match–Maker, The" (Saki), **Supp. VI:** 240

"Mater Dolorosa" (Swinburne), **V:** 325

"Mater Triumphalis" (Swinburne), **V:** 325

Materials for a Description of Capri (Douglas), **VI:** 305

Mathilda (Shelley), **Supp. III: 363–364**

"Mathilda's England" (Trevor), **Supp. IV:** 504

Matilda (Dahl), **Supp. IV:** 203, 207, 226

Matilda (film), **Supp. IV:** 203

Matisse, Henri, **Supp. IV:** 81, 154

Matisse Stories, The (Byatt), **Supp. IV:** 151, 154–155

"Matres Dolorosae" (Bridges), **VI:** 81

"Mattens" (Herbert), **II:** 127; **Retro. Supp. II:** 179

"Matter of Fact, A" (Kipling), **VI:** 193

Matthew Arnold: A Study in Conflict (Brown), **V:** 211–212, 217

Matthew Arnold: A Symposium (ed. Allott), **V:** 218

Matthews, Geoffrey Maurice, **IV:** x, xxv, 207, 208, 209, 237

Matthews, William, **I:** 68

Matthiessen, F. O., **V:** 204

Matthieu de Vendôme, **I:** 23, 39–40

Maturin, Charles, **III:** 327, 331, 333–334, 336, 345; **Supp. III:** 384

Maud (Tennyson), **IV:** xxi, 325, 328, 330–331, 333–336, 337, 338; **VI:** 420

Maude: A Story for Girls (Rossetti), **V:** 260

"Maud–Evelyn" (James), **VI:** 69

Maugham, Syrie, **VI:** 369

Maugham, W. Somerset, **VI:** xi, xiii, 200, **363–381; VII:** 318–319; list of short stories and sketches, **VI:** 379–381;

Supp. II: 7, 141, 156–157; **Supp. IV:** 9–10, 21, 500

Maumbury Ring (Hardy), **VI:** 20

Maupassant, Guy de, **III:** 340, **Supp. IV:** 500

Maurice (Forster), **VI:** xii, 397, **407–408,** 412; **Retro. Supp. II:** 145–146

Maurice, Frederick D., **IV:** 54; **V:** xxi, 284, 285

Max in Verse (Beerbohm), **Supp. II:** 44

Maxfield, James F., **Supp. IV:** 336

May Day (Chapman), **I:** 244

"May Day, 1937" (Nicholson), **Supp. VI:** 214

"May Day Song for North Oxford" (Betjeman), **VII:** 356

"May 23" (Thomas), **Supp. III:** 405

Maybe Day in Kazakhstan, A (Harrison), **Supp. V:** 164

"Mayday in Holderness" (Hughes), **Supp. I:** 344

Mayer, Carl, **III:** 342

"Mayfly" (MacNeice), **VII:** 411

Mayo, Robert, **IV:** ix

Mayor of Casterbridge: The Life and Death of a Man of Character, The (Hardy), **VI:** 3, 5, 7, 8, 9–10, 20

Maze Plays (Ayckbourn), **Supp. V:** 12

Mazeppa (Byron), **IV:** xvii, 173, 192

Mazzini, Giuseppi, **V:** 313, 314, 324, 325

Me, Myself, and I (Ayckbourn), **Supp. V:** 13

Meaning of Meaning, The (Richards and Ogden), **Supp. II:** 405, 408, **410–411,** 414

"Meaning of the Wild Body, The" (Lewis), **VII:** 77

Meaning of Treason, The (West), **Supp. III:** 440, 445

Measure for Measure (Shakespeare), **I:** 313–314, 327; **II:** 30, 70, 168; **V:** 341, 351

Measures, (MacCaig), **Supp. VI: 188–189,** 194

"Mechanical Genius, The" (Naipaul), **Supp. I:** 385

Mechanical Womb, The (Orton), **Supp. V:** 364

Medal: A Satyre Against Sedition, The (Dryden), **II:** 299, 304

Medea (Seneca), **II:** 71

Medea: A Sex–War Opera (Harrison), **Supp. V:** 164

Medieval Heritage of Elizabethan Tragedy (Farnham), **I:** 214

Meditation upon a Broom–Stick, A (Swift), **III:** 35

Meditations Collected from the Sacred Books . . . (Richardson), **III:** 92

"Meditations in Time of Civil War" (Yeats), **V:** 317; **VII:** 24; **Retro. Supp. I:** 334–335

Meditations of Daniel Defoe, The (Defoe), **III:** 12

"Mediterranean" (Redgrove), **Supp. VI:** 231

Mediterranean Scenes (Bennett), **VI:** 264, 267

"Medussa's Ankles" (Byatt), **Supp. IV:** 154–155

Medwin, Thomas, **IV:** 196, 209

Mee, Arthur, **Supp. IV:** 256

Meet My Father (Ayckbourn), **Supp. V:** 2

"Meet Nurse!" (Hope), **Supp. VII:** 151

Meeting by the River, A (Isherwood), **VII:** 317

Meeting the British (Muldoon), **Supp. IV:** 421–424

"Melancholia" (Bridges), **VI:** 80

"Melancholy" (Bridges), **VI:** 80

"Melancholy Hussar of the German Legion, The" (Hardy), **VI:** 20, 22; **Retro. Supp. I:** 116

Melchiori, Giorgio, **VI:** 208

Meleager (Euripides), **V:** 322, 323

Melincourt (Peacock), **IV:** xvii, 162, 163–164, 165, 168, 170

Melly, Diana, **Supp. IV:** 168

Melmoth Reconciled (Balzac), **III:** 334, 339

Melmoth the Wanderer (Maturin), **III:** 327, 333–334, 335, 345; **Supp. III:** 384–385

Melnikov, Konstantin, **Supp. IV:** 174

"Melon" (Barnes), **Supp. IV:** 75

Melville, Herman, **IV:** 97; **V:** xvii, xx–xxi, xxv, 211; **VI:** 363; **Supp. IV:** 160

Memento Mori (Spark), **Supp. I:** 203

"Memoir" (Scott), **IV:** 28, 30, 35–36, 39

"Memoir of Bernard Barton" (Fitz-Gerald), **IV:** 353

"Memoir of Cowper: An Autobiography" (ed. Quinlan), **III:** 220

"Memoir"of Fleeming Jenkin (Stevenson), **V:** 386, 395

Memoir of Jane Austen (Austen–Leigh), **III:** 90

"Memoir of My Father, A" (Amis), **Supp. II:** 1

Memoir of the Bobotes (Cary), **VII:** 185

Mémoire justificatif etc. (Gibbon), **III:** 233

Mémoires littéraires de la Grande Bretagne (periodical), **III:** 233

Memoirs (Amis), **Supp. IV:** 27

Memoirs (Temple), **III:** 19

Memoirs of a Cavalier, The (Defoe), **III:** 6, 13; **VI:** 353, 359; **Retro. Supp. I:** 66, 68, 71–72

Memoirs of a Midget (de la Mare), **III:** 340, 345

Memoirs of a Physician, The (Dumas père), **III:** 332

Memoirs of a Protestant, The (tr. Goldsmith), **III:** 191

Memoirs of a Survivor, The (Lessing), **Supp. I:** 249–250, 254

Memoirs of Barry Lyndon, Esq., The (Thackeray), *see Barry Lyndon*

Memoirs of Doctor Burney (Burney), **Supp. III:** 68

Memoirs of Himself (Stevenson), **V:** 396

"Memoirs of James Boswell, Esq." (Boswell), **III:** 248

Memoirs of Jonathan Swift (Scott), **IV:** 38

Memoirs of Martin Scriblerus, (Pope), **III:** 24, 77; **Retro. Supp. I:** 234

"Memoirs of M. de Voltaire" (Goldsmith), **III:** 189

Memoirs of My Dead Life (Moore), **VI:** 87, 88, 95, 96, 97, 98–99

"Memoirs of Percy Bysshe Shelley" (Peacock), **IV:** 158, 169, 170

Memoirs of the Author of A Vindication of the Rights of Woman (Godwin), **Supp. III:** 465

Memoirs of the Late Thomas Holcroft . . . (Hazlitt), **IV:** 128, 139

Memoirs of the Life of Edward Gibbon, The (ed. Hill), **III:** 221*n*, 233

Memoirs of the Life of Sir Walter Scott, Bart. (Lockhart), **IV:** 27, 30, 34, 35–36, 39

Memoirs of the Life of William Collins, Esp., R.A. (1848) (Collins), **Supp. VI:** 92, 95

Memoirs of the Navy (Pepys), **II:** 281, 288

"Memoirs of the World" (Gunn), **Supp. IV:** 264

Memoirs Relating to . . . Queen Anne's Ministry (Swift), **III:** 27

"Memorabilia" (Browning), **IV:** 354–355

Memorable Masque of the Middle Temple and Lincoln's Inn, The (Chapman), **I:** 235

Memorial, The (Isherwood), **VII:** 205, 310–311

"Memorial for the City" (Auden), **VII:** 388, 393; **Retro. Supp. I:** 8

Memorials of a Tour on the Continent (Wordsworth), **IV:** 24–25

Memorials of Edward Burne–Jones (Burne–Jones), **V:** 295–296, 306

"Memorials of Gormandising" (Thackeray), **V:** 23, 24, 38

Memorials of Thomas Hood (Hood and Broderip), **IV:** 251, 261, 267

Memorials of Two Sisters, Susanna and Catherine Winkworth (ed. Shaen), **V:** 149

Memories and Adventures (Doyle), **Supp. II:** 159

Memories and Hallucinations (Thomas), **Supp. IV:** 479, 480, 482, 483, 484, 486

Memories and Portraits (Stevenson), **V:** 390, 395

"Memories of a Catholic Childhood" (Lodge), **Supp. IV:** 363–364

"Memories of a Working Women's Guild" (Woolf), **Retro. Supp. I:** 311

Memories of the Space Age (Ballard), **Supp. V:** 24

"Memories of the Space Age" (Ballard), **Supp. V:** 33

Memories of Vailiona (Osborne and Strong), **V:** 393, 397

"Memories of Youghal" (Trevor), **Supp. IV:** 501

"Memory, A" (Brooke), **Supp. III:** 55

"Memory Man" (Ewart), **Supp. VII:** 41

Memory of Ben Jonson Revived by the Friends of the Muses, The (Digby), **Retro. Supp. I:** 166

"Memory Unsettled" (Gunn), **Supp. IV:** 277

Men and Wives (Compton–Burnett), **VII:** 64, 65, 66–67

Men and Women (Browning), **IV:** xiii, xxi, 357, 363, 374; **Retro. Supp. II:** 26, 27–28

Men at Arms (Waugh), **VII:** 304; *see also Sword of Honour* trilogy

Men Like Gods (Wells), **VI:** 226 240 244; **VII:** 204

Men on Women on Men (Ayckbourn), **Supp. V:** 3

"Men Sign the Sea" (Graham), **Supp. VII:** 110

"Men Who March Away" (Hardy), **VI:** 415, 421; **Retro. Supp. I:** 120

"Men With Coats Thrashing" (Lowry), **Supp. III:** 283

Men Without Art (Lewis), **VII:** 72, 76

"Menace, The" (du Maurier), **Supp. III:** 139

"Menace, The" (Gunn), **Supp. IV:** 261

Menand, Louis, **Supp. IV:** 305

"Menelaus and Helen" (Brooke), **Supp. III:** 52

Menaphon (Greene), **I:** 165

Mencius on the Mind (Richards), **Supp. II:** 421

Men's Wives (Thackeray), **V:** 23, 35, 38

"Mental Cases" (Owen), **VI:** 456, 457

Mental Efficiency (Bennett), **VI:** 250, 266

Merchant of Venice, The (Shakespeare), **I:** 310

Merchant's Tale, The (Chaucer), **I:** 36, 41–42

Mercian Hymns (Hill), **Supp. V:** 187, 189, 194–196

Mercier and Camier (Beckett), **Supp. I:** 50–51; **Retro. Supp. I:** 21

"Mercy" (Collins), **III:** 166

Mere Accident, A (Moore), **VI:** 86, 91

Mere Christianity (Lewis), **Supp. III:** 248

"Mere Interlude, A" (Hardy), **VI:** 22

Meredith (Sassoon), **V:** 219, 234

Meredith, George, **II:** 104, 342, 345; **IV:** 160; **V:** x, xviii, xxii–xxvi, **219–234,** 244, 432; **VI:** 2

Meredith, H. O., **VI:** 399

Meredith et la France (Mackay), **V:** 223, 234

"Meredithian Sonnets" (Fuller), **Supp. VII:** 74

Meres, Francis, **I:** 212, 234, 296, 307

Merie Tales, The, **I:** 83, 93

Meriton, George, **II:** 340

Merkin, Daphne, **Supp. IV:** 145–146

Merleau–Ponty, Maurice, **Supp. IV:** 79, 88

"Merlin and the Gleam" (Tennyson), **IV:** 329

Mermaid, Dragon, Fiend (Graves), **VII:** 264

Merope (Arnold), **V:** 209, 216

Merry England (periodical), **V:** 440

Merry Jests of George Peele, The, **I:** 194

Merry Men, and Other Tales and Fables, The (Stevenson), **V:** 395; **Retro. Supp. I:** 267

Merry Wives of Windsor, The (Shakespeare), **I:** 295, 311; **III:** 117

Merry–Go–Round, The (Lawrence), **VII:** 120

Merry–Go–Round, The (Maugham), **VI:** 372

Mescellanies (Fielding), **Retro. Supp. I:** 80

Meschonnic, Henri, **Supp. IV:** 115

Mespoulet, M., **V:** 266

"Message, The" (Donne), **Retro. Supp. II:** 90

"Message from Mars, The" (Ballard), **Supp. V:** 33

Messages (Fernandez), **V:** 225–226

"Messdick" (Ross), **VII:** 433

Messenger, The (Kinsella), **Supp. V:** 269–270

"M. E. T." (Thomas), **Supp. III:** 401

Metamorphoses (Ovid), **III:** 54; **V:** 321; **Retro. Supp. II:** 36, 215

Metamorphosis (Kafka), **III:** 340, 345

Metamorphosis of Pygmalion's Image (Marston), **I:** 238; **II:** 25, 40

Metaphysical Lyrics and Poems of the Seventeenth Century (Grierson), **Retro. Supp. II:** 173

Metempsycosis: Poêma Satyricon (Donne), **Retro. Supp. II:** 94

"Methinks the poor Town has been troubled too long" (Dorset), **II:** 262

"Method. For Rongald Gaskell" (Davie), **Supp. VI:** 106

Metrical Tales and Other Poems (Southey), **IV:** 71

Metroland (Barnes), **Supp. IV:** 65, 66–67, 71, 76

Mew, Charlotte, **Supp. V:** 97, 98–99

Meynell, Wilfred, **V:** 440, 451

MF (Burgess), **Supp. I:** 197

"Mianserin Sonnets" (Fuller), **Supp. VII:** 79

Micah Clark (Doyle), **Supp. II:** 159, 163

"Michael" (Wordsworth), **IV:** 8, 18–19

Michael and Mary (Milne), **Supp. V:** 299

Michael Robartes and the Dancer (Yeats), **VI:** 217; **Retro. Supp. I:** 331–333

"Michael X and the Black Power Killings in Trinidad" (Naipaul), **Supp. I:** 396

Michaelmas Term (Middleton), **II:** 3, 4, 21

Michelet, Jules, **V:** 346

Microcosmography (Earle), **IV:** 286

Micro–Cynicon, Six Snarling Satires (Middleton), **II:** 2–3

Midas (Lyly), **I:** 198, 202, 203

Middle Age of Mrs Eliot, The (Wilson), **Supp. I:** 160–161

Middle Ground, The (Drabble), **Supp. IV:** 230, 231, 234, 246–247, 248

"Middle of a War" (Fuller), **VII:** 429; **Supp. VII:** 69

Middle Passage, The (Naipaul), **Supp. I:** 386, 390–391, 393, 403

"Middle–Sea and Lear–Sea" (Jones), **Supp. VII:** 176

Middle Years, The (James), **VI**: 65, 69

"Middle Years, The" (Ewart), **Supp. VII**: 39

"Middle Years, The" (James), **VI**: 69

Middlemarch (Eliot), **III**: 157; **V**: ix–x, xxiv, 196–197, 200; **Supp. IV**: 243; **Retro. Supp. II**:113–114

Middlemen: A Satire, The (Brooke–Rose), **Supp. IV**: 99, 103

Middleton, D., **V**: 253

Middleton, Thomas, **II**: **1–23**, 30, 33, 68–70, 72, 83, 85, 93, 100; **IV**: 79

Midnight Oil (Pritchett), **Supp. III**: 312, 313

Midnight on the Desert (Priestley), **VII**: 209, 212

"Midnight Skaters, The" (Blunden), **VI**: 429

Midnight's Children (Rushdie), **Supp. IV**: 162, 433, 435, 436, 438, 439–444, 445, 448, 449, 456; **Supp. V**: 67, 68

"Midsummer Holiday, A, and Other Poems" (Swinburne), **V**: 332

"Midsummer Ice" (Murray), **Supp. VII**: 278

Midsummer Night's Dream, A (Shakespeare), **I**: 304–305, 311–312; **II**: 51, 281; **Supp. IV**: 198

"Mid–Term Break" (Heaney), **Retro. Supp. I**: 125

Mid–Victorian Memories (Francillon), **V**: 83

Mightier Than the Sword (Ford), **VI**: 320–321

Mighty and Their Full, The (Compton–Burnett), **VII**: 61, 62

Mighty Magician, The (FitzGerald), **IV**: 353

Miguel Street (Naipaul), **Supp. I**: 383, 385–386

"Mike: A Public School Story" (Wodehouse), **Supp. III**: 449

Mike Fletcher (Moore), **VI**: 87, 91

"Mildred Lawson" (Moore), **VI**: 98

Milestones (Bennett), **VI**: 250, 263, 264

Milford, H., **III**: 208n

"Milford: East Wing" (Murphy), **Supp. V**: 328

Military Memoirs of Capt. George Carleton, The (Defoe), **III**: 14

Military Philosophers, The (Powell), **VII**: 349

Mill, James, **IV**: 159; **V**: 288

Mill, John Stuart, **IV**: 50, 56, 246, 355; **V**: xxi–xxii, xxiv, 182, 279, 288, 343

Mill on the Floss, The (Eliot), **V**: xxii, 14, 192–194, 200; **Supp. IV**: 240, 471; **Retro. Supp. II**: 106–108

Millais, John Everett, **V**: 235, 236, 379

Miller, Arthur, **VI**: 286

Miller, Henry, **Supp. IV**: 110–111

Miller, J. Hillis, **VI**: 147

Miller, Karl, **Supp. IV**: 169

"Miller's Daughter, The" (Tennyson), **IV**: 326

Miller's Tale, The (Chaucer), **I**: 37

Millet, Jean François, **Supp. IV**: 90

Millett, Kate, **Supp. IV**: 188

Millionairess, The (Shaw), **VI**: 102, 127

"Millom Cricket Field" (Nicholson), **Supp. VI**: 216

"Millom Old Quarry" (Nicholson), **Supp. VI**: 216

Mills, C. M., pseud. of Elizabeth Gaskell

Millstone, The (Drabble), **Supp. IV**: 230, 237–238

Milne, A. A., **Supp. V**: **295–312**

"Milnes, Richard Monckton" (Lord Houghton), *see* Monckton Milnes, Richard

Milton (Blake), **III**: 303–304, 307; **V**: xvi 330; **Retro. Supp. I**: 45

Milton (Meredith), **V**: 234

"Milton" (Macaulay), **IV**: 278, 279

Milton, Edith, **Supp. IV**: 305–306

Milton in America (Ackroyd), **Supp. VI**: **11–12**, 13

Milton, John, **II**: 50–52, 113, **158–178**, 195, 196, 198, 199, 205, 206, 236, 302; **III**: 43, 118–119, 167n, 211n, 220, 302; **IV**: 9, 11–12, 14, 22, 23, 93, 95, 185, 186, 200, 205, 229, 269, 278, 279, 352; **V**: 365–366; **Supp. III**: 169; **Retro. Supp. II**: **269–289**

Milton's God (Empson), **Supp. II**: 180, **195–196**

Milton's Prosody (Bridges), **VI**: 83

Mimic Men, The (Naipaul), **Supp. I**: 383, 386, 390, 392, 393–394, 395, 399

"Mina Laury" (Brontë), **V**: 122, 123, 149, 151

Mind at the End of Its Tether (Wells), **VI**: xiii; **VI**: 228, 242

Mind Has Mountains, The (Jennings), **Supp. V**: 213, 215–216

Mind in Chains, The (ed. Day Lewis), **Supp. III**: 118

Mind of the Maker, The (Sayers), **Supp. III**: 345, 347

Mind to Murder, A (James), **Supp. IV**: 319, 321, 323–324

"Mine old dear enemy, my froward master" (Wyatt), **I**: 105

"Miner's Hut" (Murphy), **Supp. V**: 328

"Miners" (Owen), **VI**: 452, 454

Ministry of Fear, The (Greene), **Supp. I**: 10–11, 12; **Retro. Supp. II**: 157

Minor Poems of Robert Southey, The (Southey), **IV**: 71

Minpins, The (Dahl), **Supp. IV**: 204, 224

Minstrel, The (Beattie), **IV**: 198

Minstrelsy of the Scottish Border (ed. Scott), **IV**: 29, 39

"Mint" (Heaney), **Retro. Supp. I**: 133

Mint, The (Lawrence), **Supp. II**: 283, **291–294**

Minute by Glass Minute (Stevenson), **Supp. VI**: 261

Minute for Murder (Day Lewis), **Supp. III**: 130

Minutes of the Negotiations of Monsr. Mesnager, . . . (Defoe), **III**: 13

"Mirabeau" (Macaulay), **IV**: 278

"Miracle Cure" (Lowbury), **VII**: 432

Miracles (Lewis), **Supp. III**: 248, 255, 258–259

Mirèio (Mistral), **V**: 219

Mirour de l'omme (Gower), **I**: 48, 49

Mirror for Magistrates, The, **I**: 162, 214

"Mirror in February" (Kinsella), **Supp. V**: 262

Mirror of the Sea: Memories and Impressions, The (Conrad), **VI**: 138, 148

Mirror Wall, The (Murphy), **Supp. V**: 313, 329–330

Mirrour; or, Looking–Glasse Both for Saints and Sinners, A (Clarke), **II**: 251

Misadventures of John Nicholson, The (Stevenson), **V**: 396

Misalliance (Shaw), **VI**: xv, 115, 117, 118, 120, 129; **Retro. Supp. II**: 321

Misalliance, The (Brookner), **Supp. IV**: 129

Misanthrope, The (tr. Harrison), **Supp. V**: 149–150, 163

"Misanthropos" (Gunn), **Supp. IV**: 264–265, 268, 270

Miscellanea (Temple), **III**: 40

Miscellaneous Essays (St. Évremond), **III**: 47

Miscellaneous Observations on the Tragedy of Macbeth (Johnson), **III**: 108, 116, 121

Miscellaneous Poems (Marvell), **II**: 207

Miscellaneous Studies (Pater), **V**: 348, 357

Miscellaneous Works of the Duke of Buckingham, **II**: 268

Miscellaneous Works . . . with Memoirs of His Life (Gibbon), **III**: 233

Miscellanies (Cowley), **II**: 198

Miscellanies (Pope and Swift), **II**: 335

Miscellanies (Swinburne), **V**: 332

Miscellanies; A Serious Address to the People of Great Britain (Fielding), **III**: 105

Miscellanies, Aesthetic and Literary . . . (Coleridge), **IV**: 56

Miscellany (Tonson), **III**: 69

Miscellany of New Poems, A (Behn), **Supp. III**: 36

Miscellany Poems (Wycherley), **II**: 321

Miscellany Tracts (Browne), **II**: 156

Mischmasch (Carroll), **V**: 274

"Mise Eire" (Boland), **Supp. V**: 45–46

Miser, The (Fielding), **III**: 105

"Miserie" (Herbert), **II**: 128–129

Miseries of War, The (Ralegh), **I**: 158

Misfortunes of Arthur, The (Hughes), **I**: 218

Misfortunes of Elphin, The (Peacock), **IV**: xviii, 163, 167–168, 170

Mishan, E. J., **VI**: 240

"Misplaced Attachment of Mr. John Dounce, The" (Dickens), **V**: 46

"Miss Brill" (Mansfield), **VII**: 175

Miss Gomez and the Brethren (Trevor), **Supp. IV**: 507, 508–509

"Miss Gunton of Poughkeepsie" (James), **VI**: 69

Miss Herbert (The Suburban Wife) (Stead), **Supp. IV**: 473, 476

"Miss Kilmansegg and Her Precious Leg" (Hood), **IV**: 258–259

Miss Lucy in Town (Fielding), **III**: 105

Miss Mackenzie (Trollope), **V**: 101

Miss Marple's Last Case (Christie), **Supp. II**: 125

Miss Ogilvy Finds Herself (Hall), **Supp. VI:** 120–121, 128

"Miss Ogilvy Finds Herself" (Hall), **Supp. VI:** 121

"Miss Pulkinhorn" (Golding), **Supp. I:** 78–79, 80

"Miss Smith" (Trevor), **Supp. IV:** 502, 510

"Miss Tickletoby's Lectures on English History" (Thackeray), **V:** 38

"Miss Twye" (Ewart), **Supp. VII:** 36

"Missing, The" (Gunn), **Supp. IV:** 276

"Missing Dates" (Empson), **Supp. II:** 184, 190

Mistake, The (Vanbrugh), **II:** 325, 333, 336

Mistakes, The (Harris), **II:** 305

Mr. A's Amazing Mr. Pim Passes By (Milne), **Supp. V:** 299

"Mr. and Mrs. Dove" (Mansfield), **VII:** 180

"Mr. and Mrs. Frank Berry" (Thackeray), **V:** 23

"Mr. Apollinax" (Eliot), **VII:** 144

Mr. Beluncle (Pritchett), **Supp. III:** 311, 313, 314–315

Mr. Bennett and Mrs. Brown (Woolf), **VI:** 247, 267, 275, 290; **VII:** xiv, xv

"Mr. Bennett and Mrs. Brown" (Woolf), **Supp. II:** 341; **Retro. Supp. I:** 309

"Mr. Bleaney" (Larkin), **Supp. I:** 281

"Mr. Bodkin" (Hood), **IV:** 267

Mr. Britling Sees It Through (Wells), **VI:** 227, 240

"Mr. Brown's Letters to a Young Man About Town" (Thackeray), **V:** 38

Mr. Bunyan's Last Sermon (Bunyan), **II:** 253

Mr. C[olli]n's Discourse of Free–Thinking (Swift), **III:** 35

"Mr. Crabbe—Mr. Campbell" (Hazlitt), **III:** 276

"Mr. Eliot's Sunday Morning Service" (Eliot), **VII:** 145

"Mr. Feasey" (Dahl), **Supp. IV:** 214

Mr. Foot (Frayn), **Supp. VII:** 57

Mr. Fortune's Maggot (Warner), **Supp. VII:** 370, 374–375, 379

"Mr. Gilfil's Love Story" (Eliot), **V:** 190; **Retro. Supp. II:** 103–104

"Mr. Gladstone Goes to Heaven" (Beerbohm), **Supp. II:** 51

"Mr. Graham" (Hood), **IV:** 267

"Mr. Harrison's Confessions" (Gaskell), **V:** 14, 15

Mr. H (Lamb), **IV:** 80–81, 85

Mr. John Milton's Character of the Long Parliament and Assembly of Divines . . . (Milton), **II:** 176

Mister Johnson (Cary), **VII:** 186, 187, 189, 190–191

"Mr. Know–All" (Maugham), **VI:** 370

Mr. Macaulay's Character of the Clergy in the Latter Part of the Seventeenth Century Considered (Babington), **IV:** 291

"Mr. McNamara" (Trevor), **Supp. IV:** 501

Mr. Meeson's Will (Haggard), **Supp. III:** 213

Mr. Noon (Lawrence), **Retro. Supp. II:** 229–230

"Mr. Norris and I" (Isherwood), **VII:** 311–312

Mr. Norris Changes Trains (Isherwood), **VII:** xx, 311–312

Mr. Polly (Wells), *see History of Mr. Polly, The*

Mr. Pope's Welcome from Greece (Gay), **II:** 348

Mr. Prohack (Bennett), **VI:** 260, 267

"Mr. Reginald Peacock's Day" (Mansfield), **VII:** 174

"Mr. Robert Herricke His Farewell unto Poetrie" (Herrick), **II:** 112

"Mr. Robert Montgomery's Poems" (Macaulay), **IV:** 280

Mr Sampath (Naipaul), **Supp. I:** 400

Mr. Scarborough's Family (Trollope), **V:** 98, 102

"Mr. Sludge 'the Medium' " (Browning), **IV:** 358, 368; **Retro. Supp. II:** 26–27

Mr. Smirke; or, The Divine in Mode (Marvell), **II:** 219

Mr. Stone and the Knights Companion (Naipaul), **Supp. I:** 383, 389

"Mr. Tennyson" (Trevor), **Supp. IV:** 502

Mr. Waller's Speech in the Painted Chamber (Waller), **II:** 238

"Mr. Waterman" (Redgrove), **Supp. VI:** 228–229, 231, 235, 237

Mr. Weston's Good Wine (Powys), **VII:** 21

Mr. Whatnot (Ayckbourn), **Supp. V:** 2, 13

"Mr. Whistler's Ten O'Clock" (Wilde), **V:** 407

"Mrs. Acland's Ghosts" (Trevor), **Supp. IV:** 503

"Mrs. Bathurst" (Kipling), **VI:** 193–194

Mrs. Browning: A Poet's Work and Its Setting (Hayter), **IV:** 322

Mrs. Craddock (Maugham), **VI:** 367

Mrs. Dalloway (Woolf), **VI:** 275, 279; **VII:** xv, 18, 21, 24, 28–29; **Supp. IV:** 234, 246; **Retro. Supp. I:** 316–317

Mrs. Dot (Maugham), **VI:** 368

Mrs. Eckdorf in O'Neill's Hotel (Trevor), **Supp. IV:** 501, 508

Mrs. Fisher; or, The Future of Humour (Graves), **VII:** 259–260

Mrs. Harris's Petition (Swift), **Retro. Supp. I:** 283

"Mrs. Jaypher found a wafer" (Lear), **V:** 86

Mrs. Leicester's School (Lamb and Lamb), **IV:** 80, 85

Mrs. McGinty's Dead (Christie; U.S. title, *Blood Will Tell*), **Supp. II:** 135

"Mrs. Medwin" (James), **VI:** 69

"Mrs. Nelly's Complaint," **II:** 268

"Mrs. Packletide's Tiger" (Saki), **Supp. VI:** 242

Mrs. Perkins's Ball (Thackeray), **V:** 24, 38

"Mrs. Silly" (Trevor), **Supp. IV:** 502

"Mrs. Simpkins" (Smith), **Supp. II:** 470

"Mrs. Temperley" (James), **VI:** 69

Mrs. Warren's Profession (Shaw), **V:** 413; **VI:** 108, 109; **Retro. Supp. II:** 312–313

Mistral, Frederic, **V:** 219

Mistras, The (Cowley), **II:** 194, 198, 202, 236

"Mistress of Vision, The" (Thompson), **V:** 447–448

"Mists" (Redgrove), **Supp. VI:** 228

Mist's Weekly Journal (newspaper), **III:** 4

Mitford, Mary Russell, **IV:** 311, 312

Mitford, Nancy, **VII:** 290

Mithridates (Lee), **II:** 305

Mixed Essays (Arnold), **V:** 213n, 216

"Mixed Marriage" (Muldoon), **Supp. IV:** 415

Mo, Timothy, **Supp. IV:** 390

Mob, The (Galsworthy), **VI:** 280, 288

Moby–Dick (Melville), **VI:** 363

Mock Doctor, The (Fielding), **III** 105

Mock Speech from the Throne (Marvell), **II:** 207

Mock–Mourners, The: . . . Elegy on King William (Defoe), **III:** 12

"Model Prisons" (Carlyle), **IV:** 247

Modern Comedy, A (Galsworthy), **VI:** 270, 275

Modern Fiction (Woolf), **VII:** xiv; **Retro. Supp. I:** 308–309

Modern Husband, The (Fielding), **III:** 105

"Modern Love" (Meredith), **V:** 220, 234, 244

Modern Love, and Poems of the English Roadside . . . (Meredith), **V:** xxii, 220, 234

Modern Lover, A (Moore), **VI:** 86, 89, 98

Modern Movement: 100 Key Books from England, France, and America, 1880–1950, The (Connolly), **VI:** 371

Modern Painters (Ruskin), **V:** xx, 175–176, 180, 184, 282

Modern Painting (Moore), **VI:** 87

Modern Poetry: A Personal Essay (MacNeice), **VII:** 403, 404, 410

Modern Utopia, A (Wells), **VI:** 227, 234, 241, 244

"Modern Warning, The" (James), **VI:** 48, 69

Modernism and Romance (Scott–James), **VI:** 21

Modes of Modern Writing: Metaphor, Metonymy, and the Typology of Modern Literature, The (Lodge), **Supp. IV:** 365, 377

"Modest Proposal" (Ewart), **Supp. VII:** 46

Modest Proposal, A (Swift), **III:** 21, 28, 29, 35; **Supp. IV:** 482

"Moestitiae Encomium" (Thompson), **V:** 450

Moffatt, James, **I:** 382–383

Mohocks, The (Gay), **III:** 60, 67

Mohr, Jean, **Supp. IV:** 79

Moi, Toril, **Retro. Supp. I:** 312

"Moisture–Number, The" (Redgrove), **Supp. VI:** 235

Molière (Jean Baptiste Poquelin), **II:** 314, 318, 325, 336, 337, 350; **V:** 224

Moll Flanders (Defoe), **III:** 5, 6, 7, 8, 9, 13, 95; **Retro. Supp. I:** 72–73

Molloy (Beckett), **Supp. I:** 51–52; **Supp. IV:** 106; **Retro. Supp. I:** 18, 21–22

Molly Sweeney (Friel), **Supp. V:** 127

"Molly Gone" (Hardy), **Retro. Supp. I:** 118

Moly (Gunn), **Supp. IV:** 257, 266–268

"Moly" (Gunn), **Supp. IV:** 267

Molyneux, William, **III:** 27

"Moment, The: Summer's Night" (Woolf), **Retro. Supp. I:** 309

"Moment of Cubism, The" (Berger), **Supp. IV:** 79

Moments of Being (Woolf), **VII:** 33; **Retro. Supp. I:** 305, 315

Moments of Grace (Jennings), **Supp. V:** 217–218

Moments of Vision, and Miscellaneous Verses (Hardy), **VI:** 20

Monastery, The (Scott), **IV:** xviii, 39

Monckton Milnes, Richard (Lord Houghton), **IV:** 211, 234, 235, 251, 252, 254, 302, 351; **V:** 312, 313, 334; **Retro. Supp. I:** 185–186

"Monday; or, The Squabble" (Gay), **III:** 56

Monday or Tuesday (Woolf), **VII:** 20, 21, 38; **Retro. Supp. I:** 307

Money: A Suicide Note (Amis), **Supp. IV:** 26, 32–35, 37, 40

Money in the Bank (Wodehouse), **Supp. III:** 459

"Money Singing" (Motion), **Supp. VII:** 261

Monk, The (Lewis), **III:** 332–333, 335, 345; **Supp. III:** 384

Monks and the Giants, The (Frere), *see Whistlecraft*

Monks of St. Mark, The (Peacock), **IV:** 158, 169

Monk's Prologue, The (Chaucer), **II:** 70

Monk's Tale, The (Chaucer), **I:** 31

Monk's Tale, The (Lydgate), **I:** 57

"Monna Innominata" (Rossetti), **V:** 251

"Mono–Cellular" (Self), **Supp.** V: 402

Monody on the Death of the Right Hon. R. B. Sheridan . . . (Byron), **IV:** 192

Monro, Harold, **VI:** 448

Monsieur (Durrell), **Supp. I:** 118, 119

Monsieur de Pourceaugnac (Molière), **II:** 325, 337, 339, 347, 350

Monsieur d'Olive (Chapman), **I:** 244–245

"M. Prudhomme at the International Exhibition" (Swinburne). **V:** 333

Monsieur Thomas (Fletcher), **II:** 45, 61, 65

Monsignor Quixote (Greene), **Supp. I:** 18–19; **Retro. Supp. II:** 166

Monstre Gai (Lewis), **VII:** 72, 80

"Mont Blanc" (Shelley), **IV:** 198; **Retro. Supp. I:** 248

Montagu, Lady Mary Wortley, **II:** 326

Montague, John, **VI:** 220

Montaigne, Michel Eyquem de, **II:** 25, 30, 80, 104, 108, 146; **III:** 39

Monte Verité (du Maurier), **Supp. III:** 143–144, 147, 148

Montemayor, Jorge de, **I:** 164, 302

Montezuma's Daughter (Haggard), **Supp. III:** 214

Montgomery, Robert, **IV:** 280

Month (periodical), **V:** 365, 379

Month in the Country, A (tr. Friel), **Supp. V:** 124

Montherlant, Henry de, **II:** 99*n*

Monthly Review (periodical), **III:** 147, 188

Montrose, marquess of, **II:** 222, 236–237, 238

"Monument Maker, The" (Hardy), **Retro. Supp. I:** 117

Monumental Column, A. Erected to . . . Prince of Wales (Webster), **II:** 68, 85

"Monuments of Honour" (Webster), **II:** 68, 85

Monye, A. A., **Supp. II:** 350

Monypenny, W. F., **IV:** 292, 295, 300, 307, 308

Moon and Sixpence, The (Maugham), **VI:** xiii, 365, 374, **375–376**

Mooncranker's Gift (Unsworth), **Supp. VII:** 354, 356–357

Moonlight (Pinter), **Retro. Supp. I:** 226

"Moonlight Night on the Port" (Keyes), **VII:** 439

"Moonshine" (Murphy), **Supp. V:** 326

Moonstone, The (Collins), **Supp. VI:** 91, 93, **100–102**

Moorcock, Michael, **Supp. V:** 24, 25, 32

Moonstone, The (Collins), **III:** 340, 345

Moore, G. E., **Supp. I:** 217; **Supp. II:** 406–407; **Supp. III:** 46, 49

Moore, George, **IV:** 102; **V:** xxi, xxvi, 129, 153; **VI:** xii **85–99**, 207, 239, 270, 365

Moore, John Robert, **III:** 1, 12

Moore, Marianne, **IV:** 6; **Supp. IV:** 262–263

Moore, Thomas, **IV:** xvi, 193, 205; **V:** 116

"Moore's Life of Lord Byron" (Macaulay), **IV:** 281–282

"Moorings" (MacCaig), **Supp. VI:** 187

Moorland Cottage, The (Gaskell), **V:** 14, 15

Moorman, Mary, **IV:** 4, 25

Moor's Last Sigh, The (Rushdie), **Supp. IV:** 433, 438, 444, 446, 448, 451–454, 456

Moortown (Hughes), **Supp. I:** 354, 357; **Retro. Supp. II:** 211–212

"Mora Montravers" (James), **VI:** 69

Moral and Political Lecture, A (Coleridge), **IV:** 56

Moral Epistle, Respectfully Dedicated to Earl Stanhope (Landor), **IV:** 99

Moral Ending and Other Stories, A (Warner), **Supp. VII:** 379

Moral Essays (Pope), **III:** 74–75, 77, 78; **Retro. Supp. I:** 145; **Retro. Supp. I:** 235

Moralities (Kinsella), **Supp. V:** 260, 261

"Morality and the Novel" (Lawrence), **VII:** 87

Morality Play (Unsworth), **Supp. VII:** 362, 364–365

Morall Fabillis of Esope the Phrygian, The (Henryson), **Supp. VII:** 136–142, 145

More, Hannah, **IV:** 269

More, Paul Elmer, **II:** 152

More, Sir Thomas, **I:** 325; **II:** 24; **IV:** 69, **Supp. VII: 233–250**

"More a Man Has the More a Man Wants, The" (Muldoon), **Supp. IV:** 420–421, 425

More Dissemblers Besides Women (Middleton), **II:** 3, 21

"More Essex Poems" (Davie), **Supp. VI:** 110–111

More New Arabian Nights: The Dynamiter (Stevenson), **V:** 395

More Nonsense, Pictures, Rhymes, Botany (Lear), **V:** 78, 87

More Poems (Housman), **VI:** 152, 157, 161–162

More Pricks than Kicks (Beckett), **Supp. I: 45–46**; **Retro. Supp. I:** 19

More Reformation: A Satyr upon Himself . . . (Defoe), **III:** 13

More Short–Ways with the Dissenters (Defoe), **III:** 13

More Trivia (Connolly), **Supp. III:** 98

More Women than Men (Compton–Burnett), **VII:** 61–62

Morgan, Margery M., **VI:** xiii, xiv–xv, xxxiv

Morgann, Maurice, **IV:** xiv, 168

Morgante Maggiore (Pulci), **IV:** 182

Morison, James Augustus Cotter, **IV:** 289, 291

Morley, Frank, **IV:** 79, 86

Morley, John, **VI:** 2, 157, 336

Morley, Lord John, **III:** 201, 205; **IV:** 289, 291; **V:** 279, 280, 284, 290, 313, 334

"Morning" (Davie), **Supp. VI:** 112

"Morning Call" (Murphy), **Supp. V:** 326

Morning Chronicle, The (periodical), **IV:** 43, 128, 129; **V:** 41

"Morning Coffee" (Kinsella), **Supp. V:** 273

"Morning, Midday, and Evening Sacrifice" (Hopkins), **V:** 370

Morning Post (periodical), **III:** 269; **VI:** 351

Morning Star (Haggard), **Supp. III:** 214

"Morning Sun" (MacNeice), **III:** 411

Mornings in Mexico (Lawrence), **VII:** 116, 117

"Morning-watch, The" (Vaughan), **II:** 187

Moronic Inferno, The (AAnd Other Visits to America") (Amis), **Supp. IV:** 42, 43

"Morpho Eugenia" (Byatt), **Supp. IV:** 140, 153–154

Morrell, Ottoline, **VII:** 103

Morrell, Sir Charles, **V:** 111

Morris, Margaret, **VI:** 274

Morris, May, **V:** 298, 301, 305

Morris, William, **IV:** 218; **V:** ix, xi, xii, xix, xxii–xxvi, 236–238, **291–307**, 312, 365, 401, 409; **VI:** 103, 167–168, 283

Morris & Co., **V:** 295, 296, 302

"Morris's Life and Death of Jason" (Swinburne), **V:** 298

Morrison, Arthur, **VI:** 365–366

Mortal Coils (Huxley), **VII:** 200

Mortal Consequences (Symons), **Supp. IV:** 3

Morte Arthur, Le, **I:** 72, 73

Morte Darthur, Le (Malory), **I:** 67, 68–79; **V:** 294; **Retro. Supp. II:** 237–239, 240–251

"Morte d'Arthur" (Tennyson), **IV:** xx, 332–334, 336

"Mortier Water–Organ Called Oscar, The" (Redgrove), **Supp. VI:** 236

"Mortification" (Herbert), **II:** 127

Mortimer His Fall (Jonson), **Retro. Supp. I:** 166

Mosada, a Dramatic Poem (Yeats), **VI:** 221

Moseley, Humphrey, **II:** 89

Moses (Rosenberg), **VI:** 433

Moses the Lawgiver (Keneally), **Supp. IV:** 346

"Mosquito" (Lawrence), **VII:** 119

"Most Extraordinary Case, A" (James), **VI:** 69

Most Piteous Tale of the Morte Arthur Saunz Guerdon, The (Malory), **I:** 72, 77

"Mother, The" (Stevenson), **Supp. VI:** 256

Mother and Son (Compton–Burnett), **VII:** 64, 65, 68–69

Mother Bombie (Lyly), **I:** 203–204

"Mother Country" (Rossetti), **V:** 255

Mother Courage (Brecht), **VI:** 123

Mother Hubberd's Tale (Spenser), **I:** 124, 131

Mother Ireland (O'Brien), **Supp. V:** 338

"Mother of the Muses, The" (Harrison), **Supp. V:** 161

"Mother Speaks, The" (Day Lewis), **Supp. III:** 125

Mother, What Is Man? (Smith), **Supp. II:** 462

Mother's Day (Storey), **Supp. I:** 420

"Mother's Sense of Fun" (Wilson), **Supp. I:** 153, 157–158

Motion, Andrew, **Supp. VII: 251–267**

"Motions of the Earth, The" (Nicholson), **Supp. VI:** 217

Motteux, Pierre, **II:** 352, 353

Mount of Olives, The; or, Solitary Devotions . . . (Vaughan), **II:** 185, 201

Mount Zion (Betjeman), **VII:** 364

"Mount Zion" (Hughes), **Supp. I:** 341

Mountain Town in France, A (Stevenson), **V:** 396

Mountolive (Durrell), **Supp. I:** 104, 106, 108, 109

"Mourning" (Marvell), **II:** 209, 212

Mourning Bride, The (Congreve), **II:** 338, 347, 350

Mourning Muse of Alexis, The: A Pastoral (Congreve), **II:** 350

Mousetrap, The (Christie), **Supp. II:** 125, 134

Movevent, The, **Supp. IV:** 256

Moving Finger, The (Christie), **Supp. II:** 132

Moving Out (Behan), **Supp. II:** 67, 68, 70

Moving Target, A (Golding), **Supp. I:** 88

"Mower to the Glo–Worms, The" (Marvell), **II:** 209

"Mowgli's Brothers" (Kipling), **VI:** 199

Moxon, Edward, **IV:** 83, 86, 252

Much Ado About Nothing (Shakespeare), **I:** 310–311, 327

Much Obliged (Wodehouse), **Supp. III:** 460

"Mud Vision, The" (Heaney), **Supp. II:** 281

Mudlark Poems & Grand Buveur, The (Redgrove), **Supp. VI:** 236

"Mudtower, The" (Stevenson), **Supp. VI:** 253

Muggeridge, Malcolm, **VI:** 356; **VII:** 276; **Supp. II:** 118, 119

Muiopotmos (Spenser), **I:** 124

Muir, Edwin, **I:** 247; **IV:** 27, 40; **Supp. V:** 208; **Supp. VI: 197–209**

Muir, K., **IV:** 219, 236

Mulberry Bush, The (Wilson), **Supp. I:** 154–155

Mulberry Garden, The (Sedley), **II:** 263–264, 271

"Mulberry Tree, The" (Bowen), **Supp. II:** 78, 92

Mulberry Tree, The (Bowen), **Supp. II:** 80

Mulcaster, Richard, **I:** 122

Muldoon, Paul, **Supp. IV: 409–432**

Mule on the Minaret, The (Waugh), **Supp. VI:** 274

Mules (Muldoon), **Supp. IV:** 414–415

Mullan, John, **Retro. Supp. I:** 69–70

Müller, Max, **V:** 203

Mum and Mr. Armitage (Bainbridge), **Supp. VI:** 23

Mummer's Wife, A (Moore), **VI:** xii, 86, 90, 98

"Mummia" (Brooke), **Supp. III:** 52, 60

"Mummy to the Rescue" (Wilson), **Supp. I:** 153

"Mundus and Paulina" (Gower), **I:** 53–54

Mundus Muliebris; or, The Ladies–Dressing Room Unlock'd (Evelyn), **II:** 287

Mundy Scheme, The (Friel), **Supp. V:** 119

Munera Pulveris (Ruskin), **V:** 184

"Municipal Gallery Revisited, The" (Yeats), **VI:** 216; **Retro. Supp. I:** 337–338

Munnings, Sir Alfred, **VI:** 210

"Murad the Unlucky" (Brooke), **Supp. III:** 55

Murder at the Vicarage (Christie), **Supp. II:** 130, 131

"Murder Considered as One of the Fine Arts" (De Quincey), **IV:** 149–150

Murder in the Calais Coach (Christie), *see Murder on the Orient Express*

Murder in the Cathedral (Eliot), **VII:** 153, 157, 159; **Retro. Supp. II:** 132

Murder in Triplicate (James), **Supp. IV:** 320, 327

"Murder, 1986" (James), **Supp. IV:** 340

Murder of John Brewer, The (Kyd), **I:** 218

Murder of Quality, A (le Carré), **Supp. II:** 300, **302–303**

Murder of Roger Ackroyd, The (Christie), **Supp. II:** 124, 128, 135

"Murder of Santa Claus, The" (James), **Supp. IV:** 340

Murder of the Man Who Was Shakespeare, The (Hoffman), **I:** 277

Murder on the Orient Express (Christie; U.S. title, *Murder in the Calais Coach*), **Supp. II:** 128, 130, 134, 135

Murderous Michael, **I:** 218

"Murdered Drinker, The" (Graham), **Supp. VII:** 115

"Murders in the Rue Morgue, The" (Poe), **III:** 339

Murdoch, Iris, **III:** 341, 345; **VI:** 372; **Supp. I: 215–235; Supp. IV:** 100, 139, 145, 234

Murmuring Judges (Hare), **Supp. IV:** 282, 294, 296–297, 298

Murnau, F. W., **III:** 342

Murphy (Beckett), **Supp. I:** 46–47, 48, 51, 62, 220; **Retro. Supp. I:** 19–20

Murphy, Richard, **VI:** 220; **Supp. V: 313–331**

Murray, Gilbert, **VI:** 153, 273, 274

Murray, John, **IV:** 182, 188, 190, 193, 294

Murray, Les, **Supp. VII: 269–288**

Murray, Nicholas, **Supp. IV:** 171

Murray, Sir James, **III:** 113

Murry, John Middleton, **III:** 68; **VI:** 207, 375, 446; **VII:** 37, 106, 173–174, 181–182

"Muse, The" (Cowley), **II:** 195, 200

"Muse Among the Motors, A" (Kipling), **VI:** 202

"Musée des Beaux Arts" (Auden), **VII:** 379, 385–386; **Retro. Supp. I:** 8

"Muses Dirge, The" (James), **II:** 102

"Museum" (MacNeice), **VII:** 412

Museum of Cheats, The (Warner), **Supp. VII:** 380

"Music" (Owen), **VI:** 449

Music: An Ode (Swinburne), **V:** 333

Music at Night (Priestley), **VII:** 225–226

Music Cure, The (Shaw), **VI:** 129

"Music for Octopi" (Redgrove), **Supp. VI:** 234

Music of Time novel cycle (Powell), *see Dance to the Music of Time, A*

"Music on the Hill, The" (Saki), **Supp. VI:** 243–244

"Musical Instrument, A" (Browning), **IV:** 315

Musicks Duell (Crashaw), **II:** 90–91

Musil, Robert, **Supp. IV:** 70

Muslin (Moore), **VI:** 98; *see Drama in Muslin, A*

"Mute Phenomena, The" (Mahon), **Supp. VI:** 173

"Mutual Life" (MacCaig), **Supp. VI:** 188

"My Aged Uncle Arly" (Lear), **V:** 85–86

My Brother (Kincaid), **Supp. VII:** 217, 230–231

My Brother Evelyn and Other Profiles (Waugh), **Supp. VI:** 269, 276

My Child, My Sister (Fuller), **Supp. VII:** 74, 76, 77, 81

"My Company" (Read), **VI:** 437

My Cousin Rachel (du Maurier), **Supp. III:** 134, 139, 140, 141, 147

My Darling Dear, My Daisy Flower (Skelton), **I:** 83

My Dear Dorothea: A Practical System of Moral Education for Females (Shaw), **VI:** 109, 130

"My delight and thy delight" (Bridges), **VI:** 77

"My Diary": The Early Years of My Daughter Marianne (Gaskell), **V:** 15

"My Doves" (Browning), **IV:** 313

"My Dream" (Rossetti), **V:** 256

"My Dyet" (Cowley), **II:** 197, 198

My Early Life (Churchill), **VI:** 354

My Father's Trapdoors (Redgrove), **Supp. VI: 236**

"My First Acquaintance with Poets" (Hazlitt), **IV:** 126, 132

"My First Book" (Stevenson), **Retro. Supp. I:** 260

"My First Marriage" (Jhabvala), **Supp. V:** 236

"My Friend Bingham" (James), **VI:** 69

My Fellow Devils (Hartley), **Supp. VII:** 127–128, 132

"My galley charged with forgetfulness" (Wyatt), **I:** 110

My Garden Book (Kincaid), **Supp. VII:** 217, 229, 230, 231

My Guru and His Disciple (Isherwood), **VII:** 318

My House in Umbria (Trevor), **Supp. IV:** 516–517

My Idea of Fun: A Cautionary Tale (Self), **Supp. V:** 396–398

"My Joyce" (Lodge), **Supp. IV:** 364

"My Lady Love, My Dove" (Dahl), **Supp. IV:** 217

My Lady Ludlow (Gaskell), **V:** 15

"My Last Duchess" (Browning), **IV:** 356, 360, 372; **Retro. Supp. II:** 22–23

"My Life up to Now" (Gunn), **Supp. IV:** 255, 265, 266, 268, 269, 273

"My love whose heart is tender said to me" (Rossetti), **V:** 251

"My lute awake!" (Wyatt), **I:** 105–106

My Man Jeeves (Wodehouse), **Supp. III:** 455

"My Mother" (Kincaid), **Supp. VII:** 221

"My own heart let me more have pity on" (Hopkins), **V:** 375–376

"My Own Life" (Hume), **Supp. III:** 229

"My pen take pain a little space" (Wyatt), **I:** 106

"My Picture Left in Scotland" (Jonson), **Retro. Supp. I:** 152

My Sad Captains (Gunn), **Supp. IV:** 257, 262–264

"My Sad Captains" (Gunn), **Supp. IV:** 263–264

My Sister Eileen (McKenney), **Supp. IV:** 476

"My Sister's Sleep" (Rossetti), **V:** 239, 240, 242

"My Sister's War" (Thomas), **Supp. IV:** 492

My Son's Story (Gordimer), **Supp. II:** 233, 240–242

"My Spectre" (Blake), **V:** 244

"My spirit kisseth thine" (Bridges), **VI:** 77

"My true love hath my heart, and I have his" (Sidney), **I:** 169

My Uncle Oswald (Dahl), **Supp. IV:** 213, 219, 220

My Very Own Story (Ayckbourn), **Supp. V:** 3, 11, 13

My World as in My Time (Newbolt), **VI:** 75

My Year (Dahl), **Supp. IV:** 225

Myer, Valerie Grosvenor, **Supp. IV:** 230

Myers, William Francis, **VII:** xx, xxxviii

Myles Before Myles, A Selection of the Earlier Writings of Brian O'Nolan (O'Nolan), **Supp. II:** 322, 323, 324

Myrick, K. O., **I:** 160, 167

"Myself in India" (Jhabvala), **Supp. V:** 227, 229–230

Myself When Young: Confessions (Waugh), **Supp. VI:** 270

Mysteries, The (Harrison), **Supp. V:** 150, 163

Mysteries of Udolpho, The (Radcliffe), **III:** 331–332, 335, 345; **IV:** xvi, 111; **Supp. III:** 384

Mysterious Affair at Styles, The (Christie), **Supp. II:** 124, 129–130

"Mysterious Kôr" (Bowen), **Supp. II:** 77, 82, 93

Mystery of Charles Dickens, The (Ackroyd), **Supp. VI:** 13

Mystery of Edwin Drood, The (Dickens), *see Edwin Drood*

"Mystery of Sasaesa Valley" (Doyle), **Supp. II:** 159

Mystery of the Blue Train (Christie), **Supp. II:** 125

Mystery of the Charity of Charles Péguy, The (Hill), **Supp. V:** 189, 196–198

Mystery of the Fall (Clough), **V:** 159, 161

Mystery of the Sea, The (Stoker), **Supp. III:** 381

Mystery Revealed: ... Containing ... Testimonials Respecting the ... Cock Lane Ghost, The (Goldsmith), **III:** 191

Mystic Masseur, The (Naipaul), **Supp. I:** 383, 386, 387, 393

"Mysticism and Democracy" (Hill), **Supp. V:** 192–193

Myth of Modernism (Bergonzi), **Supp. IV:** 364

"Mythical Journey, The" (Muir), **Supp. VI:** 206

Mythologiae sive explicationis fabularum (Conti), **I:** 266

"Mythological Sonnets" (Fuller), **Supp. VII:** 73

"Mythology" (Motion), **Supp. VII:** 266

N.

'n Droë wit seisoen (Brink), **Supp. VI:** 50

'n Oomblik in die wind (Brink), **Supp. VI:** 49

"Naaman" (Nicholson), **Supp. VI:** 216

"Nabara, The" (Day Lewis), **Supp. III:** 127

Nabokov, Vladimir, **Supp. IV:** 26–27, 43, 153, 302

Nacht and Traüme (Beckett), **Retro. Supp. I:** 29

Nada the Lily (Haggard), **Supp. III:** 214

Nadel, G. H., **I:** 269

Naipaul, V. S., **VII:** xx; **Supp. I: 383–405; Supp. IV:** 302

Naive and Sentimental Lover, The (le Carré), **Supp. II:** 300, **310–311,** 317

Naked Warriors (Read), **VI:** 436

Name and Nature of Poetry, The (Housman), **VI:** 157, 162–164

Name of Action, The (Greene), **Supp. I:** 3

Name of the Rose, The (Eco), **Supp. IV:** 116

"Naming of Offa, The" (Hill), **Supp. V:** 195

"Naming of Parts" (Reed), **VII:** 422

Nannie's Night Out (O'Casey), **VII:** 11–12

Napier, Macvey, **IV:** 272

Napoleon of Notting Hill, The (Chesterton), **VI:** 335, 338, 343–344

Napoleon III in Italy and Other Poems (Browning), *see Poems Before Congress*

Narayan, R. K., **Supp. IV:** 440

"Narcissus" (Gower), **I:** 53–54

Nares, Edward, **IV:** 280

Narrative of All the Robberies, ... of John Sheppard, A (Defoe), **III:** 13

"Narrative of Jacobus Coetzee, The" (Coetzee), **Supp. VI:** 76, **79–80**

Narrow Corner, The (Maugham), **VI:** 375

Narrow Place, The (Muir), **Supp. VI:** 204, **206**

"Narrow Place, The" (Muir), **Supp. VI:** 206

Narrow Road to the Deep North (Bond), **Supp. I:** 423, 427, 428–429, 430, 435

"Narrow Sea, The" (Graves), **VII:** 270

"Narrow Vessel, A" (Thompson), **V:** 441

Nashe, Thomas, **I:** 114, 123, 171, 199, 221, 278, 279, 281, 288; **II:** 25; **Supp. II:** 188; **Retro. Supp. I:** 156

Nation (periodical), **VI:** 455

Nation Review (publication), **Supp. IV:** 346

National Observer (periodical), **VI:** 350

National Standard (periodical), **V:** 19

National Tales (Hood), **IV:** 255, 259, 267

"National Trust" (Harrison), **Supp. V:** 153

Native Companions: Essays and Comments on Australian Literature 1936–1966 (Hope), **Supp. VII:** 151, 153, 159, 164

"Natura Naturans" (Clough), **V:** 159–160

Natural Causes (Motion), **Supp. VII:** 254, 257–258, 263

Natural Curiosity, A (Drabble), **Supp. IV:** 231, 249–250

Natural History and Antiquities of Selborne, The, (White), **Supp. VI:** 279–284, **285–293**

Natural History of Religion, The (Hume), **Supp. III:** 240–241

"natural man," **VII:** 94

"Natural Son" (Murphy), **Supp. V:** 327, 329

Naturalist's Calendar, with Observations in Various Branches of Natural History, A (White), **Supp. VI:** 283

Naturalist's Journal (White), **Supp. VI:** 283, 292

"Naturally the Foundation Will Bear Your Expenses" (Larkin), **Supp. I:** 285

Nature of a Crime, The (Conrad), **VI:** 148

Nature of Blood, The (Phillips), **Supp. V:** 380, 391–394

Nature of Cold Weather, The (Redgrove), **Supp. VI: 227–229,** 236

"Nature of Cold Weather, The" (Redgrove), **Supp. VI:** 228,237

"Nature of Gothic, The" (Ruskin), **V:** 176

Nature of History, The (Marwick), **IV:** 290, 291

Nature of Passion, The (Jhabvala), **Supp. V:** 226

"Nature of the Scholar, The" (Fichte), **V:** 348

Nature Poems (Davies), **Supp. III:** 398

"Nature That Washt Her Hands in Milk" (Ralegh), **I:** 149

Natwar–Singh, K., **VI:** 408

Naufragium Joculare (Cowley), **II:** 194, 202

Naulahka (Kipling and Balestier), **VI:** 204

"Naval History" (Kelman), **Supp. V:** 250

"Naval Treaty, The" (Doyle), **Supp. II:** 169, 175

Navigation and Commerce (Evelyn), **II:** 287

"Navy's Here, The" (Redgrove), **Supp. VI:** 234

Naylor, Gillian, **VI:** 168

Nazarene Gospel Restored, The (Graves and Podro), **VII:** 262

Nazism, **VI:** 242

Neal, Patricia, **Supp. IV:** 214, 218, 223

Near and Far (Blunden), **VI:** 428

"Near Lanivet" (Hardy), **VI:** 17

"Near Perigord" (Pound), **V:** 304

Necessity of Art, The (Fischer), **Supp. II:** 228

Necessity of Atheism, The (Shelley and Hogg), **IV:** xvii, 196, 208; **Retro. Supp. I:** 244

"Necessity of Not Believing, The" (Smith), **Supp. II:** 467

Necessity of Poetry, The (Bridges), **VI:** 75–76, 82, 83

"Necessity's Child" (Wilson), **Supp. I:** 153–154

"Neck" (Dahl), **Supp. IV:** 217

"Ned Bratts" (Browning), **IV:** 370; **Retro. Supp. II:** 29–30

Ned Kelly and the City of the Bees (Keneally), **Supp. IV:** 346

"Ned Skinner" (Muldoon), **Supp. IV:** 415

"Need to Be Versed in Country Things, The" (Frost), **Supp. IV:** 423

Needham, Gwendolyn, **V:** 60

Needle's Eye, The (Drabble), **Supp. IV:** 230, 234, 241, 242–243, 245, 251

"Negative Love" (Donne), **Retro. Supp. II:** 93

"Neglected Graveyard, Luskentyre" (MacCaig), **Supp. VI:** 182, 189, 194

Neizvestny, Ernst, **Supp. IV:** 88

"Nelly Trim" (Warner), **Supp. VII:** 371

Nelson, W., **I:** 86

Nerinda (Douglas), **VI:** 300, 305

Nero Part I (Bridges), **VI:** 83

Nero Part II (Bridges), **VI:** 83

Nesbit, E., **Supp. II:** 140, 144, 149

"Nest in a Wall, A" (Murphy), **Supp. V:** 326

Nest of Tigers, A: Edith, Osbert and Sacheverell in Their Times (Lehmann), **VII:** 141

Nether World, The (Gissing), **V:** 424, 437

Netherwood (White), **Supp. I:** 131, 151

"Netting, The" (Murphy), **Supp. V:** 318

Nettles (Lawrence), **VII:** 118

"Netty Sargent's Copyhold" (Hardy), **VI:** 22

"Neurotic, The" (Day Lewis), **Supp. III:** 129

Neutral Ground (Corke), **VII:** 93

"Neutral Tones" (Hardy), **Retro. Supp. I:** 110, 117

New Age (periodical), **VI:** 247, 265; **VII:** 172

New and Collected Poems 1934–84 (Fuller), **Supp. VII:** 68, 72, 73, 74, 79

New and Collected Poems, 1952–1992 (Hill), **Supp. V:** 184

New and Improved Grammar of the English Tongue, A (Hazlitt), **IV:** 139

New and Selected Poems (Davie), **Supp. VI:** 108

New and Useful Concordance, A (Bunyan), **II:** 253

New Apocalypse, The (MacCaig), **Supp. VI:** 184

New Arabian Nights (Stevenson), **V:** 384n, 386, 395; **Retro. Supp. I:** 263

New Arcadia (Sidney), **Retro. Supp. II:** 332

New Atlantis (Bacon), **I:** 259, 265, 267–269, 273

"New Ballad of Tannhäuser, A" (Davidson), **V:** 318n

New Bath Guide (Anstey), **III:** 155

New Bats in Old Belfries (Betjeman), **VII:** 368–369

New Bearings in English Poetry (Leavis), **V:** 375, 381; **VI:** 21; **VII:** 234, 244–246

"New Beginning, A" (Kinsella), **Supp. V:** 270

New Belfry of Christ Church, The (Carroll), **V:** 274

New Characters . . . of Severall Persons . . . (Webster), **II:** 85

"New Cemetery, The" (Nicholson), **Supp. VI:** 219

New Cratylus, The: Notes on the Craft of Poetry (Hope), **Supp. VII:** 151, 155

New Country (ed. Roberts), **VII:** xix, 411

"New Delhi Romance, A" (Jhabvala), **Supp. V:** 236–237

New Discovery of an Old Intreague, An (Defoe), **III:** 12; **Retro. Supp. I:** 67

New Dominion, A (Jhabvala), **Supp. V:** 230–231

"New Drama" (Joyce), **Retro. Supp. I:** 170

New Dunciad, The (Pope), **III:** 73, 78; **Retro. Supp. I:** 238

"New Empire Within Britain, The" (Rushdie), **Supp. IV:** 436, 445

"New England Winter, A" (James), **VI:** 69

New Essays by De Quincey (ed. Tave); **IV:** 155

New Ewart, The: Poems 1980–82 (Ewart), **Supp. VII:** 34, 44, 45

New Family Instructor, A (Defoe), **III:** 14

"New Forge" (Murphy), **Supp. V:** 328

New Form of Intermittent Light for Lighthouses, A (Stevenson), **V:** 395

New Grub Street (Gissing), **V:** xxv, 426, 427, 429, 430, 434–435, 437; **VI:** 377; **Supp. IV:** 7

"New Hampshire" (Reid), **Supp. VII:** 326

New Inn; The Noble Gentlemen (Jonson), **II:** 65; **Retro. Supp. I:** 165

New Journey to Paris, A (Swift), **III:** 35

"New King for the Congo: Mobutu and the Nihilism of Africa" (Naipaul), **Supp. I:** 398

New Light on Piers Plowman (Bright), **I:** 3

New Lines (Conquest), **Supp. IV:** 256

New Lives for Old (Snow), **VII:** 323

New Love–Poems (Scott), **IV:** 39

New Machiavelli, The (Wells), **VI:** 226, 239, 244

New Magdalen, The (Collins), **Supp. VI:** 102

New Meaning of Treason, The (West), **Supp. III:** 440, 444

New Men, The (Snow), **VII:** xxi, 324, 328–329, 330

New Method of Evaluation as Applied to ð, The (Carroll), **V:** 274

New Monthly (periodical), **IV:** 252, 254, 258

"New Novel, The" (James), **VI:** xii

New Numbers (periodical), **VI:** 420; **Supp. III:** 47

New Oxford Book of Irish Verse, The (Kinsella), **Supp. V:** 274

New Poems (Arnold), **V:** xxiii, 204, 209, 216

"New Poems" (Bridges), **VI:** 77

New Poems (Davies), **Supp. III:** 398

New Poems (Fuller), **Supp. VII:** 76–77

New Poems (Kinsella), **Supp. V:** 266, 274

New Poems (Thompson), **V:** 444, 446, 451

New Poems by Robert Browning and Elizabeth Barrett Browning (ed. Kenyon), **IV:** 321

New Poems Hitherto Unpublished or Uncollected . . . (Rossetti), **V:** 260

New Quixote, The (Frayn), **Supp. VII:** 57

New Review (periodical), **VI:** 136

New Rhythm and Other Pieces, The (Firbank), **Supp. II:** 202, 205, 207, 222

New Satyr on the Parliament, A (Defoe), **Retro. Supp. I:** 67

New Selected Poems (Heaney), **Retro. Supp. I:** 131

New Signatures (Day Lewis), **Supp. III:** 125

New Signatures (ed. Roberts), **VII:** 411; **Supp. II:** 486

"New Song, A" (Heaney), **Supp. II:** 273

New Statesman (periodical), **VI:** 119, 250, 371; **VII:** 32; **Supp. IV:** 26, 66, 78, 80, 81

New Stories I (ed. Drabble), **Supp. IV:** 230

New Territory (Boland), **Supp. V:** 35, 36

New Testament in Modern English (Phillips), **I:** 383

New Testament in Modern Speech (Weymouth), **I:** 382

New Voyage Round the World, A (Dampier), **III:** 7, 24

New Voyage Round the World, A (Defoe), **III:** 5, 13

New Weather (Muldoon), **Supp. IV:** 412–414, 416

"New Weather" (Muldoon), **Supp. IV:** 413

New Witness (periodical), **VI:** 340, 341

New Worlds for Old (Wells), **VI:** 242

New Writings of William Hazlitt (ed. Howe), **IV:** 140

New Year Letter (Auden), **VII:** 379, 382, 388, 390, 393; **Retro. Supp. I:** 10

"New Year Wishes for the English" (Davie), **Supp. VI:** 110

"New Year's Burden, A" (Rossetti), **V:** 242

Newbolt, Henry, **VI:** 75, 417

Newby, T. C., **V:** 140

Newcomes, The (Thackeray), **V:** xxii, 18, 19, **28–31**, 35, 38, 69

Newell, K. B., **VI:** 235, 237

"Newgate" novels, **V:** 22, 47

Newman, F. W., **V:** 208*n*

Newman, John Henry, **II:** 243; **III:** 46; **IV:** 63, 64; **V:** xi, xxv, 156, 214, 283, 340; **Supp. VII: 289–305**

"News" (Traherne), **II:** 191, 194

"News from Ireland, The" (Trevor), **Supp. IV:** 504–505

News from Nowhere (Morris), **V:** xxv, 291, 301–304, 306, 409

"News from the Sun" (Ballard), **Supp. V:** 22

Newspaper, The (Crabbe), **III:** 275, 286

"Newsreel" (Day Lewis), **Supp. III:** 127

"Newstead Abbey" (Fuller), **Supp. VII:** 73

Newton, Isaac, **Supp. III:** 418–419

Newton, J. F., **IV:** 158

Newton, John, **III:** 210

"Next Time, The" (James), **VI:** 69

"Next, Please" (Larkin), **Supp. I:** 278

Nice and the Good, The (Murdoch), **Supp. I:** 226, 227

"Nice Day at School" (Trevor), **Supp. IV:** 504

"Nice to Be Nice" (Kelman), **Supp. V:** 245–246

Nice Valour, The (Fetcher and Middleton), **II:** 21, 66

Nice Work (Lodge), **Supp. IV:** 363, 366, 372, 378–380, 383, 385

Nice Work (television adaptation), **Supp. IV:** 381

Nicholas Nickleby (Dickens), **IV:** 69; **V:** xix, 42, 50–53, 54, 71

Nicholls, Bowyer, **IV:** 98

Nichols, Robert, **VI:** 419

Nicholson, Norman, **Supp. VI: 211–224**

Nichomachean Ethics (Johnson), **Retro. Supp. I:** 149

Nicoll, Allardyce, **II:** 363

Nietzsche, Friedrich Wilhelm, **IV:** 121, 179; **Supp. IV:** 3, 6, 9, 10, 12, 17, 50, 108

Nigger of the "Narcissus," The (Conrad), **VI:** 136, 137, 148; **Retro. Supp. II:** 71–73

Nigger Question, The (Carlyle), **IV:** 247, 250

Night (Harris), **Supp. V:** 138, 139

Night (O'Brien), **Supp. V:** 338

Night (Harris), **Supp. V:** 138, 139

Night (O'Brien), **Supp. V:** 338

Night Fears and Other Stories (Hartley), **Supp. VII:** 121–122

Night Feed (Boland), **Supp. V:** 50

"Night Feed" (Boland), **Supp. V:** 50

"Night Sister" (Jennings), **Supp. V:** 215

"Night Songs" (Kinsella), **Supp. V:** 261

"Nightwalker" (Kinsella), **Supp. V:** 263

Nightwalker and Other Poems (Kinsella), **Supp. V:** 262, 263–264

"1938" (Kinsella), **Supp. V:** 271

Night (Pinter), **Supp. I:** 376

"Night, The" (Vaughan), **II:** 186, 188

Night and Day (Rosenberg), **VI:** 432

Night and Day (Stoppard), **Supp. I:** 451; **Retro. Supp. II:** 352–353

Night and Day (Woolf), **VII:** 20, 27; **Retro. Supp. I:** 307, 316

"Night and the Merry Man" (Browning), **IV:** 313

Night (Harris), **Supp. V:** 138, 139

Night (O'Brien), **Supp. V:** 338

Night–Crossing (Mahon), **Supp. VI: 167–168,** 169

Night Feed (Boland), **Supp. V:** 50

"Night Feed" (Boland), **Supp. V:** 50

Night Mail (Auden), **Retro. Supp. I:** 7

"Night of Frost in May" (Meredith), **V:** 223

Night on Bald Mountain (White), **Supp. I:** 131, 136, **149–151**

"Night Out" (Rhys), **Supp. II:** 402

Night Out, A (Pinter), **Supp. I:** 371–372, 375; **Retro. Supp. I:** 223

"Night Patrol" (West), **VI:** 423

Night School (Pinter), **Supp. I:** 373, 375

"Night Sister" (Jennings), **Supp. V:** 215

"Night Songs" (Kinsella), **Supp. V:** 261

"Night Taxi" (Gunn), **Supp. IV:** 272–273, 274

Night the Prowler, The (White), **Supp. I:** 131, 132

Night Thoughts (Young), **III:** 302, 307; **Retro. Supp. I:** 43

Night to Remember, A (Ambler), **Supp. IV:** 3

Night to Remember, A (film), **Supp. IV:** 2

Night Walker, The (Fletcher and Shirley), **II:** 66

"Night Wind, The" (Brontë), **V:** 133, 142

"Nightclub" (MacNeice), **VII:** 414

Night–Comers, The (Ambler), *see State of Siege*

Night–Comers, The (film), **Supp. IV:** 3

"Nightingale and the Rose, The" (Wilde), **Retro. Supp. II:** 365

"Nightmare, A" (Rossetti), **V:** 256

Nightmare Abbey (Peacock), **III:** 336, 345; **IV:** xvii, 158, 162, 164–165, 170, 177

"Nightpiece to Julia, The" (Herrick), **II:** lll

Nightrunners of Bengal (film, Ambler), **Supp. IV:** 3

Nights at the Alexandra (Trevor), **Supp. IV:** 514–515

Nights at the Circus (Carter), **Supp. III:** 79, 87, 89–90, 91–92

"Night's Fall Unlocks the Dirge of the Sea" (Graham), **Supp. VII:** 110

Nightfishing, The (Graham), **Supp. VII:** 105, 106, 111–113, 114, 116

"Nightwalker" (Kinsella), **Supp. V:** 263

Nightwalker and Other Poems (Kinsella), **Supp. V:** 262, 263–264

Nin, Anaïs, **Supp. IV:** 110, 111

Nina Balatka (Trollope), **V:** 101

Nine Essays (Housman), **VI:** 164

Nine Experiments (Spender), **Supp. II:** 481, 486

Nine Tailors, The (Sayers), **Supp. III:** 343, 344–345

"Ninemaidens" (Thomas), **Supp. IV:** 494

1985 (Burgess), **Supp. I:** 193

Nineteen Eighty–four (Orwell), **III:** 341; **VII:** xx, 204, 274, 279–280, 284–285

1914 (Brooke), **Supp. III:** 48, 52, 56–58

"1914" (Owen), **VI:** 444

1914 and Other Poems (Brooke), **VI:** 420; **Supp. III:** 48, 55

1914. Five Sonnets (Brooke), **VI:** 420

1900 (West), **Supp. III:** 432, 445

"Nineteen Hundred and Nineteen" (Yeats), **VI:** 217; **Retro. Supp. I:** 335

"1938" (Kinsella), **Supp. V:** 271

"Nineteenth Century, The" (Thompson), **V:** 442

Nineteenth Century: A Dialogue in Utopia, The (Ellis), **VI:** 241*n*

Nip in the Air, A (Betjeman), **VII:** 357

Niven, Alastair, **VII:** xiv, xxxviii

No (Ackroyd), **Supp. VI:** 2

No Abolition of Slavery . . . (Boswell), **III:** 248

No Enemy (Ford), **VI:** 324

No Exit (Sartre), **III:** 329, 345

"No Flowers by Request" (Ewart), **Supp. VII:** 36

No Fond Return of Love (Pym), **Supp. II: 374–375,** 381

No Fool Like an Old Fool (Ewart), **Supp. VII:** 41

No Laughing Matter (Wilson), **Supp. I:** 162–163

No Man's Land (Pinter), **Supp. I:** 377

No More Parades (Ford), **VI:** 319, 329

No Name (Collins), **Supp. VI:** 91, 93–94, **97–98,** 102

No Quarter (Waugh), **Supp. VI:** 275

"No Rest for the Wicked" (Mahon), **Supp. VI:** 167

"No Road" (Larkin), **Supp. I:** 285

"No Smoking" (Ewart), **Supp. VII:** 47

No Star on the Way Back (Nicholson), **Supp. VI:** 217

"No, Thank You John" (Rossetti), **V:** 256

No Truce with Time (Waugh), **Supp. VI:** 274

No Wit, No Help Like a Woman's (Middleton), **II:** 3, 21

"No Witchcraft for Sale" (Lessing), **Supp. I:** 241, 242

"No worst, There is none" (Hopkins), **V:** 374

Noah and the Waters (Day Lewis), **Supp. III:** 118, 126, 127

Noble Jilt, The (Trollope), **V:** 102

Noble Numbers (Herrick), *see His Noble Numbers*

Nobleman, The (Tourneur), **II:** 37

Nocturnal upon S. Lucy's Day, A (Donne), **I:** 358, 359–360; **II:** 128; **Retro. Supp. II:** 91

"Nocturne" (Murphy), **Supp. V:** 325

Noh theater, **VI:** 218

Noises Off (Frayn), **Supp. VII:** 61

"Noisy Flushes the Birds" (Pritchett), **Supp. III:** 324–325

"Noisy in the Doghouse" (Pritchett), **Supp. III:** 324, 325

"Noli emulari" (Wyatt), **I:** 102

Nollius, **II:** 185, 201

"Nona Vincent" (James), **VI:** 69

"Nones" (Auden), **Retro. Supp. I:** 2

Nonsense Songs, Stories, Botany and Alphabets (Lear), **V:** 78, 84, 87

Non-Stop Connolly Show, The (Arden and D'Arcy), **Supp. II:** 28, 30, **35–38,** 39

Nooks and Byways of Italy, The (Ramage), **VI:** 298

"Noon at St. Michael's" (Mahon), **Supp. VI:** 174

"Noonday Axeman" (Murray), **Supp. VII:** 272

Norman Douglas (Dawkins), **VI:** 303–304

Norman Conquests, The (Ayckbourn), **Supp. V:** 2, 5, 9, 10, 11, 14

Normyx, pseud. of Norman Douglas

North, Thomas, **I:** 314

North (Heaney), **Supp. II:** 268, **273–275; Supp. IV:** 412, 420–421, 427; **Retro. Supp. I:** 124, 125, 129–130

North America (Trollope), **V:** 101

North and South (Gaskell), **V:** xxii, **1–6,** 8, 15

"North and South, The" (Browning), **IV:** 315

"North London Book of the Dead, The" (Self), **Supp. V:** 400

"North Sea" (Keyes), **VII:** 437

"North Sea off Carnoustie" (Stevenson), **Supp. VI:** 260

North Ship, The (Larkin), **Supp. I:** 276–277

"North Wind, The" (Bridges), **VI:** 80

Northanger Abbey (Austen), **III:** 335–336, 345; **IV:** xvii, 103, 104, 107–110, 112–114, 122; **Retro. Supp. II:** 4–6

Northanger Novels, The (Sadleir), **III:** 335, 346

"Northern Farmer, New Style" (Tennyson), **IV:** 327

"Northern Farmer, Old Style" (Tennyson), **IV:** 327

Northern Lights: A Poet's Sources (Brown), **Supp. VI:** 61, 64

Northern Memoirs (Franck), **II:** 131

Northward Ho! (Dekker, Marston, Webster), **I:** 234–235, 236, 244; **II:** 68, 85

Norton, Charles Eliot, **IV:** 346; **V:** 3, 9, 299; **VI:** 41

Norton, Thomas, **I:** 214

"Nose, The" (Gogol), **III:** 340, 345

Nosferatu (film), **III:** 342; **IV:** 180

"Nostalgia in the Afternoon" (Heaney), **Retro. Supp. I:** 126

Nostromo (Conrad), **VI:** 140–143; **Retro. Supp. II:** 77–80

Not . . . not . . . not . . . not . . . not enough oxygen (Churchill), **Supp. IV:** 181

"Not Abstract" (Jennings), **Supp. V:** 217

"Not After Midnight" (du Maurier), **Supp. III:** 135

"Not Celia, that I juster am" (Sedley), **II:** 265

Not for Publication (Gordimer), **Supp. II:** 232

Not Honour More (Cary), **VII:** 186, 194–195

Not I (Beckett), **Supp. I:** 61; **Retro. Supp. I:** 27–28

"Not Ideas, But Obsessions" (Naipaul), **Supp. I:** 399

"Not Not While the Giro" (Kelman), **Supp. V:** 246

Not Not While the Giro and Other Stories (Kelman), **Supp. V:** 242, 244–246

"Not Now for My Sins' Sake" (Reid), **Supp. VII:** 325–326

"Not on Sad Stygian Shore" (Butler), **Supp. II:** 111

"Not Palaces" (Spender), **Supp. II:** 494

"Not Proven" (Day Lewis), **Supp. III:** 130

Not-So-Stories (Saki), **Supp. VI:** 240

Not to Disturb (Spark), **Supp. I:** 200, 201, 210

Not Waving But Drowning (Smith), **Supp. II:** 463

"Not Waving But Drowning" (Smith), **Supp. II:** 467

Not Without Glory (Scannell), **VII:** 424, 426

"Not yet Afterwards" (MacCaig), **Supp. VI:** 185

"Note for American Readers" (Byatt), **Supp. IV:** 149

"Notes from a Spanish Village" (Reid), **Supp. VII:** 334, 335–336

Note on Charlotte Brontë, A (Swinburne), **V:** 332

"Note on F. W. Bussell" (Pater), **V:** 356–357

"Note on 'To Autumn,' A" (Davenport), **IV:** 227

"Note on Zulfikar Ghose's 'Nature Strategies'" (Harris), **Supp. V:** 145

"Note to the Difficult One, A" (Graham), **Supp. VII:** 115

Notebook (Maugham), **VI:** 370

"Notebook, A" (Hulme), **Supp. VI:** 135, 140, 145

Note-Book of Edmund Burke (ed. Somerset), **III:** 205

Notebook on William Shakespeare, A (Sitwell), **VII:** 127, 139, 140

Note-Books (Butler), **Supp. II:** 100, 102, 105, **108–111,** 115, 117, 118, 119

Notebooks (Thomas), **Supp. I:** 170

Notebooks of Henry James, The (ed. Matthiessen and Murdock), **VI:** 38

Notebooks of Samuel Taylor Coleridge, The (ed. Coburn), **IV:** 48, 53, 56

Notes and Index to . . . the Letters of Sir Walter Scott (Corson), **IV:** 27, 39

Notes and Observations on the Empress of Morocco (Dryden), **II:** 297, 305

Notes and Reviews (James), **V:** 199

Notes by an Oxford Chiel (Carroll), **V:** 274

Notes for a New Culture: An Essay on Modernism (Ackroyd), **Supp. VI:** 2, 12–13

"Notes from a Book of Hours" (Jennings), **Supp. V:** 211

Notes from the Land of the Dead and Other Poems (Kinsella), **Supp. V:** 266, 274

Notes of a Journey from Cornhill to Grand Cairo (Thackeray), **V:** 25, 37, 38

Notes of a Journey Through France and Italy (Hazlitt), **IV:** 134, 140

Notes of a Son and Brother (James), **VI:** 59, 65–66

Notes of an English Republican on the Muscovite Crusade (Swinburne), **V:** 332

"Notes on Being a Foreigner" (Reid), **Supp. VII:** 323

"Notes on Designs of the Old Masters at Florence" (Swinburne), **V:** 329

Notes on English Divines (Coleridge), **IV:** 56

Notes on Joseph Conrad (Symons), **VI:** 149

"Notes on Language and Style" (Hulme), **Supp. VI:** 135–136, 141–143, 146

Notes on Life and Letters (Conrad), **VI:** 67, 148

Notes on Novelists (James), **V:** 384, 392; **VI:** 149

Notes on . . . Pictures Exhibited in the Rooms of the Royal Academy (Ruskin), **V:** 184

Notes on Poems and Reviews (Swinburne), **V:** 316, 329, 332

Notes on Sculptures in Rome and Florence . . . (Shelley), **IV:** 209

"Notes on Technical Matters" (Sitwell), **VII:** 139

Notes on the Construction of Sheep–Folds (Ruskin), **V:** 184

Notes on the Royal Academy Exhibition, 1868 (Swinburne), **V:** 329, 332

Notes on "The Testament of Beauty" (Smith), **VI:** 83

Notes on the Turner Gallery at Marlborough House (Ruskin), **V:** 184

"Notes on Writing a Novel" (Bowen), **Supp. II:** 90

Notes Theological, Political, and Miscellaneous (Coleridge), **IV:** 56

Nothing (Green), **Supp. II: 263–264**

Nothing Like Leather (Pritchett), **Supp. III:** 313–314

Nothing Like the Sun (Burgess), **Supp. I:** 194, 196

Nothing Sacred (Carter), **Supp. III:** 80, 86–87

Nott, John, **II:** 102

"Nottingham and the Mining Country" (Lawrence), **VII:** 88, 89, 91, 121; **Retro. Supp. II:** 221

Nouvelles (Beckett), **Supp. I:** 49–50

Novak, Maximillian, **Retro. Supp. I:** 66–67, 68–69

Novel and the People, The (Fox), **Supp. IV:** 466

Novel Now, The (Burgess), **Supp. I:** 194

Novel on Yellow Paper (Smith), **Supp. II:** 460, 462, 469, 473, **474–476**

Novelist, The (portrait; Kitaj), **Supp. IV:** 119

Novelist at the Crossroads, and Other Essays on Fiction, The (Lodge), **Supp. IV:** 365

"Novelist at Work, The" (Cary), **VII:** 187

"Novelist Today: Still at the Crossroads?, The" (Lodge), **Supp. IV:** 367

"Novelist's Poison, The" (Keneally), **Supp. IV:** 343

Novels of E. M. Forster, The (Woolf), **VI:** 413

Novels of George Eliot: A Study in Form, The (Hardy), **V:** 201

Novels of George Meredith, and Some Notes on the English Novel, The (Sitwell), **V:** 230, 234

Novels Up to Now (radio series), **VI:** 372

"November" (Bridges), **VI:** 79–80

Novum organum (Bacon), **I:** 259, 260, 263–264, 272; **IV:** 279

"Now" (Thomas), **Supp. I:** 174

Now and in Time to Be (Keneally), **Supp. IV:** 347

"Now in the Time of This Mortal Living" (Nicholson), **Supp. VI:** 214

"Now Sleeps the Crimson Petal" (Tennyson), **IV:** 334

Now We Are Six (Milne), **Supp. V:** 295, 302–303

"Now, Zero" (Ballard), **Supp. V:** 21

Nude with Violin (Coward), **Supp. II:** 155

"Numina at the Street Parties, The" (Redgrove), **Supp. VI:** 235

Numismata: A Discourse of Medals . . . (Evelyn), **II:** 287

"Nunc Dimittis" (Dahl), **Supp. IV:** 215, 217

Nunquam (Durrell), **Supp. I: 94,** 103, **113–118,** 120

Nuns and Soldiers (Murdoch), **Supp. I:** 231, 233

Nun's Priest's Tale, The (Chaucer), **I:** 21

"Nuptiall Song, A; or, Epithalamie, on Sir Clipseby Crew and his Lady" (Herrick), **II:** 105, 106

"Nuptials of Attilla, The" (Meredith), **V:** 221

Nursery Alice, The (Carroll), **V:** 273

Nursery Rhymes (Sitwell), **VII:** 138

"Nursery Songs" (Reid), **Supp. VII:** 326

"Nurse's Song" (Blake), **III:** 292; **Retro. Supp. I:** 42

Nussey, Ellen, **V:** 108, 109, 113, 117, 118, 126, 152

"Nymph Complaining for the Death of Her Faun, The" (Marvell), **II:** 211, 215–216

"Nympholept, A" (Swinburne), **V:** 328

"O Dreams, O Destinations" (Day Lewis), **Supp. III:** 122

"O! for a Closer Walk with God" (Cowper), **III:** 210

"O happy dames, that may embrace" (Surrey), **I:** 115, 120

"O land of Empire, art and love!" (Clough), **V:** 158

O Mistress Mine (Rattigan), see *Love in Idleness*

O Rathaille, Aogan, **Supp. IV:** 418–419

"O Tell Me the Truth About Love" (Auden), **Retro. Supp. I:** 6

Ó Tuama, Seán, **Supp. V:** 266

"O World of many Worlds" (Owen), **VI:** 445

"O Youth whose hope is high" (Bridges), **VI:** 159

Oak Leaves and Lavender (O'Casey), **VII:** 7, 8

Oases (Reid), **Supp. VII:** 333–337

"Obedience" (Herbert), **II:** 126

"Obelisk, The" (Forster), **VI:** 411

"Obermann Once More" (Arnold), **V:** 210

Oberon (Jonson), **I:** 344–345

"Object Lessons" (Boland), **Supp. V:** 38–39

Object Lessons: The Life of the Woman and the Poet in Our Time (Boland), **Supp. V:** 35, 36, 37, 42, 43, 46

"Object of the Attack, The" (Ballard), **Supp. V:** 33

Objections to Sex and Violence (Churchill), **Supp. IV:** 182–183, 184, 198

O'Brien, Conor Cruise, **Supp. IV:** 449

O'Brien, E. J., **VII:** 176

O'Brien, Edna, **Supp. V: 333–346**

O'Brien, Flann, see O'Nolan, Brian

Obsequies to the Memory of Mr. Edward King (Milton), **II:** 175

"Observation Car" (Hope), **Supp. VII:** 154

Observations on a Late State of the Nation (Burke), **III:** 205

Observations on Macbeth (Johnson), see *Miscellaneous Observations on the Tragedy of Macbeth*

Observations . . . on Squire Foote's Dramatic Entertainment . . . (Boswell), **III:** 247

Observations Relative . . . to Picturesque Beauty . . . [in] the High–Lands of Scotland (Gilpin), **IV:** 36

Observations upon the Articles of Peace with the Irish Rebels . . . (Milton), **II:** 176

Observator (periodical), **III:** 41; **Supp. IV:** 121

O'Casey, Sean, **VI:** xiv, 214, 218, 314–315; **VII:** xviii, **1–15;** list of articles, **VII:** 14–15; **Supp. II:** 335–336

Occasion for Loving (Gordimer), **Supp. II:** 227, 228, 231, 232, 233

Occasional Verses (FitzGerald), **IV:** 353

Occasions of Poetry, The (ed. Wilmer), **Supp. IV:** 255, 263

Ocean of Story (Stead), **Supp. IV:** 476

O'Connor, Frank, **Supp. IV:** 514

O'Connor, Monsignor John, **VI:** 338

O'Connor, Ulick, **Supp. II:** 63, 70, 76

October and Other Poems (Bridges), **VI:** 81, 83

"October Dawn" (Hughes), **Supp. I:** 344

October Ferry to Gabriola (Lowry), **Supp. III: 284–285**

October Man, The (film, Ambler), **Supp. IV:** 3

"October Dawn" (Hughes), **Retro. Supp. II:** 203

"October Salmon" (Hughes), **Supp. I:** 363; **Retro. Supp. II:** 213–214

Odd Women, The (Gissing), **V:** 428, 433–434, 437

Oddments Inklings Omens Moments (Reid), **Supp. VII:** 327–329

Ode ad Gustavem regem. Ode ad Gustavem exulem (Landor), **IV:** 100

"Ode: Autumn" (Hood), **IV:** 255

"Ode for Music" (Gray), see "Installation Ode"

"Ode. Intimations of Immortality from Recollections of Early Childhood" (Wordsworth), **II:** 189, 200; **IV:** xvi, 21, 22

"Ode on a Distant Prospect of Eton College" (Gray), **III:** 137, 144

"Ode on a Grecian Urn" (Keats), **III:** 174, 337; **IV:** 222–223, 225, 226; **Supp. V:** 38; **Retro. Supp. I:** 195–196

"Ode on Indolence" (Keats), **IV:** 221, 225–226

"Ode on Melancholy" (Keats), **III:** 337; **IV:** 224–225

"Ode on Mrs. Arabella Hunt Singing" (Congreve), **II:** 348

Ode, on the Death of Mr. Henry Purcell, An (Dryden), **II:** 304

"Ode on the Death of Mr. Thomson" (Collins), **III:** 163, 175

"Ode on the Death of Sir H. Morison" (Jonson), **II:** 199

Ode on the Death of the Duke of Wellington (Tennyson), **II:** 200; **IV:** 338

Ode on the Departing Year (Coleridge), **IV:** 55

Ode on the Installation of . . . Prince Albert as Chancellor of . . . Cambridge (Wordsworth), **IV:** 25

"Ode on the Insurrection at Candia" (Swinburne), **V:** 313

"Ode on the Morning of Christ's Nativity" (Milton), **Retro. Supp. II:** 272

"Ode on the Pleasure Arising from Vicissitude" (Gray), **III:** 141, 145

"Ode on the Popular Superstitions of the Highlands of Scotland" (Collins), **III:** 163, 171–173, 175

Ode on the Proclamation of the French Republic (Swinburne), **V:** 332

"Ode on the Spring" (Gray), **III:** 137, 295

"Ode Performed in the Senate House at Cambridge" (Gray), **III:** 145

Ode Prefixed to S. Harrison's Arches of Triumph . . . (Webster), **II:** 85

"Ode to a Lady on the Death of Colonel Ross" (Collins), **III:** 162

"Ode to a Nightingale" (Keats), **II:** 122; **IV:** 212, 221, 222–223, 224, 226; **Retro. Supp. I:** 195–196

"Ode to Apollo" (Keats), **IV:** 221, 227

"Ode to Duty" (Wordsworth), **II:** 303

"Ode to Evening" (Collins), **III:** 166, 173; **IV:** 227

"Ode to Fear" (Collins), *see* "Fear"

Ode to Himself (Jonson), **I:** 336

Ode to Independence (Smollett), **III:** 158

"Ode to John Warner" (Auden), **Retro. Supp. I:** 8

"Ode to Liberty" (Shelley), **IV:** 203

"Ode to Master Endymion Porter, Upon his Brothers Death, An" (Herrick), **II:** 112

"Ode to May" (Keats), **IV:** 221, 222

Ode to Mazzini (Swinburne), **V:** 333

"Ode to Memory" (Tennyson), **IV:** 329

"Ode to Mr. Congreve" (Swift), **III:** 30

"Ode to Naples" (Shelley), **II:** 200; **IV:** 195

Ode to Napoleon Buonaparte (Byron), **IV:** 192

"Ode to Pity" (Collins), **III:** 164

"Ode to Psyche" (Keats), **IV:** 221–222

"Ode to Rae Wilson" (Hood), **IV:** 261, 262–263

"Ode to Sir William Temple" (Swift), **III:** 30

"Ode to Sorrow" (Keats), **IV:** 216, 224

"Ode to the Moon" (Hood), **IV:** 255

"Ode to the Setting Sun" (Thompson), **V:** 448, 449

"Ode to the West Wind" (Shelley), **II:** 200; **IV:** xviii, 198, 203

Ode to Tragedy, An (Boswell), **III:** 247

"Ode upon Dr. Harvey" (Cowley), **II:** 196, 198

"Ode: Written at the Beginning of the Year 1746" (Collins), **III:** 169

Odes (Gray), **III:** 145

Odes and Addresses to Great People (Hood and Reynolds), **IV:** 253, 257, 267

Odes in Contribution to the Song of French History (Meredith), **V:** 223, 234

Odes on Several Descriptive and Allegorical Subjects (Collins), **III:** 162, 163, 165–166, 175

Odes on the Comic Spirit (Meredith), **V:** 234

Odes to . . . the Emperor of Russia, and . . . the King of Prussia (Southey), **IV:** 71

Odette d'Antrevernes (Firbank), **Supp. II:** 199, 201, 205–206

"Odour of Chrysanthemums" (Lawrence), **VII:** 114; **Retro. Supp. II:** 232–233

"Odysseus of Hermes" (Gunn), **Supp. IV:** 275

Odyssey (Homer), **Supp. IV:** 234, 267, 428

Odyssey (tr. Cowper), **III:** 220

Odyssey (tr. Pope), **III:** 70, 77

Odyssey, The (Butler translation), **Supp. II:** 114, 115

Odyssey of Homer, The (Lawrence translation), **Supp. II:** 283, 294

Odyssey of Homer, done into English Verse, The (Morris), **V:** 306

Oedipus Tyrannus; or, Swellfoot the Tyrant (Shelley), **IV:** 208

Of Ancient and Modern Learning (Temple), **III:** 23

"Of Commerce and Society: The Death of Shelley" (Hill), **Supp. V:** 186

"Of Democritus and Heraclitus" (Montaigne), **III:** 39

"Of Discourse" (Cornwallis), **III:** 39–40

"Of Divine Love" (Waller), **II:** 235

Of Dramatick Poesie, An Essay (Dryden), *see Essay of Dramatick Poesy*

Of Education (Milton), **II:** 162–163, 175

"Of Eloquence" (Goldsmith), **III:** 186

"Of English Verse" (Waller), **II:** 233–234

"Of Essay Writing" (Hume), **Supp. III:** 231–232

"Of Greatness" (Cowley), **III:** 40

Of Human Bondage (Maugham), **VI:** xiii, 365, 373–374

Of Justification by Imputed Righteousness (Bunyan), **II:** 253

"Of Liberty" (Cowley), **II:** 198

Of Liberty and Loyalty (Swinburne), **V:** 333

Of Liberty and Servitude (tr. Evelyn), **II:** 287

Of Magnanimity and Chastity (Traherne), **II:** 202

"Of Masques" (Bacon), **I:** 268

"Of My Self" (Cowley), **II:** 195

"Of Nature: Laud and Plaint" (Thompson), **V:** 443

"Of Pacchiarotto" (Browning), **IV:** 366

"Of Plants" (Cowley), **Supp. III:** 36

"Of Pleasing" (Congreve), **II:** 349

"Of Poetry" (Temple), **III:** 23, 190

Of Prelatical Episcopacy . . . (Milton), **II:** 175

Of Reformation Touching Church Discipline in England (Milton), **II:** 162, 175

Of Style (Hughes), **III:** 40

Of the Characters of Women (Pope), *see Moral Essays*

Of the Friendship of Amis and Amile, Done into English (Morris), **V:** 306

Of the House of the Forest of Lebanon (Bunyan), **II:** 253

Of the Lady Mary (Waller), **II:** 238

Of the Law and a Christian (Bunyan), **II:** 253

Of the Laws of Ecclesiastical Polity (Hooker), **I:** 176, 179–190

Of the Trinity and a Christian (Bunyan), **II:** 253

Of the Use of Riches, an Epistle to . . . Bathurst (Pope), *see Moral Essays*

Of True Greatness (Fielding), **III:** 105

Of True Religion, Haeresie, Schism, Toleration, . . . (Milton), **II:** 176

"Offa's Leechdom" (Hill), **Supp. V:** 194

"Offa's Second Defence of the English People" (Hill), **Supp. V:** 195

Offer of the Clarendon Trustees, The (Carroll), **V:** 274

"Office for the Dead" (Kinsella), **Supp. V:** 263

"Office Friendships" (Ewart), **Supp. VII:** 39

Officers and Gentlemen (Waugh), **VII:** 302, 304; *see also Sword of Honour* trilogy

"Officers Mess" (Ewarts), **VII:** 423; **Supp. VII:** 37

Offshore (Fitzgerald), **Supp. V:** 96, 97, 98, 102

"Oflag Night Piece: Colditz" (Riviere), **VII:** 424

Ogden, C. K., **Supp. II:** 405, 406, 407–408, 409, 410, 411, 422, 424

Ogg, David, **II:** 243

O'Grady, Standish James, **Supp. V:** 36

"Oh, dreadful is the check—intense the agony" (Brontë), **V:** 116

"Oh, Madam" (Bowen), **Supp. II:** 92–93

"Oh! That 'Twere Possible" (Tennyson), **IV:** 330, 332

Oh What a Lovely War (musical), **VI:** 436

Ohio Impromptu (Beckett), **Supp. I:** 61

Okri, Ben, **Supp. V:** 347–362

"Olalla" (Stevenson), **V:** 395

Old Adam, The (Bennett), *see Regent, The*

"Old Andrey's Experience as a Musician" (Hardy), **VI:** 22

"Old Atheist Pauses by the Sea, An" (Kinsella), **Supp. V:** 261

Old Batchelour, The (Congreve), **II:** 338, 340–341, 349

"Old Benchers of the Inner Temple, The" (Lamb), **IV:** 74

Old Boys, The (Trevor), **Supp. IV:** 505–506, 507, 517

Old Calabria (Douglas), **VI:** 294, 295–296, 297, 298, 299, 305

"Old Chartist, The" (Meredith), **V:** 220

"Old Chief Mshlanga, The" (Lessing), **Supp. I:** 242

"Old China" (Lamb), **IV:** 82

"Old Church Tower and the Garden Wall, The" (Brontë), **V:** 134

"Old Crofter" (MacCaig), **Supp. VI:** 192

Old Curiosity Shop, The (Dickens), **V:** xx, 42, 53, 71

Old Debauchees, The (Fielding), **III:** 105

Old Devils, The (Amis), **Supp. II:** 3, 18–19; **Supp. IV:** 37

"Old Dispensary" (Murphy), **Supp. V:** 329

Old English (Galsworthy), **VI:** 275, 284

Old English Baron, The (Reeve), **III:** 345

"Old Familiar Faces, The" (Lamb), **IV:** 78

"Old Folks at Home" (Highsmith), **Supp. V:** 180

"Old Fools, The" (Larkin), **Supp. I:** 282–283, 285

Old Fortunatus (Dekker), **II:** 71, 89

"Old Francis" (Kelman), **Supp. V:** 249

Old French Romances, Done into English (Morris), **V:** 306

Old Gang and the New Gang, The (Lewis), **VII:** 83

"Old Garbo" (Thomas), **Supp. I:** 181

"Old Harry" (Kinsella), **Supp. V:** 261

"Old Holborn" (Kelman), **Supp. V:** 256

"Old House" (Redgrove), **Supp. VI:** 228

Old Huntsman, The (Sassoon), **VI:** 423, 430, 453

"Old John's Place" (Lessing), **Supp. I:** 240

Old Joiner of Aldgate, The (Chapman), **I:** 234, 244

Old Lady Shows Her Medals, The (Barrie), **Supp. III:** 6, 9, 16

Old Law, The (Middleton, Rowley), **II:** 21

Old Lights for New Chancels (Betjeman), **VII:** 361, 367, 368

"Old Main Street, Holborn Hill, Millom" (Nicholson), **Supp. VI:** 216–217

"Old Man" (Jennings), **Supp. V:** 210

"Old Man" (Thomas), **Supp. III:** 402

"Old Man, The" (du Maurier), **Supp. III:** 142–143

Old Man of the Mountains, The (Nicholson), **Supp. VI: 220–221,** 222

Old Man Taught Wisdom, An (Fielding), **III:** 105

Old Man's Love, An (Trollope), **V:** 102

"Old Meg" (Gunn), **Supp. IV:** 276

Old Men at the Zoo, The (Wilson), **Supp. I:** 154, 161

Old Mrs. Chundle (Hardy), **VI:** 20

Old Mortality (Scott), **IV:** 33, 39

"Old Nurse's Story, The" (Gaskell), **V:** 14, 15

Old Possum's Book of Practical Cats (Eliot), **VII:** 167

Old Pub Near the Angel, An (Kelman), **Supp. V:** 242, 244, 245

"Old Pub Near the Angel, An" (Kelman), **Supp. V:** 245

Old Reliable, The (Wodehouse), **Supp. III:** 451

Old Times (Pinter), **Supp. I:** 376–377

"Old Toy, The" (Fuller), **Supp. VII:** 79

"Old Vicarage, Grantchester, The" (Brooke), **Supp. III:** 47, 50, 54

Old Whig (periodical), **III:** 51, 53

Old Wife's Tale, The (Peele), **I:** 206–208

Old Wives' Tale, The (Bennett), **VI:** xiii, 247, 249, 250, 251, **254–257**

"Old Woman, An" (Sitwell), **VII:** 135–136

"Old Woman and Her Cat, An" (Lessing), **Supp. I:** 253–254

"Old Woman of Berkeley, The" (Southey), **IV:** 67

"Old Women, The" (Brown), **Supp. VI:** 71

"Oldest Place, The" (Kinsella), **Supp. V:** 268

Oldham, John, **II:** 259

Oley, Barnabas, **II:** 141; **Retro. Supp. II:** 170–171

Oliver, H. J., **I:** 281

"Oliver Cromwell and Walter Noble" (Landor), **IV:** 92

Oliver Cromwell's Letters and Speeches (Carlyle), **IV:** 240, 244, 246, 249, 250, 342

Oliver Newman (Southey), **IV:** 71

Oliver Twist (Dickens), **V:** xix, 42, 47–50, 51, 55, 56, 66, 71

Olney Hymns (Cowper), **III:** 210, 211, 220

Olor Iscanus . . . (Vaughan), **II:** 185, 201

Olympia (Manet), **Supp. IV:** 480

O'Malley, Mary, **Supp. IV:** 181

Oman, Sir Charles, **VI:** 387

Omega Workshop, **VI:** 118

Omen, The (film), **III:** 343, 345

Omniana; or, Horae otiosiores (Southey and Coleridge), **IV:** 71

"On a Brede of Divers Colours Woven by Four Ladies" (Waller), **II:** 233

"On a Chalk Mark on the Door" (Thackeray), **V:** 34

On a Chinese Screen (Maugham), **VI:** 371

"On a Croft by the Kirkaig" (MacCaig), **Supp. VI:** 194

"On a Dead Child" (Bridges), **VI:** 77–78

"On a Drop of Dew" (Marvell), **II:** 211

"On a Girdle" (Waller), **II:** 235

"On a Joke I Once Heard from the Late Thomas Hood" (Thackeray), **IV:** 251–252

"On a Midsummer Eve" (Hardy), **Retro. Supp. I:** 119

"On a Mourner" (Tennyson), **IV:** 332

"On a Prayer Booke Sent to Mrs. M. R." (Crashaw), **II:** 181

"On a Return from Egypt" (Douglas), **VII:** 444

"On Actors and Acting" (Hazlitt), **IV:** 137

"On Adventure" (Rushdie), **Supp. IV:** 455

On Alterations in the Liturgy (Newman), **Supp. VII:** 292

"On an Insignificant" (Coleridge), **Retro. Supp. II:** 65

On Baile's Strand (Yeats), **VI:** 218, 309

On Ballycastle Beach (McGuckian), **Supp. V:** 282, 284–286

"On Ballycastle Beach" (McGuckian), **Supp. V:** 285

"On Being English but Not British" (Fowles), **Supp. I:** 292

"On Board the *West Hardaway*" (Lowry), **Supp. III:** 285

On Christian Doctrine (Milton), **Retro. Supp. II:** 271

"On Dryden and Pope" (Hazlitt), **IV:** 217

On English Poetry (Graves), **VII:** 260

"On Fairy–Stories" (Tolkien), **Supp. II:** 521, 535

"On Familiar Style" (Hazlitt), **IV:** 138

"On First Looking into Chapman's Homer" (Keats), **IV:** 214, 215–216; **Retro. Supp. I:** 188

"On First Looking into Loeb's Horace" (Durrell), **Supp. I:** 126

On Forsyte 'Change (Galsworthy), **VI:** 270, 275

"On 'God' and 'Good' " (Murdoch), **Supp. I:** 217–218, 224–225

"On Greenhow Hill" (Kipling), **VI:** 191

"On Hearing Bartok's Concerto for Orchestra" (Fuller), **Supp. VII:** 72

"On Heaven" (Ford), **VI:** 323

"On Her Leaving Town After the Coronation" (Pope), **III:** 76

"On Her Loving Two Equally" (Behn), **Supp. III:** 38

"On Himself" (Herrick), **II:** 113

On His Grace the Duke of Marlborough (Wycherley), **II:** 322

"On Home Beaches" (Murray), **Supp. VII:** 283

"On Installing an American Kitchen in Lower Austria" (Auden), **Retro. Supp. I:** 13

"On Living for Others" (Warner), **Supp. VII:** 380

"On Living to One's–Self" (Hazlitt), **IV:** 137

"On Marriage" (Crashaw), **II:** 180

"On Men and Pictures" (Thackeray), **V:** 37

"On Milton" (De Quincey), **IV:** 146

"On Mr. Milton's 'Paradise Lost'" (Marvell), **II:** 206

"On My First Daughter" (Jonson), **Retro. Supp. I:** 155

"On My First Son" (Jonson), **Retro. Supp. I:** 155

"On My Thirty–fifth Birthday" (Nicholson), **Supp. VI:** 217

"On Not Being Milton" (Harrison), **Supp. V:** 152–153

"On Not Knowing Greek" (Woolf), **VII:** 35

"On Not Saying Anything" (Day Lewis), **Supp. III:** 130

"On Palestinian Identity: A Conversation with Edward Said" (Rushdie), **Supp. IV:** 456

"On Personal Character" (Hazlitt), **IV:** 136

"On Poetry: A Rhapsody" (Swift), **III:** 30, 36

"On Poetry in General" (Hazlitt), **IV:** 130, 138

"On Preaching the Gospel" (Newman), **Supp. VII:** 294

"On Preparing to Read Kipling" (Hardy), **VI:** 195

"On Receiving News of the War" (Rosenberg), **VI:** 432

"On Renoir's *The Grape–Pickers*" (Boland), **Supp. V:** 40

"On Ribbons" (Thackeray), **V:** 34

"On Seeing England for the First Time" (Kincaid), **Supp. VII:** 218, 225, 228

"On Seeing the Elgin Marbles" (Keats), **IV:** 212–213, 214

On Seeming to Presume (Durrell), **Supp. I:** 124

"On Sentimental Comedy" (Goldsmith), *see Essay on the Theatre . . .*

"On Silence" (Pope), **Retro. Supp. I:** 233

"On Sitting Back and Thinking of Porter's Boeotia" (Murray), **Supp. VII:** 274

"On Some Characteristics of Modern Poetry" (Hallam), **IV:** 234, 235

"On Some Obscure Poetry" (Lander), **IV:** 98

"On Spies" (Jonson), **Retro. Supp. I:** 156

"On Stella's Birthday, . . . A.D. 1718–" (Swift), **III:** 31

"On Style" (De Quincey), **IV:** 148

"On the Application of Thought to Textual Criticism" (Housman), **VI:** 154, 164

On the Black Hill (Chatwin), **Supp. IV:** 158, 168–170, 173

On the Boiler (Yeats), **Retro. Supp. I:** 337

On the Choice of a Profession (Stevenson), **V:** 396

On the Choice of Books (Carlyle), **IV:** 250

"On the City Wall" (Kipling), **VI:** 184

"On the Cliffs" (Swinburne), **V:** 327

"On the Closing of Millom Iron Works" (Nicholson), **Supp. VI:** 218

"On the Conduct of the Understanding" (Smith), **Supp. VII:** 342

On the Constitution of the Church and State (Coleridge), **IV:** 54, 55, 56; **Retro. Supp. II:** 64

On the Contrary (Brink), **Supp. VI: 56–57**

"On the Death of Dr. Robert Levet" (Johnson), **III:** 120

"On the Death of General Schomberg . . ." (Farquhar), **II:** 351

"On the Death of Mr. Crashaw" (Cowley), **II:** 198

"On the Death of Mr. William Hervey" (Cowley), **II:** 198

"On the Death of Sir Henry Wootton" (Cowley), **II:** 198

On the Dignity of Man (Mirandola), **I:** 253

"On the Discovery of a Lady's Painting" (Waller), **II:** 233

"On the Dismantling of Millom Ironworks" (Nicholson), **Supp. VI:** 218–219

On the Edge of the Cliff and Other Stories (Pritchett), **Supp. III:** 328

"On the English Novelists" (Hazlitt), **IV:** 136–137

"On the Feeling of Immortality in Youth" (Hazlitt), **IV:** 126

On the Frontier (Auden and Isherwood), **VII:** 312; **Retro. Supp. I:** 7

"On the Genius and Character of Hogarth" (Lamb), **IV:** 80

"On the Head of a Stag" (Waller), **II:** 233

On the Herpetology of the Grand Duchy of Baden (Douglas), **VI:** 300, 305

"On the Influence of the Audience" (Bridges), **VI:** 83

"On the Knocking at the Gate in 'Macbeth'" (De Quincey), **IV:** 146, 149

"On the Lancashire Coast" (Nicholson), **Supp. VI:** 216

"On the Living Poets" (Hazlitt), **IV:** 130

On the Margin (Huxley), **VII:** 201

"On the means of improving people" (Southey), **IV:** 102

"On the Medusa of Leonardo da Vinci in the Florentine Gallery" (Shelley), **III:** 337

"On the Morning of Christ's Nativity" (Milton), **II:** 199; **IV:** 222

"On the Move" (Gunn), **Supp. IV:** 259–260, 261

"On the Origin of Beauty: A Platonic Dialogue" (Hopkins), **V:** 362; **Retro. Supp. II:** 187

On the Origin of Species by Means of Natural Selection (Darwin), **V:** xxii, 279, 287; **Supp. II:** 98

"On the Periodical Essayists" (Hazlitt), **IV:** 136

On the Place of Gilbert Chesterton in English Letters (Belloc), **VI:** 345

"On the Pleasure of Painting" (Hazlitt), **IV:** 137–138

"On the Profession of a Player" (Boswell), **III:** 248

"On the Receipt of My Mother's Picture" (Cowper), **III:** 208, 220

"On the Road with Mrs. G." (Chatwin), **Supp. IV:** 165

On the Rocks (Shaw), **VI:** 125, 126, 127; **Retro. Supp. II:** 324

"On the Scotch Character" (Hazlitt), **IV:** 132

"On the Sea" (Keats), **IV:** 216

"On the Spirit of Monarchy" (Hazlitt), **IV:** 132

On the Study of Celtic Literature (Arnold), **V:** 203, 212, 216

On the Sublime and Beautiful (Burke), **III:** 195, 198, 205

"On the Table " (Motion), **Supp. VII:** 262–263, 264

On the Thermal Influence of Forests (Stevenson), **V:** 395

"On the Toilet Table of Queen Marie–Antoinette" (Nicholls), **IV:** 98

"On the Tragedies of Shakespeare . . . with Reference to . . . Stage Representation" (Lamb), **IV:** 80

"On the Victory Obtained by Blake" (Marvell), **II:** 211

"On the Western Circuit" (Hardy), **VI:** 22

"On the Wounds of Our Crucified Lord" (Crashaw), **II:** 182

"On the Zattere" (Trevor), **Supp. IV:** 502

"On This Island" (Auden), **Retro. Supp. I:** 7

"On Toleration" (Smith), **Supp. VII:** 347

On Translating Homer (Arnold), **V:** xxii, 212, 215, 216

On Translating Homer: Last Words (Arnold), **V:** 214, 215, 216

"On Wit and Humour" (Hazlitt), **II:** 332

"On Wordsworth's Poetry" (De Quincey), **IV:** 146, 148

"On Writing a Novel" (Fowles), **Supp. I:** 293

"On Yeti Tracks" (Chatwin), **Supp. IV:** 157

Once a Week (Milne), **Supp. V:** 298

"Once as me thought Fortune me kissed" (Wyatt), **I:** 102

"Once at Piertarvit" (Reid), **Supp. VII:** 327–328

"Once in a Lifetime, Snow" (Murray), **Supp. VII:** 273

Once in Europa (Berger), **Supp. IV:** 93, 94

Once on a Time (Milne), **Supp. V:** 298

"Once Upon a Time" (Gordimer), **Supp. II:** 233

"One, The" (Kavanagh), **Supp. VII:** 198

One and Other Poems (Kinsella), **Supp. V:** 267–268

"One Before the Last, The" (Brooke), **Supp. III:** 51

One Day (Douglas), **VI:** 299, 300, 305

One Fat Englishman (Amis), **Supp. II:** 10, 11, 15

One Fond Embrace (Kinsella), **Supp. V:** 272

One Foot in Eden (Muir), **Supp. VI:** 204, 206, **207–208**

One for the Grave (MacNeice), **VII:** 405, 406, 408

One for the Road (Pinter), **Supp. I:** 378, 381

One Hand Clapping (Burgess), **Supp. I:** 186

One Hundred Years of Solitude (García Márquez), **Supp. IV:** 116

One of Our Conquerors (Meredith), **V:** 232, 233, 234

"One Off the Short List" (Lessing), **Supp. I:** 244

"One Out of Many" (Naipaul), **Supp. I:** 395

"One Sea–side Grave" (Rossetti), **V:** 255

One Thing Is Needful (Bunyan), **II:** 253

One Thing More; or, Caedmon Construed (Fry), **Supp. III:** 191, 196–197

"One Thousand Days in a Balloon" (Rushdie), **Supp. IV:** 437

"One Viceroy Resigns" (Kipling), **VI:** 202

"One We Knew" (Hardy), **Retro. Supp. I:** 118

"One Who Disappeared" (Motion), **Supp. VII:** 258

One Who Set Out to Study Fear, The (Redgrove), **Supp. VI:** 231

"One Word More" (Browning), **IV:** 357

One–Way Song (Lewis), **VII:** 72, 76

O'Neill, Eugene, **Supp. III:** 12

"Only our love hath no decay" (Donne), **II:** 221

Only Problem, The (Spark), **Supp. I:** 212–213

"Only This" (Dahl), **Supp. IV:** 211

O'Nolan, Brian, **Supp. II: 321–338; Supp. IV:** 412

Open Conspiracy, The, Blueprints for a World Revolution (Wells), **VI:** 240, 242

Open Court (Kinsella), **Supp. V:** 272, 273

"Open Court" (Kinsella), **Supp. V:** 273

Open Door (Fry), **Supp. III:** 194

Open Door, The (Sillitoe), **Supp. V:** 411, 415

Open Letter to the Revd. Dr. Hyde in Defence of Father Damien, An (Stevenson), *see Father Damien*

"Open Secrets" (Motion), **Supp. VII:** 255–256

Opened Ground (Heaney), **Retro. Supp. I:** 124

"Opening a Place of Social Prayer" (Cowper), **III:** 211

Operette (Coward), **Supp. II:** 152

Opium and the Romantic Imagination (Hayter), **III:** 338, 346; **IV:** 57

Oppenheim, E. Phillips, **VI:** 249

Opus 7 (Warner), **Supp. VII:** 372

Or Shall We Die? (McEwan), **Supp. IV:** 390

"Or, Solitude" (Davie), **Supp. VI:** 110

Or Where a Young Penguin Lies Screaming (Ewart), **Supp. VII:** 41

"Oracles, The" (Housman), **VI:** 161

Orage, A. R., **VI:** 247, 265, **VII:** 172

"Orange March" (Murphy), **Supp. V:** 322

Oranges Are Not the Only Fruit (Winterson), **Supp. IV:** 541, 542, 543–545, 546, 547–548, 552, 553, 555, 557

Orators, The (Auden), **VII:** 345, 380, 382; **Retro. Supp. I:** 5

Orchard End (Redgrove), **Supp. VI:** 236

"Orchards half the way, The" (Housman), **VI:** 159

Ordeal by Innocence (Christie), **Supp. II:** 125

Ordeal of George Meredith, The, A Biography (Stevenson), **V:** 230, 234

Ordeal of Gilbert Pinfold, The (Waugh), **VII:** 291, 293, 302–303

Ordeal of Richard Feverel, The (Meredith), **V:** xxii, 225, 226–227, 234

Ordeal of Sigbjorn Wilderness, The (Lowry), **Supp. III:** 280

"Ordered South" (Stevenson), **Retro. Supp. I:** 261

"Ordination, The" (Burns), **III:** 311, 319

Oresteia, The (tr. Harrison), **Supp. V:** 163

"Orf" (Hughes), **Supp. I:** 359

"Orford" (Davie), **Supp. VI:** 110

Orford, fourth earl of, *see* Walpole, Horace

Orgel, Stephen, **I:** 237, 239

Orghast (Hughes), **Supp. I:** 354

Orient Express (Greene), **Supp. I:** *see* Stamboul Train

"Orient Ode" (Thompson), **V:** 448

"Oriental Eclogues" (Collins), *see* "Persian Eclogues"

Orientations (Maugham), **VI:** 367

Origin, Nature, and Object of the New System of Education, The (Southey), **IV:** 71

Origin of Species by Means of Natural Selection, or the Preservation of Favoured Races in the Struggle for Life (Darwin), **Supp. VII:** 17, 19, 23–25

Origin of the Family, Private Property, and the State, The (Engels), **Supp. II:** 454

Original and Progress of Satire, The (Dryden), **II:** 301

Original Letters &c of Sir John Falstaff (White and Lamb), **IV:** 79, 85

Original Michael Frayn, The (Frayn), **Supp. VII:** 51

"Original Place, The" (Muir), **Supp. VI:** 206

Original Poetry by Victor and Cazire (Shelley and Shelley), **IV:** 208

Original Power of the Collective Body of the People of England, Examined and Asserted, The (Defoe), **Retro. Supp. I:** 68

Original Sin (James), **Supp. IV:** 333–335

"Original Sins of Edward Tripp, The" (Trevor), **Supp. IV:** 503

Origine of Sciences, The (Pope), **Retro. Supp. I:** 234

Origins of the English Imagination, The (Ackroyd), **Supp. VI:** 13

Orkney Tapestry, An (Brown), **Supp. VI:** 64–65

"Orkney: The Whale Islands" (Brown), **Supp. VI:** 72

Orlando (Woolf), **VII:** 21, 28, 35, 38; **Supp. IV:** 557; **Retro. Supp. I:** 314, 318–319

Orlando furioso (Ariosto), **I:** 131, 138

Orley Farm (Trollope), **V:** xxii, 100, 101

Ormond (Edgeworth), **Supp. III:** 154, 156, **163–165**

Oroonoko: A Tragedy (Southerne), **Supp. III:** 34–35

Oroonoko; or, The Royal Slave (Behn), **Supp. III:** 21, 22–23, 32–36, 39

Orpheus (Hope), **Supp. VII:** 165

Orpheus (Hughes), **Supp. I:** 347

Orpheus and Eurydice (Henryson), **Supp. VII:** 136, 145–146

"Orpheus in Hell" (Thomas), **Supp. IV:** 493

"Orpheus; or, Philosophy" (Bacon), **I:** 267

Ortelius, Abraham, **I:** 282

Orthodoxy (Chesterton), **VI:** 336

Orton, Joe, **Supp. V: 363–378**

Orton Diaries, The (Orton), **Supp. V:** 363, 367–369

Orwell, George, **III:** 341; **V:** 24, 31; **VI:** 240, 242; **VII:** xii, xx, **273–287;** **Supp. I:** 28*n*; **Supp. III:** 96, 107; **Supp. IV:** 17, 81, 110–111, 440, 445

Osborne, John, **VI:** 101; **Supp. I: 329–340; Supp. II:** 4, 70, 139, 155; **Supp. III:** 191; **Supp. IV:** 180, 281, 283

Osbourne, Lloyd, **V:** 384, 387, 393, 395, 396, 397

Oscar Wilde. Art and Egoism (Shewan), **V:** 409, 421

O'Shaughnessy, Arthur, **VI:** 158

Othello (Shakespeare), **I:** 316; **II:** 71, 79; **III:** 116; **Supp. IV:** 285

"Other, The" (Thomas), **Supp. III:** 403

"Other Boat, The" (Forster), **VI:** 406, 411–412

Other House, The (James), **VI:** 48, 49, 67

Other House, The (Stevenson), **Supp. VI:** 263–265

"Other Kingdom" (Forster), **VI:** 399, 402

Other People: A Mystery Story (Amis), **Supp. IV:** 26, 39–40

Other People's Clerihews (Ewart), **Supp. VII:** 46

"Other People's Houses" (Reid), **Supp. VII:** 336

Other People's Worlds (Trevor), **Supp. IV:** 501, 506, 511–512, 517

Other Places (Pinter), **Supp. I:** 378

"Other Tiger, The" (tr. Reid), **Supp. VII:** 332–333

"Others, The" (Ewart), **Supp. VII:** 39, 40

Otho the Great (Keats and Brown), **IV:** 231, 235

Otranto (Walpole), *see Castle of Otranto, The*

"Otter, An" (Hughes), **Retro. Supp. II:** 204–205

Ouch (Ackroyd), **Supp. VI:** 3–4

Ounce, Dice, Trice (Reid), **Supp. VII:** 326

Our Betters (Maugham), **VI:** 368, 369

"Our Bias" (Auden), **VII:** 387

Our Corner (periodical), **VI:** 103

Our Country's Good (Keneally), **Supp. IV:** 346

Our Exagmination Round His Factification for Incamination of Work in Progress (Beckett et al.), **Supp. I:** 43*n*

Our Exploits at West Poley (Hardy), **VI:** 20

"Our Father" (Davie), **Supp. VI:** 113

Our Family (Hood), **IV:** 254, 259

Our Friend the Charlatan (Gissing), **V:** 437

"Our Hunting Fathers" (Auden), **VII:** 108

Our Man in Havana (Greene), **Supp. I:** 7, 11, 13, 14–15; **Retro. Supp. II:** 161

"Our Mother" (Kinsella), **Supp. V:** 263

Our Mother's House (Gloag), **Supp. IV:** 390

Our Mutual Friend (Dickens), **V:** xxiii, 42, 44, 55, 68–69, 72; **Supp. IV:** 247

Our Old Home (Hawthorne), **VI:** 34

"Our Parish" (Dickens), **V:** 43, 46

Our Republic (Keneally), **Supp. IV:** 347

"Our Parish" (Dickens), **V:** 43, 46

"Our Village—by a Villager" (Hood), **IV:** 257

Our Women: Chapters on the Sex–Discord (Bennett), **VI:** 267

Out (Brooke–Rose), **Supp. IV:** 99, 104, 105–106

"Out and Away" (Kavan), **Supp. VII:** 202

Out of India (Jhabvala), **Supp. V:** 235–236

Out of India (Kipling), **VI:** 204

Out of Ireland (Kinsella), **Supp. V:** 271

"Out of Ireland" (Kinsella), **Supp. V:** 271

Out of the Picture (MacNeice), **VII:** 405

Out of the Shelter (Lodge), **Supp. IV:** 364, 365, 370–371, 372

"Out of the signs" (Thomas), **Supp. I:** 174

Out of the Silent Planet (Lewis), **Supp. III:** 249, 252–253

Out of the Whirlpool (Sillitoe), **Supp. V:** 411

Out of This World (Swift), **Supp. V:** 437–438

Outback (Keneally), **Supp. IV:** 346

"Outcast, The" (Tennyson), **IV:** 329

Outcast of the Islands, An (Conrad), **VI:** 136, 137, 148; **Retro. Supp. II:** 71

Outcasts, The (Sitwell), **VII:** 138

Outcry, The (Julia), **VI:** 67

"Outdoor Concert, The" (Gunn), **Supp. IV:** 269

"Outer Planet, The" (Nicholson), **Supp. VI:** 217

Outline of History: Being a Plain History of Life and Mankind, The (Wells), **VI:** 245

"Outlook, Uncertain" (Reid), **Supp. VII:** 330

"Outpost of Progress, An" (Conrad), **VI:** 136, 148

"Outside the Whale" (Rushdie), **Supp. IV:** 455

"Outstation, The" (Maugham), **VI:** 370, 371, 380

"Ovando" (Kincaid), **Supp. VII:** 225

"Over Mother, The" (McGuckian), **Supp. V:** 288

"Over Sir John's Hill" (Thomas), **Supp. I:** 179

Over the Frontier (Smith), **Supp. II:** 462, 474

"Over the Hill" (Warner), **Supp. VII:** 380

"Over the Hills" (Thomas), **Supp. III:** 400

"Over the Rainbow" (Rushdie), **Supp. IV:** 434

Over the River (Galsworthy), **VI:** 272–275

Over the River (Gregory), **VI:** 318

Over to You: Ten Stories of Flyers and Flying (Dahl), **Supp. IV:** 208–211, 213

Overbury, Sir Thomas, **IV:** 286

"Overcoat, The" (Gogol), **III:** 340, 345

Overcrowded Barracoon, The (Naipaul), **Supp. I: 384**

"Overcrowded Barracoon, The" (Naipaul), **Supp. I:** 402

"Overloaded Man, The" (Ballard), **Supp. V:** 33

Overruled (Shaw), **VI:** 129

"Overture" (Kinsella), **Supp. V:** 270–271

"Overtures to Death" (Day Lewis), **Supp. III:** 122

Overtures to Death (Day Lewis), **Supp. III:** 118, 127–128

Ovid, **II:** 110*n*, 185, 292, 304, 347; **III:** 54; **V:** 319, 321

"Ovid on West 4th" (Mahon), **Supp. VI:** 176

"Ovid in the Third Reich" (Hill), **Supp. V:** 187

Ovid's Art of Love Paraphrased (Fielding), **III:** 105

Ovid's Banquet of Sense (Chapman), **I:** 237–238

Ovid's Epistles, Translated by Several Hands (Dryden), **Supp. III:** 36

Ovid's Fasti (tr. Frazer), **Supp. III:** 176

Owen, Wilfred, **VI:** xvi, 329, 416, 417, 419, 423, **443–460; VII:** xvi, 421; list of poems, **VI:** 458–459; **Supp. IV:** 57, 58

"Owen Wingrave," (James), **VI:** 69

"Owl, The" (Thomas), **VI:** 424; **Supp. III:** 403–404

"Owl and the Pussy–cat, The" (Lear), **V:** 83–84, 87

Owls and Artificers (Fuller), **Supp. VII:** 77

Owners (Churchill), **Supp. IV:** 179, 180, 181–182, 198

"Oxen, The" (Hardy), **VI:** 16

Oxford Book of English Verse, The (ed. Quiller–Couch), **II:** 102, 121

Oxford Book of Modern Verse, The, **VI:** 219

Oxford Book of Twentieth–Century English Verse, The (Larkin), **Supp. I:** 286

Oxford Companion to English Literature, **Supp. IV:** 229, 231, 247, 252

Oxford Lectures on Poetry (Bradley), **IV:** 216, 236

"Oxford Leave" (Ewart), **Supp. VII:** 37

"Oxford"papers (De Quincey), **IV:** 148

Oxford Poetry (eds. Day Lewis and Auden), **Supp. III:** 117; **Retro. Supp. I:** 3

"Oxford Staircase" (Murphy), **Supp. V:** 315

Oxford University Chest (Betjeman), **VII:** 356

"P. & O.," (Maugham), **VI:** 370–371

"P. D. James' Dark Interiors" (Majeske), **Supp. IV:** 330

P. R. B.: An Essay on the Pre-Raphaelite Brotherhood, 1847–1854 (Waugh), **VII:** 291

Pacchiarotto and How He Worked in Distemper (Browning), **IV:** 359, 374; *see also* "Of Pacchiarotton"

Pacific 1860 (Coward), **Supp. II:** 155

Pacificator, The (Defoe), **III:** 12; **Retro. Supp. I:** 67

"Pack Horse and the Carrier, The" (Gay), **III:** 59–60

Pack My Bag: A Self Portrait (Green), **Supp. II: 247–248,** 251, 255

Packer, Lona Mosk, **V:** 251, 252–253, 260

"Pad, Pad" (Smith), **Supp. II:** 470

"Paddiad, The" (Kavanagh), **Supp. VII:** 193–194

Paddock and the Mouse, The (Henryson), **Supp. VII:** 136, 141–142, 147

Paddy Clarke Ha Ha Ha (Doyle), **Supp. V:** 78, 89–91, 92

Pagan Mysteries in the Renaissance (Wind), **V:** 317*n*

Pagan Place, A (O'Brien), **Supp. V:** 338–339

Pagan Poems (Moore), **VI:** 98

Page of Plymouth, The (Jonson/Dekker), **Retro. Supp. I:** 157

Pageant and Other Poems, A (Rossetti), **V:** 251, 260

"Pageant of Knowledge" (Lydgate), **I:** 58

"Pageants" (Spenser), **I:** 123

Paid on Both Sides (Auden), **Retro. Supp. I:** 4–5

Painful Adventures of Pericles, Prince of Tyre (Wilkins), **I:** 321

"Painful Case, A" (Joyce), **Retro. Supp. I:** 172

"Painful Pleasure of Suspense, The" (Dahl), **Supp. IV:** 222

"Pains of Sleep, The" (Coleridge), **IV:** xvii, 48, 56

Painter, William, **I:** 297; **II:** 76

Painter of His Own Dishonour, The (tr. FitzGerald), **IV: 344–345**

Painter of Our Time (Berger), **Supp. IV:** 79, 81–84, 88

Painter's Eye, The (James), **VI:** 67

Painting and the Fine Arts (Haydon and Hazlitt), **IV:** 140

"Painting It In" (Stevenson), **Supp. VI:** 264

Pair of Blue Eyes, A: A Novel (Hardy), **VI:** 3, 4, 20; **Retro. Supp. I:** 110, 111–112

"Palace of Art, The" (Tennyson), **IV:** 331

"Palace of Pan, The" (Swinburne), **V:** 328

Palace of Pleasure (Painter), **I:** 297, 313; **II:** 76

Palace of the Peacock (Harris), **Supp. V:** 132–136

Pale Companion, The (Motion), **Supp. VII:** 252

Pale Fire (Nabokov), **Supp. IV:** 26, 27

Pale Horse, The (Christie), **Supp. II:** 125, 135

Pale View of the Hills, A (Ishiguro), **Supp. IV:** 301, 303, 304, 305–306, 307–309, 310

Paleface (Lewis), **VII:** 72, 75

Paley, William, **IV:** 144

Paley, Grace, **Supp. IV:** 151

Palgrave, Francis Turner, **II:** 208; **IV:** xxii, 196

Palicio (Bridges), **VI:** 83

Palladas: Poems (Harrison), **Supp. V:** 163

Palladis Tamia (Meres), **I:** 296

"Palladium" (Arnold), **V:** 209

Palmer, George Herbert, **Retro. Supp. II:** 173

Palmer, John, **II:** 267, 271

Palmerin of England, **II:** 49; tr. Southey, **IV:** 71

"Palmer's 'Heroides' of Ovid" (Housman), **VI:** 156

Palmyra (Peacock), **IV:** 158, 169

Pamela (Richardson), **III:** 80, **82–85,** 92, 94, 95, 98; **Retro. Supp. I:** 80, 83, 85–86

Pamphlet Against Anthologies, A (Graves), **VI:** 207; **VII:** 260–261

"Pan and Pitys" (Landor), **IV:** 96

"Pan and Thalassius" (Swinburne), **V:** 328

"Pan; or, Nature" (Bacon), **I:** 267

"Pandora" (James), **VI:** 69

Pandosto (Greene), **I:** 165, 322

"Panegerick to Sir Lewis Pemberton, A" (Herrick), **II:** 110

Panegyric to Charles the Second, Presented . . . the Day of His Coronation . . . (Evelyn), **II:** 287

Panegyrick to My Lord Protector, A (Waller), **II:** 238

Panic Spring (Durrell), **Supp. I:** 95, 96

Panofsky, Erwin, **I:** 237

"Panthea" (Wilde), **V:** 401

Paoli, Pasquale di, **III:** 235, 236, 243

Paper Men, The (Golding), **Supp. I:** 88–89; **Retro. Supp. I:** 102–103

Paper Money Lyrics, and Other Poems (Peacock), **IV:** 170

Paperbark Tree, The: Selected Prose (Murray), **Supp. VII:** 270, 271, 273, 274, 277

"Papers, The" (James), **VI:** 69

Papers by Mr. Yellowplush (Thackeray), *see Yellowplush Correspondence, The*

"Parable Island" (Heaney), **Supp. II:** 280

Paracelsus (Browning), **IV:** xix, 355, 365, 368, 373; **Retro. Supp. II:** 20

Parade's End (Ford), **VI:** 321, 324, 328, 329–330; **VII:** xv

Paradise Lost (Milton), **I:** 188–189; **II:** 158, 161, **165–171**, 174, 176, 198, 294, 302; **III:** 118, 302; **IV:** 11–12, 15, 47, 88, 93, 95, 186, 200, 204, 229; ed. Bentley, **VI:** 153; **Retro. Supp. I:** 184; **Retro. Supp. II:** 279–284

Paradise News (Lodge), **Supp. IV:** 366, 374, 381–383, 384, 385

Paradise Regained (Milton), **II:** 171–172, 174, 176; **Retro. Supp. II:** 284–285

"Paradox, The" (Donne), **Retro. Supp. II:** 91

Paradoxes and Problems (Donne), **Retro. Supp. II:** 97

"Paraffin Lamp, The" (Brown), **Supp. VI:** 69–70

Parallel of the Antient Architecture with the Modern, A (tr. Evelyn), **II:** 287

"Paraphrase on Oenone to Paris" (Behn), **Supp. III:** 36

Parasitaster (Marston), *see Fawn, The*

Parasites, The (du Maurier), **Supp. III:** 139, 143

Pardoner's Tale, The (Chaucer), **I:** 21, 42

"Parents" (Spender), **Supp. II:** 483

Parents and Children (Compton-Burnett), **VII:** 62, 65, 66, 67

Parent's Assistant, The (Edgeworth), **Supp. III:** 152

Pargiters, The (Woolf), **Retro. Supp. I:** 308, 320

Paridiso (Dante), **Supp. IV:** 439

Paris by Night (film), **Supp. IV:** 282, 292

Paris Nights (Bennett), **VI:** 259, 264

Paris Sketch Book, The (Thackeray), **V:** 22, 37

Parish Register, The (Crabbe), **III:** 275, 279, 283

Parisian Sketches (James), **VI:** 67

Parisina (Byron), **IV:** 173, 192

Parker, Brian, **II:** 6

Parker, W. R., **II:** 165*n*

Parkinson, T., **VI:** 220

Parlement of Foules (Chaucer), *see Parliament of Fowls, The*

Parleyings with Certain People of Importance in Their Day . . . (Browning), **IV:** 359, 374

Parliament of Birds (tr. FitzGerald), **IV:** 348–349, 353

Parliament of Fowls, The (Chaucer), **I:** 31, 38, 60; **Retro. Supp. II:** 39–40

Parliamentary Speeches of Lord Byron, The (Byron), **IV:** 193

Parnell, Thomas, **III:** 19

Parnell and His Island (Moore), **VI:** 86

Parochial and Plain Sermons (Newman), **Supp. VII:** 292

Parr, Samuel, **IV:** 88

Parry, William, **IV:** 191, 193

Parson's Daughter, The (Trollope), **V:** 101

"Parson's Pleasure" (Dahl), **Supp. IV:** 217

Parson's Tale, The (Chaucer), **I:** 34–35

Part of the Seventh Epistle of the First Book of Horace Imitated (Swift), **III:** 35

"Parthenogenesis" (Dhomhnaill), **Supp. V:** 40–41

Partial Portraits (James), **V:** 95, 97, 102; **VI:** x, 46

"Partie Fine, The" (Thackeray), **V:** 24, 38

"Parting" (Thomas), **Supp. III:** 305

"Partition" (Auden), **Retro. Supp. I:** 14

"Partner, The" (Conrad), **VI:** 148

Partnership, The (Unsworth), **Supp. VII:** 354–355, 356

Party Going (Green), **Supp. II: 253–254**

Pascal, Blaise, **II:** 146, 244; **V:** 339; **Supp. IV:** 160

Pascali's Island (Unsworth), **Supp. VII:** 355, 356, 357–359, 360

Pasiphaë: A Poem (Swinburne), **V:** 333

Pasmore (Storey), **Supp. I:** 408, 410, 411–412, 413, 414–415

Pasquin (Fielding), **III:** 97, 98, 104, 105; **Retro. Supp. I:** 82

Passage of Arms (Ambler), **Supp. IV:** 16

Passage to India, A (Forster), **VI:** 183, 397, 401, 401, **408–410**; **VII:** xv; **Retro. Supp. II:** 146–149

Pastoral Care (Pope Gregory), **Retro. Supp. II:** 295

Passages in the Life of an Individual (Brontë), *see Agnes Grey*

Passages of Joy, The (Gunn), **Supp. IV:** 257, 271–274

Passenger (Keneally), **Supp. IV:** 346

Passenger to Frankfurt (Christie), **Supp. II:** 123, 125, 130, 132

"Passer-by, A" (Bridges), **VI:** 78

"Passing Events" (Brontë), **V:** 122, 123, 151

Passing of the Essenes, The (Moore), **VI:** 96, 99

"Passing of the Shee, The" (Synge), **VI:** 314

Passion (Bond), **Supp. I:** 423, 429–430

"Passion, The" (Collins), **III:** 166, 168, 174

"Passion, The" (Vaughan), **II:** 187

Passion, The (Winterson), **Supp. IV:** 542, 548, 553–554, 555–556

Passion Fruit: Romantic Fiction with a Twist (Winterson), **Supp. IV:** 542

Passion of New Eve, The (Carter), **Supp. III:** 84, 85–86, 91

Passion Play, A (Shaw), **VI:** 107

Passion, Poison, and Petrification; or, The Fatal Gazogene (Shaw), **VI:** 129

Passionate Century of Love (Watson), **I:** 193

Passionate Friends, The (Ambler), **Supp. IV:** 3

"Passionate Man's Pilgrimage, The" (Ralegh), **I:** 148, 149

"Passionate Pilgrim, A" (James), **VI:** 69

Passionate Pilgrim, The, **I:** 291, 307

Passionate Pilgrim and Other Tales, A (James), **VI:** 67

Passionate Shepherd to His Love, The (Marlowe), **I:** 149, 284, 291; **IV:** 327; **Retro. Supp. I:** 203–204

"Passionate Woman, A" (Ewart), **Supp. VII:** 42

"Passions: An Ode. Set to Music, The" (Collins), **III:** 163, 175

Passions of the Mind (Byatt), **Supp. IV:** 139, 140, 141, 146, 151

"Passport to Eternity" (Ballard), **Supp. V:** 20

Passwords: Places, Poems, Preoccupations (Reid), **Supp. VII:** 324, 330, 336

Past and Present (Carlyle), **IV:** xx, 240, 244, 249, 250, 266*n*, 301

"Past ruin'd Ilion Helen lives" (Landor), **IV:** 99

"Past Ever Present, The" (Murray), **Supp. VII:** 280–281

"Paste" (James), **VI:** 69

Pastoral Lives of Daphnis and Chloë. Done into English (Moore), **VI:** 99

Pastorals (Blunden), **VI:** 427

Pastorals (Pope), **III:** 69

Pastorals of Virgil (tr. Thornton), **III:** 307

Pastors and Masters (Compton-Burnett), **VII:** 59, 65, 68

Pat and Roald (Farrell), **Supp. IV:** 223

"Pat Cloherty's Version of *The Maisie*" (Murphy), **Supp. V:** 325

"Patagonia, The," (James), **VI:** 49

Pater, Walter Horatio, **V:** xiii, xix, xxiv–xxvi, 286–287, 314, 323, 324, 329, **337–360**, 362, 400–401, 403, 408, 410, 411; **VI:** ix, 4 365

"Pater on Style" (Chandler), **V:** 359

Paterson, Banjo, **Supp. IV:** 460

"Path of Duty, The" (James), **VI:** 69

Patience (Gawain–Poet), **Supp. VII:** 83, 84, 96–98

"Patience, hard thing!" (Hopkins), **V:** 375

Patmore, Coventry, **V:** 372, 379, 441

"Patmos" (Durrell), **Supp. I:** 125

Paton, Alan, **Supp. II: 341–359**

"Patricia, Edith, and Arnold," (Thomas), **Supp. I:** 181

Patrician, The (Galsworthy), **VI:** 273, 278

"Patrick Sarsfield's Portrait" (Murphy), **Supp. V:** 323

Patriot (Johnson), **III:** 121

Patriot for Me, A (Osborne), **Supp. I:** 335, 337

"Patrol: Buonomary" (Gutteridge), **VII:** 432–433

Patronage (Edgeworth), **Supp. III:** 151, 158

Pattern of Maugham, The (Curtis), **VI:** 379

Pattern of Painful Adventures, The (Twine), **I:** 321

Patterns of Culture (Benedict), **Supp. III:** 186

Paul (Wilson), **Supp. VI:** 306

Pauli, Charles Paine, **Supp. II:** 98, 116

Pauline: A Fragment of a Confession (Browning), **IV:** xix, 354, 355, 373; **Retro. Supp. II:** 19

Paul's Departure and Crown (Bunyan), **II:** 253

Paul's Letters to His Kinsfolk (Scott), **IV:** 38

Pausanias' Description of Greece (Frazer), Supp.**III:** 172, 173

"Pause en Route" (Kinsella), **Supp. V:** 261

"Pavana Dolorosa" (Hill), **Supp. V:** 190–191

Pavic, Milorad, **Supp. IV:** 116

"Pavilion on the Links, The" (Stevenson), **V:** 395; **Retro. Supp. I:** 263

"Pawnbroker's Shop, The" (Dickens), **V:** 45, 47, 48

Paying Guest, The (Gissing), **V:** 437

Payne, W. L., **III:** 41*n*

"Peace" (Brooke), **VI:** 420; **Supp. III:** 56, 57

"Peace" (Collins), **III:** 166, 168

"Peace" (Hopkins), **V:** 370

"Peace" (Vaughan), **II:** 186, 187

Peace and the Protestant Succession, The (Trevelyan), **VI:** 392–393

Peace Conference Hints (Shaw), **VI:** 119, 129

Peace in Our Time (Coward), **Supp. II:** 151, 154

Peace of the World, The (Wells), **VI:** 244

Peaceable Principles and True (Bunyan), **II:** 253

"Peaches, The" (Thomas), **Supp. I:** 181

Peacock, Thomas Love, **III:** 336, 345; **IV:** xv, xvii–xix, xxii, **157–170**, 177, 198, 204, 306; **V:** 220; **VII:** 200, 211

Peacock Garden, The (Desai), **Supp. V:** 55, 62–63

Pearl (Arden), **Supp. II:** 39–40

Pearl (Gawain–Poet), **Supp. VII:** 83, 84, 91–96, 98

"Pearl, Matth.13. 45., The" (Herbert), **Retro. Supp. II:** 175

"Pearl Necklace, A" (Hall), **Supp. VI:** 119

Pearl'Maiden (Haggard), **Supp. III:** 214

Pearsall Smith, Logan, **VI:** 76

Peasant Mandarin, The: Prose Pieces (Murray), **Supp. VII:** 270, 271

"Peasants, The" (Lewis), **VII:** 447

Pecket, Thomas, **Supp. III:** 385

Peckham, Morse, **V:** 316, 335

Pedlar, The (Wordsworth), **IV:** 24

Peele, George, **I: 191–211**, 278, 286, 305

"Peele Castle" (Wordsworth), *see* AElegiac Stanzas, Suggested by a Picture of Peele Castle . . . A

"Peep into a Picture Book, A" (Brontë), **V:** 109

Peer Gynt (Ibsen), **Supp. III:** 195

Pegasus (Day Lewis), **Supp. III:** 118, 129–130

"Pegasus" (Kavanagh), **Supp. VII:** 193

Pelican History of English Literature, The, **I:** 102

Pell, J. P., **V:** 161

Pelles, George, **VI:** 23

"Pen, Pencil and Poison" (Wilde), **V:** 405, 407; **Retro. Supp. II:** 367–368

Pen Portraits and Reviews (Shaw), **VI:** 129

Pen Shop, The (Kinsella), **Supp. V:** 272, 273, 274

Pendennis (Tackeray), *see History of Pendennis, The*

Penelope (Maugham), **VI:** 369

Penguin Book of Contemporary British Poetry, The (ed. Motion), **Supp. VII:** 252, 254, 255, 257

Penguin Book of Lesbian Short Stories, The (ed. Winterson), **Supp. IV:** 542

Penguin Book of Light Verse (ed. Ewart), **Supp. VII:** 43, 47

Penguin Book of Modern British Short Stories (ed. Bradbury), **Supp. IV:** 304

Penguin Modern Poets II (Thomas), **Supp. IV:** 490

Penitential Psalms (Wyatt), **I:** 101–102, 108, 111

"Pennines in April" (Hughes), **Supp. I:** 344

"Penny Plain and Twopence Coloured, A" (Stevenson), **V:** 385

Penny Whistles (Stevenson), *see Child's Garden of Verses, A*

Pensées (Pascal), **Supp. IV:** 160

"Penshurst, To" (Jonson), **II:** 223

"Pension Beaurepas, The" (James), **VI:** 69

Pentameron and Pentalogia, The (Landor), **IV:** 89, 90–91, 93, 100

"Pentecost Castle, The" (Hill), **Supp. V:** 189, 190, 199

Penfriends from Portlock (Wilson), **Sup. VI:** 298, 304

"Penthouse Apartment, The" (Trevor), **Supp. IV:** 502

Pentland Rising, The (Stevenson), **V:** 395; **Retro. Supp. I:** 260

Penultimate Poems (Ewart), **Supp. VII:** 45–46

"Penwith" (Thomas), **Supp. IV:** 492

People Who Knock on the Door (Highsmith), **Supp. V:** 178

People with the Dogs, The (Stead), **Supp. IV:** 473

People's Otherworld, The (Murray), **Supp. VII:** 270, 277–279

"People's Park and the Battle of Berkeley, The" (Lodge), **Supp. IV:** 374

Pepys, Samuel, **II:** 145, 195, 273, 274, 275, 278, **280–288**, 310

Per Amica Silentia Lunae (Yeats), **VI:** 209

"Perchance a Jealous Foe" (Ewart), **Supp. VII:** 42

Percy, Thomas, **III:** 336; **IV:** 28–29

Percy Bysshe Shelley (Swinburne), **V:** 333

"Perdita" (Warner), **Supp. VII:** 379

Père Goriot (Balzac), **Supp. IV:** 238

Peregrine Pickle (Smollett), **III:** 149, 150, 152–153, 158

Perelandra (Lewis), **Supp. I:** 74; **Supp. III:** 249, 252, 253–254

Perennial Philosophy, The (Huxley), **VII:** xviii, 206

Perfect Alibi, The (Milne), **Supp. V:** 310

"Perfect Critic, The" (Eliot), **VII:** 163

Perfect Fool, The (Fuller), **Supp. VII:** 74, 75

Perfect Happiness (Churchill), **Supp. IV:** 181

Perfect Spy, A (le Carré), **Supp. II: 300–302**, 304, 305

Perfect Wagnerite, The (Shaw), **VI:** 129

"Perfect World, A" (Motion), **Supp. VII:** 265, 266

Performing Flea (Wodehouse), **Supp. III:** 460

Pericles (Shakespeare), **I:** 321–322; **II:** 48

Pericles and Aspasia (Landor), **IV:** xix, 89, 92, 94–95, 100

Pericles and Other Studies (Swinburne), **V:** 333

Peripatetic, The (Thelwall), **IV:** 103

Perkin Warbeck (Ford), **II:** 89, 92, 96, 97, 100

Perkin Warbeck (Shelley), **Supp. III:** 371

Perkins, Richard, **II:** 68

Permanent Red: Essays in Seeing (Berger), **Supp. IV:** 79, 81

Pernicious Consequences of the New Heresie of the Jesuites . . . , The (tr. Evelyn), **II:** 287

Peronnik the Fool (Moore), **VI:** 99

Perry, Thomas Sergeant, **VI:** 24

"Persian Eclogues" (Collins), **III:** 160, 164–165, 175

"Persian Passion Play, A" (Arnold), **V:** 216

Personae (Pound), **Supp. III:** 398

Personal and Possessive (Thomas), **Supp. IV:** 490

Personal Heresy, The: A Controversy (Lewis), **Supp. III:** 249

Personal History, Adventures, Experience, and Observation of David Copperfield, The (Dickens), *see David Copperfield*

Personal Landscape (periodical), **VII:** 425, 443

Personal Places (Kinsella), **Supp. V:** 272

"Personal Problem" (Kavanagh), **Supp. VII:** 198

Personal Record, A (Conrad), **VI:** 134, 148; **Retro. Supp. II:** 69

Personal Reminiscences of Henry Irving (Stoker), **Supp. III:** 381

Persons from Porlock (MacNeice), **VII:** 408

Persse, Jocelyn, **VI:** 55

Persuasion (Austen), **IV:** xvii, 106–109, 111, 113, 115–120, 122; **Retro. Supp. II:** 12–13
"Perturbations of Uranus, The" (Fuller), **Supp. VII:** 73
"Pervasion of Rouge, The" (Beerbohm), **Supp. II:** 45
"Pessimism in Literature" (Forster), **VI:** 410
Peter Bell (Wordsworth), **IV:** xviii 2
Peter Bell the Third (Shelley), **IV:** 203, 207
"Peter Grimes" (Crabbe), **III:** 283, 284–285
Peter Ibbetson (du Maurier), **Supp. III:** 134, 135, 136, 137, 138, 139
Peter Pan; or, The Boy Who Would Not Grow Up (Barrie), **Supp. III:** 2, **6–8**
Petrarch's Seven Penitential Psalms (Chapman), **I:** 241–242
Peveril of the Peak (Scott), **IV:** xviii, 36, 37, 39
Pfeil, Fred, **Supp. IV:** 94
Phaedra (Seneca), **II:** 97
"Phaèthôn" (Meredith), **V:** 224
"Phallus in Wonderland" (Ewart), **Supp. VII:** 36
Phantasmagoria (Carroll), **V:** 270, 273
Pharos, pseud. of E. M. Forster
Pharos and Pharillon (Forster), **VI:** 408
Pharsalia (tr. Marlowe), **I:** 276, 291
Phases of Faith (Newman), **V:** 208*n*
"Phebus and Cornide" (Gower), **I:** 55
Philadelphia, Here I Come! (Friel), **Supp. V:** 111, 116–118
Philanderer, The (Shaw), **VI:** 107, 109; **Retro. Supp. II:** 312
Philaster (Beaumont and Fletcher), **II:** 45, 46, **52–54**, 55, 65
Philby Conspiracy, The (Page, Leitch, and Knightley), **Supp. II:** 302, 303, 311–312
Philip (Thackeray), *see Adventures of Philip on His Way Through the World, The*
Philip Larkin (Motion), **Supp. VII:** 253
Philip Sparrow (Skelton), **I:** 84, 86–88
Philip Webb and His Work (Lethaby), **V:** 291, 292, 296, 306
Philips, Ambrose, **III:** 56
Philips, Katherine, **II:** 185
Phillips, Caryl, **Supp. V: 379–394**
Phillipps, Sir Thomas, **II:** 103
Phillips, Edward, **II:** 347
"Phillis is my only Joy" (Sedley), **II:** 265
"Phillis, let's shun the common Fate" (Sedley), **II:** 263
Phillpotts, Eden, **VI:** 266
"Philosopher, The" (Brontë), **V:** 134
"Philosopher and the Birds, The" (Murphy), **Supp. V:** 318
Philosopher's Pupil, The (Murdoch), **Supp. I:** 231, 232–233
Philosophical Discourse of Earth, An, Relating to . . . Plants, &c. (Evelyn), **II:** 287
Philosophical Enquiry into the Origin of Our Ideas of the Sublime and Beautiful, A (Burke), *see On the Sublime and Beautiful*

Philosophical Essays Concerning Human Understanding (Hume), **Supp. III:** 238
Philosophical Lectures of S. T. Coleridge, The (ed. Coburn), **IV:** 52, 56
"Philosophical View of Reform, A" (Shelley), **IV:** 199, 209; **Retro. Supp. I:** 254
"Philosophy of Herodotus" (De Quincey), **IV:** 147–148
Philosophy of Melancholy, The (Peacock), **IV:** 158, 169
Philosophy of Nesessity, The (Bray), **V:** 188
Philosophy of Rhetoric (Richards), **Supp. II:** 416, 423
Philosophy of the Unconscious (Hartmann), **Supp. II:** 108
Phineas Finn (Trollope), **V:** 96, 98, 101, 102
Phineas Redux (Trollope), **V:** 96, 98, 101, 102
Phoenix (Storey), **Supp. I:** 408, 420
Phoenix, The, **Retro. Supp. II:** 303
Phoenix, The (Middleton), **II:** 21, 30
Phoenix and the Turtle, The (Shakespeare), **I:** 34, 313
"Phoenix Park" (Kinsella), **Supp. V:** 264
"Phoenix Rose Again, The" (Golding), **Supp. I:** 66
Phoenix Too Frequent, A (Fry), **Supp. III:** 194–195, 201–202
Physicists, The (Snow), **VII:** 339–340
Physico-Theology (Derham), **III:** 49
"Pibroch" (Hughes), **Supp. I:** 350
Picasso, Pablo, **Supp. IV:** 81, 87, 88
Piccolomini; or, The First Part of Wallenstein, The (Coleridge), **IV:** 55–56
Pickering, John, **I:** 213, 216–218
Pickwick Papers (Dickens), **V:** xix, 9, 42, 46–47, 48, 52, 59, 62, 71
Pico della Mirandola, **II:** 146; **V:** 344
"Pictor Ignotus, Florence 15" A (Browning), **IV:** 356, 361; **Retro. Supp. II:** 27
"Pictorial Rhapsody, A" (Thackeray), **V:** 37
Picture and Text (James), **VI:** 46, 67
"Picture of a Nativity" (Hill), **Supp. V:** 186
Picture of Dorian Gray, The (Wilde), **III:** 334, 345; **V:** xxv, 339, 399, 410–411, 417, 419; **Retro. Supp. II:** 368
"Picture of Little T. C. in a Prospect of Flowers, The" (Marvell), **II:** 211, 215
"Picture This" (Motion), **Supp. VII:** 266
Picturegoers, The (Lodge), **Supp. IV:** 364, 367–368, 369, 371, 372, 381, 382
"Pictures" (Kelman), **Supp. V:** 250
Pictures at an Exhibition (Thomas), **Supp. IV:** 487–488
"Pictures from a Japanese Printmaker" (Redgrove), **Supp. VI:** 234
"Pictures from an Ecclesiastical Furnisher's" (Redgrove), **Supp. VI:** 234
Pictures from Italy (Dickens), **V:** 71
Pictures in the Hallway (O'Casey), **VII:** 9, 12

Picturesque Landscape and English Romantic Poetry (Watson), **IV:** 26
"Piece of Cake, A" (Dahl), **Supp. IV:** 208, 209
"Pied Beauty" (Hopkins), **V:** 367; **Retro. Supp. II:** 196
"Pied Piper of Hamelin, The" (Browning), **IV:** 356, 367
Pied Piper of Lovers (Durrell), **Supp. I:** 95
"Pier Bar" (Murphy), **Supp. V:** 328
Pier'Glass, The (Graves), **VII:** 263–264
Pierrot mon ami (Queneau), **Supp. I:** 220
Piers Plowman (Langland), **I: 1–18**
Pietrkiewicz, Jerzy, **Supp. IV:** 98
"Pig" (Dahl), **Supp. IV:** 221
"Pig, The" (Lessing), **Supp. I:** 240
Pig Earth (Berger), **Supp. IV:** 90, 92, 93
Pigeon, The (Galsworthy), **VI:** 271, 274, 287–288
"Pigeons" (Reid), **Supp. VII:** 329
"Pigs" (Murray), **Supp. VII:** 282
Pigs Have Wings (Wodehouse), **Supp. III:** 453–454, 458–459, 462
Pilgrim, The (Fletcher), **II:** 65
Pilgrim, The (Vanbrugh), **II:** 289, 305, 325, 336
Pilgrim to Compostella, The (Southey), **IV:** 71
"Pilgrimage of Pleasure, The" (Swinburne), **V:** 332
Pilgrimage of the Life of Man (Lydgate), **I:** 57
Pilgrims of Hope (Morris), **V:** 301, 306
Pilgrim's Progress, The (Bunyan), **I:** 16, 57; **II:** 240, 241, 243, 244, **245–250**, 253; **III:** 82; **V:** 27; **Supp. IV:** 242
Pilgrim's Regress, The (Lewis), **Supp. III:** 249, **250–252**, 264
Pilkington, John, **Supp. IV:** 164
"Pillar of the Cloud" (Newman), *see* "Lead, Kindly Light"
"Pillar of the Community, A" (Kinsella), **Supp. V:** 261
Pillars of Society, The (Ibsen), **V:** xxiv, 414
"Pillow hot . . . , The" (tr. McKane), **Supp. IV:** 494
"Pillow hot . . . , The" (tr. Thomas), **Supp. IV:** 494
Pincher Martin (Golding), **Supp. I:** 67, 72–75, 76, 77, 83, 218*n*; **Retro. Supp. I:** 97
Pindar, **II:** 198–199; **IV:** 95, 316
Pindaric Ode, Humbly Offer'd to the King . . . , A (Congreve), **II:** 350
"Pindaric Poem to the Reverend Doctor Burnet, A" (Behn), **Supp. III:** 41
Pindarique Ode on the victorious Progress of Her Majesties Arms, A (Congreve), **II:** 350
Pindarique Odes (Cowley), **II:** 197, 199, 202
Pinero, Arthur Wing, **V:** 413; **VI:** 269, 368
Pinter, Harold, **Supp. I: 367–382; Supp. IV:** 180, 290, 390, 437, 456; **Retro. Supp. I: 215–228**
Pinter Problem, The (Quigley), **Retro. Supp. I:** 227

Piozzi, Hester Lynch, **III:** 134, 246
Pippa Passes (Browning), **IV:** 356, 362–363, 370, 373; **Retro. Supp. II:** 20–21
Piranesi Giovanni Battista, **III:** 325, 338
Pirate, The (Scott), **IV:** 36, 39
"Pirate and the Apothecary, The" (Stevenson), **V:** 391
"Pisgah" (Nicholson), **Supp. VI: 219**
"Pit and the Pendulum, The" (Poe), **III:** 339
Pit Strike (Sillitoe), **Supp. V:** 411
Pithy, Pleasant, and Profitable Works of John Skelton, The (ed. Stow), **I:** 94
"Pity" (Collins), **III:** 166
"Pity of It, The" (Hardy), **Retro. Supp. I:** 120
Pizarro (Sheridan), **III: 267–270**
Place at Whitton, A (Keneally), **Supp. IV:** 345
Place Where Souls Are Born: A Journey to the Southwest, The (Keneally), **Supp. IV:** 343, 347, 357–358
"Placeless Heaven, The" (Heaney), **Supp. II:** 280; **Retro. Supp. I:** 131
"Places, Loved Ones" (Larkin), **Supp. I:** 278
Plain Man and His Plain Wife, The (Bennett), **VI:** 264, 267
Plain Speaker, The (Hazlitt), **IV:** 131, 134, 136, 140
Plain Tales from the Hills (Kipling), **VI:** 168, 204
Plain'Dealer, The (Wycherley), **II:** 308, **318–320,** 321, 322, 343
Plaine Mans Path'Way to Heaven, The (Dent), **II:** 241, 246
"Plains, The" (Fuller), **VII:** 430; **Supp. VII:** 69
"Plan, The" (O'Brien), **Supp. V:** 340
Plan of a Dictionary of the English Language, The (Johnson), **III:** 113, 121; *see also Dictionary of the English Language, A*
Plan of a Novel . . . With Opinions on AMansfield Park"and AEmma" . . . (Austen), **IV:** 112, 122
Plan of the English Commerce, A (Defoe), **III:** 14
"Planter of Malata, The" (Conrad), **VI:** 148
Plath, Sylvia, **Supp. I:** 346, 350; **Supp. IV:** 252, 430; **Retro. Supp. II:** 199, 200–201, 216–218
Plato, **IV:** 47–48, 54; **V:** 339; **Supp. III:** 125; **Supp. IV:** 13
Plato and Platonism (Pater), **V:** 339, 355, 356
Plato Papers: A Novel, The (Ackroyd), **Supp. VI:** 4, 11, 13
Plato Papers: A Prophesy, The (Ackroyd), **Supp. VI:** 13
"Platonic Blow, by Miss Oral" (Auden), **Retro. Supp. I:** 12
"Platonic Love" (Cowley), **II:** 197
Play (Beckett), **Supp. I:** 46, 58; **Retro. Supp. I:** 27
Play from Romania, A, see Mad Forest

Playboy of the Western World, The (Synge), **VI:** xiv, 308, 309–310, 312–313, 316; **Retro. Supp. I:** 291, 298–300
Playground of Europe, The (Stephen), **V:** 282, 289
Playing Away (Phillips), **Supp. V:** 380
"Playing with Terror" (Ricks), **Supp. IV:** 398
Playmaker, The (Keneally), **Supp. IV:** 346
"Plays" (Landor), **IV:** 98
Plays for England (Osborne), **Supp. I:** 335
Plays for Puritans (Shaw), **VI:** 109
Plays of William Shakespeare, The (ed. Johnson), **III:** 115–117, 121; **Retro. Supp. I:** 138, 144
Plays: One (Arden), **Supp. II:** 30
Plays: Pleasant and Unpleasant (Shaw), **VI:** ix, 104, **107–112; Retro. Supp. II:** 313–315
Plaza de Toros, The (Scott), **Supp. I:** 266
Plea of the Midsummer Fairies, The (Hood), **IV:** 253, 255, 261, 267
Pleasant Notes upon Don Quixote (Gayton), **I:** 279
Pleasure (Waugh), **Supp. VI:** 270
Pleasure Dome, The (Greene), **Supp. I:** 3, 9
"Pleasure Island" (Auden), **Retro. Supp. I:** 12
Pleasure of Poetry, The (Sitwell), **VII:** 129–130
Pleasure of Reading, The (Fraser), **Supp. V:** 20
Pleasure Steamers, The (Motion), **Supp. VII:** 253–255, 257
Pleasures of the Flesh (Ewart), **Supp. VII:** 38–39
Plebeian (periodical), **III:** 51, 53
Pléiade, **I:** 170
Plenty (Hare), **Supp. IV:** 282, 286–287, 293
Plot Discovered, The (Coleridge), **IV:** 56
Plotinus, **III:** 291
Plotting and Writing Suspense Fiction (Highsmith), **Supp. V:** 167, 171, 174, 177
Plough, The (Walker), **V:** 377
Plough and the Stars, The (O'Casey), **VI:** 214; **VII:** xviii, 5–6
Ploughman and Other Poems (Kavanagh), **Supp. VII:** 187–188
Ploughman, and Other Poems, A (White), **Supp. I:** 130
Ploughman's Lunch, The (McEwan), **Supp. IV:** 389, 390, 399–400
Plumb, Sir John Harold, **IV:** 290; **VI:** xv, xxxiv, 391n
Plumed Serpent, The (Lawrence), **VII:** 87–88, 91, **109–110,** 123; **Retro. Supp. II:** 231
Plutarch, **II:** 185
Plutarch's Lives (tr. Goldsmith), **III:** 191
Plutarch's Lives. The translation called Dryden's . . . (ed. Clough), **V:** 157, 170
Plutus, The God of Riches (tr. Fielding), **III:** 105

Plymley, Peter, *see* Smith, Sydney
PN Review (publication), **Supp. IV:** 256
Podro, Joshua, **VII:** 262
Poe, Edgar Allan, **III:** 329, 333, 334, 338–339, 340, 343, 345; **IV:** 311, 319; **V:** xvi, xx–xxi; **VI:** 371
"Poem About a Ball in the Nineteenth Century" (Empson), **Supp. II:** 180–181, 183
"Poem as Abstract" (Davie), **Supp. VI:** 106
"Poem from the North," (Keyes), **VII:** 439
"Poem for My Father" (Reid), **Supp. VII:** 325
"Poem in October" (Thomas), **Supp. I:** 177, 178–179
Poem in St. James's Park, A (Waller), **II:** 238
"Poem in Seven Books, A" (Blake), **Retro. Supp. I:** 37
"Poem in Winter" (Jennings), **Supp. V:** 213–214
"Poem of the Midway" (Thomas), **Supp. IV:** 493
"Poem on His Birthday" (Thomas), **Supp. I:** 179
Poem on the Late Civil War, A (Cowley), **II:** 202
Poem Sacred to the Memory of Sir Isaac Newton, A (Thomson), **Supp. III:** 411, 418–419
"Poem Upon the Death of O. C., A" (Marvell), **II:** 205, 211
"Poem with the Answer, A" (Suckling), **II:** 228
Poemata et Epigrammata, . . . (Crashaw), **II:** 201
Poemata et inscriptiones (Landor), **IV:** 100
Poems [1853] (Arnold), **V:** xxi, 165, 209, 216
Poems [1854] (Arnold), **V:** 216
Poems [1855] (Arnold), **V:** 216
Poems [1857] (Arnold), **V:** 216
Poems (Bridges), **VI:** 83
Poems (Brooke), **Supp. III: 51–53**
Poems [1844] (Browning), **IV:** xx, 311, 313–314, 321, 356
Poems [1850] (Browning), **IV:** 311, 321
Poems (Byron), **IV:** 192
Poems (Carew), **II:** 238
Poems (Clough), **V:** 170
Poems (Cowley), **II:** 194, 198, 199, 202
Poems (Crabbe), **III:** 286
Poems (Eliot), **VII:** 146, 150
Poems (Empson), **Supp. II:** 180
Poems (Gay), **III:** 55
Poems (Golding), **Supp. I:** 66
"Poems, 1912–13" (Hardy), **Retro. Supp. I:** 117
Poems (Hood), **IV:** 252, 261, 266
Poems (Jennings), **Supp. V:** 208
Poems (Keats), **IV:** xvii, 211, 213–214, 216, 235; **Retro. Supp. I:** 183, 187–188
Poems (Kinsella), **Supp. V:** 260
Poems (Lovell and Southey), **IV:** 71
Poems (Meredith), **V:** xxi, 219, 234
Poems (C. Rossetti), **V:** 260

Poems [1870] (D. G. Rossetti), **V:** xxiii, 237, 238, 245

Poems [1873] (D. G. Rossetti), **V:** 245

Poems [1881] (D. G. Rossetti), **V:** 238, 245

Poems (Ruskin), **V:** 184

Poems (Sassoon), **VI:** 429

Poems (Southey), **IV:** 71

Poems (Spender), **Supp. II:** 483, 486–487

Poems [1833] (Tennyson), **IV:** 326, 329, 338

Poems [1842] (Tennyson), **IV:** xx, 326, 333–334, 335, 338

Poems (Thompson), **V:** 439, 451

Poems (Waller), **II:** 238

Poems (Wilde), **V:** 401–402, 419; **Retro. Supp. II:** 361–362

Poems, The (Landor), **IV:** xvi, 99

Poems, The (Swift), **III:** 15n, 35

Poems, The (Thomas), **Supp. I:** 170

Poems Against Economics (Murray), **Supp. VII:** 270, 273–275

Poems and Ballads (Swinburne), **V:** xxiii, 309, 310, 313, **314–321,** 327, 330, 332

"Poems and Ballads of Goethe" (Clough), **V:** 170

Poems and Ballads: Second Series (Swinburne), **V:** xxiv, 314, 327, 332

Poems and Ballads: Third Series (Swinburne), **V:** 332

Poems and Letters of Bernard Barton (ed. FitzGerald), **IV:** 343–344, 353

Poems and Lyrics of the Joy of Earth (Meredith), **V:** 221, 224, 234

Poems and Melodramas (Davie), **Supp. VI:** 113

Poems and Metrical Tales (Southey), **IV:** 71

Poems and Prose Remains of A. H. Clough, The (ed. Clough and Symonds), **V:** 159, 170

Poems and Songs, The (Burns), **III:** 310n, 322

Poems and Songs (Ewart), **Supp. VII:** 34, 36–37

Poems and Translations (Kinsella), **Supp. V:** 264

Poems Before Congress (Browning), **IV:** 312, 315, 321

Poems by Alfred, Lord Tennyson (Lear), **V:** 78, 87

Poems by Currer, Ellis and Acton Bell (Brontës), **V:** xx, 131–134, 151

Poems by the Author of the Growth of Love (Bridges), **VI:** 83

Poems by the Way (Morris), **V:** 306

Poems by Two Brothers (Tennyson and Tennyson), **IV:** 337–338

Poems Chiefly in the Scottish Dialect (Burns), **III:** 315

Poems, Chiefly Lyrical (Tennyson), **IV:** xix, 326, 329, 331, 338

Poems Chiefly of Early and Late Years (Wordsworth), **IV:** xx, 25

Poems, Elegies, Paradoxes, and Sonnets (King), **Supp. VI:** 162

"Poems for Angus" (MacCaig), **Supp. VI:** 193

Poems for Young Ladies (Goldsmith), **III:** 191

Poems from Centre City (Kinsella), **Supp. V:** 272

Poems from the Arabic and Persian (Landor), **IV:** 99

Poems from Villon, and Other Fragments (Swinburne), **V:** 333

Poems in Prose (Wilde), **Retro. Supp. II:** 371

Poems, in Two Volumes (Wordsworth), **IV:** 22, 24

Poems, 1930 (Auden), **VII:** xix

Poems 1938–1945 (Graves), **VII:** 267–268

Poems, 1943–1947 (Day Lewis), **Supp. III:** 118, 128

Poems 1950 (Bunting), **Supp. VII:** 5, 13

Poems 1962–1978 (Mahon), **Supp. VI:** 173–174

Poems of Dedication (Spender), **Supp. II:** 489, 490

Poems of Felicity (Traherne), **II:** 191, 202

Poems of Henry Vaughan, Silurist, The (ed. Chambers), **II:** 187

Poems of John Keats, The (ed. Allott), **IV:** 223n 224, 234–235

"Poems of 1912–13" (Hardy), **VI:** 14

Poems of Ossian, The (Macpherson), **III:** 336

Poems of Wit and Humour (Hood), **IV:** 257, 266

Poems on His Domestic Circumstances (Byron), **IV:** 192

Poems on the Death of Priscilla Farmer (Lloyd and Lamb), **IV:** 78, 85

Poems on the Theatre (Brecht), **Supp. IV:** 87

Poems on Various Occasions (Byron), **IV:** 192

Poems on Various Subjects (Coleridge), **IV:** 43, 55, 78, 85

Poems Original and Translated (Byron), **IV:** 192

Poems Translated from the French of Madame de la Mothe Guion (tr. Cowper), **III:** 220

Poems upon Several Occasions: With a Voyage to the Island of Love (Behn), **Supp. III:** 36

Poems, with the Tenth Satyre of Juvenal Englished (Vaughan), **II:** 184–185, 201

"Poet, The" (Hulme), **Supp. VI:** 135

"Poet, The" (Sillitoe), **Supp. V:** 425

Poet and Dancer (Jhabvala), **Supp. V:** 223, 234, 235

"Poet Hood, The" (Blunden), **IV:** 267

Poet in the Imaginary Museum, The (Davie), **Supp. VI:** 115, 117

"Poet in the Imaginary Museum, The" (Davie), **Supp. VI:** 115

"Poet on the Island, The" (Murphy), **Supp. V:** 318

"Poet O'Rahilly, The" (Kinsella), **Supp. V:** 263

"Poet with Sea Horse" (Reid), **Supp. VII:** 328

Poetaster (Jonson), **I:** 339, 340; **Retro. Supp. I:** 158

"Poetic Diction in English" (Bridges), **VI:** 73

Poetic Image, The (Day Lewis), **Supp. III:** 118

"Poetic Imagination, The" (Muir), **Supp. VI:** 202–203

Poetic Unreason (Graves), **VII:** 257, 260

Poetical Blossomes (Cowley), **II:** 194, 202

Poetical Calendar (Fawkes and Woty), **III:** 170n

"Poetical Character, The" (Collins), **III:** 166, 168

Poetical Fragments (Swinburne), **V:** 333

Poetical Pieces (Lamb), **IV:** 74

Poetical Register (Jacob), **II:** 348

Poetical Sketches (Blake), **III:** 289, 290; **Retro. Supp. I:** 33–34

Poetical Works, The, . . . (Traherne), **II:** 201–202

Poetical Works, The (Southey), **IV:** 71

Poetical Works (Bridges), **VI:** 83

Poetical Works of George Crabbe, The (ed. Carlyle and Carlyle), **III:** 272n

Poetical Works of George Meredith, The (ed. Trevelyan), **V:** 223, 234

Poetical Works of Gray and Collins, The (ed. Poole and Stone), **III:** 161n

Poetical Works of John Gay, The (ed. Faber), **III:** 66, 67

"Poetics of Sex, The" (Winterson), **Supp. IV:** 547, 551–552, 553

Poetria nova (Geoffrey of Vinsauf), **I:** 59

"Poetry"[broadcast] (Bridges), **VI:** 83

"Poetry" (Moore), **IV:** 6

"Poetry and the Other Modern Arts" (Davie), **Supp. VI:** 115–116

Poetry and Philosophy of George Meredith, The (Trevelyan), **VI:** 383

Poetry and Prose (ed. Sparrow), **VI:** 83

"Poetry and Striptease" (Thomas), **Supp. IV:** 491

Poetry by the Author of Gebir (Landor), **IV:** 99

Poetry for Children (Lamb and Lamb), **IV:** 85

"Poetry in Public" (Motion), **Supp. VII:** 265

Poetry in the Making (Hughes), **Supp. I:** 347

Poetry of Browning, The (Drew), **IV:** 375

"Poetry of Departures" (Larkin), **Supp. I:** 277, 278–279

Poetry of Edward Thomas, The (Motion), **Supp. VII:** 252, 253, 258, 263

Poetry of Ezra Pound, The (Kenner), **VI:** 333

Poetry of Meditation, The (Martz), **V:** 366, 382

Poetry of Nonsense, The (Cammaerts), **V:** 262, 274

"Poetry of Pope, The" (De Quincey), **IV:** 146

"Poetry of Protest, A" (Davie), **Supp. VI:** 116

Poetry of the First World War (Hibberd), **VI:** 460

Poetry of Thomas Hardy, The (Day Lewis), **VI:** 21

"Poetry of W. B. Yeats, The" (Eliot), **VI:** 207*n*, 223

Poetry of W. B. Yeats, The (MacNeice), **VII:** 404

"Poetry of Wordsworth, The" (De Quincey), **IV:** 146, 148

"Poetry Perpetuates the Poet" (Herrick), **II:** 115

"Poet'Scholar, The" (Davie), **Supp. VI:** 105

"Poets Lie where they Fell, The" (Mahon), **Supp. VI:** 167

Poet's Notebook, A (Sitwell), **VII:** 127, 139

Poets of the First World War (Stallworthy), **VI:** 441

"Poet's Pilgrimage to Waterloo, The" (Southey), **IV:** 66, 71

Poet's Tongue, The (Auden and Garrett), **Supp. IV:** 256; **Retro. Supp. I:** 6–7

"Poet's Vow, The" (Browning), **IV:** 313

"Poggio" (Durrell), **Supp. I:** 126

Point Counter Point (Huxley), **VII:** xviii, 201, 202–204

"Point of It, The" (Forster), **V:** 208

Point Valaine (Coward), **Supp. II:** 152

Points of View (Maugham), **VI:** 374, 377

Pointz Hall (Woolf), **Retro. Supp. I:** 308

"Poison" (Dahl), **Supp. IV:** 206, 215

Pol Pot, **Supp. IV:** 247

Polanski, Roman, **III:** 343

Polaris (Weldon), **Supp. IV:** 521

"Police, The: Seven Voices" (Murray), **Supp. VII:** 276

Polidori, John, **III:** 329, 334, 338; **Supp. III:** 385

Polite Conversations (Swift), **III:** 36

Political Economy of Art, The (Ruskin), **V:** 184

Political Essays (Hazlitt), **IV:** 129, 139

Political History of the Devil, The (Defoe), **III:** 5, 14

Political Justice (Godwin), **IV:** 43

"Political Poem" (Ewart), **Supp. VII:** 36

Political Romance, A (Sterne), **III:** 127, 135

Political Situation, The (Schreiner), **Supp. I:** 453

Political Thought in England, 1848–1914 (Walker), **IV:** 304

Politicks of Laurence Sterne, The (Curtis), **III:** 127*n*

"Politics" (Durrell), **Supp. I:** 124

"Politics and the English Language" (Orwell), **Supp. III:** 107; **Supp. IV:** 455

"Politics of King Lear, The" (Muir), **Supp. VI:** 202

"Politics of Mecca, The" (Lawrence), **Supp. II:** 286–287

"Politics vs. Literature" (Orwell), **VII:** 273, 282

Poliziano, Angelo, **I:** 240

Poll Degree from a Third Point of View, The (Stephen), **V:** 289

Pollock, Jackson, **Supp. IV:** 80

Polly (Gay), **III:** 55, 65–67

"Polonius" (FitzGerald), **IV:** 353

Polonius: A Collection of Wise Saws and Modern Instances (FitzGerald), **IV:** 344, 353

Polychronicon (Higden), **I:** 22

"Pomegranates of Patmos, The" (Harrison), **Supp. V:** 160

Pomes Penyeach (Joyce), **VII:** 42

Pomona (Evelyn), **II:** 287

Pompeii (Macaulay), **IV:** 290

Pompey the Great (tr. Dorset et al.), **II:** 270, 271

Pooh Perplex: A Freshman Casebook (Crews), **Supp. V:** 311

Poole, A. L., **III:** 161*n*

Poole, Thomas, **IV:** 42, 43, 51

Poor Clare (Hartley), **Supp. VII:** 132

"Poor Koko" (Fowles), **Supp. I:** 303

"Poor Man and the Lady, The" (Hardy), **VI:** 2, 20; **Retro. Supp. I:** 112

Poor Man's Plea, The (Defoe), **III:** 2, 12; **Retro. Supp. I:** 74–75

"Poor Mary" (Warner), **Supp. VII:** 380

"Poor Mathias" (Arnold), **V:** 207

Poor Miss Finch (Collins), **Supp. VI:** 102–103

Poor Mouth, The (O'Nolan), **Supp. II:** **333–335**

"Poor Richard" (James), **VI:** 69

Poor Tom (Muir), **Supp. VI:** 198

Pope, Alexander, **I:** 326, 328; **II:** **195–197**, 236, 259, 261, 263, 298, 308–309, 311, 321, 332, 335, 344; **III:** 1, 19, 20, 33, 46, 50, 54, 56, 60, 62, **68–79**, 95, 118, 167*n*, 234, 278, 280–282, 288; **IV:** 104, 182, 187, 189–190, 280; **V:** 319; **Supp. III:** 421–422; **Retro. Supp. I:** 76, **229–242**

Pope's Wedding, The (Bond), **Supp. I:** 422, **423–425**, 426, 427, 435

Popery: British and Foreign (Landor), **IV:** 100

"Poplar Field, The" (Cowper), **III:** 218

Popper, Karl, **Supp. IV:** 115

"Poppy grows upon the shore, A" (Bridges), **VI:** 78

Popular Education of France with Notices of that of Holland and Switzerland, The (Arnold), **V:** 216

"Popular Fallacies" (Lamb), **IV:** 82

Porcupine, The (Barnes), **Supp. IV:** 65, 67, 68, 73, 74

"Pornography and Obscenity" (Lawrence), **VII:** 91, 101, 122

"Pornography" (McEwan), **Supp. IV:** 394–395

"Porphyria's Lover" (Browning), **IV:** 360; **V:** 315; **Retro. Supp. II:** 22

Porson, Richard, **IV:** 63

"Portico" (Murphy), **Supp. V:** 327

"Portobello Road, The" (Spark), **Supp. I:** 200

"Portrait, The" (Gogol), **III:** 340, 345

"Portrait, The" (Rossetti), **V:** 239

Portrait, The (Swinburne), **V:** 333

Portrait of a Gentleman in Slippers (Milne), **Supp. V:** 300

"Portrait of a Grandfather, The" (Bridges), **VI:** 78

"Portrait of a Lady" (Eliot), **VII:** 144

Portrait of a Lady, The (James), **V:** xxiv, 51; **VI:** 25, 26, **35–38**; **Supp. IV:** 243

"Portrait of Mr. W. H., The" (Wilde), **V:** 405–406, 419; **Retro. Supp. II:** 365–366

Portrait of Rossetti (Grylls), **V:** 247, 249, 260

"Portrait of the Artist, A" (Kinsella), **Supp. V:** 272

"Portrait of the Artist, A" (Mahon), **Supp. VI:** 168

Portrait of the Artist as a Young Dog (Thomas), **Supp. I:** 176, 180, 181, 182

Portrait of the Artist as a Young Man, A (Joyce), **VII:** xiv, **45–47**; critical studies, **VII:** 57; **Supp. IV:** 364, 371; **Retro. Supp. I:** 169, 170, 173–175

"Portrait of the Artist as Émigré" (Berger), *see Painter of Our Time, A*

"Portrait of the Engineer, A" (Kinsella), **Supp. V:** 261

Portrait of the Lakes (Nicholson), **Supp. VI:** 223

Portrait of Orkney (Brown), **Supp. VI:** 65

"Portraits" (Thomas), **Supp. IV:** 494

Portraits Contemporains (Sainte'Beuve), **V:** 212

Portraits from Memory (Russell), **VI:** 170

Portraits of Places (James), **VI:** 67

Portugal History, The; or, A Relation of the Troubles . . . in the Court of Portugal . . . (Pepys), **II:** 288

"Pose (After the Painting *Mrs. Badham* by Ingres)" (Boland), **Supp. V:** 40

Positions (Mulcaster), **I:** 122

Positives (Gunn), **Supp. IV:** 257, 264, 265, 266

Possession: A Romance (Byatt), **Supp. IV:** 139, 149, 151–153

Postal Problem, A (Carroll), **V:** 274

"Posterity" (Larkin), **Supp. I:** 282

Posthumous Fragments of Margaret Nicholson . . . (ed. Shelley), **IV:** 208

Posthumous Papers of the Pickwick Club, The (Dickens), *see Pickwick Papers*

Posthumous Poems (Day Lewis), **Supp. III:** 130

Posthumous Poems (Shelley), **IV:** 208

Posthumous Poems, The (Swinburne), **V:** 333

Posthumous Tales (Crabbe), **III:** 278, 286

Post'Mortem (Coward), **Supp. II:** 149–150, 151

"Postscript" (Fuller), **Supp. VII:** 81

"Postscript: for Gweno" (Lewis), **VII:** 444, 446

"Postscripts" (radio broadcasts), **VII:** 212

Poet Geranium, The (Nicholson), **Supp. VI:** 213, 216–217

Pot of Broth, The (Yeats), **VI:** 218

"Potato Gatherers, The" (Friel), **Supp. V:** 114

Potter, Beatrix, **Supp. III:** **287–309**

Potter, Cherry, **Supp. IV:** 181

Potting Shed, The (Greene), **Supp. I:** 13; **Retro. Supp. II:** 162

Pottle, F. A., **III:** 234*n*, 239, 240, 247, 249

Pound, Ezra, **I:** 98; **IV:** 323, 327, 329, 372; **V:** xxv, 304, 317*n*; **VI:** 207, 216, 247, 323, 417; **VII:** xiii, xvi, 89, 148, 149; **Supp. III:** 53–54, 397, 398; **Supp. IV:** 99, 100, 114–115, 116, 411, 559

Pound on Demand, A (O'Casey), **VII:** 12

"Poussin" (MacNeice), **VII:** 411

Powell, Anthony, **VI:** 235; **VII:** xxi, **343–359; Supp. II:** 4; **Supp. IV:** 505

Powell, Edgar, **VI:** 385

Powell, L F., **III:** 234*n*

Power and the Glory, The (Greene; U.S. title, *The Labyrinthine Ways*), **Supp. I:** 5, 8, 9–10, 13, 14, 18; **Retro. Supp. II:** 156–157

Power in Men (Cary), **VII:** 186, 187

Power of Grace Illustrated (tr. Cowper), **III:** 220

Powers, Mary, **Supp. IV:** 423, 428

Powys, T. F., **VII:** 21, 234

Practical Criticism (Richards), **Supp. II:** 185, 405, **418–421,** 423, 430

Practical Education (Edgeworth), **Supp. III:** 152

Practice of Piety, The (Bayly), **II:** 241

Practice of Writing, The (Lodge), **Supp. IV:** 366, 381

Praed, Winthrop Mackworth, **IV:** 269, 283; **V:** 14

Praeterita (Ruskin), **V:** 174, 175, 182, 184

"Prague Milk Bottle, The" (Motion), **Supp. VII:** 262

"Praise for Mercies, Spiritual and Temporal" (Blake), **III:** 294

"Praise for the Fountain Opened" (Cowper), **III:** 211

Praise of Age, The (Henryson), **Supp. VII:** 146, 148

"Praise of My Lady" (Morris), **V:** 295

"Praise of Pindar, The" (Cowley), **II:** 200

"Praise II" (Herbert), **II:** 129; **Retro. Supp. II:** 177

Praises (Jennings), **Supp. V:** 219

Prancing Nigger (Firbank; British title, *Sorrow in Sunlight*), **Supp. II:** 200, 202, 204, 205, 211, 213, **218–220, 222, 223**

Prater Violet (Isherwood), **VII:** 313–314

Pravda (Hare and Brenton), **Supp. IV:** 282, 283, 284, 285, 286, 293

Praxis (Weldon), **Supp. IV:** 522, 525–526, 528, 533

"Prayer, A" (Joyce), **Retro. Supp. I:** 179

"Prayer Before Birth" (MacNeice), **VII:** 415

"Prayer for My Daughter, A" (Yeats), **VI:** 217, 220; **Supp. V:** 39; **Retro. Supp. I:** 333

"Prayer 1" (Herbert), **II:** 122; **Retro. Supp. II:** 179

Prayers Written at Vailima (Stevenson), **V:** 396

Praz, Mario, **I:** 146, 292, 354; **II:** 123; **III:** 329, 337, 344–345, 346; **V:** 412, 420; **VII:** 60, 62, 70

"Precautions in Free Thought" (Butler), **Supp. II:** 99

Predictions for the Year 1708 (Swift), **III:** 35

Pre'eminent Victorian: A Study of Tennyson, The (Richardson), **IV:** 339

"Preface" (Arnold), **Supp. II:** 57

"Preface: Mainly About Myself" (Shaw), **VI:** 129

Preface to Paradise Lost, " (Lewis), **Supp. III:** 240, 265

Preface to the Dramatic Works of Dryden (ed. Congreve), **II:** 348, 350

Prefaces (Dryden), **IV:** 349

"Prefaces" (Housman), **VI:** 156

"Prefatory Letter on Reading the Bible for the First Time" (Moore), **VI:** 96

"Prefatory Poem to My Brother's Sonnets" (Tennyson), **IV:** 327, 336

Preiching of the Swallow, The (Henryson), **Supp. VII:** 136, 139–140

"Prelude" (Mansfield), **VII:** 177, 179, 180

"Prelude, A" (Lawrence), **VII:** 114

Prelude, The (Wordsworth) **IV:** ix–x, xxi, 1, 2, 3, **11–17,** 24, 25, 43, 151, 315; **V:** 310

"Prelude and History" (Redgrove), **Supp. VI:** 236

"Preludes" (Eliot), **Retro. Supp. II:** 121

Premonition to Princes, A (Ralegh), **I:** 154

Preoccupations: Selected Prose 1968–1978 (Heaney), **Supp. II:** 268–269, 272, 273

Pre'Raphaelite Imagination, The (Dixon Hunt), **VI:** 167

Pre'Raphaelitism (Ruskin), **V:** 184

Prerogative of Parliaments, The (Ralegh), **I:** 157–158

"Presage of the Ruin of the Turkish Empire, A" (Waller), **II:** 233

Presbyterians' Plea of Merit, The (Swift), **III:** 36

Prescott, William H., **VI:** 394

Present and the Past, The (Compton'Burnett), **VII:** 61, 62

"Present and the Past: Eliot's Demonstration, The" (Leavis), **VII:** 237

"Present Estate of Pompeii" (Lowry), **Supp. III:** 281–282

Present Laughter (Coward), **Supp. II:** 153–154, 156

Present Position of History, The (Trevelyan), **VI:** 383

Present State of All Nations, The (Smollet), **III:** 158

Present State of the Parties in Great Britain, The (Defoe), **III:** 13

Present State of Wit, The (Gay), **III:** 44, 67

"Present Time, The" (Carlyle), **IV:** 247–248

Present Times (Storey), **Supp. I:** 408, 419–420

"Preserved" (Ewart), **Supp. VII:** 44

President's Child, The (Weldon), **Supp. IV:** 530–531

Press Cuttings: A Topical Sketch (Shaw), **VI:** 115, 117, 118–119, 129

Press, John, **VI:** xvi, xxxiv; **VII:** xxii, xxxviii

Preston, Thomas, **I:** 122, 213

Pretty Lady, The (Bennett), **VI:** 250, 251, 259

Previous Convictions (Connolly), **Supp. III:** 110

Prévost, Antoine, **III:** 333

Price, Alan, **VI:** 314

Price, Cecil, **III:** 258*n*, 261, 264, 268, 271

Price, Cormell, **VI:** 166, 167

Price, Richard, **IV:** 126

"Price, The" (Stevenson), **Supp. VI:** 260

Price of Everything, The (Motion), **Supp. VII:** 253, 254, 260–262

Price of Salt, The (Highsmith), **Supp. V:** 167, 169–170

Price of Stone, The (Murphy), **Supp. V:** 313, 315, 316, 326–329

"Price of Stone, The" (Murphy), **Supp. V:** 327

"Price of Things, The" (Ewart), **Supp. VII:** 42

Pride and Prejudice (Austen), **III:** 91, 336; **IV:** xvii, 103–104, 108–120, 122; **Supp. IV:** 235, 521; **Retro. Supp. II:** 7–9

Pride and Prejudice (television adaptation, Weldon), **Supp. IV:** 521

Pride's Cure (Lamb), *see John Woodvie*

Priest to the Temple, A; or, The Country Parson His Character etc. (Herbert), **II:** 120, 141; **Retro. Supp. II:** 176

Priestley, J. B., **IV:** 160, 170; **V:** xxvi, 96; **VII:** xii, xviii, 60, **209–231**

Priestley, Joseph, **III:** 290

"Prima Belladonna" (Ballard), **Supp. V:** 21

"Prime Minister" (Churchill), **VI:** 349

Prime Minister, The (Trollope), **V:** xxiv, 96, 97, 98–99, 101, 102

Prime of Miss Jean Brodie, The (Spark), **Supp. I:** 200, 201, 204–206

Primer, The; or, Office of the B. Virgin Mary (Dryden), **II:** 304

Prince, F. T., **VII:** xxii 422, 427

Prince Caspian (Lewis), **Supp. III:** 248, 260

Prince Hohenstiel'Schwangau, Saviour of Society (Browning), **IV:** 358, 369, 374

Prince Otto (Stevenson), **V:** 386, 395

Prince Prolétaire (Swinburne), **V:** 333

"Prince Roman" (Conrad), **VI:** 148

"Prince's Progress, The" (Rossetti), **V:** 250, 258, 259

Prince's Progress and Other Poems, The (Rossetti), **V:** 250, 260

Princess, The (Tennyson), **IV:** xx, 323, 325, 328, 333–334, 336, 338

Princess Casamassima, The (James), **VI:** 27, 39, **41–43,** 67

Princess Zoubaroff, The (Firbank), **Supp. II:** 202, 204, 205, **215–216**

Principia Ethica (Moore), **Supp. III:** 49

Principles and Persuasions (West), **VI:** 241

Principles of Literary Criticism (Richards), **Supp. II:** 405, **411–417**

Pringle, David, **Supp. V:** 32

Prior, Matthew, **II:** 265

Prioress's Prologue, The (Chaucer), **I:** 37

Prioress's Tale, The (Chaucer), **I:** 22, 34

"Prison" (Murphy), **Supp. V:** 329

"Prisoner, The" (Brontë), **V:** 142, 143, 254

"Prisoner, The" (Browning), **IV:** 313–314

Prisoner of Chillon, The (Byron), **IV:** 180, 192

Prisoner of Grace (Cary), **VII:** 186, 194–195

Prisoners (Stevenson), **Supp. VI:** 265

Prisoners of Mainz, The (Waugh), **Supp. VI:** 269

"Prisoner's Progress" (MacNeice), **VII:** 406

Prisons We Choose to Live Inside (Lessing), **Supp. I:** 239, 254–255

Pritchett, V. S., **IV:** 120, 298, 306; **Supp. III:** 99, 102, 211, **311–331**

"Private, A" (Thomas), **Supp. III:** 403, 404, 406

Private Ear, The (Shaffer), **Supp. I:** 317–318, 322, 323, 327

"Private Life, The" (James), **VI:** 48, 67, 69; **Retro. Supp. I:** 2

Private Life of Henry Maitland, The (Roberts), **V:** 425, 427, 438

Private Lives (Coward), **Supp. II:** 139, **147–149,** 155–156

Private Papers of Henry Ryecroft, The (Gissing), **V:** 424, 425, 427, **430–432,** 436, 437

Private Papers of James Boswell . . . , The (ed. Pottle and Scott), **III:** 234n, 247, 249

"Private Place, The" (Muir), **Supp. VI:** 206

"Private Tuition by Mr. Bose" (Desai), **Supp. V:** 65

Private View, A (Brookner), **Supp. IV:** 135

Privy Seal (Ford), **VI:** 324, 326

"Pro and Con on Aragon" (Stead), **Supp. IV:** 466

Pro populo anglicano defensio . . . (Milton), **II:** 176

Pro populo anglicano definsio secunda (Milton), **II:** 176

"Probable Future of Metaphysics, The" (Hopkins), **V:** 362

"Problem, The" (Swift), **III:** 32

Problem of Pain, The (Lewis), **Supp. I:** 71; **Supp. III:** 248, 255–256

"Problem of Prose, The" (Leavis), **VII:** 248

"Problem of Thor Bridge, The" (Doyle), **Supp. II:** 172, 174

Process of Real Freedom, The (Cary), **VII:** 186

"Procrastination" (Crabbe), **III:** 281, 285

Prodigal Child, A (Storey), **Supp. I:** 408, 419

"Proferred Love Rejected" (Suckling), **II:** 227

Professional Foul (Stoppard), **Supp. I:** 451, 453; **Retro. Supp. II:** 351–352

"Professions for Women" (Woolf), **Retro. Supp. I:** 310

Professor, The (Brontë), **V:** xxii, 112, 122, 123, 125, 132, **134–137,** 148, 150, 151, 152; **Retro. Supp. I:** 52

"Professor, The" (Thackeray), **V:** 21, 37

"Professor Fargo" (James), **VI:** 69

Professors and Gods (Fuller), **Supp. VII:** 77

Professor's Love Story, The (Barrie), **Supp. III:** 4

"Profile of Arthur J. Mason, A" (Ishiguro), **Supp. IV:** 304

Profitable Meditations . . . (Bunyan), **II:** 253

"Programme Note" (Fuller), **Supp. VII:** 80

Progress and Poverty (George), **VI:** viii

Progress of Julius, The (du Maurier), **Supp. III:** 139, 140, 144

"Progress of Poesy" (Gray), **II:** 200; **III:** 140

"Progress of Poesy, The" (Arnold), **V:** 209

"Progress of the Soul, The" (Donne), **II:** 209

Progymnasmata (More), **Supp. VII:** 236

"Project for a New Novel" (Ballard), **Supp. V:** 21

Project for the Advancement of Religion . . . , A (Swift), **III:** 26, 35, 46

"Proletariat and Poetry, The" (Day Lewis), **Supp. III:** 120

Prolific and the Devourer, The (Auden), **Retro. Supp. I:** 10

Prologue (Henryson), **Supp. VII:** 136

"Prologue to an Autobiography" (Naipaul), **Supp. I:** 385

Prometheus Bound (Aeschylus), **IV:** 199

Prometheus Bound, Translated from the Greek of Aeschylus (Browning), **IV:** 310, 321

Prometheus on His Crag (Hughes), **Supp. I:** 354–355, 363

Prometheus the Firegiver (Bridges), **VI:** 83

Prometheus Unbound (Shelley), **III:** 331; **IV:** xviii, 176, 179, 196, 198, **199–201,** 202, 207, 208; **VI:** 449–450; **Supp. III:** 370; **Retro. Supp. I:** 250, 251–253

"Promise, The" (James), **VI:** 49

Promise and Fulfillment (Koestler), **Supp. I:** 33

Promos and Cassandra (Whetstone), **I:** 313

Promus of Formularies and Elegancies, A (Bacon), **I:** 264, 271

"Propagation of Knowledge" (Kipling), **VI:** 200

Proper Marriage, A (Lessing), **Supp. I:** 238, 244

Proper Studies (Huxley), **VII:** 198, 201

"Property of Colette Nervi, The" (Trevor), **Supp. IV:** 500

Prophecy (Seltzer), **III:** 345

Prophecy of Dante, The (Byron), **IV:** 193

Prophesy to the Wind (Nicholson), **Supp. VI:** **221–222**

Prophetess, The (Fletcher and Massinger), **II:** 55, 66

"Prophets, The" (Auden), **Retro. Supp. I:** 9

"Prophet's Hair, The" (Rushdie), **Supp. IV:** 438

Proposal for Correcting . . . the English Tongue, A (Swift), **III:** 29, 35

Proposal for Giving Badges to the Beggars . . . of Dublin, A (Swift), **III:** 36

Proposal for Making an Effectual Provision for the Poor, A (Fielding), **III:** 105; **Retro. Supp. I:** 81

Proposal for Putting Reform to the Vote, A (Shelley), **IV:** 208

Proposals for an Association of . . . Philanthropists . . . (Shelley), **IV:** 208

Proposals for Publishing Monthly . . . (Smollett), **III:** 148

Proposals for the Universal Use of Irish Manufacture . . . (Swift), **III:** 27–28, 35

Propositions for the Advancement of Experimental Philosophy, A (Cowley), **II:** 196, 202

Prose Works, The (Swift), **III:** 15n 35

Proserpine, The (Rossetti), **V:** 295

Prosody of A Paradise Lost" and A Samson Agonistes," The (Bridges), **VI:** 83

Prospero's Cell (Durrell), **Supp. I:** 96, 100, 110–111

Protestant Monastery, The; or, A Complaint against the Brutality of the Present Age (Defoe), **III:** 14

"Proteus; or, Matter" (Bacon), **I:** 267

Prothalamion (Spenser), **I:** 124, 131

"Proud word you never spoke, but you will speak" (Landor), **IV:** 99

Proust, Marcel, **V:** xxiv, 45, 174, 183; **Supp. I:** 44–45; **Supp. IV:** 126, 136, 139

Proust Screenplay, The (Pinter), **Supp. I:** 378

Provence (Ford), **VI:** 324

"Proverbs of Hell" (Blake), **III:** 298; **Retro. Supp. I:** 38

Providence (Brookner), **Supp. IV:** 124–125, 131

"Providence" (Herbert), **Retro. Supp. II:** 177

"Providence and the Guitar" (Stevenson), **V:** 395

Provincial Pleasures (Nicholson), **Supp. VI:** 223

Provok'd Husband, The (Cibber), **II:** 326, 337

Provok'd Wife, The (Vanbrugh), **II:** 325, **329–332,** 334, 336, 360

Provost, The (Galt), **IV:** 35

Prussian Officer, The, and Other Stories (Lawrence), **VII:** 114

Pryce-Jones, Alan, **VII:** 70

Prynne, William, **II:** 339; **Supp. III:** 23

"Psalm of Montreal, A" (Butler), **Supp. II:** 105

"Psalms of Assize" (Hill), **Supp. V:** 193

Pseudodoxia Epidemica (Browne), **II:** 149–150, 151, 155, 156, 345n

Pseudo-Martyr (Donne), **I:** 352–353, 362; **Retro. Supp. II:** 97

Psmith Journalist (Wodehouse), **Supp. III:** 450

Psyche's Task (Frazer), **Supp. III:** 185
Psycho (film), **III:** 342–343
Psycho Apocalypté, a Lyrical Drama (Browning and Horne), **IV:** 321
Psychoanalysis and the Unconscious (Lawrence), **VII:** 122; **Retro. Supp. II:** 234
"Psychology of Advertising, The" (Sayers), **Supp. III:** 345
Psychology of the Unconscious (Jung), **Supp. IV:** 3
"Psychopolis" (McEwan), **Supp. IV:** 395–396
Puberty Tree, The (Thomas), **Supp. IV:** 490
"Puberty Tree, The" (Thomas), **Supp. IV:** 492–493
Public Address (Blake), **III:** 305
Public Burning, The (Coover), **Supp. IV:** 116
Public Eye, The (Shaffer), **Supp. I:** 317, 318–319, 327
Public Image, The (Spark), **Supp. I:** 200, 208–209, 218n
Public Ledger (periodical), **III:** 179, 188
Public School Life: Boys, Parents, Masters (Waugh), **Supp. VI:** 267, 270
"Public Son of a Public Man, The" (Spender), **Supp. II:** 483
Publick Employment and an Active Life Prefer'd to Solitude (Evelyn), **II:** 287
Publick Spirit of the Whigs, The (Swift), **III:** 35
Puck of Pook's Hill (Kipling), **VI:** viii, 169, 204
Puffball (Weldon), **Supp. IV:** 531, 533–534
Pulci, Luigi, **IV:** 182, 188
Pumpkin Eater, The (Pinter), **Supp. I:** 374
Punch (periodical), **IV:** 263; **V:** xx, 19, 23, 24–25; **VI:** 367, 368; **Supp. II:** 47, 49
Punch's Prize Novelists (Thackeray), **V:** 22, 38
"Pupil, The" (James), **VI:** 49, 69
Purcell, Henry, **Retro. Supp. II:** 196
Purcell Commemoration Ode (Bridges), **VI:** 81
Purchas's Pilgrimage, **IV:** 46
Pure Poetry. An Anthology (Moore), **VI:** 99
Purgatorio (Dante), **Supp. IV:** 439
Purgatorio (Heaney), **Retro. Supp. I:** 124
Purgatorio II (Eliot), **VII:** 151
Purgatory (Yeats), **VI:** 219
Puritan, The (anonymous), **I:** 194; **II:** 21
Puritan and the Papist, The (Cowley), **II:** 202
Purity of Diction in English Verse (Davie), **Supp. VI:** 107, **114**
"Purple" (Owen), **VI:** 449
Purple Dust (O'Casey), **VII:** 7, 8
"Purple Jar, The" (Edgeworth), **Supp. III:** 153
Purple Plain, The (Ambler), **Supp. IV:** 3
Pushkin, Aleksander, **III:** 339, 345; **Supp. IV:** 484, 495

Put Out More Flags (Waugh), **VII:** 290, 297–298, 300, 313
Puttenham, George, **I:** 94, 114, 119, 146, 214
Puzzleheaded Girl, The (Stead), **Supp. IV:** 476
"Pygmalion" (Gower), **I:** 53–54
Pygmalion (Shaw), **VI:** xv, 108, 115, 116–117, 120; **Retro. Supp. II:** 322
"Pylons, The" (Spender), **Supp. II:** 48
Pym, Barbara, **Supp. II: 363–384**
Pynchon, Thomas, **Supp. IV:** 116, 163
Pynson, Richard, **I:** 99
Pyramid, The (Golding), **Supp. I:** 81–82; **Retro. Supp. I:** 100–101
"Pyramis or The House of Ascent" (Hope), **Supp. VII:** 154
"Pyramus and Thisbe" (Gower), **I:** 53–54, 55
"Qua cursum ventus" (Clough), **V:** 160
Quadrille (Coward), **Supp. II:** 155
"Quaint Mazes" (Hill), **Supp. V:** 191
"Quality of Sprawl, The" (Murray), **Supp. VII:** 278–279
Quality Street (Barrie), **Supp. III:** 6, 8
"Quantity Theory of Insanity, The" (Self), **Supp. V:** 402
Quantity Theory of Insanity, The: Together with Five Supporting Propositions (Self), **Supp. V:** 395, 400–402
Quare Fellow, The (Behan), **Supp. II:** 65, **68–70,** 73
Quaritch, Bernard, **IV:** 343, 346, 348, 349
Quarles, Francis, **II:** 139, 246
Quarterly Review (periodical), **IV:** xvi, 60–61, 69, 133, 204–205, 269–270; **V:** 140
Quartermaine, Peter, **Supp. IV:** 348
Quartet (Rhys), **Supp. II:** 388, **390–392,** 403
Quartet in Autumn (Pym), **Supp. II: 380–382**
Queen, The; or, The Excellency of Her Sex (Ford), **II:** 88, 89, 91, 96, 100
"Queen Annelida and False Arcite" (Browning), **IV:** 321
Queen Is Crowned, A (Fry), **Supp. III:** 195
Queen Mab (Shelley), **IV:** xvii, 197, 201, 207, 208; **Retro. Supp. I:** 245–246
Queen Mary (Tennyson), **IV:** 328, 338
Queen of Corinth, The (Field, Fletcher, Massinger), **II:** 66
Queen of Hearts, The (Collins), **Supp. VI:** 95
"Queen of Spades, The" (Pushkin), **III:** 339–340, 345
Queen of the Air, The (Ruskin), **V:** 174, 180, 181, 184
Queen of the Dawn (Haggard), **Supp. III:** 222
Queen Sheba's Ring (Haggard), **Supp. III:** 214
Queen Victoria (Strachey), **Supp. II: 512–514**
Queen Was in the Parlor, The (Coward), **Supp. II:** 141, 146
Queen Yseult (Swinburne), **V:** 333
Queenhoo'Hall (Strutt), **IV:** 31

"Queenie Fat and Thin" (Brooke–Rose), **Supp. IV:** 103
Queen'Mother, The (Swinburne), **V:** 312, 313, 314, 330, 331, 332
Queen's Tragedy, The (Swinburne), **V:** 333
Queery Leary Nonsense (Lear), **V:** 87
Quennell, Peter, **V:** xii, xviii, 192, 193, 194; **VI:** 237; **Supp. III:** 107
Quentin Durward (Scott), **IV:** xviii, 37, 39
"Quest, The" (Saki), **Supp. VI:** 249
Quest sonnets (Auden), **VII:** 380–381; **Retro. Supp. I:** 2, 10
"Question, A" (Synge), **VI:** 314
"Question, The" (Shelley), **IV:** 203
"Question in the Cobweb, The" (Reid), **Supp. VII:** 326
"Question of Place, A" (Berger), **Supp. IV:** 92
Question of Proof, A (Day Lewis), **Supp. III:** 117, 131
Question of Upbringing, A (Powell), **VII:** 343, 347, 350, 351
Questions about the . . . Seventh'Day Sabbath (Bunyan), **II:** 253
"Questions in a Wood" (Graves), **VII:** 268
"Qui laborat orat" (Clough), **V:** 160
"Quiddite, The" (Herbert), **Retro. Supp. II:** 179
Quiet American, The (Greene), **Supp. I:** 7, 13, 14; **Supp. IV:** 369; **Retro. Supp. II:** 160–161
Quiet Life, A (Bainbridge), **Supp. VI:** 17, 21–22, 26–27
Quiet Memorandum, The (Pinter), **Supp. I:** 374
"Quiet Neighbours" (Warner), **Supp. VII:** 371
Quiet Wedding (Rattigan), **Supp. VII:** 311
"Quiet Woman of Chancery Lane, The" (Redgrove), **Supp. VI:** 235, 237
Quigley, Austin E., **Retro. Supp. I:** 227
Quiller'Couch, Sir Arthur, **II:** 121, 191; **V:** 384
Quillinan, Edward, **IV:** 143n
Quinlan, M. J., **III:** 220
Quinn Manuscript, **VII:** 148
Quintessence of Ibsenism, The (Shaw), **VI:** 104, 106, 129
"Quintets for Robert Morley" (Murray), **Supp. VII:** 278, 283
Quinx (Durrell), **Supp. I:** 119, 120
"Quip, The" (Herbert), **II:** 126
"Quis Optimus Reipvb. Status (What Is The Best Form of the Commonwealth?)" (More), **Supp. VII:** 238
"Quite Early One Morning" (Thomas), **Supp. I:** 183
Quoof (Muldoon), **Supp. IV:** 418–421, 422, 423, 425
"R.I. P." (Gissing), **V:** 43
R.L.S. and His Sine Qua Non (Boodle), **V:** 391, 393, 397
"Rabbit Catcher, The" (Hughes), **Retro. Supp. II:** 217–218

Rabelais, François, **III:** 24; **Supp. IV:** 464

Rachel Papers, The (Amis), **Supp. IV:** 26, 27, 28–29, 30

Rachel Ray (Trollope), **V:** 101

Racine, Jean Baptiste, **II:** 98; **V:** 22

Racing Demon (Hare), **Supp. IV:** 282, 294–296, 298

Radcliffe (Storey), **Supp. I:** 408, 410, 414, 415–416, 418–419

Radcliffe, Ann, **III:** 327, 331–332, 333, 335–338, 345; **IV:** xvi, 30, 35, 36, 111, 173, 218; **Supp. III:** 384

Radiant Way, The (Drabble), **Supp. IV:** 231, 234, 247–249, 250

Radical Imagination, The (Harris), **Supp. V:** 140, 145

Rafferty, Terrence, **Supp. IV:** 357, 360

Raffety, F. W., **III:** 199*n*

Raft of the Medusa, The (Géricault), **Supp. IV:** 71–72

"Rage for Order" (Mahon), **Supp. VI:** 170

Rage of the Vulture, The (Unsworth), **Supp. VII:** 356, 357, 359–360

Raiders' Dawn (Lewis), **VII:** 445, 448

Rain (Maugham), **VI:** 369

"Rain" (Thomas), **VI:** 424; **Supp. III:** 400, 401

"Rain Charm for the Duchy" (Hughes), **Supp. I:** 365; **Retro. Supp. II:** 214

"Rain Horse, The" (Hughes), **Supp. I:** 348

"Rain in Spain, The" (Reid), **Supp. VII:** 328

"Rain Stick, The" (Heaney), **Retro. Supp. I:** 132–133

Rain upon Godshill (Priestley), **VII:** 209, 210

Rainbow, The (Lawrence), **VI:** 232, 276, 283; **VII:** 88, 90, 93, **98–101; Retro. Supp. II:** 227–228

Raine, Kathleen, **III:** 297, 308

"Rainy Night, A" (Lowry), **Supp. III:** 270

Raj Quartet (Scott), **Supp. I:** 259, 260, 261–262, **266–272**

"Rajah's Diamond, The" (Stevenson), **V:** 395

Rajan, B., **VI:** 219

Rake's Progress, The (Auden/Kallman), **Retro. Supp. I:** 10

Raknem, Ingwald, **VI:** 228

Ralegh, Sir Walter, **I: 145–159**, 277, 278, 291; **II:** 138; **III:** 120, 122, 245; **VI:** 76, 157; **Retro. Supp. I:** 203–204

Raleigh, Sir Walter, *see* Ralegh, Sir Walter

Ralph the Heir (Trollope), **V:** 100, 102

Rambler (Newman), **Supp. VII:** 299

Rambler (periodical), **II:** 142; **III:** 94, 110–111, 112, 119, 121; **Retro. Supp. I:** 137, 140–141, 149

Rambles Among the Oases of Tunisia (Douglas), **VI:** 305

Ramillies and the Union with Scotland (Trevelyan), **VI:** 392–393

Ramsay, Allan, **III:** 312, 313; **IV:** 28

Ramsay, Andrew, **III:** 99, 100

Randall, H. S., **IV:** 275

Randolph, Thomas, **II:** 222, 237, 238

Rank and Riches (Collins), **Supp. VI:** 93

Ranke, Leopold von, **IV:** 288

Rao, Raja, **Supp. IV:** 440; **Supp. V:** 56

Rape of Lucrece, The (Shakespeare), **I:** 306–307, 325; **II:** 3

Rape of the Lock, The (Pope), **III:** 70–71, 75, 77; **Retro. Supp. I:** 231, 233

"Rape of the Sherlock, The" (Milne), **Supp. V:** 297

Rape upon Rape (Fielding), **III:** 105

"Rapparees" (Murphy), **Supp. V:** 323

"Rapture, A" (Carew), **II:** 223

Rash Act, The (Ford), **VI:** 319, 331

"Raspberry Jam" (Wilson), **Supp. I:** 154, 157

Rat Trap, The (Coward), **Supp. II:** 146

"Ratcatcher, The" (Dahl), **Supp. IV:** 214

Ratchford, Fannie, **V:** 133, 151, 152

"Rats, The" (Sillitoe), **Supp. V:** 424

Rats and Other Poems, The (Sillitoe), **Supp. V:** 409, 424

Rattigan, Terence, **Supp. VII: 307–322**

Raven, The (Poe), **V:** xx, 409

"Ravenna" (Wilde), **V:** 401, 409

"Ravenswing, The" (Thackeray), **V:** 23, 35, 36

Raw Material (Sillitoe), **Supp. V:** 411, 414–415, 422, 423

"Rawdon's Roof" (Lawrence), **VII:** 91

Rawley, William, **I:** 257

Ray, G. N., **V:** 37, 39

Ray, Satyajit, **Supp. IV:** 434, 450

Raymond Asquith: Life and Letters (Jolliffe), **VI:** 428

Raysor, T. M., **IV:** 46, 51, 52, 56, 57

Razor's Edge, The (Maugham), **VI:** 374, 377–378

Read, Herbert, **III:** 134; **VI:** 416, 436–437; **VII:** 437

Reade, Winwood, **Supp. IV:** 2

Reader (periodical), **III:** 50, 53

Reader's Guide to G. M. Hopkins, A (MacKenzie), **V:** 374, 382

Reader's Guide to Joseph Conrad, A (Karl), **VI:** 135

Readie & Easie Way to Establish a Free Commonwealth . . . (Milton), **II:** 176; **Retro. Supp. II:** 271

"Reading and Writhing in a Double Bind" (Lodge), **Supp. IV:** 385

"Reading Lesson, The" (Murphy), **Supp. V:** 316, 325

Reading of Earth, A (Meredith), **V:** 221, 234

Reading of George Herbert, A (Tuve), **II:** 124, 130; **Retro. Supp. II:** 174

Reading of Life, A, and Other Poems (Meredith), **V:** 234

"Reading the Elephant" (Motion), **Supp. VII:** 260, 263

Reading Turgenev (Trevor), **Supp. IV:** 516

Readings in Crabbe's "Tales of the Hall" (Fitzgerald), **IV:** 349, 353

Reagan, Ronald, **Supp. IV:** 485

"Real and Made–Up People" (Amis), **Supp. II:** 10

Real Inspector Hound, The (Stoppard), **Supp. I:** 443–444; **Retro. Supp. II:** 345–346

Real Robert Louis Stevenson, The, and Other Critical Essays (Thompson), **V:** 450, 451

"Real Thing, The" (James), **VI:** 48, 69

Real Thing, The (Stoppard), **Supp. I:** 451–452; **Retro. Supp. II:** 353–354

Realists, The (Snow), **VII:** 338–339

Realms of Gold, The (Drabble), **Supp. IV:** 230, 232, 243–245, 246, 248, 251

"Realpolitik" (Wilson), **Supp. I:** 154, 157

Reardon, Derek, **Supp. IV:** 445

"Rear–Guard, The" (Sassoon), **VI:** 431; **Supp. III:** 59

Reason and Sensuality (Lydgate), **I:** 57, 64

Reason of Church Government Urg'd Against Prelaty, The (Milton), **II:** 162, 175; **Retro. Supp. II:** 269, 276

"Reason our Foe, let us destroy" (Wycherley), **II:** 321

Reasonable Life, The: Being Hints for Men and Women (Bennett), *see Mental Efficiency*

Reasons Against the Succession of the House of Hanover (Defoe), **III:** 13

Rebecca (du Maurier), **Supp. III:** 134, 135, 137–138, 139, 141, 142, 143, 144, 145–146, 147

Rebecca and Rowena: A Romance upon Romance (Thackeray), **V:** 38

"Recantation, A" (Kipling), **VI:** 192–193

"Receipt to Restore Stella's Youth . . . , A" (Swift), **III:** 32

"Recessional" (Kipling), **VI:** 203

Recklings (Hughes), **Supp. I:** 346, 348

"Recollections" (Pearsall Smith), **VI:** 76

Recollections of Christ's Hospital (Lamb), **IV:** 85

"Recollections of Solitude" (Bridges), **VI:** 74

Recollections of the Lake Poets (De Quincey), **IV:** 146*n*, 155

"Reconcilement between Jacob Tonson and Mr. Congreve, The" (Rowe), **II:** 324

"Record, The" (Warner), **Supp. VII:** 371

"Record of Badalia Herodsfoot, The" (Kipling), **VI:** 167, 168

Record of Friendship, A (Swinburne), **V:** 333

Record of Friendship and Criticism, A (Smith), **V:** 391, 396, 398

Records of a Family of Engineers (Stevenson), **V:** 387, 396

Recoveries (Jennings), **Supp. V:** 211

"Recovery, The" (Vaughan), **II:** 185

Recruiting Officer, The (Farquhar), **II:** 353, 358–359, 360, 361, 362, 364

Rectory Umbrella and Mischmasch, The (Carroll), **V:** 264, 273

"Red" (Hughes), **Retro. Supp. II:** 218

Red Badge of Courage, The (Crane), **Supp. IV:** 116

Red Cotton Night–Cap Country (Browning), **IV:** 358, 369, 371, 374

Red Days and White Nights (Koestler), **Supp. I:** 23

"Red Front" (Warner), **Supp. VII:** 372
Red Harvest (Hammett), **Supp. II:** 130
Red House Mystery, The (Milne), **Supp. V:** 310
Red Peppers (Coward), **Supp. II:** 153
"Red, Red Rose, A" (Burns), **III:** 321
Red Roses for Me (O'Casey), **VII:** 9
"Red Rubber Gloves" (Brooke–Rose), **Supp. IV:** 104
"Redeeming the Time" (Hill), **Supp. V:** 186
"Redemption" (Herbert), **II:** 126–127
Redgauntlet (Scott), **IV:** xviii, 31, 35, 39
Redgrove, Peter, **Supp. VI: 225–238**
"Red–Headed League, The" (Doyle), **Supp. II:** 170
Redimiculum Matellarum [A Necklace of Chamberpots] (Bunting), **Supp. VII:** 4
"Redriff" (Jones), **Supp. VII:** 176
"Reed, A" (Browning), **IV:** 313
Reed, Henry, **VII:** 422–423, 449
Reed, J. W., **III:** 249
Rees–Mogg, W., **II:** 288
Reeve, C., **III:** 345
Reeve, Clara, **III:** 80
Reeve's Tale, The (Chaucer), **I:** 37, 41
"Reflection from Anita Loos" (Empson), **Supp. II:** 183–184
Reflections (Greene), **Retro. Supp. II:** 166–167
"Reflections of a Kept Ape" (McEwan), **Supp. IV:** 394
"Reflections on a Peninsula" (Koestler), **Supp. I:** 34
Reflections on Hanging (Koestler), **Supp. I:** 36
"Reflections on Leaving a Place of Retirement" (Coleridge), **IV:** 44
"Reflections on the Death of a Porcupine" (Lawrence), **VII:** 103–104, 110, 119
Reflections on the French Revolution (Burke), **III:** 195, 197, 201–205; **IV:** xv, 127; **Supp. III:** 371, 467, 468, 470
Reflections on the Late Alarming Bankruptcies in Scotland (Boswell), **III:** 248
Reflections on the Psalms (Lewis), **Supp. III:** 249, 264
Reflections on Violence (Hulme), **Supp. VI:** 145
Reflections upon Ancient and Modern Learning (Wotton), **III:** 23
Reflections upon the Late Great Revolution (Defoe), **Retro. Supp. I:** 64
Reflector (periodical), **IV:** 80
Reformation of Manners (Defoe), **III:** 12
"Refusal to mourn, A" (Thomas), **Supp. I:** 178
Refutation of Deism, in a Dialogue, A (Shelley), **IV:** 208
"Refutation of Philosophies" (Bacon), **I:** 263
"Regency Houses" (Day Lewis), **Supp. III:** 127–128
Regeneration (Barker), **Supp. IV:** 45, 46, 57–59
Regeneration (Haggard), **Supp. III:** 214
"Regeneration" (Vaughan), **II:** 185, 187
Regent, The (Bennett), **VI:** 259, 267

Regicide, The (Smollett), **III:** 158
"Regina Cara" (Bridges), **VI:** 81
Reginald (Saki), **Supp. VI:** 240–242
"Reginald at the Theatre" (Saki), **Supp. VI:** 241–242
Reginald in Russia and Other Sketches (Saki), **Supp. VI:** 243–246
"Reginald on the Academy" (Saki), **Supp. VI:** 240
"Reginald's Choir Treat" (Saki), **Supp. VI:** 241, 249
"Regret" (Swinburne), **V:** 332
Rehabilitations (Lewis), **Supp. III:** 249
Rehearsal, The (Buckingham), **II:** 206, 294
Rehearsal Transpros'd, The (Marvell), **II:** 205, 206–207, 209, 218, 219; **Retro. Supp. II:** 257–258, 264–266
Reid, Alastair, **Supp. VII: 323–337**
Reid, J. C., **IV:** 254, 267
Reign of Sparrows, The (Fuller), **Supp. VII:** 79
Rejected Address (Smith), **IV:** 253
"Relapse, The" (Vaughan), **II:** 187
Relapse, The; or, Virtue in Danger (Vanbrugh), **II:** 324, 326–329, 332, 334, 335, 336; **III:** 253, 261
Relation Between Michael Angelo and Tintoret, The (Ruskin), **V:** 184
Relationship of the Imprisonment of Mr. John Bunyan, A (Bunyan), **II:** 253
Relative Values (Coward), **Supp. II:** 155
Relatively Speaking (Ayckbourn), **Supp. V:** 2, 4, 13
"Relativity" (Empson), **Supp. II:** 182
Religio Laici; or, A Layman's Faith (Dryden), **I:** 176, 189; **II:** 291, 299, 304
Religio Medici (Browne), **II:** 146–148, 150, 152, 156, 185; **III:** 40; **VII:** 29
"Religion" (Vaughan), **II:** 189
Religious Courtship: . . . Historical Discourses on . . . Marrying . . . (Defoe), **III:** 13
"Religious Musings" (Coleridge), **IV:** 43; **Retro. Supp. II:** 52
Reliques of Ancient English Poetry (Percy), **III:** 336; **IV:** 28–29
Reliquiae Wottonianae, **II:** 142
"Remain, ah not in youth alone" (Landor), **IV:** 99
Remains (Newman), **Supp. VII:** 295
Remains of Elmet (Hughes), **Supp. I:** 342; **Retro. Supp. II:** 210–211
Remains of Sir Walter Ralegh, The, **I:** 146, 157
Remains of the Day, The (Ishiguro), **Supp. IV:** 301–302, 304, 305, 306, 307, 311–314
Remake (Brooke–Rose), **Supp. IV:** 98, 99, 102
"Remarkable Rocket, The" (Wilde), **Retro. Supp. II:** 365
Remarks on Certain Passages of the 39 Articles (Newman), **Supp. VII:** 295–296
Remarks Upon a Late Disingenuous Discourse (Marvell), **II:** 219; **Retro. Supp. II:** 266

"Rembrandt's Late Self–Portraits" (Jennings), **Supp. V:** 211
Remede de Fortune (Machaut), **Retro. Supp. II:** 37
"Remember" (Rossetti), **VII:** 64
Remember Me (Weldon), **Supp. IV:** 535–536
"Remember Me When I Am Gone Away" (Rossetti), **V:** 249
"Remember Young Cecil" (Kelman), **Supp. V:** 245
"Remembering Old Wars" (Kinsella), **Supp. V:** 263
Remembering Sion (Ryan), **VII:** 2
"Remembering the 90s" (Mahon), **Supp. VI:** 177
"Remembering the Thirties" (Davie), **Supp. VI:** 106
Remembrances of Words and Matter Against Richard Cholmeley, **I:** 277
Reminiscences (Carlyle), **IV:** 70n, 239, 240, 245, 250
"Reminiscences of Charlotte Brontë" (Nussey), **V:** 108, 109, 152
Reminiscences of the Impressionistic Painters (Moore), **VI:** 99
Remorse (Coleridge), **IV:** 56
Remorse: A Study in Saffron (Wilde), **V:** 419
Renaissance: Studies in Art and Poetry, The (Pater), *see Studies in the History of the Renaissance*
Renan, Joseph Ernest, **II:** 244
Renegade Poet, And Other Essays, A (Thompson), **V:** 451
"Repentance" (Herbert), **II:** 128
"Rephan" (Browning), **IV:** 365
Replication (Skelton), **I:** 93
Reply to the Essay on Population, by the Rev. T. R. Malthus, A (Hazlitt), **IV:** 127, 139
"Report from Below, A" (Hood), **IV:** 258
"Report on a Threatened City" (Lessing), **Supp. I:** 250n
"Report on an Unidentified Space Station" (Ballard), **Supp. V:** 33
"Report on Experience" (Blunden), **VI:** 428
Report on the Salvation Army Colonies (Haggard), **Supp. III:** 214
"Reported Missing" (Scannell), **VII:** 424
Reports on Elementary Schools, 1852–1882 (Arnold), **V:** 216
Reprinted Pieces (Dickens), **V:** 72
Reprisal, The (Smollett), **III:** 149, 158
Reproof: A Satire (Smollett), **III:** 158
"Requiem" (Stevenson), **V:** 383; **Retro. Supp. I:** 268
"Requiem" (tr. Thomas), **Supp. IV:** 494–495
"Requiem for the Croppies" (Heaney), **Retro. Supp. I:** 127–128
"Requiescat" (Arnold), **V:** 211
"Requiescat" (Wilde), **V:** 400
Required Writing (Larkin), **Supp. I:** 286, 288
"Re–Reading Jane" (Stevenson), **Supp. VI:** 262
Rescue, The (Conrad), **VI:** 136, 147
Resentment (Waugh), **Supp. VI:** 270

"Resignation" (Arnold), **V:** 210

"Resolution and Independence" (Wordsworth), **IV:** 19–20, 22; **V:** 352

"Resound my voice, ye woods that hear me plain" (Wyatt), **I:** 110

Responsibilities (Yeats), **VI:** 213; **Retro. Supp. I:** 330

"Responsibility" (MacCaig), **Supp. VI:** 189

Responsio ad Lutherum (More), **Supp. VII:** 242–243

Ressoning betuix Aige and Yowth, The (Henryson), **Supp. VII:** 146, 147

Ressoning betuix Deth and Man, The (Henryson), **Supp. VII:** 146, 147

Restoration (Bond), **Supp. I:** 423, 434, 435

Restoration of Arnold Middleton, The (Storey), **Supp. I:** 408, 411, 412–413, 414, 415, 417

"Resurrection, The" (Cowley), **II:** 200

Resurrection, The (Yeats), **VI:** xiv, 222

"Resurrection and Immortality" (Vaughan), **II:** 185, 186

Resurrection at Sorrow Hill (Harris), **Supp. V:** 144

Resurrection of the Dead, The, . . . (Bunyan), **II:** 253

"Retaliation" (Goldsmith), **III:** 181, 185, 191

"Reticence of Lady Anne, The" (Saki), **Supp. VI:** 245

"Retired Cat, The" (Cowper), **III:** 217

"Retirement" (Vaughan), **II:** 187, 188, 189

"Retreat, The" (King), **Supp. VI:** 153

"Retreate, The" (Vaughan), **II:** 186, 188–189

"Retrospect" (Brooke), **Supp. III:** 56

"Retrospect: From a Street in Chelsea" (Day Lewis), **Supp. III:** 121

"Retrospective Review" (Hood), **IV:** 255

"Return, The" (Conrad), **VI:** 148

"Return, The" (Muir), **Supp. VI:** 207

Return from Parnassus, The, part 2, **II:** 27

"Return from the Freudian Islands, The" (Hope), **Supp. VII:** 155–156, 157

"Return from the Islands" (Redgrove), **Supp. VI:** 235

Return of Eva Peron, The (Naipaul), **Supp. I:** 396, 397, 398, 399

Return of the Druses, The (Browning), **IV:** 374

"Return of the Iron Man, The" (Hughes), **Supp. I:** 346

Return of the King, The (Tolkien), **Supp. II:** 519

Return of the Native, The (Hardy), **V:** xxiv, 279; **VI:** 1–2, 5, 6, 7, 8; **Retro. Supp. I:** 114

Return of the Soldier, The (West), **Supp. III:** 440, 441

Return of Ulysses, The (Bridges), **VI:** 83

Return to Abyssinia (White), **Supp. I:** 131

Return to My Native Land (tr. Berger), **Supp. IV:** 77

Return to Oasis (Durrell), **VII:** 425

Return to Yesterday (Ford), **VI:** 149

Returning (O'Brien), **Supp. V:** 339

"Returning, We Hear the Larks" (Rosenberg), **VI:** 434–435

Revaluation (Leavis), **III:** 68; **VII:** 234, 236, 244–245

"Reveille" (Hughes), **Supp. I:** 350

Revelations of Divine Love (Juliana of Norwich), **I:** 20–21

Revenge for Love, The (Lewis), **VII:** 72, 74, 81

Revenge Is Sweet: Two Short Stories (Hardy), **VI:** 20

Revenge of Bussy D'Ambois, The (Chapman), **I:** 251–252, 253; **II:** 37

Revenger's Tragedy, The, **II:** 1–2, 21, 29, **33–36,** 37, 39, 40, 41, 70, 97

Revengers' Comedies, The (Ayckbourn), **Supp. V:** 3, 10

Reverberator, The (James), **VI:** 67

"Reverie" (Browning), **IV:** 365

Reveries over Childhood and Youth (Yeats), **VI:** 222

Reversals (Stevenson), **Supp. VI:** 255–256

"Reversals" (Stevenson), **Supp. VI:** 256

Review (periodical), **II:** 325; **III:** 4, 13, 39, 41, 42, 51, 53

Review of some poems by Alexander Smith and Matthew Arnold (Clough), **V:** 158

Review of the Affairs of France, A . . . (Defoe), **III:** 13; **Retro. Supp. I:** 65

Review of the State of the British Nation, A (Defoe), **Retro. Supp. I:** 65

"Reviewer's ABC, A" (Aiken), **VII:** 149

Revised Version of the Bible, **I:** 381–382

Revolt in the Desert (Lawrence), **Supp. II:** 288, 289–290, 293

Revolt of Aphrodite, The (Durrell), *see Tunc; Nunquam*

Revolt of Islam, The (Shelley), **IV:** xvii, 198, 203, 208; **VI:** 455; **Retro. Supp. I:** 249–250

"Revolt of the Tartars" (De Quincey), **IV:** 149

"Revolution" (Housman), **VI:** 160

Revolution in Tanner's Lane, The (Rutherford), **VI:** 240

Revolutionary Epick, The (Disraeli), **IV:** 306, 308

Revolving Lights (Richardson), **Retro. Supp. I:** 313–314

Revue des Deux Mondes (Montégut), **V:** 102

"Revulsion" (Davie), **Supp. VI:** 110, 112

"Rex Imperator" (Wilson), **Supp. I:** 155, 156

"Reynard the Fox" (Masefield), **VI:** 338

Reynolds, G. W. M., **III:** 335

Reynolds, Henry, **Supp. IV:** 350

Reynolds, John, **II:** 14

Reynolds, John Hamilton, **IV:** 215, 221, 226, 228, 229, 232, 233, 253, 257, 259, 281

Reynolds, Sir Joshua, **II:** 336; **III:** 305

"Rhapsody of Life's Progress, A" (Browning), **IV:** 313

"Rhapsody on a Windy Night" (Eliot), **Retro. Supp. II:** 121–122

Rhetor (Harvey), **I:** 122

"Rhetoric" (De Quincey), **IV:** 147

"Rhetoric" (Jennings), **Supp. V:** 218

"Rhetoric and Poetic Drama" (Eliot), **VII:** 157

"Rhetoric of a Journey" (Fuller), **Supp. VII:** 72

Rhetoric of the Unreal: Studies in Narrative and Structure, Especially of the Fantastic, A (Brooke–Rose), **Supp. IV:** 97, 99, 115, 116

"Rhineland Journal" (Spender), **Supp. II:** 489

Rhoda Fleming (Meredith), **V:** xxiii, 227n, 234

"Rhodian Captain" (Durrell), **Supp. I:** 124

Rhododaphne (Peacock), **IV:** 158, 170

Rhyme? and Reason? (Carroll), **V:** 270, 273

Rhyme Stew (Dahl), **Supp. IV:** 226

Rhys, Jean, **Supp. II: 387–403; Supp. V:** 40; **Retro. Supp. I:** 60

"Rhythm and Imagery in British Poetry" (Empson), **Supp. II:** 195

"Ribblesdale" (Hopkins), **V:** 367, 372; **Retro. Supp. II:** 191

Ribner, Irving, **I:** 287

Riccoboni, Luigi, **II:** 348

Riceyman Steps (Bennett), **VI:** 250, 252, 260–261

Rich, Barnaby, **I:** 312

Rich Get Rich (Kavan), **Supp. VII:** 208–209

Richard II (Shakespeare), **I:** 286, 308

Richard III (Shakespeare), **I:** 285, 299–301

"Richard Martin" (Hood), **IV:** 267

Richard Rolle of Hampole, **I:** 20

Richards, I. A., **III:** 324; **V:** 367, 381; **VI:** 207, 208; **VII:** xiii, 233, 239; **Supp. I:** 185, 193, **405–431**

Richard's Cork Leg (Behan), **Supp. II:** 65, 74

Richards, Grant, **VI:** 158

Richardson, Betty, **Supp. IV:** 330

Richardson, Dorothy, **VI:** 372; **VII:** 20; **Supp. IV:** 233; **Retro. Supp. I:** 313–314

Richardson, Elaine Cynthia Potter, *see* Kincaid, Jamaica

Richardson, Joanna, **IV:** xxv, 236; **V:** xi, xviii

Richardson, Samuel, **III: 80–93,** 94, 98, 333; **VI:** 266 **Supp. II:** 10; **Supp. III:** 26, 30–31; **Supp. IV:** 150; **Retro. Supp. I:** 80

Ricks, Christopher, **Supp. IV:** 394, 398

"Riddle of Houdini, The" (Doyle), **Supp. II:** 163–164

Riddle of Midnight, The (film, Rushdie), **Supp. IV:** 436, 441

"Ride from Milan, The" (Swinburne), **V:** 325, 333

Riders in the Chariot (White), **Supp. I:** 131, 132, 133, 136, **141–143,** 152

Riders to the Sea (Synge), **VI:** xvi, 308, 309, 310–311; **Retro. Supp. I:** 296

Riding, Laura, **VI:** 207; **VII:** 258, 260, 261, 263, 269; **Supp. II:** 185; **Supp. III:** 120

Riding Lights (MacCaig), **Supp. VI:** 181, **185–186,** 190, 194

Riffaterre, Michael, **Supp. IV:** 115

Rigby, Elizabeth, **V:** 138

Right at Last and Other Tales (Gaskell), **V:** 15

Right Ho, Jeeves (Wodehouse), **Supp. III:** 458, 461

Right to an Answer, The (Burgess), **Supp. I:** 187, 188–189, 190, 195, 196

Righter, Anne, **I:** 224, 269, 329

Rilke, Rainer Maria, **VI:** 215; **Supp. IV:** 480

Rimbaud, Jean Nicolas, **Supp. IV:** 163

"Rime of the Ancient Mariner, The" (Coleridge), *see* "Ancient Mariner, The"

Riming Poem, The, **Retro. Supp. II:** 304

Ring, The (Wagner), **V:** 300

Ring and the Book, The (Browning), **IV:** xxiii, 358, 362, 369, 373, 374; **Retro. Supp. II:** 28–29

Ring Round the Moon (Fry), **Supp. III:** 195, 207

"Ringed Plover by a Water's Edge" (MacCaig), **Supp. VI:** 192

Rings on a Tree (MacCaig), **Supp. VI:** 190

Ripley Under Ground (Highsmith), **Supp. V:** 171

Ripley Under Water (Highsmith), **Supp. V:** 171

Ripley's Game (Highsmith), **Supp. V:** 171

Ripple from the Storm, A (Lessing), **Supp. I:** 244–245

Rise and Fall of the House of Windsor, The (Wilson), **Sup. VI:** 308

"Rise of Historical Criticism, The" (Wilde), **V:** 401, 419

Rise of Iskander, The (Disraeli), **IV:** 308

"Rising Five" (Nicholson), **Supp. VI: 216**

Rising of the Moon, The (Gregory), **VI:** 315, 316

Rise of the Russian Empire, The (Saki), **Supp. VI:** 239

Ritchie, Lady Anne, **V:** 10

"Rite and Fore–Time" (Jones), **Supp. VII:** 176

Rites of Passage (Golding), **Supp. I:** 86–87; **Retro. Supp. I:** 103–104

"Rites of Passage" (Gunn), **Supp. IV:** 266

"Ritual of Departure" (Kinsella), **Supp. V:** 264

"Rival, The" (Warner), **Supp. VII:** 371

Rival Ladies, The (Dryden), **II:** 293, 297, 305

Rivals, The (Sheridan), **III:** 253, **257–259,** 270

Rive, Richard, **Supp. II:** 342–343, 350

River (Hughes), **Supp. I:** 363; **Retro. Supp. II:** 212–214

"River, The" (Muir), **Supp. VI:** 206

River Dudden, The, a Series of Sonnets (Wordsworth), **IV:** 24

"River God, The" (Smith), **Supp. II:** 472

River Town, A (Keneally), **Supp. IV:** 347, 348

River War, The (Churchill), **VI:** 351

Rivers, W. H. R., **Supp. IV:** 46, 57, 58

Riverside Chaucer, The (ed. Benson), **Retro. Supp. II:** 49

Riverside Villas Murder, The (Amis), **Supp. II:** 12

Riviere, Michael, **VII:** 422, 424

"Road from Colonus, The" (Forster), **VI:** 399

"Road These Times Must Take, The" (Day Lewis), **Supp. III:** 126–127

"Road to Emmaus, The" (Brown), **Supp. VI:** 70

"Road to the Big City, A" (Lessing), **Supp. I:** 240

Road to Volgograd (Sillitoe), **Supp. V:** 409

Road to Wigan Pier, The (Orwell), **VII:** 274, 279–280

Road to Xanadu, The (Lowes), **IV:** 47, 57

"Road Uphill, The," (Maugham), **VI:** 377

"Roads" (Stevenson), **V:** 386

"Roads" (Thomas), **Supp. III:** 404, 406

Roald Dahl's Revolting Rhymes (Dahl), **Supp. IV:** 226

Roaring Girl, The (Dekker and Middleton), **II:** 3, 21

Roaring Queen, The (Lewis), **VII:** 82

Rob Roy (Scott), **IV:** xvii, 33, 34, 39

Robbe–Grillet, Alain, **Supp. IV:** 99, 104, 115, 116

Robbery Under Law (Waugh), **VII:** 292, 294

Robbins, Bruce, **Supp. IV:** 95

Robe of Rosheen, The (O'Casey), **VII:** 12

Robene and Makyne (Henryson), **Supp. VII:** 146, 147

Robert Bridges and Gerard Manley Hopkins (Ritz), **VI:** 83

Robert Bridges 1844–1930 (Thompson), **VI:** 83

"Robert Bridges: His Work on the English Language" (Daryush), **VI:** 76

Robert Browning (ed. Armstrong), **IV:** 375

Robert Browning (Chesterton), **VI:** 344

Robert Browning (Jack), **IV:** 375

Robert Browning: A Collection of Critical Essays (Drew), **IV:** 375

Robert Burns (Swinburne), **V:** 333

Robert Graves: His Life and Work (Seymour–Smith), **VII:** 272

Robert Louis Stevenson (Chesterton), **V:** 391, 393, 397; **VI:** 345

Robert Louis Stevenson (Cooper), **V:** 397, 398

Robert Louis Stevenson. An Essay (Stephen), **V:** 290

Robert Louis Stevenson: Man and Writer (Stewart), **V:** 393, 397

Robert Macaire (Stevenson), **V:** 396

Robert of Sicily: Opera for Children (Fry and Tippett), **Supp. III:** 194

Robert Southey and His Age (Carnall), **IV:** 72

Robert the Second, King of Scots (Jonson/Chettle/Dekker), **Retro. Supp. I:** 157

Roberts, Michael, **VII:** xix, 411

Roberts, Morley, **V:** 425, 427, 428, 438

Robertson, Thomas, **V:** 330; **VI:** 269

Robin Hood: A Fragment, by the Late Robert Southey, and Caroline Southey, **IV:** 71

Robinson, Henry Crabb, **IV:** 11, 52, 56, 81

Robinson, Henry Morton, **VII:** 53

Robinson, Lennox, **VI:** 96

Robinson (Spark), **Supp. I:** 201, 202–203

Robinson Crusoe (Defoe), **III:** 1, 5, 6, 7, 8, 10–12, 13, 24, 42, 50, 95; **Supp. I:** 73; **Retro. Supp. I:** 65–66, 68, 70–71

"Robinson Tradition, The" (Milne), **Supp. V:** 304

Roche, Denis, **Supp. IV:** 115

Roche, Maurice, **Supp. IV:** 116

Rochester, earl of, **II:** 208n, 255, 256, **257–261, 269–270;** **Supp. III:** 39, 40, 70

Rock, The (Eliot), **VII:** 153

"Rock, The" (Hughes), **Supp. I:** 341, 342; **Retro. Supp. II:** 199

Rock Face (Nicholson), **Supp. VI:** 213, **216–217**

Rock Pool, The (Connolly), **Supp. III:** **98–100**

Rockaby (Beckett), **Supp. I:** 61; **Retro. Supp. I:** 28–29

"Rocking–Horse Winner, The" (Lawrence), **Supp. IV:** 511

Roderick Hudson (James), **VI:** 24, **26–28,** 42, 67

Roderick Random (Smollett), **III: 150–152,** 158

Roderick, The Last of the Goths (Southey), **IV:** 65–66, 68, 71

Rodker, John, **VI:** 327

"Roger Ascham and Lady Jane Grey" (Landor), **IV:** 92

Roger Fry (Woolf), **Retro. Supp. I:** 308

Rogers, Charles, **III:** 249

Rogers, Woodes, **III:** 7

"Rois Fainéants" (Auden), **Retro. Supp. I:** 14

Rojas Zorilla, Francisco de, **II:** 325

Rokeby (Scott), **IV:** 38

Roland Whately (Waugh), **Supp. VI:** 270

"Roll for Joe, A" (Kelman), **Supp. V:** 244–245

"Rolling English Road, The" (Chesterton), **I:** 16

Rollins, Hyder, **IV:** 231, 232, 235

Rollo, Duke of Normandy (Chapman, Fletcher, Jonson, Massinger), **II:** 45, 66

Roman de la rose, **I:** 28, 49; tr. Chaucer, **I:** 28, 31

Roman de Troie (Benoît de Sainte–Maure), **I:** 53

Roman expérimental (Zola), **V:** 286

Roman Forgeries . . . (Traherne), **II:** 190, 191, 201

Roman History, The (Goldsmith), **III:** 180, 181, 191

Roman Quarry and Other Sequences, The (Jones), **Supp. VII:** 167, 171

Romance (Conrad and Ford), **VI:** 146, 148, 321

"Romance" (Sitwell), **VII:** 132–133

"Romance in Ireland" (Yeats), **Retro. Supp. I:** 330

"Romance of Certain Old Clothes, The" (James), **VI:** 69

Romantic Adventures of A Milkmaid, The (Hardy), **VI:** 20, 22

Romantic Agony, The (Praz), **III:** 337, 346; **V:** 412, 420

Romantic Image (Kermode), **V:** 344, 359, 412

Romantic Poetry and the Fine Arts (Blunden), **IV:** 236

"Romanticism and Classicism" (Hulme), **Supp. VI:** 135, 138, 142–145

"Romaunt of Margaret, The" (Browning), **IV:** 313

Romeo and Juliet (Shakespeare), **I:** 229, 305–306, 320; **II:** 281; **IV:** 218

Romola (Eliot), **V:** xxii, 66, 194–195, 200; **Retro. Supp. II:** 110–111

Romulus and Hersilia; or, The Sabine War (Behn), **Supp. III:** 29

Rondeaux Parisiens (Swinburne), **V:** 333

"Roof-Tree" (Murphy), **Supp. V:** 329

Rookwood (Ainsworth), **V:** 47

Room, The (Day Lewis), **Supp. III:** 118, 129–130

"Room, The" (Day Lewis), **Supp. III:** 130

Room, The (Pinter), **Supp. I:** 367, 369; **Retro. Supp. I:** 216, 218, 221–222

"Room Above the Square" (Spender), **Supp. II:** 494

Room at the Top (Braine), **Supp. IV:** 238

Room of One's Own, A (Woolf), **VII:** 22–23, 25–26, 27, 38; **Supp. III:** 19, 41–42; **Supp. V:** 36; **Retro. Supp. I:** 310–314

Room with a View, A (Forster), **VI:** 398, 399, **403–404**; **Retro. Supp. II:** 141–143

"Rooms of Other Women Poets, The" (Boland), **Supp. V:** 37

Rootham, Helen, **VII:** 129

Roots of Coincidence (Koestler), **Supp. I:** 39

"Roots of Honour, The" (Ruskin), **V:** 179–180

Roots of the Mountains, The (Morris), **V:** 302, 306

Roppen, G., **V:** 221*n*

Rosalind and Helen (Shelley), **IV:** 208

Rosalynde (Lodge), **I:** 312

Rosamond, Queen of the Lombards (Swinburne), **V:** 312–314, 330, 331, 332, 333

Rose, Ellen Cronan, **Supp. IV:** 232

"Rose, The" (Southey), **IV:** 64

Rose, The (Yeats), **Retro. Supp. I:** 330

Rose and Crown (O'Casey), **VII:** 13

Rose and the Ring, The (Thackeray), **V:** 38, 261

Rose Blanche (McEwan), **Supp. IV:** 390

Rose in the Heart, A (O'Brien), **Supp. V:** 339

"Rose in the Heart of New York, A" (O'Brien), **Supp. V:** 340–341

"Rose Mary" (Rossetti), **V:** 238, 244

Rosemary's Baby (film), **III:** 343

Rosenberg, Bruce, **Supp. IV:** 7

Rosenberg, Eleanor, **I:** 233

Rosenberg, Isaac, **VI:** xvi, 417, 420, **432–435**; **VII:** xvi; **Supp. III:** 59

Rosenberg, John, **V:** 316, 334

Rosencrantz and Guildenstern Are Dead (Stoppard), **Supp. I: 440–443**, 444, 451; **Retro. Supp. II:** 343–345

Rosenfeld, S., **II:** 271

"Roses on the Terrace, The" (Tennyson), **IV:** 329, 336

"Rosiphelee" (Gower), **I:** 53–54

Ross (Rattigan), **Supp. VII:** 320, 321

Ross, Alan, **VII:** xxii, 422, 433–434

Ross, John Hume (pseud., Lawrence), **Supp. II:** 286, 295

Rossetti, Christina, **V:** xi–xii, xix, xxii, xxvi, **247–260; Supp. IV:** 139

Rossetti, Dante Gabriel, **IV:** 346; **V:** ix, xi, xii, xviii, xxiii–xxv, **235–246**, 247–253, 259, 293–296, 298, 299, 312–315, 320, 329, 355, 401; **VI:** 167

Rossetti, Maria **V:** 251, 253

Rossetti, William, **V:** 235, 236, 245, 246, 248–249, 251–253, 260

Rossetti (Waugh), **VII:** 291

Rossetti and His Circle (Beerbohm), **Supp. II:** 51

"Rossetti's Conception of the 'Poetic' " (Doughty), **V:** 246

Røstvig, Maren-Sofie, **I:** 237

"Rosyfingered, The" (MacCaig), **Supp. VI:** 186

"Rot, The" (Lewis), **VII:** 73

Rotting Hill (Lewis), **VII:** 72

Rough Shoot (film, Ambler), **Supp. IV:** 3

Round and Round the Garden (Ayckbourn), **Supp. V:** 2, 5

Round of Applause, A (MacCaig), **Supp. VI: 187–188**, 190, 194–195

Round Table, The (Hazlitt), **IV:** xvii, 129, 137, 139

Round Table, The; or, King Arthur's Feast (Peacock), **IV:** 170

Round the Sofa (Gaskell), **V:** 3, 15

Roundabout Papers (Thackeray), **V:** 34, 35, 38

Roundheads, The; or, The Good Old Cause (Behn), **Supp. III:** 25

Rousseau, Jean Jacques, **III:** 235, 236; **IV:** xiv, 207; **Supp. III:** 239–240

Rover, The (Conrad), **VI:** 144, 147, 148

Rover, The; or, The Banish'd Cavaliers (Behn), **Supp. III:** 26, 27–29, 31

Rowe, Nicholas, **I:** 326

Rowley, Hazel, **Supp. IV:** 459, 460

Rowley, William, **II:** 1, 3, 14, 15, 18, 21, 66, 69, 83, 89, 100

Roxana (Defoe), **III:** 8–9, 14; **Retro. Supp. I:** 69, 74

Roy, Arundhati, **Supp. V:** xxx, 67, 75

Royal Academy, The (Moore), **VI:** 98

Royal Beasts, The (Empson), **Supp. II:** 180, 184

Royal Combat, The (Ford), **II:** 100

Royal Court Theatre, **VI:** 101

Royal Hunt of the Sun, The (Shaffer), **Supp. I:** 314, **319–322**, 323, 324, 327

"Royal Jelly" (Dahl), **Supp. IV:** 221

"Royal Man" (Muir), **I:** 247

"Royal Naval Air Station" (Fuller), **Supp. VII:** 69

Royal Pardon, The (Arden and D'Arcy), **Supp. II:** 30

Rubáiyát of Omar Khayyám, The (FitzGerald), **IV:** xxii, 342–343, **345–348**, 349, 352, 353; **V:** 318

Rubin, Merle, **Supp. IV:** 360

Rudd, Margaret, **VI:** 209

Rudd, Steele, **Supp. IV:** 460

Rude Assignment (Lewis), **VI:** 333; **VII:** xv, 72, 74, 76

Rudolf II, Emperor of Holy Roman Empire, **Supp. IV:** 174

Rudyard Kipling, Realist and Fabulist (Dobrée), **VI:** 200–203

Rudyard Kipling to Rider Haggard (ed. Cohen), **VI:** 204

Ruffhead, O., **III:** 69*n*, 71

Ruffian on the Stair, The (Orton), **Supp. V:** 367, 370, 372, 373

"Rugby Chapel" (Arnold), **V:** 203

Ruin, The, **Retro. Supp. II:** 305

Ruined Boys, The (Fuller), **Supp. VII:** 74, 75

"Ruined Cottage, The," (Wordsworth), **IV:** 23, 24

"Ruined Maid, The" (Hardy), **Retro. Supp. I:** 120

Ruins and Visions (Spender), **Supp. II:** 486, 489

Ruins of Time, The (Spenser), **I:** 124

Rukeyser, Muriel, **Supp. V:** 261

Rule a Wife and Have a Wife (Fletcher), **II:** 45, 65

Rule Britannia (du Maurier), **Supp. III:** 133, 147

"Rule, Britannia" (Thomson), **Supp. III:** 412, 425

"Rules and Lessons" (Vaughan), **II:** 187

Rules for Court Circular (Carroll), **V:** 274

"Rummy Affair of Old Biffy, The" (Wodehouse), **Supp. III:** 455, 457

Rumors of Rain (Brink), **Supp. VI: 49–50**

Rumour at Nightfall (Greene), **Supp. I:** 3

"Run" (Motion), **Supp. VII:** 259

Running Wild (Ballard), **Supp. V:** 30–31

Rural Denmark (Haggard), **Supp. III:** 214

Rural England (Haggard), **Supp. III:** 214

Rural Minstrel, The (Brontë), **V:** 107, 151

Rural Sports: A Poem (Gay), **III:** 67

Rushdie, Salman, **Supp. IV:** 65, 75, 116, 157, 160, 161, 162, 170–171, 174, 302, **433–456; Supp. V:** 67, 68, 74

Rushing to Paradise (Ballard), **Supp. V:** 31

Ruskin, John, **IV:** 320, 346; **V:** xii, xviii, xx–xxii, xxvi, 3, 9, 17, 20, 85–86, **173–185**, 235, 236, 291–292, 345, 362, 400; **VI:** 167

Ruskin's Politics (Shaw), **VI:** 129

Russell, Bertrand, **VI:** xi, 170, 385; **VII:** 90

Russell, G. W. E., **IV:** 292, 304

Russell, John, **Supp. IV:** 126

Russia House, The (le Carré), **Supp. II:** 300, 310, 311, 313, **318–319**

Russian Interpreter, The (Frayn), **Supp. VII:** 52–53, 54

Russian Nights (Thomas), **Supp. IV:** 483–486

Rusticus (Poliziano), **I:** 240

"Ruth" (Crabbe), **V:** 6

Ruth (Gaskell), **V:** xxi, 1, 6–7, 15

"Ruth" (Hood), **IV:** 255

Ryan, Desmond, **VII:** 2

Rymer, James Malcolm, **Supp. III:** 385

Rymer, Thomas, **I:** 328

Ryskamp, C., **III:** 249

S. T. Coleridge (ed. Brett), **IV:** 57

"Sabbath Morning at Sea, A" (Browning), **IV:** 313

"Sabbath Park" (McGuckian), **Supp. V:** 283–284

Sackville, Charles, *see* Dorset, earl of

Sackville, Thomas, **I:** 169, 214

Sackville–West, Edward, **VI:** 35, 59

Sacred and Profane Love Machine, The (Murdoch), **Supp. I:** 224

Sacred Flame, The (Maugham), **VI:** 369

Sacred Fount, The (James), **VI:** 56–57, 67

Sacred Hunger (Unsworth), **Supp. VII:** 353, 357, 361, 363–364

Sacred Wood, The (Eliot), **I:** 293; **V:** 310, 334; **VII:** 149, 164; **Retro. Supp. I:** 166

"Sacrifice" (Kinsella), **Supp. V:** 267

"Sacrifice, The" (Herbert), **II:** 124, 128

"Sad Fortunes of the Reverend Amos Barton, The" (Eliot), **Retro. Supp. II:** 103

Sad One, The (Suckling), **II:** 226

Sad Shepherd, The (Jonson), **Retro. Supp. I:** 166

"Sad Steps" (Larkin), **Supp. I:** 284

"Sadak the Wanderer" (Shelley), **IV:** 20

Sade, marquis de, **V:** 316–317

Sadeian Woman, The: An Exercise in Cultural History (Carter), **Supp. III:** 87–88

Sadleir, Michael, **III:** 335, 346; **V:** 100, 101, 102

"Sadness of Cricket, The" (Ewart), **Supp. VII:** 45–46

"Safe as Houses" (Drabble), **Supp. IV:** 231

"Safety" (Brooke), **Supp. III:** 57

Saga Library, The (Morris, Magnusson), **V:** 306

Sagar, Keith, **VII:** 104

Sage, Lorna, **Supp. IV:** 346

"Sage to the Young Man, The" (Housman), **VI:** 159

Said, Edward, **Supp. IV:** 164, 449

Saigon: Year of the Cat (Hare), **Supp. IV:** 282, 289

Sail Away (Coward), **Supp. II:** 155

Sailing Alone Around the World (Slocum), **Supp. IV:** 158

Sailing to an Island (Murphy), **Supp. V:** 317–320

"Sailing to an Island" (Murphy), **Supp. V:** 319

"Sailing to Byzantium" (Yeats), **Retro. Supp. I:** 333–334

"Sailor, What of the Isles?" (Sitwell), **VII:** 138

"Sailor's Mother, The" (Wordsworth), **IV:** 21

"Saint, The" (Maugham), **VI:** 377

"Saint, The" (Pritchett), **Supp. III:** 315, 318–319

"St. Alphonsus Rodriquez" (Hopkins), **V:** 376, 378

"St. Anthony's Shirt" (Day Lewis), **Supp. III:** 115

St. Augustine (West), **Supp. III:** 433

St Bartholomew's Eve: A Tale of the Sixteenth Century in Two Cantos (Newman), **Supp. VII:** 289

Sainte–Beuve, Charles, **III:** 226, 230; **V:** 212

"St. Botolph's" (Hughes), **Retro. Supp. II:** 217

St. Catherine's Clock (Kinsella), **Supp. V:** 271

St. Évremond, Charles de, **III:** 47

St. Francis of Assisi (Chesterton), **VI:** 341

Saint Ignatius Loyola (Thompson), **V:** 450, 451

St. Irvine (Shelley), **III:** 338

St. Irvyne; or, The Rosicrucian (Shelley), **IV:** 208

St. Ives (Stevenson and Quiller–Couch), **V:** 384, 387, 396

Saint Joan (Shaw), **VI:** xv, 120, **123–125**; **Retro. Supp. II:** 323–324

St. Joan of the Stockyards (Brecht), **VI:** 123

St. Leon (Godwin), **III:** 332

"St. Martin's Summer" (Browning), **IV:** 369

"Sainte Mary Magdalene; or, The Weeper" (Crashaw), *see* AWeeper, The"

"St. Mawr" (Lawrence), **VII:** 115; **Retro. Supp. II:** 232

"St. Patrick's Day" (Mahon), **Supp. VI:** 178

St. Patrick's Day (Sheridan), **III:** 253, 259, 270

St. Paul and Protestantism (Arnold), **V:** 216

St. Paul's boys' theater, **I:** 197

St. Ronan's Well (Scott), **IV:** 36, 37, 39

"St. Simeon Stylites" (Tennyson), **IV:** xx, 332

St. Thomas Aquinas (Chesterton), **VI:** 341

St. Valentine's Day (Scott), **IV:** 39

"St. Winefred's Well" (Hopkins), **V:** 371

Saint's Knowledge of Christ's Love, The (Bunyan), **II:** 253

Saint's Privilege and Profit, The (Bunyan), **II:** 253

Saint's Progress (Galsworthy), **VI:** 272, 279, 280–281

Saintsbury, George, **II:** 211; **IV:** 271, 282, 306; **V:** 31, 38; **VI:** 266

Saki (H. H. Munro), **Supp. II:** 140–141, 144, 149; **Supp. VI:** **239–252**

Salámón and Absál . . . Translated from . . . Jámí (FitzGerald), **IV:** 342, 345, 353

Salih, Tayeb, **Supp. IV:** 449

Salinger, J. D., **Supp. IV:** 28

"Salisbury Plain"poems (Wordsworth), **IV:** 2, 3, 4, 5–6, 23, 24

Sally Bowles (Isherwood), **VII:** 311

"Salmon Eggs" (Hughes), **Supp. I:** 363, 364; **Retro. Supp. II:** 213

Salomé (Wilde), **V:** xxvi, 412–413, 419; **Retro. Supp. II:** 370–371

Salsette and Elephanta (Ruskin), **V:** 184

Salt Lands, The (Shaffer), **Supp. I:** 314

"Salt of the Earth, The" (West), **Supp. III:** 442

"Salt Stream, The" (Redgrove), **Supp. VI:** 231–232

Salt Water (Motion), **Supp. VII:** 259, 262–264

Salter, F. M., **I:** 82

"Salutation, The" (Traherne), **II:** 191

Salutation, The (Warner), **Supp. VII:** 379–380

"Salvation of Swithin Forsyte, The" (Galsworthy), **VI:** 274, 277

"Salvatore" (Maugham), **VI:** 370

Salve (Moore), **VI:** 99

Salzburg Tales, The (Stead), **Supp. IV:** 461

"Same Day" (MacCaig), **Supp. VI:** 186

Samson Agonistes (Milton), **II:** 165, 172–174, 176; **Retro. Supp. II:** 285–288

Samuel Johnson (Krutch), **III:** 246

Samuel Johnson (Stephen), **V:** 281, 289

"Samuel Johnson and John Horne (Tooke)" (Landor), **IV:** 92

Samuel Pepys's Naval Minutes (ed. Tanner), **II:** 288

Samuel Pepys's APenny Merriments". . . Together with Comments . . . (ed. Thompson), **II:** 288

Samuel Taylor Coleridge: A Biographical Study (Chambers), **IV:** 41, 57

Samuel Titmarsh and the Great Hoggarty Diamond (Thackeray), *see Great Hoggarty Diamond, The*

Sanchez, Nellie, **V:** 393, 397

Sand, George, **V:** 22, 141, 207

"Sand–Between–the–Toes" (Milne), **Supp. V:** 302

"Sand Coast Sonnets, The" (Murray), **Supp. VII:** 283

Sandboy, The (Frayn), **Supp. VII:** 58

Sandcastle, The (Murdoch), **VII:** 66; **Supp. I:** 222–223, 225

Sanders, M. F., **V:** 250, 260

Sanderson, Robert, **II:** 136–137, 140, 142

Sandison, Alan G., **VI:** xi, xxxiv

Sanditon (Austen), **IV:** 108, 110, 122

Sandkastele (Brink), **Supp. VI:** **57**

Sandra Belloni (Meredith), **V:** 226, 227, 234

"Sandro Botticelli" (Pater), **V:** 345, 348

"Sandstone Keepsake" (Heaney), **Supp. II:** 277

Sanity of Art, The (Shaw), **VI:** 106–107, 129

Sans (Beckett), **Supp. I:** *see Lessness*

Santal (Firbank), **Supp. II:** 202, 204, **214–215**, 223

Sapho and Phao (Lyly), **I:** 198, 201–202

"Sapho to Philænis" (Donne), **Retro. Supp. II:** 92–93

Sapper, **Supp. IV:** 500

"Sapphics" (Swinburne), **V:** 321

Sappho (Durrell), **Supp. I:** 126–127

"Sappho to Phaon" (Ovid), **V:** 319

Saramago, Jose, **Supp. V:** xxx

Sardanapalus (Byron), **IV:** xviii, 178–179, 193

Sarraute, Nathalie, **Supp. IV:** 99

Sarton, May, **Supp. II:** 82

Sartor Resartus (Carlyle), **IV:** xii, xix, 231, 239–240, 242–243, 249, 250

Sartre, Jean-Paul, **III:** 329, 345; **Supp. I:** 216, 217, 221, 222, 452–453; **Supp. III:** 109; **Supp. IV:** 39, 79, 105, 259

Sartre: Romantic Rationalist (Murdoch), **Supp. I:** 219–220, 222

Sassoon, Siegfried, **V:** 219, 234; **VI:** xvi, 416, **429–431,** 451, 454, 456–457; **VII:** xvi; **Supp. III:** 59; **Supp. IV:** 57–58

"Satan in a Barrel" (Lowry), **Supp. III:** 270

Satan in Search of a Wife (Lamb), **IV:** 84, 85

Satanic Verses, The (Rushdie), **Supp. IV:** 116, 433, 434, 436, 437, 438, 445–450, 451, 452, 456

Satire and Fiction (Lewis), **VII:** 72, 77

Satire on Satirists, A, and Admonition to Detractors (Landor), **IV:** 100

Satires (Donne), **I:** 361; **Retro. Supp. II:** 86

Satires (Wyatt), **I:** 100, 101–102, 111

Satires of Circumstance (Hardy), **VI:** 14, 20; **Retro. Supp. I:** 117

Satires of Circumstance (Sorley), **VI:** 421

"Satiric Muse, The " (Hope), **Supp. VII:** 163

"Satisfactory, The" (Pritchett), **Supp. III:** **319–320**

Saturday Life, A (Hall), **Supp. VI:** 120–122

"Saturday Night" (Gunn), **Supp. IV:** 269

Saturday Night and Sunday Morning (Sillitoe), **Supp. V:** 409, 410, 413, 416–419

Saturday Review (periodical), **V:** 279; **VI:** 103, 106, 366; **Supp. II:** 45, 48, 53, 54, 55

"Saturday; or, The Flights" (Gay), **III:** 56

"Saturnalia" (Gunn), **Supp. IV:** 269

"Saturnalia" (Wilson), **Supp. I:** 158

"Satyr Against Mankind, A" (Rochester), **II:** 208n, 256, 260–261, 270

"Satyrical Elegy on the Death of a Late Famous General, A" (Swift), **III:** 31

Saucer of Larks, The (Friel), **Supp. V:** 113

"Saul" (Browning), **IV:** 363

Saunders, Charles, **II:** 305

Sauter, Rudolf, **VI:** 284

Sauve Qui Peut (Durrell), **Supp. I:** 113

Savage, Eliza Mary Ann, **Supp. II:** 99, 104, 111

Savage, Richard, **III:** 108

Savage Gold (Fuller), **Supp. VII:** 70

Savage Pilgrimage, The (Carswell), **VII:** 123

Save It for the Minister (Churchill, Potter, O'Malley), **Supp. IV:** 181

Save the Beloved Country (Paton), **Supp. II:** 359, 360

Saved (Bond), **Supp. I:** 421, 422–423, 425–426, 427, 435

Saved By Grace (Bunyan), **II:** 253

Savile, George, *see* Halifax, marquess of

Saville (Storey), **Supp. I:** 419

Saviour of Society, The (Swinburne), **V:** 333

"Savonarola Brown" (Beerbohm), **Supp. II:** 51, 56

Savonarola e il priore di San Marco (Landor), **IV:** 100

Savrola (Churchill), **VI:** 351

"Say not of me that weakly I declined" (Stevenson), **V:** 390

"Say not the struggle nought availeth" (Clough), **V:** 158–159, 165, 166, 167

Sayers, Dorothy L., **III:** 341; **VI:** 345; **Supp. II:** 124, 126, 127, 135; **Supp. III:** **333–353; Supp. IV:** 2, 3, 500

"Scale" (Self), **Supp. V:** 403–404

Scandal (Wilson), **Supp. VI:** 302–303, 308

"Scandal in Bohemia, A" (Doyle), **Supp. I:** 173

Scandal of Father Brown, The (Chesterton), **VI:** 338

Scandalous Woman, A (O'Brien), **Supp. V:** 339

Scannell, Vernon, **VII:** 422, 423–424

Scapegoat, The (du Maurier), **Supp. III:** 136, 139, 140–141

"Scapegoat, The" (Pritchett), **Supp. III:** 312, 317–318

Scapegoats and Rabies (Hughes), **Supp. I:** 348

Scarcity of Love, A (Kavan), **Supp. VII:** 213, 214

"Scarecrow in the Schoolmaster's Oats, The" (Brown), **Supp. VI:** 71

Scarlet Tree, The (Sitwell), **VII:** 128–129

Scarperer, The (Behan), **Supp. II:** 67

Scarron, Paul, **II:** 354

"Scenes" (Dickens), **V:** 44–46

Scenes from Italy's War (Trevelyan), **VI:** 389

"Scenes from the Fall of Troy" (Morris), **V:** 297

Scenes of Clerical Life (Eliot), **V:** xxii, 2, 190–191, 200; **Retro. Supp. II:** 103–104

Sceptick (Ralegh), **I:** 157

Schelling, Friedrich Wilhelm, **V:** 347

Scheme and Estimates for a National Theatre, A (Archer and Barker), **VI:** 104, 113

Schepisi, Fred, **Supp. IV:** 345

Schiller, Friedrich von, **IV:** xiv, xvi 173, 241

Schindler's Ark (Keneally), *see Schindler's List*

Schindler's List (Keneally), **Supp. IV:** 343, 346, 348, 354–357, 358

Schirmer Inheritance, The (Ambler), **Supp. IV:** 4, 13–16, 21

Schlegel, A. W., **I:** 329; **IV:** vii, xvii; **V:** 62

Schneider, Elizabeth, **V:** 366, 382

"Scholar and Gypsy" (Desai), **Supp. V:** 65

"Scholar Gipsy, The" (Arnold), **V:** xxi, 209, 210, 211, 216

School for Husbands (Mahon), **Supp. VI:** 175

School for Wives (Mahon), **Supp. VI:** 175

School for Scandal, The (Sheridan), **III:** 97, 100, 253, **261–264,** 270

School of Abuse (Gosson), **I:** 161

School of Donne, The (Alvarez), **II:** 125n

"School of Eloquence, The" (Harrison), **Supp. V:** 150, 151–157

"School Stories" (Wodehouse), **Supp. III:** 449

"School Story, A" (Trevor), **Supp. IV:** 502

Schoolboy Verses (Kipling), **VI:** 200

"Schoolboys" (McEwan), **Supp. IV:** 393

Schools and Universities on the Continent (Arnold), **V:** 216

Schopenhauer, Arthur, **Supp. IV:** 6

Schreber's Nervous Illness (Churchill), **Supp. IV:** 181

Schreiner, Olive, **Supp. II:** **435–457**

Science and Poetry (Richards), **VI:** 207, 208; **Supp. II:** 405, 412, 413, 414, **417–418,** 419

Science of Ethics, The (Stephen), **V:** 284–285, 289

"Science of History, The" (Froude), **IV:** 324

Science of Life, The (Wells), **VI:** 225

Scilla's Metamorphosis (Lodge), **I:** 306

"Scipio, Polybius, and Panaetius" (Landor), **IV:** 94

Scoop (Waugh), **VII:** 297

Scornful Lady, The (Beaumont and Fletcher), **II:** 65

Scorpion and Other Poems (Smith), **Supp. II:** 463

Scorpion God, The (Golding), **Supp. I:** 82–83

Scot, William, **Supp. III:** 20, 22, 23

"Scotch Drink" (Burns), **III:** 315

"Scotland" (Reid), **Supp. VII:** 331

Scots Musical Museum (Johnson), **III:** 320, 322

Scott, Geoffrey, **III:** 234n, 238, 249

Scott, John, **IV:** 252, 253

Scott, Paul, **Supp. I:** **259–274; Supp. IV:** 440

Scott, Robert Falcon, **II:** 273

Scott, Sir Walter **II:** 276; **III:** 146, 157, 326, 335, 336, 338; **IV:** viii, xi, xiv, **27–40,** 45, 48, 102, 111, 122, 129, 133–136, 167, 168, 173, 254, 270, 281; **V:** 392; **VI:** 412; **Supp. III:** 151, 154, 167

Scott Moncrieff, Charles, **VI:** 454, 455

Scottish Journey (Muir), **Supp. VI:** 198, 201

Scott–James, Rolfe Arnold, **VI:** x, xxxiv, 1

Scott–Kilvert, Ian Stanley, **VI:** xvi, xxxiv; **VII:** xxii

Scott–King's Modern Europe (Waugh), **VII:** 301

Scotus, Duns, *see* Duns Scotus, John

Scourge of Villainy, The (Marston), **II:** 25, 26, 40

Scrapbook (Mansfield), **VII:** 181

Screams and Other Poems, The (Richards), **Supp. II:** 407, 427

Screwtape Letters, The (Lewis), **Supp. III:** 248, 255, 256–257

"Script for an Unchanging Voice" (McGuckian), **Supp. V:** 292

Scriptorum illustrium maioris Britanniae catalogus (Bale), **I:** 1

Scrutiny (periodical), **VII:** 233, 238, 243, 251–252, 256; **Supp. III:** 107

Scudéry, Georges de, **III:** 95

Sculptura; or, The History . . . of Chalcography and Engraving in Copper (Evelyn), **II:** 287

Scum of the Earth (Koestler), **Supp. I:** 26

"Scylla and Charybdis" (Kinsella), **Supp. V:** 261

Sea, The (Bond), **Supp. I:** 423, 427, 432–433, 435

Sea, The Sea, The (Murdoch), **Supp. I:** 231, 232

Sea and Sardinia (Lawrence), **VII:** 116–117

Sea and the Mirror, The (Auden), **VII:** 379, 380, 388, 389; **Retro. Supp. I:** 11

"Sea and the Skylark, The" (Hopkins), **V:** 367

"Sea in Winter, The" (Mahon), **Supp. VI:** 173, 175

"Sea Limits" (Rossetti), **V:** 241

Sea Gull, The (tr. Frayn), **Supp. VII:** 61

Sea to the West (Nicholson), **Supp. VI:** 213, **218–219**

"Sea to the West" (Nicholson), **Supp. VI:** 219

Sea Voyage, The (Fletcher and Massinger), **II:** 43, 66

Seafarer, The, **Retro. Supp. II:** 303–304

"Seafarer, The" (Pound), **Supp. IV:** 100, 115

Sea–King's Daughter and *Eureka!, The* (Brown), **Supp. VI:** 71–73

"Seals at High Island" (Murphy), **Supp. V:** 324

"Sea–Mists of the Winter, The" (Lewis), **VII:** 84

Sean O'Casey: The Man Behind the Plays (Cowasjee), **VII:** 4

Search, The (Snow), **VII:** 321–322, 323–324

"Search, The" (Vaughan), **VII:** 187

"Search After Happiness, The" (Brontë), **V:** 110

"Seaside Walk, A" (Browning), **IV:** 313

Season at Sarsaparilla, The (White), **Supp. I:** 131, 149

Season in Purgatory (Keneally), **Supp. IV:** 346

Season Songs (Hughes), **Supp. I:** 357–359; **Retro. Supp. II:** 208–209

Seasonable Counsel; or, Advice to Sufferers (Bunyan), **II:** 253

Season's Greetings (Ayckbourn), **Supp. V:** 3, 10, 13, 14

Seasons, The (Thomson), **Supp. III:** 409, 410, 411, **412–419,** 420, 428; **Retro. Supp. I:** 241

Sebastian (Durrell), **Supp. I:** 120

Seccombe, Thomas, **V:** 425, 437

"Second Best, The" (Arnold), **V:** 209

"Second Best" (Brooke), **Supp. III:** 49

Second Book of Odes (Bunting), **Supp. VII:** 13–14

"Second Coming, The" (Yeats), **VI:** xiv; **Retro. Supp. I:** 332–333

Second Curtain, The (Fuller), **Supp. VII:** 71, 72, 81

Second Defence of the People of England, The (Milton), **II:** 164; **Retro. Supp. II:** 270

Second Epistle of the Second Book (Pope), **Retro. Supp. I:** 230

Second Funeral of Napoleon, The (Thackeray), **V:** 22, 38

"Second Hut, The" (Lessing), **Supp. I:** 240–241

Second Journal to Eliza, The, **III:** 135

Second Jungle Book, The (Kipling), **VI:** 204

Second Maiden's Tragedy, The (Middleton), **II:** 2, 3, **8–10,** 21

Second Mrs. Tanqueray, The (Pinero), **V:** 413

Second Nun's Tale, The (Chaucer), **I:** 31, 34, 43

Second Part of Mr. Waller's Poems, The (Waller), **II:** 238

Second Part of Pilgrim's Progress, The (T. S.), **II:** 248

Second Part of the Bloody Conquests of Mighty Tamburlaine, The (Marlowe), *see Tamburlaine, Part 2*

Second Part of The Rover, The (Behn), **Supp. III:** 27

2nd Poems (Graham), **Supp. VII:** 109–110

Second Satire (Wyatt), **I:** 111

Second Sex, The (Beauvoir), **Supp. IV:** 232

Second Treatise on Government (Locke), **Supp. III:** 33

"Second Visit, A" (Warner), **Supp. VII:** 380

Second World War (Churchill), **VI:** 359–360

Secord, Arthur Wellesley, **III:** 41

"Secret Agent, The" (Auden), **Retro. Supp. I:** 3

Secret Agent (Conrad), **Supp. IV:** 1

Secret Agent, The (Conrad), **VI: 143–144,** 148; **Retro. Supp. II:** 80–81

Secret Brother, The (Jennings), **Supp. V:** 216

Secret Dispatches from Arabia (Lawrence), **Supp. II:** 295

"Secret Garden, The" (Kinsella), **Supp. V:** 263

Secret Glass, The (Bainbridge), **Supp. VI:** 20

Secret History of the White Staff, The, . . . (Defoe), **III:** 13

"Secret History of World War 3, The" (Ballard), **Supp. V:** 33

Secret Ladder, The (Harris), **Supp. V:** 132, 135, 139

Secret Love; or, The Maiden Queen (Dryden), **II:** 305

Secret Narratives (Motion), **Supp. VII:** 255–256, 257, 263

Secret of Father Brown, The (Chesterton), **VI:** 338

Secret Pilgrim, The (le Carré), **Supp. II:** 319

Secret Rapture, The (Hare), **Supp. IV:** 282, 292, 293–294, 296

Secret Rose (Yeats), **VI:** 222

"Secret Sharer, The" (Conrad), **VI: 145–147**

"Secret Sharer, The" (Gunn), **Supp. IV:** 256, 259

Secret Water (Ransome), **Supp. I:** 68

Secular Lyrics of the XIVth and XVth Centuries (Robbins), **I:** 40

"Secular Masque, The" (Dryden), **II:** 289, 290, 305, 325

"Sedge–Warblers" (Thomas), **Supp. III:** 406

Sedley, Sir Charles, **II:** 255, 261, **263–266,** 271

"Seductio ad Absurdam" (Lowry), **Supp. III:** 285

"Seed Growing Secretly, The" (Vaughan), **II:** 189

"Seed Picture, The" (McGuckian), **Supp. V:** 281, 285

Seeing Things (Heaney), **Retro. Supp. I:** 124, 131–132

Seek and Find (Rossetti), **V:** 260

"Seesaw" (Gunn), **Supp. IV:** 275–276

Seicentismo e Marinismo in Inghilterra (Praz), **II:** 123

Sejanus (Jonson), **I:** 235, 242, 249, 345–346; **Retro. Supp. I:** 161, 164

Self Portrait (Kavanagh), **Supp. VII:** 197–198

Select British Poets; or, New Elegant Extracts from Chaucer to the Present Time (Hazlitt), **IV:** 139

Select Collection of Original Scottish Airs (Thomson), **III:** 322

Select Poets of Great Britain (Hazlitt), **IV:** 139

Selected Essays of Cyril Connolly, The (ed. Quennell), **Supp. III:** 107

Selected Letters of Edwin Muir (Muir), **Supp. VI:** 203

Selected Life, A (Kinsella), **Supp. V:** 267

Selected Plays [of Lady Gregory] (ed. Coxhead), **VI:** 317

Selected Poems (Gunn and Hughes), **Supp. IV:** 257

Selected Poems (Harrison), **Supp. V:** 150, 157, 160

Selected Poems (Hope), **Supp. VII:** 156, 159

Selected Poems (Hughes), **Supp. I: 364–365**

Selected Poems (Mahon), **Supp. VI:** 166–167, 169–174Selected Poems (Mahon), Supp. VI: 166-167, 169-174

Selected Poems (Muldoon), **Supp. IV:** 413

Selected Poems (Murray), **Supp. VII:** 270

Selected Poems (Smith), **Supp. II:** 463

Selected Poems (Spender), **Supp. II:** 486, 489

Selected Poems (Stevenson), **Supp. VI:** 256, 261–263

Selected Poems (Thomas), **Supp. IV:** 490, 494

Selected Poems of Malcolm Lowry (tr. Birney), **Supp. III:** 282

Selected Poems 1954–1992 (Brown), **Supp. VI:** 70–72

Selected Poems 1976–1997 (Motion), **Supp. VII:** 252, 257

Selected Prose (Housman), **VI:** 154

Selected Speeches (Disraeli), **IV:** 308

Selected Stories (Friel), **Supp. V:** 113

Selected Stories (Gordimer), **Supp. II:** 231, 232, 234, 242

Selection of Kipling's Verse (Eliot), **VI:** 202

Self, Will, **Supp. IV:** 26; **Supp. V: 395–408**

Self and Self–Management (Bennett), **VI:** 264

Self Condemned (Lewis), **VII:** 74, 81–82

"Self Justification" (Harrison), **Supp. V:** 155–156

"Self Portrait: Nearing Sixty" (Waugh), **Supp. VI:** 276

"Selfish Giant, The" (Wilde), **Retro. Supp. II:** 365

"Self–Release" (Kinsella), **Supp. V:** 270

"Self–Renewal" (Kinsella), **Supp. V:** 270

"Self–Scrutiny" (Kinsella), **Supp. V:** 270

"Self–Unseeing, The" (Hardy), **VI:** 13; **Retro. Supp. I:** 118

"Self's the Man" (Larkin), **Supp. I:** 281

Selimus, **I:** 220

Seltzer, David, **III:** 343, 345

"Selves" (Gunn), **Supp. IV:** 272

Selvon, Samuel, **Supp. IV:** 445

"Semi–Monde," (Coward), **Supp. II:** 146

"Semiology and Rhetoric" (de Man), **Supp. IV:** 114

"Send–Off, The" (Owen), **VI:** 447, 452

Seneca, **I:** 214–215; **II:** 25, 28, 71, 97

Sense and Sensibility (Austen), **III:** 91, 336; **IV:** xvii, 108, 109, 111, 112, **114–122**; **Retro. Supp. II:** 6–7

Sense of Detachment, A (Osborne), **Supp. I:** 339

Sense of Movement, The (Gunn), **Supp. IV:** 257, 259–262

Sense of the Past, The (James), **VI:** 64–65

Sense of the World, A (Jennings), **Supp. V:** 210, 212, 214

"Sensitive Plant, The" (Shelley), **IV:** 203

"Sentence, The" (tr. McKane), **Supp. IV:** 494–495

"Sentence, The" (tr. Thomas), **Supp. IV:** 494–495

"Sentimental Blues" (Ewart), **Supp. VII:** 36

"Sentimental Education, The" (Ewart), **Supp. VII:** 40

Sentimental Journey, A (Sterne), **III:** 124, 127, 132–134, 135

Sentimental Tommy (Barrie), **Supp. III:** 3

Sentiments of a Church–of–England Man, The (Swift), **III:** 26

"Sentry, The" (Owen), **VI:** 448, 451

Separate Tables: Table by the Window and Table Number Seven (Rattigan), **Supp. VII:** 313, 318–319

"September 1, 1939" (Auden), **Retro. Supp. I:** 10, **Retro. Supp. I:** 14

"September Song" (Hill), **Supp. V:** 187

September Tide (du Maurier), **Supp. III:** 143

"Sepulchre" (Herbert), **II:** 128

Sequence for Francis Parkman, A (Davie), **Supp. VI:** 108–109, 115

"Sequence in Hospital" (Jennings), **Supp. V:** 214

Sequence of Sonnets on the Death of Robert Browning, A (Swinburne), **V:** 333

Serafino Aquilano, **I:** 103, 105, 110

"Seraph and the Zambesi, The," (Spark), **Supp. I:** 199

"Seraphim, The" (Browning), **IV:** 312, 313

Seraphim, The, and Other Poems (Browning), **IV:** xix, 311, 312–313, 321

"Serenade" (Sitwell), **VII:** 135

Sergeant Lamb (Graves), **VII:** 258

Serious and Pathetical Contemplation of the Mercies of God, A . . . (Traherne), **II:** 201

Serious Money (Churchill), **Supp. IV:** 179, 180, 184, 192–195, 198

Serious Reflections During . . . A Robinson Crusoe" (Defoe), **III:** 12, 13; **Retro. Supp. I:** 71

Serjeant Musgrave's Dance (Arden), **Supp. II: 25–28,** 29, 30, 35, 38

"Sermon, The" (Redgrove), **Supp. VI:** 228–229, 232, 235, 237

Sermon Preached at Pauls Crosse, the 25. Of November. 1621, A (King), **Supp. VI:** 152

"Sermon to Our Later Prodigal Son" (Meredith), **V:** 223

Sermons (Donne), **I:** 364–366; **II:** 142; **Retro. Supp. II:** 96

Sermons: An Exposition upon the Lord's Prayer (King), **Supp. VI:** 152, 155, 158, 161

Sermons and Devotional Writings of Gerard Manley Hopkins, The (ed. Devlin), **V:** 372, 381

Sermons, Chiefly on the Theory of Religious Belief, Preached Before the University of Oxford (Newman), **Supp. VII:** 296

"Serpent–Charm, The" (Gissing), **V:** 437

Servant, The (Pinter), **Supp. I:** 374; **Retro. Supp. I:** 226

"Servant Boy" (Heaney), **Retro. Supp. I:** 128

"Servant Girl Speaks, A" (Lawrence), **VII:** 118

"Servants' Quarters, The" (Hardy), **Retro. Supp. I:** 121

"Serving Maid, The" (Kinsella), **Supp. V:** 263

Sesame and Lilies (Ruskin), **V:** 180, 184

"Session of the Poets, A" (Suckling), **II:** 229

"Sestina of the Tramp Royal" (Kipling), **VI:** 202, 203

Set of Six, A (Conrad), **VI:** 148

Seton, Ernest Thempson, **Supp. IV:** 158

"Setteragic On" (Warner), **Supp. VII:** 380

Setting the World on Fire (Wilson), **Supp. I:** 165–166

"Seven Ages, The" (Auden), **Retro. Supp. I:** 11

Seven at a Stroke (Fry), **Supp. III:** 194

"Seven Conjectural Readings" (Warner), **Supp. VII:** 373

Seven Days in the New Crete (Graves), **VII:** 259

"Seven Good Germans" (Henderson), **VII:** 426

Seven Journeys, The (Graham), **Supp. VII:** 111

Seven Lamps of Architecture, The (Ruskin), **V:** xxi, 176, 184

Seven Lectures on Shakespeare and Milton (Coleridge), **IV:** 56

"Seven Letters" (Graham), **Supp. VII:** 111

Seven Men (Beerbohm), **Supp. II:** 55–56

Seven Men and Two Others (Beerbohm), **Supp. II:** 55

Seven Men of Vision: An Appreciation (Jennings), **Supp. V:** 217

"7, Middagh Street" (Muldoon), **Supp. IV:** 411, 422, 424

Seven Pillars of Wisdom (Lawrence), **VI:** 408; **Supp. II:** 283, 284, 285, 286, **287–291**

"Seven Poets, The" (Brown), **Supp. VI:** 69

Seven Poor Men of Sydney (Stead), **Supp. IV:** 461–464

"Seven Rocks, The" (Nicholson), **Supp. VI: 216–217**

"Seven Sages, The" (Yeats), **Supp. II:** 84–85

Seven Seas, The (Kipling), **VI:** 204

Seven Short Plays (Gregory), **VI:** 315

Seven Types of Ambiguity (Empson), **I:** 282; **II:** 124, 130; **VII:** 260; **Supp. II:** 179, 180, 183, **185–189,** 190, 197

Seven Winters (Bowen), **Supp. II:** 77–78, 91

Seven Women (Barrie), **Supp. III:** 5

"1740" (Kinsella), **Supp. V:** 271

Seventh Man: Migrant Workers in Europe, A (Berger), **Supp. IV:** 79

Several Perceptions (Carter), **Supp. III:** 80, 81, 82–83

"Several Questions Answered" (Blake), **III:** 293

Severed Head, A (Murdoch), **Supp. I:** 215, 224, 225, 228

Severn and Somme (Gurney), **VI:** 425

"Sex That Doesn't Shop, The" (Saki), **Supp. VI:** 246

Sexing the Cherry (Winterson), **Supp. IV:** 541, 542, 545, 547, 549, 552, 554, 556, 557

"Sexton's Hero, The" (Gaskell), **V:** 15

Sexual Politics (Millett), **Supp. IV:** 188

Seymour–Smith, Martin, **VII:** xviii, xxx-viii

Shabby Genteel Story, A (Thackeray), **V:** 21, 35, 37

Shade Those Laurels (Connolly), **Supp. III:** 111–112

Shadow Dance (Carter), **III:** 345; **Supp. III:** 79, 80, 81, 89

Shadow of a Gunman, The (O'Casey), **VI:** 316; **VII:** xviii, 3–4, 6, 12

"Shadow of Black Combe, The" (Nicholson), **Supp. VI:** 218

Shadow of Cain, The (Sitwell), **VII:** xvii, 137

Shadow of Dante, A (Rossetti), **V:** 253n

Shadow of Hiroshima, The (Harrison), **Supp. V:** 164

Shadow of Night (Chapman), **I:** 234, 237

Shadow of the Glen, The (Synge), **VI:** 308, 309, 310, 316

Shadow of the Sun, The (Byatt), **Supp. IV:** 140, 141, 142–143, 147, 148, 149, 155

Shadow Play (Coward), **Supp. II:** 152–153

Shadow–Line, The: A Confession (Conrad), **VI:** 135, 146–147, 148

"Shadows" (Lawrence), **VII:** 119

"Shadows in the Water" (Traherne), **II:** 192

Shadows of the Evening (Coward), **Supp. II:** 156

Shadowy Waters, The (Yeats), **VI:** 218, 222

Shadwell, Thomas, **I:** 327; **II:** 305, 359

"Shadwell Stair" (Owen), **VI:** 451

Shaffer, Anthony, **Supp. I:** 313

Shaffer, Peter, **Supp. I: 313–328**

Shaftesbury, earl of, **Supp. III:** 424

Shaftesbury, seventh earl of, **IV:** 62

Shaftesbury, third earl of, **III:** 44, 46, 198

Shahnameh (Persian epic), **Supp. IV:** 439

Shakes Versus Shav (Shaw), **VI:** 130

Shakespear, Olivia, **VI:** 210, 212, 214

Shakespeare, William, **I:** 188, **295–334; II:** 87, 221, 281, 302; **III:** 115–117; **IV:** 149, 232, 352; **V:** 41, 328; and Collins, **IV:** 165, 165n, 170; and Jonson, **I:** 335–337, **II:** 281; **Retro. Supp. I:** 158, 165; and Kyd, **I:** 228–229; and Marlowe, **I:** 275–279, 286; and Middleton, **IV:** 79–80; and Webster, **II:** 71–72, 74–75, 79; influence on English literature, **II:** 29, 42–43, 47, 48, 54–55, 79, 82, 84; **III:** 115–116, 167n; **IV:** 35, 51–52; **V:** 405; **Supp. I:** 196, 227; **Supp. II:** 193, 194; **Supp. IV:** 158, 171, 283, 558

Shakespeare (Swinburne), **V:** 333

"Shakespeare and Stage Costume" (Wilde), **V:** 407

Shakespeare and the Allegory of Evil (Spivack), **I:** 214

Shakespeare and the Goddess of Complete Being (Hughes), **Retro. Supp. II:** 202

Shakespeare and the Idea of the Play (Righter), **I:** 224

"Shakespeare and the Stoicism of Seneca" (Eliot), **I:** 275

"Shakespeare as a Man" (Stephen), **V:** 287

Shakespeare Wallah (Jhabvala), **Supp. V:** 237–238

Shakespeare's Sonnets Reconsidered (Butler), **Supp. II:** 116

Shall We Join the Ladies? (Barrie), **Supp. III:** 6, 9, 16–17

"Shamdev; The Wolf–Boy" (Chatwin), **Supp. IV:** 157

Shame (Rushdie), **Supp. IV:** 116, 433, 436, 440, 443, 444–445, 448, 449

Shamela (Fielding), **III:** 84, 98, 105; **Retro. Supp. I:** 80; **Retro. Supp. I:** 82–83

Shape of Things to Come, The (Wells), **VI:** 228, 241

"Shapes and Shadows" (Mahon), **Supp. VI:** 178

Shards of Memory (Jhabvala), **Supp. V:** 233, 234–235

"Sharp Trajectories" (Davie), **Supp. VI:** 116

Sharp, William, **IV:** 370

Sharrock, Roger, **II:** 246, 254

Shaving of Shagpat, The (Meredith), **V:** 225, 234

Shaw, George Bernard, **III:** 263; **V:** xxii, xxv, xxvi, 284, 301, 305–306, 423, 433; **VI:** viii, ix, xiv–xv, **101–132,** 147, 343; **Supp. II:** 24, 45, 51, 54, 55, 117–118, 288, 296–297; **Supp. III:** 6; **Supp. IV:** 233, 288, 292; **Retro. Supp. II: 309–325**

Shaw Gives Himself Away: An Autobiographical Miscellany (Shaw), **VI:** 129

Shaw–Stewart, Patrick, **VI:** 418–419, 420

She (Haggard), **Supp. III:** 211, 212, 213, 219–222, 223–227

She Stoops to Conquer (Goldsmith), **II:** 362; **III:** 177, 181, 183, 188, 191, 256

She Wou'd if She Cou'd (Etherege), **II:** 266, 268, 271

Sheaf of Verses, A (Hall), **Supp. VI:** 119

"Sheep" (Hughes), **Retro. Supp. II:** 209

Sheep and the Dog, The (Henryson), **Supp. VII:** 136, 138–139, 141

"Sheepdog Trials in Hyde Park" (Day Lewis), **Supp. III:** 130

"She's all my fancy painted him" (Carroll), **V:** 264

Shelf Life (Powell), **Supp. IV:** 258

Shelley, Mary Wollstonecraft, **III: 329–331,** 336, 341, 342, 345; **IV:** xv, xvi, xvii, 118, 197, 201, 202, 203; **Supp. III: 355–373,** 385; **Supp. IV:** 546; **Retro. Supp. I:** 246

Shelley, Percy Bysshe, **II:** 102, 200; **III:** 329, 330, 333, 336–338; **IV:** vii–xii, 63, 132 158–159, 161, 163, 164, 168–169, 172, 176–179, 182, **195–210,** 217, 234, 281, 299, 349, 354, 357, 366, 372; **V:** 214, 330, 401, 403; **VI:** 453; **Supp. III:** 355, 357–358, 364–365, 370; **Supp. IV:** 468; **Retro. Supp. I: 243–257**

Shelley (Swinburne), **V:** 333

Shelley (Thompson), **V:** 450, 451

Shelley: A Life Story (Blunden), **IV:** 210

Shelley and Keats as They Struck Their Contemporaries (Blunden), **IV:** 210

Shelley's Idols of the Cave (Butler), **IV:** 210

"Shelley's Skylark" (Hardy), **Retro. Supp. I:** 119

Shelmalier (McGuckian), **Supp. V:** 280, 290–292

"Shelmalier" (McGuckian), **Supp. V:** 291

Shelter, The (Phillips), **Supp. V:** 380

Shepheardes Calendar (Spenser), *see Shepherd's Calendar, The*

Shepheard's Oracles, The (Quarles), **II:** 139

Shepherd, Ettrick, *see* Hogg, James

"Shepherd and the Nymph, The" (Landor), **IV:** 96

Shepherd of the Giant Mountains, The (tr. Smedley), **V:** 265

"Shepherd's Brow, The" (Hopkins), **V:** 376, 378n

Shepherd's Calendar, The (Spenser), **I:** 97, 121, 123, 124–128, 162

"Shepherd's Carol" (Nicholson), **Supp. VI:** 214–215

Shepherd's Life, A (Hudson), **V:** 429

Shepherd's Week, The (Gay), **III:** 55, 56, 67

Sheppey (Maugham), **VI:** 377

Sherburn, George, **III:** 73, 78

Sheridan, Richard Brinsley, **II:** 334, 336; **III:** 32, 97, 101, **252–271**

Sheridan, Susan, **Supp. IV:** 459

"Sherthursdaye and Venus Day" (Jones), **Supp. VII:** 177

Shewan, R., **V:** 409n, 421

Shewing–Up of Blanco Posnet, The: A Sermon in Crude Melodrama (Shaw), **VI:** 115, 117, 124, 129

"Shian Bay" (Graham), **Supp. VII:** 110–111

"Shield of Achilles, The" (Auden), **VII:** 388, 390–391, 397–398; **Retro. Supp. I:** 10

Shikasta (Lessing), **Supp. I:** 250, 251, 252, 253

Shining, The (King), **III:** 345

"Ship That Found Herself, The" (Kipling), **VI:** 170

Shipman's Tale, The (Chaucer), **I:** 36

Shipwreck (Fowles), **Supp. I:** 292

Shipwrecked, The (Greene), *see England Made Me*

Shires, The (Davie), **Supp. VI:** 111–112

Shirley, James, **II:** 44, 66, 87

Shirley (Brontë), **V:** xxi, 12, 106, 112, **145–147,** 152; **Retro. Supp. I:** 53, 54, 60

Shirley Sanz (Pritchett), **Supp. III:** 313

Shrimp and the Anemone, The (Hartley), **Supp. VII:** 119, 124–125

"Shoals Returning, The" (Kinsella), **Supp. V:** 263

Shoemaker of Merano, The (Hall), **Supp. VI:** 130

Shoemaker's Holiday, The (Dekker), **II:** 89

"Shooting an Elephant" (Orwell), **VII:** 273, 276, 282

Shooting Niagara (Carlyle), **IV:** xxii, 240, 247

"Shore Road, The" (MacCaig), **Supp. VI:** 187, 195

Short Account of a Late Short Administration, A (Burke), **III:** 205

Short Character of . . . [the Earl of Wharton], A (Swift), **III:** 35

Short Historical Essay . . . , A (Marvell), **II:** 219

"Short History of British India, A" (Hill), **Supp. V:** 191

"Short History of the English Novel, A" (Self), **Supp. V:** 403

Short History of the English People (Green), **VI:** 390

Short Stories, Scraps, and Shavings (Shaw), **VI:** 129

"Short Story, The" (Bowen), **Supp. II:** 86

Short View of the Immorality and Profaneness of the English Stage, A (Collier), **II:** 303, 325, 338, 340, 356; **III:** 44

Short View of the State of Ireland, A (Swift), **III:** 28, 35; **Retro. Supp. I:** 276

Short Vindication of "The Relapse" and "The Provok'd Wife," . . . by the Author (Vanbrugh), **II:** 332, 336

Shortened History of England, A (Trevelyan), **VI:** 395

Shorter, Clement, **V:** 150, 151–153

Shorter Finnegans Wake, A (Burgess), **Supp. I:** 197

Shorter Poems (Bridges), **VI:** 72, 73, 81

Shortest Way to Peace and Union, The (Defoe), **III:** 13

Shortest Way with the Dissenters, The (Defoe), **III:** 2, 3, 12–13; **Retro. Supp. I:** 64–65, 67

"Shot, The" (Jennings), **Supp. V:** 210

"Shot Down over Libya" (Dahl), **Supp. IV:** 202, 207–208, 209

"Should lanterns shine" (Thomas), **Supp. I:** 174

Shoulder of Shasta, The (Stoker), **Supp. III:** 381

Shout, The (Graves), **VII:** 259

"Show me, dear Christ, thy spouse" (Donne), **I:** 367, 368

"Show Saturday" (Larkin), **Supp. I:** 283, 285

Shrapnel Academy, The (Weldon), **Supp. IV:** 529–530, 531

Shropshire Lad, A (Housman), **VI:** ix, xv, 157, 158–160, 164

Shroud for a Nightingale (James), **Supp. IV:** 319, 320, 323, 326–327

"Shrove Tuesday in Paris" (Thackeray), **V:** 22, 38

Shuttlecock (Swift), **Supp. V:** 429–431

"Sibylla Palmifera" (Rossetti), **V:** 237

Sibylline Leaves (Coleridge), **IV:** 56

"Sic Vita" (King), **Supp. VI:** 162

Sicilian Carousel (Durrell), **Supp. I:** 102

Sicilian Romance, A (Radcliffe), **III:** 338

"Sick King in Bokhara, The" (Arnold), **V:** 210

Sidgwick, Henry, **V:** 284, 285

Sidhwa, Bapsi, **Supp. V:** 62

Sidley, Sir Charles, *see* Sedley, Sir Charles

Sidney, Sir Philip, **I:** 123, **160–175;** **II:** 46, 48, 53, 80, 158, 221, 339; **III:** 95; **Retro. Supp. I:** 157; **Retro. Supp. II: 327–342**

Siege (Fry), **Supp. III:** 194

Siege of Corinth, The (Byron), **IV:** 172, 192; *see also* Turkish tales

Siege of London, The (James), **VI:** 67

Siege of Pevensey, The (Burney), **Supp. III:** 71

Siege of Thebes, The (Lydgate), **I:** 57, 61, 65

"Siena" (Swinburne), **V:** 325, 332

"Sierra Nevada" (Stevenson), **Supp. VI:** 254–255

"Sighs and Grones" (Herbert), **II:** 128

Sign of Four, The (Doyle), **Supp. II:** 160, 162–163, 164–165, 167, 171, 173, 176

Sign of the Cross, The (Barrett), **VI:** 124

Signal Driver (White), **Supp. I:** 131, 151

"Signpost, The" (Thomas), **Supp. III:** 403, 404

"Signs" (Stevenson), **Supp. VI:** 263

Signs of Change (Morris), **V:** 306

"Signs of the Times" (Carlyle), **IV:** 241–242, 243, 249, 324; **V:** viii

Sigurd the Volsung (Morris), *see Story of Sigurd the Volsung and the Fall of the Niblungs, The*

Silas Marner (Eliot), **V:** xxii, 194, 200; **Retro. Supp. II:** 108–110

"Silecroft Shore" (Nicholson), **Supp. VI:** 216

Silence (Pinter), **Supp. I:** 376

Silence Among the Weapons (Arden), **Supp. II:** 41

Silence in the Garden, The (Trevor), **Supp. IV:** 505, 506, 515–516, 517

"Silent One, The" (Gurney), **VI:** 427

Silent Passenger, The (Sayers), **Supp. III:** 335

"Silent Voices, The" (Tennyson), **IV:** 329

Silent Woman, The (Jonson), **Retro. Supp. I:** 163

Silex Scintillans: . . . (Vaughan), **II:** 184, 185, 186, 201

Sillitoe, Alan, **Supp. V: 409–426**

Silmarillion, The (Tolkien), **Supp. II:** 519, 520, 521, 525, 527

Silver, Brenda, **Retro. Supp. I:** 305

"Silver Blaze" (Doyle), **Supp. II:** 167

Silver Box, The (Galsworthy), **VI:** 273, 284–285

Silver Bucket, The (Orton), **Supp. V:** 364

Silver Chair, The (Lewis), **Supp. III:** 248

Silver Spoon, The (Galsworthy), **VI:** 275

Silver Tassie, The (O'Casey), **VII:** 6–7

Silverado Squatters, The (Stevenson), **V:** 386, 395; **Retro. Supp. I:** 262

"Silvia" (Etherege), **II:** 267

Simenon, Georges, **III:** 341

Simmons, Ernest, **V:** 46

Simmons, James, **Supp. IV:** 412

"Simon Lee" (Wordsworth), **IV:** 7, 8–9, 10

Simonetta Perkins (Hartley), **Supp. VII:** 122–123, 126

Simonidea (Landor), **IV:** 100

Simple and Religious Consultation (Bucer), **I:** 177

"Simple Susan" (Edgeworth), **Supp. III:** 153

Simpleton of the Unexpected Isles, The (Shaw), **VI:** 125, 126, 127, 129

Simplicity (Collins), **III:** 166

"Simplify Me When I'm Dead" (Douglas), **VII:** 440

Simpson, Alan, **Supp. II:** 68, 70, 74

Simpson, Percy, **I:** 279

Simpson, Richard, **IV:** 107, 122

Sinai Sort, The (MacCaig), **Supp. VI: 186–187**

"Since thou, O fondest and truest" (Bridges), **VI:** 74, 77

"Sincerest Critick of My Prose, or Rhime" (Congreve), **II:** 349

Singer, S. W., **III:** 69

"Singing, 1977" (Fuller), **Supp. VII:** 79

Single Man, A (Isherwood), **VII:** 309, 316–317

Sing-Song (Rossetti), **V:** 251, 255, 260

Singular Preference, The (Quennell), **VI:** 237, 245

Sinjohn, John, pseud. of John Galsworthy

Sins of the Fathers and Other Tales (Gissing), **V:** 437

Sir Charles Grandison (Richardson), **III:** 80, 90–91, 92; **IV:** 124

"Sir Dominick Ferrand" (James), **VI:** 69

"Sir Edmund Orme" (James), **VI:** 69

"Sir Eustace Grey" (Crabbe), **III:** 282

Sir Gawain and the Carl of Carlisle, **I:** 71

Sir Gawain and the Green Knight, (Gawain–Poet), **I:** 2, 28, 69, 71; **Supp. VII:** 83, 84–91, 94, 98

Sir George Otto Trevelyan: A Memoir (Trevelyan), **VI:** 383, 391

Sir Harry Hotspur of Humblethwaite (Trollope), **V:** 100, 102

Sir Harry Wildair, Being the Sequel of AThe Trip to the Jubilee" (Farquhar), **II:** 352, 357, 364

Sir Hornbook; or, Childe Launcelot's Expedition (Peacock), **IV:** 169

Sir John Vanbrugh's Justificahon of . . . the Duke of Marlborough's Late Tryal (Vanbrugh), **II:** 336

Sir Launcelot Greaves (Smollett), **III:** 149, 153, 158

Sir Martin Mar–All; or, The Feign'd Innocence (Dryden), **II:** 305

Sir Nigel (Doyle), **Supp. II:** 159

Sir Proteus, a Satirical Ballad (Peacock), **IV:** 169

Sir Thomas More; or, Colloquies on the Progress and Prospects of Society (Southey), **IV:** 69, 70, 71, 280

Sir Thomas Wyatt (Dekker and Webster), **II:** 68

Sir Tristrem (Thomas the Rhymer), **IV:** 29

"Sir Walter Scott" (Carlyle), **IV:** 38

Sir Walter Scott: The Great Unknown (Johnson), **IV:** 40

"Sir William Herschel's Long Year" (Hope), **Supp. VII:** 164–165

"Sire de Maletroit's Door, The" (Stevenson), **V:** 395

Siren Land (Douglas), **VI:** 293, 294, 295, 297, 305

"Sirens, The" (Manifold), **VII:** 426

Sirian Experiments, The: The Report by Ambien II, of the Five (Lessing), **Supp. I:** 250, 252

Sirocco (Coward), **Supp. II:** 141, 146, 148

"Siskin" (Stevenson), **Supp. VI:** 256

Sisson, C. J., **I:** 178*n*, 326

Sister Anne (Potter), **Supp. III:** 304

"Sister Helen" (Rossetti), **IV:** 313; **V:** 239, 245

"Sister Imelda" (O'Brien), **Supp. V:** 340

"Sister Maude" (Rossetti), **V:** 259

Sister Songs (Thompson), **V:** 443, 449, 450, 451

Sister Teresa (Moore), **VI:** 87, 92, 98

Sisterly Feelings (Ayckbourn), **Supp. V:** 3, 6, 10, 11–12, 13, 14

"Sisters" (Kinsella), **Supp. V:** 261

Sisters, The (Conrad), **VI:** 148

"Sisters, The" (Joyce), **Retro. Supp. I:** 171–172

Sisters, The (Swinburne), **V:** 330, 333

"Sitting, The" (Day Lewis), **Supp. III:** 128–129

Situation of the Novel, The (Bergonzi), **Supp. IV:** 233

Sitwell, Edith, **I:** 83; **III:** 73, 78; **VI:** 454; **VII:** xv–xvii, **127–141**

Sitwell, Osbert, **V:** 230, 234; **VII:** xvi, 128, 130, 135; **Supp. II:** 199, 201–202, 203

Sitwell, Sacheverell, **VII:** xvi, 128

Six Distinguishing Characters of a Parliament–Man, The (Defoe), **III:** 12

Six Dramas of Calderón. Freely Translated (FitzGerald), **IV:** 342, 344–345, 353

Six Epistles to Eva Hesse (Davie), **Supp. VI:** 111

"Six o'clock in Princes Street" (Owen), **VI:** 451

Six of Calais, The (Shaw), **VI:** 129

Six Poems (Thomas), **Supp. III:** 399

Six Stories Written in the First Person Singular (Maugham), **VI:** 374

"Six Weeks at Heppenheim" (Gaskell), **V:** 14, 15

"Six Years After" (Mansfield), **VII:** 176

"Six Young Men" (Hughes), **Supp. I:** 344; **Retro. Supp. II:** 203–204

"Sixpence" (Mansfield), **VII:** 175, 177

Sixteen Self Sketches (Shaw), **VI:** 102, 129

Sixth Beatitude, The (Hall), **Supp. VI:** 120, 122, **130**

Sixth Heaven, The (Hartley), **Supp. VII:** 124, 125, 127

"Sixth Journey, The" (Graham), **Supp. VII:** 109

Sizemore, Christine Wick, **Supp. IV:** 336

"Skating" (Motion), **Supp. VII:** 251, 256

Skeat, W. W., **I:** 17

"Skeleton, The" (Pritchett), **Supp. III:** 325

Skelton, John, **I: 81–96**

"Sketch, A" (Rossetti), **V:** 250

Sketch Book (Irving), **III:** 54

"Sketch from Private Life, A" (Byron), **IV:** 192

"Sketch of the Great Dejection, A" (Gunn), **Supp. IV:** 274

"Sketch of the Past, A" (Woolf), **Retro. Supp. I:** 314–315

Sketches and Essays (Hazlitt), **IV:** 140

Sketches and Reviews (Pater), **V:** 357

Sketches and Travels in London (Thackeray), **V:** 38

Sketches by Boz (Dickens), **V:** xix, 42, 43–46, 47, 52, 71

"Sketches for a Self–Portrait" (Day Lewis), **Supp. III:** 128

Sketches from Cambridge, by a Don (Stephen), **V:** 289

Sketches of the Principal Picture–Galleries in England (Hazlitt), **IV:** 132, 139

"Skin" (Dahl), **Supp. IV:** 216

Skin Game, The (Galsworthy), **VI:** 275, 280, 288

Skriker, The (Churchill), **Supp. IV:** 179, 180, 197–198

Skull Beneath the Skin, The (James), **Supp. II:** 127; **Supp. IV:** 335–336, 337

"Sky Burning Up Above the Man, The" (Keneally), **Supp. IV:** 345

"Skylarks" (Hughes), **Retro. Supp. II:** 206

Skylight (Hare), **Supp. IV:** 282, 298–299

"Skylight, The" (Heaney), **Retro. Supp. I:** 132

Slag (Hare), **Supp. IV:** 281, 283

"Sleep" (Cowley), **II:** 196

"Sleep, The" (Browning), **IV:** 312

"Sleep and Poetry" (Keats), **IV:** 214–215, 217, 228, 231; **Retro. Supp. I:** 184, 188

Sleep Has His House (Kavan), see *House of Sleep, The*

Sleep It Off, Lady (Rhys), **Supp. II:** 389, 401, 402

Sleep of Prisoners, A (Fry), **Supp. III:** 194, 195, 199–200

Sleep of Reason, The (Snow), **VII:** 324, 331–332

Sleepers of Roraima (Harris), **Supp. V:** 132

Sleep of the Great Hypnotist, The (Redgrove), **Supp. VI:** 231

"Sleeping at Last" (Rossetti), **V:** 251–252, 259

Sleeping Beauty, The (Sitwell), **VII:** 132

Sleeping Fires (Gissing), **V:** 437

Sleeping Lord and Other Fragments, The (Jones), **Supp. VII:** 167, 170, 178–180

Sleeping Murder (Christie), **Supp. II:** 125, 134

Sleeping Prince, The (Rattigan), **Supp. VII:** 318–319

Sleepwalkers, The: A History of Man's Changing Vision of the Universe (Koestler), **Supp. I:** 37–38

Sleuths, Inc. (Eames), **Supp. IV:** 3

Slight Ache, A (Pinter), **Supp. I:** 369, 371; **Retro. Supp. I:** 222–223

"Slips" (McGuckian), **Supp. V:** 281–282

Slocum, Joshua, **Supp. IV:** 158

Slot Machine, The (Sillitoe), **Supp. V:** 411

"Slough" (Betjeman), **VII:** 366

"Slumber Did My Spirit Seal, A" (Wordsworth), **IV:** 18

"Small Boy" (MacCaig), **Supp. VI:** 194

Small Boy and Others, A (James), **VI:** 65

Small Family Business, A (Ayckbourn), **Supp. V:** 3, 12, 14

Small g: A Summer Idyll (Highsmith), **Supp. V:** 179

Small House at Allington, The (Trollope), **V:** xxiii, 101

"Small Personal Voice, The" (Lessing), **Supp. I:** 238

Small Place, A (Kincaid), **Supp. VII:** 217, 225–226, 230, 231

Small Town in Germany, A (le Carré), **Supp. II:** 300, **303–305**, 307

Small World: An Academic Romance (Lodge), **Supp. IV:** 363, 366, 371, 372, 374, 376–378, 384, 385

"*Small World:* An Introduction" (Lodge), **Supp. IV:** 377

Smeaton, O., **III:** 229*n*

"Smile" (Thomas), **Supp. IV:** 491–492

"Smile of Fortune, A" (Conrad), **VI:** 148

Smile Please (Rhys), **Supp. II:** 387, 388, 389, 394, 395, 396

Smiles, Samuel, **VI:** 264

Smiley's People (le Carré), **Supp. II:** 305, 311, **314–315**

Smith, Adam, **IV:** xiv, 144–145; **V:** viii

Smith, Alexander, **IV:** 320; **V:** 158

Smith, Edmund, **III:** 118

Smith, George, **V:** 13, 131, 132, 147, 149, 150, 279–280

Smith, Henry Nash, **VI:** 24

Smith, James, **IV:** 253

Smith, Janet Adam, **V:** 391, 393, 395–398

Smith, Logan Pearsall, **Supp. III:** 98, 111

Smith, Nichol, **III:** 21

Smith, Stevie, **Supp. II: 459–478**

Smith, Sydney, **IV:** 268, 272; **Supp. VII: 339–352**

Smith, William Robertson, **Supp. III:** 171

Smith (Maugham), **VI:** 368

Smith and the Pharaohs and Other Tales (Haggard), **Supp. III:** 214, 222

Smith of Wootton Major (Tolkien), **Supp. II:** 521

Smithers, Peter, **III:** 42, 53

"Smoke" (Mahon), **Supp. VI:** 177

Smollett, Tobias, **III: 146–159;** **V:** xiv 52

Smyer, Richard I., **Supp. IV:** 338

"Snail Watcher, The" (Highsmith), **Supp. V:** 180

Snail Watcher and Other Stories, The (Highsmith), **Supp. V:** 180

"Snake" (Lawrence), **VII:** 119; **Retro. Supp. II:** 233–234

Snake's Pass, The (Stoker), **Supp. III:** 381

"Snap–dragon" (Lawrence), **VII:** 118

Snapper, The (Doyle), **Supp. V:** 77, 82–85, 88

"Snayl, The" (Lovelace), **II:** 231

"Sneaker's A (Mahon), **Supp. VI:** 175–176

"Sniff, The" (Pritchett), **Supp. III:** 319, **320–321**

"Sniper, The" (Sillitoe), **Supp. V:** 414

Snobs of England, The (Thackeray), *see Book of Snobs, The*

Snodgrass, Chris, **V:** 314

Snooty Baronet (Lewis), **VII:** 77

Snow, C. P., **VI:** 235; **VII:** xii, xxi, 235, **321–341**

"Snow" (Hughes), **Supp. I:** 348

"Snow" (MacNeice), **VII:** 412

Snow on the North Side of Lucifer (Sillitoe), **Supp. V:** 424, 425

Snow Party, The (Mahon), **Supp. VI:** 169, **172–173**

"Snow Party, The" (Mahon), **Supp. VI:** 172

"Snowmanshit" (Redgrove), **Supp. VI:** 234

Snowstop (Sillitoe), **Supp. V:** 411

"Snow–White and the Seven Dwarfs" (Dahl), **Supp. IV:** 226

"So crewell prison howe could betyde, alas" (Surrey), **I:** 113

So Lovers Dream (Waugh), **Supp. VI:** 272

"So On He Fares" (Moore), **VI:** 93

"So sweet love seemed that April morn" (Bridges), **VI:** 77

"So to Fatness Come" (Smith), **Supp. II:** 472

"Soap–Pig, The" (Muldoon), **Supp. IV:** 423

"Social Life in Roman Britain" (Trevelyan), **VI:** 393

Social Rights and Duties (Stephen), **V:** 289

Socialism and the Family (Wells), **VI:** 244

Socialism: Its Growth and Outcome (Morris and Box), **V:** 306

"Socialism: Principles and Outlook" (Shaw), **VI:** 129

Society for Pure English Tracts, **VI:** 83

"Sociological Cure for Shellshock, A" (Hibberd), **VI:** 460

"Sofa in the Forties, A" (Heaney), **Retro. Supp. I:** 133

Soft Side, The (James), **VI:** 67

Soft Voice of the Serpent and Other Stories, The (Gordimer), **Supp. II:** 226

"Sohrab and Rustum" (Arnold), **V:** xxi, 208, 209, 210, 216

"Soil Map, The" (McGuckian), **Supp. V:** 282

"Soldier, The" (Brooke), **VI:** 420, 421; **Supp. III:** 57, 58

"Soldier, The" (Hopkins), **V:** 372

Soldier and a Scholar, A (Swift), **III:** 36

Soldier of Humour (ed. Rosenthal), **VII:** 73

Soldier, Soldier (Arden), **Supp. II:** 28

Soldier's Art, The (Powell), **VII:** 349

"Soldiers Bathing" (Prince), **VII:** xxii 427

"Soldier's Declaration, A" (Sassoon), **Supp. IV:** 57

Soldier's Embrace, A (Gordimer), **Supp. II:** 232

"Soldiers of the Queen" (Kipling), **VI:** 417

Soldiers Three (Kipling), **VI:** 204

"Sole of a Foot, The" (Hughes), **Supp. I:** 357

Solid Geometry (McEwan), **Supp. IV:** 390, 398

"Solid House, A" (Rhys), **Supp. II:** 402

Solid Mandala, The (White), **Supp. I:** 131, **143–145**, 148, 152

"Solid Objects" (Woolf), **VII:** 31

"Soliloquies" (Hill), **Supp. V:** 187

Soliloquies (St. Augustine), **Retro. Supp. II:** 297

"Soliloquy by the Well" (Redgrove), **Supp. VI:** 230

"Soliloquy of the Spanish Cloister" (Browning), **IV:** 356, 360, 367

Soliman and Perseda, **I:** 220

"Solitary Confinement" (Koestler), **Supp. I:** 36

"Solitary Reaper, The" (Wordsworth), **IV:** 22

"Solitude" (Carroll), **V:** 263

"Solitude" (Milne), **Supp. V:** 303

"Solitude" (Traherne), **II:** 192

Sollers, Philippe, **Supp. IV:** 115, 116

Solomon, Simeon, **V:** 312, 314, 320

Solomon's Temple Spiritualized (Bunyan), **II:** 253

Solon, **II:** 70

Solstices (MacNeice), **VII:** 416

"Solution, The" (James), **VI:** 69

Some Advice . . . to the Members of the October Club (Swift), **III:** 35

Some Arguments Against Enlarging the Power of the Bishop (Swift), **III:** 35

Some Do Not (Ford), **VI:** 319

Some Early Impressions (Stephen), **V:** 278, 281, 290

Some Free Thoughts upon the Present State of Affairs (Swift), **III:** 27, 36

Some Gospel–Truths Opened According to the Scriptures (Bunyan), **II:** 253

Some Imagist Poets (ed. Lowell), **Supp. III:** 397

Some Observations upon a Paper (Swift), **III:** 35

Some Papers Proper to Be Read Before the Royal Society (Fielding), **III:** 105

Some Passages in the Life of Major Gahagan (Thackeray), *see Tremendous Adventures of Major Gahagan, The*

Some Popular Fallacies About Vivisection (Carroll), **V:** 273

Some Reasons Against the . . . Tyth of Hemp . . . (Swift), **III:** 36

Some Reasons to Prove That No Person Is Obliged . . . as a Whig, etc. (Swift), **III:** 35

Some Recent Attacks: Essays Cultural and Political (Kelman), **Supp. V:** 257

Some Remarks on the Barrier Treaty (Swift), **III:** 35

Some Remarks upon a Pamphlet (Swift), **III:** 35

Some Reminiscences (Conrad), **VI:** 148

Some Tame Gazelle (Pym), **Supp. II:** **366–367**, 380

Some Time Never: A Fable for Supermen (Dahl), **Supp. IV:** 211, 213, 214

Some Versions of Pastoral (Empson; US. title, *English Pastoral Poetry*), **Supp. II:** 179, 184, 188, **189–190**, 197

Someone Like You (Dahl), **Supp. IV:** 206, 214, 215

Somers, Jane, *see Diaries of Jane Somers, The*

Somerset Maugham (Brander), **VI:** 379

Somerset Maugham (Curtis), **VI:** 379

Somervell, Robert, **VI:** 385

Something Childish, and Other Stories (Mansfield), **VII:** 171

"Something Else" (Priestley), **VII:** 212–213

Something Fresh (Wodehouse), *see Something New*

Something New (Wodehouse), **Supp. III:** 452, 453

"Something the Cat Dragged In" (Highsmith), **Supp. V:** 180

"Sometime I fled the fire that me brent" (Wyatt), **I:** 103–104

Somewhere Is Such a Kingdom: Poems, 1952–1971 (Hill), **Supp. V:** 184

Somnium Scipionis (Cicero), **IV:** 189

"Son, The" (Swift), **Supp. V:** 432–433

Son of Frankenstein (film), **III:** 342

"Sonatas in Silence" (Owen), **VI:** 449, 451, 454

Sone and Air of the Foirsaid Foxe, called Father wer, The: Alswa the Parliament of fourfuttit Beistis, halden be the Lyoun (Henryson), *see Trial of the Fox, The*

"Song" (Blake), **III:** 290

"Song" (Collins), **III:** 170

"Song" (Congreve, two poems), **II:** 347–348

"Song" (Ewart), **Supp. VII:** 36

"Song" (Goldsmith), **III:** 184–185

"Song" (Lewis), **VII:** 446

"Song" (Nicholson), **Supp. VI:** 216

"Song" (Tennyson), **IV:** 329

"Song, A" (Rochester), **II:** 258

"Song [3]" (Thomas), **Supp. III:** 401

"Song, The" (Muir), **Supp. VI:** 208

"Song at the Beginning of Autumn" (Jennings), **Supp. V:** 214

Song at Twilight, A (Coward), **Supp. II:** 156–157

Song for a Birth or a Death (Jennings), **Supp. V:** 213, 215

"Song for a Birth or a Death" (Jennings), **Supp. V:** 215

"Song for a Corncrake" (Murphy), **Supp. V:** 324

"Song for a Phallus" (Hughes), **Supp. I:** 351

"Song for the Four Seasons" (Reid), **Supp. VII:** 326

"Song for the Swifts" (Jennings), **Supp. V:** 218

Song for St. Cecilia's Day, A (Dryden), **II:** 304

"Song for Simeon, A" (Eliot), **VII:** 152

"Song from Armenia, A" (Hill), **Supp. V:** 189

"Song from Cymbeline, A" (Collins), **III:** 163, 169–170

"Song in Storm, A" (Kipling), **VI:** 201

"Song in the Songless" (Meredith), **V:** 223

"Song of a Camera" (Gunn), **Supp. IV:** 273

Song of Hylas (Morris), **VII:** 164

Song of Italy, A (Swinburne), **V:** 313, 332

Song of Liberty, A (Blake), **III:** 307

Song of Los, The (Blake), **III:** 307; **Retro. Supp. I:** 44

"Song of Poplars" (Huxley), **VII:** 199

"Song of Rahero, The" (Stevenson), **V:** 396

Song of Roland, **I:** 69

Song of Songs (Redgrove), **Supp. VI:** 233

"Song of the Amateur Psychologist" (Empson), **Supp. II:** 181

"Song of the Bower" (Rossetti), **V:** 243

Song of the Cold, The (Sitwell), **VII:** 132, 136, 137

"Song of the Militant Romance, The" (Lewis), **VII:** 79

"Song of the Night" (Kinsella), **Supp. V:** 269

Song of the Night and Other Poems (Kinsella), **Supp. V:** 269

"Song of the Rat" (Hughes), **Supp. I:** 348

"Song of the Shirt, The" (Hood), **IV:** 252, 261, 263–264

"Song. To Celia" (Jonson), **Retro. Supp. I:** 164

"Song Written at Sea . . ." (Dorset), **II:** 261–262, 270

"Songbook of Sebastian Arrurruz, The" (Hill), **Supp. V:** 187, 188–189

Songlines, The (Chatwin), **Supp. IV:** 157, 158, 160, 161, 162, 163, 170–173, 174

Songs, The (Burns), **III:** 322

Songs and Sonnets (Donne), **I:** 357, 358, 360, 368

Songs Before Sunrise (Swinburne), **V:** xxiii, 313, 314, 324–325, 331, 332

"Songs for Strangers and Pilgrims" (Rossetti), **V:** 251, 254n, 260

"Songs in a Cornfield" (Rossetti), **V:** 258

Songs of Chaos (Read), **VI:** 436

Songs of Enchantment (Okri), **Supp. V:** 348–349, 350, 353, 358–359

Songes and Sonnettes . . . (pub. Tottel), see Tottel's Miscellany

Songs of Experience (Blake), **III:** 292, 293, 294, 297; **Retro. Supp. I:** 34, 36–37

Songs of Innocence (Blake), **III:** 292, 297, 307

Songs of Innocence and of Experience (Blake), **III:** 290, 299, 307; **V:** xv, 330; **Retro. Supp. I:** 36, 42–43

Songs of the Psyche (Kinsella), **Supp. V:** 270

"Songs of the PWD Man, The" (Harrison), **Supp. V:** 151

Songs of the Springtides (Swinburne), **V:** 332

Songs of Travel (Stevenson), **V:** 385, 396

Songs of Two Nations (Swinburne), **V:** 332

Songs Wing to Wing (Thompson), see Sister Songs

"Songster, The" (Smith), **Supp. II:** 465

"Sonnet, A" (Jennings), **Supp. V:** 207

"Sonnet, 1940" (Ewart), **VII:** 423

"Sonnet on the Death of Richard West" (Gray), **III:** 137

"Sonnet to Henry Lawes" (Milton), **II:** 175

"Sonnet to Liberty" (Wilde), **V:** 401

"Sonnet to Mr. Cyriack Skinner Upon His Blindness" (Milton), **II:** 164

"Sonnet to my Friend with an identity disc" (Owen), **VI:** 449

sonnets (Bridges), **VI:** 81

sonnets (Shakespeare), **I:** 307–308

"Sonnets for August 1945" (Harrison), **Supp. V:** 161–162

"Sonnets for August 1945" (Harrison), **Supp. V:** 161–162

"Sonnets for Five Seasons" (Stevenson), **Supp. VI:** 262

"Sonnets from Hellas" (Heaney), **Retro. Supp. I:** 133–134

"Sonnets from the Portuguese" (Browning), **IV:** xxi, 311, 314, 320, 321

Sonnets of William Wordsworth, The, **IV:** 25

Sonnets to Fanny Kelly (Lamb), **IV:** 81, 83

Sons and Lovers (Lawrence), **VII:** 88, 89, 91, 92, **95–98**; **Retro. Supp. II:** 227

"Sons of the Brave" (Kinsella), **Supp. V:** 261

"Sorrow" (Muir), **Supp. VI:** 207

Sort of Freedom, A (Friel), **Supp. V:** 115

"Son's Veto, The" (Hardy), **VI:** 22

Sophonisba (Marston), see Wonder of Women, The

Sordello (Browning), **IV:** xix, 355, 371, 373

Sorel, Georges, **VI:** 170

Sorley, Charles Hamilton, **VI:** xvi, 415, 417, 420, **421–422**

Sorrow in Sunlight (Firbank), see Prancing Nigger

"Sorrow of true love is a great sorrow, The" (Thomas), **Supp. III:** 396

Sorrows of Young Werther, The (Goethe), **IV:** xiv, 59; **Supp. IV:** 28

"Sort of" (Fuller), **Supp. VII:** 80

"Sort of Exile in Lyme Regis, A" (Fowles), **Supp. I:** 292

"Sospetto d'Herode" (Crashaw), **II:** 180, 183–184

Sotheby, William, **IV:** 50

Sot–Weed Factor, The (Barth), **Supp. IV:** 116

Soul and Body I, **Retro. Supp. II:** 301

Soul for Sale, A: Poems (Kavanagh), **Supp. VII:** 193, 199

Soul of Man Under Socialism, The (Wilde), **V:** 409, 413, 415, 419

"Soul of Man Under Socialism, The" (Wilde), **Supp. IV:** 288; **Retro. Supp. II:** 367

Souls and Bodies (Lodge), see How Far Can You Go?

"Soul's Beauty," (Rossetti), **V:** 237

"Soul's Expression, The" (Browning), **IV:** 313

Souls of Black Folk, The (Du Bois), **Supp. IV:** 86

"Soul's Travelling, The" (Browning), **IV:** 313

Sound Barrier, The (Rattigan), **Supp. VII:** 318

"Sound Machine, The" (Dahl), **Supp. IV:** 214–215

"Sound of the River, The" (Rhys), **Supp. II:** 402

"Sounds of a Devon Village" (Davie), **Supp. VI:** 113

"Sounds of the Day" (MacCaig), **Supp. VI:** 189

Soursweet (film), **Supp. IV:** 390, 399

Soursweet (Mo), **Supp. IV:** 390, 400

South Africa (Trollope), **V:** 102

South Sea Bubble (Coward), **Supp. II:** 155

South Seas, The (Stevenson), **V:** 396

South Wind (Douglas), **VI:** 293, 294, 300–302, 304, 305; **VII:** 200

Southam, Brian Charles, **IV:** xi, xiii, xxv, 122, 124, 337

Southern, Thomas, **II:** 305

"Southern Night, A" (Arnold), **V:** 210

Southerne, Thomas, **Supp. III:** 34–35

Southey, Cuthbert, **IV:** 62, 72

Southey, Robert, **III:** 276, 335; **IV:** viii–ix, xiv, xvii, 43, 45, 52, **58–72**, 85, 88, 89, 92, 102, 128, 129, 162, 168, 184–187, 270, 276, 280; **V:** xx, 105, 121; **Supp. IV:** 425, 426–427

"Southey and Landor" (Landor), **IV:** 93

"Southey and Porson" (Landor), **IV:** 93, 97

"Southey's Colloquies" (Macaulay), **IV:** 280

Southey's Common–place Book (ed. Warter), **IV:** 71

"South–Sea House, The" (Lamb), **IV:** 81–82

"South–Wester The" (Meredith), **V:** 223

Souvenirs (Fuller), **Supp. VII:** 67, 81

Sovereignty of Good, The (Murdoch), **Supp. I:** 217–218, 225

"Soviet Myth and Reality" (Koestler), **Supp. I:** 27

Space Vampires (Wilson), **III:** 341

"Spain 1937" (Auden), **VII:** 384; **Retro. Supp. I:** 8

Spanish Curate, The (Fletcher and Massinger), **II:** 66

Spanish Fryar, The; or, The Double Discovery (Dryden), **II:** 305

Spanish Gipsy, The (Middleton and Rowley), **II:** 100

Spanish Gypsy, The (Eliot), **V:** 198, 200

"Spanish Military Nun, The" (De Quincey), **IV:** 149

Spanish Tragedy, The (Kyd), **I:** 212, 213, 218, 220, **221–229; II:** 25, 28–29, 69

Spanish Virgin and Other Stories, The (Pritchett), **Supp. III:** 316, 317

Spanner and Pen (Fuller), **Supp. VII:** 67, 68, 74, 81

Spark, Muriel, **Supp. I: 199–214; Supp. IV:** 100, 234

"Sparrow" (MacCaig), **Supp. VI:** 192

Sparrow, John, **VI:** xv, xxxiv; **VII:** 355, 363

Sparrow, The (Ayckbourn), **Supp. V:** 2

"Spate in Winter Midnight" (MacCaig), **Supp. VI:** 187

"Spätlese, The" (Hope), **Supp. VII:** 157

Speak, Parrot (Skelton), **I:** 83, 90–91

"Speak to Me" (Tennyson), **IV:** 332

Speaker (periodical), **VI:** 87, 335

"Speaking a Foreign Language" (Reid), **Supp. VII:** 330

Speaking Likenesess (Rossetti), **V:** 260

"Special Type, The" (James), **VI:** 69

"Specimen of an Induction to a Poem" (Keats), **IV:** 214

Specimens of English Dramatic Poets (Lamb), **IV:** xvi 79, 85

Specimens of German Romance (Carlyle), **IV:** 250

Specimens of Modern Poets: The Heptalogia . . . (Swinburne), **V:** 332

Speckled Bird, The (Yeats), **VI:** 222; **Retro. Supp. I:** 326

Spectator (periodical), **III:** 39, 41, 44, **46–50,** 52, 53; **V:** 86, 238; **VI:** 87; **Supp. IV:** 121

Spectatorial Essays (Strachey), **Supp. II:** 497, 502

"Spectre of the Real, The" (Hardy), **VI:** 20

Speculations (Hulme), **Supp. VI:** 134, 140

Speculative Instruments (Richards), **Supp. I:** 426

Speculum hominis (Gower), **I:** 48

Speculum meditantis (Gower), **I:** 48

Speculum Principis (Skelton), **I:** 84

Spedding, James, **I:** 257n, 259, 264, 324

Speech Against Prelates Innovations (Waller), **II:** 238

Speech . . . Against Warren Hastings (Sheridan), **III:** 270

Speech . . . for the Better Security of the Independence of Parliament (Burke), **III:** 205

Speech, 4 July 1643 (Waller), **II:** 238

Speech . . . in Bristol upon . . . His Parliamentary Conduct, A (Burke), **III:** 205

Speech on American Taxation (Burke), **III:** 205

Speech . . . on Mr. Fox's East India Bill (Burke), **III:** 205

Speech on Moving His Resolutions for Conciliation with the Colonies (Burke), **III:** 205

Speech on Parliamentary Reform (Macaulay), **IV:** 274

Speech on the Anatomy Bill (Macaulay), **IV:** 277

Speech on the Army Estimates (Burke), **III:** 205

Speech on the Edinburgh Election (Macaulay), **IV:** 274

Speech on the People's Charter (Macaulay), **IV:** 274

Speech on the Ten Hours Bill (Macaulay), **IV:** 276–277

Speech Relative to the Nabob of Arcot's Debts (Burke), **III:** 205

Speech to the Electors of Bristol (Burke), **III:** 205

Speeches on Parliamentary Reform (Disraeli), **IV:** 308

Speeches on the Conservative Policy of the Last Thirty Years (Disraeli), **IV:** 308

Speeches, Parliamentary and Miscellaneous (Macaulay), **IV:** 291

Speedy Post, A (Webster), **II:** 69, 85

Spell, The: An Extravaganza (Brontë), **V:** 151

Spell for Green Corn, A (Brown), **Supp. VI: 72–73**

Spell of Words, A (Jennings), **Supp. V:** 219

"Spelt from Sybil's Leaves" (Hopkins), **V:** 372–373

Spence, Joseph, **II:** 261; **III:** 69, 86n

Spencer, Baldwin, **Supp. III:** 187–188

Spencer, Herbert, **V:** 182, 189, 284

Spender, Stephen, **VII:** 153, 382, 410; **Supp. II: 481–495; Supp. III:** 103, 117, 119; **Supp. IV:** 95

Spengler, Osvald, **Supp. IV:** 1, 3, 10, 11, 12, 17

Spenser, Edmund, **I: 121–144,** 146; **II:** 50, 302; **III:** 167n; **IV:** 59, 61, 93, 205; **V:** 318

Sphinx (Thomas), **Supp. IV:** 485

"Sphinx, The" (Rossetti), **V:** 241

Sphinx, The (Wilde), **V:** 409–410, 415, 419; **Retro. Supp. II:** 371

"Sphinx; or, Science" (Bacon), **I:** 267

Spider (Weldon), **Supp. IV:** 521

Spielmann, M. H., **V:** 137, 152

Spiess, Johann, **III:** 344

Spingarn, J. E., **II:** 256n

"Spinster Sweet-Arts, The" (Tennyson), **IV:** 327

Spiral, The (Reid), **Supp. VII:** 330

Spire, The (Golding), **Supp. I:** 67, **79–81,** 83; **Retro. Supp. I:** 99–100

"Spirit Dolls, The" (McGuckian), **Supp. V:** 292

"Spirit is Too Blunt an Instrument, The" (Stevenson), **Supp. VI:** 256

Spirit Level, The (Heaney), **Retro. Supp. I:** 132–133

Spirit of Man, The (ed. Bridges), **II:** 160; **VI:** 76, 83

Spirit of the Age, The (Hazlitt), **III:** 276; **IV:** xi, 39, 129, 131, 132–134, 137, 139

Spirit of Whiggism, The (Disraeli), **IV:** 308

Spirit Rise, A (Warner), **Supp. VII:** 380

Spirits in Bondage (Lewis), **Supp. III:** 250

Spiritual Exercises (Loyola), **V:** 362, 367, 371, 373n; **Retro. Supp. II:** 188

Spiritual Exercises (Spender), **Supp. II:** 489

"Spiritual Explorations" (Spender), **Supp. II:** 489, 490

"Spite of thy hap hap hath well happed" (Wyatt), **I:** 103

Spitzer, L., **IV:** 323n, 339

Spivack, Bernard, **I:** 214

Spivak, Gayatri, **Retro. Supp. I:** 60

Splitting (Weldon), **Supp. IV:** 535

Spoils, The (Bunting), **Supp. VII:** 5, 7–9

Spoils of Poynton, The (James), **VI: 49–50**

"Spoilt Child, The" (Motion), **Supp. VII:** 251

Sport of Nature, A (Gordimer), **Supp. II:** 232, 239–240, 241, 242

Spottiswoode, John, **II:** 142

Sprat, Thomas, **II:** 195, 196, 198, 200, 202, 294; **III:** 29

"Spraying the Potatoes" (Kavanagh), **Supp. VII:** 190

Spreading the News (Gregory), **VI:** 309, 315, 316

"Sprig of Lime, The" (Nichols), **VI:** 419

"Spring, The" (Carew), **II:** 225

"Spring, The" (Cowley), **II:** 197

"Spring" (Hopkins), **V:** 368

Spring (Thomson), **Supp. III:** 413–414, 415, 416,

"Spring and Fall" (Hopkins), **V:** 371–372, 381; **Retro. Supp. II:** 196–197

Spring Days (Moore), **VI:** 87, 91

Spring Fever (Wodehouse), **Supp. III:** 451

"Spring Hail" (Murray), **Supp. VII:** 272, 279, 281

"Spring Morning" (Milne), **Supp. V:** 302

"Spring Nature Notes" (Hughes), **Supp. I:** 358

"Spring 1942" (Fuller), **VII:** 429

"Spring Offensive" (Owen), **VI:** 455, 456, 458

"Spring Song" (Milne), **Supp. V:** 309–310

Spring, Summer, Autumn, Winter (Hughes), **Supp. I:** 357

sprung rhythm, **V:** 363, 365, 367, 374, 376, 379, 380

Spy in the Family, A (Waugh), **Supp. VI:** 276

Spy Story, The (Cawelti and Rosenberg), **Supp. IV:** 7

Spy Who Came In from the Cold, The (le Carré), **Supp. II:** 299, 301, 305, **307–309,** 313, 315, 316, 317

Square Cat, The (Ayckbourn), **Supp. V:** 2

Square Egg and Other Sketches, The (Saki), **Supp. VI:** 242, 250–251

Square Rounds (Harrison), **Supp. V:** 164

Squaring the Circle (Stoppard), **Supp. I:** 449–450, 451

"Squarings" (Heaney), **Retro. Supp. I:** 132

"Squaw, The" (Stoker), **Supp. III:** 382–383

"Squire Hooper" (Hardy), **Retro. Supp. I:** 121

418, 420Squire, J. C., **VII:** xvi

"Squire Petrick's Lady" (Hardy), **VI:** 22

Squire Trelooby (Congreve, Vanbrugh, Walsh), **II:** 325, 336, 339, 347, 350

Squire's Tale, The (Chaucer), **I:** 23, 24

"Sredni Vashtar" (Saki), **Supp. VI:** 245–246

"Stabilities" (Stevenson), **Supp. VI:** 256

Stade, George, **Supp. IV:** 402

"Staff and Scrip, The" (Rossetti), **V:** 240

Staffordshire Sentinel (periodical), **VI:** 248

"Stag in a Neglected Hayfield" (MacCraig), **Supp. VI:** 192

Stage Coach, The, **II:** 353, 358, 364

Stalin, Joseph, **Supp. IV:** 82

Stalky & Co. (Kipling), **VI:** 204; **Supp. IV:** 506

Stallworthy, Jon, **VI:** 220, 438

Stallybrass, Oliver, **VI:** 397

Stamboul Train (Greene; US. title, *Orient Express*), **Supp. I:** 3, 4–5; **Retro. Supp. II:** 152

Standard of Behavior, A (Trevor), **Supp. IV:** 505

Standing Room Only (Ayckbourn), **Supp. V:** 2, 11

Stanley, Arthur, **V:** 13, 349

Stanley and Iris (film), **Supp. IV:** 45

Stanley and The Women (Amis), **Supp. II:** 17–18

Stans puer ad mensam (Lydgate), **I:** 58

"Stanzas" (Hood), **IV:** 263

"Stanzas from the Grande Chartreuse" (Arnold), **V:** 210

"Stanzas in Memory of the Author of 'Obermann' " (Arnold), **V:** 206

"Stanzas Written in Dejection" (Shelley), **IV:** 201

Staple of News, The (Jonson), **Retro. Supp. I:** 165

Star (periodical), **VI:** 103

Star over Bethlehem (Fry), **Supp. III:** 195

Star Turns Red, The (O'Casey), **VII:** 7–8

Stares (Fuller), **Supp. VII:** 81

"Stare's Nest by My Window, The" (Yeats), **VI:** 212

Staring at the Sun (Barnes), **Supp. IV:** 65, 67, 70–71

"Starlight Night, The" (Hopkins), **V:** 366, 367; **Retro. Supp. II:** 190

"Stars" (Brontë), **V:** 133, 142

Stars of the New Curfew (Okri), **Supp. V:** 347, 348, 352, 355, 356–357

Start in Life, A (Brookner), *see Debut, The*

Start in Life, A (Sillitoe), **Supp. V:** 410, 413

Starting Point (Day Lewis), **Supp. III:** 118, 130–131

State of France, . . . in the IXth Year of . . . , Lewis XIII, The (Evelyn), **II:** 287

State of Independence, A (Phillips), **Supp. V:** 380, 383–384

State of Innocence, The (Dryden), **II:** 290, 294, 305

"State of Poetry, The" (Jennings), **Supp. V:** 215

"State of Religious Parties, The" (Newman), **Supp. VII:** 294

State of Siege (Ambler; formerly *The Night-Comers*), **Supp. IV:** 4, 16

States of Emergency (Brink), **Supp. VI:** 53–54

Statesman's Manual, The (Coleridge), **IV:** 56; **Retro. Supp. II:** 64

"Statements, The" (Ewart), **Supp. VII:** 39

Station Island (Heaney), **Supp. II:** 268, 277–279

"Station Island" (Heaney), **Supp. II:** 277–278; **Retro. Supp. I:** 124, 130–131

Stations (Heaney), **Retro. Supp. I:** 129

"Statue and the Bust, The" (Browning), **IV:** 366

"Statue in Stocks-Market, The" (Marvell), **II:** 218

"Statues, The" (Yeats), **VI:** 215

Staying On (Scott), **Supp. I:** 259, 272–274

Stead, Christina, **Supp. IV:** 459–477

"Steam Washing Co., The" (Hood), **IV:** 267

"Steel, The" (Murray), **Supp. VII:** 278

Steel Glass, The (Gascoigne), **I:** 149

Steele, Richard, **II:** 359; **III:** 7, 18, 19, 38–53

"Steep and her own world" (Thomas), **Supp. III:** 401

Steep Holm (Fowles), **Supp. I:** 292

Steevens, G. W., **VI:** 351

Steevens, George, **I:** 326

Steffan, Truman Guy, **IV:** 179, 193

Stein, Arnold, **Retro. Supp. II:** 181

Stein, Gertrude, **VI:** 252; **VII:** 83; **Supp. IV:** 416, 542, 556, 557–558

Steiner, George, **Supp. IV:** 455

"Stella at Wood-Park" (Swift), **III:** 32

"Stella's Birth Day, 1725" (Swift), **III:** 32

"Stella's Birthday . . . A.D. 1720–21" (Swift), **III:** 32

"Stella's Birthday, March 13, 1727" (Swift), **III:** 32

Stella's Birth-Days: A Poem (Swift), **III:** 36

Stendhal, **Supp. IV:** 136, 459

Step by Step (Churchill), **VI:** 356

Stephen, Janus K., **IV:** 10–11, 268

Stephen, Leslie, **II:** 156, 157; **III:** 42; **IV:** 301, 304–306; **V:** xix, xxv, xxvi, 277–290, 386; **VII:** xxii, 17, 238

Stephen Hero (Joyce), **VII:** 45–46, 48

Stephens, Frederick, **V:** 235, 236

Stephens, James, **VI:** 88

Steps to the Temple. Sacred Poems, with Other Delights of the Muses (Crashaw), **II:** 179, 180, 184, 201

Sterling, John, **IV:** 54

Stern, Gladys Bronwen, **IV:** 123; **V:** xiii, xxviii, 395

Stern, J. B., **I:** 291

Stern, Laurence, **III:** 124–135, 150, 153, 155, 157; **IV:** 79, 183; **VII:** 20; **Supp. II:** 204; **Supp. III:** 108

Steuart, J. A., **V:** 392, 397

Stevens, Wallace, **V:** 412; **Supp. IV:** 257, 414; **Supp. V:** 183

Stevenson, Anne, **Supp. VI:** 253–268

Stevenson, L., **V:** 230, 234

Stevenson, Robert Louis, **I:** 1; **II:** 153; **III:** 330, 334, 345; **V:** xiii, xxi, xxv, vxvi, 219, 233, 383–398; **Supp. IV:** 61; **Retro. Supp. I:** 259–272

Stevenson and Edinburgh: A Centenary Study (MacLaren), **V:** 393, 398

Stevenson Companion, The (ed. Hampden), **V:** 393, 395

Stevensoniana (ed. Hammerton), **V:** 393, 397

Stewart, J. I. M., **I:** 329; **IV:** xxv; **VII:** xiv, xxxviii

Stiff Upper Lip (Durrell), **Supp. I:** 113

Still Centre, The (Spender), **Supp. II:** 488, 489

"Still Falls the Rain" (Sitwell), **VII:** xvii, 135, 137

Still Life (Byatt), **Supp. IV:** 139, 145, 147–149, 151, 154

Still Life (Coward), **Supp. II:** 153

Stirling, William Alexander, earl of, *see* Alexander, William

"Stoic, A" (Galsworthy), **VI:** 275, 284

Stoker, Bram, **III:** 334, 342, 343, 344, 345; **Supp. III:** 375–391

Stokes, John, **V:** xiii, xxviii

Stolen Bacillus, The, and Other Incidents (Wells), **VI:** 226, 243

"Stolen Child, The" (Yeats), **Retro. Supp. I:** 329

Stone, C., **III:** 161*n*

"Stone Mania" (Murphy), **Supp. V:** 326

Stone Virgin (Unsworth), **Supp. VII:** 355, 356, 357, 360–361, 362, 365

Stones of Venice, The (Ruskin), **V:** xxi, 173, 176–177, 180, 184, 292

"Stony Grey Soil "(Kavanagh), **Supp. VII:** 189–190

Stoppard, Tom, **Supp. I:** 437–454; **Retro. Supp. II:** 343–358

Storey, David, **Supp. I:** 407–420

Storey, Graham, **V:** xi, xxviii, 381

Stories, Dreams, and Allegories (Schreiner), **Supp. II:** 450

Stories from "Black and White" (Hardy), **VI:** 20

Stories of Red Hanrahan (Yeats), **VI:** 222

Stories, Theories and Things (Brooke-Rose), **Supp. IV:** 99, 110

"Stories, Theories and Things" (Brooke-Rose), **Supp. IV:** 116

"Storm" (Owen), **VI:** 449

"Storm, The" (Brown), **Supp. VI:** 70–71

"Storm, The" (Donne), **Retro. Supp. II:** 86

Storm, The; or, A Collection of . . . Casualties and Disasters . . . (Defoe), **III:** 13; **Retro. Supp. I:** 68

Storm and Other Poems (Sillitoe), **Supp. V:** 424

"Storm Bird, Storm Dreamer" (Ballard), **Supp. V:** 26

"Storm is over, The land hushes to rest, The" (Bridges), **VI:** 79

"Stormpetrel" (Murphy), **Supp. V:** 315

"Storm–Wind" (Ballard), **Supp. V:** 22

"Story, A" (Thomas), **Supp. I:** 183

Story and the Fable, The (Muir), **Supp. VI:** 198

"Story in It, The" (James), **VI:** 69

"Story of a Masterpiece, The" (James), **VI:** 69

Story of a Non–Marrying Man, The (Lessing), **Supp. I:** 253–254

"Story of a Panic, The" (Forster), **VI:** 399

"Story of a Year, The" (James), **VI:** 69

Story of an African Farm, The (Schreiner), **Supp. II:** 435, 438, 439, 440, 441, **445–447,** 449, 451, 453, 456

Story of Fabian Socialism, The (Cole), **VI:** 131

Story of Grettir the strong, The (Morris and Magnusson), **V:** 306

Story of Rimini, The (Hunt), **IV:** 214

Story of San Michele, The (Munthe), **VI:** 265

Story of Sigurd the Volsung and the Fall of the Niblungs, The (Morris), **V:** xxiv, 299–300, 304, 306

Story of the Glittering Plain, The (Morris), **V:** 306

Story of the Injured Lady, The (Swift), **III:** 27

Story of the Malakand Field Force (Churchill), **VI:** 351

Story of the Sundering Flood, The (Morris), **V:** 306

"Story of the Three Bears, The" (Southey), **IV:** 58, 67

"Story of the Unknown Church, The" (Morris), **V:** 293, 303

Story of the Volsungs and . . . Songs from the Elder Edda, The (Morris and Magnusson), **V:** 299, 306

Story So Far, The (Ayckbourn), **Supp. V:** 2

"Storyteller, The" (Berger), **Supp. IV:** 90, 91

Story–Teller, The (Highsmith), **Supp. V:** 174–175

Storyteller, The (Sillitoe), **Supp. V:** 410

Story–Teller's Holiday, A (Moore), **VI:** 88, 95, 99

Stout, Mira, **Supp. IV:** 75

Stovel, Nora Foster, **Supp. IV:** 245, 249

Stowe, Harriet Beecher, **V:** xxi, 3

Strachey, J. St. Loe, **V:** 75, 86, 87

Strachey, Lytton, **III:** 21, 28; **IV:** 292; **V:** 13, 157, 170, 277; **VI:** 155, 247, 372, 407; **VII:** 34, 35; **Supp. II:** **497–517**

Strado, Famiano, **II:** 90

Strafford: An Historical Tragedy (Browning), **IV:** 373

Strait Gate, The . . . (Bunyan), **II:** 253

"Strand at Lough Beg, The" (Heaney), **Supp. II:** 278

Strange and the Good, The (Fuller), **Supp. VII:** 81

"Strange and Sometimes Sadness, A" (Ishiguro), **Supp. IV:** 303, 304

Strange Case of Dr. Jekyll and Mr. Hyde, The (Stevenson), **III:** 330, 342, 345; **V:** xxv, 383, 387, 388, 395; **VI:** 106; **Supp. IV:** 61; **Retro. Supp. I:** 263, 264–266

"Strange Comfort Afforded by the Profession" (Lowry), **Supp. III:** 281

Strange Fruit (Phillips), **Supp. V:** 380

"Strange Meeting" (Owen), **VI:** 444, 445, 449, 454, 457–458

Strange Necessity, The (West), **Supp. III:** 438

"Strange Ride of Morrowbie Jukes, The" (Kipling), **VI:** **175–178**

Strange Ride of Rudyard Kipling, The (Wilson), **VI:** 165; **Supp. I:** 167

Stranger, The (Kotzebue), **III:** 268

Stranger Still, A (Kavan), **Supp. VII:** 207–208, 209

Stranger With a Bag, A (Warner), **Supp. VII:** 380

Strangers and Brothers cycle (Snow), **VII:** xxi, 322, **324–336**

Strangers on a Train (Highsmith), **Supp. V:** 167, 168–169

Strapless (film), **Supp. IV:** 282, 291–292

"Strategist, The" (Saki), **Supp. VI:** 243

"Stratton Water" (Rossetti), **V:** 239

Strauss, Richard, **Supp. IV:** 556

"Strawberry Hill" (Hughes), **Supp. I:** 342

Strayed Reveller, The (Arnold), **V:** xxi, 209, 216

"Street in Cumberland, A" (Nicholson), **Supp. VI:** 216

Street Songs (Sitwell), **VII:** 135

"Streets of the Spirits" (Redgrove), **Supp. VI:** 235

"Strephon and Chloe" (Swift), **III:** 32; **Retro. Supp. I:** 284, 285

Strickland, Agnes, **I:** 84

Strictures on A Coningsby" (Disraeli), **IV:** 308

"Strictures on Pictures" (Thackeray), **V:** 37

Striding Folly (Sayers), **Supp. III:** 335

Strife (Galsworthy), **VI:** xiii, 269, 285–286

Strike at Arlingford, The (Moore), **VI:** 95

Strindberg, August, **Supp. III:** 12

Stringham, Charles, **IV:** 372

Strings Are False, The (MacNeice), **VII:** 406

Strode, Ralph, **I:** 49

Strong, Roy, **I:** 237

Strong Poison (Sayers), **Supp. III:** 339, 342, 343, 345

Stronger Climate, A: Nine Stories (Jhabvala), **Supp. V:** 235

Structure and Distribution of Coral Reefs, On the (Darwin), **Supp. VII:** 19

Structural Analysis of Pound's Usura Canto: Jakobson and Applied to Free Verse, A (Brooke–Rose), **Supp. IV:** 99, 114

Structural Transformation of the Public Sphere, The (Habermas), **Supp. IV:** 112

Structure in Four Novels by H. G. Wells (Newell), **VI:** 245, 246

Structure of Complex Words, The (Empson), **Supp. II:** 180, **192–195,** 197

Struggle of the Modern, The (Spender), **Supp. II:** 492

Struggles of Brown, Jones and Robinson, The (Trollope), **V:** 102

Strutt, Joseph, **IV:** 31

Strutton, Bill, **Supp. IV:** 346

Struwwelpeter (Hoffman), **I:** 25; **Supp. III:** 296

Stuart, D. M., **V:** 247, 256, 260

"Stubb's Calendar" (Thackeray), *see A Fatal Boots, The"*

Studies in Classic American Literature (Lawrence), **VII:** 90; **Retro. Supp. II:** 234

Studies in Ezra Pound (Davie), **Supp. VI:** 115

Studies in Prose and Poetry (Swinburne), **II:** 102; **V:** 333

Studies in Song (Swinburne), **V:** 332

Studies in the History of the Renaissance (Pater), **V:** xxiv, 286–287, 323, 338–339, **341–348,** 351, 355–356, 400, 411

Studies in the Prose Style of Joseph Addison (Lannering), **III:** 52

Studies in Words (Lewis), **Supp. III:** 249, 264

Studies of a Biographer (Stephen), **V:** 280, 285, 287, 289

"Studio 5, the Stars" (Ballard), **Supp. V:** 26

Study in Scarlet, A (Doyle), **Supp. II:** 159, 160, 162, 163, 164, 167, 169, 170, 171, 172, 173, 174, 176

Study in Temperament, A (Firbank), **Supp. II:** 201, 206–207

Study of Ben Jonson, A (Swinburne), **V:** 332

Study of Shakespeare, A (Swinburne), **V:** 328, 332

"Study of Thomas Hardy" (Lawrence), **VI:** 20; **Retro. Supp. II:** 234

Study of Victor Hugo, A (Swinburne), **V:** 332

"Style" (Pater), **V:** 339, 347, 353–355

Stylistic Development of Keats, The (Bate), **Retro. Supp. I:** 185

Subhuman Redneck Poems (Murray), **Supp. VII:** 271, 283–284

Subject of Scandal and Concern, A (Osborne), **Supp. I:** 334

"Sublime and the Beautiful Revisited, The" (Murdoch), **Supp. I:** 216–217, 223

"Sublime and the Good, The" (Murdoch), **Supp. I:** 216–217, 218, 220

Subsequent to Summer (Fuller), **Supp. VII:** 79

Substance of the Speech . . . in Answer to . . . the Report of the Committee of Managers (Burke), **III:** 205

Substance of the Speeches for the Retrenchment of Public Expenses (Burke), **III:** 205

"Suburban Dream" (Muir), **Supp. VI:** 207

Success (Amis), **Supp. IV:** 26, 27, 31–32, 37

"Success" (Empson), **Supp. II:** 180, 189

Success and Failure of Picasso, The (Berger), **Supp. IV:** 79, 88

Such (Brooke–Rose), **Supp. IV:** 99, 104, 105, 106–108

"Such Darling Dodos" (Wilson), **Supp. I:** 154

"Such nights as these in England . . . A (Swinburne), **V:** 310

Such Stuff as Dreams Are Made On (tr. FitzGerald), **IV:** 349, 353

Such, Such Were the Joys (Orwell), **VII:** 275, 282

Such Was My Singing (Nichols), **VI:** 419

Suckling, Sir John, **I:** 337; **II:** 222, 223, **226–229**

"Sudden Light" (Rossetti), **V:** 241, 242

Sue, Eugène, **VI:** 228

Suffrage of Elvira, The (Naipaul), **Supp. I:** 386–387, 388

"Sufism" (Jennings), **Supp. V:** 217

Sugar and Other Stories (Byatt), **Supp. IV:** 140, 151

Sugar and Rum (Unsworth), **Supp. VII:** 357, 361–363, 366

"Suicide Club, The" (Stevenson), **V:** 395; **Retro. Supp. I:** 263

Suite in Three Keys (Coward), **Supp. II:** 156–157

Sultry Month, A: Scenes of London Literary Life in 1846 (Hayter), **IV:** 322

Sum Practysis of Medecyn (Henryson), **Supp. VII:** 146, 147

Summer (Bond), **Supp. I:** 423, 434–435

Summer (Thomson), **Supp. III:** 411, 414, 416, 417, 418, 419

Summer Before the Dark, The (Lessing), **Supp. I:** 249, 253

Summer Bird–Cage, A (Drabble), **Supp. IV:** 230, 234–236, 241

Summer Day's Dream (Priestley), **VII:** 229

Summer Islands (Douglas), **VI:** 295, 305

"Summer Lightning" (Davie), **Supp. VI:** 112–113

Summer Lightning (Wodehouse), *see Fish Preferred*

"Summer Night, A" (Auden), **Retro. Supp. I:** 6

"Summer Waterfall, Glendale" (MacCaig), **Supp. VI:** 182

Summer Will Show (Warner), **Supp. VII:** 376

"Summerhouse on the Mound, The" (Bridges), **VI:** 74

Summers, M., **III:** 345

Summing Up, The (Maugham), **VI:** 364, 374

Summit (Thomas), **Supp. IV:** 485, 489

Summoned by Bells (Betjeman), **VII:** 355, 356, 361, 373–374

Sumner, Rosemary, **Retro. Supp. I:** 115

"Sun and the Fish, The" (Woolf), **Retro. Supp. I:** 308

Sun Before Departure (Sillitoe), **Supp. V:** 424, 425

"Sun used to shine, The" (Thomas), **Supp. III:** 395

"Sun Valley" (Thomas), **Supp. IV:** 493

"Sunburst" (Davie), **Supp. VI:** 110

"Sunday" (Hughes), **Supp. I:** 341–342, 348

"Sunday Afternoon" (Bowen), **Supp. II:** 77

"Sundew, The" (Swinburne), **V:** 315, 332

"Sunlight" (Gunn), **Supp. IV:** 268

"Sunlight on the Garden" (MacNeice), **VII:** 413

"Sunne Rising, The" (Donne), **II:** 127; **Retro. Supp. II:** 88–89, 90–91

"Sunny Prestatyn" (Larkin), **Supp. I:** 285

Sunny Side, The (Milne), **Supp. V:** 298

"Sunrise, A" (Owen), **VI:** 449

Sun's Darling, The (Dekker and Ford), **II:** 89, 100

Sun's Net, The (Brown), **Supp. VI:** 69

Sunset and Evening Star (O'Casey), **VII:** 13

Sunset at Blandings (Wodehouse), **Supp. III:** 452–453

"Sunset on Mount Blanc" (Stephen), **V:** 282

"Sunsets" (Aldington), **VI:** 416

"Suntrap" (Murphy), **Supp. V:** 328

"Sunup" (Murphy), **Supp. V:** 325

"Super Flumina Babylonis" (Swinburne), **V:** 325

"Superannuated Man, The" (Lamb), **IV:** 83

Supernatural Horror in Literature (Lovecraft), **III:** 340

Supernatural Omnibus, The (Summers), **III:** 345

"Superstition" (Bacon), **III:** 39

"Superstitious Man's Story, The" (Hardy), **VI:** 22

Supper at Emmaus (Caravaggio), **Supp. IV:** 95

Supplication of Souls (More), **Supp. VII:** 244–245

"Supports, The" (Kipling), **VI:** 189

"Supposed Confessions of a Second–rate Sensitive Mind in Dejection" (Owen), **VI:** 445

Supposes (Gascoigne), **I:** 298, 303

"Sure Proof" (MacCaig), **Supp. VI:** 191

"Surface Textures" (Desai), **Supp. V:** 65

Surgeon's Daughter, The (Scott), **IV:** 34–35, 39

Surprised by Joy: The Shape of My Early Life (Lewis), **Supp. III:** 247, 248

"Surrender, The" (King), **Supp. VI:** 151, 153

Surrey, Henry Howard, earl of, **I:** 97, 98, 113

Surroundings (MacCaig), **Supp. VI: 189–190**, 195

Survey of Experimental Philosophy, A (Goldsmith), **III:** 189, 191

Survey of Modernist Poetry, A (Riding and Graves), **VII:** 260; **Supp. II:** 185

"Surview" (Hardy), **VI:** 13

"Survivor" (Kinsella), **Supp. V:** 267

Survivor, The (Keneally), **Supp. IV:** 345

"Survivors" (Ross), **VII:** 433

Suspense (Conrad), **VI:** 147

Suspension of Mercy, A (Highsmith), **Supp. V:** 174–175

"Suspiria de Profundis" (De Quincey), **IV:** 148, 153, 154

"Swallow, The" (Cowley), **II:** 198

Swallow (Thomas), **Supp. IV:** 483, 484–485

"Swan, The" (Dahl), **Supp. IV:** 207, 223, 224

Swan Song (Galsworthy), **VI:** 275

"Swans on an Autumn River" (Warner), **Supp. VII:** 380

Swearer's Bank, The (Swift), **III:** 35

Swedenborg, Emanuel, **III:** 292, 297; **Retro. Supp. I:** 39

Sweeney Agonistes (Eliot), **VII:** 157–158

"Sweeney Among the Nightingales" (Eliot), **VII:** xiii, 145

Sweeney Astray (Heaney), **Supp. II:** 268, 277, 278; **Retro. Supp. I:** 129

"Sweeney Erect" (Eliot), **VII:** 145

Sweeney poems (Eliot), **VII:** 145–146; *see also* "Sweeney Among the Nightingales"; "Sweeney Erect"

"Sweeney Redivivus" (Heaney), **Supp. II:** 277, 278

Sweet Dove Died, The (Pym), **Supp. II: 378–380**

Sweet Dreams (Frayn), **Supp. VII:** 56, 58–60, 61, 65

Sweet Smell of Psychosis (Self), **Supp. V:** 406

Sweet–Shop Owner, The (Swift), **Supp. V:** 427–429

"Sweet Things" (Gunn), **Supp. IV:** 272

Sweet William (Bainbridge), **Supp. VI:** 18, 20–22, 24

"Sweet William's Farewell to Black–ey'd Susan" (Gay), **III:** 58

"Sweetheart of M. Brisieux, The" (James), **VI:** 69

Sweets of Pimlico, The (Wilson), **Supp. VI:** 297, **298–299**, 301

Swift, Graham, **Supp. IV:** 65; **Supp. V: 427–442**

Swift, Jonathan, **II:** 240, 259, 261, 269, 273, 335; **III: 15–37**, 39, 44, 53, 55, 76; **IV:** 160, 257, 258; **VII:** 127; **Retro. Supp. I: 273–287**

"Swift has sailed into his rest" (Yeats), **III:** 21

"Swifts" (Hughes), **Retro. Supp. II:** 208–209

"Swifts" (Stevenson), **Supp. VI:** 265

"Swim in Co. Wicklow, A" (Mahon), **Supp. VI:** 178

Swinburne, Algernon Charles, **II:** 102; **III:** 174; **IV:** 90, 337, 346, 370; **V:** xi, xii, 236, 284, 286, 298–299, **309–335**, 346, 355, 365, 401

Swinburne: The Portrait of a Poet (Henderson), **V:** 335

"Swing, The" (Heaney), **Retro. Supp. I:** 133

"Swing of the Pendulum, The" (Mansfield), **VII:** 172

Swinging the Maelstrom (Lowry), **Supp. III:** 272

Swinnerton, Frank, **VI:** 247, 268; **VII:** 223

Switch Bitch (Dahl), **Supp. IV:** 219

Sword of Honour trilogy (Waugh), **VII:** xx–xxi, 303–306; *see also Men at Arms; Officers and Gentlemen; Unconditional Surrender*

Sybil (Disraeli), **IV:** xii, xx, 296, 300, 301–302, 305, 307, 308; **V:** viii, x, 2, 4

Sycamore Tree, The (Brooke–Rose), **Supp. IV:** 99, 101–102

"Sydney and the Bush" (Murray), **Supp. VII:** 276

Sykes Davies, Hugh, **IV:** xii, xxv; **V:** x, xxviii, 103

Sylva (Cowley), **II:** 202

Sylva; or, A Discourse of Forest–Trees (Evelyn), **II:** 275, 287

Sylva sylvarum (Bacon), **I:** 259, 263, 273

Sylvae (ed. Dryden), **II:** 301, 304

Sylvia's Lovers (Gaskell), **V:** 1, 4, 6, 7–8, 12, 15

Sylvie and Bruno (Carroll), **V:** 270–271, 273

Sylvie and Bruno Concluded (Carroll), **V:** 271, 273

Symbolic Logic (Carroll), **V:** 271, 274

Symbolist Movement in Literature, The (Symons), **VI:** ix

Symonds, John Addington, **V:** 83

Symons, Arthur, **VI:** ix

Symons, Julian, **Supp. IV:** 3, 339

"Sympathy in White Major" (Larkin), **Supp. I:** 282

Synge, John Millington, **II:** 258; **VI:** xiv, **307–314,** 317; **VII:** 3, 42; **Retro. Supp. I: 289–303**

Synge and Anglo–Irish Drama (Price), **VI:** 317

Synge and the Ireland of His Time (Yeats), **VI:** 222, 317

Syntactic Structures (Chomsky), **Supp. IV:** 113–114

"Syntax of Seasons, The" (Reid), **Supp. VII:** 330

Syrie Maugham (Fisher), **VI:** 379

System of Logic (Mill), **V:** 279

System of Magick, A; or, A History of the Black Art (Defoe), **III:** 14

Systema medicinae hermeticae generale (Nollius), **II:** 201

Syzygies and Lanrick (Carroll), **V:** 273–274

T. E. Hulme: The Selected Writings (Hulme), **Supp. VI:** 135–136, 138, 140, 142, 143

T. E. Lawrence: The Selected Letters (Lawrence), **Supp. II:** 283, 286, 289, 290, 293, 295, 296, 297

T. Fisher Unwin (publisher), **VI:** 373

T. S. Eliot (Ackroyd), **Supp. VI:** 5–6, 8

T. S. Eliot (Bergonzi), **VII:** 169

"T. S. Eliot" (Forster), **VII:** 144

"T. S. Eliot and Ezra Pound" (Ewart), **Supp. VII:** 45

"T. S. Eliot as Critic" (Leavis), **VII:** 233

"Table, The" (Trevor), **Supp. IV:** 500

Table Book (Hone), **IV:** 255

Table Manners (Ayckbourn), **Supp. V:** 2, 5

Table Near the Band, A (Milne), **Supp. V:** 309

Table Talk (Hazlitt), **IV:** xviii, 131, 137, 139

Table Talk, and Other Poems (Cowper), **III:** 220

Tables Turned, The (Morris), **V:** 306

"Tables Turned, The" (Wordsworth), **IV:** 7, 225

Taburlaine the Great, Part I (Marlowe), **Retro. Supp. I:** 204–206

Taburlaine the Great, Part II (Marlowe), **Retro. Supp. I:** 206–207

Tagore, Rabindranath, **Supp. IV:** 440, 454

Tailor of Gloucester, The (Potter), **Supp. III:** 290, 301–302

Taill of Schir Chantecleir and the Foxe, The (Henryson), see *Cock and the Fox, The*

Taill of the Uponlondis Mous and the Burges Mous, The (Henryson), see *Two Mice, The*

Táin, The (Kinsella), **Supp. V:** 264–266

Take a Girl Like You (Amis), Supp. II: 10–11, 18

Taken Care of (Sitwell), **VII:** 128, 132

Takeover, The (Spark), **Supp. I:** 211–212

"Taking Down the Christmas Tree" (Stevenson), **Supp. VI:** 262

Taking Steps (Ayckbourn), **Supp. V:** 3, 12, 13

Talbert, E. W., **I:** 224

"Talbot Road" (Gunn), **Supp. IV:** 272, 273–274

"Tale, The" (Conrad), **VI:** 148

Tale of a Town, The (Martyn), **VI:** 95

"Tale of a Trumpet, A" (Hood), **IV:** 258

Tale of a Tub, A (Swift), **II:** 259, 269; **III:** 17, 19, **21–23,** 35; **Retro. Supp. I:** 273, 276, 277–278

Tale of Balen, The (Swinburne), **V:** 333

Tale of Benjamin Bunny, The (Potter), **Supp. III:** 290, 299

Tale of Beowulf, Done out of the Old English Tongue, The (Morris, Wyatt), **V:** 306

Tale of Ginger and Pickles, The (Potter), **Supp. III:** 290, 299

Tale of Jemima Puddle–Duck, The (Potter), **Supp. III:** 290, 303

Tale of Johnny Town–Mouse, The (Potter), **Supp. III:** 297, 304, 307

Tale of King Arthur, The (Malory), **I:** 68

Tale of Little Pig Robinson, The (Potter), **Supp. III:** 288, 289, 297, 304–305

Tale of Mr. Jeremy Fisher, The (Potter), **Supp. III:** 298, 303

Tale of Mr. Tod, The (Potter), **Supp. III:** 290, 299

Tale of Mrs. Tiggy–Winkle, The (Potter), **Supp. III:** 290, 301–302

Tale of Mrs. Tittlemouse, The (Potter), **Supp. III:** 298, 301

Tale of Paraguay, A (Southey), **IV:** 66–67, 68, 71

Tale of Peter Rabbit, The (Potter), **Supp. III:** 287, 288, 290, 293, **295–296,** 299

Tale of Pigling Bland, The (Potter), **Supp. III:** 288–289, 290, 291, 304

Tale of Rosamund Gray and Old Blind Margaret, A (Lamb), **IV:** 79, 85

Tale of Samuel Whiskers, The (Potter), **Supp. III:** 290, 297, 301, 305

Tale of Sir Gareth of Orkeney that was called Bewmaynes, The (Malory), **I:** 72, 73; **Retro. Supp. II:** 243, 247

Tale of Sir Lancelot and Queen Guinevere (Malory), **Retro. Supp. II:** 243, 244

Tale of Sir Thopas, The (Chaucer), **I:** 67, 71

"Tale of Society As It Is, A" (Shelley), **Retro. Supp. I:** 245

Tale of Squirrel Nutkin, The (Potter), **Supp. III:** 288, 290, 301

Tale of the House of the Wolflings, A (Morris), **V:** 302, 306

Tale of the Noble King Arthur that was Emperor himself through Dignity of his Hands (Malory), **I:** 69, 72, 77–79

Tale of the Pie and the Patty–Pan, The (Potter), **Supp. III:** 290, 299

Tale of the Sankgreal, The (Malory), **I:** 69; **Retro. Supp. II:** 248–249

Tale of the Sea, A (Conrad), **VI:** 148

Tale of Timmy Tiptoes, The (Potter), **Supp. III:** 290

"Tale of Tod Lapraik, The" (Stevenson), **Retro. Supp. I:** 267

Tale of Tom Kitten, The (Potter), **Supp. III:** 290, 299, 300, 302, 303

Tale of Two Bad Mice, The (Potter), **Supp. III:** 290, 300–301

Tale of Two Cities, A (Dickens), **V:** xxii, 41, 42, 57, 63, 66, 72

"Talent and Friendship" (Kinsella), **Supp. V:** 270

Talented Mr. Ripley, The (Highsmith), **Supp. V:** 170

Tales (Crabbe), **III:** 278, 285, 286; *see also Tales in Verse; Tales of the Hall; Posthumous Tales*

"Tales" (Dickens), **V:** 46

Tales and Sketches (Disraeli), **IV:** 308

Tales from a Troubled Land (Paton), **Supp. II: 344–345,** 348, 354

Tales from Angria (Brontë), **V:** 151

Tales from Ovid (Hughes), **Retro. Supp. II:** 202, 214–216

Tales from Shakespeare (Lamb and Lamb), **IV:** xvi, 80, 85

Tales in Verse (Crabbe), **III:** 275, 278, 279, 281, 286

Tales of a Grandfather (Scott), **IV:** 38

Tales of All Countries (Trollope), **V:** 101

Tales of Good and Evil (Gogol), **III:** 345

Tales of Hearsay (Conrad), **VI:** 148

Tales of Hoffmann (Hoffmann), **III:** 334, 345

Tales of Mean Streets (Morrison), **VI:** 365

Tales of My Landlord (Scott), **IV:** 39

Tales of Natural and Unnatural Catastrophes (Highsmith), **Supp. V:** 179

Tales of St. Austin's (Wodehouse), **Supp. III:** 449–450

Tales of Sir Gareth (Malory), **I:** 68

Tales of the Crusaders (Scott), **IV:** 39

Tales of the Five Towns (Bennett), **VI:** 253

Tales of the Hall (Crabbe), **III:** 278, 285, 286; **V:** xvii, 6
"Tales of the Islanders" (Brontë), **V:** 107, 114, 135
Tales of Three Cities (James), **VI:** 67
Tales of Unrest (Conrad), **VI:** 148
Talfourd, Field, **IV:** 311
Talisman, The (Scott), **IV:** 39
Talk Stories (Kincaid), **Supp. VII:** 217, 231
Talking Bronco (Campbell), **Supp. III:** 119
Talking It Over (Barnes), **Supp. IV:** 65, 67, 68, 72–74
Talking of Jane Austen (Kaye–Smith and Stern), **IV:** 123
"Talking to Myself" (Auden), **Retro. Supp. I:** 13
"Tam o' Shanter" (Burns), **III:** 320
Tamburlaine the Great (Marlowe), **I:** 212, 243, 276, 278, 279–280, **281–282; II:** 69, 305
Tamburlaine, Part 2 (Marlowe), **I:** 281–282, 283
"Tamer and Hawk" (Gunn), **Supp. IV:** 258
Taming of the Shrew, The (Shakespeare), **I:** 298, 302, 303, 327; **II:** 68
Tamworth Reading Room, The (Newman), **Supp. VII:** 294
Tancred (Disraeli), **IV:** 294, 297, 300, 302–303, 307, 308
Tancred and Gismund (Wilmot), **I:** 216
Tancred and Sigismunda (Thomson), **Supp. III:** 411, 423, 424
Tangier Papers of Samuel Pepys, The (ed. Chappell), **II:** 288
Tangled Tale, A (Carroll), **V:** 273
Tanner, Alain, **Supp. IV:** 79, 95
Tanner, J. R., **II:** 288
Tanner, Tony, **VI:** xxxiv
Tannhäuser and Other Poems (Clarke), **V:** 318n
Tao of Pooh, The (Hoff), **Supp. V:** 311
"Tapestry Moths" (Redgrove), **Supp. VI:** 235–236
"Tapestry Trees" (Morris), **V:** 304–305
"Tardy Spring" (Meredith), **V:** 223
Tarr (Lewis), **VII:** xv, 72
"Tarry delight, so seldom met" (Housman), **VI:** 161
Tarry Flynn (Kavanagh), **Supp. VII:** 186, 194–195, 199
Task, The (Cowper), **III:** 208, **212–217,** 220; **IV:** xv, 184
Tasso, Torquato, **II:** 49; **III:** 171
"Taste" (Dahl), **Supp. IV:** 215, 217
Taste for Death, A (James), **Supp. IV:** 320, 330–331
Taste of Honey, A (Rattigan), **Supp. VII:** 320
Tate, Nahum, **I:** 327; **II:** 305
Tatler (periodical), **II:** 339; **III:** 18, 29, 30, 35, 39, **41–45,** 46, 51, 52, 53
Tausk, Victor, **Supp. IV:** 493
Tawney, R. H., **I:** 253
Taxation No Tyranny (Johnson), **III:** 121; **Retro. Supp. I:** 142–143
Taylor, A. L., **V:** 270, 272, 274
Taylor, A. J. P., **IV:** 290, 303

Taylor, Henry, **IV:** 62n
Taylor, Jeremy, **Supp. IV:** 163
Taylor, John, **IV:** 231, 233, 253
Taylor, Mary, **V:** 117
Taylor, Thomas, **III:** 291
Taylor, Tom, **V:** 330
Te of Piglet, The (Hoff), **Supp. V:** 311
"Tea" (Saki), **Supp. VI:** 244
Tea Party (Pinter), **Supp. I:** 375
"Tea with an Artist" (Rhys), **Supp. II:** 390
"Tea with Mrs. Bittell" (Pritchett), **Supp. III:** 328–329
Teapots and Quails (Lear), **V:** 87
"Tear" (Kinsella), **Supp. V:** 274
"Teare, The" (Crashaw), **II:** 183
"Tears" (Thomas), **VI:** 424
"Tears" (Vaughan), **II:** 187
"Tears, Idle Tears" (Hough), **IV:** 323n, 339
"Tears, Idle Tears" (Tennyson), **IV:** 329–330, 334
"'Tears, Idle Tears' Again" (Spitzer), **IV:** 323n, 339
Tears of Amaryllis for Amyntas, The: A Pastoral. (Congreve), **II:** 350
Tears of Peace, The (Chapman), **I:** 240–241
"Teasers, The" (Empson), **Supp. II:** 190
Tea–Table (periodical), **III:** 50
Tea–Table Miscellany, The (Ramsay), **III:** 312; **IV:** 28–29
Tebbit, Norman, **Supp. IV:** 449
"Technical Manifesto of Futurist Literature" (Marinetti), **Supp. III:** 396
Technical Supplement, A (Kinsella), **Supp. V:** 268–269
"Technological Crisis, The" (Richards), **Supp. II:** 426
"'Teem'" (Kipling), **VI:** 169, 189
Teeth 'n' Smiles (Hare), **Supp. IV:** 282, 283–284
Tel Quel circle, **Supp. IV:** 115
"Tell me, Dorinda, why so gay" (Dorset), **II:** 262–263
"Tell me no more how fair she is" (King), **Supp. VI:** 151
"Tell me not here, it needs not saying" (Housman), **VI:** 160
"Tell me what means that sigh" (Landor), **IV:** 98
Tell Me Who to Kill (Naipaul), **Supp. I:** 395, 396
Tellers and Listeners: The Narrative of Imagination (Hardy), **V:** 73
Tellers of Tales (Maugham), **VI:** 372
"Telling Myself" (Motion), **Supp. VII:** 256
"Temper, The" (Herbert), **II:** 125
Tempest, The (Shakespeare), **I:** 323–324; **II:** 55; **III:** 117
Tempest, The; or, The Enchanted Island (Dryden), **II:** 305
Temple, Sir William, **III:** 16, 19, 23, 40, 190
Temple, The (Herbert), **II:** 119, 121–125, 128, 129, 184; **Retro. Supp. II:** 172, 173, 174–182
"Temple, The" (Herrick), **II:** 113

Temple, The (Spender), **Supp. II:** 485, 493
Temple Bar (Forster), **VI:** 399
Temple Beau, The (Fielding), **III:** 96, 98, 105
Temple of Fame, The (Pope), **III:** 71, 77; **Retro. Supp. I:** 233
Temple of Glass, The (Lydgate), **I:** 57, 62, 65
Temporary Kings (Powell), **VII:** 352
Temporary Life, A (Storey), **Supp. I:** 408, 410, 411, 412, 413, 414–415, 416, 417–418, 419
"Temporis Partus Masculus" (Bacon), **Supp. III:** 361
ten Brink, Bernard, **I:** 98
Ten Burnt Offerings (MacNeice), **VII:** 415
"Ten Lines a Day" (Boswell), **III:** 237
Ten Little Indians, see Ten Little Niggers
Ten Little Niggers (Christie; US. title, *"nd Then There Were None*), **Supp. II:** 131, 132, 134
"Ten Memorial Poems" (Fuller), **Supp. VII:** 72
Ten Novels and Their Authors (Maugham), **VI:** 363–364
"Ten O'Clock Lecture" (Whistler), **V:** 407; **VI:** 103
Ten Times Table (Ayckbourn), **Supp. V:** 3, 10, 14
Tenant of Wildfell Hall, The (Brontë), **V:** xxi, 130, 153; **Supp. III:** 195; **Retro. Supp. I:** 50, 52, 53, 54, 55–56
Tender Only to One (Smith), **Supp. II:** 462
Tenebrae (Hill), **Supp. V:** 189–192, 199
Tenniel, John, **V:** 266, 267
"Tennis Court, The" (Trevor), **Supp. IV:** 504
Tennyson, Alfred Lord, **II:** 200, 208; **IV:** viii, xii–xiii, 196, 240, 292, 310, 313, **323–339,** 341, 344, 351, 352, 371; **V:** ix, 77–79, 85, 182, 285, 299, 311, 327, 330, 365, 401; **VI:** 455–456
Tennyson, Emily, **V:** 81
Tennyson, Frederic, **IV:** 350, 351
Tennyson, Hallam, **IV:** 324, 329, 332, 338
"Tennyson and Picturesque Poetry" (McLuhan), **IV:** 323n, 338, 339
"Tennyson and the Romantic Epic" (McLuhan), **IV:** 323n, 339
Tennyson: Poet and Prophet (Henderson), **IV:** 339
Tenth Man, The (Greene), **Supp. I:** 1, 11
Tenth Satire (Juvenal), **Retro. Supp. I:** 139
Tenure of Kings and Magistrates, The (Milton), **II:** 176
Teresa of Watling Street (Bennett), **VI:** 249
"Teresa's Wedding" (Trevor), **Supp. IV:** 503
"Tereus" (Gower), **I:** 54
"Terminal Beach, The" (Ballard), **Supp. V:** 23, 25, 34
Terminal Beach, The (Ballard), **Supp. V:** 23
Terminations (James), **VI:** 49, 67

"Terminus" (Emerson), **IV:** 81

"Terra Incognita" (Lawrence), **VII:** 119

Terra Nostra (Fuentes), **Supp. IV:** 116

"Terrapin, The" (Highsmith), **Supp. V:** 180

Terrible Sonnets (Hopkins), **Retro. Supp. II:** 197–198

"Territorial" (Motion), **Supp. VII:** 260

Territorial Rights (Spark), **Supp. I:** 211, 212

"Terrors of Basket Weaving, The" (Highsmith), **Supp. V:** 180

Terrors of Dr. Trevils, The (Redgrove), **Supp. VI:** 230

Terry, Ellen, **VI:** 104

Terry Hogan, an Eclogue (Landor), **IV:** 100

Teseide (Boccaccio), **I:** 30

Tess of the d'Urbervilles: A Pure Woman Faithfully Presented (Hardy), **VI:** 5, 9, 20; **Supp. IV:** 243, 471; **Retro. Supp. I:** 115–116

"Test Case" (Kinsella), **Supp. V:** 261

"Test of Manhood, The" (Meredith), **V:** 222

Testament (Lydgate), **I:** 65

Testament of Beauty, The (Bridges), **VI:** 72, 73, 74, 75, 82

Testament of Cresseid, The (Henryson), **Supp. VII:** 135, 136, 142–145, 146

Testament of Love, The (Usk), **I:** 2

"Tête à Tête (Kinsella), **Supp. V:** 260

Tetrachordon: . . . (Milton), **II:** 175

Textermination (Brooke–Rose), **Supp. IV:** 97, 100, 112

Texts and Pretexts (Huxley), **VII:** 204; **Retro. Supp. II:** 182

Texts for Nothing (Beckett), **Supp. I:** 51, 53, 60

Thackeray, Anne Isabella, **VI:** 4

Thackeray, Bal, **Supp. IV:** 438

Thackeray, William Makepeace, **II:** 363; **III:** 124, 125, 146; **IV:** 240, 251, 254, 257, 266, 272, 301, 306, 340; **V:** ix, **17–39**, 56, 62, 68, 69, 139, 140, 147, 179, 191, 279; **Supp. IV:** 238, 244

Thackeray (Trollope), **V:** 102

Thackeray: Prodigal Genius (Carey), **V:** 39

Thalaba the Destroyer (Southey), **III:** 335; **IV:** 64, 65, 71, 197, 217

"Thalassius" (Swinburne), **V:** 327

Thalia Rediviva (Vaughan), **II:** 185, 201

"Thank You, Fog" (Auden), **Retro. Supp. I:** 14

Thank You, Jeeves (Wodehouse), **Supp. III:** 455, 460

"Thanksgiving for a Habitat" (Auden), **Retro. Supp. I:** 13

Thanksgiving Ode, 18 January 1816 (Wordsworth), **IV:** 24

Thanksgivings (Traherne), **II:** 190–191

That American Woman (Waugh), **Supp. VI:** 272

That Hideous Strength (Lewis), **Supp. III:** 249, 252, 254–255

"That Morning" (Hughes), **Supp. I:** 364

"That Nature Is a Heraclitean Fire" (Hopkins), **V:** 376, 377

"That Now Is Hay Some–tyme Was Grase" (Lydgate), **I:** 57

"That the Science of Cartography Is Limited" (Boland), **Supp. V:** 43–44, 46

That Time (Beckett), **Supp. I:** 61; **Retro. Supp. I:** 28

That Uncertain Feeling (Amis), **Supp. II:** 7–8

Thatcher, Margaret, **Supp. IV:** 74–75, 437

"Thaw, A" (Redgrove), **Supp. VI:** 234

Thealma and Clearchus (Chalkhill), **II:** 133

Theatre (periodical), **III:** 50, 53

"Theatre of God's Judgements" (Beard), **Retro. Supp. I:** 204

Theatrical Companion to Maugham (Mander and Mitchenson), **VI:** 379

Theatrum Orbis Terrarum (Ortelius), **I:** 282

Theatrum Poetarum (Phillips), **II:** 347

"Their Finest Hour" (Churchill), **VI:** 358

"Their Lonely Betters" (Auden), **VII:** 387

"Their Quiet Lives" (Warner), **Supp. VII:** 380

"Their Very Memory" (Blunden), **VI:** 428

Thelwall, John, **IV:** 103

Themes and Conventions of Elizabethan Tragedy (Bradbrook), **I:** 293; **II:** 78

"Then dawns the Invisible . . . " (Brontë), **V:** 143; *see also* "Prisoner, The"

Theobald, Lewis, **I:** 324, 326; **II:** 66, 87; **III:** 51

"Theodolinde" (James), **VI:** 69

Theodore (Boyle), **III:** 95

"Theology" (Hughes), **Supp. I:** 350

Théophile (Swinburne), **V:** 333

Theophrastus, **II:** 68, 81; **III:** 50

Theory of Permanent Adolescence, The (Connolly), **Supp. III:** 97

Theory of the Leisure Class, The (Veblen), **VI:** 283

Therapy (Lodge), **Supp. IV:** 366, 381, 383–385

"There is a hill beside the silver Thames" (Bridges), **VI:** 78

"There Is a House Not Made with Hands" (Watts), **III:** 288

"There Is No Conversation" (West), **Supp. III:** 442

There Is No Natural Religion (Blake), **III:** 292, 307; **Retro. Supp. I:** 35

"There Is Nothing" (Gurney), **VI:** 426–427

"There was a Saviour" (Thomas), **Supp. I:** 177, 178

"There was a time" (Thomas), **Supp. III:** 404

"There was an old Derry down Derry" (Lear), **V:** 82

"There Was an Old Man in a Barge" (Lear), **V:** 83

"There Was an Old Man of Blackheath" (Lear), **V:** 86

"There Was an Old Man of Three Bridges" (Lear), **V:** 86

"There was never nothing more me pained" (Wyatt), **I:** 103

"There Will Be No Peace" (Auden), **Retro. Supp. I:** 13

"There's Nothing Here" (Muir), **Supp. VI:** 208

"Thermal Stair, The" (Graham), **Supp. VII:** 114

"These Summer–Birds did with thy Master stay" (Herrick), **II:** 103

These the Companions (Davie), **Supp. VI:** 105, 109, 111, 113, 117

These Twain (Bennett), **VI:** 258

"Theses on the Philosophy of History" (Benjamin), **Supp. IV:** 87

Thespian Magazine (periodical), **III:** 263

"They" (Kipling), **VI:** 199

"They" (Sassoon), **VI:** 430

"They All Go to the Mountains Now" (Brooke–Rose), **Supp. IV:** 103

"They Are All Gone into the World of Light!" (Vaughan), **II:** 188

They Came to a City (Priestley), **VII:** 210, 227

"They flee from me" (Wyatt), **I:** 102

"They Shall Not Grow Old" (Dahl), **Supp. IV:** 210, 224

They Walk in the City (Priestley), **VII:** 217

They Went (Douglas), **VI:** 303, 304, 305

"Thief" (Graves), **VII:** 267

Thierry and Theodoret (Beaumont, Fletcher, Massinger), **II:** 66

Thieves in the Night (Koestler), **Supp. I:** 27–28, 32–33

Things That Have Interested Me (Bennett), **VI:** 267

Things That Interested Me (Bennett), **VI:** 267

Things We Do for Love (Ayckbourn), **Supp. V:** 3–4, 12–13

Things Which Have Interested Me (Bennett), **VI:** 267

"Thinking as a Hobby" (Golding), **Supp. I:** 75

"Thinking of Mr. D." (Kinsella), **Supp. V:** 260

Thinking Reed, The (West), **Supp. III:** 442

Thiong'o, Ngugi wa, **Supp. V:** 56

"Third Journey, The" (Graham), **Supp. VII:** 109

Third Man, The (Greene), **Supp. I:** 11; **Retro. Supp. II:** 159

"Third Person, The" (James), **VI:** 69

Third Policeman, The (O'Nolan), **Supp. II:** 322, **326–329**, 337, 338

Third Satire (Wyatt), **I:** 111

Thirteen Such Years (Waugh), **Supp. VI:** 272–273

Thirteenth Tribe, The (Koestler), **Supp. I:** 33

"38 Phoenix Street" (Kinsella), **Supp. V:** 268

Thirty–Nine Steps, The (Buchan), **Supp. II:** 299, 306; **Supp. IV:** 7

36 Hours (film), **Supp. IV:** 209

"Thirty–Three Triads" (Kinsella), **Supp. V:** 264

"This Be the Verse" (Larkin), **Supp. I:** 284

"This bread I break" (Thomas), **Supp. I:** 174

"This England" (Thomas), **Supp. III:** 404

This England: An Anthology from Her Writers (ed. Thomas), **Supp. III: 404–405**

This Gun for Hire (Greene), *see Gun for Sale, A*

This Happy Breed (Coward), **Supp. II:** 151, 154

"This Is No Case of Petty Right or Wrong" (Thomas), **VI:** 424; **Supp. III:** 395

This Is Where I Came In (Ayckbourn), **Supp. V:** 3, 11, 13

"This Is Your Subject Speaking" (Motion), **Supp. VII:** 257

"This Last Pain" (Empson), **Supp. II:** 184–185

This Life I've Loved (Field), **V:** 393, 397

"This Lime Tree Bower My Prison" (Coleridge), **IV:** 41, 44; **Retro. Supp. II:** 52

This Misery of Boots (Wells), **VI:** 244

This Real Night (West), **Supp. III:** 443

This Sporting Life (Storey), **Supp. I:** 407, **408–410,** 414, 415, 416

This Sweet Sickness (Highsmith), **Supp. V:** 172–173

This Was a Man (Coward), **Supp. II:** 146

"This was for youth, Strength, Mirth and wit that Time" (Walton), **II:** 141

This Was the Old Chief's Country (Lessing), **Supp. I:** 239

This Year of Grace! (Coward), **Supp. II:** 146

"Thistles" (Hughes), **Retro. Supp. II:** 205–206

Thom Gunn and Ted Hughes (Bold), **Supp. IV:** 256, 257

"Thom Gunn at 60" (Hall), **Supp. IV:** 256

Thomas, D. M., **Supp. IV: 479–497**

Thomas, Dylan, **II:** 156; **Supp. I: 169–184; Supp. III:** 107; **Supp. IV:** 252, 263

Thomas, Edward, **IV:** 218; **V:** 313, 334, 355, 358; **VI:** 420–421, **423–425; VII:** xvi, 382; **Supp. III: 393–408**

"Thomas Bewick" (Gunn), **Supp. IV:** 269

"Thomas Campey and the Copernican System" (Harrison), **Supp. V:** 151

Thomas Carlyle (Campbell), **IV:** 250

Thomas Carlyle (Froude), **IV:** 238–239, 250

Thomas De Quincey: A Biography (Eaton), **IV:** 142, 156

Thomas De Quincey: His Life and Writings (Page), **IV:** 152, 155

"Thomas Gray" (Arnold), **III:** 277

Thomas Hardy: A Bibliographical Study (Purdy), **VI:** 19

Thomas Hardy and British Poetry (Davie), **Supp. VI:** 115

Thomas Hobbes (Stephen), **V:** 289

Thomas Hood (Reid), **IV:** 267

Thomas Hood and Charles Lamb (ed. Jerrold), **IV:** 252, 253, 267

Thomas Hood: His Life and Times (Jerrold), **IV:** 267

Thomas Love Peacock (Priestley), **IV:** 159–160, 170

Thomas Nabbes (Swinburne), **V:** 333

Thomas Stevenson, Civil Engineer (Stevenson), **V:** 395

Thomas the Rhymer, **IV:** 29, 219

Thompson, E. P., **Supp. IV:** 95, 473

Thompson, Francis, **III:** 338; **V:** xxii, xxvi, **439–452**

Thompson, R., **II:** 288

Thomson, George, **III:** 322

Thomson, James, **III:** 162, 171, 312; **Supp. III:** 409–429; **Retro. Supp. I:** 241

Thor, with Angels (Fry), **Supp. III:** 195, 197–198

"Thorn, The" (Wordsworth), **IV:** 6, 7

Thornton, R. K. R., **V:** 377, 382

Thornton, Robert, **III:** 307

Thorsler, Jr., P. L., **IV:** 173, 194

Those Barren Leaves (Huxley), **VII:** 79, 199, 202

Those Were the Days (Milne), **Supp. V:** 298

Those Were the Days: The Holocaust through the Eyes of the Perpetrators and Bystanders, **Supp. IV:** 488

Those Who Walk Away (Highsmith), **Supp. V:** 175

"Thou art an Atheist, *Quintus,* and a Wit" (Sedley), **II:** 265–266

"Thou art fair and few are fairer" (Shelley), **IV:** 203

"Thou art indeed just, Lord" (Hopkins), **V:** 376, 378

"Thou damn'd Antipodes to Common sense" (Dorset), **II:** 263

"Thou that know'st for whom I mourne" (Vaughan), **II:** 187

"Though this the port and I thy servant true" (Wyatt), **I:** 106

"Though, Phillis, your prevailing charms,"**II:** 257

"Thought" (Lawrence), **VII:** 119

Thought Power (Besant), **VI:** 249

"Thought–Fox, The" (Hughes), **Supp. I:** 347

Thoughts and Details on Scarcity . . . (Burke), **III:** 205

Thoughts in the Wilderness (Priestley), **VII:** 212

"Thoughts of a Suicide" (Tennyson), *see* "Two Voices, The"

"Thoughts on Criticism, by a Critic" (Stephen), **V:** 286

Thoughts on the Ministerial Commission (Newman), **Supp. VII:** 291

Thoughts on South Africa (Schreiner), **Supp. II:** 453, 454, 457

Thoughts on the Cause of the Present Discontents (Burke), **III:** 197

Thoughts on the Education of Daughters; . . . (Wollstonecraft), **Supp. III:** 466

Thoughts on the . . . Falkland's Islands (Johnson), **III:** 121; **Retro. Supp. I:** 142

"Thoughts on the Shape of the Human Body" (Brooke), **Supp. III:** 52–53

"Thoughts on Unpacking" (Gunn), **Supp. IV:** 262

Thrale, Hester, *see* Piozzi, Hester Lynch

"Thrawn Janet" (Stevenson), **V:** 395; **Retro. Supp. I:** 267

Thre Deid Pollis, The (Henryson), **Supp. VII:** 146, 148

"Three Aquarium Portraits" (Redgrove), **Supp. VI:** 234, 236

"Three Baroque Meditations" (Hill), **Supp. V:** 187, 188

"Three Blind Mice" (Christie), **Supp. II:** 134

Three Brothers, The (Muir), **Supp. VI:** 198

Three Cheers for the Paraclete (Keneally), **Supp. IV:** 345

Three Clerks, The (Trollope), **V:** 101

Three Continents (Jhabvala), **Supp. V:** 233–234, 235

Three Dialogues (Beckett), **Retro. Supp. I:** 18–19, 22

Three Essays, Moral and Political (Hume), **Supp. III:** 239

Three Friends (Bridges), **VI:** 72, 83

Three Glasgow Writers (Kelman), **Supp. V:** 241

Three Guineas (Woolf), **VII:** 22, 25, 27, 29, 38; **Supp. IV:** 399; **Retro. Supp. I:** 308, 311

Three Hours After Marriage (Gay), **III:** 60, 67

Three Letters, Written in Spain, to D. Francisco Riguelme (Landor), **IV:** 100

"Three Little Pigs, The" (Dahl), **Supp. IV:** 226

"Three Lives of Lucie Cabrol, The" (Berger), **Supp. IV:** 92–93, 94

Three Memorials on French Affairs . . . (Burke), **III:** 205

Three Men in New Suits (Priestley), **VII:** 218

Three Northern Love Stories (Morris and Magnusson), **V:** 306

Three of Them (Douglas), **VI:** 300, 305

Three Plays for Puritans (Shaw), **VI:** 104, 112, 129; **Retro. Supp. II:** 315–317

"Three Poems in Memory of My Mother, Miriam Murray neé Arnall" (Murray), **Supp. VII:** 278

"Three Poems of Drowning" (Graham), **Supp. VII:** 110

Three proper, and witty, familiar Letters (Spenser), **I:** 123

Three Sermons (Swift), **III:** 36

Three Sisters, The (tr. Frayn), **Supp. VII:** 61

Three Sisters, The (tr. Friel), **Supp. V:** 124

"Three Songs for Monaro Pubs" (Hope), **Supp. VII:** 158

"Three Strangers, The" (Hardy), **VI:** 20, 22

Three Sunsets and Other Poems (Carroll), **V:** 274

Three Voices of Poetry, The (Eliot), **VII:** 161, 162

Three Wayfarers, The: A Pastoral Play in One Act (Hardy), **VI:** 20

"Three Weeks to Argentina" (Ewart), **Supp. VII:** 45

"Three Women's Texts and a Critique of Imperialism" (Spivak), **Retro. Supp. I:** 60

Three Years in a Curatorship (Carroll), **V:** 274

Threnodia Augustalis (Goldsmith), **III:** 191

Threnodia Augustalis: A Funeral . . . Poem to . . . King Charles II (Dryden), **II:** 304

"Through the Looking Glass" (Auden), **VII:** 381

Through the Looking-Glass and What Alice Found There (Carroll), **V:** xxiii, 261, 262, 264, 265, 267–269, 270–273

Through the Panama (Lowry), **Supp. III:** 269, 280, 282, 283

"Through These Pale Gold Days" (Rosenberg), **VI:** 435

Thru (Brooke-Rose), **Supp. IV:** 98, 99, 105, 109–110, 112

"Thrush in February, The" (Meredith), **V:** 222

"Thrushes" (Hughes), **Supp. I:** 345

"Thunder and a Boy" (Jennings), **Supp. V:** 218

Thurley, Geoffrey, **Supp. II:** 494

"Thursday; or, The Spell" (Gay), **III:** 56

Thursday's Child: A Pageant (Fry), **Supp. III:** 194

Thus to Revisit (Ford), **VI:** 321, 323

Thyestes (Seneca), **I:** 215; **II:** 71

"Thyrsis" (Arnold), **V:** 157–158, 159, 165, 209, 210, 211; **VI:** 73

Thyrza (Gissing), **V:** 437

"Tiare Tahiti" (Brooke), **Supp. III:** 56

Tickell, Thomas, **III:** 50

Ticonderoga (Stevenson), **V:** 395

Tide and Stone Walls (Sillitoe), **Supp. V:** 424

Tietjens tetralogy (Ford), **VI:** xii, 319, **328–331; VII:** xxi; *see also Last Post; Man Could Stand Up, A; No More Parades; Some Do Not*

Tiger at the Gates (Fry), **Supp. III:** 195

"Tiger! Tiger!" (Kipling), **VI:** 199

Tigers Are Better-Looking (Rhys), **Supp. II:** 389, 390, 401, 402

Tiger's Bones, The (Hughes), **Supp. I:** 346–347

"Till September Petronella" (Rhys), **Supp. II:** 401–402

Till We Have Faces (Lewis), **Supp. III:** 248, **262–264,** 265

Tillotson, Kathleen, **IV:** 34; **V:** 73

Timber (Jonson), **Retro. Supp. I:** 166

Timbuctoo (Tennyson), **IV:** 338

Time and the Conways (Priestley), **VII:** 212, 224–225

Time and Tide (O'Brien), **Supp. V:** 341

Time and Tide by Weare and Tyne (Ruskin), **V:** 184

Time and Time Again (Ayckbourn), **Supp. V:** 2, 4–5, 9, 10, 13–14

Time and Western Man (Lewis), **VII:** 72, 74, 75, 83, 262

"Time Disease, The" (Amis), **Supp. IV:** 40

Time Flies: A Reading Diary (Rossetti), **V:** 260

Time for a Tiger (Burgess), **Supp. I:** 187

Time Imported (Warner), **Supp. VII:** 370, 371–372

Time in a Red Coat (Brown), **Supp. VI:** 66, 69–70

Time in Rome, A (Bowen), **Supp. II:** 80, 94

Time Machine, The: An Invention (Wells), **VI:** ix, xii, 226, 229–230

Time Must Have a Stop (Huxley), **VII:** 205

Time of Hope (Snow), **VII:** xxi, 321, 324–325

Time of My Life (Ayckbourn), **Supp. V:** 3, 8, 10, 11, 13, 14

"Time of Plague, The" (Gunn), **Supp. IV:** 277

Time of the Angels, The (Murdoch), **III:** 341, 345; **Supp. I:** 225–226, 227, 228

"Time of Waiting, A" (Graves), **VII:** 269

Time Present (Osborne), **Supp. I:** 338

"Time the Tiger" (Lewis), **VII:** 74

Time to Dance, A (Day Lewis), **Supp. III:** 118, 126

Time to Go, A (O'Casey), **VII:** 12

Time to Keep, A (Brown), **Supp. VI:** 64, 70

Time Traveller, The: The Life of H. G. Wells (MacKenzie and MacKenzie), **VI:** 228, 246

"Timer" (Harrison), **Supp. V:** 150

Time's Arrow; or The Nature of the Offence (Amis), **Supp. IV:** 40–42

Time's Laughingstocks and other Verses (Hardy), **VI:** 20

Times (periodical), **IV:** xv, 272, 278; **V:** 93, 279

Times Literary Supplement, **Supp. IV:** 25, 66, 121

"Time-Tombs, The" (Ballard), **Supp. V:** 21

Timon of Athens (Shakespeare), **I:** 318–319, 321; **II:** 70

Tin Drum, The (Grass), **Supp. IV:** 440

Tin Men, The (Frayn), **Supp. VII:** 51–52, 64

Tinker, C. B., **III:** 234*n*, 249, 250

"Tinker, The" (Wordsworth), **IV:** 21

Tinker, Tailor, Soldier, Spy (le Carré), **Supp. II:** 306, **311–313,** 314

Tinker's Wedding, The (Synge), **VI:** 311, 313–314; **Retro. Supp. I:** 296–297

"Tintern Abbey" (Wordsworth), *see* "Lines Composed a Few Miles Above Tintern Abbey"

Tiny Tears (Fuller), **Supp. VII:** 78

"Tipperary" (Thomas), **Supp. III:** 404

"Tirade for the Mimic Muse" (Boland), **Supp. V:** 49

Tireless Traveller, The (Trollope), **V:** 102

"Tiresias" (Tennyson), **IV:** 328, 332–334, 338

"Tiriel" (Blake), **III:** 298, 302; **Retro. Supp. I:** 34–35

"Tirocinium; or, A Review of Schools" (Cowper), **III:** 208

'Tis Pity She's a Whore (Ford), **II:** 57, 88, 89, 90, 92–93, 99, 100

"Tithon" (Tennyson), **IV:** 332–334; *see also* "Tithonus"

"Tithonus" (Tennyson), **IV:** 328, 333

Title, The (Bennett), **VI:** 250, 264

Title and Pedigree of Henry VI (Lydgate), **I:** 58

Titmarsh, Michael Angelo, pseud. of William Makepeace Thackeray

Titus Andronicus (Shakespeare), **I:** 279, 305; **II:** 69

"Titus Hoyt, I A" (Naipaul), **Supp. I:** 385

"To a Black Greyhound" (Grenfell), **VI:** 418

"To a Brother in the Mystery" (Davie), **Supp. VI:** 113–114

"To a Butterfly" (Wordsworth), **IV:** 21

"To a Cretan Monk in Thanks for a Flask of Wine" (Murphy), **Supp. V:** 318

"To a Cold Beauty" (Hood), **IV:** 255

"To a Comrade in Flanders" (Owen), **VI:** 452

"To a Devout Young Gentlewoman" (Sedley), **II:** 264

"To a *Fine Singer,* who had gotten a *Cold;* . . ." (Wycherley), **II:** 320

"To a Fine Young *Woman . . .*" (Wycherley), **II:** 320

"To a Friend in Time of Trouble" (Gunn), **Supp. IV:** 274, 275

"To A. L." (Carew), **II:** 224–225

"To a Lady in a Letter" (Rochester), **II:** 258

To a Lady More Cruel Than Fair (Vanbrugh), **II:** 336

"To a Lady on Her Passion for Old China" (Gay), **III:** 58, 67

"To a Lady on the Death of Colonel Ross . . ." (Collins), **III:** 166, 169

"To a Louse" (Burns), **III:** 315, 317–318

"To a Mountain Daisy" (Burns), **III:** 313, 315, 317, 318

"To a Mouse" (Burns), **III:** 315, 317, 318

"To a Nightingale" (Coleridge), **IV:** 222

"To a Skylark" (Shelley), **III:** 337

"To a Snail" (Moore), **Supp. IV:** 262–263

"To a Very Young Lady" (Etherege), **II:** 267

"To Althea from Prison" (Lovelace), **II:** 231, 232

"To Amarantha, That She Would Dishevell Her Haire" (Lovelace), **II:** 230

"To Amoret Gone from Him" (Vaughan), **II:** 185

"To Amoret, of the Difference 'twixt Him, . . ." (Vaughan), **II:** 185

"To an English Friend in Africa" (Okri), **Supp. V:** 359

"To an Old Lady" (Empson), **Supp. II:** 182–183

"To an Unborn Pauper Child" (Hardy), **Retro. Supp. I:** 121

"To an Unknown Reader" (Fuller), **Supp. VII:** 78

"To and Fro" (McEwan), **Supp. IV:** 395

"To Anthea" (Herrick), **II:** 105–106, 108

"To Any Dead Officer" (Sassoon), **VI:** 431

To Asmara (Keneally), **Supp. IV:** 346

"To Augustus" (Pope), **Retro. Supp. I:** 230–231

"To Autumn" (Keats), **IV:** 221, 226–227, 228, 232

To Be a Pilgrim (Cary), **VII:** 186, 187, 191, 192–194

"To Be a Poet" (Stevenson), **Supp. VI:** 260

"To Be Less Philosophical" (Graves), **VII:** 266

"To Blossoms" (Herrick), **II:** 112

"To Call Paula Paul" (McGuckian), **Supp. V:** 286

To Catch a Spy (Ambler), **Supp. IV:** 4, 17

"To cause accord or to agree" (Wyatt), **I:** 109

"To Celia" (Johnson), **IV:** 327

"To Charles Cowden Clarke" (Keats), **IV:** 214, 215

"To Certain English Poets" (Davie), **Supp. VI:** 110

"To Charles Cowden Clarke" (Keats), **Retro. Supp. I:** 188

"To Constantia Singing" (Shelley), **IV:** 209

"To Daffodills" (Herrick), **II:** 112

"To Deanbourn" (Herrick), **II:** 103

"To Dianeme" (Herrick), **II:** 107, 112

"To E. Fitzgerald" (Tennyson), **IV:** 336

"To Edward Thomas" (Lewis), **VII:** 445

"To E. L., on his Travels in Greece" (Tennyson), **V:** 79

"To Electra" (Herrick), **II:** 105

"To Everlasting Oblivion" (Marston), **II:** 25

"To Fanny" (Keats), **IV:** 220–221

"To George Felton Mathew" (Keats), **IV:** 214

"To Germany" (Sorley), **VI:** 421

"To God" (Gurney), **VI:** 426

"To Helen" (Thomas), **Supp. III:** 401

"To His Coy Mistress" (Marvell), **II:** 197, 198, 208–209, 211, 214–215; **Retro. Supp. II:** 259–261

"To his inconstant Friend" (King), **Supp. VI:** 151

"To His Love" (Gurney), **VI:** 426

"To His Lovely Mistresses" (Herrick), **II:** 113

To His Sacred Majesty, a Panegyrick on His Coronation (Dryden), **II:** 304

"To His Sweet Savior" (Herrick), **II:** 114

"To His Wife" (Hill), **Supp. V:** 189

"To Hope" (Keats), **Retro. Supp. I:** 188

"To Ireland in the Coming Times" (Yeats), **Retro. Supp. I:** 330

"To J. F. H. (1897–1934)" (Muir), **Supp. VI:** 206

"To Julia, The Flaminica Dialis, or Queen–

To Keep the Ball Rolling (Powell), **VII:** 351

"To King Henry IV, in Praise of Peace" (Gower), **I:** 56

"To Leonard Clark" (Graham), **Supp. VII:** 116

To Let (Galsworthy), **VI:** 272, 274, 275, 282

To Lighten My House (Reid), **Supp. VII:** 325–327

"To Live Merrily, and to Trust to Good Verses" (Herrick), **II:** 115

To Live with Little (Chapman), **I:** 254

"To Lizbie Browne" (Hardy), **VI:** 16

"To Lord Stanhope" (Coleridge), **IV:** 43

"To Louisa in the Lane" (Thomas), **Supp. IV:** 493

"To Lucasta, Going to the Warres" (Lovelace), **II:** 229

"To Marguerite—Continued" (Arnold), **V:** 211

"To Mary Boyle" (Tennyson), **IV:** 329, 336

"To Mr. Dryden" (Congreve), **II:** 338

To Mr. Harriot (Chapman), **I:** 241

"To Mr. Hobs" (Cowley), **II:** 196, 198

To Mistress Anne (Skelton), **I:** 83

"To My Brother George" (Keats), **IV:** 214

"To My Brothers" (Keats), **IV:** 215

"To My Daughter in a Red Coat" (Stevenson), **Supp. VI:** 254

"To my dead friend Ben: Johnson" (King), **Supp. VI:** 157

To My Fellow Countrymen (Osborne), **Supp. I:** 330

"To My Friend, Mr. Pope, . . . " (Wycherley), **II:** 322

"To My Inconstant Mistris" (Carew), **II:** 225

To My Lady Morton (Waller), **II:** 238

To My Lord Chancellor . . . (Dryden), **II:** 304

"To My Lord Northumberland Upon the Death of His Lady" (Waller), **II:** 233

To My Mother on the Anniversary of Her Birth, April 27, 1842 (Rossetti), **V:** 260

"To My Sister" (Wordsworth), **IV:** 8

"To Night" (Lovelace), **II:** 231

"To Nobodaddy" (Blake), **III:** 299

"To Olga Masson" (tr. Thomas), **Supp. IV:** 495

"To One Who Was with Me in the War" (Sassoon), **VI:** 431

"To Penshurst" (Jonson), **Retro. Supp. I:** 164

"To Perilla" (Herrick), **II:** 113

"To P. H. T" (Thomas), **Supp. III:** 401

"To Please His Wife" (Hardy), **VI:** 20, 22

"To Poet Bavius" (Behn), **Supp. III:** 40

To Present the Pretense (Arden), **Supp. II:** 30

"To R. B." (Hopkins), **V:** 376, 378

"To Rilke" (Lewis), **VII:** 446

"To Room Nineteen" (Lessing), **Supp. I:** 248

"To Saxham" (Carew), **III:** 223

To Scorch or Freeze (Davie), **Supp. VI:** 113–115

"To seek each where, where man doth live" (Wyatt), **I:** 110

"To seem the stranger lies my lot" (Hopkins), **V:** 374–375

"To Sir Henry Cary" (Jonson), **Retro. Supp. I:** 154

To Sir With Love (Braithwaite), **Supp. IV:** 445

"To Sleep" (Graves), **VII:** 267

"To Sleep" (Keats), **IV:** 221

"To Solitude" (Keats), **IV:** 213–214

"To Stella, Visiting Me in My Sickness" (Swift), **III:** 31

"To Stella, Who Collected and Transcribed His Poems" (Swift), **III:** 31

"To Stella . . . Written on the Day of Her Birth . . . " (Swift), **III:** 32

To the Air, **Supp. IV:** 269

"To the Athenian Society" (Defoe), **Retro. Supp. I:** 67

"To the Author of a Poem, intitled, Successio" (Pope), **Retro. Supp. I:** 233

"To the Coffee Shop" (Kinsella), **Supp. V:** 274

"To the Evening Star" (Blake), **Retro. Supp. I:** 34

"To the fair Clarinda, who made Love to Me, imagin'd more than Woman" (Behn), **Supp. III:** 8

"To the High Court of Parliament" (Hill), **Supp. V:** 192, 193

"To the King" (Waller), **II:** 233

To the King, upon His . . . Happy Return (Waller), **II:** 238

To the Lighthouse (Woolf), **V:** 281; **VI:** 275, 278; **VII:** xv, 18, 21, 26, 27, 28–29, 36, 38; **Supp. IV:** 231, 246, 321; **Supp. V:** 63; **Retro. Supp. I:** 308, 317–318

"To the Master of Balliol" (Tennyson), **IV:** 336

To the Memory of Charles Lamb (Wordsworth), **IV:** 86

"To the Memory of My Beloved, the Author Mr William Shakespeare" (Jonson), **Retro. Supp. I:** 165

"To the Memorie of My Ever Desired Friend Dr. Donne" (King), **Supp. VI:** 156

"To the Muses" (Blake), **III:** 289; **Retro. Supp. I:** 34

"To the Name of Jesus" (Crashaw), **II:** 180

"To the Nightingale" (McGuckian), **Supp. V:** 283

To the North (Bowen), **Supp. II:** 85, 88–89

"To the Pen Shop" (Kinsella), **Supp. V:** 274

"To the Queen" (Tennyson), **IV:** 337

To the Queen, upon Her . . . Birthday (Waller), **II:** 238

"To the Reader" (Jonson), **Retro. Supp. I:** 165

"To the Reader" (Webster), **I:** 246

"To the Reverend Shade of His Religious Father" (Herrick), **II:** 113

"To the Rev. W. H. Brookfield" (Tennyson), **IV:** 329

"To the Royal Society" (Cowley), **II:** 196, 198

"To the Sea" (Larkin), **Supp. I:** 283, 285

"To the Shade of Elliston" (Lamb), **IV:** 82–83

"To the Slow Drum" (Ewart), **Supp. VII:** 42

"To the Small Celandine" (Wordsworth), **IV:** 21

"To the (Supposed) Patron" (Hill), **Supp. V:** 184

"To the Virgins, to Make Much of Time" (Herrick), **II:** 108–109

To the Wedding (Berger), **Supp. IV:** 80

To This Hard House (Friel), **Supp. V:** 115

"To Thom Gunn in Los Altos, California" (Davie), **Supp. VI:** 112

"To True Soldiers" (Jonson), **Retro. Supp. I:** 154

"To Vandyk" (Waller), **II:** 233

"To Virgil" (Tennyson), **IV:** 327

"To wet your eye withouten tear" (Wyatt), **I:** 105–106

"To what serves Mortal Beauty?" (Hopkins), **V:** 372, 373

"To Whom It May Concern" (Motion), **Supp. VII:** 264

To Whom She Will (Jhabvala), **Supp. V:** 224–226

"To William Camden" (Jonson), **Retro. Supp. I:** 152

"To William Godwin" (Coleridge), **IV:** 43

"To X" (Fuller), **Supp. VII:** 74

"To Yvor Winters, 1955" (Gunn), **Supp. IV:** 261

"Toads" (Larkin), **Supp. I:** 277, 278, 281

"Toads Revisited" (Larkin), **Supp. I:** 281

"Toccata of Galuppi's, A" (Browning), **IV:** 357

To–Day (periodical), **VI:** 103

Todhunter, John, **V:** 325

Todorov, Tzvetan, **Supp. IV:** 115–116

Together (Douglas), **VI:** 299–300, 304, 305

Tolkien, J. R. R., **Supp. II: 519–535; Supp. IV:** 116; **Retro. Supp. II:** 291

"Tollund Man, The" (Heaney), **Supp. II:** 273, 274; **Retro. Supp. I:** 128

Tolstoy (Wilson), **Supp. VI:** 304

Tolstoy, Leo, **Supp. IV:** 94, 139

"Tom Brown Question, The" (Wodehouse), **Supp. III:** 449

Tom Brown's Schooldays (Hughes), **V:** xxii, 157, 170; **Supp. IV:** 506

Tom Jones (Fielding), **III:** 95, 96–97, 100–102, 105; **Supp. II:** 194, 195; **Retro. Supp. I:** 81, 86–89, 90–91; **Retro. Supp. I:** 81, 86–89, 90–91

Tom Thumb (Fielding), **III:** 96, 105

"Tom–Dobbin" (Gunn), **Supp. IV:** 267

Tomlin, Eric Walter Frederick, **VII:** xv, xxxviii

"Tomlinson" (Kipling), **VI:** 202

"Tomorrow" (Conrad), **VI:** 148

"Tomorrow" (Harris), **Supp. V:** 131

"Tomorrow Is a Million Years" (Ballard), **Supp. V:** 26

Tomorrow Morning, Faustus! (Richards), **Supp. II:** 427–428

"Tom's Garland" (Hopkins), **V:** 376

"Tone of Time, The" (James), **VI:** 69

Tonight at 8:30 (Coward), **Supp. II:** 152–153

Tono–Bungay (Wells), **VI:** xii, 237–238, 244

Tonson, Jacob, **II:** 323; **III:** 69

"Tony Kytes, The Arch–Deceiver" (Hardy), **VI:** 22

"Tony White's Cottage" (Murphy), **Supp. V:** 328

"Too Dearly Bought" (Gissing), **V:** 437

Too Good to Be True (Shaw), **VI:** 125, 127, 129

"Too Late" (Browning), **V:** 366, 369

Too Late the Phalarope (Paton), **Supp. II:** 341, **351–353**

Too Many Husbands (Maugham), **VI:** 368–369

"Too Much" (Muir), **Supp. VI:** 207

"Toot Baldon" (Motion), **Supp. VII:** 253

Top Girls (Churchill), **Supp. IV:** 179, 183, 189–191, 198

Topkapi (film), **Supp. IV:** 4

"Torridge" (Trevor), **Supp. IV:** 501

"Tortoise and the Hare, The" (Dahl), **Supp. IV:** 226

Tortoises (Lawrence), **VII:** 118

Tortoises, Terrapins and Turtles (Sowerby and Lear), **V:** 76, 87

"Torturer's Apprenticeship, The" (Murray), **Supp. VII:** 280

"Tory Prime Minister, Maggie May . . . , A" (Rushdie), **Supp. IV:** 456

Totemism (Frazer), **Supp. III:** 171

"Totentanz" (Wilson), **Supp. I:** 155, 156, 157

Tottel's Miscellany, **I:** 97–98, 114

Touch (Gunn), **Supp. IV:** 257, 264, 265–266

"Touch" (Gunn), **Supp. IV:** 265–266

Touch and Go (Lawrence), **VII:** 120, 121

Touch of Love, A (screenplay, Drabble), **Supp. IV:** 230

Tour Thro' the Whole Island of Great Britain (Defoe), **III:** 5, 13; **Retro. Supp. I:** 75–76

Tour to the Hebrides, A (Boswell), *see Journal of a Tour to the Hebrides*

Tourneur, Cyril, **II:** 24, 33, **36–41,** 70, 72, 85, 97

Toward Reality (Berger), *see Permanent Red: Essays in Seeing*

"Toward the Imminent Days" (Murray), **Supp. VII:** 274

"Towards an Artless Society" (Lewis), **VII:** 76

Towards the End of Morning (Frayn), **Supp. VII:** 53–54, 65

Towards the Mountain (Paton), **Supp. II:** 346, 347, 351, 359

Towards Zero (Christie), **Supp. II:** 132, 134

Tower, The (Fry), **Supp. III:** 194, 195

Tower, The (Yeats), **VI:** 207, 216, 220; **Retro. Supp. I:** 333–335

Towers of Silence, The (Scott), **Supp. I:** 267–268

Town (periodical), **V:** 22

"Town and Country" (Brooke), **VI:** 420

"Town Betrayed, The" (Muir), **Supp. VI:** 206

Townley plays, **I:** 20

Townsend, Aurelian, **II:** 222, 237

Townsend Warner, George, **VI:** 485

Town–Talk (periodical), **III:** 50, 53

"Track 12" (Ballard), **Supp. V:** 21

Trackers of Oxyrhyncus, The (Harrison), **Supp. V:** 163, 164

Tract 90 (Newman), *seeRemarks on Certain Passages of the 39 Articles*

"Tractor" (Hughes), **Retro. Supp. II:** 211

Tracts for the Times (Newman), **Supp. VII:** 291, 293

"Traction–Engine, The" (Auden), **Retro. Supp. I:** 3

"Tradition and the Individual Talent" (Eliot), **VII:** 155, 156, 163, 164

"Tradition of Eighteen Hundred and Four, A" (Hardy), **VI:** 22

Tradition of Women's Fiction, The (Drabble), **Supp. IV:** 231

Tradition, the Writer and Society (Harris), **Supp. V:** 145, 146

Traffics and Discoveries (Kipling), **VI:** 204

"Tragedy and the Essay, The" (Brontë), **V:** 135

Tragedy of Brennoralt, The (Suckling), **II:** 226

Tragedy of Byron, The (Chapman), **I:** 233, 234, 241n, 251

Tragedy of Count Alarcos, The (Disraeli), **IV:** 306, 308

Tragedy of Doctor Faustus, The (Marlowe), **Retro. Supp. I:** 200, 207–208

"Tragedy of Error, A" (James), **VI:** 25

Tragedy of Sir John Van Olden Barnavelt, The (Fletcher and Massinger), **II:** 66

Tragedy of Sophonisba, The (Thomson), **Supp. III:** 411, 422, 423, 424

Tragedy of the Duchess of Malfi, The (Webster), *see Duchess of Malfi, The*

Tragedy of Tragedies; or, The Life . . . of Tom Thumb, The (Fielding), *see Tom Thumb*

"Tragedy of Two Ambitions, A" (Hardy), **VI:** 22

Tragic Comedians, The (Meredith), **V:** 228, 234

Tragic History of Romeus and Juliet, The (Brooke), **I:** 305–306

Tragic Muse, The (James), **VI:** 39, **43–55,** 67

"Tragic Theatre, The" (Yeats), **VI:** 218

Tragical History of Doctor Faustus, The (Hope), **Supp. VII:** 160–161

Tragical History of Dr. Faustus, The (Marlowe), **III:** 344

Traherne, Thomas, **II:** 123, **189–194, 201–203**

Trail of the Dinosaur, The (Koestler), **Supp. I:** 32, 33, 36, 37

Traill, H. D., **III:** 80

Train of Powder, A (West), **Supp. III:** 439–440

Trained for Genius (Goldring), **VI:** 333

Traité du poeme épique (Le Bossu), **III:** 103

"Trampwoman's Tragedy, The" (Hardy), **VI:** 15; **Retro. Supp. I:** 120

transatlantic review (periodical), **VI:** 324

Transatlantic Sketches (James), **VI:** 67

"Transfiguration, The" (Muir), **Supp. VI:** 207

Transformed Metamorphosis, The (Tourneur), **II:** 37, 41

"Transients and Residents" (Gunn), **Supp. IV:** 271, 273

Transitional Poem (Day Lewis), **Supp. III:** 117, 121–123

Translations (Friel), **Supp. V:** 123–124

Translations and Tomfooleries (Shaw), **VI:** 129

"Translations from the Early Irish" (Kinsella), **Supp. V:** 264

Translations of the Natural World (Murray), **Supp. VII:** 281–282

"Transparencies" (Stevenson), **Supp. VI:** 262

Traps (Churchill), **Supp. IV:** 179, 180, 183–184, 188, 198

Traulus (Swift), **III:** 36

Travelers (Jhabvala), **Supp. V:** 230

"Traveller" (Kinsella), **Supp. V:** 263

Traveller, The (Goldsmith), **III:** 177, 179, 180, 185–186, 191; **Retro. Supp. I:** 149

"Traveller, The" (Stevenson), **Supp. VI:** 254, 265

Travelling Behind Glass (Stevenson), **Supp. VI:** 256–257

"Travelling Behind Glass" (Stevenson), **Supp. VI:** 257, 261

"Travelling Companion, The" (Kinsella), **Supp. V:** 261

"Travelling Companions" (James), **VI:** 25, 69

Travelling Grave, The (Hartley), see *Killing Bottle, The*

"Travelling Letters" (Dickens), **V:** 71

Travelling Sketches (Trollope), **V:** 101

Travels in Arabia Deserta (Doughty), **Supp. II:** 294–295

Travels in Italy (Addison), **III:** 18

Travels in Nihilon (Sillitoe), **Supp. V:** 410

Travels Through France and Italy (Smollett), **III:** 147, **153–155,** 158

Travels with a Donkey in the Cevennes (Stevenson), **V:** 389, 395; **Retro. Supp. I:** 262

Travels with My Aunt (Greene), **Supp. I:** 2, 13, 16; **Retro. Supp. II:** 161

Travesties (Stoppard), **Supp. I:** 438, 445, 446, **447–449,** 451; **Retro. Supp. II:** 349–351

"A Treading of Grapes" (Brown), **Supp. VI:** 70

Treasure Island (Stevenson), **V:** xxv, 383, 385, 386, 394, 395; **Retro. Supp. I:** 263

"Treasure of Franchard, The" (Stevenson), **V:** 395

"Treasure, The" (Brooke), **Supp. III:** 57, 58

"Treatise for Laundresses" (Lydgate), **I:** 58

Treatise of Civil Power in Ecclesiastical Causes . . . , The (Milton), **II:** 176

Treatise of Human Nature, A (Hume), **IV:** 138; **Supp. III:** 229, 230–231, **232–237,** 238

Treatise of the Fear of God, A (Bunyan), **II:** 253

Treatise of the Soul, A (Ralegh), **I:** 157

Treatise on Method (Coleridge), **IV:** 56

Treatise on the Astrolabe, A (Chaucer), **I:** 31

Treatise on the Passion (More), **Supp. VII:** 245

Trebitsch, Siegfried, **VI:** 115

Tree, Herbert Beerbohm, **Supp. II:** 44, 46, 53–54, 55

"Tree, The" (Thomas), **Supp. I:** 180

"Tree of Knowledge, The" (James), **VI:** 69

Tree of Man, The (White), **Supp. I:** 129, 131, 134, 136, 137–138, 143

Tree of Strings (MacCaig), **Supp. VI:** 192–193

Tree of the Sun, The (Harris), **Supp. V:** 139–140

Tree on Fire, A (Sillitoe), **Supp. V:** 409, 410, 414, 421, 422–423

"Tree Unleaved, The" (Warner), **Supp. VII:** 371

"Trees, The" (Larkin), **Supp. I:** 284, 285

Trelawny, Edward, **IV:** xiv, 203, 207, 209

Tremaine (Ward), **IV:** 293

Trembling of the Veil, The (Yeats), **VI:** 210

Tremendous Adventures of Major Gahagan, The (Thackeray), **V:** 22, 37

Tremor of Forgery, The (Highsmith), **Supp. V:** 175–176

Tremor of Intent (Burgess), **Supp. I:** 185, 191–192

"Trenches St. Eloi" (Hulme), **Supp. VI:** 140

Trespasser, The (Lawrence), **VII:** 89, 91, 93–95; **Retro. Supp. II:** 227

Trevelyan, G. M., **I:** 375; **V:** xxiv, 223, 227, 234; **VI:** xv, 347, **383–396;** list of works, **VI:** 394–396

Trevenen (Davie), **Supp. VI:** 111

Trevor, William, **Supp. IV:** **499–519**

Trevor–Roper, Hugh, **Supp. IV:** 436

Trial, The (Kafka), **III:** 340

Trial of a Judge (Spender), **Supp. II:** 488

Trial of Elizabeth Cree: A Novel of the Limehouse Murders, The (Ackroyd), **Supp. VI:** 10

Trial of the Fox, The (Henryson), **Supp. VII:** 136, 138, 139, 140

Trial of the Honourable Augustus Keppel, The (Burke), **III:** 205

"Tribune's Visitation, The" (Jones), **Supp. VII:** 175, 179–180

Tributes (Jennings), **Supp. V:** 216

Trick of It, The (Frayn), **Supp. VII:** 61–62

Trick to Catch the Old One, A (Middleton), **II:** 3, 4–5, 21

"Trickster and the Sacred Clown, Revealing the Logic of the Unspeakable, The" (Belmonte), **Supp. IV:** 15–16

Trilby (du Maurier), **Supp. III:** 134, 135, 136

Trilogy (Beckett), **Retro. Supp. I:** 18, 20–23

Trilogy of Death (James), **Supp. IV:** 328, 329, 335, 337

"Trinity at Low Tide" (Stevenson), **Supp. VI:** 264

Trinity College (Trevelyan), **VI:** 383, 393

Trip to Scarborough, A (Sheridan), **II:** 334, 336; **III:** 253, 261, 270

Triple Thinkers, The (Wilson), **VI:** 164

"Triple Time" (Larkin), **Supp. I:** 279

"Tristram and Iseult" (Arnold), **V:** 210

"Tristram and Iseult: Prelude of an Unfinished Poem" (Swinburne), **V:** 332

Tristram Shandy (Sterne), **III:** 124, 126, **127–132,** 135, 150, 153; **IV:** 183; **Supp. II:** 204, 205

Triumph and Tragedy (Churchill), **VI:** 361

Triumph of Death (Fletcher), **II:** 66

Triumph of Gloriana, The (Swinburne), **V:** 333

Triumph of Honour (Field), **II:** 66

"Triumph of Life, The" (Shelley), **IV:** xi, 197, 206–207, 209; **Retro. Supp. I:** 256

Triumph of Love (Field), **II:** 66

Triumph of Love, The (Hill), **Supp. V:** 183, 189, 198–199, 202

Triumph of the Four Foster Children of Desire (Sidney), **Retro. Supp. II:** 329–330

Triumph of Time (Fletcher), **II:** 66

"Triumph of Time, The" (Swinburne), **V:** 311, 313, 318–319, 331

"Triumphal March" (Eliot), **VII:** 152–153

"Triumphs of Odin, The" (Gray), **III:** 142

"Triumphs of Sensibility" (Warner), **Supp. VII:** 371

Triumphs of Truth, The (Middleton), **II:** 3

Triumphs of Wealth and Prosperity, The (Middleton), **II:** 3

Trivia (Connolly), **Supp. III:** 98

Trivia; or, The Art of Walking the streets of London (Gay), **III:** 55, 57, 67

"Troglodyte, The" (Brooke-Rose), **Supp. IV:** 103

Troilus and Cressida (Dryden), **II:** 293, 305

Troilus and Cressida (Shakespeare), **I:** 313, 314; **II:** 47, 70; **IV:** 225; **V:** 328

Troilus and Criseyde (Chaucer), **I:** 24, 30, 31, 32–34, 41, 43, 44; **IV:** 189; **Retro. Supp. II:** 40–45

Trollope, Anthony, **II:** 172–173; **IV:** 306; **V:** x, xvii, xxii–xxv, 11, **89–103; VII:** xxi; **Supp. IV:** 229, 230

Trollope, Frances, **V:** 89

Trollope: A Commentary (Sadleir), **V:** 100, 102

"Trollope and His Style" (Sykes Davies), **V:** 103

Trooper Peter Halket of Mashonaland (Schreiner), **Supp. II:** 454

"Troopship" (Fuller), **Supp. VII:** 69

"Troopship in the Tropics, A" (Lewis), **VII:** 446

Tropic Seed (Waugh), **Supp. VI:** 275

Troubled Eden, A, Nature and Society in the Works of George Meredith (Kelvin), **V:** 221, 234

Troublesome Reign of John, King of England, The, **I:** 301

"Troy" (Muir), **Supp. VI:** 206

Troy Park (Sitwell), **VII:** 138

Troy–book (Lydgate), **I:** 57, 58, 59–65, 280

"Truce of the Bear, The" (Kipling), **VI:** 203

True Born Irishman, The (Friel), **Supp. V:** 126

"True Function and Value of Criticism, The" (Wilde), **Retro. Supp. II:** 367

True Heart, The (Warner), **Supp. VII:** 370, 375

True History (Lucian), **III:** 24

True History of Squire Jonathan and His Unfortunate Treasure, The (Arden), **Supp. II:** 31

True Patriot, The (Fielding), **III:** 105; **Retro. Supp. I:**

True Relation of the Apparition of . . . Mrs. Veal . . . to . . . Mrs. Bargrave . . . (Defoe), **III:** 13

True State of the Case of Bosavern Penlez, A (Fielding), **III:** 105

True Widow, The (Shadwell), **II:** 115305

True-Born Englishman, The (Defoe), **III:** 3, 12; **Retro. Supp. I:** 64, 67

Trumpet-Major, The: A Tale (Hardy), **VI:** 5, 6–7, 20; **Retro. Supp. I:** 114

"Truth" (Bacon), **III:** 39

"Truth" (Cowper), **III:** 212

Truth About an Author (Bennett), **VI:** 264–265

Truth About Blayds, The (Milne), **Supp. V:** 299

"Truth in the Cup" (Warner), **Supp. VII:** 381

"Truth of Masks, The" (Wilde), **Retro. Supp. II:** 368

"Truthful Adventure, A" (Mansfield), **VII:** 172

Trying to Explain (Davie), **Supp. VI:** 115

"Tryst at an Ancient Earthwork, A" (Hardy), **VI:** 22

Trystram of Lyonesse (Swinburne), **V:** 299, 300, 314, 327–328, 332

Tsvetayeva, Marina, **Supp. IV:** 493

Tucker, Abraham, pseud. of William Hazlitt

Tudor trilogy (Ford), **VI:** 319, 323, 325–327; *see also Fifth Queen, The; Fifth Queen Crowned, The; Privy Seal*

"Tuesday; or, The Ditty" (Gay), **III:** 56

"Tulips" (McGuckian), **Supp. V:** 281

Tumatumari (Harris), **Supp. V:** 136, 137

Tumble–down Dick (Fielding), **III:** 105

Tunc (Durrell), **Supp. I:** 113–118, 120

"Tunnel" (Barnes), **Supp. IV:** 75, 76

Tunning of Elinour Rumming, The (Skelton), **I:** 82, 86–87, 92

"Tunstall Forest" (Davie), **Supp. VI:** 110

Turkish Delight (Churchill), **Supp. IV:** 181

Turkish Mahomet and Hiren the Fair Greek (Peele), **I:** 205

Turkish tales (Byron), **IV:** x, 172, 173–175

"Turn for the Better, A" (Nicholson), **Supp. VI:** 217

Turn of the Screw, The (James), **III:** 334, 340, 345; **V:** xxvi, 14; **VI:** 39, **52–53,** 69; **Supp. IV:** 97, 116, 503, 511

Turn of the Years, The (Pritchett), **Supp. III:** 311

Turner, J. M. W., **V:** xix, xx, 174–175, 178

"Turns" (Harrison), **Supp. V:** 154–155

Tutchin, John, **III:** 3

"Tutelar of the Place, The" (Jones), **Supp. VII:** 179–180

Tuve, Rosamund, **II:** 124, 130; **Retro. Supp. II:** 174

"Twa Dogs, The" (Burns), **III:** 315, 316

"Twa Herds, The" (Burns), **III:** 311, 319

Twain, Mark, **IV:** 106; **V:** xix, xxiv–xxv

Twelfth Night (Shakespeare), **I:** 312, 320

Twelve Adventurers and Other Stories (Brontë), **V:** 151

Twelve Apostles (Ewart), **Supp. VII:** 40

Twelve Months in a Curatorship (Carroll), **V:** 274

Twelve Pound Look, The (Barrie), **Supp. III:** 6, 8, 9, 15–16

"Twelve Songs" (Auden), **VII:** 383, 386

"Twentieth Century Blues" (Coward), **Supp. II:** 147

"Twenty Pounds" (Gissing), **V:** 437

Twenty five (Gregory), **VI:** 309

Twenty–five Poems (Thomas), **Supp. I:** 174, 176, 180

"Twenty–four years" (Thomas), **Supp. I:** 177

"24th March 1986" (Ewart), **Supp. VII:** 46

"Twenty–Seven Articles, The" (Lawrence), **Supp. II:** 287

Twilight Bar (Koestler), **Supp. I:** 25

Twilight in Italy (Lawrence), **VII:** 116

Twin Rivals, The (Farquhar), **II:** 353, 357–358, 364

Twine, Laurence, **I:** 321

Twitchell, James B., **Supp. III:** 383

Twits, The (Dahl), **Supp. IV:** 205, 207, 223

'Twixt Land and Sea: Tales (Conrad), **VI:** 148

"Two Analogies for Poetry" (Davie), **Supp. VI:** 115

Two Autobiographical Plays (Arden), **Supp. II:** 31

Two Biographical Plays (Arden), **Supp. II:** 31

"Two Blond Flautists" (Fuller), **Supp. VII:** 79

Two Cheers for Democracy (Forster), **VI:** 397, 411

"Two Chorale–Preludes" (Hill), **Supp. V:** 199

"Two Countries" (James), **VI:** 69

Two Destinies, The (Collins), **Supp. VI:** 102

Two Drovers, The (Scott), **IV:** 39

"Two Early French Stories" (Pater), **V:** 344

"Two Faces, The" (James), **VI:** 69

Two Faces of January, The (Highsmith), **Supp. V:** 173–174

Two Foscari, The (Byron), **IV:** xviii, 178, 193

"Two Fragments: March 199–" (McEwan), **Supp. IV:** 395

"Two Frenchmen" (Strachey), **Supp. II:** 500, 502

"Two Fusiliers" (Graves), **VI:** 452

"Two Gallants" (Joyce), **VII:** 44

Two Generals, The (FitzGerald), **IV:** 353

Two Gentlemen of Verona (Shakespeare), **I:** 302, 311–312

Two Great Questions Consider'd, The (Defoe), **III:** 12

Two Guardians, The (Yonge), **V:** 253

Two Heroines of Plumplington, The (Trollope), **V:** 102

"Two Houses" (Thomas), **Supp. III:** 399

"Two Impromptus" (Amis), **Supp. II:** 15

"Two in the Campagna" (Browning), **IV:** 357, 369

"Two Kinds of Motion" (Stevenson), **Supp. VI:** 255

"Two Kitchen Songs" (Sitwell), **VII:** 130–131

"Two Knights, The" (Swinburne), **V:** 315, 333

Two Letters on the Conduct of Our Domestic Parties (Burke), **III:** 205

Two Letters on the French Revolution (Burke), **III:** 205

Two Letters . . . on the Proposals for Peace (Burke), **III:** 205

Two Letters . . . to Gentlemen in the City of Bristol . . . (Burke), **III:** 205

Two Lives (Trevor), **Supp. IV:** 516

Two Magics, The (James), **VI:** 52, 69

Two Mice, The (Henryson), **Supp. VII:** 136, 137, 140

Two Noble Kinsmen, The (Shakespeare), **I:** 324, 325; **II:** 43, 66, 87

Two of Us, The (Frayn), **Supp. VII:** 57

Two on a Tower: A Romance (Hardy), **VI:** 4, 5, 20; **Retro. Supp. I:** 114

Two or Three Graces (Huxley), **VII:** 201

Two Paths, The (Ruskin), **V:** 180, 184

"Two Peacocks of Bedfont, The" (Hood), **IV:** 256, 267

Two People (Milne), **Supp. V:** 310

"Two Races of Men, The" (Lamb), **IV:** 82

"Two Spirits, The" (Shelley), **IV:** 196

"2000: Zero Gravity" (Motion), **Supp. VII:** 266

"2001: The Tennyson/Hardy Poem" (Ewart), **Supp. VII:** 40

Two Towers, The (Tolkien), **Supp. II:** 519

Two Voices (Thomas), **Supp. IV:** 490

"Two Voices, The" (Tennyson), **IV:** 329

"Two Ways of It" (MacCaig), **Supp. VI:** 187

Two Worlds and Their Ways (Compton–Burnett), **VII:** 65, 66, 67, 69

"Two Year Old" (MacCaig), **Supp. VI:** 192

Two–Part Inventions (Howard), **V:** 418

"Two–Party System in English Political History, The" (Trevelyan), **VI:** 392

"Two–Sided Man, The" (Kipling), **VI:** 201

Twyborn Affair, The (White), **Supp. I:** 132, 148–149

"Tyes, The" (Thomas), **Supp. III:** 401

"Tyger, The" (Blake), **III:** 296; **Retro. Supp. I:** 42–43

Tyler, F. W., **I:** 275n

Tylney Hall (Hood), **IV:** 254, 256, 259, 267

Tynan, Katherine, **V:** 441

Tynan, Kenneth, **Supp. II:** 70, 140, 147, 152, 155; **Supp. IV:** 78

Tyndale, William, **I:** 375–377

"Typhoon" (Conrad), **VI:** 136, 148

Tyrannicida (tr. More), **Supp. VII:** 235–236

Tyrannick Loce; or, The Royal Martyr (Dryden), **II:** 290, 294, 305

"Tyronic Dialogues" (Lewis), **VII:** 82

Udolpho (Radcliffe), *see Mysteries of Udolpho, The*

Ulick and Soracha (Moore), **VI:** 89, 95, 99

"Ultima" (Thompson), **V:** 441

"Ultima Ratio Regum" (Spender), **Supp. II:** 488

Ultramarine (Lowry), **Supp. III:** 269, 270, **271–272,** 280, 283, 285

Ulysses (Butler), **Supp. II:** 114

Ulysses (Joyce), **V:** 189; **VII:** xv, 42, 46–47, 48–52; **Retro. Supp. I:** 169, 176–179; critical studies, **VII:** 57–58; **Supp. IV:** 87, 370, 390, 426

"Ulysses" (Tennyson), **IV:** xx, 324, 328, 332–334

"Umbrella Man, The" (Dahl), **Supp. IV:** 221

"Un Coeur Simple" (Flaubert), **Supp. IV:** 69

Un Début dans la vie (Balzac), **Supp. IV:** 123

"Unarmed Combat" (Reed), **VII:** 422–423

"Unattained Place, The" (Muir), **Supp. VI:** 206

Unbearable Bassington, The (Saki), **Supp. VI:** **245–248**

Uncensored (Rattigan), **Supp. VII:** 311

Unclassed, The (Gissing), **V:** 437

Uncle Bernac (Doyle), **Supp. II:** 159

"Uncle Ernest" (Sillitoe), **Supp. V:** 414

Uncle Fred in the Springtime (Wodehouse), **Supp. III:** 460–461

Uncle Silas (Le Fanu), **III:** 345; **Supp. II:** 78–79, 81

Uncle Vanya (tr. Frayn), **Supp. VII:** 61

Unclouded Summer (Waugh), **Supp. VI:** 274

Uncollected Essays (Pater), **V:** 357

Uncollected Verse (Thompson), **V:** 451

Uncommercial Traveller, The (Dickens), **V:** 72

Unconditional Surrender (Waugh), **VII:** 303, 304; *see also Sword of Honour trilogy*

Unconscious Memory (Butler), **Supp. II:** 107–108

Unconsoled, The (Ishiguro), **Supp. IV:** 301, 302, 304, 305, 306–307, 314–316

"Uncovenanted Mercies" (Kipling), **VI:** 175

"Under a Lady's Picture" (Waller), **II:** 234–235

"Under Ben Bulben" (Yeats), **VI:** 215, 219–220; **Retro. Supp. I:** 338

"Under Brinkie's Brae" (Brown), **Supp. VI:** 64

"Under Carn Brea" (Thomas), **Supp. IV:** 492

Under Milk Wood (Thomas), **Supp. I:** 183–184

Under Plain Cover (Osborne), **Supp. I:** 335–336

Under the Greenwood Tree: A Rural Painting of the Dutch School (Hardy), **VI:** 1, 2–3, 5, 20; **Retro. Supp. I:** 112–113

Under the Hill (Beardsley), **VII:** 292

Under the Hill (Firbank), **Supp. II:** 202

Under the Microscope (Swinburne), **IV:** 337; **V:** 329, 332, 333

Under the Net (Murdoch), **Supp. I:** 220, 222, 228, 229–230

Under the Sunset (Stoker), **Supp. III:** 381

Under the Volcano (Lowry), **Supp. III:** 269, 270, 273, **274–280,** 283, 285

Under the Reservoir (Redgrove), **Supp. VI:** 236

Under Western Eyes (Conrad), **VI:** 134, 144–145, 148; **Retro. Supp. II:** 81–82

"'Under Which King, Bezonian?'" (Leavis), **VII:** 242

Undergraduate Sonnets (Swinburne), **V:** 333

"Understanding the Ur–Bororo" (Self), **Supp. V:** 401–402

Undertones of War (Blunden), **VI:** 428, 429

Underwood (Jonson), **Retro. Supp. I:** 166

Underwood, Dale, **II:** 256n

Underwoods (Stevenson), **V:** 390n, 395; **Retro. Supp. I:** 267–268

Undine (Schreiner), **Supp. II:** **444–445**

"Undiscovered Planet, The" (Nicholson), **Supp. VI:** 217

Undying Fire, The (Wells), **VI:** 242

Unfinished Portrait (Christie), **Supp. II:** 133

"Unfortunate" (Brooke), **Supp. III:** 55

"Unfortunate Lover, The" (Marvell), **II:** 211

Unfortunate Traveller, The (Nashe), **I:** 114, 281

"Ungratefulnesse" (Herbert), **II:** 127

Unguarded Hours (Wilson), **Supp. VI:** 299, 308

"Unhappy Families" (Carter), **Supp. IV:** 459

Unhappy Favorite, The (Banks), **II:** 305

Unholy Trade, The (Findlater), **VII:** 8–9, 14

Unicorn, The (Murdoch), **III:** 341, 345; **Supp. I:** 215, 225, 226, 228

Unicorn, The (Rosenberg), **VI:** 433

Unicorn from the Stars, The (Yeats and Gregory), **VI:** 318

"Unimportant Fire, An" (Rushdie), **Supp. IV:** 445

Union of the Two Noble and Illustre Families of Lancaster and York, The (Hall), **I:** 299

"Union Reunion" (Wilson), **Supp. I:** 153, 155, 157

Union Street (Barker), **Supp. IV:** 45, 46–50, 57

Universal Chronicle (periodical), **III:** 111

Universal Gallant, The (Fielding), **III:** 105

"University of Mainz, The" (Waugh), **Supp. VI:** 269

"University Feud, The: A Row at the Oxford Arms" (Hood), **IV:** 258

Unjust War: An Address to the Working-men of England (Morris), **V:** 305

Unknown, The (Maugham), **VI:** 369

"Unknown Bird, The" (Thomas), **Supp. III:** 402

"Unknown Shores" (Thomas), **Supp. IV:** 490

Unlimited Dream Company, The (Ballard), **Supp. V:** 28–29

Unlit Lamp, The (Hall), **Supp. VI:** 120–122, **123–125**

"Unluckily for a Death" (Thomas), **Supp. I:** 178

Unnamable, The (Beckett), **Supp. I:** 45, 51, 52, 53–54, 55, 56, 60; **Supp. IV:** 106; **Retro. Supp. I:** 22–23

Unnatural Causes (James), **Supp. IV:** 320, 321, 324–326

Unnatural Death (Sayers), **Supp. II:** 135; **Supp. III:** 338–339, 340, 343

Unofficial Rose, An (Murdoch), **Supp. I:** 222, 223–224, 229, 232

Unpleasantness at the Bellona Club, The (Sayers), **Supp. III:** 330, 340

Unprofessional Tales (Douglas), **VI:** 293, 305

Unpublished Early Poems (Tennyson), **IV:** 338

Unquiet Grave, The: A Word Cycle by Palinurus (Connolly), **Supp. III: 103–105**

Unrelenting Struggle, The (Churchill), **VI:** 356

"Unremarkable Year, The" (Fuller), **Supp. VII:** 78

Unruly Times: Wordsworth and Coleridge in Their Time (Byatt), **Supp. IV:** 145

"Unseen Centre, The" (Nicholson), **Supp. VI:** 217

"Unsettled Motorcyclist's Vision of His Death, The" (Gunn), **Supp. IV:** 260

Unsocial Socialist, An (Shaw), **VI:** 103, 104, 105, 106, 129

"Unstable dream" (Wyatt), **I:** 103, 109

Unsuitable Attachment, An (Pym), **Supp. II: 375–377**

Unsuitable Job for a Woman, An (James), **Supp. IV:** 320, 335, 336

Unsworth, Barry, **Supp. VII: 353–367**

"Until My Blood Is Pure" (Chatwin), **Supp. IV:** 173

Untilled Field, The (Moore), **VI:** 88, 93, 98

Untitled Sea Novel (Lowry), **Supp. III:** 280

Unto This Last (Ruskin), **V:** xii, xxii, 20, 179–180

"Unusual Young Man, An" (Brooke), **Supp. III:** 50–51

Up Against It (Orton), **Supp. V:** 363, 366, 369–370

"Up and Awake" (Kinsella), **Supp. V:** 268

"Up and Down" (Smith), **Supp. II:** 470

"Up at a Villa—Down in the City" (Browning), **IV:** 360

Up the Rhine (Hood), **IV:** 254, 259, 267

Up to Midnight (Meredith), **V:** 234

Updike, John, **Supp. IV:** 27, 136, 480, 483

"Upon a Child That Dyed" (Herrick), **II:** 115

"Upon a Cloke Lent Him by Mr. J. Ridsley" (Vaughan), **II:** 184

Upon a Dead Man's Head (Skelton), **I:** 84

"Upon Ancient and Modern Learning" (Temple), **III:** 40

"Upon Appleton House" (Marvell), **II:** 208, 209–210, 211, 212–213; **Retro. Supp. II:** 261–262

Upon Cromwell's Return from Ireland (Marvell), **II:** 199

Upon Her Majesty's New Buildings (Waller), **II:** 238

"Upon Heroick Virtue" (Temple), **III:** 40

"Upon Julia's Clothes" (Herrick), **II:** 107

"Upon Julia's Fall" (Herrick), **II:** 107

"Upon Julia's Unlacing Herself" (Herrick), **II:** 106

"Upon Julia's Voice" (Herrick), **II:** 107

"Upon Nothing" (Rochester), **II:** 259, 270

"Upon Our Late Loss of the Duke of Cambridge" (Waller), **II:** 233

"Upon Poetry" (Temple), **III:** 40

"Upon the Death of a Gentleman" (Crashaw), **II:** 183

"Upon the Death of Mr. R. W . . . ." (Vaughan), **II:** 184

"Upon the Earl of Roscommon's Translation of Horace" (Waller), **II:** 234

"Upon the Gardens of Epicurus" (Temple), **III:** 40

Upon the Late Storme, and of the Death of His Highnesse (Waller), **II:** 238

"Upon the Lonely Moor" (Carroll), **V:** 265, 267

Upstairs Downstairs (teleplay, Weldon), **Supp. IV:** 521

Upton, John, **I:** 121

Ure, Peter, **VI:** 220

Urgent Copy (Burgess), **Supp. I:** 186, 190, 194, 197

Use of Poetry and the Use of Criticism, The (Eliot), **VII:** 153, 158, 164; **Retro. Supp. II:** 65–66

Useful and Instructive Poetry (Carroll), **V:** 263, 264, 273

Uses of Literacy, The (Hoggart), **Supp. IV:** 473

"Uses of the Many–Charactered Novel" (Stead), **Supp. IV:** 466

Using Biography (Empson), **Supp. II:** 180

Usk, Thomas, **I:** 2

U.S. Martial (Harrison), **Supp. V:** 163

"Usura Canto," *see* "Canto 45"

Utility Player, The (Keneally), **Supp. IV:** 347

Utopia (More), **III:** 24; **Supp. VII:** 233, 235, 236, 238–240, 243, 248

"Utter Rim, The" (Graves), **VII:** 270

Utz (Chatwin), **Supp. IV:** 159, 163, 173, 174–175

"V." (Harrison), **Supp. V: 153, 157–160**

V. (Pynchon), **Supp. IV:** 116

V. and Other Poems (Harrison), **Supp. V:** 160

V. C. O'Flaherty (Shaw), **VI:** 119–120, 129

Vagrant Mood, The (Maugham), **VI:** 374

Vailima Letters (Stevenson), **V:** 391, 396

Vain Fortune (Moore), **VI:** 87, 91

Vainglory (Firbank), **Supp. II:** 201, 203–204, 205, 208–209

Val D'Arno (Ruskin), **V:** 184

Vala; or, The Four Zoas (Blake), *see Four Zoas, The*

Vale (Moore), **VI:** 99

"Valediction, A: Forbidding Mourning" (Donne), **II:** 185, 197; **Retro. Supp. II:** 87–88

"Valediction, A: Of Weeping" (Donne), **II:** 196

"Valediction of my name, in the window, A" (Donne), **Retro. Supp. II:** 92

Valentinian (Fletcher), **II:** 45, 58–60, 65

Valentinian: A Tragedy . . . (Rochester), **II:** 270

Valiant Scot, The (Webster), **II:** 69, 85

Valley of Bones, The (Powell), **VII:** 349

"Valley of Couteretz" (Tennyson), **IV:** 330

Valley of Fear, The (Doyle), **Supp. II:** 162, 163, 171, 172, 173, 174

Valmouth: A Romantic Novel (Firbank), **Supp. II:** 199, 201, 202, 205, **213–214**

"Value of Money, The" (Berger), **Supp. IV:** 92

Vamp Till Ready (Fuller), **Supp. VII:** 81

Vampirella (Carter), **III:** 341

Vampyre, The (Polidori), **III:** 329, 334; **Supp. III:** 385

"Van Gogh among the Miners" (Mahon), **Supp. VI:** 168

Van, The (Doyle), **Supp. V:** 78, 85–87

Van Vechten, Carl, **Supp. II:** 200, 203, 218

Vanbrugh, Sir John, **II:** 289, **323–337**, 339, 347, 360; **III:** 253, 261

Vandaleur's Folly (Arden and D'Arcy), **Supp. II:** 35, 39

"Vanitie" (Herbert), **II:** 127

Vanity Fair (Thackeray), **IV:** 301; **V:** xxi, 17, 19, 20, 23, **25–28**, 30, 31, 35, 38; **Supp. IV:** 238

"Vanity of Human Wishes, The" (Johnson), **III:** 109–110, 121, 280, 281; **IV:** 188; **Supp. IV:** 271; **Retro. Supp. I:** 139, 148

"Vanity of Spirit" (Vaughan), **II:** 185

"Vaquero" (Muldoon), **Supp. IV:** 415

Vargas Llosa, Mario, **Supp. IV:** 440

Variation of Public Opinion and Feelings, The (Crabbe), **III:** 286

"Variations of Ten Summer Minutes" (MacCaig), **Supp. VI:** 193

Variation on a Theme (Rattigan), **Supp. VII:** 315, 319–320

"Variations and Excerpts" (Ewart), **Supp. VII:** 43

Variations on a Time Theme (Muir), **Supp. VI:** 204

"Variations on a Time Theme" (Muir), **Supp. VI:** 205

Varieties of Parable (MacNeice), **VII:** 405

Varma, D. P., **III:** 338, 346

Varney the Vampire (Pecket and Rymer), **Supp. III:** 385

Vasari, Georgio, **V:** 346

"Vastness" (Tennyson), **IV:** 329, 330

Vathek (Beckford), **III: 327–329**, 345; **IV:** xv, 230

Vaughan, Henry, **II:** 123, 126, **184–189**, 190, **201–203**, 221; **Retro. Supp. II:** 172

Vaughan, Thomas, **II:** 184, 185

"Vauxhall Gardens by Day" (Dickens), **V:** 47n

"Velvet Glove, The" (James), **VI:** 69

Venables, Robert, **II:** 131, 137

Vendor of Sweets, The (Naipaul), **Supp. I:** 400

Venerable Bede, The, **I:** 374–375

Venetia (Disraeli), **IV:** xix, 298, 299, 307, 308

Veni, Creator Spiritus (Dryden), **II:** 300

Venus and Adonis (Shakespeare), **I:** 291, 306, 325; **IV:** 256

Venus and Tannhäuser (Beardsley), **V:** 318n

Venus and the Rain (McGuckian), **Supp. V:** 277, 282–284, 287

"Venus and the Rain" (McGuckian), **Supp. V:** 277–278

"Venus and the Sun" (McGuckian), **Supp. V:** 283

"Venus Fly–trap" (MacCaig), **Supp. VI:** 192

Venus Observed (Fry), **Supp. III:** 195, 202–203, 207, 208

"Venus Smiles" (Ballard), **Supp. V:** 26

Venusberg (Powell), **VII:** 344, 345

Vera; or, The Nihilists (Wilde), **V:** 401, 419; **Retro. Supp. II:** 362

Veranilda (Gissing), **V:** 435, 437

Verbivore (Brooke–Rose), **Supp. IV:** 100, 111–112

Vercelli Book, **Retro. Supp. II:** 301–303

Vergil, **II:** 292, 300, 304; **III:** 222, 311, 312; **IV:** 327; **Supp. III:** 415–416, 417

Vergil's Gnat (Spenser), **I:** 123

Vérité de la réligion Chrétienne (tr. Sidney), **I:** 161

Verlaine, Paul, **V:** 404, 405

Vermeer, Jan, **Supp. IV:** 136

Vernacular Republic, The (Murray), **Supp. VII:** 270

Verne, Jules, **III:** 341; **VI:** 229

Veronese, Paolo, **V:** 179

"Vers de Société" (Larkin), **Supp. I:** 282, 285

Vers d'Occasion (Day Lewis), **Supp. III:** 130

Verse (Murray), **Supp. VII:** 270

"Verse from an Opera—The Village Dragon" (Ewart), **Supp. VII:** 37

Verses (Rossetti), **V:** 260

Verses, in the Character of a Corsican (Boswell), **III:** 248

Verses Lately Written upon Several Occasions (Cowley), **II:** 202

Verses on the Death of Dr. Swift (Swift), **III:** 21, 32; **Retro. Supp. I:** 274

"Verses . . . to Sir Thomas Hanmer" (Collins), **III:** 160, 175

Vertical Man: Sequel to A Selected Life (Kinsella), **Supp. V:** 267

Very Fine Clock, The (Spark), **Supp. I:** 213

Very Private Eye, A: An Autobiography in Diaries and Letters (Pym), **Supp. II:** 363, 374

Very Private Life, A (Frayn), **Supp. VII:** 54–56

Very Woman, A (Fletcher and Massinger), **II:** 66

"Vespers" (Auden), **Retro. Supp. I:** 13

"Vespers" (Milne), **Supp. V:** 301–302

Vexilla Regis (Jones), **Supp. VII:** 180

Vexilla Regis (Skelton), **I:** 84

Via Media, The (Newman), **Supp. VII:** 295, 302

"Via Portello" (Davie), **Supp. VI:** 107

"Vicar, The" (Praed), **V:** 14

Vicar of Bullhampton, The (Trollope), **V:** 102

Vicar of Sorrows, The (Wilson), **Supp. VI:** 308

Vicar of Wakefield, The (Goldsmith), **III:** 177, 178, 179, 180, **181–184,** 185, 188, 191

Viceroy of Ouidah, The (Chatwin), **Supp. IV:** 158, 165–168, 173

Victim of Circumstances, A, and Other Stories (Gissing), **V:** 437

Victim of the Aurora, A (Keneally), **Supp. IV:** 346, 352–354

"Victor Hugo" (Swinburne), **V:** 333

Victoria, queen of England, **IV:** 303–304, 305; **V:** xvii, xix, xxv–xxvi, 77, 114, 117

Victoria Station (Pinter), **Supp. I:** 378

Victorian Age in Literature (Chesterton), **VI:** 337

Victorian and Edwardian London from Old Photographs (Betjeman), **VII:** 358

Victorian Lady Travellers (Middleton), **V:** 253

Victorian Ode for Jubilee Day, 1897 (Thompson), **V:** 451

Victorian Romantic, A: D. G. Rossetti (Doughty), **V:** 246, 297n, 307

Victory (Conrad), **VI:** 144, 146, 148; **Supp. IV:** 250; **Retro. Supp. II:** 82

"Victory, The" (Stevenson), **Supp. VI:** 256, 264

Vidal, Gore, **Supp. IV:** 546

Vienna (Spender), **Supp. II:** 486, 487

"Vienna. Zürich. Constance" (Thomas), **Supp. IV:** 493

"Vienne" (Rhys), **Supp. II:** 388, 389–390

Viet Rock (play), **Supp. IV:** 435

"Vietnam Project, The" (Coetzee), **Supp. VI:** 76, **78–79,** 80

"View of Exmoor, A" (Warner), **Supp. VII:** 380

"View of Poetry, A" (Muir), **Supp. VI:** 202–203

View of the Edinburgh Theatre . . . , A (Boswell), **III:** 247

View of the English Stage, A (Hazlitt), **IV:** 129, 139

View of the Present State of Ireland (Spenser), **I:** 139

Views and Reviews (James), **VI:** 67

Views in Rome and Its Environs (Lear), **V:** 76, 87

Views in the Seven Ionian Islands (Lear), **V:** 87

"Vigil of Corpus Christi, The" (Gunn), **Supp. IV:** 266

Vigny, Alfred de, **IV:** 176

Vile Bodies (Waugh), **VII:** 289, 290–291

Villa Rubein (Galsworthy), **VI:** 277

Village, The (Crabbe), **III:** 273, 274, 275, 277–278, 283, 286

"Village, The" (Reid), **Supp. VII:** 325

Village Betrothal (Greuze), **Supp. IV:** 122

Village by the Sea (Desai), **Supp. V:** 55, 63, 68–69

Village Wooing (Shaw), **VI:** 127, 129

Villainy of Stock–Jobbers Detected, The (Defoe), **III:** 12

"Villanelle" (Empson), **Supp. II:** 183

Villette (Brontë), **V:** xxi, 112, 125–126, 130, 132, 136, 145, **147–150,** 152; **Retro. Supp. I:** 53, 54, 60–61

Villiers, George, *see* Buckingham, duke of

Villon (Bunting), **Supp. VII:** 3, 6

Villon, François, **V:** 327, 384

Vinaver, Eugéne, **Retro. Supp. II:** 242, 246

Vindication &c., The (Dryden), **II:** 305

Vindication of a Natural Diet . . . , A (Shelley), **IV:** 208

Vindication of . . . Lord Carteret, A (Swift), **III:** 35–36

Vindication of Natural Society, A (Burke), **III:** 195, 198, 205

Vindication of . . . Some Gospel–Truths, A (Bunyan), **II:** 253

Vindication of Some Passages in . . . the Decline and Fall . . . , A (Gibbon), **III:** 233

Vindication of the English Constitution (Disraeli), **IV:** 298, 308

Vindication of the Rights of Men, A (Wollstonecraft), **Supp. III: 467–470,** 474, 476

Vindication of the Rights of Women, A (Wollstonecraft), **IV:** xv, 118; **Supp. III:** 465, **470–473,** 476

Vindiciae Ecclesiae Anglicanae: Letters to Charles Butler . . . (Southey), **IV:** 71

Vinegar Tom (Churchill), **Supp. IV:** 181, 184–186, 198

Vinland (Brown), **Supp. VI:** 67

Vintage London (Betjeman), **VII:** 358–359

"Vintage to the Dungeon, The" (Lovelace), **II:** 231

Violent Effigy, The: A Study of Dickens's Imagination (Carey), **V:** 73

"Violent Noon, The" (Ballard), **Supp. V:** 20

Viper and Her Brood, The (Middleton), **II:** 3, 33

Virchow, Rudolf, **V:** 348

Virgidemiarum (Hall), **II:** 25

Virgil, *see* Vergil

Virgin and the Gipsy, The (Lawrence), **VII:** 91, 115

Virgin in the Garden, The (Byatt), **Supp. IV:** 139, 145–147, 149

"Virgin Mary to the Child Jesus, The" (Browning), **IV:** 313

Virginia (O'Brien), **Supp. V:** 334

Virginia Woolf: A Biography (Bell), **VII:** 38; **Retro. Supp. I:** 305

Virginia Woolf Icon (Silver), **Retro. Supp. I:** 305

Virginians, The (Thackeray), **V:** 29, **31–33,** 38

Virginibus Puerisque and Other Papers (Stevenson), **V:** 395; **Retro. Supp. I:** 262

Vision, A (Yeats), **VI:** 209, 213, 214, 222

"Vision, The" (Burns), **III:** 315

"Vision and Prayer" (Thomas), **Supp. I:** 178

Vision of Bags, A (Swinburne), **V:** 333

Vision of Battlements, A (Burgess), **Supp. I:** 185, 187, 195–196

Vision of Delight, The (Jonson), **Retro. Supp. I:** 165

Vision of Don Roderick, The (Scott), **IV:** 38

Vision of Gombold Proval, The (Orton), **Supp. V:** 365–366, 370

Vision of Judgement, A (Southey), **IV:** 61, 71, 184–187

Vision of Judgment, The (Byron), **IV:** xviii, 58, 61–62, 132, 172, 178, **184–187,** 193

"Vision of Poets, A" (Browning), **IV:** 316

"Vision of the Last Judgment, A" (Blake), **III:** 299

"Vision of the Mermaids, A" (Hopkins), **V:** 361, 381

Vision of the Three T's, The (Carroll), **V:** 274

"Vision of that Ancient Man, The" (Motion), **Supp. VII:** 260, 261

Vision of William Concerning Piers the Plowman . . . , The (ed. Skeat), **I:** 17

Visions of the Daughters of Albion (Blake), **III:** 307; **Retro. Supp. I:** 39–40

"Visit in Bad Taste, A" (Wilson), **Supp. I:** 157

"Visit to Grandpa's, A" (Thomas), **Supp. I:** 181

"Visit to Morin, A" (Greene), **Supp. I:** 15, 18

"Visitation, The" (Jennings), **Supp. V:** 212

Visitations (MacNeice), **VII:** 416

"Visiting Hour" (Kinsella), **Supp. V:** 273

"Visiting Hour" (Murphy), **Supp. V:** 326

Visiting Mrs. Nabokov and Other Excursions (Amis), **Supp. IV:** 42, 43

"Visiting Rainer Maria" (McGuckian), **Supp. V:** 286

"Visitor, The" (Bowen), **Supp. II:** 81

"Visitor, The" (Dahl), **Supp. IV:** 219–220

Visitor, The (Orton), **Supp. V:** 363, 367

"Visitors, The" (Fuller), **Supp. VII:** 77

"Visits, The" (James), **VI:** 49, 69

"Visits to the Cemetery of the Long Alive" (Stevenson), **Supp. VI:** 264

Vita Nuova (tr. Rossetti), **V:** 238

"Vitaï Lampada" (Newbolt), **VI:** 417

Vittoria (Meredith), **V:** 227–228, 234

Vivian (Edgeworth), **Supp. III:** 158

Vivian Grey (Disraeli), **IV:** xvii, 293–294, 297, 299, 308

Vivisector, The (White), **Supp. I:** 132, 145–146

Vizetelly (publisher), **VI:** 86

"Voice, The" (Brooke), **Supp. III:** 52

"Voice, The" (Hardy), **VI:** 18

"Voice from the Dead, A" (Connolly), **Supp. III:** 111

"Voice of Nature, The" (Bridges), **VI:** 79

"Voice of the Ancient Bard, The" (Blake), **Retro. Supp. I:** 37

"Voice of Things, The" (Hardy), **Retro. Supp. I:** 121

Voice Over (MacCaig), **Supp. VI:** 194

Voices in the City (Desai), **Supp. V:** 54, 59–60, 72

"Voices of Time, The" (Ballard), **Supp. V:** 22, 24, 29, 34

Volpone (Jonson), **I:** 339, 343–344, 348; **II:** 4, 45, 70, 79; **V:** 56; **Retro. Supp. I:** 163, 164

Voltaire, **II:** 261, 348; **III:** 149, 235, 236, 327; **IV:** xiv, 290, 295, 346; **Supp. IV:** 136, 221

"Voltaire at Ferney" (Auden), **Retro. Supp. I:** 8

"Volunteer, The" (Asquith), **VI:** 417

Volunteers (Friel), **Supp. V:** 111, 112, 121–122

Vonnegut, Kurt, Jr., **III:** 341; **Supp. IV:** 116

Vortex, The (Coward), **Supp. II:** 139, 141–143, 144, 149

Voss (White), **VII:** 31; **Supp. I:** 130, 131, **138–141,** 142

Votive Tablets (Blunden), **IV:** 86

Vox clamantis (Gower), **I:** 48, 49–50

"Vox Humana" (Gunn), **Supp. IV:** 261–262

Voyage, The (Muir), **Supp. VI:** 204, **206–207**

Voyage In the Dark (Rhys), **Supp. II:** **394–396**

Voyage of Captain Popanilla, The (Disraeli), **IV:** 294–295, 308

"Voyage of Mael Duin," **Supp. IV:** 415–416

Voyage of the Dawn Treader, The (Lewis), **Supp. III:** 248, 260

Voyage Out, The (Woolf), **VII:** 20, 27, 37; **Retro. Supp. I:** 307, 315–316

Voyage That Never Ends, The (Lowry), **Supp. III:** 276, 280

Voyage to Abyssinia, A (tr. Johnson), **III:** 107, 112, 121; **Retro. Supp. I:** 139

Voyage to New Holland, A (Dampier), **III:** 24

Voyage to the Island of Love, A (Behn), **Supp. III:** 37

Voyage to Venus (Lewis), **Supp. III:** 249

Voyages (Hakluyt), **I:** 150, 267; **III:** 7

"Voyages of Alfred Wallis, The" (Graham), **Supp. VII:** 110

Vulgar Errors (Browne), *see Pseudodoxia Epidemica*

Vulgar Streak, The (Lewis), **VII:** 72, 77

"Vulgarity in Literature" (Huxley), **V:** 53; **VII:** 198

"Vulture, The" (Beckett), **Supp. I:** 44

W. B. Yeats, Man and Poet (Jeffares), **VI:** 223

W. B. Yeats: The Critical Heritage (Jeffares), **VI:** 224

"W. Kitchener" (Hood), **IV:** 267

W. Somerset Maugham and the Quest for Freedom (Calder), **VI:** 376n

Waagen, Gustav Friedrich, **III:** 328

Wager, William, **I:** 213

Waggoner, The (Wordsworth), **IV:** 24, 73

"Wagner" (Brooke), **Supp. III:** 53

Wagner the Werewolf (Reynolds), **III:** 335

Wagstaff, Simon, pseud. of Jonathan Swift

Waif Woman, The (Stevenson), **V:** 396

Wain, John, **VI:** 209

Wainewright, Thomas, **V:** 405

Waingrow, W., **III:** 249

Waith, Eugene, **II:** 51, 64

"Waiting" (Self), **Supp. V:** 402

"Waiting at the Station" (Thackeray), **V:** 25

"Waiting for Breakfast" (Larkin), **Supp. I:** 277

"Waiting for Columbus" (Reid), **Supp. VII:** 334

Waiting for Godot (Beckett), **I:** 16–17; **Supp. I:** 51, 55–56, 57, 59; **Supp. IV:** 281, 429; **Retro. Supp. I:** 17–18, 20–21, 23–24; **Retro. Supp. II:** 344

"Waiting for J." (Ishiguro), **Supp. IV:** 303

Waiting for the Barbarians (Coetzee), **Supp. VI:** 75–76, **81–82**

"Waiting Grounds, The" (Ballard), **Supp. V:** 21, 22

Waiting in the Wings (Coward), **Supp. II:** 155

Waiting Room, The (Harris), **Supp. V:** 136, 137–138, 140

"Waiting Supper, The" (Hardy), **VI:** 22

"Waking Father, The" (Muldoon), **Supp. IV:** 416–417

"Waking in a Newly Built House" (Gunn), **Supp. IV:** 263

Waldegrave, Frances, **V:** 77, 80, 81

Waldere, **Retro. Supp. II:** 306–307

Walk in Chamounix, A, and Other Poems (Ruskin), **V:** 184

Walk on the Water, A (Stoppard), **Supp. I:** 437, 439

Walker, Ernest, **IV:** 304

Walker, London (Barrie), **Supp. III:** 4

Walker, R. S., **III:** 249

Walker, Shirley, **Supp. IV:** 347

"Walking to the Cattle Place" (Murray), **Supp. VII:** 274–275, 280, 281

"Walking with God" (Cowper), **III:** 212

"Walking Wounded" (Scannell), **VII:** 423

"Wall, The" (Jones), **Supp. VII:** 175

Wall of the Plague, The (Brink), **Supp. VI:** **52–53**

Waller, Edmund, **II:** 138, 222, **232–236,** 256, 271

Walpole, Horace, **III:** 324, **325–327,** 336, 345; **Supp. III:** 383–384

Walpole, Hugh, **VI:** 55, 247, 377; **VII:** 211

Walpole, Robert, **Retro. Supp. I:** 235–236

"Walrus and the Carpenter, The" (Carroll), **V:** 268

Walsh, William, **II:** 325, 337, 339, 347; **Retro. Supp. I:** 232

Walter Pater: A Critical Study (Thomas), **V:** 355, 358; **VI:** 424

Walter Pater: The Idea in Nature (Ward), **V:** 347, 359

Walter Savage Landor: A Biography (Forster), **IV:** 87, 100

Walton, Izaak, **I:** 178; **II:** 118, 119, 130, **131–144; Retro. Supp. II:** 171–172

Walton, William, **VII:** xv

Walts, Janet, **Supp. IV:** 399

Waltz: An Apostrophic Hymn by Horace Hornem, Esq. (Byron), **IV:** 192

Wanderer, The, **Retro. Supp. II:** 304

Wanderer, The (Auden), **VII:** 380

"Wanderer, The" (Smith), **Supp. II:** 465

Wanderer, The; or, Female Difficulties (Burney), **Supp. III:** 64, 67, 74, 75, 76–77

"Wandering Angus, The" (Yeats), **Supp. IV:** 424

Wandering Islands, The (Hope), **Supp. VII:** 153–156, 157, 159

Wandering Jew, The (Shelley), **IV:** 209

"Wanderings of Brendan," **Supp. IV:** 415

Wanderings of Oisin, The (Yeats), **IV:** 216; **VI:** 220, 221; **Supp. V:** 36; **Retro. Supp. I:** 325

Want of Wyse Men, The (Henryson), **Supp. VII:** 146–147

Wanting Seed, The (Burgess), **Supp. I:** 186, 190, 192–193

War (Doyle), **Supp. V:** 77, 87, 88–89

War and Common Sense (Wells), **VI:** 244

"War Death in a Low Key" (Ewart), **Supp. VII:** 44

War Fever (Ballard), **Supp. V:** 33

"War Fever" (Ballard), **Supp. V:** 33

War in Samoa (Stevenson), **V:** 396

War in South Africa, The: Its Cause and Conduct (Doyle), **Supp. II:** 161

War in the Air . . . , The (Wells), **VI:** 234, 244

War Issues for Irishmen (Shaw), **VI:** 119

War of the Worlds, The (Wells), **VI:** 226, 233–234

War Plays, The (Bond), **Supp. I:** 423, 434

War Speeches (Churchill), **VI:** 361

"War That Will End War, The" (Wells), **VI:** 227, 244

"War–time" (Ewart), **Supp. VII:** 38

Ward, A. C., **V:** xiii, xxviii, 85, 86, 347, 348, 349

Ward, Edward, **III:** 41

Ward, Mrs. Humphry, **VI:** 387

Ward, R. P., **IV:** 293

"Ward 1G" (Fuller), **Supp. VII:** 80

"Ward 9" (Self), **Supp. V:** 401

Warden, The (Trollope), **V:** xxii, 92, 93, 101

"Warden's Daughter, The" (Gissing), **V:** 437

Ware the Hawk (Skelton), **I:** 88

"Waring" (Browning), **IV:** 356

Warner, Sylvia Townsend, **Supp. VII:** 369–383

"Warning to Children" (Graves), **VII:** 265

Warren, Austin, **II:** 155, 332*n*

"Warriors of the North, The" (Hughes), **Supp. I:** 342, 350

"Warriors Soul, The" (Conrad), **VI:** 148

War's Embers (Gurney), **VI:** 425

Warton, Joseph, **III:** 162, 170*n*

"Was He Married?" (Smith), **Supp. II:** 468

"Was, Is, Will Be" (Reid), **Supp. VII:** 327

Washington Square (James), **VI: 32–33**

Wasp in a Wig, The (Carroll), **V:** 274

"Waste Land, The" (Eliot), **VI:** 137, 158; **VII:** xv, 143, **147–150; Supp. III:** 122; **Supp. IV:** 58, 249, 377; **Retro. Supp. I:** 3; **Retro. Supp. II:** 120, 121, 124–129

"Waste Land, The" (Paton), **Supp. II:** 345

Wasted Years, The (Phillips), **Supp. V:** 380

Wat Tyler (Southey), **IV:** 59, 62, 66, 71, 185

"Watch, The" (Swift), **Supp. V:** 433–434

Watch and Ward (James), **VI:** 24, 26, 67

Watch in the Night, A (Wilson), **Supp. VI:** 307

Watched Pot, The (Saki), **Supp. VI:** 250

"Watching Post" (Day Lewis), **Supp. III:** 128

Watchman, The (periodical), **IV:** 43, 55, 56

"Water Cinema" (Redgrove), **Supp. VI:** 236

"Water Lady, The" (Hood), **IV:** 255

"Water–Lady" (Redgrove), **Supp. VI:** 230

Water of Life, The (Bunyan), **II:** 253

Water of the Wondrous Isles, The (Morris), **V:** 306

Waterfall, The (Drabble), **Supp. IV:** 230, 239–241

"Waterfall of Winter" (Redgrove), **Supp. VI:** 234

"Waterglass, The" (Reid), **Supp. VII:** 326

"Waterkeeper's Bothy" (Murphy), **Supp. V:** 328

Waterland (Swift), **Supp. V:** 427, 434–437

Waters of Babylon, The (Arden), **Supp. II:** 21, 22, 23–24, 25, 29

"Watershed, The" (Auden), **Retro. Supp. I:** 3

"Water–Witch, Wood–Witch, Wine–Witch" (Redgrove), **Supp. VI:** 234

Watson, George L., **VI:** 152

Watson, John B., **Supp. II:** 451

Watson, John Richard, **IV:** ix, xxv, 26, 375

Watson, Peter, **Supp. III:** 102–103, 105, 109

Watson, Richard, **III:** 301

Watson, Sir William, **VI:** 415

Watson, Thomas, **I:** 193, 276

Watsons, The (Austen), **IV:** 108, 122

Watson's Apology (Bainbridge), **Supp. VI:** 23

Watt, Ian, **VI:** 144; **Retro. Supp. I:** 70

Watt (Beckett), **Supp. I:** 46, **47–49,** 50, 51; **Retro. Supp. I:** 17, 20

Watteau (Brookner), **Supp. IV:** 122

Watteau, Jean–Antoine, **Supp. IV:** 122

Watter's Mou', The (Stoker), **Supp. III:** 381

"Wattle Tent" (Murphy), **Supp. V:** 329

Watts, Isaac, **III:** 118, 211, 288, 294, 299, 300

Watts–Dunton, Theodore, **V:** 314, 334

Waugh, Alec, **Supp. VI: 267–277**

Waugh, Evelyn, **V:** 33; **VII:** xviii, xxxi, **289–308; Supp. II:** 4, 74, 199, 213, 218; **Supp. III:** 105; **Supp. IV:** 27, 281, 287, 365, 505

Waverly novels (Scott), **IV:** 28, 30–34, 38

Waverly; or, 'Tis Sixty Years Since (Scott), **III:** 335; **IV:** xvii, 28, 30–31, 37, 38; **Supp. III:** 151, 154

Waves, The (Woolf), **VI:** 262; **VII:** xv, 18, 22, 27, 38; **Supp. III:** 45; **Supp. IV:** 461, 557; **Retro. Supp. I:** 308, 314, 319–320

"Waxwing Winter" (McGuckian), **Supp. V:** 289

"Way of Literature: An Apologia, The" (Brown), **Supp. VI:** 70

"Way It Came, The" (James), **VI:** 69

Way of All Flesh, The (Butler), **VI:** ix; **Supp. II:** 97, 98, 99, 104, **111–114,** 117, 119

Way of Being Free, A (Okri), **Supp. V:** 353, 359, 360

"Way of Imperfection, The" (Thompson), **V:** 451

Way of Looking, A (Jennings), **Supp. V:** , 210, 211, 214

"Way of the Cross, The" (du Maurier), **Supp. III:** 147

Way of the Spirit (Haggard), **Supp. III:** 214, 222

Way of the World, The (Congreve), **II:** 339, **343–346,** 347, 350

Way to the Stars, The (Rattigan), **Supp. VII:** 313, 319

"Way up to Heaven, The" (Dahl), **Supp. IV:** 218–219

Way Upstream (Ayckbourn), **Supp. V:** 3, 10, 14

Way We Live Now, The (Trollope), **IV:** 307; **V:** xxiv, 98–99, 100, 102

Ways and Means (Coward), **Supp. II:** 153

Ways of Escape (Greene), **Supp. I:** 3, 7, 11, 18

Ways of Seeing (Berger), **Supp. IV:** 79, 82, 88–90

Ways of Telling: The World of John Berger (Dyer), **Supp. IV:** 81

"Wayside Station, The" (Muir), **Supp. VI:** 206

"We Are Seven" (Wordsworth), **IV:** 8, 10

"We have a pritty witty king" (Rochester), **II:** 259

"We lying by seasand" (Thomas), **Supp. I:** 176

"We Must Act Quickly" (Paton), **Supp. II:** 359

We Were Dancing (Coward), **Supp. II:** 153

Wealth of Mr. Waddy, The (Wells), *see Kipps*

Wealth of Nations, The (Smith), *see Inquiry into the Nature & Causes of the Wealth of Nations*

Wearieswa': A Ballad (Swinburne), **V:** 333

Weatherboard Cathedral, The (Murray), **Supp. VII:** 270, 272–273, 282

Weathering (Reid), **Supp. VII:** 323, 330–331

Webb, Beatrice, **VI:** 227, 241; **Supp. IV:** 233

Webb, Mary, **Supp. IV:** 169

Webb, Philip, **V:** 291, 296

Webb, Sidney, **VI:** 102; **Supp. IV:** 233

Webber, Andrew Lloyd, **Supp. V:** 3

Webster, John, **II:** 21, 31,, 33, **68–86,** 82359, 97, 100; **Supp. IV:** 234

Webster: "The Dutchess of Malfi" (Leech), **II:** 90*n*

Wedd, Nathaniel, **VI:** 398, 399

"Wedding Gown, The" (Moore), **VI:** 93

"Wedding Morning" (Kinsella), **Supp. V:** 261

"Wedding Wind" (Larkin), **Supp. I:** 277, 285

Wedding–Day, The (Fielding), **III:** 105

"Weddings" (Thomas), **Supp. IV:** 491

Weddings at Nether Powers, The (Redgrove), **Supp. VI:** 235

Wedgwood, Tom, **IV:** 127–128

Wednesday Early Closing (Nicholson), **Supp. VI:** 212, 214

"Wednesday; or, The Dumps" (Gay), **III:** 56

Wee Willie Winkie (Kipling), **VI:** 204

"Weeds" (Nicholson), **Supp. VI:** 219

Weekend with Claude, A (Bainbridge), **Supp. V:** 17–19, 24

Weekly Journal (newspaper), **III:** 7

"Weeper, The" (Crashaw), **II:** 180, 181, 183

"Weighing" (Heaney), **Retro. Supp. I:** 133

"Weights" (Murray), **Supp. VII:** 278

Weil, Simone, **Supp. I:** 217

Weinraub, Judith, **Supp. IV:** 345

Weir of Hermiston, The (Stevenson), **V:** 383, 384, 387, 390, 392, 396; **Retro. Supp. I:** 270

Weis, C. McC., **III:** 249

Weismann, August, **Supp. II:** 108

Welch, Denton, **Supp. III:** 107

"Welcome, The" (Cowley), **II:** 196

"Welcome to Sack, The" (Herrick), **II:** lll

Weldon, Fay, **Supp. IV: 521–539**

Well at the World's End, The (Morris), **V:** 306

Well of Loneliness, The (Hall), **VI:** 411; **Supp. VI:** 119–120, 122, **125–128,** 129, 131

Well of Lycopolis, The (Bunting), **Supp. VII:** 4

"Well of Pen–Morta, The" (Gaskell), **V:** 15

Well of the Saints, The (Synge), **VI:** 308, 311, 312–313; **Retro. Supp. I:** 297–298

Well–Beloved, The: A Sketch of a Temperament (Hardy), **VI:** 14, 20; **Retro. Supp. I:** 114–115

"Wellington College" (Murphy), **Supp. V:** 328

Wells, H. G., **III:** 341; **V:** xxiii, xxvi, 388, 426–427, 429, 438; **VI:** x–xiii, 102, **225–246,** 287; **VII:** xiv, 197; list of works and letters, **VI:** 243–246; **Supp. II:** 295; **Supp. III:** 434; **Supp. IV:** 256

"Wells, Hitler, and the World State" (Orwell), **VII:** 274

"Wells, The" (Redgrove), **Supp. VI:** 234, 237

Well–Wrought Urn, The (Brooks), **IV:** 323n, 339

Welsh Ambassador, The, **II:** 100

Welsh, Irvine, **Supp. IV:** 26

Welsh Opera, The (Fielding), **III:** 105

We're Not Going to Do Anything (Day Lewis), **Supp. III:** 118

"Werewolf, The" (Carter), **Supp. III:** 88

Werner, J., **III:** 249

Werner: A Tragedy (Byron), **IV:** 193

Werther (Goethe), *see Sorrows of Young Werther, The*

Wesker, Arnold, **VI:** 101

Wesley, Charles, **III:** 211

Wesley, John, **II:** 273

Wessex Poems (Hardy), **VI:** 14; **Retro. Supp. I:** 110

Wessex Tales: Strange, Lively and Commonplace (Hardy), **VI:** 20

West, Anthony, **VI:** 241, 242

West, Arthur Graeme, **VI:** 423

West, Moris, **Supp. IV:** 343

West, Rebecca, **VI:** 226, 227, 252, 371; **Supp. II:** 146–147; **Supp. III:** 431–445

"West Indies, The" (Macaulay), **IV:** 278

West Indies and the Spanish Main, The (Trollope), **V:** 101

West of Suez (Osborne), **Supp. I:** 339

West Window, The (Hartley), see *Shrimp and the Anemone, The*

"Westland Row" (Kinsella), **Supp. V:** 263

"Westland Well" (Swinburne), **V:** 333

Westmacott, Mary (pseud., Christie), **Supp. II:** 123, 133

"Westminster Abbey" (Arnold), **V:** 208–209

Westminster Alice, The (Saki), **Supp. VI:** 239

Westminster Review, The (periodical), **V:** xviii, 189

Westward Ho! (Dekker and Webster), **II:** 68, 85

Wet Fish (Arden), **Supp. II:** 28

"Wet Night, A" (Beckett), **Supp. I:** 45; **Retro. Supp. I:** 19

"Wet Snow" (MacCaig), **Supp. VI:** 186

Wetherby (Hare), **Supp. IV:** 282, 289–290

"What a Misfortune" (Beckett), **Supp. I:** 45

What Am I Doing Here (Chatwin), **Supp. IV:** 157, 163, 173

What Became of Jane Austen? (Amis), **Supp. II:** 1, 2, 11

What D'Ye Call It, The (Gay), **III:** 58, 60, 67

"What Do Hippos Eat?" (Wilson), **Supp. I:** 156–157

"What Does It Matter?" (Forster), **VI:** 411

What Every Woman Knows (Barrie), **Supp. III:** 6, 9, **10–11**

"What Gets Lost *Lo Que Se Pierde*" (Reid), **Supp. VII:** 331

"What Happened to Blake?" (Hare), **Supp. IV:** 281, 283

What Happened to Burger's Daughter: or How South African Censorship Works (Gordimer), **Supp. II:** 237

"What I Believe" (Spender), **Supp. II:** 494

"What I Have Been Doing Lately" (Kincaid), **Supp. VII:** 221

What I Really Wrote About the War (Shaw), **VI:** 129

What Is He? (Disraeli), **IV:** 308

"What Is the Language Using Us For?" (Graham), **Supp. VII:** 115

"What Is There to Discuss?" (Ramsey), **VII:** 240

What Maisie Knew (James), **VI: 50–52,** 67

"What meaneth this?" (Wyatt), **I:** 104

What Mrs. McGillicuddy Saw (Christie), *see 4.50 from Paddington*

"What rage is this" (Wyatt), **I:** 104

What the Black Mirror Saw (Redgrove), **Supp. VI:** 236

What the Butler Saw (Orton), **Supp. V:** 367, 371, 377–378

What the Public Wants (Bennett), **VI:** 263–264

"What the Shepherd Saw" (Hardy), **VI:** 22

"What the Thrush Said" (Keats), **IV:** 225

"What the Thunder Said" (Eliot), **Retro. Supp. II:** 128–129

"What Then?" (Yeats), **Retro. Supp. I:** 337

What Where (Beckett), **Supp. IV:** 284

"What will they do?" (Thomas), **Supp. III:** 400, 401

What You Will (Marston), **II:** 29–30, 40

Whately, Richard, **IV:** 102, 122

What's Become of Waring? (Powell), **VII:** 346, 353

Wheatcroft, Geoffrey, **Supp. IV:** 173

"Wheel of Time, The" (James), **VI:** 69

Wheels of Chance, The: A Holiday Adventure (Wells), **VI:** 231–232, 244

"When a Beau Goes In" (Ewart), **VII:** 423; **Supp. VII:** 37

"When all my five and country senses see" (Thomas), **Supp. I:** 176

"When Earth's Last Picture Is Painted" (Kipling), **VI:** 169

"When I Am Dead, My Dearest" (Rossetti), **V:** 249

"When I Have Fears" (Keats), **IV:** 221

When Is a Door Not a Door? (Arden), **Supp. II:** 29

"When Israel came out of Egypt" (Clough), **V:** 160

"When My Girl Comes Home" (Pritchett), **Supp. III:** 312, **321–324**

When My Girl Comes Home (Pritchett), **Supp. III:** 313, 321

"When the Camel Is Dust it Goes Through the Needle's Eye" (Stevenson), **Supp. VI:** 264

When the Moon Has Set (Synge), **VI:** 310n; **Retro. Supp. I:** 294

When the Sleeper Wakes (Wells), **VI:** 234

When the Wicked Man (Ford), **VI:** 319, 332

When We Dead Awaken (Ibsen), **VI:** 269; **Retro. Supp. I:** 170, 175

"When we that were dear . . . A (Henley), **V:** 392

When We Were Very Young (Milne), **Supp. V:** 295, 301–302

When William Came (Saki), **Supp. VI: 248–250**

"When Windsor walles sustained my wearied arm" (Surrey), **I:** 113

"When You Are Old" (Yeats), **Retro. Supp. I:** 329

"When you see millions of the mouthless dead" (Sorley), **VI:** 422

Where Angels Fear to Tread (Forster), **VI:** 400–401; **Retro. Supp. II:** 136–139

"Where once the waters of your face" (Thomas), **Supp. I:** 173–174

Where Shall We Go This Summer (Desai), **Supp. V:** 53, 55, 63–64, 66, 73

"Where Tawe Flows" (Thomas), **Supp. I:** 180

Where There Is Darkness (Phillips), **Supp. V:** 380

"Where They Are Wrong" (Paton), **Supp. II:** 360

Whereabouts: Notes on Being a Foreigner (Reid), **Supp. VII:** 323, 335–336

"Whereto Art Thou Come" (Thompson), **V:** 444

Whether a Dove or Seagull (Warner), **Supp. VII:** 370, 371, 372–373, 376

Whetstone, George, **I:** 282, 313

Whibley, Charles, **II:** 259

"Which New Era Would Be?" (Gordimer), **Supp. II:** 242

Whig Examiner (periodical), **III:** 51, 53

Whig Interpretations of History, The (Butterfield), **IV:** 291

While the Sun Shines (Rattigan), **Supp. VII:** 313

Whims and Oddities (Hood), **IV:** 253, 255, 257, 267

Whimsicalities (Hood), **IV:** 254, 267

Whirlpool, The (Gissing), **V:** 437

"Whisperer, The" (Nicholson), **Supp. VI:** 218

Whispering Roots, The (Day Lewis), **Supp. III:** 116, 118, 129–130

"Whispers" (Tennyson), **IV:** 332

"Whispers of Immortality" (Eliot), **VII:** 145

Whistlecraft (Frere), **IV:** 182–183

Whistler, James McNeill, **V:** 238, 245, 320, 407

White, Gilbert, **Supp. VI: 279–295**

White, James, **IV:** 79

White, Norman, **V:** 379*n*

White, Patrick, **Supp. I: 129–152; Supp. IV:** 343

White, Tony, **Supp. IV:** 256, 272, 273–274

White Bird, The (Berger), **Supp. IV:** 89

White Bird, The (MacCaig), **Supp. VI:** 192

White Cockade, The (Gregory), **VI:** 315

White Company, The (Doyle), **Supp. II:** 159, 163

White Devil, The (Webster), **I:** 246; **II:** 68, 70, 72, 73–75, 76, 79, 80–85, 97; **Supp. IV:** 234–235

White Doe of Rylstone, The (Wordsworth), **IV:** xvii, 24

White Goddess, The (Graves), **VII:** xviii, 257, 259, 261–262

White Horseman, The (MacCaig), **Supp. VI:** 184

White Hotel, The (Thomas), **Supp. IV:** 479, 481–483, 486, 490, 493

"White Island, The; or, Place of the Blest" (Herrick), **II:** 113

White Liars (Shaffer), **Supp. I:** 322–323

White Lies (Shaffer), **Supp. I:** 322

White Monkey, The (Galsworthy), **VI:** 274

"White Negro, The" (Mailer), **Supp. IV:** 17–18

White Peacock, The (Lawrence), **VII:** 88, 89, **91–93; Retro. Supp. II:** 222–223, 226

"White Queen, The" (Harrison), **Supp. V:** 151

"White Ship, The" (Rossetti), **V:** 238, 244

"White Stocking, The" (Lawrence), **VII:** 114

White Threshold, The (Graham), **Supp. VII:** 110–111

"White Windsor Soap" (McGuckian), **Supp. V:** 288

White Writing: On the Culture of Letters in South Africa (Coetzee), **Supp. VI: 84–85**

White–Eagles over Serbia (Durrell), **Supp. I:** 100

Whitehall, Harold, **V:** 365, 382

Whitelock, Derek, **Supp. IV:** 348

"Whitewashed Wall, The" (Hardy), **Retro. Supp. I:** 120

Whitman, Walt, **IV:** 332; **V:** 418; **VI:** 55, 63; **Supp. IV:** 163, 487

Whitsun Weddings, The (Larkin), **Supp. I:** 276, **279–281,** 285

"Whitsun Weddings, The" (Larkin), **Supp. I:** 285

"Whitsunday" (Herbert), **II:** 125

"Whitsunday in Kirchstetten" (Auden), **VII:** 396, 397

"Who Are These Coming to the Sacrifice?" (Hill), **Supp. V:** 191

Who Are You? (Kavan), **Supp. VII:** 214

"Who Goes Home?" (Day Lewis), **Supp. III:** 130

Who Is Sylvia? (Rattigan), **Supp. VII:** 317

Who Was Oswald Fish? (Wilson), **Supp. VI: 300–301**

Whole Armour, The (Harris), **Supp. V:** 132, 134, 135

Whole Duty of Man, The (Allestree), **III:** 82

"Whole Truth, The" (Motion), **Supp. VII:** 256

Whole Works of Homer, The (Chapman), **I:** 235

Whoroscope (Beckett), **Supp. I:** 43; **Retro. Supp. I:** 19

"Who's Who" (Auden), **Retro. Supp. I:** 2

Whose Body? (Sayers), **Supp. III:** 334, 336–338, 340, 350

"Whose Endless Jar" (Richards), **Supp. II:** 426, 429

Whose Is the Kingdom? (Arden and D'Arcy), **Supp. II:** 39, 40–41

"Whoso list to hunt" (Wyatt), **I:** 101, 109

"Why Brownlee Left" (Muldoon), **Supp. IV:** 409, 410, 415, 418, 426

Why Come Ye Not to Court? (Skelton), **I:** 92–93

Why Do I Write? (Bowen), **Supp. II:** 80, 81, 91

Why Frau Frohmann Raised Her Prices and Other stories (Trollope), **V:** 102

"Why Has Narrative Poetry Failed" (Murphy), **Supp. V:** 320–321

"Why I Have Embraced Islam" (Rushdie), **Supp. IV:** 437

"Why I Ought Not to Have Become a Dramatic Critic" (Beerbohm), **Supp. II:** 54

"Why Not Take Pater Seriously?" (Fletcher), **V:** 359

"Why She Would Not" (Shaw), **VI:** 130

"Why Should Not Old Men Be Mad?" (Yeats), **Retro. Supp. I:** 337

Why So, Socrates? (Richards), **Supp. II:** 425

"Why the Novel Matters" (Lawrence), **VII:** 122

"Why We Are in Favour of This War" (Hulme), **Supp. VI:** 140

"Wicked Tunge Wille Sey Amys, A" (Lydgate), **I:** 57

Wide Sargasso Sea (Rhys), **Supp. II:** 387, 389, **398–401,** 441; **Retro. Supp. I:** 60

Widow, The (Middleton), **II:** 3, 21

Widow Ranter, The (Behn), **Supp. III:** 34

Widow Ranter, The (Belin), **II:** 305

"Widower in the Country, The" (Murray), **Supp. VII:** 271

Widower's Son, The (Sillitoe), **Supp. V:** 410, 414, 415, 425

Widowers' Houses (Shaw), **VI:** 104, 107, 108, 129; **Retro. Supp. II:** 310–312

"Widowhood System, The" (Friel), **Supp. V:** 113

Widowing of Mrs. Holroyd, The (Lawrence), **VII:** 120, 121

Widow's Tears, The (Chapman), **I:** 243–244, 245–246

Widsith, **Retro. Supp. II:** 304

Wiene, Robert, **III:** 342

Wife for a Month (Fletcher), **II:** 65

Wife of Bath, The (Gay), **III:** 60, 67

Wife of Bath's Prologue, The (Chaucer), **I:** 24, 34, 39, 40

Wife of Bath's Tale, The (Chaucer), **I:** 27, 35–36

"Wife Speaks, The" (Day Lewis), **Supp. III:** 125

Wife's Lament, The, **Retro. Supp. II:** 305

Wilberforce, William, **IV:** 133, 268; **V:** 277

Wild Ass's Skin, The (Balzac), **III:** 339, 345

"Wild Boar and the Ram, The" (Gay), **III:** 59

Wild Body, The (Lewis), **VII:** 72, 77, 78, 79

Wild Duck, The (Ibsen), **VI:** ix

"Wild Flowers" (Howard), **V:** 48

Wild Gallant, The (Dryden), **II:** 305

Wild Garden, The; or, Speaking of Writing (Wilson), **Supp. I:** 153, 154–155, 156, 158, 160

Wild Goose Chase, The (Fletcher), **II:** 45, 61–62, 65, 352, 357

Wild Honey (Frayn), **Supp. VII:** 61

Wild Knight, The (Chesterton), **VI:** 336

Wild Swans at Coole, The (Yeats), **VI:** 207, 213, 214, 217; **Retro. Supp. I:** 331

"Wild with All Regrets" (Owen), **VI:** 446, 452, 453

Wilde, Oscar, **III:** 334, 345; **V:** xiii, xxi, xxv, xxvi, 53, 339, **399–422; VI:** ix, 365; **VII:** 83; **Supp. II:** 43, 45–46, 48, 50, 51, 53, 54, 141, 143, 148, 155; **Supp. IV:** 288; **Retro. Supp. II:** 314–315, **359–374**

Wilder Hope, The: Essays on Future Punishment . . . (De Quincey), **IV:** 155

"Wilderness, The" (Keyes), **VII:** 439

Wilderness of Zin (Woolley and Lawrence), **Supp. II:** 284

Wildest Dreams (Ayckbourn), **Supp. V:** 3, 10, 12, 14

"Wilfred Owen and the Georgians" (Hibberd), **VI:** 460

Wilfred Owen: War Poems and Others (Hibberd), **VI:** 446, 459

"Wilfred Owen's Letters" (Hibberd), **VI:** 460

Wilhelm Meister (Goethe), **IV:** 241; **V:** 214

Wilhelm Meister's Apprenticeship (tr. Carlyle), **IV:** 241, 250

Wilkes, John, **IV:** 61, 185

Wilkes, Thomas, **II:** 351, 363

Wilkie, David, **IV:** 37

Wilkins, George, **I:** 321

Wilkinson, Martin, **Supp. IV:** 168

"Will, The" (Donne), **Retro. Supp. II:** 91

Will Drew and Phil Crewe and Frank Fane . . . (Swinburne), **V:** 333

"Will o' the Mill" (Stevenson), **V:** 395

Will Warburton (Gissing), **V:** 435, 437

Willey, Basil, **II:** 145, 157; **Supp. II:** 103, 107, 108

"William and Mary" (Dahl), **Supp. IV:** 218, 219

William B. Yeats: The Poet in Contemporary Ireland (Hone), **VI:** 223

William Blake (Chesterton), **VI:** 344

William Blake (Swinburne), **V:** 313, 314, 317, 329–330, 332

William Cobbett (Chesterton), **VI:** 341, 345

"William Cobbett: In Absentia" (Hill), **Supp. V:** 183

"William Congreve" (Swinburne), **V:** 332

William Morris (Bloomfield), **V:** 306

William Morris, Artist, Writer, Socialist (Morris), **V:** 301, 305

"William Morris as I Knew Him" (Shaw), **VI:** 129

William Pitt . . . an Excellent New Ballad . . . (Boswell), **III:** 248

William Posters trilogy (Sillitoe), **Supp. V:** 410, 413, 421–424

William Wetmore Story and His Friends (James), **VI:** 67

"William Wordsworth" (De Quincey), **IV:** 146

William Wordsworth: A Biography (Moorman), **IV:** 4, 25

Williams, Basil, **VI:** 234

Williams, H., **III:** 15*n*, 35

Williams, Hugo, **Supp. IV:** 168

Williams, Iolo, **VII:** 37

Williams, Raymond, **Supp. IV:** 95, 380

Williams, William Carlos, **Supp. IV:** 257, 263

Williams Manuscript and the Temple, The (Charles), **Retro. Supp. II:** 174

Willis, W., **III:** 199*n*

"Willowwood"sonnets (Rossetti), **V:** 243, 259

Willy Wonka and the Chocolate Factory (film), **Supp. IV:** 203

Wilmot, John, *see* Rochester, earl of

Wilson, A. N., *see* Wilson, Angus

Wilson, Angus, **V:** 43, 72; **VI:** 165; **Supp. I: 153–168; Supp. II:** 92; **Supp. IV:** 229, 231, 234, 346; **Supp. VI: 297–310**

Wilson, Colin, **III:** 341

Wilson, Dover, *see* Wilson, J. Dover

Wilson, Edmund, **IV:** 27; **V:** 66, 69, 72; **VI:** 56, 62, 363; **VII:** 53; **Supp. II:** 57, 118, 124, 200, 204, 223; **Supp. III:** 95, 101, 105

Wilson, F. A. C., **VI:** 208, 220

Wilson, F. P., **I:** 286

Wilson, J. Dover, **I:** 326; **III:** 116*n*; **V:** 287, 290

Wilson, J. H., **II:** 257, 271

Wilson, John, **IV:** 11

Wilson, Rae, **IV:** 262

Wimsatt, M. K., Jr., **III:** 249

Winckelman, Johann, **V:** 341, 343, 344

"Winckelmann" (Pater), **V:** 341, 343, 344

Wind, Edgar, **I:** 237; **V:** 317*n*

"Wind" (Hughes), **Supp. I:** 343–344

Wind Among the Reeds, The (Yeats), **VI:** 211, 222

Wind from Nowhere, The (Ballard), **Supp. V:** 22

"Windhover, The" (Hopkins), **V:** 366, 367; **Retro. Supp. II:** 190, 191, 195–196

Winding Stair, The (Yeats), **Supp. II:** 84–85; **Retro. Supp. I:** 336–337

Winding Stair, The: Francis Bacon, His Rise and Fall (du Maurier), **Supp. III:** 139

Windom's Way (Ambler), **Supp. IV:** 3

"Window, The" (Moore), **VI:** 93

Window in Thrums, A (Barrie), **V:** 392; **Supp. III:** 3

Windows (Galsworthy), **VI:** 269

"Windows, The" (Herbert), **Retro. Supp. II:** 176

"Wind's on the World, The" (Morris), **V:** 305

"Windscale" (Nicholson), **Supp. VI:** 218

Windsor Forest (Pope), **III:** 70, 77; **Retro. Supp. I:** 231

Wine, A Poem (Gay), **III:** 67

Wine, Water and Song (Chesterton), **VI:** 340

"Wingless" (Kincaid), **Supp. VII:** 220, 221, 226

Wings of the Dove, The (James), **VI:** 32, 55, **59–60,** 320; **Supp. IV:** 243

Winkworth, Catherine, **V:** 149

Winnie-the-Pooh (Milne), **Supp. V:** 295, 303–307

"Winning of Etain, The" (Boland), **Supp. V:** 36

"Winnowers, The" (Bridges), **VI:** 78

Winslow Boy, The (Rattigan), **Supp. VII:** 307, 313–315

"Winter" (Blake), **Retro. Supp. I:** 34

"Winter" (Brontë), **V:** 107

Winter (Thomson), **Supp. III:** 411, 412–413, 417, 418

Winter Apology (Bainbridge), **Supp. VI: 22–23**

Winter Fuel (Millais), **V:** 379

Winter Garden (Bainbridge), **Supp. VI: 22–23,** 24

"Winter in Camp" (Fuller), **Supp. VII:** 70

"Winter in England" (Fuller), **Supp. VII:** 70

"Winter in July" (Lessing), **Supp. I:** 240

Winter in the Air (Warner), **Supp. VII:** 380

"Winter Landscape near Ely, A" (Davie), **Supp. VI:** 110

"Winter, My Secret" (Rossetti), **V:** 256

"Winter Night" (Fuller), **Supp. VII:** 72

Winter Pilgrimage, A (Haggard), **Supp. III:** 214

Winter Pollen: Occasional Prose (Hughes), **Retro. Supp. II:** 202

Winter Tales (Brown), **Supp. VI:** 68–70

"Winter with the Gulf Stream" (Hopkins), **V:** 361, 381

Winter Words, in Various Moods and Metres (Hardy), **VI:** 20

Wintering Out (Heaney), **Supp. II:** 268, 272–273; **Retro. Supp. I:** 125, 128

Winters, Yvor, **VI:** 219; **Supp. IV:** 256–257, 261; **Retro. Supp. I:** 335

"Winters and the Palmleys, The" (Hardy), **VI:** 22

"Winter's Tale, A" (Thomas), **Supp. I:** 177, 178

Winter's Tale, The (Chaucer), **I:** 25

Winter's Tale, The (Shakespeare), **I:** 166*n*, 302, 322–323, 327

"Winter's Talents" (Davie), **Supp. VI:** 112

Winterslow: Essays and Characters Written There (Hazlitt), **IV:** 140

Winterson, Jeanette, **Supp. IV: 541–559**

"Wires" (Larkin), **Supp. I:** 278, 285

"Wisdom Literature", **Retro. Supp. II:** 304

Wisdom of Father Brown, The (Chesterton), **VI:** 338

Wisdom of Solomon Paraphrased, The (Middleton), **II:** 2

Wisdom of the Ancients (Bacon), *see De sapientia veterum*

Wise, T. J., **V:** 150, 151

Wise Children (Carter), **Supp. III:** 90–91

Wise Virgins (Wilson), **Supp. VI:** 297, **301,** 303

Wise Wound, The (Redgrove), **Supp. VI:** 230, 233

"Wish, The" (Cowley), **II:** 195, 198

"Wish, The" (Dahl), **Supp. IV:** 206, 221

"Wish House, The" (Kipling), **VI:** 169, 193, 196, **197–199**

"Wish in Spring" (Warner), **Supp. VII:** 373

"Wishes to His (Supposed), Mistresse" (Crashaw), **II:** 180

Wit at Several Weapons, **II:** 21, 66

Wit Without Money (Fletcher), **II:** 66

Witch, The (Middleton), **II:** 3, 21; **IV:** 79

"Witch of Atlas, The" (Shelley), **IV:** 196, 204

Witch of Edmonton, The (Dekker, Ford, Rowley), **II:** 89, 100

Witches, The (Dahl), **Supp. IV:** 204, 213, 215, 225–226

Witches, The (film), **Supp. IV:** 203

Witch's Head, The (Haggard), **Supp. III:** 213

With My Little Eye (Fuller), **Supp. VII:** 70–71

"With my Sons at Boarhills" (Stevenson), **Supp. VI:** 260

Wither, George, **IV:** 81

"Withered Arm, The" (Hardy), **VI:** 22; **Retro. Supp. I:** 116

Within the Gates (O'Casey), **VII:** 7

Within the Tides: Tales (Conrad), **VI:** 148

"Without Benefit of Clergy" (Kipling), **VI:** 180–183

"Without Eyes" (Redgrove), **Supp. VI:** 235

"Without the Option" (Wodehouse), **Supp. III:** 456

Witlings, The (Burney), **Supp. III:** 64, 71, 72, 75

"Witness, The" (Lessing), **Supp. I: 244**

Witness for the Prosecution (Christie), **Supp. II:** 125, 134

Wit's Treasury (Meres), **I:** 296

Wittig, Monique, **Supp. IV:** 558

Wives and Daughters (Gaskell), **V:** xxiii, 1–4, 8, 11–13, 14, 15

Wizard of Oz, The (Baum), **Supp. IV:** 450

Wizard of Oz, The (film), **Supp. IV:** 434, 443, 448, 450, 455

Wizard of Oz, The (Rushdie), **Supp. IV:** 434

Wodehouse, P. G., **Supp. III: 447–464**

Wodwo (Hughes), **Supp. I:** 343, 346, **348–350,** 363; **Retro. Supp. II:** 205–206

Woefully Arrayed (Skelton), **I:** 84

Wolf and the Lamb, The (Henryson), **Supp. VII:** 136, 141

Wolf and the Wether, The (Henryson), **Supp. VII:** 136, 140–141

Wolf, Friedrich, **IV:** 316–317

Wolf, Lucien, **IV:** 293

Wolf Leader, The (Dumas *père*), **III:** 339

Wolf that gat the Nekhering throw the wrinkis of the Foxe that begylit the Cadgear, The (Henryson), see *Fox, the Wolf, and the Cadger, The*

Wolfe, Tom, **Supp. IV:** 454

Wolff, S. L., **I:** 164

"Wolfhound, The" (Murphy), **Supp. V:** 323

Wolfwatching (Hughes), **Retro. Supp. II:** 214

Wollstonecraft, Mary, **Supp. III: 465–482; Retro. Supp. I:** 39

Wolves and the Lamb, The (Thackeray), **V:** 35

Woman (periodical), **VI:** 249

Woman, The (Bond), **Supp. I:** 423, 434, 435

"Woman, The Place, The Poet, The" (Boland), **Supp. V:** 35

Woman and Labour (Schreiner), **Supp. II:** 444, **454–456**

"Woman at the Shore, The" (Mansfield), **VII:** 173

Woman–Captain, The (Shadwell), **II:** 359

Woman Hater, The (Beaumont and Fletcher), **II:** 46, 65

Woman–Hater, The (Burney), **Supp. III:** 64

"Woman in His Life, The" (Kipling), **VI:** 193

Woman in Mind (Ayckbourn), **Supp. V:** 3, 6–7, 10, 11, 13, 15

Woman in the Moon, The (Lyly), **I:** 204–205

Woman in White, The (Collins), **III:** 340, 345; **Supp. VI:** 91–94, **95–97,** 100, 102–103

Woman Killed With Kindness, A (Heywood), **II:** 19

Woman of No Importance, A (Wilde), **V:** xxvi, 414, 419; **Retro. Supp. II:** 369

"Woman of No Standing, A" (Behan), **Supp. II:** 66

"Woman of the House, The" (Murphy), **Supp. V:** 313, 318–319

Woman of the Inner Sea (Keneally), **Supp. IV:** 347, 348, 358–360

"Woman out of a Dream, A" (Warner), **Supp. VII:** 373

Woman Pleased (Fletcher), **II:** 45, 65

"Woman! When I behold thee flippant, vain" (Keats), **Retro. Supp. I:** 188–189

"Woman Who Rode Away, The" (Lawrence), **VII:** 87–88, 91, 115

Woman Who Walked into Doors, The (Doyle), **Supp. V:** 78, 88, 91–92

Womanhood, Wanton, Ye Want (Skelton), **I:** 83

"Womans constancy" (Donne), **Retro. Supp. II:** 89

"Woman's Last Word, A" (Browning), **IV:** 367; **Retro. Supp. II:** 24

Woman's Prize, The; or, The Tamer Tamed (Fletcher), **II:** 43, 45, 65

"Woman's Song" (Warner), **Supp. VII:** 373

Womb of Space: The Cross–Cultural Imagination (Harris), **Supp. V:** 140, 146

"Women, The" (Boland), **Supp. V:** 50–51

"Women, The" (Stevenson), **Supp. VI:** 254

Women Beware Women (Middleton), **II:** 1, 3, 8, **10–14,** 19

Women in Love (Lawrence), **IV:** 119; **VI:** 276; **VII:** 87–88, 89, 91, 98, **101–104;** **Retro. Supp. II:** 228–229

"Wonder" (Traherne), **II:** 191

Wonder of Women, The; or, The Tragedie of Sophonisba (Marston), **II:** 25, 30–31, 40, 305

"Wonderful Story of Henry Sugar, The" (Dahl), **Supp. IV:** 223

Wonderful Tennessee (Friel), **Supp. V:** 126–127

Wonderful Visit, The (Wells), **VI:** 226, 228, 230, 243

Wondrous Tale of Alroy, The (Disraeli), see *Alroy*

Wood, Anthony à, **II:** 185

Wood Beyond the World, The (Morris), **V:** 306

"Wood Fire, The" (Hardy), **Retro. Supp. I:** 121

"Wooden Chair with Arms" (MacCaig), **Supp. VI:** 192

Woodhouse, Richard, **IV:** 230, 232, 233

Woodman, Thomas, **Supp. IV:** 364

Woods, Helen Emily, see Kavan, Anna

"Woods of Westermain, The" (Meredith), **V:** 221

"Woodsman" (MacCaig), **Supp. VI:** 192

"Woodspurge, The" (Rossetti), **V:** 241, 242, 314–315

Woodstock (Scott), **IV:** xviii, 27, 39

Woodward, Benjamin, **V:** 178

Woolf, Leonard, **VI:** 415; **VII:** 17

Woolf, Virginia, **I:** 169; **IV:** 107, 320, 322; **V:** xxv, 226, 256, 260, 281, 290; **VI:** 243, 252, 275, 411; **VII:** xii, xiv–xv, **17–39;** **Supp. II:** 341–342, 487, 501–502; **Supp. III:** 19, 41–42, 45, 49, 60, 103, 107, 108; **Supp. IV:** 231, 233, 246, 399, 407, 461, 542, 558; **Supp. V:** 36, 63; **Retro. Supp. I:** 59, **305–323**

Woolley, Hannah, **Supp. III:** 21

Woolley, Leonard, **Supp. II:** 284

"Word, The" (Thomas), **Supp. III:** 406

Word Child, A (Murdoch), **Supp. I:** 228

Word for the Navy, A (Swinburne), **V:** 332

Word over All (Day Lewis), **Supp. III:** 118, 128

Word–Links (Carroll), **V:** 274

"Words" (Gunn), **Supp. IV:** 267

Words and Music (Beckett), **Supp. I:** 53, 60

Words and Music (Coward), **Supp. II:** 152

Words of Advice (Weldon), **Supp. IV:** 536–537

Words upon the Window Pane, The (Yeats), **VI:** 219, 222

Wordsworth, Dorothy, **II:** 273; **IV:** 1–4, 10, 19, 49, 128, 143, 146

Wordsworth, William, **II:** 188–189; **III:** 174; **IV:** viii–xi, **1–26,** 33, 70, 73, 95–96, 111, 137, 178, 214, 215, 281, 311, 351, 352; **V:** 287, 311, 331, 351–352; **VI:** 1; and Coleridge, **IV:** 43–45, 50, 51, 54; **Retro. Supp. II:** 62, 63–64; and DeQuincey, **IV:** 141–143, 146, 154; and Hazlitt, **IV:** 126–130, 133–134, 137, 138; and Keats, **IV:** 214, 215, 225, 233; and Shelley, **IV:** 198, 203, 207; and Tennyson, **IV:** 326, 329, 336; literary style, **III:** 304, 338; **IV:** 95–96, 154, 336; verse forms, **II:** 200; **V:** 224; **Supp. II:** 269; **Supp. IV:** 230, 252, 558

"Wordsworth" (Pater), **V:** 351–352

"Wordsworth and Byron" (Swinburne), **V:** 332

"Wordsworth's Ethics" (Stephen), **V:** 287

"Work" (Lamb), **IV:** 83

Work in Progress (Lowry), **Supp. III:** 280

Work in Progress (Redgrove), **Supp. VI:** 231

"Work of Art, A" (Warner), **Supp. VII:** 380

"Work of My Own, A" (Winterson), **Supp. IV:** 558

"Work of Water, The" (Redgrove), **Supp. VI:** 235

Work Suspended (Waugh), **VII:** 298–299

Work, Wealth and Happiness of Mankind, The (Wells), **VI:** 225

"Work without Hope" (Coleridge), **Retro. Supp. II:** 65

Workers in the Dawn (Gissing), **V:** 424, 435, 437

Workes of Edmund Waller in This Parliament, The (Waller), **II:** 238

"Workhouse Clock, The," (Hood), **IV:** 261, 264

Workhouse Donkey, The (Arden), **Supp. II:** 28, 30

Workhouse Ward, The (Gregory), **VI:** 315, 316

Working Novelist, The (Pritchett), **VI:** 290

Working of Water, The (Redgrove), **Supp. VI:** 235–236

Working with Structuralism: Essays and Reviews on Nineteenth– and Twentieth–Century Literature (Lodge), **Supp. IV:** 365, 377

Works (Congreve), **II:** 348

Works (Cowley), **II:** 195

Works (Swift), **III:** 24

Works of Art and Artists in England (Waagen), **III:** 328

Works of Charles Lamb, The, **IV:** 73, 81, 85

Works of Henry Fielding, The (ed. Stephen), **V:** 290

Works of Henry Vaughan, The (Martin), **II:** 184

Works of Max Beerbohm, The (Beerbohm), **Supp. II:** 45, 46, 47

Works of Morris and Yeats in Relation to Early Saga Literature, The (Hoare), **V:** 299, 306

Works of Samuel Johnson, The, **III:** 108n, 121

Works of Sir John Vanbrugh, The (ed. Dobrée and Webb), **II:** 323n

Works of Sir Thomas Malory, The (ed. Vinavier), **I:** 70, 80

Works of the English Poets (Johnson), **Retro. Supp. I:** 143

Works of Thomas Lodge, The (Tyler), **VI:** 102

Works of Virgil, The (tr. Dryden), **II:** 304

Works of William Blake, The (ed. Yeats), **VI:** 222

World (periodical), **VI:** 103, 104

"World, The" (Vaughan), **II:** 185, 186, 188

World Crisis, The (Churchill), **VI:** 353–354

World I Breathe, The (Thomas), **Supp. I:** 176, 180–181

World in the Evening, The (Isherwood), **VII:** 309, 314–315

World of Charles Dickens, The (Wilson), **Supp. I:** 166

World of Difference, A (MacCaig), **Supp. VI:** 193–194

"World of Light, A" (Jennings), **Supp. V:** 210

World of Light, A (Sarton), **Supp. II:** 82

World of Light, The (Huxley), **VII:** 201

World of Love, A (Bowen), **Supp. II:** 77, 79, 81, 84, 94

World of Paul Slickey, The (Osborne), **Supp. I:** 333–334

World of Strangers, A (Gordimer), **Supp. II:** 227, 231, 232, 236, 243

World Set Free, The: A Story of Mankind (Wells), **VI:** 227, 244

World Within World (Spender), **Supp. II:** 482, 483, 484, 485, 486, 487, 488, 490

Worldliness (Moore), **VI:** 95, 98

Worlds, The (Bond), **Supp. I:** 423, 434

World's Desire, The (Haggard and Lang), **Supp. III:** 213, 222

"World's End, The" (Empson), **Supp. II:** 182

World's Room, The (MacCaig), **Supp. VI:** 192

"Worlds That Flourish" (Okri), **Supp. V:** 356

Worm and the Ring, The (Burgess), **Supp. I:** 186, 187, 188, 189

Worm of Spindlestonheugh, The (Swinburne), **V:** 333

Wormwood (Kinsella), **Supp. V:** 262–263

"Wormwood" (Kinsella), **Supp. V:** 262

Worst Fears (Weldon), **Supp. IV:** 538

"Worst of It, The" (Browning), **IV:** 369

"Worstward Ho" (Beckett), **Supp. I:** 62; **Retro. Supp. I:** 29–30

Worthies of England (Fuller), **II:** 45

Worthies of Westminster (Fuller), **Retro. Supp. I:** 152

Wotton, Sir Henry, **II:** 132, 133, 134, 138, 140, 141, 142, 166

Wotton, William, **III:** 23

Wotton Reinfred (Carlyle), **IV:** 250

Woty, W., **III:** 170n

"Wound, The" (Gunn), **Supp. IV:** 259

"Wound, The" (Hughes), **Supp. I:** 348

"Wreath for Tom Moore's Statue" (Kavanagh), **Supp. VII:** 193

"Wreaths" (Hill), **Supp. V:** 186

"Wreck" (MacCaig), **Supp. VI:** 186

Wreck of the Archangel, The (Brown), **Supp. VI:** 71

"Wreck of the Deutschland, The" (Hopkins), **V:** 361, 362, **363–366,** 367, 369, 370, 375, 379, 380, 381; **Retro. Supp. II:** 189, 191–194

"Wreck of the Deutschland, The": A New Reading (Schneider), **V:** 366, 382

Wreck of the Mary Deare, The (film, Ambler), **Supp. IV:** 3

Wrecked Eggs (Hare), **Supp. IV:** 282, 293

Wrecker, The (Stevenson), **V:** 383, 387, 396

Wrens, The (Gregory), **VI:** 315–316

"Wrestling" (Rossetti), **V:** 260

Wretched of the Earth, The (Fanon), *see Les Damnés de la terre*

Wright, William Aldis, **IV:** 343, 353

Write On: Occasional Essays, '65–'85 (Lodge), **Supp. IV:** 366

Writer and the Absolute, The (Lewis), **VII:** xv, 71, 72, 73–74, 76

Writers and Their Work series, **VII:** xi, xxii

Writer's Britain: Landscape in Literature, A (ed. Drabble), **Supp. IV:** 230, 252

Writer's Diary, A (Woolf), **V:** 226

"Writer's Friends, A" (Stead), **Supp. IV:** 461, 466

Writer's Ireland: Landscape in Literature, A (Trevor), **Supp. IV:** 514

Writer's Notebook, A (Maugham), **VI:** 365, 366

"Writers Take Sides, The" (Stead), **Supp. IV:** 463, 466

"Writing" (Auden), **Retro. Supp. I:** 13

"Writing" (Motion), **Supp. VII:** 256

"Writing as a Woman" (Stevenson), **Supp. VI:** 257

Writing Game: A Comedy, The (Lodge), **Supp. IV:** 366, 381

Writing in a State of Seige (Brink), **Supp. VI:** 47, 49

Writing Left–Handed (Hare), **Supp. IV:** 282, 283

"Written After the Death of Charles Lamb" (Wordsworth), **IV:** 73

"Written in My Lady Speke's Singing Book" (Waller), **II:** 234

Written on the Body (Winterson), **Supp. IV:** 542, 547, 549–551, 552, 553, 555, 557

Wrong Box, The (Stevenson and Osbourne), **V:** 387, 396

Wulf and Eadwacer, **Retro. Supp. II:** 305

Wulfstan, Archbishop, **Retro. Supp. II:** 298

Wurzel–Flummery (Milne), **Supp. V:** 298–299

Wuthering Heights (Brontë), **III:** 333, 338, 344, 345; **V:** xx, 113, 114, 127, 128, 131, 133–135, 140, **141–145,** 254; **Supp. III:** 144, 145; **Supp. IV:** 231, 452, 462, 513; **Retro. Supp. I:** 50, 52, 53, 54, 57–58

Wyatt, Sir Thomas, **I:** **97–112,** 113, 115

"Wyatt resteth here, that quick could never rest" (Surrey), **I:** 115

Wycherley, William, **II:** **307–322,** 343, 352, 360

Wycliffe, John, **I:** 375

Wymer, T. L., **V:** 324, 335

"Wyncote, Pennsylvania: A Gloss" (Kinsella), **Supp. V:** 274

Wyndham, Francis, **Supp. IV:** 159, 161, 304

Wyndham, John, **Supp. V:** 22

Wyndham Lewis: A Memoir (Eliot), **VII:** 77

Wyndham Lewis: His Theory of Art and Communication (McLuhan), **VII:** 71n

Xmas v. Mastermind (Ayckbourn), **Supp. V:** 2

Xorandor (Brooke-Rose), **Supp. IV:** 100, 111

XX Poems (Larkin), **Supp. I:** 277

"Yaddo Letter, The" (Mahon), **Supp. VI:** 176

Yan Tan Tethera (Harrison), **Supp. V:** 150, 164

Yangtse Incident (film, Ambler), **Supp. IV:** 3

Yard of Sun, A (Fry), **Supp. III:** 191, 194, 195, 204–205

"Yardley Oak" (Cowper), **III:** 218

"Yarrow" (Muldoon), **Supp. IV:** 429–432

Yarrow Revisited, and Other Poems (Wordsworth), **IV:** 25

Yates, Edmund, **V:** 20

Yates, Frances M., **I:** 237

"Ye happy youths, whose hearts are free" (Etherege), **II:** 267

Yealland, Lewis, **Supp. IV:** 58–59

Year of the Whale, The (Brown), **Supp. VI:** 71

Year In, Year Out (Milne), **Supp. V:** 309, 310–311

"Year of the Sloes, For Ishi, The" (Muldoon), **Supp. IV:** 414

Year to Remember: A Reminiscence of 1931, A (Waugh), **Supp. VI:** 273

Years, The (Woolf), **VII:** 18, 22, 24, 27, 28, 36, 38; **Retro. Supp. I:** 308

Years Between, The (Kipling), **VI:** 204

"Years Later" (Murphy), **Supp. V:** 313, 320

Years of the Young Rebels, The (Spender), **Supp. II:** 493

Yeast (Kingsley), **V:** 4

"Yeats, Berkeley, and Romanticism" (Davie), **Supp. VI:** 107

Yeats, William Butler, **II:** 78; **III:** 21, 36, 184; **IV:** 196, 216, 323, 329; **V:** xxiii, xxv, xxvi, 301, 304, 306, 311, 318, 329–330, 355, 356, 404; **VI:** ix, xiii–xiv, 55–56, 86, 88, **207–224,** 307, 308, 309, 314; **VII:** 1, 3, 42, 404; **Supp. II:** 84–85, 275, 332, 487; **Supp. III:** 102, 121, 124; **Supp. IV:** 257, 409, 412, 413, 414, 419, 423–424, 480; **Supp. V:** 36, 39; **Retro. Supp. I:** 170–171, 290, **325–339**

"Yeats in Civil War" (Boland), **Supp. V:** 36

Yellow Book (periodical), **VI:** 248, 365

Yellow Book, The (Mahon), **Supp. VI:** 176, **177**

"Yellow Girl, The" (Sitwell), **VII:** 138

"Yellow Streak, The" (Maugham), **VI:** 371

Yellow Wallpaper, The (du Maurier), **Supp. III:** 147

Yellowplush Correspondence, The (Thackeray), **V:** 21, 22, 37

Yes and No (Greene), **Supp. I:** 2

Yglesias, Jose, **Supp. IV:** 460

Yogi and the Commissar, The (Koestler), **Supp. I:** 26–27, 35

"Yongy-Bonghy-Bo" (Lear), **V:** 84–86

Yorkshire Tragedy, The, **II:** 3, 21

"You and Me and the Continuum" (Ballard), **Supp. V:** 21

You Make Your Own Life (Pritchett), **Supp. III:** 313, 316, 317

You Never Can Tell (Coward), **Supp. II:** 141

You Never Can Tell (Shaw), **VI:** 109, 111–112; **Retro. Supp. II:** 314–315

You Only Live Twice (Fleming), **Supp. IV:** 212–213

You Only Live Twice (screenplay, Dahl), **Supp. IV:** 212–213

"You praise the firm restraint with which they write" (Campbell), **IV:** 320

"You that in love find luck and abundance" (Wyatt), **I:** 104

"You Went Away" (MacCaig), **Supp. VI:** 185

Young Adolph (Bainbridge), **Supp. VI:** 18, **21–22,** 24

"Young Blades" (Ewart), **Supp. VII:** 38

"Young Dragon, The" (Southey), **IV:** 67

Young Duke, The (Disraeli), **IV:** 293, 295–296, 308

Young, Edward, **III:** 302, 307, 336; **Retro. Supp. I:** 43

Young George du Maurier, The: A Selection of His Letters, 1860–1867 (du Maurier), **Supp. III:** 135–136

Young, G. M., **IV:** 277, 290, 291, 295; **V:** 228, 262

"Young Him" (Nicholson), **Supp. VI:** 216

Young Idea, The (Coward), **Supp. II:** 141

Young, Kenneth, **IV:** xii, xxv; **VI:** xi–xii, xiii, xxxiv; **VII:** xviii, xxxix

"Young King, The" (Wilde), **V:** 406

"Young Love Lies Sleeping" (Rossetti), **V:** 249

"Young Parson Richards" (Shelley), **IV:** 209

Young Pobble's Guide to His Toes, The (Ewart), **Supp. VII:** 45

Young, Richard B., **I:** 170

Young Samuel Johnson (Clifford), **III:** 244n

"Young Soldier with Bloody Spurs, The" (Lawrence), **VII:** 118

Young Visitors, The (Ashford), **V:** 111, 262

"Young Woman Visitor, The" (Murray), **Supp. VII:** 280

"Young Women with the Hair of Witches" (Redgrove), **Supp. VI:** **232–233,** 236

Your Five Gallants (Middleton), **II:** 3, 21

"Your Philosophies Trouble Me" (Paton), **Supp. II:** 360

Youth (Conrad), **VI:** 135, 137; **Retro. Supp. II:** 73

Youth (Rosenberg), **VI:** 432

"Youth" (Tennyson), **IV:** 329

"Youth and Art" (Browning), **IV:** 369

Youth and the Peregrines (Fry), **Supp. III:** 193, 194

"Youth in Memory" (Meredith), **V:** 222, 234

"Youth of Man, The" (Arnold), **V:** 210

"Youth of Nature, The" (Arnold), **V:** 210

"Youth Revisited" (Fuller), **Supp. VII:** 73

Zaillian, Steven, **Supp. IV:** 346

Zapolya (Coleridge), **IV:** 56

Zastrozzi: A Romance (Shelley), **III:** 338; **IV:** 208

ZBC of Ezra Pound, A (Brooke-Rose), **Supp. IV:** 99, 114–115

Zeal of Thy House, The (Sayers), **Supp. III:** 335–336, 348–349

Zee & Company (O'Brien), **Supp. V:** 334

Zhdanov, Andrei, **Supp. IV:** 82

Zola, Émile, **V:** xxiv–xxvi, 286; **VI:** viii; **Supp. IV:** 136, 249

Zoo (MacNeice), **VII:** 403

Zoo Story, The (Albee), **Supp. IV:** 435

Zuleika Dobson; or, An Oxford Love Story (Beerbohm), **Supp. II:** 43, **56–59**

Zweig, Paul, **Supp. IV:** 356